VOWELS

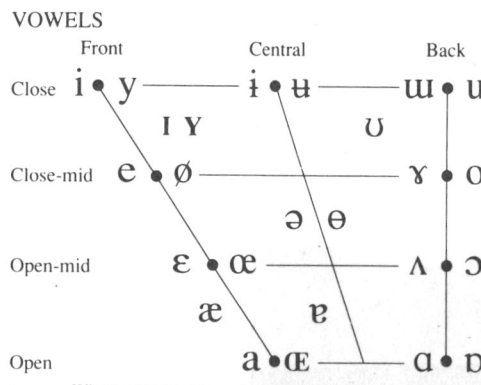

	Front	Central	Back
Close	i • y	ɨ • ʉ	ɯ • u
	ɪ ʏ		ʊ
Close-mid	e • ø		ɤ • o
		ə θ	
Open-mid	ɛ • œ	ɜ • ɞ	ʌ • ɔ
	æ	ɐ	
Open		a • ɶ	ɑ • ɒ

Where symbols appear in pairs, the one to the right represents a rounded vowel.

SUPRASEGMENTALS

ˈ	Primary stress	ˌfoʊnəˈtɪʃən
ˌ	Secondary stress	
ː	Long	eː
ˑ	Half-long	eˑ
̆	Extra-short	ĕ
.	Syllable break	ɹi.ækt
ǀ	Minor (foot) group	
‖	Major (intonation) group	
‿	Linking (absence of a break)	
↗	Global rise	
↘	Global fall	

OTHER SYMBOLS

ʍ	Voiceless labial-velar fricative
w	Voiced labial-velar approximant
ɥ	Voiced labial-palatal approximant
ʜ	Voiceless epiglottal fricative
ʢ	Voiced epiglottal fricative
ʡ	Epiglottal plosive
ɕ ʑ	Alveolo-palatal fricatives
ɺ	Additional mid central vowel
ʘ	Bilabial click
ǀ	Dental click
ǃ	(Post)alveolar click
ǂ	Palatoalveolar click
‖	Alveolar lateral click
ɺ	Alveolar lateral flap
ɧ	Simultaneous ʃ and x

Affricates and double articulations can be represented by two symbols joined by a tie bar if necessary.

k͡p t͡s

TONES & WORD ACCENTS

LEVEL			CONTOUR		
e̋ or ˥	Extra high		ě ˩˥	Rising	
é ˦	High		ê ˥˩	Falling	
ē ˧	Mid		e᷄ ˧˥	High rising	
è ˨	Low		e᷅ ˩˧	Low rising	
ȅ ˩	Extra low		e᷈	Rising-falling	
				etc.	
↓	Downstep				
↑	Upstep				

THE WORLD'S WRITING SYSTEMS

THE WORLD'S WRITING SYSTEMS

Edited by
Peter T. Daniels
and
William Bright

New York   Oxford
OXFORD UNIVERSITY PRESS
1996

OXFORD UNIVERSITY PRESS

Oxford   New York
Athens   Auckland   Bangkok   Bombay
Calcutta   Cape Town   Dar es Salaam   Delhi
Florence   Hong Kong   Istanbul   Karachi
Kuala Lumpur   Madras   Madrid   Melbourne
Mexico City   Nairobi   Paris   Singapore
Taipei   Tokyo   Toronto

and associated companies in
Berlin   Ibadan

Published by Oxford University Press, Inc.,
198 Madison Avenue, New York, NY 10016

Oxford is a registered trademark of Oxford University Press

Library of Congress Cataloging-in-Publication Data
The world's writing systems / edited by Peter T. Daniels and William Bright
p.   cm.
Includes bibliographical references and index.
ISBN 0-19-507993-0
1. Writing.   2. Alphabet.   3. Graphemics.
I. Daniels, Peter T., 1951– .   II. Bright, William, 1928– .
P211.W714   1995
411—dc20   95-2247
CIP
r952
Rev.

Printing (last digit):   9   8   7   6   5   4   3   2   1
Printed in the United States of America
on acid-free paper

In memory of my father,

who taught me to read;

and

in honor of my mother,

who taught me to write

—P.T.D.

To Robert Thiel,

oldest friend

and companion in the study of language

—W.B.

Contents

Part IV East Asian Writing Systems

Part VI South Asian Writing Systems

Part VII Southeast Asian Writing Systems

Part VIII Middle Eastern Writing Systems

Part IX Scripts Invented in Modern Times

Part XI Sociolinguistics and Scripts

Part XIII Imprinting and Printing

Contributors

HOWARD I. ARONSON is Professor of Slavic Linguistics at the University of Chicago.

GERHARD AUGST is Professor of Linguistics, University of Siegen (Germany). He has published numerous articles on the German writing system and spelling reform.

TISTA BAGCHI is Reader in Linguistics at the University of Delhi, India. In addition to holding degrees in linguistics from the Universities of Calcutta, Delhi, and Chicago, she has published articles on various aspects of the grammar of Bengali.

DRAGANA BARAC-CIKOJA holds degrees in psychology from the University of Connecticut. She has taught at the University of Split in Zadar and at Wesleyan University in Connecticut; she is currently a postdoctoral fellow at Gallaudet University.

THOMAS BAUER holds degrees in Islamic and Semitic studies and teaches at the University of Erlangen (Germany). He has published monographs and articles on Classical Arabic literature and philology.

JOHN BENDOR-SAMUEL has degrees from Oxford and London Universities. He is a member of the Summer Institute of Linguistics and has a special interest in West African languages. He was editor of the *Journal of West African Languages*, 1982–1993, and edited *The Niger-Congo Languages*, the current reference book on this family.

EMMETT L. BENNETT is Professor Emeritus of Classical Studies, University of Wisconsin–Madison. He has published the Linear B inscriptions from Pylos, and articles on their interpretation, with special attention to the elucidation of the differences between the Linear A and Linear B scripts. He edited *Nestor* for 21 years.

WILLIAM G. BOLTZ is Associate Professor of Classical Chinese at the University of Washington, Seattle, working and teaching primarily in the area of early texts.

LARISSA BONFANTE is Professor of Classics at New York University and author of numerous books and articles on Etruscan language and culture.

WILLIAM BRIGHT is Professor Emeritus of Linguistics, University of California, Los Angeles, and Adjunct Professor, University of Colorado. Among his principal interests are sociolinguistics and the languages of North America and South Asia; he was editor of *Language* for 22 years and is currently editor of *Language in Society*.

BRUCE CAIN recently spent several years in the Maldives collecting Dhivehi language material. He co-authored a Dhivehi language course to help expatriates learn the language. He is currently pursuing a Ph.D. in linguistics at Cornell University.

BERNARD COMRIE was educated at the University of Cambridge and taught Russian and Linguistics there before moving to the University of Southern California, where he is now Professor of Linguistics. His main interests are language universals and typology, historical linguistics, and linguistic fieldwork. His publications include *Aspect* (Cambridge, 1976), *Language Universals and Linguistic Typology* (Oxford, 1981), *The Languages of the Soviet Union* (Cambridge, 1981), and *Tense* (Cambridge, 1985). He is also editor of *The World's Major Languages* (London/New York, 1987) and is managing editor of the journal *Studies in Language*.

JERROLD S. COOPER is an Assyriologist in the Department of Near Eastern Studies at the Johns Hopkins University. His specialty is Sumerian literature and history, and he has a long-standing interest in the origins of writing and writing systems.

CHRISTOPHER COURT is in charge of the Thai and Cambodian (Khmer) language programs at Monash University and has taught Thai at the University of California, Berkeley, and Stanford University. With a doctorate in linguistics from Berkeley, he has written on Iu-mien (Yao) grammar and is interested in tonal phenomena in Southeast Asia (including the Austronesian languages of South Thailand); he is also interested in the indigenous writing systems of Southeast Asian languages.

PAUL CUBBERLEY is Associate Professor of Russian at the University of Melbourne. His main interests apart from Slavic scripts are the phonology and word-formation of the Slavic languages. He is the foundation and current editor of *Australian Slavonic and East European Studies*.

PETER T. DANIELS holds degrees in linguistics from Cornell University and the University of Chicago; he has taught at the University of Wisconsin–Milwaukee and Chicago State University. He has published numerous articles and reviews on writing systems, Semitic languages, and languages of the world.

ANTHONY DILLER is Reader in the Faculty of Asian Studies, Australian National University, and has taught extensively in Thailand. He holds degrees in classics from Williams College and in linguistics from Cornell University; his publications focus on Thai linguistics.

ERNST EBBINGHAUS, Professor Emeritus of German, Pennsylvania State University, received a Ph.D. in Scandinavian philology from the University of Marburg. His principal interests are Old Germanic languages and paleography, and he is editor-in-chief of *General Linguistics*.

RALPH W. V. ELLIOTT, of the Australian National University, Canberra, is Emeritus Professor of English. He has taught at two British and three Australian universities and has written widely on aspects of the history of English, including runes, the language of Chaucer and Middle English topography, and Thomas Hardy's English.

ROBERT ENGLUND is Assistant Professor of Near Eastern Studies at the Free University of Berlin. His research interests include work on the decipherment of proto-cuneiform and on administrative forms in third-millennium B.C.E. Mesopotamia.

BRENDA FARNELL is a Visiting Assistant Professor of Anthropology at the University of Iowa. Among her principal interests are human movement and dance and the embodiment of social theory and linguistics. She has published widely on Plains Indian Sign Language in Assiniboine (Nakota) storytelling performance, and is co-editor of the *Journal for the Anthropological Study of Human Movement.*

LAURIE BETH FELDMAN is an Associate Professor of Psychology at the State University of New York at Albany. Among her principal research interests are the processes that underlie reading and the perception of words, and how those processes vary across writing systems.

JAMES W. GAIR is Professor of Linguistics at Cornell University. He has worked extensively in South Asian linguistics, concentrating on Sinhala, but working and publishing also on other languages, including Tamil, Hindi, Marathi, and Dhivehi/Mahal.

GETATCHEW HAILE, Ph.D., F.B.A., is cataloguer of Oriental manuscripts and Regents Professor of Medieval Studies at St. John's University, Collegeville, Minnesota. He holds degrees in theology from Coptic Theological College in Cairo, in social sciences from the American University in Cairo, and in Semitic philosophy from the University of Tübingen. He taught for many years at the Haile Sellassie I (now Addis Ababa) University. He has published many articles and several monographs in the field of Ethiopian studies.

HARJEET SINGH GILL is Professor of Linguistics at Jawaharlal Nehru University, New Delhi. After his earlier work in structural linguistics at Hartford, he spent several years in France as a Fellow of the Centre National de la Recherche Scientifique, Paris. Since then he has been engaged in the study of the philosophy of language and semiotics in the French tradition of the medieval philosopher Pierre Abelard, and the Cartesian thinkers of conceptual constructs.

ALLAN GLEASON, Professor Emeritus of Linguistics at the University of Toronto, wrote the classic textbook *An Introduction to Descriptive Linguistics* in 1955, and has long been associated with missionary linguistics. Recently, he has been involved in the computerization of scripts.

RICHARD GOERWITZ (M.A., Yale Divinity School; Ph.D., University of Chicago) is currently a lecturer in Northwest Semitic at the University of Chicago, working primarily on historical linguistics, computational phonology, Unix system programming, and full text retrieval systems.

GENE B. GRAGG is Professor of Near Eastern Languages and Linguistics at the Oriental Institute of the University of Chicago. His main interest is the pre- and early history of Afroasiatic (Cushitic) and the peripheral languages of the ancient Near East.

ERIC P. HAMP is Robert Maynard Hutchins Distinguished Service Professor Emeritus for Linguistics, Psychology, Slavic Languages and Linguistics, and Committee on the Ancient Mediterranean World at the University of Chicago. Among his many areas of expertise is Indo-European linguistics, with Celtic as a subspecialty. He is also the linguistic consultant and analyst for the Braille Reading and Language Program.

BENJAMIN HARY is Director of the Department of Near Eastern Studies, Emory University. He has published extensively on Judeo-Arabic language and linguistics, Arabic linguistics and dialectology, the history of Judaic languages, and proficiency-based teaching of Hebrew and Arabic.

ROBERT D. HOBERMAN is Associate Professor of Judaic Studies and Linguistics at the State University of New York at Stony Brook. He holds a doctorate in linguistics from the University of Chicago. His principal interests are in phonology and morphology and in modern Aramaic, Arabic, and Hebrew.

DEE ANN HOLISKY is Associate Professor at George Mason University in Fairfax, Virginia. Her primary research has focused on verbal morphology in Georgian and Tsova-Tush (a Nakh language spoken in Georgia), but she has also published two books on English vocabulary for ESL students and a textbook on English grammar for ESL teachers.

WOLFGANG JENNIGES holds degrees in classical and Oriental philology from the University of Leuven. He is currently doing research work in the Oriental Department of the University of Leuven.

GYÖRGY KARA is Professor of Mongolian in the Department of Central Eurasian Studies, Indiana University, Bloomington, and Professor of the Department of Inner Asian Studies, Loránd Eötvös University of Budapest.

ALAN S. KAYE is Professor of Linguistics and Arabic and Director of the Laboratory for Phonetic Research at California State University, Fullerton. In addition to publishing several books, his work in Arabic, Semitic, and general linguistics has appeared in over sixty journals.

KOSTAS KAZAZIS is Professor of Linguistics at the University of Chicago. His interests include Balkan linguistics and Greek diglossia.

ROSS KING is Assistant Professor of Korean Language and Literature, University of British Columbia. His principal research interests are Korean linguistics and philology, the Koreans of the former Soviet Union and their language, and Altaic comparative linguistics.

STAN KNIGHT has a degree in fine art from Leeds University, England, and is an internationally known scribe and teacher. He is on the faculty of Cornish College of the Arts in Seattle. The author of *Historical Scripts* and joint author of *A Book of Formal Scripts*, he has written numerous articles on the history and current practice of calligraphy.

JOEL KUIPERS is Associate Professor of Anthropology at George Washington University in Washington, D.C. He has researched and written extensively about the language and culture of the Weyewa of the eastern Indonesian island of Sumba.

EVGENIJ I. KYCHANOV is a member of the St. Petersburg Branch of the Institute of Oriental Studies of the Russian Academy of Sciences.

MICHAEL K. C. MACMAHON is Senior Lecturer in English Language at the University of Glasgow, Scotland, and a member of the Interational Phonetic Association's council. One of his research interests is the history of phonetics during the eighteenth and nineteenth centuries, especially in Britain and Europe; he has published extensively on this topic.

MARTHA J. MACRI is Associate Professor in the Departments of Native American Studies and Anthropology at the University of California, Davis, where she is the director of the Native American Language Center. Her primary research interests are non-alphabetic writing systems and the linguistic prehistory of the Americas.

B. P. MAHAPATRA holds degrees in linguistics from Deccan College Postgraduate and Research Institute, Poona; the University of London; and Calcutta University. At present, he is head of the Language Division, Government of India, Calcutta. He is the chief author of *The Written Languages of India,* vols. 1 and 2, jointly produced by the Government of India and the International Centre for Research on Bilingualism and Language Planning, University of Laval, Québec. He has published many articles on Dravidian, Munda, and Indo-Aryan languages and sociolinguistics. He is also a member of the Executive Committees of the Linguistic Society of India and the Dravidian Linguistics Association of India.

VICTOR H. MAIR is Professor of Chinese Language and Literature, Department of Oriental Studies, University of Pennsylvania. Among his publications are translations of the *Tao te Ching* and other Chinese classics; he edits *Sino-Platonic Papers* and co-edited *Characters and Computers*.

COLIN P. MASICA is a professor in the Departments of South Asian Languages and Civilizations and Linguistics at the University of Chicago. His interests have included the cultural history of South Asia, cultural history in general, cultural geography, South Asia as a linguistic convergence area, other convergence areas, modern and medieval Indo-Aryan and Dravidian languages and literatures, and the history of religions and world-hypotheses, in general and as pertaining to South Asia in particular.

JAMES D. McCAWLEY is Andrew MacLeish Distinguished Service Professor of Linguistics and of East Asian Languages and Civilizations at the University of Chicago. He has published extensively on syntax and semantics and less extensively on phonology, writing systems, history of linguistics, and philosophy of science.

RAY McDERMOTT is a Professor of Education and Anthropology at Stanford University. He has written widely on the role of talking, reading, and writing in the organization of social interaction and learning.

DAMIAN McMANUS is Lecturer in the Irish Department and Fellow of Trinity College, Dublin. In addition to various articles on linguistic aspects of Primitive and Old Irish, he is the author of *A Guide to Ogham* (1991) and co-editor of *Stair na Gaeilge* (1994), a comprehensive history of the Irish language, to which he contributed the chapter on Classical Modern Irish.

H. CRAIG MELCHERT is Professor of Linguistics at the University of North Carolina at Chapel Hill. A specialist in Indo-European linguistics, particularly the Anatolian subgroup, he is the author of *Anatolian Historical Phonology* and lexica of the Cuneiform Luvian and Lycian languages.

PIOTR MICHALOWSKI is George G. Cameron Professor of Ancient Near Eastern Languages and Civilizations, University of Michigan. His principal interests include Sumerian and Akkadian languages, literatures, history, and society. A notable volume is *The Lamentation over the Destruction of Sumer and Ur* (Eisenbraun's, 1989).

N. B. MILLET is a curator in the Egyptian Department of the Royal Ontario Museum in Toronto, and a full professor in the Department of Near Eastern Studies at the University of Toronto. He is an Egyptologist, trained in Egyptian philology, who developed his interest in the ancient Meroitic language while excavating in Nubia in the 1960s.

P. J. MISTRY is Professor of Linguistics, California State University, Fresno, and has been Section Head of Indic Linguistics for the MLA International Bibliography since 1978. He has published several articles on Gujarati.

K. P. MOHANAN has taught in the departments of linguistics at MIT, the University of Texas at Austin, and Stanford University. He currently teaches in the Department of English Language and Literature, National University of Singapore. Though he is known for his work on lexical phonology, his interests include various other aspects of theoretical linguistics, as well as the structure of Malayalam.

JOHN MOUNTFORD taught classics before qualifying in general linguistics and in applied linguistics at Edinburgh University. His interest in writing systems stems from applying linguistics in the teaching of English to native speakers of English. His current concern, after some years as a teacher-trainer, is with the teaching of spelling—starting with English spelling.

NGUYỄN ĐÌNH-HOÀ is Professor Emeritus of Linguistics and Foreign Languages and Literatures at Southern Illinois University at Carbondale. At SIU-C he was instrumental in the development of academic courses and research programs coordinated by the Center for Vietnamese Studies between 1969 and 1990.

JOHN D. NICHOLS is Professor of Native Studies and Linguistics, University of Manitoba, and holds graduate degrees in linguistics from Harvard University. His research interests are in the North American indigenous languages (especially Ojibwe, Cree, and other languages of the Algonquian family), oral literature, and traditional arts.

M. O'CONNOR is Associate Professor of Hebrew and Biblical Studies at the Union Theological Seminary in the City of New York. He is the author of *Hebrew Verse Structure* (1980) and *An Introduction to Biblical Hebrew Syntax* (with Bruce K. Waltke, 1989).

ASKO PARPOLA has been Professor of South Asian Studies at the University of Helsinki since 1982. His major research interests include the Indus script, correlating the linguistic prehistory of South Asian languages with archeological evidence, Sāma-vedic texts, and the history of Indian religions.

JOHN SÖREN PETTERSSON holds a licentiate degree in general linguistics from Uppsala University, where he is at present a doctoral candidate. He also holds a B.A. in mathematics from Uppsala University.

MARTHA RATLIFF is Associate Professor of Linguistics, Wayne State University. Her principal interests and publications are in the fields of historical linguistics, phonology (especially tonology), and typology; the description of individual Hmong-Mien languages; and the reconstruction of the Hmong-Mien protolanguage.

ROBERT K. RITNER, having previously studied and taught at the University of Chicago, is the first Marilyn K. Simpson Assistant Professor of Egyptology at Yale University. He is a specialist in the Demotic language and script and associate editor of the Demotic Dictionary Project of the University of Chicago.

RICHARD SALOMON, Professor of Asian Languages (Sanskrit) at the University of Washington, is a specialist in Indian epigraphy and paleography. His *Indian Epigraphy: A Guide to the Study of Inscriptions in Sanskrit, Prakrit, and the Other Indo-Aryan Languages* is published by Oxford University Press.

AVEDIS K. SANJIAN is Narekatsi Professor Emeritus of Armenian Studies, University of California, Los Angeles. Among his principal interests are medieval Armenian cultural and literary history and paleography. He edited the first five annual volumes of the *Journal of the Society for Armenian Studies*. He holds degrees from the American University of Beirut and the University of Michigan. He has also taught Armenian language and literature at Harvard University. He has authored and/or edited ten books and has written more than forty articles on a large variety of Armenian topics.

JANINE SCANCARELLI is Associate Professor of English at the College of William and Mary. Her publications and presentations have explored the relationship between grammar and discourse structure, the grammar and historical development of the Cherokee language, and the cultural significance of Cherokee literacy and language use.

ERIC SCHILLER holds a Ph.D. in linguistics from the University of Chicago; he has taught at Wayne State University and the University of Chicago. He has written extensively on Khmer, Southeast Asian languages, and autolexical theory, with particular emphasis on serial verb constructions.

WAYNE M. SENNER, a professor of German and Scandinavian at Arizona State University, is the author of *The Reception of German Literature in Iceland, 1770–1850* (1985) and other books, and is editor of *The Origins of Writing* (1989).

DINGXU SHI holds degrees in linguistics from the University of Pittsburgh and the University of Southern California; he taught at the University of California at Irvine and teaches at the Hong Kong Polytechnic University. He publishes mainly in syntax, semantics, language typology, and language change.

JOHN VICTOR SINGLER is Associate Professor of Linguistics at New York University. His research focuses on pidgin and creole studies, sociolinguistics, phonology, and the languages of West Africa and the Caribbean.

PRODS OKTOR SKJÆRVØ is Aga Khan Professor of Iranian at Harvard University. His field of interest covers pre-Islamic Iran: languages, literatures (especially medieval inscriptions), and religions, as well as modern Iranian dialects.

JANET S. (SHIBAMOTO) SMITH is a Professor of Anthropology, University of California, Davis. Among her principal interests are Japanese sociolinguistics, language and gender, and non-alphabetic writing systems. Publications include *Japanese Women's Language* (1985) and numerous articles on Japanese language and society, including use of a multi-scriptal writing system.

SANFORD B. STEEVER holds degrees in linguistics from Cornell University and the University of Chicago, as well as a diploma in Tamil from Madurai-Kamaraj University. He has published three books and numerous articles on morphology, syntax, pragmatics, historical linguistics, Tamil, and Dravidian linguistics.

JOHN STEVENS is Professor of Buddhist Studies at Tohoku Fukushi University in Sendai, Japan. An avid student and practitioner of Asian calligraphy, he has been involved in arranging exhibitions of calligraphic art in the United States and Europe, and he is the author of *Sacred Calligraphy of the East*.

PIERRE SWIGGERS is Professor of Linguistics and Romance Languages at the University of Leuven, Research Director of the Belgian National Science Foundation, and Co-director of the Centre International de Dialectologie Générale (Louvain). He has published numerous books and articles in the fields of general and descriptive linguistics (Indo-European, Semitic, and occasionally Bantu), writing, semiotics, and the philosophy of language.

DAVID D. TESTEN holds a joint doctorate in linguistics and Near Eastern languages and civilizations from the University of Chicago. He works primarily in the historical phonology and morphology of the Semitic and Iranian languages.

LESLIE THREATTE holds degrees from Oberlin College and Harvard University and studied at the American School of Classical Studies, Athens. He has taught at Cornell University and since 1970 at the University of California, Berkeley. He is the author of *The Grammar of Attic Inscriptions*.

EDWARD F. TUTTLE is Professor of Italian and Romance Linguistics, University of California, Los Angeles. Having reached linguistics via Romance philology, including comparative medieval literatures, he is currently examining typologic relationships between language and culture observed within the prism of Italian dialects—his prime research area.

LEONARD W. J. VAN DER KUIJP is Professor of Tibetan at the University of Washington, Seattle.

JULIAN K. WHEATLEY is a senior lecturer in the Department of Modern Languages and Linguistics, Cornell University, and director of the modern Chinese and Burmese language programs there. His principal interests are the languages and linguistics of mainland Southeast Asia and China.

NORMAN ZIDE is Professor Emeritus of Linguistics and of South Asian Languages and Civilizations at the University of Chicago. His main interests are Munda languages and cultures and general Indological topics; he has worked on poetic language and writing systems, among other topics.

Preface

Why a book on the world's writing systems? There have been several surveys of the world's languages, attempts by individual scholars to cover all the languages of the world as well as collaborative volumes and series by specialists on individual languages and families. Occasionally such surveys include tables of the alphabets of some of those languages, and occasionally they include examples of what those languages look like in print. Almost never, though, do they include information about how the scripts represent the languages.

There have also been several surveys of the world's scripts—with one exception, the noble work of dedicated individuals: David Diringer, Hans Jensen, James-G. Février, Marcel Cohen; Charles Fossey edited a valuable volume. These usually include facsimiles of ancient inscriptions and old manuscripts, tables of the alphabets, and a discussion of the historical relationships among the scripts. Again, they don't include information about how the scripts represent the languages.

This book is different: each contributor was asked to provide a historical sketch and the table of signforms in their standard order and their variations, but the bulk of their work was to be a description of *how the script actually works*—how the sounds of a language are represented in writing, along with a brief text in the language(s) the script is used for. For each script, the standard transliteration is shown. This is the system used by scholars, and by governments and libraries, for representing the script in a Roman alphabet with various modifications. Furthermore, since the Roman letters and associated marks have often been used with different meanings in different parts of the world, for each script a transcription is given using the symbols of the 1989 revision of the International Phonetic Alphabet (see the endpapers, and, for an explanation, SECTION 71). This provides a uniform frame of reference and ensures that the reader can make a rather accurate attempt at pronouncing any text written with a phonetic script. (In practical terms, this means that among modern languages only the Chinese/Japanese/Korean sphere is not fully presented here.) For each text, the transliteration and transcription are accompanied by an item-by-item literal translation (the gloss) as well as a free translation, to give some idea of how the language works.

This book is organized into thirteen parts, by writing system and chronology, and coincidentally by region—not by language family. After a discussion of the study of writing systems, *grammatology*, in Part I, the scripts described in Part II are the oldest known: those of the ancient Near East. There follows in Part III an account of the recovery of ancient languages, with individual reports on certain obscure scripts whose interpretation is becoming more and more clear. Next oldest is the script of China, and it is followed in Part IV with its derivatives down to the present.

At the root of the single tree of all the scripts that serve the rest of the world is the Canaanite. Its first derivative, the Greek alphabet, and its descendants, the alphabets of Europe, are described in Part V. Part VI covers the scripts used for Sanskrit, along with its relatives and their neighbors in South Asia, and Part VII deals with its further offshoots in Southeast Asia. Historically, the latest flowering of the Canaanite branch took place in its home region, so the last of the historical parts, VIII, covers the scripts of the Middle East.

Writing has come to unlettered cultures in two ways, described in Parts IX and X: either some individual genius observes a visitor writing in some language and determines to provide such a boon for the local language; or such a visitor provides an adaptation of an existing script that fits the new language more or less well. Part XI addresses some examples of interrelations between scripts within particular societies. Within Western civilization, writing has been adapted to record phenomena beyond everyday language—the minutiae of speech production, speech recorded accurately as it is spoken, numbers, music, movement—and such systems are the subject of Part XII. And while writing is inherently a unitary phenomenon, Part XIII covers means of multiple production of recorded texts.

The first page or two of each part is an overview of its contents, written by the volume editors or by the contributor of its first section. These opening pages place the writing systems in their historical and linguistic contexts, and they can be read in sequence as an initial orientation to the place of writing through the past and in the contemporary world.

A book like this would have been impossible ten or even five years ago. To typeset all the characters of all the languages involved would have required the labor of numerous specially trained compositors at a number of different printing houses. But the implementation of multiscript technologies by Apple Computer has made it feasible, if not exactly simple, to prepare the entire manuscript electronically on a Macintosh IIci system. It is Lloyd B. Anderson, proprietor of Ecological Linguistics, who deserves the greatest credit for making this project possible. He assembled custom software incorporating both the right-to-left scripts and the "character"-based (two-byte) scripts—making it possible to mix, say, Arabic and Korean writing in a single document. He has also uncomplainingly met all requests for obscure and difficult fonts for obscure and difficult languages, ancient and modern, coming up with ingenious schemes to make typing them almost easy, even for someone who knows nothing of the languages involved beyond their transliterations. (A list of Ecological Linguistics fonts employed herein is included in the colophon.)

We are grateful to Cleo Huggins for the use of her Egyptian Hieroglyphic fonts, based on the Gardiner types held by Oxford University Press and utilized by the Oriental Institute, University of Chicago. Robert K. Ritner provided the Demotic font used at the Oriental Institute. Asko Parpola has made available his own font of Indus

Valley characters, © Asko Parpola, Tuomo Saarikivi, and Bertil Tikkanen, Department of Asian and African Studies, University of Helsinki. Paul Cubberley supplied a pair of shareware fonts of Old Cyrillic forms—known, appropriately enough, as Constantin and Methodius. The text of the book is set in Adobe Times Roman and Times Small Caps & Old Style Figures; Adobe's Wittenberger Fraktur and Helvetica appear in examples, as does SoftKey Software's script font Koffee.

Jan Nattier made several useful recommendations of contributors, and one of her recruits, György Kara, in turn suggested several topics we had omitted, as well as scholars to treat them. To both of them go our thanks. Jack Cella, manager of Seminary Cooperative Bookstore, Chicago, made sure that Daniels was aware of interesting new books.

Joan Greenfield created an elegant and flexible design that has proved quite adaptable to the unprecedentedly diverse demands made by this project. Peter T. Daniels, frequently using computer files supplied by the contributors—and, for many of the South Asia sections, by William Bright—prepared the electronic manuscript. The basic software is FrameMaker 4, and the parts involving right-to-left and two-byte scripts were first done in NisusWriter. The sales and tech support representatives—Greg Nisius and Raquel Romano, respectively—at Nisus Software Inc. have been unfailingly helpful, and Lester LaPierre of Frame User's Network–Chicago came up with useful tips early on. The music examples in SECTION 72 were prepared with MusicPrinter Plus 4.0, courtesy of Anne Heider, director, His Majestie's Clerkes (Chicago). Brenda Farnell made the Labanotation examples in SECTION 73 with LabanWriter 3.1. PostScript files were created by Daniels, and high-resolution camera-ready output of Part IV (which uses Apple Language Kit TrueType fonts) was prepared by Eisenbrauns, Winona Lake, Indiana. Special thanks go to Jim Eisenbraun and Sam Heldenbrand.

I. J. Gelb (1907–1985), a pioneer in the field of grammatology (and Daniels's teacher at the University of Chicago), kept a list of future projects. Among them was a "treasure-book of writing," which would gather both descriptive and theoretical accounts of writing systems. We hope that this collection will go partway toward realizing Gelb's intention.

—Peter T. Daniels and William Bright

Abbreviations, Conventions, and Definitions

1	first person
2	second person
abecedary	a text listing the characters of an abjad or alphabet in their traditional or standard order (even if that order does not begin with the equivalent of *a* and *b*)
abjad	a type of writing system that denotes only consonants
ABL	ablative
ABS	absolutive
abugida	a type of writing system whose basic characters denote consonants followed by a particular vowel, and in which diacritics denote the other vowels
ACC	accusative
ACT	active
ADJ	adjective, adjectival
ADV	adverbial
AGR	agreement
allograph	conditioned or free variant of a character, e.g. the distinctive forms of five Hebrew letters used at the end of a word (conditioned), the differing forms of *a/a*, *g/g* that can be intermixed in handwriting (free)
alphabet	a type of writing system that denotes consonants and vowels
alphasyllabary	a writing system in which vowels are denoted by subsidiary symbols not all of which occur in a linear order (with relation to the consonant symbols) that is congruent with their temporal order in speech
ambisyllabic	of certain consonants, interpretable as either the end of one syllable or the beginning of the next, or both

<angle brackets> used commonly in the study of writing, but not in this book, to enclose transliterations or, where confusion is possible, sequences of roman letters to be taken as orthography

AOR aorist

*asterisk marks nonexistent (unattested) items, either reconstructions of probable ancestral forms (e.g. Indo-European *abel-, which became *apple*), or forms that do not occur in ordinary speech (e.g. *breaked*)

AUX auxiliary

B.C.E. Before the Common Era, a nonsectarian year designation equivalent to B.C. 'before Christ'

boustrophedon a style of writing a document in which lines of text read alternately left to right and right to left (or vice versa); of practical value when a monumental inscription occupies a very broad wall, and of psychological value because the eye need not hunt for the beginning of each succeeding line; however, no script formerly written boustrophedon has retained the style

c. century

ca. circa 'approximately'

C.E. Common Era, a nonsectarian year designation equivalent to A.D. *anno domini* 'in the year of the Lord'

character 1. general term for any self-contained element of a writing system; 2. conventional term for a unit of the Chinese writing system in East Asian scripts

CLF classifier

COMP comparative, complementizer

CONJ conjunctive

CONN connector

consonant a brief portion of an utterance in which obstruction to the air stream is created in the vocal tract; also, a character designating such a sound

COP copula

cursive flowing, showing the influence of the motion of the hand in writing, often with joined characters

DAT dative

DECL declension

DEF   definitizer

DEMONST   demonstrative

DERIV   derivational affix

derivation   grammatical process in which a distinct word is formed from another, e.g. *friendly* is derived from *friend*, *song* from *sing*

DET   determiner

diacritic   a mark added to a character to indicate a modified pronunciation (or sometimes to distinguish homophonous words)

digraph   a pair of letters denoting a single sound, e.g. *ph*, *sh*

DIR   direct

DISP   displaced

ductus   an individual style of handwriting, characteristic of a small group of scribes or sometimes a single person

EMPH   emphatic

ENCL   enclitic

epigraphy   the study of texts inscribed on hard surfaces, usually by incising; cf. paleography

ERG   ergative

featural script   a type of writing system whose characters denote phonetic features

FEM   feminine

fortis   of certain consonants, pronounced with more energy (opposed to lenis); e.g., English voiceless stops

FUT   future

GEN   genitive

GER   gerund

grammatogeny   the invention of a writing system

grammatology   the discipline that studies writing systems

grapheme   term intended to designate a unit of a writing system, parallel to phoneme and morpheme, but in practice used as a synonym for letter, diacritic, character (2), or sign (2)

HON   honorific

HORT   hortatory

iconic of a sign, bearing some nonconventional, visual relationship to what is referred to

IMP imperative

IMP(F) imperfect

IMPFV imperfective

IMV imperative

INDEF indefinite

INF(IN) infinitive

inflection grammatical process resulting in forms of a single word, e.g. *friends* is an inflected form of *friend*; also, the morpheme that marks it, here *-s*

INTENS intensifier

INTENT intentional

italics in this book indicate transcriptions and normalizations (in the tables and sample texts, replaced by upright type since they do not need to be distinguished from the context)

ITER iterative

lenis of certain consonants, pronounced with less energy (opposed to fortis); e.g., English voiced stops

letter a self-contained unit of an abjad, alphabet, or abugida

ligature a composite character in which the components are recognizable, e.g *Æ, Œ*

LOC locative

LOC'NAL locational

logogram a character that denotes the meaning but not the pronunciation of a morpheme

logosyllabary a type of writing system whose characters denote morphemes, and a subset of whose characters can be used for their phonetic syllabic values without regard to their semantic values

markedness a property (associated with a particular theory of the organization of knowledge/culture) that correlates with lower frequency, higher complexity, less generality

MOD modal

morpheme a minimal stretch of speech that has a meaning, either grammatical (*-s*) or independent (*friend*)

morphophonemic	of orthography, spellings that remain constant when a morpheme undergoes changes in pronunciation (*photograph, photography, photographic*)
NEG	negative
NOM	nominalizer, nominative
NONFIN	nonfinite
normalization	in this book, for scripts that are not fully explicit, a conjectural interpretation that supplies, e.g., the vocalization of languages written with an abjad (based on comparison with related languages and reconstruction of earlier forms)
OBJ	object
OBL	oblique
OPT	optative
orthography	conventional spelling of texts, and the principles therefor
paleography	the study of texts inscribed on (usually) flexible surfaces, usually with ink; cf. epigraphy
PART	particle, participle
PASS	passive
PAST	past
PCPL	participle
PERF	perfect
phoneme	a minimal sound of speech that distinguishes words in a particular language; usually discovered by examining "minimal pairs" such as *fuss*/*bus*, *bus*/*buzz*, *thing*/*sing*, *thigh*/*thy*
PL	plural
POSS	possessive
PREF	prefix
PRES	present
PRON	pronoun
PTCL	particle
QUOT	quotative
REDUP	reduplication
REFL	reflexive

REL   relative

sandhi   interaction between sounds at the end of one word and the beginning of the next

script   in this book, equivalent to *writing system*

serif   a small protrusion, not in itself distinguishing two characters, at the end of a stroke of a writing instrument; the historic origin was in the brush strokes traced to guide Roman inscription carvers, and subsequently it served to strengthen the edges of characters in printing type

SG   singular

shwa   a neutral vowel produced with the vocal organs in rest position

sign   1. a unit in a communicative system comprising a signifier (what carries the meaning) and a signified (what is meant); 2. conventional term for a self-contained unit of cuneiform script

signary   general term for a determined collection of characters (or signs), used to avoid specifying abjad, alphabet, etc.

'single quotes'   enclose glosses (translations)

/slant brackets/   enclose phonemic transcriptions

sloped roman   in this book, used (with an asterisk) for reconstructed ancestral forms of attested materials, e.g. Indo-European, Archaic Chinese

SMALL CAPITALS   in this book, used for cross references; in the study of Romance languages, used for reconstructed Vulgar Latin forms; with logo-syllabic scripts, used to transliterate logograms

SOC   sociative

[square brackets]   enclose phonetic transcriptions

SUBJ   subject, subjunctive

SUP(ERL)   superlative

syllabary   a type of writing system whose characters denote syllables, with no deliberate graphic similarity between characters denoting phonetically similar syllables

TOP   topic

transcription   an interpretation of a written text that supplies information not explicit in the text; in this book, limited to a (broad) phonetic transcription using the characters and conventions of the International Phonetic Alphabet

transliteration   a one-to-one transposition of the signs of a text into the signs of another writing system; in this book, following the conventions of individual fields of study (thus the transliteration *ṭ* has different interpretations in Semitic and Indic studies)

UNKN   unknown

VOC   vocative

vowel   a brief portion of an utterance in which no obstruction to the air stream is created throughout the vocal tract; also, a character designating such a sound

writing system   a signary together with an associated orthography

Part I: Grammatology

HUMANKIND IS DEFINED BY LANGUAGE; but civilization is defined by writing. Writing made historical records possible, and writing was the basis for the urban societies of the Old World. All humans speak; only humans in civilizations write, so speech is primary, and writing is secondary. Nonetheless, written rather than spoken language has received attention from scholars since antiquity: standards were codified and rules were formulated. An educated minority attempted to speak as they wrote, and they assumed special prestige with command of these artificial rules and standards. All the while, the majority who spoke as they had learned from the cradle maintained their native tongues in their evolving vitality and vibrancy. Language changes continually, but writing cannot keep up, both because of social conservatism and because permanent documents remain as a continual reminder of the past standards.

Linguistics, the modern science of language, has properly taken spoken language and its structure as its main object of study. (Philology, a science with a distinguished pedigree, studies civilizations as revealed in their documents: it is the counterpart of archeology, which investigates cultures through their physical remains. An archeologist who discovers a text entrusts it to a philologist for interpretation.) Written language itself (the medium as opposed to the content of documents) has of late been taken into the scope of linguistics. But writing systems per se, the marks that record the languages of the documents produced by the civilizations, have absorbed the attention of only a very few linguists. No name for this field of study has even become widely accepted; "grammatology," proposed in the mid twentieth century, is better than most.

Grammatology, like linguistics in general, must be descriptive, historical, and theoretical. The characters of each writing system must be inventoried and their use and interpretation ascertained. Since many writing systems of the past have survived, this process can enter greater time depth with more security than is possible for the linguistics that studies spoken, necessarily contemporary, languages. Nonetheless, of course, the historical record is far from complete, so interrelationships among contemporary scripts and those known from earlier times need to be puzzled out, just as with languages.

Writing differs from language, though, in a very fundamental way. Language is a natural product of the human mind—the properties of people that make it possible for everyone to learn any language, provided they start at a young enough age—while writing is a deliberate product of human intellect: no infant illiterate absorbs its script along with its language; writing must be studied. Language continually develops and changes without the conscious interference of its speakers, but writing can be petrified or reformed or adapted or adopted at will. It is thus in the theoretical realm that grammatology differs most from the rest of linguistics—the theory of writing must be very different from the theory of language. It is not to be expected that patterns or principles that describe language should apply to writing, but little attention has yet been paid to that fact.

Languages, perpetually changing and accompanying their speakers through population expansions, migrations, and conquests, have one past; scripts, perpetuated by civilizations and intellectuals with a penchant for going among "savages" to bestow the "blessings of civilization" upon them, have a different history. While all human languages probably own a common ancestor (albeit so long ago that there is no hope of determining its substance), there seem to have been at least three—and possibly as many as seven—distinct, independent origins of writing in the ancient world. Earliest was probably the cuneiform writing devised for Sumerian (or even some other language, of which all trace has been lost), which seems to have been the inspiration for Egyptian Hieroglyphic. The second of the three was Chinese, which came to be adopted in Japan and Korea, and imitated in other areas under China's influence. The third took place in Mesoamerica, culminating in the Maya script that has begun to be understood by modern scholars.

Egyptian hieroglyphic in turn probably inspired the Canaanite script, whose offshoots became the scripts of all of Europe and most of Asia. At the root of this tree is a system that recorded consonants only, one per character, what I call the Semitic *abjad*. Perhaps nearly simultaneously at the eastern and western extremes of the ancient Near East, this system was augmented with notations for vowels on quite different principles: In the Mediterranean, they came to be written with individual characters, resulting in the Greek alphabet that underlies all the scripts of Europe and its worldwide extensions. In India, they became appendages to the consonants, in the Brahmi writing system that in turn underlies all the scripts of South and Southeast Asia. (Scions of both branches penetrated Inner Asia, and the script of Ethiopia seems to represent a blending of the two.) Some centuries later, the abjads themselves—Syriac, Hebrew, Arabic—added vocalizations that did not impinge on the consonantal text and remain optional.

No fewer than six different ways of relating the signs of a script to the sounds of a language have arisen, through human ingenuity. Such variety, not reducible to any underlying unity, is further evidence that writing cannot be treated in the same way as language. The outlines of a science of writing systems are presented below.

— PETER T. DANIELS

The Study of Writing Systems

PETER T. DANIELS

___

Grammatology

The word *grammatology* was adopted by I. J. Gelb, author of the first linguistically sound theoretical study of writing systems (1952), to refer—in preference to *graphology*, which was already used for the practice of reading a person's character by handwriting analysis—to the science he pioneered. (The term was subsequently taken over, with acknowledgment, in a very different sense by the philosopher Jacques Derrida.) The name parallels *phonology* and *morphology*, the branches of linguistics that study sounds and meaningful units.

A science begins with the identification and definition of its object of study. In the case of *writing*, we must distinguish several senses—here we are not concerned with writing as the motions the hand makes in creating written symbols ("That calligrapher writes beautifully"), nor with writing as the careful arrangement of language ("That essayist writes beautifully"). Rather, writing is defined as *a system of more or less permanent marks used to represent an utterance in such a way that it can be recovered more or less exactly without the intervention of the utterer.* By this definition, writing is bound up with language; consequently, the widespread practice of recording by means of pictures (*pictograms*) of *ideas* that are not couched in a specific linguistic form is excluded. Such pictograms are often designated *forerunners* of writing (e.g. Gelb 1952), but in fact writing systems (or *scripts*) do not develop from them (DeFrancis 1989).

Pictography is not writing, because languages include many things that cannot be represented by pictures: not only obvious things like abstract notions and many verbs, but also grammatical inflections and particles, and names. Even if the drawing skill of communicators in a language were such that identifiable portraits of individual people (and animals and places and so on) could be created whenever the individuals were mentioned, the significance of such drawings would soon be lost. It is thus necessary for a writing system to represent the *sounds* of a language.

A term often used in connection with writing is *grapheme*. This word is modeled on the linguistic terms *phoneme* and *morpheme* (significant units of sound and of meaning); but because of the fundamental difference between writing and language

---

ACKNOWLEDGMENTS: For comments on drafts of SECTIONS 1, 2, and/or 52, I am grateful to William Bright, Jerry Cooper, Piotr Michalowski, Michael Patrick O'Connor, Pierre Swiggers, and especially Sara Mandell.

(see page 2), the usual understanding of the suffix *-eme* does not apply (it marks units in a language—or in a culture generally—that "make a difference": [θ] and [s] are distinct phonemes in English, cf. *thing/sing*, but not in French). Too many attributes of phonemes find no parallel among "graphemes," and many attributes of the units of writing systems are not paralleled in sound systems (Daniels 1991, 1994; Kohrt 1986 summarizes his massive 1985). Most obviously, linguistics finds that, however different two languages may sound, in some fundamental way all languages are essentially the same—humans in general, regardless of ancestry, can learn any language; and specifically, that the same principles of phonology apply to all languages, however much they differ in their inventory of phonemes.

On the other hand, half a dozen fundamentally different types of writing systems have been devised with respect to how symbols relate to the sounds of language (and there's no reason more types could not be invented). In a *logosyllabary*, the characters of a script denote individual words (or morphemes) as well as particular syllables. In a *syllabary*, the characters denote particular syllables, and there is no systematic graphic similarity between the characters for phonetically similar syllables. In a consonantary, here called an *abjad* as a parallel to "alphabet" (the word is formed from the first letters of the most widespread example, the Arabic script, in their historic order; cf. SECTION 68), the characters denote consonants (only). In an *alphabet*, the characters denote consonants and vowels. In an *abugida*, each character denotes a consonant accompanied by a specific vowel, and the other vowels are denoted by a consistent modification of the consonant symbols, as in Indic scripts. (The word is Ethiopic, from the first four consonants and the first four vowels of the traditional order of the script, cf. SECTION 68; the type has been called neosyllabary [Février], pseudo-alphabet [Householder], and semisyllabary [Diringer].* But these terms misleadingly suggest that the abugida is a subtype, or hybrid, of alphabet or syllabary—a notion that has led to unfortunate historical/evolutionary notions about the history of writing.) In a *featural* system, like Korean or "phonotypic" shorthand, the shapes of the characters correlate with distinctive features of the segments of the language.

Note that purely *logographic* writing is not possible: for a script to adequately represent a language, it must not only represent its words, but also must be able to represent names and foreign words—even if it were possible to have a character for every word in a language, it would still be necessary to be able to represent its sounds so that such items from outside the system could be communicated. It is also noteworthy that virtually every extant syllabary represents syllables comprising (besides a vowel alone) a consonant (C) followed by a vowel (V), rather than VC or CVC syllables.

---

*Bright's *alphasyllabary* (see SECTION 31) is apparently not intended as an equivalent of these functional terms, but refers to the formal property of denoting vowels by marks that are not of the same status as consonants, and do not occur in a linear order corresponding to the temporal order of utterance.

The study of diverse writing systems requires some acquaintance with the pho-netics of the world's languages. In this work, the International Phonetic Alphabet is taken as a reference standard, and all discussion of the sounds of languages uses its symbols as revised in 1989 (see ENDPAPERS). The articulatory correlates of the sym-bols (i.e., how one pronounces the world's linguistic sounds) are beyond our scope; see SECTION 71 for a summary, and John Laver's monumental *Principles of Phonet-ics* (1994) for a full treatment. The reader who is not familiar with the field would do better to turn to the standard works of the three teachers Laver acknowledges: Aber-crombie (1967) has a special interest in phonetic notation systems; Ladefoged (1975) is the classroom standard; and Catford (1988) gives nearly sure-fire instructions for properly pronouncing any sound used in language.

It is often supposed that writing was devised for the purpose of communicating at a distance—in order to send messages that did not rely upon the memory of the messenger. But this seems to be a case of overlooking the obvious: the sending of messages, and the writing of books for posterity, are happily accidental byproducts. The earliest uses of writing seems to be to communicate things that really don't have oral equivalents (Cooper 1989: 323f., 329f.). In Mesopotamia, the earliest documents are business records: quantities of livestock, lists of workers and their rations and tasks. In China, the oldest writing is found in oracles addressing queries to the gods (though it has been inferred that commercial applications that have not survived ap-peared a little earlier and underlie the oracles; Keightley 1989). In Mesoamerica, as-tronomical, life cycle, and other calendrical information is the primary topic of the many texts that can be interpreted.

History of the study of writing

From earliest times, in Mesopotamia and in Classical Greece, the grammatical study of language meant the study of written language (Lepschy 1994, vols. 1–2). But the writing systems themselves were overlooked, or looked right through. The Greeks be-lieved their alphabet had been brought to them by a Phoenician named Cadmus. The Sumerians believed their script was an invention of the gods (SECTION 3), and the closest they came to historical investigation was the compilation of lists of obsolete signforms, so that ancient documents could be read (and, on occasion, forged: Gelb 1949 shows that a large stela that looks Old Akkadian was actually written much lat-er).

The European Renaissance awoke interest in the study of early Greek and Latin manuscripts; explorers brought back both antiquities and contemporary manuscripts bearing writing in exotic scripts; subsequently, colonial administrators needed to un-derstand their subjects' texts and to publish their own edicts in native languages. From the sixteenth century, specimens of such exotica found their way into illustra-tions and even type, and from the late seventeenth, the modern institution of the schol-arly journal was in place. In such publications as the *Transactions of the Royal*

Society, the *Mémoires de l'Académie des Inscriptions et Belles Lettres*, and *Asiatick Researches*, scholars such as Edmond Halley, Jean-Jacques Barthélemy, and William Jones presented pioneering work on scripts of ancient and modern Asia (SECTION 9). The *Journal Asiatique, Zeitschrift der Deutschen Morgenländischen Gesellschaft*, and *Journal of the Royal Asiatic Society* (with branches in many lands), among many others, began to carry reports of explorers and missionaries about the languages and scripts they were encountering.

Western scholars cautiously freed themselves from literal interpretations of the biblical account of the Tower of Babel (though the Bible is silent on the institution of writing), and began to trace the historical relationships among languages and among writing systems. It took some doing to keep those two topics separate: early interpreters of Mesopotamian cuneiform were led astray by the supposition that—if the language it recorded was Semitic (a reasonable, and correct, guess)—then the script must, like those of the Semitic languages Hebrew and Arabic, record only consonants. This hypothesis had to be abandoned before progress could be made (SECTION 9). One of the most influential scholars in the early nineteenth century, whose name is now absent from the histories of philology—perhaps he has been forgotten because he was a generalist—is Ulrich Friedrich Kopp. His *Bilder und Schriften der Vorzeit* (1821) is a very rare book, but it includes pioneering investigations in many fields, including European and Semitic antiquities. His work would well repay careful study, though no single modern scholar would be competent to evaluate it in its entirety.

Toward the end of the nineteenth century, scholars began to devote entire books to writing systems. The earliest is Karl Faulmann's *Geschichte der Schrift* (1880, with a companion volume of specimens, *Buch der Schrift*). The coverage is very broad, but the sensibility is premodern and rather mystical. The first book on writing from a scientific perspective is Isaac Taylor's *The Alphabet* (1883). Fully half of it is devoted to the scripts of India, and some of the factual material included thereon can be found nowhere else. It seems to be Taylor who first laid out (vol. 1, p. 6) the tripartite typology of writing systems—logographic, syllabic, alphabetic—that has dominated grammatology for more than a century, though it has been attributed to Edward Burnett Tylor, "father of anthropology" (1865). This may be a simple confusion of the more familiar name with the more obscure, for Tylor seems not to have made any finer distinction than picture-writing vs. phonetic writing (e.g., 1881, chap. 7).

The twentieth century has brought a number of popular treatments of writing, many of which are still to be found in public libraries and used-book stores. Readily available—and often cited—are such works as Clodd 1904, Mason 1920, Ogg 1948, Moorhouse 1953, and Ober 1965. Volumes like these often include attractive illustrations, but they tend to perpetuate misinformation. In a different class are Diringer 1958, 1962, and Gaur 1992. These are works by scholars for the general public (Gaur's is superbly illustrated from the collections of the British Museum and Library). Still another type of writing-book is the collection of specimens: *The Book of a Thousand Tongues* (Nida 1972), which celebrates the translation work of the United

Bible Societies, includes a wealth and variety of information on its hundreds of non-Roman specimens. Nakanishi (1980) presents whatever will fit onto a single page of the actual workings of twenty-nine scripts (the criterion for inclusion being use in a daily newspaper), along with samples of dozens of others. The details may occasionally go astray, but this is a valuable resource. Lastly, there have been a number of coffee-table books, in various languages, with sumptuous illustrations and dubious textual value; on the other hand, the catalogs of museum exhibitions increasingly lead to the next category, with both beautiful photographs *and* essays by competent experts (but they tend to achieve limited distribution, so none are listed here).

Modern scholarly books on writing fall in two classes. There are historical catalogs: Cohen 1958, Diringer 1968, Février 1959, Fossey 1948, Friedrich 1966, Jensen 1969. Of this group, Février tends to exhibit the soundest judgment, Friedrich's is the easiest to use, and Jensen provides the most copious bibliography. Cohen includes the most information, but if there is any organization to the material, it is not obvious. Diringer's treatment is very readable, but bibliographic references are absent or inadequate. Fossey's many specialists are reliable, and their remarks are orientated toward practical advice for typesetters of the languages of the Orient. Driver 1976 is wide-ranging and copiously illustrated. A bridge to the next category is the work of Harald Haarmann (1990), who presents the essential materials for the history of writing but in a conceptual, rather than strictly chronological, order.

In 1952, I. J. Gelb published the first linguistically informed study of writing. Like all the books mentioned below, it is shaped by its author's specialties, Gelb's being the earliest stages of the Semitic language Akkadian (as a very young man, he had also led in the decipherment of Luvian hieroglyphs). Gelb was also a great systematizer: he was never happier than when finding patterns in disparate phenomena, and this mindset on occasion led him to *over*systematize, as happened in his evolutionary explanation of the tripartite typology of writing. Gelb claimed that syllabaries could only develop from logographies, and that alphabets could only develop from syllabaries, and that these steps could be neither skipped nor reversed. He called this sequence the "principle of unidirectional development," and this principle has become the accepted view. The difficulties arising from it are described in the next subsection.

Gelb always said he intended his book to be the first, not the last, word on the theory of writing. But it was more than three decades before successors appeared—Sampson 1985, Coulmas 1989, DeFrancis 1989—and Gelb did not live to see them. Sampson's work is tendentious, and he includes the "forerunners" in his catalog of writings; his accounts of Linear B and of Korean script are especially good. Coulmas concentrates on the place of writing in society. DeFrancis debunks notions of the "forerunners" of writing and of the "ideographic" nature of Chinese writing. DeFrancis is a specialist in Chinese, and Gaur in the languages of India; Sampson and Coulmas do not demonstrate a bias in their materials from which a specialty can be identified. All four authors seem to make up for Gelb's orientation (and errors) by misstating assorted bits of information regarding ancient Near Eastern scripts.

The typology of writing systems

As has already become clear, a variety of typologies of scripts have been proposed. The tripartite scheme of logography, syllabary, alphabet was the first real one and has remained the most popular; but it led to certain unlikely suggestions about the nature of certain scripts, and several alternatives have been offered.

Gelb's insistence on the principle of unidirectional development led him to proclaim that the Phoenician script (from which the Greek alphabet developed) was not an alphabet, as it was commonly known, but rather a syllabary with indeterminate vowels; and that the Ethiopic script (which developed from it via the South Arabian script) is not a syllabary, but that its classification is problematic. Both of these assertions are counterintuitive and seemingly counterfactual: the Phoenician script *does not* identify syllables, and the Ethiopic script *does*! Owing to the importance of Gelb's work, one nowadays regularly finds the West Semitic scripts referred to as syllabaries by authors who have not made a special study of the topic.

There are two sources for the awkwardness of this nomenclature. One is the unquestioning acceptance of the tripartite typology: the problem disappears when scripts need no longer be assigned to only three classes. (Justeson and Stephens 1993 believe they have refuted Gelb's theory by adducing an impressive collection of examples of "syllabaries" derived from "alphabets"; but the refinement of the typology renders the exercise unnecessary.) It must simply be recognized (Daniels 1990) that abjads are not (any longer) syllabaries and not (yet) alphabets, and that abugidas—though they denote syllables—are not like syllabaries, since vowels receive identification equivalent to that for consonants.

The other source of difficulty is the notion of applying the concept of *evolution* to products of the human mind. As normally understood, evolution is the result of natural selection operating on random variation. So, while evolution can be understood as the source of human linguistic ability, and a metaphorical extension of the term applies to the diversification of human languages, it cannot be taken as appropriate to the history of writing. Changes in scripts are successive *improvements* (or at least attempts at improvement), rather than evolutions. Only the change in the shapes of characters with successive generations might be seen as evolution, but they are always held in check by the authority of the teacher and by the need to be able to read older documents.

Note that Gelb, as well as DeFrancis (cf. Sampson 1994) and this volume, exclude from the category of writing systems those graphic expressions that do not reflect the sounds of the language. The Soviet scholar Viktor Istrin (1953, 1957) defines writing as serving to transmit *language* at a distance in space or time; on this basis he admits a four-way typology of pictographic, ideographic, syllabic, and phonetic writing. But since pictography records "an entire sentence, proposition, or communication, not yet clearly divided by signs into separate words" (1972 [1953]: 362), how can it be said to transmit language at all? Istrin's "ideograms" do not in fact record "ideas" (Gelb rightly banished the term from our science, preferring *logogram*) but rather individual words or their significant parts. He notes, therefore, that the sound of the word can be linked to the logogram or not (the latter as in the determinatives of Mesopotamian cuneiform or Egyptian, the Sumerograms of Akkadian or Hittite, or the mathematical signs of English). Istrin does not mention any examples of what are here called abugidas, so it is unclear whether he would count them as syllabaries. He usefully identifies three kinds of alphabetic writing: phonetic, where the orthography of words corresponds to their current pronunciation (e.g. schemes of phonetic transcription); phonologico-morphological, which we would call morphophonemic, with unique orthography of phonemes—and of morphemes as well—even when, for phonetic reasons, their pronunciation varies in different grammatical forms (e.g. Russian); and historico-traditional, where the orthography of words corresponds to their former pronunciation (e.g. French and English—though it is now clear that the conservatism of these orthographies is advantageous, in that much morphophonemic information, the result of change in the language, is organized in their apparent chaos). Istrin mentions a further possible classification of scripts, grouping them into families of common origin; moreover, such a scheme has been worked out, using synchronic characteristics as well as awareness of their history, for a wide range of scripts, in Herrick 1974.

A. A. Hill (1967) classifies scripts according to their relation to the units of the different "levels" at which language is studied in descriptive linguistics: discourse systems, morphemic systems, and phonemic systems. Since all systems omit some of the linguistic structure from the record (morphemic systems omit phonemic information; phonemic systems omit stress and usually pitch), it's not odd to say that discourse systems—what are here called pictographic—omit *all* the linguistic structure! "Discourse systems are unique only in that they do not demand that the reader know the language of the recorded utterance, and rely instead to a very heavy extent on knowledge of the non-linguistic background" (p. 94)—even though "the purpose of writing can be said to be unique identification of an utterance" (p 93).

A different approach to typology, looking at letters rather than languages, is taken by Voegelin and Voegelin (1961, wherein *alphabet* apparently refers to *any* phonographic script). They begin with the characters of scripts and consider the systems that comprise them. There are four kinds: CVD, *consonant* signs which distinguish adjacent *vowels* by graphemic *dissimilarity*; CVS, consonant signs which distinguish adjacent vowels by graphemic *similarity* for a particular consonant [and, of course, for particular vowels]; IC, *independent* consonant signs; and IV, independent *vowel* signs. The five attested combinations of such units—CVD+IV (syllabaries), IC (abjads), IC+CVD (the only example is Ugaritic), IC+IV (alphabets), and CVS+IV (abugidas)—are called *self-sufficient alphabets*; they are opposed to *alphabet included logographic systems* (Chinese, Egyptian, Luvian, Maya) and to *alphabet excluded mnemonic systems*, encompassing pictographic writing (though *writing* itself goes undefined!) as well as quipus and "motion languages" (i.e. Plains Indian Sign Language, rather than sign languages of the deaf, which are languages fully equal in structure and complexity to spoken languages and not a transference into gesture of any spoken language). Voegelin and Voegelin are caught up in the euphoria ensuing from the decipherment of Linear B, and they are nearly prescient in recognizing the significance of the nascent decipherment of Maya glyphs. Their article still deserves perusal for their remarks on many aspects of the study of writing.

T. V. Gamkrelidze (1994) applies the Saussurean notions of *paradigmatic* and *syntagmatic* relations (respectively, mutual substitutability in a particular position in an utterance, and relations among successive elements of an utterance) to the description of script types: an alphabet encodes segments in both ways, while an abjad encodes segments paradigmatically and syllables syntagmatically.

The study of writing

The fortunes of writing in modern linguistics have fallen and risen. When the focus of linguistics shifted from historical philology, which investigated the development of (primarily) the Indo-European languages on the basis of ancient records and of comparison of attested tongues, to the description of new-met languages that had never been written—a shift largely occasioned by the American encounter with exotic, and dying, indigenous populations—writing itself was concomitantly devalued: if unfamiliar languages could, as it turned out, be fully described without the intermediary of historic records, did that not show that writing was secondary, and all languages should be described in purely oral mode? The outcome was *descriptive linguistics*, which strove to present language as it is used (see page 12 on F. de Saussure; the *locus classicus* is Bloomfield 1933). Bound up with this enterprise was insistence on lack of value judgments. The languages of those who had been called "savages" proved as rich and expressive as any European language, however different they appeared to be; it was hard to maintain claims of mental or racial inferiority before such evidence. This attitude was reimported to the study of, say, English (e.g. the polemics of Hall 1950), resulting in reference works that were *descriptive* rather than *prescriptive* (e.g. reaction to the publication of the Merriam-Webster *Third New International Dictionary*: Sledd and Ebbitt 1962, Morton 1994): language as it *is* rather than as it *should be*; language is not *correct* or *incorrect*—it is *appropriate* or *inappropriate*. Prescriptivists, on the other hand, tend to insist that only written language can be formal language, and that only formal language can be correct; spoken language is consequently devalued. Such reaction has preoccupied indignant "language police" or "language mavens" who, apparently without considering the basis of descriptivism, insist that it is the cause, rather than the reflection, of what they regard as the "corruption" of the language. They would forbid (as if it were possible) traits of colloquial speaking from entering written discourse. No linguist, however, would deny that a more formal register of speech is appropriate in a more formal situation.

Another productive approach to linguistics emerged when Joseph Greenberg discovered "implicational universals" of language, which are statements along the lines of "If a language usually puts its verbs before its objects, then it probably also usually puts prepositions before its nouns" (as in English; compare Japanese, with the opposite patterns). His disciple John Justeson (1976) came up with a series of statements reagarding writing systems, such as "[1] All writing systems distinguishing any phonemes contain signs distinguishing some consonantal phonemes," "[7] Alphabets are more likely to represent loan-word phonemes separately than are syllabaries," and "[32] If /l/ is not represented in a script, neither is /r/." These are empirical findings, and they would repay study to discover whether they are accidental or bear on the nature of the relations between script and language.

Orthography has found its way into linguistics in the discipline called *generative phonology*, developed by Morris Halle and taken up by Noam Chomsky. This system accounts for the varying phonological shapes of words (and morphemes) by, in effect, asserting that individual speakers recapitulate the chronological sequence of changes in the sound system of their language: what they hold in their heads is a lexicon of "underlying forms" and a set of rules that change them—and the underlying forms, not surprisingly, correspond very closely to the orthographic forms of the words, leading to the valid claim that "English orthography turns out to be rather close to an optimal system for spelling English" (Chomsky and Halle 1968: 184 n. 19).

More generally, it ought to be kept in mind that what even the purest descriptive linguistics analyzes nearly always *is* a written text—the product of, ideally, careful transcription of casual speech (which became more feasible with the introduction of sound recording), or sometimes, careful correction of a text in cooperation with native-speaker consultants (Murray 1983). There is also a field of Native American philology, whose business is to reconstruct the pronunciation of the texts and isolated words and phrases collected by writers in the Colonial period, recorded more or less accurately using the sound–spelling correspondence conventions of the English, Spanish, or French of the time (Goddard 1973). What we have in all these cases is descriptive grammars of spoken language *written down*.

Largely outside the United States, there is a tradition of studying written language as a register of language that is taken to be qualitatively *different from*, albeit not *superior to*, spoken language. The principal names in the field are the Czech scholar Josef Vachek, whose *Written Language Revisited* (1989) collects a half century of articles; and the British-Australian linguist M. A. K. Halliday, whose systemic linguistics seeks to involve patterns of discourse well beyond the level of sentence at which descriptive linguistics (encompassing both Leonard Bloomfield and Noam Chomsky, with all the apparent diversity of their many disciples; Matthews 1993) until recently called a halt to analysis. Linguists in the American tradition who have gone on to larger stretches of language continue to focus on spoken dialogue, whereas Halliday has also investigated the structure of written prose. Halliday and Martin

1993 includes several chapters written for non-linguists and represents perhaps the most accessible entrée to the approach.

The theoretical underpinnings of descriptive (which became structural) linguistics were laid down in the second decade of the twentieth century by Ferdinand de Saussure (1916), who had done revolutionary work on Indo-European. He codified the distinction between historical and descriptive linguistics, and firmly established that writing is secondary to speaking; for Saussure, language comprises *signs*, which embody a *signifier* (sound) and a *signified* (meaning), and these signs are *arbitrary* and *linear*. These postulates have been axiomatic ever since, but Roy Harris (1990, most clearly) challenges them all. He is unwilling to separate the current state of a language from its past, or its spoken from its written form (or language as a whole from other forms of communication). The denial of linearity—succession of spoken elements in a single temporal dimension—is most relevant to the linguistics of writing. On the one hand, the existence of complete texts, written down, means that stretches of language can be referred to out of the sequence of their production. On the other, and most importantly for writing systems, Harris reminds us (1986) that phonetics has shown the stream of speech not to be segmentable into units corresponding to letters—that is, into phonemes; syllables are the smallest linguistic units with physical existence (cf. SECTION 52). For Harris, the phenomenon of phonemes is an artifact of alphabetic writing. One need not accept his deconstruction of the field of linguistics, but his proposal deserves serious consideration.

Related topics

Beyond the scope of *The World's Writing Systems*, but too important to go unmentioned, are two fertile fields of scholarship, concerned with the psychology of reading and with the phenomenon of literacy. A collection reporting a pioneering conference of both linguists and psychologists is Kavanagh and Mattingly (1972), and a selection of papers from a 1988 conference on linguistics and literacy is published by Downing, Lima, and Noonan (1992). The acquisition of written language—i.e., learning to read—is one of the most important tasks of modern youth. This has been one of the most intensely studied areas of psycholinguistics (e.g. Gibson and Levin 1975, Henderson 1982; Kennedy 1984 and McLane and McNamee 1990 address the general reader), and a source of endless controversy among educationists. Indeed, psycholinguists overall have a tendency to investigate the performance of subjects on tasks involving written language, and to assume that they are discovering how human minds process language in general. This assumption seems to be not quite legitimate, in part at least because it is difficult to understand how any part of the human brain can have evolved to specialize in writing (as opposed to talking): such a process—operating over the last five thousand years or so—would have required some reproductive advantage to be connected with literacy, and it is not the case that literate humans have produced offspring at the expense of non-literate ones.

TABLE 1.1: *Studies in the History of Western Literacy*

Period	References
Classical Greece	Thomas 1989, 1992
Classical Rome	Harris 1989
Medieval Europe	Chaytor 1945, McKitterick 1989, 1990
Medieval England	Clanchy 1979
European Renaissance	Febvre and Martin 1976, Eisenstein 1979
Elizabethan England	Goldberg 1990
Early United States	Simpson 1986, Murray 1991

The study of literacy falls into two parts. There is the problem of illiteracy in the modern world, both in the technologically advanced nations, and in the developing countries where no tradition—or claim—of universal literacy exists. Some useful readings—excluding the large literature on language planning—include de Castell, Luke, and Egan 1986; Graubard 1991; Kintgen, Kroll, and Rose 1988; Olson and Torrance 1991; Olson, Torrance, and Hildyard 1985; Pattison 1982; Street 1984; and Stubbs 1980. This is the domain of, again, educationists, but also of politicians and political scientists, of economists and business executives. We may hope that enhanced knowledge of writing systems may at least inform their deliberations.

The history of literacy, in Western civilization at least, has in the last few decades been well studied—nearly every era has been examined in monographic works (the references in TABLE 1.1 are not claimed to be exhaustive), and general syntheses have begun to appear that show the importance of written materials through the course of European and American culture (Graff 1987, Martin 1988, Olson 1994). Baines (1983) and Michalowski (1994) have done pioneering work on literacy in the ancient Near East. Anthropologists and philosophers consider the impact of the written word in the modern world, affecting both previously nonliterate cultures (e.g. Goody 1968, 1977, 1986, 1987; Scribner and Cole 1981; Street 1993) and the modern West (e.g. Ong 1977, 1982; Illich and Sanders 1988). Marshall McLuhan, e.g. 1962, is notorious, and found a disciple in Logan 1986; the similar suppositions of Eric Havelock are discussed in SECTION 2. Barton (1994) provides an integrated, though simplified, overview. As with some topics noted earlier, for general historians it seems that the written word is too close at hand to be noticed at all. The very documents that make history possible have been studied for their content, but not for themselves.

Bibliography

GRAMMATOLOGY AND ITS HISTORY

Abercrombie, David. 1967. *Elements of General Phonetics*. Edinburgh: Edinburgh University Press; Chicago: Aldine.

Catford, J. C. 1988. *A Practical Introduction to Phonetics*. Oxford: Clarendon.

Clodd, Edward. 1904. *The Story of the Alphabet*. New York: Appleton.

Cohen, Marcel. 1958. *La grande invention de l'écriture et son évolution.* 3 vols. Paris: Imprimerie Nationale.

Cooper, Jerrold S. 1989. "Writing." *International Encyclopedia of Communications.* New York: Oxford University Press.

Coulmas, Florian. 1989. *The Writing Systems of the World.* Oxford: Blackwell.

Daniels, Peter T. 1991. "Is a Structural Graphemics Possible?" *LACUS Forum* 18: 528–37.

———. 1994. "Reply to Herrick." *LACUS Forum* 21: 425–31.

DeFrancis, John. 1989. *Visible Speech: The Diverse Oneness of Writing Systems.* Honolulu: University of Hawaii Press.

Diringer, David. 1958. *The Story of the Aleph Beth.* New York: Philosophical Library.

———. 1962. *Writing* (Ancient People and Places 25). New York: Praeger.

———. 1968. *The Alphabet: A Key to the History of Mankind,* 3rd ed. 2 vols. New York: Funk & Wagnalls.

Driver, Godfrey Rolles. 1976. *Semitic Writing: From Pictograph to Alphabet* (Schweich Lectures of the British Academy, 1944), 3rd ed., ed. Simon A. Hopkins. London: Oxford University Press.

Faulmann, Karl. 1880. *Das Buch der Schrift, enthaltend die Schriftzeichen und Alphabeten aller Zeiten und aller Völker des Erdkreises,* 2nd ed. Vienna: K.K. Hof- und Staatsdruckerei. Repr. Nördlingen: Greno, 1985.

———. 1880. *Illustrierte Geschichte der Schrift: Populär-wissenschaftliche Darstellung der Entstehung der Schrift der Sprache und der Zahlen sowie der Schriftsysteme aller Völker der Erde.* Vienna. Repr. Nördlingen: Greno, 1989.

Février, James-Germain. 1959. *Histoire de l'écriture,* 2nd ed. Paris: Payot.

Fossey, Charles, ed. 1948. *Notices sur les caractères étrangers anciens et modernes.* Paris: Imprimerie Nationale.

Friedrich, Johannes. 1966. *Geschichte der Schrift unter besonderer Berücksichtigung ihrer geistigen Entwicklung.* Heidelberg: Winter.

Gaur, Albertine. 1992. *A History of Writing.* rev. ed. London: British Library; New York: Abbeville.

Gelb, I. J. 1949. "The Date of the Cruciform Monument of Maništušu." *Journal of Near Eastern Studies* 8: 346–48.

———. 1952. *A Study of Writing.* Chicago: University of Chicago Press. Rev. ed., 1963.

Haarmann, Harald. 1990. *Universalgeschichte der Schrift.* Frankfurt: Campus Verlag.

Householder, Fred W., Jr. 1959. "More on Mycenean" [review article]. *Classical Journal* 54: 379–83.

Jensen, Hans. 1969. *Sign, Symbol and Script,* 3rd ed., trans. George Unwin. London: George Allen & Unwin; New York: Putnam's.

Keightley, David N. 1989. "The Origins of Writing in China: Scripts and Cultural Contexts." In *The Origins of Writing,* ed. Wayne M. Senner, pp. 171–202. Lincoln: University of Nebraska Press.

Kohrt, Manfred. 1985. *Problemgeschichte des Graphembegriffs und des frühen Phonembegriffs* (Reihe Germanistische Linguistik 61). Tübingen: Niemeyer.

———. 1986. "The Term 'Grapheme' in the History and Theory of Linguistics." In *New Trends in Graphemics and Orthography,* ed. Gerhard Augst, pp. 80–96. Berlin: de Gruyter.

Kopp, Ulrich Friedrich. 1821. *Bilder und Schriften der Vorzeit.* 2 vols. Mannheim.

Ladefoged, Peter. 1975. *A Course in Phonetics.* New York: Harcourt Brace Jovanovich.

Laver, John. 1994. *Principles of Phonetics* (Cambridge Textbooks in Linguistics). Cambridge: Cambridge University of Press.

Lepschy, Giulio C., ed. 1994– . *History of Linguistics.* 4 vols. London: Longmans. (Italian original, 1990.)

Mason, William A. 1920. *A History of the Art of Writing.* New York: Macmillan.

Moorhouse, Alfred C. 1953. *The Triumph of the Alphabet: A History of Writing.* New York: Schuman.

Nakanishi, Akira. 1980. *Writing Systems of the World: Alphabets · Syllabaries · Pictograms.* Rutland, Vt.: Tuttle. (Japanese original, 1975.)

Nida, Eugene, ed. 1972. *Book of a Thousand Tongues,* 2nd ed. London: United Bible Societies.

Ober, J. Hamilton. 1965. *Writing: Man's Greatest Invention.* Baltimore: Peabody Institution.

Ogg, Oscar. 1948. *The 26 Letters.* New York: Crowell.

Sampson, Geoffrey. 1985. *Writing Systems.* London: Hutchinson; Stanford: Stanford University Press.

Taylor, Isaac. 1883. *The Alphabet: An Account of the Origin and Development of Letters.* 2 vols. London: Kegan Paul, Trench.

Tylor, Edward Burnett. 1865. *Researches into the Early History of Mankind and the Development of Civilization.* London.

———. 1881. *Anthropology: An Introduction to the Study of Man and Civilization.* London. Repr. New York: Appleton, 1898 (International Scientific Series).

TYPOLOGY OF WRITING

Daniels, Peter T. 1990. "Fundamentals of Grammatology." *Journal of the American Oriental Society* 110: 727–31.

Gamkrelidze, Thomas V. 1994. *Alphabetic Writing and the Old Georgian Script: A Typology and Provenience of Alphabetic Writing Systems.* Delmar, N.Y.: Caravan Books. (Georgian and Russian original, 1989.)

Istrin, Viktor Aleksandrovich. 1953. "Nekotorye voprosy teorii pis'ma: Tipy pis'ma i ix sviaz' s jazykom." *Voprosy jazykoznanija* 4: 109–21. = "Relations entre les types d'écriture et la langue," trans. David Cohen. *Recherches internationales à la lumière du marxisme* 7 (1958): 35–60. Repr. in *Readings in Modern Linguistics: An Anthology,* ed. Bertil Malmberg, pp. 359–82. Stockholm: Läromedelsförlagen; The Hague: Mouton.

———. 1957. "L'écriture, sa classification, sa terminologie et les régularités de son développement." *Journal of World History* 4: 15–39.

Herrick, Earl M. 1974. "A Taxonomy of Alphabets and Scripts." *Visible Language* 8: 5–32.

Hill, Archibald A. 1967. "The Typology of Writing Systems." In *Papers in Linguistics in Honor of Léon Dostert* (Janua Linguarum Series Major 25), ed. William M. Austin, pp. 93–99. The Hague: Mouton.

Justeson, John, and Laurence D. Stephens. 1993. "The Evolution of Syllabaries from Alphabets: Transmission, Language Contrast, and Script Typology." *Die Sprache* 35: 2–46.

Sampson, Geoffrey. 1994. "Chinese Script and the Diversity of Writing Systems." *Linguistics* 32: 117–32.

Voegelin, C. F., and F. M. Voegelin. 1961. "Typological Classification of Systems with Included, Excluded and Self-Sufficient Alphabets." *Anthropological Linguistics* 3/1: 55–96.

STUDY OF WRITING

Bloomfield, Leonard. 1933. *Language.* New York: Holt.

Chomsky, Noam, and Morris Halle. 1968. *The Sound Pattern of English.* New York: Harper & Row.

Goddard, Ives. 1973. "Philological Approaches to the Study of North American Indian Languages: Documents and Documentation." In *Current Trends in Linguistics,* ed. Thomas A. Sebeok, vol. 10, *Linguistics in North America,* pp. 727–45. The Hague: Mouton.

Hall, Robert A., Jr. 1950. *Leave Your Language Alone!* Ithaca, N.Y.: Linguistica. Repr. as *Linguistics and Your Language,* Garden City, N.Y.: Doubleday Anchor, 1960.

Halliday, Michael A. K., and J. R. Martin. 1993. *Writing Science: Literacy and Discursive Power.* Pittsburgh: University of Pittsburgh Press.

Harris, Roy. 1986. *The Origin of Writing.* London: Duckworth; La Salle, Ill.: Open Court.

———. 1990. "On Redefining Linguistics." In *Redefining Linguistics,* ed. Hayley G. Davis and Talbot J. Taylor, pp. 18–52. London: Routledge.

Justeson, John. 1976. "Universals of Language and Universals of Writing." In *Linguistic Studies Offered to Joseph Greenberg,* ed. Alphonse Juilland, vol. 1, *General Linguistics,* pp. 57–94. Saratoga, Calif.: Anma Libri.

Matthews, Peter Hugoe. 1993. *Grammatical Theory in the United States from Bloomfield to Chomsky* (Cambridge Studies in Linguistics 67). Cambridge: Cambridge University Press.

Morton, Herbert C. 1994. *The Story of Webster's Third: Philip Gove's Controversial Dictionary and Its Critics.* Cambridge: Cambridge University Press.

Murray, Stephen O. 1983. "The Creation of Linguistic Structure." *American Anthropologist* 83: 356–62.

Saussure, Ferdinand de. 1916. *Cours de linguistique générale,* posthumous publication from students' lecture notes, ed. Charles Bally and Albert Sechehaye. Paris: Payot. Trans., as *Course in General Linguistics,* by Wade Baskin, New York: Philosphical Library, 1959 (repr. New York: McGraw-Hill, 1966); by Roy Harris, London: Duckworth, 1983 (repr. La Salle, Ill.: Open Court, 1986). Critical edition of the sources, ed. Rudolf Engler, Wiesbaden: Harrassowitz, 1967–74.

Sledd, James, and Wilma R. Ebbitt, eds. 1962. *Dictionaries and* That *Dictionary: A Casebook on the Aims of Lexicographers and the Targets of Reviewers.* Chicago: Scott, Foresman.

Vachek, Josef. 1989. *Written Language Revisited,* ed. Philip A. Luelsdorff. Amsterdam: Benjamins.

RELATED TOPICS

Baines, John. 1983. "Literacy and Ancient Egyptian Society." *Man* n.s. 18: 572–99.

Barton, David. 1994. *Literacy: An Introduction to the Ecology of Written Language.* Oxford: Blackwell.

Chaytor, Henry J. 1945. *From Script to Print: An Introduction to Medieval Vernacular Literature.* Cambridge: Cambridge University Press. Repr. Cambridge: Heffer., 1966.

Clanchy, M. T. 1979. *From Memory to Written Record: England, 1066–1307.* London: Arnold; Cambridge: Harvard University Press.

de Castell, Suzanne, Allan Luke, and Kieran Egan, eds. 1986. *Literacy, Society, and Schooling: A Reader.* Cambridge: Cambridge University Press.

Downing, Pamela, Susan D. Lima, and Michael Noonan, eds. 1992. *The Linguistics of Literacy* (Typological Studies in Language 21). Amsterdam: Benjamins.

Eisenstein, Elizabeth L. 1979. *The Printing Press as an Agent of Change: Communications and Cultural Transformations in Early-modern Europe.* 2 vols. Cambridge: Cambridge University Press.

Febvre, Lucien, and Henri-Jean Martin. 1976. *The Coming of the Book: The Impact of Printing 1450–1800.* London: NLB. (French original, 1958.)

Gibson, Eleanor J., and Harry Levin. 1975. *The Psychology of Reading.* Cambridge: MIT Press.

Goldberg, Jonathan. 1990. *Writing Matter: From the Hands of the English Renaissance.* Stanford: Stanford University Press.

Goody, Jack. 1977. *The Domestication of the Savage Mind.* Cambridge: Cambridge University Press.

———. 1986. *The Logic of Writing and the Organization of Society.* Cambridge: Cambridge University Press.

———. 1987. *The Interface between the Written and the Oral.* Cambridge: Cambridge Univ. Press.

Goody, Jack, ed. 1968. *Literacy in Traditional Societies.* Cambridge: Cambridge University Press.

Graff, Harvey J. 1987. *The Legacies of Literacy: Continuities and Contradictions in Western Culture and Society.* Bloomington: Indiana University Press.

Graubard, Stephen R., ed. 1991. *Literacy: An Overview by 14 Experts.* New York: Hill and Wang (=

Daedalus 119/2).

Harris, William V. 1989. *Ancient Literacy.* Cambridge: Harvard University Press.

Henderson, Leslie. 1982. *Orthography and Word Recognition in Reading.* London: Academic Press.

Illich, Ivan, and Barry Sanders. 1988. *ABC: The Alphabetization of the Popular Mind.* San Francisco: North Point Press. Repr. New York: Random House, 1989.

Kavanagh, James F., and Ignatius G. Mattingly, eds. 1972. *Language by Ear and by Eye: The Relationships between Speech and Reading.* Cambridge: MIT Press.

Kennedy, Alan. 1984. *The Psychology of Reading.* London: Methuen.

Kintgen, Eugene R., Barry M. Kroll, and Mike Rose, eds. 1988. *Perspectives on Literacy.* Carbondale: Southern Illinois University Press.

Logan, Robert K. 1986. *The Alphabet Effect: The Impact of the Phonetic Alphabet on the Development of Western Civilization.* New York: Morrow.

Martin, Henri-Jean. 1994. *The History and Power of Writing,* trans. Lydia G. Cochrane. Chicago: University of Chicago Press. (French original, 1988.)

McKitterick, Rosamond. 1989. *The Carolingians and the Written Word.* Cambridge: Cambridge University Press.

McKitterick, Rosamond, ed. 1990. *The Uses of Literacy in Early Mediaeval Europe.* Cambridge: Cambridge University Press.

McLane, Joan Brooks, and Gillian Dowley McNamee. 1990. *Early Literacy* (The Developing Child). Cambridge: Harvard University Press.

McLuhan, Marshall. 1962. *The Gutenberg Galaxy: The Making of Typographic Man.* Toronto: University of Toronto Press.

Michalowski, Piotr. 1994. "Writing and Literacy in Early States: A Mesopotamianist Perspective." In *Literacy: Interdisciplinary Conversations,* ed. Deborah Keller-Cohen. Cresskill, N.J.: Hampton.

Murray, David. 1991. *Speech, Writing and Representation in North American Indian Texts.* Bloomington: Indiana University Press.

Olson, David R. 1994. *The World on Paper: The Conceptual and Cognitive Implications of Writing and Reading.* Cambridge: Cambridge University Press.

Olson, David R., and Nancy Torrance, eds. 1991. *Literacy and Orality.* Cambridge: Cambridge University Press.

Olson, David R., Nancy Torrance, and Angela Hildyard, eds. 1985. *Literacy, Language, and Learning: The Nature and Consequences of Reading and Writing.* Cambridge: Cambridge Univ. Press.

Ong, Walter J., S.J. 1977. *Interfaces of the Word: Studies in the Evolution of Consciousness and Culture.* Ithaca, N.Y.: Cornell University Press.

———. 1982. *Orality and Literacy: The Technologizing of the Word.* London: Methuen.

Pattison, Robert. 1982. *On Literacy: The Politics of the Word from Homer to the Age of Rock.* New York: Oxford University Press.

Scribner, Sylvia, and Michael Cole. 1981. *The Psychology of Literacy.* Cambridge: Harvard University Press.

Simpson, David. 1986. *The Politics of American English, 1776–1850.* New York: Oxford Univ. Pr.

Street, Brian V. 1984. *Literacy in Theory and Practice.* Cambridge: Cambridge University Press.

Street, Brian V., ed. 1993. *Cross-cultural Approaches to Literacy.* Cambridge: Cambridge University Press.

Stubbs, Michael. 1980. *Language and Literacy: The Sociolinguistics of Reading and Writing.* London: Routledge & Kegan Paul.

Thomas, Rosalind. 1989. *Oral Tradition and Written Record in Classical Athens.* Cambridge: Cambridge University Press.

———. 1992. *Literacy and Orality in Ancient Greece.* Cambridge: Cambridge University Press.

Part II: Ancient Near Eastern Writing Systems

PREHISTORY ISN'T LIKE A "VEIL" OR A "CURTAIN" that "lifts" to reveal the pre-set "stage" of history. Rather, prehistory is an *absence* of something: an absence of writing. So a better image of the "dawn of history" might be an AM radio in the pre-dawn hours: you recognize wisps of words or music across the dial, interblending, and noise obscures even the few clear-channel stations. With the coming of the daylight, the static fades away, and signals emerge. The first ones we find, when we switch on the radio of history about 3200 B.C.E., come from Mesopotamia, and those from Egypt soon emerge. Eventually the neighboring lands produce records, with the effect that the ancient Near East is probably the best documented civilization before the invention of printing.

The earliest scribes we know about wrote on shaped lumps of clay—the durability of which is the reason we know about them—indenting wedge-shaped marks with a square corner of a reed stylus. They wrote in Sumerian, a language related to no other of which traces have survived. Scholars have debated for over a century why and whence they were gradually superseded by writers of a Semitic language, Akkadian (which appears in the main varieties Assyrian and Babylonian). The cultural influence of this civilization led to its script being adapted (and simplified) in neighboring realms for a variety of languages that, other than the Indo-European Hittite, remain difficult because of the paucity of materials and because they are not related to better known ones.

Contemporary with the entire duration of Mesopotamian civilization was that of Egypt in the Nile Valley. Egyptians wrote their language—distantly related to Akkadian—with ink on papyrus, using recognizable pictures (beside developments therefrom) for three thousand years. Between the fertile valleys of Egypt and Mesopotamia, in the hills and deserts of Syria and Palestine, dozens of small kingdoms rose and fell. Somehow, perhaps around 1500 B.C.E., for a range of Semitic languages (the most important would prove to be Hebrew and Aramaic) they came to use an abjad or consonantal script which may find its forebears to both the east and the south, and which, carrying Aramaic, was to be used from India to Egypt. Used to record other languages, it reached to the western edge of Europe.

In the far northwest of the ancient Near East, in Anatolia and on Aegean and Mediterranean islands, again from the mid second millennium, Indo-European languages (and apparently some others) have been found to use a pair of pictographic scripts that may or may not reflect Egyptian influence. The Luvian hieroglyphs record a language similar to Hittite. Linear B was the script of a form of Greek older by perhaps five hundred years than any that has survived from the Classical era. A seeming descendant of it was used in Cyprus a thousand years later, but other than that neither Luvian nor Linear B lived long enough to be directly superseded by the alphabetic scripts that were to occupy their territories in the first millennium B.C.E.

The first script we know to have been invented, rather than developed out of another, was that devised for the monumental inscriptions of the Persian Empire (last of the great pre-Classical realms). In appearance it imitates Mesopotamian cuneiform; in inner form it resembles Aramaic script; but in function it was severely circumscribed—not one private document or record using it has been found from the full geographical extent and temporal range of the realm.

— PETER T. DANIELS

The First Civilizations

PETER T. DANIELS

"Civilization" has been used in several ways. To the anthropologist, it is a term to avoid, since it can be (and was) taken to contrast the "civilized" nations of Europe (and occasionally China) with the "savages" in the rest of the world. For the archeologist, civilization begins with the advent of agriculture and permanent settlement ("villagization," perhaps, long predating urbanization), as early as 10,000 B.C.E. But in popular use—and this is the sense taken over by literacy scholars—civilization is marked by the appearance of writing in a culture. Jack Goody's recent musings on the written and the oral end thus (1987: 300): "Cognitively as well as sociologically, writing underpins 'civilization', the culture of cities."

"Forerunners" of writing

The full range of scripts of the ancient Near East are or appear to be related to each other by immediate adaptation or by direct, conscious influence. There are, in addition, remains of two recording devices that have been hypothesized to underlie Sumerian cuneiform, the earliest true writing system: the Vinča signs and the Near Eastern clay tokens.

The Vinča signs

The Vinča culture, found in the central Balkans and dating to 5300–4300 B.C.E., is named for the Serbian site southeast of Belgrade, Yugoslavia, where it was initially excavated during the first third of the twentieth century (Gimbutas 1991: 62–70, with bibliography, describes the culture and places it in its Balkan and wider contexts). Numerous objects—what Gimbutas notes as "religious items only" (p. 308)—bear graphic marks that look as though they might be elements of a script (pp. 308–21); often an object displays a series of such marks. According to an analysis by Winn (1973/1981), there are 210 signs; 30 are core signs, with the remainder being variants and combinations (Gimbutas, figures 8-1 and 8-2). Gimbutas supposes (as Winn apparently does not) that these marks are a writing system that records the pre–Indo-European language of her "Old European" civilization. She goes so far as to (facetiously) compare Old European signs with those of Linear A (her figure 8-22) and the Cypriote syllabary (figure 8-23; for both, see SECTION 7). Had Gimbutas not included

21

the proviso "for our amusement" (p. 320), she would have committed the oldest fallacy in the study of writing systems: the comparison of shapes alone without attention to sound values. Researchers must, therefore, not be misled by such charts into retrojecting the Greek values to a putative Old European language. Moreover, no claim seems to have been put forward that any recurring sequences of signs have been identified, and the first step in any linguistic analysis is the identification of strings that are the same or partly the same. It seems, then, most improbable that the marks represent a language, either logographically or phonetically. Thus on the current evidence it is not possible to recognize a Vinča writing system. A sober study of these and related materials, e.g. the "Tartaria tablets," by a scholar of the Aegean scripts—not cited by Gimbutas—is Masson 1984.

Near Eastern tokens

Firmly associated with the name of Denise Schmandt-Besserat—though the theory had been adumbrated by A. Leo Oppenheim and Pierre Amiet—is the notion that the thousands of "small clay objects" that have been recovered at sites from Palestine to eastern Iran dating back to 8000 B.C.E., and which have come to be known as *tokens*, represent the starting-point of cuneiform writing. (Many of Schmandt-Besserat's long series of articles, which began in 1977, are gathered and adapted in volume 1 of *Before Writing*, 1992.)

It was Oppenheim (1959) who noted that the inscription on the outside of a hollow, spheroidal clay object from second-millennium Nuzi listed a quantity of animals that corresponded to the number of "pebbles" (according to the excavators) that had been enclosed in the object. Amiet (1966) reported the discovery at Susa of similar objects (known as *envelopes*) that were some two thousand years older: they contained variously shaped clay artifacts (rather than pebbles), they dated from a prehistoric period ("protoliterate"), and some bore markings that resembled the contents (but, Amiet noted, there was not so great a variety of markings as of enclosed tokens). For only a handful of the two hundred or so known envelopes is the corresponding complement of tokens known, and only some of them have markings; but for these, the number of markings corresponds to the number of associated tokens, and they seem to have been made by impressing the tokens on the surface of the envelope before enclosing them within (Schmandt-Besserat 1992: 110–28, especially tables 1–4 and pp. 127–28).

Schmandt-Besserat associates the different shapes of tokens with different commodities that figured in protoliterate culture, such as species of domestic animals, textiles, and metal goods. Since the "pebbles" formerly contained in the only known inscribed envelope are lost, there is no possibility of associating their shapes with whatever original meaning they may have had; Schmandt-Besserat compares their geometric shapes with early stylized cuneiform signs that do not seem to have a pictographic background, and suggests that the signs developed from the impressions of the tokens; e.g., a disk with an incised cross is compared with a sign (TABLE 3.1 on page 39, line 6) that inexplicably means 'sheep' (pp. 139–54). Schmandt-Besserat now distinguishes two types of token, *simple* and *complex*, and associates the adoption of their use with the spread of agriculture. She connects the simple tokens with the numeral signs of cuneiform tablets (SECTION 69) and the complex tokens with logographic signs; the two kinds of sign are indeed quite different.

Schmandt-Besserat's theory of the origin of writing received great attention during the 1980s and has been uncritically incorporated into ancient histories and linguistics textbooks. But almost at once voices of dissent from those few who were in a position to evaluate the Sumerological evidence were raised, notably that of the late Steve Lieberman (1980), who seems to be responsible for the distinction between simple and complex tokens. Michalowski (1990, cf. 1993) addresses Schmandt-Besserat's theories from a variety of viewpoints, including the full range of ancient Near Eastern civilization as well as literacy studies, and finds them wanting. He has moreover developed an understanding of a very localized origin of cuneiform writing that renders the great temporal and geographic range of tokens irrelevant (see SECTION 3). The most convincing refutation of Schmandt-Besserat eventuated with the publication of a full catalog of the objects which her theory describes (1992, vol. 2). Paul Zimansky (1993) reanalyzed her database and found that the data do not support the analysis: from everything known about the lifestyle of the region, the aforementioned 'sheep' token ought to be among the most common; yet there are just 15 examples covering seven thousand years. The two most common tokens are those said to signify 'nail' and 'work, build'—"Is it really credible that these early villagers would leave more evidence of keeping accounts on nails and work days than livestock?" (p. 516). Zimansky also finds it incredible that tokens can have had uniform meanings over so vast an attested range. He suggests that "various people at various times exploited the few geometric shapes that are relatively easy to make in clay and used them as counters or for whatever other purposes they, as individuals, chose" (ibid.). Zimansky's review is absolutely essential for anyone interested in the topic.

Interconnections

There are not now, if there ever were, any scholars well enough versed in more than one ancient civilization to speak authoritatively about connections between them or their scripts at their very earliest stages, when by definition there are no historical records to refer to. The notoriety attached to the name of Martin Bernal (who arrived with, perhaps, the *advantage* of being a specialist in neither of the civilizations he would relate: the Egyptian and the Classical Greek) pertains less to his mishandling of archeological and philological data—which are, after all, of interest only to specialists (1990; 1987–91, vol. 2)—than to his demonstration of the antisemitism pervasive in Oriental studies (1986; 1987–91, vol. 1). Likewise it pertains to what was perceived as assent to pan-African sentiment deriving mainly from the title *Black Ath-*

ena (see the preface to 1987–91, vol. 2). Lost in the fuss was his tribute to two schol-ars who faced similar dismissive responses, the industrious Michael Astour and the visionary Cyrus Gordon. Both investigated influences of the Near East on Greece (Astour 1967, Gordon 1962); and both have been marginalized. The former meticu-lously establishes ancient geographic patterns, while the latter as early as the 1930s was a pioneer in the study of the Ugaritic language, though he also has championed the claims of American finds of Phoenician and Runic texts. (When questioned as to whether he really believed in ancient connections between the Old World and the New, he replied, "Well, it *might* be so.") One must thus tread lightly in this area.

I begin with the two civilizations that are best attested and longest studied: the Mesopotamian and the Egyptian. It is universally recognized that the cuneiform (SECTION 3) and hieroglyphic (SECTION 4) writing systems are sufficiently dissimi-lar (one logosyllabic, the other logoconsonantal) that one could not have been adapted directly from the other. But the similarities of earliest attestation (ca. 3200 B.C.E.) and the combination of logography, phonography, and determinatives are sufficient to convince Egyptologists (e.g. Fischer 1977: 1189) or suggest to them (e.g. Schenkel 1984: 725) that the *idea* of writing came from the Sumerians to the Egyptians. Early contacts between the two peoples are documented by Fischer (nn. 3–4) and Micha-lowski (1990 n. 23).

In the nineteenth century, with the decipherment of hieroglyphs and cuneiform and the recognition of their logographic nature, the notion grew of a connection be-tween the Near Eastern and Far Eastern scripts. But the few signs of cuneiform and archaic Chinese (SECTION 14) that shared a form and a meaning (e.g. 'sun', 'tree', 'water') pertained to such basic and simple concepts (as already noted in 1927 by Arthur Ungnad) that their depiction could hardly be other than very similar. Of equal significance is the recognition that, at the time of the development of Chinese logo-graphic writing from pictograms, the pictographic origin of cuneiform had been com-pletely forgotten (Daniels 1992B). If Chinese writing was stimulated by, or imitated from, Mesopotamian cuneiform, then it should have emerged as a syllabary or a logo-syllabary, rather than as a nearly pure logography with pervasive phonetic comple-mentation. Recently, there have been proposals of direct influence from the Semitic abjad on the 22 Chinese calendrical signs (Mair 1992, Gordon 1994: 37–45; for a so-ber account of the data, see Pulleyblank 1991). Their evaluation must await the full publication of the evidence.

Historically, the next pair of scripts (and civilizations) that could be connected is the Anatolian hieroglyphs (SECTION 6) and the Aegean group (SECTION 7). Note that this pair falls across the great divide between Classical and Orientalist scholarship, so the question of possible interrelations has not received sufficient attention. The lead-ing authority on Luvian writing, David Hawkins (1986: 374), suggests that the picto-rial character of both, their original use on stamp seals, and their typological similarity in comprising only logograms and CV(CV) signs indicate some sort of in-fluence, probably from the Aegean to Anatolia (these characteristics also render unlikely a cuneiform inspiration for the Luvian script). Moreover, "The unsuitability of both the Linear B and Anatolian syllabaries for writing the Indo-European languages Greek and Hittite has been often noted, and this factor points to both systems, though indigenous constructs, being ultimately dependent on an external model, i.e. Egyptian Hieroglyphic" (ibid.).

The origin of the Semitic abjad (and hence the Greek and European alphabet) has ethnocentrically received great attention for centuries (SECTION 5). In more recent decades, it seems that each time a new script was discovered or deciphered, it was taken to be the direct ancestor of the Canaanite script: Egyptian Hieratic, Proto-Sinaitic, Linear A or B, pseudo-hieroglyphs of Byblos have all been placed in that exalted line. The truth is that insufficient materials from the earliest phases of writing in the Levant and neighboring regions are available; every new discovery adds a new piece to the puzzle and potentially could be the key to the entire development.

The most commonly presented scenario has West Semitic mine workers in the Sinai taking the idea of consonantal writing and the shapes of the letters from hieroglyphs, and writing dedicatory inscriptions in their language on religious objects. The values of the letters are not as in Egyptian. Rather, they are supposed to have been assigned on the *acrophonic* principle, whereby a letter stands for the initial sound in the word for the object of which it is a picture. This new script is then supposed to have been taken into use in the Canaanite area. Aside from the sociological objections mentioned in SECTION 5, this theory requires the proposed decipherment of the Proto-Sinaitic inscriptions to be valid, which is a dubious assumption (see below).

What needs to be recognized is the intellectual achievement in passing from a syllabary, the most perspicuous form of phonetic writing (see SECTION 52), to a consonantary. Someone had to recognize that *ta*, *ti*, and *tu* have something in common; and moreover that *at*, *it*, and *ut* have that very same something in common. It has often been claimed that the structure of the Semitic languages (wherein the consonantal roots are important and the vowels merely add variations to the root meanings) is responsible for this recognition, but this won't work—because Akkadian, which never adapted syllabic cuneiform into a consonantal or alphabetic script, shares exactly the same structural property. It is conceivable that the very frequent *plene* writing of vowels in Hittite cuneiform (page 65)—CV_i-V_i—made it possible to regard the CV sign as representing *only* the C of its syllable (potentially the inspiration of the abjad), with the vowel expressed *only* by the V sign (the similarly written Hurrian is attested too late to be relevant; note that it was in use in the Levant in the mid second millennium).

Ultimately the most successful adaptations of earlier scripts for Indo-European languages were those that allowed the expression of vowels (and by definition also the absence of vowels) independently of the signs for the consonants. Two such adaptations happened—and they may have been nearly simultaneous, if certain arguments from silence be accepted. In the west, the abjad was applied to Greek, with letters for Semitic consonants not found in Greek adapted to represent vowels (SECTION 21). In the east, marks for the vowels of Prakrit were added to the consonant letters to produce the Indic abugida (SECTION 30). In Ethiopia (SECTION 51), over a millennium later, a similar device was introduced (along with Christianity) to vocalize the inherited version of the Semitic abjad. (In Ethiopia, the vowel marks are more integrated into the consonant letters than in India, and there is no unambiguous way of indicating a vowelless syllable.) The idea of vocalization cannot have been introduced by Syriac-using missionaries, since at the time Syriac had no vowel signs (SECTION 47); nor by Coptic missionaries, or vocalization would presumably have followed the Greek model and used separate letters. Rather, there must have been some contact—however ephemeral—with the Christian community of western India, established in legend by the apostle Thomas himself (Daniels 1992A).

Syriac script became vocalized in several stages and regions. The earliest schemes seem to have been indigenous; but in the portion of the Syriac civilization that accepted Greek ecclesiastical influence, tiny Greek vowels were placed above or below the line of consonants that constituted the text. Each vowel is placed with the consonant it follows. Again, there is no unambiguous mark for a vowelless syllable. The native Syriac vocalization system apparently was the stimulus for the adoption of similar schemes for both Hebrew and Arabic—again, crossing deep cultural divides—yet in both these systems there are explicit indications of vowellessness.

Religion plays a part, too, in the latest examples of cross-civilizational script influence. In Korea (SECTION 17), *hankul* emerged from King Seycong's desire to turn his country from Confucian to Buddhist ideals. While the presence or degree of influence from the Tibetan-based 'Phags pa script on Korean is disputed, it is clear that Seycong or his linguistic consultants could use as a model the alphabetic or abugidic scripts of India and Inner Asia in which Buddhist scriptures were preserved.

In modern times, it was the entrepreneurs who sent out expeditions to all corners of the globe, but it was usually the missionaries who introduced writing or the idea of writing to the cultures they met (PART IX).

The significance of the alphabet

As outlined in SECTION 1, for more than a century the accepted view of script typology has admitted logography, syllabary, and alphabet. The descriptive adequacy of this scheme has already been dealt with; here my concern is with its implications. The sequence has usually been taken as not merely one of historical development, but also as representing "progress"—as if the alphabet is the best possible kind of writing system, ostensibly because it (ideally) provides one symbol of the script for each phoneme of the language. In fact, it is probably because the alphabet is "our" kind of writing: the vehicle of the "best" culture (or of "civilization" in the judgmental sense). This attitude may have reflected unthinking, nearly harmless chauvinism, and it can be refuted fairly simply: each type of script entails about the same amount of effort to record the same amount of information. Since a logographic system must distinguish several thousand characters, the characters, in the aggregate, are necessarily quite complex (though the most common ones tend to be simpler). The characters of a syllabary, numbering on the order of a hundred, are more complicated—take longer to write—than those of an abjad or alphabet, which number in the tens, while those of an abugida are again somewhat more elaborate. Undoubtedly, average reading speed is uniform across script types.

Moreover, language changes continually but writing is generally fixed. So, however perfectly phonemic an alphabet was when it was first applied to a language, every phonological system changes over time (sometimes over a very short time; witness the Great English Vowel Shift, which overtook standard English just as English spelling was being codified with the introduction of printing to England). Then the original writing system comes to reflect an earlier historical stage of the language, and in effect becomes morphophonemic rather than phonemic. Only when spelling has very recently been introduced or ruthlessly reformed is an alphabet likely to be phonemic.

Additionally, there are languages for which an alphabet is *not* an ideal writing system. The Semitic abjads really do fit the structure of Hebrew, Aramaic, and Arabic very well, and the abugida really is more appropriate to Ethiopic languages than an alphabet would be, since the spelling ensures that each root looks the same through its plethora of inflections and derivations. The supplemental vowel markings on the abjads serve to remove ambiguity among words with the same consonants which cannot be resolved from the context. And it is not only Semitic languages for which an abjad is appropriate (Daniels 1995).

(It is often argued that Chinese logography is ideal for that language because of the large number of homonyms. Note, though, that the exceptional homonymy is largely illusory, since it results from phonetic change by which final consonants were lost. Modern Standard Chinese compensated in ordinary ways—e.g. syntactic and morphological elaboration—differently in different regions, so that the literary and vernacular languages grew quite distinct and a Classical written text cannot be read as colloquial Chinese; see SECTION 15.)

No, it is not unthinking chauvinism that renders pernicious the teleological view of the perfect alphabet. It is ignorance and prejudice. Although we can deal more easily with ignorance, prejudice is also formative: too many scholars of writing or literacy know and want to know nothing of the civilizations that preceded the Classical. The study of Hebrew (and Arabic and Syriac) is admittedly not easy; the study of Akkadian, and moreso of Sumerian, is very difficult (not least because so few people have ever taken it up). But it ought to be possible for the classicist or the literary scholar to at least gain some familiarity with what came before.

Bernal exposed the antisemitism that pervaded Orientalism at least until the mid twentieth century. It is shocking to find it operative forty years later; but what else can be made of the following statements by Eric Havelock? Havelock was a Classicist, originally from Toronto, who held that the great divide in human history falls between orality and literacy, a view that is now common but mistaken, or at least oversimplified (Olson 1994, chap. 1). For Havelock, though, literacy began only with the introduction of the Greek alphabet—the tool that made possible Greek literature, Greek philosophy, Greek thought.

Not content with elevating Greek belles lettres, Havelock depreciated, denigrated, all that had come before. He knew the Bible and cuneiform literature only in translation (for the latter, Speiser's deiberately archaizing and poetic translation, 1969), and made these assessments: "A stark contrast appeared between the sheer richness of Greek orality as transcribed and the caution of its competitors. A wealth of detail and depth of psychological feeling contrasted with an economy of vocabulary and a cautious restriction of sentiment which seemed to be specific properties of all Near Eastern and Hebrew literature" (1986: 9). "Selfhood and the soul, when expressed in Greek, conjure up convictions which in the West have been powerfully reinforced by two thousand years of Christianity (though it is worth notice that the same conceptions seem to be lacking in the Old Testament)" (pp. 120f.). "… We need only turn to the so-called literatures of the ancient Near East as they have been translated for us. We have first to discount the inevitable tendency of the modern translator to overtranslate his original, relieving its verbal repetitions, for example, by variation, and removing ambiguities by using his version to impose a single choice among many possible ones. … When all allowance is made for the simple grandeur of conception or refinement of design, the basic complexity of human experience is not there. … [This is] not literature in the Graeco-Roman sense. … One need only compare what is narrated in the so-called Epic of Gilgamesh with what is narrated in Homer, or, for that matter, expounded in Hesiod, to realize the difference" (1976: 33f. = 1982: 71f.).

The Mesopotamians and Hebrews were preliterate, Havelock asserts, because they did not use an alphabet; to this deficiency in their writing system is to be attributed the defects of their written remains—in 1979 he even added the "Hindu Vedic literature [sic]" to the preliterate corpus (1982: 9).

Undeciphered scripts

A scattering of documents has been recovered from the ancient Near East in scripts that remain undeciphered (cf. SECTION 9). In each case, the small amount of text is primarily responsible for the difficulty; usually there is also no clue as to the linguistic affinity of the language(s) involved.

Scripts from the Aegean and Cyprus

The epigraphic remains from what was to be the Greek world are described in SECTION 7. Here I simply mention some of the more impressive attempts to interpret them. In 1930–32 there appeared a volume of posthumous *Mediterranean Studies* by the American Anglicist and Germanist George Hempl (1859–1921). These interrelated studies bring togther Hittite, Etruscan, Venetic (see SECTION 23), and the Minoan and Mycenean scripts (Linear A and B) in an ambitious effort to interpret what was unknown among them. Emmett Bennett regards Stawell (1931) as an early effort worth mentioning, and reports that F. G. Gordon (1931), with considerable ingenuity, uncovered a very nice (at least in the English translation) Basque poem in a Linear B tablet. The Czech scholar Bedřich Hrozný, who was the first to interpret Hittite as Indo-European, late in his life produced a massive synthesis regarding the pictographic and hieroglyphic scripts of the Aegean area (1944–49). All these works were rendered moot, of course, by the successful decipherment of Linear B in 1952 (SECTION 9).

Four of the mysterious scripts of this area have been interpreted as expressing Northwest Semitic by Cyrus Gordon in a 1966 monograph and many subsequent articles. He considers Eteocypriote, Eteocretan, Linear A, and the Phaistos Disk, calling the language revealed "Minoan." The lack of acceptance which this work found may be attributed in part to the aforementioned reluctance of Classical scholars to admit to Semitic influence in their realm, but more likely it results from the tiny amount of material concerned in three of the scripts and the failure to provide a complete corpus (fully analyzed with exhaustive scholarly apparatus!) of the Linear A materials. Problems arise because Gordon's readings of the signs are determined by ascribing to Linear A signs the values they have in Linear B, a procedure that could be validated only by indisputable results, and for that the full corpus really does need to be inspected.

Proto-Sinaitic

In 1905, a handful of votive objects were discovered at Serābît el-Khâdem, Sinai, that bore inscriptions in a script that looked something like a forerunner of the Semitic abjad. (It is called "Proto-Sinaitic" to distinguish it from the "Sinaitic" inscriptions, in a late form of Nabatean.) The first attempt at decipherment, Gardiner 1916, which is taken over in the standard treatment of the script, Albright 1966, focused on sequences of signs that seemed to acrophonically represent *lb 'lt* 'to the lady'. As its most systematic critic points out, this solution involves at least four assumptions: this is an alphabetic script; the signs have Egyptian prototypes; the letters are pictographic and acrophonic; and the language is Semitic (Sznycer 1975: 91). Furthermore, most of the occurrences of *lb 'lt* are restorations. Gardiner took a snake-shaped character to be *n* because the modern Ethiopic name for the letter is *nahas*, and the corresponding word in Hebrew, *nāḥāš*, means 'snake'. But it seems very likely that the modern Ethiopic letter names date no further back than the sixteenth century C.E., and so are irrelevant to the investigation of Proto-Sinaitic (Daniels 1991).

Pseudo-hieroglyphs of Byblos

The ancient city of Byblos—a center for the distribution of papyrus and the source of the Greek word for 'book' and hence the word *Bible*—has yielded a number of very important epigraphic documents, as well as a handful of enigmatic texts in an unknown script (dubbed "pseudo-hieroglyphic" because its pictograms resemble Egyptian hieroglyphs) of which the most extensive are two on bronze tablets. Dunand (1945) published all the texts, and classified the 1038 characters found on them into 114 signs, with no suggestions as to interpretation. There have been four significant attempts at decipherment.

Dhorme (1946) assumed the language was Phoenician. He focused on a set of seven marks at the end of Text C, supposing that they represented a date numeral so that the four letters preceding them were the word *bšnt* 'in the year'. Upon substituting these four values into other occurrences of those letters, he found in the first line of the text *n?š*; since the text is written on bronze, he took that word to be *nḥš* 'bronze'. Texts, however, do not often refer to the material on which they are written, so his methodology is immediately suspect; so are his results, which give five letters for *y* but do not distinguish *ḥ* from *ḫ* or *z* from *ṣ*—surprising in a Semitic language.

Sobelman (1961), prescinding from the phonetic values of the letters, applied the techniques of descriptive linguistics to the corpus to identify word boundaries and uncover grammatical patterns. His results should be taken into account in all future work on these texts.

Malachi Martin, originally a skilled paleographer, later a novelist and critic of the Roman Catholic church, published only the first part of his work on the pseudo-hieroglyphs (1962). He reanalyzed the corpus of characters into just 27 "classes." It is clear from the descriptions attached and from certain remarks in the text that he was trying to make the script into an ordinary alphabet (i.e. abjad). The absence of further publications suggests that the attempt was not successful.

Mendenhall (1985) received the most attention for his work, because he labored at it for 37 years and had used his findings in his historical and biblical publications for at least fifteen years before its publication. Unfortunately, although he gives full texts, translations, and apparatus for what he calls Old Coastal Semitic documents, his description of the decipherment process is so inexplicit (and unreconstructible) that no credence can be given to the results. The texts themselves have been received with incredulity by those competent to study them, as they conform entirely too closely to Mendenhall's idiosyncratic view of Levantine history.

Bibliography

Albright, William Foxwell. 1966. *The Proto-Sinaitic Inscriptions and Their Decipherment* (Harvard Theological Studies 12). Cambridge: Harvard University Press.

Amiet, Pierre. 1966. "Il y a 5000 ans les Elamites inventaient l'écriture." *Archeologia* 12: 20–22.

Astour, Michael. 1967. *Hellenosemitica: An Ethnic and Cultural Study in West Semitic Impact on Mycenaean Greece*. Leiden: Brill.

Bernal, Martin. 1986. "Black Athena Denied: The Tyranny of Germany over Greece." *Comparative Criticism* 8: 3–69.

———. 1987–91. *Black Athena: The Afroasiatic Roots of Classical Civilization*, vol. 1: *The Fabrication of Ancient Greece 1785–1985*; vol. 2, *The Archaeological and Documentary Evidence*.

New Brunswick, N.J.: Rutgers University Press.

———. 1990. *Cadmean Letters: The Transmission of the Alphabet to the Aegean and Further West before 1400 B.C.* Winona Lake, Ind.: Eisenbrauns.

Daniels, Peter T. 1991. "Ha, La, Ḥa or Hōi, Lawe, Ḥaut: The Ethiopic Letter Names." In *Semitic Studies in Honor of Wolf Leslau on the Occasion of His Eighty-fifth Birthday,* ed. Alan S. Kaye, pp. 275–88. Wiesbaden: Harrassowitz.

———. 1992A. "Contacts between Semitic and Indic Scripts." In *Contacts between Cultures: Selected Papers from the 33rd International Congress of Asian and North African Studies, Toronto, August 15–25, 1990,* vol. 1, *West Asia and North Africa,* ed. Amir Harrak, pp. 146–52. Lewiston, N.Y.: Edwin Mellen.

———. 1992B. "What Do the 'Paleographic' Tablets Tell Us of Mesopotamian Scribes' Knowledge of the History of Their Script?" *Mār Šipri: Newsletter of the Committee on Mesopotamian Civilization, ASOR* 5/1: 1–4.

———. 1995. "The Protean Arabic Abjad." In *Humanism, Culture, and Language in the Near East: Studies in Honor of Georg Krotkoff,* ed. Asma Afsaruddin and A. H. Mathias Zahniser. Winona Lake, Ind.: Eisenbrauns.

Dhorme, Édouard. 1946. "Déchiffrement des inscriptions pseudo-hiéroglyphiques de Byblos." *Syria* 25: 1–35.

Dunand, Maurice. 1945. *Byblia grammata: Documents et recherches sur le développement de l'écriture en Phénicie.* Beirut: Ministry of Education of Lebanon.

Fischer, Henry George. 1977. "Hieroglyphen" [in English]. *Lexikon der Ägyptologie,* vol. 2, cols. 1189–99. Wiesbaden: Harrassowitz.

Gardiner, Alan H. 1916. "The Egyptian Origin of the Semitic Alphabet." *Journal of Egyptian Archaeology* 3: 1–16.

Gimbutas, Marija. 1991. *The Civilization of the Goddess: The World of Old Europe.* San Francisco: HarperCollins.

Goody, Jack. 1987. *The Interface between the Written and the Oral.* Cambridge: Cambridge University Press.

Gordon, Cyrus H. 1962. *Before the Bible: The Common Background of Greek and Hebrew Civilizations.* New York: Harper & Row.

———. 1966. *Evidence for the Minoan Language.* Ventnor, N.J.: Ventnor Publishers.

———. 1994. "The Background to Jewish Studies in the Bible and in the Ancient East: The Abe and Ida Miller Lecture presented by the Jewish Studies Program at Purdue University December 4, 1991." *Shofar* 12/4: 1–46 (separatim as PUJSP Occasional Publication 1).

Gordon, Frank G. 1931. *Through Basque to Minoan.* London: Oxford University Press

Havelock, Eric A. 1976. *Origins of Western Literacy.* Toronto: Ontario Institute for Studies in Education. Repr. in Havelock 1982: 39–76, 314–50.

———. 1982. *The Literate Revolution in Greece and Its Cultural Consequences.* Princeton, N.J.: Princeton University Press.

———. 1986. *The Muse Learns to Write: Reflections on Orality and Literacy from Antiquity to the Present.* New Haven, Conn.: Yale University Press.

Hawkins, David. 1986. "Writing in Anatolia: Imported and Indigenous Systems." *World Archaeology* 17: 363–76.

Hempl, George. 1930–32. *Mediterranean Studies,* ed. Frederick Anderson (Stanford University Publications, University Series, Language and Literature 5). No. 1, *I. The Genesis of European Alphabetic Writing, II. Minoan Seals,* 1930; no. 2, *III. Three Papers on the History and Language of the Hittites,* 1931; no. 3, *IV. Etruscan, V. Venetic,* 1932. Repr. New York: AMS Press, 1967.

Hrozný, Bedřich. 1944–49. "Kretas und Vorgriechenlands Inschriften, Geschichte und Kultur. I. Ein

Entzifferungsversuch." *Archív Orientální* 14 (1944): 1–117. "Les inscriptions crétoises II. Essai de déchiffrement." *Archív Orientální* 15 (1946): 158–302. "Liste des signes crétois et de leurs valeurs d'après notre déchiffrement." *Archív Orientální* 16 (1949): 162–84.

Lieberman, Stephen J. 1980. "Of Clay Pebbles, Hollow Clay Balls, and Writing: A Sumerian View." *American Journal of Archaeology* 84: 339–58.

Mair, Victor H. 1992. "West Eurasian and North African Influences on the Origin of Chinese Writing." In *Contacts between Cultures: Selected Papers from the 33rd International Congress of Asian and North African Studies, Toronto, August 15–25, 1990*, vol. 3, *Eastern Asia: Literature and Humanities*, ed. Bernard Hung-Kay Luk, pp. 335–38. Lewiston, N.Y.: Edwin Mellen.

Martin, Malachi. 1962. "Revision and Reclassification of the Proto-Byblian Signs." *Orientalia* 31: 250–71, 339–63.

Masson, Emilia. 1984. "L'écriture' dans les civilisations danubiennes néolithiques." *Kadmos* 23: 89–123.

Mendenhall, George E. 1985. *The Syllabic Inscriptions from Byblos.* Beirut: American University of Beirut.

Michalowski, Piotr. 1990. "Early Mesopotamian Communicative Systems: Art, Literature, and Writing." In *Investigating Artistic Environments in the Ancient Near East*, ed. Ann C. Gunther, pp. 53–69. Washington, D.C.: Smithsonian Institution, Arthur M. Sackler Gallery.

———. 1993. "Tokenism" [review of Schmandt-Besserat 1992]. *American Anthropologist* 95: 996–99.

Olson, David R. 1994. *The World on Paper: The Conceptual and Cognitive Implications of Writing and Reading.* Cambridge: Cambridge University Press.

Oppenheim, A. Leo. 1959. "On an Operational Device in Mesopotamian Bureaucracy." *Journal of Near Eastern Studies* 18: 121–28.

Pulleyblank, Edwin G. 1991. "The *Ganzhi* as Phonograms and Their Application to the Calendar." *Early China* 16: 39–80.

Schenkel, Wolfgang. 1984. "Schrift." *Lexikon der Ägyptologie*, vol. 5, cols. 713–35. Wiesbaden: Harrassowitz.

Schmandt-Besserat, Denise. 1992. *Before Writing*, vol. 1: *From Counting to Cuneiform;* vol. 2, *A Catalog of Near Eastern Tokens.* Austin: University of Texas Press.

Sobelman, Harvey. 1961. "The Proto-Byblian Inscriptions: A Fresh Approach." *Journal of Semitic Studies* 6: 226–45.

Speiser, Ephraim Avigdor. 1969. "Akkadian Myths and Epics." In *Ancient Near Eastern Texts Relating to the Old Testament*, ed. James B. Pritchard, 3rd ed., pp. 60–119. Princeton, N.J.: Princeton University Press (1st ed., 1950).

Stawell, F. Melian. 1931. *A Clue to the Cretan Scripts.* London: Bell.

Sznycer, Maurice. 1975. "Les inscriptions protosinaïtiques." In *Le déchiffrement des écritures et des langues (Colloque du XXIXe Congrès International des Orientalistes)*, ed. Jean Leclant, pp. 84–93. Paris: Asiathèque.

Ungnad, Arthur. 1927. "Sumerische und chinesische Schrift." *Wiener Zeitschrift für die Kunde des Morgenlandes* 34: 76–86.

Winn, Shan M. M. 1981. *Pre-Writing in Southeast Europe: The Sign System of the Vinča Culture, ca. 4000 B.C.* Calgary: Western Publishers (original dissertation, 1973).

Zimansky, Paul. 1993. Review of Schmandt-Besserat 1992. *Journal of Field Archaeology* 20: 513–17.

Mesopotamian Cuneiform

Origin

PIOTR MICHALOWSKI

What is probably the first known writing system in the world, conventionally called *proto-cuneiform*, was used in Mesopotamia at the end of the fourth millennium B.C.E., in the latter part of what is known as the Uruk Period. It is still a matter of debate whether the first Egyptian writings were contemporary, slightly later, or perhaps even earlier than the Uruk tablets. In southern Mesopotamia this was a time of rapid urbanization, population growth, and dramatic increase in the division of labor and political development. The first writing is part of this sudden expansion of Mesopotamian civilization; it cannot be ascribed to any single cause, but must be viewed as an element in a rapidly diversifying human environment. There can be little doubt that the primary context for the first writing was administrative necessity, but an invention of this magnitude, which required a realignment of all communicative systems within a small but important segment of society, also had complex symbolic and psychological roots. The script can be "understood" in some sense, but it cannot be fully read; although there has been some doubt concerning the language that was the basis for this written expression, there is clear evidence that it was Sumerian.

History of discovery

The first written texts derive from excavations in the southern Mesopotamian city of Uruk, from the period of roughly 3200–3000 B.C. Almost 5000 tablets and fragments inscribed with proto-cuneiform have been found there. All these tablets were found in secondary context, mainly in dumps and fill areas. Whereas the exact chronology as well as the original location of the tablets is unknown, the texts undoubtedly came from large organizations, conventionally designated as "palaces" or "temples." On typological grounds these have been divided into two periods, Uruk III and IV, on the model of the stratigraphy of that part of Uruk, the ceremonial area which was named Eana in antiquity (archeological strata are numbered in the order they are uncovered, so Uruk IV is older than Uruk III). Recently, Hans Nissen (Green and Nissen 1987), who heads the Berlin team that is publishing these materials, has proposed a more precise dating of tablets into smaller subdivisions. The stratigraphy of the archaic Uruk finds is currently being revised, and it possible that the dating of many of the texts may have to be changed accordingly (Englund 1994: 16).

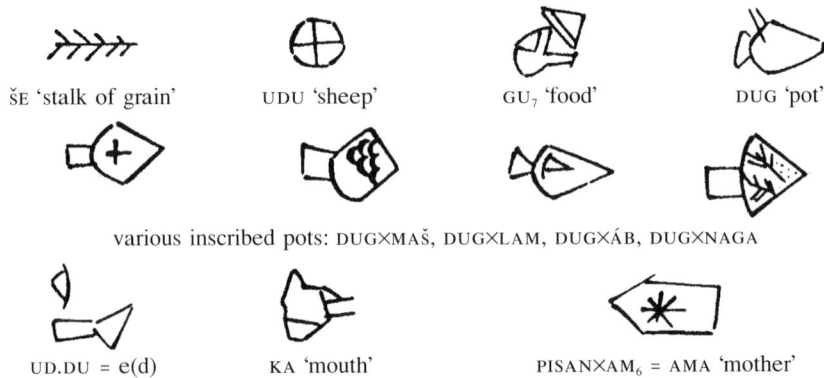

ŠE 'stalk of grain'   UDU 'sheep'   GU₇ 'food'   DUG 'pot'

various inscribed pots: DUG×MAŠ, DUG×LAM, DUG×ÁB, DUG×NAGA

UD.DU = e(d)   KA 'mouth'   PISAN×AM₆ = AMA 'mother'

FIGURE I. Proto-cuneiform signs
(Green and Nissen 1987, nos. 511, 575, 235, 88, 108, 106, 89. 109, 132, 271, 28).

The Uruk IV period texts are unparalleled elsewhere, while the period III ones are roughly contemporary with tablets found at other Mesopotamian sites. Although we are at the mercy of chance discoveries and there is no way of establishing the earlier history of the system, there are reasons to believe that the period IV tablets from Uruk are not far removed from the invention of the script.

Structure

The archaic system consisted of approximately 800 separate symbols, of which more than sixty or seventy were number signs. The exact number of discrete symbols is difficult to establish; it depends on how one defines certain complex and compound signs, and there is still some debate concerning similar-looking symbols. Many of the signs were pictographic, for example a drawing of a stalk of barley or wheat for 'grain'; others, such as a cross within a circle ('sheep') were abstract depictions (see FIGURE I). To avoid multiplying shapes, new signs were created by combining two or three signs (SAG + SILA₃ 'head' + 'ration bowl' = GU₇ 'food, to eat'); by inscribing one within another (various types of clay vessels denoted by the 'pot' sign differently inscribed); by combining two or more signs (UD.DU = *e(d)*), or by modifying existing ones with hatching (SAG + hatching = KA 'mouth'). Another way of forming signs is represented by a subset that was used for writing the names of major Sumerian cities. In these a stylized representation of some symbol of the major deity of the city was combined with a sign that was a classifier for 'city' and had no phonetic value. Thus Zabala was written MUŠ₃ (stylized drawing of the symbol of the goddess Inanna) and CITY. The name of Uruk was written simply as CITY, which may suggest that writing, or the version of writing that spread throughout Mesopotamia, was invented in Uruk, whose inhabitants may have viewed their home as "the city" par excellence (Michalowski 1993). Some of these representations of divine symbols are known from seal designs and other artistic representations.

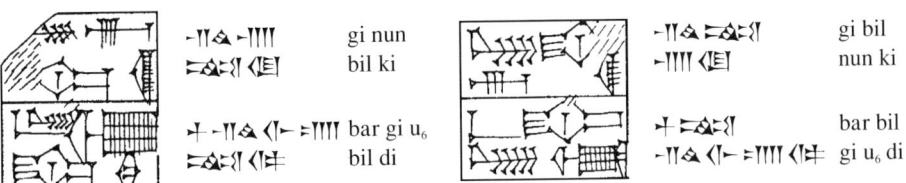

FIGURE 2. Two copies of lines 152–53 of the za.me hymn, with Neo-Assyrian equivalents and transliterations. The meaning is obscure, but there is no doubt that they represent the same text: (152) bil.gi nun^{ki} (153) bar bil.gi u$_6$ di (Biggs 1974: 50; *left*, pl. 117, no. 265; *right*, pl. 122, no. 268; reproduced with permission).

Unlike in early Chinese and Egyptian writing, there is only sporadic evidence for phonetic complementation, which was used more frequently in later phases of the writing system. Nevertheless, there are a few cases of phonetic complementation already in the earliest stages of cuneiform, and these, as Krispijn (1991–92), Krebernik (1994), and Steinkeller (IN PRESS) have recently observed, leave little doubt that the underlying language of the earliest texts was indeed Sumerian. Thus the sign AMA, which was the Sumerian word for 'mother', was rendered with a sign we transliterate as PISAN ('box') inscribed with AM$_6$, which indicates the range of pronunciation. Some had double glosses, as demonstrated by the writing Ú.NAGA.GA.MUŠEN for *uga* 'raven', which consists of a basic sign, NAGA, bracketed by the glosses *ú* and *ga*, followed by the bird name classifier MUŠEN.

Although the majority of individual symbols represented whole words—because Sumerian was predominantly monosyllabic—these same words could function as syllables in other contexts (BA 'ration' = /ba/). The syllabic spellings were needed for the expression of personal names and later for the writing of grammatical elements. Homophony was used to produce syllabic writings, but rarely for creating other word signs through the rebus principle. There were also a series of preposed and postposed classifiers that delimited semantic classes, such as GIŠ 'wood'. The visual layout of tablets also had semantic value. The arrangement of cases and columns enclosing signs was different for different types of transactions and for different parts of the text, such as for the final total of goods. This variety of arrangements disappeared later on as the system became more flexible and more linked to natural language. On the early tablets, signs were arranged in random order within cases that were ordered vertically, from our point of view. There are indications that the tablets were held at a different angle than in later times. The random order of signs within the cases continued down to Early Dynastic times when the first literary texts are attested; in this period, duplicate passages of the same composition could be written with signs in completely different order (see FIGURE 2).

The structure and logic of the system indicate that it was invented as a whole and did not develop gradually. Individual elements were borrowed from existing communicative devices: the number signs may have been adapted from small clay counters that were used independently, or impressed on tablets. Certain cult symbols, as well as other signs were probably used earlier in cylinder seal designs, but the system as such was designed in one fell swoop. Those who favor an evolutionary model of the development of writing cite certain "antecedents" to proto-cuneiform: rough clay containers ("bullae") that enclosed simple counters and were impressed with the shape of the counters, and sealed; as well as the so-called numerical tablets; that is, clay tablets with the impressions of counters. It has been proposed that the hollow bullae were flattened, and this produced the first tablets. These, in turn, were impressed with the shape of the clay counters (Schmandt-Besserat 1992). The inventor or inventors of proto-cuneiform drew on a variety of such ideas, but the quantum leap to the conceptualization of the earliest writing system was without precedent.

The only other contemporary writing system was the hitherto undeciphered Proto-Elamite script used over a wide area of southwest and central Iran. The first tablets in Proto-Elamite are slightly later than proto-cuneiform—conventionally they are regarded as contemporary with Uruk III—and the relation between the two systems is unclear. Both use the same numerical notation, and they share at least one sign; but other than that, there is little that one can say about the differences and similarities between the two (see SECTION 10).

Distribution and contents

Aside from the tablets found at Uruk, archaic texts of period III have been found further north at Jemdet Nasr, possibly at nearby Tell Uqair, and at Fara; and some, of unknown provenance, have been purchased on the antiquities market. This means that the writing conventions first attested, and perhaps invented, at Uruk were rapidly adopted by other Mesopotamian polities. The largest group of over 200 tablets, from Jemdet Nasr (Englund and Grégoire 1991), consists of texts that are very similar to the Uruk III materials.

The majority of Uruk archaic texts are administrative documents. These comprise texts dealing with such matters as animal husbandry, grain distribution, land, animal and personnel management, and the processing of fruits and cereals. Approximately 15% are not economic: these are lists of words arranged by semantic class and by sign design, commonly known as lexical lists (Englund and Nissen 1993). There are lists of wooden objects, professional names, fish, plants, and other subjects. These differ from the accounts in a number of respects: they are preserved in multiple copies (as many as 163 for the professions list), some duplicates were found outside Uruk, and they were copied by later scribes for hundreds of years. These lexical texts have been interpreted in a variety of ways, but most scholars agree that they were manuals for the teaching of writing. This demonstrates that from the beginning there was a concern for the structured transmission of the system from generation to generation, and that the method of instruction was passed on along with the practical knowledge of the script.

Sumerian and Akkadian

JERROLD S. COOPER

Cuneiform script was used to represent the Sumerian language (Thomsen 1984) in southern Mesopotamia from ca. 3200 B.C.E., and was adapted to write Semitic dialects in Mesopotamia and Syria by 2500. Although Sumerian had become extinct as a spoken language by the early second millennium, it continued to be used for religious and legal purposes, and was studied and written until the beginning of the current era. Cuneiform texts in the Semitic dialect family we call Akkadian (Reiner 1966) appear in southern Mesopotamia beginning around 2350 (the dialect is called Old Akkadian); and after 2000, texts are written in two dialects, the Babylonian, originating in southern Mesopotamia, and Assyrian, originating in northern Mesopotamia. These are chronologically distinguished as Old Babylonian/Assyrian, Middle Babylonian/Assyrian, and Neo-Babylonian/-Assyrian, representing the dialects of, roughly, the first half of the second millennium, the second half of the second millennium, and the first half of the first millennium respectively. The Akkadian cuneiform that continued to be used into the Seleucid period in Babylonia is called Late Babylonian, and the language used for literary and commemorative inscriptions in the late second and the first millennium is known as Standard Babylonian; cuneiform texts were written as late as the first century C.E. In addition, during the second millennium, Sumerian and Akkadian cuneiform texts were produced at various times in various areas peripheral to Mesopotamia, in an arc stretching from southwestern Iran up to Anatolia and down through Syria and the Levant into Egypt. The few cuneiform texts from southern Mesopotamia written in Semitic before 2350, in a dialect that was probably a precursor to Old Akkadian—and the many thousands from Ebla in Syria, representing a language related to, but probably different from, the precursor of Old Akkadian (Gelb 1987)—is not considered here.

Sumerian and Akkadian are not only dead languages, but unlike Sanskrit, Biblical Hebrew, ancient Greek, or Latin, they are languages without a continuous tradition of study. Akkadian is a Semitic language, but Sumerian is a language isolate of a very different type, and with a very different phonemic inventory. The values we give to cuneiform signs in Sumerian texts are based on Akkadian values and on ancient glosses. Since most of these glosses date from periods when Sumerian was no longer spoken, i.e. from a milieu speaking Akkadian or other Semitic languages, it is said that we view Sumerian phonology through Akkadian glasses. However, since the signs used to write Akkadian had been adapted from an originally Sumerian system of cuneiform writing, we might also say that our Akkadian glasses were made by a Sumerian optician.

Cuneiform writing

Cuneiform characters, commonly called *signs*, are configurations of impressions made by a reed stylus on wet clay. The earliest signs (3100 B.C.E.) were linear—that is, they were *drawn* with a pointed stylus—but it was quickly realized that *impressing* the stylus in short, quick strokes was both more efficient and more esthetic. The strokes making up a single sign are varied in length and impressed at various angles. Each stroke has a wedge-shaped head, formed by the angular head of the stylus, and a straight tail. Short angular strokes lost their tails by the end of the third millennium; and by the same time, scribes abandoned the practice of using a separate stylus with a round cross-section (or the butt-end of the normal stylus?) to write numbers (SEC-TION 67). The native terms for 'cuneiform' refer to impression of the stroke (Sumerian *gu-sum* = Akkadian *miḫiṣtu/miḫiltu*) or the appearance of the stroke (Sumerian *santak* = Akkadian *santakku*). In a Sumerian epic text that includes an etiology of writing (Vanstiphout 1989), the purported first recipient of a cuneiform message exclaims, "It's wedge-like!"

Clay cuneiform tablets vary in size from 2 × 2 cm to 30 × 30 cm, and their shapes (round, rounded corners, sharp corners, relatively thick or thin) and orientation ("portrait" or "landscape") have varied both diachronically and synchronically (according to text type and function). Because of the effect of gravity on the wet clay, the obverse of an inscribed tablet will be flat (it sits on a flat surface while the reverse is being written and/or while drying), and the reverse slightly convex. Tablets could be fired in a kiln for enhanced durability, but this was normally done only in special circumstances, as in the case of the beautifully written exemplars in the library of Ashurbanipal (king of Assyria, 668–627); many more tablets were unintentionally baked when conflagrations destroyed their storage places in antiquity. For commemorative purposes, clay cones, prisms, cylinders, pots, and bricks were also inscribed. These last were also stamped by the thousands with ceramic or wooden stamps that had the entire text of a short inscription carved in reverse.

It is clear from the pictographic signs in the first column of TABLE 3.1 that the original orientation of writing had been 90° clockwise from the position that the cuneiform signs classically assumed. The shift in orientation is generally supposed to have to do with a change in the way the tablet was held, probably for ergonomic reasons. The time of the shift is a matter of controversy; it quite possibly had occurred by the middle of the third millennium, most certainly by the beginning of the second, although the original orientation was maintained on stone stelas until the middle of the second millennium.

From the archaic stage onward, signs were grouped into boxes called *cases*, and these could be arranged in vertical columns (in the "classical" orientation); cases were read from top to bottom, and the columns from left to right (see FIGURE 3 on page 44). By the middle of the third millennium, tablets were turned over vertically, and the reverse was inscribed in columns beginning on the right, so that the last (right-

TABLE 3.1: *The Formation and Evolution of Cuneiform Signs*

			Archaic Uruk ca. 3000	Presargonic Lagash, ca. 2400	Neo-Assyrian ca. 700
I	SAG	'head'			
2	KA	'mouth'			
3	GU₇	'to eat'			
4	EME	'tongue'			
5	DU	'to go'			
6	UDU	'sheep'			
7	UD₅	'goat'			
8	GUD	'bull'			
9	GEME₂	'female slave'			
IO	GI	'reed, to render'			
II	SAR	'plant, to write'			

most) column of the obverse bordered the same edge of the tablet as the first column of the reverse. A writer or reader finishing the obverse turned the tablet and continued writing or reading in a column contiguous to the one just finished. Within cases, signs could be arranged randomly, but after the mid third millennium, they were written in the order in which they were read. Over time, the cases broadened into lines of signs, and the columns necessarily broadened as well, so that in later periods texts would rarely have more than three columns per side, whereas in earlier periods some tablets have up to fifteen columns per side. In the second and first millennia, the majority of tablets have just one column per side, representing a single transaction, a letter, or an extract of a literary text.

The only medium other than clay suitable for cuneiform writing was wax, and wax-covered writing boards—made usually of wood, but also of ivory or other precious materials—which could be hinged together to form polyptychs, are attested in texts from the end of the third millennium onward. A set of writing boards has been found in a late second millennium shipwreck off the Turkish coast, but it is impossible to determine whether they had been inscribed with cuneiform or some other script (Symington 1991). Although they were used in large numbers in first-millennium Mesopotamia, only one complete writing board in ivory, and fragments of others in ivory and wood, have been found at the Assyrian royal city Kalakh (modern Nimrud). The cover of the ivory board identified it as a copy of an astrological text intended for the palace of Sargon II (721–705), and fragments of the wax surface found with it were indeed inscribed with that very text.

Other media were used only for commemorative, decorative, or legal purposes. Cuneiform signs were laboriously incised on stone from early in the third millennium onward, on objects ranging in size from tiny cylinder seals to tall stelas (e.g. the Code of Hammurabi) to the walls of Assyrian palaces. Cuneiform was also worked in metal and wood, and painted on a variety of surfaces. Except in the early periods, the distinctive wedge shape of the strokes was painstakingly imitated in these other media.

The cuneiform signs themselves underwent great change over time, and show significant regional variation as well. (The cuneiform typeface used in this book is based on the sign forms found on tablets from the time of Ashurbanipal. Compare the illustrations throughout this section with the sometimes very different forms printed in the figure legends and the text samples.) An experienced cuneiformist can roughly date and localize a tablet by its paleography alone. The major trends in the evolution of cuneiform signs, as can be seen from TABLE 3.1, are the straightening of curved lines, the broadening of the head of each stroke, the diminution in the number of strokes per sign, the restriction of the possible orientation of the strokes, the replacement of angled strokes by horizontals, and, in Assyria, the resolution of certain groups of angular wedges into groups of parallel horizontals. As a result, almost all pictorial content disappears after the archaic stage. The number of signs diminished by about one half: in the earliest repertoire, there were around 1200 signs, counting compounds and significant variants; the number drops to 800 or less by the middle of the third millennium, and in the second and first millennia there were about 600 signs. Even though many signs in the early repertories disappeared and others merged, new signs and sign combinations continued to be created, and some older signs even split into distinctive shapes for different meanings. The native names for the signs, attested in the second and first millennia, derive from a Sumerian or Akkadian value of a sign, or, in the case of compound, complex, and altered signs, describe the way a sign has been composed or altered.

Cuneiform signs

TABLE 3.1 reveals the pictographic basis of cuneiform, which in C. S. Peirce's terminology was both *iconic* (a head used to write the word "head" [3.1.1]) and *indexical* (a bull's head to write "bull" [3.1.8], a foot used to write "to go" and "to stand" [3.1.5]; the latter type of index is also called *semantic association* herein). But there were also a number of purely symbolic signs, such as the cross in a circle for "sheep," and other related signs for gendered and age-graded categories of sheep and goats (3.1.6–7). Possibly because drawing or impressing the stylus on clay did not lend itself to detailed representation without sacrificing the rapidity necessary for the writing system to be a useful administrative tool, the vast majority of signs are quite schematic even in their earliest versions, and the specific basis of many that are clearly intended to be representations of something remains obscure.

Using around 300 basic signs, and even fewer discrete elements, the archaic scribes elaborated a system of over 1,000 signs that was capable of representing the vocabulary necessary for recording bureaucratic transactions, including personal and place names. New signs were created by altering and combining these basic signs. Conventions for altering signs included adding lines or hatching, inversion, writing the sign at an angle, writing multiples of the sign, and making a cross of the sign and its duplicate. *Compound* signs were formed by writing one sign joined or very close to another, *complex* signs by putting one sign inside another. Many of the archaic compounds became complex signs in later periods.

Thus, the SAG sign* (TABLE 3.1.1), a pictogram of a head (Sum. *sag* 'head'), had some lines added where the mouth would be to create the sign for Sum. *ka* 'mouth' (3.1.2; used as well to write Sum. *zú* 'tooth', *kir₄* 'nose', *inim* 'word', *gù* 'voice, sound', and *dug₄* 'to say'). The sign for 'food' (Sum. *ninda*) was adjoined to SAG to create the sign for Sum. *gu₇* 'to eat' (3.1.3); in subsequent periods, the sign GU₇ was built on KA, and the food moved inside, becoming a complex sign (KA×NINDA) rather than a compound one (SAG+NINDA). The sign for 'woman', a pubic triangle, is joined to the sign for 'mountains, foreign lands' to form a compound for Sum. *geme₂* 'female slave' (3.1.9) because slaves were obtained in raids on foreign lands in the mountainous northeast. All these modifications and combinations are based on semantic association; after the archaic period, combinations that join phonetic to semantic elements were created, such as KA×ME = Sum. *eme* 'tongue' (3.1.4), or ⵈ ⵝ ⵛ PA.TE.SI = *ensi₂* 'ruler'.

This last example illustrates an important tendency in matching the repertory of signs to the lexicon. Rather than creating ever more compound, complex, and altered

---

*The Assyriological convention is to refer to a sign by one of its common values written in small capitals. Actual Sumerian and Akkadian words are in *italics* (or, Sumerian is presented in s p a c e d r o m a n type). The components of compound signs are joined by +, those of complex signs by ×; individual signs in clusters are separated by periods. Homophones are distinguished by subscript index numbers, except that on monosyllables ₂ is replaced by an acute accent and ₃ by a grave accent. Signs making up a single word are joined by hyphens.

signs, clusters of two or more signs (selected on a semantic, or, less frequently, semantic plus phonetic, basis) were written serially and read as a single Sumerian word.
This prevented what would have otherwise been an enormous inflation in the number
of signs as the application of writing was extended to various and different contexts.

Rebus writing, too, made it possible to represent a large number of lexemes with
a relatively small number of signs, and was a way of representing lexemes that could
not be easily indicated by iconic or indexical signs. Sumerian has a large number of
homonyms and near homonyms—so many, in fact, that scholars have assumed that
Sumerian must have been a tone language. It was thus particularly well suited for rebus substitution. Curiously, the principle of rebus writing was understood in the archaic period but hardly used. Examples include ⊢ᴇᴵ BA, probably a pictogram of a
tool called *ba* in Sumerian, used to mean 'to distribute', also *ba*, and ⊢ᴵᴵ⊿ GI
(TABLE 3.1.10), a pictogram of a reed (Sum. *gi*), used to represent *gi* 'to render' and
in the archaic period probably also used for *sigi* 'yellow'. Massive exploitation of rebus writing quickly developed in subsequent periods. A very few examples (giving
the Sumerian word, the meaning represented originally by the sign, and the homonym
represented by rebus extension): ⊾ᴱᴵᴵ *su* 'body' and 'to replace', ⊢ᴵᴵ *si* 'horn' and
'to fill', ⊨ᴵᴵ *e* 'dike' and 'to speak', ⊨ᴱᴸᴵ *sar* 'plant' and 'to write' (3.1.11). Rebus
phoneticism—that is, the use of a sign to represent not a homonym of the word represented by the sign, but only the sound of that word in order to write phonetically—
also seems to have been understood in the archaic period, but again is very rare. Consider archaic ⊱⊿⊢ᴵ ⊰ᴵᴵᴵ NE+RU *erim₂* 'evil', and later ᵼᵼᵸ⊢ᴱᴵ *ha-la* 'share' or ⊢ᴱᴵ⊢ᴷᴵ
ba-al 'to dig'. NE.RU is probably an attempt to render the sound [erim]; in each case,
the semantic values of the individual signs have nothing to do with the meanings of
the words.

The mixture of semantic association and rebus writing resulted in a very inconsistent system of representation. Whereas ⊾ᴱᴵᴵ SU represents the homonyms 'body'
and 'to replace', to represent *sù(d)* 'distant' the sign for semantically associated ✕⊢
gíd 'long' was altered with additional strokes and the resulting sign ✕⊢ᵼᵼᵼ SUD was
used as well for *sù(g)* 'empty, naked', based on both semantic association and rebus,
and for *sù* 'to sprinkle', based on rebus alone. The word for 'beard', *su₆*, is written
KA×SA, a complex sign combining semantic association (⊢ᴱᴸᴵ *ka* = 'mouth') and a
rebus phonetic indicator (⊼ᵼᵼ SA). Although rebus writing was employed with increasing frequency after about 2900, the majority of compound and complex signs and
sign clusters are semantically based, without any phonetic reading clue. Consider the
long and certainly post-archaic ⟨ᴱᴵ ⊾ᴱᴵᴵ ᴱᴵᴵ ᴱᴵ ᵠ KI.SU.LU.ÚB.GAR ('place where
the water bag is put?') *ugnim* 'army', or ⊢ᵼᵼᵼ⊢ ⟨ᴱᴵ ⊾ᴱᵼ ⊢ᵼᵼᵼ⊰ Ú.KI.SÌ.GA ('put together
grass?') *gùd* 'nest'.

Sumerian homonymy and the primacy of semantic association in the mapping of
the lexicon onto the sign system are responsible for the notorious homophony and polyphony of cuneiform signs, features that complicated the initial decipherment and
were the source of considerable resistance to the decipherment once it was accom-

plished. Over twenty different signs can be read /du/, and the sign ►ᴴ KA has several times the half-dozen readings mentioned above.

Sumerian cuneiform

The transformation of a writing system that used language strictly as an administrative tool into one that could adequately express natural language in a broad range of contexts—letters, commemorative inscriptions, legal documents, literary texts, technical literature—was effected by the increasing use of rebus phoneticism to write grammatical affixes. Sumerian is an agglutinative language in which nouns take suffixes and verbs both prefixes and suffixes. Virtually no trace of these affixes can be found in the early archaic texts, but they begin appearing after 2900 B.C.E. Curiously, they are used in what can only be described as a skeletal way for centuries; and only in the early second millennium, when Sumerian was probably extinct and spoken only in the schools, are the affixes fully expressed. The example in FIGURE 3 comes from a collection of sayings preserved in manuscripts from ca. 2500 and ca. 1800 (Alster 1974). The cuneiform signs added by the later version to express the affixes are here shown in smaller type.

The earlier version, using what is sometimes referred to as *nuclear writing*, omits the genitive and dative suffixes of the nominal complex, as well as the verbal prefix, root reduplication (for imperfective), and second person singular suffix of the verb. Note that the genitive suffix *-a(k)* is written *-ra* after *engar* 'farmer', illustrating the regular convention of using a CV sign to write a vocalic suffix after a consonant, which helps (along with contextual features) to disambiguate the sign APIN, which could be read *apin* 'plow' or *uru₄* 'to cultivate' in addition to *engar* 'farmer'. (How and to what extent the grammatical affixes expressed in written Sumerian found phonological expression in Sumerian is a vexing problem that cannot be broached here.)

Sumerian cuneiform, then, is what Gelb (1963) termed a logosyllabic writing system. Unbound morphemes are represented by logograms (single signs or sign clusters); bound morphemes are expressed by rebus-derived syllabograms, usually V, CV, or VC (but note ►ᴵᴸᵡ NAM in FIGURE 3, late version). In addition, beginning in the archaic period Sumerian texts employ a series of semantic classifiers called *determinatives* that had no phonological realization and were probably developed to help disambiguate polyvalent signs. Some precede and some follow the word they determine, and in transliterations they are generally written as superscripts, for which purpose the very common determinatives ►╂ AN for *dingir* 'god', ⌐ DIŠ preceding a male personal name, and ⌁ SAL for *munus* 'woman' preceding a female name are abbreviated ᵈ, ᵐ, and ᶠ respectively. Thus, in the sample passage below, ⌁ ►⟨⟨⟨ ⌐⟨ᴱⳆ *kul-ab₄*ᵏⁱ is the city Kulab followed by the determinative *ki* 'place', and ►╂ ⌐ᵈ*utu* is Utu, the sun god, preceded by the determinative *dingir* 'god'.

In literary texts, lines are generally complete clauses; and in archival texts, a line constitutes a single entry. When a clause or entry doesn't fit on a single line, it is con-

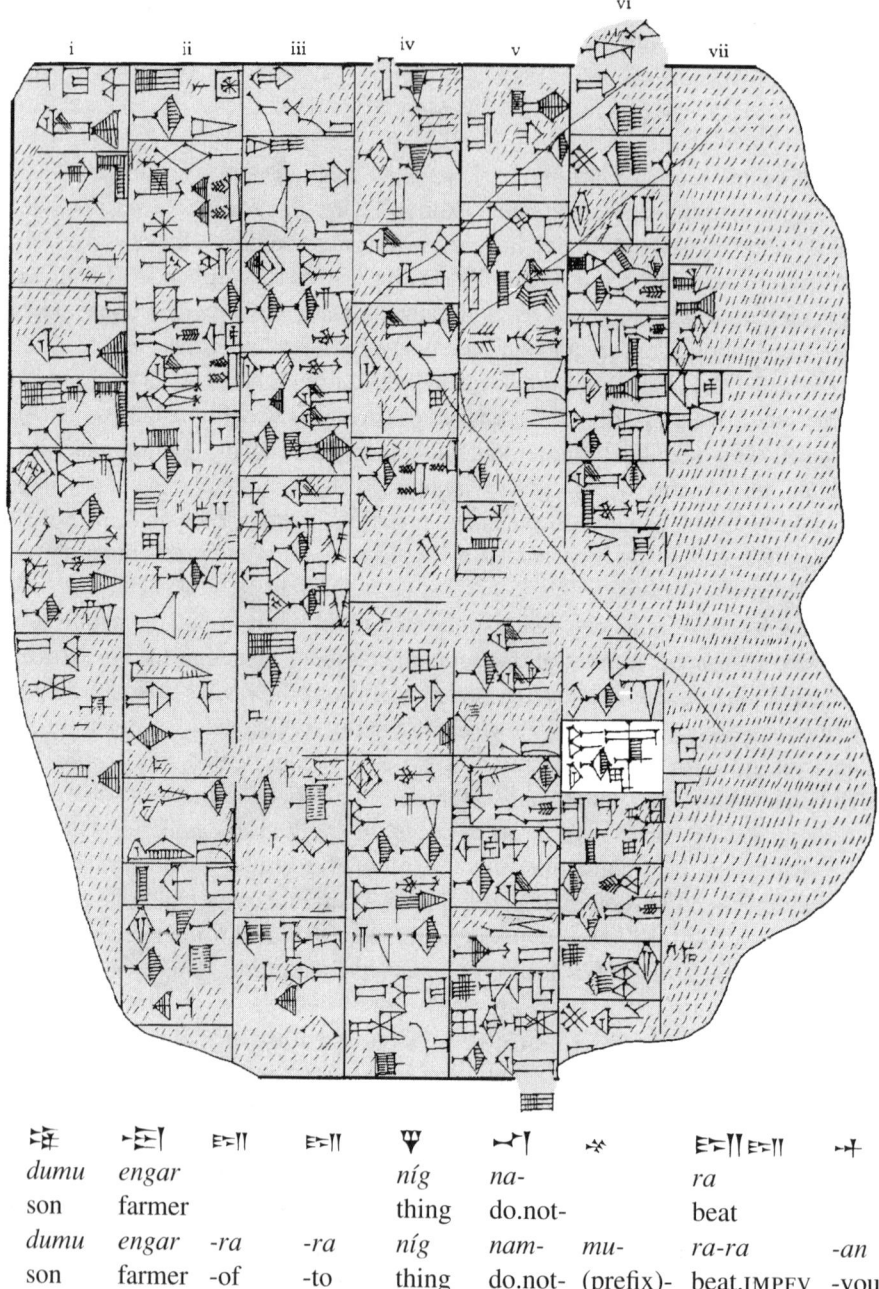

𒁷	𒂗	𒂊𒈠	𒂊𒈠	𒐊	𒈾	𒅗	𒂊𒈠𒂊𒈠	𒀀
dumu	*engar*			*níg*	*na-*		*ra*	
son	farmer			thing	do.not-		beat	
dumu	*engar*	*-ra*	*-ra*	*níg*	*nam-*	*mu-*	*ra-ra*	*-an*
son	farmer	-of	-to	thing	do.not-	(prefix)-	beat.IMPFV	-you

'Do not beat a farmer's son.'

FIGURE 3. Copy of cuneiform tablet with early version of saying.
The example quoted is the fifth-from-bottom case in column vi (Biggs 1974, no. 256).

tinued, indented, just beneath, before a new line is begun at the column's left edge. If space permits, words or phrases may be grouped together; if there is too much space, the last sign or two are moved to the right, even though it breaks up the word, so that the last sign on the line is at the line's right edge. In no instance, at least after the middle of the third millennium, are words split between two lines.

SAMPLE OF SUMERIAN

1. Sumerian:

2. Transliteration: kin-gi₄-a   ka-ni   dugud šu

3. Gloss: messenger   mouth-his   heavy AUX

1.

2. nu-mu-un-da-an-gi₄-gi₄   en   kul-ab₄ᵏⁱ-a-ke₄   im-e   šu

3. not-PREF-able-he-repeated   lord Kulab-DET-of-ERG   clay-on hand

1.

2. bí-in-ra   inim   dub-gim   bí-in-gub   u₄-bi-ta   inim

3. PREF-he-struck word   tablet-like PREF-he-put   day-that-from word

1.

2. im-ma   gub-bu   nu-ub-ta-gál-la

3. clay-on   put   not-that-from-existed-COP

> 'The messenger's mouth was heavy, he could not repeat the message. The Lord of Kulab patted some clay, he put the words on it as on a tablet. Before that time, words put on clay had never existed.'
> —*From manuscript of ca. 1800 B.C.E. of the Sumerian tale "Enmerkar and the Lord of Aratta" (Vanstiphout 1989).*

Akkadian cuneiform

The Old Akkadian syllabary (Gelb 1961) developed ca. 2350 B.C.E. based on the same principle of rebus-based syllabic writing used to express grammatical affixes in Sumerian cuneiform, which had been used as well to write Semitic and other non-Sumerian names for centuries. Many of the same syllabic signs were used, and many more were added, based either on Sumerian values or on the Akkadian translation of the Sumerian meaning of a sign.† For example, KAL = /dan/ because that sign was used to write Sumerian *kalg* 'strong', which is *dannu* in Akkadian; or GIŠ = /is, iṣ, iz/ because Sumerian *giš* 'tree' = Akkadian *iṣu*. Most of the signs chosen represent open syllables (V, CV, VC); but CVC signs were also used from the beginning, constituting from five to fifty percent or more of the syllabary, depending on period,

---

†In transcribing Akkadian, a macron indicates a historically long vowel or length compensating for loss of a consonant, and a circumflex indicates a long vowel derived via contraction of vowels. Logograms are transliterated in small capitals; in a transcription, logographic vs. syllabic writing is not indicated.

place, and the kind of text being written. (For the question of CVCV signs, see Reiner 1973.) In addition to syllabic orthography, Akkadian writing can also use signs with their Sumerian lexical values as logograms; e.g. the sign ⟨𒈗⟩ LUGAL (Sumerian *lugal* 'king') would be read as the contextually appropriate allomorph of Akkadian *šarru* 'king'. But Akkadian cuneiform writing was from the beginning primarily syllabic—no doubt because as an inflecting language, Akkadian was ill suited to the kind of logosyllabic writing used for Sumerian. (Sumerian-style logosyllabic writing was in fact tried on a Semitic language at Ebla and other northwestern sites, but was later abandoned in favor of the syllabic writing developed for Old Akkadian.)

INVENTORY. In the Old Akkadian syllabary, the phonological features voiced, voiceless, and "emphatic" are not distinguished at all. Only one CV sign each is used to represent a labial, dental, or velar stop followed by a given vowel. Either this was a way to hold down the number of signs in the syllabary, or the actual phonological basis of the distinction made between the Sumerian stops that we transcribe as voiced vs. voiceless (*b, d, g* vs. *p, t, k*) was heard differently than the distinction made between Akkadian voiced, voiceless, and emphatic stops (represented as *b-p*-[no emphatic labial], *d-t-ṭ*, and *g-k-q*). So for example, ⟨𒁕⟩ DA = /da, ta, ṭa/, ⟨𒋾⟩ TI = /di, ti, ṭi/, ⟨�⟩ GA = /ga, ka, qa/, ⟨𒁍⟩ BU = /bu, pu/. By the early second millennium, when Sumerian was no longer spoken outside the schools, scribes began to use the signs for distinct Sumerian stops to represent voiced and voiceless syllable-initial Akkadian stops, in what appears to be a reinterpretation of the stop system of the now dead Sumerian language in terms of the system of Akkadian. The emphatic series was represented by the voiced or voiceless sign (⟨𒁕⟩ DA = /da, ṭa/, ⟨𒆠⟩ KI = /ki, qi/), or else emphatic values were given to separate signs (e. g. ⟨𒌈⟩ TÙN = /ṭu/; ⟨𒄣⟩ GUM = /qu/; ⟨𒄭⟩ ḪI = /ṭa/ because ḪI was used to write Sumerian DÙG 'good', which is *ṭābu* in Akkadian). The tendency over time is to increasingly distinguish stops in CV signs, but in no period was this done consistently. The representation of sibilants developed similarly, though it was very much more complicated at the beginning because Old Akkadian preserved more sibilants than later stages of the language and tried to distinguish among them (see Gelb 1961 for the problem of Old Akkadian sibilants, laryngeals, and pharyngeals).

In syllable-final position, Sumerian never distinguished between voiced and voiceless stops (probably only voiced stops were allowed in that position), and Akkadian writing never makes that distinction either. In all periods, ⟨𒀜⟩ AD = /ad, at, aṭ/, etc. (similarly, in the sibilants, ⟨𒊻⟩ UZ = /uz, us, uṣ/, etc.). In CVC signs, the initial stop may be distinguished (⟨𒁉𒅕⟩ DIR = /dir, ṭir/, but ⟨𒋻⟩ TIR = /tir/), but never final stops (⟨𒁖⟩ DAG = /dag, dak, daq/).

As in Sumerian writing, the Akkadian syllabary generally distinguishes three primary vowels, /a, i, u/, and distinguishes a fourth vowel /e/ (see Reiner 1973) in some signs, but usually the signs incorporating the /i/ vowel are used for /e/ as well (e.g. the pairs /id, ed/, /gir, ger/, etc. are written with one sign each). Exceptions occur with weak consonants and glides: ⸲⎹⎼ PI can be used to represent /w/ + any vowel, or any vowel + /w/—and also, in some syllabaries, /y/ + any vowel, or any vowel + /y/ (which in other syllabaries is represented by ⎬⏊ I+A). ⸲⊷⫲ AḪ = any vowel + /ḫ/, and in earlier periods ʾ + any vowel; in later periods a separate sign derived from AḪ, ⸲⊷⊦, is used for ʾ + any vowel, or any vowel + ʾ. In some CVC signs, too, the V can represent more than one primary vowel; thus, for different reasons in each case, ⸲⎬ ḪAR = /ḫar, ḫir, ḫur/, ⟨⊏⎹ NIM = /nim, num/, and ⫐⎬ LU = /dib, dab/.

With rare exceptions in certain syllabaries, there is one sign each for the vowels /a, e, i/ and three for /u/. In Old Akkadian, ⟨ U = /yu/, ⊢⎹⎹⎹⊢ Ú = /u/, and ⟨⎹⊦⫐⎹ Ù = /ʔu/; in the early second millennium, U dropped out of the syllabary, Ú was used for /u/, and Ù was specialized to write the conjunction *u* 'and'. In the first millennium, Ú and Ù retain those same functions, but U returns as an alternate for either.

In theory, Akkadian could be written perfectly well with a concise set of V, CV, and VC signs, since the digraph CV-VC is equivalent in the system to CVC. Yet CVC signs were in the Akkadian syllabary from the beginning, probably because of the association of the signs with Sumerian CVC readings; and their number and use increase over time. But even the latest periods do not have CVC signs for every possible syllable: for example, from Old Akkadian onward, CVC signs can be used to write /dan/ or /maš/, but there are never CVC signs to write /lan/ or /baš/. There is a small amount of homophony in the early Akkadian syllabaries, but the choice of homophones is seldom free; it is, rather, contextually determined. In Old Akkadian, ⊏⸲⎹ NE = /bi/ when it is etymologically /biʔ/. At Mari, ⫐⊏⎹ AB is commonly used with the value *is* to write /is/; but in a sequence /issV/, if /ss/ is etymologically *ns*, then /is/ is written with ⫐⎹ GIŠ = *is*. Only after the middle of the second millennium, and especially in the first, do we find cases of free variation (though still, often, with a degree of predictability) of values like ⫐⎬⎹ *ad* and ⊷⫐⎹⎹⎹ *ád*, ⸲⊷ *pu* and ⟨⎹ *pú*, and even CVC signs like ⊏⎹⎹⎹⎹ *dub* and ⫐⎹⊏⎹ *dúb*. Similarly, although a small amount of polyphony exists in the early syllabaries, it is only in the first millennium that it becomes rampant. ⸲⊷ KUR can be read *mad, nat, lad, šad, sad, kur*; ⎹⊢⎹ UR is *ur, lik, tàn, taš/s, tís*; ⸲⊏ SAL is *s/šal, rag, mim, mám*, and so on. Whereas a scholar at the court of Ashurbanipal would have mastered ca. 600 cuneiform signs with their syllabic and/or logographic values (as well as hundreds more compound logograms), scribes writing Akkadian in most periods had a working repertoire of between two and three hundred signs, and a scribe or merchant in an Old Assyrian trading firm (ca. 1800 B.C.E.) could do very well with around one hundred syllabic signs and a handful of logograms.

TABLE 3.2 presents a cuneiform syllabary of the first millennium, known as Syllabary A (edited by Richard T. Hallock, in Landsberger 1955: 1–45; cf. Cavigneaux 1983). This would have been the first list of signs and their values for a student scribe to master in Nineveh during the age of Ashurbanipal. It is presented in the order of the original manuscripts, and the values are supplied with accents and index numbers according to modern scholarly conventions. Only the values given in the syllabary are listed here (with some minor adjustments). Where the sign values have not been preserved on the ancient manuscripts, they have been restored. In the manuscripts, the values are expressed using a very limited inventory of CV and VC signs; these are gathered in TABLE 3.4 on page 57, which will also serve as a phonetic key to the cuneiform syllabary and to the subsequent tables.

As set forth above (page 46), all syllable-final stops and sibilants (except /š/) can be used for voiced, voiceless, or emphatic segments (thus sign 3 could be used to write /šug, šuk, šuq/), but in syllable-initial position this is not necessarily the case (sign 2 is /sur/ but never /zur, ṣur/, for which see sign 82; sign 22 is /za, ṣa/ but rarely /sa/, which is usually written with sign 108). Note that this ancient beginners' syllabary does not always give all the current values of each sign it lists, and there are some relatively common signs that it entirely omits (TABLE 3.3 on page 52). A few signs appear in two different places in the list, because the sign current in seventh-century Assyria represented two or more earlier signs whose forms had coalesced.

Syllabary A begins with the sign A because a different beginners' syllabary, used a thousand years earlier, also began with A. The succession of signs is determined by phonetic, graphic, and semantic factors, but not all transitions are explicable. Thus, sign 2 SUR follows A possibly because Sumerian *a* is 'water' and *sur* is 'to press out, drip liquid'. Sign 3 is graphically similar to sign 2, and sign 4 was attracted because of the rhyme of /mur/ and /sur/ (no. 2). Signs 5 and 6 are graphically related to 4, sign 7 was attracted because /ḫu/ is the inverse of no. 5 /uḫ/, and sign 8 is formed by adding a single vertical wedge to sign 7. Cavigneaux stresses that not only Sumerian meanings come into play (signs 9 and 10 are both third person singular suffixes), but the phonetic similarities of the Akkadian equivalents of the signs can be relevant as well (166–168: GEME₂ = *amtu*, AMA = *ummu*, EŠ = *amūtu*).

TABLE 3.3 lists some common signs that were not included in Syllabary A by the ancients. The list is adapted from Landsberger 1955: 45, with the most frequent values added using the same typographic scheme as TABLE 3.2.

ORTHOGRAPHY. Rules of Akkadian orthography vary chronologically and geographically; the following represents standard practices and trends that do not (necessarily) apply to Old Akkadian or late Akkadian dialects. Within a word, a consonant-final sign cannot be followed by a vowel-initial sign: *parāsu* 'to decide' would be written 𒈨𒊏𒋢 *pa-ra-su*, never *par-as-u* or the like. There are two exceptions. This rule is sometimes violated at a morpheme boundary: *iprusam* < *iprus* 'he decided' + ventive suffix *-am* may be written �𒊒𒊬𒄠 *ip-ru-us-am*. Otherwise, the C-V juncture is used to indicate a glottal stop: *im ᵓidu* 'they have become many' is written 𒅎𒄿𒁺 *im-i-du*. Double consonants may or may not be expressed, but in most orthographies a double consonant can only be written if grammatically justified. Similarly, long vowels may or may not be indicated (by adding the appropriate V sign after a CV sign), but are usually grammatically justified when written, and are almost always expressed in word-final position when derived from the contraction of etymologically dissimilar consonants. Thus 𒅗𒇻 *ka-lu* can be either *kallu* 'bowl' or

TABLE 3.2: *Syllabary A*[a] TABLE 3.2: *Syllabary A*[a] *(continued)*

I	𒀀	a
2		sur
3		šug
4		mur, ḫar, KIKKIN
5		uḫ
6		i', UMUN₄
7		ḫu, u₁₁, *pag*, MUŠEN
8		ri, dal
9		bi, kaš
10		ni, zal, *lí*
11		bu, sír
12		sù
13	[b]	ku, šè, zì, dúr, tukul
14	[c]	lu, dib, UDU
15		ru, šub, GEŠPU
16		ḫa, a₇, ku₆
17		kir, peš
18		li
19		la
20		lum
21		zu
22		za
23		su, kuš
24		nu
25		na
26		ba
27		zi
28		ge
29		ge₄
30		gim, dím
31		ma
32		mu
33		taḫ
34		iz, giš
35		gá, MÀ, *mal*, PISAN

36		gán
37		en
38		in
39		eri
40		*el*, SIKIL
41		*ši*, *lim*, LIB₄, BAD₅, igi
42		IGI₂
43		ḫi, *tí*, šár, DÙG
44		DU₁₅, kam
45		an, *il*, DINGIR, SA₈
46		BULUḪ, ḫal
47		ur, *lik*, taš
48		ne, dè, bí, bil, kúm, ṣaḫ, IZI
49		GIBIL
50		ka, *pi₄*, INIM, DU₁₁, ZÚ, KIR₄
51		sag
52		súr
53		du, ša₄, rá, gub
54		SUḪ₆
55		KAŠ₄
56		i
56A		*ya*
57		šu
58		šà
59		ša
60		úḫ
61		aš, *rù*, dil
62		ERIM, zab
63		u₄, ud, tam, *par*, laḫ, ZALAG
64		ad
65		da
66		ta
67		ti
68		um
69		dub

a. Values transcribed in lower-case roman would have been used both for syllabic Akkadian writing and logo-graphically, italicized values would have been used only in syllabic writing, and values in small capitals are only logograms or hypothetical values that are never found in context. Cf. FIGURE 9 on page 147.

b. Compare no. 200.

c. Compare no. 91.

TABLE 3.2: *Syllabary A*[a] *(continued)*   TABLE 3.2: *Syllabary A*[a] *(continued)*

70	𒈩	mes
71	M98	urudu
72	𒄠	am
73	𒅎	im
74	𒅖	iš, *mil*, SAḪAR
75	𒃲	gal
76	𒉣	nun
77	𒈨	me
78	𒈪	mi, *ṣíl*, GÍG
79	𒂂	dugud
80	𒁷	din
81	𒌷	GEŠTIN
82	𒈥	*zur*, AMAR
83	𒋃	siskur
84	�	uz
85	𒆪	KU₄, tu, ḪUDUŠ
86	𒌈	tum, íb
87	𒄀	egir
88	𒁴	dim
89	𒈤	mar
90	𒊏	*rad*
91	𒁲[d]	dib
92	𒆷	ḫab, *kìr*, rim, LAGAB
93	𒋰	tab
94	𒊍	kas
95	𒇲	*làḫ*, SUKKAL
96	𒆗	*dan*, kal, *líb*, GURUŠ
97	𒄖	gu
98	𒂵	ga
99	𒌒	ub, ár
100	𒇴	lam
101	𒉿	pi, *me₈*, à, tál, GELTAN
102	𒂆	dù, rú, gag
103	�ir	ir
104	𒊏	ra
105	𒆠	ki

106	𒁲	di, sá, SÌM
107	�	šar, mú, NIŠA, NISI
108	𒊓	sa
109	𒁉	*bir₅*, sim, nam
110	𒀊	ab, èš
111	𒄞	GU₄, GUD
112	�	ul
113	𒊻	az
114	𒊬	ug, PIRIG₃
115	𒀲	ANŠE₂, ḪÚŠ, PIRIG, GÌR
116	𒉄	ALIM
117	𒍽	ḫuš
118	𒆧	kiš
119	𒀲	ANŠE
120	𒎏	lib, *paḫ*, nar
121	𒉀	NAGAR
122	𒄥	gur
123	𒃮	gàr
124	𒁈	dar
125	𒉆	*ríg*, ṣum
126	𒊮	ŠA₉, *qu*, gum
127	𒂰	gaz
128	𒉘	ÁG
129	𒅆	kúr, pap
130	𒁓	bur
131	𒁇[e]	bar
132	𒋛	si
133	𒉈	SI₄
134	𒉺	pa
135	𒌋	u
136	𒅇	ù
137	𒈦[f]	maš
138	𒊮	*šá*, gar, MU₈, NINDA, NITA₄
139	𒀠	al
140	𒅋	il
141	𒌑	ú

d. Repeated from no. 14, because originally different sign.

e. Compare no. 137.

f. Sign originally different from no. 131.

TABLE 3.2: *Syllabary A*ᵃ *(continued)*

142		lál
143		làl
144		*id*
145		ṣi
146		SIMUG
147		uš, ús, *nit*, NITA, GÌŠ
148		KU₇
149		sì
150		KI₄, saḫ, líl, kid
151		bar₄, dàg
152		e, ÉG
153		é
154		BUR₆, LEL₄, KISAL
155		ká
156		ar
157		muš, ṣir
158		úr
159		sis, šeš, URI₃
160		ib, URAŠ, DARA₂
161		tag, šum
162		sal, *rag*, *mín*
163		nin, *min₄*, eriš
164		ag, ME₆
165		ig, gál
166		GEME₂
167		AMA, DAGAL
168		eš
169		zib
170		kur, *šad*, *lad*, *mad*, *nad*
171		*qa*, SILA₃
172		tar, ḫaš, kud, sil
173		*be*, til, úš, bad g
174		kù
175		sa₆
176		BÀN, BANDA₃, DUMU, tur

TABLE 3.2: *Syllabary A*ᵃ *(continued)*

177		un, KALAM
178		gú
179		dur
180		sig
181		SIG₅
182		te, TEMEN
183		kar
184		bal
185		šul
186		šaḫ
187		lú
188		LUGAL, *šarru*
189		maḫ
190		ḫul
191		gul
192		áš, ZÍZ
193		ÍL, GÙR
194		gab, duḫ, DU₈
195		NITA₂, ìr, ARAD
196		ARAD₂
197		šìr, ḫir, EZEN
198		IDIM
199		še
200		ŠÈ i
201		nim, *tum₄*, ELAM
202		tùm
203		nir
204		zag
205		ḫé
206		kab
207		*kib*
208		ter
209		tuk
210		tag₄
211		bár, ŠAR₆

g. Compare no. 198.
h. Sign originally different from no. 173.
i. Sign originally different from no. 13.

TABLE 3.3: *Additional Signs*[a]

3		mug
7		šen, *šun*, *rug*
9		gír, *ád*
10		BÚR, *búl*
24		GIŠGAL
14		ITI
28		APIN, ENGAR, *pin*
37		kád
44		šir
45		NUMUN, kul
56		mud
69		mun
74		muš, *suḫ*
88		má
89		dir
94		*nab*
95		mul
111		rab
118		EDIN
128		zíb, *zig*, *ḫáš*
141		šim, *rig*

TABLE 3.3: *Additional Signs*[a] *(continued)*

154		šab
155		SIPA, síb
164		dug, lud
188		lil
198		mir, AGA, NIMGIR
210		gam, gúr
220		*liš*, DILIM₂
237		bir, ELLAG₂, GIRIŠ
244		áb, *lid*
256		pan
262		pà
274		man, mìn, *mam*, *mìm*, niš
276		diš, *dáš*, GIŠ, *ana*
277		lal, lá
283		túl, pú, ḪÁB
284		bul, TUK₄
285		sug, AMBAR
294		kin, *qi*
296		šú
301		dam
322		GÍN, TÙN, *tu*

a. The succession of the signs follows the order used in modern scholarly sign lists: taking the strokes from left to right, one and more horizontal wedges, one and more oblique wedges, one and more angle wedges, one and more vertical wedges. The numbers on the left are those of von Soden and Röllig 1967–76.

kalu 'all', whereas ⟨signs⟩ *ka-al-lu* or ⟨signs⟩ *kal-lu* could only be *kallu*, and ⟨signs⟩ *ka-lu-u* would be *kalû* 'lamentation priest'. ⟨signs⟩ *ka-ru* might be *kāru* 'dock' or *karru* 'pommel', but ⟨signs⟩ *ka-a-ru* would be only the former, and ⟨signs⟩ *kar-ru* or ⟨signs⟩ *ka-ar-ru* only the latter.

Logograms were used regularly for some very common lexemes, like 'king', 'field', 'silver', 'barley', 'scribe', etc., and for numerous technical terms as well. Logograms can be followed by phonetic complements, which can contain both grammatical information and clues to the proper Akkadian reading of the logogram. Logograms are generally used for nouns and adjectives; but verbs, too, at least in certain kinds of inscriptions, could already be written logographically in Old Akkadian—a practice which, together with the logographic writing of prepositions, becomes common in certain first millennium texts. In this case, phonetic complements may also precede the verbal logogram. In discursive texts of all kinds, the amount of logography seldom exceeds 15%, and is usually much more limited. Administrative texts, with their long lists and repetitive formulas, always employed a much greater amount of logography. Scientific and technical texts have some logography in the early second millennium; but in the late second and especially in the first millennium, the use of logograms in these texts expands enormously: divinatory and astronomical texts can be 85% logographic. This increase in the use of signs with their Sumerian-derived lexical values to write Akkadian was in part a scholarly affectation that made facility in the specialized use of the vocabulary of a long-dead language prerequisite to an academic career; but once mastered, logography was very useful. It often reduced the number of signs needed to write a given word or phrase, and it resulted in easy-to-scan texts, in which specific phenomena could quickly be located (FIGURE 4).

In the first millennium, a few common bisyllabic logograms were actually used as syllabograms in writing Akkadian, but this was done either in restricted contexts or as a scribal pun. So the sign 𒆪 for the Sumerian word *tukul* 'weapon' was used to spell forms of Akkadian *tukultu* 'trust', as in 𒆪𒋾 *tukul-ti* 'my trust'. Or the name of the Sumerian moon god Nanna is found in a playful writing of the Akkadian word *inanna* 'now': 𒄿𒀭𒈾𒆪 *i-ᵈnanna*.

Determinatives occur with logograms, but also with words written syllabically; they are transliterated in superscript (as in Sumerian) or can be written in small capitals with a logogram they modify. Thus, the logogram 𒄑𒆪, for Akkadian *kakku* 'weapon' preceded by the determinative for 'wood', can appear in transliteration as ᵍⁱˢTUKUL or GIŠ.TUKUL. Besides the use of phonetic complements, the grammatical realization of logographic writings can be indicated by reduplication, by the addition of plural markers derived from Sumerian, or by the dual marker 𒈫 (the numeral two), sometimes written by the scribe as a small superscript. The numeral two, often preceded by the sign 𒆠 KI, can also be used as a ditto sign, and the Sumerian-derived suffix 𒃶 KAM following a numeral indicates that it is to be read as an ordinal. Glosses and variant readings are set off by one or more angled wedges, known by the German term *Glossenkeil*.

In some Old Assyrian texts, a vertical wedge 𒁹 is used as a word divider, but never consistently. Otherwise, words are not separated or grouped in letters, legal texts, or commemorative texts. As in Sumerian, words and phrases may be grouped together in literary and technical texts, and words are never carried over to a new line; again as in Sumerian, the remainder of a word (or phrase in a literary text) will be indented below the line on which it began and considered the prolongation of that line. In poetry, a line is a whole stich, and in technical texts, a line is normally a complete entry (e.g. a protasis together with its apodosis in an omen collection). As in Sumerian writing, short lines are spaced so that the last sign reaches the right margin.

Just as Sumerian cuneiform writing was slow—even, it seems, reluctant—to exploit rebus phoneticism to fully express Sumerian grammatical affixes or provide phonetic indications for the pronunciation of Sumerian signs, so Akkadian cuneiform never exploited the potential for either a concise and consistent syllabary, or fully syllabic writing. Much like Japanese writing in its relationship with Chinese, Akkadian cuneiform relished the vestiges of its Sumerian origins, using Sumerian values to add

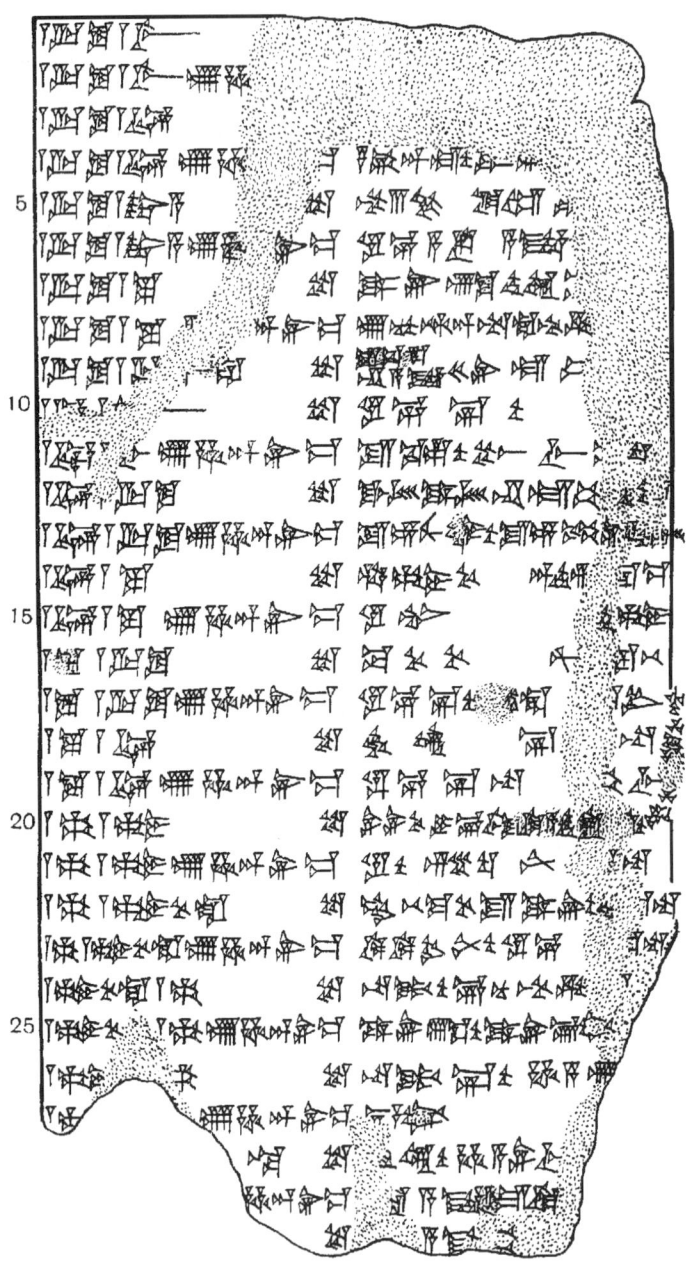

FIGURE 4. A first-millennium Akkadian omen text in Babylonian script. The omens are derived from the behavior of various animals. The initial wedge 𒁹 in each line is logographic for Akkadian *šumma* 'if', which is followed by the logogram for the animal in question: 1–9 𒌨𒄀 UR.GI₇ 'dog', 10–15 � ŠAH 'pig', 16–19 𒇻 UDU 'sheep', 20–23 𒄞 GUD 'ox', and 24–27 𒀲𒆳𒊏 ANŠE.KUR.RA 'horse' (Gadd 1926, pl. 26).

to the stock of superfluous CVC signs, and making ever increasing use of Sumerian-derived logograms. Literacy in cuneiform was never to be reduced to the mastery of a syllabary and some orthographic rules; "Sumerian culture," acquired over years of study and zealously cultivated by the academics who controlled the curriculum and established the canon, was the ticket of admission to literate society. Neither efficiency nor convenience played an important role in the development of Akkadian cuneiform.

SAMPLE OF AKKADIAN

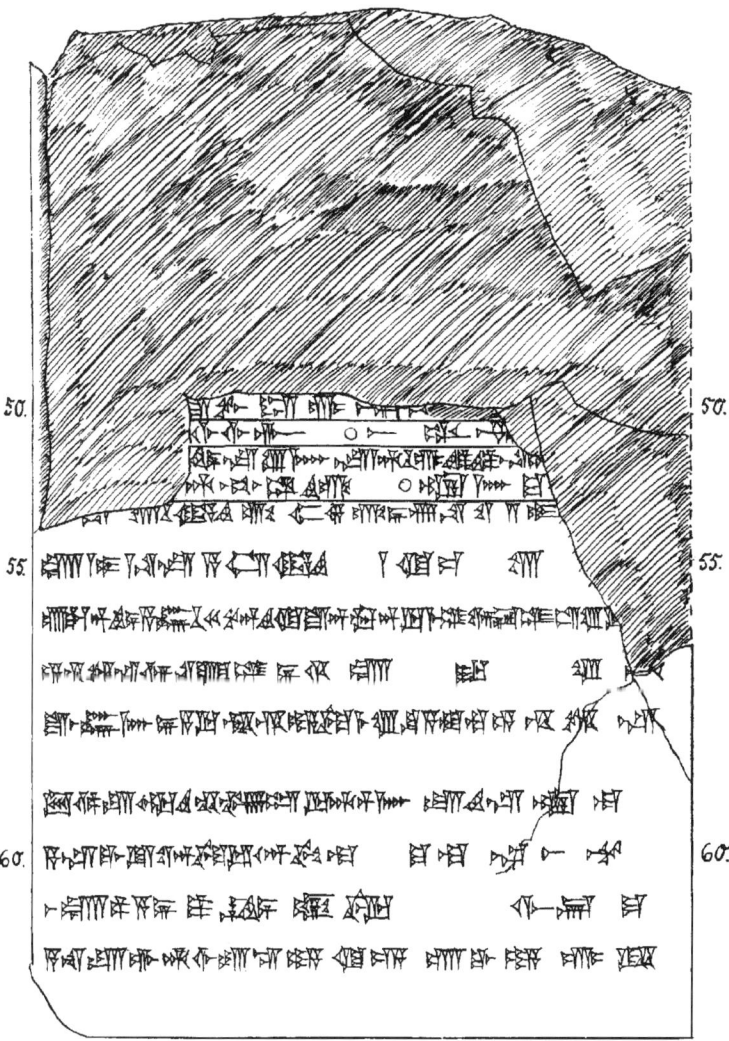

1. Akkadian: (cuneiform)

2. Transliteration:	[56] É.GAL	[m]AN.ŠÁR.DÙ.A	LUGAL	ŠÚ	MAN	KUR
3. Transcription:	ekal	Aššur-bān-apli	šar	kiššati	šar	māt
4. Gloss:	palace.of	Ashurbanipal	king.of	totality	king.of	land.of

2.	AN.ŠÁR[ki]	ša	[d]NÀ	[d]taš-me-tu₄	GEŠTUG[II]	DAGAL-tu₄
3.	Aššur	ša	Nabû	Tašmētu	uznē	rapaštu
4.	Ashur	whom	Nabû	Tašmetu	ears/wisdom	broad

2.	iš-ru-k[u-uš]	[57] e-ḫu-uz-zu	IGI[II]	na-mir-tu₄	ni-siq
3.	išrukuš	ēḫuzu	īnē	namirtu	nisiq
4.	they.gave.him	he.acquired	eyes	sharp	best.of

2.	ṭup-šar-ru-ti	[58] ša	AŠ	LUGAL.MEŠ-ni	a-lik	maḫ-ri-ya
3.	ṭupšarr-ūti	ša	ina	šarr-āni	ālik	maḫr-iya
4.	scribe-ship	which	among	kings	goer.of	front-my

2.	mám-ma	šip-ru	šu-a-tú	la	e-ḫu-uz-zu	[59] bul-ṭi	TA	muḫ-ḫi
3.	mamma	šipru	šuātu	la	ēḫuzu	bulṭī	ultu	muḫḫi
4.	any	work	this	not	he.learned	remedies	from	top.of.head

2.	EN	UMBIN	liq-ti	BAR.MEŠ	ta-ḫi-zu	nak-la
3.	adi	ṣupri	liqtī	aḫûti	tāḫizu	nakla
4.	to	nail	selections	other	teaching	clever

2.	[60] a-zu-gal-lu-ut	[d]nin-urta	u	[d]gu-la	ma-la	ba-aš-mu
3.	azugall-ūt	Ninurta	u	Gula	mala	bašmu
4.	chief.physician-ship.of	Ninurta	and	Gula	whatever	pertains

2.	[61] AŠ	ṭup-pa-a-ni	áš-tur	as-niq	IGI.KÁR-ma	[62] a-na
3.	ina	ṭuppāni	a-šṭur	a-sniq	a-bre-ma	ana
4.	on	tablets	I-wrote	I-checked	I-collated-and	for

2.	ta-mar-ti	ši-ta-si-ya	qé-reb	é.gal-ya	ú-kin
3.	tāmarti	šitassī-ya	qereb	ekalli-ya	u-kīn
4.	perusal	reading-my	within	palace-my	I-deposited

'Palace of Ashurbanipal, king of totality, king of Assyria, whom (the gods)
Nabû and Tashmetum gave broad wisdom, who acquired sharp eyes: The best
of the scribal art, such works as none of the kings who went before me had ever
learned, remedies from the top of the head to the toenails, non-canonical selec-
tions, clever teachings, whatever pertains to the medical mastery of (the gods)
Ninurta and Gula, I wrote on tablets, checked and collated, and deposited
within my palace for my perusal and reading.'

> —*From a colophon on a medical text from the library of Ashurbanipal, king of
> Assyria, 668–627 (Hunger 1968, no. 329). Bottom of the last column, most of
> which is destroyed. Beneath the last horizontal rule is the catchline for the next
> tablet in the series, followed (line 55) by the identification of the tablet as the
> first in the series "If a man is sick with a cough" (drawing, Küchler 1904, pl. 5).*

Basic cuneiform syllabary

TABLE 3.4: *Inventory of Basic Signs Used in the Pronunciation Column of Syllabary A[a]*

	_a	_e	_i	_u	a_	e_	i_	u_
p b								
t d ṭ								
k g q								
s z ṣ								
š								
m n								
l r								
w y								
ḫ ʾ								
Ø								

a. The following CVC signs are also used: dim, dím, gír, ḫar, kal, kil,
kin, kul, lag, lam, rig, suk, tan, tin. Table prepared by P. T. Daniels.

Other languages

Gene B. Gragg

By the mid third millennium B.C.E., the cuneiform writing system, now adapted to both Sumerian and Akkadian, had evolved into its near-definitive inventory of some 600 mixed syllabic-logographic signs with their characteristic polyphony (most signs are associated with a set of syllabic and/or logographic values) and homophony (most syllabic and some logographic values can be represented by more than one sign). No one implementation of cuneiform used all 600-plus signs, nor all possible values of the signs it did use, and the history of cuneiform is the history of the variable selection made by different periods, places, and genres, adding some values, pruning many, with characteristic local adjustments in the ductus and complexity of the sign-forms (usually in the direction of simplification and reduction in number of possible "sign components"). As Mesopotamian institutions (including the cuneiform writing system) became normal vehicles of West Asian cultural expression, the adaptation of the cuneiform writing system took on a dimension of adjustment to new linguistic environments—sometimes for proper names (Amorite) or isolated glosses (Kassite) or texts in related Semitic languages (Eblaite, Canaanite; even a single known Aramaic incantation text), but eventually for full notation of a corpus of texts in languages completely distinct from Sumerian and Akkadian. There are four privileged cases of this adaptation: Hittite, Elamite, Hurrian, and Urartian. (A possible fifth case, involving Hattic, the non–Indo-European language of the predecessors of the Hittites in their capital Hattusha, involves too many unknowns—not the least of which is uncertainty about the reliability of the knowledge of Hattic on the part of the Hittite-speaking scribes from whom we have all our Hattic texts.)

In the tables that follow, the row labels give the probable consonant (phoneme or allophone) value in the target language, with following or preceding vowels as column labels. Each syllable in the cells is a standard transliteration value of the cuneiform sign used to represent the combination of the consonant(s) in question with the particular vowel(s)—the transliteration value which is the closest available one to the presumed target language syllable. Thus the sign ⸢𒍣⸣, which can be transliterated *zí*, is used for the Elamite syllables /zi/ and /ze/, or perhaps /či/ and /če/. Where the transliteration value is less familiar (e.g. ⸢𒅗⸣ *ka₄*), its usual designation is added in small capitals. Less common values are given in italics.

Elamite cuneiform

Elamite has no known linguistic affiliations (a link with Dravidian has been suggested, but never widely accepted). Spoken by the southeastern neighbors of Sumerian on the Iranian coastal plain and associated highlands, it has a history of cuneiform ex-

TABLE 3.5: *Achaemenid Elamite Syllabic Signs and Values*

	_a	_e	_i	_u	a_	e_	i_	u_
p	pa		pi	pu	ap		ip, íp	up
b	ba	be						
k	ka_4(QA)		ki	ku	ak		ik	uk
g			gi					
t	da	te	ti	tu, tu_4	at			ut
d				du				
š	šá, šà	še	ši	šu	áš		íš	
s	sa		si	su	as/z		is/z	
z (=č?)	za		zí					
y	ya							
l	la		li	lu				ul
m	ma	me	mi	mu	am			um
n	na		ni	nu	an	en	in	un
r	ra		ri	ru			ir	ur
h	ḫa		ḫi	ḫu	aḫ			
Ø	a	e	i	u, ú				

pression, ca. 2500–331 B.C.E., almost as long as that of Akkadian. After abandoning an indigenous cuneiform-like writing system which had achieved widespread use on the Iranian plateau by the early third millennium (SECTION 10), the Elamites began using an Old Akkadian form of cuneiform to write at first Akkadian, but eventually monumental inscriptions, letters, and administrative documents in their own language. Soon after the initial adaptation, sign forms began to take on a recognizably Elamite ductus, and for texts of the final periods there are many signs that cannot be easily recognized by scholars who have not spent time working specifically in this area of cuneiform.

The Elamite adaptation of the cuneiform script is characterized by a radical reduction in the inventory of cuneiform signs. For the whole period only 206 signs are used, and in any given period (Old, Middle, Neo-, and Achaemenid) the total number of signs used remains remarkably constant—at about 130 (Stève 1992). What changes from period to period is the complexity of the syllabary and the number of logograms. In the earliest texts very few logograms are used, but almost all common syllabic CV and VC values from the Old Akkadian syllabary are taken over. In each successive period the syllabary becomes sparser, while, for unrelated reasons (probably because of the increased frequency of list-like administrative and economic texts) the number of logograms increases.

TABLE 3.5 (adapted from Paper 1955) gives the relatively compact syllabary of CV and VC signs achieved in the royal monumental inscriptions of the final period, Achaemenid Elamite (539–331 B.C.E.).

As is obvious from the table, the polyphony and homophony of the cuneiform syllabary have been almost (but not entirely) eliminated in a syllabic inventory reduced to 47 (C)V and 23 VC signs. In addition, almost no distinction is made between voiced and voiceless stops in CV signs (the same lack of distinction in VC signs is inherent in the cuneiform writing system, and probably corresponded to a phonological feature of Sumerian)—to such an extent that the distinctiveness of this feature for Achaemenid Elamite has frequently been called into question. However, where there is a distinction in signs, many words are consistently spelled with one or the other sign; consequently we cannot be certain that a simple phonological generalization can be drawn from the orthography in this respect. The /z ~ s/ distinction is more consistently made, but from Old Persian loanwords it seems likely that graphic z may in fact have been [tʃ], [dʒ], or [ts]. The hV signs are in frequent variation with the corresponding V signs, so that /h/ may have been in the process of disappearing. A few common CVC signs (about 40) are also used on occasion; it has been noted that their primary function seems to be to represent only the two consonants in question, with the vowel value frequently ignored: thus words are written in some contexts indifferently with the CVC signs whose conventional value is *tar* ⟶ or *tur* 𒋻, and in other contexts with writings of the form *ti-rV*. Writings of the form VC_1-C_1V seem to be in free variation with V-CV writings (e.g. 𒀊𒉺 *ap-pa* ~ 𒀀𒉺 *a-pa*), so that gemination may not be distinctive in the language. The most unusual feature of Achaemenid Elamite is the phenomenon of *broken writing*, whereby a sequence $C_1V_1C_2$ is represented as C_1V_1-V_2C_2, without regard for the quality of V_2: thus 𒁺𒈾𒀸 ~ 𒁺𒈾𒅖 *du-na-áš ~ du-na-iš* 'he gave', 𒋗𒊌𒁕 ~ 𒋗𒅅𒁕 *šu-uk-da ~ šu-ik-da* 'Sogdian', 𒊓𒀜𒁕𒆪𒅖 ~ 𒊓𒌓𒁕𒆪𒅖 *sa-ad-da-ku-iš ~ sa-ud-da-ku-iš* 'Satagydian'. Although it is possible that these writings may be a sporadic representation of vowel length or glide formation, it now seems more probable that this represents a quasi-alphabetic reinterpretation of Elamite, whereby the V_2C_2 in fact represents C_2, i.e. the pure, isolated consonantal value. The use of the masculine personal name determinative 𒁹 m is greatly expanded—it is even used with pronouns. In addition a new determinative ⟶ h is used for place names, but also for many nouns. The general cuneiform plural determinative 𒈨𒌍 MEŠ is regularly used without the connotation of plurality to indicate that the previous sign is a logogram.

SAMPLE OF ELAMITE

𒁹 𒂊𒁹 𒀪𒈫𒄷 𒂊𒀫 𒋼𒅖 ⟨ 𒁹𒐊 𒁹 𒐊𒐊𒐊 𒄴𒁹 𒀪𒁹 𒀪𒈫𒄷 𒐋 ⟨
⟨𒂊𒀪 𒂊𒂊𒀪 𒀪𒁹 ⟨ 𒀪𒂊𒐊𒀪 𒀀 𒂊𒁹 𒄴𒁹 𒁹 𒂊𒐊𒐊 ⟶ 𒂊𒀪𒀪 𒂊𒀪 𒐊
𒂊𒁹 𒀀 𒂊𒄷 𒀪𒐊𒀪 ⟨𒐊𒀪 𒀪𒈫 𒄴 𒂊𒁹 𒀪𒂊𒀪 𒀪𒈫𒄷 𒂊𒂊𒄷 𒂊𒀫

1. *Cuneiform:*	𒁹𒀭𒊑𒅀𒈠𒌋𒅖		𒁹𒂗	𒈾𒀭𒊑
2. *Transliteration:*	ᵐDa-ri-ia-ma-u-iš		ᵐSUNKI	na-an-ri
3. *Transcription:*	daryamauʃ		sunki	na-n-ri
4. *Gloss:*	Darius		king	speak-PART-SG

1.	𒅀𒌋𒍝𒂷𒌍	𒁕𒌋𒊏𒈦𒁕𒈾	𒈬	𒄷𒁾𒉿𒈨	𒁕𒀀𒂊
2.	za-u-mi-in	ᵈU-ra-maš-da-na	ᵐú	ʰtup-pi-me	da-a-e
3.	ʧaumin	uramaʃta-na	u	tuppi-me	daae
4.	grace	Ahuramazda-of	I	tablet-DERIV	other

1.	𒅅𒆠	𒄷𒌓𒁕	𒄯𒊑𒅀𒈠
2.	ik-ki	ḫu-ud-da	Ḫar-ri-ia-ma
3.	ikki	hutta	harriya-ma
4.	on	make	Aryan-in

'Darius the king said: "By the grace of Ahuramazda I made another inscription in Aryan (Iranian)."'

— *Trilingual inscription of Darius on the cliff at Behistun, § 70: 1–3*

(King and Thompson 1907: 167).

Hurrian cuneiform

Hurrian, related to Urartian but otherwise an isolate (a hypothesis of Northeast Caucasian affiliation has been proposed), is attested from the third millennium on, in northern Syria and those parts of modern Iraq and Turkey now inhabited by Kurds. The adaptation of the cuneiform syllabary to Hurrian is attested in a monumental inscription from the end of the third millennium and in many contemporary and subsequent proper names. Many religious texts in Hurrian have been found in Syria and, especially, incorporated into Hittite rituals in texts found in Anatolia. In the middle of the second millennium a Hurrian kingdom in northern Syria, Mitanni, was a major player with the Assyrians, Hittites, and Egyptians on the international scene, and carried on a vigorous diplomatic correspondence with the Egyptian Pharaoh. Most of these letters were in Akkadian, but one long letter (almost 500 lines—written on what is physically the largest cuneiform tablet in existence) is in Hurrian, drawn up by the Mitanni chancery in one of the most original and consistent adaptations of the cuneiform syllabary ever made. (Other fragmentary instances of letters in the same Mitanni chancery orthography have been discovered—it is generally supposed that there exists or existed a major archive in the as yet undiscovered Mitanni capital city, Waššukani.) The Hurrians disappear abruptly from the ancient Near Eastern world toward the end of the second millennium.

TABLE 3.6 gives the Mitanni Hurrian (C)V (43 signs) and VC (34) syllabary (the system also contained a few CVC signs and a very limited number of the most standard cuneiform determinatives and logograms). One major feature of Mitanni Hurrian, its treatment of the voiced/voiceless distinction, is a systematization of tendencies present in earlier attempts to write Hurrian: these earlier orthographies, which tend to use the full range of voiced and voiceless CV signs available in the Old Babylonian and Middle Babylonian syllabaries, consistently show voiceless CV writings such as 𒉺 𒄩 *pa-ḫi* in initial position, voiced in intervocalic (C)V-CV as in 𒆠 𒁀 *ki-ba*, but

TABLE 3.6: *Mitanni Hurrian Syllabic Signs and Values*

	_a	_e	_i	_o	_u	a_	e_	i_	o_	u_
p~b, pp	pa	pè	pí(BI)	pu		ap	e/ip		up	
t~d, tt	ta	te	ti	tù		at	e/it		ut	
k~g, kk	ka	ké	ki	ku	ku₈	ak	e/ik		uk	
f~v/w, ff?	wa/e/i/u(PI)					aw(AB)	e/iw(IB)		uw(UB)	
(see text)	ú-a	ú-e	ú-i	ú-u	ú-ú?	a-ú	e-ú	i-ú	u-ú	ú-ú?
ts~dz, tsts	sa	si/e		su						
s~z, ss	sà	sé/sí		sú		as	es/is		us	
š~ž, šš	ša	še	ši	šu		aš	eš	iš	uš	
x~ğ, xx	ḫa	ḫé	ḫi	ḫu		a/e/i/uḫ				
l, ll	la	le/i		lu		al	el	il	ul	
r	ra	re/i		ru		ar	e/ir		ur	
m, mm	ma	me	mi	mu		am	e/im		um	
n	na	né/i		nu		an	en	in	un	
Ø	a	e	i	u	ú					

again voiceless in intervocalic geminates of the type VC-CV as in ⸢ḫu-up⸣ *ḫu-up-pa*. Apparently in Hurrian, then, the basic distinction in consonants is not voiced/voiceless, but geminate/ non-geminate; initial consonants can only occur non-geminate and are realized as voiceless, as are intervocalic geminates, while intervocalic non-geminates are realized with a voiced allophone. This principle seems to be explicitly incorporated into the Mitanni syllabary, whose organization tends generally toward absolute minimization, if not complete elimination, of polyphony/homophony. For each vowel V and each articulatory position, only one of the possible voiced/voiceless pair of CV signs is chosen, usually the more common one. This sign was then presumably pronounced with the (redundant) voiced allophone when occurring intervocalically and non-geminate, voiceless otherwise.

For back rounded vowels, Mitanni used both ⟨ U and ⸢ Ú, but never as variants—words and affixes are consistently spelled with one or the other; therefore they must represent two different vowels, presumably /u/ and /o/ (Ú, which can also be used for /w/, is assigned to the former, and U to the latter). In the velar series, the orthography, which has chosen ⟨E⟩ KI and E KU for the values *ki, gi, ku, gu*, goes so far as to take the unassigned signs ⸢ GI and ⸢ GU and use them without exception for values which are clearly *ke, ge, ko, go* (this can be verified in instances where stem-final *g, (k)k* is followed by *e, o*). Note, however, that although they could have done this also for the dental series by employing the unused ⸢ TU, they did not; the labial series in cuneiform in any case does not afford two signs for the values *pu, bu*. Writings of the form CV$_1$-V$_1$, with "*plene*" or "redundant" writing of the vowel inherent in the CV sign, are especially abundant. Opinion is divided as to whether this is an indication of vowel length, absence of a cluster, or an attempt to make explicit vowel quality distinctions (*e* vs. *i* and *o* vs. *u*) not consistently made by the syllabary.

The Mitanni syllabary needed additional innovations in order to represent what seems to have been a voiced/voiceless labial continuant pair, probably either [f, v] or [f, w]. For these in CV signs, the Mitanni syllabary uses the sign ⟨𒉿⟩ PI, which is already quasi-alphabetic with the values *wa, we, wi, wu* in the standard cuneiform syllabary. In view of the general avoidance of homophony, the fact that the ⟨𒀊⟩ AB, ⟨𒅁⟩ IB, ⟨𒌒⟩ UB series is used for this labial continuant VF may mean a genuine neutralization of the stop/continuant distinction in geminates. ⟨𒌑⟩ Ú is also used with preceding or following vowel for a sequence involving a labial continuant. It is not clear how, if at all, the value of these Ú writings differs from that of the PI, AB, IB, UB writings—although the tendency to avoid homophony would seem to indicate a priori that it should. Elsewhere in spirants, the ⟨𒍝⟩ ZA, ⟨𒍣⟩ ZI, ⟨𒍪⟩ ZU series is used for *s, z*, whereas the ⟨𒊓⟩ SA, ⟨𒋛⟩ SI, ⟨𒋢⟩ SU series seems to be used for an affricate, perhaps *ts, dz*. Similarly, the š- and ḫ-series enable representation of *š, ž* and *x, γ*.

SAMPLE OF HURRIAN

1. Cuneiform:	𒁹𒆤𒇷𒀸𒊭𒀀𒀭	𒉺𒀸𒅆𒀉𒄭𒅇𒉿𒍑
2. Transliteration:	ᵐKè-li-[i]-aš-ša-a-an	pa-aš-ši-i-it-ḫi-iw-wu-uš
3. Transcription:	kelia-ʃ-(nn)a-an	paʃʃ-itxi-iffu-ʃ
4. Gloss:	Kelia-ERG-it(OBJ)-and	send-NOMINALIZER-my-ERG

1.				
2.	ti-we	an-ti	ku₈-lu-u-ša	ma-a-an-[na]-a-am	ḫi-il-li
3.	tive	andi	kul-oʒ-a	manna-an	xill-i
4.	word	this	say-PAST-3SG(SUBJ)	PRONOMINAL-and	speak-PART

1.			
2.	še-e-na-wu-ša-an	ᵐNi-im-mu-u-ri-i-aš	ᵏᵘʳMi-sí-ir-re-e-we-né-eš
3.	ʃena-f-ʃ-an	nimmoria-ʃ	misir(i)-(n)e-ve-ne-ʃ
4.	brother-your-ERG-and	Nimmoria-ERG	Egypt-DEF-of-DEF-ERG

1.				
2.	ew-ri-iš	ta-še	ap-li	ta-a-a-nu-u-ša
3.	evre-ʃ	taʒe	apli	tan-oʒ-a
4.	lord-ERG	gift	great(?)	make-PAST-3SG(SUBJ)

'And Kelia, my messenger, said this word: thus speaking, "Your brother, Nim-moria, the lord of Egypt, made a great(?) gift."'

—*Mitanni letter lines 83–85 (Schroeder 1915, no. 200).*

Urartian cuneiform

Urartian, a reasonably close relative of Hurrian, is attested on a large number of monumental inscriptions (and a much smaller corpus of other kinds of texts) from the highlands around Lake Van in southeastern Turkey between about 830 and 650 B.C.E. Although the language may have lasted into the first centuries C.E., by the time of the Persian Empire the Urartians had been replaced by the Armenians as the politically and culturally dominant group in the area. As opposed to the Elamite and Hurrian cuneiform adaptations, the Urartian syllabary does not go back to roots in the Old Akkadian period. In values and sign-shape, it seems to have been adapted directly from current Neo-Assyrian cuneiform, and shows no trace of having been influenced by the writing practice for Hurrian (from whose phonological system Urartian shows significant differences in any case).

As can be seen from TABLE 3.7, Urartian cuneiform, like the previous two, shows a "reduced inventory" sign system. It has more (C)V signs (59), but fewer VC signs (18) than the others. In addition it has a small number of CVC signs (22), but a

TABLE 3.7: *Urartian Syllabic Signs and Values*

	_a	_e	_i	_u	a_	e_	i_	u_
p *b*	pa ba	be	pi bi	p/bu	ap/b	ip/b		up/b
t *d* *t꞉* (t^h?)	ta da	te tè(NE)	ti tí(ḪI)	tu, tú du ṭu	at/d	it/d		
k *g* *k?* (k^h?)	ka ga qa		ki gi qi	ku gu qu	ak/g/q			
s *z* *ts*	sa z/ṣa		si zi ṣi	su zu ṣu				
š	ša	še	ši	šú, *šu*	áš		iš	uš
x	ḫa	ḫé	ḫi	ḫu				
m *n*	ma na	me	ni	mu nu	am *an*			
l *r*	l ra		li ri	lu ru	al ar, ár(UB)	el	il ir	ul ur
Ø	a	e	i	u, ú				

larger inventory of logograms than Hurrian: 106 signs, of which 20 also have syllabic values and 15 are commonly used as determinatives. Urartian has frequent *plene* writings of vowels, and many "broken" writings of the type C*i-e* and C*e-i*; there are, however, virtually no geminate writings of the form VC$_1$-C$_1$V—a fact which perhaps explains the relatively low number of VC signs (which are thus only used for true clusters). Unlike Hurrian, Urartian systematically uses the cuneiform emphatic series ṭ- and q- for what seem to be glottalized (or aspirated) dentals and velars. It is possible that the same manner of articulation existed in the labial series as well, but could not readily be represented by the syllabary.

SAMPLE OF URARTIAN

1. *Cuneiform:*			
2. *Transliteration:*	ᵈḪal-di-ie	e-ú-ri-i-e	ᵐIš-pu-ú-i-ni-še
3. *Transcription:*	xaldi-ie	evri-ie	iʃpuini-ʃe
4. *Gloss:*	Xaldi-DAT	lord-DAT	Ishpuini-ERG

1.			
2.	ᵐᵈSàr-du-ri-e-ḫi-ni-še	ᵐMe-nu-a-še	ᵐIš-pu-ú-i-ni-ḫi-ni-še
3.	sarduri-xi-ni-ʃe	menua-ʃe	iʃpuini-xi-ni-ʃe
4.	Sarduri-ADJ-DEF-ERG	Menua-ERG	Ishpuini-ADJ-DEF-ERG

1.			
2.	ᵈḪal-di-e-i	su-si	ši-di-iš-tú-ni
3.	xaldi-ei	susi	ʃid-iʃt-uni
4.	Xaldi-of	shrine	build-DERIV-3SG.SUBJ+3SG.OBJ

'For lord Haldi, Ishpuni son of Sarduri (lit. 'the Sardurian one') and Menua son of Ishpuini built Haldi's shrine.
—*Dedicatory inscription on a shrine, line 1 (König 1955 no. 8).*

Hittite cuneiform

Of the cases being considered here, Hittite is the only one in which cuneiform has been adopted by a language belonging to a well-known and widely distributed family, Indo-European, and attested in a varied, extensive, and well-studied corpus of texts of literary, religious, historical, and legal content. The Hittite corpus is larger, but more concentrated in time, than either the Hurrian or the Elamite. Although it may have been written as early as the seventeenth century B.C.E., the bulk of the material in our possession, more than 600 compositions preserved on several thousand tablets, comes from the fifteenth through the thirteenth centuries, and was found in the various archives of the Hittite capital, Hattusha (modern Boghazköi).

The Hittite writing system uses at least 375 cuneiform signs, of which 86 are employed in the core syllabary of CV, V, and VC signs. These are given in TABLE 3.8. In addition to these values, Hittite cuneiform also took over a number of CVC values. The most recent syllabary, Rüster and Neu (1989), lists 74 signs with a total of 89 CVC values (nine of these signs also occur in TABLE 3.8 with VC and CV values). Besides the syllabic CV signs of TABLE 3.8, the scribes of Boghazköy evolved five complex CV signs made by inserting a small V sign 𒀀 *a*, 𒂊 *e*, 𒄿 *i*, 𒌋 *u*, 𒌑 *ú* inside (under the horizontal of) 𒉿 PI, a sign which in a number of cuneiform systems could be used by itself in the values *wa, wi, we, wu* (compare e.g. TABLE 3.6). These signs, however (transcribed wa_a, we_e, wi_i, wu_u, $wú_ú$), were only used in the writing of Hurrian, Hattic, Luvian, and Palaic passages. Moreover, in Boghazköy Hurrian at least, the signs were used redundantly in a large number of their occurrences—i.e. in writings of the sort *-wa_a-a-*, *-we_e-e-*, etc.

Following a pattern already observed in the other adaptations of cuneiform, the Hittite writing system shows its own ambivalence about the rendering of voiced and voiceless stops. In the stop series, for a given articulatory position and vowel, the choice of a voiced or voiceless consonant value (i.e. a sign whose conventional Akkadian value is voiced or voiceless) seems to be a question of at most orthographic habit, and many words can be written with either variant: thus 𒁕𒈠𒅖 *da-ma-iš* or 𒋫𒈠𒅖 *ta-ma-iš* 'other', 𒂊𒍑𒍪 *e-eš-tu* or 𒍪𒌅 *eš-du* 'let him be', 𒄀𒂊� *gi-e-nu* 'knee (nom.sg.)' versus 𒆠𒉡𒉿𒀸 *ki-nu-wa-aš* 'knee (dat.pl.)'. Hittite does, however, show a tendency to write etymologically voiceless stops double "where the cuneiform syllabary makes this possible" (i.e. between vowels). This relationship between gemination and voicelessness is known as Sturtevant's Law; it can be seen in words such as 𒀝𒋫 *kat-ta* 'with, along, down' (cf. Greek κατά *katâ*) and 𒋼𒅅𒆪𒍑�𒈪 *te-ek-ku-uš-ša-mi* 'I show, I present' (cf. Latin *dīcō* 'I say', Greek δείκνυμι *deíknumi* 'I show'), as opposed to words for 'eat' like 𒀀𒌅𒂊𒉌 *a-tu-e-ni* 'we eat', 𒀀𒁕𒀭�zi *a-da-an-zi* 'they eat', where the stem is invariably written with a single *tV* or *dV* sign (cf. Latin *edō* 'I eat').

For the continuants, the relationship between gemination and voicing is much less clear. To begin with, Hittite apparently only had one continuant in the dental-alveolar region, and its phonetics is very uncertain. This phoneme is always rendered by signs conventionally transcribed with *š* in the cuneiform syllabary—a phenomenon undoubtedly connected with the generally complex and shifting relationship between the *sV* and *šV* signs throughout the history of cuneiform. There was no /z/ in Hittite, but the cuneiform *zV* and *Vz* signs are used to represent an alveolar or dental affricate /ts/, a palatalization of /t/ before /i/ or /e/: e.g. in the third person singular present ("primary") ending *-zi* (as opposed to *-ti* in the closely related Luvian). Since

TABLE 3.8: *Hittite Syllabic Signs and Values*

	_a	_e	_i	_u	a_	e_	i_	u_
p, b	pa / ba	be	bi	bu	ab	ib		ub
t, d	ta / da	te	di / ti	tu / du	ad	id		ud
k, g	ka / qa / ga		ki / gi	ku / gu		ag	ig	ug
ts	za	zé	zi	zu	az	iz		uz
s	ša	še	ši	u, šú	aš	eš	iš	uš
x (, x₂?)	ḫa	ḫé	ḫi	ḫu	a/i/uḫ			
m	ma	me	mi	mu	am	im		um
n	na	ne	ni	nu	an	en	in	un
l	la		li	lu	al	el	il	ul
r	ra		ri	ru	ar	ir		ur, úr
w	wa		wi₅					
y	ya							
Ø	a	e	i	u, ú				

the *ḫV* and *Vḫ* signs occur both single and geminate, it is thought that Hittite may have preserved at least two spirants, voiced and voiceless, in the so-called "laryngeal" range—an important class of consonants first postulated for Proto-Indo-European solely on the basis of complex historical reconstructions (Saussure 1879), and subsequently discovered in Hittite, the only Indo-European language to have preserved them directly as distinct consonants.

For any of the adaptations of cuneiform, it is a priori plausible that the phonological system of the borrowing language could show a certain lack of fit with the representation possible in the borrowed writing system. For Hurrian, Elamite, and Urartian, lacking any independent access to the languages' phonological structure, we can only guess at areas where this might be the case. In the case of Hittite, a member of a familiar language family, we are in a much better position to judge. Thus, in the cuneiform syllabary, word-initial and word-final clusters of more than one consonant cannot be directly represented; nor can word-internal clusters of more than two consonants. It seems probable, however, that at least some of each of these cluster types are possible in Hittite, and that VC and CV signs are sometimes used to represent single consonants. Thus ⬚⬚⬚⬚ *pa-ra-a* 'forward' presumably represents /pra/ (cf. Latin *prō*); ⬚⬚⬚⬚ *li-in-ik* (stem *link-*) 'swear!' and ⬚⬚⬚⬚ *ša-an-ḫa* (or ⬚⬚⬚⬚ *ša-a-aḫ*, stem *šanḫ-*) 'seek!' represent /link/ and /sanx/; and ⬚⬚⬚⬚ *kar-ab-zi* 'he lifts' seems to represent /karptsi/. On the other hand, although the standard cuneiform syllabary permits an unambiguous distinction between /i/ and /e/ at least in a limited number of contexts, for example, before /š/ and after /n/ (⟨sign⟩ *iš* vs. ⟨sign⟩ *eš*; ⟨sign⟩ *ni* vs. ⟨sign⟩ *ne*), the distinction is not consistently observed in the corpus from which most of our texts come. Thus 'blood' is written both ⟨signs⟩ *e-eš-ḫar* and ⟨signs⟩ *iš-ḫar*. Finally, although geminate (so-called *plene*) writing of vowels can be used for long vowels in Akkadian, the frequent, but sometimes inconsistent, writing of double vowels in Hittite does not seem to correlate with length. On the one hand, the consistent ⟨signs⟩ *e-eš-zi* 'is' corresponds to a short vowel in Indo-European (cf. Latin *est*), but on the other hand there are many words with variations of the type ⟨signs⟩ *pa-aḫ-ḫu-ur* ~ ⟨signs⟩ *pa-a-aḫ-ḫur* ~ ⟨signs⟩ *pa-aḫ-ḫu-u-ur* 'fire'.

Signs functioning as syllabograms account for the bulk of running Hittite text. However, in addition to syllabographic function (which in any case, as we have seen, only involves about 150 of the 375 signs), as in contemporary Akkadian, each of the cuneiform signs used in Hittite has at least one, and sometimes several, logographic values, and 41 signs function additionally as determinatives. The largest number of logographic values are carried over either directly from Sumerian, or from the scholastic elaboration of Sumerian in the Akkadian scribal schools. For example, the sign ⟨sign⟩ *šá* has, in addition to its syllabic value, the logographic values NÍG 'thing; four', NINDA 'bread', and GAR 'set, put'—moreover, these values themselves figure in compound expressions such as ⟨signs⟩ NÍG.SI.SÁ 'justice', ⟨signs⟩ NÍG.BA 'gift', ⟨signs⟩ NINDA.KU₇ 'sweet bread', and ⟨signs⟩ NINDA.KASKAL 'voyage provisions'. These logograms are referred to as *Sumerograms*, and are usually printed in capital letters in Hittite transliterations. More than 1500 Sumerograms are known, of which several hundred were in common use. In addition to the Sumerograms, the Hittite scribes also used a smaller number (about 150) of *Akkadograms*, syllabically written Akkadian words or word elements (such as suffixed possessive pronouns), usually printed in capital italics in transliterations: ⟨signs⟩ *I-NA* 'in' (= Hittite *anda*), ⟨signs⟩ *IŠ-PUR* 'he sent' (= Hittite *ḫatrāiš*), ⟨signs⟩ *DI-NAM* 'judgment (acc.sg.)' (= Hittite *ḫanneššar*). For a number of expressions written only in logograms, the underlying Hittite lexical items are unknown or uncertain.

Finally, a number of Hittite words are written in a mixed logographic-syllabic system, whereby a Sumerogram or Akkadogram can be followed by a syllabogram (sometimes referred to as a *phonetic complement*), usually representing inflectional information—either Akkadian or Hittite. A variety of combinations are possible (where SG = "Sumerogram," AG = "Akkadogram," PC$_{akk}$ = "Akkadian phonetic complement," PC$_{hit}$ = "Hittite phonetic complement"):

SG + PC$_{akk}$	⟨signs⟩ ŠU-*TI* 'hand (gen.)'
	(Akk. *QA-TI*, Hit. *ki-eš-ša-ra-aš*)
SG + PC$_{hit}$	⟨signs⟩ LUGAL-*uš* 'king (nom.)'
	(Hit. *ḫa-aš-šu-uš*)
AG + PC$_{hit}$	⟨signs⟩ *EL-LAM-aš* 'free (nom.)'
	(Hit. *a ra-wa-aš*; N.B.: Akk. *ellam* is accusative)

SG + PC_{akk} + PC_{hit}   ⟦cuneiform⟧ DINGIR-*LIM-ni* 'god (dat.)'
(Hit. *ši-ú-ni*; N.B.: Akk. *ilim* is genitive)

As a final refinement, these mixed logographic-syllabic writings standing for Akkadian words can themselves be used in a syllabic function (so-called *rebus writing*, in proper names). On the one hand, the Sumerogram ⟦cuneiform⟧ ^{giš}PA 'scepter', which stands for the Akkadian word /ḫaṭṭu/, is given the syllabic value /ḫaṭṭu/; on the other hand, ⟦cuneiform⟧ DINGIR-*LIM*, which stands for the genitive of 'god' in Akkadian, earlier /ilim/ but later /ili/, is given the syllabic value /ili/—as a result the writing ⟦cuneiform⟧ ^{giš}PA-*ši*-DINGIR-*LIM-iš* is to be interpreted as *ḫaṭṭu-ši-ili-iš*, and can be used to write the name of the ruler Hattusili (which can also be written more conventionally ⟦cuneiform⟧ *ḫa-at-tu-ši-li-iš*).

SAMPLE OF HITTITE

⟦cuneiform text⟧

In the Analysis, Akkadograms and Sumerograms are marked with subscript Akk and Sum respectively, and determinatives are superscript.

1. Cuneiform:	⟦cuneiform⟧	⟦cuneiform⟧ ⟦⟧	⟦cuneiform⟧
2. Transliteration:	A-BU-YA-ma-kán	I-NA KUR	^{URU}Mi-it-ta-an-ni
3. Analysis:	abu_{Akk}-ya_{Akk}-ma-kan	ina_{Akk} kur_{Sum}	^{city}Mittanni
4. Gloss:	father-my-but-LOC'NAL	in land	Mitanni

1.	⟦cuneiform⟧	⟦cuneiform⟧ ⟦cuneiform⟧	⟦cuneiform⟧
2.	ku-it	an-da	a-ša-an-du-le-eš-ki-it	na-aš-kán
3.	kuit	anda	ašandul-eške-t	n(u)-aš-kan
4.	because	in	camp-ITERATIVE-3SG(PAST)	and-he-LOC'NAL

1.	⟦cuneiform⟧	⟦cuneiform⟧	⟦cuneiform⟧	⟦cuneiform⟧	⟦cuneiform⟧
2.	a-ša-an-du-li	an-da	iš-ta-an-da-a-it	ŠA	^dUTU
3.	ašandul-i	anda	ištantāi-t	ša_{Akk}	^{god}utu_{Sum}
4.	camp-LOC	in	delay-3SG(PAST)	of	sun.god

1.	⟦cuneiform⟧	⟦cuneiform⟧	⟦cuneiform⟧
2.	^{URU}A-ri-in-na-ma-kán	GAŠAN-YA	EZEN^{ḪI.A}
3.	^{city}Arinna-ma-kan	gašan_{Sum}-ya_{Akk}	ezen^{plural}_{Sum}
4.	Arinna-but-LOC'NAL	lady-my	festivals

1.	⟦cuneiform⟧
2.	ša-ku-wa-an-da-re-eš-ki-ir
3.	šakuwandar-ešk-ir
4.	go.unobserved-ITER-3PL(PAST)

'But because my father remained camped in the land Mitanni, and delayed in the camp, the festivals of my Lady the sun goddess of Arinna went unobserved.'
—*Excerpt from the "Ten-Year Annals" of Mursili II (ca. 1353–1325 B.C.E.), found in Boghazköi (Figulla and Weber 1919, no. 4, lines 16–18).*

Bibliography

ORIGIN

Biggs, Robert D. 1974. *The Inscriptions from Tell Abū Ṣalābīkh* (Oriental Institute Publications 99). Chicago: University of Chicago Press.

Cooper, Jerrold S. 1989. "Cuneiform." *International Encyclopedia of Communications* 1: 439–43. Oxford: Oxford University Press.

Englund, Robert K. 1994. *Archaic Administrative Texts from Uruk: The Early Campaigns.* Berlin: Gebr. Mann.

Englund, Robert K., and Jean-Pierre Grégoire. 1991. *The Proto-Cuneiform Texts from Jemdet Nasr.* Berlin: Gebr. Mann.

Englund, Robert K., and Hans J. Nissen 1993. *Die lexikalischen Listen der archaischen Texte aus Uruk.* Berlin: Gebr. Mann.

Green, Margaret W. 1981. "The Construction and Implementation of the Cuneiform Writing System." *Visible Language* 15: 345–72.

Green, Margaret W., and Hans J. Nissen. 1987. *Zeichenliste der archaischen Texte aus Uruk* (Ausgrabungen der Deutschen Forschungsgemeinschaft in Uruk-Warka 11). Berlin: Gebr. Mann.

Krebernik, Manfred. 1994. Review of Green and Nissen 1987. *Orientalistische Literaturzeitung* 89: 380–86.

Krispijn, Th. J. H. 1991–92 [pub. 1993]. "The Early Mesopotamian Lexical Lists and the Dawn of Linguistics." *Jaarbericht "Ex Oriente Lux"* 32: 12–22.

Michalowski, Piotr. 1990. "Early Mesopotamian Communicative Systems: Art, Literature and Writing." In *Investigating Artistic Environments in the Ancient Near East,* ed. Anne C. Gunter, pp. 53–69. Washington, D.C.: Smithsonian Institution.

———. 1993. "On the Early Toponymy of Sumer: A Contribution to the Study of Early Mesopotamian Writing." In *kinattūtu ša dārāti: Raphael Kutscher Memorial Volume* (Tel Aviv Occasional Publications 1), ed. Anson F. Rainey, pp. 119–33. Tel Aviv: Institute of Archaeology.

Nissen, Hans J. 1986. "The Archaic Texts from Uruk." *World Archaeology* 17: 317–34.

Nissen, Hans J., Peter Damerow, and Robert K. Englund. 1993. *Archaic Bookkeeping: Writing and Techniques of Economic Administration in the Ancient Near East.* Chicago: University of Chicago Press.

Schmandt-Besserat, Denise. 1992. *Before Writing,* vol. 1: *From Counting to Cuneiform.* Austin: University of Texas Press.

Szarzyńska, Krystyna. 1987–88. "Some of the Oldest Cult Symbols in Archaic Uruk." *Jaarbericht "Ex Oriente Lux"* 30: 3–21.

Steinkeller, Piotr. IN PRESS. Review of Green and Nissen 1987. *Bibliotheca Orientalis.*

SUMERIAN AND AKKADIAN

Alster, Bendt. 1974. *The Instructions of Suruppak* (Mesopotamia 2). Copenhagen: Akademisk Forlag.

Buccellati, Giorgio. 1979. "Comparative Graphemic Analysis of Old Babylonian and Western Akkadian." *Ugarit-Forschungen* 11: 89–100.

Cavigneaux, Antoine. 1983. "Lexikalische Listen" [in French]. *Reallexikon der Assyriologie und vorderasiatischen Archäologie* 6: 609–41.

Civil, Miguel. 1973. "The Sumerian Writing System: Some Problems." *Orientalia* 42: 21–34.

———. 1994. "Sumerian." In "Linguistics in the Ancient Near East," ed. Erica Reiner, pp. 76–87. In *History of Linguistics,* ed. Giulio Lepschy, vol. 1: *The Eastern Traditions of Linguistics,* pp. 61–96. London: Longman. (Original publication in Italian, 1990.)

Cooper, Jerrold S. 1992. "Cuneiform." *Anchor Bible Dictionary,* vol. 1, pp. 1212–18. New York: Doubleday.

———. 1993. "Bilingual Babel: Cuneiform Texts in Two or More Languages from Ancient Mesopotamia and Beyond." *Visible Language* 27: 69–96.

Edzard, Dietz Otto. 1980. "Keilschrift." *Reallexikon der Assyriologie und vorderasiatischen Archäologie* 5: 544–69.

Gadd, Cyril J. 1926. *Cuneiform Texts from Babylonian Tablets, &c., in the British Museum,* part 39. London: British Museum.

Gelb, I. J. 1961. *Old Akkadian Writing and Grammar,* 2nd ed. (Materials for the Assyrian Dictionary 2). Chicago: University of Chicago Press.

———. 1963. *A Study of Writing,* 2nd ed. Chicago: University of Chicago Press.

———. 1987. "The Language of Ebla in the Light of the Sources from Ebla, Mari and Babylonia." In *Ebla 1975–1985* (Series Minor 27), ed. Luigi Cagni, pp. 49–74. Naples: Istituto Universitario Orientale, Dipartimento di Studi Asiatici.

Gong, Y. 1993. *Studien zur Bildung und Entwicklung der Keilschriftzeichen.* Munich: Kovač.

Hunger, Hermann. 1968. *Babylonische und assyrische Kolophone* (Alter Orient und Altes Testament 2). Kevelaer: Butzon & Bercker.

Küchler, Friedrich. 1904. *Beiträge zur Kenntnis der assyrisch-babylonischen Medizin* (Assyriologische Bibliothek 18). Leipzig: Hinrichs.

Labat, René. 1988. *Manuel d'épigraphie akkadienne,* 6th ed., ed. Florence Malibran-Labat. Paris: Geuthner.

Landsberger, Benno, ed. 1955. *Materialien zum sumerischen Lexikon 3.* Rome: Pontifical Biblical Institute.

Lieberman, Stephen. 1977. *The Sumerian Loanwords in Old-Babylonian Akkadian* (Harvard Semitic Studies 22). Missoula, Mont.: Scholars Press.

Reiner, Erica. 1966. *A Linguistic Analysis of Akkadian* (Janua Linguarum Series Practica 21).The Hague: Mouton.

———, 1973. "How We Read Cuneiform Texts." *Journal of Cuneiform Studies* 25: 3–58.

Symington, D. 1991. "Late Bronze Age Writing-Boards and Their Uses: Textual Evidence from Anatolia and Syria." *Anatolian Studies* 41: 111–23.

Thomsen, Marie-Louise. 1984. *The Sumerian Language* (Mesopotamia 10). Copenhagen: Akademisk Forlag.

Vanstiphout, Herman. 1989. "Enmerkar's Invention of Writing Revisited."In *DUMU-E$_2$-DUB-BA-A: Studies in Honor of Åke W. Sjöberg* (Occasional Publications of the Samuel Noah Kramer Fund 11), ed. Hermann Behrens et al., pp. 515–24. Philadelphia: University Museum.

von Soden, Wolfram, and Wolfgang Röllig. 1967–76. *Das Akkadische Syllabar,* 2nd ed., *samt Ergänzungsheft* (Analecta Orientalia 42–42A). Rome: Pontifical Biblical Institute. (1st ed., 1948.)

Walker, Christopher B. F. 1987. *Cuneiform* (Reading the Past). London: British Museum Publications; Berkeley and Los Angeles: University of California Press.

OTHER LANGUAGES

Benedict, Warren C. 1958. "Urartian Phonology and Morphology." Ph.D. dissertation, University of Michigan.

Bush, Frederic W. 1964. "A Grammar of the Hurrian Language." Ph.D. dissertation, Brandeis University.

Diakonoff, Igor M. 1971. *Hurrisch und Urartäisch,* trans. Karl Sdrembek. Munich: Kitzinger.

Figulla, Hugo H., and Otto Weber. 1919. *Keilschrifttexte aus Boghazköi,* vol. 3. Leipzig: Hinrichs.

Friedrich, Johannes. 1960. *Hethitisches Elementarbuch I: Kurzgefasste Grammatik,* 2nd ed. Heidelberg: Winter.

Goetze, Albrecht. 1933. *Die Annalen des Mursilis* (Mitteilungen der Vorderasiatisch-Aegyptische Gesellschaft 38). Leipzig: Hinrichs.

Güterbock, Hans Gustav, and Harry Hoffner, eds. 1980– . *The Hittite Dictionary of the Oriental Institute of the University of Chicago.* Chicago: Oriental Institute.

King, Leonard W., and Reginald Campbell Thompson. 1907. *The Sculptures and Inscriptions of Darius the Great on the Rock of Behistun in Persia.* London: British Museum.

König, Friedrich W. 1955. *Handbuch der chaldischen Inschriften* (Archiv für Orientforschung Beiheft 8). Osnabrück: Biblio-Verlag.

Paper, Herbert H. 1955. *The Phonology and Morphology of Royal Achaemenid Elamite.* Ann Arbor: University of Michigan Press.

Reiner, Erica. 1969. "The Elamite Language." In *Altkleinasiatische Sprachen* (Handbuch der Orientalistik, division 1, vol. 2), pp. 54–118. Leiden: Brill.

Rüster, Christel, and Erich Neu. 1989. *Hethitisches Zeichenlexikon.* Wiesbaden: Harrassowitz.

Saussure, Ferdinand de. 1879. *Mémoire sur le système primitif des voyelles dans les langues indo-européennes.* Leipzig: Teubner. Repr. Hildesheim: Olms, 1987.

Schroeder, Otto. 1915. *Die Tontafeln von El-Amarna* (Vorderasiatische Schriftdenkmäler 12). Leipzig: Hinrichs.

Stève, Marie-Joseph. 1992. *Syllabaire élamite: Histoire et paléographie.* Neufchatel and Paris: Recherches et Publications.

Sturtevant, Edgar. 1951. *A Comparative Grammar of the Hittite Language,* rev. ed. New Haven: Yale University Press.

Wilhelm, Gernot. 1992. "EA 24: A Letter in Hurrian about Marriage and Friendship." In *The Amarna Letters,* by William Moran, pp. 63–71. Baltimore: Johns Hopkins University Press.

Egyptian Writing

ROBERT K. RITNER

The Egyptian script tradition is one of the world's longest, extending from the end of the fourth millennium B.C.E. to at least the tenth century C.E. During these four thousand years, four distinct but interrelated scripts were developed, often in complementary usage: Hieroglyphic, Hieratic, Demotic, and Coptic (see SECTION 22).

Hieroglyphic

Of these various scripts, none was as long-lived, or has so captured the public imagination (Iverson 1993), as Egyptian hieroglyphs. Indeed, hieroglyphs represent the fundamental Egyptian writing system, from which Hieratic, Demotic, and (to a lesser extent) Coptic are cursive derivatives. The common designation "Hieroglyphic" (from Greek τὰ ἱερογλυφικά *tà hierogluphiká* 'sacred carvings') was first applied by Clement of Alexandria (*Stromata* V.IV.20–21), while Herodotus termed the script τὰ ἱερά (γράμματα) *tà hierá (grámmata)* 'the sacred (letters)' (II.36). Such terminology corresponds to that of the native language, in which hieroglyphs were styled ⸗‖‖‖ *mdw-nṯr* 'god's-words', in recognition of the divine origin of writing, the invention of Thoth, the god of wisdom.

The Hieroglyphic script is pictographic in nature and was developed by the rebus principle at or just before the beginning of the First Dynasty (ca. 3100 B.C.E.) in close conjunction with a nascent artistic tradition. Bas-relief and accompanying text form an interdependent unit, in which depicted actions and individuals may be "read" as "ideograms" or "determinatives" for phonetically written names or titles. This representational character of Egyptian writing was continually exploited by scribes and theologians, resulting in the late misconception by outsiders that the script was purely "symbolic" and not phonetic. The development of writing in Egypt may be the result of "stimulus diffusion" by which Egypt gained the "notion of writing" through trade with Sumerians. However, it must be stressed that the Egyptian system is quite alien to the Sumerian and represents a distinctly local creation.

The distinguishing feature of the Hieroglyphic script is its consonontal basis. Unlike Sumerian, Egyptian pictograms are not syllabic, i.e. they neither write vowels nor indicate their presence. The contrary suggestion of a syllabic basis for Egyptian by the linguist Gelb (1963: 72–81) has found no Egyptological support (Schenkel 1984, cols. 717–18). The omission of vowels probably results from syllabic shifts such as are characteristic of the related Semitic languages, in which grammatical inflection is indicated by internal vowel variation around generally invariable consonontal word roots. Egyptian writing thus provides word "skeletons" to which the reader would add the appropriate vowels, obvious from the context to native speakers.* Evidence from Coptic further indicates that Egyptian syllables with sonants often lacked vowels altogether. Special techniques for representing the unfamiliar syllabic character of foreign loanwords ("group writing") are discussed below.

Not all hieroglyphs represent consonants, however, for Egyptian is a "mixed system" in which certain signs convey sounds (*phonograms*) while others indicate meaning (*semograms*). Though there is a fairly consistent core of about 700 standard signs used to write the classical stage of the language (Middle Egyptian, Dynasties XI–XII, ca. 2000–1650), no strictures were placed on either the form or the number of signs. Despite the often conservative character of scribal schools, some signs were "updated" (Old Kingdom ᴗ > Middle Kingdom ⌐ 'axe') and innovations were acknowledged with new signs (New Kingdom ⍦ *wrry.t* 'chariot'). The generation of new hieroglyphs accelerates in the Late Period (Dynasties XXVI–XXX, 664–332), resulting in over 5,000 signs in the Greco-Roman eras (332 B.C.E. – ca. 400 C.E.).

The simplest element of the hieroglyphic repertoire is the "logogram" or "ideogram," by which a word is represented with a corresponding picture: ☉ *rꜥ* 'sun', ⌐ *ꜥbꜣ* 'mace', ⌀ *msḏr* 'ear', ⍦ *mnhd* 'scribal outfit'. Extended usage of this picture writing permits ideograms to stand for affiliated notions and actions: ☉ *hrw* 'day', ⌐ *hrp* 'govern', ⌀⍦ *sḏm* 'hear', ⍦ *sš* 'write'. Exclusively logographic writing is relatively rare in Egyptian, and, as in the examples above, instances of nouns are usually followed by a stroke (ı) as a determinative. From the logograms derive all other hieroglyphs, whether semographic determinatives or phonograms. The association of individual pictures with characteristic sound values led to the use of such signs as purely phonetic elements, so that the sign ◇ *ḥr* 'face' is used in writing the homophonous ◇⌐ *ḥr* 'upon' and ◇⌐⇌ *ḥr* 'be distant'.

Phonograms in Egyptian are divided into three categories on the basis of the number of consonants represented by the individual sign. The most basic of these are the 26 "alphabetic" or uniconsonontal signs (TABLE 4.1). Classical (Middle) Egyptian recognizes 24 consonants. An alternate sign for *y* (ᴗ) derives from the archaic dual ending, while that for *s* (⇌) originally indicated a lost consonant *z*, still distinguished in Old Egyptian. The phonemic structure of classical Egyptian probably represents the spoken dialect of the capital Memphis. Later dialectal spellings reveal the widespread existence of an *l*, conflated with *r* (less often *n*) in Middle Egyptian. The consonants ⍦ *ꜣ*, ⌐ *i*, ⍦ *y*, and ⍦ *w* are weak, readily assimilated to preceding vowels, and frequently omitted in final position. The order of the Egyptian "alphabet" given

---

*Conventionally, the sound [ɛ] is inserted into words for convenience in pronunciation, but with no claim of accuracy or authenticity. In transcriptions of Egyptian, periods link gender and number affixes, tilted double hyphens link personal affixes, and hyphens link members of compound words.

TABLE 4.1: *Uniconsonantal or "Alphabetic" Hieroglyphs*

	ꜣ	[ʔ]		ḥ	[ħ]
	i	affinity to *i*, otherwise [j]		ḫ	[x]
	y	usually word-final		ẖ	perhaps [ç]
	y	word-final		s	variant of following, originally *z*
	ʿ	[ʕ]		s	
	w	affinity to *u*, otherwise [w]		š	[ʃ]
	b			q	[q]
	p			k	[k]
	f			g	[g]
	m			t	
	n	may substitute for *l*		ṯ	[tʃ]
	r	may substitute for *l*		d	
	h			ḏ	[dʒ]

in TABLE 4.1 follows modern scholarly convention; native classification is known to begin with the letter ▢ *h*, but is not fully attested (Johnson 1994: 67–68).

Although Egyptians could thus compose purely alphabetic texts, and did attempt such experiments in the Late Period, preference was given to mixed writings that actually increase legibility (Davies 1987: 35). Thus the alphabetic ▢◡ *pr* is ambiguous as to meaning, while ▢ *pr* 'house' and ▢◡∧ *pr* 'go forth' are clear.

The largest category of Egyptian phonograms comprises the biliterals, or combinations of two consonants. About eighty common biliterals are used, and several have more than one possible sound value. The full inventory is shown in TABLE 4.2. Whether or not alternative readings are possible, biliterals are usually accompanied by alphabetic signs acting as *phonetic complements*: 𓏞𓅢 [b]*bꜣ*[ꜣ], 𓅓𓂋 *mr*[mr], 𓏏𓊌 [ꜣ]*bb*[b]. More than one biliteral may have the same phonetic value, but in practice biliterals are rarely interchangeable for the choice of biliteral is typically dependent upon word root.

The remaining phonographic category includes the approximately seventy triliterals, or signs comprising three consonants; they are given in TABLE 4.3. Since many Egyptian words are based on triliteral roots, the distinction between triliteral and logogram is often blurred (Gardiner 1957: 45). As with biliterals, triliterals may be accompanied by alphabetic phonetic complements which serve to specify the reading of a pictogram with more than one signification: 𓌅𓏏𓋴 *wꜣs* 'scepter'; 𓂧𓏤 *ḏꜣm*[m] 'electrum'. More often, the phonetic elements are redundant and optional: 𓋹 or 𓋹𓈖 *ʿnḫ*[(nḫ)] 'life'. Phonetically redundant elements nonetheless function calligraphically, facilitating the arrangement of signs within invisible square spaces or "quadrants."

TABLE 4.2: *Biliteral Hieroglyphs*

	-ꜣ	-i	-ꜥ	-w	-b	-p	-m	-n
ꜣ-				ꜣw	ꜣb			
i-				iw			im	in
ꜥ-	ꜥꜣ							
w-	wꜣ		wꜥ			wp		wn / wn
b-	bꜣ							
p-	pꜣ							
m-	mꜣ	mi / mi		mw				mn
n-				nw / nw	nb		nm	nn
r-				rw				
ḥ-	ḥꜣ			ḥw			ḥm	ḥn
ḫ-	ḫꜣ		ḫꜥ	ḫw				
ẖ-	ẖꜣ							ẖn / ẖn
s-	sꜣ / sꜣ			sw				sn
š-	šꜣ			šw				šn
q-								
k-	kꜣ					kp	km	
g-							gm	
t-	tꜣ	ti					tm	
ṯ-	ṯꜣ							
ḏ-	ḏꜣ			ḏw				

Completing the inventory of hieroglyphic signs are the "semographic" determinatives, which are placed after the phonetic elements and add precision to a word's meaning (TABLE 4.4). Determinatives are often the only distinguishing features among homonyms. Thus, the concluding "book-roll" determinative characterizes the word 𓏞 *sš* 'writing' in contrast to 𓏞 *sš* 'scribe', determined with a seated man. While some determinatives are specific to individual words (∧ in *nḥḥw* 'flail'), most are generic indicators of a word's nature (*taxograms*). The number of commonly used generic determinatives is quite large, indicating, for example, specif-

TABLE 4.2 (*continued*)

	-r	-ḥ	-s	-q	-k	-t	-d	-ḏ
ꜣ-								
i-	ir		is					
ꜥ-				ꜥq				ꜥḏ
w-	wr							wḏ
b-		bḥ						
p-	pr	pḥ						
m-	mr / mr	mḥ	ms			mt / mt		
n-		nḥ	ns					nḏ
r-								
ḥ-	ḥr		ḥs					ḥḏ
ḫ-						ḫt		
ẖ-	ẖr							
s-					sk	st		
š-			šs				šd	
q-							qd	
k-								
g-			gs					
t-								
ṯ-								
ḏ-	ḏr						ḏd	

ic fields of action, classifications, and materials (Gardiner 1957: 31–33). Words often have more than one determinative to add clarity or nuance, e.g. ⟨image⟩ *gsꜣ* 'anoint' with JUG and FORCE determinatives. Some determinatives provide further, extra-linguistic, information. Thus by the addition of ⟨image⟩ STICK, ⟨image⟩ CRUCIBLE, or ⟨image⟩ SLAB to the writing of ⟨image⟩ *ꜥfḏ.t* 'box/chest', the reader would be informed of its composition in wood, metal, or stone. Determinatives are a most significant aid to legibility, being readily identifiable word dividers.

TABLE 4.3: *Triliteral Hieroglyphs*

	ꜣbw		biꜣ		sbq
	iꜣm		bit		spr
	iʿb		pds		smꜣ
	iwʿ		mꜣʿ		smn
	iwn		mnw		sḫm
	ibꜣ		msn		sḫm
	imi		mdḥ		sšm
	isw		nni		sšm
	idn		nḥb		sšr
	idr		nṯr		stp
	ʿwt		nḏm		stꜣ
	ʿbꜣ		rwd, rwḏ		sḏb
	ʿpr		ḥfn		sḏm
	ʿnḫ		ḥry		šbn
	ʿrq		ḥtm		šmʿ
	ʿḥʿ		ḫbs		šnʿ
	ʿšꜣ		ḫpr		šsp
	wꜣḥ		ḫnt		šsm
	wꜣs		ḫnt		qmi
	wꜣḏ		ḥrw		kꜣp
	wʿr		ḫsf		kfꜣ
	wbn		hꜣr		ghs
	wḥm		hnm		tyw
	wsr		sꜣh		tpy
	wsḫ		siꜣ		ṯmꜣ
	wsḫ		sin		dšr
	wšm		swꜣ		dʿm
	bꜣs		swn		dbꜣ
	biꜣ		sbꜣ		dbʿ

Despite the variety of signs and potential combinations, words are rarely written in all possible combinations. Though never rigidly standardized, the spelling of individual words regularly crystallizes around a core of specific sign combinations. As elsewhere in the ancient Near East, scribes learned to write by memorizing word

TABLE 4.4: *Generic Determinatives*[a]

𓀀	man, person		🌳	tree
𓁐	woman		🌿	plant, flower
𓀀𓁐	people		🍇	vine, fruit, garden
𓀔	child, young		⌒	wood, tree
𓀛	old man, old, lean upon		🌾	corn
𓀜	official, man in authority		∘∘∘	grain
𓀢	exalted person, the dead		⎯	sky, above
𓀭	god, king		⊙	sun, light, time
𓀽 or 𓀾	king		🌙	night, darkness
𓀞	god, king		✶	star
𓁷 or 𓁷	goddess, queen		🔥	fire, heat, cook
𓀠	high, rejoice, support		𓊽	air, wind, sail
𓀡	praise, supplicate		▭	stone
𓀢	force, effort		𓋊	copper, bronze
𓀁	eat, drink, speak, think, feel		∘∘∘	sand, minerals, pellets
𓀦	lift, carry		〰	water, liquid, related actions
𓀐	weary, weak		▭	sheet of water
𓀢	enemy, foreigner		𓈗	irrigated land
𓀜	enemy, death		⌓	land (later often replaces 𓈗)
𓀾 or 𓀿	lie down, death, bury		𓂻	road, travel, position
𓀾	mummy, likeness, shape		𓈊	desert, foreign country
𓁀	head, nod, throttle		〉	foreign (country or person)
𓄿	hair, mourn, forlorn		𓊖	town, village, Egypt
𓁹	eye, see, actions of eye		𓉐	house, building
𓁻	actions or conditions of eye		⌓	door, open
𓂀[b]	nose, smell, joy, contempt		𓋬	box, coffin
𓂋	ear, states or activities of ear		𓉗	shrine, palanquin, mat
𓂧	tooth, actions of teeth		𓊛	boat, ship, navigation
𓂡	force, effort[c]		𓊝	sacred bark
𓂢	substitute for 𓂡 in hieratic[d]		𓋳	clothe, linen
𓂤	offer, present		⌒	bind, document
𓂝	arm, bend arm, cease		𓏌	rope, actions with cord or rope

TABLE 4.4: *Generic Determinatives*[a] (Continued)

〇	envelop, embrace		↘	knife, cut
⌐	phallus, beget, urinate		⊤	hoe, cultivate, hack up
ʃ	leg, foot, actions of foot		×	break, divide, cross
⋏	walk, run		▽	cup
⋏	move backwards		♁	vessel, anoint
◊	limb, flesh		♁[e]	pot, vessel, beverages
◯	tumors, odors, disease		θ	bread, cake
◇	bodily discharges		⊂◯ or ⊂◯	loaf, cake, offering
𓃾 and 𓃿	cattle		▽	festival
𓄂	savage, Typhonian		⌐[f]	book, writing, abstract
𓄹	skin, mammal		▭	royal name, king
𓅭	bird, insect		ı	one; the object depicted
𓅪	small, bad, weak		ı ı ı[g]	several, plural
𓆛	fish		＼	substitute for hard-to-draw signs[h]
𓆙	snake, worm			

a. After Gardiner 1957: 31–33. Listed in the conceptual order used for hieroglyphs in modern lists.
b. Less accurately ⌡.
c. Interchangeable with 𓄂.
d. Less often in hieroglyphic.
e. Less accurately 〇.
f. Also vertically ⌡, older form ⌐.
g. Also ∘∘∘.
h. Mostly hieratic.

groups, and this communal practice resulted in a high degree of consistency and clarity.

  Hieroglyphic texts are composed in either vertical columns or horizontal lines. With few exceptions ("retrograde"), the direction of reading is toward the face of human or animal pictograms, i.e. the signs are turned toward the beginning of the inscription. Vertical columns are read from top to bottom, while horizontal texts may be oriented either from right to left or left to right. In practice, a distinct preference is shown for right-to-left orientation. Reversal of this norm is usually based on an artistic desire for symmetry (flanking inscriptions on doorways, etc.), or to coordinate the text with a represented figure facing left (Fischer 1977, cols. 1192–93). Artistic considerations may also dictate a rearrangement of the expected sequence of signs, so that tall thin signs typically precede birds: 𓈅𓏏 for 𓈅𓏏 *ꜣḥ.t* (never *ḥꜣ.t*) 'field'. Honorific transposition is accorded to terms of exceptional prestige in written sequences, with divine and royal terms written first though pronounced in inverted order: ЛШ *mdw-nṯr*, written <nṯr-mdw> (< ⌐ 'flag' + ⌐ 'word') 'god's-words' (cf. English *$1,000*). "Orthograms" (calligrams) and ligatures represent additional artistic and theological influence on the script. Calligraphic "filler strokes" eliminate blank spaces in textual arrangement. The use of ligatured "composite signs" increases with time, either for harmonious arrangement (ℬ = 𝔸 *m* + ⌐ '; 𝔗 = ⌐ *š* + ⌐ COME in 𝔗𝔸⌐ *šm* 'go') or for "magical" considerations due to the representational nature of the signs (✷; see Ritner 1993: 163–67).

A particular subset of hieroglyphic writing is the so-called "group writing" by which foreign names and terms are rendered in combinations of biliterals and sign groupings, as in 𝔩𝔩𝔩𝔩𝔩 *'Ihi* not *'*I̯ḥwiw* (Gardiner 1957: 52). This system was termed a syllabic orthography by Albright (1934), and despite initial opposition this interpretation is now dominant (Iverson 1993: 34–36; Schenkel 1985). Though the system was in common usage only in the Middle and New Kingdoms, a Demotic text of Persian date uses similar principles for transcribing not isolated words, but an extensive manuscript composed in Aramaic (Steiner and Nims 1985: 65–68).

Of great importance for the later history of hieroglyphs are the occasional cryptographic writings, in which common signs or modified variants represent atypical phonetic values on the basis of visual puns, acrophony, or other reasons. Such writings occur rarely even in the Old Kingdom, but become common in royal funerary texts of the New Kingdom, where they are often accompanied by a parallel, normal "translation." Many of these individual spellings and values survive into the Greco-Roman eras, when the application of traditional cryptographic principles led to the formation of thousands of new signs and the misperception by outsiders that the script was purely symbolic.

Hieratic

Like the Hieroglyphic script of which it is a direct cursive equivalent, Hieratic ("priestly") received its name from Clement of Alexandria, in whose time its use was restricted to religious compositions. Native terminology does not distinguish Hieratic from hieroglyphs. Both forms were invented and developed almost simultaneously, with Hieratic being but a linear simplification of the complex hieroglyphs. Hieratic, however, is written exclusively from right to left. As Hieroglyphic served as a monumental script, Hieratic was designed for more rapid and often less exalted purposes on ostraca (see FIGURE 3) and papyrus: dockets, accounts, and letters. Only rarely was late Hieratic engraved on stone. Developing Hieratic produced a variety of distinctive writing styles, with the mundane "business hand" displaying increased use of ligatures, while elaborate calligraphic flourishes characterize the "book hand" later used for literary and religious compositions. Literary Hieratic may include punctuation in the form of "verse points." Regional variations are also notable, so that by the Twenty-fifth Dynasty the chancery styles of the south (Abnormal Hieratic) and north (Demotic) were no longer mutually legible. With Demotic accorded royal preference

TABLE 4.5: *Demotic Uniconsonantal "Alphabetic" Signs*

Sign	Value	Sign	Value
2͜ or ʔ	ꜣ	ꜣ or ꜣ	ḥ
ꞁ	i	6	ḫ
‖	e	ꜣ	ẖ
ꗃ‖	y	ꓺ or ꜣ	h
ꜣ or ꜣ	ꜥ	ꜣ, ꜣꞁ, ꜣ, or ꜩ‖	s
ꜣ or ꜣ	w	ꜣ or ꜣ	š
ꞁ꜊ or ꞁꜩ	b	ꜣ	q
ꜣ or ꜣ	p	ꜣ	k
ꜣ	f	ꜣ	g
ꜣ or ꜣ	m	ꜣ	t
— or ꜣ	n	ꜣ	ṯ
ꜣ or ꜣ	r	ꜣ	t
ꜣ	l	ꜣ or ꞁ꜊	d
ꜣ	h		

in the Twenty-sixth Dynasty, only calligraphic Hieratic survived as a traditional script for religious texts.

Demotic

Designated "Demotic" ('popular') by Herodotus, the script was termed *sš-šꜥ.t* "letter writing" in the native language, and thus "Epistological" by Clement. As noted, Demotic derives from the "business hand" of the Delta and was in continuous use from the seventh century B.C.E. to the fifth century C.E. Though ultimately descended from hieroglyphs, Demotic is characterized by numerous abbreviated writings and ligatured word groupings, making identifications with precise hieroglyphic renderings difficult or impossible. Thus the common ligature ꜣ may derive historically from a variety of phonetic combinations: ꜥ and ꜥ, ꜥ and *n*, *r* and *n*, *t* and *n*, etc. Within Demotic orthography, such ligatures acquire almost independent status as "logograms" used to represent words, with specific readings indicated by accompanying phonetic complements or other visual markers. Demotic still retains "alphabetic" signs, however (shown in TABLE 4.5), and purely "alphabetic" spellings are common for loanwords. Like Hieratic, Demotic is read only from right to left. Unlike Hieratic, however, Demotic was regularly inscribed on stone from the Ptolemaic Period onward, the most famous example being the Rosetta Stone used in the decipherment of the Egyptian scripts.

With the demise of Demotic, Egyptian scripts survived only vestigially in Coptic as a means for writing the Egyptian language. However, Egyptian writing had a dominant influence on both the Meroitic and Proto-Sinaitic scripts, and through the latter, Egyptian may serve as the direct ancestor of the contemporary Latin alphabet.

HIERATIC SELECTION

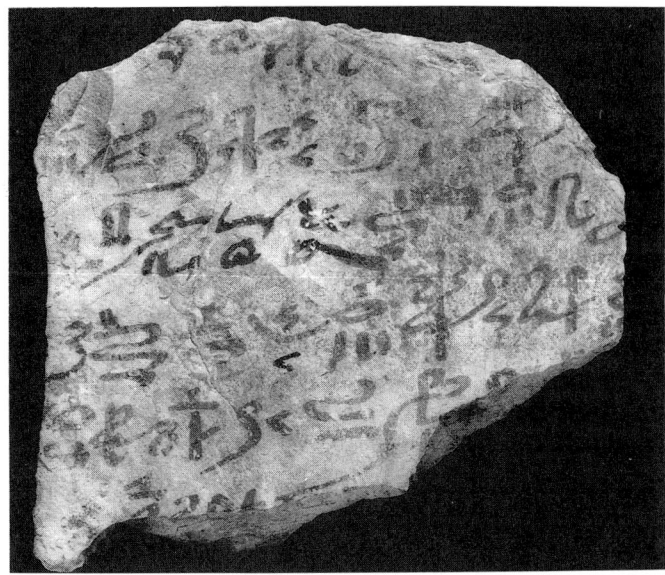

FIGURE 3. Ostracon bearing part of the following text (Oriental Institute Museum 25329;
photo courtesy of The Oriental Institute of The University of Chicago).

HIEROGLYPHIC TRANSCRIPTION

1. *Hieroglyphs:*				
2. *Explanation:*	d-d-k	HEART-/-k	m-sȝ-/	SCRIBAL KIT-W-SCROLL-PL-•
3. *Transcription:*	dd⸗k	ib⸗k	m-sȝ	sš.w
4. *Gloss:*	set-you	heart-your	after	writings

1.				
2.	d-g-ȝ-EYE-n-I SG	n-ḥm-m-w-SCROLL-MAN W. STICK	ḥr-/	bȝ-k-w-SCROLL-PL-•
3.	dgȝ.n⸗y	nḥm.w	ḥr	bȝk.w
4.	since-have-seen-I	those-saved	concerning	work-their

1.				
2.	m-(ʿ)-k-y-SCROLL	n-n	wn-n	m ḥȝ-ȝ-w	SCRIBAL KIT-W-SCROLL-PL-•
3.	mk	nn	wn	m ḥȝw	sš.w
4.	behold	not	there.is	in excess.of	writings

1. [hieroglyphs]

2. mi̯-t-t-SCROLL ḥr-/ mw p-w-• d-(i)-1SG

3. mit.t ḥr mw pw di̯ ≠i

4. likeness on water they-are may-cause-I

1. [hieroglyphs]

2. mr-y-MAN W. HAND TO MOUTH-k SCRIBAL KIT-W-SCROLL-PL r

3. mry≠k sš.w r

4. that.love-you writings more.than

1. [hieroglyphs]

2. mwt-t-SEATED WOMAN-k-• d-(i)-1SG ʿq-q-WALKING LEGS nfr-/-SCROLL-PL-s

3. mw.t≠k di̯ ≠i ʿq nfr.w ≠s

4. mother-your let.cause-I enter beauty-its

1. [hieroglyphs]

2. m ḥr-/-k-• wr-r sw-w g-r-t r i-ꜣ-w-t-STANDARD-SCROLL-PL

3. m ḥr≠k wr sw grt r iꜣw.t

4. into face-your great it then more.than office

1. [hieroglyphs]

2. nb-t-• n-n wn-n mi̯-t-t-SCROLL-s m EARTH-/-LAND-•

3. nb.t nn wn mit.t≠s m tꜣ

4. any not there.is likeness-its in land

'Set your thoughts just on writings, for I have seen people saved by their labor. Behold, there is nothing greater than writings. They are like a boat on water. Let me cause you to love writing more than your mother. Let me usher its beauty into your sight. For it is greater than any office. There is nothing like it on earth.' — *From the Teaching of Dua-khety, IIa–IIId (Helck 1970: 19–21, 29–29).*

The Meroitic Script

N. B. MILLET

The script used by the ancient Meroites, or inhabitants of the ancient empire of Meroë in the Sudan, was apparently devised in the third century B.C.E. and remained in use until after the fall of that empire in the first half of the fourth century C.E. There is some evidence to suggest that it was employed to write the Nubian languages of the successor kingdoms that grew up amidst the ruins of the old imperial power, although no actual texts have survived. It was finally displaced by the coming of Christianity to the Nubian Nile and the adoption of the Coptic alphabet in the sixth century.

TABLE 4.6: *The Meroitic Script*

Hieroglyph	Cursive	Transliteration	Hieroglyph	Cursive	Transliteration
𓏤	𐦧𐦲	initial a	𓂝	𐦧	l
𓏭	𐦧	e	⬭, ⬭	𐦡	ḫ
𓐍	/	o	☊	𐦣	ẖ
𓏲	𐦧	i	♯	𐦶	se
𓏐𓏐	///	y	𓇳	𐦡	s
𓆱	𐦢	w	𓅭	𐦲	k
𓅓	𐦪	b	△	13	q
𓈍	𐦣	p	𓅬	𐦧	t
𓀀	𐦦	m	𓊪	𐦤𐦧	te
𓈖	𐦨	n	𓂧	𐦦	to
𓍲	𐦣	ne	𓂀	𐦦	d
▱, ◧	𐦧	r	⋮	:	word divider

The Meroitic script existed in two variants, a "cursive" or linear version for general use, and a pictorial "hieroglyphic" lapidary style for monumental purposes on temple walls and other royal monuments. This duality reflects the age-old Egyptian scribal traditions, from which both forms of the Meroitic script had in fact been derived by their inventors.

The individual characters of the hieroglyphic variant are simply pictorial substitutions for those of the cursive system, most of the forms being explainable as drawn directly from the Egyptian hieroglyphic system which the Meroites had themselves been using for hundreds of years. The signs of the parallel cursive script are also generally traceable to Egyptian Demotic (cursive) prototypes.

Meroitic writing is written from right to left and occasionally, in the case of hieroglyphic, in columns for decorative effect. The system is essentially alphabetic and makes use of a word divider with varying degrees of regularity. There are fifteen consonantal signs and three vowel signs, besides a sign to indicate the presence of the initial vowel 𐦧𐦲 *a*. For reasons not understood, but possibly having to do with the existence of dialect differences, the devisers of the system created four further characters to express the syllables 𐦨 *ne*, 𐦶 *se*, 𐦤𐦧 *te*, and 𐦦 *to*. Absence of a written vowel after a consonant implied the vowel *a*. Certain syllable-closing consonants such as *s* and *n* were not necessarily noted. In the cursive variant, the sign for the vowel *i* is usually written in ligature with the preceding consonant.

The phonetic values of the signs of the script were ascertained in 1910 by the English Egyptologist F. Ll. Griffith (see SECTION 9); but since no true bilinguals have ever come to light, and no surviving related languages have been identified, the language itself remains in the main undeciphered. Place and personal names, a few divine names, and a mere handful of words can be identified with any certainty.

SAMPLE OF MEROITIC

:/13	4WW453	:4W/3	:44513A4III A453	:313←
: oq	irrtew	: iros	: ileqeniyentew	: sow←

4815324W/←	4452 4W/←	:5III 25W134III	48/135III5J1
iwolekiret	ilekiret	: eykerqiy	iwoqeyemt

1544/←-X/3/3	4815S<X/←	445<X/←	:5III5W14X3
beletenosos	iwolehdet	ilehdet	: eyertidk

4815SX 175 III	5III 353	X<ξW<	4815SX 175 III
iwoledmtey	eyosek	enhprh	iwoledmtey

:4815SX 175 III	5341513 III	III 451 X52	:/←-4W5ξ
: iwoledmtey	ekiteqes	silbda	: etirep

1. *Transliteration:*	wos :	wetneyineqeli :		sori :	wetrri	
2. *Gloss:*	O Isis	[epithet]		O Osiris	[epithet]	

1.	qo :	tmeye-qowi		yiqrekye :	terikeli
2.	The noble	Tameye-the.noble.one.it.is		(of) Yiqarekaye	begotten

1.	terikelowi	kditreye :		tedheli	tedhelowi
2.	begotten.he.was	(of) Kaditareye		born	born.he.was

1.	sosoneteleb	yetmdelowi		hrphne	kesoye
2.	(to) *sosonete*-officers	related.he.was;		(to) the.city.governor	Keshoye

1.	yetmdelowi	perite :		adblis	seqetike yetmdelowi :
2.	related.he.was	(to) the.agent		of.the.*adb*	Seqetike related.he.was

'O … Isis! O … Osiris! Here lies the noble Tameye; Yiqarekaye was his father, Kaditareye was his mother; he was related to *sosonete*-officers, to the city governor Keshoye, and to the *adb* agent Seqetike.'

— *Opening lines of a sandstone tombstone from Qasr Ibrim in Lower Nubia, ca. 300 B.C.E. (Mills 1982: 69).*

Bibliography

EGYPTIAN

Albright, William F. 1934. *The Vocalization of the Egyptian Syllabic Orthography* (American Oriental Series 5). New Haven: American Oriental Society (repr. Millwood, N.Y.: Kraus Reprints, 1974).

Davies, W. V. 1987. *Egyptian Hieroglyphs* (Reading the Past). Berkeley and Los Angeles: University of California Press; London: British Museum.

Fischer, Henry G. 1977. "Hieroglyphen" [in English]. *Lexikon der Ägyptologie,* vol. 2, cols. 1189–99.

Gardiner, Sir Alan. 1957. *Egyptian Grammar,* 3rd ed. Oxford: Griffith Institute.

Gelb, I. J. 1963. *A Study of Writing,* 2nd ed. Chicago: University of Chicago Press.

Helck, Wolfgang. 1970. *Die Lehre des Dwꜣ-Ḥtjj.* Wiesbaden: Harrassowitz.

Helck, Wolfgang, Eberhard Otto, and Wolfhart Westendorf, eds. 1975–89. *Lexikon der Ägyptologie.* 7 vols. Wiesbaden: Harrassowitz.

Iverson, Erik. 1993. *The Myth of Egypt and Its Hieroglyphs.* Princeton, N.J.: Princeton University Press (1st ed. Copenhagen, 1961).

Johnson, Janet H. 1994. "Ancient Egyptian Linguistics." In "Linguistics in the Ancient Near East," ed. Erica Reiner, pp. 63–76. In *History of Linguistics,* ed. Giulio C. Lepschy, vol. 1, *The Eastern Traditions of Linguistics,* pp. 61–96. London: Longman (original Italian publication, 1990).

Lüddeckens, Erich. 1974. "Demotisch." *Lexikon der Ägyptologie,* vol. 1, cols. 1052–56.

Osing, Jürgen. 1980. "Lautsystem." *Lexikon der Ägyptologie,* vol. 3, cols. 944–49.

Ritner, Robert K. 1993. *The Mechanics of Ancient Egyptian Magical Practice* (Studies in Ancient Oriental Civilization 54). Chicago: Oriental Institute.

Satzinger, Helmut. 1977. "Hieratisch." *Lexikon der Ägyptologie,* vol. 2, cols. 1187–89.

Schenkel, Wolfgang. 1984. "Schrift." *Lexikon der Ägyptologie,* vol. 5, cols. 713–35.

———. 1985. "Syllabische Schreibung." *Lexikon der Ägyptologie,* vol. 6, cols. 114–22.

Steiner, Richard C., and Charles F. Nims. 1985. "Ashurbanipal and Shamash-Shum-Ukin: A Tale of Two Brothers from the Aramaic Text in Demotic Script." *Revue Biblique* 82: 60–81.

MEROITIC

Griffith, Francis Ll. 1911. *Karanog: The Meroitic Inscriptions of Shablul and Karanog.* Philadelphia: University Museum.

———. 1912. *Meroitic Inscriptions II.* London: Egypt Exploration Fund.

Hintze, Fritz. 1974. "Some Problems of Meroitic Philology." In *Studies in Ancient Languages of the Sudan,* ed. Abdelgadir Mahmoud Abdalla, pp. 73–78. Khartoum: Khartoum University Press.

Mills, A. J. 1982. *Cemeteries of Qasr Ibrim* (Excavation Memoir 51). London: Egypt Exploration Society.

Priese, Karl-Heinz. 1973. "Zur Entstehung der Meroitischen Schrift." In *Sudan in Altertum* (Meroitica 1), ed. Fritz Hintze, pp. 273–306. Berlin: Akademie-Verlag.

Epigraphic Semitic Scripts

M. O'CONNOR

The Semitic languages are spoken across major sections of the Old World (Asia, Africa, and southern Europe). In ancient times they were spoken in the area of southwestern Asia known nowadays as the Near East or the Middle East, from the banks of the Tigris in the east to the Mediterranean in the west, and from the Armenian mountains in the north to the Arabian peninsula in the south; then, as now, they were used alongside a variety of languages from other families. Beginning in ancient times the Semitic languages spread into Africa, initially North Africa and later Ethiopia, and to islands in the Mediterranean and off the Arabian Peninsula.

The forerunner of the alphabet was invented to notate the consonants of the Semitic languages, specifically the West Semitic languages, which comprise the Canaanite group (Hebrew and Phoenician, and numerous local dialects; Ugaritic may be an early form of Canaanite), the Aramaic group, the Arabic group, and the southern group (South Arabian and Ethiopic).

The term "alphabet" is controversial (SECTION 1): some scholars have proposed that the Semitic script, which is purely consonantal at base and does not fully notate vowels (and is thus an abjad in the terms of Daniels 1990), prior to the development of a system of more or less independent diacritics, is not a "true alphabet," but a syllabary. On this understanding, pioneered by I. J. Gelb, each sign of a syllabary notates a syllable; the Ethiopic, Indic, and Japanese syllabaries record an entire syllable, while the Semitic "syllabaries" record the initial consonant of the syllable and leave the remainder unspecified. This proposal may be arguable on linguistic grounds (Gelb 1963, Swiggers 1983, 1984), but it is counterintuitive (Daniels 1990) and has been misused as a way of privileging the distinctive role of Greek consciousness in a way that makes no linguistic or historical sense (e.g. Havelock 1976, 1982). The standard practice of referring to the West Semitic scripts as "alphabets" could be defended on the grounds that no writing system notates everything relevant to language: the difference between what a Semitic script notates and what the Greek alphabet notates is a real difference, but a difference of degree and thus hardly grounds for explaining the unquestioned Greek contribution to the growth of the Western tradition.

The name of a language and the name of a script may be different, but it is common and sometimes unavoidable, even among careful scholars, to muddle the terms; some confusion must be expected in both popular and scholarly treatments. The history of forms of the script is a different matter from the history and relationship of the

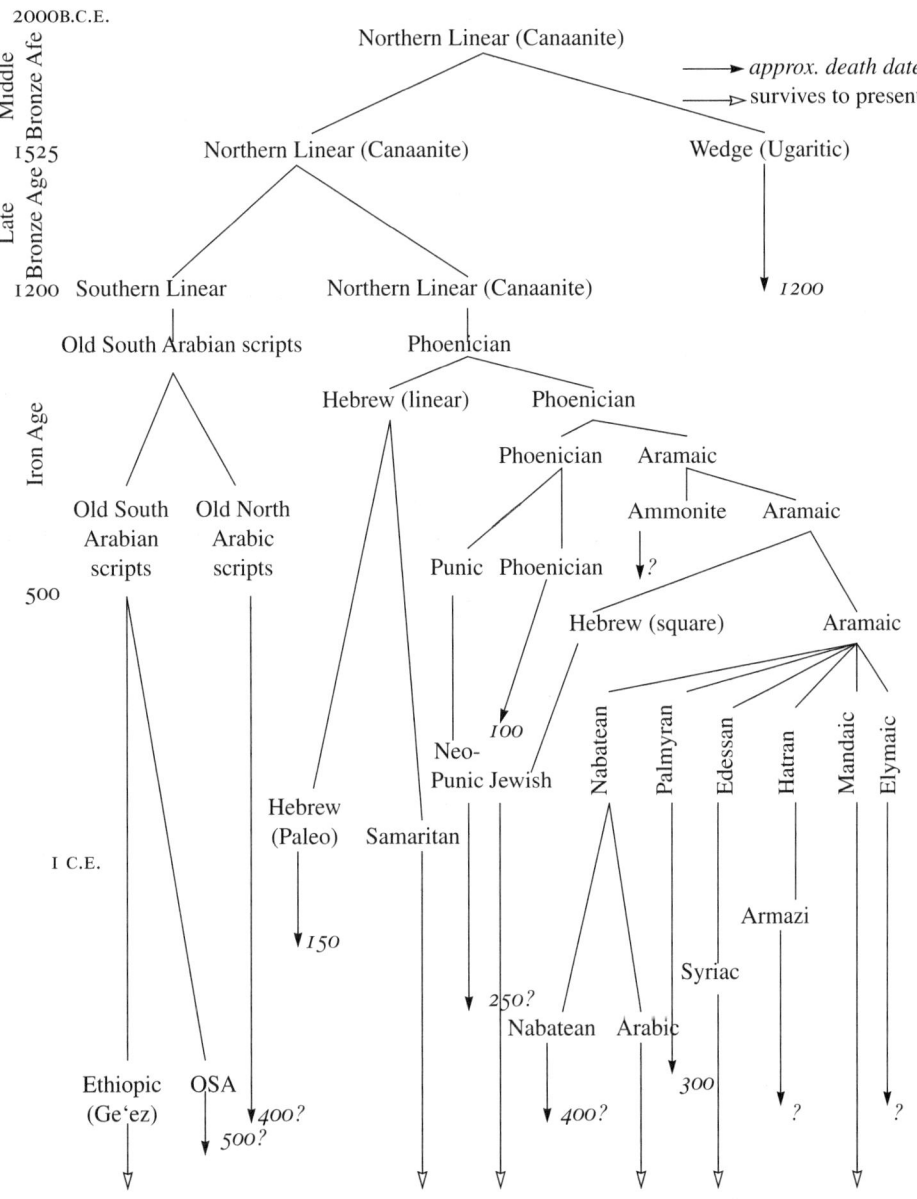

FIGURE 4. Family tree of ancient Semitic scripts

languages, even within the comparatively small compass of West Semitic (FIGURE 4).
Consider two examples: (a) the earliest text in the Ammonite language is written in
the Aramaic script (a form of the northern linear abjad first attested in Aramaic-language texts), while later texts in Ammonite are written in the Ammonite script (which
is derived from the Aramaic script)—even though the Ammonite language is more
closely affiliated to Hebrew than to Aramaic (Herr 1978); (b) the Classical Arabic

script developed from Nabatean, a form of the Aramaic script (Gruendler 1993), though the epigraphic scripts used earlier for languages closely related to Classical Arabic derived from a distinct, southern linear form of the abjad.

The study of the ancient written records of the Semitic languages is important because of their cultural and historical importance and because of the many innovations in the history of writing associated with the Semitic languages. Ancient written records can be divided into three categories based on the material used for the writing. (a) *Paleographic* records are those written on soft or perishable materials; these records lead into the great manuscript traditions of the three monotheistic religions, Judaism, Christianity, and Islam, though not all paleographic records are literary. (b) *Argillographic* records are those written on clay, the medium of choice for wedge writing; nearly all Akkadian (cuneiform) records are preserved on clay; many of the wedge-abjad records of Ugaritic are also preserved on clay. Both these categories include many literary texts. (c) *Epigraphic* texts are those written on durable materials (stone, including living rock as well as precious and semi-precious stones; ceramic; metal, including coins). They do not excite much love but are nonetheless crucial for historical and linguistic purposes and exhibit some points of literary interest.

Scripts in the Bronze Age (2000–1200 B.C.E.)

The abjad was invented during the Middle Bronze Age (2000–1525) and came into increasingly broad use during the succeeding Late Bronze Age (1525–1200). The process by which it came into being has been much disputed, and there is little historical evidence. On the one hand, there can be no doubt that speakers of West Semitic languages were exposed to a variety of writing systems in the cultural ambience of the ancient Near East; the Egyptian models were of more immediate importance than the Mesopotamian models (see Sass 1991). (The role of Aegean models is uncertain, as is the character of the early Middle Bronze Age "pseudo-hieroglyphic" texts from Byblos.) On the other hand, there is a longstanding and plausible tradition of regarding writing as an invention, i.e. as something that reflects the work of one person at one time.

A small and difficult body of texts called the Proto-Sinaitic inscriptions, dating from the end of the Middle Bronze period, seems to be relevant to the prehistory of the alphabet. Despite various attempts, it cannot be said that they have been deciphered. These rock-cut graffiti are from a turquoise-mining area in the Sinai peninsula, Serābît el-Khâdem; the setting is noteworthy, since the workers were prisoners of war from southwestern Asia and thus probably West Semitic speakers. The texts, as they have been deciphered, appear to be religious, specifically votive, texts. The Proto-Sinaitic texts thus raise two questions that recur at every stage of the history of writing: (a) Are writing systems developed for religious or for economic (and social) purposes? (b) Are writing systems before the European Renaissance chiefly a concern of elites? One argument against current proposals for reading the Proto-Sinaitic texts

TABLE 5.1: *The Earliest Linear Scripts (Garbini 1979, fig. 1)*[a]

	I	II	III	IV	V
ʾ	ҝ ҝ		ҝҝ	⅄ ⅄	⅄
b	৭ ৭	৭	৭Ყ	Ყ	৭
g	⅄		⅂		
d	△		◁ ◁	▷ ◁	△
h			⅂ ⅂		
w			ϒ Υ		Υ Υ
z	I		I	I	I
ḥ	⊟ ⊟	⊟	⊟ ⊟	I⊟ ⊞	⊟⊟
ṭ			⊕		
y	⅄ ⅃		⅄ ⅃		⅄ ⅃
k	↓ ↓		↓		↓
l	⌣	⌣	⌇ ⌇	⌇⌇ ⌇	⌇⌇
m		⅀	⅀ ⅀		⅀
n	⅄ ⅄	⅀	⅀ ⅀		
s			⅄		⅄
ʿ	∘ ◇ ∘	∘	∘	⊙	∘
p			⑀⑀⑀		⑀
ṣ	⤳ ⅄ ⅄			⊢⊢ ⌐	⊢⌇
q					⅌
r	৭		৭৭৭		৭৭
š			ᴡ	ᴡ	ᴡ
t			✛ ✚ ✕	✛	✕

a. Col. I, Arrowheads from Lebanon; col. II, Byblos 7765; col. III, Aḥiram inscription; col. IV, Inscriptions from Palestine; col. V, Gezer calendar.

TABLE 5.2: *The Ugaritic Script, with Hebrew Equivalents*[a]

à	b	g	ḫ	d	h	w	z	ḥ	ṭ	y	k	š	l	m	d̲	n	ẓ	s	ʿ	p	ṣ	q	r	ṭ	ġ	t	i	ù	s
ʔa	b	g	x	d	h	w	z	ħ	ŧ	j	k	ʃ	l	m	ð	n	ð̣	s	ʕ	p	ş	q	r	θ	ɣ	t	ʔi	ʔu	ʔ
א	ב	ג		ד	ה	ה	ו	ז	ח	ט	י	כ	שׁ	ל	מ		נ		ס	ע	פ	צ	ק	ר		ת			

a. Ugaritic uses a word divider in the form of a small vertical wedge ˈ. The second row of the table shows a standard transliteration scheme, and the third gives a plausible IPA transcription. The last line gives Hebrew equivalents.

(or reading them as the earliest alphabetic texts) is that miners seeking to honor a deity would not have come up with a writing system; this is plainly open to question, though the proposals are unsatisfactory on other grounds.

In the Late Bronze Age texts, two forms of signs are used: the linear (i.e. composed of lines) form (TABLE 5.1), the ancestor of all later forms, and the wedge or cuneiform form, used for Ugaritic (TABLE 5.2); wedge-abjad texts have been found at Ugarit and a few other Late Bronze sites. The wedge form of the abjad developed under the influence of cuneiform (logo- and syllabographic) writing: writing with a stylus on clay worked better with wedges than with the simple strokes that make up the forms of the linear abjad, and so the scribes at Ugarit adapted the script. These scribes also adapted it to record vowels in a limited way, specifically vowels following the glottal stop: the abjad, developed for West Semitic languages, was purely consonantal in origin, but the need to record words, especially names, that originated in other languages led to the notation of some vowels. The wedge script thus replaces the glottal stop sign (ˈaleph) with three "ˈalephs," for the combinations ˈ + *a*, ˈ + *u*, and ˈ + *i* (probably also used when no vowel followed the ˈ). The wedge script also used an extra sign for a sibilant whose sound value is unclear; it may represent a sound articulated between [s] and [ʃ]. Wedge-letter writing, unlike most other Semitic forms of the abjad, was oriented from left to right. The Ugaritic script is recorded in two different orders, one similar to the order known for the Phoenician and another similar to the order known for the Arabic (SECTION 68). The wedge script records an inventory of sounds that is closer to that found in Classical Arabic (ca. 28 sounds) than to that found in Biblical Hebrew (ca. 22 sounds).

From the Bronze Age there are also various linear-script texts from the Levant, the "Proto-Canaanite" texts (TABLE 5.1, col. I). It is difficult to place these linguistically, since the structure of the language family at this time is uncertain and the material is slight. By convention, texts dated on other grounds to the period before 1050 are called Canaanite (Old Canaanite, Proto-Canaanite), while texts from the ensuing period are called Phoenician (Naveh 1987). For some transitional texts from Byblos, including the inscribed clay handle Byblos 7765, cited in TABLE 5.1, see Cross and McCarter 1973.

TABLE 5.3: *Northern Linear Cursive Scripts (Garbini 1979, fig. 4)*[a]

	VI	VII	VIII	IX	X	XI
ʾ						
b						
g						
d						
h						
w						
z						
ḥ						
ṭ						
y						
k						
l						
m						
n						
s						
ʿ						
p						
ṣ						
q						
r						
š						
t						

a. Col. VI, Mozia, 6th c. B.C.E., stela, Punic; col. VII, Malta, 3rd–2nd c. C.E., ostraca, Late Phoenician cursive; col. VIII, Sidon, 5th c. B.C.E., Phoenician; col. IX, Phoenician papyrus, 4th–3rd c. B.C.E.; col. X, Samaria, mid 8th c. B.C.E., ostraca, Hebrew cursive; col. XI, Aramaic papyrus, 465 B.C.E.

———

Scripts in the Iron Age and later times (from 1200 B.C.E.)

Phoenician and related scripts

During the Iron Age, the linear script flourished and spread. There are two principal forms of linear abjad, the northern (usually called Phoenician) and the southern form. The latter is sometimes thought to have broken off from the northern form before the end of the Late Bronze Age, ca. 1300 B.C.E., though no texts that old are known.

The northern linear abjad (TABLES 5.1, 5.3) has a smaller consonantal inventory (ca. 22 sounds) than the southern linear form (ca. 28 sounds) and was used to represent a language like Phoenician that had undergone certain sound changes by ca. 1200. (Aramaic underwent similar changes several centuries later.) Since the earliest major texts are in fact Phoenician, the script of the period 1050–850 is called Phoenician. The argument has been made that various forms of the Bronze Age linear abjad survived into the Iron Age (Kaufman 1986). The contention that the use of the term Phoenician is therefore not justified does not follow (pace Kaufman 1986: 3–4); since the texts show the smaller consonantal inventory, they are linguistically closer to Phoenician (if they are not actually Phoenician) than to Aramaic (Naveh 1987). The number of texts is in any case small, and the diagnostic points for both language and script are sparsely attested. The oldest Aramaic applications of the Phoenician script show polyvalence, i.e. the writing of two related but distinct sounds with a single sign. There were four Aramaic "ghost sounds" and thus four cases of polyvalence (/ð/, written z but later written ḏ; /θ/, written š but later written ṯ; /ð̣/, written q but later written ʿ; /θ̣/ written ṣ but later written ṭ).

The southern form of the linear script retained throughout its history the original, purely consonantal structure, while the northern form over the ninth to fifth centuries developed various ways of notating vowels with *matres lectionis* 'mothers of reading', consonantal signs used to indicate the presence of a vowel.* Earliest notated were long vowels at the ends of words, followed almost immediately by word-internal long vowels; short-vowel notation came later. (West Semitic words never begin with vowels.) This process of vowel notation apparently began among the Arameans and later spread to Canaanite scribes. The shift to the use of vowel letters was not universal among the West Semitic script traditions: Phoenician was written in a purely consonantal orthography with no trace of vowel letters as late as the first century B.C.E., though its descendant language Punic had developed vowel letters centuries before.

The Phoenician form of the linear abjad was widely diffused as a result of Mediterranean colonization, and it is customary to refer to the Phoenicians as the "inven-

---

*In transliterations of West Semitic texts, it is customary to mark the presence of a *mater lectionis* with a circumflex accent on the letter for the vowel it indicates, while a macron marks a long vowel not indicated by a *mater*. Northwest Semitic texts are usually transliterated into Hebrew letters, so that the scholar is not forced to resolve ambiguities inherent in the consonantal script that cannot be conveniently reproduced in Roman letters.

TABLE 5.4: *Northern Linear Monumental Scripts (Garbini 1979, fig. 5)[a]*

	XII	XIII	XIV	XV	XVI
ʾ					
b					
g					
d					
h					
w					
z					
ḥ					
ṭ					
y					
k					
l					
m					
n					
s					
ʿ					
p					
ṣ					
q					
r					
š					
t					

a.   Col. XII, Siloam inscription, Hebrew; col. XIII, Hebrew seals; col. XIV, Mesha inscription, Moabite; col. XV, Ammonite script; col. XVI, Hasmonean coins and Abba inscription, 2nd–1st c. B.C.E., "Paleo-Hebrew" script.

tors and propagators of the alphabet." This is misleading. There were no Phoenicians as such in the Bronze Age, and so the Phoenicians did not "invent" the alphabet. A variety of scripts (and peoples) were involved in the diffusion of the alphabet around the region, even if the Phoenicians played a major role in the process.

As the northern linear script spread through the Levant (modern Syria, Lebanon, Israel, and Jordan) and neighboring regions, and was used to write the various Northwest Semitic languages, it took on different shapes. These identities, which are "scripts" in themselves, chiefly reflect geography, but language, chronology, writing medium, and the purpose of the writing are also revelant in describing them.

The Phoenician script was the base from which the other varieties (and later subvarieties) developed. Texts are found in various Canaanite languages from the eleventh century B.C.E. on. In the central and southern Levant, the most notable script variety is linear Hebrew (TABLE 5.4), used also for that language's lesser known relatives, Moabite and Philistine (the Semitic language of the Philistine area, Naveh 1985, not the language of the ruling military elite from the Aegean). The colonies of the Phoenician homeland and its cultural dependencies throughout the Mediterranean at first used the Phoenician script and later developed local varieties of it; the most important were Punic and its lineal offspring Neo-Punic.

Aramaic

In the northern Levant and in neighboring, Aramean-influenced areas (southern Anatolia and northern Mesopotamia), and sporadically elsewhere, Aramaic speakers (and writers) used the Phoenician script during the ninth and early eighth centuries; a distinctive Aramaic script developed by the mid eighth century B.C.E. By 700, Aramaic was the preeminent language of the region, and the Persian Empire, established in the mid sixth century, confirmed that position by adopting it as its official language. The official status of Imperial Aramaic provided a stability and uniformity for both the language and the script that outlasted the empire. Extant materials include not only many epigraphs but also several caches of manuscripts from Egypt. Aramaic script was a major influence on the developing scripts of the Transjordanian region: the earliest Ammonite texts are in Aramaic script, probably as a result of contacts with Damascus. Hebrew continued to be written with the linear Hebrew abjad during the exilic period (597–539 B.C.E.), when it was gradually replaced by a form of the Aramaic script. The older ("linear") Hebrew abjad remained in intermittent use, nationalistically or religiously motivated, until 135 C.E.; during this later phase it is called Paleo-Hebrew script. This abjad is the basis of the Samaritan script, which emerged during the first century B.C.E. and is still used for religious purposes. Post-biblical Hebrew scripts, the Jewish (also called square or Assyrian) scripts, develop from the exilic, Aramaic script (SECTION 46).

The Aramaic script continued its dominance after the collapse of the Achaemenid Empire, spreading far to the east, through Iran to South and Central Asia. The earliest,

TABLE 5.5: *Scripts Derived from Aramaic Script (Garbini 1979, fig. 7)*[a]

	XVII	XVIII	XIX	XX
ʾ				
b				
g				
d				
h				
w				
z				
ḥ				
ṭ				
y				
k				
l				
m				
n				
s				
ʿ				
p				
ṣ				
q				
r				
š				
t				

a. Col. XVII, Hebrew square script; col. XVIII, Palmyrene script; col. XIX, Nabatean script; col. XX, Ancient Arabic script.

Semitic phase of this post-imperial history begins with the breakdown of the uniformity of Imperial Aramaic script around 250 B.C.E. (TABLE 5.5). In the western half of the old empire, in addition to the Jewish scripts, the Arabic-speaking Nabateans developed their own Aramaic script; the texts are found in Palestine, Transjordan, the Sinai, and northern Arabia. In the eastern half of the imperial territory, there were a number of developments. The trading oasis of Palmyra in the Syrian desert developed its own script, which may have had some influence in later Iranian developments. Northern Mesopotamian local scripts are attested both in the old Assyrian heartland (at Hatra and Assur) and to the west, at Edessa. The Old Edessan texts are unvocalized and epigraphic or legal in character; their script eventually developed into the Syriac script used to record the literary and religious texts of a large part of Christianity (SECTION 47). In southern Mesopotamia an unattested local script gave rise to the writing system used by Mandean gnostics of the marsh regions. Under the broad heading of Arsacid Aramaic scripts may be gathered texts from the Parthian period texts (200 B.C.E.–200 C.E.): texts from the far north, Armenia and Georgia (Armazi), reflect the Hatran script, while texts from the far south, in the Iranian province of Elymais (ancient Elam), reflect the same origins as the Mandean script. The Elymaic script, though poorly attested, is the chief predecessor of the adaptations of the Aramaic script used to write a range of Iranian dialects in the ensuing Sassanid period and later (SECTION 48).

Arabia

Among the languages of the Arabian peninsula, understood broadly to extend northward into the wildernesses of the Levant and westward into the Horn of Africa, there is great diversity. From early in the first millennium B.C.E. (perhaps ca. 900) there are texts in several varieties of Arabic (or North Arabic) and corresponding scripts, including a dialect more or less identical to Classical Arabic, as well as in Dedanite, Lihyanite, Safaitic, and Thamudic; the interrelations among these languages/dialects and their writing systems remain under study (TABLE 5.6). The South Arabian branch of the Semitic family includes both the languages associated with the south of the Peninsula, the South Arabian languages proper, and their close relatives, the Ethiopic languages. There are several living South Arabian languages, but these are not identified with the ancient languages attested epigraphically: Minean, Sabean, Qatabanian, Hadramauti. The southern linear abjad was the source for the scripts used for the (North) Arabic and South Arabian languages and for inscriptional Ethiopic script (TABLE 5.7). Some forty texts written on wooden slats in a cursive South Arabian script (Ryckmans 1986) have recently come to light; sixteen are now published (Ryckmans, Müller, and Abdullah 1994).

The Ethiopic epigraphic finds, from the early first millennium C.E., are in a form of the major northern Ethiopic language, Ge'ez, the language of Ethiopian Christianity; the early inscriptions are consonantal, while in the later texts the Ge'ez syllabary

TABLE 5.6: *North Arabic Scripts (Garbini 1979, fig. 9)*[a]

	XXI	XXII	XXIII	XXIV	XXV	XXVI
ʾ						
b						
g						
d						
h						
w						
z						
ḥ						
ṭ						
y						
k						
l						
m						
n						
s						
ʿ						
p						
ṣ						
q						
r						
š						
t						

a. Col. XXI, Dedanite; col. XXII, Late Liḥyanite; cols. XXIII–XXV, Thamudic (XXIII, Teima; XXIV, Hejaz; XXV, Tabuk); col. XXVI, Safaitic.

(the abugida) has developed (SECTION 51). The southern form of the linear abjad died out in Asia during the first millennium C.E.; classical Arabic script developed from Nabatean script (SECTION 50).

Starting with the late Second Temple period of Judaism (ca. 200 B.C.E.–70 C.E.), with the establishment of Eastern (Aramaic-speaking) Christianity (ca. 400 C.E.), and with the establishment of Islam (ca. 700 C.E.), epigraphic texts in Hebrew, Aramaic (Syriac and various other forms of Jewish and Christian Aramaic), and Arabic are influenced by and reflect the scriptures of those religions. Full cursives develop more extensively in this later period, although cursive scripts had appeared earlier; the use of final forms in Hebrew and various ligatures in Nabatean are related phenomena, preliminary to the ligatured cursive scripts of Arabic and Syriac.

In the northern and southern forms of the linear abjad, various numbering systems were used, some native, notably the use of letters with numeral values ('aleph = 1, beth = 2, etc.), and some borrowed. In Hebrew, the Egyptian hieratic numerals were used; "Arabic numerals" are in origin from South Asia and are called by the Arabs "Hindu numerals."

Salient features of various groups of texts

What features make the various corpora of ancient Semitic epigraphic texts distinctive? Pride of numerical place goes to the North Arabic texts, mostly short graffiti and numbering in the many thousands. Pride of historical place goes to the Aramaic texts, since Aramaic was the most widely used language of the ancient Near East, the international language from the seventh or perhaps even eighth century B.C.E. and the official language of the Persian empire (550–330 B.C.E.). Pride of geographical place may be awarded either to the Aramaic texts, a corpus extending far to the East (the six Official Aramaic inscriptions of the 3rd-century Indian emperor Ashoka are found in Afghanistan and Pakistan), or to the Phoenician texts, which are found far to the west of the Levantine homeland, as early as the ninth century, in Cyprus, Crete, Sardinia, Spain, and most famously North Africa.

As texts, the most beautiful ancient Semitic epigraphs are the monumental Old South Arabian texts, with their large and perfectly formed letters; these are distinctive in exhibiting the greatest variation in writing direction: some are left-to-right, others right-to-left, still others boustrophedon. The most beautiful epigraphs as works of art are the Syro-Hittite texts from northern Syria, some written in Phoenician, including our example text, the Kilamuwa inscription (ca. 825 B.C.E.), and some in Aramaic, such as the Fekheriye bilingual (ca. 850), also represented below.

TABLE 5.7: *Monumental Scripts of Yemen and Ethiopia (Garbini 1979, fig. 10)*[a]

	XXVII	XXVIII	XXIX	XXX
ʾ	ḥ	ḥ	ḥ ḥ ʌ	ḥ ʌ
b	⊓	⨅ ⋈	⊓ ⊓	⊓
g	⌐(φ)	1	⌐	1 ⌐
d	⋈	⋈	◁ ᴫ	Ρ Υ
ḏ	⊟	⋈	# ⊟	
h	Υ(Υ)	Υ	Υ Υ	∨
w	⊙	⊕ ∞	⊖ ⊕	⊕ ▽
z	⊠	⊠	⊟	⊟
ḥ	ψ(Υ)	ψ	Υ ⋔	⋔
ḫ	Υ(ϟ)	Υ̸	ϟ	ϟ
ṭ	⊞	⊟	⊞ ⋔	⋔
ẓ	φφ φ	ϟ	♁	φ φ Ρ
y	φ	φ	φ Υ	φ Υ Ρ
k	⋔	⋔	⋔ ʰ	⋔ ʰ
l	1	1	1 ⌐	∧
m	⊴	⟩	⧈ ⧈ ᴔ ᴔ	ᴔ ⟁
n	ʮ	⟊	ʮ	⟊
s¹	⋔	⋔	⋔ ʌ	⋔
ʿ	○	○	○	○ ▽
ǵ	⊓⌐	⊓⌐ ⌐		⊲ ⊿
p	◇	φ	○	⊲ ⊿
ṣ	⋔(ϟ)	⋔	⊻ ▽	⊻
ḍ	⊟	⊟	⊟	
q	φ	φ	φ	φ ψ
r	⊃	⟩ ε	⊃	⊂ <
s²	⧊	⧊⧈	⧊	W
s³	χ	χ		+ χ
t	×	×	+ ×	
ṯ	φ(✳)	φ	○—○	

a. Col. XXVII, Epigraphic South Arabian script (forms in parentheses are of the North Arabic type, found in some older inscriptions); col. XXVIII, Later South Arabian script; col. XXIX, "Thamudic" type of Ethiopic script; col. XXX, Ethiopic consonantal script. The order of letters in this table is artificially based on the North Semitic order; for the ancient South Semitic order, see SECTION 68.

Samples of West Semitic

Ugaritic text

1. Ugaritic: 𒀭 (cuneiform)

2. Transliteration:	²⁴ ltbrknn	ltr .	il	àby
3. Normalization:	lā+tubarrikan(a)na	li+t̠ôru	ʾIlu	ʾābuya
4. Transcription:	la:-tu-barrikan(a)na	li-θo:ru	ʔilu	ʔa:bu-ja
5. Gloss:	NEG-you-bless	O-bull	ʾIlu	father-my

1.					
2.	²⁵ tmrnn .	lbny .	bnwt	²⁶ wykn .	bnh bbt .
3.	tamurran(a)na	li+bānayu	banawāti	wa+yakuna	binuhu ba+bēti
4.	ta-murran(a)na	li-ba:naju	banawa:ti	wa-ya-kuna	binu-hu ba-be:ti
5.	you-strengthen	O-creator	creatures	and-he-is	son-his in-house

1.						
2.	šrš .	bqrb	²⁷ hklh .	nṣb .	skn . ilibh .	bqdš
3.	šuršu	bi+qirbi	hēkalihi	nāṣibu	sikna ʾIliʾibihi	bi+qaduši
4.	ʃurʃu	bi-qirbi	he:kali-hi	na:ṣibu	sikna ʔiliʔibihi	bi-qaduʃi
5.	root	in-midst	palace-his	erector	stela ʾIlʾib	in-sanctuary

1.						
2.	²⁸ ztr .	ʿmh .	lȧrṣ .	mšṣu̇ .	qtrh	²⁹ lʿpr .
3.	zittara	ʿammihi	li+ʾarṣi	mušīṣiʾu	qittarahu	li+ʿapri
4.	zittara	ʕammi-hi	li-ʔarṣi	muʃi:ṣiʔu	qittira-hu	li-ʕapri
5.	solar.disk	people-his	in-earth	causer.to.go.forth	incense-his	in-dirt

1.						
2.	dmr .	ʾtrh .	ṭbq .	lht	³⁰ niṣh .	grš d .
3.	d̠āmiru	ʾaṯrahu	ṭābiqu	laḥāta	nāʾiṣihi	gārišu dā
4.	ða:miru	ʔaθra-hu	ṭa:biqu	laḥa:ta	na:ʔiṣi-hi	ga:riʃu da:
5.	singer	step(s)-his	smasher(?)	jaws	attacker-his	expeller him.who

1.						
2.	ʿšy .	lnh	³¹ àḫd . ydh .	bškrn .	mʿmsh	
3.	ʿāsiya	lônahu	ʾāḫidu yadahu	bi+šikkaruni	muʿammisuhu	
4.	ʕa:siya	lo:na-hu	ʔa:xidu jada-hu	bi-ʃikkaruni	muʕammisu-hu	
5.	obscures	face-his	seizer hand-his	in-drunkenness	carrier-his	

1.							
2.	³² [k]šbʿ	yn .	spu̇ .	ksmh .	bt .	bʿl	³³ [wm]nth bt .
3.	ki+šabʿi	yēni	sāpiʾu	kussimahu	bēta	baʿala	wa+manattahu bēta
4.	ki-ʃabʕi	je:ni	sa:piʔu	kussima-hu	be:ta	baʕala	wa-manatta-hu be:ta
5.	when-sated	wine	eater(?)	emmer-his	house	Baʿlu	and-gift-his house

1. 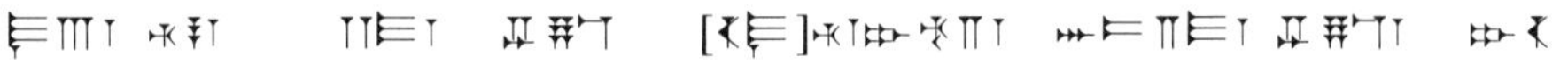

2.	il̓ .	ṯḫ̮ .	ggh .	bym	[34] [ṯi̓]ṯ .	rḥṣ .	npṣh .	bym .	rṯ
3.	ʾili	ṯāḫ̮u	gagahu	biyōmi	ṯaʾiṯi	rāḥiṣu	nipāṣahu	biyōmi	riṯi
4.	ʔili	ŧa:xu	gagahu	bi-jo:mi	θaʔiŧi	ra:ħis̶u	nipa:s̶ahu	bi-jo:mi	riθi
5.	’Ilu	plasterer	his roof	in-day	mud	washer	his-cloak	in-day	slime

‘Will you not bless him, Bull ’Ilu, my Father,
(And) strengthen him, Creator of Creatures,
So there may be a son of his in the house,
A scion in his palace,
To erect the stela of the family god,
(And) the clan solar disk in the sanctuary,
To burn incense for him on the (temple?) ground(s),
To sing his achievements(?) out in the yard(?),
To smash the jaws of those who abuse him,
To drive off those who darken(?) his face(?),
To hold his hand when he’s drunk,
To carry him (home) when he’s full of wine,
To eat food for him at the Ba‘lu temple,
And a gift on his behalf at the Ilu temple,
To fix his roof in bad weather,
To wash his clothes when he’s slipped in the mud?’

—A petition, ca. 1250 B.C.E., requesting a son for the king Dan’ilu offered by the god Ba‘lu, from the Legend of Aqhatu (CTA 17, KTU 1.17, lines 24–34).

ARAMAIC TEXT

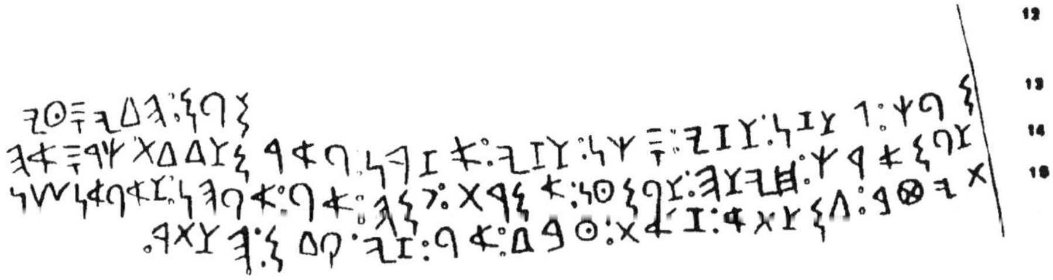

FIGURE 5. From the Fekheriye Assyrian–Aramaic bilingual (Abou-Assaf, Bordreuil, and Millard 1982, fig. 3).

←צלם: הדיסעי 12
y‘sydh :mlṣ←

מלכ: גזנ: וזי: סכנ: וזי: ארזנ לארמ ורדת כרסאה 13
hʾsrk tdrw mrʾl nzrʾ :yzw :nks :yzw :nzg :klm

ולמארכ: חיוה: ולמענ: אֹמרת: פמה: אל: אֹלכנ: ואל: אנשנ 14
nšnʾ :lʾw :nhlʾ :lʾ :hmp :trmʾ :n‘mlw :hwyḥ :krʾmlw

תיטב: דמותא: זאת: עבד: אל: זי: קדמ: הותר 15
rtwh :mdq :yz :lʾ :db‘ :tʾz :ʾtwmd :bṭyt

1. Transliteration: ṣlm: hdysʿy   mlk: gzn: wzy: skn: wzy:
2. Normalization: ṣalm   Had-Yiṯʿī   malk   Gozani wa+dī Sikani wa+dī
3. Transcription: ṣalm   had-yiθʕi: malk gozani wa-ði: sikani wa-ði:
4. Gloss: image.of Had-Yithʿi king.of Gozan and-of Sikan and-of

1. ʾrzn   lʾrm   wrdt: krsʾh   wlmʾrk: ḥywh:
2. ʾAzrani li+ʾAram wa+darat kars(ʾ)ohi wa+li+maʾrak   ḥayyōhi
3. ʔazrani li-ʔaram wa-darat kars-ohi wa-li-maʔrak   ħajj-o:hi
4. Azran to-Aram ?   throne-his and-for-lengthening.of life-his

1. wlmʿn: ʾmrt: pmh: ʾl: ʾlhn: wʾl: ʾnšn tytb:
2. wa+li+maʿn   ʾimrat pim-ohi ʾel ʾēlahīn wa+ʾel ʾanasīn tēṭab
3. wa-li-maʕn   ʔimrat pim-ohi ʔel ʔe:lahi:n wa-ʔel ʔana:ʃi:n te:ṭab
4. and-for-because word.of mouth-his to gods   and-for people it.is.good

1. dmwtʾ: zʾt: ʿbd: ʾl: zy: qdm: hwtr
2. damutaʾ ḏo(ʾ)t ʿabad ʾel dī   qadam hōtīr
3. damuta: ðot   ʕabad ʔel ði: qadam ho:ti:r
4. image-the this he.made for what before being-exceeding

'The image of Had-Yithʿi, King of Gozanu and of Sikanu and of Azranu to
Aram … his throne and to lengthen his life and so that the speech of his mouth
for gods and for people might be good, he made this likeness, improving on
what it once was.'
       —*Opening of the second section of the Aramaic portion, ca. 850 B.C.E.*
                         (Abou-Assaf, Bordreuil, and Millard 1982).

PHOENICIAN TEXTS

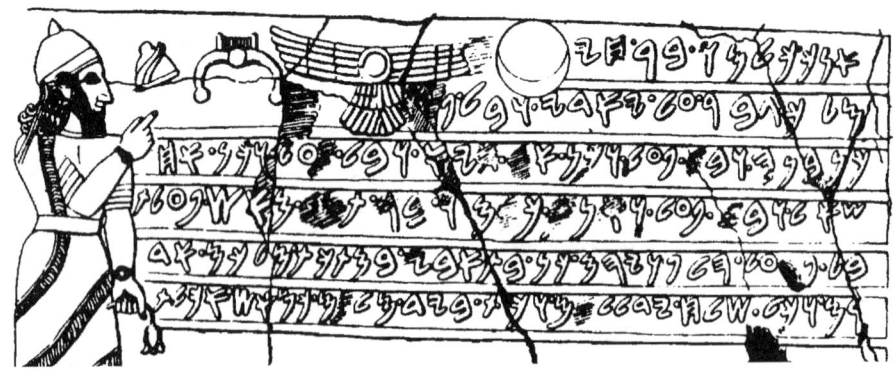

FIGURE 6. From the Kilamuwa inscription
(after Birnbaum 1957, vol. 1, no. 014).

            [א]חי . בר . כלמו . אנכ←
            [ʾ]yḥ . rb . wmlk . knʾ←

₂ מלך . גבר . על . יאדי . ובל . פ[על]

[lʿ]p . lbw . ydʾy . lʿ . rbg . klm

₃ כן . במה . ובל . פעל . וכן . אבי . חיא . ובל . פעל . וכן   אח

ḥʾ . nkw . lʿp . lbw . ʾyḥ . ybʾ . nkw . lʿp . lbw . hmb   nk

₄ שאל . ובל . פעל . ואנ[ך] . כלמו . בר . תם . מאש פעלת

tlʿp . šʾm . ʾmt . rb . wmlk . [k]nʾw . lʿp . lbw . lʾš

₅ בל . פעל . הלפנים . כן . בתאבי . במתכת . מלכם . אד   רם ₆

mr   dʾ . mklm . tktmb . ybʾ tb . nk . mynplh . lʿp . lb

1. *Transliteration:* ʾnk .   klmw .   br .   ḥy[ʾ]   mlk .   gbr .
2. *Normalization:* ʾanōkī .   Kilamuwa .   bir .   Ḥayyaʾ mālak .   Gabbar .
3. *Transcription:* ʔano:ki: kilamuwa   bar   ħajjaʔ   ma:lak   gabbar
4. *Gloss:*   I   Kilamuwa   son.of   Hayya   he.ruled   Gabbar

1. ʿl .   yʾdy .   wbl .   p[ʿ]l   kn   bmh .   wbl .   pʿl .
2. ʿal . Yaʾudi(?) .   wa+bal .   pāʿal   kēn   Bamah .   wa+bal .   pāʿal .
3. ʕal   yaʔudi   wa-bal   pa:ʕal   ke:n   bamah   wa-bal   pa:ʕal
4. over   Yaʾudi   and-NEG   he.did   he.was   Bamah   and-NEG   he.did

1. wkn .   ʾby .   ḥyʾ .   wbl .   pʿl .   wkn .   ʾḥ
2. wa+kēn .   ʾābiya .   Ḥayya . wa+bal .   pāʿal   wa+kēn .   ʾaḥiya
3. wa-ke:n   ʔa:b-ija   ħajja   wa-bal   pa:ʕal   wa-ke:n   ʔaħ-ija
4. and-he.was   father-my   Hayya   and-NEG   he.did   and-he.was   my brother

1. šʾl .   wbl .   pʿl .   wʾn[k] .   klmw .   br .   tmʾ .
2. Šāʾūl(?) .   wa+bal .   pāʿal .   wa+ʾanōkī .   Kilamuwa .   bar .   tōm(?) .
3. ʃa:ʔu:l   wa-bal   pa:ʕal   wa-ʔano:ki: kilamuwa   bar   to:m(?)
4. Saul   and-NEG   he.did   and-I   Kilamuwa   son.of   virtue(?)

1. mʾš .   pʿlt   bl . pʿl .   hlpnym .   kn .   bt
2. maʾēš .   pāʿaltī   bal . pāʿalū ,   halipanniyyīm   kēn .   bēt
3. ma-ʔe:ʃ   pa:ʕal-ti   bal   pa:al-u: ha-lipannijj-i:m   ke:n   be:t
4. what-which   did-1SG   NEG   did-3PL   the-former.one-PL   it.was   house.of

1. ʾby .   bmtkt .   mlkm .   ʾdrm
2. ʾabiya .   ba+mitōket .   milākīm .   ʾaddirīm
3. ʔab-ija   ba-mito:ket   mila:k-i:m   ʔaddir-i:m
4. my-father   in-the.midst.of   king-PL   mighty-PL

'I am Kilamuwa Bir [son of] Hayya. Gabbar ruled over Yaudi and did nothing. Bamah was (king) and did nothing and Hayya my father was (king) and did nothing and my brother Saul was (king) and did nothing and I, Kilamuwa, a virtuous man—that which I did (my) predecessors did not do. My father's house was surrounded by kings (more) powerful (than I).'

—From the Kilamuwa inscription (ca. 825 B.C.E.), lines 1–5
(Donner and Röllig 1971 no. 24; O'Connor 1977).

THE PHOENICIAN TEXT FROM PYRGI (illustrated in FIGURE 36 on page 300)

שׁדק רׁשׁא לעשׁתרת לרבת→			1
šdq rš᾽ trtš῾l tbrl←			
נתן ואשׁ פעל אשׁ עז			2
nty š᾽w l῾p š᾽ z᾽			
תבריא • ולנשׁ מלכ אל			3
l῾ klm šnlw • ᾽yrbt			
כישׁריא • בׁירח • זבח			4
ḥbz • ḥryb • ᾽yršyk			
נבו אבבת במתנ שׁמשׁ			5
nbw tbb᾽ ntmb šmš			
בדי • כאשׁתרת • אׁרשׁ • תו			6
ydb • šr᾽ • trtš᾽k • wt			
בי ‖‖ שׁלשׁ שׁנת למלכי			7
yb III šlš tnš yklml			
קבר בימ • כרר • רח			8
rbq myb • rrk ḥr			
אלמ למאשׁ ושׁנת אלמ			9
ml᾽ š᾽ml tnšw ml᾽			
הככבמ כמ שׁנת רבתי			10
mbkkh mk tnš ytbr			
אל			11
l᾽			

1. *Transliteration:* lrbt l᾽štrt ᾽šr qdš ᾽z ᾽š p῾l
2. *Normalization:* la+rabbat la+῾aštarat ᾽ašar qōdīš ᾽az ᾽iš pā῾al
3. *Transcription:* la-rabbat la-ʕaʃtarat ʔaʃar qoːdiːʃ ʔaz ʔiʃ paːʕal
4. *Gloss:* for-lady for-Astarte place holy this which he.made

1. w᾽š ytn tbry᾽ • wlnš mlk ῾l kyšry᾽ • byrḥ • zbḥ
2. wa+᾽iš yātan Tabariya Walunaš melek ῾al Kaysriya bi+yariḥ zebaḥ
3. wa-ʔiʃ jaːtan tabarija walunaʃ melek ʕal kajsrija bi-jariḥ zebaḥ
4. and-he gave Thefarie Velianas king over Caere in-month sacrifice

1.	šmš	bmtn	ʾbbt	wbn	tw •	kʾštrt •	ʾrš •	bdy
2.	šemeš	bi+MTN	ʾabi+bēt	wa+bānā	taw	ka+ʿaštarat	ʾerreša	bodiyo
3.	ʃemeʃ	bi …	ʔabi-beːt	wa-baːnaː	taw	ka-aʃtarat	ʔerreʃa	bo-di-jo
4.	sun	in-MTN	in-temple	and-he.built	room	as-Ashtarat	asked	in-his-hand

1.	lmlky	šnt	šlš ///	b-yrḥ	krr •	bym	qbr	ʾlm
2.	li+molkiyo	šanat	šaluš ///	bi+yariḥ	KRR	bi+yōm	qibbur	ʾilim
3.	li-molk-ijo	ʃanat	ʃaluʃ	bi-jariħ	…	bi-joːm	qibbur	ʔilim
4.	for-rule-I	years	three 3	in-month	KRR	on-day.of	burial.of	deity

1.	wšnt	lmʾš	ʾlm	rbty	šnt	km	hkkbm	ʾl
2.	wa+šanat	li+muʾiš	ʾilim	rabbotay	šanat	kima	ha+kokabīm	ʾelle
3.	wa-ʃanat	li-muʔiʃ	ʔilim	rabbotaj	ʃanat	kima	ha-kokab-iːm	ʔelle
4.	and-years	for-statue.of	deity	many	years	like	the-star-PL	these

'For the Lady, for Ashtarat is this holy place that Thefarie Velunas, king over Caere, made and donated to (the) temple, in the Month of the Solar Sacrifice (which is called?) MTN, and he built (a/ the?) cella as Ashtarat had asked of him during the third year of his reign, in the Month of KRR on the Day of the God's Burial. And may the years of the god's statue be as many as these stars.'

—Phoenician text from Pyrgi (Donner and Röllig 1968–73, no. 277; Guzzo Amadasi 1967; Schmitz 1995).

Old South Arabian texts

1.	*South Arabian:*	𐩡𐩨𐩬𐩺	𐩤𐩪𐩷	𐩧𐩬𐩵	𐩢𐩹𐩫
2.	*Transliteration:*	lbny	qs^{1}ṭ	rnd	ḥḏk
3.	*Normalization:*	lubāniyyu	qos^{1}ṭu	randu	?
4.	*Transcription:*	lubaːnijju	qoʃt'u	randu	?
5.	*Gloss:*	frankincense	costum	nard	(type of incense)

—The words appear (one to a side) on limestone incense altars, ca. 300–100 B.C.E. The first two are from Pritchard 1969, no. 579; the others, from no. 581.

Philological notes:

Frankincense is a gum resin from trees of the genus *Boswellia*; the English term involves an obsolete sense of *frank* 'first rate, high quality'. The Semitic terms for frankincense are derived from the root *lbn* 'to be white', though actually the resin is yellowish: Arabic *lubān*, Hebrew *ləbônâ*; from the latter comes Greek *libanos*, ultimately the source of archaic English *olibanum*.

Costum is the name for a variety of incense ingredients, some also used as spices, including in at least some cases a root. *Qs^{1}ṭ*, which may not be Semitic, appears as well in Greek, *kostos*; and Latin, *costum*, *costos*. The Latin term has left various traces in English, notably *costmary*, an herb.

Nard is the extract of plants of the genus *Valeriana*; for incense use the term *nard* is preferred, while for the medical, mostly sedative, uses, the term *valerian* is used. The word *nard* is derived from Sanskrit *naladâ*, perhaps via Persian *nârdîn*, as the spikenard is imported from India via Persia. The Biblical Hebrew term *nērd* is found only in the Song of Songs. The English term is from the Greek *nardos*. The Classical Arabic form *rand* shows the same metathesis as the Old South Arabian.

Nothing is known of *ḥḏk*.

The Iberian Scripts

PIERRE SWIGGERS

Iberian (or *Paleo-Hispanic*) is the term used for the speech and script varieties of the *(H)iberi* (Gk. Ἴβηρες) who lived in the south and northeast of Spain and in Portugal during the second and first millennia B.C.E. These varieties include a number of non–Indo-European languages or dialects (with "Iberian" serving as their general designation) and one Indo-European—more specifically, Celtic—dialect, Celtiberian. The Iberian varieties are attested in four scripts: (a) a Northeast Iberian script (also called, somewhat misleadingly, "Iberian" script), (b) a South Iberian script (also called "South Lusitanian" script), (c) the Ionic Greek alphabet, and (d) the Latin alphabet. This subsection discusses the first two; for the others, see SECTIONS 22 and 23.

The geographical distribution of the scripts is as follows: (1) In the northeast Iberian peninsula (Catalonia, Aragon, and the Valencia region up to the Júcar), the Northeast Iberian script was used almost exclusively and in a uniform way; it is also attested in inscriptions from southern France. (2) South of the Júcar, down to the Segura, three scripts are attested: Northeast Iberian (in Alcoy, Benidorm, Alicante), South Iberian (in Mogente, Elche, and the province of Albacete), and Greek (in Alcoy, Campello, Cigarralejo). (3) In Andalusia, most of the inscriptions are in the South Iberian writing system, but the Northeast Iberian script is sporadically attested, occasionally with slight variants, as in Iliberris, in eastern Andalusia.

The Northeast Iberian is the best attested variety, with, in most cases, at least two variants for each letter. The Celtiberians adapted it around the turn of the third to the second century B.C.E.; they used this adapted form (beside the Latin alphabet) for the inscriptions in their Indo-European language. They made a number of formal changes, such as the use of a diacritic to distinguish *r* and *ŕ*, and the reintroduction of the Ionic Ⲙ for *ś*; and some structural changes, such as the use of five consonantal signs B, Δ, T, Γ, K instead of the fifteen syllabograms of the Northeast Iberian script.

In the southwest corner of Spain, inscriptions are attested in a script variety often labeled "Tartessian"; the underlying language is unknown. This "Tartessian" or "Southwest" script (see Correa 1985) can be assigned to the South Iberian variety, although there are a few signs by which these two scripts differ (for a juxtaposition of the two inventories, see Untermann 1990, 3/1: 141–42). Typologically the Iberian script varieties can be traced to one basic Paleo-Hispanic type. In view of this, it is preferable to avoid script designations based on the names of the Iberian tribes who once inhabited a particular region (e.g. Tartessian, Turdetanian, etc.). It is better to speak of Northeastern and Southern varieties of Paleo-Hispanic (with "Southern" comprising Southeastern and Southwestern), rather than "Iberian" script; however, this usage is not yet established, and the term "Iberian" is maintained here.

TABLE 5.8: *The Iberian Scripts*

	Northeast	*South*	
a	Ρ Δ Ρ Ρ	Α	
e	ʢ Ε Ϝ Ϝ	ο Ϙ	
i/i̯	ᴙ	ᴟ	
o	Η	⧻ ⊤	
u/u̯	↑ ʌ	Ч Ч	
l	ʌ ʃ	𐌂	
m	ᛉ		
m̄	V Υ Ϝ		
n	ᴎ	ᴟ	
r	◁ ◁ ◁	٩	
ŕ	◇ ϙ ϙ ϙ	Ж	(?)
s	ϟ ϟ ϟ ϟ	⧻ ⊤	
ś	ᛘ	ᛘ	
pa/(ba)	Ι ᶜ, Ω	⌐	(?)
pe/(be)	⬦ ⬦ ⅏ ⅏ ⅏	⇛	(?)
pi/(bi)	⌐ ⌐	↑	
po/(bo)	✻ ✳	⋈	
pu/(bu)	▢		
ka/ga	ʌ ʌ ʌ	ʌ	
ke/ge	ᑕ ᑕᑕᑕ ᑕ ᵡ	⋊ ⋊	
ki/gi	ʃ ʄ ʄ ⥾ ⥾	⥾	
ko/go	⅀ ⅀	⋈	
ku/gu	◈ ⊙		
ta/da	Χ	✝ Χ	
te/de	⬦ ⬦ ⬦ ⊘ ⊗		
ti/di	ψ Ψ V Ψ	⬦	
to/do	⊔ V ⨄		
tu/du	Δ Δ	Δ Δ	

Description

The Iberian script varieties have the following characteristics: (a) They combine monophonemic ("alphabetic") and syllabic characters: the vowels and all the continuants are represented by single signs, whereas the stops are written together with a following vowel. (b) Some of the syllabic signs show variations, both geographic and chronological, but it is unclear whether these variations reflect an attempt at phonetic discrimination. It is best to transcribe these variants using diacritics, as is done by Untermann (1975–90) in the definitive edition of the inscriptions. It should be noted that variants of one sign occur in some inscriptions, while other signs show no variations in the same inscriptions. (c) The syllabic signs for the stops distinguish place of artic- ulation (labial, dental, velar), but do not mark a voicing contrast; the Iberian inscrip- tions in the Latin and Greek alphabets, however, show a distinction between voiced and unvoiced stops (except in the labials?), which must be accepted as phonemic.

In the few texts that are more than one word long, word division is marked by centered single or double dots. Graphically separate elements can be taken to be words (i.e. unbound morphemes, or a lexical construct of morphemes).

Inventory and commentary

TABLE 5.8 gives an inventory of the Northeast and South Iberian characters with their values (see also Untermann 1990, 3/1; Lejeune 1993: 55).

Northeast Iberian inscriptions are written from left to right (with one boustrophe- don inscription), and South Iberian inscriptions from right to left. The differences be- tween the sign shapes do not show any consistent pattern: *a* and *i* are identical in Northeast and South Iberian, but *e* and *u* differ completely. The signs for *l, r, ś*, and *n* are almost identical, but *s* and *ŕ* are very divergent. Some signs of the South Iberian script are still unidentified, and the representations of [pu], [ku], [te], and [to] are un- known. Roughly, the Iberian language(s) underlying these scripts can be phonologi- cally characterized as having five vowel timbres *a, e, i, o, u*; two or three pairs of voiced and voiceless stops (velar, dental, and perhaps only one labial); six dento- alveolar or post-alveolar resonants *l, n, r, ŕ* (velarized, flapped, or geminated *r*?); and *s, ś* (affricated or palatalized). Under Celtic influence, two shapes, 'Ṭ' and Y, were added, but it is not clear whether they denote *m* and another nasal, or whether they are simply variants of a single letter (the distribution is too complicated to be explained in geographic terms).

Problems

There are two types of problems concerning the Iberian script varieties: structural and historical.

The *structural* problems arise from the fact that the Iberian inscriptions are as yet uninterpreted—the values of the letters are known from bilingual and biscriptal in- scriptions, from parallel texts in Latin and Greek, and from Iberian-language texts in Latin and Greek script, but we cannot offer a grammatical and semantic analysis. Our knowledge is limited to (a) identification of proper names, on external grounds; and (b) a very limited contextual and interlinguistic recognition of the sometimes still hy- pothetical value of sequences such as *aretake/areteike*, corresponding to Latin *hic est situs* 'here is located', or *tebanen*, corresponding to the parallel Latin *coerav*[*it*] 'he procured/arranged for himself' in a bilingual text.

The *historical* problems—a subject of ongoing debate—concern the origin of the Iberian writing system. (a) Did the Iberian script originate, in the sixth or seventh century B.C.E., in the south(west) and then spread through the south, and later, in the fifth century, to the north? If so, we should reckon with the fact that the Southwest ("Tartessian") variety was used to note a language of which we know almost nothing.

(b) How is the mixture of "alphabetic" and syllabic signs to be explained? This problem is of course linked with the first, but it is wider in scope (apart from its general linguistic relevance, and its typological oddity in the history of writing systems). Should the Iberian writing system be viewed as a simultaneous integration of a Semitic and a Greek model (with some letter shapes closer to the Greek, others closer to the Semitic model)? as the refurbishing of a Greek model? or as an original Paleo-Hispanic adaptation of a Phoenician signary, leading to a solution analogous to the Greek adaptation? This problem has divided scholars into pro-Greek and pro-Semitic camps. Whatever position one takes, it remains to be explained how a partial syllabary could have been conceived (on what basis? for what reasons?) and why it was limited to the stop series.

(c) Is it possible to distinguish various scribal schools and traditions that flourished during the first millennium in the Iberian peninsula, and to correlate with these the variants observed in the Iberian scripts?

Sample of Northeast Iberian

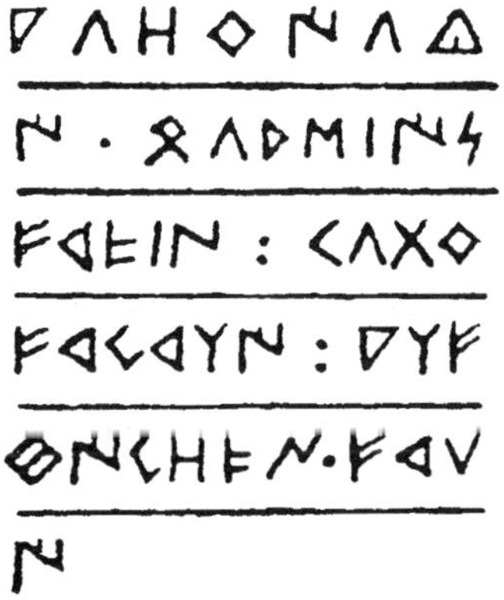

1. Iberian:	ᐁΛH◇ᛗΛΔᛗ·	ᛟΛᐅMIᛗᛊᚠᐊ	⊢Iᛗ:
2. *Transliteration:*	alof́iltu/i .	belaśbais/er	eban :
2. *Interpretation:*	alof́iltun	belaśbaiser	eban
3. Gloss:	Alof́iltu-	Belaśbais-	has.dedicated/built

1. ᐸΛX◇ᚠᐊᒪᐊYᛗ:	ᐁY*ᚠ◇ᛗᒪHᚠᛗ·	ᚠᐊVᛗ
2. keltaf́/erkerm̃i:	am̃e/teikeoen .	er-m̃/i
3. keltaf́erker-m̃i	areteike-oen	er-m̃i
4. for (to).Keltaf́erk-	this.(is the) place-UNKN	for.him

'Aloŕiltu (son of) Belaśbais has dedicated this resting place for Keltaŕerk.'
—*Northeast Iberian inscription found in 1894 in Pilaret de Santa Quiteria*
(Fita 1894: 259–61; Untermann 1990, 3/2: 171–72).

*Y *m̄* is a scribal error for ◁ *r* or ◇ *ŕ*.

The Berber Scripts

M. O'CONNOR

The diverse but closely related Berber languages, a branch of the Afro-Asiatic phylum, are spoken across North Africa, from the far west of Egypt (in the Ṣiwâ oasis) through Libya, Tunisia, and Algeria, to the far northwestern margins of the African continent in Morocco. The major living Berber languages are Tamazight (four million speakers in Morocco and Algeria) and Kabyle (two and a half million speakers in Algeria and France), both belonging to the Northern Berber subfamily, and the various Tamasheq languages, whose speakers are collectively known as the Tuareg, who live on both sides of the Sahara, in southern Algeria and Morocco and on the upper reaches of the Niger River (in Mali and Niger).

The term *Berber*, though well established, is Greek in origin and pejorative, akin to English 'barbarian'. *Numidia* is the ancient Roman term for the Algerian home of the ancient Berber kingdom; this too is Greek, a form of νομάς *nomás* 'nomad', and indeed some Berber groups are in modern times true nomads. The local term is Massilian or *Maššuli*.

An ancient Berber language (or perhaps several) is preserved in the ancient Berber script (or scripts), sometimes called Numidian, Libyan, or Libyco-Berber.

The Berber languages have always existed on the margins of literate nations and empires: the Carthaginians and Romans dominated the Berbers, while the Muslims incorporated them to the degree possible—Berber Islam is distinctive in various ways. Thus the Berber languages have never regularly been used as written languages; they are not regularly written today.

Ancient Berber

The ancient Berber script (TABLE 5.9) is based on and derived from a Semitic prototype, probably Punic. The geometrical character of the letterforms suggests that Old South Arabian scripts (and the related North Arabian scripts) may also be relevant (cf. Rössler 1979A), but Berber forms are more consistently symmetrical. (In this connection, Rössler remarks [p. 91], "From the point of view of the history of writing, it is noteworthy that a drive toward symmetry is not an archaic feature in the shaping of writing signs.") The idea of consonantal writing has been borrowed, along with a few of the letters. There are twenty-two letters; words are never broken over lines; word spacing is erratic, as is line-internal word division by dots or puncts (in some texts the punct seems to have a second, obscure function as well). The earliest date proposed for the script, the sixth century B.C.E., is possible, given that Phoenician colonization may go back to the eighth or even ninth century, but it seems dubious.

The major datable inscriptions come from the period of Numidian independence in the second century B.C.E., a time associated with a contest between Carthage and Rome in the late third and second centuries; ultimately Carthage lost and Rome won, but there was a brief opening for Numidian independence, seized by the kings Gaia (*Gaya*), Massinissa (d. 148 B.C.E.; *Masinisan*), Micipsa (*Mikiwsan*), and Jugurtha, who played the two enemies off against one another.

Most of the inscriptions—Chabot's corpus (1940–41) includes over 1100 texts—are from western Tunisia and Algeria, with Morocco yielding a few texts (Galand 1966 has 27 texts); Dougga and Maktar in western Tunisia are major sources. Among the Berber texts, monumental inscriptions are rare; the bulk of the inscriptions are non-official funeral texts, repetitive and thus poor in linguistic information. The basic orientation of these texts is from below upward, starting from either the right or the left; an upward orientation is extremely rare among the writing systems of the world. In monumental texts (and some others), this orientation is abandoned for a horizontal orientation from right to left, on a Punic model. Perhaps related is the great variation in the orientation of individual letters.

A group of three Berber–Punic bilingual texts is worth noting (see Rössler in Donner and Rollig 1968–73 [*KAI*]). Two of these, both from Dougga (Latin *Thugga*, Berber *Tubgag* [sic!]), are from the time of the Numidian kings. One is dated to 139 B.C.E., during the reign of Micipsa, commemorating his predecessor Massinissa (*KAI* 101). The other is a tomb building inscription (*KAI* 100, photo in Rössler 1979B; cf. Rössler's suggestion [1979A] that this may be the oldest Berber inscription). The latest of these bilinguals is a tomb inscription (*KAI* 153); the Semitic text is Neo-Punic (the stage of Punic written after the fall of Carthage), and the Berber section is badly damaged.

The script continued in use through the following Roman period, as is shown by Berber–Latin bilinguals, probably extending through the third century C.E.; there is no way to guess at the date of apparently late, isolated graffiti, written on desert stones in a distinctive spiral shape.

On the basis of one of the bilinguals, F. de Saulcy in 1843 established the decipherment that is still basically accepted, yielding recognizable Berber names and words. Nonetheless, the question remains, Has the ancient Berber script been deciphered? Two points are relevant. First, the writing system exhibits a good deal of variability, so that it may represent several related scripts, perhaps two: an eastern, the script of the Dougga texts; and a western. Second, no single modern Berber language can be identified with the language of the script; thus the term "Berber" is used here

TABLE 5.9: *The Berber Scripts*

	ANCIENT BERBER		TIFINIGH	
	Horizontal	*Vertical*	*Letter*	*Ligature with -t*
ʾ	.	.	.	
b	⊙	⊙ ⊡	⊕ ⊞	⊣⊟
ǧ[a]	Γ	V ∧	·╀ ╼	·╀
d	Π	⊐ ⊏	Π ∧	
h		‖‖	⁝	
w	=	‖	⁝	
z	—	—	#	#
ž	H	H Ⲏ	Ⲏ	
ẕ	⋀	Ш	Ж ⋈	
ḥ	Ⱶ	⊥ ⊤	∷	
ṭ, ḏ[b]	⊱	⊓	Ⴈ E Ш	
y	Z	N Z	⟨ ⟩	
k	⇐	⇑	·⁚	
l	‖	=	‖	Ⲏ
m	⊐	⊔ ∪	⊐ ⊏	⊣⊒
n	|	|	|	╀ (╀ *nk*)
s	X	X 8	⊙ ⊡	⊣⊡
s²	⊏ ⟨ ⟨	⊓		
ǵ	≡ ÷	‖‖ ·╀·	⁝	
f[c]	X	X ɤ	Ⴈ Ⴖ	
q		≡	⋯	
g			⋊ ⋉	⊣⋈
r	◯	◯ □	◯ □	⊞
š	⋜	M ⋜	Ɜ Ͻ	⊣⊒
t[d]	+ ×	+	+	
t²	⊒	Ш		

a. The modern Berber form is *ǰ*, the ancient perhaps *g*.

b. The pronunciation is uncertain; the sounds in question are not native to Berber, occurring in Punic and Arabic loans.

c. Modern Berber has *f* in Arabic loanwords. The ancient Berber realization is uncertain.

d. The second form is used finally.

to refer to one or more unspecified languages not identified with living tongues. Galand has gone so far as to propose that the script is undeciphered, though he does not deny that it is alphabetic and that it could be related to a Berber language. Most other scholars are not so skeptical—the Berber character of the ancient kingdoms is guaranteed by the attested names (though the kingdoms used Punic and Greek rather than Berber script on their coinage).

The texts from the Canary Islands may be Berber (Álvarez Delgado 1964); it has been proposed that the extinct indigenous language of the islands, Guanche, was a Berber language. The Celtiberian coinage of the first century B.C.E. seems to use Berber letters.

The Islamic period: Silence; modern use

The Berber languages in medieval and modern times, down to the present, have been written in the Arabic script; Berber texts written in Arabic script are known from the 12th century C.E. on, and there is a translation of the Qur'an into Berber from the medieval period. During the Middle Ages, various quasi-Islamic, local Berber religions developed, several with their own Berber scriptures, written in Arabic script. Since there are Berber Jews, there are also Berber texts written in Hebrew script, mostly prayerbooks and ritual texts (e.g., Passover haggadoth).

There are no references to Berber script during the medieval and early modern periods, but something of the ancient script has endured in the Tifinigh (TABLE 5.9) used by the Tuareg for playful purposes, for love letters, family notes, and domestic ornamentation (two examples in Cohen 1958, vol. 2, plates 39–40) by both men and women, often in settings where the women are not able to read Arabic. The remarkable continuity of the ancient and modern scripts remains unexplained. This modern Berber script is never (in Chaker's formulation) used to support collective memory, be it historical, literary, or institutional—such is the role of Arabic. Recent attempts to adapt Tifinigh for serious use in the writing of other Berber languages, prompted by pan-Berber political aspirations, have failed.

The most striking feature of this writing system is its name, Tifinigh (sometimes Tifinagh), which is the feminine plural (ti- is a Berber feminine marker) of the Latin word *Punicus* 'Phoenician'; thus *Tifinigh* means 'the Phoenician (letters)'. (Another view associates it with Greek πίναξ *pínaks* 'writing tablet', Rössler 1979A: 93). Tifinigh uses about forty letters. The script is written without word dividers or spacing; but distinctive ligatures, linking the feminine ending -*t* to whatever precedes it (cf. the Arabic *tā' marbūṭa*), and a single sign, apparently read as -*a* unless after *y* or *w* when it is read -*i* or -*u*, serve to mark the ends of some words. The fullest illustration of the Berber scripts is in Friedrich 1966: 94–95 with figures 166–73.

SAMPLES OF BERBER

ANCIENT BERBER

⊢-Χ⋛	Χ‖‖‖—=	⊒∏‖Γ	ΖΖΓ=	⊒∏‖Γ	ΙΧΙΧ⊐	Η⋛ΧΙ⊙	ΓΓ⊙+	⊢⇐⊢←
[t]ṭpš	nsllzw	tdlg	yygw	tdlg	nsnsm	nštpnb	ggbt	nkṣ←

ⵏⵅ=ⵌⵔ   ⵏⵉⵍⴳ   ⵎⵅⵣⵅ   ⴲⵏⴳⵛ   ⵎⵏⵉⵛⵔⵛ
nswkm   dlg   'sys   tdgś   'dnśbś

1. Transliteration: ṣkn   tbgg   bnp'ṭ'šn'   msnsn   gldt   wgyy
2. Normalization: (e)ṣək-n   Tubgag   bn-pṭš-n   Msnsn-i   gəllidt   w-Gyy
3. Gloss: built-3PL   Thugga   tent-?-this   Massinissa-DAT   king   son-Gaia

1. gldt   wzllsn   špt[t]   śbśnd'   śgdt   sys'   gld   mkwsn
2. gəllidt   w-Zllsn   šft   šwâš-nd'sugasdenn   s-yusa'   gəllidMikiwsan
3. king   son-Zllsn   *shuphet*   year-?   after   that-come.3SGking Mikiwsan

> 'The Thuggans built this sacred place for King Massinissa, son of King Gaia,
> son of the shuphet Zllsn, in the year of the Jubilee(?) after Micipsa became
> king."   *—From the Punic–Numidian bilingual KAI 101, lines 1–2.*

MODERN BERBER: FROM A TUAREG LETTER

1. Tifinigh: : Ⅰ·: ⵊⵈ∧∧: +Ⅰ+ ⁞Ⅱ⁝Ⅰ ⵕⵊⴺ ⵙ:ⵅ   ⵉⵞ Ⅱ:ⵕⵟ ·
2. Transliteration: w   nk   fddw   tnt   hlǵn   šf   swy   hd   lǵšb'
3. Transcription: awanək fədudu   tənnat huləɣin ʃif   siwi   hid   elɣəʃaba
4. Gloss: this I   Fedudu   saying I.salute   chief send.me   here   garment

> 'I, Fedudu, greet the chief and request a garment.'
>   *—After Cohen 1958, pl. 39, line 1.*

Bibliography

EPIGRAPHIC SEMITIC WRITING

Abou-Assaf, Ali, Pierre Bordreuil, and Alan R. Millard. 1982. *La statue de Tell Fekherye et son in-scription bilingue assyro-araméenne* (Études assyriologiques, Cahiers 7). Paris: Éditions Recherche sur les Civilisations.

Birnbaum, Solomon A. 1954–71. *The Hebrew Scripts.* Part 1, *The Text.* Leiden: Brill, 1971. Part 2, *The Plates.* London: Palaeographica, 1954–57.

Colless, Brian E. 1988. "Recent Discoveries Illuminating the Origin of the Alphabet." *Abr-Nahrain* 26: 30–67.

Cross, Frank Moore, Jr. 1961. "The Development of the Jewish Scripts." In *The Bible and the Ancient Near East: Essays in Honor of William Foxwell Albright,* ed. G. Ernest Wright, pp. 133–202. Garden City, N. Y.: Doubleday. Repr. Winona Lake, Ind.: Eisenbrauns, 1979.

Cross, Frank Moore, Jr., and P. Kyle McCarter, Jr. 1973. "Two Archaic Inscriptions on Clay Objects from Byblos." *Rivista di studi fenici* 1: 3–8.

CTA = Andrée Herdner. 1963. *Corpus des tablettes en cunéiformes alphabétiques* (Mission de Ras Shamra 10). Paris: Geuthner.

Daniels, Peter T. 1990. "Fundamentals of Grammatology." *Journal of the American Oriental Society* 110: 727–31.

Dietrich, Manfried, and Oswald Loretz. 1989. "The Cuneiform Alphabets of Ugarit." *Ugarit-Forschungen* 21: 101–12.

Donner, Herbert, and Wolfgang Röllig. 1968–73. *Kanaanäische und aramäische Inschriften,* 3 vols. Wiesbaden: Harrassowitz.

Garbini, Giovanni. 1979. *Storia e problemi dell'epigrafia semitica* (*Annali dell'Istituto Orientale di Napoli,* Supplement 19, to 39/2). Naples.

Gelb, I. J. 1963. *A Study of Writing: The Foundations of Grammatology,* 2nd ed. Chicago: University of Chicago Press.

Gibson, John C. L. 1973–82. *Textbook of Syrian Semitic Inscriptions,* 3 vols. Oxford: Oxford University Press.

Gruendler, Beatrice. 1993. *The Development of the Arabic Scripts from the Nabatean Era to the First Islamic Century According to Dated Texts* (Harvard Semitic Studies 43). Atlanta: Scholars Press.

Guzzo Amadasi, M. G. 1967. *Le iscrizioni fenicie e puniche delle colonie in Occidente* (Studi Semitici 28). Rome: Istituto di studi del Vicino Oriente.

Havelock, Eric A. 1976. *Origins of Western Literacy.* Toronto: The Ontario Institute for Studies in Education. Repr. in Havelock 1982: 39–88, 314–50.

———. 1982. *The Literate Revolution in Greece and Its Cultural Consequences.* Princeton: Princeton University Press.

Herr, Larry G. 1978. *The Scripts of Ancient Northwest Semitic Seals* (Harvard Semitic Monographs 18). Missoula, Mont.: Scholars Press.

KTU = Manfried Dietrich, Oswald Loretz, and J. Sanmartín. 1976. *Die keilalphabetischen Texte aus Ugarit,* vol. 1: *Transkription* (Alter Orient und Altes Testament 24/1). Kevelaer and Neukirchen-Vluyn: Verlag Butzon und Bercker and Neukirchener Verlag.

Kaufman, Stephen A. 1986. "The Pitfalls of Typology: On the Early History of the Alphabet." *Hebrew Union College Annual* 57: 1–14.

Naveh, Joseph. 1982. *Early History of the Alphabet.* Jerusalem: Magnes.

———. 1985. "Writing and Scripts in Seventh-century B.C.E. Philistia: The New Evidence from Tell Jemmeh. *Israel Exploration Journal* 35: 8–21.

———. 1987. "Proto-Canaanite, Archaic Greek, and the Script of the Aramaic Text on the Tell Fakhariyah Statue." In *Ancient Israelite Religion: Essays in Honor of Frank Moore Cross,* ed. P. D. Miller, Jr., et al., pp. 101–14. Philadelphia: Fortress.

O'Connor, M. 1977. "The Rhetoric of the Kilamuwa Inscription." *Bulletin of the American Schools of Oriental Research* 226: 15–29.

Pritchard, James B. 1969. *The Ancient Near East in Pictures Relating to the Old Testament,* 2nd ed. Princeton, N.J.: Princeton University Press.

Puech, Emile. 1986. "Origine de l'alphabet: documents en alphabet linéaire et cunéiforme du IIe millénaire." *Revue biblique* 93: 161–213.

Ryckmans, Jacques. 1986. "Une écriture minuscule sud arabe antique récemment découverte." In *Scripta Signa Vocis: Studies about Scripts, Scriptures, Scribes and Languages in the Near East, Presented to J. H. Hospers by His Pupils, Colleagues and Friends,* ed. H. L. J. Vanstiphout, K. Jongeling, F. Leemhuis, and G. J. Reinink, pp. 185–99. Groningen: Forsten.

Ryckmans, Jacques, W. W. Müller, and Yusuf Abdullah. 1994. *Textes du Yémen antique inscrits sur bois.* Louvain-La-Neuve, Belgium: Institut Orientaliste.

Sass, Benjamin. 1991. *Studia Alphabetica: On the Origin and Early History of the Northwest Semitic, South Semitic and Greek Alphabets* (Orbis biblicus et orientalis 102). Freiburg, Switzerland: Universitätsverlag.

Schmitz, Philip C. 1995. "The Phoenician Text from the Etruscan Sanctuary at Pyrgi." *Journal of the American Oriental Society* 115.

Seger, Joe D. 1983. "The Gezer Jar Signs: New Evidence of the Earliest Alphabet." In *The Word of the Lord Shall Go Forth: Essays in Honor of David Noel Freedman,* ed. Carol L. Meyers and M. O'Connor, pp. 477–95. Winona Lake, Ind.: Eisenbrauns.

Segert, Stanislav. 1984. *A Basic Grammar of the Ugaritic Language.* Berkeley and Los Angeles:

University of California Press.

Swiggers, Pierre. 1983. "Some Remarks on Gelb's Theory of Writing." *General Linguistics* 23: 198–201.

———. 1984. "On the Nature of West-Semitic Writing Systems." *Aula Orientalis* 2: 149–51.

Virolleaud, Charles. 1936. *La légende phénicienne de Danel* (Mission de Ras Shamra 1). Paris: Geuthner.

THE IBERIAN SCRIPTS

Anderson, James M. 1988. *Ancient Languages of the Hispanic Peninsula.* Lanham, Md.: University Press of America.

Caro Baroja, Júlio. 1946. "Sobre la historia del desciframiento de las escrituras hispánicas." *Actas y Memorias, Sociedad Española de Antropología, Etnografía y Prehistoria* 21: 151–71.

———. 1954. "La escritura en la España prerromana (Epigrafía y numismática)." In *Historia de España*, ed. Ramón Menéndez Pidal, vol. 1/3, pp. 679–812. Madrid: Espasa-Calpe.

Correa, José A. 1983. "Escritura y lengua prerromanas en el sur de la Península Ibérica." In *Actas del VI Congreso Español de Estudios Clásicos (Sevilla, 6–11 de abril de 1981)*, vol. 1, pp. 397–411. Madrid: Gredos.

———. 1985. "Consideraciones sobre las inscripciones tartesias." In *Actas del III Colóquio sobre lenguas y culturas paleohispánicas (Lisboa, 8 noviembre 1980)*, pp. 377–95. Salamanca: Ediciones Universidad de Salamanca.

de Hoz, Javier. 1979. "On Some Problems of Iberian Script and Phonetics." In *Actas del II Colóquio sobre lenguas y culturas prerromanas de la Península Ibérica (Tübingen, 17–19 junio 1976)*, pp. 257–71. Salamanca: Ediciones Universidad de Salamanca.

———. 1983A. "Origine ed evoluzione delle scritture ispaniche." *AIΩN* 5: 27–63.

———. 1983B. "Las lenguas y la epigrafía prerromanas de la Península Ibérica." *Actas del VI Congreso Español de Estudios Clásicos (Sevilla, 6–11 de abril de 1981)*, vol. 1, pp. 351–96. Madrid: Gredos.

———. 1985. "El origen de la escritura del S.O." *Actas del III Colóquio sobre lenguas y culturas paleohispánicas (Lisboa, 5–8 noviembre 1980)*, pp. 423–64. Salamanca: Ediciones Universidad de Salamanca.

———. 1986. "Escritura fenicia y escrituras hispánicas: Algunos aspectos de su relación." *Aula Orientalis* 4: 73–84.

———. 1991. "The Phoenician Origin of the Early Hispanic Scripts." In *Phoinikeia Grammata: Lire et écrire en Méditerranée*, ed. Claude Baurain, Corinne Bonnet, and Véronique Krings, pp. 669–82. Namur, Belgium: Société des Études Classiques.

———. 1993. "De la escritura meridional a la escritura ibérica levantina." In *Sprachen und Schriften des antiken Mittelmeerraums: Festschrift für Jürgen Untermann*, ed. Frank Heidermanns, Helmut Rix, and Elmar Seebold, pp. 175–89. Innsbruck: Innsbrucker Beiträge zur Sprachwissenschaft.

Février, James G. 1957. "Remarques sur l'écriture ibéro-tartessienne." *Rivista degli Studi Orientali* 32: 719–30.

Fita, F. 1894. "Fraga: Inscripciones romanas e ibéricas." *Boletín de la Real Academia de la Historia* 25: 257–304.

Fletcher Valls, Domingo. 1983. "Lengua y epigrafía ibéricas." In *Arqueología del País Valenciano: panorama y perspectivas*, pp. 281–305. Alicante: Universidad de Alicante.

Friedrich, Johannes. 1956. "Zur iberischen Schrift." *Minos* 4: 172–75.

Gómez-Moreno, Manuel. 1943. *Misceláneas: Historia, arte, arqueología I*. Madrid: Aguirre [esp. pp. 219–330]

Lafon, René. 1952. "Les écritures anciennes en usage dans la péninsule ibérique." *Bulletin hispanique* 54: 165–83.

———. 1975. "Les écritures ibériques." In *Colloque du XXIXe Congrès international des Orienta-listes: Le déchiffrement des écritures et des langues,* pp. 11–14. Paris: L'Asiathèque.

Lejeune, Michel. 1993. *Notice biographique et bibliographique, suivie de l'exposé "D'Alcoy à Es-panca: Réflexions sur les écritures paléo-hispaniques."* Louvain: Centre international de dia-lectologie générale.

Maluquer de Motes, Juan. 1968. *Epigrafía prelatina de la Península Ibérica.* Barcelona: Univer-sidad de Barcelona.

Michelena, Luis. 1979. "La langue ibère." In *Actas del II Colóquio sobre lenguas y culturas pre-rromanas de la Península Ibérica (Tübingen, 17–19 junio 1976),* pp. 23–39. Salamanca: Edi-ciones Universidad de Salamanca.

Schmoll, Ulrich. 1961. *Die südlusitanischen Inschriften.* Wiesbaden: Harrassowitz.

———. 1962. "Zur Entzifferung der südhispanischen Schrift." *Madrider Mitteilungen* 3: 85–100.

Siles, Jaime. 1985. *Léxico de inscripciones ibéricas.* Madrid: Ministerio de Cultura.

Tovar, Antonio. 1961. *The Ancient Languages of Spain and Portugal.* New York: Vanni.

———. 1975. "Les écritures de l'ancienne Hispania." In *Colloque du XXIXe Congrès international des Orientalistes: Le déchiffrement des écritures et des langues,* pp. 15–23. Paris: L'Asia-thèque.

Untermann, Jürgen. 1962. "Das silbenschriftliche Element in der iberischen Schrift." *Emerita* 30: 281–94.

———. 1983. "Die althispanischen Sprachen." *Aufstieg und Niedergang der Römischen Welt* II.29/2, 791–818. Berlin: de Gruyter.

———. 1984. "La lengua ibérica." *Varia* 3: 249–72.

———. 1975–90. *Monumenta Linguarum Hispanicarum.* Wiesbaden: Harrassowitz. [See vol. 3/1 (1990) for bibliography, indexes, and a general philological-historical and linguistic descrip-tion].

THE BERBER SCRIPTS

Álvarez Delgado, Juan. 1964. *Inscripciones líbicas de Canarias: Ensayo de interpretación líbica.* La Laguna: Universidad de la Laguna.

Chabot, Jean-Baptiste. 1940–41. *Recueil des inscriptions libyques.* Paris: Gouvernement Général de L'Algérie.

Chaker, Salem. 1984. *Textes en linguistique berbère: Introduction au domaine berbère* (Laboratoire d'Anthropologie et de Préhistoire des Pays de la Méditerranée Occidentale, L.A. 164, Aix-en-Provence). Paris: Éditions du Centre Nationale de la Recherche Scientifique.

Cohen, Marcel. 1958. *La grande invention de l'écriture et son évolution.* Paris: Klincksieck.

Friedrich, Johannes. 1966. *Geschichte der Schrift.* Heidelberg: Winter.

Galand, Lionel. 1966. "Inscriptions libyques." In *Inscriptions antiques du Maroc* by L. Galand et al., pp. 9–80 (Publications de la Section antiquité du Centre de recherches sur l'Afrique Médi-terranéenne, Faculté des Lettres, 13, Aix-en-Provence). Paris: Éditions du Centre Nationale de la Recherche Scientifique.

———. 1979. *Langue et littérature berbères: Vingt cinq ans d'études* (Chroniques de l'Annuaire de l'Afrique du Nord). Paris: Éditions du Centre Nationale de la Recherche Scientifique.

Horn, Heinz Gunter, and Christoph B. Rüger, eds. 1979. *Die Numider: Reiter und Könige nordlich der Sahara.* (Kunst und Altertum am Rhein 96). Cologne: Rheinland-Verlag; Bonn: Rudolf Ha-belt.

KAI = Donner and Röllig 1968–73.

Rössler, Otto. 1979A. "Die Numider: Herkunft—Schrift—Sprache." In Horn and Rüger 1979: 89–97.

———. 1979B. "Bilingue von Thugga." In Horn and Rüger 1979: 576–77.

Anatolian Hieroglyphs

H. CRAIG MELCHERT

Usage and history

Hieroglyphs were used in central, western, and southern Anatolia and in parts of what is now modern Syria during the third and second millennia B.C.E. They first appear on personal seals from the ancient capital of the Hittite Empire, Hattusha (modern Boğazköy). Virtually all later use is also found in the cultural sphere of the Hittites. The system therefore has been and continues to be known widely as the "Hittite Hieroglyphs."

The inscriptions on seals consist only of names, titles, and sometimes good-luck symbols such as that for 'well-being'. It is inappropriate to view these as texts in a given language. I follow Marazzi (1990) and others in treating this use of the hieroglyphs as "ideographic." They stand not for sounds or words in a particular language, but for concepts which may be "read" in any language. One may compare the present world-wide use of Arabic numerals.

All actual texts written in the hieroglyphs are in Luvian, an Indo-European language closely related to, but distinct from, cuneiform Hittite (for an orientation to the Anatolian languages, see SECTION 22, "The Anatolian Alphabets" on page 281). A form of Luvian is also attested in cuneiform from Hattusha, and the phonological interpretations of hieroglyphic spellings given below are largely based on Cuneiform Luvian. We do have a handful of one-word Urartian glosses (see Klein 1974) on pithoi (storage jars), and at the Hittite shrine at Yazılıkaya several divine names are written with the hieroglyphs in specifically Hurrian form.

The Luvian texts are mostly monumental inscriptions on stone, on either natural rock faces or man-made structures. There are also a few letters and economic documents inscribed on soft lead strips. There are references in the Hittite cuneiform texts to writing on wooden tablets (*gulzattana-*/GIŠ.ḪUR). It remains an open question whether any of these were inscribed with hieroglyphs, and if so, whether the language was Luvian or Hittite.

General characteristics

The direction of writing is variable, but the text is most commonly arranged in a series of horizontal panels or "registers." The text begins in the top left or right corner of the top register, with each register reading alternately left-to-right and right-to-left in a

TABLE 6.1: *The Logograms, Equivalents, and Translations (after Hawkins 1975: 153)*

ANNUS 'year'		DOMINUS 'lord'		LUNA 'moon'		REGIO 'kingdom'	
ARHA ᵃ 'away'		DOMUS 'house'		MAGNUS 'great'		REX 'king'	
AUDIRE 'hear'		EGO 'I'		MALLEUS 'hammer'		SARMA ᵃ 'Sarruma'	
AVIS 'bird'		EQUUS 'horse'		MALUS 'bad'		SCALPRUM 'chisel'	
AVUS 'ancestor'		EXERCITUS 'army'		MANUS 'hand'		SCRIBA 'clerk'	
BONUS 'good'		FEMINA 'woman'		MONS 'mountain'		SOL 'sun'	
BOS 'cattle'		FINES 'boundary'		NEG(ative)		SOLIUM 'seat'	
CAELUM 'heaven'				NEG₂, NEG₃		STELE 'stela'	
CAPUT 'head'		FRONS 'forehead'		NEPOS 'descendant'		SUPER 'above'	
CASTRUM 'camp'		HALPA ᵃ 'Aleppo'		OCCIDENS 'west'		TERRA 'land'	
CERVUS 'stag'		HEROS 'hero'		OMNIS 'all'		THRONUS 'throne'	
CERVUS₂		INFANS 'child'		ORIENS 'east'		TONITRUS 'thunder'	
CORNU 'horn'		INFRA 'below'		OVIS 'sheep'		URBS 'city'	
CRUS 'leg'		IRA 'wrath'		PANIS 'bread'		VAS 'vase'	
CRUX 'cross'		LEPUS 'hare'		PES 'foot'		VERSUS 'toward'	
CULTER 'knife'		LIBARE 'offer'		PES₂		VIA 'road'	
CUM 'with'		LINGUA 'tongue'		PONERE 'put'		VINUM 'wine'	
CURRUS 'chariot'		LITUUS 'staff'		POST 'after'		VIR 'man'	
DARE 'give'				PRAE 'before'		VIS 'strength'	
DEUS 'god'		LOQUI 'speak'		PUGNUS 'fist'			

a.   Three of the equivalents are Luvian rather than Latin words.

boustrophedon pattern. Signs with a distinct left–right orientation face into the direction from which one reads: right for reading right-to-left and vice versa. Within each register, the signs are arranged in a series of roughly vertical columns. However, one esthetic principle of the scribes was that all available space should be filled in a balanced way, and the reading order of the signs is not always strictly vertical nor unambiguous to the modern reader. The texts are written continuously without word breaks. There is a word divider ᴰᴵ, but it is not employed consistently.

TABLE 6.2: *The Regular Syllabary (after Hawkins 1975: 154–55)*

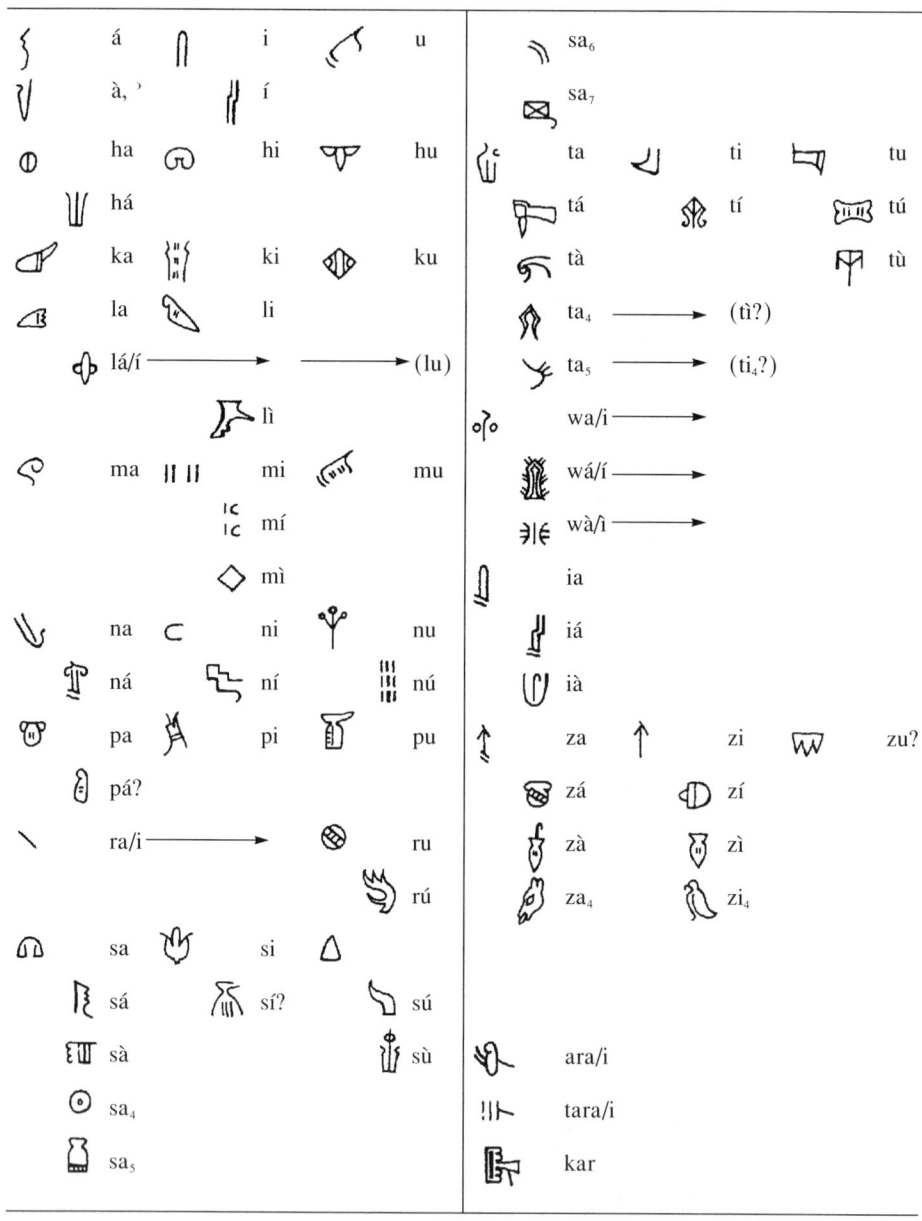

In their fully developed form, the Anatolian hieroglyphs are employed in a mixed logographic–phonographic system. Words may be written logographically, phonographically, or logographically with a *phonetic complement*. The word [wawis] 'cow' may thus be written as BOS, as *wa/i-wa/i-(i)-sa*, or as BOS-*wa/i-sa* (by a convention established in 1974, most logograms are transliterated with Latin equivalents;

TABLE 6.1). One also finds the logograms preceding or following a complete phonological spelling, thus functioning as determiners: (BOS)*wa/i-wa/i-sa*. Some signs are used exclusively logographically or phonographically, but many serve in both functions. There is a sign ⟩ ⟨ (transliterated with quotation marks) which explicitly marks logographic use, but it appears only sporadically.

The phonographic portion of the system is syllabic (TABLE 6.2). There are signs for vowel (V) and for consonant+vowel (CV), and a few complex signs for CVCV. There are no VC or CVC signs. Final consonants and all consonant clusters must thus be spelled using "empty" vowels: *wa/i-wa/i-s(a)* = [wawis] 'cow', *á-s(a)-ta* = [asta] 'was'. For some syllables there are several homophonous signs, distinguished in transliteration by accents and subscript numbers: *sa, sá, sà, sa₄*, etc., all equal [sa]. The system does not distinguish single versus geminate consonants, or voicing in stops. The signs transliterated *ta₄* and *ta₅* may be used consistently for [da], but this is not certain, and other signs such as *ta* are used for both [ta] and [da]. Preconsonantal [n] is not indicated in spelling: *à-ta* = [anda] 'into'.

For syllables beginning with [r], there is a separate sign only for *ru* ([ra] and [ri] do not occur word-initially). All other instances of [r] are indicated by adding an oblique stroke or "tang" \ to a V or CV sign. Such combinations may be read with an [a] or [i] vowel before or after the [r] or both: *i+ra/i* = [iri] 'goes', *i+ra/i-hi-* = [irhi-] 'boundary', *pa+ra/i-na* = [par(r)an] 'in front', *pa+ra/i-na-* = [parna-] 'house', *i-sà-ta+ra/i-* = [istri-] 'hand'.

There are distinct hieroglyphic signs for *a, i,* and *u* and likewise for many combinations C*a*, C*i*, and C*u*. However, for some consonants, particularly in early texts from the second millennium, there is a single sign for C*a* and C*i*; hence the rather awkward transliterations C*a/i* above. There is no indication of vowel length in the Anatolian hieroglyphs. The only function of CV-V spellings (such as *-tu-u* 'to him/her') is esthetic (filling space, as mentioned above).

Signs

Most of the signs are clearly pictorial in origin, representing human figures, body parts, plants and animals, and everyday objects. Unsurprisingly, as the signs came to be used for syllabic values, they became more stylized and less easily recognizable as representational drawings.

In many clear cases the syllabic values are derived by acrophony, i.e. by taking the first syllable(s) of the word represented by a logogram. For example, the sign *tara/i* is derived from [tarri-] 'three', that for *ta* from [targasna-] 'ass, donkey', and so on. Our knowledge of the Luvian lexicon is quite limited, and it is likely that nearly all syllabic values are derived in this manner. The fact that all known cases are derived from specifically Luvian words suggests that the system was invented for writing Luvian (cf. Hawkins 1986). Resemblances to Egyptian hieroglyphs are of a typological sort, and there is little if any influence from cuneiform.

SAMPLE OF LUVIAN

1. Transliteration:	. à-wa/i	á-mi-za	. (DIES)ha-li-ia-za	. á-tana-wa/i-ní-zi (URBS)	
2. Transcription:	a-wa	amints	haliyants	Adanawannintsi	
3. Gloss:	CONJ-PTCL	my	days	Adanian	

1.	FINES-zi	'MANUS'-la-tara/i-ha	. zi-na	. 'OCCIDENS'-pa-mi
2.	irhintsi	ladaraha	tsin	ipami
3.	boundaries	I.extended	on.this.side	west

1.	. VERSUS-ia-na	. zi-pa-wa/i	'ORIENS'-ta-mi	VERSUS-na
2.	tawiyan	tsin-pa-wa	isatami	tawiyan
3.	toward	on.this.side-but-PTCL	east	toward

'In my days I extended the Adanian territory toward the west on this side, and toward the east on this side.'
— *From the Karatepe Luvian–Phoenician bilingual (Bossert 1950–51: 270).*

■■■

Bibliography

Bossert, H. Th. 1950–51. "Die phönizisch-hethitischen Bilinguen von Karatepe. 3. Fortsetzung." *Jahrbuch für kleinasiatische Forschung* 1: 264–95.

Hawkins, J. David. 1975. "The Negatives in Hieroglyphic Luwian." *Anatolian Studies* 25: 119–56.

———. 1986. "Writing in Anatolia: Imported and Indigenous Systems." *World Archaeology* 17: 363–76.

Hawkins, J. David, Anna Morpurgo Davies, and Günter Neumann. 1974. *Hittite Hieroglyphs and Luwian: New Evidence for the Connection. Nachrichten der Akademie der Wissenschaften, Göttingen, philol.-hist. Kl.*, 1973/6.

Klein, Jeffrey J. 1974. "Urartian Hieroglyphic Inscriptions from Altıntepe." *Anatolian Studies* 24: 77–94.

Marazzi, Massimiliano. 1990. *Il geroflico anatolico: Problemi di analisi e prospettive di ricerca.* Rome: Univ. "La Sapienza".

The following works also remain useful, especially for their complete repertoire of signs, but their readings of many syllabic signs must be revised in the light of the work of Hawkins et al. 1974:

Laroche, Emmanuel. 1960. *Les hiéroglyphes hittites I.* Paris: Éditions du Centre National de la Recherche Scientifique.

Meriggi, Piero. 1962. *Hieroglyphen-hethitisches Glossar.* Wiesbaden: Harrassowitz.

Aegean Scripts

EMMETT L. BENNETT

Most of the five scripts considered in this section are confined to the Aegean islands, Crete, and mainland Greece, and to the second millennium B.C.E.; those from Cyprus have often been described as derivative from those in the Aegean. The proliferation of names for them may be confusing. Listing them in order of discovery, "Cypriote" is simply an indigenous script of Cyprus. The Hieroglyphic script was "Cretan" because the first examples were put on the antiquities market as coming from Crete. It was first named "Pictographic" from its almost three-dimensional signs. When clay tablets whose signs were drawn with simple lines were excavated in Crete (initially at Knossos by Arthur Evans), these became "Cretan Linear"—and "Pictographic" became "Cretan Hieroglyphic." It was soon apparent that there were two "Linear" scripts. These became "A" and "B": earlier and simpler, later and sophisticated. These three may be "Minoan," since that name was given to the Bronze Age culture of Crete; but the mainland connections, or even origin, of Linear B have suggested that it might really be "Mycenaean" Linear B. "Cypro-Minoan" reflects the possibilities that this script is both derivative from a Minoan script and ancestral to the Cypriote script. For only two of these scripts, Linear B and Cypriote, can comprehensive descriptions be offered, inasmuch as they have been deciphered (SECTION 9). Until the others are deciphered, any description must be incomplete.

Linear B

The Greek mainland and Crete, ca. 1550–1200 B.C.E.

The best-known pictographic script of the Aegean is the Mycenaean script *Linear B*. Since the principal texts are accounting records, the phonographic and sematographic elements are of equal importance (Bennett 1963). These are respectively a syllabary and a large repertory of nonphonetic signs, including punctuation, numerals, and signs for commodities and measures, usually called *ideograms* (they are not used as logograms in writing sentences).

The texts are regularly drawn with a stylus on clay tablets; some are written on clay pressed into the surface of a basket, as a label, while others are written on lumps of clay formed around a knot and impressed with a seal. A few are drawn with paint

TABLE 7.1: *The Basic Syllabary of Linear B*

a		e		i		o		u
da		de		di		do		du
ja		je				jo		ju
ka		ke		ki		ko		ku
ma		me		mi		mo		mu
na		ne		ni		no		nu
pa		pe		pi		po		pu
qa		qe		qi		qo		
ra		re		ri		ro		ru
sa		se		si		so		su
ta		te		ti		to		tu
wa		we		wi		wo		
za		ze				zo		

and brush on pots. The sign-groups are written horizontally from left to right. Except in narrow tablets of one or two lines, the text is normally written in the space above a ruled line. Words are separated by a word-divider, by a change in the height of the signs, or by a space. In transcription the signs of a word are joined by a hyphen, the words divided by a comma. Words are rarely carried over from one line to the next. Emphatic words of a text are frequently indicated by the height of their signs. When a series of parallel statements or items follows on several lines of a text, a columnar arrangement is frequent.

In the fundamental syllabary of 59 signs (TABLE 7.1), there are signs for each of the five vowels, plus 54 signs for the consonant–vowel (CV) combinations of twelve consonant series. It is assumed that the syllabary is adapted for writing an early Greek dialect. It must be emphasized that these transcriptions are a modern convention and correspond exactly only to the shape, and not to any pronunciation or phonemic value of the sign. The five vowel signs are used primarily at the beginnings of words. But sometimes one does occur in a sequence of signs of the form CV_1-V_1 (𐀞𐀀 *pa-a*). This does not represent a single syllable with a long vowel, but two syllables; the second could begin with aspiration, or be in hiatus. In the sequences C*a-u*, C*e-u*, C*o-u* (𐀞𐀄 *pa-u*, 𐀟𐀄 *pe-u*, 𐀡𐀄 *po-u*), the diphthongs *au*, *eu*, *ou* may be represented.

It is assumed that the *d*- and *t*-series represent syllables beginning with a dental stop, the *k*-series with gutturals, the *p*- with labials, the *q*-series with labiovelars; the *r*-series with either liquid, *r* or *l*. The nature of the consonant in the *z*-series is unclear. Voiced and unvoiced, aspirated and unaspirated consonants are represented by the same signs. In the conventional transcription, *j*- and *w*- represent English *y* and *w*.

Spoken syllables beginning with a consonant cluster are represented by two or more signs, e.g., $C_1C_2V_1$ (*pra*) is written C_1V_1-C_2V_1 (𐀞𐀨 *pa-ra*), and are thus not distinguishable from the sequence of two syllables C_1V_1-C_2V_1 (*pa-ra*). Some probable instances of C_1V_1-$C_2C_3V_2$ (*pa-tro*) written as C_1V_1-C_2V_1-C_3V_2 (𐀞𐀲𐀫 *pa-ta-ro*) do occur beside the normal C_1V_1-C_2V_2-C_3V_2 (𐀞𐀵𐀫 *pa-to-ro*). Any double consonants are apparently represented in the single sign.

In conventional transcription, syllabic signs have only open syllables (V, CV; 𐀀 *a*, 𐀞 *pa*), but they may also represent certain types of closed syllables, as well as syllables with a diphthong in *iota* (cf. SECTION 22; *pan*, *pai*). The syllabic codas are limited to those normally permitted in Classical Greek. These are a sibilant *sigma*, a nasal *nu*, and a liquid *lambda*, *rho*. Syllables in any position in the word, including the final, may be interpreted in this way. Two words, where the first ends in one of these codas, and the next word begins in a vowel, sometimes are written as single sign-group, with the coda and initial vowel joined in one sign. Enclitics and proclitics are regularly included in the sign-group as, e.g., in 𐀅𐀂𐀕𐀆𐀖𐀖 *da-mo-de-mi* (*da:mos de min*) 'damos but her'.

There are also sixteen signs transcribed either with diacritics (e.g., 𐁀 *a₂*, 𐀨 *ra₂*), perhaps indicating diphthongs or aspiration, or double consonants, e.g., 𐀺 *nwa*, 𐀠 *pte*). Unless some of these indicate vowel length, it is nowhere indicated. These signs may be used in the frequent variations of spelling, perhaps reflecting differences of idiolect, of local dialect, or of date. Eleven further signs occur so rarely that no transcription has been agreed upon (Ruijgh 1967: 21–34).

The sample text presents the longest sentence known in Linear B. It occurs in two versions, one copied from the other, with additions and changes. Note that any phonemic transcription is speculative, and especially one of a unique text; this follows Ruijgh 1967: 314–15. In names (as in the name of the priestess, *e-ri-ta*), transcription is entirely arbitrary. The spelling rules of Linear B allow 𐀁𐀪𐀲 *e-ri-ta* to represent *Eritha, *Eritta, *Erita, *Erintha, *Erista, *Elitha, *Elintha, or *Elista, etc.

The sentence ends with the record of a quantity of GRANUM, which in Eb 297 stands in apposition to 𐀁𐀵𐀛𐀍 *e-to-ni-jo* and 𐀃𐀙𐀵 *o-na-to*. In most of these texts, and in Ep 704, the quantity stands in apposition to the phrase 𐀵𐀰𐀟𐀗 *to-so pe-mo*. All the surviving texts in Linear B are, like this one, accounting documents. In most texts the indication of the nature of the transaction, which might be expressed as a verbal predicate, is absent. The very frequent simplest form of record is a name, followed by an ideogram, followed by a number. The type of transaction in a text is frequently recognized only through the context of the group of tablets to which it belongs. Very few surviving records do not include an ideogram. Many ideograms are certainly, others possibly, pictographic in origin. The species and quantity represented by the ideograms and numbers are an integral part of the text. It is important to note that sematograms have a morphology and syntax of their own.

The ideograms in TABLE 7.2 represent a few of the commodities important in the Mycenaean economy. The decimal numerals are written from left to right, larger to

TABLE 7.2: *Selected Ideograms (sematographic signs) of Linear B*

Category	Sign, Transliteration, Gloss	Example	Gloss
Word divider	⎮		
Numerals, decimal	◇ '1000', ○ '100', ‒ '10', ⎮ '1'		
Dry volume: Unit measures for cereals, etc., implied		𐂇 ⦀	GRANUM 3 units
Fractional measures	⎺ T '¹⁄₁₀', ◁ V '¹⁄₆₀', ∾ Z '¹⁄₂₄₀'	𐂁 ⎮ ⎺ ⎮ ◁ ⎮	NI $1^{17}/_{60}$
Liquid volume: Unit measures for wine, etc., implied		▨ ‖	VINUM 2 units
Fractional measures	⍑ S '¹⁄₃', ◁ V '¹⁄₁₈', ∾ Z '¹⁄₇₂'	⚦ ⎮ ◁ ⎮ ∾ ⎮	OLEUM $1^{7}/_{60}$
Weight: Unit measure for metals, etc.	𐄗 L	⊨ 𐄗 ‖‖	AES 4 units
Fractional measures	₂̌ M '¹⁄₃₀', ╫ N '¹⁄₁₂₀'	⊨ ₂̌ ⎮ ╫ ⎮	AES $^{1}/_{24}$
Unit measure for wool implied, fractional units	₂̌ M '¹⁄₃', ╫ N '¹⁄₁₂'	𐂴 ⎮ ₂̌ ⎮ ╫ ⎮	LANA $1^{5}/_{12}$
Cereals, plants	𐂇 GRANUM 'grain', 𐂁 NI 'figs', 𐂎 ARB 'tree'		
Extracts	⚦ OLEUM 'oil', ▨ VINUM 'wine', 𐂝 FAR 'flour'		
Metals	⊨ AES 'bronze'		
Other materials	𐂴 LANA 'wool', ☌ CORNU 'horn'		
Artifacts Vessels	𐃡 'phial', 𐃭 'bull's head rhyton'		
Vehicles	𐃇 BIGAE 'chariot', ⊕ ROTA 'wheel'		
Weapons	⚲ 'sword', ⤳ HASTA 'spear', ← SAGITTA 'arrow'		
Animals	𐂶 OVIS 'ovine' (𐂷 'ram', 𐂸 'ewe'),		
	𐂿 CAPER 'caprine' (𐃀 'he-goat', 𐃁 'she-goat'),		
	𐃂 BOS 'bovine' (𐃃 'bull', 𐃄 'cow'),		
	𐃅 SUS 'suine' (𐃆 'boar', 𐃇 'sow'),		
	𐃺 EQUUS 'equine' (𐃻 'stallion', 𐃼 'mare')		
Humans	𐂃 VIR 'male', 𐂄 MULIER 'female', 𐀏𐀷 ko-wa 'girl', 𐀏𐀺 ko-wo 'boy'		
Syllabograms used as ideograms or to abbreviate names of commodities	𐂁 NI 'figs', 𐀭 SA sa-sa-ma 'sesame', 𐀖 MA ma-ra-tu-wo 'fennel', 𐀎 KU ku-mi-no 'cumin', 𐁋 ZE <*ze-u-ko> (cf. ze-u-ke-si) 'pair' (example: 𐃺𐁋 ⎮ EQUUS ZE I '2 horses')		
Adjuncts, parallel to the use of different stems to distinguish male & female animals	𐃞 PELLIS + 𐀒 KO 𐃞 'oxhide', 𐃰 VAS + 𐀡 PO 𐃰 'type of vessel', 𐃚 TELA + 𐀿 ZO 𐃚 'type of cloth'		
Monograms	𐂻 KAPO ka-po 'fruit',		
	𐂼 AREPA a-re-pa 'ointment',		
	𐂽 MERI me-ri-(to) 'honey'		

smaller. The place of the ideogram is sometimes taken by a word followed directly by a number, e.g., 𐀒𐀷 III *ko-wa 6*. In others a word spelled out is repeated in an ideogram, which occasionally is an abbreviation, e.g., 𐀮 *SA* for 𐀮𐀮𐀔 *sa-sa-ma* 'sesame', or a monogram, e.g., *AREPA* for 𐀀𐀩𐀞 *a-re-pa* 'ointment'.

For commodities which occur in distinct varieties, the ideogram may be modified by various devices. The support of an animal ideogram varies with sex, transcribed BOS^f, BOS^m. For many pictographic signs, the addition of specific detail to the drawing is found. E.g., one may draw a vase with three or four handles, or a chariot at successive stages of manufacture.

For things counted, e.g. humans, animals, and artifacts, the ideogram represents the unit of counting. For things measured by dry measure or liquid measure, the ideogram generally represents not only the commodity but also the unit of measure. For weight, however, the sign for the commodity is always followed by the largest sign required by the quantity, whether L for bronze, or N or even the smaller fraction P for gold. But the sign for wool, *LANA*, indicates a special unit equal to M 3. By an extension of this system to a team of horses, EQUUS with *ZE I* records one pair, and with an additional *MO*, a single additional horse.

Obviously the repertory of syllabic signs used by any one scribe, at any one center, or in any one period of time, will be finite. Since new abbreviations, new monograms, and new pictograms could be introduced at any time, the sematographic repertory is open-ended.

These inscriptions have been found at Pylos (Bennett and Olivier 1977); Mycenae, Thebes, and Tiryns on the Greek mainland; and at Knossos (Chadwick et al. 1986) and Khania in Crete; inscribed pots are found elsewhere as well. The language of the texts is an early dialect of Greek; among the personal names some are of normal Greek formation, but many cannot be characterized as Greek (Chadwick 1987).

Two sentences from Pylos

1. Linear B:	𐀂𐀋𐀩𐀊 𐄀	𐀁𐀐𐀤 𐄀	𐀁𐀄𐀐𐀵𐀤 𐄀	𐀁𐀵𐀛𐀍 𐄀
2. Transliteration:	i-je-re-ja ,	e-ke-qe ,	e-u-ke-to-qe ,	e-to-ni-jo ,
3. Transcription:	hijereja	hekhej k^{w}e	eukhetoj k^{w}e	eto:nijon
4. Gloss:	priestess	has	swears-and	special.land.grant

1.	𐀁𐀐𐀁 𐄀	𐀳𐀃	𐀒𐀵𐀜𐀃𐀒𐀆 𐄀	𐀒𐀵𐀙𐀃 𐄀
2.	e-ke-e ,	te-o	ko-to-no-o-ko-de ,	ko-to-na-o ,
3.	hekhehen	theo:j	ktojnohokhoj de	ktojna:ho:n
4.	to.have	for.the.god	landholders-but	of.cultivable.lands

1.	𐀐𐀐𐀕𐀙𐀃 𐄀	𐀃𐀙𐀲 𐄀	𐀁𐀐𐀁	III T IIIII IIII V III
2.	ke-ke-me-na-o ,	o-na-ta ,	e-ke-e	GRANUM 3 T 9 V 3
3.	khekhemena:ho:n	ona:ta	hekhehen	GRANUM 3 T 9 V 3
4.	of.communal	land.grants	to.have:	GRANUM 3 57/60 measures

1.	𒀸𒑱𒀸	𒅀𒊭𒀸𒂍	𒀸𒐊	𒀸𒊏𒊭𒋾𒀸	𒀸𒋾𒅀𒊺	𒀸𒊭𒀸
2.	e-ri-ta ,	i-je-re-ja ,	e-ke ,	e-u-ke-to-qe ,	e-to-ni-jo ,	e-ke-e ,
3.	*eritha	hijereja	hekhej	eukhetoj kʷe	eto:nijon	hekhehen
4.	*Eritha	priestess	has	swears-and	special.land.grant	to.have

1.	𒋼𒀸	𒁕𒈬𒁖𒈨	𒉺𒋛	𒅗𒌅𒈾𒀸	𒋼𒅗𒈨𒈾𒀸
2.	te-o ,	da-mo-de-mi ,	pa-si ,	ko-to-na-o ,	ke-ke-me-na-o ,
3.	theo:j	da:mos de min	pha:si	ktojna:ho:n	khekhemena:ho:n
4.	for-the-god	damos-but-her	says	of-cultivable-lands	of-communal

1.	𒍢𒈾𒋫	𒀸𒊭𒀸	𒋫𒈬	𒉿𒈬	𒀸 III 𒋫 IIIII / IIIII
2.	o-na-to ,	e-ke-e ,	to-so	pe-mo	GRANUM 3 T 9
3.	ona:ton	hekhehen	tosson	spermo:	GRANUM 3 T 9
4.	land-grant	to-have	so-much	seed:	GRANUM 3 ⁹⁄₁₀

'The priestess has and swears she has a special-land-grant for the god, but the landholders <say> that she has 3.95 land measures in land-grants of communal lands.'   —*PY Eb 297*.

'*Eritha, the priestess, has and swears she has a special-land-grant for the god, but the *dāmos* (community) says that she has 3.9 land measures in a land-grant of communal lands.'   —*Ep 704.5–.6*.

Scripts of Cyprus

Cyprus, ca. 800–200 B.C.E.

The *Cypriote syllabary*, used primarily in Greek inscriptions of ca. 800–200 B.C.E., shares many of the features of Linear B (Masson 1983). The sign forms (TABLE 7.3) are clearly not pictographic; they seem to be derived from Cypro-Minoan scripts. Cypriote is written from right to left, with conventions similar to those of Linear B. The chief difference is that all syllables ending in liquids or sibilants (*par*, *pas*), and those with nasals final in the word (*pan*), are written with two syllabograms, CV-C*e* (cf. ✳𒅅𒀸 *a-no-ko-ne* ἄνωγον [ano:gon] 'they ordered' and ✕𒑱✕ *i-ta-i* ιν ται [in ta:i] 'in the') (Chadwick 1987, Baurain 1991).

Cyprus, ca. 1500–1200 B.C.E.

No consensus has been reached on the interpretation of the very limited corpus of *Cypro-Minoan* inscriptions. Many signs resemble those of Cypriote, except that they are written by impressing the stylus rather than drawing with the stylus; the appearance of a text is often reminiscent of Linear A signs. It has naturally been suggested that the Cypriote is descended from Cypro-Minoan, which in turn is descended from Linear A (Chadwick 1987, Palaima 1989).

TABLE 7.3: *The Cypriote Syllabary*

	a		e		i		o		u
	ja						jo		
	ka		ke		ki		ko		ku
	la		le		li		lo		lu
	ma		me		mi		mo		mu
	na		ne		ni		no		nu
	pa		pe		pi		po		pu
	ra		re		ri		ro		ru
	sa		se		si		so		su
	ta		te		ti		to		tu
	wa		we		wi		wo		
	xa		xe				xo		
	ga								

SAMPLE OF GREEK IN CYPRIOTE SYLLABARY (WITH CLASSICAL EQUIVALENT)

1. Syllabary:				
2. Transliteration:	a-no-ko-ne	o-na-si-lo-ne ,		to-no-na-si-ku-po-ro-ne
3. Classical:	Ἄνωγον	Ὠνασίλον		τὸν Ὠνασικύπρων
4. Transcription:	áno:gon	onasílon		ton onasikúpro:n
5. Gloss:	they.ordered	Onasilos		the of.Onasikupros

2.	to-ni	ja-te-ra-ne ,	ka-se ,	to-se ,	ka-si-ke-ne-to-se
3.	τὸν	ἰατῆραν	κὰς	τὸς	κασιγνήτος
4.	ton	iatê:ran	kas	tos	kasigné:tos
5.	the	physician	and	the	brothers

2.	i-ja-sa-ta-i ,	to-se ,	a-to-ro-po-se ,	to-se ,	i	ta-i
3.	ἰᾶσθαι	τὸς	ἀνθρώπος	τὸς	ἰν	τᾶι
4.	iâsthai	tos	anthró:pos	tos	in	ta:i
5.	to heal	the	men	those	in	the

2.	ma-ka-i ,	i-ki-ma-me-no-se ,	a-ne-u ,	mi-si-to-ne
3.	μάχαι	ικμαμένος	ἄνευ	μισθῶν.
4.	mákha:i	ikmaménos	áneu	misthô:n
5.	battle	wounded	without	fee

'They ordered Onasilos the (son) of Onasikupros the physician and the brothers to heal the men wounded in the battle without fee.'
— *From the Idalion inscription, after Chadwick 1987: 56, with permission.*

Minoan Linear A

Crete and Aegean islands, ca. 1800–1450 B.C.E.

Linear A is apparently a syllabic script, and Linear B is to some extent affiliated to it. The phonetic signs in A which are similar in shape to those of B (e.g. *da, ro, pa*) are a majority, about 50 out of 60 phonetic signs, and about 40 of the 60 sematographic. Many of the signs for commodities (e.g. GRA, AES, *NI*) are similar. These are also found with modifications indicating varieties. There is, however, no consensus on a standard transliteration of the phonetic signs and ideograms. The language of the texts is still to be identified. Some attempts at decipherment are mentioned in SECTION 2.

Most of the texts are the accounting tablets. Linear A tablets are smaller and more carefully made than Linear B tablets; but the writing is less careful. The direction of writing is left to right, and words are sometimes separated by word dividers. Sign-groups are regularly carried over from one line to the next, divided by the edge of the tablet at any point. There is no ruling to divide successive lines of text, but lines are often drawn to make fields for different records. Small clay objects of various shapes with minimal inscriptions and ill-defined accounting functions also occur. There are several inscriptions, without ideograms, on objects of stone or metal. These texts may have a different function, and they share few of the sign-groups occurring in the clay tablets (Godart and Olivier 1976, Chadwick 1983, Duhoux 1989).

The pictographic or Cretan Hieroglyphic script

Crete, ca. 1750–1600 B.C.E.

This script is most often found on sealstones, or on their impressions on clay. It also may possibly be syllabic; the signs on the seals seem to be in regular sequence, and a simple mark may indicate the end of a word. There are some clay tablets, or other shapes, with linear signs closely resembling the pictographic signs rather than Linear A signs, and with ideograms and numerals employed very much in the style of Linear A. There is even less material preserved for this script than for Linear A (Chadwick 1987).

The Phaistos Disk

The notorious Phaistos Disk, found in Crete, is unique. Although the circumstances of its discovery make it impossible to determine when it was made, it has been dated to about 1700 B.C.E. There can be no certainty that it was made in Crete. Its script is certainly pictographic. It is a clay disk on whose two faces 242 clear impressions were made by 45 different stamps. They appear in the 31 fields drawn on the one face and the 30 on the other, and each field has from two to seven impressions. Those figures suggest that the script was syllabic, but nothing suggests that a verifiable decipherment will ever be achieved (Olivier 1975, Duhoux 1977, Chadwick 1987).

Bibliography

Baurain, Claude. 1991. "L'Écriture syllabique à Chypre." In *Phoinikeia Grammata: Lire et écrire en Méditerranée*, ed. Claude Baurain, Corinne Bonnet, and Véronique Krings, pp. 389–424. Namur, Belgium: Société des Études Classiques.

Bennett, Emmett L. 1963. "Names for Linear B writing and its signs." *Kadmos* 2: 98–123.

Bennett, Emmett L., and Jean-Pierre Olivier. 1973. *Pylos Tablets Transcribed, I* (Incunabula Graeca 51). Roma: Edizioni dell'Ateneo.

Chadwick, John. 1987. *Linear B and Related Scripts* (Reading the Past). Berkeley and Los Angeles: University of California Press.

Chadwick, John, et al. 1986–89. *Corpus of Mycenaean Inscriptions of Knossos*. 2 vols. Cambridge: Cambridge University Press.

Duhoux, Yves. 1977. *Le disque de Phaistos*. Louvain: Peeters.

———. 1989. "Le linéaire A: Problèmes de déchiffrement." In Duhoux et al. 1989: 59–119.

Duhoux, Yves, Thomas G. Palaima, and John Bennet, eds. 1989. *Problems in Decipherment* (Bibliothèque des Cahiers de l'Institut de Linguistique de Louvain 49). Louvain: Peeters.

Godart, Louis, and Jean-Pierre Olivier. 1976–85. *Receuil des inscriptions en linéaire A*. 5 vols. (École Française d'Athènes, Études Crétoises 21). Paris: Geuthner.

Masson, Olivier. 1983. *Les inscriptions chypriotes syllabiques*, 2nd ed. (École Française d'Athènes, Études Chypriotes 1). Paris: Boccard.

Olivier, Jean-Pierre. 1975. *Le disque de Phaistos*. Paris: Boccard.

———. 1989. "The Possible Methods in Deciphering the Pictographic Cretan Script." In Duhoux et al. 1989: 39–58.

Palaima, Thomas G. 1989. "Cypro-Minoan Scripts: Problems of Historical Context." In Duhoux et al. 1989: 121–87.

Ruijgh, C. J. 1967. *Études sur la grammaire et le vocabulaire du Grec mycénien.* Amsterdam: Hakkert.

Old Persian Cuneiform

DAVID D. TESTEN

The Old Persian script is found in a small number of royal inscriptions in the Old Persian language dating from the Achaemenid Empire. The most extensive and important of these is the trilingual monument of Darius I at Bisitun (Behistun), which, in addition to playing a central role in Old Persian studies, served as a "Rosetta stone" in the deciphering of cuneiform (SECTION 9).

Although inspired by cuneiform, the Old Persian script is essentially an alphabetic writing system—its only clear relation to cuneiform lies in the sign ᚆ for the non-Persian sound /l/, the character for which is clearly based on cuneiform ⊢ᛂᚍ *la* (Paper 1956). The development of the Old Persian script remains a matter of debate. It is likely that this writing system was invented early in the reign of Darius I (522–486 B.C.E.), although some investigators maintain that it reaches back to the reign of Cyrus II (539–530), the founder of the empire. The discussion of the history of the script has mainly centered on the interpretation of the brief inscription CMa—which may or may not date back to Cyrus's time—and on the ambiguous lines IV:88–92 of the Bisitun inscription (known as "paragraph 70"), in which Darius makes a statement suggesting, in the opinion of many researchers, that he was responsible for first putting Old Persian into written form. In any event, there is no unambiguous evidence for the existence of the script prior to Darius's time (see Nylander 1967, Hinz 1973: 15–21, Schmitt 1989: 61–62, and Stronach 1990).

The script runs from left to right and, in addition to thirty-six phonetic characters, employs seven ideograms, a set of numerals, and a word divider (TABLE 8.1).

In transcriptions of Old Persian, the letters *v* and *y* stand for the semivowels [w] and [j]; the sound *ç* (< Iranian **θr*) is a sibilant of undetermined quality which corresponds to Modern Persian *s*. Raised characters are sometimes used in transcriptions to represent the sounds left unexpressed by the writing system.

The script contains three vowel signs ᚏᚏ *a*, ᚏᚏ *i*, ᚏᚏ *u*. In word-initial position these indicate the vowels *ă̄, ĭ̄, ŭ̄*, with length unexpressed. In medial position ᚏᚏ *a* indicates that the preceding consonant is followed by *ā*. Medial ᚏᚏ *i*, ᚏᚏ *u* represent *ĭ*, *ŭ*, respectively, although a long *ī* or *ū* is occasionally represented by ᚏᚏᚏ *i-y*, ᚏᚏᚏ *u-v*[a]. Outside of initial position, there is no marker for short *a*, the consonant signs of the *(a)*-series (see below) containing an inherent *a*; since a consonant sign of this series may also be read without a vowel, ambiguity is not uncommon (e.g., ᚆ *b* = [b], [ba]).

TABLE 8.1: *Old Persian Characters*

VOWEL SIGNS		
𒀀 a	𒄿 i	𒌋 u

CONSONANTS WHOSE SHAPE IS INDEPENDENT OF A FOLLOWING VOWEL		
p		č
b		
f	θ	
	s	š
	z	
ç	h	y	l

CONSONANTS WHOSE SHAPE IS GOVERNED BY A FOLLOWING VOWEL		
$C^{(a)}$	C^i	C^u
$d^{(a)}$	d^i	d^u
$m^{(a)}$	m^i	m^u
	$t^{(a-i)}$	t^u
	$n^{(a-i)}$	n^u
	$r^{(a-i)}$	r^u
$k^{(a)}$	—	k^u
$g^{(a)}$	—	g^u
$j^{(a)}$	j^i	—
$v^{(a)}$	v^i	—

IDEOGRAMS		
	xšāyaθiya	'king'
	dahyāuš	'land'
	baga	'god'
	būmiš	'earth'
	A(h)uramazdā	divine name
	„	„
	A(h)uramazdāha	divine name (genitive)

WORD BOUNDARY: ⸜

Consonant signs are of two types. For consonants of the first type (p, b, $č$, f, θ, x, s, z, $š$, $ç$, h, y, l), the following vowel is indicated solely by a vowel sign (𒀀 a, 𒄿 i, 𒌋 u; the absence of a vowel sign = short /a/ or vowellessness): p-a = [pa:]; p-i = [pi(:)]; = [pa], [p]. Each of the remaining consonants (d, m, j, v, k, g, t, n, r) has a different shape depending on the nature of the following vowel. The consonants d and m each have three distinct shapes (e.g. $d^{(a)}$, d^i, d^u), which correlate

TABLE 8.2: *Attested Numerals*

𐏑	‘1’	𐏓	‘10’	𐏔	‘20’	𐏔𐏔	‘40’
𐏒	‘2’	𐏓𐏒	‘12’	𐏔𐏒	‘22’	𐏔𐏔𐏔	‘60’
𐏒𐏒𐏑	‘5’	𐏓𐏒𐏑	‘13’	𐏔𐏒𐏑	‘23’	𐏕𐏔	‘120’
𐏒𐏒𐏒𐏑	‘7’	𐏓𐏒𐏒	‘14’	𐏔𐏒𐏒𐏑	‘25’		
𐏒𐏒𐏒𐏒	‘8’	𐏓𐏒𐏒𐏑	‘15’	𐏔𐏒𐏒𐏒	‘26’		
𐏒𐏒𐏒𐏒𐏑	‘9’	𐏓𐏒𐏒𐏒𐏒	‘18’	𐏔𐏒𐏒𐏒𐏑	‘27’		
		𐏓𐏒𐏒𐏒𐏒𐏑	‘19’				

with the following vowel (*a*/Ø, *i*, *u*, respectively). *T*, *n*, and *r* have two shapes, distinguishing a following *u* from any other vowel (i.e. 𐎬 t^{u} vs. 𐎫 $t^{(a\text{-}i)}$). Similarly, there is only a two-way distinction with *k*, *g*, *j*, *v* (𐎣 $k^{(a)}$, 𐎤 k^{u}; 𐎥 $g^{(a)}$, 𐎦 g^{u}; 𐎩 j^{a}, 𐎪 j^{i}; 𐎺 $v^{(a)}$, 𐎻 v^{i}), although this may be due to the fact that the sequences *ki*, *gi*, *ju*, *vu* are not attested in Old Persian.

The vowel signs are rarely omitted, even when the preceding consonant sign indicates the nature of the vowel—i.e., [di(:)] is spelled 𐎮𐎡 d^{i}-*i*. The vowel signs are also used in diphthongs, which in medial position are thus graphically distinct from pure vowels only when following a consonant capable of marking a distinction in vowel quality—[dai] 𐎭𐎡 $d^{(a)}$-*i* differs from [di] 𐎮𐎡 d^{i}-*i*, but 𐎫𐎡 $t^{(a\text{-}i)}$-*i* represents both [tai] and [ti]—although the vowel sign 𐎠 *a* was infrequently used to distinguish a diphthong from a simple vowel (𐎨𐎡𐏁𐎱(𐎠)𐎡𐏁 *č-i-š-p-(a)-i-š* [ʧiʃpaiʃ]). The long diphthongs *āi*, *āu* contain the vowel sign 𐎠 *a* (𐎠𐎡 *a-i*, 𐎠𐎢 *a-u*). It is not clear why, in word-final position, [i(j)], [u(w)], and the diphthongs were written with an extra semivowel (𐎠𐎿𐎫𐎡𐎹 *a-s-*$t^{(a\text{-}i)}$*-i-y* = *asti(y)* ‘is’, 𐎲𐎠𐎲𐎡𐎼𐎢𐎺 *b-a-b-i-*$r^{(a\text{-}i)}$*-u-*$v^{(a)}$ = *bābirau(v)* ‘in Babylon’).

In syllable-final position, *n* and (before medial stops) *m* are not reflected in the script (𐎣𐎲𐎢𐎪𐎡𐎹 $k^{(a)}$*-b-u-*j^{i}*-i-y-* [kaᵐbuʤija-] ‘Cambyses’). *H* is left unexpressed before *u* (𐎢 *u-* [ʰu-] ‘good-’) and, generally, *m* (𐎠(𐏃)𐎷𐎡𐎹 *a-(h)-*m^{i}*-i-y* [ahmi(y)] ‘am’). With a few exceptions, the vowel 𐎡 *i* is not written immediately after 𐏃 *h*, perhaps indicating a lowering of the vowel in this environment: 𐏃𐏀𐎠𐎴𐎶 *h-z-a-*$n^{(a\text{-}i)}$*-*$m^{(a)}$ ‘tongue (acc.)’ < **hizā-* (Hoffmann 1976: 642–43). Syllabic [r̥] is not graphically distinguished from [ar].

The attested numerals are shown in TABLE 8.2.

SAMPLE OF OLD PERSIAN

1. Old Persian:	𐎰𐎠𐎫𐎡𐎹𐏐	𐎭𐎠𐎼𐎹𐎺𐎢𐏁𐏐	𐎧𐏁𐎠𐎹𐎰𐎡𐎹𐏐
2. Transliteration:	θ-a-ti-i-y .	da-a-ra-y-va-u-š .	x-š-a-y-θ-i-y .
3. Transcription:	θāti	dārayavahuš	xšāyaθiya
4. Gloss:	says	Darius	king

1.	𐎹𐎮𐎡𐎹𐏐	𐎡𐎶𐎠𐎶𐏐	𐎮𐎡𐎱𐎡𐎶𐏐	𐎺𐎡𐎴𐎠𐏃[𐎹𐏐]	𐎡𐎶𐎡𐎺𐎠𐏐
2.	y-di-i-y .	i-ma-a-m .	di-i-p-i-m .	va-i-na-a-h-[y .]	i-ma-i-va-a .
3.	yadi	imām	dipim	vaināhi	imai-vā
4.	if	this	inscription	(you) see	these-or

1.	𐎱𐎫𐎡𐎣𐎼𐎠𐏐	𐎴𐎡𐎹𐎮𐎡𐏁𐏐	𐎻𐎣𐎴𐎠𐏃𐎹𐏐	𐎢𐎫𐎠𐎫𐎡𐎹𐏐
2.	p-ti-i-ka-ra-a .	na-i-y-di-i-š .	vi-ka-na-a-h-y .	u-ta-a-ta-i-y .
3.	patikarā	nai(y)-diš	vikanāhi	utā-tai
4.	sculptures	not-them	(you) destroy	and-to.you

1.	𐎹𐎠𐎺𐎠𐏐	𐎫𐎢𐎶𐎠[𐏐	𐎠𐏃𐎫𐎡𐎹𐏐]	𐎱𐎼𐎡𐎲𐎼𐎠𐏃𐎮𐎡𐏁𐏐
2.	y-a-va-a .	ta-u-ma-a[.	a-h-ti-i-y .]	p-ri-i-b-ra-a-h-di-i-š .
3.	yāvā	taumā	ahati	paribarāhi-diš
4.	as.long.as	strength	(there) be	(you) preserve-them

1.	𐎠𐎢𐎼𐎶𐏀𐎭𐎠𐏐	𐎰𐎢𐎺𐎠𐎶𐏐	𐎭𐎢𐏁𐎫𐎠𐏐	𐎲𐎡𐎹𐎠𐏐
2.	a-u-ra-ma-z-da-a .	θ-u-va-a-m .	da-u-š-ta-a .	b-i-y-a .
3.	ahuramazdā	θuvām	dauštā	biyā
4.	Ahuramazdā	you	friend	may (he) be

'Says Darius, the king: If you look at this inscription or these sculptures, (and) do not destroy them (but), as long as there is strength to you, you care for them, may Ahuramazdā be friendly to you.'

—*Bisitun IV: 72–75, according to the reading of Schmitt 1991: 43–44.*

Bibliography

Hallock, Richard T. 1970. "On the Old Persian Signs." *Journal of Near Eastern Studies* 29: 52–55.

Hinz, Walther. 1973. *Neue Wege im Altpersischen.* (Veröffentlichungen des Sonderforschungsbereiches Orientalistik an der Georg-August-Universität Göttingen, ser. 3, Iranistik, vol. 1). Wiesbaden: Harrassowitz.

Hoffmann, Karl. 1976. "Zur altpersischen Schrift." In his *Aufsätze zur Indoiranistik*, vol. 2, pp. 620–45. Wiesbaden: Reichert.

Kent, Roland G. 1953. *Old Persian: Grammar, Texts, Lexicon.* (American Oriental Series 33) New Haven: American Oriental Society.

Nylander, Carl. 1967. "Who Wrote the Inscriptions at Pasargadae? Achaemenid Problems. III." *Orientalia Suecana* 16: 135–80.

Paper, Herbert H. 1956. "The Old Persian /l/ Phoneme." *Journal of the American Oriental Society* 76: 24–26.

Schmitt, Rüdiger. 1989. "Altpersisch." In *Compendium Linguarum Iranicarum*, ed. Rüdiger Schmitt, pp. 56–85. Wiesbaden: Reichert.

———. 1991. *The Bisitun Inscription of Darius the Great: Old Persian Text* (Corpus Inscriptionum Iranicarum 1/1). London: School of Oriental and African Studies.

Stronach, David. 1990. "On the Genesis of the Old Persian Cuneiform Script." In *Contributions à l'histoire d'Iran: Mélanges offerts à Jean Perrot*, ed. François Vallat, pp. 195–203. Paris: Editions Recherches sur les Civilisations.

Windfuhr, Gernot L. 1970. "Notes on the Old Persian Signs." *Indo-Iranian Journal* 12: 120–25.

Part III: Decipherment

MORE THAN SIX THOUSAND LANGUAGES have been catalogued as spoken in the world today. The most optimistic prediction of survival rates for these languages as living tongues is 50% by the end of the twenty-first century. Not all "language death" results from replacement by the languages of dominant cultures (as has happened many times, for instance, in the Western Hemisphere, with the encroachment of Spanish, Portuguese, French, and English); often, communities have simply dwindled away, or their inhabitants have mingled with the populations of neighboring groups and adopted the language of their new homes.

Another sort of "ecology" of language is the pattern of multilingualism. The United States is quite unusual in this respect. In most of the world, most people are familiar with and regularly use more than one language: people of one village speak somewhat—or very—differently from the people in a neighboring village, yet regularly interact with them; the language of an administrative center can become a de facto standard for a region, and so be used in interactions with bureaucracy and in primary education—writ large, the pattern in Western Europe; regional lingua francas, sometimes spoken natively by no one in a region, help unify nations whose political boundaries do not correspond to ethnic borders, and facilitate communication between neighboring nations; and "metropolitan" languages of former colonial or similar powers, notably the set used as official languages by the United Nations, make possible international commerce and cultural interaction.

There is no reason to suppose that the dual phenomena of great linguistic diversity and pervasive multilingualism, with the attendant passing out of use of numerous tongues, have not obtained throughout the human career. At any moment after the human species had expanded from its original home and begun to spread around the globe, thousands of distinct forms of speech must have been employed—as soon as communities fragment, their languages diverge. And of those thousands, most must be lost forever.

We now enjoy the good fortune that a small number of cultures, or civilizations, since vanished from the earth, have left behind written records of their languages, from which some information can be determined and much else can be deduced.

But—except in the few cases where the writings of long-gone peoples have been maintained in an unbroken tradition, as with Latin, Hebrew, Chinese, and the relative handful of other Classical languages—those written records must be recovered.

Recovery has two aspects: inscriptions must be discovered, and texts must be deciphered. Discovery can be accidental, as with the Rosetta Stone, or deliberate, either by archeological excavation or by illicit prospecting for materials to be sold on the antiquities market (or taken home as souvenirs). The latter sort of discovery makes an item virtually worthless: shorn of its context, an object may be difficult or impossible to identify, and can make little contribution to the understanding of the people who produced it; an inscription, even if the language and script are identifiable, may be all but uninterpretable. Every possible clue must be available to the decipherer.

The decipherment of a newly discovered or perennially mysterious text is the most glamorous aspect of the study of writing systems. Whether two centuries ago or today, decipherment makes headlines. Decipherers are like mathematicians, in that they manipulate pure patterns and combinations. Also like mathematicians, they tend to do their major work when they are young. Cyrus Gordon, himself an investigator of little-known languages, divides all scholars who work on unknown scripts into those who are decipherers and those who aren't, based on whether they can have an original idea, stick to it when it seems to defy conventional wisdom, and abandon preconceptions when necessary. A true decipherer must have all three capacities—although the second and third might seem to exclude each other. Examples of each are easily found in the chronicle of decipherment: An original idea was the notion that Coptic would be useful in reading Egyptian. An unlikely idea held on to was the notion that Ugaritic could have more than one letter for aleph. An abandoned preconception was that Linear B must be Etruscan.

Perhaps popular acclaim yields scholarly disdain: it is surprisingly difficult to find accounts of how a decipherment was accomplished. To be sure, there are lavishly illustrated books with lush photos of the Rosetta Stone and old engravings of the cliff at Behistun; but such volumes rarely reveal the details of a scholar's labors.

Nonetheless, nearly every ancient writing system whose interpretation is taken for granted today had to be read for the first time, and those first readings had to be defended and submitted to scholarly scrutiny, criticism, and refutation or acceptance. The initial publications were of necessity addressed to the tiny community of learned contemporaries who were competent to evaluate them; they are found in scholarly journals of limited circulation, and some of the relevant volumes seem not to have been opened in more than a century. Each generation has an obligation to remember the contributions of its forebears, especially when later generations have allowed the achievements, and even the names, of those forebears to slip into obscurity.

Not all surviving inscriptions have been interpreted, of course; four fairly extensive corpora—Proto-Elamite, Indus, Maya, Easter Island—seem amenable to new approaches that may yet unlock the meanings they held for their users and hold for us.

— PETER T. DANIELS

Methods of Decipherment

PETER T. DANIELS

———

Types of decipherment

In popular usage, whenever Assyriologists or Egyptologists read a cuneiform tablet or a hieroglyphic inscription, they are engaged in deciphering. As a technical term, *decipherment* refers to determining the relation between some writing not hitherto understood and the language it represents. TABLE 9.1 is adapted from the typology of possible decipherments devised by I. J. Gelb (1973: 268 = 1975A: 73 = 1975B: 96, see Gelb's note p. 95).

Type O comprises everyday documents in a familiar language in its ordinary script—as well as phenomena like Punic texts written in Greek letters, or Indian names in Chinese Buddhist compositions, which can present knotty problems for the philologist and must indeed count as deciphering words.

Type IA refers to such decipherments as those of Phoenician and Ugaritic. Both languages were readily identifiable—it was always known that certain inscriptions scattered about Europe and North Africa had been left by the Phoenicians—but it was not obvious that both would be quite similar to Hebrew. Indeed, it probably was less obvious than hindsight suggests that the Ugaritic script concealed a Semitic language, for the first dates provided by the archeologists for the Ugaritic materials—ca. 1500 B.C.E.—were half a millennium earlier than the earliest known Phoenician and Hebrew inscriptions (Harris 1939). The dating has since been adjusted, according to mentions in Ugaritic texts of otherwise known rulers, to ca. 1380–1180 (Yon, Pardee, and Bordreuil 1992), so that they are nearly contemporary with the composition of the earliest Biblical passages (though not with the earliest Hebrew inscriptions).

Type IB designates familiar languages in unknown scripts, including such cases as Linear B (SECTION 7) and Maya glyphs (SECTION 12).

Type II includes two different situations. The first is cryptanalysis, where the identity of the concealed language may be known, but it is written in some fashion

TABLE 9.1: *Typology of Decipherment*

	WRITING	
LANGUAGE	*Known*	*Unknown*
Known	O	IA, IB
Unknown	II	III

devised to confound the reader not in possession of the key. Cryptanalysts, followed by Gelb, distinguish between *codes* and *ciphers*, the former operating at a semantic level, the latter at a phonetic (or, more likely, graphic) level (Kahn 1967: xiv). The other kind of Type II is languages that are pronounceable but unintelligible. The scripts have, if necessary, been deciphered, but the languages need to be *interpreted*. Examples (see SECTION 3, "Other languages" on page 58) include Sumerian and Elamite; Hittite might count as a language that has been successfully interpreted. How these languages were learned is an interesting and useful study, but not an aspect of grammatology.

Type III is where most decipherments start out; they move into one of the other types as inspiration or toil provides the impetus. The most impressive example is the decipherment of Mesopotamian cuneiform.

It might be surmised that the work of deciphering is rather like the work of learning a new language. Superficially, in both cases a speaker of some language is confronted with an alien communication system. But it is interesting to discover that the filling-in of details seems to work the same way in both situations: first the broad concepts are elucidated, then the grammatical details on various levels. Investigation of the parallels could prove enlightening. Voegelin and Voegelin (1963) note several times that decipherers were often keen polyglots. Their article applies a number of novel concepts to the study of decipherment, including their script typology discussed in SECTION 1. Unfortunately for information on decipherment they rely almost exclusively on Doblhofer 1961, a breezy, biographically oriented narrative that perpetuates a number of errors.

Processes in decipherment

It might seem unnecessary at the present time to stress that the single most important requisite for a decipherment is *accurate copies* of the inscriptions under study. Nowadays, photography is at everyone's fingertips, but during the quarter millennium after 1600, when scientific study of antiquities captured the imagination of Europe, only the artist's eye and hand could record the materials, and their publication involved the additional step of having the drawing reproduced by an engraver or (later) a lithographer. The process was subjective, and wildly divergent renditions of the same inscription could be offered (see examples in Daniels 1988).

A preliminary step in deciphering an unknown script is compiling a *catalog* of all the apparently different characters that occur in the texts, and attempting to identify the permissible variations each character may undergo. The *number* of different characters can be a clue to the type of script involved. A small number, around 30, suggests an abjad or an alphabet; greater variety, 100 or so, suggests a syllabary or an abugida; and several hundred or more, a logosyllabary (or a logography—though no purely logographic script, if such has ever truly existed, has been deciphered).

On the borderline between decipherment and normal philological study are cases where a seemingly unreadable script, on careful examination of the catalog of characters, proves to be a *variety* of some known script. This has happened with several descendants of the Semitic script.

Nearly all successful decipherments have involved a language that was *familiar*, or very like a known language. Since language isolates such as Sumerian and Etruscan are preserved in scripts that can already be read, they are available for interpretation; but the pseudo-hieroglyphs of Byblos, for instance (SECTION 2), will probably not be deciphered unless further materials turn up.

Helpful in determining the possible identity of the unknown language is *distributional analysis*: do certain signs occur frequently at the beginnings or ends of words? Are there patterns of substitution, suggesting patterns of grammatical inflection?

The must useful stretches of language for pursuing decipherments have proven to be *proper names*. These tend to be familiar from historical accounts preserved by neighboring peoples with whom the unknowns interacted.

The most useful tool overall, though, is a *bilingual* inscription. It sometimes happened that ancient monarchs would post accounts of their mighty deeds, or dedicatory inscriptions, or other important matters in the language of imperial administration as well as in local languages. When texts of similar length in different scripts are inscribed together, it is usually safe to assume they express the same content. If one of the parallel versions can be read, the content of the other can be deduced, along with its form of expression.

Unfortunately, readable bilinguals are not terribly common. Most often, texts occur in just one language; rarely, inscriptions will turn up with parallel texts that are written in more than one unknown script. In these cases, the ingenuity of the scholar is called upon to discover some external linguistic object that might plausibly be represented in the unreadable text. Such a surmised parallel may be called a *virtual bilingual*. Poor choice of a virtual bilingual is what most commonly dooms a failed decipherment—yet it is uncommonly difficult to decouple an unsuccessful decipherer from a false virtual bilingual.

Accounts of decipherment

Several books on decipherment can be recommended—in increasing detail, Friedrich 1957, Gordon 1982, and Pope 1975—though none is ideal (their accounts of the decipherment of Mesopotamian cuneiform are incomplete). Friedrich's English version has been reprinted without taking into account the revised German edition, so it does not cover Linear B. Gordon's is an enticingly personal account; the 1982 edition largely replaces the discussion of his eastern Mediterranean work with a discussion of (the interpretation of) Eblaite. Pope's is well illustrated and includes a number of references to primary sources. See Daniels 1995 for a general overview. Deuel 1965 is a popular, but reliable, narrative of the recovery of (primarily) manuscripts.

TABLE 9.2: *Publications and Accounts of Decipherments and Interpretations*

Script	Original Work	Description
LOGOSYLLABARIES		
Egyptian (Hieroglyphic, Demotic)	Young 1818; Champollion 1822, 1828; Lepsius 1837; Hincks 1846B, 1859	Ray 1990/91, Davies 1987
Cuneiform		
Elamite	Westergaard 1844A, 1844B; Hincks 1846A; Norris 1852; Sayce 1874	
Mesopotamian	Hincks 1846C, 1847, 1849, 1850, 1852, 1853, 1863; Rawlinson 1850, 1851, 1851; "Comparative Translations" 1857	Fossey 1904, Rogers 1916, Daniels 1994
Urartian	Hincks 1848, Sayce 1880B	
Sumerian	Hincks 1850, 1856; Haupt 1878	Weissbach 1898, Cooper 1991
Hittite	Hrozný 1915	
Luvian	Sayce 1880A, 1903–4, 1907; Gelb 1931, 1935, 1942; Forrer 1932; Meriggi 1937; Hawkins, Morpurgo-Davies, and Neumann 1974	
Maya	Knorosov 1952, 1963; Berlin 1958; Proskouriakoff 1960; Lounsbury 1973	Lounsbury 1989
SYLLABARIES		
Old Persian	Grotefend 1802, 1817; Burnouf 1836; Lassen 1836; Hincks 1846A; Rawlinson 1846	
Cypriote	Smith 1871, Schmidt 1874	
Linear B	Kober 1945, Ventris 1951–52	Chadwick 1967, 1973, 1987
ABJADS		
Palmyrene	Barthélemy 1759; Swinton 1755	Daniels 1988
Phoenician	Barthélemy 1764	
Imperial Aramaic	Berthélemy 1768	
Sassanian	Silvestre de Sacy 1787–91	
Himyaritic	Rödiger 1837, 1841, 1842; Gesenius 1841A, 1841B	Hommel 1893, Daniels 1986
Nabatean (Sinaitic)	Beer 1840	
Ugaritic	Virolleaud 1929, 1931; Bauer 1930, 1932; Dhorme 1930; Friedrich 1933	Corré 1966
ALPHABETS		
Avestan	Burnouf 1833	
Orkhon runes	Thomsen 1893, 1894	
Meroitic	Griffith 1909, 1911	
ABUGIDAS		
Brahmi	Prinsep 1834, 1837	Hoernle 1884, Daniels 1987
Kharoshthi	Prinsep 1838	

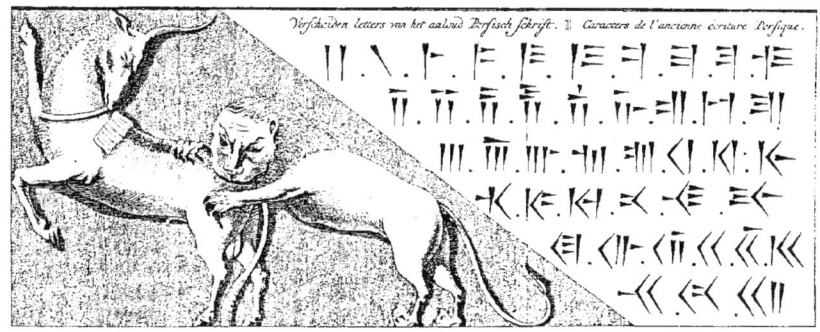

FIGURE 7. The inventory of Old Persian characters, as identified by Niebuhr; cf. TABLE 8.1
(1778, pl. 23; retouched in the French edition of 1780).

The best-known decipherments are those of Old Persian cuneiform, Egyptian hieroglyphs, and Linear B, and they are described well in the books just mentioned, as well as elsewhere. A number of other decipherments are equally interesting, and many have never been brought to general attention. Some are presented here chronologically; TABLE 9.2 (which see for all references) is organized by script family.

In chronicling decipherment, it is common to list the characters that each investigator "got right." This is a meaningless exercise—because at every stage, the decipherment had to stand or fall as a whole. Subsequent researchers could not know a priori which of the values were reliable and which should be rejected; only the full coherence of the system and of the underlying language—founded on demonstrable, replicable method—is probative of a decipherment.

Palmyrene

The first decipherment exemplifies many of the principles and processes enumerated above. "Copies" of Palmyrene script had been available in print since 1616; but not until 1756, when English travelers published accurate copies of paired inscriptions in Greek and Palmyrene, could the script be deciphered. Accounts by various Church Fathers had mentioned that the Palmyrene language was similar to Syriac. The first word in one of the inscriptions is the name *Septimios*, and literally overnight the Abbé Jean-Jacques Barthélemy (1716–1795) was able to match the Palmyrene letters with the Greek (as well as to discover that they were recognizably similar to both Hebrew and Syriac, see TABLE 5.5 on page 97, col. XVIII).

Cuneiform

The first decent copies of trilingual—Old Persian, Elamite, and a late, odd form of Akkadian—cuneiform inscriptions from the awesome ruins of Persepolis were published by Carsten Niebuhr in 1772–78, who also set out the characters of the Old Persian script (FIGURE 7; cf. SECTION 8). Expecting that inscriptions from Persepolis

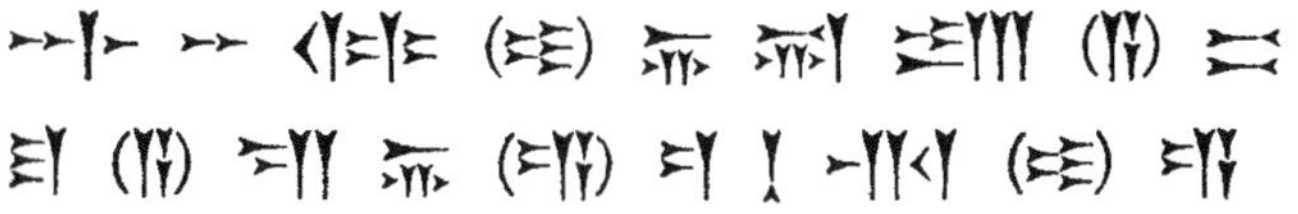

FIGURE 8. Hincks's summary of the formulary introducing the annals of Argishti (1848: 388).
The passage is now read ᵈḪal-di(-i)-ni u-ta(-a)-bi ma(-a)-si-ni(-e) GIŠ-šu-ri(-i)-e
'the god Haldi set out with his own weapons' (interpretation prepared by G. Gragg).

would include Persian rulers' names (known in Greek guise from Herodotus), and familiar with Silvestre de Sacy's recent reading of the formulary of Sassanian inscriptions (SECTION 48), Georg Friedrich Grotefend (1775–1853), in what seems to be the first use of a virtual bilingual, supposed that the names would appear in the style "Darius, great king, son of Xerxes, great king, son of Hystaspes"—who was not a king. There is sufficient repetition of sounds among the names that Grotefend could be fairly sure he was on the right track, and he identified the language as Persian. The Iranists Rasmus Rask, Eugène Burnouf, and Christian Lassen contributed significantly to the rigor of the description of the language in its Iranian context.

An important contribution to the study of cuneiform was Henry Creswicke Rawlinson's copying and eventual publication of what is by far the longest trilingual cuneiform inscription, incised over several years during the reign of Darius the Great on an inaccessible cliff at Behistun, Iran. Rawlinson (1810–1895), then a British Army major stationed in Baghdad, apparently replicated Grotefend's decipherment after learning of the virtual bilingual (he could not read German). But the frequently repeated assertion that Rawlinson deciphered Mesopotamian cuneiform is incorrect; the third version of the Behistun inscription was even published too late to play any part in the decipherment. What is telling is that he was never able, in after years, to describe his process of "deciphering" the scripts. Much of what he published was derived from work he was kept abreast of, via an efficient postal service, that was laboriously carried out by a self-effacing Irish cleric, Edward Hincks.

Hincks (1792–1866) was already middle-aged when he turned from his main interest, Egyptian, to cuneiform—he expected it would shed light on the Hieroglyphic texts; between 1846 and 1852 he produced a series of significant monographs. Successively, he demonstrated that the Old Persian script was (semi-)syllabic rather than strictly consonantal; that the second and third versions were written with respectively less and more elaborate inventories of the same signary; that the rather different-looking cuneiform scripts on objects brought from Babylonia and Assyria were in fact equivalent (thus greatly augmenting the materials available for analysis); that Mesopotamian cuneiform, though it probably represented (in the third version) a Semitic language, combined syllabic and logographic but not consonantal elements; that most or all of the signs had more than one phonetic reading, probably because the script had been devised for a non-Semitic language; that most or all of the signs had logographic as well as phonetic readings; and that Biblical personages were named in the Assyrian records.

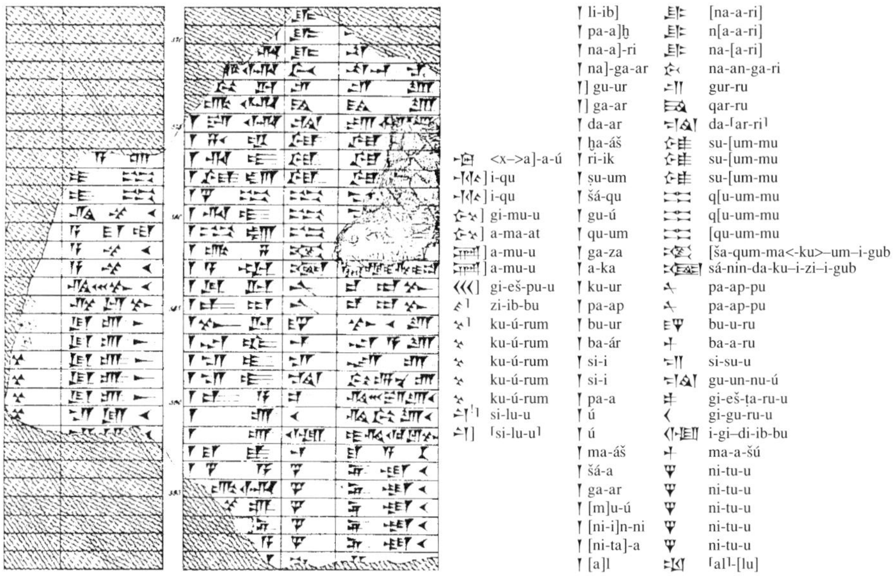

	li-ib]		[na-a-ri]
	pa-a]ḫ		n[a-a-ri]
	na-a]-ri		na-[a-ri]
	na]-ga-ar		na-an-ga-ri
	gu-ar		gur-ru
	ga-ar		qar-ru
	da-ar		da-[ar-ri]
	ḫa-áš		su-[um-mu]
	<x->a]-a-ú	ri-ik	su-[um-mu]
	i-qu	su-um	su-[um-mu]
	i-qu	šá-qu	q[u-um-mu]
	gi-mu-u	gu-ú	q[u-um-mu]
	a-ma-at	qu-um	[qu-um-mu]
	a-mu-u	ga-za	[ša-qum-ma<-ku>—um–i-gub
	a-mu-u	a-ka	sá-nin-da-ku–i-zi–i-gub
	gi-eš-pu-u	ku-ur	pa-ap-pu
	zi-ib-bu	pa-ap	pa-ap-pu
	ku-ú-rum	bu-ur	bu-u-ru
	ku-ú-rum	ba-ár	ba-a-ru
	ku-ú-rum	si-i	si-su-u
	ku-ú-rum	si-i	gu-un-nu-ú
	si-lu-u	pa-a	gi-eš-ṭa-ru-u
	[si-lu-u]	ú	gi-gu-ru-u
		ú	i-gi–di-ib-bu
		ma-áš	ma-a-šú
		šá-a	ni-tu-u
		ga-ar	ni-tu-u
		[m]u-ú	ni-tu-u
		[ni-i]n-ni	ni-tu-u
		[ni-ta]-a	ni-tu-u
		[a]l	[al]-[lu]

FIGURE 9. K.62, the fragment of Syllabary A identified by Hincks; from its first publication (Rawlinson and Norris 1866, pl. 3; cf. TABLE 3.2 on page 49, lines 164–71, 120–39). Transliteration from Hallock 1955, lines 309–22, 230–60 (that the later column is at the left shows that this fragment is from the reverse of a tablet).

Hincks's initial approach to the second and third versions was through the personal and place names revealed in the first version, but he soon turned to the grammatical patterning that he could transfer from known Semitic languages. The most important of his articles, though, is probably that of 1848, published in the prestigious *Journal of the Royal Asiatic Society,* which deals not with Akkadian, but with Urartian. He had just received a copy of the inscriptions from near Lake Van, collected at the price of his life by Fr. Ed. Schultz in the late 1820s and published in Paris in 1840. The most extensive inscription is a royal annal, covering some thirteen years, in which each year's account begins with the same formula. Hincks noted that the formulaic repetition is not exact: certain signs seemed to be omissible (FIGURE 8) as, apparently, required by the space available on the surface where the inscription was carved. He rightly took these to be optional vowel signs; since he already knew some of their values from the Persepolis trilinguals, he could identify the vowel inherent in each preceding CV sign. Grammatical investigation of the Urartian language (which he believed was Indo-European) resulted in a tolerably full signlist, with values from Assyrian and Babylonian as well as Urartian sources. Hincks also brought an end (in 1852) to the decipherment phase of Assyriology, by correctly interpreting the first of thousands of fragments of lists of signs that give their pronunciations (it was, in fact, a portion of Syllabary A, FIGURE 9). He went on to publish grammatical studies of Assyrian, as well as articles on a wide variety of Egyptian and Assyrian topics.

M. *SPECIMENS OF PHRASES. ROS. INSCR. LAST LINE.*

FIGURE 10. Young's comparison of the three versions of a Rosetta Stone passage (1818, pl. 78).

Egyptian

Thanks to misunderstandings on the part of various Greek and Roman authors, it was believed until the European Enlightenment that the hieroglyphs of Egypt were esoteric signs concealing sacred mysteries. An English polymath, Thomas Young (1773–1829), and a French monomaniac, Jean-François Champollion (1790–1832), share the credit for determining that the ancient Egyptian language was written with scripts very like other scripts. Both held that Coptic, the liturgical language of Egyptian Christians, would reflect the ancient language. The impetus for their decipherment was the discovery by Napoleon's army, in 1799 near Rashid (Rosetta), Egypt, of a large chunk of basalt bearing a long inscription in three scripts—Hieroglyphic, Demotic, and Greek. The Greek inscription was easily read, and it was immediately recognized that here lay the key to the mysterious hieroglyphs. (Its importance was such that in 1802 it was made part of the booty upon a British victory, and it has remained in the British Museum ever since.) Unfortunately, only seven Hieroglyphic lines were preserved, versus nearly all of the Demotic and Greek passages.

Decades earlier, Barthélemy had suggested that the cartouches observed in Hieroglyphic inscriptions might enclose royal names (cf. TABLE 4.4 on page 79). This could now be seen to be the case; unfortunately, the preserved portions of the Hieroglyphic version contain only cartouches corresponding to the name *Ptolemy* in the Greek, so any guesses about the values of signs comprising it could not be confirmed.

Young, therefore, turned to the Demotic passage, and began by identifying a number of stretches of text—*Alexander, Alexandria, and, king, Ptolemy, Egypt*—with their counterparts in the Greek; he also noted that some of the Demotic signs related in shape to correspondingly situated hieroglyphs (FIGURE 10). But he had no way of determining their pronunciation, and indeed continued to believe that the script was primarily semasiographic, and phonographic only when representing names. Budge's discussion of Young (1929: 198–216) is more responsible than his presentation of the decipherment of cuneiform as Rawlinson's work (1925); in both books, his chief purpose seems to be to promote the claims of English over French scholars.

Champollion may well have known of Young's work, but took it immeasurably further. The name of *Cleopatra* turned up on a bilingually inscribed obelisk brought to England in 1813, and there was enough overlap of letters with *Ptolemy* to confirm the values of many signs. Other names could be brought into play, and when a sun-shaped sign (Coptic *rē*) appeared in a cartouche before an unknown sign and two *s*'s,

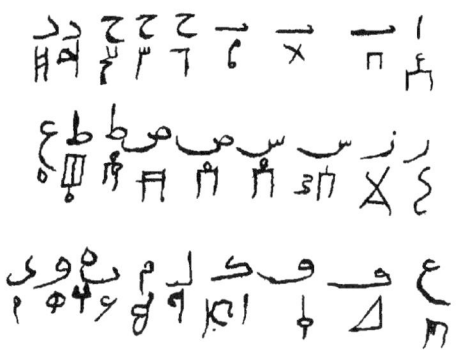 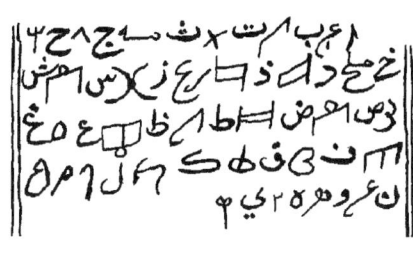

FIGURE 11. Supposed Himyaritic alphabets found in two unrelated manuscripts in the Königliche Bibliothek, Berlin (*left,* ms. 110, Arabic, written in Arabia, dated 856 A.H./1452 C.E.; *right,* ms. 248, Persian, written in India, early 18th century). Arabic key and South Arabian letters (*right to left*):

ا ب ت ث ج ح خ د ذ ر ز س ش ص ض ط ظ ع غ ف ق ك ل م ن ه و ي

𐩠 𐩡 𐩢 𐩣 𐩤 𐩥 𐩦 𐩧 𐩨 𐩩 𐩪 𐩫 𐩬 𐩭 𐩮 𐩯 𐩰 𐩱 𐩲 𐩳 𐩴 𐩵 𐩶 𐩷

(Rödiger 1837, plate).

Champollion recognized the well-known name *Ramesses.* He then had the courage to defy the common wisdom that hieroglyphs couldn't be phonetic, and tried to read Coptic—in which he had immersed himself from boyhood—in the hieroglyphs to which he could assign phonetic values.

Thus many of the principles of decipherment came into play in the Egyptian case: bilinguals, familiar language, proper names, flash of insight all featured in Champollion's work. He died young; it fell to Richard Lepsius to discover that signs could contain more than one consonant, and to Edward Hincks to show that they could not contain any vowels.

Himyaritic

Again two rivals competed to decipher inscriptions found in southern Arabia, again as a result of British operations overseas. Wilhelm Gesenius (1786–1842) was the greatest Hebraist of his age—updated editions of his grammar and dictionary remain the standard today—and Emil Rödiger (1801–1874) was his most distinguished pupil (and editor of the first posthumous versions of those two works). Several Islamic manuscripts record alphabets of various alleged infidels; these were often fanciful, but Rödiger found two tolerably similar ones, both said to represent the writing of South Arabian peoples, that apparently derived from independent traditions (FIGURE 11). He relied on these, and on his enormous command of Semitic philology, to interpret the inscriptions; Gesenius put more faith in a newly reported Semitic language from the same area. Both made important contributions to the decipherment of the inscriptions, but they are particularly obscure and difficult—it turns out that the first sizable text contained almost nothing but proper names, names not familiar from other sources and not accompanied by a version in another script.

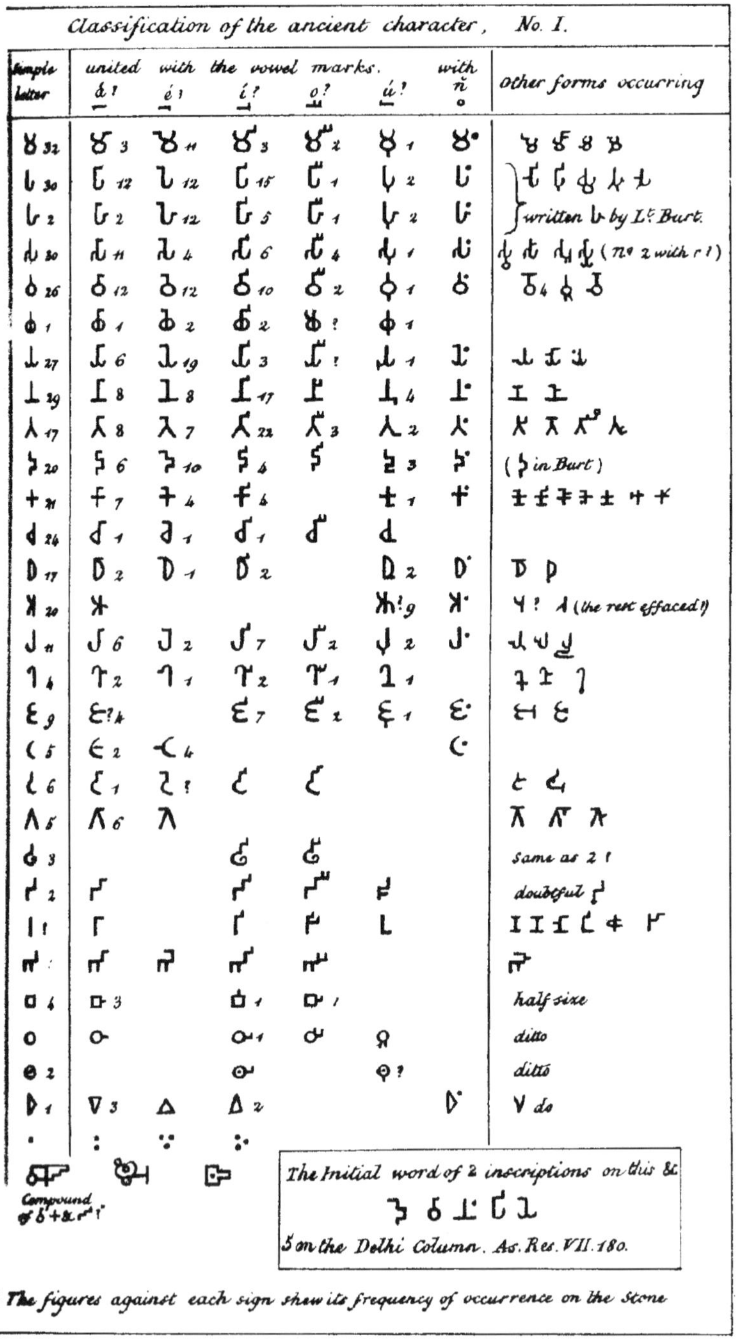

FIGURE 12. Prinsep's chart of the Brahmi characters found on the Allahabad pillar (1834, pl. 5).

Brahmi

The Brahmi script of Ashokan India (SECTION 30) is another that was deciphered largely on the basis of familiar language and familiar related script—but it was made possible largely because of the industry of young James Prinsep (1799–1840), who inventoried the characters found on the immense pillars left by Ashoka and arranged them in a pattern like that used for teaching the Ethiopian abugida (FIGURE 12). Apparently, there had never been a tradition of laying out the full set of aksharas thus—or anyone, Prinsep said, with a better knowledge of Sanskrit than he had had could have read the inscriptions straightaway, instead of after discovering a very minor virtual bilingual a few years later.

Cypriote

Barthélemy deciphered Phoenician on the basis of bilingual coin legends in the 1760s. That language repaid its debt by in turn serving as the key to the Cypriote syllabary (TABLE 7.3), thanks to the bilingual from Idalion (page 131) discovered in 1869. It was an Assyriologist—a protégé of Rawlinson, George Smith (1840–1876)—who determined that the script was syllabic, and a specialist in Greek, Moriz Schmidt, who proved that the language was Greek. He searched for signs that could represent each of the necessary consonants with each of the five vowels, thus using the property of a syllabary as a tool.

Turkic runes

With the simultaneous publication of reliable editions of bilingual inscriptions—two of them major—in Chinese and the vaguely known script found by the Orkhon River near Karakorum, Mongolia, it became possible for Vilhelm Thomsen (1842–1927) to decipher the latter. The first problem was to determine the unusual layout of the lines of writing—right to left, and bottom to top; except that on the bilinguals, the script ran vertically, with the columns reading top to bottom, taken right to left like Chinese. The second problem was that it was clear from the number of words in the two versions that one was not a translation of the other. The number of different characters was 38 (see TABLE 49.1), suggesting a syllabary or a script representing subphonemic distinctions. Thomsen began by identifying the vowel letters: in a pattern xyx, if x is a consonant, then y is a vowel, and vice versa; it is very unlikely that x and y are both consonants or both vowels. Three vowel letters, ⟩ u, Γ i, Ν $ü$, were thus isolated. The small number of vowels coupled with the large number of consonants suggested that the script was expressing vowel harmony (within a word, all vowels must belong to one of two classes, $a/y/o/ö$ or $ä/i/u/ü$) by varying the accompanying consonant.

Unable to use the sense of the Chinese inscriptions in interpreting the Orkhon, Thomsen searched for words that could serve as virtual bilinguals. The most common word in both inscriptions, he surmised, represented part of the royal titulary, ᚱᛏᚌᚼ *tengri* 'heaven, god', which is common to Mongolian and all of Turkic. There was one word that occurred frequently in one of the inscriptions, but not the other; Thomsen identified this with the name of the person honored by the Chinese version, *K'iueh-ti(k)-k'in* = ᚅᛂᚱᚻᚤᛁᚤ *Köl-tigin*. This gave him another common word, ᚱᛏᚤᚼ *türk* 'Turk', confirming the nature of the language. He filled in the known letters as in an acrostic, recognized more and more Turkic words (the fourth vowel letter, ᚤ *a*, occurred only finally), and eventually could read these inscriptions as well as others.

Meroitic

Meroitic inscriptions were observed by explorers in Nubia and the Sudan from about 1820, primarily Richard Lepsius's expedition of 1843–44. Lepsius noted some equations between Egyptian and Meroitic cartouches, which were to provide the first few phonetic values of the characters. F. Ll. Griffith's study of the materials began with compiling the list of 23 letters (see TABLE 4.6 on page 85); he was able to establish the equivalences between the hieroglyphic and demotic forms (he shuns the term "cursive" because except for ᛘ *i* the letters are not joined) thanks to the very formulaic content of the many funerary inscriptions, written now in one, now in the other script. Positional analysis followed: Griffith found that ᛋᛉoccurred only initially; ᛋ, ⁄, and ᛘ did not occur before or after each other, or after ᛗ, ᚾ, ᚸ, or ᛢ. The first four signs would seem to be vowels, and the last four—in a rather surprising suggestion—CV syllables. From a list of the names of places where inscriptions were found, and from other likely equations with names and titles known from Egyptian and Greek accounts of Nubian civilization, Griffith determined the value of each letter.

Luvian

The pioneer in interpreting Luvian hieroglyphs was the immensely prolific Archibald H. Sayce (1845–1933)—he seems to have intuited that they represented the distinctive product of Hittite civilization—but sufficient materials were never available to him. Among the several contributors to the decipherment, the most explicit as to method was I. J. Gelb (1907–1985). From Sayce, he knew the determinatives, the word divider, and the indicator of logograms (see SECTION 6). Like decipherers before him, he gathered the words accompanied by the COUNTRY determinative from inscriptions found at places whose ancient names were known, he insisted that the signs were strictly syllabic, and he isolated the vowel signs by finding that they were optional. He made judicious use of personal names and of the few bilinguals; and he analyzed the grammar with full knowledge of Hittite (which Bedřich Hrozný had recognized as Indo-European in 1915). Gelb found that the languages were not identical, and accepted Johannes Friedrich's identification of the hieroglyphic language with cuneiform Luvian. Other scholars have further refined the decipherment.

Ugaritic

The three scholars who worked on Ugaritic (SECTION 5), language of a large corpus of texts originally found by accident at a site on the Syrian coast, chose different virtual bilinguals. The excavator, Charles Virolleaud (1879–1968), noted that an inscription on certain adzes was also found at the beginning of a clay tablet, with one additional sign preceding it; he suggested that the tablet was a message to the owner of the adzes, and the extra sign was the prefix *l-* 'to' in Semitic. On what seemed to be an accounts tablet, he found a word of the pattern (rare in Semitic) *?l?*; this had to be 'three' (Hebrew *šlš*, Arabic *ṯlṯ*). Hans Bauer (1878–1937) isolated the letters that seemed to be prefixes and suffixes, and assigned them to the limited number of sounds that are used as such in Semitic (*l, m, n, t*). Édouard Dhorme (1881–1966) worked along similar lines, and there was exemplary cooperation among the three.

The most unusual feature of Ugaritic is that all the letters represent consonants, except for the three that represent *ʾ* [ʔ] plus each of the vowels (transliterated *ȧ, i̇, u̇*). Bauer, confronted by irrefutable evidence that two different letters had to stand for *ʾ*, even though this was unparalleled in Semitic, declared that indeed they did—and Virolleaud soon added a third. Bauer tried to differentiate the three alephs according to the following vowel, but he had worked out an account of Hebrew vocalization involving different stages of the language, and within that framework he could not get the vowels to come out right. It was Johannes Friedrich who explained them correctly. (Bauer did not dispute the solution, but he did not publish the second volume of his monumental Hebrew grammar, Bauer and Leander 1918–22, perhaps because he would have had to reconceptualize so much of the undocumented history of the language.)

Linear B

As has been described in SECTION 2, the Aegean scripts fascinated generations of scholars, who were unable to succeed in reading them. As soon as sufficient materials were adequately published, Alice Kober (1907–1950) undertook distributional analysis, finding words that were identical but for the last sign or two; she took these to represent inflections. Her untimely death left the field to Michael Ventris (1922–1956), who built on her work, constructing charts of mutually substitutable signs, setting presumed consonants against presumed vowels. (Barber 1974 is—without saying so, and without a single actual example—a mathematical generalization of the Kober–Ventris technique.) In a now familiar pattern, he matched place names with inscriptions found at particular sites. Yet just as for his predecessors, work was hampered for Ventris by inability to suppose that some form of Greek could have been spoken centuries before the earliest remains of the Classical era. On a whim, he said, he tried reading the texts as an archaic form of Greek—and knew immediate success.

Maya

The decipherment of Maya glyphs has proceeded in two separate phases. The interpretation of the numerical, astronomical, and calendrical information included on the monuments was the work of the nineteenth century, and belongs more to the history of mathematics than to the history of decipherment. Primary credit is assigned to Ernst Förstemann (1822–1906; Thompson 1971: 29–30), whose work was based on the few surviving pre-Conquest astronomical codices.

Though virtually all knowledge of Maya script was extirpated by the Conquistadores, along with those who commanded such knowledge, there was one Spanish bishop, Diego de Landa, who took an interest in the dying civilization. Among the data he recorded from the few surviving intellectuals was what he called the "alphabet" of the Maya glyphs. His work, though, went unknown until 1864, and meanwhile Americanists, like Europeans faced with Egyptian hieroglyphs, convinced themselves that the impossibly ornate glyphs could be at best an ideography, and despaired of ever understanding it.

Over the decades, order was brought to the overwhelming variation in sign appearance, and equivalences established between completely different signs (various items could be expressed by distinctive heads, or by full-square glyphs, or by appendages to glyphs, for instance). This kind of information was codified in the works of J. Eric S. Thompson (1898–1975). It fell to a Soviet linguist, Yuri Knorosov (who became aware of Maya literature when he rescued a sumptuous edition of the surviving codices from the ruins of a burning Berlin library in 1945), to take seriously Bishop Landa's "alphabet." Knorosov tried reading some words as (modern) Mayan using the handful of values Landa assigned to glyphs, comparing them with pictures in the codices, and the results were encouraging enough to convince some scholars (though never Thompson) that actual language might be concealed in the Maya inscriptions.

The next step was taken by Heinrich Berlin (1915–1987), who discovered that particular "emblem glyphs" are associated with specific sites; when a different site's emblem glyph turns up in an inscription, presumably some sort of interaction between the places is described. About the same time, Tatiana Proskouriakoff (1909–1985) discovered that certain inscriptions bore dates that did not obviously relate to astronomical cycles, and she noted that they often occurred in triplets, spaced suitably to number birth, coronation, and death of a ruler. These discoveries constituted the first evidence that the monuments could concern mundane as well as celestial events.

Finally, it is the linguist Floyd Lounsbury who has led in linguistic interpretation of the glyphs as syllabic and logographic. It is difficult to point to a single breakthrough article; he tends to publish in great detail on a single glyph or group of glyphs at a time. This is the pattern of progress in Maya research, to which numerous scholars continue to contribute. (Coe 1992, though useful for certain historical information, cannot be recommended as an account of the decipherment, since it omits essential details of methodology, and is marred by a pervasive, inexplicably personal animosity toward Thompson.)

Even from this brief summary of the ongoing decipherment of Mayan, several techniques that are by now recognizable from previous decipherments are apparent—familiar languages, place names, combinatorial analysis, willingness to renounce preconceptions and to embrace unlikely propositions. One can only wonder whether, had the methods of other decipherers been familiar to Mayanists, they might not have achieved far more in a far shorter time. Within the neglected study of writing systems, the study of decipherment has been attended to the least.

Bibliography

Barber, Elizabeth J. W. 1974. *Archaeological Decipherment: A Handbook.* Princeton, N.J.: Princeton University Press.

Barthélemy, Jean-Jacques. 1759. "Réflexions sur l'alphabet et sur la langue dont on se servoit autrefois à Palmyre." *Mémoires de l'Académie des Inscriptions et Belles Lettres* 26: 577–97.

———. 1764. "Réflexions sur quelques monuments phéniciens, et sur les alphabets qui en résultent." *Mémoires de l'Académie des Inscriptions et Belles Lettres* 30: 405–26.

———. 1768. "Explication d'un bas-relief égyptien, et de l'inscription phénicienne qui l'accompagne." *Mémoires de l'Académie des Inscriptions et Belles Lettres* 32: 725–38.

Bauer, Hans. 1930. *Entzifferung der Keilschrifttafeln von Ras Schamra.* Halle/Saale: Niemeyer.

———. 1932. *Das Alphabet von Ras Schamra: Seine Entzifferung und seine Gestalt.* Halle/Saale: Niemeyer.

Bauer, Hans, and Pontus Leander. 1918–22. *Historische Grammatik der hebräischen Sprache des Alten Testaments.* Halle/Saale: Niemeyer. Repr. Hildesheim: Olms, 1962.

Beer, E. F. F. 1840. *Inscriptiones veteres litteris et lingua hucusque incognitis ad montem Sinai magno mumero servatae ....* Leipzig: Barth.

Berlin, Heinrich. 1958. "El glifo 'emblema' en las inscripciones mayas." *Journal de la Société des Américanistes* 47: 111–19.

Budge, E. A. Wallis. 1925. *The Rise and Progress of Assyriology.* London: Martin Hopkinson.

———. 1929. *The Rosetta Stone ....* London: The Religious Tract Society. Repr. New York: Dover, 1989.

Burnouf, Eugène. 1833. *Commentaire sur le Yaçna.* Paris: Imprimerie Royale.

———. 1836. *Mémoire sur deux Inscriptions cunéiformes trouvées près d'Hamadan.* Paris: Imprimerie Royale.

Chadwick, John. 1967. *The Decipherment of Linear B,* 2nd ed. Cambridge: Cambridge University Press.

———. 1973. "Linear B." In *Current Trends in Linguistics,* vol. 11, *Diachronic, Areal, and Typological Linguistics,* ed. Thomas A. Sebeok, pp. 537–68. The Hague: Mouton.

———. 1987. *Linear B and Related Scripts* (Reading the Past). London: British Museum; Berkeley and Los Angeles: University of California Press.

Champollion, Jean-François. 1822. *Lettre à M. Dacier.* Repr. in Champollion 1828: 41–89.

———. 1828. *Précis du système hiéroglyphique des anciens Égyptiens,* 2nd ed. Paris: Imprimerie Royale (1st ed., 1825).

"Comparative Translations, by W. H. Fox Talbot, Esq., F.R.S., The Reverend E. Hincks, D.D., Dr. Oppert, and Lieut.-Col. Sir Henry C. Rawlinson, K.C.B., of the Inscription of Tiglath Pileser I." 1857. *Journal of the Royal Asiatic Society* 18: 150–220.

Coe, Michael D. 1992. *Breaking the Maya Code.* New York: Thames and Hudson.

Cooper, Jerrold S. 1991. "Posing the Sumerian Question: Race and Scholarship in the Early History of Assyriology." *Aula Orientalis* 9: 47–66.

Corré, Alan D. 1966. "Anatomy of a Decipherment." *Proceedings of the Wisconsin Academy of Sciences, Arts and Letters* 55: 11–20.

Daniels, Peter T. 1986. "'To Prove Him with Hard Questions': The Decipherment of Himyaritic." Paper presented at the North American Conference on Afroasiatic Linguistics, New Haven. Appendix 1 of Daniels TO APPEAR.

———. 1987. "'To Be Engraved on Rocks … To Be Engraved on Stone Pillars': The Decipherment of Brahmi." Paper presented at the annual meeting of the American Oriental Society, Los Angeles. Appendix 2 of Daniels TO APPEAR.

———. 1988. "'Shewing of Hard Sentences and Dissolving of Doubts': The First Decipherment." *Journal of the American Oriental Society* 108: 419–36.

———. 1994. "Edward Hincks's Decipherment of Mesopotamian Cuneiform." In *The Edward Hincks Bicentenary Lectures,* ed. Kevin J. Cathcart, pp. 30–57. Dublin: University College, Department of Near Eastern Languages.

———. 1995. "The Decipherments of Near Eastern Scripts." In *Civilizations of the Ancient Near East,* ed. Jack M. Sasson et al., vol. 1, pp. 81–93. New York: Scribners.

———. TO APPEAR. "How to Decipher a Script." In *Writing/Écriture* (La Pensée Linguistique), ed. Pierre Swiggers and Willy Van Hoecke. Louvain: Peeters.

Davies, W. V. 1987. *Egyptian Hieroglyphs* (Reading the Past). London: British Museum; Berkeley and Los Angeles: University of California Press.

Deuel, Leo. 1965. *Testaments of Time: The Search for Lost Manuscripts and Records.* New York: Knopf.

Dhorme, Édouard. 1930. "Un nouvel alphabet sémitique." *Revue biblique* 39: 571–77.

Doblhofer, Ernst. 1961. *Voices in Stone: The Decipherment of Ancient Scripts and Writings.* London: Souvenir Press. (German orig., 1957.)

Forrer, Emil. 1932. *Die hethitische Bilderschrift* (Studies in Ancient Oriental Civilization 3). Chicago: University of Chicago Press.

Fossey, Charles. 1904. *Manuel d'assyriologie,* vol. 1. Paris: Leroux.

Friedrich, Johannes. 1933. "Zu den drei Aleph-Zeichen des Ras-Schamra-Alphabets." *Zeitschrift für Assyriologie* 41: 305–13.

———. 1957. *Extinct Languages,* trans. Frank Gaynor. New York: Philosophical Library. (German orig., 1954; 2nd ed., 1966.)

Gelb, I. J. 1931, 1935, 1942. *Hittite Hieroglyphs I–III* (Studies in Ancient Oriental Civilization 2, 14, 21). Chicago: University of Chicago Press.

———. 1973. "Written Records and Decipherment." In *Current Trends in Linguistics,* ed. Thomas A. Sebeok, vol. 11: *Diachronic, Areal, and Typological Linguistics,* pp. 253–84. The Hague: Mouton.

———. 1975A. "Records, Writing, and Decipherment." In *Language and Texts: The Nature of Linguistic Evidence,* ed. Herbert H. Paper, pp. 59–86. Ann Arbor: The University of Michigan, Center for Coördination of Ancient and Modern Studies.

———. 1975B. "Methods of Decipherment." *Journal of the Royal Asiatic Society,* pp. 95–104.

Gesenius, Wilhelm. 1841A. "Himjaritische Sprache und Schrift, und Entzifferung der letzteren." *Allgemeine Literatur-Zeitung* 123–26: 369–99 + *Ergänzungsblätter* 64: 511–12.

———. 1841B. Review of Rödiger 1841. *Allgemeine Literatur-Zeitung* 221–22: 545–51, 556–60.

Gordon, Cyrus H. 1982. *Forgotten Scripts: Their Ongoing Discovery and Decipherment,* rev. and enl. ed. New York: Basic Books (1st ed., 1968).

Griffith, Francis Llewellyn. 1909. "Meroitic Inscriptions." In *Areika* (University of Pennsylvania, Publications of the Egyptian Department of the University Museum, Eckley B. Coxe Junior Expedition to Nubia 1), by D. Randall MacIver and C. Leonard Woolley, pp. 43–54. Oxford:

Oxford University Press.

———. 1911. *Karanòg: The Meroitic Inscriptions of Shablûl and Karanòg* (University of Pennsylvania, Egyptian Department of the University Museum, Eckley B. Coxe Junior Expedition to Nubia 6). Philadelphia: University Museum.

Grotefend, Georg Friedrich. 1802. "Praevia de cuneatis, quas vocant, inscriptionibus Persepolitanis legendis et explicandis relatio." *Göttinger gelehrte Anzeigen* 3: 1481–87.

———. 1817. "Über die Erklärung der Keilschriften, und besonders der Inschriften von Persepolis." In *Ideen über die Politik, den Verkehr und den Handel der vornehmsten Völker der alten Welt,* part 1: *Asiatische Völker,* section 1, *Einleitung; Perser,* by Arnold H. L. Heeren, pp. 397–433. Vienna: Härter. English trans., "On the Cuneiform Character, and Particularly the Inscriptions at Persepolis," in *Historical Researches into the Politics, Intercourse, and Trade of the Principal Nations of Antiquity,* pp. 313–60. Oxford: David Alphonso Talboys, 1833. Repr. in *Historical Researches ...,* vol. 2: *Asiatic Nations, Scythians, Indians, Appendixes,* pp. 319–49. London: Henry G. Bohn, 1854.

Hallock, Richard T. 1955. "Syllabary A." In *Materialen zum sumerischen Lexikon 3.* Rome: Pontifical Biblical Institute.

Harris, Zellig S. 1939. *Development of the Canaanite Dialects: An Investigation in Linguistic History* (American Oriental Series 16). New Haven: American Oriental Society. Repr. Millwood, N.Y.: Kraus Reprint, 1978.

Haupt, Paul. 1878. *Die sumerischen Familiengesetze ....* Leipzig: Hinrichs.

Hawkins, J. D., Anna Morpurgo-Davies, and Günter Neumann. 1974. "Hittite Hieroglyphs and Luwian: New Evidence for the Connection." *Nachrichten der Akademie der Wissenschaften in Göttingen, I, Philologisch-Historische Klasse* 1973 no. 6.

Hincks, Edward. 1846A. "On the First and Second Kinds of Persepolitan Writing." *Transactions of the Royal Irish Academy* 21 *Polite Literature* 114–31.

———. 1846B. "An Attempt to Ascertain the Number, Names, and Powers, of the Letters of the Hieroglyphic, or Ancient Egyptian Alphabet; Grounded on the Establishment of a New Principle in the Use of Phonetic Characters." *Transactions of the Royal Irish Academy* 21 *Polite Literature* 132–232.

———. 1846C. "On the Three Kinds of Persepolitan Writing, and on the Babylonian Lapidary Characters." *Transactions of the Royal Irish Academy* 21 *Polite Literature* 233–48.

———. 1847. "On the Third Persepolitan Writing, and on the Mode of Expressing Numerals in Cuneatic Characters." *Transactions of the Royal Irish Academy* 21 *Polite Literature* 249–56.

———. 1848. "On the Inscriptions at Van." *Journal of the Royal Asiatic Society* 9: 387–449.

———. 1849. "On the Khorsabad Inscriptions." *Transactions of the Royal Irish Academy* 22 *Polite Literature* 3–72.

———. 1850. "On the Language and Mode of Writing of the Ancient Assyrians." *Report of the Twentieth Meeting of the British Association for the Advancement of Science,* p. 140.

———. 1851. "Nimrud Obelisk." *The Athenaeum* no. 1251 (27 December): 1384–85.

———. 1852. "On the Assyro-Babylonian Phonetic Characters." *Transactions of the Royal Irish Academy* 22 *Polite Literature* 293–370.

———. 1853. "The Nimrûd Obelisk." *The Dublin University Magazine* 42: 420–26.

———. 1856. "Brief des Herrn Dr. Edw. Hincks an Prof. Brockhaus." *Zeitschrift der Deutschen Morgenländischen Gesellschaft* 10: 516–18.

———. 1859. "On the Grounds for Supposing That the Name of the Tribe of Issachar Occurs in Egyptian Inscriptions." *Proceedings of the Royal Irish Academy* 7: 172–78.

———. 1863. "On the Polyphony of the Assyro-Babylonian Cuneiform Writing." *The Atlantis* 4: 57–112.

Hoernle, A. F. Rudolf. 1884. *Centenary Review of the Asiatic Society of Bengal from 1774–1883,* part 2, *Archæology, History, Literature, &c.* Calcutta: Asiatic Society of Bengal.

Hommel, Fritz. 1893. *Süd-arabische Chrestomathie.* Munich: Franz.

Hrozný, Bedřich. 1915. "Die Lösung des hethetischen Problems." *Mitteilungen der Deutschen Orient-Gesellschaft* 56 (December) 17–50.

Kahn, David. 1967. *The Codebreakers: The Story of Secret Writing.* New York: Macmillan.

Knorosov [Knorozov], Yuri V. 1952. "Drevnjaja pis'mennost' Tsentral'noi Ameriki" [Ancient writing of Central America]. *Sovetskaja Etnografia* 1952/3. Moscow: Academy of Sciences.

———. 1963. *Pis'mennost' indejtsev Majia* [The writing of the Maya Indians]. Moscow: Academy of Sciences. Partial trans., *Selected chapters from ...*, by Sophie Coe (Harvard University, Peabody Museum of Archaeology and Ethnology, Russian Translation Series 4), Cambridge, 1967.

Kober, Alice E. 1945. "Evidence of Inflection in the 'Chariot' Tablets from Knossos." *American Journal of Archaeology* 49: 143–51.

Lassen, Christian. 1836. *Die altpersischen Keil-Inschriften von Persepolis. Entzifferung des Alphabets und Erklärung des Inhalts.* Bonn: Weber.

Lepsius, Richard. 1837. "Lettre à M. le Professeur H. Rosellini sur l'alphabet hiéroglyphique." *Annali dell'Instituto archeologico di Roma* 9/1: 5–100.

Lounsbury, Floyd. 1973. "On the Derivation and Reading of the 'Ben-Ich' Prefix." In *Mesoamerican Writing,* ed. Elizabeth P. Benson, pp. 99–143. Washington, D.C.: Dumbarton Oaks Research Library and Collections.

———. 1989. "The Ancient Writing of Middle America." In *The Origins of Writing,* ed. Wayne M. Senner, pp. 203–37. Lincoln: University of Nebraska Press.

Meriggi, Piero. 1937. "Listes des hiéroglyphes hittites." *Revue hittite et asianique* 4: 69–114, 157–200.

Niebuhr, Carsten. 1772–78. *(Reise)beschreibung von Arabien.* 3 vols. Copenhagen.

Norris, Edwin. 1852. "Memoir on the Scythic Version of the Behistun Inscription." *Journal of the Royal Asiatic Society* 15: 1–213, 431–33.

Pope, Maurice. 1975. *The Story of Archaeological Decipherment: From Egyptian Hieroglyphs to Linear B.* London: Thames & Hudson.

Prinsep, James A. 1834. "Notes on Inscription No. 1 of the Allahabad Column." *Journal of the Asiatic Society of Bengal* 3: 114–23.

———. 1837. "Note on the Facsimiles of Inscriptions from Sanchá near Bhilsa." *Journal of the Asiatic Society of Bengal* 6: 451–77.

———. 1838. "Additions to Bactrian Numismatics, and Discovery of the Bactrian Alphabet." *Journal of the Asiatic Society of Bengal* 7: 636–55.

Proskouriakoff, Tatiana. 1960. "Historical Implications of a Pattern of Dates at Piedras Negras." *American Antiquity* 25: 454–75.

Rawlinson, Henry Creswicke. 1846. *The Persian Cuneiform Inscription at Behistun, Decyphered and Translated; with a Memoir on Persian Cuneiform Inscriptions in General, and on That of Behistun in Particular. Journal of the Royal Asiatic Society* 10 (entire volume).

———. 1850. "A Commentary on the Cuneiform Inscriptions of Babylonia and Assyria; Including Readings of the Inscription on the Nimrud Obelisk, and a Brief Notice of the Ancient Kings of Nineveh and Babylon." *Journal of the Royal Asiatic Society* 12: 401–83.

———. 1851. *Memoir on the Babylonian Translation of the Great Persian Inscription at Behistun. Journal of the Royal Asiatic Society* 14 (entire volume).

Rawlinson, Henry Creswicke, and Edwin Norris. 1866. *A Seliection from the Miscellaneous Inscriptions of Assyria* (Cuneiform Inscriptions of Western Asia 2). London: British Museum.

Ray, John. 1990/91. "The Name of the First: Thomas Young and the Decipherment of Egyptian Writing." *Journal of the Ancient Chronology Forum* 4: 49–53.

Rödiger, Emil. 1837. "Notiz über die himjaritische Schrift nebst doppeltem Alphabet derselben."

Zeitschrift für die Kunde des Morgenlandes 1: 332–40.

———. 1841. *Versuch über die himjaritischen Schriftmonumente.* Halle: Waisenhaus.

———. 1842. "Exkurs über die von Lieut. Wellsted bekannt gemachten himjaritischen Inschriften." In *J. R. Wellsted's Reisen in Arabien,* ed. and trans. E. Rödiger, vol. 2, pp. 352–411. Halle: Waisenhaus.

Rogers, R. W. 1915. *History of Babylonia and Assyria,* vol. 1, *Babylonia,* 6th ed. New York.

Sayce, Archibald H. 1874. "The Languages of the Cuneiform Inscriptions of Elam and Media." *Transactions of the Society of Biblical Archaeology* 3: 465–85.

———. 1880A. "The Bilingual Hittite and Cuneiform Inscription of Tarkondêmos." *Transactions of the Society of Biblical Archaeology* 7: 294–308.

———. 1880B. "The Cuneiform Inscriptions at Van, Deciphered and Translated." *Journal of the Royal Asiatic Society* N.S. 14: 377–732.

———. 1903–4. "The Decipherment of the Hittite Inscriptions." *Proceedings of the Society of Biblical Archaeology* 25: 141–56, 173–94, 277–87, 305–10, 347–56; 26: 17–24, 235–50.

———. 1907. "Hittite Inscriptions: The Method, Verification, and Results of My Decipherment of Them." *Proceedings of the Society of Biblical Archaeology* 29: 207–13, 253–59.

Schmidt, Moriz. 1874. *Die Inschrift von Idalion und das kyprische Syllabar.* Jena: Mauke.

Silvestre de Sacy, Antoine Isaac. 1787–91. *Mémoires sur diverses antiquités de la Perse.* Paris: Imprimerie Nationale, 1793.

Smith, George. 1871. "On the Reading of the Cypriote Inscriptions." *Transactions of the Society of Biblical Archaeology* 1: 129–44.

Swinton, John. 1755. "An Explication of All the Inscriptions in the Palmyrene Language and Character Hitherto Publish'd." *Philosophical Transactions of the Royal Society of London* 48/2: 690–756.

Thompson, J. Eric S. 1971. *Maya Hieroglyphic Writing: An Introduction,* 3rd ed. Norman: University of Oklahoma Press.

Thomsen, Vilhelm. 1893. "Déchiffrement des inscriptions de l'Orkhon et de l'Iénisséi." *Bulletin de l'Académie Royale des Sciences et des Lettres de Danemark,* pp. 285–99. Augmented repr. in Thomsen 1922: 3–19.

———. 1894. "L'alphabet runiforme turc." In his *Inscriptions de l'Orkhon déchiffrées* (Mémoires de la Société Finno-ougrienne 5), pp. 7–54. Helsinki. Revised repr. in Thomsen 1922: 27–91.

———. 1922. *Samlede Afhandlinger,* vol. 3. Copenhagen: Gyldendalske Boghandel.

Ventris, Michael. 1951–52. "Work Notes on Minoan Language Research," nos. 1–20. In his *Work Notes on Minoan Language Research and Other Unedited Papers* (Incunabula Graeca 90), ed. Anna Sacconi, pp. 135–333. Rome. Ateneo, 1988.

Virolleaud, Charles. 1929. "Les inscriptions cunéiformes de Ras Shamra." *Syria* 10: 304–40.

———. 1931. "Le déchiffrement des tablettes alphabétiques de Ras-Shamra." *Syria* 12: 15–23.

Voegelin, C. F., and F. M. Voegelin. 1963. "Patterns of Discovery in the Decipherment of Different Types of Alphabets." *American Anthropologist* 65: 1231–53.

Weissbach, Franz H. 1898. *Die sumerische Frage.* Leipzig: Hinrichs.

Westergaard, Niels Louis. 1844A. "On the Deciphering of the Second Achæmenian or Median Species of Arrowheaded Writing." *Mémoires de la Société Royale des Antiquaires du Nord,* pp. 271–439.

———. 1844B. "Zur Entzifferung der achämenidischen Keilschrift zweiter Gattung." *Zeitschrift für die Kunde des Morgenlandes* 6: 337–466.

Yon, Marguerite, Dennis Pardee, and Pierre Bordreuil. 1992. "Ugarit." In *Anchor Bible Dictionary* 6: 695–721. Garden City, N.Y.: Doubleday.

Young, Thomas. 1818. "Egypt." *Supplement to the Fourth, Fifth, and Sixth Editions of the Encyclopædia Britannica* 4 (1824) 38–74.

The Proto-Elamite Script

ROBERT K. ENGLUND

The ideographic writing system conventionally called Proto-Elamite was developed and used in western and southern Persia at the end of the fourth through the beginning of the third millennium B.C.E., a historical phase generally considered to correspond to the Jemdet Nasr and the Early Dynastic I periods in Mesopotamia (Le Brun 1971; Damerow and Englund 1989: 1–4). The region of Persia designated "Elam" in later Mesopotamian cuneiform sources lent its name by association to the language spoken there; Old Elamite/Old Akkadian bilinguals employing the partially deciphered linear Elamite and Old Akkadian cuneiform date this language of unknown linguistic affiliation (Reiner 1969) no earlier than ca. 2300 B.C.E. "Proto-Elamite" is the name used for the writing system of the earliest documents from the region—texts on clay tablets which are assumed to represent a precursor of Old Elamite (Hinz 1975; Meriggi 1971: 184–220; André and Salvini 1989). The earlier language has not, however, been identified; the phonological structure of the archaic script is thus entirely unknown. However, contextual analyses and the formal similarity of Proto-Elamite documents to better-understood proto-cuneiform tablets from Mesopotamia dating to ca. 3200–3000 B.C.E. make possible a substantive assessment of the ideographic nature and the fields of application of the indigenous Persian writing system.

History of decipherment

Since the first archaic texts were discovered at the turn of the twentieth century, some 1500 Proto-Elamite tablets have been published, the great majority excavated at Susa on the Kerkha river east of Babylonia, but including in smaller numbers tablets found in sites reaching to the southeast across to Shahr-i Sokhta on the Afghanistan border (Damerow and Englund 1989: 1–2). The tablets are administrative documents, to the near total exclusion of either literary or lexical texts.

Syllabic sign readings adduced from an assumed link between Proto-Elamite and the ostensibly related linear Elamite (see above) have not led to successful decipherment of the archaic script. A preliminary graphotactical analysis of the Proto-Elamite texts has also met with only modest success (Meriggi 1975: 105, 1971: 172–84; Brice 1962–63: 28–33; Gelb 1975). To be sure, scholars have with mixed success established some graphic and semantic connections between Proto-Elamite and proto-cuneiform, the first writing stage of which predates that of Proto-Elamite by some 100

Direction of script

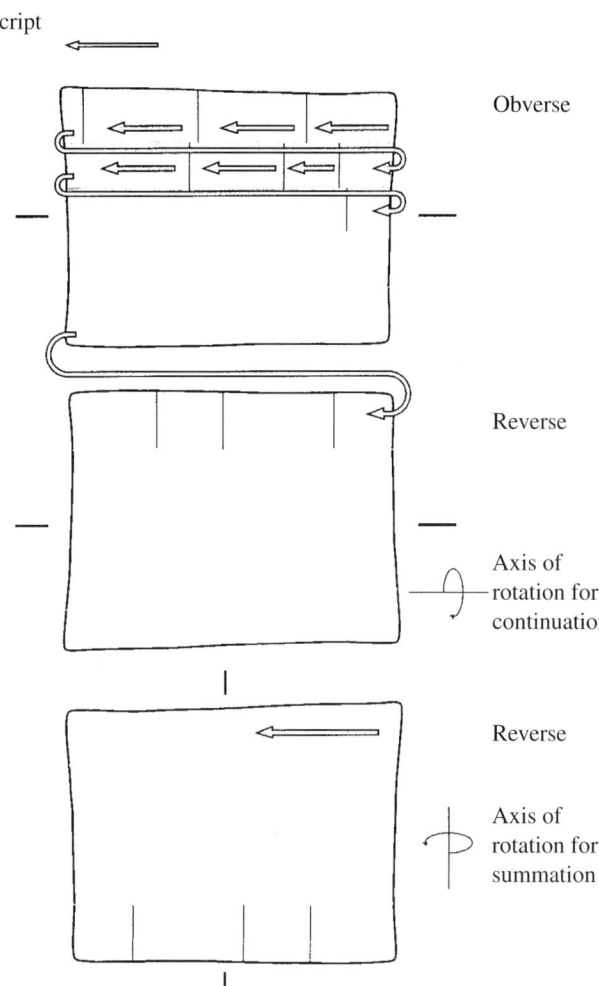

Obverse

Reverse

Axis of
rotation for
continuation

Reverse

Axis of
rotation for
summation

FIGURE 13. Complex rotation of the Proto-Elamite account Scheil 1905, no. 4997 (all figures depict tablets and signs in true orientation; see Damerow and Englund 1989: 11–12, n. 30). Proto-Elamite tablets were rotated around their horizontal axis to inscribe additional individual entries on the reverse, if necessary; summations were also entered on the reverse face of tablets, but in this case the accounts were rotated around their vertical axis.

years (Langdon 1928: viii; Mecquenem 1949: 147; Gelb 1963: 217–20; Meriggi 1969: 156–63; Damerow and Englund 1989: 11–28). However, a lack of necessary philological tools, above all a dependable sign list purged of redundant sign variants, continues to hinder progress in this work.

Basic characteristics of Proto-Elamite script and texts

A preliminary study of the entire text corpus suggests that the Proto-Elamite sign repertory was comparable to that of proto-cuneiform, using less than 1000 individual

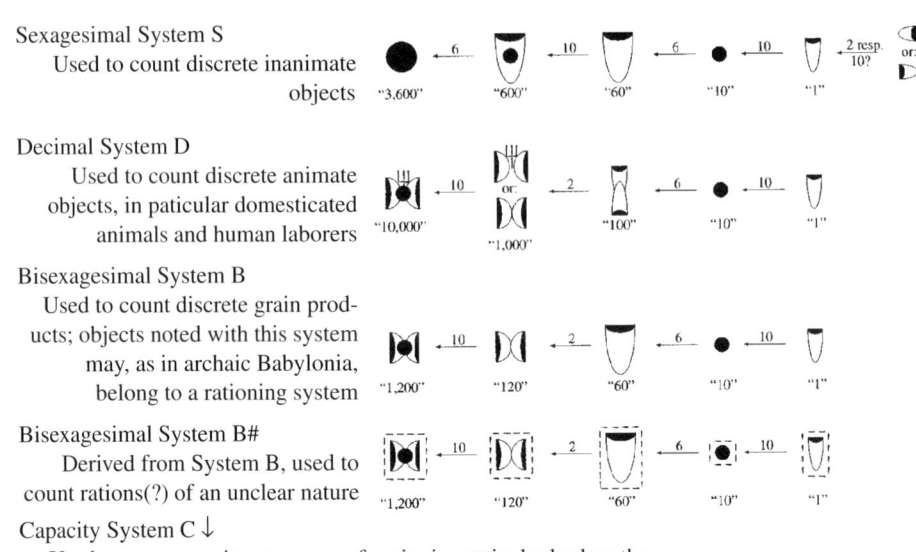

Sexagesimal System S
    Used to count discrete inanimate
                            objects

Decimal System D
    Used to count discrete animate
    objects, in paticular domesticated
        animals and human laborers

Bisexagesimal System B
    Used to count discrete grain prod-
    ucts; objects noted with this system
    may, as in archaic Babylonia,
    belong to a rationing system

Bisexagesimal System B#
    Derived from System B, used to
count rations(?) of an unclear nature

Capacity System C ↓
    Used to note capacity measures of grain, in particular barley; the
small units also designate bisexagesimally counted cereal products.

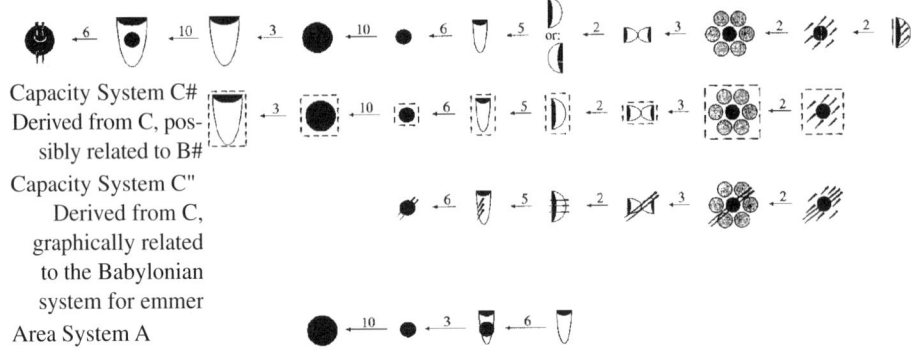

Capacity System C#
Derived from C, pos-
sibly related to B#

Capacity System C''
    Derived from C,
    graphically related
    to the Babylonian
    system for emmer

Area System A

FIGURE 14. Numerical sign systems attested in the Proto-Elamite text corpus (Damerow and Englund 1989: 18–30; the numbers above the arrows indicate how many respective units are replaced by the next higher unit). In the capacity system, the basic sign (*middle column*; = "1" in the systems qualifying discrete units) may have represented ca. 25 liters of grain.

signs and thus in the range of logo- or ideographic writing systems (Damerow and Englund 1989: 4–7). Superficially, a large number of signs seem entirely abstract—which, considering the probability that the script developed explosively during the Jemdet Nasr Period (ca. 3050–3000 B.C.E.), suggests that its developers consciously chose geometric and other nonpictorial shapes and introduced them into conventional usage. The extent to which pictography may have been represented in a dead script is, however, difficult to discern.

    The first serious work on a formal description of the Proto-Elamite texts was done in the 1960s and early 1970s (Brice 1962–63, 1963; Meriggi 1971–74; Vaiman 1972). Proto-Elamite documents were written in a linearized script from right to left,

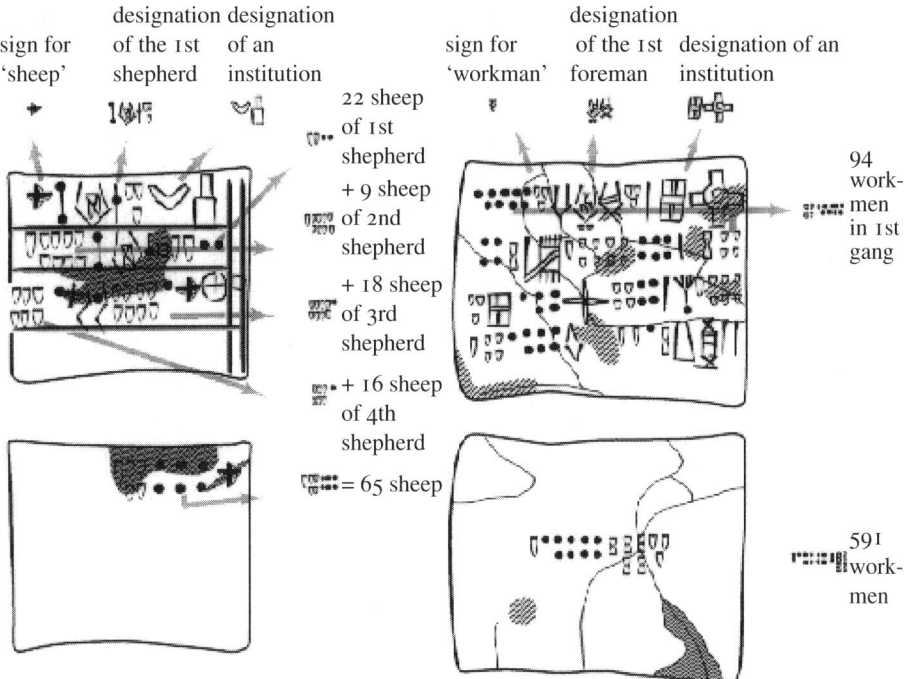

FIGURE 15. Proto-Elamite administrative accounts. *Left*: Account of four sheep herds (Scheil 1905, no. 212). The graphic form and the large numerical notations, as well as the association of the cross-shaped ideogram with other signs that bear a strong graphic resemblance to proto-cuneiform signs known to represent domestic animals (the circled cross and derived signs), make plausible the interpretation of this sign as 'sheep and goats'. The fact that the signs are on the whole abstract forms may be suggestive either of a set of symbols commonly shared in Mesopotamia and Susiana for domestic animals prior to the inception of written documents (so-called tokens), or—and this seems more likely—of a defective borrowing of signs already in use in Uruk (Schmandt-Besserat 1992; Damerow and Englund 1989: 53–55). *Right:* Account of seven labor gangs (Scheil 1923, no. 45). The sign for 'workman' is the most common sign used as a symbol qualifying Proto-Elamite names. All the names in a text may be introduced by this sign; for the most part, however, only the first entry of a text is (Damerow and Englund 1989: 53–55).

in lines from top to bottom. The first signs on a Proto-Elamite tablet generally express the purpose and acting person or institution of the text, followed by individual entries, without the formal arrangement of the tablet into the columns known in proto-cuneiform (see FIGURE 13). Each entry normally includes an ideographic notation representing persons/institutions or quantified objects or both, followed by a numerical notation. That all entries in Proto-Elamite texts seem to contain a numerical notation suggests they represent more the structure of a system of bookkeeping than the division of a spoken language into distinct sentences or comparable semantic units. Continuing analysis of the Proto-Elamite numerical systems (see FIGURE 14), which derived from the systems developed earlier in Mesopotamia, has been a powerful tool in recent semantic identifications of a number of signs and sign combinations, including those for animals, for grain products and, it seems, for humans (Meriggi 1971; Vaiman 1972; Friberg 1978; Damerow and Englund 1987: 117–21, 1989: 18–30, 53–55; Nissen, Damerow, and Englund 1993: 75–79; see FIGURE 15).

Bibliography

André, B., and Mirjo Salvini. 1989. "Réflexions sur Puzur-Inšušinak." *Iranica Antiqua* 24: 53–72.

Brice, William. 1962–63. "The Writing System of the Proto-Elamite Account Tablets of Susa." *Bulletin of the John Rylands Library* 45: 15–39.

Carter, Elizabeth, and Matthew W. Stolper. 1984. *Elam: Surveys of Political History and Archaeology*. Berkeley and Los Angeles: University of California Press.

Damerow, Peter, and Robert Englund. 1987. "Die Zahlzeichensysteme der Archaischen Texte aus Uruk." In *Zeichenliste der Archaischen Texte aus Uruk*, by Margaret W. Green and Hans Nissen, pp. 117–66. Berlin: Mann.

———. 1989. *The Proto-Elamite Texts from Tepe Yahya* (American School of Prehistoric Research Bulletin 39). Cambridge: Harvard University Press.

Friberg, Jöran. 1978. *The Early Roots of Babylonian Mathematics*, vol. 1. Göteborg: Chalmers Technical University, University at Göteborg.

Gelb, I. J. 1963. *A Study of Writing*, 2nd ed. Chicago: University of Chicago Press.

———. 1975. "Methods of Decipherment." *Journal of the Royal Asiatic Society* 95–104.

Hinz, Walter. 1975. "Problems of Linear Elamite." *Journal of the Royal Asiatic Society* 106–15.

Langdon, Stephen. 1928. *Pictographic Inscriptions from Jemdet Nasr* (Oxford Editions of Cuneiform Texts 7). London: Oxford University Press.

Le Brun, Alain. 1971. "Recherches stratigraphiques à l'Acropole de Suse, 1969–1971." *Cahiers de la Délégation Archéologique Française en Iran* 1: 163–216.

Mecquenem, Roland de. 1949. *Epigraphie proto-élamite* (Mission de la Délégation en Perse 31). Paris: Presses Universitaires de France.

Meriggi, Piero. 1969. "Altsumerische und proto-elamische Bilderschrift." *Zeitschrift der Deutschen Morgenländischen Gesellschaft* Supp. 1: 156–63.

———. 1971–74. *La scrittura proto-elamica*. 3 vols. Rome: Accademia Nazionale dei Lincei.

———. 1975. "Der Stand der Erforschung des Proto-elamischen." *Journal of the Royal Asiatic Society* 105.

Nicholas, Ilene. 1981. "Investigating an Ancient Suburb." *Expedition* 23: 39–47.

Nissen, Hans, Peter Damerow, and Robert Englund. 1993. *Archaic Bookkeeping: Writing and Techniques of Economic Administration in the Ancient Near East.* Chicago: Univ. of Chicago Press.

Reiner, Erica. 1969. "The Elamite Language." In *Altkleinasiatische Sprachen* (Handbuch der Orientalistik division 1, vol. 2, part 1–2, fascicle 2), pp. 54–118. Leiden: Brill.

Scheil, Vincent. 1900. *Textes élamites-sémitiques* (Mission de la Délégation en Perse 2). Paris: Leroux.

———. 1905. *Documents en écriture proto-élamite* (MDP 6). Paris: Leroux.

———. 1923. *Textes de comptabilité proto-élamites* (MDP 17). Paris: Leroux.

———. 1935. *Textes de comptabilité proto-élamites* (MDP 26). Paris: Leroux.

Schmandt-Besserat, Denise. 1992. *Before Writing*. Austin: University of Texas Press.

Stolper, Matthew W. 1985. "Proto-Elamite Texts from Tall-i Malyan." *Kadmos* 24: 1–12.

Sumner, William. 1976. "Excavations at Tall-i Malyan (Anshan) 1974." *Iran* 14: 103–14.

Vaiman, A. A. 1972. "A Comparative Study of the Proto-Elamite and Proto-Sumerian Scripts" [in Russian]. *Vestnik Drevnej Istorii* 1972–73: 124–33. English summary, p. 133; German translation in *Baghdader Mitteilungen* 20 (1989): 101–14.

The Indus Script

ASKO PARPOLA

Historical background and development

From the fourth millennium until about 2600 B.C.E., the Early Harappan cultures of eastern Baluchistan and the Indus Valley used "potters' marks" but had no real writing. The Indus script came into being during the short transition period that led to the emergence of the literate Indus Civilization around 2500. The adoption of naval transport changed the volume and direction of internal and external trade. Towns along the old land routes to Inner Asia and Iran withered, while new settlements were founded on the coast. Between ca. 2400 and 1900, the Harappans traded in the Gulf and Mesopotamia, as evidenced by forty seals with Indus script found in the Near East (Parpola 1994A). The first seafaring Indus merchants probably saw writing being used by their western trade partners, who had become literate much earlier. Instead of copying foreign script signs, however, the Harappans devised their own; some at least go back to local Early Harappan symbols. (There is a parallel in the sudden emergence of a mature writing system based on local art traditions in Upper Egypt, ca. 3000 B.C.E., evidently triggered by the influence of Sumerians or Proto-Elamites; see Ray 1986: 308–11, Amiet 1980: 38–39.)

So far, we have not seen the Indus script in its formative phase; in its fully developed form, it has no obvious genetic affinity with any other known script. There is little diachronic or regional development in the script until it disappears around 1900 B.C.E. with the collapse of the urban civilization that created and used it. At the remote southern site of Daimabad, in Maharashtra, the script lingered on until about 1700. There is no connection whatsoever with the earliest scripts of historical South Asia, Brahmi and Kharoshthi, which were created on the basis of Semitic and Greek alphabets and used from the third century B.C.E.

Obstacles to decipherment

The Indus script has withstood more than fifty attempts at decipherment made since a stamp seal from Harappa, containing the first known sample of it, was published in 1875. A principal reason is the total lack of translations into known scripts and languages. Even historical information, such as names and genealogies of kings (which helped to decipher cuneiform script), is absent. Nor do we have any definite information on the affinity of the Harappan language(s). In addition, all the approximately 4000 texts are short; word division is not specifically indicated; and sign forms have often been simplified beyond pictorial recognition.

Characteristics

Direction of writing

There is fair agreement about the direction of writing in the Indus script. Normally the texts are to be read from right to left; in the case of inscribed seal stamps, this applies to their impressions. But occasionally the direction may be reversed, particularly in early "miniature tablets" from Harappa. Overlaps of lines in pottery graffiti indicate in which order and direction the signs were drawn. Other external criteria are provided by orientation and spacing of the components in asymmetric signs and uneven distribution of the text on the available writing space. Most important is the internal evidence of sign distribution: some signs and sequences are characteristic of the beginning, others of the end of inscriptions. The frequency patterns of sign sequences also show that some of the rare multi-line texts run in alternate directions (boustrophedon).

The means of distinguishing words

The average length of the Indus texts is five signs. The minimum length is one sign, and the longest known have 28 signs (divided into three lines on three sides of a prismatic amulet), 17 signs (divided into three lines on one side of a seal), and 14 signs (a single continuous line). Word division does not appear to have been marked in any way. Distributional analysis does not confirm the hypothesis that signs consisting of single or double short vertical strokes may be markers of word division. The only reliable means of distinguishing words is comparative study of partially identical complete texts of different length. Normal word length seems to vary from one to three signs. A few signs have been suspected of representing declensional suffixes, but these identifications remain uncertain.

Type of the script and orthography

Widely diverging estimates of the number of characters in the Indus script have been made, but 400 different signs should be close to the truth; see TABLE 11.1. Some signs have a great number of graphic variants. Occasionally it is hard to say whether two nearly similar signs are distinct symbols or merely allographs of one symbol, particularly if they have a low frequency of occurrence. Together with the short word length and the great age of the script, the number of characters strongly suggests that the Indus script is a logosyllabic writing system.

TABLE 11.1: *Inventory of Signs*

Many compound signs occur in the Indus script, consisting of two or more elements that may or may not occur also as separate signs. A compound sign and one of the signs forming it can replace each other in identical or nearly identical contexts (TABLE 11.2); this suggests some kind of redundancy for the added component(s). There is reason to believe that some of these "redundant" elements are determinatives, as known from other logosyllabic scripts, i.e. auxiliary signs specifying the semantic or phonetic reading of the main sign. Some signs, such as that apparently depicting 'man' or 'human being', enter into a whole series of compound signs. They may denote compound words representing occupational titles (such as for example *police-man* or *fisher-man* in English), with an optional second member of the compound.

The iconic nature of some Indus signs constitutes one of the chief keys to their interpretation. Unfortunately the pictorial meaning of most Indus signs is not clear. As in many other scripts, the demand for fluency in writing led to a radical simplification of their shapes.

Numerals belong to the few Indus signs whose function and meaning can be deduced with fair certainty, partly from their form (they consist of groups of vertical strokes, as in many other scripts), and partly from their mutual interchangeability in fixed positions: the numerals regularly occur before specific signs. The fact that the head word is preceded and not followed by the numeral attribute is a typological feature that helps in the identification of the Indus language.

Current state of decipherment

The failure to solve the Indus puzzle is also the result of methodological weaknesses. Most commonly, Indus signs have been equated with similar-looking signs of other readable ancient scripts, and the phonetic values of the latter have been transferred to the Indus signs. However, this method has a chance of success only when the scripts compared are closely related.

In the early logosyllabic scripts, many signs were originally pictures denoting the objects or ideas they represented. Such an ideographically used pictogram may be roughly understood directly from its iconic shape, irrespective of how any word corresponding to the sign's meaning was pronounced. But in order to express things that are impossible to represent by pictures in an unambiguous way, the meaning of a pictogram or ideogram was extended from the word for the depicted object to all its homophones. A valid methodology for deciphering a logosyllabic script phonetically can be devised on the basis of this use of the rebus principle. It may be possible to identify the language underlying the script and to decipher some of the pictograms if four conditions are simultaneously fulfilled: (a) the object depicted in a given pictogram can be recognized; (b) the pictogram has been used phonetically for a word with the same sound as, but a meaning different from, the object it represents; (c) this intended meaning (expressed by punning) can be deduced from the context; and (d) a

TABLE 11.2: *Texts in the Indus Script with Partially Identical Sign Sequences*[a]

A. 'Man' Ligatures

3266[b]	
1077	
0488	
2519	
1087	
2027	
2226	
2466[c]	

2366	
1037	
4113	

2434	
2088	
3651	
1542	

3412	
3458	
3372	
3419	

B. Other Signs

1052	
8527	

6020	
2657	

3086	
5056	

2331	
0732	

2535	
2511	

1296	
6140	
1104	
2655	

a. After Parpola 1994, fig. 5.3. Texts cited from Koskenniemi and Parpola 1979, 1980, 1982.
b. Cf. also 2466.
c. Cf. also 3266.

TABLE 11.3: *Interpretations of Indus Signs and Sign Combinations*[a]

Sign or Combination	Pictorial Meaning	Shared Phonetic Shape in Dravidian	Intended Meaning
𝍭	'fish'	mīn	'star'
𝍭	'roof' + 'fish'	mēy/may + mīn	'black' + 'star' (= Saturn)
𝍭	'halving, dividing' + 'fish'	pacu + mīn	'green' + 'star' (= Mercury)
𝍭 ‖	'(intervening) space' + 'fish'	veḷi/veḷ(ḷi) + mīn	'white (bright, star)' + 'star' (= Venus)
𝍭 ♨	'fig tree' + 'fish'	vaṭa + mīn	'north' + 'star'
‖♨	'fig tree' + 'space'	vaṭa + veḷḷi	'north' + 'star'
𝍭 ‖‖‖	'six' + 'fish'	caṟu + mīn	'six' + 'star' (= Pleiades)

a. After Parpola 1988: 132.

linguistically satisfactory homophony with these two meanings exists in a likely language. If an opening can be effected, the order of the operations can be permuted.

Besides the question concerning the type of writing, the other principal problem connected with the Indus script concerns the genetic affinity of its language. The Dravidian language family, nowadays distributed throughout South India and in isolated pockets of Baluchistan and North India, is the most likely candidate historically. Dravidian loanwords are found in the Rigveda, which was composed in the northern Indus Valley during the latter half of the second millennium B.C.E. This hypothesis seems to be confirmed by interlocking interpretations of a small number of Indus pictograms, whose intended meaning can be deduced from the contexts to some extent (TABLE 11.3): Pictograms (col. 1) can be interpreted as representing (Proto-)Dravidian words (cols. 2–3) which are homophonous with compound words attested in Dravidian languages as names of heavenly bodies (cols. 3–4), which in turn are assumed to represent divinities (as in the ancient Near Eastern and later Hindu religions); for detailed arguments on some two dozen tentative readings, see Parpola 1994B. The other main contestant for the language of the Indus script in attempts at decipherment is Sanskrit or more broadly Indo-Aryan, spoken in the Indus Valley since the second millennium B.C.E. but probably not earlier (see Mahadevan 1982, Norman 1984).

While amulet tablets and pottery graffiti stand out among the categories of texts, more than sixty percent of the surviving texts are seal inscriptions. Their content appears to be similar to the readable inscriptions on the Near Eastern seals used by the trade partners of the Harappans: the latter contain personal names and titles of office (with names of divinities as important components). The texts transcribed in TABLE 11.2 include seal inscriptions and small tablets; spaces within texts reflect breaks between lines or sides within inscriptions.

Bibliography

Amiet, Pierre. 1980. *La glyptique mésopotamienne archaïque,* 2nd ed. Paris: Editions du Centre National de la Recherche Scientifique.

Joshi, Jagat Pati, and Asko Parpola, eds. 1987. *Corpus of Indus Seals and Inscriptions,* vol. 1: *Collections in India* (Annales Academiae Scientiarum Fennicae B 239; Memoirs of the Archaeological Survey of India 86). Helsinki: Suomalainen Tiedeakatemia.

Koskenniemi, Kimmo, and Asko Parpola. 1979. *Corpus of Texts in the Indus Script* (University of Helsinki, Department of Asian and African Studies, Research Reports 1).

———. 1980. *Documentation and Duplicates of the Texts in the Indus Script* (University of Helsinki, Department of Asian and African Studies, Research Reports 2).

———. 1982. *A Concordance to the Texts in the Indus Script* (University of Helsinki, Department of Asian and African Studies, Research Reports 3).

Krishna Rao, M. V. N. 1982. *Indus Script Deciphered.* Delhi: Agam Kala Prakashan.

Mahadevan, Iravatham. 1977. *The Indus Script: Texts, Concordance and Tables* (Memoirs of the Archaeological Survey of India 77). New Delhi: Archaeological Survey of India.

———. 1982. "S. R. Rao's Decipherment of the Indus Script." *The Indian Historical Review* 8/1–2: 58–73.

Mitchiner, John E. 1978. *Studies in the Indus Valley Inscriptions.* Delhi: Oxford University Press.

Norman, K. R. 1984. "The Decipherment of the Indus Valley Script" [Review of Mitchiner 1978, Krishna Rao 1982, and Rao 1982]. *Lingua* 63: 313–24.

Parpola, Asko. 1975. "Tasks, Methods and Results in the Study of the Indus Script." *Journal of the Royal Asiatic Society,* pp. 178–209.

———. 1986. "The Indus Script: A Challenging Puzzle." *World Archaeology* 17: 399–419.

———. 1988. "Religion Reflected in the Iconic Signs of the Indus Script: Penetrating into Long-forgotten Picto+graphic Messages." *Visible Religion* 6: 114–35.

———. 1994A. "Harappan Inscriptions: An Analytical Catalogue of the Indus Inscriptions from the Near East." In *Qala'at al-Bahrain, 1: The Northern City Wall and the Islamic Fortress* (Jutland Archaeooogical Society Publications 30:1), by Flemming Højlund and H. Hellmuth Andersen, pp. 304–15, 483–92. Aarhus: Aarhus University Press.

———. 1994B. *Deciphering the Indus Script.* Cambridge: Cambridge University Press.

Rao, S. R. 1982. *The Decipherment of the Indus Script.* Bombay: Asia Publishing House.

Ray, John D. 1986. "The Emergence of Writing in Egypt." *World Archaeology* 17: 307–16.

Shah, Sayid Ghulam Mustafa, and Asko Parpola, eds. 1991. *Corpus of Indus Seals and Inscriptions,* vol. 2: *Collections in Pakistan* (Annales Academiae Scientiarum Fennicae B 240; Memoirs of the Department of Archaeology and Museums, Government of Pakistan 5). Helsinki: Suomalainen Tiedeakatemia.

Maya and Other Mesoamerican Scripts

MARTHA J. MACRI

Archeological, linguistic, and ethnographic data confirm that the peoples of Meso-america have been interacting with each other for thousands of years. Although many centuries separate the stone inscriptions of the Mayas and the Zapotecs, the pictorial manuscripts of the Mixtecs and the Aztecs, and the Quiché Popol Vuh (written in the Roman alphabet), each records shared knowledge and beliefs about the world which have astounded modern scholars (e.g. Freidel and Schele 1993). Associated with de-tailed political histories is a knowledge of solar, lunar, stellar, and planetary phenom-ena that can only be the result of centuries of recorded observation. Just as writing in ancient Mesopotamia developed within the context of commerce, writing in Meso-america is inextricably connected with an intricate calendar and seems to have devel-oped partially in response to the desire to record astronomical observations.

Mesoamerican cultures shared a vigesimal counting system, a count of 13 days, a set of 20 day names, combining them into a 260 day cycle; and a year of 18 named months of 20 days each, plus a period of 5 days; and a combination of the 260- and 365-day cycles into a Calendar Round of 52 years. Several groups, including the Maya and the Epi-Olmec, recorded Long Count dates (the total number of days since the beginning of the current era in 3114 B.C.E. in groups of days, 20 days, 360 days, 20×360 days, 400×360 days, etc.; Sharer 1994).

The ancient Olmec civilization known from the sites of Tres Zapotes, La Venta, and San Lorenzo along the Gulf of Mexico had a complex iconography but left no written texts. A column of three symbols on Monument 13, the *Ambassador,* from La Venta hints that this civilization might have had a writing system (Marcus 1976: 47–48). True writing is first attested in Oaxaca, the Gulf Coast region, and the Guatema-lan Pacific Piedmont and Highlands between 500 B.C.E. and 150 C.E. (Justeson et al. 1985; Marcus 1976). The development of writing from an intricate iconography into a script with increasingly larger logographic and phonetic components remains a fa-vored hypothesis of the origin of Mesoamerican scripts. However, the relationships between the scripts is not well understood, and there is lack of agreement about which is the earliest.

A conservative estimate of the number of distinct writing systems identified in pre-Columbian Mesoamerica is fifteen—many known only from a single inscription. Scripts for which a sufficient corpus remains to allow a meaningful analysis can be grouped into logographic/syllabic scripts and codified pictorial systems. Features

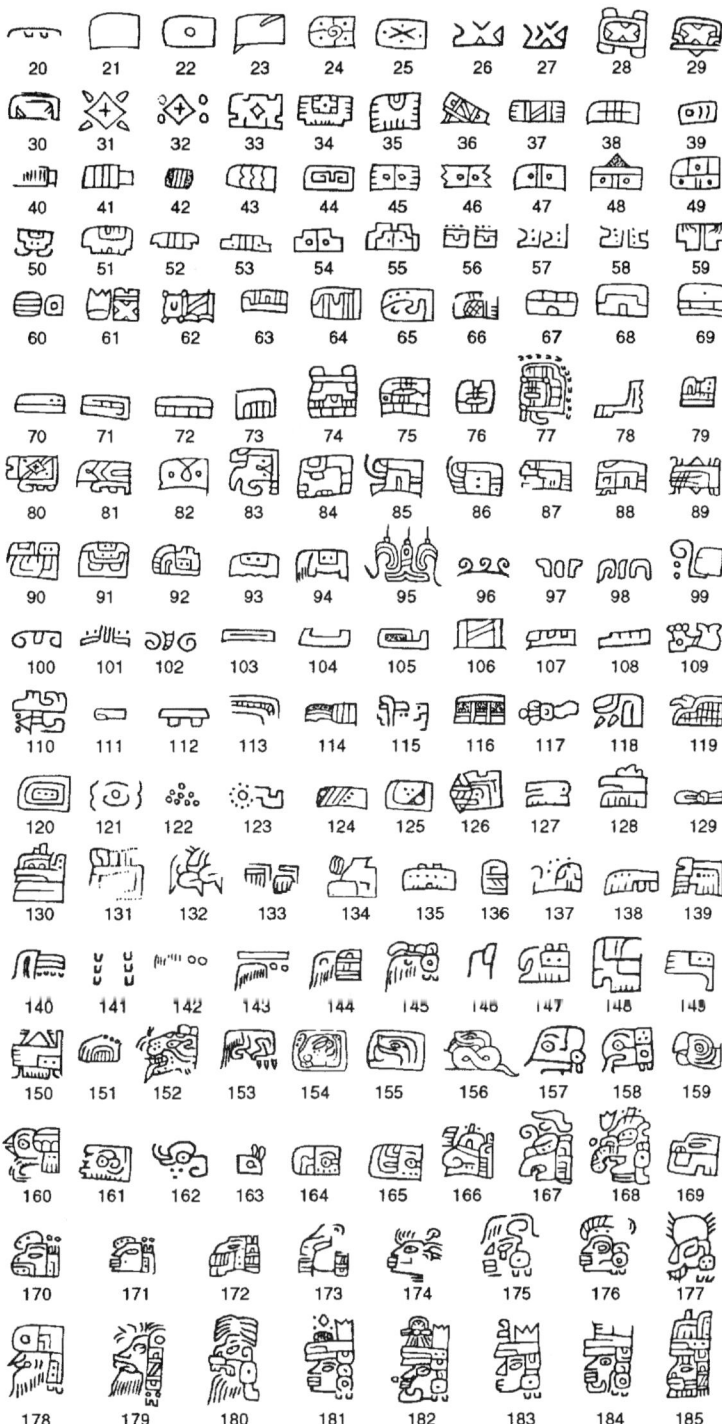

FIGURE 16. Sign list for La Mojarra Stela 1 and the Tuxtla Statuette
(Macri and Stark 1993, signs after drawing by George Stuart (Winfield Capitaine 1988)).

used in comparisons of these scripts include arrangement of symbols (boustrophedon, single or double column format), enlarged calendrical statements, numbers (dots only, or bar/dot combinations for numbers over five), Long Count dates (Justeson et al. 1985: 40), and the placement of bar/dot numbers with respect to day signs (vertically with bars closest to the sign, horizontally, beneath the sign with dots above bars, or beneath the sign with the bars above the dots).

Logographic/syllabic scripts

Three logographic/syllabic traditions existed in pre-Columbian Mesoamerica: the Zapotec, the Epi-Olmec, and the Maya. Writing first appears at the Zapotec site of Monte Albán on Stelas 12 and 13 about 500–400 B.C.E. (Marcus 1976: 45–47). Although the study of Zapotec writing is in its infancy (Marcus 1992: 72), the arrangement of signs and the abstract form of many of them suggest the script is analogous to the logographic/syllabic Epi-Olmec and Maya scripts. Texts from Monte Albán I and II (500 B.C.E. – 100 C.E.) have signs of regular width closely stacked in columns. Numbers are placed beneath calendrical signs with dots above bars. Later texts from Monte Albán III (after 100 C.E.), such as Stela 1 (Marcus 1992, fig. 10.11) and the Lápida de Bazán (Marcus 1983B, fig. 6.7), have less regularly shaped signs placed farther apart and have numbers beneath calendrical signs with bars above the dots. This may reflect influence from Central Mexico.

The Epi-Olmec script is known principally from two inscriptions from Veracruz. The Tuxtla Statuette and La Mojarra Stela 1, dated at 163 C.E. and 156 C.E. respectively (Holmes 1907; Winfield Capitaine 1988), contain both historical and astronomical data (Justeson and Kaufman 1993). The length of the La Mojarra text (over 500 signs) and the pattern of repetition of certain characters support the identification of the script as mixed logographic and phonetic. The sign list (FIGURE 16) shows simple, abstract signs which are probably phonetic (e.g. MS 22, 38, 63) and more complex representational signs that are probably logographic (e.g. MS 152, 168). Other related monuments from Veracruz and Chiapas, some with even earlier dates, such as Tres Zapotes Stela C, dated at 32 B.C.E., bore inscriptions which are missing or are no longer readable. Eroded texts from Cerro de las Mesas, arranged in a similar columnar format, are later examples of the same script tradition.

Maya writing

The earliest Maya writing dates from before 250 C.E., but it probably has origins at least as early as those of the Epi-Olmec script. The incised glyphic text on Kaminaljuyu Stela 10 (200 B.C.E. – 200 C.E.) stands in an ambiguous intermediate position between the Epi-Olmec and the Classic Maya scripts (Macri 1991). FIGURE 17 shows several shared characters of similar form.

FIGURE 17. A comparison of Maya *(left)* and La Mojarra *(right)* signs with those on Kaminaljuyu Stela 10 *(center)* (after Macri 1991).

Maya writing, though not completely deciphered, is the best understood of all Mesoamerican scripts, known from hundreds of sculptures as well as painted pottery, and four bark paper codices. The first bishop of the Yucatan, Bishop Landa, attests that it was still in use among speakers of Yucatec Maya in the sixteenth century.

The last several decades have seen rapid development in its decipherment (Coe 1992, G. Stuart 1992). This has been due to a number of factors, including Yuriy Knorozov's assertion that the script is composed of logographic and syllabic signs (1963, 1967), Proskouriakoff's proof of the historic content of the texts (1960, 1963), improved access to texts such as the Corpus of Maya Hieroglyphic Inscriptions edited by Ian Graham et al. (1975–), and detailed structural analysis of texts such as those of Palenque (Mathews and Schele 1974). Histories of various sites are summarized in Houston 1993, Schele and Freidel 1990, and Tate 1992. The Maya Hieroglyph Database Project (University of California, Davis) estimates the total number of characters at fewer than 600. TABLE 12.1 is a chart of signs for which syllabic readings have

TABLE 12.1: *Maya Glyphs with Syllabic Values*[a]

	i	e	a	o	u
›					
p					
t					
k					
b'					
t'					
k'					
m					
n					

TABLE 12.1: *Maya Glyphs with Syllabic Values[a] (Continued)*

	i	*e*	*a*	*o*	*u*
ts					
ch					
ts'					
ch'					
s					
x					
h					
l					
w					
y					

a. Redrawn by Judy Alexander after Thompson 1962. For a more complete syllabary see Schele and Grube 1995: 16–17.

FIGURE 18. Symbols in the Maya script based on hands; beneath each one appears the grapheme conde and the Thompson catalog number(drawing by Judy Alexander after Thompson 1962).

been proposed. Glyphs are usually read from left to right in double columns from top to bottom. Signs within glyph blocks read loosely from upper left corner to lower right corner, with generous allowances for artistic convention. FIGURE 18 contains signs consisting of hands, many of which have known phonetic values.

SAMPLE OF MAYA SCRIPT

Transcription and translation by Macri based on previous work by several epigraphers (e.g. Berlin 1963; Bricker 1986: 129, 1989; Macri 1988; Mathews 1979; Schele 1978–93; D. Stuart 1987, 1990). Logograms (shown in uppercase letters) appear in combination with CV syllabic signs. Variations of a single sign, as well as substitutions of equivalent signs, are frequent in Maya texts. In this passage, for example, there are five different variants for the third person marker *u*. The clause is part of a longer text commemorating the ritual dressing of the ruler Pakal at twenty year ceremonies. Although this clause contains a list of ritual costuming of which Kawil is the

k'a ya wa	u pi	*1. Interp.:* y-ak'aw u-pi(s) *2. Gloss:* he.presents his-cycle
WINIK hun ki	xo pi la	1. hun winik pixol 2. one twenty hat
u hu na SAK la	u ha	1. u-sak hunal u-ha(l) 2. his-white headband his-necklace
ch'u YAX li	CHAN TUN? na	1. yax ch'ul chan tun 2. green sacred sky stone
tu u pa	YAX u	1. u-tup yax 2. his-earrings green
KAWAW u wa	ch'o ko	1. u-kawaw ch'ok 2. his-helmet young.one
ka wi	k'a ya wa	1. Kawil y-ak'a-w 2. Kawil it.is.given

named possessor, it is not clear whether Kawil is also the subject of the sentence, or whether the subject of this entire passage is the ruler Pakal. The presence of the third person ergative subject marker (*u-* before consonant-initial roots, *y-* before vowels) on the verb *ak'* 'give, present, offer' suggests an active-voice, ergative construction. The postfix *-wa* is not well understood.

> 'He presents young Kawil's [a mythological personage] cycle of twenty, the hat, his white headband, his heavenly greenstone (jade) necklace, his green earrings, and his helmet.'
> —*From the middle panel of the Temple of the Inscriptions at Palenque (K3–K9).*

Codified pictorial systems

The Ñuiñe script of the Mixteca Baja region of Oaxaca, known primarily from stones and urns bearing short inscriptions, dating from 400 to 700 C.E., shows more similarity to Monte Albán inscriptions than to those from any other Mesoamerican site. Moser (1977) numbers 142 motifs (actually over 200 different elements).

Teotihuacan, which flourished approximately from 200 B.C.E. to 650 C.E., left no evidence of a script, but its artists clearly distinguished between pictorial imagery and iconographic signs. Langley (1991) lists 120 signs as having clear notational significance. Berlo (1989: 44) sees Teotihuacan as the source for the highly conventionalized system which later spread throughout Central Mexico.

By the time of the European invasion in the sixteenth century, the Aztecs of Tenochtitlan, the Mixtecs of southern Puebla and northern Oaxaca (Byland 1993: xiii–xv; Jansen 1990; Smith 1983), and the Zapotecs of Oaxaca (Marcus 1992: 69–75) had hundreds of paper manuscripts which recorded both history and mythic traditions. However, these manuscripts, containing more logographic than phonetic signs, relied heavily on context—on learned cultural conventions—for resolving ambiguities; this limits the ability of modern scholars to reconstruct precise word-for-word transcriptions. Thus we speak of the *interpretation* of these texts rather than of their *decipherment*. Glass (1975A, 1975B) offers a survey of both pre- and post-colonial pictorial manuscripts, along with detailed ethnohistoric and bibliographic sources.

The culture of literacy played an important role in the history of Mesoamerica. Every language family has names for 'paper', 'book', 'scribe', and 'writing'. Unfortunately, what we know of these scripts is based on a very small, and usually not representative, sample of the texts that once existed. But even from this shadowy picture we see the fascinating variety of graphic communication which existed in this region.

Bibliography

Berlin, Heinrich. 1963. "The Palenque Triad." *Journal de la Société des Américanistes* (Paris) 52: 91–99.

Berlo, Janet Catherine. 1989. "Early Writing in Central Mexico: *In Tlilli, In Tlapalli* before A.D. 1000." In *Mesoamerica after the Decline of Teotihuacan A.D. 700–900,* ed. Richard A. Diehl and Janet Catherine Berlo, pp. 19–47. Washington, D.C.: Dumbarton Oaks Research Library and Collection.

Bricker, Victoria R. 1986. *A Grammar of Mayan Hieroglyphs* (Middle American Research Institute Publications 56). New Orleans: Tulane University.

———. 1989. "Notes on Classic Maya Metrology." In *Fifth Palenque Round Table, 1983,* vol. 7, ed. Virginia M. Fields, pp. 189–92. San Francisco: Pre-Columbian Art Research Institute.

Byland, Bruce E. 1993. "Introduction and Commentary." In *The Codex Borgia: A Full-Color Restoration of the Ancient Mexican Manuscript,* by Gisele Díaz and Alan Rodgers, pp. xiii–xxxii. New York: Dover.

Coe, Michael D. 1992. *Breaking the Maya Code.* New York: Thames and Hudson.

Freidel, David, and Linda Schele. 1993. *Maya Cosmos: Three Thousand Years on the Shaman's Path.* New York: Morrow.

Glass, John B. 1975A. "A Survey of Native Middle American Pictorial Manuscripts." In *Guide to Ethnohistorical Sources,* part 3 (Handbook of Middle American Indians 14), ed. Howard F. Cline, pp. 3–80. Austin: University of Texas Press.

———. 1975B. "A Census of Native Middle American Pictorial Manuscripts." In *Guide to Ethno-historical Sources,* part 3 (Handbook of Middle American Indians 14), ed. Howard F. Cline, pp. 81–252. Austin: University of Texas Press.

Graham, Ian, et al. 1975– . *Corpus of Maya Hieroglyphic Inscriptions.* Cambridge: Harvard University, Peabody Museum of Archaeology and Ethnology.

Greene Robertson, Merle. 1983. *The Sculpture of Palenque*, vol. 1: *The Temple of the Inscriptions.* Princeton: Princeton University Press.

Holmes, W. H. 1907. "On a Nephrite Statuette from San Andres Tuxtla, Vera Cruz, Mexico." *American Anthropologist* 9: 691–701.

Houston, Stephen D. 1989. *Maya Glyphs* (Reading the Past). London: British Museum; Berkeley and Los Angeles: University of California Press.

———. 1993. *Hieroglyphs and History at Dos Pilas: Dynastic Politics of the Classic Maya.* Austin: University of Texas Press.

Jansen, Maarten. 1990. "The Search for History in Mixtec Codices." *Ancient Mesoamerica* 1: 99–112.

Justeson, John S., and Terrence Kaufman. 1993. "A Deciferment of Epi-Olmec Hieroglyphic Writing." *Science* 259: 1703–11.

Justeson, John S., William M. Norman, Lyle Campbell, and Terrence Kaufman. 1985. *The Foreign Impact on Lowland Mayan Language and Script* (Middle American Research Institute, Publication 53). New Orleans: Tulane University.

Knorozov, Yuriy V. 1963. *Pis'mennost' indejcev maija.* Moscow and Leningrad: Academy of Sciences. Chs. 1, 6, 7, and 9 trans. by Sophie Coe as *Selected Chapters from The Writing of the Maya Indians* (Russian Translation Series 4). Cambridge: Harvard University, Peabody Museum of Archaeology and Ethnology, 1967.

Langley, James C. 1991. "The Forms and Usage of Notation at Teotihuacan." *Ancient Mesoamerica* 2: 285–98.

Lounsbury, Floyd. 1989. "The Ancient Writing of Middle America." In *The Origins of Writing,* ed. Wayne M. Senner, pp. 203–37. Lincoln: University of Nebraska Press.

Macri, Martha J. 1988. "A Descriptive Grammar of Palenque Mayan." Ph.D. dissertation, University of California, Berkeley.

———. 1991. "The Script on La Mojarra Stela 1 and Classic Maya Writing." In *Literacies: Writing Systems and Literate Practices,* ed. David L. Schmidt and Janet S. Smith, pp. 11–23 (Davis Working Papers in Linguistics 4). University of California, Davis.

Macri, Martha J., and Laura M. Stark. 1993. *A Sign Catalog of the La Mojarra Script* (Pre-Columbian Art Research Institute, Monograph 5). San Francisco.

Marcus, Joyce. 1976. "The Origins of Mesoamerican Writing." *Annual Review of Anthropology* 5: 35–67.

———. 1983A. "The First Appearance of Zapotec Writing and Calendrics." In *The Cloud People: Divergent Evolution of the Zapotec and Mixtec Civilizations*, ed. Kent V. Flannery and Joyce Marcus, pp. 91–96. New York: Academic Press.

———. 1983B. "Teotihuacán Visitors on Monuments and Murals." In *The Cloud People: Divergent Evolution of the Zapotec and Mixtec Civilizations*, ed. Kent V. Flannery and Joyce Marcus, pp. 175–81. New York: Academic Press.

————. 1992. *Mesoamerican Writing Systems: Propoganda, Myth, and History in Four Ancient Civilizations.* Princeton: Princeton University Press.

Mathews, Peter. 1979. "The Glyphs on the Ear Ornaments from Tomb A-1/1." In *Excavations at Altun Ha, Belize, 1964–1970,* ed. David Pendergast, vol. 1, pp. 79f.. Toronto: Royal Ontario Museum.

Mathews, Peter, and Linda Schele. 1974. "Lords of Palenque: The Glyphic Evidence." In *Primera Mesa Redonda de Palenque,* part 1, ed. Merle Greene Robertson, pp. 63-76. Pebble Beach, Calif.: Robert Louis Stevenson School.

Moser, Christopher L. 1977. *Ñuiñe Writing and Iconography of the Mixteca Baja* (Vanderbilt University Publications in Anthropology 19). Nashville.

Proskouriakoff, Tatiana. 1960. "Historical Implications of a Pattern of Dates at Piedras Negras, Guatemala." *American Antiquity* 25: 454–75.

————. 1963. "Historical Data in the Inscriptions of Yaxchilan." *Estudios de Cultura Maya* 4: 177–202.

Schele, Linda. 1978–93. *Notebooks for the Maya Hieroglyphic Writing Workshop at Texas.* Austin: University of Texas, Institute of Latin American Studies.

Schele, Linda, and David Freidel. 1990. *A Forest of Kings: The Untold Story of the Ancient Maya.* New York: Morrow.

Schele, Linda, and Nikolai Grube. 1995. *Notebook for the XIXth Maya Hieroglyphic Workshop at Texas.* Austin: University of Texas.

Schele, Linda, Peter Mathews, and Floyd Lounsbury. 1990. "Untying the Headband." *Texas Notes on Precolumbian Art, Writing, and Culture,* No. 4.

Sharer, Robert J. 1994. *The Ancient Maya,* 5th ed. Stanford: Stanford University Press.

Smith, Mary Elizabeth. 1983. "The Mixtec Writing System." In *The Cloud People: Divergent Evolution of the Zapotec and Mixtec Civilizations,* ed. Kent V. Flannery and Joyce Marcus, pp. 238–45. New York: Academic Press.

Stuart, David. 1987. *Ten Phonetic Syllables* (Research Reports on Ancient Maya Writing 14). Washington, D.C.: Center for Maya Research.

————. 1990. "The Decipherment of 'Directional Count Glyphs' in Maya Inscriptions." *Ancient Mesoamerica* 1: 213–24.

Stuart, George E. 1992. "Quest for Decipherment: A Historical and Biographical Survey of Maya Hieroglyphic Investigation." In *New Theories on the Ancient Maya* (University Museum Symposium Series 3), ed. Elin C. Danien and Robert J. Sharer, pp. 1–63. Philadelphia: University of Pennsylvania, University Museum.

Tate, Carolyn. 1992. *Yaxchilan: The Design of a Maya Ceremonial City.* Austin: University of Texas Press.

Thompson, J. Eric S. 1962. *A Catalog of Maya Hieroglyphs.* Norman: University of Oklahoma Press.

————. 1971. *Maya Hieroglyphic Writing: An Introduction,* 3rd ed. Norman: University of Oklahoma Press.

Winfield Capitaine, Fernando. 1988. *La Estela 1 de La Mojarra, Veracruz, Mexico* (Research Reports on Ancient Maya Writing 16). Washington, D.C.: Center for Maya Research.

Rongorongo of Easter Island

MARTHA J. MACRI

Easter Island, over 3600 km west of Chile and 2600 km east of the island of Manga-reva, was first visited by European sailors in 1722. In 1862 Peruvian ships kidnapped over 1400 islanders, speakers of Rapanui (a Polynesian language). By the time European missionaries began to notice the *rongorongo* (lit. 'recitation') boards covered with rows of incised characters, knowledge of how to read and write them had been lost. In addition to classical rongorongo script, Barthel (1971) notes the presence of two other scripts on the island: the *ta'u* and *mama* scripts, which had separate inventories of signs. Fischer (1993B) lists 26 rongorongo texts, 6 ta'u texts, and 2 mama texts. Only classical script is discussed here.

Progress in decipherment

Florentin Étienne Jaussen, the Catholic bishop in Tahiti in 1866—working with Metoro Taouaouré, an Easter Islander in Tahiti—created a list of several hundred signs grouped according to subject matter, with French and Rapanui translations (Heyerdahl and Ferdon 1965, figs. 83–94). In 1956 a manuscript containing rongorongo signs with Rapanui translations in roman script, belonging to Esteban Atan, was shown to members of the Norwegian expedition (ibid., figs. 97–121). Examination of both of these sources suggests only that the writing was pictographic, giving no evidence of relationships between signs with similar features and words or phrases with similar sounds or meanings.

One of the earliest observations based purely on the structure of the script was published posthumously by Borja Kudrjavtsev (1949), a young Russian who observed a repeated sequence in the two St. Petersburg tablets (RR 17–18 in Fischer 1993B), later also observed in two additional tablets (Butinov 1990: 268). Butinov and Knorozov (1957) called attention to a sequence of signs which they said was a genealogy. The tablets are read left to right, from bottom to top, in reverse boustrophedon fashion. Barthel (1958) provided scholars with line drawings of the entire corpus arranged in lines reading from left to right. He provides a list of several hundred signs (numbers go to 778, but not all slots are filled). Barthel (1963) lists a sign inventory of 150, and later (Barthel 1971) 120 signs. Twenty years later, Barthel writes (1993: 175) that he considers as much as ninety percent of his earlier work to be correct.

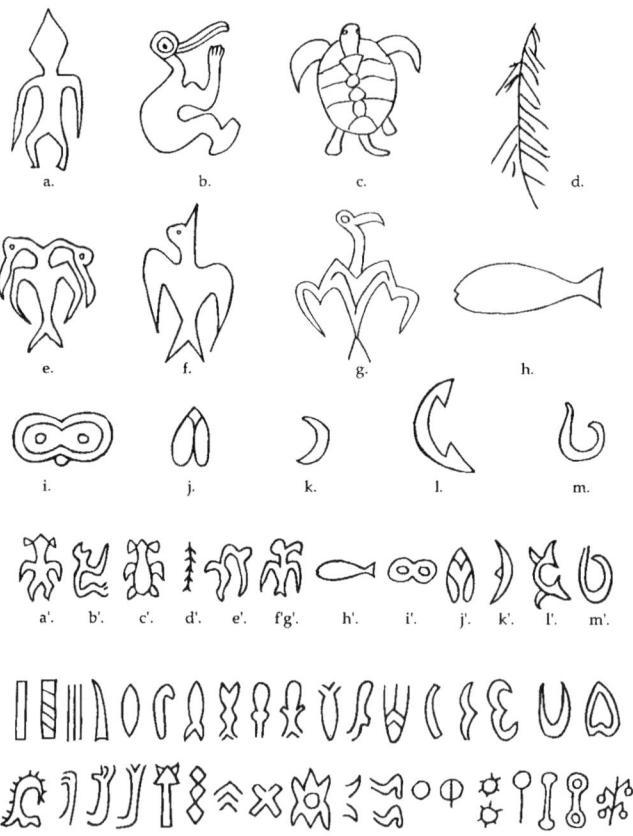

FIGURE 19. Petroglyph motifs with corresponding Rongorongo symbols *(marked with ')*, drawings by Judy Alexander after Lee 1992: *(a)* Anthropomorphic figure (fig. 3.5:2), *(b)* Bird man (fig. 3.7:2), *(c)* Turtle (fig. 3.9:9), *(d)* Plant (fig. 3.15:2), *(e)* Two-headed frigate bird (fig. 3.8.4, rotated slightly and flipped on vertical axis), *(f)* Tern (fig. 3.8:2), *(g)* Frigate bird (fig. 3.8.4), *(h)* Fish (fig. 3.9.1), *(i)* Eye mask (fig. 3.6:4), *(j)* Vulva (fig. 3.6:8), *(k)* Lunate (fig. 3.14:10), *(l)* Rei miro, a crescent-shaped wooden pectoral (fig. 3.11:1, rotated 90°), *(m)* Fishhook (fig. 3.13:1). *(bottom)* Partial list of other symbols.

Viktor Krupa identified signs for 'moon', 'lizard', and the god Tane, and produced a frequency chart of human figures with varying head forms (1971, 1972, 1973, 1974). Jacques Guy of the Australian National University has contributed an interesting discussion of fused glyphs (1982) and notes a sequence from the Tahua tablet (RR 1) which occurs on three other tablets (1985).

Sergej Rjabchikov of Krasnodar claimed the script is "typical of other mixed ideographic and phonetic writing systems, relying on ideograms proper, phonograms, and generic determinatives" (1987: 361). He notes allographic variations of several glyphs (1988). Criticizing his work, Guy (1988) cautions that only the Marmari tablet (RR 2), which Barthel showed was a lunar calendar, is understood beyond reasonable doubt. He rejects assigning readings at this stage but characterizes the script as a mixed ideographic and phonetic system.

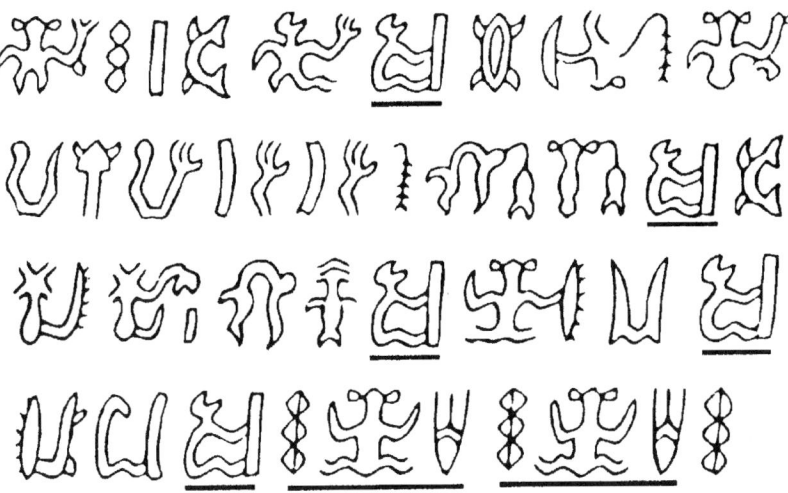

FIGURE 20. One line of text from the Keiti tablet (RR 6) (after Barthel 1958: Ev3).
Two repeated sequences are underlined.

In spite of impressive contributions by international scholars, Vignes (1990) observes correctly that the script remains undeciphered, and that we are still at the beginning of rongorongo studies. In fact, many of these scholars have suggested, in
otherwise useful publications, all manner of fanciful interpretations.

A linguistic approach to decipherment

I propose a sign analysis which is both rigorous and systematic (Macri IN PREPARA-
TION). It begins with an examination of the art of the island (Lee 1992), observing
similarities between the written symbols and those found carved on stone or wood.
FIGURE 19a–m' is not an exhaustive list, but does establish beyond any doubt that the
script belongs to Easter Island. Even a cursory examination shows that most of the
signs are composed of fairly simple forms which appear in a number of combinations
(FIGURE 19n, FIGURE 20). However, signs which some researchers have considered
basic are, in fact, products of doubling (FIGURE 21), concatenation (FIGURE 22a)—
sometimes in boustrophedon fashion, reduction of size (FIGURE 22b), rotation
(FIGURE 22a, e), and finally, of complex conflation of two or more signs
(FIGURE 22b–e). Four symbols (FIGURE 19a', b', e', and f'g'), and perhaps more, have
the quality of undergoing loss of many of their elements when combined with other
symbols.

Invoking these principles, the texts can be accounted for with fewer than 70 symbols—a number consistent only with a syllabary. Rapanui has 10 consonants [p t k ʔ
m n ŋ h r v] and 5 vowels [i e a o u], so only 55 signs are required to represent all
syllables composed of a single vowel or of a consonant + vowel. In addition to the 55
signs required by a syllabary, some signs, such as the lunar crescent and the lizard,
were probably used logographically.

FIGURE 21. Doubled symbols (drawing by Judy Alexander).

This analysis is consistent with the assertion of islanders that each graphic unit (composed of one to four or five syllabic elements) represents a single word, and with the correlation between the number of symbols and the number of possible syllables in the Rapanui language. Complete decipherment can only be accomplished through the cooperative efforts of Rapanui speakers, art historians, archeologists, and linguists. Texts need to be assembled and redrawn (Dederen and Fischer 1993), individ-

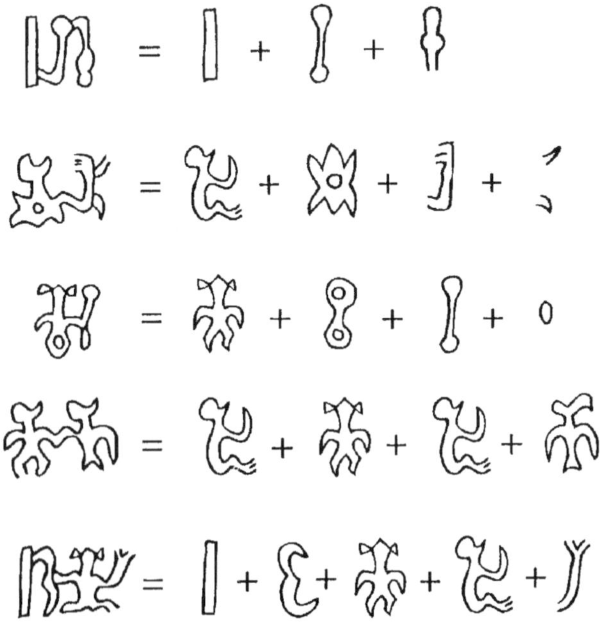

FIGURE 22. Composite signs showing full forms of constituent symbols (drawing by Judy Alexander).

ual symbols identified, and syllabic and/or logographic values demonstrated. Vignes's (1990) suggestion of a computer database will be an essential part of such an analysis.

───────

Bibliography

Barthel, Thomas S. 1958. *Grundlagen zur Entzifferung der Osterinselschrift* (Abhandlungen aus dem Gebiet der Auslandskunde 64, series B, vol. 36). Hamburg: Cram, de Gruyter.

───────. 1963. "Rongorongo-Studien (Forschungen und Fortschritte bei der weiteren Entzifferung der Osterinselschrift)." *Anthropos* 58: 372–436.

───────. 1971. "Pre-contact Writing in Oceania." In *Current Trends in Linguistics,* ed. Thomas A. Sebeok, vol. 8: *Linguistics in Oceania,* pp. 1165–86. The Hague: Mouton.

───────. 1993. "Perspectives and Directions of the Classical Rapanui Script." In Fischer 1993A: 174–76.

Butinov, N. A. 1990. "Decipherment of the Easter Island Script." In *Culture and History in the Pacific,* ed. Jukka Siikala, pp. 267–82. Helsinki: Suomen Antropologisen Seura.

Butinov, N. A., and Yuriy V. Knorozov. 1957. "Preliminary Report on the Study of the Written Language of Easter Island." *Journal of the Polynesian Society* 66/1: 5–17.

Dederen, François, and Steven Roger Fischer. 1993. "The Traditional Production of the Rapanui Tablets." In Fischer 1993A: 182–84.

Fischer, Steven Roger, ed. 1993A. *Easter Island Studies: Contributions to the History of Rapanui in Memory of William T. Mulloy* (Oxbow Monograph 32). Oxford: Oxbow Books.

───────. 1993B. "A Provisional Inventory of the Inscribed Artifacts in the Three Rapanui Scripts." In Fischer 1993A: 177–81.

Guy, Jacques B. 1982. "Fused Glyphs in the Easter Island Script." *Journal of the Polynesian Society* 91: 445–47.

───────. 1985. "On a Fragment of the 'Tahua' Tablet." *Journal of the Polynesian Society* 94: 367–88.

───────. 1988. "Rjabchikov's Decipherments Examined." *Journal of the Polynesian Society* 97: 321–23.

Heyerdahl, Thor, and Edwin N. Ferdon, Jr., eds. 1965. *Reports of the Norwegian Archaeological Expedition to Easter Island and the East Pacific,* vol. 2: *Miscellaneous Papers* (Monographs of the School of American Research and the Museum of New Mexico 24/2). Chicago: Rand McNally.

Krupa, Viktor. 1971. "'Moon' in the Writing of Easter Island." *Oceanic Linguistics* 10: 1–10.

───────. 1972. "Some Human Figures and Hand Forms in the Writing of Easter Island." *Asian and African Studies* 8: 19–26.

───────. 1973. "Tane in the Easter Island Script." *Asian and African Studies* 9: 115–19.

───────. 1974. "The Symbol for Lizard in the Writing of the Easter Island." *Asian and African Studies* 10: 61–67.

Kudrjavtsev, Borja. 1949. "Pis′mennost′ Ostrova Paschi" [Writing of Easter Island]. *Sbornik Muzeja Antropologii i Etnografii* (Leningrad) 2: 176–221.

Lee, Georgia. 1992. *Rock Art of Easter Island: Symbols of Power, Prayers to the Gods* (Monumenta Archaeologica 17). Los Angeles: U.C.L.A. Institute of Archaeology.

Macri, Martha J. IN PREPARATION. "The Easter Island Tablets: A Phonetic Script."

Rjabchikov, Sergej V. 1987. "Progress Report on the Decipherment of the Easter Island Writing System." *Journal of the Polynesian Society* 96: 361–67.

───────. 1988. "Allographic Variations of Easter Island Glyphs." *Journal of the Polynesian Society*

97: 313–20.

Vignes, Jacques. 1990. "Is a New Approach to the Decipherment of Rongorongo Writing Necessary?" In *State and Perspectives of Scientific Research in Easter Island Culture*, ed. Heide-Mar-
  garet Esen-Baur, pp. 115–19. Frankfurt: Courier Forschungsinstitut Senchkenberg.

Part IV: East Asian Writing Systems

THE EAST ASIAN SCRIPTS COVERED IN THIS SECTION are all traceable one way or another to Chinese as their source. This is a consequence of the pervasive cultural dominance that Chinese civilization has consistently enjoyed throughout East Asia from the earliest historical period. The modern Chinese script, of course, as well as Japanese (kanji and kana alike) and Korean (except for the Hankul letters) are all either varieties of, or derived from, Chinese characters. Before the Koreans and Japanese used Chinese characters to write their own languages (which may be related to each other and in turn to the Altaic group but are not related to Chinese), they adopted the Chinese language as the linguistic vehicle for the composition of their own literary texts, and in this they of course used Chinese characters. It was therefore a natural next step, when they began to write their native languages, to use Chinese characters there as well. Because these scripts arise directly from the Chinese, we may designate them, along with Chinese proper, by the general term Sinitic. An adaptation of Chinese script was also used in Vietnam, under the name *chữ nôm*, until it was replaced by the Roman alphabet in the seventeenth century.

Medieval scripts of Inner Asia—such as those of Tangut (Tibeto-Burman) and of Khitan and Jurchin (Altaic)—and scripts used for certain languages of South China, such as Yi (of the Tai family), are only impressionistically based on the appearance of Chinese characters, and bear no genuine evolutionary or cognate relation to Chinese writing. As with the spatial arrangement of Korean hankul letters, the external shape of the graphic complexes in these scripts reflects the influence of Chinese characters, even though the internal structure of the graphs proper has no connection with Chinese; the scripts themselves are in no way actual descendants of Chinese orthography. Scripts of this type we call Siniform because they take the outward form of the Chinese script as their basis, but are otherwise unrelated to it.

Chinese writing is the oldest of any East Asian script and is the only one to have arisen ex nihilo, first appearing in north-central China in the second half of the second millennium B.C.E. There is no persuasive evidence for any fully developed kind of

189

writing system, Chinese or other, in East Asia prior to this time, nor is there any indication of outside influence, e.g. from the ancient Near East, on the invention of the Chinese script.

In recent centuries, the Siniform scripts (except for a few examples like the Yi) have been replaced by syllabic or alphabetic scripts. The Sinitic scripts, by contrast, have endured as viable writing systems throughout China and Japan, yielding neither to Indic aksharas nor to European alphabets in spite of extensive cultural contacts with both. The traditional Korean mixed script with its heavy component of Chinese characters was replaced in North Korea in the 1940s, largely for political reasons, by writing exclusively in hankul. In South Korea, use of the traditional mixed script lasted until very recently and has still not been entirely supplanted by an exclusively hankul writing system, although the clear tendency is to use fewer Chinese characters as time goes on.

— WILLIAM G. BOLTZ

Early Chinese Writing

WILLIAM G. BOLTZ

We know from direct archeological evidence that Chinese writing arose no later than the last quarter of the second millennium B.C.E. in north-central China. This is the locale of the first historically attested period of Chinese civilization, the Shang or Yin dynasty; the two names refer to the same political and cultural entity.

The first appearance of what we recognize unequivocally to be Chinese writing comes in the form of inscribed ox scapulas and turtle plastrons from sites near modern Ānyáng 安陽 on the northern border of Henan province. These inscribed objects, which date from about 1200 B.C.E. to the end of the Shang state 150 years later, are records of royal divinations performed at the Shang court and are therefore often referred to as "oracle bone inscriptions." There is no proof that the Shang Chinese were solely responsible for the origin of writing in China; but neither is there evidence of recognizable Chinese writing from any earlier time or any other place.

It is true that Chinese archeologists have uncovered numerous neolithic pottery fragments, some dating back to ca. 4800 B.C.E., that carry incised marks of one kind or another (e.g. Cheung 1983); but none of these marks can be successfully identified with the characters of the Shang inscriptions, or in any other way as Chinese writing. Apart from the near impossibility of deciphering a few scattered graphs occurring outside a known linguistic context, the sheer extent of time (close to 3500 years in some cases) precludes these marks from being direct forerunners of Shang characters. Neither is there any indication that writing was imported into China from any civilization in Western Asia, or from anywhere else.

The Chinese characters in use today are the direct descendants of the Chinese script of the Shang period. In outward appearance, to be sure, modern characters differ substantially from those of the Shang inscriptions, so that the latter are not readable by someone who knows only the modern forms; nevertheless, the basic structural principles that underlie the Shang writing system are fundamentally the same as for later stages of the Chinese script, including the modern script.

The Shang writing system is logographic; i.e., each character stands for a single word (technically, for a single syllabic morpheme), and each character can therefore be called a logogram. Formally there are two different kinds: those that consist of one graphic element alone and cannot be divided into component parts, called unit characters, and those that are made up of two or more component parts, called compound characters.

TABLE 14.1: *Shang Unit Characters*

1.		'person'	人	rén
2.		'large'	大	dà
3.		'eye'	目	mù
4.		'sun, day'	日	rì
5.		'mouth, orifice'	口	kǒu
6.		'ear'	耳	ěr
7.		'hand'	又	yòu
8.		'moon, month'	月	yuè
9.		'rain'	雨	yǔ
10.		'water'	水	shuǐ
11.		'ox'	牛	niú
12.		'boat'	舟	zhōu
13.		'king'	王	wáng
14.		'woman'	女	nǚ
15.		'cowrie shell'	貝	bèi
16.		'top of the head'	丁	dīng
17.		'growing grain'	禾	hé

Unit characters

Examples of *unit characters* of the Shang script, with modern equivalents and readings, are given in TABLE 14.1. A few of them, when we already know what words they stand for, seem pictographically realistic, e.g., TABLE 14.1:4, 5, 8, 9, and 14. This suggests that the first steps of the Chinese toward a script entailed drawing realistic pictures of easily depictable things and letting the picture stand for the name of the thing in question. Thus  (no. 8) was in origin presumably a pictographic representation of a crescent moon; and  (no. 14) portrayed a kneeling human figure, arms crossed in front (presumably a woman, since this is the precursor of the modern character 女 for *nǚ* 'woman').

These graphs convey meaning in Shang inscriptions by standing for the names of the objects they depict, i.e. for the words denoting those objects. Number 13, for example, stands for the word *wáng* (or more precisely, for the Old Chinese word that has become modern Chinese *wáng*). (When the Old Chinese pronunciation is pertinent to the discussion, I give it with an asterisk; otherwise I use modern Chinese).* Since the word *wáng* means 'king', the graph conveys that meaning, but only through the medium of the word. There is nothing remotely suggestive of a 'king' in the

*The reconstruction of Old Chinese follows that of Norman (1994), except that pharyngealization is marked with ˤ rather than ʻ.

graphic shape 土 alone. By the same token, ⑺ (no. 15) stands for the word *bèi* 'cowrie shell', and means 'cowrie shell' only by virtue of standing for that word. Once we know that ⑺ is used to write the word *bèi* 'cowrie shell', we may be inclined to see an image of a cowrie shell in the character; but this is surely only after the fact.

The first important consequence of this use of graphs was the recognition that a graph could be used to stand for a second word, pronounced like the first, but with a different and often unrelated meaning, especially one that did not lend itself to direct pictographic representation. This is what is commonly called the rebus use of graphs. Thus 土 (no. 13) was used to write the verb *wǎng* 'go toward'. This word had no semantic link to *wáng* 'king'; it just happened to be pronounced very nearly the same way. In the same way ⑺, standing for *bèi* 'cowrie shell', was used to write the verb *bài* 'defeat', and ▭ (no. 16) *dīng* (Old Chinese *ᶜ*ting*) 'top of the head', was used to write the nearly homophonous word *zhēng* (Old Chinese *ting*) 'to mount a military expedition'. The rebus use of characters increased the effectiveness of the writing system significantly. Hundreds of words with meanings that were not amenable to pictographic representation could now be written by the rebus principle.

If a graph could be used to stand for a semantically unrelated but phonetically similar word, it could also stand for a phonetically unrelated but semantically related word. This is called the polyphonic use of a graph; like the rebus principle, this allowed the writing of numerous words that could not otherwise be written. The word *míng* 'call out', for example, was written with ㅂ (no. 5), which presumably depicted an orifice of some kind, and which represented the word *kǒu* 'mouth'. The words *míng* 'call out' and *kǒu* 'mouth' clearly have nothing in common in pronunciation; but just as clearly they are linked semantically. Similarly, ☞ (no. 3) was used to write the verb *jiàn* 'to see'. The character ⏉ (no. 8), standing originally for *yuè* 'moon', was used to write the semantically related word *míng* 'brighten'.

These two extended uses of characters, by the rebus principle and by polyphony, are simply two converse ways of doing the same thing. In both cases the graphs still stand for words, and can still properly be called logograms, even though the words are not necessarily those for which they were originally created. This is called by the general term *graphic multivalence*.

Graphic multivalence introduced considerable versatility into the nascent Chinese writing system, providing a way to write words that would not otherwise be writable because their meanings did not lend themselves to direct graphic depiction. At the same time it perforce introduced a significant measure of ambiguity—semantic or phonetic. Often, of course, the context of a passage would readily determine which possibility was intended. But there must have been an unwelcome abundance of cases when the context was not sufficient to resolve the ambiguity. Hence some other recourse was needed to keep the writing system from succumbing to an unmanageable burden of ambiguity.

Compound characters

To solve the problem of ambiguity, the Chinese scribes appended secondary graphic components, called *determinatives*, to ambiguous primary graphs; such components specify either the intended meaning or the pronunciation. The addition of these secondary graphs to potentially ambiguous primary graphs gave rise to *compound characters*.

In cases of semantic ambiguity, like that attending 土, which could stand for *wáng* 'king' or *wǎng* 'go toward', the determinative serves to indicate which of the two words is intended. When 土 was used for the word *wǎng* 'go toward', the secondary graph 止 (止/之), standing independently for *zhǐ* 'step, stop/go', was added, yielding a compound graph 往 (往). Similarly, when 貝 was used to stand for *bài* 'defeat' as opposed to *bèi* 'cowrie shell', the secondary graph 攴 (攴), standing independently for the word *pū* 'strike', was appended, giving a compound graph 敗 (敗). The secondary graphs function as semantic determinatives. The rationale for their use is based on meaning alone; their pronunciation has no bearing on their usage here.

Phonetic ambiguity was resolved in a comparable way: secondary graphs were appended to phonetically ambiguous primary graphs, to indicate which of two or more possible pronunciations was intended in a particular case. The character 口 could stand for either *kǒu* 'mouth' or *míng* 'to speak, call out'. In the latter usage, the secondary graph 夕, pronounced *míng* (with the meaning 'brighten'), was appended to specify the pronunciation *míng* as opposed to *kǒu*; the result was the compound graph 名 (名). Similarly, 禾 (no. 17), which could stand either for the word *hé* 'growing grain' or for the semantically akin but phonetically distinct word *nián* 'harvest' (> 'year'), was written 年 (年) with the graph 人 (人) *rén* (Old Chinese *znen) added underneath to determine the pronunciation *nián* (Old Chinese *ʿznen) unambiguously. The secondary graphs function as phonetic determinatives; their intrinsic meaning is irrelevant to these usages.

Like unit characters, compound characters could be used either polyphonically or as rebuses; thus they were susceptible of receiving additional added components as determinatives. The graph 名 *míng* 'call out', consisting of two components, was used as a rebus for the homophonous word *míng* 'inscription (on a bronze vessel)'; later it acquired the semantic determinative 金 referring to 'metal', thus coming to be written 銘 with three graphic components in all. (Characters can in theory have an unlimited number of components, in practice as many as five or six, e.g. 贏 *luǒ* 'naked' with five, 鬱 *yù* 'worried' with six; characters with more than six are distinctly uncommon.) Early scribes, sensing the structural principles that underlay the emerging writing system, probably created additional new compound characters outright, even if the underlying unit character had not actually been used multivalently before.

Examples of compound characters in the Shang script, with modern equivalents and readings, are given in TABLE 14.2.

TABLE 14.2: *Shang Compund Characters*

1.		'go toward'	往	wǎng
2.		'defeat'	敗	bài
3.		'harvest, year'	年	nián
4.		'call out, name'	名	míng
5.		'mount a military expedition'	征	zhēng
6.		'dusk'	莫	mù
7.		'catch'	隻	zhī
8.		'illness'	嫉	jí
9.		'male animal'	牡	mǔ
10.		'spring season'	春	chūn
11.		'dream'	夢	mèng
12.		'change'	易	yì

With the versatility that compound characters brought to the script—together with the fact that they, like unit characters, could be used multivalently—the Chinese writing system achieved a form that allowed for full expression of the language, while still remaining fundamentally logographic. In a given written context any character, compound or unit, stood for a single syllable, and as far as we know, that syllable always corresponded to a single word. Some characters always stood for the same word; others, thanks to the multivalent feature of the script, could stand for one of several possibilities, depending on context. No character ever stood for an "idea" independently of a word. Chinese characters stood, and continue to stand, for words, and only by extension for the ideas those words convey. The word "ideogram" (or "ideograph") is thus inapplicable to Chinese characters.

Apart from a few oracle texts, texts from the early Zhou are known only in the form of inscriptions cast on bronze vessels. Cast inscriptions, because they are made initially in soft clay, impose fewer constraints on the execution of the characters than incised inscriptions; thus the outward appearance of the script of bronze inscriptions differs substantially from that of the Shang oracle bone texts. Later texts came to be written in ink on bamboo, wood, and silk, allowing for the same orthographic versatility as the bronzes. This greater latitude in executing characters, combined with innumerable idiosyncratic and independent regional developments, gave rise to a large number of different ways for writing the same words from text to text and place to place. None of this diversity affected the basic structural rules of the writing system.

Orthographic irregularity had become so widespread by the end of the third century B.C.E., when the state of Qin succeeded in uniting all of China for the first time into a single empire, that standardization of the script became one of the Qin emperor's earliest social goals. The Emperor's Grand Councillor Lǐ Sī is credited with establishing and promulgating a type of script intended to serve as a standard, called the

"Small Seal" or sometimes the "Qin Seal" script, in contrast to an earlier "Large Seal" script. Both scripts were ostensibly used, as their names imply, for seals, i.e. signets, of officials and noblemen.

The actual orthographic consequences of this official policy are not clear. The evidence of recently discovered silk manuscripts dating from around 200 B.C.E. suggests that, even a generation after the Qin attempts at standardization, the writing system was still characterized by much orthographic instability and variation. Some of these manuscripts even hint at impending desemanticization of a few graphs, which would have allowed them to function almost as syllabograms. Had this tendency fulfilled itself, it might have added a genuine syllabary to the Chinese writing system. But that did not happen. The tendency toward desemanticization was arrested by a conscientious use of semantic determinatives as an intrinsic part of a character's structure, almost as if the intellectuals of the time were consciously committed to thwarting any movement in the direction of a syllabary and to reaffirming the logographic structure of the script.

Tangible evidence of a genuine orthographic standardization does not appear until 100 C.E., when the *Shuō wén jiě zì* 説文解字 'Explaining the unit characters and analyzing the compound characters', a lexicon of about 9,500 characters, was compiled by Xǔ Shèn 許慎. Taking the Small Seal form of characters as basic, Xǔ explains and analyzes nearly the entire inventory of known characters of his time within a framework of structural categories that constitutes a de facto standardization of the script. Against this framework he is able to identify nonstandard forms of characters, implicitly curbing their use.

The *Shuō wén jiě zì* classifies characters at three different levels. The most fundamental is the bipartite distinction between unit characters (*wén* 文) and compound characters (*zì* 字); this classification is implicit but unambiguous. The next is according to a set of 540 different graphic elements, which we now call *semantic classifiers*. One of these 540 occurs in the graphic structure of every character, and this component is deemed indicative of the semantic class of the word for which the character stands. The character is therefore entered in the lexicon under that classifier. Characters often contain more than one of these components, but only one of them is taken as the primary semantic indicator, i.e. the semantic classifier under which the character will be entered.

While this seems at first to produce a 540-way classification scheme, it is in fact a way of rendering all compound characters bipartite, regardless of how many components the character actually has, by singling out a single component as the semantic classifier. This in effect imposes a hierarchy on the components of compound characters with more than two elements; simultaneously, it ratifies earlier efforts to ensure that semantic constituents remain an integral part of characters and thus that the characters themselves remain unfalteringly invested with meaning as well as sound. The effect is to preclude any further movement toward desemanticization and the development of syllabograms.

At the third level, Xǔ Shèn ascribes characters to one of six different classes; four are based on graphic structure, and two on usage. These classes are known traditionally as the *liù shū* 六書, the 'six [classes of] script'; they do not recapitulate the actual historical development of the writing system, although it is sometimes claimed that they do. Instead they constitute a set of explicitly descriptive, and perhaps implicitly prescriptive, rules accounting for the graphic structure and usage of characters in the writing system of the first century C.E.

(1) *Zhǐ shì* 指事 'indicating the matter'; unit characters that are graphically suggestive in some impressionistic sense of the meaning of the word they write, e.g. 上 *shàng* 'above', 下 *xià* 'below'.

(2) *Xiàng xíng* 象形 'representing the form'; unit characters that are ostensibly graphic representations of the thing in question, e.g. 目 *mù* 'eye', 耳 *ěr* 'ear'.

(3) *Xíng shēng* 形聲 'forming the sound'; compound characters comprising a semantic determinative and a sound-bearing element, e.g. 敗 *bài* 'defeat' (from 貝 *bèi*), 征 *zhēng* 'mount a military expedition' (from 正 *zhēng*).

(4) *Huì yì* 會意 'conjoining the sense'; compound characters that are analyzed as if the meaning of the word for which they stand were reflected by the combination of graphic constituents in the character, e.g. 信 *xìn* 'trustworthy' (as if from 人 *rén* 'person' and 言 *yán* 'speech', "a person keeping his word"), 武 *wǔ* 'martial' (as if from 止 *zhǐ* 'stop' and 戈 *gē* 'spear', "putting a stop to the use of weapons"). In origin actual characters are never formed this way; this is an artificial, retrospective category.

(5) *Zhuǎn zhù* 轉注 'redirected characters'. This and the next are classes of usage, not of character structure; it is not clear what exactly the process of "redirecting" characters was, but it seems to have had to do with writing etymologically related words with related, but not identical, characters. The usual example is 考 *kǎo* 'aged' and 老 *lǎo* 'old'; the process that this is intended to exemplify is not obvious.

(6) *Jiǎ jiè* 假借 'borrowed characters'. Like the above, this is not a description of graphic structure. It is a name for the use of a character to write a word different from, but homophonous or nearly homophonous with, the word that the character in question conventionally writes. For example, 令 *lìng* 'command' used to write *liáng* 'fine' (usually written 良).

The Small Seal script that Xǔ Shèn took as basic did not become the quotidian script of his time; but it did devolve into a simplified form called *lì shū* 隸書 'clerical script', which was widely used in administrative contexts. It is this script that underlies virtually all subsequent forms of the Chinese writing system. For comparison of character forms, see TABLE 14.3.

By the Qing dynasty (1644–1911), the number of Chinese characters had grown to several tens of thousands. In 1710 the Kangxi Emperor appointed a panel of scholars to prepare a new comprehensive dictionary; this was completed in 1716, and is known as the *Kāngxī zìdiǎn* 康熙字典 'The Kāngxī character dictionary'. It was ar-

TABLE 14.3: *Comparison of Script Forms*[a]

Oracle bone inscription	Bronze inscription	Small Seal script	Clerical script	Modern character	Pronunciation	Meaning
				五	wǔ	'five'
				令	lìng	'command'
				命	mìng	'fate'
				先	xiān	'prior'
				克	kè	'conquer'
				毓	yù	'parturition'
				孝	xiào	'filiality'
				事	shì	'affair'
				受	shòu	'receive'
				更	gēng	'change'
				逐	zhú	'expel'
				進	jìn	'advance'
				相	xiàng	'inspect'
				取	qǔ	'take'
				祭	jì	'sacrifice'
				獸	shòu	'animal'
				干	gān	'stalk'
				買	mǎi	'buy'
				盟	méng	'covenant'
				鼎	dǐng	'cauldron'
				武	wǔ	'martial'
				方	fāng	'area'
				安	ān	'settled'
				去	qù	'depart'
				在	zài	'located'

a. Columns 1–3 from Gāo Míng 1980; column 4 from the *Qín Hàn Wèi Jìn zhuàn lì zì xíng biǎo* (1985).

ranged according to a scheme of 214 semantic classifiers, a considerable reduction from the 540 of Xǔ Shèn's *Shuō wén jiě zì*. Conversely, it contains over 47,000 characters, as compared to the approximately 9,500 in the *Shuō wén*. Within each semantic classifier category, classifiers are entered in order of increasing number of residual strokes, i.e. number of strokes in that part of the character exclusive of the classifier. The Kangxi dictionary has become the standard authority for the whole range of Classical Chinese literature, and its scheme of 214 semantic classifiers, now commonly called *radicals*, remains basic for Chinese reference works of all kinds, in spite of recent sporadic and arbitrary efforts at simplification.

Bibliography

Boltz, William G. 1986. "Early Chinese Writing." *World Archaeology* 17: 420–36.

———. 1994. *The Origin and Early Development of the Chinese Writing System* (American Oriental Series 78). New Haven: American Oriental Society.

Cheung Kwong-yue. 1983. "Recent Archaeological Evidence Relating to the Origin of Chinese Characters." In *The Origins of Chinese Civilization*, ed. David N. Keightley, pp. 323–91. Berkeley and Los Angeles: University of California Press.

DeFrancis, John. 1984. *The Chinese Language: Fact and Fantasy.* Honolulu: University of Hawaii Press.

Gāo Míng 高明. 1980. *Gǔ wén zì lèi biān* [Tables of ancient characters] 古文字類編. Peking: Zhōng huá 中華.

Karlgren, Bernhard. 1940. *Grammata Serica.* Bulletin of the Museum of Far Eastern Antiquities (Stockholm) 12.

———. 1957. *Grammata Serica Recensa.* Bulletin of the Museum of Far Eastern Antiquities (Stockholm) 29.

Keightley, David N. 1989. "The Origins of Writing in China: Scripts and Cultural Contexts." In *The Origins of Writing*, ed. Wayne M. Senner, pp. 171–202. Lincoln: University of Nebraska Press.

Norman, Jerry. 1994. "Pharyngealization in Early Chinese." *Journal of the American Oriental Society* 114: 397–408.

Qín Hàn Wèi Jìn zhuàn lì zì xíng biǎo [Tables of the 'seal' and 'clerical' characters from the Qín, Hàn, Wèi, and Jìn periods] 秦漢魏晉篆隸字形表. 1985. Chéngdū: Sìchuān cí shū 四川辭書.

Tsien, Tsuen-hsuin. 1962. *Written on Bamboo and Silk.* Chicago: University of Chicago Press.

Modern Chinese Writing

VICTOR H. MAIR

Since the great codification of the Chinese writing system at the end of the first century C.E. in Xǔ Shèn's *Shuō wén jiě zì* 'Explanation of simple and compound graphs', the number of sinograms ('characters'; *hànzi*, Jpn. *kanji*, Kor. *hanja*) has continued to grow steadily. Xǔ's dictionary included a total of 9,353 characters. In succeeding centuries, lexicographic works contained the following numbers of characters: 11,520 (compiled during the period 227–239); 12,824 (in 400); 13,734 (in 500); 22,726 (in 534); 26,911 (in 753); 31,319 (in 1066); 33,179 (in 1615); 47,043 (in 1716). The most recent dictionary of single graphs published in China, *Hànyǔ dà zìdiǎn* (1986–90) lists about 60,000.

So long as the script is actively used, the number of sinograms will continue to grow because, unlike a phonetic script, the traditional Chinese writing system is open-ended. This is due to the fact that, as in any language, words are constantly being added to the lexicon. Since the representation of these words is fundamentally logographic—or, more precisely, morphosyllabic—new sinograms must be invented when new morphemes arise in the Chinese languages or enter through borrowings.

Although the characters are made up of recurring components, their shapes and proportions change in combination; hence each character is a distinct entity and must be stored as a separate unit in memories or fonts. But of course the number of characters in daily use is at least a factor of ten smaller than the total number in existence.

Massive statistical studies of a wide variety of reading material in China during the last two decades have repeatedly demonstrated that 1,000 sinograms cover approximately 90% of all occurrences in typical texts, 2,400 sinograms cover 99%, 3,800 cover 99.9%, 5,200 cover 99.99%, and 6,600 cover 99.999%. The percentages are intriguingly similar for earlier periods of Chinese history when only Classical Chinese texts were normally composed and written (written Vernacular Chinese, a relatively late phenomenon, had not yet come into existence; see Mair 1994). It would appear that there is a natural upper limit to the number of unique forms that can be tolerated in a functioning script. For most individuals, this amount seems to lie in the range of approximately 2,000–2,500. Still, the command of 2,400 diverse signs—the number considered by educators as essential for basic reading and writing skills—is a formidable task.

The vast majority of the graphs found in the largest Chinese character dictionaries are extremely rare. Many are so obscure that neither the sound nor the meaning is known, only the shape; others may only have been used once or twice in all of history. Unfortunately, they cannot be completely ignored by font-makers, lexicographers, and classicists.

Many scholars, especially linguists and Sinologists, now agree that the Chinese script may be described as an enormously large but phonetically imprecise syllabary, with strong visual and semantic qualities (DeFrancis 1984, 1989). A few philosophers still insist that the Chinese writing system is pictographic and "ideographic" (Hansen 1993), but their views have been effectively countered by empirical and historical evidence (Unger 1990, 1993). Nonetheless, it must be admitted that Chinese characters function differently from a purely phonetic script in that they have a powerful ability to carry semantic weight in and of themselves—i.e., without entering into combinations, as is necessary for the elements of phonetic scripts to convey meaning. This can be seen in the semantic dissonance that occurs when they are used for transcriptional purposes. Thus, because of semantic interference, readers frequently misinterpret such expressions as 特納廣播電台 *Tènà Guǎngbó Diàntái* as 'Special Acceptance Broadcasting Station' instead of as 'Turner Broadcasting Station'.

All Chinese characters, whether they have one stroke or sixty-four strokes, are designed to fit into the same square frame; hence they are sometimes called *fāngkuàizì* 'tetragrams' by the Chinese. (Chinese characters were not always written as single syllabic units occupying a square; but for over two thousand years there has been a fixed convention of writing each character, no matter how complex, in the same size square.) In premodern times, all genres of texts, including poetry, were customarily written from top to bottom, right to left, in long strips of unbroken, equidistantly spaced characters, with no indication of word breaks or punctuation. Punctuation became common in the twentieth century, although it remains unstandardized and not fully utilized. Except for a few unpublicized experiments, no attempt has been made to group syllables into words. There are still no established conventions for such things as emphasis and distinguishing proper names, although various devices (such as types of underlining or sidelining) have been invented. The direction of writing has largely shifted so that most Chinese books and journals now read horizontally from left to right, by way of accommodation to international usage.

Examination and analysis of the 8,075 sinograms in the extremely popular *Xīnhuá zìdiǎn* 'New China character dictionary' reveal that 1,348 (17% of the total) may function independently or as semantic or phonetic components of other characters, but 6,542 (81%) are made up of a phonetic component plus a semantic "radical," of which there are approximately 200 (the number varies with different dictionaries). Only 185 (2%) do not function as components in other graphs and are not composed of such components (Zhou 1992: 179).

It must be pointed out that neither the semantic nor the phonetic components of the sinograms provide an exact indication of meaning or sound, but only give a vague approximation. Thus, 蹩 *bié* 'sprain [ankle]' is a combination of the radical 足 *zú* 'foot' with the phonetic 敝 *bì* 'shabby'—which, in combination with other semantic elements, gives the pronunciations *biē*, *bié*, *piē*, *piě*. Readers must guess or memorize the appropriate sound of the phonetic for each character in which it occurs; they must also associate the graph with a word that they already know. Only then can they arrive at the meaning of the sinogram in question. In many cases, phonetic components have much wider latitude than in *bié* 'sprain'; some have as many as a dozen or more different pronunciations depending on the characters in which they are found. Often a large number of pronunciations exist for the same sinogram, e.g., 碨 has the following possibilities in MSM: *wèi*, *kǎi*, *nái*, *wéi*, *yí*, *jī*, *kāi*, *ái*, *mò*, *gài*. In such cases, the variant pronunciations may indicate multiple meanings of the graph. Conversely, hundreds of different characters may be used to represent the same sound, though with different meanings. For example, *yī* is the MSM pronunciation of 一 or 壹 'one', 衣 'clothing', 依 'depend on', 銥 'iridium', 伊 'he/she' (used regionally), also a surname, 咿 part of a word meaning 'squeak' or 'babble', 醫 'physician', 繄 'tantamount to', 揖 'to bow with hands clasped in front', 噫 'alas' (interjection), 椅 or 漪 'ripple', 黟 name of a district, and so on. In earlier times, many of these sinograms would have had distinctive pronunciations, but through a long and complicated process of phonetic reduction, they have collapsed into a single sound.

Relationship to the Chinese languages

One of the most difficult problems in dealing with Chinese characters (*zì*) is that they are frequently confused with words (*cí*), the assumption being that Sinitic languages are exclusively monosyllabic (allegedly, one graph = one syllable = one word). On the contrary, even in the artificial classical or literary written language (passages are not intelligible when read aloud unless previously memorized), there were many polysyllabic words. The *Liánmián* and *Cítōng* dictionaries compiled in the twentieth century list thousands of examples drawn from ancient texts, such as *húdié* 'butterfly', *zhīzhū* 'spider', *shānhú* 'coral', *wēiyí* 'self-possessed, nonchalant', and *wēichí* 'sinuous, winding'. The latter two words can both be written with many different combinations of characters; this demonstrates the primacy of sound over symbol, and of word over graph, even in Chinese where the characters are so powerful.

In modern Mandarin, the average length of a word has been shown to be almost exactly two syllables. Typical words are *fēijī* 'airplane', *dǎzìjī* 'typewriter', *jīngjì* 'economics', *yóuyǒng* 'to swim', *cuīféi* 'to fatten', *fěicuì* 'jadeite, halcyon', and *tuífèi* 'decadent'. The non-monosyllabic nature of Sinitic languages is even reflected in some deviant features of the script itself, where unofficial but widely used characters such as 圕 *túshūguǎn* 'library', 瓩 *qiānwǎ* 'kilowatt', and 问 *wèntí* 'question' show that speakers clearly recognize these words as polysyllabic, in spite of the strongly monosyllabic features of the script.

The script is well suited for writing Classical Chinese, but it is poorly equipped to record the vernaculars and the regional variants (*fāngyán*). This defect was already evident toward the end of the second century C.E., when the first attempts were made

TABLE 15.1: *Phonological Variation through Time*

	600 B.C.E.	600 C.E.	1008	1250	1993	
道 'way, track'	*drog	taw˚	tʰiaw˚	daw˙	dào	[dɑu]
德 'virtue, doughtiness'	*dugh	təjˇ	təǎk	tək	dé	[də]
經 'classic, file'	*gwing	kiŋ	kjiajŋ	kɛjŋ	jīng	[d̠ʒɪŋ]

TABLE 15.2: *Phonological Variation through Space*

	MSM (Northern)		Suzhou	Wenzhou	Canton	Amoy
茶 'tea'	chá	[tsʰɑ]	꞉zo	꞉dzo	꞉ʨá	꞉ta/꞉te
千 'thousand'	qiān	[tɕʰiɛn]	꞉tsʼiɪ	꞉tɕʼiˈ	꞉ʦʼin	꞉ʦʼin
伯 'uncle'	bó/bái	[b̥ɤ/b̥aɪ̯]	poʔꞋ	poꞋ	pɔkꞋ	pɔkꞋ/pakꞋ

by Buddhists to write integral vernacular texts (Mair 1994). Before that time, only the barest snatches of vernacular ever appeared in writing, and there were really no conventions for composing anything other than Literary Sinitic. Still today, and even for Pekingese (which is the current foundation for Mandarin, the lingua franca), authors complain that it is impossible to write out all their favorite expressions in characters. In the nonstandard, regional languages, it is all the more difficult to write out unadulterated speech in characters, since many of the most frequently used morphemes are not represented in the standard set of 60,000 sinograms. Consequently, to write languages such as Cantonese, Taiwanese, and Shanghainese, it is necessary to invent numerous nonce characters—or simply to resort to romanization, as has often been done since the late nineteenth century, particularly under the influence of Western missionaries.

Another difficult problem caused by the sharp disjunction between spoken word and written script in China is that the latter has remained relatively stable for over two millennia—while the former, like all living languages, has evolved steadily. Although there have been stylistic variations since the standardization of the characters during the Qin dynasty (221–207 B.C.E.), their basic shapes and construction have changed little. In contrast, the sounds of the Sinitic languages, and consequently the pronunciations assigned to individual graphs, have changed dramatically through time and space (see TABLES 15.1 and 15.2; diacritics preceding and following syllables indicate tone).

Reform

Various Chinese scholars, since at least the twelfth century, have recognized the cumbersomeness of their morphosyllabic script and the superior efficiency of phonetic scripts for conveying the sounds of language (Mair 1993). However, because of a general conservatism of the culture and a strong emotional attachment to the characters, they never developed a fully functioning phonetic script of their own.

Around the end of the Ming dynasty (first half of the 16th century), with the arrival of the Jesuits in China, many progressive ideas became current, including the concept of romanization. The first schemes were created by Matteo Ricci (1605) and Nicolas Trigault (1625). During the ensuing centuries, the notion of phonetic scripts for Sinitic languages matured, especially with their widespread adoption by Christian missionaries for the previously unwritten regional varieties. Around the end of the nineteenth century, there was a great wave of protest against the moribund policies of the Manchu government in the face of foreign encroachment, and a vigorous push for reform in all areas of intellectual, political, and social life took place; many proposals for phonetic scripts were then put forward by Chinese patriots as means for the salvation of their country (to make China "wealthy and strong," as they put it). The first such proposal was advanced in 1892 by Lu Zhuangzhang (1854–1928). Lu's alphabet was keyed to the language of his native Amoy, but he declared that it could be applied to Mandarin and all the other varieties.

The fall of the Manchu government, and with it the dynastic structures that had lasted for more than two thousand years, came quickly (1911). Soon thereafter, the new Republican government replaced Classical Chinese with Mandarin as the official written language of the state, thus setting the stage for further linguistic reforms.

One of the most influential script reforms was the creation of a National Phonetic Alphabet (*Guóyīn Zìmŭ*, also called *Bōpōmōfō*; TABLE 15.3) under the Republic of China in 1913. This has been very useful in the movement to extend the use of Mandarin nationwide; many books, newspapers, and journals published in Taiwan still employ it in a Japanese furigana-like fashion, as a sound-annotating device for the characters.

With the founding of the People's Republic of China in 1949, script reform in the 1950s and thereafter basically took a two-pronged approach: simplification of the characters, and application of romanization to more and more spheres of activity. Simpler variants of the characters had been used among the populace for many centuries as a way to cope with their time-consuming script. Thus they used 宝 for 寶 *bǎo* 'precious', 拟 for 擬 *nǐ* 'consider', 体 for 體 *tǐ* 'body', and so on. The Communists made simplification a matter of state policy and promoted it energetically, with the result that thousands of characters and their components took on a wholly new look. Since most of the Chinese outside of the mainland still use the complicated forms of the characters, the script has assumed a very different appearance (see "Comparison of Sinitic Characters" on page 252). It has now become a task for the people of China to read and write the unfamiliar complicated forms of the characters. In contrast, it is hard for the people of Taiwan to read and write the alien simplified script of China.

The commonest romanization used for Mandarin in the West (and to some extent in China) was for many years the Wade-Giles system. However, the official PRC romanization known as *pīnyīn* has made great strides in specific applications during recent decades. It is now used for Chinese Braille, telegraphy, shipboard semaphore, road signs, brand names, computer input, elementary education, and a host of other

TABLE 15.3: *Bōpōmōfō, with Pinyin Equivalents (Chinese Language Library 1985)*

Initials		Finals							
ㄅ	b			一	i	ㄨ	u	ㄩ	ü
ㄆ	p	ㄚ	a	一ㄚ	ia	ㄨㄚ	ua		
ㄇ	m	ㄛ	o			ㄨㄛ	uo		
ㄈ	f	ㄜ	e	一ㄝ	ie			ㄩㄝ	üe
ㄉ	d	ㄞ	ai			ㄨㄞ	uai		
ㄊ	t	ㄟ	ei			ㄨㄟ	uei		
ㄋ	n	ㄠ	ao	一ㄠ	iao				
ㄌ	l	ㄡ	ou	一ㄡ	iou				
ㄍ	g	ㄢ	an	一ㄢ	ian	ㄨㄢ	uan	ㄩㄢ	üan
ㄎ	k	ㄣ	en	一ㄣ	in	ㄨㄣ	uen	ㄩㄣ	ün
ㄏ	h	ㄤ	ang	一ㄤ	iang	ㄨㄤ	uang		
ㄐ	j	ㄥ	eng	一ㄥ	ing	ㄨㄥ	ueng		
ㄑ	q	ㄨㄥ	ong	ㄩㄥ	iong				
ㄒ	x	ㄦ	er						
ㄓ	zh								
ㄔ	ch			Tones					
ㄕ	sh	一	$\bar{}$ = 1	╱	$\acute{}$ = 2	ˇ	$\check{}$ = 3	╲	$\grave{}$ = 4
ㄖ	r	high level		high rising		low dipping		high falling	
ㄗ	z								
ㄘ	c								
ㄙ	s								

uses (for comparison of pinyin and Wade-Giles romanization, see TABLE 15.4). Pinyin has been recognized by both the United Nations and the International Standards Organization as the standard form of romanization for Mandarin. With the elaboration of an official set of orthographical rules (Yin and Felley 1990; Zhou 1992: 289–301), pinyin is now poised to take on the role of a full-fledged script. For political and practical reasons, the government cannot now advocate such a move. Yet the facts are inescapable: while not yet securely established as an auxiliary script, pinyin has long been widely accepted as a handy notational system, and China may be said already to have entered a policy of digraphia, with pinyin and the sinograms used in complementarity. Whether or not pinyin gradually displaces sinograms remains to be seen.

The pressures of technology and information processing pose severe challenges for all users of sinograms (Unger 1987). While valiant efforts are being made by linguists, engineers, and programmers to meet these challenges, it is inevitable that economies of cost effectiveness will require additional adjustments in the script. Nonetheless, whatever exciting developments take place during the twenty-first century, they are unlikely to bring about the total elimination of the traditional characters, which will certainly always be used in classical studies.

TABLE 15.4: *Mandarin Transcription Systems*[a]

Pinyin	W-G	IPA	
a	e	[ɛ]	In *ian* = ien = [i̯ɛn]
	a	[ɑ]	before *ng, u*: *lao* = lao = [lau̯]
	a	[a]	elsewhere
b	p	[b̥]	
c	tz'	[tsʰ]	Before *i*: *ci* = tz'ŭ = [tsʰɨ]
	ts'		elsewhere: *cu* = tz'ŭ = [tsʰu]
ch	ch'	[tʂʰ]	Note *chi* = ch'ih = [tʂʰɻ]
d	t	[d̥]	
e	ê	[ə]	Before nasals: *ben* = pên = [b̥ən]
	eh	[ɛ]	after *i, ü, y*: *tie* = t'ieh = [tʰi̯ɛ]
	e	[e]	before *i*: *wei* = wei = [wɛi̯]
	ê/o	[ɤ]	elsewhere: *he* = hê/ho = [χɤ]
f	f	[f]	
g	k	[g̊]	
h	h	[χ]	
i	ih	[ɻ]	After *ch, r, sh, zh*: *chi* = ch'ih = [tʂʰɻ]
	ŭ	[ɨ]	after *c, s, z*: *ci* = tz'ŭ = [tsʰɨ]
	i	[ɪi̯]	after *gu, ku*: *kui* = k'uei = [kʰu̯ɪi̯]
	i	[i̯]	before/after vowels: *lai* = lai = [lai̯]
	i	[ɪ]	before *n, ng*: *bin* = pin = [b̥ɪn]
	i	[i]	elsewhere: *li* = li = [li]
j	ch	[d̥z]	Before *i, u*: *ju* = chü = [d̥zy]
k	k'	[kʰ]	
l	l	[l]	

Pinyin	W-G	IPA	
m	m	[m]	
n	n	[n]	
ng	ng	[ŋ]	
o	o	[u̯]	After *a*: *lao* = lao = [lau̯]
	o	[o]	before *u*: *tou* = t'ou = [tʰou̯]
	u	[ʊ]	before *ng*: *zhong* = chung = [d̥ʐʊŋ]
	o	[ɤ]	elsewhere: *po* = p'o = [pʰɤ]
p	p'	[pʰ]	
q	ch'	[tɕʰ]	Before *i, u*: *qu* = ch'ü = [tɕʰy]
r	rh	[ɻ]	Final: *er* = erh = [ɤɻ]
	j	[ɻ]	elsewhere; note *ri* = jih = [ɻ]
s	ss/sz	[s]	Before *i*: *si* = ssŭ = [sɨ]
	s	[s]	elsewhere: *su* = su = [su]
sh	sh	[ʂ]	Note *shi* = shih = [ʂɻ]
t	t'	[tʰ]	
u	ü	[y]	After *q, j, x, y*: *qu* = ch'ü = [tɕʰy]
	u	[ou̯]	after *i*: *diu* = tiu = [d̥i̯ou̯]
	u	[u̯]	before a vowel: *kua* = k'ua = [kʰu̯a]
	u	[ʊ]	before *n*: *sun* = sun = [sʊn]
	u	[u]	elsewhere: *mu* = mu = [mu]
ü	ü	[y]	After *l, n*: *nü* = nü = [ny]
w	w	[w]	
x	hs	[ɕ]	Before *i, u*: *xu* = hsü = [ɕy]
y	y	[y]	
z	tz	[d̥z]	Before *i*: *zi* = tzŭ = [d̥zɨ]
	ts		before *u*: *zu* = tsu = [d̥zu]
zh	ch	[d̥ʒ]	Note *zhi* = chih = [d̥ʐɻ]

a. The four basic tones are written ā, á, ǎ, à in pinyin, a[1], a[2], a[3], a[4] in Wade-Giles (W-G). Pinyin is italicized here for clarity.

SAMPLE OF CHINESE

1. Sinograms:	嘗	念	中	國	文	字	最	為	美
2. Pinyin:	cháng	niàn	Zhōng	guó	wén	zì,	zuì	wéi	měi
3. Transcription:	tsʰáŋ	nìɛ̰n	dʐōŋ	gṵó	wə́n	dʐɨ̰	dʐṵèḭ	wéi	mḛḭ
4. Gloss:	PAST	think	China		script		most	be	beautiful

1.	備	亦	最	繁	難	倉	史	以	降	孳 乳
2.	bèi,	yì	zuì	fán	nán.	Cāng	Shǐ	yǐ	jiàng,	zī rǔ
3.	bḛḭ̀	jì	dʐṵèḭ	fán	nán	tsʰāŋ	ʂḭ̌	jǐ	dʐàŋ	dʐɨ̰ ɹǔ
4.	prepare	also	most	manifold	difficult	Cang	scribe	since		multiply

1.	日	多	字	典	所	收	四 萬	餘	字	士 人
2.	rì	duō.	zì	diǎn	suǒ	shōu,	sì wàn	yú	zì.	shì rén
3.	ɹ̰	dṵ5	dʐɨ̰	dḭɛ̌n	sṵǒ	ʂōu	sɨ̄ wàn	jɤ́	dʐɨ̰	ʂɨ̰ ɹə́n
4.	day	many	dictionary	REL	receive		40,000	surplus	graph	scholar

1.	讀 書	畢	生	不	能	盡	識
2.	dú shū,	bì	shēng	bù	néng	jìn	shí.
3.	dú ʂū	bḭ̀	ʂə̄ŋ	bù	nə́ŋ	dʐìn	ʂɨ̰́
4.	study	lifelong		not	can	complete	recognize

'I have thought that, while Chinese characters are the most beautiful and complete, they are also the most complicated and difficult. Since the time of Cang Jie [the mythical inventor of Chinese characters], they have grown and multiplied day by day. Those which are gathered in dictionaries are more than 40,000. Scholars who read books for their whole lives cannot recognize all of them.'
                                            —*Preface to Cài Xīyǒng 1896, cited in Ní Hǎishǔ 1959: 34.*

Cài Xīyǒng (1847–1897) was a scholar, diplomat, educator, and reformer in the late Qing dynasty.

Bibliography

Cài Xīyǒng 蔡錫勇. 1896. *Chuányīn kuàizì* [Rapid graphs for transmitting sounds] 傳音快字. Húběi Guān Shūjú: woodblock. Repr. Beijing: Wénzì Gǎigé Chūbǎnshè, 1956.

Chinese Language Library. 1985. *Chinese Characters: Unsimplified, Simplified, plus Pinyin Romanization.* Beijing: Foreign Languages Press.

DeFrancis, John. 1950. *Nationalism and Language Reform in China.* Princeton: Princeton University Press. Repr. New York: Octagon, 1972.

———. 1984. *The Chinese Language: Fact and Fantasy.* Honolulu: University of Hawaii Press.

———. 1989. *Visible Speech: The Diverse Oneness of Writing Systems.* Honolulu: University of Hawaii Press.

Hansen, Chad. 1993. "Chinese Ideographs and Western Ideas." *Journal of Asian Studies* 52: 373–99.

Hànyǔ dà zìdiǎn Biānjí wěiyuánhuì [Editorial committee for the Great character dictionary of Sinitic] 漢語大字典編輯委宛會. 1986–90. *Hànyǔ dà zìdiǎn* [Great character dictionary of Sinitic] 漢語大字典, 8 vols. Wǔhàn: Húběi Císhū and Sìchuān Císhū.

Mair, Victor H. 1989. "Script Reform in China." *The World & I* (October): 635–43.

————. 1993. "Cheng Ch'iao's Understanding of Sanskrit: The Concept of Spelling in China." In *A Festschrift in Honour of Professor Jao Tsung-i on the Occasion of His Seventy-fifth Anniversary*, pp. 331–41. Hong Kong: Chinese University of Hong Kong.

————. 1994. "Buddhism and the Rise of the Written Vernacular in East Asia: The Making of National Languages." *Journal of Asian Studies* 53: 707–51.

Mair, Victor H., and Yongquan Liu, eds. 1991. *Characters and Computers.* Amsterdam: IOS Press.

Ní Hǎishǔ 倪海曙. 1959. *Qīng-mò hànyǔ pīnyīn yùndòng (Qièyīnzì yùndòng) biānniánshǐ* [Yearly chronology of the Late Qing Sinitic spelling movement (tomogrammic movement)] 清末汗語拼音杴動（切音字運動）編年史. Shanghai: Shànghǎi rénmín chūbǎnshè.

Norman, Jerry. 1988. *Chinese.* Cambridge: Cambridge University Press.

Pulleyblank, Edwin. 1991. *Lexicon of Reconstructed Pronunciation in Early Middle Chinese, Late Middle Chinese, and Early Mandarin.* Vancouver: University of British Columbia Press.

Ramsey, S. Robert. 1987. *The Languages of China.* Princeton: Princeton University Press.

Schuessler, Axel. 1987. *A Dictionary of Early Zhou Chinese.* Honolulu: University of Hawaii Press.

Unger, J. Marshall. 1987. *The Fifth Generation Fallacy: Why Japan Is Betting Its Future on Artificial Intelligence.* New York: Oxford University Press.

————. 1990. "The Very Idea: The Notion of Ideogram in China and Japan." *Monumenta Nipponica* 45: 391–411.

————. 1993. Communication to the Editor. *Journal of Asian Studies* 52: 949–54.

Xīnhuá zìdiǎn [New China character dictionary] 新華字典. 1957, 1992. Beijing: Shangwu.

Yin Binyong and Mary Felley. 1990. *Chinese Romanization: Pronunciation and Orthography.* Peking: Sinolingua.

Zhōu Yǒuguāng 周有光. 1992. *Zhōngguó yǔwén zònghéng tán* [Desultory discussions of Chinese language and writing] 中國語文縱橫談. [Beijing]: Rénmín jiàoyù.

Japanese Writing

JANET S. (SHIBAMOTO) SMITH

Modern Japanese is written in a mixture of three basic scripts: *kanji*, a logo/morphographic script; and *hiragana* and *katakana*, two syllabaries. Additionally, *rōmaji* 'romanization', *eimoji* 'English script' (roughly, non-Japanese words written in their [native] alphabetic script), and a variety of *kigō* 'symbols' are commonly interspersed in texts.

Kanji

Kanji are graphic elements, mostly derived from Chinese, representing logo/morphological units. These characters were introduced, probably by way of Korea, from around the third century C.E. The same character may stand, as a homograph, for several different morphemes (each with its specific meanings and "reading," or pronunciation). *On*-readings are those based on the pronunciation of the character in Chinese, at the time of borrowing. *Kun*-readings represent a Japanese morpheme corresponding to the meaning of a particular character. Thus the character 人 'person' has *on*-readings that include *jin* and *nin* (cf. Mandarin *rén*), but the *kun*-reading is *hito*.

The characters, when used to represent morphemes of Chinese origin, sometimes contain a clue to their pronunciation. Thus the characters 五 'five', 吾 'I', and 語 'language' all have the *on*-reading *go*. However, no more than 25% of the approximately 2000 general-use kanji contain useful phonological clues to the pronunciation of one of their *on*-morphemes (Paradis et al. 1985: 11).

Kanji are used to encode primary lexical categories: nouns, verb stems, adjective stems, and some adverbs. Polymorphemic words are represented by more than one kanji. *Kun*-readings occur in compound (multi-kanji) words as well as in single-kanji words; *on*-readings occur much more often in compound kanji. However, all combinations are possible. In principle, compound words are written/read with all *on* or all *kun* pronunciations, but there are numerous exceptions. *Yutō-yomi* refers to cases in which the first element of the compound form has a *kun* reading while the second has an *on* reading (夕刊 *yūkan* 'evening newspaper' from 夕 *seki/yū* 'evening' + 刊 *kan/–* 'publish', 見本 *mihon* 'sample' from 見 *ken/mi* 'see' + 本 *–/moto* 'origin'). *Jūbako-yomi* refers to the opposite case—*on*-reading followed by *kun*-reading (本箱 *honbako* 'bookshelf' from 本 *hon/–* 'book' + 箱 *shō/bako* 'box', 毎朝 *maiasa* 'every morning' from 毎 *mai/-goto* 'every' + 朝 *chō/asa* 'morning'). *Ateji* are multi-kanji words whose component characters are pronounced in accordance with a standard pronunciation but whose usual meanings are irrelevant to the meaning of the word (珈琲 *kōhii* 'coffee' from 珈 *kō* 'ornamental hatpin' + 琲 *hii* 'string of many pearls'). *Jukujikun* are multi-character words whose pronunciation is independent of any pronunciation of the component characters (大人 *otona* 'adult' from 大 *dai/ōkī* 'big' + 人 *jin/hito* 'person').

Japanese contains a great number of homophones. These are disambiguated in writing via different kanji for each meaning (科学 *kagaku* 'science', 化学 *kagaku* 'chemistry' from 科 *ka* 'division', 化 *ka* 'change', and 学 *gaku* 'study'). That this function is indispensable for the reading of Japanese is one of the reasons commonly adduced for not eliminating kanji entirely in favor of one of the kana syllabaries.

Since World War II, the government has issued two sets of "guidelines" as to which kanji are considered as being in common use and thus appropriate to include in the compulsory education curriculum, to use in public or official documents, etc. These are the *tōyō*-kanji list (1946, rev. 1948; 1,850 kanji) and the current *jōyō*-kanji list (1981; 1,945 kanji). These represent characters suggested for official use. The number of different kanji employed in newspapers and magazines in general, however, is approximately 3200–3300 (Kokuritsu Kokugo Kenkyūjo 1962–64, 1976). One reason that kanji proportions in texts have not dropped below this higher general level of use is that place and family names are written with characters not otherwise used, increasing the number of characters needed in many texts (Seeley 1991: 157). Also, Japanese is written without spaces between the words; thus visual cues to morphological segmentation, afforded by kanji, are critical. When texts are written entirely in kana or in romaji, phrases or words, respectively, are segmented by leaving spaces between the relevant units, but such texts are not typical. Nomura (1988) reports a continuous decrease throughout this century in the use of kanji for (in temporal order) the grammatical morphemes used in *kanbun* 'Chinese writing by/for Japanese'; deictics, conjunctions, and adverbs; prefixes (御/お *o-* 'honorific'), formal nouns (事/こと *koto* 'thing, fact'), and pronouns; and indigenous Japanese words. Writers are apparently resolving potential problems of morphological segmentation that result from the reduction in the proportion of kanji used, by employing a mixture of the two kana syllabaries, plus a sprinkling of romaji, eimoji, and other symbols (Nomura 1988, Smith and Schmidt 1995).

Hiragana and katakana

In addition to kanji, Japanese uses two syllabaries: hiragana and katakana. The two kana syllabaries are phonographic characters derived in the ninth century from the borrowed logo/morphographic kanji. Kana are complete orthographies (Faber 1992); anything that can be said in Japanese can be written in either of the kana syllabaries. Even sounds and sound sequences such as ヴィ /vi/ and ティ /ti/, which are not na-

TABLE 16.1: *Japanese Syllabaries and Romanization*[a]

		(C)V Combinations					CyV Combinations		
		a	*i*	*u*	*e*	*o*	*ya*	*yu*	*yo*
Ø	Hi.	あ	い	う	え	お			
	Ka.	ア	イ	ウ	エ	オ			
k-	Hi.	か	き	く	け	こ	きゃ	きゅ	きょ
	Ka.	カ	キ	ク	ケ	コ	キャ	キュ	キョ
g-	Hi.	が	ぎ	ぐ	げ	ご	ぎゃ	ぎゅ	ぎょ
	Ka.	ガ	ギ	グ	ゲ	ゴ	ギャ	ギュ	ギョ
s-	Hi.	さ	し	す	せ	そ	しゃ	しゅ	しょ
	Ka.	サ	シ	ス	セ	ソ	シャ	シュ	ショ
			(H. shi)				(H. sha)	(H. shu)	(H. sho)
z-	Hi.	ざ	じ	ず	ぜ	ぞ	じゃ	じゅ	じょ
	Ka.	ザ	ジ	ズ	ゼ	ゾ	ジャ	ジュ	ジョ
			(H. ji)				(H. ja)	(H. ju)	(H. jo)
t-	Hi.	た	ち	つ	て	と	ちゃ	ちゅ	ちょ
	Ka.	タ	チ	ツ	テ	ト	チャ	チュ	チョ
			(H. chi)	(H. tsu)			(H. cha)	(H. chu)	(H. cho)
d-	Hi.	だ	ぢ	づ	で	ど	ぢゃ	ぢゅ	ぢょ
	Ka.	ダ	ヂ	ヅ	デ	ド	ヂャ	ヂュ	ヂョ
			(H. ji)	(H. zu)			(H. ja)	(H. ju)	(H. jo)
n-	Hi.	な	に	ぬ	ね	の	にゃ	にゅ	にょ
	Ka.	ナ	ニ	ヌ	ネ	ノ	ニャ	ニュ	ニョ
h-	Hi.	は	ひ	ふ	へ	ほ	ひゃ	ひゅ	ひょ
	Ka.	ハ	ヒ	フ	ヘ	ホ	ヒャ	ヒュ	ヒョ
				(H. fu)					
b-	Hi.	ば	び	ぶ	べ	ぼ	びゃ	びゅ	びょ
	Ka.	バ	ビ	ブ	ベ	ボ	ビャ	ビュ	ビョ
p-	Hi.	ぱ	ぴ	ぷ	ぺ	ぽ	ぴゃ	ぴゅ	ぴょ
	Ka.	パ	ピ	プ	ペ	ポ	ピャ	ピュ	ピョ
m	Hi.	ま	み	む	め	も	みゃ	みゅ	みょ
	Ka.	マ	ミ	ム	メ	モ	ミャ	ミュ	ミョ
y-	Hi.	や	–	ゆ	–	よ			
	Ka.	ヤ	–	ユ	–	ヨ			
r-	Hi.	ら	り	る	れ	ろ	りゃ	りゅ	りょ
	Ka.	ラ	リ	ル	レ	ロ	リャ	リュ	リョ
w-	Hi.	わ	–	–	–	を			
	Ka.	ワ	–	–	–	ヲ			

a. Hi., hiragana; Ka., katakana. The romanization used to label the rows and columns is kunreishiki; Hepburn romanization, where it differs, is indicated with (H.). The syllabic nasal (Hi. ん, Ka. ン) comes at the end of the list.

Vowel length is indicated in kana by doubling, or more often with a following dash: ああ or あー is kunreishiki *aa*, Hepburn *ā*. Geminate consonants are written in kana with a preceding subscript つ *tu* (Ka. ッ); thus Hi. あっか *akka* (Ka. アッカ).

tive to Japanese but do occur in words borrowed from other languages, can be written in kana (Sampson 1985: 184).

Hiragana 'kana without angles' grew out of an increasingly simplified set of cursively written kanji used as *man'yōgana* 'Chinese characters used phonetically to write Japanese' (TABLE 16.1). The hiragana syllabary consists of 46 characters, supplemented with a set of diacritics. Today's hiragana forms were fixed by the Ministry of Education's 1900 regulations on standard kana signs and usage. Typical Japanese texts are written in a mixture of kanji and kana, primarily hiragana. Hiragana is used for particles, auxiliary verbs, and the inflectional affixes of nouns, adjectives, and verbs—in sum, the grammatical elements of sentences.

Okurigana are hiragana added after kanji to encode inflectional elements. The present guidelines for okurigana were issued in the Cabinet Notification "*Okurigana no tsukekata*" in 1973. Issues surrounding okurigana have to do with how much of the verb stem and the inflectional material is encoded explicitly in the kana following the kanji verb stem versus how much material is left implicit. For example, *wakar-anai* '[I] understand-NEG' can be written several ways:

判からない	WA.*ka.ra.na.i*
判らない	WAKA.*ra.na.i*
判ない	WAKARA.*na.i*

These are three possibilities for material written in hiragana as okurigana. In this example, successively less material is provided to give the reader phonographic cues to the relationship between the kanji and the kana portions of the word. Traditionally, the implicit options have been favored for school texts, while increasingly explicit encoding via okurigana occurs in popular texts (Seeley 1991: 158).

Like hiragana, katakana derived from man'yogana. At the beginning of the Heian Period (794–1192), small script that could be written between characters and/or between lines was needed in order to write down readings of, or exegetic commentary on, Buddhist sutras (Ogawa 1982: 481). *Katakana* 'simple, incomplete kana' were created by taking parts of established man'yogana, sometimes but not always the same man'yogana that were the source for the counterpart hiragana syllable. The present forms and conventions of use for katakana were fixed in 1900, at the same time as hiragana. Katakana is used in contemporary texts to write foreign names and loanwords, onomatopoeic and mimetic words, exclamations, and some specialized scientific terminology. It is also used for words usually written in kanji or hiragana to give special emphasis, indicate an ironic tone, signal euphemisms, and the like; young people are particularly likely to incorporate katakana into their script mix, perhaps to give a "conversational" tone to their written productions (Nakamura 1983; Satake 1989, 1990).

The canonical order of kana is traditionally that in which they occur in a short poem, the "*Iroha*," which uses each symbol just once (FIGURE 34 on page 250). However, most modern dictionaries use the alternate order, shown in TABLE 16.1, based on that of Indic script: first vowels, then occlusives (starting with *k*), and then sonorants (see SECTION 30). The differences between voiceless and voiced consonants, and between full and subscript symbols, are ignored in the ordering. Both scripts are used as *furigana*: small kana put to the side of or above kanji in order to indicate the pronunciation or meaning of the kanji used.

Romaji

Rōmaji includes the Roman alphabet and Arabic numerals. Japanese texts use these alphanumeric symbols to write train station names, street and highway signs, company names; and Roman capitals are used to produce acronyms like OL 'office lady' (i.e. female office worker), 2DK 'two [rooms] plus a dining-kitchen'. Arabic numerals are frequently used in texts, particularly those written horizontally (e.g. scientific texts). From the Meiji Period onward there has been debate—sometimes heated— about the desirability of writing Japanese entirely in romaji, but this idea has never taken strong hold.

There are two transliteration systems for writing Japanese alphabetically: (1) the Hepburn system (*Hebon-shiki*), a system based on English spelling pronunciation developed by American missionary James Curtis Hepburn (1815–1911), and used in this volume; and (2) *kunreishiki* (Cabinet Ordinance system), a phonemic system promulgated by the Japanese government (TABLE 16.1). In all, 19 syllables differ. Hepburn uses *ji* for kunreishiki *zi*, and *j-* for *zy-*. For vowel length, kunreishiki and Hepburn use a circumflex accent or macron (ああ or あー = *â, ā*), or doubling in the case of capital letters or *i*. Geminate consonants are written in both systems by doubling. Hepburn double *ch* is *tch*. The syllabic nasal ん/ン is romanized by kunreishiki as *n* everywhere; but by Hepburn as *m* before labials, *n* elsewhere. Medially, syllabic *n* is followed by an apostrophe to distinguish it from consonantal *n*. When the revised kunreishiki system was issued (1954), the government stipulated that it was to be used in transcribing the Japanese language, with the caveat that the Hepburn system might continue to be used if a change would seriously affect customs and considerations of international relations. Hepburn transliterations are required, for instance, in passports and many official application forms. Thus the Japanese, in alphabetic as well as non-alphabetic inscription, maintain a complexly organized, multi-scriptal (or multi-orthographic) system.

Other script elements

In commercial writing (Haarmann 1989) and in the writing of the young (Satake 1990, 1991), *eimoji* 'English (or other foreign language) letters' and various symbols such as ♥ and ☆ are used:

日経 Woman: 働く女性の情報誌
Nikkei Woman: Hataraku Josei no Jōhōshi
　'Nikkei "Woman": News for the Working Woman'

TABLE 16.2: *Common Japanese Punctuation*

○	maru	period
、	ten	comma
「」	kagi	quotation marks
『』	futaekagi	double quotation marks; used for quotation-internal quotations, book titles, etc.
・	nakaten	used optionally in place of comma in lists of nouns
-	dasshu	dash, hyphen
?	gimonfu	question mark
!	kantanfu	exclamation mark

美江ちゃんなんて、ホントかわいー子♥
Mie-chan nante, honto kawaii ko ♥
  'Mie is really cute ♥'   (Satake 1990: 2)

Eimoji are used to give overtones of international sophistication. Such symbols, allied with an extensive set of punctuation and other marks indicating stress, expressive lengthening, etc., convey the intonation and feeling of spoken communication.

Direction, punctuation, and organization of texts

Vertical writing, with columns written right to left (*tategaki*), is still the norm in Japan, but many texts are horizontally printed or written from left to right (*yokogaki*). In neither case is space left between words. Segmentation cues afforded by the normal mixture of scripts are supplemented by numerous punctuation devices (TABLE 16.2).

Conclusion

Throughout this century, no writing system has been written about so pejoratively as Japanese (e.g. Sansom 1928: 44; Miller 1967: 91–140; Coulmas 1989: 122–23, 133). Two apparent reasons are: (a) the multiscriptal nature of Japanese, seen as unnecessary by many analysts since the kana syllabaries can encode in writing anything that can be said in Japanese; and (b) the complexities of kanji use, involving multiple potential readings for each character, choice among which is dependent on the lexical—or sometimes even the larger textual—environment. The Japanese writing system, however, is associated with a highly literate and successful society, with a rich written tradition which makes full use of its multi-scriptal potentialities for the creation of nuanced, graphically vital texts. The high degree of literacy of Japan and the high consumption of published material suggest that the writing system is fully functional.

SAMPLES OF JAPANESE

PASSAGE FROM A CONTEMPORARY ESSAYIST

1. *Japanese:* ところが、 若い 人たち から くる
2. *Transliteration:* tokoro ga, WAKA.i HITO.tachi kara kuru
3. *Transcription:* tokoro ga waka-i çito-taʧi kara kurɯ
4. *Gloss:* however young-ADJ person-PL from come

1. 手紙 は、 大半 が 横書き な の である。
2. TE-KAMI wa, TAI-HAN ga YOKO-KA.ki na no de aru.
3. tegami wa taihaŋ ga joko-ga-ki na no de aru
4. letter TOP majority SUBJ horizontally-write-ADJ NOM is/are

1. 字 も、 お習字 で 習った 字 と
2. JI mo, o-SHŪ-JI de NARA.tta JI to
3. ʤi mo oʃu:ʤi de narat-ta ʤi to
4. characters too calligraphy in learn-PAST character(s) QUOT

1. いう より、 イラスト である。 劇画 の 画面 の
2. iu yori, irasuto de aru. GEKI-GA no GA-MEN no
3. iɯ jori, irasuto de arɯ gekiga no gameṇ no
4. say/call (rather) than illustration is/are cartoon GEN picture GEN

1. 吹き出し で、 「ギャハ！」 など と 書いて ある、
2. FU.ki-DA.shi de "gyaha" nado to KA.ite aru,
3. ɸukidaʃi de gjaha nado to kai-te arɯ
4. balloon in "eek!" etc. QUOT write-GER be

1. あんな 字 な の である。 中 に は
2. anna JI na no de aru. NAKA ni wa
3. aṇna ʤi na no de arɯ naka ni wa
4. that.kind.of character ADJ NOM is/are inside in TOP

1. イラスト入り の もの も あるし、 赤 や
2. irasuto-I.ri no mono mo aru shi, AKA ya
3. irasɯto-iri no mono mo arɯ ʃi aka ja
4. illustration-containing GEN thing(s) also be and red and

1. グリーン など さまざま な ペン で 書き分けた
2. guriin nado samazama na pen de KA.ki-WA.keta
3. gɯri:n nado sama-zama na peṇ de kaki-wake-ta
4. green etc. various-REDUP ADJ pen with write-divide-PAST

1. の も ある。
2. no mo aru.
3. no mo arɯ
4. one(s) also be

'However, the majority of the letters that come from young people are written horizontally. The characters, too, aren't the characters we learned in calligraphy (classes); rather, they're graphics. They're the kind of characters you see in the dialog balloons in the comics, saying "Eek!" or things like that. Among them, there are ones with (real) graphics mixed in and ones with (the words) separated by writing with various pens, like red or green pens.'   —*Mukōda 1980: 40–41.*

CARTOON

1. コン　コン
2. kon kon
3. koṇ koṇ
4. knock knock

1. う～～～～～～～ん
2. u~~~~~~~~~~~~n
3. ɯ::::ṇ
4. hmmmm …

1. なん　　だーっ
2. nan　　da—(tsu)
3. naṇ　　da:
4. what　is

1. うるさいのよっ！！
2. urusai no yo(tsu)!!
3. ɯrɯsai no jo
4. bothersome PART PART

1. ドーーモ　　スミマセン
2. dō—mo　　sumimasen
3. do::mo　　sɯmimaseṇ
4. indeed　　inexusable

1. 素直　　デ　　ヨロシイ！
2. sunao　de　yoroshii
3. sɯnao　de　yoroʃi:
4. docile　is　all.right

1. あつ　　いらっしゃい
2. a　　irasshai
3. a　　iraʃʃai
4. ah　welcome

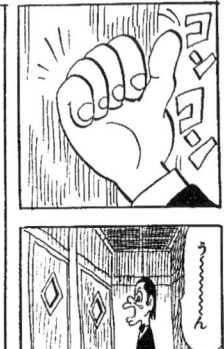

VISITOR: 'Knock-knock —Hmmmm … —What is this??!! —KINDŌ-SAN: Go away!! (lit., Stop bothering [me]) —VISITOR: I'm sorry. —KINDŌ-SAN: Good, you're submissive [enough]. —DŌ-SAN: Ah, welcome.'

—*Kamogawa 1979: 94.*

Note: Some of the humor represented in this excerpt involves the inappropriate linguistic behavior of the character in work clothes addressing the character in a suit in a way proper only to the third character, perhaps the employer.

Bibliography

Coulmas, Florian. 1989. *The Writing Systems of the World.* Oxford: Blackwell.

Faber, Alice. 1992. "Phonemic Segmentation as Epiphenomenon: Evidence from the History of Alphabetic Writing." In *The Linguistics of Literacy* (Typological Studies in Language 21), ed. Pamela Downing, Susan D. Lima, and Michael Noonan, pp. 111–34. Amsterdam: Benjamins.

Haarmann, Harald. 1989. *Symbolic Values of Foreign Language Use: From the Japanese Case to a General Sociolinguistic Perspective.* Berlin: Mouton de Gruyter.

Habein, Yaeko Sato. 1984. *The History of the Japanese Written Language.* Tokyo: University of Tokyo Press.

Kajima Tadao. 1979. *Nihon no Moji—Hyōki Taikei o Kangaeru* [Japanese script: Considering the inscription system]. Tokyo: Iwanami Shinsho.

Kamogawa Tsubama. 1979. "Makaroni hōrensō" [Macaroni spinach]. *Shūkan Shōnen Champion* [Weekly youth champion] 35: 91–102. Tokyo: Akita Shoten.

Kokuritsu Kokugo Kenkyūjo. 1962–64. *Gendai Zasshi Kyūjusshu no Yōgo Yōji* {Translation goes here]. 3 vols. Tokyo: Shūei Shuppan.

———. 1976. *Gendai Shimbun no Kanji* [Contemporary newpaper kanji]. Tokyo: Shūei Shuppan.

Miller, Roy Andrew. 1967. *The Japanese Language.* Chicago: University of Chicago Press.

Mukōda Kuniko. 1980. *Mumei Kamei Jinmeibo* [Directory of anonyms and pseudonyms]. Tokyo: Bungei Shunju.

Nakamura Kumiko. 1983. "Joshi kōsei no tegamibun—sono eigo shikō to hyōkijō no tokuchō" [Letters of high school girls: Their inclination toward English and their special orthographic characteristics]. *Gengo Seikatsu* 380/8: 88–96.

Nomura Masaaki. 1988. *Kanji no Mirai* [The future of kanji]. Tokyo: Chikuma Shobo.

Ogawa Yoshio. 1982. *Nihongo Kyōiku Jiten* [Japanese language education dictionary]. Tokyo: *Taishūkan* Shoten.

Paradis, Michel, Hiroko Hagiwara, and Nancy Hildebrandt. 1985. *Neurolinguistic Aspects of the Japanese Writing System.* New York: Academic Press.

Sampson, Geoffrey. 1985. *Writing Systems.* Stanford: Stanford University Press.

Sansom, George B. 1928. *An Historical Grammar of Japanese.* Oxford: Oxford University Press.

Satake, Hideo. 1989. "Statistical Method to Analyze the Writing Form Variation of Japanese Words." In *Japanese Quantitative Linguistics* (Quantitative Linguistics 39), ed. Shizuo Mizutani, pp. 119–29. Bochum: Brockmeyer.

———. 1990. "Junia shōsetsu to fan reta" ["Junior" novels and fan letters]. *Mukogawa Joshi Daigaku Gengo Bunka Kenkyūjo Nenpō* 2: 1–11.

———. 1991. "Shin-genbun-itchitai no keiryōteki bunseki" [Quantitative analysis of the new colloquial style]. *Mukogawa Joshi Daigaku Gengo Bunka Kenkyūjo Nenpō* 3: 1–14.

Sato Kiyoji, et al., eds. *Kanji Kōza* [Kanji series]. 12 vols. Tokyo: Meiji Shoin.

Seeley, Christopher. 1991. *A History of Writing in Japan.* Leiden: Brill.

———. ed. 1984. *Aspects of the Japanese Writing System* (special issue). *Visible Language* 18/3.

Smith, Janet S. (Shibamoto), and David L. Schmidt. 1995. "Variability in Written Japanese: Towards a Sociolinguistics of Script Choice." *Visible Language* 29/4.

Twine, Nanette. 1991. *Language and the Modern State: The Reform of Written Japanese.* London: Routledge.

Unger, J. Marshall. 1987. *The Fifth Generation Fallacy: Why Japan Is Betting Its Future on Artifical Intelligence.* New York: Oxford University Press.

Korean Writing

ROSS KING

Chinese writing in Korea

Chinese writing was probably known in Korea before Han times, and was used in the Han administration of their commanderies in northern Korea from 108 B.C.E. to 313 C.E. The first evidence of the use of Chinese by Koreans is on a stone inscription of 414 C.E. The Koreans later developed three different, but related, ways to use Chinese characters to write Korean: Hyangchal, Kwukyel, and Itwu.

The *Hyangchal* system, preserved in lyric texts, is reminiscent in some ways of the Japanese man'yogana, on which it doubtless had a formative influence. The abbreviated characters of the *Kwukyel* system, a transcription for interpretation and translation of Chinese texts, resemble the Japanese kana in some ways, just as the Kwukyel system for annotating Chinese texts resembles Japanese *kambun* traditions. The *Itwu* 'clerk readings' were a system of prose transcription used widely in administrative contexts. At the time of the promulgation of the *Hwunmin cengum* (1446; see below), the Hyangchal system was moribund, but Kwukyel and Itwu were still in use long after the invention of the Korean alphabet.

Given their long experience with Chinese writing, it is not surprising that the Koreans have added specifically Korean readings and/or meanings to certain genuinely Chinese characters. But the Koreans have also invented a number of "Chinese" characters; Sasse (1980) lists over 150 such characters indigenous to Korea, but they are all quite rare, and were used in traditional times chiefly for the rendering of native Korean words as well as in personal names and place names.

Even after the promulgation of Hankul, the indigenous Korean script (see below), in the fifteenth century, Chinese writing continued to dominate written culture in Korea until the second decade of the twentieth century. Hankul was associated with the uneducated—women and children—and was accorded low status. With the spread of Western-style education and mass media, a Sino-Korean "mixed script" style emerged whereby any and all morphemes of Chinese origin could be, and often were, written in Chinese characters; native Korean words and grammatical endings were written in Hankul. Formerly, Chinese-character transcriptions of Old Korean poetry could include representations of morphemes meant to be read in their native guise; but this practice (seen in modern Japanese) is not used in modern Korean.

Since Liberation from Japan in 1945, Korea has accorded a much less important role to Chinese characters than in traditional, or even pre-Liberation, times. North Korea abolished the use of Chinese characters in public writing in 1949, but continues to teach a limited number in schools. South Korean policy has been less consistent; certain government ministries use Chinese characters more than others, but most major daily newspapers still use them, and students learn approximately 1800 characters before leaving high school. The role of Chinese characters in Korean writing is a matter of heated public debate in the Republic of Korea in the 1990s.

Hankul: General characteristics

Hankul (in the Yale romanization)* designates the native Korean script; it is written 한글 in Korean, Han'gŭl in McCune-Reischauer, [hangïl] in IPA, lit. 'Han [= Korean] writing'. It is one of the most scientifically designed and efficient scripts in the world. Invented by the sage King Seycong (r. 1419–1450). It is one of the earliest known examples of "sophisticated grammatogeny" (Daniels 1992; SECTION 52).

The original name of the Korean script was 訓民正音 *Hwunmin cengum* 'The correct sounds for the instruction of the people', this also being the title of the work which promulgated the script in 1446. Until 1910, the script was also known as *cengum* 'correct sounds', *enmun* 'vulgar script', or *kwukmun* 'national writing'. The name Hankul is a neologism created by Cwu Si-kyeng (1876–1914), a Korean linguist active in the movement to reform and promote the Korean language and script.

Hankul is a phonemically based alphabet with the following interesting, often unique, features.

1. Hankul has always been written in syllable blocks, rather than having its letters arranged in a row from left to right and written side by side—a feature usually attributed to influence from the equidimensional geometry of Chinese characters (Kōno 1969). This feature, more than others, makes Hankul distinctive, and has prompted Taylor (1979) to call it an "alphabetic syllabary."

2. Hankul appeared out of the blue. With no warning, the *Veritable Records of the Cosen Dynasty* announce its invention in the 12th month of Seycong's 25th year (approximately January 1444).

3. Hankul is original. It was the product of deliberate, linguistically informed planning (Ledyard 1966). Despite numerous theories attempting to link it to, or derive it from, other scripts (there are no less than ten different "origin theories"), the most convincing theory of letter shape origins remains that given in the *Hwunmin cengum haylyey* (HCH) 'Explanations and examples of the correct sounds for the instruction of the people', which was lost and not rediscovered until 1940. According to the

---

*There are now two widely accepted schemes for romanizing Korean in the scholarly world: the McCune-Reischauer system (see McCune and Reischauer 1939), and the Yale system (see Martin 1992). Linguists prefer the Yale system, and it is used in this book.

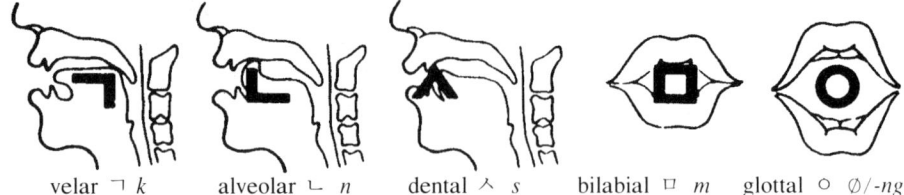

velar ㄱ *k*   alveolar ㄴ *n*   dental ㅅ *s*   bilabial ㅁ *m*   glottal ㅇ *Ø/-ng*

FIGURE 1. Origin of shapes of basic Hankul consonants (from Kim Jin-p'yŏng 1983).

HCH, the basic consonant shape for each of the five places of articulation is based on a graphic representation of the speech organ involved (FIGURE 1).

The vowel signs were organized on a completely different basis, and given a metaphysical rationale. Each vowel sign was made up of one or more of the three elements Man, Earth, and Heaven (FIGURE 2).

4. Hankul is scientific. Its invention rested on an elaborate phonological analysis of fifteenth-century Korean, and transcended Chinese-based theories of phonology of the time. In particular, the tripartite division of the syllable into initial (onset), medial (peak), and final (coda) and the systematic treatment of vowels mark Hankul as the "high peak which the eastward currents of the alphabetic system of writing attained" (Lee Ki-moon 1983: 76).

5. Hankul keeps consonants and vowels apart conceptually and graphically.

6. Hankul has an additive structure. By doubling, or adding strokes to, the five basic consonant shapes for *k*, *n*, *s*, *m*, *ng*, one derives the shapes for the aspirates, tense unaspirates, affricates, etc. (In pre-modern Korean, the doubled letters represented the voiced stops and affricates of Chinese.) Likewise, the three basic fifteenth-century vowel shapes of vertical line, horizontal line, and dot combine to give all the possible vowels, as well as diphthongal combinations. This has led Sampson (1985) to call Hankul a featural system.

7. Hankul's combination of the typological features of alphabet and syllabary is simple and efficient. Both Vos (1963) and Sampson (1985) note that the simplicity of its graphic elements promotes learnability, while its syllabic organization enhances efficiency in processing and reading. However, there have been few psycholinguistic tests of these claims. Hankul is currently used in the Republic of Korea (South Korea) and the Democratic People's Republic of Korea (North Korea). However, the term

Symbol of Heaven: round dot   Symbol of Earth: horizontal line   Symbol of Man: vertical line

FIGURE 2. Origin of shapes of basic Hankul vowels (after Kim Jin-p'yŏng 1983).

TABLE 17.1: *Vowels*

SIMPLE VOWELS								
ㅣ	i	[i]	ㅡ	u	[ɨ]	ㅜ	wu	[u]
ㅔ	ey	[e]	ㅓ	e	[ʌ]	ㅗ	o	[o]
ㅐ	ay	[æ]				ㅏ	a	[a]
DIPHTHONGS								
			ㅢ	uy	[ɨj]	ㅟ	wuy	[wi]
						ㅚ	oy	[we]
*y*V								
						ㅠ	ywu	[ju]
ㅖ	yey	[je]	ㅕ	ye	[jʌ]	ㅛ	yo	[jo]
ㅒ	yay	[jæ]				ㅑ	ya	[ja]
*w*V								
ㅞ	wey	[we]	ㅞ	we	[wʌ]			
ㅙ	way	[wæ]				ㅘ	wa	[wa]

Hankul is not used in North Korea, where the script is referred to as *cosenkul* 'Korean script' or *wuli kulca* 'our script'. Hankul also serves Korean communities in the People's Republic of China, Russia and the former Soviet Union, and elsewhere.

The symbols

The modern vowels

The simple vowel symbols, and those that are built up from combinations of the simple symbols, are shown in TABLE 17.1. Diphthongs are formed by adding the vertical stroke of ㅣ *i* to the signs for *o*, *wu*, and *u*. In origin, the simple vowels *ay* and *ey* were also diphthongs built in the same way, by adding *i* to *a* and *e*; but through sound change they have become simple vowels in the modern language. By adding an additional stroke to the six vowel signs *a*, *e*, *o*, *wu*, *ay*, *ey*, the combination *y* + V is formed. Lastly, adding *wu* (to the mid vowels) or *o* (to the low vowels) results in the combination *w* + V.

The modern consonants

The consonant symbols are shown in TABLE 17.2. Taking the schemata of FIGURE I as basic, something of the original designs can be discerned: an additional stroke makes *t* from *n* and *c* from *s*, another stroke forms *th ch kh* from *t c k*. Symbols are doubled to write the "tense," unaspirated series (here transcribed with an apostrophe).

TABLE 17.2: *Consonants*

ㄱ	k	[k]	ㄴ	n	[n]	ㅅ	s	[s]	ㅁ	m	[m]	ㅇ	Ø/ng	[Ø/-ŋ]
			ㄷ	t	[t]	ㅈ	c	[ʧ]	ㅂ	p	[p]			
ㅋ	kh	[kʰ]	ㅌ	th	[tʰ]	ㅊ	ch	[ʧʰ]	ㅍ	ph	[pʰ]	ㅎ	h	[h]
ㄲ	kk	[k']	ㄸ	tt	[t']	ㅆ	ss	[s']	ㅃ	pp	[p']			
						ㅉ	cc	[ʧ']						
			ㄹ	l	[l, r]									

Middle Korean pitch accent

Korean of the fifteenth and early sixteenth centuries was a pitch-accent language, and the *Hwunmin cengum* included a set of dots for recording the three Middle Korean surface "tones": High, Low, and Rising (composite of Low + High). The dots were written to the left of the syllable, as shown in TABLE 17.3 (Low was unmarked). Syllables with the old Rising tone have a long vowel in modern Seoul standard, but this distinctive vowel length is not indicated orthographically. In this respect, Hankul underdifferentiates in its representation of spoken Korean.

Forming orthographic syllables

Any written syllable in Hankul must begin with a consonant sign. In order for the vowel signs to form the nucleus of a syllable block, they must attach to the side of or below a consonant sign, using the following principles of stroke order. (a) Everything "horizontal" moves from left to right. This applies to the movement of individual strokes, as well as to writing a sequence of letters (e.g. the consonant first, then the vowel): 바 *pa* 'rope', 밤 *pam* 'night'. (b) Everything "vertical" moves from top to bottom: 소 *so* 'cow', 손 *son* 'hand'.

When the spoken syllable begins with a vowel, one must begin the written syllable with the Ø sign representing a "zero" consonant: 아 *a*, 와 *wa*, 야 *ya*, etc. This "zero sign" has an alter ego: at the end of a syllable it represents the sound [ŋ]. Thus, 옹 *ong*, 앙 *ang*, etc. Since Korean has no basic syllables of the type [ŋ] + V, this is a clever economy and a good example of the ingenuity of Hankul. Korean also writes the following syllable-final consonant clusters: ㄳ *ks*, ㄵ *nc*, ㄺ *lk*, ㄻ *lm*, ㄼ *lp*, ㄽ *ls*, ㄾ *lth*, ㄿ *lph*, ㅀ *lh*, ㅄ *ps*; e.g. 읽다 *ilkta* 'read', 밟다 *palpta* 'treads on'.

TABLE 17.3: *Tone Marking*

	15th c.		20th c.		
Low	죽	cywuk	죽	cwuk	'rice gruel'
High	•신	•sin	신	sin	'shoes'
Rising	：죵	••cyong	죵	cōng	'slave'

Orthography and letter shapes

The 500-year history of Hankul has seen a number of changes in Korean writing, both in its orthographic principles and in the letters and letter shapes themselves.

The history of Korean orthography is characterized by a tug-of-war between phonemicists and morphophonemicists. Phonemicists wrote Korean as it was pronounced, taking into account its many automatic sound changes, while morphophonemicists strove to write verb and noun bases in one constant shape, ignoring automatic sound changes. Although King Seycong himself seems to have favored morphophonemic writing, and adopted this policy in his *Welin chenkang ci kok* (1449), other fifteenth-century texts are all phonemic in their orthography.

Hankul orthography drifts from a more or less consistently phonemic approach, in the fifteenth century, to an increasingly morphophonemic one by the twentieth century. This trend was more pronounced in nouns than in verbs. Thus the development in spelling *nimkum-i* 'lord-NOMINATIVE' (using contemporary lettershapes):

15th c.	16th c.	18th/19th c.
님그미	님금미	님금이
nim.ku.mi	*nim.kum.mi*	*nim.kum.i*

is earlier and more widespread than that in spelling *cap-a* 'catch-INFINITIVE':

자바	잡바	잡아
ca.pa	*cap.pa*	*cap.a*

The morphophonemic solution did not win out until the adoption in 1933 by the Korean Language Society (later renamed the Hankul Society) of the *Draft Plan for a Unified Orthography*, and constituted nonetheless a sharp break with earlier spelling traditions. Since Liberation from Japan in 1945, this Unified Orthography (with minor changes and amendments along the way) has served both the DPRK and the ROK to the present day.

The twentieth century has witnessed a number of attempts to reform various aspects of Korean writing. Critics often point out the typographical problems imposed by writing in syllable blocks; and the alternative of taking apart the Hankul syllable blocks and writing the Korean letters side by side (한글 would become 하ㄴㄱㅡㄹ) was already advocated in the 1910s by Cwu Si-kyeng himself, many of whose ideas are reflected in the 1933 Draft Plan. The side-by-side idea still has a small following today. The Soviet authorities tried unsuccessfully in the early 1930s to abolish Hankul and replace it with a Latinized script for use by the Korean minority in the Soviet Far East, but this attempt failed. North Korea experimented with various reforms, including side-by-side writing and the invention of new letters, but these experiments were discontinued in the late 1950s.

Letters and letter shapes (TABLE 17.4) have changed since the fifteenth century, too. Through sound change, a number of graphs promulgated with the *Hwunmin Cengum* have disappeared, e.g. • 'lower *a*', △ *z*, ᄫ 'light *p*', ㆁ glottal stop, and *p*-clus-

TABLE 17.4: *The Korean Alphabet Today*[a]

Hankul	Yale	McCune-Reischauer	IPA	Name
ㄱ	k	k, g	[k, g]	ki(y)ek
ㄲ	kk	kk	[k']	ssang ('double') ki(y)ek
ㄴ	n	n	[n]	niun
ㄷ	t	t, d	[t, d]	tikut
ㄸ	tt	tt	[t']	ssang ('double') tikut
ㄹ	l	l, r	[l, r]	liul
ㅁ	m	m	[m]	mium
ㅂ	p	p, b	[p, b]	piup
ㅃ	pp	pp	[p']	ssang ('double') piup
ㅅ	s	s	[s]	sios
ㅆ	ss	ss	[s']	ssang ('double') sios
ㅇ	-ng	-ng	[∅/-ŋ]	iung
아	a	a	[a]	
애	ay	ae	[æ]	
야	ya	ya	[ja]	
얘	yay	yae	[jæ]	
어	e	ŏ	[ʌ]	
에	ey	e	[e]	
여	ye	yŏ	[jʌ]	
예	yey	ye	[je]	
오	o	o	[o]	
요	yo	yo	[jo]	
와	wa	wa	[wa]	
왜	way	wae	[wæ]	
외	oy	oe	[we]	
우	wu	u	[u]	
워	we	wŏ	[wʌ]	
웨	wey	we	[we]	
위	wi	wi	[wi]	
유	yu	yu	[ju]	
으	u	ŭ	[ɨ]	
의	uy	ŭi	[ɨj]	
이	i	i	[i]	
ㅈ	c	ch, j	[ʧ, ʤ]	ciuc
ㅉ	cc	tch	[ʧ']	ssang ('double') ciuc
ㅊ	ch	ch'	[ʧʰ]	chiuch
ㅋ	kh	k'	[kʰ]	khiukh
ㅌ	th	t'	[tʰ]	thiuth
ㅍ	ph	p'	[pʰ]	phiuph
ㅎ	h	h	[h]	hiuh [hiɨt]

a. The table follows the order in which Hankul letters appear in ROK dictionaries, and also follows the ROK names. North Korea has introduced a new alphabetical order and new letter names.

ters like 몽ㅅ. In addition, the original squarish, geometrical, and symmetrical shapes of the *Hwunmin cengum* began to change within a decade of their promulgation. The original letterforms soon gave way to the pressures of brush writing, and evolved into forms more amenable to writing with the hand. The first such change joined the dots of *wo, wu, e, a*, etc., to the vertical and horizontal lines: ㅇ·ㅣ > 어 *e*, ㅇ:ㅣ > 여 *ye*, etc.

This development is responsible, for example, for the addition of the serif to the tip of certain consonants, and the creation of asymmetrical forms, in modern Korean writing:

	15th c.	20th c.
s	∧	ㅅ
c	∧̄	ㅈ
Ø	○	○
-ng	ㆁ	○

Note that the modern-day zero/*-ng* symbol is a merger of two different Middle Korean symbols. In early days it was possible to write ØaØ and *ngang* as well as Ø*ang* and *nga*Ø, though the final *-*Ø fell into disuse almost immediately.

The relationship of Hankul to other scripts

Before the discovery of the original document explaining the rationale of the Hankul letter shapes, numerous theories came and went about the origins or antecedents of various Korean graphs. The Koreans' own explanation is almost too ingenious to doubt, but King Seycong and his scholars certainly knew of other writing systems, and there may still be reason to believe they looked to scripts of Indic descent for the alphabet idea, to Mongolian 'Phags pa writing for some of the letter shapes (Ledyard 1966, building on Hope 1957; SECTION 40), as well as to Chinese writing for the idea of writing in syllabic blocks, and perhaps even for some individual graphs.

Most accounts of Korean writing dwell on its possible antecedents, and present the *Hwunmin cengum* of the fifteenth century as the final link in a long chain of script connections. However, there is also evidence to suggest that Hankul, in its turn, had an influence on the Manchus when they set out to adopt Mongolian writing to their language (King 1987; SECTION 49).

SAMPLE OF KOREAN

1. Sino-Korean:	우리	나라의	말은	中 國의	말과
2. Hankul:	우리	나라의	말은	중국의	말과
3. Transliteration:	wuli	nalauy	malun	cwungkwukuy	malkwa
4. Transcription:	uri	nara-e	mar-ɨn	tʃuŋgug-e	mal-gwa
5. Gloss:	our	country-'s	language-TOP	China-'s	language-with

1. 달라서,	漢字와는	서로	잘	通하지
2. 달라서,	한자와는	서로	잘	통하지
3. tallase	hancawanun	selo	cal	thonghaci
4. tall-asʌ	hanʧʼa-wa-nɨn	sʌro	ʧal	tʰoŋha-ʤi
5. different-so	characters-with-contrast	mutually	well	communicate-COMP

1. 아니	한다.	그러므로	어리석은	百姓들이	나타내고자
2. 아니	한다.	그러므로	어리석은	백성들이	나타내고자
3. ani	hanta.	kulemulo	elisekun	payksengtuli	nathanaykoca
4. ani	ha-n-da	kɨrʌmɨro	ʌrisʌg-ɨn	pæksʌn-dɨr-i	natʰanæ-goʤa
5. not	do	therefore	foolish-MOD	peasant-PL-NOM	express-INTENT

1. 하는	일이	있어도		...	
2. 하는	일이	있어도	마침내	제	생각을
3. hanun	ili	isseto	machimnay	cey	sayngkakul
4. ha-nɨn	ir-i	isʼ-ʌ-do	maʧʰimnæ	ʧe	sæŋgag-ɨl
5. do-MOD	thing-NOM	exist-even-though	ultimately	self's	thought-ACC

2. 얻어	내어	펴지	못	하는	사람이
3. et-e	naye	phyeci	mos	hanun	salami
4. ʌdʌ	næʌ	pʰyʌ-ʤi	mo	tʰa-nɨn	saram-i
5. obtain-and	express-and	unfold-COMP	cannot	do-MOD	person-NOM

2. 많을	것이다.	나는	이들을	불쌍하게	생각하여
3. manhul	kesita.	nanun	itulul	pulssanghakey	sayngkakhaye
4. man-ɨl	kʌʃ-ida	na-nɨn	i-dɨr-ɨl	pulsʼaŋha-ge	sæŋgakʰa-ja
5. many-MOD	thing-be	I-TOP	this-PL-ACC	pitiful-ly	think-and

2. 새로	스물	여덟	자를	만들었는데
3. saylo	sumwul	yetelp	calul	mantulessnuntey
4. særo	sɨmul	yʌdʌl	ʧʼa-rɨl	mandɨr-ʌn-nɨnde
5. newly	twenty	eight	graph-ACC	make-PAST-and

'Our country's language is different from that of China and thus does not correspond well with characters. Therefore, even should the foolish people have something they wish to express, those ultimately unable to express and develop their ideas are bound to be many. I have taken pity on these people, and newly created 28 letters.'

— *Modern Korean version (Kang 1990) of the first lines of King Seycong's Preface to the Hwunmin cengum.*

Bibliography

Buzo, Adrian. 1980. "Early Korean Writing Systems." *Transactions of the Korea Branch of the Royal Asiatic Society (Seoul)* 55: 35–62.

Daniels, Peter T. 1992. "The Syllabic Origin of Writing and the Segmental Origin of the Alphabet." In *The Linguistics of Literacy* (Typological Studies in Language 21), ed. Pamela Downing, Susan D. Lima, and Michael Noonan, pp. 83–110. Amsterdam: Benjamins.

Gale, James Scarth. 1912. "The Korean Alphabet." *Transactions of the Korean Branch of the Royal Asiatic Society* 4/1: 13–61.

Hope, E. R. 1957. "Letter Shapes in Korean Önmun and Mongol hPhags-pa Alphabets." *Oriens* 10: 150–59.

Kang Sin-hang. 1990. *Hwunmin cengum yenkwu* {Research on the *Hwunmin cengum*]. Seoul: Sengkyunkwan University Press.

Kim Jin-p'yŏng. 1983. "The Letterforms of Han'gŭl." In Korean National Commission for UNESCO 1983: 80–102.

Kim-Renaud, Young-Key, ed. 1996. *The Korean Writing System: Its History and Structure.* Honolulu: University of Hawaii Press.

King, Ross. 1987. "The Korean Elements in the Manchu Script Reform of 1632." *Central Asiatic Journal* 31: 197–217.

Kōno Rokurō. 1969. "The Chinese Writing and Its Influences on the Scripts of the Neighbouring Peoples: With Special Reference to Korea and Japan." *Memoirs of the Research Department of the Tōyō Bunko* 27: 83–140.

Kontsevich, L. R. 1969. "The First monument of Korean Writing (Essay in Critical Translation)." In *Asia in Soviet Studies*, pp. 335–64. Moscow.

Korean National Commission for UNESCO, eds. 1983. *The Korean Language.* Seoul: Si-sa-yong-o-sa.

Ledyard, Gari Keith. 1966. "The Korean Language Reform of 1446: The Origin, Background and Early History of the Korean Alphabet." Ph.D. dissertation, University of California, Berkeley.

Lee Ki-moon. 1963. English resumé of *Kwuke Phyoki-pep uy Yeksa-cek Kochal* [Historical studies of the Korean writing system]. Seoul: Hankwuk Yenkwu-wen.

———. 1983. "Foundations of Hunmin Chŏngŭm." In Korean National Commission for UNESCO 1983: 71–79.

———. 1996. "The Inventor of the Korean Alphabet." In Kim-Renaud 1996.

Martin, Samuel E. 1992. *A Reference Grammar of Korean.* Tokyo: Tuttle.

McCune, G. M., and Edwin O. Reischauer. 1939. "The Romanization of the Korean Language." *Transactions of the Korea Branch of the Royal Asiatic Society* 38: 121–28.

Sampson, Geoffrey. 1985. *Writing Systems: A Linguistic Introduction.* Stanford: Stanford University Press.

Sasse, Werner. 1980. "'Chinesische' Zeichen erfunden in Korea." *Asiatische Studien* 34: 189–205.

Shin Sang-Soon, Lee Don-Ju, and Lee Hwan-Mook, eds. 1990. *Understanding Hunmin-jŏng.ŭm.* Seoul: Hanshin.

Taylor, Insup. 1979. "The Korean Writing System: An Alphabet? A Syllabary? A Logography?" In *Processing of Visible Language 2*, ed. Paul A. Kolers, Merald E. Wrolstad, and Herman Bouma, pp. 67–82. New York: Plenum.

Vos, Fritz. 1963. "Korean Writing: Idu and Han'gŭl." In *Papers of the CIC Far Eastern Language Institute*, ed. Joseph K. Yamagiwa, pp. 29–34. Ann Arbor: University of Michigan.

Siniform Scripts of Inner Asia

―――――

Tangut

E. I. KYCHANOV

The Tangut script, used to write a now extinct Tibeto-Burman language, was introduced in 1036 in the Tangut (西夏 Xīxià) state, located in the present northwestern Chinese provinces of Gansu and Shenxi. The script was probably invented by "the Teacher Iri" (野利任顯 Yělì Rèn-yóng in Chinese) under the Imperial supervision of the Emperor 李元昊 Lǐ Yuán-hào (1003–1047). It is a logographic script, for which the Chinese characters were used as a model. Only a partial phonological reconstruction of Tangut vocabulary has been done; but we know it was a tone language (with level and rising tones) and abounded in homonyms. Thus, apart from Chinese cultural influence, the logographic script was suited to the nature of the language.

Every Tangut character, like Chinese characters, is designed to fit in a square. Some of these units are the result of deliberate alteration of Chinese characters (or parts of them; TABLE 18.1). This group of Tangut characters also performs functions like that of the Chinese determinatives; but some of them are used as independent characters, e.g. 𗾑 'man' from 人.

All the main structures of the Chinese script (SECTION 14) may be found in the Tangut script. Thus the character 𗢍 'gate' may be classified as "figurative" (xiàngxíng); it is explained in a Tangut dictionary, *The Sea of Characters* (12th century, cf. Kychanov 1980), as follows: "by its appearance it resembles a gate." A symbol 𗰔 'to ride (a horse)' can be explained in terms of a transition from figurative symbols to logographic ones (huì yì). It consists of two parts, 𗾑 'man' and 𗵗 'horse'; the character simply "portrays" a man riding a horse. Many logograms are

TABLE 18.1: *Chinese Sources of Tangut Characters*

Tangut	Gloss	Chinese Source
𗾔	dog	犬 *quǎn* in its combining form as seen at the left of 狗 *gǒu* 'dog'
𗵗	horse	馬 *mǎ*
𗳉	stone	石 *shí*
𗾑, 𗾔	word	言 *yún*
𗾍, 𗾏	sheep, cow	羊 *yáng* 'sheep'

made in this way: ◻ 'grass' plus ◻ 'water' = ◻ 'rush', i.e. 'grass which grows in water'; ◻ 'red' plus ◻ 'stone' = ◻ 'red mineral, cinnabar'; 'red' plus ◻ 'metal' = ◻ 'red metal, copper'.

The "phonetic" logograms of the *xíng shēng* group form the next category. They are based on homonyms: one part of the character indicates its pronunciation, and the other its meaning. The homonyms ◻ 'cherry' and ◻ 'cream' are constructed on the basis of the homonymic character ◻ 'terrestrial spirit, divinity' with the addition of the determinatives ◻ 'tree' and ◻ 'water'.

A number of characters in the Tangut script can be classified in the Chinese tradition as "inverted" (*zhuánzhù*), e.g. ◻ 'man' and ◻ 'heart, soul'.

Some characters can be attributed to the "indicatory" category of Chinese characters (*zhǐ shì*). Among these are family names; thus a part of ◻ 'ear' plus part of ◻ 'kin, family' is used in the family name ◻.

A special group is formed by characters made for transcription of Chinese syllables; here the "indicatory" principle is also implied. So Tangut writes the Chinese syllable *fen* with the character ◻; the lower part is ◻ 'to divide', corresponding to Chinese 分 *fēn*.

Another group of transcription symbols consists of the logograms used in Buddhist texts to transcribe Sanskrit mantras: ◻ *om*, ◻ *ya*, ◻ *vi*, etc. The character ◻ *ken* 'celestial sound' is formed from from the left part of ◻ 'sound' + part of the character ◻ 'stone'. A method similar to Chinese *fǎnqiè* is also used, in which the phonetic value of a Chinese character is rendered by a pair of other characters, the first showing the pronunciation of the initial, the second indicating the "rhyme," i.e. the rest (vowel + tone + final consonant, if any). Thus Tangut ◻ *iei* is formed from ◻ *ie* 'alas!' plus ◻ *viei* 'to be in the middle'.

Finally, numerical characters form a special group. They are complex, and only in a few cases can a Chinese basis be traced. In ◻ 'one', the upper part is perhaps Chinese 一. ◻ 'two' is from the determinative ◻ 'doubling', with Chinese 二 as part of the character. In ◻ 'three', the upper right part shows the modified characters 三 or ◻. In ◻ 'eight', ◻ perhaps = Chinese 八. In ◻ 'nine', ◻ is possibly Chinese 九. The authors of the dictionary *The Sea of Characters* found it difficult to explain the numerical characters: ◻ 'eight' is explained as ◻ 'seven' without its top, then the structure of the character ◻ 'seven' is explained in a completely artificial way— it is figure ◻ 'eight' with parts of the characters ◻ 'clean' and ◻ 'method'.

There are approximately 6,600 characters in the Tangut script. Sometime in the middle of the twelfth century, when the script had been developing for over a hundred years, the structure of nearly every character was explained in the dictionary *The Sea of Characters*. The determinatives in the dictionary are used as parts of a limited set of characters. In the process of script invention, characters were divided into basic and derivative. Presumably the character ◻ 'rice' (which is not in the dictionary) was derived from ◻ 'cereal' (a modification of Chinese 米) and ◻ 'heart, soul' (perhaps from Chinese 心), suggesting 'cereal pleasant for the heart'. From ◻, the characters 粥 'rice porridge' and 糜 'rice broth' were produced. The use of logographic principles and characters of phonetic value made it possible to create chains of characters such as 頭 'head', 統 'initial', 統先 'first, previous', 髮頭 'hair and head, hair style', and 額 'forehead'. Such chains of logograms are in part reflected in *The Sea of Characters*, and in part reconstructable by scholars.

The Tangut script remained in use after the fall of the Tangut state, since the Tangut language was still the language of Buddhist texts. But with completion of this process of Chinese assimilation, probably in the second part of the sixteenth century, the script went out of use.

Kitan and Jurchin

GYÖRGY KARA

The Kitan Scripts

The Kitan (Khitan) dynasty flourished in the area of Manchuria from 916 to 1125 C.E.; it was known to the Chinese as Liao. In 920, a Siniform writing system was established for the Altaic (probably Mongolic) Kitan language. Chinese sources mention it as the "large script." Another system, called "small script," was created by the Kitan scholar Diela following his acquaintance with "the Uyghur language and script" during the visit of an Uyghur embassy in the Kitan court (924 or 925). This is why some thought the small script was a variety of the Uyghur alphabet (SECTION 49); but in fact, the not too numerous epigraphic monuments preserve two distinct scripts, both resembling Chinese writing (similar graphic elements, in vertical lines from right to left). The relatively simple characters of one of them (now equated with the large script) are written one below the other, leaving equal spaces between them. In the other system (now identified as the small script), the characters forming a word in the text are assembled in blocks. These blocks contain two to seven characters, usually arranged pairs below pairs. An odd-numbered final character is centered below the last pair; the first element of a pair is on the left side. In the headings of some epitaphs, the same symbols appear in the "linear" style of the large script. Up to now no character common to the two scripts has been identified with certainty.

The "large script" consists of logograms; see TABLE 18.2. Some of them are taken from Chinese, modified or unchanged ('month', 'day', 'emperor', 'horse', 'south', etc.), but many of them cannot be identified with any Chinese sign. Some were later borrowed into the Jurchin scripts (e.g., the Kitan large script character for 'year' received an additional dot in the Jurchin small script). It is possible that the large script also had ideograms for grammatical functions, perhaps syllabograms, but more monuments would be necessary for the fuller decipherment of this system.

TABLE 18.2: *Kitan "Large Script"*

Kitan	Gloss	Chinese	Kitan	Gloss	Chinese
禾	heaven	天	馬	horse	馬
日	day	日	髙	high	高
月	month	月	亜	west	西
米	year	_ a	方	direction	方
	one	一		dragon?	
一	two	二	夂	ten	十
二	five	五	十	twenty	廿
五			卅		

a. Cf. Jurchin.

The "assembled" or "small script" (see TABLE 18.3) is a complex of logograms, syllabograms, and perhaps other phonograms (marking single sounds). Not only suffixes are written in syllabograms, but also some stems. Syllables may be rendered by a set of syllabograms, with one character for the initial, one for the medial, and one for the final sound(s)—as in some deciphered Kitan transcriptions of Chinese names and terms (cf. the Chinese *fǎnqiè* method). External similarity of a small script character to a Chinese character does not help reading; thus the Kitan logogram for 'gold' has the shape of the Chinese character for 'mountain'. However, if the meaning of a Kitan character is known, it is sometimes possible to find its Chinese source (cf. 'heaven'). Some 370 characters (and variants) of this small script are known from large imperial and other epitaphs as well as minor inscriptions. A third of them have been partially deciphered by the Mongolian scholar Chinggeltei and his team (Qingge'rtai et al. 1985) with the aid of the more or less parallel Chinese text of some monuments (logograms of numerals, names of animals of the Twelve-year Cycle and other calendar terms, 'year', 'month', 'day', 'time', 'heaven', 'emperor', 'great', etc.). Logograms were also used as syllabograms; thus the character for 'year' also occurs as a final phonogram marking *ai*, while the character for *tau* 'five' is the first syllabogram in the block meaning *taula* 'hare'). There is no graphic difference between logograms and phonograms. The small script is attested in calligraphic and cursive styles. The two Kitan scripts seem to have been used concurrently, and survived the fall of the Liao Empire. The Jurchins wrote in the Kitan script until 1191, when it was suppressed by imperial order.

FIGURE 25. An inscription of 1041 in Kitan Large Script (Chén Shù 1982).

TABLE 18.3: *Kitan "Small Script"*

1	2	3	4	5 *tau*	

7	8	9 *ši?*	10	20	30

100 *jau*	heaven	day *nair*	month *sair*	year *ai*	time *po*

order *s.l.b.*	rat *...γa?*	ox	hare *tau.l.a*	dragon	snake *m.γ.o*

horse *m.r.*	goat *im.a*	hen *t.q.a*	dog *n.q.*	crow *γa.γ.*	gold *jürgü*

silver *m.ng.*	great *m.o*	big *m.o*	holy *m.n.*	emperor *xwang di*[a] + n. (GEN)	

lady *pu.ši.n*[a]	general *s.iang g.iun*[a]		name *i.r.*	empress *xwang tai xeu*[a]	

a. Chinese element.

SAMPLE OF KITAN SMALL SCRIPT

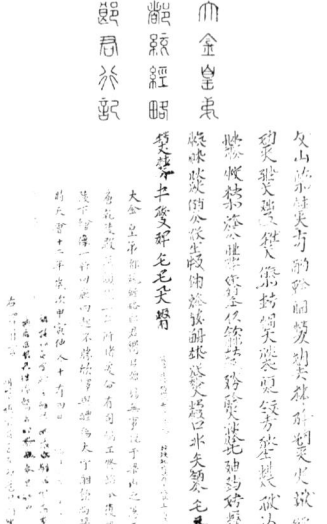

FIGURE 26. Inscription of 1134. With Chinese heading and translation *(text on the left side)* (cf. Qingge'rtai et al. 1985, Kane 1989).

1.	po	?		t. iu.	?	?	?	s. iau	?
2.	time	Heaven	gathering		ten	two		*jia* [blue/wood]

1.	qa. γa	?	ai	d(a). ur.	?	u. ul	?
2.	*yan* [tiger]		year	middle		winter	ten

1.	?	?	b(i). o.	?
2.	four	day	[verb of existence?]

'The time [of his return] is [the same?] jia yan twelfth year [of the period of] Gathering by Heaven [= Chinese Tianhui], the fourteenth day of the midwinter [month.]'

                                           —*Qingge'rtai et al. 1985.*

FIGURE 27. Kitan Small Script. Seal Script Style, 1101.

Jurchin Script

The Jurchin language (also called Jurchi or Jurchen, Southern Tungusic) of the Golden Empire (Jin, 1115–1234) received its first writing system in 1120 when Wanyan Xiyin established the Jurchin "large script" following the Kitan model. With Emperor Xizong's "small characters" added, the new script was officially introduced in 1145; see TABLE 18.4. Like the large script of the Kitans, this system borrowed numerous Chinese characters, sometimes adding a "diacritical" dot (see, e.g., 'month' and 'day'), sometimes distorting the original (e.g., 'capital city', 'summer', etc.). The same happened with characters adapted from the Kitan large script. This system is known from manuscript fragments and epigraphic monuments of the Jurchin Empire, from the Sino–Jurchin glossary and documents of the Ming Bureau of Translators, and from a Ming stone inscription of 1413; it contains logograms, syllabograms, and perhaps other phonetic symbols (e.g. for rendering final consonants). The Jurchin script is "linear" like the Kitan large script. Jin Qizong (1984) lists 1,384 characters and variants from all available sources. The Ming Sino–Jurchin glossary with Jurchin script contains some 720 characters (see Kiyose 1977; Dorji/Dao'rji and Heshig/ Hexige 1983).

TABLE 18.4: *Jurchin Script*

abka heaven	*na* earth	*edu* wind	*towo* fire	*mu* water	*moo* tree
inenggi day	*ania* year	*jua* summer	*bolo* autumn	*tuwe* winter	*nienie* spring
bia month	*eri* season	*nialma* man	*weile* deed	*guru=un* empire	*nienie=eri* springtime
mudu=r dragon	*inda=xun* dog	*muri=in* horse	*gin* capital city[a]	*guru=un=ni* empire (GEN)	*amba=an* great
emu one	*duyin* four	*nadan* seven	*juwa* ten	*tobuxon* fifteen	*tanggu* hundred
juwe two	*sunja* five	*jakun* eight	*omšo* eleven	*orin* twenty	*minggan* thousand
ilan three	*ninggu* six	*uyewun* nine	*jirxon* twelve	*gušin* thirty	*tumen* ten thousand

a. *Cf. Chinese 京.

SAMPLE OF JURCHIN

1. Jurchin   2. Transliteration   3. Gloss

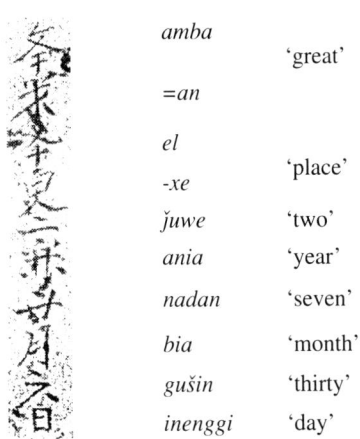

amba	
	'great'
=an	
el	
	'place'
-xe	
ǰuwe	'two'
ania	'year'
nadan	'seven'
bia	'month'
gušin	'thirty'
inenggi	'day'

'The (period of) Great Peace, second year, seventh moon, thirtieth day.'
—*Jurchin inscription of Aotun, 1210 (Jīn and Jīn 1980).*

Bibliography

TANGUT

Grinstead, Eric. 1972. *Analysis of the Tangut Script* (Scandinavian Institute of Asian Studies Monograph 10). Lund: Studentlitteratur.

Kwanten, Luc. 1982. *The Timely Pearl: A 12th Century Tangut Chinese Glossary.* vol. 1, *The Chinese Glosses* (Indiana University Uralic and Altaic Series 142). Bloomington: Indiana University.

Kwanten, Luc, and Susan Hesse. 1980. *Tangut (Hsi Hsia) Studies: A Bibliography* (Indiana University Uralic and Altaic Series 137). Bloomington: Indiana University.

Kychanov, E. I. 1964. *K izucheniju struktury tangutskoj pis'mennosti* [On the study of the structure of Tangut script] (Kratkie soobščeniya Instituta Narodov Azii AN SSSR 68). Moscow: Nauka.

———. 1980. "Tangutskoe pis'mo v istolkovanii samix tangutov" [Tangut script in the interpretation of the Tanguts themselves]. In *Razyskanija po obščemu i kitajskomu jazykoznaniju*, pp. 209–23. Moscow: Nauka.

Nishida, Tatsuo. 1964–66. "Reconstruction of the Hsi-Hsia Language and Decipherment of the Hsi-Hsia Script." In his *Seikago no kenkyû* [Research into the Tangut language], vol. 2, pp. 509–600. Tokyo: Zauho Kankokai.

———. 1967. *Seika moji* [The Tangut script]. Tokyo: Kinokuniya.

———. 1981. *Seika no moji* [The Tangut script]. Tokyo: Taishukan Shoten.

———. 1989. *Seika moji no hanashi* [The language of the Tangut script]. Tokyo: Taishukan Shoten.

KITAN AND JURCHIN

Chén Shù. 1982. *Jīn Liáo wén* [Jin and Liao literature]. Beijing: Zhōngguó shūjú.

Dorji/Dao'rji and Heshig/Hexige. 1983. *Nüzhen yiyu yanjiu [Research on the Sino-Jurchen vocabulary of the Bureau of Translators].* Höhhot.

Jīn Guăngpíng and Jīn Qĭzóng. 1980. *Nǚzhēn yǔyán wénzì yánjiū* [Research on the Jurchin language and script]. Beijing: Wénwù chūbǎn shè.

Jīn Qǐzóng. 1984. *Nǚzhēnwén cìdiǎn* [Dictionary of Jurchin characters]. Beijing.

Kane, Daniel. 1989. *The Sino-Jurchen Vocabulary of the Bureau of Interpreters.* Bloomington: Indian University

Kiyose, Gisaburo N. 1977. *A Study of the Jurchen Language and Script: Reconstruction and Decipherment.* Kyoto: Horitsubunka-sha.

Krippes, Karl A. 1988. "The Decipherment of the Jurchen Language Reconsidered." *LACUS Forum* 15: 402–15.

Qingge'rtai, Liú Fēngzhū, Chén Nǎixióng, Yú Bǎolín, and Xíng Fùlǐ. 1985. *Qìdān xiǎozì yánjiū* [Research on the Kitan small characters]. Beijing: Zhōngguó shèhuì kēxué chūbǎn shè.

The Yi Script

DINGXU SHI

Several Siniform scripts, which resemble Chinese characters in overall shape, are found in southwest China. Some of these were created with components taken directly from Chinese characters, such as the Geba and Malimasa scripts used for Naxi (or Nakhi, a Tibeto-Burman language) and the script used for Lisu (also Tibeto-Burman). Other Siniform scripts, such as that of Yi (or Lolo, also a Tibeto-Burman language), were invented more independently.

Classic Yi

The Yi characters, also known as Cuan [tswen] script or Wei writing, have an attested history of five hundred years and an estimated history of up to five thousand years. The term "classic" Yi script is applied to the characters used before the 1970s, when an official campaign of modernization started. The total number of different characters in existing classic Yi records is estimated at eight to ten thousand.

Classic Yi characters are syllabic logographs; that is, each character represents a syllable which is also a morpheme. They are written in a vertical pattern in which each page starts at the left-hand side, and each line goes from top to bottom.

Yi characters apparently evolved from hieroglyphs, like the Chinese characters. In classic Yi writing, a number of pictographs have kept, at least in part, their original shape, e.g. ☡ $sə^{33}$ 'snake', ☺ na^{33} 'eye', and �335 so^{34} 'fir'. (Tones are transcribed here in terms of numbered levels, with 5 the highest.) Some other classic Yi characters represent abstract concepts with self-explanatory symbols; thus ☂ mi^{21} 'sky' has the shape of an overhead dome supported by a pillar.

Internal borrowing among homophonous words is another way to convey abstract meanings in classic Yi writing. The character ☡ $t'ɤ^{21}$ 'ground' is also employed to mean 'speak'; and ☡ represents 'gold', 'yellow', and 'hereditary (son)', in addition to its original meaning of 'snake'.

There are five basic strokes in Yi writing: the dot, the horizontal line, the vertical line, the arch, and the circle. Each basic stroke has a number of variations. The horizontal line, for example, can be wavy or hooked. Strokes are combined to form simple units called radicals, which are usually also characters, like ☡ $p'a^{33}$ 'half'; however, these elements do not have constant semantic value to the extent that they do in Chinese. Complex characters are formed by adding strokes to a radical, as in ☡ $ʔʊ^{33}$ 'ridge/head'. The added stroke occasionally carries semantic information; thus

TABLE 19.1: *The Modern Yi Syllabary (Dīng et al. 1991: 446)*

	–	p	ph	b	mb	m̥	m	f	v	t	th	d	nd	n̥	n	ɬ	l	k	kh	g	ŋg	h
i																						
e																						
a																						
ɔ																						
o																						
ə																						
u																						
ʉ																						
ɿ																						
ʅ																						

the circle at the right shoulder of ⸜ *bɤ³³* 'flow, noise made by flowing water' signifies a hole from which ⸝ *zi²¹* 'water' emerges. New characters can also be formed by combining several radicals; e.g., 罜 *tsʼʋ⁵⁵* 'accompany' consists of 世 'ground' beneath ⸎ 'half'. Sometimes a radical is doubled to create a new character, such as 舙 *ti³⁴* 'certain', a doubling of ⸎ 'half'.

In certain cases, radicals are combined or doubled in such a way that the meaning of the new character can be derived from the combination of the components. Thus 逵 *ta³³* 'hug or hold with both hands' is formed by doubling 扗 *la³⁴* 'hand'. In rare cases, semantic radicals carry phonetic information as well. The positions of strokes and radicals in a given character cannot be altered. If the dot in 千 *tu³³* 'thousand' is moved from the top right position to the bottom right, the character 干 *ti³³* 'one' is created.

Modern Yi

Because of the geographic separation of Yi tribes, classic Yi writing was not always a unified system, and internal variation is not uncommon. The character for 'stomach', for example, has about forty different forms. An effort is being made to stan-

TABLE 19.1 *(Continued)*

ŋ	x	ɣ	ts	tsh	dz	ndz	s	z	tʂ	tʂh	dʐ	ndʐ	ʂ	ʐ	tɕ	tɕh	dʑ	ndʑ	ɲ	ɕ	ʑ	
																						55
																						33
																						21

dardize Yi characters. A popular proposal, supported by the local government, is to transform Yi characters into a pure syllabary, in which a single character represents all morphemes with the same pronunciation. The total number of characters can thus be reduced. The proposed modern Yi script has 819 characters, chosen from the classic writing. Of the four tones of a given syllable, the high level (55), mid level (33), and low falling (21) are represented by different characters. The character for the mid level tone is also used for the mid rising tone (34), but with an arch — above it. This version has a horizontal writing pattern, in which each page starts at the top and each line goes from left to right. It also has a printed style, with four basic strokes: horizontal, vertical, curve, and circle (see TABLE 19.1).

SAMPLES OF YI

PRAYER TO THE GOD OF AGRICULTURE IN CLASSIC YI SCRIPT

1. Yi:	𖽑	𖼺	丑	𖽘	𖾕
2. Transcription:	gu33	zu21	m̩21	t'a21	ŋi21
3. Gloss:	plow	sow	do	one	day

1.	𖼴	𖽑	𖾇	𖽘	𖾔
2.	ga34	gu33	ʔhĩ21	t'a21	p'u55
3.	valley	plow	wind	no	encounter

1.	𖽲	𖽑	甘	𖽘	𖾁
2.	ndi21	gu33	tsz̩55	t'a21	t'i34
3.	plain	plow	dew	no	lose

1.	∋	𖾘	𖾙	𖽘	𖽾
2.	die21	ɣo34	sə33	t'a21	tɕy33
3.	edge	inside	snake	no	curl

'When the season of plowing and sowing comes, may the field plowed in the valley not encounter wind, may the field plowed in the plain not lose rain and dew, may the field not be infested with snakes.'

—*Adapted from Mǎ 1986: 277.*

PHRASES IN PRINTED YI

1.	𖽯	𖼧	𖽯	𖾨
2.	ts'o33	de34	ts'o34	hmo33
3.	person	make	person	do

'apology'

1.	H	Ø	H	𖾋
2.	m̩33	pe33	m̩33	tɕ'e33
3.	horse	kick	horse	jump

'a horse that is kicking and jumping'

—*Adapted from Chén 1986: 285.*

Bibliography

Chén Kāng. 1986. "Liángshān Yíyǔ sìyīncí císù yìyì de dápèi" [The semantic collocation of the four morpheme words in Liangshan Yi]. In *Zhōngguó mínzú yǔyán lùnwén jí* [Papers on minority languages in China], ed. Fù Màojī, pp. 264–85. Chengdu: Sichuan Press of Nationalities.

Coyaud, Maurice. 1984. *Langues et écritures en Chine et alentour,* 2nd ed. Paris: "Pour l'Analyse du Folklore."

Dīng Chūnshòu, Zhū Wénxù, Lǐ Shēngfú, Zhū Jiànxīn, Dīng Jīnyǔ, and Chén Shìliáng. 1991. *Xiàndài Yíyǔ* [Modern Yi]. Beijing: Press of the Central College for Nationalities.

Mǎ Xuéliáng. 1986. *Cuànwén cóngkè* [Anthology of Cuan characters]. Chengdu: Sichuan Press of Nationalities.

Nishida, Tatsuo. 1980. *A Study of the Lolo-Chinese Vocabulary Lolo I-Yu: The Structure and Lineage of Shui-Liao Lolo.* Tokyo: Shokado.

Zhōngyāng Mínzú Xuéyuàn Shǎoshù Mínzú Yǔyán Yánjiūsuǒ [Institute of Minority Languages under the Central College for Nationalities]. 1987. *Zhōngguó shǎoshù mínzú yǔyán* [Minority languages in China]. Chengdu: Sichuan Press of Nationalities.

Zhōngyāng Mínzú Xuéyuàn Yíwén Wénxiàn Biānyì Shǐ [Office for Collecting and Translating Yi Records under the Central College for Nationalities]. 1993. *Yíwén wénxiàn yánjiū* [The study of Yi records]. Beijing: Press of the Central College for Nationalities.

Asian Calligraphy

JOHN STEVENS

Throughout Asia, the aesthetic configuration of a script is often as highly valued as its linguistic content. Calligraphy, an essential element of traditional Asian culture, remains an important art form in many areas today, and it has also attracted the attention of connoisseurs in the West.

Arabic was one of the last languages to be put into written form, but its calligraphy eventually became the principal art motif in the Muslim world, an area that stretched from India to Spain. Since pictorial representation was largely discouraged in Islam, calligraphy was the main vehicle for artistic representation. From the seventh century on, Arabic letters (SECTION 50) were shaped into an incredible variety of scripts and styles, ranging from monumental Kufic designs employed in the decoration of buildings (such as the Taj Mahal) to tiny *ghubar* 'dust script' used to write the Muslim profession of faith on a grain of rice (see FIGURE 28). (The six classical scripts of Islamic calligraphy are *Thuluth, Naskhī, Muḥaqqaq, Rayḥānī, Riqʿā*, and *Tawqīʿ*.) Calligraphy adorned nearly everything in the Muslim world: books, coins, ceramics, brocades, buildings, furniture, rugs, garments, belts, hats, funeral shrouds, pills and other forms of medicine, and even skin—Muslim women in certain areas decorated their cheeks and foreheads with verses calligraphed in henna. Each letter of the Arabic script was believed to be a work of Allah, and thus calligraphy was the most potent of talismans. Calligraphers were venerated in Islamic culture—it was said that the "angel" of each letter appeared to pious scribes—and the finest examples of calligraphy were likened to the purest gold, the most delectable feast, and the sweetest wine. (For numerous examples of Islamic calligraphy, see Khatibi 1977 and Schimmel 1984.)

While some calligraphic masterpieces have been produced in Devanagari script—usually in the realm of Tantric and Jain art—India is primarily an oral culture and there is not a strong tradition of Hindu artistic calligraphy (as opposed to Mughal art, which inherited Islam's veneration for the written word). However, it was in India that the Siddhaṃ script developed, a script that was destined to "migrate to other countries, travel to other lands, go to other worlds, always displaying the holy, abiding in the hearts of all" (*Akṣamālikopaniṣad*, I, i).

The symmetrical and refined Siddhaṃ letters, stemming from the western branch of the Brahmi alphabet (SECTION 30), were adopted by the Buddhists for their holy texts, and even when the sutras were translated into Chinese, *mantra* (esoteric formu

FIGURE 28. A Qurʾānic passage in a variety of calligraphic styles (Zakariya 1978: 103):
ʾinna ḫalaqnākum min ḏakarin wa ʾunṭā 'Behold, we have created you male and female'
(Sura 49:13).

las) were reproduced in the Siddhaṃ script (FIGURE 29). Siddhaṃ script was similarly introduced into Korea and Japan through the vehicle of Buddhism, and the study
and calligraphic representation of this script became well established in East Asia.

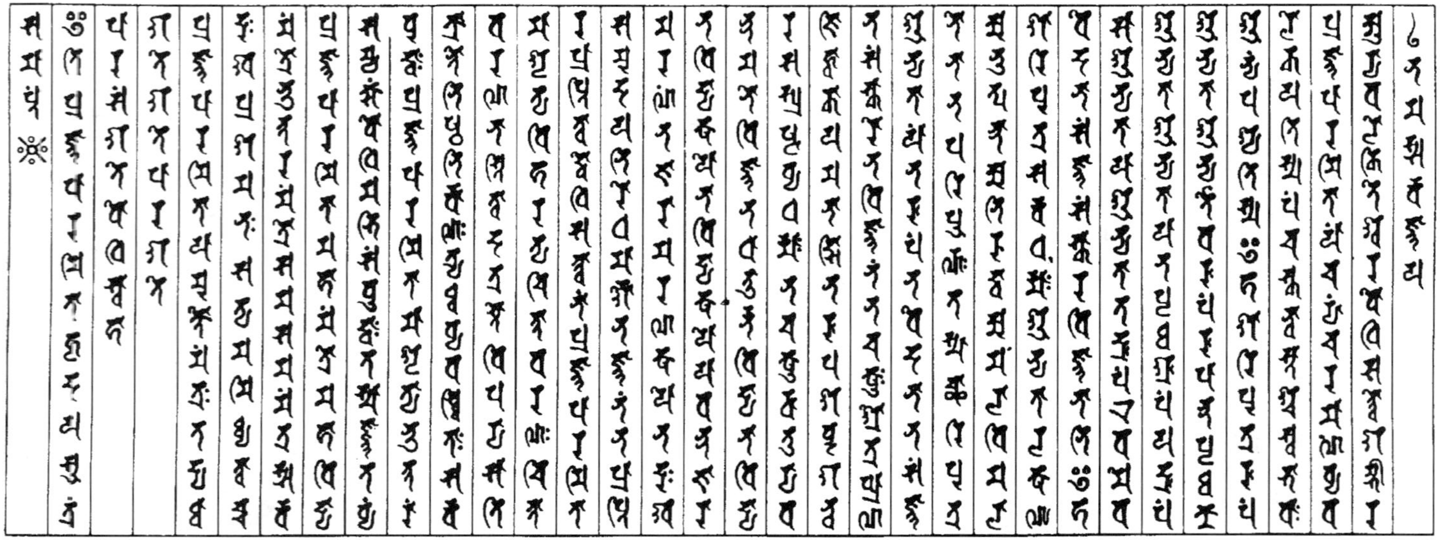

FIGURE 29. The "Heart Sutra" in Sanskrit, brushed by Kijun Tokuyama in siddham characters. Transliteration and translation of the first few lines: *namaḥ sarvajñāya // āryāvalokiteśvaro bodhisattvo gambhīrāyāṃ prajñāpāramitāyāṃ caryāṃ caramāṇo vyavalokayati sma // pañca skandhāḥ // tāṃś ca svabhāva-śunyān paśyati sma // iha śāriputra rūpaṃ śūnyatā śūunyataiva rūpaṃ rūpān na pṛthak śūnyatā śūnyatāyā na pṛthag rūpaṃ yad rūpaṃ sā śūnyatā tad rūpam // ...* 'Avalokitesvara, the Bodhisattva of compassion, doing deep Prajna Paramita, clearly saw that the five skandhas are Sunyata, thus transcending misfortune and suffering. O Shariputra, form is no other than Sunyata, Sunyata is no other than form. Form is exactly Sunyata, Sunyata exactly form. Feeling, thought, volition and consciousness are likewise like this' (Stevens 1988: 120, 131, calligraphy unpublished; cf. p. 119, same text in horizontal lines).

FIGURE 30. The sacred mantra *oṃ mani padme hūṃ* written in the Tibetan styles Lentsa, Uchen, Drutsa, and Ume (Stevens 1988: 77).

East Asian Buddhists had little affinity for the intricacies of Sanskrit grammar or pronunciation, though, and the use of Siddhaṃ script was entirely calligraphic—it was venerated for its beauty and magic. One finds Siddhaṃ script displayed all over East Asia in *mantra* and as *bīja* (seed syllables). During the twentieth century in Japan, there has even been a Siddhaṃ renaissance: the practice of Siddhaṃ calligraphy is widespread among both Buddhist priests and lay believers, and several outstanding Siddhaṃ calligraphers have mounted elaborate exhibitions which attracted large crowds. (For guidance in writing Siddhaṃ script, see Stevens 1988: 31–69.)

The entrancing scripts of Tibet, too (SECTION 40), are based on Gupta forms which eventually branched into the following calligraphic styles (FIGURE 30): *Uchen* (*dbu-can*), standard block script; *Ume* (*dbu-med*), cursive hand script; *Bamyik* (*'bamyig*), decorative script for official documents; *Drutsa* (*'brutsha*), another type of decorative script; *Lentsa* (*lan-tsha*), sacred script; and *Chuyik* (*'khyug-yig*), handwriting script for general use. Senior monks and government officials were expected to be expert calligraphers, and penmanship figured prominently in Tibetan education (FIGURE 31). A well-produced Tibetan text, brushed in gold, silver, and black ink on blue paper, is truly a delight to behold and an example of the finest religious art. (For guidance in writing calligraphic Tibetan, see Stevens 1988: 81–91.)

It was in China (SECTIONS 14–15) that the calligraphic approach reached a pinnacle. Calligraphy, considered by the Chinese to be the ultimate art form, has been appreciated there for over two thousand years. The five basic scripts, each with its own "flavor," are: bold and elegant *juàn shū*, seal script; dignified and serious *lì shū*, clerical script; formal and controlled *kǎi shū*, standard script (FIGURE 32); graceful and polished *xíng shū*, running script; and fluid, individualistic *cǎo shū*, grass script.

Early on, the Chinese recognized that "Calligraphy *is* the person"—that is, a calligrapher's character is clearly revealed in the brushstrokes. Thus, specimens of calligraphy by statesmen, philosophers, scholars, generals, famous beauties, and monks and nuns were more highly valued than pieces by professional calligraphers. Indeed, the Chinese truly treasured calligraphy. One emperor, for instance, was so enamored of the celebrated "Preface Written at the Orchid Pavilion" (*Lán Tīng Xù*) by the renowned general-calligrapher Wang Xi-ji (321–379) that he offered the owner any other treasure in his palace in exchange for it. When the owner refused, the emperor resorted to subterfuge, finally obtaining his heart's desire. Later, the emperor insisted

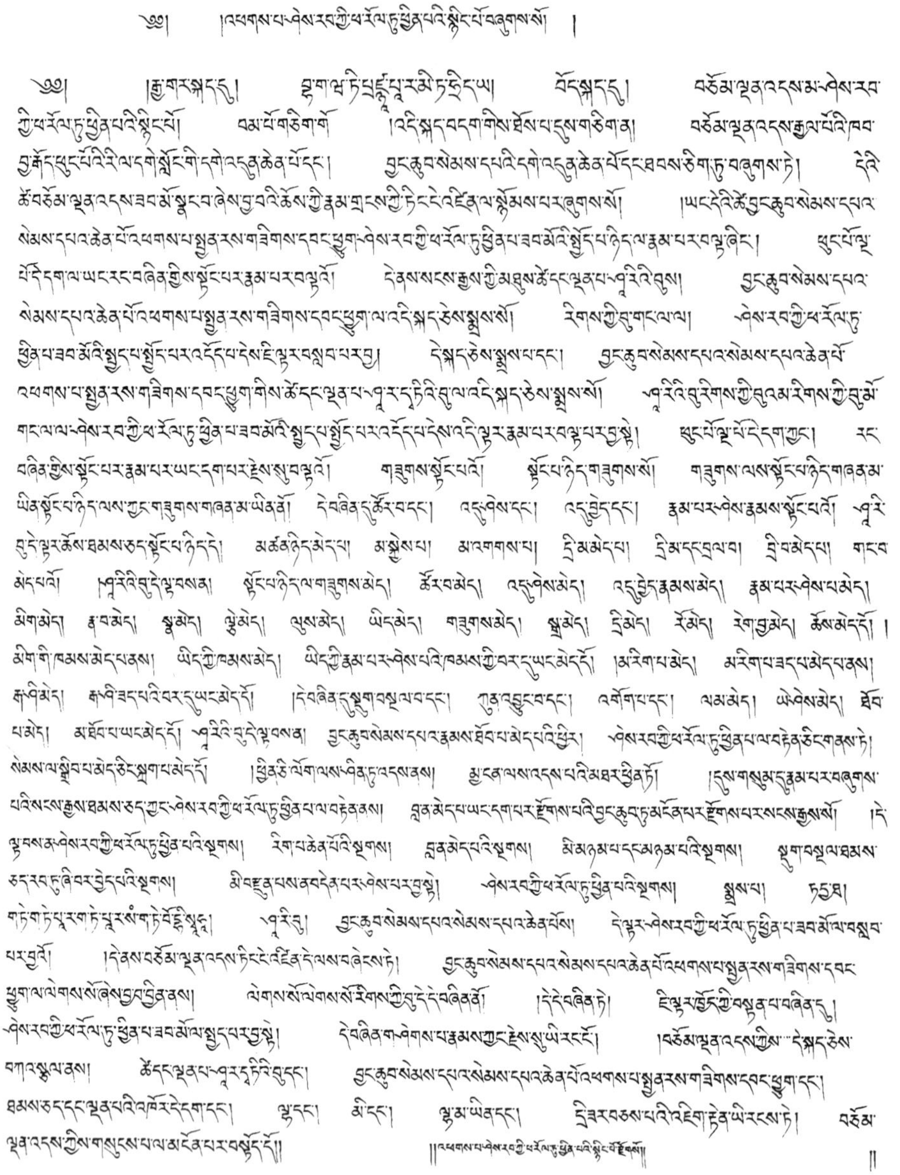

FIGURE 31. The Heart Sutra in Tibetan—Uchen script (Stevens 1988: 128).

on being buried with the masterpiece. (Wang Hsi-chi himself described his favorite pieces of calligraphy as being orchestras of movement, replete with billowing clouds, falling rocks, brass hooks, venerable vines, and swift couriers.) Calligraphy in China also supported a huge industry to supply calligraphers with the four treasures: brush, ink, inkstone, and paper. (For guidance in writing Chinese characters, see Fazzioli 1986.)

般若心経
羯諦羯諦　波羅羯諦　波羅僧羯諦　菩提薩婆呵
多呪即説呪曰
呪能除一切苦真実不虚故説般若波羅蜜
多是大神呪是大明呪是無上呪是無等等
得阿耨多羅三藐三菩提故知般若波羅蜜
想究竟涅槃三世諸佛依般若波羅蜜多故
罣礙無罣礙故無有恐怖遠離一切顛倒夢
所得故菩提薩埵依般若波羅蜜多故心無
亦無老死尽無苦集滅道無智亦無得以無
無意識界無無明亦無無明尽乃至無老死
耳鼻舌身意無色声香味触法無眼界乃至
不増不減是故空中無色無受想行識無眼
是舍利子是諸法空相不生不滅不垢不浄
異色色即是空空即是色受想行識亦復如
蘊皆空度一切苦厄舍利子色不異空空不
観自在菩薩行深般若波羅蜜多時照見五
摩訶般若波羅蜜多心経

FIGURE 32. The Heart Sutra in standard Chinese script (*kǎi shū*; Stevens 1988: 123).

In Confucian Korea, calligraphy traditionally employed Chinese characters, but in modern times some fine brush calligraphy is being done with *Hankul* letters (SECTION 17; FIGURE 33). Japan maintains a calligraphic tradition as rich as that of China (and indeed, many masterpieces of Chinese calligraphy are preserved in that country). In addition to classical *kanji* calligraphy, delicate brushwork in *kana* script is favored by female calligraphers (SECTION 16; FIGURE 34), and, as mentioned above, there are a number of outstanding Siddhaṃ calligraphers in Japan. Dynamic Zen calligraphy—"brushstrokes of enlightenment"—has had a profound impact on Japanese aesthetics, and masterpieces by a figure such as Hakuin (1685–1768) continue to inspire modern artists, East and West. (For guidance in creating Zen calligraphy, see Ōmori and Terayama 1983: 89–97.)

Mention should also be made of *shakyō* 'sutra copying'. Brushing sacred texts has always been a popular form of devotion for pious Buddhists throughout East Asia, and many splendid examples have been produced. Since each character of a sacred text is felt to represent a "Buddha," the calligrapher takes special care with each stroke and the resulting brushwork is "written prayer." (For a guide to *shakyō*, see Stevens 1988: 116–31.)

Compared to East Asian countries, calligraphy in Southeast Asian lands was basically an auxiliary art. Outstanding examples of such art include highly stylized, decorative square script used on Burmese lacquer and gilt ordination texts for Buddhist monks; texts in Cambodian Mul script; and finely detailed Javanese (SECTION 45) and Malay manuscripts. It should also be noted that calligraphic talismans are frequently employed as tattoo designs in Asia, especially in Thailand and Japan.

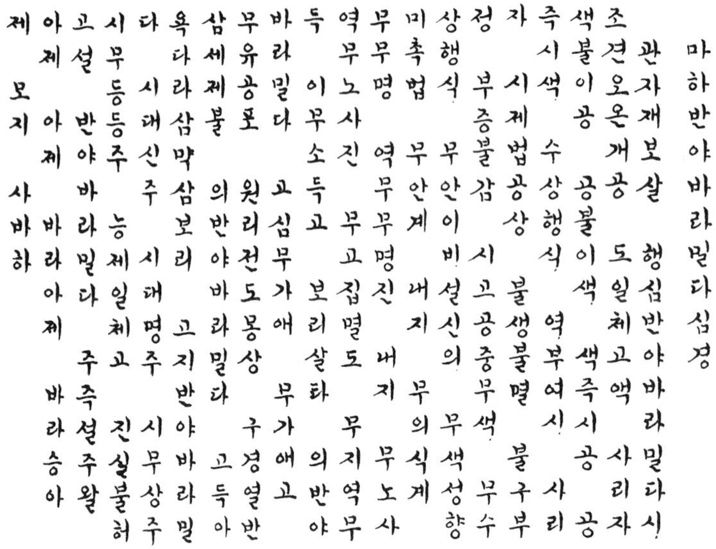

마하반야바라밀다심경

관자재보살 행심반야바라밀다시 조견오온개공 도일체고액 사리자 색불이공 공불이색 색즉시공 공즉시색 수상행식 역부여시 사리자 시제법공상 불생불멸 불구부정 부증불감 시고공중무색 무수상행식 무안이비설신의 무색성향미촉법 무안계 내지 무의식계 무무명 역무무명진 내지 무노사 역무노사진 무고집멸도 무지역무득 이무소득고 보리살타 의반야바라밀다고 심무가애 무가애고 무유공포 원리전도몽상 구경열반 삼세제불 의반야바라밀다고 득아뇩다라삼먁삼보리 고지반야바라밀다 시대신주 시대명주 시무상주 시무등등주 능제일체고 진실불허 고설반야바라밀다주 즉설주왈 아제아제 바라아제 바라승아제 모지 사바하

FIGURE 33. The Heart Sutra in Korean (Stevens 1988: 129).

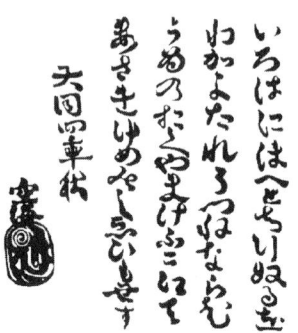

FIGURE 34. The traditional arrangement of Japanese hiragana (each character is used once, to spell out the following poem, attributed to the Buddhist monk Kūkai):
いろはにほへとちりぬるをわかよたれそつねならむうゐのおくやまけふこえてあさきゆ
めみしゑひもせす

Iro wa nioedo chirinuru wo waga yo tare zo tsune naran ui no okuyama kyō koete asaki
yume miji ei mo sezu

'The colorful [flowers] are fragrant, but they must fall. Who in this world can live forever? Today cross over the deep mountains of life's illusions and there will be no more shallow dreaming, no more drunkenness'
(Stevens 1988: 185; from the Zentsuji Treasury).

Bibliography

Billeter, Jean François. 1990. *The Chinese Art of Writing*. New York: Rizzoli.

Chiang, Yee. 1973. *Chinese Calligraphy: An Introduction to Its Aesthetics and Technique*, 3rd ed. Cambridge: Harvard University Press.

Douglas, Nik. 1978. *Tibetan Tantric Charms and Amulets*. New York: Dover.

Fazzioli, Edoardo. 1987. *Chinese Calligraphy*. New York: Abbeville.

Gallop, Annabel T. 1991. *Golden Letters: Writing Traditions of Indonesia*. London: British Library.

Khatibi, Abdelkebir, and Mohammed Sijelmassi. 1977. *The Splendour of Islamic Calligraphy*. New York: Rizzoli.

Lai, T. C. 1975. *Chinese Calligraphy: An Introduction*. Seattle: University of Washington Press.

Losty, Jeremiah P. 1982. *The Art of the Book in India*. London: British Library.

Mookerjee, Ajit. 1975, *Yoga Art*. London: Thames and Hudson.

Nakata, Yujiro. 1976. *The Art of Japanese Calligraphy*. New York and Tokyo: Weatherhill/Heibon-sha.

Ōmori Sōgen, and Terayama Katsujō. 1983. *Zen and the Art of Calligraphy*. London: Routledge and Kegan Paul.

Sadafi, Yasin H. 1978. *Islamic Calligraphy*. Boulder, Colo.: Shambhala.

Schimmel, Annemarie. 1984. *Calligraphy and Islamic Culture*. New York: New York University Press.

Stevens, John. 1988. *Sacred Calligraphy of the East*. Boston: Shambhala.

Van Gulik, R. H. 1980. *Siddham*. New Delhi: Mrs. Sharada Rani.

Zakariya, Mohamed U. 1978. "Observations on Islamic Calligraphy." *Fine Print* 4: 97–103.

———. 1979. *The Calligraphy of Islam: Reflections on the State of the Art*. Washington, D.C.: Georgetown Univerwity, Center for Contemporary Arab Studies.

Comparative Table of Sinitic Characters

The following list is intended to give a sampling of Chinese characters that have more than one form in current use: Traditional (used in Taiwan, Hong Kong, Singapore, and other overseas Chinese communities), Simplified (used in the People's Republic of China), and Japanese. In addition, the list illustrates the differences in pronunciation that are found as one goes from Mandarin Chinese (in pinyin romanization) to Japanese *on* and *kun* readings (in the Hepburn romanization) and to Korean (Yale system). Items are arranged alphabetically by the pinyin forms. Data were provided by Victor H. Mair, Janet S. (Shibamoto) Smith, and Ross King.

PY	Tr.	Si.	Chinese Gloss	Jp.	On	Kun	Jpn. Gloss if diff.	Korean
ái	獃	呆	silly obstinacy	呆	(hō)			—
ài	愛	爱	love	愛	ai			āy
bìng	並	并	together, moreover	並	hei	nami naraberu narabu narabi ni	line up, equal	pyēng
bǔ	補	补	supplement	補	ho	oginau		pō
cái	纔	才	just, then	纔	(san /zan/sai)	(wazukani)	a little, a small quantity	cay
cān	參	参	blend, confused	参	san	mairu	three	cham
chān	鑱	馋	cut into, carve		(sen)	(surudoi)	going, coming	(chan)
chán	纏	缠	bind up, involve	纏	(ten)	(matou)		cen
chǎn	產	产	produce, estate	産	san	umu umareru ubu	+ childbirth	sān
chàn	懺	忏	to regret, ritual	懺	(zan)			cham
cháng	嘗	尝	to taste, past	嘗	(shō)	(nameru)		sāng
cháng	腸	肠	intestines	腸	chō			cang
cháng, zhǎng	長	长	long, to grow	長	chō	nagai		cang
chǎng	廠	厂	shed,storehouse,factory	廠	(shō)			chang
chē	車	车	cart, car	車	sha	kuruma		cha, ke
chén	塵	尘	dust	塵	chin jin	chiri gomi		cin
chèn	襯	衬	inner garments	襯	(shin)			chūn
chèn, chèng	稱	称	fitting, suitable	稱	(shō)		name, title	ching
chí	遲	迟	slow, late	遲	chi	okureru okurasu osoi		ci
chǐ	齒	齿	teeth	齒	shi	ha		chi

PY	Tr.	Si.	Chinese Gloss	Jp.	On	Kun	Jpn. Gloss if diff.	Korean
chōng	衝	冲	collide, rush against	衝	shō			chwung
chǒng	寵	宠	kindness, grace	寵	(chō)		favor, affection	chōng
chǒu	醜	丑	deformed	醜	shū	minikui	ugliness	chwu
chǔ	處	处	place	処	sho			chē
cóng	從	从	follow, from	從	jū	shitagau		cong
					shō	shitagaeru		
					ju			
dǎng	黨	党	political party	党	tō			tang
dì	遞	递	hand in/to, exchange	逓	tei			chey
dōng	東	东	east	東	tō	higashi		tong
dòng	動	动	to move	動	dō	ugoku		tōng
						ugokasu		
ér	兒	儿	infant, boy	児	ji			a
èr	貳	贰	two, second	弐	ni			ī
fā	發	发	put forth, start	発	hatsu			pal
					hotsu			
fǎ	髮	发	hair (of the head)	髪	hatsu	kami		pal
fēi	飛	飞	to fly	飛	hi	tobu		pi
						tobasu		
fēng	風	风	wind	風	fū	kaze		phwung
					fu	kaza		
fēng	豐	丰	abundant	豊	hō	yutaka		phwung
fén	墳	坟	grave, cemetery	墳	fun			pwun
fèn	奮	奋	spirited, earnest	奮	fun	furū		pwūn
fèng	鳳	凤	phoenix	鳳	(hō)			pong
fó	佛	佛	Buddha	仏	futsu	hotoke		pwul
fū	膚	肤	skin	膚	fu			pwu
fù	覆	复	cover	覆	fuku	ōu	+ overthrow;	pok
					kutsugaesu		overturn	
					kutsugaeru			
fù	復	复	again, repeat	復	fuku			pok
fù	複	复	double garment	複	fuku		double	pok
fù	婦	妇	woman, wife	婦	fu			pwu
gān	乾	干	dry	乾	kan	kawaku		kan/ken
						kawakasu		
gàn	幹	干	attend to, tree trunk	幹	kan	miki	tree trunk	kan
gè	個,	个	a measure word	個	ko			kay
	箇							
gǔ	穀	谷	grain	穀	koku			kok
guā	颳	刮	to blow (of wind)	颳	katsu/			—
					kechi			
guǎng	廣	广	broad	広	kō	hiroi		kwāng
						hiromaru		
						hiromeru		
						hirogaru		
						hirogeru		
guó	國	国	country, kingdom	国	koku	kuni		kwuk

PY	Tr.	Si.	Chinese Gloss	Jp.	On	Kun	Jpn. Gloss if diff.	Korean
guò	過	过	pass by, exceed	過	ka	sugiru sugosu ayamatsu ayamachi	error; excess	kwa
há	蝦	虾	frog	蛙	(a)	(kaeru)		ha 'shrimp'
hái	還	还	still	還	kan		return	hwan 'return'
hàn	漢	汉	Chinese	漢	kan			han
hào	號	号	appellation, mark	号	gō			ho
héng	恆	恒	constant, persevering	恒	kō			hang
hòu	後	后	after	後	go kō	nochi		hwu
hòu	后	后	queen	后	(kō/go)	(kisaki)		hwu
huá	華	华	splendor, China	華	ka ke	hana	+ flower	hwa
huà	畫	画	picture	画	ga kaku			hwā hoyk 'stroke'
huà	劃	划	to carve, mark	劃	(kaku)			hoyk
huái	懷	怀	bosom, to cherish	懷	kai	futokoro natsukashii natsukashimu natsuku natsukeru		hoy
huān	歡	欢	rejoice, happy	歡	kan			hwan
huì	會	会	assemble, meet	会	kai e	au		hōy
huò	穫	获	to reap	穫	kaku			hoyk
huǒ	夥	伙	comrade, partner	夥	(ka)	obitadashii	immense	kwā
jī	機	机	a mechanism	機	ki	hata		ki
jī		鳩	chicken	鶏	kei	niwatori		kyey
jī	積	积	accumulate	積	seki	tsumu tsumoru		cek
jī	擊	击	attack, beat	擊	geki	utsu		kyek
jí	極	极	utmost, extreme	極	kyoku goku	kiwameru kiwamaru kiwami		kuk
jǐ	幾	几	how many, a few	幾	ki	iku		ki
jì	際	际	border, limit	際	sai	kiwa	+ time, occasion	cey
jì	繼	继	connect, continue	継	kei	tsugu		kyēy
jiā	挾	挟	clasp under the arm	挟	kyō	hasamu hasamaru	+ put between, insert	hyep
jiǎ	假	假	false, borrow	仮	ka ke	kari	vanity; temporary, provisional	kā
jià	價	价	price, value	価	ka	atai		ka
jiān	艱	艰	hardship, calamity	艱	(kan)	(nayamu)		kan
jiān	堅	坚	firm, hard	堅	ken	katai		kyen
jiān	監	监	prison, oversee	監	kan		official; director	kam
jiǎn	儉	俭	frugal, economical	険	ken	kewashii	steep; severe	kēm

PY	Tr.	Si.	Chinese Gloss	Jp.	On	Kun	Jpn. Gloss if diff.	Korean
jiǎn	繭	茧 cocoon		繭	(ken)	(mayu)		kyen
jiǎn	柬	柬 visiting card, to select		柬	(kan/ken)	(erabu)		kan
jiàn	薦	荐 introduce, recommend		薦	sen	susumeru		chēn
jiàn	見	见 see		見	ken	miru		kyēn
						mieru		
						miseru		
jiāng	將	将 take, presently		将	shō		+ commander	cǎng
jiāng	薑	姜 ginger		薑	(kyō)	(hajikami)		kang
jiǎng	講	讲 explain, lecture		講	kō			kāng
jiē	階	阶 steps, levels		階	kai			kyey
jié	傑	杰 heroic, eminent		傑	ketsu		excellence	kel
jié	節	节 joint, festival		節	setsu	fushi		cel
					sechi			
jǐn	僅	仅 barely, just		僅	(kin)	(wazuka)		kun
jǐn	儘	尽 barely, utmost		儘	jin	mama	as it is	} cin
jìn	盡	尽 exhaust, uttermost		尽	jin	tsukusu		
jìn	進	进 advance, enter		進	shin	susumu		cin
						susumeru		
jīng	經	经 past, a classic		経	kei	heru	longitude; sutra; pass, elapse	kyeng
					kyō			
jīng	驚	惊 terrify, alarm		驚	kyō	odoroku	+ surprise	kyeng
						odorokasu		
jiù	舊	旧 old		旧	kyū	kwū		
jué	覺	觉 perceive, feel		覚	kaku	oboeru	+ remember;	kak
						samasu		awake
						sameru		
kāi	開	开 open		開	kai	hiraku		kay
						hirakeru		
						aku		
						akeru		
lái	來	来 come		来	rai	kuru		ˡnay
						kitaru		
						kitasu		
liǎng	兩	两 two, tael		両	ryō			ˡyang, nyang
lǘ		驴 donkey		驢	(ro)			ˡye
mǎi	買	买 to buy		買	bai	kau		may
mài	麥	麦 wheat		麦	baku	mugi		mayk
mài	賣	卖 to sell		売	bai	uru		may
						ureru		
mén	門	门 door		門	mon	kado		mwun
nǎo	惱	恼 vexed, resentful		悩	nō	nayamu	distress; illness	noy
						nayamasu		
qí	齊	齐 equal, even		斉	sei			cey
qǐ	豈	岂 how (rhetorical)		豈	(ki)			ki, kay
qǐ	啟	启 to open, divide		啓	(kei)			kyēy

PY	Tr.	Si.	Chinese Gloss	Jp.	On	Kun	Jpn. Gloss if diff.	Korean
qì	棄	弃	reject, discard	棄	(ki)			ki
qì	氣	气	breath, air, temper	気	ki			ki
					ke			
qiān	遷	迁	to ascend, transfer	遷	sen			chēn
qiǎn	淺	浅	shallow	浅	sen	asai		chen
qiāng	鎗	枪	rifle	鎗	(sō)		spear, lance	l
qiáng	牆	墙	wall	墙	(shō)	(kaki)		cang
qiáo	橋	桥	bridge	橋	kyō	hashi		kyo
qiào	竅	窍	aperture	竅	(kyō)			kyu
qiè	竊	窃	steal, pilfer	窃	setsu		secret, stealthy	cel
qīn	親	亲	relation(ship)	親	shin	oya	intimacy;	chin
						shitashii	parents, relative	
						shitashimu		
qìng	慶	庆	congratulate, lucky	慶	kei			kyēng
qióng	窮	穷	poor, exhausted	窮	kyū	kiwameru		kwung
						kiwamaru		
quán	權	权	authority, power	権	ken			kwen
						gon		
quē	缺	缺	deficient, vacancy	欠	ketu	kakeru		kyel
						kaku		
qū	區	区	region, to distinguish	区	ku			kwu
ràng	讓	让	waive, yield	讓	jō	yuzuru		yāng
rào	繞	绕	wind around	繞	(jō)		surround	yō
rè	熱	热	hot	熱	netsu	atsui		yel
rèn	認	认	recognize	認	nin	mitomeru		in
shēng	聲	声	sound	声	sei	koe		seng
					shō	kowa		
shòu	壽	寿	longevity	寿	shu	kotobuki		swu
shǔ	屬	属	belong to	属	zoku			sok
suì	碎	碎	bits, petty	碎	sai	kudaku	break, smash	swāy
						kudakeru		
tiáo	條	条	strip, twig	条	jō		article, clause	co
tiě	鐵	铁	iron	鉄	tetsu			chel
tīng	廳	厅	hall	庁	chō		gov'ment office	cheng
wéi	圍	围	to surround, enclose	囲	i	kakomu		wi
						kakou		
wéi	為	为	to do, make	為	i	(tame)	+ welfare	wi
wú	無	无	not, without	無	mu	nai		mwu
					bu			
xī	犧	牺	sacrifice	犠	gi			huy
xí	習	习	practice, habit	習	shū	narau		sup
xì	戲	戏	joke, theater	戯	gi	tawamureru		hūy
xián	鹹	咸	salty	鹹	(kan)			ham
xián	閒	闲	leisure, idle	間	kan	aida	interval, space	han
					ken	ma		
xiǎn	顯	显	obvious	顕	ken			hyēn
xiàn	獻	献	contribute	献	ken			hēn

PY	Tr.	Si.	Chinese Gloss	Jp.	On	Kun	Jpn. Gloss if diff.	Korean
					kon			
xiàn	縣	县	district	県	ken			hyen
xiàn	憲	宪	constitution	憲	ken			hēn
xiāng	鄉	乡	village	鄉	kyō		+ native place	hyang
					gō			
xiǎng	響	响	noise, echo	響	kyō	hibiku		hyang
xié	協	协	mutual, to aid	協	kyō			hyep
xiě	寫	写	to write	写	sha	utsuru	copy, picture	să
						utsusu		
xīng	興	兴	prosper, originate	興	kō	okoru	+ interest, enter-	hūng
					kyō	okosu	tainment; revive	
xuǎn	選	选	elect	選	sen	erabu		sēn
xué	學	学	learn, study	学	gaku	manabu		hak
xún	尋	寻	seek	尋	jin	tazuneru	+ ask	sim
yǎ	亞	亚	ugly, inferior	亜	a		rank next	ā
yī	醫	医	medicine	医	i			uy
yī	壹	弌	one	壱	ichi			il
yí	儀	仪	etiquette, rites	儀	gi			uy
yì	譯	译	interpret, translate	訳	yaku	wake		yek
yì	義	义	righteousness, mng.	義	gi			ūy
yīng	應	应	ought, correspond	応	ō			ūng
yú	魚	鱼	fish	魚	gyo	uo		e
						sakana		
yuán	圓	圆	circular, a dollar	円	en	marui		wēn
yùn	運	运	transport	運	un	hakobu		wūn
zhá	箚	札	write out, a memorial	札	satsu	fuda	paper money	cap/cha; chal
zhái	齋	斋	abstain, foot, a shop	斎	sai			cāy
zhài	債	债	owe, a debt	債	sai			chay
zhān	氈	毡	rough felt, as for rugs	氈	(sen)			cēn
zhàn	戰	战	alarmed, to fight, war	戦	sen	ikusa		cēn
						tatakau		
zhào	趙	赵	hasten to, a surname	趙	(chō)			co
zhé	摺	折	to fold, document	折	setsu	oru		cep
						ori		
						oreru		
zhè	這	这	this	這	(sha)		crawl, creep	cē
zhēng	徵	征	testify, summon	征	sei			cing
zhěng	爭	争	wrangle, contest	争	sō	arasou		cayng
zhèng	鄭	郑	a surname	鄭	(tei)			cēng
zhī	隻	只	measure word	只	(si)	(tada)	only; free	chek
zhí	執	执	seize, grasp	執	shitsu	toru		cip
						shū		
zhí	職	职	office, official duty	職	shoku			cik
zhǐ	祇	只	only	祇	(gi)		national god	ci 'respect'
zhōng	鍾	钟	cup	鍾	(shō)		gather; collect	cong
zhōng	鐘	钟	bell, clock	鐘	shō	kane		cong
zhǒng	種	种	kind, seed	種	shu	tane		cōng

PY	Tr.	Si.	Chinese Gloss	Jp.	On	Kun	Jpn. Gloss if diff.	Korean
zhòng	眾	众	crowd	衆	shū			cwūng
					shu			
zhòu	晝	昼	daytime	昼	chū	hiru		cwu
zhòu	縐,	绉	crape, wrinkled					
	皺			皺	(shū)	(shiwa)		chwu
zhú	築	筑	construct	築	chiku	kizuku		chwuk
zhuān	專	专	special	專	sen	moppara	mainly, solely	cen
zhuāng	莊	庄	sedate, estate	莊	sō			cang 'villa'
					shō			
				εθ		shō 'level'		
zhuì	墜	坠	to fall, sink	墜	tsui			chwu
zhuó	濁	浊	turbid, stupid	濁	daku	nigoru		thak
						nigosu		

Kokuji

The following are characters created in Japan, following the structural principles of Chinese character formation (more or less); some of them have on-readings.

Jpn.	On	Kun	Gloss
		A. ON THE JŌYŌ-KANJI LIST	
働	dō	hataraki	work, effect
		hataraku	
峠		to¢ge	mountain pass
畑		hata	field, one's specialty
		hatake	
込		komu	be crowded; get into,
		komeru	include, concentrate on
枠		waku	frame, framework
		B. NOT ON THE JŌYŌ-KANJI LIST	
躾		shitsuke	upbringing
裃		kamishimo	samurai; ceremonial garb of samurai
裄		yuki	sleeve length
裳		tsuma	skirt

Part V: European Writing Systems

LITERACY SPREAD GRADUALLY ACROSS EUROPE, initially with the Phoenicians and then, when writing was adopted by the Greeks—who (at a date which remains hotly disputed in the scholarly community) reinterpreted certain consonant symbols as pure vowel letters, creating the alphabet—with their trading colonies and settlements. Alphabetic inscriptions in several scripts, dating to the early and mid first millennium B.C.E., are found in the Anatolian, Balkan, Italian, and Iberian peninsulas, representing both Indo-European languages and those spoken before the arrival of Indo-European–speakers. The Greek communities were founded before the script was standardized, and there is considerable variety in the alphabets and their use; in Italy, the Etruscans wrote a very limited range of inscriptions in a fairly uniform Greek-derived script, from which the Latin script evolved over a short time into a form well suited to its language. The relative prosperity and stability of the Roman Republic and then Empire afforded its artisans the luxury to bring to what many consider esthetic perfection the monumental capital letters used on official inscriptions such as Trajan's Column. (In Greece, the development was more toward geometric regularity.)

With the expansion of Roman rule across Europe, their administrators and subsequently their Christian missionaries brought writing to the periphery of the continent. In the Germanic- and Celtic-speaking areas, apparently, they were anticipated by local adaptations, Runes and Ogham respectively—perhaps inspired by contact with the Romans. Throughout Western Europe, local chanceries and scriptoria developed local variations of the Roman alphabet; rare episodes of political unification brought with them standardizations over lesser or wider areas. The spread of printing in the fifteenth century finally had the result that Roman writing became almost homogeneous in appearance, although national differences in favored typeface and layout design remain apparent.

In Eastern Europe, by contrast, beyond the farthest reach of Rome, as well as into Egypt, it was the Church rather than governments that was the primary vehicle of literacy, and individual cultures adopted strictly local scripts. These generally emulated the model of the Greek scriptures they received: Coptic, Armenian, Georgian, and Gothic, as well as Glagolitic and Cyrillic (in the Slavic areas). Of these, Gothic, Glagolitic, and Coptic sooner or later died out with their vehicular languages (the last two persist in liturgical context). But Armenian and Georgian have survived to the present in the formidable mountains of the Caucasus; and Cyrillic spread with the Orthodox church among the eastern Slavic languages. As so frequently, Russia's hegemony brought standardization, and successive regimes brought successive script reforms.

— Peter T. Daniels

Transmission of the Phoenician Script to the West

PIERRE SWIGGERS

Semitic consonantal writing, as developed and attested in the North Semitic scripts, was the ancestor of three geographically and linguistically diversified developments: one spreading toward India and southern Asia; the second—an offspring of the Aramaic consonantal script—toward Mongolia and the Manchu Empire; and the third spreading toward the west, where it led to the creation of fully alphabetic writing systems for the Indo-European languages. It is this last development which is commonly described as the transmission, with several adaptations, of the Phoenician consonantal script (22 signs) to the Greeks (see Burzachechi 1976; Healey 1990; Heubeck 1979; Jeffery 1982; Naveh 1987; Sass 1988, 1991).

The derivation of the Greek alphabet from the Phoenician script is evident from: the shapes of the letters, obvious despite reflection, elaboration, or simplification; their ordering; their numerical value; and their names (see TABLE 21.1). These names have meanings only in Phoenician (or Semitic in general), not in Greek (or Indo-European). An additional argument is the use as writing materials of leather, stone, wood, and papyrus, as opposed to the clay of Minoan-Mycenean practice (SECTION 7): these are also the materials used in the North Semitic area, where the quality of clay was poor. Herodotus (V, 58) speaks of the Greek letters as φοινικήια γράμματα 'Phoenician characters'; the word φοινικήια is attested in a fifth century inscription from Teos (*SIG* 38, l. 37) as the designation of characters. The Greeks created an alphabet capable of transcribing all the segmental components of the Greek language by adding signs with vocalic value to the consonantal inventory of Phoenician (SECTION 5). The signs of the Greek alphabet constitute the basis of all alphabets that developed in the West.

Geographical and chronological aspects

The adoption and adaptation of the Phoenician writing system by the Greeks is geographically diversified, but structurally unified, with specific variants for the various local states (for surveys, see Kirchhoff 1887, still a basic reference, and Jeffery 1990, who speaks of "primary transmission" with respect to the borrowing of the alphabet from Semites, and of "secondary transmission throughout Greece" with respect to the

TABLE 21.1: *Comparison of the Phoenician Consonantal Signs and the Letters of the Greek Alphabet*

PHOENICIAN		GREEK		
Name	*ca. 900 B.C.E.*	*800–600 Attic (400)*		*Name*
ʾālef	K K X	Λ Λ Λ	A	alpha
bēt	9 9	ꓥ Ᏸ B	B	bēta
gīmel	ᐱ ᐝ	Γ ᒉ C	Γ	gamma
dālet	Δ ᐊ ᐊ	ᐅ Δ D	Δ	delta
hē	Ⴈ Ⴈ	ᕓ ᕓ E	E	e psilon
wāw	Y Y ᐟ	F F Ϲ		(digamma)
zajin	I ⲭ I	I ⲭ I	I	zēta
ḥēt	᎑ ᎑ ᎑	᎑ ᕽ H	H	ēta
ṭēt	⊗ ⊕	⊗ ⊕ ⊙	Θ	thēta
yōd	⳼ ⳼ ⳼	⟨ ⟩ I	I	iōta
kaf	ᴗ ᴠ ᴪ	K Ƙ k	K	kappa
lāmed	⌐ L L	↳ ⌐ ∧	∧	labda
mēm	⳼ ⳼ ⳼	ⳝ ⳝ M	M	mu
nūn	ⳝ ⳝ ⳝ	ⳝ ⳝ N	N	nu
sāmek	ꓻ	ꓻ ꓻ ꓻ	Ξ	ksi
ʿayin	O	O	O	o mikron
pē	⟩ ⳝ	ⳝ Γ	Γ	pi
ṣādē	ꜧ ꜯ	M		(san)
qōf	Ϙ Ϙ φ	Ϙ Ϙ		(qoppa)
rēš	ꓢ 4	P D Ꝿ	P	rhō
śin/šin	W	⟨ ⳝ ⟨	⟨	sigma
tāw	+ X	T	T	tau
		ⳝ Y V	Y	u psilon
		φ Φ ⳝ	Φ	phi
		X +	X	chi
		Ψ ꙍ	Ψ	psi
		ꙍ Ω Ω	Ω	ō mega

diffusion of the Greek alphabet). The diversity can be reduced to an archaic stage, comprising the Dorian alphabets of Thera, Melos (largely identical to that of Thera), and Crete (TABLE 21.2); and two branches, Eastern and Western—the Western, according to some scholars, younger than the Eastern—each having a number of varieties (TABLE 21.3). The Eastern alphabets, including the Ionic scripts, comprise the alphabets of Asia Minor and the adjacent islands, of the Cyclades and Attica, of Megara, Corinth, Sicyon, and Argos, and the Ionian colonies of Magna Graecia. The Western alphabets include the Chalcidian alphabets, and the alphabets of Boeotia, Phocis, Locri, Thessaly, most of the Peloponnesus, and the non-Ionian colonies of

TABLE 21.2: *General Comparative Table of Early Greek Alphabets (8th–7th c. B.C.E.)*

	Athens	Thera	Crete	Naxos	Corcyra	Boeotia	
a							A
b							B
g							Γ
d							Δ
e							E
v/υ							F
z							Z
h(ē)							H
tʰ							Θ
i							I
k							K
l							Λ
m							M
n							N
ks							Ξ
o							O
p							Π
s							Μ
q							Ϙ
r							Ρ
s							Σ
t							T
u							Y
kʰ							X
pʰ							Φ

Magna Graecia. A variety of the Western Greek script, in which the shape X has the value [ks], Ψ has the value [kʰ], and there is no Ξ, underlies the Etruscan and Italic scripts. The transmission to Italy took place at a time when the Greek writing direction was from right to left: this is the direction attested in the oldest Etruscan, Umbrian, Oscan, and Faliscan inscriptions (SECTION 23).

Several variants of the Greek alphabet continued to exist for more than three centuries; in 403/402 B.C.E., the Ionic alphabet of Miletus was officially adopted as a

TABLE 21.3: *Detailed Comparison of Eastern and Western Alphabets*

| | EASTERN ALPHABETS | | | WESTERN ALPHABETS | | | |
	Athens	*Miletus*	*Corinth*	*Boeotia*	*Laconia*	*Arcadia*	
a	↗A	ᐃA	ᐃᐃ	ᐃAᴎ	ᐃA	ᐃA	a
b	ßB		ᒉᒋ	ßB	ß		b
g	∧∧	Γ	‹C	∧Γ	∧	‹C	g
d	ΔD	Δ	Δ▷	ΔᐁD	ΔD	ᐁΔD	d
e	Ⅎ⅀	Ⅎϵ	Ⅎℬℷ	Ⅎℇϵ	Ⅎϵ	Ⅎϵ	e
υ		ℲϜ	ℲϜ	Ϝℾ	Ϝ	Ϝ	υ
z	Ɪ	Ɪ	⍑	Ɪ			z
h(ē)	Hᗒ	Hᗒ	ᗒ	ᗒH	ᗒ	ᗒ	h
tʰ	⊕⊗	⊗⊕	⊕⊗	⊗⊕ᗒ	⊗⊕	⊕	tʰ
i	⌇ǀ	ǀ	⌇ℇ	ǀ	ǀ	ǀ	i
k	K	KϜ	K	K	K	K	k
l	Lℾ	∧∧	ℾ∧	ᒪ	∧	∧∧	l
m	ᴍ∧	M	ᴘ	ᴍ∧	M	M	m
n	∧ɴ	ᴎɴ	ᴘ	ᴎɴ	ᴘᴎ	N	n
ks		⧻Ɪ	Ɪ	+	X	+	ks
o	O	O	O	ᕲᗷ	O	O	o
p	ℾℾ	ℾⵀ	ℾℾ	ℾᴍ⟩	ℾⵀℾ	ℾⵀ	p
s			M				s
q	Ϙ	(Ϙ)	Ϙ			Ϙ	q
r	ℙℝD	ℙℙD	ℙℙℝ	ℙℙℝ	ℙℙℝ	ℝℝ	r
s	⌇‹⌇	⌇ℇ		⌇‹⌇	⅄‹⌇	⅄Σ	s
t	Τⵝ	Τ	Τ	Τⵝ	Τ	Τ	t
u/ü	VY	V	VY	Vᴘᴘ	Yℾ∨	V	u
pʰ	⊕Φ	Ⓞ	Φφ	⊕φ	φ		pʰ
kʰ	X+	X	X+	Vⵝ	VⵝY	↓	kʰ
ps		VY	YΨ			⚹)⚹	ps
ō		Ω					ō

standard in Athens, and this is what we know as the classical Greek alphabet (SEC-
TION 22). By that time the left-to-right direction had prevailed.

Linguistic aspects

The Greeks, in adapting the Phoenician script, realized two types of innovations:
structural and *local*.

Structural innovation

The consonantal writing system became a fully alphabetic writing system that notates both consonants and vowels (but usually not word division, and then never with any sort of mark). The Greeks, in achieving this innovation, exploited the potential of a system in which consonant letters were used as "reading aids" (*matres lectionis*) to transcribe long vowels (SECTION 5). In a first stage, Phoenician *ʾālef* was used for *alpha* [a], Phoenician *hē* for *e psilon* [e], Phoenician *ʿayin* for *o mikron* [o], and Phoenician *yōd* for *iōta* [i]. Later (6th century B.C.E., starting in Miletus), the Greek alphabet was enriched with two signs to distinguish long from short *e* and *o* vowels: *ēta* was distinguished from *e psilon*, with a shape derived from Phoenician *ḥēt*, which had been used to denote the rough breathing in some Western Greek alphabets; and *ō mega* was distinguished from *o mikron*—a new sign was created, perhaps on the basis of the sign used for *o mikron*. This structural innovation was a major step in the history of writing: it made possible the exhaustive representation of the linear sequence of the sound segments constituting a message, and thus allowed the direct, continuous reading of any text, not requiring any grammatical information to be supplied by the reader.

Local innovations

A number of consonantal signs of the Phoenician script were used for sounds in Greek phonologically similar to those denoted in Phoenician: *wāw* was used to render Greek *digamma* [u̯], and also the vowel [u]; *ṭēt* was used for Greek *thēta* [tʰ]; *qōf* was used for Greek *koppa*, a back variant of the voiceless velar stop; and *zajin* was used for Greek *zēta* [dz].

Letters were later added to the inventory (after the letter T) in order to notate sounds unknown in Phoenician: Φ [pʰ], Ψ [ps], X [kʰ], and Ξ [ks]; the origin (Semitic, Cypriote, or internal creation) of these added letters is disputed.

The number of signs for the sibilants was reduced. This is an intricate matter, since there is no one-to-one correspondence among the signs within Semitic scripts, and since different traditions were at play in the transmission (involving a redistribution of values among the signs for sibilants and the signs for aspirated stops; see TABLE 21.4). The Phoenician *sāmek* ‡ survives in the Eastern Ionic alphabet with the value [ks]; elsewhere it dropped out of the alphabet. The sign for the voiceless spirant [s] in Greek takes its (Ionic) name *sigma*, but not its form, from Phoenician *sāmek*. It is attested in two shapes, which derive, in parallel traditions, from Phoenician *ṣādē* (the Greek prototype letter resulting from *ṣādē* was called *san* by the Dorians), or from Phoenician *šin*. Originally these two sign shapes were probably used as free variants or as geographically or chronologically determined alternates; in some archaic Greek abecedaries the two *s*-signs, descending from *ṣādē* and *šin*, occur together, but apparently with one of them being retained as a non-functional unit in the

TABLE 21.4: *Signs for Sibilants and for Aspirated Stops in Greek Alphabets*

	Euboean	Attic	Corinthian	Thera	Melos	Cretan	Naxos	Ionic
[k]	K:Ϙ	K:Ϙ	K:Ϙ	k:Φ	K	K:Φ	K:Ϙ	K:Ϙ
[kʰ]	Ψ	X	X	KΘ:ΦΘ	kH	K	X	+X
[ks]	X	XϚ	‡	kM	kM	kM:ΦM	□Ϛ	Ξ
[pʰ]	Φ	Φ	Φ	ΓΘ	ΓH	Γ	Φ	Φ
[ps]	ΦϚ	ΦϚ	Ψ	ΓM	ΓM	ΓM	ΓϚ	Ψ
[dz]	I	I	I(:Ŧ)	‡	--	I	--	I
[s]	Ϛ	Ϛ	M	M	M	M	Ϟ	Ϟ

inventory. Eventually only one sign for [s], that deriving from Phoenician *šin*, was maintained. In Ionic inscriptions from Asia we sporadically find a sign ⊓ (later called σανπεî *sanpeî* 'quasi-π', because of its shape resembling that of Π *p*), which probably served to notate a voiceless affricate [t͜s], and for which we cannot exclude Phoenician *ṣādē* as the formal model. The reassignment of values by the Greeks to the sibilant signs calls for a reconstructive study in phonological perception (see Brixhe 1991, Swiggers 1991).

Problems

Much debate has taken place, and still does, on the *agents*, the *date*, and the *place* of transmission (for recent surveys see Amadasi Guzzo 1991 and Isserlin 1991).

Agents

The commonly held opinion, found already in ancient Greek sources, is that the Phoenicians transmitted their consonantal writing system to the Greeks, who transformed it into a fully alphabetic script. But some scholars have claimed that the agents of transmission were other Semitic groups—Arameans (Segert 1963, Knauf 1987) or "North Syrians" (Helck 1979)—or even non-Semitic groups in Asia Minor (Phrygia, Cilicia), who served as intermediaries between the Semitic and the Greek worlds (Jeffery 1982, Brixhe 1991, Lemaire 1991). It should be noted, however, that the Greek letter names *iōta* and *rhō* point to a transmission from a Phoenician source (since in Phoenician *ā* > *ō*, while this shift is absent from Aramaic); and even if there were an Asia Minor connection, the source would still have been the Phoenician writing system. It had been adopted by the Cilicians, but they used it only for writing inscriptions in Phoenician, which contain autochthonous onomastic material.

Date

The date of the transmission has been the subject of a major controversy between Classicists and Semitists (for a historiographic survey see McCarter 1975; for a list of the datings and the scholars who proposed them, see Heubeck 1979: 75–76, who notes all these: 1500–1400, 1400, 1200–1100, 1100–750, 1100–1000, 1000–900, 900, 900–800, 900–850, 800, 800–750, 750–700). Two considerations serve as guiding principles, though to be used with some flexibility: (a) the dating of the oldest Greek inscriptions, and (b) correspondences between the oldest Greek scripts and lettershapes of datable Phoenician (or Semitic) inscriptions. The available materials lead to somewhat convergent dates: the first Greek inscriptions are from around 750 B.C.E. (or 770–750), and for the oldest Greek sign shapes we find neat correspondences with the characters of Phoenician inscriptions dated between 800 and 750. This was basically the position of Carpenter (1933, adoption of the alphabet around 720–700), albeit slightly modified on the basis of new datings.

Specialists who approach the history of the alphabet from a Greek angle generally agree that the beginnings of Greek alphabetic writing go back to the (mid) eighth century (at most 800 B.C.E.; Wachter 1989). This view avoids the difficulty of assuming a (problematic) coexistence of the Mycenean syllabic script and the Greek alphabetic script, and reckons with a "dark age" of illiteracy between the collapse of the Mycenean civilization and the earliest Greek alphabetic inscriptions.

Semitists, who base themselves on comparisons of letter shapes between Semitic scripts (Phoenician, and more generally Canaanite, or even Aramaic), have tended to set the date of transmission much higher. Bernal (1987, 1990) even goes so far as to propose a date around 1500–1400, postulating a wave-like spread of "alphabetic," i.e. consonantal, scripts emanating from a Proto-Phoenician model, with successive influences from the Phoenician homeland. A lower date, but still much higher than the traditionally accepted one, has been proposed by Naveh (1973) and his followers, who reckon with a transmission around 1100 from Proto-Canaanite (consonantal writing) to archaic Greek (alphabetic writing). Their arguments are twofold: (a) the use of all possible directions (left to right, right to left, and boustrophedon) in the oldest Greek inscriptions; and (b) the lapidary features and variable inclinations of the archaic Greek letters (as can be seen in TABLES 21.1, 21.2, and 21.3).

Argument (a) is weak, since such a situation can be typical of the initial stage of any adapted writing system (moreover, the oldest Greek inscriptions are mostly written from right to left, as is the case in Semitic); such early stages are characterized by the slow emergence of scribal tradition and by geographic and individual diversity in the absence of a fixed norm. Argument (b), considered in the light of our present knowledge of Semitic epigraphy, has no solid foundation. The best parallels for archaic Greek letters are found in Phoenician inscriptions from the late 9th or early 8th century (except for *bēta*, which in any event is problematic to explain, especially in view of its many local variations; see Jeffery 1990: 23). Moreover, Naveh's hypothesis does not explain the early shape of *mu* ᛘ; his supposition of a "secondary borrowing" (in a later period) of the forms for *kappa* and *u psilon* is not substantiated. Finally, examination of the North Semitic epigraphic corpus shows a non-rectilinear progress of the writing systems.

It is of interest to note that the fairly recently found Aramaic inscription of Tell Fekheriye (9th century; FIGURE 5 on page 103) shows an archaic script, at least for several letters, and this has led some Semitists to propose a date coming nearer the Classicists' view, and perhaps involving a transmission on the continent (North Syria or Asia Minor; see Kaufman 1987). As a result, an unbiased comparison of Greek archaic scripts with North Semitic scripts, and the highly plausible hypothesis of a rather restricted period of experimentation with the alphabet among the Greeks, lead to the conclusion that the transmission of the Phoenician script and the constitution of a fully alphabetic script should be placed in Greece between 800 and 775 B.C.E.

Place

A number of hypotheses, linked with views on the agents of transmission, have been offered concerning the place of transmission of the Phoenician script to the West. (There is no convincing archeological evidence which allows us to settle the question.) According to some scholars, this would have happened in Greece, more specifically on the islands of Crete (or Thera, less likely Melos) or Rhodes, but probably not Cyprus (Cypriot Greeks had a syllabary of their own). These are the territories where truly alphabetic scripts were formed—whether without the additional letters, as in the oldest inscriptions from Thera, Melos, and Crete; or with them, as in the archaic Greek script, in both its eastern and western branches. In these areas, especially on the islands—important points on the east–west trade route—there were sustained contacts between Phoenicians and Greeks (cf. Coldstream 1982). Others have situated the origin of the process in Asia Minor or Northern Syria. The hypothesis of a multiple geographical origin of the alphabet, which in principle could account for the various local varieties, is less credible, given that everywhere the same consonant signs of the Phoenician alphabet were used to notate the same Greek vowels.

Observations

Although no definite answer can be given to the problem of the place and date of transmission, the following principles should be observed in the discussion.

It must be assumed that the adaptation of the Phoenician script to the Greek language met basic social needs: the transmission must have taken place in a social context in which political, economic, literary, and educational needs urged the creation of a proper notation system for the varieties of Greek.

Within this context, there must have been a certain symbiosis (i.e. not just sporadic contacts) between Greek-speaking and Phoenician-speaking (or Phoenician-writing) communities, possibly in the higher circles of society, i.e. circles having a certain level of education.

The adoption of the Phoenician script went hand in hand with adaptation, and therefore involves a "phonological" stance—in fact, a comparative phonological analysis—on the part of the first adapter(s); for a study of this phonological stance we would need access to the "psychological reality" of Phoenician and Greek in the perception of the possibly bilingual inventor(s) of the alphabet. (For a promising start in this direction, see Rosén 1984 and Brixhe 1991.)

In the process of adaptation, we must distinguish between internal modifications affecting the *structure* of the writing system, which were irreversible, and more external adaptations affecting the *use* of the writing system, which allowed for free alternations, or alternations conditioned by the nature of the materials on which inscriptions were written, in the absence of normative scribal conventions. Among internal modifications are (a) the introduction of signs for vowels (derived from signs for consonants in Phoenician), which included the splitting of Phoenician *wāw* into a semiconsonant *digamma* and a vowel *u psilon*; and (b) the redistribution of the sibilant signs. To external adaptation we can assign the direction of writing.

The adaptation must have taken place in a restricted circle, but may have involved the cooperation of several scholars, and must have spread to other communities, each developing particular scribal traditions (a process involving, in its early stage, a number of "mistakes"). This is the only plausible explanation for the relationship between a core of constant sign values and the variance in sign shapes and direction of writing; we later find the same situation in the Etruscan and Italic scripts.

Bibliography

Allen, W. Sidney. 1987. *Vox Graeca,* 3rd ed. Cambridge: Cambridge University Press.

Amadasi Guzzo, Maria Giulia. 1991. "'The Shadow Line': Réflexions sur l'introduction de l'alphabet en Grèce." In Baurain et al. 1991: 293–311.

Baurain, Claude, Corinne Bonnet, and Véronique Krings, eds. 1991. *Phoinikeia Grammata: Lire et écrire en Méditerranée* (Collection d'études classiques 6). Namur, Belgium: Société des Études Classiques.

Bernal, Martin. 1987. "On the Transmission of the Alphabet to the Aegean before 1400 B.C." *Bulletin of the American Schools of Oriental Research* 267: 1–19.

———. 1990. *Cadmean Letters: The Transmission of the Alphabet to the Aegean and Further West before 1400 B.C.* Winona Lake, Ind.: Eisenbrauns.

Brixhe, Claude. 1991. "De la phonologie à l'écriture: Quelques aspects de l'adaptation de l'alphabet cananéen au grec." In Baurain et al. 1991: 313–56.

Burzachechi, Mario. 1976. "L'adozione dell'alfabeto nel mondo greco." *Parola del Passato* 31: 82–102.

Carpenter, J. Rhys. 1933. "The Antiquity of the Greek Alphabet." *American Journal of Archaeology* 37: 8–29.

Coldstream, J. N. 1982. "Greeks and Phoenicians in the Aegean." In *Phönizier im Westen,* ed. H. G. Niemeyer, pp. 261–72. Mainz: von Zabern.

Healey, John F. 1990. *The Early Alphabet* (Reading the Past). London: British Museum; Berkeley and Los Angeles: University of California Press.

Helck, Wolfgang. 1979. *Die Beziehungen Ägyptens und Vorderasiens zur Ägäis bis ins 7. Jahrhundert v. Chr.* Darmstadt: Wissenschaftliche Buchgesellschaft.

Heubeck, Adolf. 1979. *Schrift* (Archaeologia Homerica 3/10). Göttingen: Vandenhoeck & Ruprecht.

Isserlin, Benedikt S. J. 1983. "The Antiquity of the Greek Alphabet." *Kadmos* 22: 151–63.

———. 1991. "The Transfer of the Alphabet to the Greeks: The State of Documentation." In Baurain et al. 1991: 283–91.

Jeffery, Lilian Hamilton. 1982. "Greek Alphabetic Writing." *Cambridge Ancient History* 3/1: 819–33. Cambridge: Cambridge University Press.

———. 1990. *The Local Scripts of Archaic Greece: A Study of the Origin of the Greek Alphabet and Its Development from the Eighth to the Fifth Centuries B.C.,* 2nd ed. revised by A. W. Johnston. Oxford: Clarendon. [1st ed., 1961.]

Johnstone, William. 1978. "Cursive Phoenician and the Archaic Greek Alphabet." *Kadmos* 17: 151–66.

Kaufman, Stephen A. 1987. "The Pitfalls of Typology: On the Earliest History of the Alphabet." *Hebrew Union College Annual* 57: 1–13.

Kirchhoff, Adolf. 1887. *Studien zur Geschichte des griechischen Alphabets.* Gütersloh: Bertelsmann. Repr. Amsterdam: Gieben, 1970.

Knauf, Ernst Axel. 1987. "Haben Aramäer den Griechen das Alphabet vermittelt?" *Welt des Orients* 18: 45–48.

Lemaire, André. 1991. "L'écriture phénicienne en Cilicie et la diffusion des écritures alphabétiques." In Baurain et al. 1991: 133–46.

McCarter, P. Kyle. 1975. *The Antiquity of the Greek Alphabet and the Early Phoenician Scripts.* Missoula, Mont.: Scholars Press.

Millard, Alan R. 1976. "The Canaanite Linear Alphabet and its Passage to the Greeks." *Kadmos* 15: 130–44.

Naveh, Joseph. 1973. "Some Semitic Epigraphical Considerations on the Antiquity of the Greek Alphabet." *American Journal of Archaeology* 77: 1–8.

———. 1987. *Early History of the Alphabet,* 2nd ed. Leiden: Brill.

Röllig, Wolfgang. 1989. "Über die Anfänge unseres Alphabets." *Das Altertum* 31: 83–91.

Rosén, Haiim B. 1984. "Le transfert des valeurs des caractères alphabétiques et l'explication de quelques habitudes orthographiques grecques archaïques." *Aux origines de l'hellénisme: La Crète et la Grèce,* 225–36. Paris: Publications de la Sorbonne.

Sass, Benjamin. 1988. *The Genesis of the Alphabet and Its Development in the Second Millennium B.C.* Wiesbaden: Harrassowitz.

———. 1991. *Studia alphabetica: On the Origin and Early History of the Northwest Semitic, South Semitic and Greek Alphabets.* Freiburg: Universitätsverlag.

Segert, Stanislav. 1963. "Altaramäische Schrift und Anfänge des griechischen Alphabets." *Klio* 41: 38–57.

SIG = W. Dittenberger, ed. 1915–24. *Sylloge Inscriptionum Graecarum,* 3rd ed. Leipzig.

Swiggers, Pierre. 1991. "Linguistic Considerations on Phoenician Orthography." In Baurain et al. 1991: 115–29.

Wachter, Rudolf. 1989. "Zur Vorgeschichte des griechischen Alphabets." *Kadmos* 28: 19–78.

The Greek Alphabet

LESLIE THREATTE

The Greek alphabet is currently employed to write all extant Greek texts produced in the more than 2700 years in which it has been in continuous use; it serves also for all purposes, literary and nonliterary, of writing in the modern world, since Greek is the national language of Greece and is spoken by more than ten million people. In the Archaic Period (ca. 750–480 B.C.E.), when Greek alphabetic writing first appears, there is considerable dialectal differentiation, also well documented in the classical (480–323) and earlier Hellenistic (323–31) periods. But from ca. 350 B.C.E. a common dialect, or Koine (from κοινὴ διάλεκτος *koinè diálektos* 'common dialect'), began to evolve, and it developed rapidly in the Hellenistic period, when the old dialects did not survive well in the new Greek cities outside Greece. The Koine developed from the Attic dialect, a result of Athens's cultural dominance in the fifth and fourth centuries, but with significant infusions from other dialects, chiefly Ionic. Except in literature and in cases of artificial archaization, the old dialects had largely been replaced by the Koine by the mid-Roman period (200 C.E.). Medieval and modern Greek developed from the Koine; and while there is dialectal differentiation today (see Newton 1972: 13–15), no modern Greek dialect evolved from an ancient one, except for Tsakonian, by now probably extinct but once spoken by a small isolated population in eastern Laconia and certainly descended from ancient Laconian.

The Greek script was a true alphabet from the beginning, and the names and order of the letters were taken from Phoenician (SECTION 21). Some of the earliest texts are written from right to left or boustrophedon, but left-to-right writing has been standard since ca. 500 B.C.E. (see Jeffery 1990: 43–50, 429; Threatte 1980: 52–57). In the first few centuries of writing, the scripts of the various Greek cities differ; this is the reason for the differences between the Roman and Greek alphabets, as the former is derived from a different Greek script from the one which became standard in Greece. These local or *epichoric* scripts (see Jeffery 1990) fall into larger groups (TABLE 22.1), sometimes still designated as *green* (lacking the letters Ξ, Φ, X, and Ψ); *blue*, the type ancestral to the Greek alphabet of today; or *red*, the type ancestral to the Latin alphabet (the colors are from the map at the end of Kirchhoff 1887). The epichoric scripts had been replaced by the eastern Ionic alphabet nearly everywhere by the early fourth century: Athens officially abandoned its own local script in 403 B.C.E. Despite a certain conservatism—e.g., most capital letters in use today are virtually identical to those in use in the fourth century B.C.E.—writing practices have evolved greatly since

TABLE 22.1: *Principal Groupings of Greek Epichoric Alphabets*

	[pʰ]	[kʰ]	[ks]	[ps]	Locations
Green	Π or ΠΗ	K or KH	ΚΣ	ΠΣ	Crete, Thera, Melos
Blue	Φ	X	Ξ or ΧΣ	Ψ or ΦΣ	Athens, Argos, Corinth, Ionia
Red	Φ	Ψ	X	ΦΣ	Euboea, most of mainland, western colonies

the classical period: in Plato's day, Greek was written with letters of only one size, with no diacritical marks or word separation, and little or no punctuation. The introduction of the Byzantine minuscule script after 800 C.E. was the most significant of many changes: the modern small letters derive from this script, itself the result of a lengthy development from cursive styles of writing employed in non-literary papyri of ancient and early Byzantine times. Modern writing and printing practices are virtually the same for ancient and modern Greek; they continue the practices of the first printed Greek books produced in Italy in the later fifteenth century, which themselves continued the practices of manuscripts of the late Byzantine period (after ca. 1250). The use of these modern writing practices for ancient texts is thus to a large degree conventional. A schematic view of the dates of the principal developments is given in TABLE 22.2.

There are two pronunciations employed today for ancient Greek: the modern Greek pronunciation, normal within Greece and employed by a few scholars elsewhere; and the one more general outside Greece, an approximate recreation of the classical Attic pronunciation (e.g. ca. 450–350)—often called "Erasmian," as it is nearly identical to that proposed by Erasmus in his 1528 treatise *De recta Latini et Graeci sermonis pronuntiatione* (see Pfeiffer 1976: 88–89). Erasmus had some precursors, but it had been usual before his treatise to employ the modern Greek pronunciation for Greek of all periods. The use of an artificially recreated ancient pronunciation has pedagogical advantages, for it represents Greek at a stage when the alphabet was, with only minor exceptions, phonetic—a one-symbol-per-sound script. But numerous phonological developments have made the Greek alphabet no longer phonetic; e.g., the seven ancient Greek spellings ει, η, ῃ, ι, οι, υ, υι, each representing a different sound in fifth-century Attic, are all pronounced [i] today. In contrast to the Classical period, the Hellenistic and Roman periods were characterized by much phonological change, and most of the features of modern Greek pronunciation were already in place by the second or third century C.E., some of them quite a bit earlier (for these developments see Threatte 1980, Allen 1987, Sturtevant 1940). Thus the period in which the Greek alphabet was truly phonetic was fairly short, and the use of the classical Attic pronunciation for later ancient Greek writers is in a number of details inaccurate and artificial.

In only a very few instances does the Greek alphabet break the one-symbol-per-sound rule for the classical Attic pronunciation: the vowels α *a*, ι *i*, and υ *u* represent both long and short vowels; ει *ei* and ου *ou* no longer represent diphthongs (see

TABLE 22.2: *Developments in Greek Writing*

Ca. 740 B.C.E.	Earliest example of Greek alphabetic writing (see Jeffery 1990: 426)
Ca. 450–350	Ionic alphabet replaces epichoric scripts in most Greek cities
By 350	Most letters in use approximate in appearance the modern capital letters
By ca. 200 B.C.E.	Diacritical marks for accents and breathings probably invented
By ca. 400 C.E.	Standard book hand is formal rounded majuscule known as uncial
835 C.E.	Date of the Uspensky Gospels (see Barbour 1981: 4, no. 13), earliest preserved example of the Byzantine minuscule script into which all ancient materials were eventually recopied: systematic use of accent marks and breathings (creating impression of word division and lessening need for it), some punctuation, development of minuscule letters
13th century	Iota subscript appears
1470s	First Greek books printed in Italy, some ligatures still employed
18th century	Abandonment of ligatures, word division systematically employed
1982	Presidential decree adopts the monotonic system, in widespread use since 1976: breathings and circumflex accent abandoned for printing most modern Greek

TABLE 22.4); the velar nasal [ŋ] has no separate symbol and is written γ *g*; σ *s* was pronounced [z] before voiced stops and [m]; there was often no symbol for [h].

The symbols

All the symbols and their pronunciation in classical Attic and modern Greek are given in TABLE 22.3. There were five short and seven long vowels (with α *a*, ι *i*, and υ *u* representing both long and short vowels). The more open η *e* and ω *o* were usually inherited from the parent language Indo-European, while the close ει *ei* and ου *ou* were of two, originally distinct, origins: (a) monophthongized diphthongs, e.g. εἰμι *eîmi* [e:mi] 'I go' (IE *$e\underset{.}{i}mi$), βοῦς *boûs* [bu:s] 'cow' (IE *$g^w\bar{o}\underset{.}{u}s$), etc.; (b) various vowel contractions and compensatory lengthenings, e.g. γένους *génous* [génu:s] 'of the clan' from γένεος *géneos* [géneos]; εἰς *eis* [e:s] 'into' from ἐνς *ens* [ens], τούς *toús* [tú:s] 'the' (acc.pl.masc.) from τόνς *tóns* [tóns], etc. In Attica and many other parts of Greece, ει *ei* and ου *ou* were originally employed only for (a), while the sounds of (b) were written ε *e* and ο *o*. The current practice was gradually introduced ca. 450–325 B.C.E. (see Threatte 1980: 172, 238). For the remaining diphthongs see TABLE 22.4. Because [a:j], [ε:j], and [ɔ:j] were early monophthongized to [a:], [ε:], and [ɔ:], the iota in αι ηι ωι was frequently omitted in antiquity, as it normally is in the earlier Byzantine manuscripts. The practice of writing this iota as a *subscript* beneath the vowel, ᾳ ῃ ῳ, first appears in the thirteenth century and has become usual for most ancient Greek. Iota subscript cannot occur with capital letters, when it must be written on the line (called *adscript*), e.g. Αι *Ai*, Ηι *Ēi*, Ωι *Ōi*, and diacritical marks cannot occur over this iota adscript, thus ᾦ *hōi*, Ηὖ *Êu*, but Ὠι *Ôi*.

TABLE 22.3: *The Greek Alphabet*

Letter		Name	Transliteration[a]	Classical Attic	Modern Greek
A	α	álpha	a	[a], [a:]	[a]
B	β	bêta	b	[b]	[v]
Γ	γ	gámma	g	[g], [ŋ]/_[k, g, x, (m)]	[ɣ], [j]/_[e, i]; [ŋ]/_[k, g, χ]
Δ	δ	délta	d	[d]	[ð]
E	ε	eî, é; later è psilón	e	[e]	[e]
Z	ζ	zêta	z	[zd], later [z]	[z]
H	η	êta	ē	[ɛ:]	[i]
Θ	θ	thêta	th	[tʰ]	[θ]
I	ι	iôta	i	[i], [i:]	[i]
K	κ	káppa	k	[k]	[k]
Λ	λ	lámbda	l	[l]	[l]
M	μ	mû	m	[m]	[m]
N	ν	nû	n	[n]	[n]
Ξ	ξ	kseî (xi)	ks, x	[ks]	[ks]
O	o	oû, ó; later ò mikrón	o	[o]	[o]
Π	π	peî (pi)	p	[p]	[p]
P	ρ	rhô̂	r, rh initially	[r]	[r]
Σ[b]	σ,[b] ς finally	sígma	s	[s], [z] /_ [b, d, g, m]	[s], [z] /_ [v, ð, ɣ, l, m]
T	τ	taû	t	[t]	[t]
Y	υ	û; later û psilón	u, y	[y], [y:]	[i]
Φ	φ	pheî (phi)	ph	[pʰ]	[f]
X	χ	kheî (chi)	kh, ch	[kʰ]	[χ]
Ψ	ψ	pseî (psi)	ps	[ps]	[ps]
Ω[c]	ω	ō̂; later ō̂ méga	ō	[ɔ:]	[o]

a. There is no standard system of transliteration, but systems differ in only a few details. That employed here assigns the same value to a letter in all situations and one symbol to each letter. Where variants are given in the table, the first is employed here, and the second also enjoys considerable currency. Long α, ι, and υ are often transliterated with a macron, here unnecessary because of the accompanying phonetic transcriptions.

For Modern Greek, there is even less standardization than for ancient Greek. The transliteration employed here assigns a separate symbol to each letter in all situations; but often phonetically based systems are employed, i.e. *i* is used for ει, η, ι, οι, and υ; *e* for αι; *v* for β; *y* for [j]; etc.

b. Or C, c. Lunate letters like c and ∈ probably did not occur before the Hellenistic period. They are sometimes useful in printing ancient Greek, partly because there is only one form of small sigma, useful in printing fragmentary texts when the ends of words cannot be determined. The use of -ς in word-final position grew out of certain practices of cursive and was established by late Byzantine times.

c. The letters Ϝ, Ϙ, and ϡ survived as numerals (see TABLE 22.5).

In modern Greek it is especially in the spelling of the vowels that the alphabet is not phonetic: the five modern Greek (isochronic) vowels and their possible spellings are: [a] α *a*; [e] ε *e*, αι *ai*; [i] ι *i*, ει *ei*, η *ē*, οι *oi*, υ *u*, υι *ui*; [o] ο *o*, ω *ō*; [u] ου *ou*. In the diphthongs αυ *au* and ευ *eu*, the second element has been desyllabified, becoming [f] before the six voiceless stops and [v] elsewhere, αὐτό *autó* [af'to] 'it', κραύγαζε *kraúgaze* ['kravɣaze] 'he shouted'. Numerous new diphthongs have arisen in the modern language, e.g. πονάει *ponáei* [po'naj] 'he is in pain', σόι *sói* ['soj] 'lineage', etc. Although diphthongal pronunciations are certainly normal in all but the most deliberate speech, such spellings are not considered to be diphthongs by Greeks, who adhere to the ancient terminology, e.g. Greek children are told that πονάει *ponáei* has three syllables (and ει *ei* [i] is taught as a "diphthong"!), although no one says [po.'na.i] rather than [po.'naj].

Ancient Greek had nine stops (modern scholars usually pronounce φ θ χ as fricatives [f θ x] rather than true aspirates [pʰ tʰ kʰ]) and three nasals ([ŋ] only before [k], [ks], [kʰ], [g], and perhaps [m]; without its own symbol and normally written γ *g*). Of the remaining consonants, only ρ *r* and ζ *z* require comment: initial ρ *r* always has the rough breathing (ῥ *rh*) and was probably voiceless (from original *sr*- or *wr*-), and the original [zd] pronunciation of ζ *z* had become [zz] or [z] by ca. 350 B.C.E. (see Threatte 1980: 25, 546–47). The laryngeal phoneme /h/ existed in initial position, but it is best treated with the diacritical marks. Attic had no phoneme /w/, but the letter Ϝ *w*, called *digamma*, continued to be used for [w] in dialects which preserved it and survived as a numeral.

Before the end of antiquity φ, β, θ, δ, χ, and γ acquired their current fricative pronunciations [f v θ ð x ɣ]. The remaining consonants have stayed the same, except that initial ρ *r* is now voiced and always written without the rough breathing, and after a nasal π, τ, κ are voiced and β, δ, γ do not become fricatives, e.g. ἔντομο *éntomo* ['endomo] 'insect'; στον πατέρα μου *ston patéra mou* [ston ba'tera mu] 'to my father'; άντρας *ántras* ['andras] 'man' (from ancient Greek ἄνδρα). With syncope of an initial vowel, a new series of voiced stops [b], [d], and [g] was created in word-initial position written μπ *mp*, ντ *nt*, γκ *gk*, e.g. μπώ *mpó* ['bo] 'I enter', ντροπή *ntropḗ* [dro'pi] 'shame', etc. These are also used for [b], [d], and [g] in foreign borrowings, e.g. μπέης *mpéēs* ['bejs] 'bey', Μπόντ *Mpónt* ['bond] 'Bond', ντιβάνι *ntibáni* [di'vani] 'divan', γκέτο *gkéto* ['geto] 'ghetto'. No ancient Greek dialect had /j/ or any rising diphthongs of the [ja] type, but [j] is frequent in modern Greek: γ = [j] before [i] and [e], and initial [j] before [a], [o], [u] is written γι *gi*, γει *gei*, or ι *i*, e.g. γιά *giá* ['ja 'for', γειά *geiá* ['ja] 'salut!' (shortened from υγεία *ugeía* [i'jia] 'health'), γιός *giós* ['jos] 'son' (from ancient Greek υἱός), ιατρός *iatrós* [ja'tros] 'doctor'. After consonant and before vowel, [j] has various spellings of [i], e.g. ποδιά *podiá* [po'ðja] 'apron', ποιός *poiós* ['pjos] 'who'. In modern borrowings, [w] is rendered ου *ou*, e.g. Ουάσιγκτον *Ouásigkton* ['wasiŋkton] 'Washington'; [ts] or [tʃ] is rendered τσ *ts* [ts], e.g. τσελεπής *tselepḗs* [tsele'pis] 'kind', πιάτσα *piátsa* ['pjatsa] 'piazza'; [dʒ] is rendered τζ *tz*, pronounced either [dz] or [dʒ], e.g. Τζέϊμς *Tzéïms* ['dzejms] or ['dʒejms]

TABLE 22.4: *Diphthongs, Monophthongized Diphthongs, Long Vowels of Later Origin*

Letters	Transliteration	Classical Attic	Modern Greek
αι	ai	[aj]	[e]
ᾳ, αι	ai	[aːj]	–
ει	ei	[eː]	[i]
η, ηι	ēi	[ɛːj]	–
οι	oi	[oj]	[i]
ῳ, ωι	ōi	[ɔːj]	–
υι	ui, yi	[yj]	[i]
αυ	au	[aw], [aːw]	[af], [av]
ευ	eu	[ew]	[ef], [ev]
ηυ	ēu	[ɛːw]	–
ου	ou	[oː], later [uː]	[u]

'James', τζαμί *tzamí* [dzaˈmi] or [ʤaˈmi] 'mosque'; [ʃ] is borrowed as [s], e.g. Σικάγκο *Sikágko* [siˈkago] 'Chicago', σόκ *sók* [ˈsok] 'shock'.

Diacritical marks and punctuation

The diacritical marks are the rough (ʽ) and smooth (ʼ) breathings; the acute (´), circumflex (ˆ), and grave (ˋ) accents; the coronis (ʼ); and the diaeresis or trema (¨). The grave accent and the coronis are usually not used in modern Greek. The breathings and accent marks, first appearing in papyri of the second century B.C.E., had probably been invented by the third (Turner 1971: 13–14; Pfeiffer 1968: 180); but all diacritical marks occur only sporadically in ancient writing, more often in papyri than inscriptions. Only a few manuscripts of the very end of classical antiquity show increased use of accents and breathings, sometimes in a different hand from the lettering, and the modern consistent use of them on every word was probably only introduced by the Byzantines after 800 C.E. (see Barbour 1981: xxvii–xxviii).

The phoneme /h/ survived in Attic and many Greek dialects, whose epichoric scripts employed the letter H *e* for it; but others, including Ionic, lost [h] early (called *psilosis*) and employed H *e* as a vowel. Thus when the Ionic alphabet became standard elsewhere, there was often no symbol for [h]. The *breathings*, which are thought to be derived from the letter H divided in half (ʽ from ⊢, ʼ from ⊣), were the Greeks' way of dealing with /h/, which occurred only initially except in compounds: to them all words beginning in vowels were either δασύς *dasús* [dasýs] 'rough' (= initial [h] + V), or ψιλός *psilós* [psilós] 'bare, smooth' (= V without [h]). In transliterating ancient Greek, *h* is used for ʽ , e.g. ἡμέρα *hēméra* [heːméraː] 'day', and ʼ is ignored, ἀνήρ *anḗr* [anéːr] 'man'.

The ancient Greek accent contained elements of pitch and stress, but pitch was the significant element in the earlier period. Even the late grammatical literature continues to describe the accent in terms of pitch, although stress predominates in the accent of the modern language, and the process of change from a pitch to a stress accent had probably begun before the end of the Hellenistic period. The workings of the pitch accent are poorly understood today, but the acute accent (´) clearly denoted a high pitch, the circumflex (ˆ) a high and a fall within a single syllable (hence it could not occur over a short vowel), and the grave (`) either a falling or a level pitch. The acute and circumflex functioned as word accents and were an integral part of each word, but the grave seems to have been associated with unaccented syllables, not necessarily final ones. The system of the Byzantines, followed today, restricts the use of the grave accent to replacing an acute on the final syllable of a word when an accented word follows, when presumably there was no high pitch because of the flow of speech, e.g. καλός *kalós* [kalós] 'beautiful' in isolation, but καλὸς ἀνήρ *kalòs anḗr* [kalos anέːr] 'beautiful man'. Accent marks are not always indicated in transliterations; and when pronouncing ancient Greek, most modern scholars pronounce the acute and circumflex as a stress accent and ignore the grave.

Until the late 1970s the acute and circumflex accents and breathings were always used when printing modern Greek—although almost two millennia had passed since initial [h] ceased to be sounded, and the pitch distinctions between the acute and circumflex accents were replaced with a uniform stress accent. Recently this artificiality has been largely given up for something called the μονοτονικό σύστημα *monotonikó sústēma* 'the monotonic system', which simply places an acute accent on any syllable actually stressed. Widespread in printing since 1976, it was officially adopted by presidential decree in April 1982. The first few words of the sample of Modern Greek below were printed thus in an edition of 1974 according to the older system (still preferred by some writers): Τώρα πού ἔχουν πεθάνει ὅλες οἱ γριές, γιαγιάδες καί παραγιαγιάδες, τώρα βρῆκαν ...

A mark called the *coronis* was used by the ancients to indicate crasis, the coalescing of two vowels into one over a word boundary. In modern printing it is usually identical to the smooth breathing and not indicated in transliteration, e.g. κἄκ *kak* [ka:k] from καὶ ἐκ *kai ek*, ἐγῷδα *egôida* [egôːjda] from ἐγὼ οἶδα *egṑ oîda*, χοἰ *khoi* [kʰoj] from καὶ οἱ *kai hoi*, etc. The coronis is omitted when the first of the two coalescing words has a rough breathing, e.g. οὑν *houn* [hu:n] from ὁ ἐν *ho en*. The *diaeresis* or trema (¨) occurs over ι *i* and υ *u* to show that they begin a new syllable, e.g. ancient Greek ἐλαύνω *elaúnō* [e.láw.no] 'I drive', but πραΰνω *praǘnō* [pra:.ý.nɔ:] 'I soothe'; modern Greek καυγάς *kaugás* [kav'ɣas] 'quarrel', but καϋμός *kaümós* [kaj'mos] 'grief'.

The breathings (and coronis) go underneath the circumflex accent (ἧ, ἦ) and to the left of the acute and grave accents (ἥ, ἥ, ἣ, ἣ); all diacritical marks go above the diaeresis (πραΰνω), to the left of single capital letters ('Α, ῎Ε, ῞Η, ῏Ω), and over the second element of diphthongs (αἰ, εὔ, Εὖ, Ηὖ)—with one exception: when the initial letter of a diphthong containing iota subscript is a capital, it forces the writing of the iota as adscript, and the diacritial marks must go to the left of the initial capital, not over the iota adscript, e.g. ῎Αιδης *haídēs* [há:jde:s] 'Hades'. Text entirely in capitals never contains any diacritical marks in either ancient or modern Greek, e.g. ΕΓΕΝΕΤΟ *egéneto* [egéneto] 'it became'.

In printing ancient and modern Greek, the period (.), comma (,), semi-colon (·), question mark (;), quotation marks (form varies according to country of printing), and apostrophe (' for indicating elision) are used. Modern Greek also employs exclamation points (!). In printing ancient Greek, change of speaker can be indicated by a dash (—); capital letters are sparingly used, for proper nouns and at the beginnings of paragraphs or quotations, but not at the beginning of each sentence. Modern Greek employs capital letters and punctuation in a manner comparable to other modern European languages.

Numerals

Two numeral systems were used in ancient Greece (see Smyth 1963: 104.348A; Threatte 1980: 110ff.): the acrophonic, with I for the unit and the first letter of the numeral name for others, e.g. Π = 5 (πέντε *pénte* 'five'), Δ = 10 (δέκα *déka* 'ten'), including combinatory symbols, e.g. 𐅏 = 50 (from Π = 5 + Δ = 10); and the still occasionally used alphabetic ("Milesian"), which assigns a numerical value for units, tens, and hundreds to each letter of the alphabet (augmented by the three disused letters Ϝ, Ϙ, and ϡ to get the necessary 27) as in TABLE 22.5. The order was usually higher to lower and the numeral set off by an acute accent, ρκθ´ = 129; thousands are denoted by a subscript acute before, ͵βσλα = 2231. The Arabic numeral system as employed in Western Europe is practically universal in Greece today; alphabetic numerals occur occasionally in learned publications (for pagination, plate numbers, etc.).

TABLE 22.5: *Alphabetic Numerals*

α	1	ι	10	ρ	100
β	2	κ	20	σ	200
γ	3	λ	30	τ	300
δ	4	μ	40	υ	400
ε	5	ν	50	φ	500
Ϝ or ς or στ	6	ξ	60	χ	600
ζ	7	ο	70	ψ	700
η	8	π	80	ω	800
θ	9	Ϙ	90	ϡ	900

SAMPLE OF ANCIENT GREEK

1. Greek:	Θουκυδίδης	Ἀθηναῖος	ξυνέγραψε	τὸν
2. Transliteration:	Thoukudídēs	Athēnaîos	ksunégrapse	tòn
3. Transcription:	tʰu:kydíd-ɛ:s	atʰe:nâ:j-os	ksynégrap-se	t-òn
4. Gloss:	Thucydides-NOM.SG	Athenian-NOM.SG	write-AOR.3.SG	the-ACC.SG

1.	πόλεμον	τῶν	Πελοποννησίων	καὶ	Ἀθηναίων,	ὡς
2.	pólemon	tôn	Peloponnēsíōn	kaì	Athēnaíōn,	hōs
3.	pólem-on	t-ɔ̂:n	peloponnɛ:sí-o:n	kàj	atʰe:náj-ɔ:n	hɔ:s
4.	war-ACC.SG	the-GEN.PL	Peloponnesian-GEN.PL	and	Athenian-GEN.PL	how

1.	ἐπολέμησαν	πρὸς	ἀλλήλους,	ἀρξάμενος	εὐθὺς
2.	epolémēsan	pròs	allḗlous,	arksámenos	euthùs
3.	epolémɛ:-san	pròs	allé:l-u:s	ark-sámen-os	ewtʰỳs
4.	fight-AOR.3.PL	against	each other-ACC.PL	begin-AOR.PART-NOM.SG	immediately

1.	καθισταμένου	καὶ	ἐλπίσας	μέγαν	τε
2.	kathistaménou	kaì	elpísas	mégan	te
3.	katʰista-mén-u:	kàj	elpí-sa:-s	méga-n	te
4.	arise-PRES.PART-GEN.SG	and	expect-AOR.PART-NOM.SG	great-ACC.SG	both

1.	ἔσεσθαι	καὶ	ἀξιολογώτατον	τῶν	
2.	ésesthai	kaì	aksiologṓtaton	tôn	
3.	ése-stʰaj	kàj	aksiologó:-tat-on	t-ɔ̂:n	
4.	be.FUT-INFIN	and	worthy.of.note-SUPERL-ACC.SG	the-GEN.PL	

1.	προγεγενημένων	τεκμαιρόμενος	ὅτι
2.	progegenēménōn	tekmairómenos	hóti
3.	pro-gegenɛ:-mén-ɔ:n	tekmajr-ómen-os	hóti
4.	before-occur-PERF.PART-GEN.PL	witness-PRES.PART-NOM.SG	that

1.	ἀκμάζοντές	τε	ἦσαν	ἐς	αὐτὸν ...
2.	akmázontés	te	êisan	es	autòn
3.	akmázd-ont-és	te	ê:j-san	es	awt-òn
4.	be.at.the.peak-PRES.PART-NOM.PL	both	go-IMP.3.PL	into	it-ACC.SG

'Thucydides (the) Athenian wrote up the war of the Peloponnesians and Athenians, (recording) how they fought with one another, having begun immediately as it began and expecting (that) it would both be great and more worthy of note than those which had occurred before, both bearing witness to the fact that the two sides went into it at their peak....'   —*Thucydides, 1.1.1.*

SAMPLE OF MODERN GREEK

1. Greek: Τώρα   πού   έχουν   πεθάνει   όλες
2. Transliteration: Tṓra   poú   ékhoun   pethánei   óles
3. Transcription: 'tora pu   'eχ-un   pe'θan-i   'ol-es
4. Gloss: now   that have-PRES.3.PL die.PAST-PART.ACT all-NOM.PL

1. οι   γριές,   γιαγιάδες   και παραγιαγιάδες,
2. oi   griés,   giagiádes   kai paragiagiádes,
3. i   γri-'es   ja'jað-es   ke   para-ja'jað-es
4. the-NOM.PL old woman-NOM.PL grandma-NOM.PL   and over-grandma-NOM.PL

1. τώρα βρήκαν   να ξεφυτρώσουν   μέσα   μου   ένα
2. tṓra brḗkan   na ksephutrṓsoun   mésa   mou   éna
3. 'tora 'vrik-an   na ksefi'tros-un   'mesa   m-u   'en-a
4. now   find-AOR.3.PL to sprout up-AOR.SUBJ.3.PL inside I-GEN.SG a-ACC.SG

1. σωρό   απορίες   βαθιές   για πρόσωπα   και
2. sōró   aporíes   bathiés   gia prósōpa   kai
3. so'r-o   apo'ri-es   va'θj-es   ja   'prosop-a   ke
4. heap-ACC.SG   perplexities-ACC.PL deep-ACC.PL   for person-ACC.PL   and

1. πράγματα   παλιά   και για πάντα σβησμένα.
2. prágmata   paliá   kai gia pánta sbēsména.
3. 'praγmat-a   pa'lj-a   ke   ja 'panda zviz-'men-a
4. thing-ACC.PL old-ACC.PL and for always extinguish-PAST.PART.PASS-ACC.PL

1. Όσο   ζούσαν   εκείνες,   δεν ξέρω   γιατί,
2. Óso   zoúsan   ekeínes,   den ksérō   giatí,
3. 'oso   'zu-san   e'kin-es   ðeŋ 'gser-o   ja'ti
4. As.long.as live-IMP.3.PL that-NOM.PL   not know-PRES.1.SG why

1. σχεδόν   τίποτε   δεν ήθελα   να ρωτήσω.
2. skhedón   típote   den éthela   na rōtḗsō.
3. sχe'ðon   'tipote   ðen 'iθel-a   na ro'tis-o
4. practically nothing   not want-AOR.1.SG to ask-AOR.SUBJ.1.SG

'Now that all the old women have died, grandmas and assorted persons of that
ilk, now they have managed to engender within me a heap of profound perplex-
ities about persons and things old and extinguished forever. As long as they
were alive, I don't know why, I practically never wanted to ask.'

—*Begininng of Ioannou 1974.*

The Anatolian Alphabets

PIERRE SWIGGERS AND WOLFGANG JENNIGES

Anatolian is a geographic designation for languages spoken in Asia Minor, from the third millennium B.C.E. into the first millennium C.E. A number of languages were introduced into this area as official languages, and are attested in their own scripts during this period: Akkadian, Phoenician, Aramaic, and later Greek and Latin. The "Anatolian" languages include both non–Indo-European languages (often called *Asianic*; see SECTION 3, "Other languages" on page 58)—Hattic, Mitannic, and Hurrian—and Indo-European ones.

The earlier Indo-European languages can be divided into three groups: (1) Palaic (written in the Anatolian adaptation of cuneiform); (2) Hittite-Nesite (also written in cuneiform; see SECTION 3, "Hittite cuneiform" on page 65); (3) Luvian, the language of southern Anatolia first attested in cuneiform but during the first millennium written in its own hieroglyphs (see SECTION 6). The historical relationships between these groups and the later attested languages of (especially southwestern) Asia Minor are not clear—although it is clear that Lycian shows the most resemblance to Luvian; these later attested languages, whose internal relationship is also problematic, include Lycian, Lydian, Pisidian, Sidetic, Pamphylian, Phrygian, and Carian. They are all attested in an alphabetic script based on the Greek writing system, as is clear from the number (the Y being included in all Anatolian alphabets) and shape of the signs in these *epichoric* ('local') scripts; some of them are in fact identical with one of the archaic Greek alphabets. The details of the development of these Anatolian alphabets remain unclear, but there is evidence that these scripts were secondary, or even tertiary within the area: the oldest writing system of Asia Minor was hieroglyphic (the ancestor of the Luvian?), and this was replaced by a syllabic script (traces are found on Anatolian coins). The borrowing of the Greek script or a prototype took place around the seventh century B.C.E.

The order of presentation here reflects increasing distance from the Greek model (Pamphylian basically uses the old Greek alphabet, illustrated in TABLE 21.3 on page 264, left side), and the increasing difficulty of interpreting the texts. Carian inscriptions constitute a major problem, given the internal variation of the script, the historical complexities of its attestations, and the uncertainties surrounding the type of language underlying the inscriptions. The Anatolian alphabets—which are all traceable to one of the ancient Greek alphabets, but underwent influences from non-Greek scripts—are treated on their own in histories of writing, and are separated from the main Greek lineage here. Two minor writing systems of Asia Minor, Pisidian and the so-called Mysian, are discussed briefly at the end.

Phrygian

Both the Old Phrygian inscriptions (7th–6th century B.C.E.) and those of Neo-Phrygian (2nd–3rd century C.E.), reflecting an Indo-European language, use the Greek alphabet; the Old Phrygian alphabet is basically the archaic Greek script (TABLE 22.6) and belongs to Kirchhoff's "red" group (use of Y for χ). It contains all the signs added by the Greeks to the Phoenician alphabet; it is also used in the problematic inscription of Lemnos. Neo-Phrygian inscriptions are written in the common classical Greek script.

Pamphylian and Sidetic

The Pamphylian alphabet is the same as the Old Greek alphabet of the Eastern type (Kirchhoff's "blue" group); it sometimes has the proto-form of the Greek digamma ꓶ and contains, at least in a later stage, the Greek additional letters, with **+** or X as the sign of aspiration. In the city of Side, a special writing system was used, attested on coins and in a very small number of inscriptions, most of them in *scriptio continua* (without word division), which has been shown to be an alphabet; this "Sidetic" script is not fully deciphered, and its precise origin is still unknown (although a few letters can be related to those of the Old Greek alphabet).

Lycian

The Lycian alphabet (TABLE 22.7), attested in some 180 inscriptions of the fifth and fourth centuries B.C.E., is borrowed from a Doric variant of the archaic Greek script (Kirchhoff's "red" group). Lycian, nearly always written from left to right, has 29 signs (6 vowels and 23 consonants and semivowels); there are local differences in the *ẽ* shapes, but no major chronological variation (except for the nasal vowels *ẽ* and *ã*). More than 80% of the letters can be traced to their Greek prototype; the remaining signs, denoting Lycian sounds absent from Greek, are either original creations or, less probably, borrowings from other writing systems—signs for *q, ã, ẽ, τ* (or *T*, interpretation uncertain), and *ñ*. The value of the signs ◊ and ᵚ is still a matter of debate: the former is transcribed as Greek *kappa* or as *h(e)*; the latter, traditionally transcribed as Greek *bēta*, probably denotes a labiovelar (*kʷ* or *gʷ*). Vowel length is not noted (intervocalic *-h-* can suggest that a contraction of vowels has taken place); word division is generally indicated by :, but particles and pronominal proclitics are written in *scriptio continua*. Although the grammar of the language is still insufficiently known, we can interpret several inscriptions and the coin legends, the latter on the basis of historical information, the former on the basis of the stereotypical wording and with the help of bilingual texts. A second dialect of Lycian, Lycian B or Milyan, is written in the same alphabet; it is distinguished from Lycian A by the almost total absence of the sign for *q*, and phonetically by changes in the dental series.

TABLE 22.6: *The Old Phrygian Alphabet*

A	a
B B	b
Γ	g
Δ	d
E E	e
F F	ʋ
≶	z
I	i
K K	k
Λ	l
M M	m
N	n
O	o
Π Π	p
P P	r
Σ Σ	s
T	t
Y	u
Φ	p^h
Ψ	k^h, χ

TABLE 22.7: *The Lycian Alphabet*

𐊀	a
𐊁	e
𐊂	b
𐊃	β
𐊄	g
𐊅	d
𐊆	i
𐊇	w
𐊈	z
𐊉	θ
𐊊	y
𐊋	k
𐊌	q
𐊍	l
𐊎	m
𐊏	n
𐊐	m̃
𐊑	ñ
𐊒	u
𐊓	p
𐊔	κ
𐊕	r
𐊖	s
𐊗	t
𐊘	τ, T
𐊙	ã
𐊚	ẽ
𐊛	h
𐊜	χ

TABLE 22.8: *The Lydian Alphabet*

𐤠	a
𐤡	b
𐤣	d
𐤤	e
𐤥	v
𐤦	i
𐤧	y
𐤨	k
𐤩	l
𐤪	m
𐤫	n
𐤬	o
𐤭	r
𐤳	s
𐤮	ś
𐤯	t
𐤰	u
𐤱	f
𐤲	q
𐤵	ã
𐤴	τ
𐤶	ẽ
𐤷	λ
𐤸	ν
𐤹	c
𐤢	g

LYCIAN–GREEK BILINGUAL

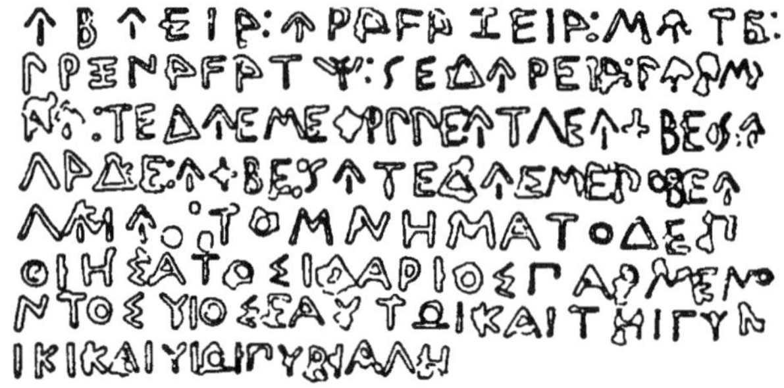

↑ Ᏽ ↑ Ɛ Ι Ρ : ↑ Ρ Ɒ ᖴ Ꝑ 𝚺 Ɛ Ι Ρ : Μ Ꝑ ↑ Ᏽ :
Ꮁ Ρ 𝚺 Ͷ Ꝑ ᖴ Ꝑ ↑ Ψ : ⌠ Ɛ Ꝺ ↑ Ρ Ɛ Ᏼ : Ꝑ ꝙ Ꝺ Ϻ
Ꙋ ꞈ . ⊤ Ɛ Ꝺ ハ Ɛ Μ Ɛ ᖯ Ꝑ Ꝑ Ɛ ↑ ⊤ ハ Ɛ ↑ ⅃ Ᏽ Ɛ ꝰ Ꝺ
ハ Ρ Ꝺ Ɛ ↑ �
 Ᏽ Ɛ Ꝥ ↑ ⊤ Ɛ Ꝺ ハ Ɛ Μ Ɛ Ρ ᖯ Ɛ ↑
ハ Ꙋ ↑ ꞈ ⊤ Ꝺ Μ ハ Ͷ Ꮁ Μ Ꝺ ⊤ Ꝺ Ꝺ Ɛ ⅊ Ꝑ
Ꝺ Ι Ꮁ Ɛ Ꝺ ⊤ Ꝺ 𝚺 Ι Ꝺ Ꝺ Ρ Ι Ꝺ 𝚺 Ρ Ꝺ ꝙ ハ Ɛ Ͷ Ꝺ
Ͷ ⊤ Ꝺ 𝚺 Y Ι Ꝺ 𝚺 Ɛ Ꝺ Y ⊤ Ꝺ Ι Ꝙ Ꝺ Ι ⊤ ꞩ Ι ᖰ Y Ꮁ
Ι Ꝙ Ι Ꝙ Ꝺ Ι Y Ꝙ ꝰ Ρ Y ᏸ Ꝺ ハ Ꮁ

	1. Lycian:	ebeija :	erawazija :	me	ti : /	prñnawatē :	siderija :
	2. Greek:	TO	MNHMA	TOΔ		ΕΠ/ΟΙΗΣΑΤΟ	ΣΙΔΑΡΙΟΣ
	3. Gloss:	this	monument	he	who	built	Siderija

	1.	parm[n]/[ah] :		tideimi [:	h]rppi :	etli	ehbi	se /	ladi :	ehbi :
	2.	ΠΑΡΜΕΝΟ/ΝΤΟΣ	ΥΙΟΣ		ΕΑΥΤΩΙ			ΚΑΙ	ΓΥΝ[Α]/	ΙΚΙ
	3.	Parmna's		son	for	him	own	and	wife	own

	1.	se	tideimi :	pubie/leje :
	2.	ΚΑΙ	ΥΙΩΙ	ΠΥΒΙΑΛΗΙ
	3.	and	son	Pubiele

'This monument was built by Siderija, son of Parmna, for himself, and for his wife, and for his son Pubiele.'

—*Epitaph on a sarcophagus from Limyra (the only bilingual with fully parallel texts; the Greek begins in line 5 after ∴), in Kalinka 1901 no. 117, with a new reading from Neumann 1985.*

Lydian

The Lydian alphabet (TABLE 22.8), attested in more than 100 inscriptions and graffiti from the fifth and fourth centuries B.C.E., is also based on a variant of the ancient Greek script of the "red" group, as can be seen from the shape of the signs for *k*, *n*, and *s*. Of its 26 signs, 16 can be traced to their Greek model; the others are local additions, most often for sounds peculiar to Lydian. A special feature of the Lydian alphabet is the sign 8/8 for *f*, a remarkable coincidence with the Etruscan alphabet (SECTION 23). The phonetic values of some Lydian signs (especially ꝙ, probably borrowed from Carian; value [j]?) are still unclear. Lydian is written from right to left (a few inscriptions are written from left to right).

LYDIAN–GREEK BILINGUALS

ΤΙΙΤΊΤ9Α ΕΙΙΑΗΙ9Α8 ΊΑΊΊΑΊ

ΝΑΝΝΑΣΔΙΟΝΥΣΙΚΛΕΟΣΑΡΤΕΜΙΔΙ

λumitra silavikab śannan←

Lydian:	nannaś	bakivalis	artimuλ
Greek:	ΝΑΝΝΑΣ	ΔΙΟΝΥΣΙΚΛΕΟΣ	ΑΡΤΕΜΙΔΙ
Gloss:	Nannas	the.one.of.Bakiva	to.Artemis

'Nannas, the son of Bakiva (i.e. Bacchus/Dionysus) (dedicates this statue) to Artemis.'   — *From Sardis (Gusmani 1964–86, no. 20).*

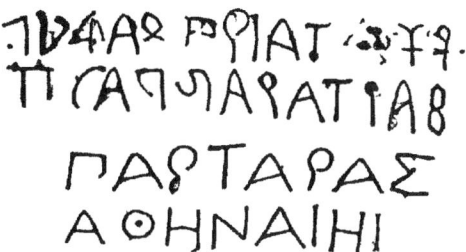

livcav caat vsv←
titaś śaratrab←

Lydian:	vsv	taac	vacvil	bartaraś	śatit
Greek:			ΠΑΡΤΑΡΑΣ ΑΘΗΝΑΙΗΙ		
Gloss:	this	statue/pillar(?)	to.Acvi	Bartara	has.built

'Bartara has built this statue/pillar to Asni(?) (= Athena).'
— *From Pergamon (Gusmani 1964–86, no. 40; Neumann 1967; Gusmani 1986a).*

Carian

Carian inscriptions have been found in Caria, in southwestern Asia Minor, and in Egypt, where the Carians, a non–Indo-European ethnic group mentioned in ancient sources (Homer, Herodotus, Thucydides), served as mercenaries under Psammetichus I or II. The inscriptions, written both left to right and right to left, include characters which formally recall signs of the proto-Greek alphabet (albeit with different values) and also of the Cretan alphabet and the Cypriote syllabary (SECTION 7), but they also contain several signs unparalleled among later ancient Greek writing systems. Despite bilingual inscriptions (with Egyptian hieroglyphic equivalents for Carian signs), the Carian script has not yet been fully deciphered. It is now accepted that its script, consisting of 45 signs with variants, is alphabetic, rather than a mixture of

syllabic and monophonemic signs. In recent years the "bilingual" approach, combined with a careful study of graphic alternation, has led to a revision of the values
traditionally assigned to Carian signs; a start has been made with the study of Carian
grammar (Ray 1990). In the present state of our knowledge (see Schürr 1992), it
seems possible to identify Carian signs for some nine vowels and semivowels (transcribed as: *a, e, i, í/i̯, o, u, ú, ù* (value *u̯*?), *w/ə*), two labials (*b, p*), three velars (*χ, q,
k*), three dentals (*t, d, τ = t̯*), three sibilants (*s, ś, š*), three liquids (*r, l, λ*), and three
nasals (*m, n, ñ*). In TABLE 22.9 the more or less acceptable identifications are given;
values for the remaining signs cannot yet be assigned.

TABLE 22.9: *The Letters of the Carian Alphabet*[a]

I	A ▷ ∧	a
3	⟨	d
4	△	l
5	Ḟ E	ù (alternating with sign 28)
6	F Ϲ Ϲ	r
7	I I	λ
9	⊕	q
10	Γ ⌐ ∧	b
11	Ͷ N	m
12	O	o (corresponding to Greek ω)
14	Ϙ	t
15	◁ ◖ ◖	š
17	Ϻ Ϻ	s
19	Y V	u (/u̯)
20	♦	ñ
21	x +	χ
22	Ϋ Ѵ	n
24	⋀⋀ ⋀⋀	p
25	⊕ ⊖	ś
26	◖ ◔ ◇	i
27	▢	e (corresponding to Greek η)
28	Ϙ	w (/ə) (alternating with sign 5)
29, 30	▽ Ͷ ⋎	k
32	⊓ ᴍ	ú (or ü)
38	Ⱶ	í (/i̯)
40	↑ ┼	τ (t̯)
41	ⱶⱶ	variant of 28

a. Omitted numbers refer to signs included in decipherment lists for
which no established value can yet be given.

Other languages

Brief mention must be made of *Pisidian* inscriptions, written in the Greek alphabet of the Roman period. The inscriptions (word dividers are used) contain mostly proper names. The language underlying these inscriptions is unknown; it seems to lack aspirated consonants (given the absence of χ, θ, φ) and is characterized by the presence of diphthongs and triphthongs. In 1926 an inscription was found in Uyujik whose right-to-left script seems to be a mixture of Phrygian and Lydian; the language (4th or 3rd century B.C.E.?) could be *Mysian*, which according to Strabo (XII 8, 3) was a "Lydian-Phrygian" mixture.

The Coptic Alphabet

ROBERT K. RITNER

"Coptic" designates the final stage of the ancient Egyptian language and script, which flourished in Egypt from the fourth through the tenth centuries C.E. and still survives in restricted liturgical use by the Coptic Orthodox Church. The term "Coptic" means simply 'Egyptian', and derives from the Arabic rendering (*Qubti*) of the Greek term Ἀιγύπτιος *Aigúptios*, a phonetic approximation of the native theological name of Memphis (*Ḥw.t-k3-Ptḥ*), the primary city of ancient Egypt. While the prominence of Coptic is due to its use as a vehicle for the vernacular translation of the Bible and other Christian texts, its initial development occurred within traditional temple circles. By virtue of the script's use of vowels, Old Coptic glosses served to clarify the pronunciation of exotic magical names in late ritual papyri (Johnson 1977: 87–88, 93–97).

The Coptic script represents a distinct break with earlier Egyptian writing systems by its general abandonment of pictographic characters, substituting instead the 24 letters of the Greek alphabet (TABLE 22.10). Many of these borrowed letters do not correspond to Coptic phonology, which has neither *d* nor *z*; does not distinguish *k* from *g*; and treats ⲑ as shorthand for *t + h*, ⲭ for *k + h*, ⲝ for *k + s*, ⲫ for *p + h*, and ⲯ for *p + s*. Standard written Coptic (Sahidic dialect) has 21 phonemes: five voiceless and unaspirated stops (ⲡ *p*, ⲧ *t*, ⲝ *ḏ* [ʤ], ϭ *q*, and ⲕ *k*), four voiceless spirants (ⲥ *s*, ϥ *f*, ϣ *š* [ʃ], and ϩ *h*), five sonants (ⲃ *v*, ⲗ *l*, ⲙ *m*, ⲛ *n*, and ⲣ *r*), four long vowels (ⲏ *ē*, ⲓ *i*, ⲩ *u*, and ⲱ *ō*), and three short vowels (ⲁ *a*, ⲉ *e*, and ⲟ *o*).

What distinguishes the Coptic from the Greek script, however, is the former's retention of several traditional signs for phonemes not represented in Greek. These supplementary signs are taken from the preceding Demotic script (7th century B.C.E.–

TABLE 22.10: *The Sahidic Coptic Alphabet*

Letter	Transcription	Phonetic Value	Name[a]	Greek/Demotic Source
ⲁ	a	[a]	alpha	A
ⲃ	v	[v]	vēta	B
ⲅ	k	[k]	kamma	Γ
ⲇ	t	[t]	talta	Δ
ⲉ	e	[e]	ei	E
ⲍ	s	[s]	sata	Z
ⲏ	ē	[e:]	hata	H
ⲑ	th	[th]	thita	Θ
ⲓ	i	[i]	iōta	I
ⲕ	k	[k]	kappa	K
ⲗ	l	[l]	lauta/lole	Λ
ⲙ	m	[m]	mē/me/mi	M
ⲛ	n	[n]	ne	N
ⲝ	ks	[ks]	ksi	Ξ
ⲟ	o	[o]	ou	O
ⲡ	p	[p]	pi	Π
ⲣ	r	[r]	rō	P
ⲥ	s	[s]	sēmma	Σ
ⲧ	t	[t]	tau	T
ⲩ	u	[u]	he/ue	Y
ⲫ	ph	[ph]	phi	Φ
ⲭ	kh	[kh]	khi	X
ⲯ	ps	[ps]	psi	Ψ
ⲱ	ō	[o:]	ō	ⲱ
ⲩ	š	[ʃ]	šai	Ꙃ
ϥ	f	[f]	fai	⟩
ϩ	h	[h]	hori	?
ϫ	ḏ	[ʤ]	danḏia	IⱢ
ϭ	q	[q]	qima	⸑
†	ti	[ti]	ti	⥾

a. Examples collected in Crum 1939, and cf. Vergote 1973, vol. 1a: 7, citing Worrell 1942; and Kasser 1991.

5th century C.E.), in declining use when Coptic was devised. The number of such additional signs varies widely according to dialect, particularly during the formative stages known as "Old Coptic." In the primary standardized dialect of Sahidic they amount to six (lower portion of TABLE 22.10). To the Sahidic unvoiced spirant ϩ *h*, an unvoiced fricative velar *ḫ* ([x]) is added in the Bohairic (ϩ) and Akhmimic (ϧ) dialects.

By adopting the Greek alphabet, Coptic entails several further innovations in Egyptian writing. Contrary to earlier preference (and initial "Old Coptic"), standard Coptic is written from left to right. More importantly, Coptic is the only native script of Egypt to indicate vowels. The importance of this feature in the script's development is noted above. Syllables containing sonants are often vowelless, however, and in Sahidic such syllables are indicated by a supralinear stroke: ⲦⲘⲚⲦⲢⲘⲚⲔⲎⲘⲈ *t̄mn̄t̄r̄mn̄kēme* 'Egyptian language'. Following Greek, Coptic no longer retains the ancient Egyptian system of "determinatives" to indicate word division, nor does it have punctuation between sentences. Some scribal schools do employ limited diacritics: dieresis over ⲓ and ⲩ at the beginning of a syllable (ⲉⲣⲟⲓ̈ *eroï* 'to me'; ⲙⲱⲩ̈ⲥⲏⲥ *mōüsēs* 'Moses'), apostrophe to indicate the end of phonological words and clitics (ⲉⲣϣⲁⲛⲧⲃⲁϣⲟⲣ' ⲁϣⲕⲁⲕⲉⲃⲟⲗ'ⲁⲛ' *ershantvashor' ashkakevol'an'* 'not if the jackal cries out'), and a circumflex on vowels forming independent syllables (post seventh century, ⲧⲏⲏ̂ⲃⲉ *tēêve* 'finger').

SAMPLE OF COPTIC

1. *Coptic:*	ⲦⲞⲦⲈ	ⲚⲢⲘⲚⲔⲎⲘⲈ		ⲐⲎⲢⲞⲨ	ⲚⲀⲘⲞⲨ	ⲀⲨⲱ ⲔⲎⲘⲈ
2. *Transliteration:*	tote	n̄rm̄n̄kēme		tērou	namou	awō kēme
3. *Transcription:*	tote	n̩-rm̩-n̩-kemə		teru	na-mu	awo kemə
4. *Gloss:*	then	the-men-of-Egypt		all	FUT-die	and Egypt

1. ⲚⲀϢⲰⲠⲈ	ⲈϤϢⲎϤ		ⲚⲚⲞⲨⲦⲈ	ⲘⲚ	ⲚⲢⲘⲚⲔⲎⲘⲈ		ⲚⲦⲞⲔ
2. našōpe	efšēf		n̄noute	m̄n	n̄rm̄n̄kēme		n̄tok
3. na-ʃopə	ɛf-ʃef		n̩-n̩-nutə	mn̩	n̩-rm̩-n̩-kemə		ntok
4. FUT-become	it.being-deserted		by-the-gods	and	the-men-of-Egypt		you

1. ⲆⲈ	ⲱ̂ ⲠⲒⲈⲢⲞ	ⲞⲨⲚ	ⲞⲨϨⲞⲞⲨ	ⲚⲀϢⲰⲠⲈ	ⲚⲢϨⲈⲦⲈ	ⲚⲤⲚⲞϤ
2. te	ô piero	oun̄	ouhoou	našōpe	n̄khetie	n̄snof
3. te	o piero	wun̩	u-hou	na-ʃopə	n̩-kʰeti	n̩-snof
4. but	O river	there.is	a-day	will-occur	and-you.flow	with-blood

1. ⲚϨⲞⲞⲨ	ⲈⲠⲘⲞⲞⲨ	ⲀⲨⲱ	ⲚⲤⲰⲘⲀ	ⲈⲦⲘⲞⲞⲨⲦ
2. n̄hoou	epmoou	awō	n̄sōma	etmoout
3. n̩-hou	e-p-mou	awo	n̩-soma	et-mout
4. in-excess	than-the-water	and	the-bodies	REL-are.dead

1. ⲤⲈⲚⲀϢⲰⲠⲈ	ⲈⲨϪⲞⲤⲈ	ⲚϨⲞⲨⲞ	ⲀⲚⲐⲎⲚⲈ	ⲀⲨⲱ
2. senašōpe	euḏose	n̄houo	antēne	awō
3. se-na-ʃopə	eu-ʤosə	n̩-hou	an-tenə	awo
4. they-FUT-be	they.being-high	in-excess	in-dams	and

I. ⲤⲈⲚⲀⲢⲓⲘⲈ	ⲀⲚ	ⲘⲠⲈⲦⲘⲞⲞⲨⲦ	ⲚⲐⲈ	ⲘⲠⲈⲦⲞⲚϨ	
2. senarime	an	m̄petmoout	n̄the	m̄petonh̄	
3. se-na-rimə	an	ṃ-p-et-mout	n̩-t-he	ṃ-p-et-onh	
4. they-FUT-weep	not	for-them-REL-are.dead	in-the-way	of-him-REL-lives	

I. ⲤⲈⲚⲀⲘⲈⲈⲨⲈ	ⲘⲈⲚ	ⲈⲢⲞϤ	ⲆⲈ	ⲞⲨⲢⲘⲚⲔⲎⲘⲈ	ⲠⲈ
2. senameeue	men	erof	de	ourm̄ñkēme	pe
3. se-na-mewe	men	ero-f	ʤe	u-rm-n-kemə	pe
4. they-FUT-think	then	regarding-him	that	a-man-of-Egypt	he.is

I. ⲈⲦⲂⲈ	ⲦⲈϤⲀⲤⲠⲈ
2. etve	tefaspe
3. etvə	t-ef-aspə
4. because.of	the-his(FEM)-language

'Then all the Egyptians will die, and Egypt will be deserted by the Gods and the Egyptians. But as for you, O river, a day will come when you will flow with blood more than with water, and the dead bodies will be higher than the dams. And one will not weep over him who is dead so much as him who is living. They will even think about him that he is an Egyptian because of his language.'
— *Asclepius, Nag Hammadi VI, 71, lines 14–25 (Krause and Labib 1971: 196).*

The Gothic Alphabet

ERNST EBBINGHAUS

The language of the East Germanic tribe of the Goths obtained historical importance in the age of the Great Migrations by which came about the expansion of the Germanic tribes in the fourth and fifth centuries C.E. It is known only through a small number of manuscripts, containing fragments of a translation of the Bible into Gothic. The ecclesiastical historians Philostorgius (*Historia ecclesiastica* II,5), Socrates (*Historia ecclesiastica* IV,33), and Sozomen (*Historia ecclesiastica* VI,37), writing in the fifth century C.E., report that the Gothic bishop Wulfila († 383) invented the "Gothic letters" (γράμματα γοτθικά), in order to write down his translation of the Bible into Gothic. That information, preserved through the Middle Ages (Streitberg 1919: xxivf.), has been accepted by all modern students of the Gothic language (Braune and Ebbinghaus 1981: 11–18). The script is variously referred to as Gothic or Visigothic; since these terms have a traditional meaning in palaeography, I prefer the term "Wulfila's script."

It is generally acknowledged that Wulfila did not invent his script ex nihilo but that he adapted one or more existing scripts to his purpose. Greek, Latin, and the Germanic runes have been proposed as sole models or in varying combinations in a long-lasting debate (Bibliographia Gotica 1950, nos. 617ff.). It has been shown in recent times that it is sufficient to assume the Greek alphabet as the only source (Boüüaert 1950; Ebbinghaus 1979, 1988–89; Agud Aparicio and Fernández Álvarez 1982: 10–11).

Wulfila's own hand is not preserved. Descended from it and preserved in manuscripts not older than the sixth century are two closely related types of script. The older of these types I have proposed to call the Sigma Type (Braune and Ebbinghaus 1981: 12; Ebbinghaus 1978: 100f.). It uses nasal suspension (the leaving out of a nasal consonant symbol) only for *n*, as Greek does, and its *s* has the shape of a minuscule Greek sigma. The Sigma Type exists in two forms; one of them is well known through, e.g., the Gothic text of Codex Ambrosianus S. 45, while the other is known only as an alphabet in Codex Vindobonensis 795 (Ebbinghaus 1978: 93–102). The second and younger type of Wulfila's script, which I have proposed to call the S Type, shows Latin influence. It uses nasal suspension for both *m* and *n* as Latin does, and its *s* has the shape of the Latin capital *s*. The S Type is best known through the calligraphically executed Codex Argenteus in Uppsala.

———

Special features

Wulfila's script is a phonetically based alphabetic script, written from left to right. The script does not separate words (*scriptio continua*); however, sentences and distinctive members of sentences are separated by space (*spatium*), centered dot (medial point), or colon. A few manuscripts show colometric writing; i.e., every colon (distinctive member of a sentence, such as a subordinate clause) occupies a separate line.

Every consonant is signaled by one letter (TABLE 22.11); for vowels a single letter or a digraph is used (TABLE 22.12). Vowel symbols distinguish quality, not quantity.

Nasal suspension is rare and occurs mostly at the end of lines; the suspended nasal is signaled by a macron above the preceding letter (e.g., **ѰΛ** *þā = þan*). Ligatures, i.e. the combining of letters with the omission of certain strokes (like & for *et*), are even rarer. Regular is the contraction of the *nomina sacra*: **ІⅠꙄ** *ius* 'Jesus', **ХⅠꙄ** *xus* 'Christ', **FΛ** *fa* < **FRΛⅡGΛ** *frauja* 'Lord'; these contractions show inflection for case.

The tenth letter **І** *i* is used with diaeresis **Ï** *ï* (a) in word-initial position, (b) in syllable-initial position after a vowel, and (c) in compounds with a verb as second member.

Wulfila adopted the Greek "Milesian system," in which every letter of the alphabet has a numerical value. If letters are employed as numbers, they are preceded and followed by centered dots or are marked by horizontal strokes above and/or below, e.g. •Ϭ• ·*e*· '5', G̲ J̲ '60' (von der Gabelentz and Loebe 1846: 17; Braune and Ebbinghaus 1981: 13).

TABLE 22.11: *The Gothic Alphabet*

S Type	Σ Type	Transliteration	Phonetic Value	Numerical Value
ᚨ	λ	a	[a/aː]	1
B	ʙ	b	[b]	2
Γ	Γ	g	[g]	3
ᕍ	ᕍ	d	[d/ð]	4
Ɇ	F	e	[e/eː]	5
u	ʊ	q	[kʷ]	6
Z	ᶻ	z	[z]	7
ʜ	ʰ	h	[h]	8
Ψ	⍦	þ	[θ]	9
ı ï	ı ı̈	i ï	[i/iː]	10
R	ʀ	k	[k]	20
λ	λ	l	[l]	30
ʜ	ʰ	m	[m]	40
N	ᴎ	n	[n]	50
Ᏻ	Ꞩ	j	[j]	60
ʘ	ʼʼ	u	[u/uː]	70
ᴨ	ᴨ	p	[p]	80
Ц		—		90
ʀ	ʀ	r	[r]	100
S	ε	s	[s]	200
T	ᴛ	t	[t]	300
Y	Y	w	[w/y]	400
ϝ	ʄ	f	[f]	500
X	×	x	[kʰ]	600
Θ	(·)	ƕ	[ʍ]	700
Ω	ᴙ	o	[o/oː]	800
↑		—		900

TABLE 22.12: *Gothic Digraphs*

Open Vowels			Close Vowels		
ᚨı	ai	æ/æː	Ɇı	ei	i/iː
ᚨᴨ	au	ɔ/ɔː			

That Wulfila's script was also used for profane material is shown by the Latin–
Gothic Deed of Naples (Papyrus Marini 119) of the sixth century (Tjäder 1982: 91ff.
and plates 116ff.). Otherwise, the preserved manuscripts contain fragments of the
Gothic translation of the gospels, the Pauline epistles, three chapters of the book of
Nehemiah, and a commentary on the gospel of John.

Wulfila's script has not had any offspring or influence on other scripts. It must have died out with the Gothic language, at a time that remains undetermined. The alphabet and Gothic fragments in Codex Vindobonensis 795 of the ninth century (close to 800?) must be attributed to the antiquarian interest of the time.

All the preceding remarks should be taken as preliminary. A comprehensive study of Wulfila's script is still lacking.

SAMPLE OF GOTHIC

1. Gothic:	NI	ｈｕｒＧＡＩψ	ＧＩ	ｕＧＭＧＡＮ	ＧＡＴＡＩＲＡＮ
2. Transliteration:	ni	hugjaiþ	ei	qemjau	gatairan
3. Transcription:	ni	hugjæθ	i:	kʷe:mjɔ	gatæran
4. Gloss:	not	think	that	I.have.come	to.destroy

1.	ＹＩＴΩψ	ＡＩψψＡＵ	ＤＲＡＵＦＧＴＵＮＳ	NI	ｕＡＭ	ＧＡＴＡＩＲＡＮ
2.	witoþ	aiþþau	praufetuns	ni	qam	gatairan
3.	wito:θ	æθθɔ	prɔfe:tuns	ni	kʷam	gatæran
4.	the.law	or	the.prophets	not	I.have.come	to.destroy

1.	ＡＲ	ｕＳＦｕＬＬＪＡＮ	ＡＭＧＮ	ＡｕＲ	ｕＩψＡ	ＩＺＹＩＳ	ｕＮＤ	ψＡＴＧＩ
2.	ak	usfulljan	amen	auk	qiþa	izwis	und	þatei
3.	ak	usfulljan	ame:n	ɔk	kʷiθa	izwis	und	θati:
4.	but	to.fulfill	truly	but	I.say	to.you	until	that

1.	ｕＳＡＧＩψＩψ	ｈＩＭＩＮＳ	ＧＡｈ	ＡＩＲψＡ	ＧΩＴＡ	ＡＩＮＳ	ＡＩψψＡＮ	ＡＩＮＳ
2.	usleiþiþ	himins	jah	airþa	jota	ains	aiþþau	ains
3.	usli:θiθ	himins	jah	ærθa	jo:ta	æns	æθθɔ	æns
4.	vanishes	heaven	and	earth	iota	one	or	one

1.	ＳＴＲＩＲＳ	NI	ｕＳＡＧＩψＩψ	ＡＦ	ＹＩＴΩＪＡ	ｕＮＴＧ	ＡＬＬＡＴＡ	ＹＡＩＲψＩψ
2.	strikɛ	ni	usleiþiþ	af	witoda	unte	allata	wairþiþ
3.	striks	ni	usli:θiθ	af	wito:ða	unte	allata	wærθiθ
4.	stroke	not	vanishes	from	the.law	until	all	becomes

'Do not think that I have come to abolish the law or the prophets; I have come not to abolish but to fulfill. For truly I tell you, until heaven and earth pass away, not one letter, not one stroke of a letter,will pass from the law until all is accomplished.'   —*Matthew 5:17–18 [New Revised Standard Version].*

Bibliography

THE GREEK ALPHABET

Allen, W. Sidney. 1987. *Vox Graeca: The Pronunciation of Classical Greek,* 3rd ed. Cambridge: Cambridge University Press.

Barbour, Ruth. 1991. *Greek Literary Hands A.D. 400–1600.* Oxford: Oxford University Press.

Buck, Carl Darling. 1955. *The Greek Dialects.* Chicago: University of Chicago Press.

Ioannou, Iorgos. 1974. *Ē mónē klēronomiá* [The sole inheritance]. Athens: Hermes.

Jeffery, Lilian H. 1990. *The Local Scripts of Archaic Greece,* rev. ed. with supp. by A. W. Johnston. Oxford: Clarendon.

Kirchhoff, Adolf. 1887. *Studien zur Geschichte des griechischen Alphabets,* 4th ed. Gütersloh: Bertelsmann. Repr. Amsterdam: Gieben, 1970.

Newton, Brian. 1972. *The Generative Interpretation of Dialect: A Study of Modern Greek Phonology* (Cambridge Studies in Linguistics 8). Cambridge: Cambridge University Press.

Pfeiffer, Rudolf. 1968. *History of Classical Scholarship from the Beginnings to the End of the Hellenistic Age.* Oxford: Oxford University Press.

———. 1976. *History of Classical Scholarship from 1300 to 1850.* Oxford: Oxford University Press.

Powell, Barry B. 1987. "The Origin of the Puzzling Supplementals Φ, X, Ψ." *Transactions and Proceedings of the American Philological Association* 117: 1–20.

Reynolds, Leighton D., and Nigel G. Wilson. 1991. *Scribes and Scholars,* 3rd ed. Oxford: Oxford University Press.

Roberts, Colin H. 1955. *Greek Literary Hands 350 B.C. – A.D. 400.* Oxford: Oxford University Press.

Smyth, Herbert Weir. 1963. *Greek Grammar,* 2nd ed., rev. Gordon M. Messing. Cambridge: Harvard University Press.

Sturtevant, Edgar H. 1940. *The Pronunciation of Greek and Latin,* 2nd ed. Philadelphia: Linguistic Society of America. Repr. Groningen: Bouma, 1968.

Threatte, Leslie. 1980. *The Grammar of Attic Inscriptions 1: Phonology.* Berlin: de Gruyter.

Turner, Eric G. 1971. *Greek Manuscripts of the Ancient World.* Oxford: Clarendon.

ANATOLIAN ALPHABETS

Adiego, Ignacio-J. 1990. "Deux notes sur l'écriture et la langue cariennes." *Kadmos* 29: 133–37.

Altkleinasiatische Sprachen. 1969. (Handbuch der Orientalistik Division 1, vol. 2/2). Leiden: Brill.

Brixhe, Claude. 1988. "La langue des inscriptions épichoriques de Pisidie." In *A Linguistic Happening in Memory of Ben Schwartz,* ed. Yoël Arbeitman, pp. 131–55. Louvain: Peeters.

Bryce, Trevor R. 1987. "Some Observations on the Pronunciation of Lycian." *Kadmos* 26/1: 84–97.

Carruba, Onofrio. 1978. "La scrittura licia." *Annali della Scuola Normale Superiore di Pisa,* ser. 3, vol. 8: 849–67.

Deroy, Louis. 1955. "Les inscriptions cariennes de Carie." *L'Antiquité Classique* 24: 305–55.

Eichner, Heiner. 1986. "Neue Wege im Lydischen I." *Zeitschrift für vergleichende Sprachforschung* 90: 203–19.

Faucounau, Jean. 1984. "À propos de récents progrès dans le déchiffrement de l'écriture carienne." *Bulletin de la Société de Linguistique de Paris* 79: 229–38.

———. 1989. "À propos de la lecture des inscriptions cariennes." *Kadmos* 28: 174–75.

Friedrich, Johannes. 1932. *Kleinasiatische Sprachdenkmäler.* Berlin: de Gruyter.

Gardthausen, Victor. 1921. "Kleinasiatische Alphabete." *Paulys Realencyclopädie der classischen Altertumswissenschaft* 11/1, cols. 601–12.

Gusmani, Roberto. 1964–86. *Lydisches Wörterbuch mit grammatischer Skizze und Inschriftensammlung + Ergänzungsband* (3 fascicles). Heidelberg: Winter.

———. 1981. "Il lidio." In *Nuovi materiali per la ricerca indoeuropeistica,* ed. Enrico Campanile, pp. 107–16. Pisa: Giardini.

———. 1986A. "Zur Lesung der lydischen Inschrift aus Pergamon." *Kadmos* 25: 155–61

———. 1986B. "Die Erforschung des Karischen." In *Im Bannkreis des Alten Orients,* ed. Wolfgang Meid and H. Trenkwalder, pp. 55–67. Innsbruck: Innsbrucker Beiträge zur Sprachwissenschaft, Universität Innsbruck.

———. 1988. "Karische Beiträge." *Kadmos* 27: 139–49.

———. 1989–90. "Lo stato delle ricerche sul milíaco." *Incontri linguistici* 13: 69–78.

Kalinka, Ernst. 1901. *Tituli Asiae Minoris,* part 1, *Tituli Lyciae lingua Lycia conscripti.* Vienna: Hölder.

Lejeune, Michel. 1969. "Discussions sur l'alphabet phrygien." *Studi micenei egeo-anatolici* 10: 19–47.

———. 1970. "Les inscriptions de Gordion et l'alphabet phrygien." *Kadmos* 9: 51–74.

Masson, Olivier. 1973. "Que savons-nous de l'écriture et de la langue des Cariens?" *Bulletin de la Société de Linguistique de Paris* 68: 187–213.

Neumann, Günter. 1967. "Der lydische Name der Athena." *Kadmos* 25: 155–61.

———. 1978. "Die sidetische Schrift." *Annali della Scuola Normale Superiore di Pisa,* ser. 3, vol. 8: 869–86.

———. 1979. *Neufunde lykischer Inschriften seit 1901.* Vienna: Österreichische Akademie der Wissenschaften.

———. 1983. "Zur Erschliessung des Lykischen." In *Le lingue indoeuropee di frammentaria attestazione/Die indogermanischen Restsprachen,* ed. Edoardo Vineis, pp. 135–61. Pisa: Giardini.

———. 1985. "Beiträge zum Lykischen VII." *Die Sprache* 31: 243–48.

———. 1988A. "Lydien." *Reallexikon der Assyriologie und der vorderasiatischen Archäologie* 7: 184–86. Berlin: de Gruyter.

———. 1988B. "Lykien." *Reallexikon der Assyriologie und der vorderasiatischen Archäologie* 7: 189–91. Berlin: de Gruyter.

Nollé, Johannes. 1988. "Mitteilungen zu sidetischen Inschriften." *Kadmos* 27: 57–62.

Ray, John D. 1982. "The Carian Script." *Proceedings of the Cambridge Philological Society* 208: 77–90.

———. 1990. "An Outline of Carian Grammar." *Kadmos* 29: 54–73.

———. 1992. "New values in Carian." *Kadmos* 31: 40–42.

Schürr, Diether. 1992. "Zur Bestimmung der Lautwerte des karischen Alphabets 1971–1991." *Kadmos* 31: 127–56.

Ševoroškin, Vitalij. 1968. "Zur Entstehung und Entwicklung der kleinasiatischen Buchstabenschriften." *Kadmos* 7: 150–73.

———. 1975. "Zur sidetischen Schrift." *Kadmos* 14: 154–66.

Woudhuizen, Fred C. 1984–85A. "Lydian: Separated from Luwian by Three Signs." *Talanta* 16–17: 91–113.

———. 1984–85B. "Origins of the Sidetic Script." *Talanta* 16–17: 115–27.

Zgusta, Ladislav. 1957. "Die pisidischen Inschriften." *Archív Orientální* 25: 570–610.

THE COPTIC ALPHABET

Crum, Walter E. 1939. *A Coptic Dictionary.* Oxford: Clarendon.

Johnson, Janet H. 1977. "Louvre E 3229: A Demotic Magical Text." *Enchoria* 7: 55–102.

Kasser, Rodolphe, ed. 1991. *Appendix: Linguistics,* vol. 8 of *The Coptic Encyclopedia,* ed. Aziz S. Atiya. New York: Macmillan.

Krause, Martin. 1979. "Koptische Sprache." In *Lexikon der Ägyptologie,* ed. Wolfgang Helck, Eberhard Otto, and Wolfhart Westendorf, vol. 3, cols. 731–37. Wiesbaden: Harrassowitz.

Krause, Martin, and Pahor Labib. 1971. *Gnostische und hermetische Schriften aus Codex II und Codex VI* (Abhandlungen des Deutschen Archäologischen Instituts, Kairo, Koptische Reihe 2). Glückstadt: Augustin.

Quaegebeur, Jan. 1982. "De la préhistoire de l'écriture copte." *Orientalia Lovaniensia Periodica* 13:

125–36.

Till, Walter C. 1955. *Koptische Grammatik.* Leipzig: Harrassowitz, pp. 29–53.

Vergote, Josef. 1973–83. *Grammaire copte.* 2 vols. in 4 parts. Louvain: Peeters.

Worrell, William H. 1942. *Coptic Texts in the University of Michigan Collection* (University of Michigan Studies, Humanistic series 46). Ann Arbor.

THE GOTHIC ALPHABET

Agud Aparicio, Ana, and Pilar Fernández Álvarez. 1982. *Manual de lengua gótica.* Salamanca: Universidad de Salamanca.

"Bibliographia Gotica." 1950–74. *Mediaeval Studies* 12: 237–324 (Fernand Mossé), 15: 169–83 (Mossé), 19: 174–96 (James W. Marchand); 29 (1967): 328–43 (E. A. Ebbinghaus), 36: 199–214 (Ebbinghaus).

Boüüaert, J. 1950. "Oorsprong en vorming van het gotisch alphabet." *Revue belge de philolologie et d'histoire* 20: 423–37.

Braune, Wilhelm, and Ernst A. Ebbinghaus. 1981. *Gotische Grammatik,* 19th ed. Tübingen: Niemeyer.

de Vries, Jan, ed. 1936. *Wulfilae codices Ambrosiani rescripti epistularum evangelicarum textum exhibentes phototypice,* vol. 2. Turin: Molfese.

Ebbinghaus, Ernst A. 1978. "The Gotica of Codex Vindobonensis 795." In *Germanic Studies in Honor of Otto Springer,* ed. Stephen J. Kaplowitt, pp. 93–102. Pittsburgh: K & S Enterprises.

———. 1978–79. "The study of Wulfila's alphabet." *Journal of the Department of English* (Calcutta) 1: 34–39.

———. 1979. "The Origin of Wulfila's Alphabet." *General Linguistics* 19: 15–29.

———. 1992. "Some Remarks on the Life of Bishop Wulfila." *General Linguistics* 32: 95–104.

———. 1994. "Wulfila's Script: Facts and Inferences." *General Linguistics* 34.

Friesen, Otto von, et al., eds. 1927. *Codex argenteus Upsaliensis jussu senatus universitatis phototypice editus.* Uppsala: Almqvist & Wiksell.

Philostorgius. 1913. *Kirchengeschichte,* ed. Joseph Bidez. Leipzig: Hinrichs.

Socrates. 1864. *Historia ecclesiastica,* ed. J.-P. Migne (Patrologia Graeca 67). Paris: Migne.

Sozomenus. 1960. *Kirchengeschichte,* ed. Joseph Bidez and Günther Christian Hansen. Berlin: Akademie Verlag.

Streitberg, Wilhelm. 1919. *Die gotische Bibel I.* Heidelberg: Winter.

Tjäder, Jan-Olof. 1982. *Die nichtliterarischen lateinischen Papyri Italiens aus der Zeit 445–470.* Stockholm: Gleerup.

von der Gabelentz, Hans C., and Julius Loebe. 1846. *Ulfilas* II,2. Leipzig: Brockhaus.

The Scripts of Italy

LARISSA BONFANTE

Etruscan

The Etruscan alphabet (TABLE 23.1) derives from the Greek, which derives from the Phoenician alphabet; the Latin alphabet derives from the Greek by way of Etruscan. The Etruscan alphabet originated from a Western Greek alphabet, that of the Euboeans, the first Western Greeks, who settled in Pithekoussai and Cumae. There are some 13,000 Etruscan inscriptions, making Etruscan second only to Latin in Italy in amount of documentation, and first until ca. 200 B.C.E.

Etruscan did not have the voiced consonants *b*, *g*, *d*, and soon expelled their letters from its alphabet; nor did it have *o*, which also disappeared. Various inscribed alphabets, including one from Marsiliana d'Albegna (mid 7th century B.C.E.; FIGURE 35), still preserve the Greek ("model") alphabet (26 signs, including *b*, *g*, *d*, and *o*, though they were never used in inscriptions).

The sign ⊟ *heth* (Greek H, *eta*) kept its old value of [h].

For the sound [k], archaic Etruscan used three letters, corresponding to three slightly different pronunciations depending on the following vowel: *ka*, *ce* and *ci*, *qu*. During the course of the fifth century B.C.E., orthography came to be simplified and only *C* was used; *K* was sometimes used in northern Etruria.

The model alphabet of Marsiliana d'Albegna had four signs for sibilants: M *ṣade* (sideways *sigma*), ⊞ *samech*, ⸳ *sigma*, and X (like Latin X). This system was then somewhat simplified: only two were used, aside from M, a sibilant of which we do not know the exact pronunciation (it may have been pronounced [ʃ]). The different Etruscan cities varied in their use of the signs for the sibilants.

The voiceless stops ⟩ *k*, T *t*, ᒣ *p*, and Y *χ* (Greek *ch* or *kh*) alternate with the aspirates in many words (*sec* : *seχ*), without any clear reason. But after the liquids ⎪ *l*, ᒣ *r*, M *m*, ᒣ *n*, only Y *χ* was used.

The Etruscans had a sound [f] which at first they expressed with ⊢⊟ *wh* (as was also done in Venetic); but in the sixth century a new sign **8** was (apparently) invented and added at the end of the letter order.

Etruscan Z always had the voiceless sound [ts].

ACKNOWLEDGMENT: I would like to thank my father, Giuliano Bonfante, for his valuable assistance in preparing this section.

297

TABLE 23.1: *Etruscan and Latin-Faliscan Alphabets (after Morandi 1982: 29)*

| | ETRUSCAN | | FALISCAN | LATIN | |
	Marsiliana	*Archaic & Recent*			
a	Ⱥ	Ⱥ	Ⱥ Я	Ⱥ	a
b	℈				b
c/g	⅂	)	C	C	c/g
d	◁		D	D	d
e	∃	∃	E	E	e
v	⅂	⅂			v
z [ts]	⫶	⫶	I Ɫ		z [ts]
h	目	目⊘	▯目	目	h
th	⊗	⊗⊙	⊙		th
i	l	l	l	l	i
k	⅄	⅄	k	K	k
l	↓	↓	L	↳	l
m	⋎	⋎ ⋔⋏	⋔ ⋔	⋏⋏	m
n	⅄	⅄ H	⋔ H	⋏	n
š	⊞				š
o	O		O	O	o
p	⌐	⌐	Γ	Γ	p
ś	M	M⋈			ś
q	Ϙ	Ϙ	Φ	Ϙ	q
r	⅃	⅂◁	P Я	P	r
s	⟩	⟨⟩	⟩ ⟨⟨	⟩	s
t	T	Ⱦ	Ⱦ	Ⱦ	t
u	Y	YV	V	YV	u
ṡ, x	X	X	X	X	ṡ, x
ph	Φ	φ ⊕			ph
ch	Ψ	Ψ ⱴ			ch
f		Ⱶ目,8	↑	Ⱶ	f

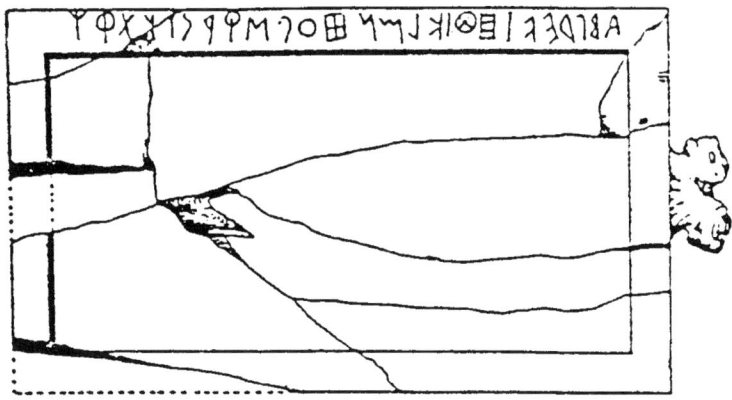

FIGURE 35. Model (Greek) alphabet on ivory tablet from Marsiliana d'Albegna
(Bonfante and Bonfante 1983, fig. 11, source 1).

Etruscan writing usually runs from right to left, except in some late inscriptions influenced by Latin. Archaic inscriptions, however, could also run from left to right, or they could be written boustrophedon, as was a funerary stela from Lemnos of the sixth century B.C.E., in a language very close to archaic Etruscan.

The earliest Etruscan inscriptions were written using *scriptio continua*, in which the words are not divided from each other: *miavileśtiteiuchsiemulenike*, that is, *mi aviléś titei uchsie mulenike* 'I [belong to] Aulus Titus, Uchsie dedicated [me]'. In the sixth and fifth centuries B.C.E. there appeared in southern Etruria and Campania a syllabic punctuation which set off with a dot the letters that were not part of an open syllable, that is, the consonants or vowels that did not fit a syllabic system (see Peruzzi 1980: 142–49). Such punctuation was normal in the Venetic alphabet, which was, curiously, derived from the archaic southern, rather than from a northern Etruscan alphabet. From the sixth century B.C.E., it became customary to separate words by means of one or two dots.

The earliest Etruscan inscriptions date from the seventh century B.C.E.; in the first century B.C.E. the use of Etruscan as a written language disappears.

SAMPLE OF ETRUSCAN

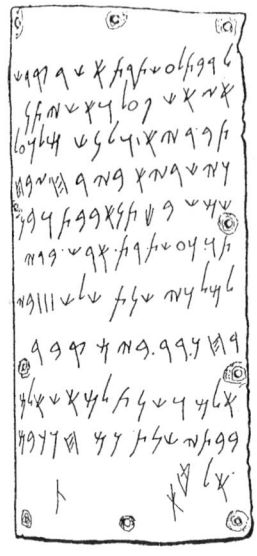

FIGURE 36. The Pyrgi tablets, with Phoenician *(left)* and Etruscan inscriptions.

For the analysis of the Phoenician text, see page 106.

1. Etruscan:	ita •	tmia •	icac •	he/ramasva •	vatieche /
2. Gloss:	this	sacred.place	and this	statue	dedicated

1.	unialastres •	themia/sa • mech •	thuta •	thefa/riei •	velianas •	sal /
2.	to Uni-Astarte	he.placed lord	people	Thefarie	Velianas	?

1.	cluvenias •	turu/ce •	munistas •	thuvas /
2.	?	he.gave.it	this.place	of.this.sacred.place

1.	ilacve • /	tulerase •	nac •	ci •	avi/l •	churvar •
2.	on.the.one.hand	established	because	three	year(s)	?

tameresca •
promoter

tesiameit/ale •
?

1.	ilacve •	alsase [•] /	nac •	atranes •	zilac/al •
2.	on.the.other.hand	dedicated?	because	of.the.temple	"king"

seleitala •
?

1.	acnasv/ers •	itanim •	heram/ve •	avil •	eniaca •	pul/umchva •
2.	gave.in.possession	this	statue	year(s)	?	stars

> *Etruscan:* 'This the sacred place and this the statue dedicated to Uni (Juno)
> Astarte the lord ruler of the people, Thefarie (Tiberius) Velianas ... placed
> (here); he gave this place, he, the caretaker of this sacred place, on the one hand
> because she established him for three years ... and on the other hand because
> he, the chief magistrate of the temple, gave her in possession this statue(?); and
> may its years be as many as the stars.'

Phoenician: 'For the Lady, for Ashtarat is this holy place that Thefarie Velunas, king over Caere, made and donated to (the) temple, in the Month of the Solar Sacrifice (which is called?) MTN, and he built (a/ the?) cella as Ashtarat had asked of him during the third year of his reign, in the Month of KRR on the Day of the God's Burial. And may the years of the god's statue be as many as these stars.'

— Three gold tablets excavated in 1964 at Pyrgi, a harbor of Cerveteri. Ca. 500 B.C.E. 18.5 x 8 cm. Only a few of the Etruscan words, aside from the names, are known with certainty (ci 'three', zilac 'king/magistrate', avil 'year', and some others). After Bonfante and Bonfante 1983: 53–56.

Other languages and scripts of Italy

The Etruscan alphabet was widely used—by non-Etruscans as well as Etruscans—in Etruria, in territories conquered by the Etruscans (Campania, Emilia), and in those influenced by Etruscan culture. Other inscriptions from pre-Roman Italy—with the exception of southern Italy and Sicily, which took their alphabets directly from Greek—were written with characters derived from the Etruscan alphabet (Umbrian, Oscan, etc.). Unlike Etruscan, the languages of these other peoples of Italy, including Latin, were Indo-European.

Latin

An Etruscan influence on the Latin alphabet (TABLE 23.1) can be seen in the third letter, Greek *gamma*, which took the voiceless sound C before *a* (as in Latin *Caesar* [kajsar]). Unlike the Etruscans, the Romans had the sound [g]; and since the Greek gamma, Γ or C, was already being used to represent [k], which the Romans also needed, Spurius Carvilius Rufa invented, in the early third century B.C.E., a new letter, G, simply by adding a stroke to the existing C. This new sign was inserted in the alphabet following the letter F, in the slot formerly occupied by the Greek letter Z, which was at this time not used in Latin. When, in the first century B.C.E., the Romans needed the Z to write Greek words, they reintroduced it; but it went to the end of the line, as the last letter of the alphabet, so as to preserve the original order of the alphabet. The Romans did not need the Greek letters Θ [tʰ] or Ξ [ks], or those which had been added at the end of the Greek alphabet, Φ [pʰ], X [kʰ], Ψ [ps], and Ω [oː]; so these letters dropped out.

Greek Y [u/y], in the form V (as in Etruscan), was used for both [u/y] and [v], while I stood for [i] and the consonant [j]. When Y was reintroduced as a separate letter in the first century B.C.E., to be used in words of Greek origin, it too was put at the end of the alphabet, immediately before Z. The last sign to be added in antiquity, the cross, had the value [ks] in the western Greek scripts, whence Latin X, rather than the value [kʰ] (Greek [x]) as in the eastern Greek script (from which came classical and

modern Greek X [kʰ]). Latin X thus had the sound of Greek Ξ [ks]. The Roman alphabet was therefore as follows: A, B, C (= [k]), D, E, F, G, H, I, K, L, M, N, O, P, Q,
R (instead of Greek P), S, T, V, X, Y, Z. The Greek and Latin scripts differed in other
ways, too—Latin D, in contrast to Greek Δ; C (and G) as against Γ; L versus Λ; S
versus Σ—no doubt because the Latin forms were western variants, which had come
into Etruscan and Latin from the Euboean colonies.

Not until the Renaissance was U distinguished from V and consonantal J from I
(and not until Noah Webster's 1806 *Compendious Dictionary of the English Language* were they separated in alphabetical lists). The sound [f], which did not exist in
Greek—Φ *ph* [pʰ] was not pronounced [f] until Roman times—was perhaps introduced to Europe by the Etruscans. This sound was at first written in Latin, as in early
Etruscan, with FH *wh*. The classic example for this usage had long been the seventh-
century B.C.E. fibula from Praeneste, near Rome, a gold pin of Etruscan style engraved with what was considered the earliest Latin inscription: *Manios : med : fhe :
fhaked : Numasioi* 'Manios made me for Numasios (Numerius)'. That this inscription
is a forgery (on a genuinely antique artifact) has recently been demonstrated (Gordon
1983: 76), though the inscription's characters and language agree with what we
would expect in this early period. By the fourth century B.C.E. the F was used alone
for [f], as in the inscription on the lid of the Ficoroni cista, an engraved bronze toilet
box from Praeneste (FIGURE 37). The earliest Latin inscriptions were retrograde or
boustrophedon (Castor and Pollux dedication, Duenos vase, Forum cippus). Associated with Praenestine (and other) Latin is *syllabic notation*, where a consonant letter
represents the consonant plus a vowel, often the letter's name (Vine 1993: 323–44).

SAMPLE OF LATIN

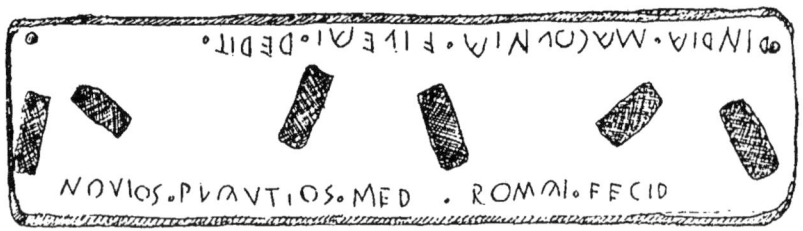

FIGURE 37. Ficoroni cista: Latin inscription on lid. Fourth century B.C.E.
(Manino 1981: 131, fig. 36).

| *1. Latin:* | Novios | Plautios | med | Romai | fecid / |
| *2. Gloss:* | Novios | Plautios | me | Rome.LOC | made |

| *1.* | Dindia | Macolnia | fileai | dedit |
| *2.* | Dindia | Macolnia | daughter.DAT | gave |

'Novios Plautios made me in Rome—Dindia Macolnia gave [me] to her daughter.'   —*Mansuelli 1950–51.*

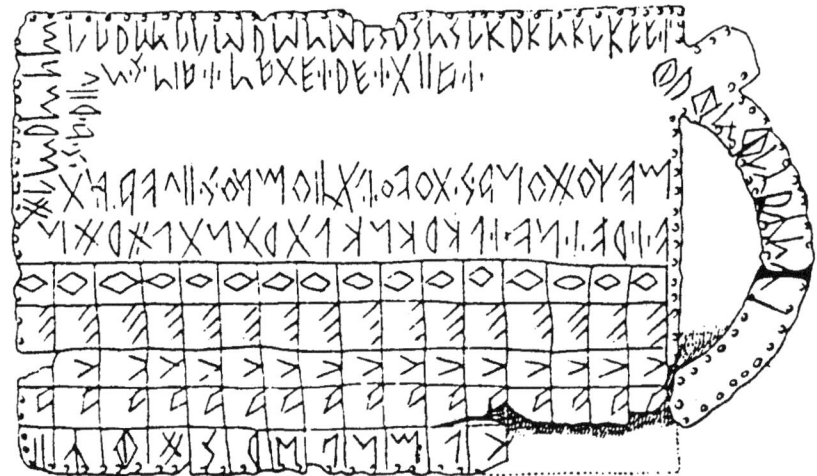

FIGURE 38. Venetic alphabet and writing exercises, including the signs ALCEO and syllable practice, on a bronze votive tablet from Este. Third century B.C.E. (Bonfante 1981, fig. 119).

Etruscan influence in the north

Etruscan merchants came to northern Europe long before the arrival of the Romans (from *Arretium* 'Arezzo' is derived German *Erz* 'ore'), and they brought writing: according to most scholars, the northern runes (SECTION 25) derive from the Etruscan alphabet.

In northern Italy (TABLE 23.2), most inscriptions are relatively late. Ligurian and Lepontic inscriptions were found in the region between eastern Piedmont, Lombardy, the southern part of the Canton Ticino and Liguria, and the Lake region (Como, Lugano, Maggiore, and d'Orta). As in Etruscan, no distinction is made between voiceless velar [k] and voiced [g]; the sign used, as in northern Etruscan, is K.

Only three Gallic inscriptions have been found, from Briona (Novara), Cureggio (Vercelli), and Todi: they are late, third to first century B.C.E.

Rhaetic inscriptions, belonging mostly to the third century B.C.E., have been found in the northern Tyrol and in the valleys of the Dolomites, at Verona, Sondrio and Padua.

Somewhat different are the more than forty inscriptions of the Val Camuna (now Valcamonica), mostly scratched on the rock walls.

There are over 250 Venetic inscriptions, dating from the sixth to the second centuries B.C.E. These are characterized by the presence of F, as in Etruscan; by the presence of the letter O, which distinguishes them from the Etruscan model; by the angular shape of the letters; by a syllabic punctuation (open syllables are not punctuated); and by the use of the Greek and Etruscan letters X, Φ, and Z for the voiced [g], [b̲], and [d̲].

TABLE 23.2: *Alphabets of Northern Italy (after Morandi 1982: 176)*

	Venetic	Rhaetic	Lepontic	Gallic	
a	𐌀𐌀	𐌀𐌀	𐌀𐌀	𐌓	a
b					b
c/g	〉	〉			c/g
d					d
e	𐌄	𐌄 𐌄	𐌄	𐌓	e
v	𐌅	𐌅	𐌅		v
z [ts]	𐌆	𐌆	𐌆		z [ts]
h	𐌇	𐌇			h
th	⊙		⊙		th
i	I	I	I	I	i
k	𐌊	𐌊	𐌊	k	k
l	𐌋	𐌋	𐌋	𐌋	l
m	𐌌𐌌𐌌	𐌌	𐌌		m
n	𐌍𐌍	𐌍	𐌍𐌍	𐌍	n
o	◇		O	O	o
p	𐌐	𐌐	𐌐	𐌐	p
ś	M	𐌞	𐌞𐌞	𐌞	ś
q					q
r	𐌓	𐌓	𐌓	D	r
s	𐌔𐌔	𐌔𐌔	𐌔𐌔	𐌔𐌔	s
t	✕𐌕	✕𐌕	𐌕✕	✕	t
u	V	V	𐌖V	V	u
ph	𐌘	𐌘			ph
ch	𐌙	𐌙	𐌙		ch
t'		↑𐌆			t'

EXAMPLES OF PUNCTUATED VENETIC

fo.u.vo.s eneijo.s doto dono. m. rumusijate. i.
Fouvos / son of Ene / gave / as a gift / to [the god] Trumusiate

'Fouvos, son of Ene, gave [this] as a gift to [the god] Trumusiate.'

mego doto vhu.g.siia volna śa.i.nale.i.re.i.tiia.i.o.p.vo.l.tiio.leno
me / gave / Fugsia / Volna / to Śainati [?] / [the goddess] Reitiia / as a voluntary / act

(The object speaks): 'Fugsia Volna gave me to [the goddess] Śainati (epithet?)
Reitiia as a voluntary act.'

SAMPLES OF VENETIC

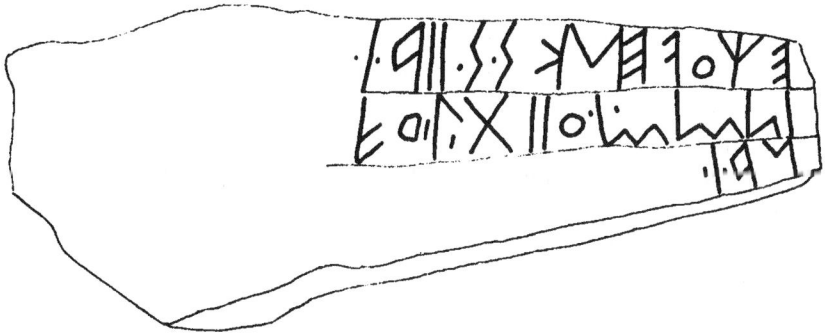

FIGURE 39. Bronze stylus (writing implement) from a votive stips at Este.
Este, Museo Nazionale Atestino.

Transliteration:	vza.n.	vhuxia.	ur.kle.i.na/	re.i.tie.i	zona.s.to
Transcription:	vdan	Fugia	Urkleina	Reitiei	donasto
Gloss:	object	Fugia	Urkleina	to.Reitia	gives

'Fugia Urkleina gives this object to (the goddess) Reitia.'
                                                                —*After Morandi 1982: 184.*

Note: *vdan* is the name of the Venetic alphabet (Lejeune 1974: 134).

FIGURE 40. Stone (trachite) cippus from the necropolis of Este, found in 1959.
Este, Museo Nazionale Atestino. Fourth century B.C.E. Boustrophedon.

.i.aiis.s.k.uhvoχ.e.←
→vo.l.tiio.m.mni.
                    .i.an←

Transliteration: .e.χo   vhu.k.s.siia.i.   vo.l.tiio.m.mni.na.i.
Transcription: ego   Fukssiai   Voltiommmninai
Gloss: I   Fukssia.DAT   Voltiommnina.DAT

'I [belong] to Fukssia Voltiommnina.'   —*After Morandi 1982: 184.*

Central and southern Italy

Faliscan, closely related to Latin, is documented by inscriptions dating from the seventh to the second centuries B.C.E. Peculiarly Faliscan (TABLE 23.1) are the shape of the letter A, which in later times looks like an R, and an arrow-shaped sign for [f]. B and Q are rarely used.

Northern Picene inscriptions (TABLE 23.3) come from Novilara, Fano, and Pesaro. *Southern Picene* inscriptions are close to Osco-Umbrian: 23 are known, from Macerata, Chieti, l'Aquila, etc. (including the one on the life-size statue of the so-called Capestrano Warrior). Much of the Southern Picene alphabet derives from the Etruscan, but two unusual characters definitely do not: A single dot (·) has the value [o] (it therefore derives not from Etruscan—since Etruscan had no O—but from Greek). Two dots (:) has the value [f]. The Southern Picene alphabet is now almost completely deciphered.

Oscan and *Umbrian* are linguistically closely related; their rich epigraphic documentation (TABLE 23.3) includes some unusual signs, and monuments handsomely inscribed with regular, squared, rubricated letters. Of the seven famous bronze Iguvine tablets from the Umbrian city of Gubbio (ca. 200–100 B.C.E.) containing instructions for religious ceremonies and rituals, the earliest are written in an Etruscan type of alphabet, the later in Latin. Oscan, the language used by several peoples of central and southern Italy, in particular the Samnites, is known to us from the bronze tablet from Agnone (in the British Museum), as well as inscriptions from Pompeii and Herculaneum; inscriptions have been found from the Abruzzi to Messina, in an area including Campania and Lucania. Three types of alphabet were used: Etruscan (on the Agnone tablet), with modifications (the use of *b, d,* and *g,* and two special signs for open *i* and *u,* transcribed *í/ú*); Greek; and Latin. In Lucania, below Taranto, *Messapic* (several hundred inscriptions, from the 6th to the 1st century B.C.E.) is written in a Greek alphabet.

TABLE 23.3: *Alphabets of Southern Italy (after Morandi 1982: 66)*

	Oscan	Umbrian	North Picene	Middle Adriatic	Messapic	
a						a
b						b
c/g						c/g
d						d
e						e
v						v
z [ts]						z [ts]
h						h
th						th
i						i
k						k
l						l
m						m
n						n
o						o
p						p
ś						ś
q						q
r						r
s						s
t						t
u						u
ṡ, x						ṡ, x
ph						ph
ch						ch
f						f

Oscan: í, ú
Umbrian: ř, ç
North Picene: ú
Middle Adriatic: í, ú
Messapic: t'

SAMPLE OF OSCAN

 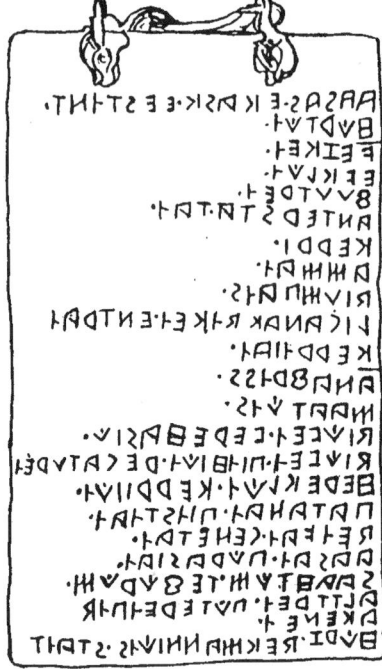

FIGURE 41. Tablet from Agnone with Oscan inscription, front *(left)* and back. Ca. 250 B.C.E.
British Museum.

1. Oscan: statús •   pús •   set • húrtín • /   kerríín •   vezkeí •
2. Gloss: ritual.places which   are   in.enclosure of.Ceres   for.Vensicus

1. statíf • /   evklúí statíf • kerrí • statíf • / futreí •   kerríiaí • státíf • /
2. stopping-place … (see translation)

1. anter • stataí • statíf • / ammaí • kerríiaí • statíf • / diumpaís • kerríiaís •

1. statíf • /   líganakdikeí • entraí • statíf • / anafríss • kerríiúís •

1. statíf • /   maatúís • kerríiúís • statíf • / díúveí • verehasiúi • statíf • /

1. díúveí • regatureí •   statíf • / hereklúí • kerríiúí • statíf • / patanaí •

1. piístíaí • statíf • / deívaí • genetaí • statíf • / aasaí • purasiaí • / saahtúm •
2.   at.altar of.fire   holy

1. tefúrúm • alttreí • / pútereípíd • akeneí • / sakahíter • / fiuusasiaís •
2. offering   other   be.sanctified to.Florae

1. az •   húrtúm • / sakarater • /   pernaí •   kerríiaí •   statíf • /   ammaí •

2. at   enclosure   be.sacrifice.SUBJ ... (see translation)

1. kerríiaí • statíf • / fluusaí •   kerríiaí •   statíf • / evklúí • patereí •   statíf • /

Reverse: 1. aasas • ekask • eestínt • /   húrtúí • / vezkeí • evklúí • /   fuutreí • /

            2. altars   these   stand   in.enclosure ... (see translation)

1. anterstataí • /   kerrí • / ammaí • / diumpaís • /   líganakdíkeí •   entraí /

1. kerríiaí • /   anafríss • /   maatúís • /   diúveí • verehasiú • /   diúveí • piíhiúí •

1. regatureí • / hereklúí • kerríiúí • / patanaí •   piístíaí • /   deívaí • genetaí • /

1. aasaí •   purasiaí • /   saahtúm • tefúrúm • /   alttreí •   pú.tereípíd • /

2. at.altar   of.fire   holy   offering   other

1. akeneí • /   húrz •   dekmanniúís •   staít •

2.   enclosure for.Decimani   stands

'The established ritual places which are in the enclosure of Ceres: The stopping-place for Vensicus; the stopping-place for Euclus; the stopping-place for Ceres; the stopping-place for Ceres' Daughter; the stopping-place for Interstita; the stopping-place for Amma; the stopping-place for the Nymphs of Ceres; the stopping-place for Liganacdix Interna; the stopping-place for the Rains of Ceres; the stopping-place for the Matis of Ceres; the stopping-place for Jupiter Juvenal; the stopping-place for Jupiter Rector, or Irrigator; the stopping-place for Hercules of Ceres; the stopping-place for Patana Pistis; the stopping-place for the Goddess Genita. At the Altar of Fire let a holy burnt offering be sanctified every other year; to the Florae by the enclosure let there be a sacrifice; the stopping-place for Perna of Ceres; the stopping-place for Amma of Ceres; the stopping-place for Flora of Ceres; the stopping-place for Euclus the Father.'

Reverse: 'These altars stand in the enclosure: for Vensicus; for Euclus; for the Daughter; for Interstita; for Ceres; for Amma; for the Nymphs; for Liganacdica Interna of Ceres; for the Rains; for the Matis; for Jupiter Juvenalis; for Jupiter Pius Rector; for Heracles of Ceres; for Patina Pistia; for Divine Genita; at the Altar of Fire a holy burnt offering every other year. The enclosure is at the disposal of the Decimani.   —*After Bonfante 1990b.*

SAMPLE OF UMBRIAN

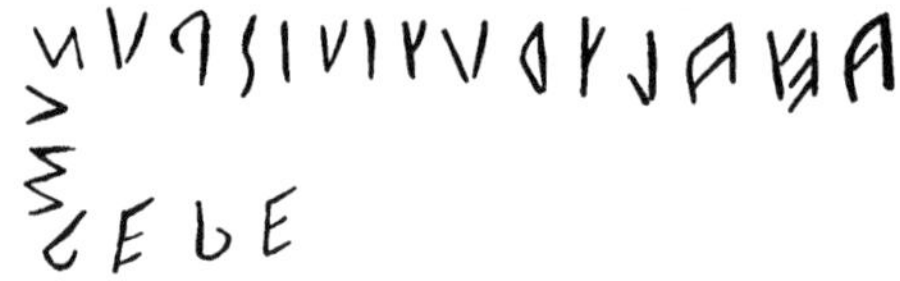

FIGURE 42. Mars from Todi: Umbrian inscription on lappet of cuirass.
Vatican, Museo Etrusco Gregoriano. Fourth century B.C.E.

Umbrian:	ahal	trutitis	dunum	dede
Gloss:	Ahal	Trutitius	gift	gave

'Ahal Trutitius gave as a gift.'   *—After Morandi 1982: 73.*

Bibliography

GENERAL

Amadasi Guzzo, Maria Giulia. 1987. *Scritture alfabetiche.* Rome: Valerio Levi Editore.
Manino, Luciano. 1981. *Antologia di testi epigrafici etruschi e italici.* Turin: Giappichelli Editore.
Morandi, Alessandro. 1982. *Epigrafia Italica.* Rome: L'Erma di Bretschneider.
Prosdocimi, Aldo L., ed. 1978A. *Popoli e civiltà dell'Italia antica,* vol. 6: *Lingue e dialetti dell'Italia antica.* Rome: Biblioteca di Storia Patria.
Reading the Past: Ancient Writing from Cuneiform to the Alphabet. 1990. Introduction by J. T. Hooker. London: British Museum; Berkeley and Los Angeles: University of California Press.

ETRUSCAN

Bonfante, Giuliano, and Larissa Bonfante. 1983. *The Etruscan Language: An Introduction.* Manchester: Manchester University Press; New York: New York University Press.
Bonfante, Larissa. 1981. *Out of Etruria: Etruscan Influence North and South* (BAR International Series 103). Oxford: British Archaeological Reports.
———. 1990A. *Etruscan* (Reading the Past). London: British Museum; Berkeley and Los Angeles: University of California Press. Repr. in *Reading the Past* 1990: 321–78.
Cristofani, Mauro. 1978. "L'alfabeto etrusco." In Prosdocimi 1978: 401–68.
———. 1979. "Recent Advances in Etruscan Epigraphy and Language." In *Italy before the Romans,* ed. David Ridgway and Francesca Serra Ridgway, pp. 373–412. London: Academic Press.
Healey, John F. 1990. *The Early Alphabet* (Reading the Past). London: British Museum; Berkeley and Los Angeles: University of California Press. Repr. in *Reading the Past* 1990: 197–258.
Pallottino, Massimo. 1978. "The Etruscan Language." In his *The Etruscans,* ed. David Ridgway, pp. 187–234. Bloomington: Indiana University Press.
Peruzzi, Emilio. 1980. *Mycenaeans in Early Latium* (Incunabula Graeca 75). Rome: Edizioni dell'Ateneo & Bizzarri.
Pfiffig, Ambros. 1969. *Die etruskische Sprache: Versuch einer Gesamtdarstellung.* Graz: Akademische Druck- und Verlagsanstalt.

EARLY LATIN

Gordon, Arthur E. 1983. *Illustrated Introduction to Latin Epigraphy.* Berkeley and Los Angeles: University of California Press.
Mansuelli, Guido. 1950–51. "L'incisore Novios Plautios." *Studi Etruschi* 21: 401–6.

Vine, Brent. 1993. *Studies in Archaic Latin Inscriptions* (Innsbrucker Beiträge zur Sprachwissenschaft 75). Innsbruck: Universität Innsbruck, Institut für Sprachwissenschaft.

Oscan and Umbrian

Bonfante, Larissa. 1990B. "Oscan: The Agnone Tablet." In Bonfante 1990A: 53–57.

Buck, Carl Darling. 1928. *A Grammar of Oscan and Umbrian, with a Collection of Inscriptions and a Glossary,* 2nd ed. Boston: Ginn. Repr. Hildesheim: Olms, 1974.

Conway, R. S., J. Whatmough, and S. E. Johnson, 1933. *The Prae-Italic Dialects of Italy.* 3 vols. Cambridge: Harvard University Press.

Prosdocimi, Aldo. 1978B. "L'umbro." In Prosdocimi 1978A: 585–788.

———. 1978C. "L'osco." In Prosdocimi 1978A: 825–912.

Vetter, Emil. 1953. *Handbuch der italischen Dialekte,* vol. 1. Heidelberg: Winter.

Other Italic Dialects

Giacomelli, Gabriella. 1978. "Il falisco." In Prosdocimi 1978A: 505–42.

Lejeune, Michel. 1974. *Manuel de la langue vénète.* Heidelberg: Winter.

Marinelli, Anna. 1985. *Le iscrizioni sudpicene,* vol. 1, *Testi.* Florence: Olschki.

Morandi, Alessandro. 1978. "Le iscrizioni medio-adriatiche." In Prosdocimi 1978A: 559–84.

Prosdocimi, Aldo L. 1978D. "Il venetico." In Prosdocimi 1978A: 256–380.

———. 1983. "Puntuazione sillabica e insegnamento della scrittura nel venetico e nelle fonti etrusche." *AIΩN* 5: 75–126.

Santoro, Ciro. 1983–84. *Nuovi studi messapici.* 3 vols. (Saggi e testi. Sez. di glottologia e dialettologia 24–26). Galatina, Italy: Congedo.

Tibiletti Bruno, Maria Grazia. 1978A. "Ligure, leponzio e gallico." In Prosdocimi 1978A: 129–208.

———. 1978B. "Camuno, retico e pararetico." In Prosdocimi 1978A: 209–55.

The Roman Alphabet

STAN KNIGHT

There is a popular notion that the evolution of the Roman script can be plotted out like a family tree, showing a single line of development from Roman times to the present day. Its history, however, is far too ancient, too complex, and too widespread for that. A multitude of influences—political, religious, esthetic, economic, or pragmatic—have been brought to bear on the way that the Roman script has been formed throughout the ages.

The original manner in which the Latin language was written down was devised over 2000 years ago (SECTION 23). Since then, Roman scripts have been used not only for Latin but also for the majority of the world's languages (SECTION 59).

The scope of this survey allows only an indication of the historical highlights in the development of the Roman script, and a hint of the more obvious causes and influences that created change.

———

Ancient Roman scripts

The earliest examples we have of Latin letters are of those carved in stone, some dating from the sixth or even seventh century B.C.E. Early Roman letters were monoline capitals of distinct form (FIGURE 43A), derived from earlier Greek models. Sometimes the text was *retrograde*, i.e. read from right to left.

By the first century C.E. the carved capitals had developed a level of sophistication and legibility which has ensured their survival to modern times in both typography and calligraphy. The detailing of these incised letters (FIGURE 43B), in the balance of their thin and thick strokes and the subtle serifing, was clearly due to preliminary planning with an edged pen or brush (see Catich 1968).

The scripts of ancient Rome can be grouped according to their use and their character: *Cursive* scripts, the informal styles used for minor documents and the everyday handwriting of the intelligentsia, most usually written with a blunt, pointed pen or stylus; and *Calligraphic* or *Book* scripts, those more formal scripts written by professional scribes for large-scale literary manuscripts, using a specially cut edged pen which produces the characteristic thick and thin strokes.

A. Vatican. Dedication to Hercules. ca. 144 B.C.E.

B. Rome, Appian Way. 1st or 2nd century C.E.

C. British Library, Papyrus 229. 166 C.E. (*nomine abban quem eutychon sive quo alio nomine*).

D. Vatican Library, Ms. Pal.Lat.1631. 4th or 5th century.

E. Oxford, Bodleian Library, Ms. Auct.T.2.26. Mid 5th century.

F. Bamberg, Staatsbibliothek, Ms.Patr.87. 6th century.

G. Vatican Library, Vat.Lat.3256. 4th or 5th century.

H. British Library, Papyrus 447. ca. 345 C.E. (*crum comitatum vestrum tirones ex provincia*).

FIGURE 43. Ancient Roman scripts. A. Monoline capitals. B. Inscriptional capitals. C. Old Roman Cursive. D. Rustic capitals. E. Uncials. F. Half Uncials. G. Square capitals. H. New Roman Cursive.

Old Roman Cursive

The earliest known handwritten Latin document can be traced to the first century B.C.E. Old Roman Cursive dates from some time before that and lasts into the third century C.E. (FIGURE 43C). The script bears some features of the earliest Latin inscriptions; but since it is written quickly (*cursive* means 'running') and inconsistently, there is a loss of legibility. Some letters were remodeled, others became linked together (in *ligatures*), and abbreviations are common. Following the epigraphic pattern, little or no word space is allowed. This script was ideally suited for the stylus and wax tablet, and can even be seen in the graffiti of Pompeii (see Aris 1990: I.4).

Rustic Capitals

The earliest fully developed Latin book script was Rustic Capitals, and we know of examples from the first century C.E. The Gallus Fragment may even date from as early as 22 B.C.E. (see Knight 1984, Introduction). Despite its unsophisticated name, this is a mature, calligraphic script used for many deluxe manuscripts (FIGURE 43D). It has narrow letterforms and a very steep pen angle (the edge of the pen held at almost 90° to the writing line). Following Old Roman Cursive, the **A** often lacks a crossbar, the **M** is widely spread, and the bowl of **R** overlaps the vertical stem. The words are divided with a centered point in the epigraphic manner.

Uncial scripts

Uncial was a popular script in common use from the fourth to eighth centuries for the text of books (FIGURE 43E). Most of the earliest surviving Uncial manuscripts have their origins in northern Africa. The oldest datable Uncial script is from Hippo and was written some time between 396 and 426 (see Lowe 1934–72 Suppl.: vii–x, also Knight 1984: B4). Later, Uncials were used in Italy (particularly in Rome) mostly for biblical texts; and through missionary activity the script spread to other parts of the Empire, including Britain, where it reached a very high level of accomplishment. However, the notion that Uncials were deliberately devised as a Christian book hand, to replace Rustic and Square Capitals used for "pagan" classics, cannot be maintained (see Woodcock and Knight 1992: 38).

Uncials did not evolve directly from Rustic Capitals; Rustics are constructed differently, using a much steeper pen angle—compare the forms of **A**, **D**, **E**, and **R**. The particular characteristics of Uncial scripts include **A** with a bowl, round forms of **D**, **E**, **H**, **M**, ascenders for **D**, **H**, **K**, **L**, and descenders for **F**, **G**, **P**, **Q**.

Half Uncial scripts

These scripts were first called Half Uncials in the mistaken idea that they were a degenerate form of Uncials. However, early Uncials used a slanted, natural pen angle evolving from scripts like that of the *De Bellis Macedonis* fragment (written perhaps as early as 100 C.E.). This shows a mixed script with discernible Uncial characteristics (see M. Brown 1990: 22–23; Knight 1984: Intro. fig. 5).

Early Half Uncials, which appeared in the fourth century, derived from scripts like that of the fragment of Livy's *Epitome* written early in the third century (Aris 1990: II,2; Knight 1984: Intro. fig. 1). Both use a flattened pen angle (the edge of the pen held parallel to the writing line).

The characteristics of Half Uncials (FIGURE 43F) are long ascenders **b, d, f, h, l** and descenders **f, g, p, q**; long **s**; round forms of **a** and **t**; "figure 5" **g**; **m** with a straight first stroke and curving end stroke; and "capital" form of **N**.

Square Capitals

Written versions of Imperial carved letters were employed for the text of prestigious manuscripts of Virgil in the fourth and fifth centuries (FIGURE 43G). They follow the inscriptional capitals in letterform and generous spacing, but their detailed character was extremely difficult for the scribe and slowed down the writing. T. J. Brown (pers. comm.) rightly regarded the use of such capitals for manuscript texts as "a late idea and a bad one"!

Only two ancient Square Capital manuscripts survive, both in fragments: Codex Sangallensis (St. Gallen, Stiftsbibliothek, Ms.Cod. 1394, pp. 7–49) and Codex Augusteus (four folios in the Vatican, Ms.Lat. 3256, and three folios in Berlin, Deutsche Staatsbibliothek, Ms.Lat. F.416).

New Roman Cursive

This rapid script, the result of a reform of Old Roman Cursive (completed by the 4th century), was the administration and correspondence script of Late Antiquity (FIGURE 43H). The speed of writing, together with the greater use of ligatures and cursive loops (a minimal **a**, and diagonal headstrokes on certain letters like **c** and **e**), make this a difficult script to read.

New Roman Cursive, however, was widely used and would play an important part in the development of the later Regional scripts.

Regional hands

These are the various scripts which arose in local centers as, in the fifth century, the control of the Roman Empire declined. New Roman Cursive mixed with Half Uncial

A. British Library, Add. Ms.11878. Mid 8th century (*citr^u quia unus quisque praedicator arro*).

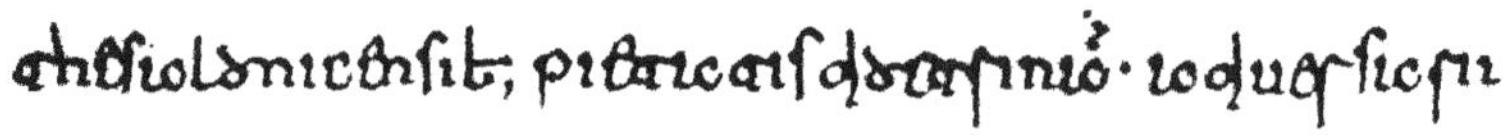

B. British Library, Harley Ms.3063. End 8th century (*thesalonicensib(us), pietatis doctrina(m) adversarii*).

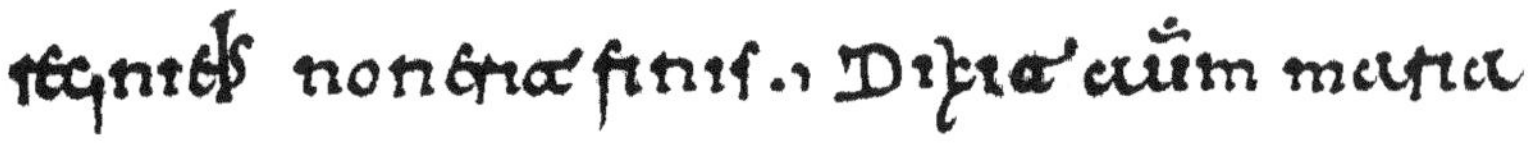

C. British Library, Add. Ms.30844. 10th century (*regnieis non estia finis. Dixit au(te)m maria*).

D. Briish Library, Add. Ms. 16413. Early 9th century (*dixit caelo esse qui nos creavit et dicimus*).

FIGURE 44. Regional scripts. A. Luxeuil Minuscule. B. Corbie ab. C. Visigothic Minuscule.
D. Beneventan Minuscule.

formed the main ingredients of these diverse minuscule scripts, which generally flourished from the fifth through the eighth centuries (see M. Brown 1990: 32–47). We can survey here only the most important.

Luxeuil Minuscule

This script was developed at the end of the seventh and early eighth centuries at the French abbey founded by the Irish missionary Columbanus. It was E. A. Lowe (1972: 2.389–98) who identified the original source of this very distinctive script.

Luxeuil Minuscule (FIGURE 44A) is a rather angular script with many unusual letterforms—a like double c, tall, ampersand-like e, g with a looped top, and a high-shouldered r. The use of looping ligatures, e.g. er, ro, rs, te, and tr, adds to the difficulty in deciphering this script. It derives from New Roman Cursive (by way of the Merovingian chancery) with some Half Uncial features. By this time, word separation was fairly consistently used.

Corbie ab

Another French minuscule is linked with the Abbey of Corbie, founded from Luxeuil ca. 661 C.E. The Corbie connection, however, has been questioned (see Ganz 1990).

Corbie ab has many of the features of Luxeuil Minuscule, but a and b are particularly distinctive (FIGURE 44B). The a looks more like u, b like a tall t. In addition, e is tall, the strokes of **o** often cross at the top (especially when ligatured), it has a long **r**, tall **s**, and a looped entrance to **t**. Word separation is inconsistent.

Visigothic Minuscule

This Spanish local script depends more on Half Uncial than New Roman Cursive and this, together with the use of some Uncial letters (e.g. **D** and **G**), makes it an altogether more legible script (FIGURE 44C).

A few simple ligatures persist. The letter **a** is open like a double c, **t** has a large looped entrance stroke which could be confused with a round a. Other features include the distinctive abbreviation marks, heavy triangular serifs on the ascenders, and ornate versions of **x** and **z**.

Because of its comparative isolation, Visigothic Minuscule had a long life, surviving until the twelfth century.

Beneventan Minuscule

Developed in southern Italy from the middle of the eighth century, this script survived locally until early in the fourteenth century, even in some places until the fifteenth century. It derives some features from New Roman Cursive, but most from Half Uncial. E. A. Lowe (1980) made a special study of this script.

Beneventan Minuscule is a self-consciously stylish script (FIGURE 44D). The letter **a** has a closed double c form, **d** is "uncial," **e** looks more like an ampersand, and **t** has a large, looped entrance. Some simple ligatures are retained. Overall there is a wavy aspect to the script, particularly in **i**, **m**, **n**, and **u**, most prominent in eleventh-century examples due to the steeper pen angle used then.

Insular scripts

Following the departure of the Romans from Britain, there developed an extensive and coherent pattern of scripts, originating in Christian Ireland. Vigorous Irish missionary activity took the scripts to northern England and eventually many parts of Europe. Later, fine versions of Roman Uncials were incorporated into the system (but never in Ireland).

The term *Insular* refers to scripts of the British Isles up to the mid ninth century and is often used when Anglo-Saxon or Irish origin is uncertain.

Insular Minuscule

A system of minuscule scripts deriving from such everyday cursive hands as that of St. Boniface (see Lowe 1934–72, vol. 2, p. 237) reached (by the 8th century) a mature enough form to be used for fine manuscript books (FIGURE 45A). Word division and

* Etur continuo disciplina divinae legis*

A. Oxford, Ms.Bodl.819. 2nd half 8th century (*etur continuo disciplina divinae legis*).

scribserunt awritton lucas evangelista ðe godspellere

B. British Library, Cotton Ms.Nero.D.iv. ca. 698 C.E (*scribserunt* awritton *lucas evangelista* ðe godspellere).

Dixit inimicus perssequens comprehenda partibo

C. British Library, Add. Ms. 37517. Ca. 1000 C.E. (*Dixit inimicus perssequens comprehenda(m) partibo*).

FIGURE 45. Insular scripts. A. Insular Minuscule. B. Insular Half Uncial; Anglo-Saxon Cursive (in the glosses to the Latin text). C. Anglo-Saxon Square Minuscule.

punctuation are quite consistent. Numerous ligatures and abbreviations occur. **a** and **d** are open; **c** and **e** are tall (especially in ligature); **p**, **r**, and **s** all have descenders and are very similar in appearance. Overall, the aspect is of a compressed letterform written with a steeply slanted pen.

Insular Half Uncial

These more formal book scripts, so characteristic of Insular manuscripts, probably originated in Ireland as a modification of the Roman Half Uncial. One of the earliest known Irish manuscripts, ca. 600 C.E., reveals a script somewhere between the two (see Lowe 1934–72, vol. 2, p. 271).

The majestic script of the Gospels written at Lindisfarne, ca. 698 C.E., shows Insular Half Uncial at its most developed stage (FIGURE 45B). These are heavy, rounded letters written with a flattened pen angle. The characteristic forms are **a**, **b**, **g**, **l**, and **n**. Alternative "uncial" forms of **A**, **D**, **N**, **R**, and **S** occur, perhaps due to the influence of the nearby Wearmouth-Jarrow scriptoria and their magnificent Uncial scripts. The interlinear gloss, added in the mid tenth century in Anglo-Saxon Cursive, is the earliest surviving English translation of the Gospels.

Anglo-Saxon Minuscules

From the middle of the tenth century, Carolingian Minuscule was used in England for Latin texts. Old English texts continued to be written in Anglo-Saxon Pointed Minuscule, a script which survived until the mid twelfth century. Anglo-Saxon Square Minuscules of the tenth and early eleventh centuries were perhaps an attempt to incorporate some Carolingian influence into the local script (FIGURE 45C).

Carolingian Minuscule

The reforms of Charlemagne, in the late eighth and early ninth centuries, encouraged the use of a legible and beautiful book script which emerged in the calligraphic centers under his influence in France. Carolingian Minuscule evolved from the ancient Roman Half Uncial script and incorporated certain features from local minuscule scripts. Early manuscripts from the Abbey at Corbie show how Half Uncial could be modified to a more minuscule form (FIGURE 46A).

Compared to the many barely readable cursive and over-elaborate regional scripts, the mature Carolingian Minuscule was a disciplined and formal script, capable of maintaining legibility even at extremely small sizes (FIGURE 46B).

The general aspect is of a flowing, rounded script with long ascenders and descenders, creating a very even texture. It employs a slightly slanted pen angle (rather than the flattened angle of the Half Uncial) and maintains a more defined body height. Certain letterforms were improved—Uncial **a** soon replaced the Half Uncial form, and the distinctive looped **g** (like the one used in Luxeuil Minuscule) replaced the "figure 5" form. Very few ligatures are used; in some Carolingian manuscripts there are none.

The emergence of the Carolingian Minuscule is one of the most important developments in the history of Western calligraphy. It became an international script and was copied and adapted in succeeding centuries by scribes in all areas under Carolingian rule.

A. Amiens, Bibliothèque Municipale, Ms. 11. ca. 772–781 C.E.

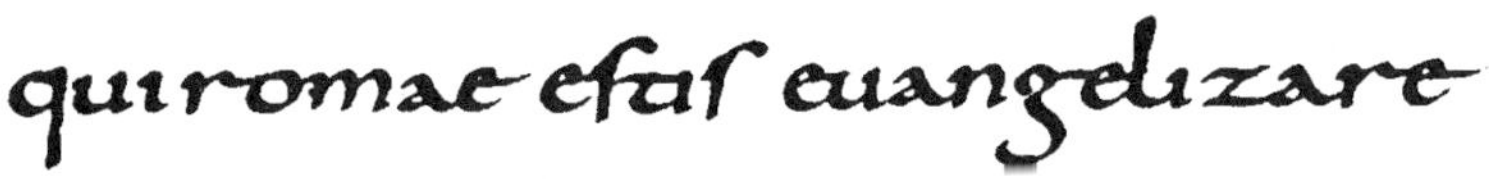

B. British Library, Add. Ms.10546. ca. 834–843 C.E.

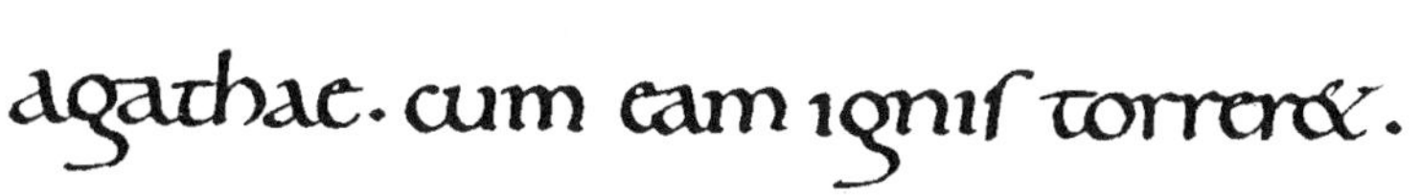

C. British Library, Add. Ms.49598. Ca. 963–984 C.E.

D. Private collection, Life of St. Ursula. Mid 12th century.

FIGURE 46. Carolingian Minuscule. A. Modified Half Uncial. B. Carolingian Minuscule. C. English Carolingian Minuscule. D. Italian Carolingian Minuscule.

English Carolingian Minuscule

Following ecclesiastical reforms in the mid tenth century, English scribes wrote a very distinctive version of Carolingian Minuscule (FIGURE 46C). Larger in scale and more formal in structure, it maintains many of the features of the earlier French Carolingian Minuscule—"uncial" **a** and **h**, looped **g**, long **s**, and "half uncial" **t**. The use of **&** to represent *-et-* within a word seems peculiar to Anglo-Saxon manuscripts. A number of cursive ligatures occur and abbreviation is common.

English Carolingian Minuscule at its best is a supremely legible and calligraphic script. It was generally reserved for Latin texts and lasted to the end of the eleventh century.

Italian Carolingian Minuscule

Carolingian Minuscule reached Italy at an early stage. (Charlemagne was crowned Holy Roman Emperor in the year 800.) It was used for books and documents from the ninth through the thirteenth centuries, alongside Beneventan Minuscule and other more cursive scripts, such as the Papal Documentary (see M. Brown 1990: 116–21).

Italian Carolingian Minuscule (FIGURE 46D) reached its peak in the twelfth century and rivals the achievements of English tenth-century scribes. The round, upright letters are quite heavy, but they are well constructed and confidently written. Discreet serifs were added to the base of the first stems of **m** and **n**.

This is the script which, later, was revived by Humanist scholars and printers.

Gothic scripts

The rise of the secular universities and the expansion of the monastic system in the twelfth century prompted the need for many more books. Different grades of scripts were employed during this period to cope with the demand (see M. Brown 1990: 80–115).

Transitional Gothic

Gothic scripts developed directly from Carolingian Minuscule, and the period of transition from the mid eleventh century through the end of the twelfth produced scripts of increasing compression and angularity, sometimes referred to as *Protogothic* (FIGURE 47A).

The letterforms of Transitional Gothic are narrow, with a hint of angularity. The "waistline" serifs are heavy, and the base terminations are more elaborate than before.

A. British Library, Cotton Ms.Tib. B.viii. Late 12th century.

B. British Library, Royal Ms.2. B.vii. Ca. 1310–20.

C. Cambridge, Fitzwilliam Museum, Ms.298. Ca. 1300.

D. Private collection, Carvajal Missal. Ca. 1520.

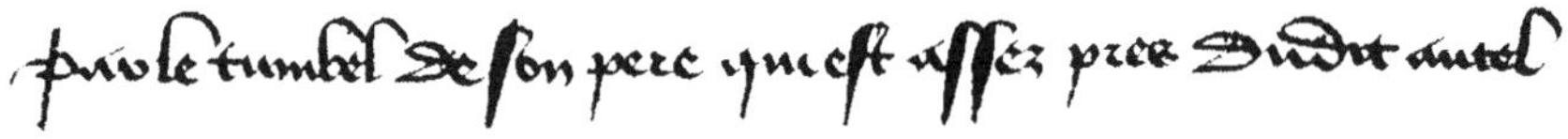

E. British Library, Harley Ms.1319. Early 15th c. (*pao le tumbel de son pere qui est assez pres sudit autel*).

F. British Library, Royal Ms. 19.C.viii. Ca. 1496. (*Roes de son fait La premiere*).

FIGURE 47. Gothic scripts. A. Transitional Gothic. B. Gothic Prescissus. C. Gothic Quadrata. D. Gothic Rotunda. E. Secretary script. F. Gothic Bâtarde.

Gothic Prescissus

The features of fully developed Gothic book scripts from the end of the twelfth century are lateral compression, heavy weight, and sharp angularity. Additional details include the usual use of the "figure 2" **r** (when following **o** and other curved letters), and the sharing of stems (*biting*) of certain letters (e.g. **b**, **d**, and **p** before **e** or **o**).

Prescissus scripts are high-grade, sophisticated scripts whose letter stems (e.g. **m** and **n**) are cut off square at the baseline (FIGURE 47B). Numerous alternative forms are used—**d** in both round and upright forms, **r** in branching and "figure 2" shapes, and **s** both round and long.

Gothic Quadrata

Another sophisticated series of scripts, which have consistently angled baseline terminations (FIGURE 47C). The letter **i**, for example, is made in three movements. That **i** shape is repeated as part of so many letters that it results in the "picket fence" effect so characteristic of Gothic scripts.

Fifteenth- and sixteenth-century versions of this script became extremely difficult to read because they are even more compressed, and the baseline terminations are invariably made with elaborate, overlapping lozenge-shaped strokes.

Gothic Rotunda

In Spain and Italy, rigidly angular Gothic scripts were largely avoided. Instead, a book script evolved in the thirteenth century (continuing in places until the 18th century) which was truly Gothic, but was more rounded. Gothic Rotunda (FIGURE 47D) was widely used for liturgical texts, ranging from tiny, personal Books of Hours to enormous ceremonial manuscripts (often with musical notation).

This script has the texture and heavy appearance of the northern Gothics, but it maintains the roundness of the Carolingian minuscule. The letters **D** and **h** take Uncial form. Both forms of **r** and **s** are used (round **s** is reserved for word endings). The unusual form of **g** is unique to Gothic Rotunda. Like all Gothic scripts, Rotunda is written with a slanted pen angle, the square baseline terminations being completed with a corner of the pen.

Gothic Bâtarde

The Gothic period saw a revival of true cursive scripts, introduced first in England at the end of the twelfth century. Many of these scripts incorporate impressive calligraphic flourishes and other decorative features. The Secretary script, as its name implies, was primarily used for correspondence and other informal documents (FIGURE 47E). This script has an angular, pointed look with mannered pen flourishes and a swelling applied to certain ascending letters (especially **f** and long **s**). From the end of the thirteenth century, cursives were accepted for use as book scripts, especially those intended for universities.

Later in the Gothic period, a number of mixed scripts appeared, combining elements of cursive and book scripts, e.g. Bastard Secretary (see M. Brown 1990: 108f.).

The formalized book script evolving from Secretary, Gothic Bâtarde, is particularly associated with the Court at Burgundy in northern France (FIGURE 47F). It retains many of the vanities and peculiar letterforms of the Secretary Script (e.g. **r** and short **s**), while having the formality and texture of other Gothic book scripts.

Humanist scripts

Humanist scholars at the beginning of the fifteenth century began a reformation of scripts, in a conscious effort to improve legibility and elegance in book design. That Humanist approach was deliberately opposed to the prevailing Gothic style of northern Europe.

Humanist Minuscule

Poggio Bracciolini of Florence has been credited with the revival, in 1402–1403, of Carolingian Minuscule based on twelfth-century Italian models. Undoubtedly he worked in collaboration with other scholars (see Ullman 1932: 140–43, Aris 1990: 21, Knight 1984: F3).

Humanist Minuscule is usually written small, with lengthened ascenders and descenders (FIGURE 48A). Carolingian characteristics are retained—Uncial **h**, long **s**, and **ct** and **st** ligatures. Later Humanist Minuscule includes short **s** at word endings.

Humanist Cursive

A quickly written form of Humanist Minuscule was devised by Niccolò Niccoli, ca. 1420. This new book script, which we now refer to as Italic, has a more cursive aspect than the minuscule—a forward slant, and some letter joins (FIGURE 48B).

Humanist Italic

Formal versions of this Cursive script were developed by Papal Chancery scribes, like Ludovico degli Arrighi (FIGURE 48C). The names they gave to these scripts varied

A. British Library, Yates Thompson Ms.7. Ca. 1515.

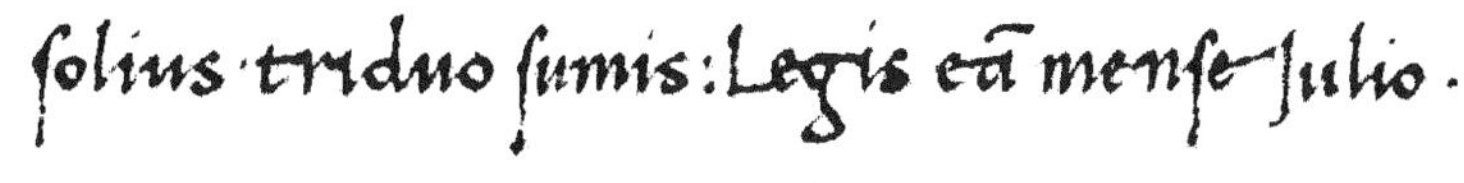

B. British Library, Add. Ms.21115. Late 15th century.

C. British Library, Royal Ms. 12.C.viii. Ca. 1517.

FIGURE 48. Humanist scripts. A. Humanist Minuscule. B. Humanist Cursive. C. Humanist Italic.

from scribe to scribe. The writing master Bernardino Cantaneo distinguished two major types: Cancellaresca Formata, with rounded arches on **m** and **n** and serifed ascenders; and Cancellaresca Corsiva, with narrower, pointed arches and hooked ascenders.

Cursive writing from the sixteenth century

Humanist Cursive, following the *cancellaresca* style of the writing masters such as Arrighi, was the handwriting of choice for Europe's intelligentsia and nobility in the sixteenth century. Cellini, Raphael, the left-handed Michelangelo, even Queen Elizabeth I (FIGURE 49A) all wrote in the "Italian" manner.

The Secretary Hand, a cursive lightweight Gothic script, evolved in England during the first half of the sixteenth century and endured for business use for more than a century. A variety of Gothic cursive first seen in the sixteenth century, Kurrentschrift, was taught in Germany and Austria as everyday handwriting until the end of World War II (SECTION 63). In France the Ronde style was introduced ca. 1650, retaining a few Gothic letterforms, and it survived in certain places in France to the late twentieth century.

G. F. Cresci, in his manual of 1570, introduced a rather mannered version of *cancellaresca*. It was rounder, with greater slope, looser texture, and "blobbed" ascenders. Varieties of this "Italian Round Hand" were popular in the seventeenth century in the American Colonies and many European countries.

The pointed pen

The evolution of copperplate printing for book illustrations led to the use of a flexible, pointed pen (rather than the edged pen) to produce strongly contrasted thick and thin strokes (FIGURE 49B). John Ayres' *Writing Book*, published in England in 1680, illustrated the new Copperplate style with its looping flourishes and ligatures, and its rather over-ornate capitals.

Early American manuals, like that of Benjamin Franklin (1748), relied heavily on imported European models. It was not until one hundred years later that the uniquely American Spencerian style emerged. P. R. Spencer developed, as a "Commercial Cursive," a monoline copperplate hand with occasional, almost random, use of thick strokes. Numerous attempts to simplify the Spencerian approach followed (FIGURE 49C). The two most publicized, by C. P. Zaner (1895) and Austin Palmer (1901), retained their influence and popularity in USA school systems throughout the twentieth century. Their only competitor was Manuscript, recommended in 1924 by Marjorie Wise, a skeletal Roman form taught to young children as unjoined letters (FIGURE 49D).

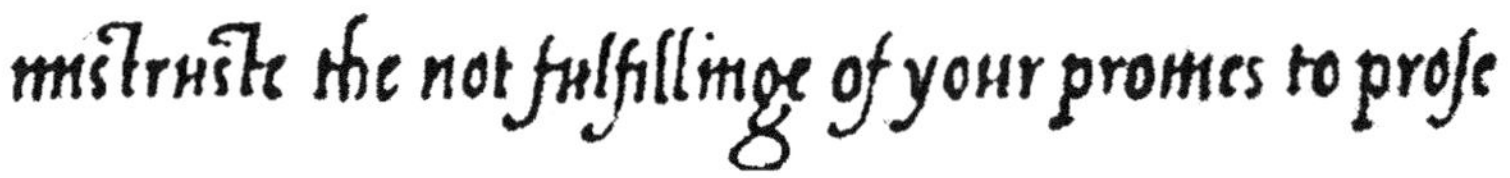

mistrust the not fulfilling of your promes to prose

A. Letter written by Queen Elizabeth I of England when a young girl. 1548.

am well pleasd wᵗʰ yo̓ performance in Writing

B. George Shelley, from *Penmanship in Its Utmost Beauty*. London, 1731.

It was during one of my sum

C. H. W. Ellsworth, from *The Penman's Art Journal*. New York, 1907.

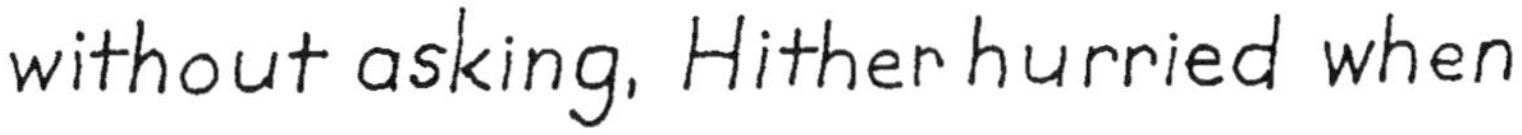

without asking, Hither hurried when

D. Marjorie Wise, from *On the Technique of Manuscript Writing*. New York, 1924.

FIGURE 49. Cursive writing from the sixteenth century. A. Cancellaresca. B. Copperplate. C. Commercial cursive. D. Manuscript.

In England in the early twentieth century, simplified Copperplate models, like that of Vere Foster, were the most common in educational use, though a type of Manuscript or Printscript superseded them.

Italic revival

A return to *cancellaresca* was pioneered by Alfred Fairbank with his *Handwriting Manual* (1932). This italic revival has gained ground in many British schools and has spread to certain parts of Europe, the British Commonwealth, and the USA. Along with an English Carolingian Minuscule favored by the British pioneer, Edward Johnston (1872–1944), *cancellaresca* underlies the craft of calligraphy that has won increasing popularity through the twentieth century.

The printed word

The invention of printing by movable metal type in the fifteenth century was, eventually, to bring to an end the very long tradition of copying books by hand. Significantly, the early printers relied heavily on the methods, *mise-en-page*, and letterforms of calligraphy they knew. Some scribes became involved in the new technology by hand-lettering initials in printed books, and even by designing typefaces.

Mainz

Johann Gutenberg's experiments with movable type in Mainz, as early as 1436, led the way in the development of a practical method for making books by means of printing. His first printed work, the so-called 42-line Bible (ca. 1456), uses the format, style, and late Gothic Quadrata script of contemporary German manuscripts (FIGURE 50A). He followed the calligraphic practice of abbreviations, ligatures, and even biting. Marginal initials and other letters were written in by hand (usually in red, hence *rubricated*).

Johann Fust and his son-in-law Peter Schöffer, a French calligrapher, using Gutenberg's machinery (and perhaps his types), produced one of the most beautifully printed books of all time, the Mainz Psalter of 1457 (FIGURE 50B). It incorporates a magnificent Gothic Quadrata typeface, large two-color initials, and small capitals rubricated by hand. Some of the copies were actually printed on vellum.

The invasion of the city of Mainz in 1462, causing the dispersion of printers, among others, hastened the spread of printing to other cities in Europe, most significantly to Venice.

The typeface used in the first printing in England, by William Caxton (dated 13 December 1476), was based on the popular Gothic Bâtarde script.

Venice

As in Germany, the first printers in Venice looked to contemporary scribal manuscripts for their models. Thus Humanist Minuscule (ultimately derived from the ancient Carolingian Minuscule) provided the inspiration for the first Italian typefaces, and the *mise-en-page* reflected the airiness and elegance of Humanist manuscripts. Capitals were based on calligraphic examples of classical Roman Square Capital forms.

Nicolas Jenson, a Frenchman who moved to Venice (probably via Mainz), produced the first Roman type for his Eusebius of 1470 (FIGURE 50C).

Three years later, Aldus Manutius established himself as a printer in Venice. He refined Jenson's approach and improved the presswork, using lighter inking. He collaborated with Francesco Griffo, a scribe and punchcutter, who designed type with capitals slightly shorter than the ascenders (as in calligraphy) to produce a better balanced page of text. This Venetian "white page" typography set the pattern which is followed to this day.

Griffo also designed a Chancery Italic type, based on his own writing. It was first used in an edition of Virgil's *Opera*, printed by Aldus in 1501 (FIGURE 50D). The italic was not used just for emphasis, as today. It was designed to condense the text and make books a more convenient size to handle. Other scribes, most notably Ludovico degli Arrighi, also designed italic typefaces.

Dñuicie xp̃ianoꝝ.Ⱥi habes ĩ poteſtate

A. Gutenberg, 42-line Bible. Ca. 1456.

obꝓobriũ hp̃m ꝫ abiectio plebis Ⓞ ñies

B. Schöffer & Fust, Mainz Psalter. 1457.

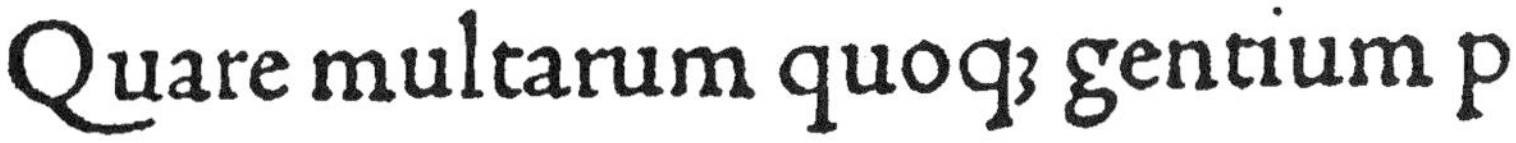

Quare multarum quoqꝫ gentium p

C. Jenson, Eusebius. 1470.

P rincipio, ſedes apibus, ſtatio᷎qꝫ petenda

D. Manutius and Griffo, Virgil. 1501.

FIGURE 50. Historical type specimens. A, B. Early types from Mainz. C. The first Roman type. D. The first Italic type.

Garamond

During the second quarter of the sixteenth century, the leadership in typography passed to France. The new Roman type was primarily the work of the typefounder Claude Garamond. It was still Venetian in character, but more refined and less mannered. The fitting of the letters was much smoother. The typeface was conceived as a harmonious family of capitals, lowercase, and italics. The italics were intended not as a separate book face, but to be used within the text for emphasis and contrast.

Modern versions of the Garamond style often mistakenly follow the later types of Jean Jannon. The most "authentic" modern revival is the Adobe Garamond of 1989 (FIGURE 51A), based on an original Garamond specimen sheet of 1492. The Adobe italics, also derived from the 1492 sheet, were originally designed by Robert Granjon, a colleague of Garamond.

Caslon

An Englishman, William Caslon, much improved on the imported Dutch types of the time. His first specimen sheet of 1734 showed Roman letters with more personality than previously (FIGURE 51B). His italic, supplied with many Baroque flourishes and swash capitals, was more dependent on pointed than edged pen calligraphy. It has an especially flamboyant **&**. It is noteworthy that the first printings of the American Declaration of Independence and the United States Constitution used Caslon's type.

Baskerville

John Baskerville, another energetic Englishman, designed a lighter, more elegant Roman typeface, used first for the printing of Virgil's *Georgicon* in 1757 (FIGURE 51C). His background as a writing teacher shows especially in his italics. To be able to print it properly he had to devise machinery, new ink, and even a smoother paper.

Baskerville typefaces are usually described as *Transitional*—moving away from the sixteenth-century *Old Style* of Garamond (with diagonal accent, heavy thin strokes, and angled serifs), toward the late eighteenth century *Modern* of Didot and Bodoni (with vertical accent, hairline thin strokes, and horizontal serifs).

Bodoni

Radically different Roman typestyles emerged in France in the mid eighteenth century from the typefoundries of Fournier and Didot. These were copied and refined by Giambattista Bodoni of Parma, Italy (FIGURE 51D). His typefaces were dark in color yet razor-sharp, requiring very smooth paper like that of Baskerville. They were characterized by a strong thick-and-thin contrast, flat hairline serifs, and a horizontal accent (i.e. the thickest parts of the **O** occur at 9 o'clock and 3 o'clock).

The nineteenth century

Typography was greatly influenced in the nineteenth century by commercial advertising's demand for large, bold letters. (The first sans serif letters in type were produced by the William Caslon Company in 1816.) Three typical styles emerged: Egyptians, with slab or slab-bracketed serifs (e.g. Clarendon, Rockwell, and Playbill; FIGURE 51E); Ornates and Fat Faces (e.g. Thorowgood Italic, Ultra Bodoni, and numerous decorative capitals); and "Gothics," heavy sans serif letters (e.g. Franklin Gothic and Grotesque 216).

The twentieth century

Roman type in the twentieth century has evolved in two ways: First, in the search for "authentic" versions of classic typefaces like Bruce Rogers's Centaur (Monotype, 1929), a Jenson revival (FIGURE 51F); Slimbach's Garamond (Adobe, 1989); Louis Hoell's Bodoni (Bauer, 1924); and Adrian Frutiger's Univers (Deberny and Peignot, 1957), a harmonized family of "Gothic" sans serif typefaces. Second, in innovation, for example like Paul Renner's Futura (Bauer, 1928), a sans serif based on geometric shapes; and Eric Gill's Gill Sans (Monotype, 1928), a sans serif following the proportions of Roman capitals. There are also unusual serif faces like Gill's epigraphic Perpetua (Monotype, 1929); Hermann Zapf's Melior (Stempel, 1952), with its

ABCDEFGHIJKLMNOPQRSTUVWXYZ

abcdefghijklmnopqrstuvwxyz &

abcdefghijklmnopqrstuvwxyz

A. Adobe Garamond, Robert Slimbach. 1989.

ABCDEFGHIJKLMNOPQRSTUVWXYZ

abcdefghijklmnopqrstuvwxyz &

abcdefghijklmnopqrstuvwxyz

B. Adobe Caslon, Carol Twombly. 1990.

ABCDEFGHIJKLMNOPQRSTUVWXYZ

abcdefghijklmnopqrstuvwxyz &

abcdefghijklmnopqrstuvwxyz

C. Monotype Baskerville. 1923.

ABCDEFGHIJKLMNOPQRSTUVWXYZ

abcdefghijklmnopqrstuvwxyz &

abcdefghijklmnopqrstuvwxyz

D. Bauer Bodoni, Louis Hoell. 1924.

ABCDEFGHIJKLMNOPQRSTUVWXYZ

abcdefghijklmnopqrstuvwxyz &

E. Stephenson Blake Playbill. 1938.

ABCDEFGHIJKLMNOPQRSTUVWXYZ

abcdefghijklmnopqrstuvwxyz &

F. Monotype Centaur, Bruce Rogers. 1929.

ABCDEFGHIJKLMNOPQRSTUVWXYZ

abcdefghijklmnopqrstuvwxyz &

G. Linotype Optima, Hermann Zapf. 1958.

FIGURE 51. Contemporary versions of traditional and modern typefaces.

extraordinary elliptical shape; and Zapf's Optima (Stempel, 1958), a serifless Roman (FIGURE 51G).

Fundamentally, little has changed. The capital letters we use still follow the Classical Roman forms of 2000 years ago, and our lowercase letters depend heavily on the ninth-century Carolingian Minuscule from France.

Bibliography

GENERAL

Anderson, Donald M. 1969. *The Art of Written Forms*. New York: Holt, Rinehart and Winston.
Aris, Rutherford. 1987. "A Sequence of Scripts." *The Scribe* (London) 41: 7–12.
———. 1990. *Explicatio Formarum Litterarum*. St. Paul, Minn.: The Calligraphy Connection.
Bischoff, Bernhard. 1990. *Latin Palaeography: Antiquity and the Middle Ages*, trans. Dáibhí Ó Cróinín and David Ganz. Cambridge: Cambridge University Press. (German original, 1979.)
Boyle, Leonard E. 1984. *Medieval Latin Palaeography: A Bibliographical Introduction*. Toronto: University of Toronto Press.
Brown, Michelle P. 1990. *A Guide to Western Historical Scripts from Antiquity to 1600*. London: The British Library.
Brown, T. Julian. 1974. "Palaeography." *New Cambridge Bibliography of English Literature*, vol. 1, cols. 209–20. Cambridge: Cambridge University Press.
———. 1993A. *A Palaeographer's View: Selected Writings of Julian Brown*, ed. Janet Bately, Michelle P. Brown, and Jane Roberts. London: Harvey Miller; New York: Oxford University Press.
———. 1993B. "Aspects of Palaeography." In Brown 1993A: 47–78.
Diringer, David. 1968. *The Alphabet*, 3rd ed. 2 vols. London: Hutchinson; New York: Funk & Wagnalls.
Knight, Stan. 1984. *Historical Scripts*. London: A. & C. Black; New York: Taplinger.
Lowe, E. A., ed. 1934–72. *Codices Latini Antiquiores: A Palaeographical Guide to Latin Manuscripts Prior to the Ninth Century*. 11 vols plus Supplement. Oxford: Clarendon.
———. 1969. *Handwriting: Our Medieval Legacy*. Rev. ed. Rome: Edizioni di Storia e Letteratura. (Orig. pub. in *The Legacy of the Middle Ages*, ed. Charles G. Crump. Oxford: Clarendon, 1926.)
———. 1972. *Palaeographical Papers (1907–1965)*, ed. Ludwig Bieler. 2 vols. Oxford: Clarendon.
Morison, Stanley. 1972. *Politics and Script*, ed. Nicolas Barker. Oxford: Clarendon.
Thompson, E. Maunde. 1912. *Introduction to Greek and Latin Palaeography*. Oxford: Oxford University Press.
Woodcock, John, and Stan Knight. 1992. *A Book of Formal Scripts*. London: A. & C. Black; Boston: Godine.

ROMAN SCRIPTS

Catich, Edward M. 1961. *The Trajan Inscription in Rome*. Davenport, Iowa: Catfish Press.
———. 1968. *The Origin of the Serif*. Davenport, Iowa: Catfish Press.
Lowe, E. A. 1960. *English Uncial*. Oxford: Clarendon.
Mallon, Jean. 1952. *Paléographie romaine*. Madrid: Consejo Superior de Investigaciones Científicas, Instituto Antonio de Nebrija de Filología.
Ullman, Berthold L. 1932. *Ancient Writing and Its Influence*. New York: Longmans Green. Repr. Cambridge: MIT Press, 1969.

REGIONAL SCRIPTS

Ganz, David. 1990. *Corbie and the Carolingian Renaissance*. Paris: German Historical Institute.

Lowe, E. A. 1953. "The 'Script of Luxeuil': A Title Vindicated." In *Palaeographical Papers* (1972), 2:389–98.

———. 1980. *The Beneventan Script: A History of the South Italian Minuscule*, 2nd ed., ed. Virginia Brown. 2 vols. Rome: Edizioni di Storia e Letteratura. (Orig. ed. Oxford: Clarendon, 1929.)

INSULAR SCRIPTS

Backhouse, Janet. 1981. *The Lindisfarne Gospels*. Oxford: Phaidon.

Brown, T. Julian. 1993C. Part 2 of Brown 1993A, pp. 93–134, 179–241.

Henry, Françoise. 1976. *The Book of Kells*, 2nd ed. London: Thames and Hudson.

CAROLINGIAN MINUSCULE

Bischoff, Bernhard. 1965. "Die Karolingische Minuskel." In *Karl der Grosse: Werk und Wirkung*, an exhibition at Aachen. Dusseldorf: Schwann.

Bishop, T. A. M. 1971. *English Caroline Minuscule*. Oxford: Clarendon.

Ganz, David. 1987. "The Preconditions for Caroline Minuscule." *Viator* 18: 23–44.

Knight, Stan. 1988–90. "Scripts of the Grandval Bible." *The Scribe* (London) 44: 13–14, 45: 6–12, 48: 3–7.

Rand, E. K. 1929. *A Survey of the Manuscripts of Tours*. Cambridge, Mass.: Medieval Academy of America.

GOTHIC SCRIPTS

Ker, Neil R. 1960. *English Manuscripts in the Century after the Norman Conquest*. Oxford: Clarendon.

Parkes, Malcolm B. 1969. *English Cursive Bookhands*. Oxford: Clarendon.

Thomson, S. Harrison. 1969. *Latin Bookhands of the Later Middle Ages*. Cambridge: Cambridge University Press.

HUMANIST SCRIPTS

de la Mare, Albinia C. 1973. *The Handwriting of the Italian Humanists*. London: Oxford University Press for L'Association Internationale de Bibliophilie, Paris.

Fairbank, Alfred J., and Berthold Wolpe. 1960. *Renaissance Handwriting*. London: Faber and Faber.

Harvard, Stephen, ed. 1981. *An Italic Copybook: the Cataneo Manuscript*. New York: Taplinger.

Knight, Stan. 1987. "Varieties of Humanist Minuscule." *The Scribe* (London) 33: 11–13.

Osley, Arthur S., ed. 1965. *Calligraphy and Palaeography*. London: Faber and Faber [esp. pp.47–68, 75–79].

Wardrop, James. 1963. *The Script of Humanism*. Oxford: Clarendon.

Ullman, Berthold L. 1974. *The Origin and Development of Humanistic Script*, 2nd ed. Rome: Edizioni di Storia e Letteratura.

CURSIVE WRITING FROM THE SIXTEENTH CENTURY

Barbe, Walter B., Virginia H. Lucas, and Thomas M. Wasylyk, eds. 1984. *Handwriting: Basic Skills for Effective Communication*. Columbus, Ohio: Zaner-Bloser.

Blunt, Wilfrid. 1952. *Sweet Roman Hand*. London: Barrie.

Fairbank, Alfred J. 1932. *A Handwriting Manual*. Leicester: Dryad. 9th ed., New York: Watson-Guptill, 1975.

Heal, Sir Ambrose. 1931. *The English Writing-Masters and Their Copy-books.* Cambridge: Cambridge University Press.

Johnston, Edward. 1906. *Writing, & Illuminating, & Lettering.* London: Pitman [frequent reprints].

Lehman, Charles L. 1976. *Handwriting Models for Schools.* Portland, Ore.: Alcuin.

Nash, Ray. 1959. *American Writing Masters and Copybooks.* Boston: Colonial Society of America.

Whalley, Joyce Irene. 1969. *English Handwriting, 1540–1853.* London: Her Majesty's Stationery Office.

THE PRINTED WORD

Blumenthal, Joseph. 1973. *Art of the Printed Book, 1455–1955.* New York: The Pierpont Morgan Library; Boston: Godine.

Carter, Sebastian. 1987. *Twentieth Century Type Designers.* New York: Taplinger.

Chappell, Warren. 1970. *A Short History of the Printed Word.* New York: Knopf.

Morison, Stanley. 1943. "Early Humanistic Script and the First Roman Type." *The Library,* 4th Series, 24: 1–29.

Osley, Arthur S., ed. 1965. *Calligraphy and Palaeography.* London: Faber and Faber [esp. pp.107–33].

Sutton, James, and Alan Batram. 1988. *An Atlas of Typeforms,* 2nd ed. Secaucus, N.J.: Chartwell.

Updike, Daniel Berkeley. 1937. *Printing Types: Their History, Forms, and Use,* 2nd ed. Cambridge: Harvard University Press. Repr. New York: Dover, 1980.

The Runic Script

RALPH W. V. ELLIOTT

The runic futhark, so named from the first six symbols (þ *th* = runic ᚦ) in the traditional common Germanic sequence of its letters, is of uncertain origin. It may have been the creation of an individual familiar both with the Roman alphabet, as there are many formal parallels, and with some northern Italic alphabet or alphabets which share some more unusual runic forms as well as the variable directions of writing found in some runic inscriptions, but not in Latin. That the futhark was invented in Denmark has been argued strongly by Moltke (1985: 64–65).

The earliest runic inscriptions from Denmark and Schleswig-Holstein are all on portable objects dating from the first century C.E. Others, also using the common Germanic futhark, belong to the period of the Germanic migrations and have been found in various parts of central Europe. Despite some minor formal variations, they all show remarkable uniformity of lettering and variable direction of writing. Their language has been called "Runic" or, better, "Northwest Germanic."

The common Germanic futhark consisted of 24 runes (TABLE 25.1). The value of rune 13 ᛃ remains uncertain. The continental inscriptions suggest a high front vowel between [e] and [i], here written *ï*; but in Anglo-Saxon inscriptions the same rune represents both vocalic [i] and consonantal [ç] and [x]. The twofold function appears to be acknowledged in a tenth-century manuscript where the letters *ih* are written alongside this rune. According to Antonsen (1989: 150), ᛃ represents [æ:], a sound not represented in the oldest inscriptions.

TABLE 25.1: *The Common Germanic Futhark*

1	2	3	4	5	6	7	8
ᚠ	ᚢ	ᚦ	ᚨ	ᚱ	ᚲ	ᚷ	ᚹ
f	u	þ	a	r	k	g	w

9	10	11	12	13	14	15	16
ᚺ	ᚾ	ᛁ	ᛃ	ᛇ	ᛈ	ᛉ	ᛊ
h	n	i	j	ï	p	z	s

17	18	19	20	21	22	23	24
ᛏ	ᛒ	ᛖ	ᛗ	ᛚ	ᛜ	ᛞ	ᛟ
t	b	e	m	l	ng	d	o

TABLE 25.2: *The Germanic Rune Names*

ᚠ	*fehu	'wealth'
ᚢ	*ūruz	'aurochs'
ᚦ	*þurisaz	'giant'
ᚨ	*ansuz	'god'
ᚱ	*raiþō	'riding'
ᚲ	*kaunaz *kēnaz *kanō	'ulcer' 'torch' 'skiff'
ᚷ	*gebō	'gift'
ᚹ	*wunjō	'joy'
ᚺ	*hagalaz	'hail'
ᚾ	*nauþiz	'need, necessity, hardship'
ᛁ	*isa-	'ice'
ᛃ	*jēra-	'year, fruitful year, harvest'
ᛇ	*eihwaz	'yew tree'
ᛈ	*perþ-	meaning unknown
ᛉ	*algiz	possibly 'sedge'
ᛋ	*sōwulō	'sun'
ᛏ	*teiwaz	the god Tyr, Old English Tiw
ᛒ	*berkana-	'birch twig'
ᛖ	*ehwaz	'horse'
ᛗ	*mannaz	'man'
ᛚ	*laguz	'water'
ᛜ	*inguz	the god Ing
ᛞ	*đagaz	'day'
ᛟ	*ōþila	'inherited land or possession'

Individual runes had names based on the acrophonic principle, except for runes 15 ᛉ and 22 ᛜ. The original Germanic names are here reconstructed (TABLE 25.2), as indicated by *, based on the names of the Scandinavian and Anglo-Saxon runes preserved in several poems and other manuscript sources. These differ in several instances. The Anglo-Saxon *Runic Poem* adds five further names, for the runes ᚠ *āc* 'oak', ᚫ *æsc* 'ash', ᚣ *ȳr* 'bow', ᛠ *ēar* 'earth, grave', and a twenty-ninth rune ᛡ *īar* 'eel', inserted between *ȳr* and *ēar*.

Direction of writing is mostly left to right, less commonly right to left or boustrophedon. Ligatures ("bindrunes"), facilitated by the uniformly epigraphic character of the script, occur. In early runic inscriptions writing is generally continuous, although separate words or sense units are occasionally indicated by one or more dots between runes. In two mid-sixth century Swedish bracteates (ornaments of thinly beaten metal), dots separate the three groups of eight runes forming the futhark into what, following later Icelandic tradition, are generally known as *ættir* 'families'. Geminate symbols, especially consonants, even when belonging to different words, are rarely indicated in the older Germanic inscriptions. Suprasegmental phonemes are not written.

The epigraphic character of runic lettering, with its avoidance of curves, may have resulted from initial scratching of runes into wood for such purposes as sending messages or casting of lots. The use of wooden message sticks (Old Norse *rúnakefli*) is attested from the sixth century, although actual survivals are fortuitous—and mostly much later, like the numerous *rúnakefli* belonging to the period ca. 1150 to 1350 discovered in Bergen, Norway, after a disastrous fire in 1955.

Later developments

From its continental homeland, runic writing spread north into Scandinavia and west to the British Isles. During the Viking Age, the use of runes spread as far west as Iceland and Greenland, and Viking inscriptions have been found in the British Isles and in parts of eastern and southern Europe. The several disputed "runic" inscriptions found in North America are generally regarded as modern forgeries, albeit not without some spirited attempts at their defense.

Scandinavia

Inscriptions in the common Germanic futhark continued to be made in Norway and Sweden in the seventh and eighth centuries. In Denmark the eighth century witnessed a radical reduction of the 24-letter futhark to sixteen runes, known as the "Danish" futhark, in which ten runes retain more or less their older forms, but the runes ᛕ *k*, ᚼ *h*, and ᛘ *m* acquired different shapes. In addition, the Germanic ᛃ *j* now became ᛏ with the value [a], reflecting the Scandinavian loss of initial *j-*. The Germanic ᚠ *a* rune is retained but now represents nasalized [ã], generally transcribed *ą*, while the ᛦ *z* rune represents uvular [ʀ], transcribed *R*.

The Danish futhark of sixteen runes, as inscribed on the Gørlev stone from Zealand, Denmark, is given in TABLE 25.3.

This shortened futhark underwent further developments from the ninth century. In Norway and southern Sweden a simplified 16-letter futhark was used in the ninth and tenth centuries; it is known as the "Swedish-Norwegian" or "short-twig" runes,

TABLE 25.3: *The Danish Futhark*

ᚠ	ᚢ	ᚦ	ᚨ	ᚱ	ᚴ	ᚼ	ᚾ	ᛁ	ᛅ	ᛦ	ᛏ	ᛒ	ᛘ	ᛚ	ᛦ
f	u	þ	ą	r	k	h	n	i	a	s	t	b	m	l	R

TABLE 25.4: *The Rök Runes*

ᚠ	ᚢ	ᚦ	ᚭ	ᚱ	ᚴ	ᚽ	ᚿ	ᛁ	ᛆ	ᛌ	ᛐ	ᛓ	ᛙ	ᛚ	ᛧ
f	u	þ	ą	r	k	h	n	i	a	s	t	b	m	l	R

and is often referred to as the "Rök runes" after its best known inscription, on the Rök stone of the first half of the ninth century in Sweden's Östergötland (TABLE 25.4).

Other developments occurred in different parts of Scandinavia, including a localized futhark found in a handful of inscriptions from the early eleventh century in Sweden's Hälsingland—in which most of the vertical staves were discarded, producing a kind of shorthand, known as the "staveless" or "Hälsinge" runes. During the Viking Age, to which the great majority of surviving runic inscriptions belong (mainly in the form of memorials carved onto standing stones), a mixture of the Danish and Swedish-Norwegian futharks emerged in Norway in the early eleventh century, known as the "Norwegian" futhark (TABLE 25.5).

The several 16-letter futharks were inadequate for indicating phonological distinctions in many cases. The several sound values which certain runes denoted are shown in TABLE 25.6.

The inadequacy of representing phonetic values led, from the eleventh century, to a more conscious, albeit gradual, attempt to distinguish the different phonemes in Scandinavian usage, culminating in a system of "pointed" or "dotted" runes, known in Danish as *stungne runer*. This system led to an expansion of the 16-letter futhark until it came to resemble a runic "alphabet" such as was employed on an inscription of the early thirteenth century from Sweden's Västergötland (TABLE 25.7).

TABLE 25.5: *The Norwegian Futhark*

ᚠ	ᚢ	ᚦ	ᚯ	ᚱ	ᚴ	ᚼ	ᚿ	ᛁ	ᛅ	ᛌ ᛋ	ᛐ	ᛒ	ᛘ	ᛚ	ᛦ
f	u	þ	ą	r	k	h	n	i	a	s	t	b	m	l	R, y

TABLE 25.6: *Phonetic Values*

ᚠ	f, v	ᛁ	i, e
ᚢ	u, y, o, ø, w	ᛆ	a, æ
ᚦ	θ, ð, d	ᛋ	s
ᚬ	ã; o from ca. 1050	ᛏ	t, d, nt, nd
ᚱ	r	ᛒ	b, p, mb, mp
ᚴ	k, g, ŋ, ŋk	ᛘ	m
ᚼ	h, x	ᛚ	l
ᚿ	n	ᛦ	z, R; y from 11th c.

TABLE 25.7: *Medieval Runes*

ᛆ	ᛒ	ᛎ	ᚦ	ᚧ	ᚠ	ᚠ	ᚵ	ᛁ	ᚴ	ᛚ	ᛘ	ᚿ	ᚮ	ᛒ
a	b	c	d	e	f, v	g	h, x	i, j	k	l	m	n	o	p
		ᚠ	ᚱ	ᛌ	ᛏ	ᚦ	ᚢ	ᛦ	ᛎ	ᛐ	ᛨ			
		kw	r	s	t	θ, ð	u, w	y	z	æ	ø			

As runic writing gave way to the Latin alphabet, the futhark became increasingly a matter of antiquarian interest; however, in some more remote regions of Sweden, knowledge of runes survived into modern times (see Jansson 1987: 174–75).

The British Isles

The Anglo-Saxons brought to Britain a version of the common Germanic futhark; but contrary to the development in Scandinavia, the number of runes increased in Anglo-Saxon England, initially to twenty-eight and reaching a total of thirty-one in epigraphic use. A manuscript codex of the tenth century records two further runes.

The Anglo-Saxon futhorc, so called because of the changed values of the fourth and sixth runes, reflects phonetic changes undergone in the transition from Germanic through a transitional Anglo-Frisian phase into Old English. Some of the new runes, among them ᚠ *o*, are also found in Frisian inscriptions of the fifth to seventh centuries.

The only complete epigraphic Anglo-Saxon futhorc is inscribed on a short sword, *scramasax*, of the ninth century, found in the river Thames (TABLE 25.8). A second futhorc, with only minor variations, is preserved in a manuscript codex now in Vienna, probably copied in the tenth century from a northern English prototype of perhaps two centuries earlier (Derolez 1954: 52ff.).

Comparison of TABLE 25.8 with TABLE 25.1 shows that, in the Thames futhorc, phonetic changes have altered the values of runes 6, 15, 24, and 26; that formal modifications have occurred in runes 9, 12, 16, and 21; and that new runes 4, 25, 27, and 28 have been added. Especially noteworthy are the runes ᚠ and ᚠ, which occur only in Frisian and Anglo-Saxon inscriptions; the rune H with its regular two transverse bars; the vocalic and consonantal values, mentioned earlier, of rune 13 ᛚ suggested by the letters *ih* in the Vienna futhorc; the combination of what appears to be the traditional *u* rune with a small *i* rune inside it ᚫ, suggesting the Old English *i*-mutation of *u* to [y]; and the representation of the diphthong *ea* by a single rune.

In a later development, restricted to the north and northwest of England, the Anglo-Saxon futhorc was augmented by three further runes intended to distinguish between the Old English front and back pronunciation of Germanic [g] and [k]. The rune X now represents [j], as its Old English name *gyfu* 'giving, gift' implies; the rune ᚻ now represents [ʧ], its name being *cen* 'torch'. The new rune ᚷ, with the name *gar* 'spear', represents velar [g], and the new rune ᛣ, with the name *calc* 'shoe, sandal', represents velar [k]. A further allophonic refinement ᚸ is found in the inscription of

TABLE 25.8: *The Anglo-Saxon Futhorcs*

Thames scramasax

1	2	3	4	5	6	7	8	9	10	11	12	13	14	15	16	17	18
ᚠ	ᚢ	ᚦ	ᚩ	ᚱ	ᚳ	ᚷ	ᚹ	ᚻ	ᚾ	ᛁ	ᛄ	ᛇ	ᛈ	ᛉ	ᛋ	ᛏ	ᛒ
f	u	þ	o	r	c	g	w	h	n	i	j	ï	p	x [ks]	s	t	b

19	20	21	22	23	24	25	26	27	28
ᛖ	ᛝ	ᛞ	ᛚ	ᛗ	ᛟ	ᚪ	ᚫ	ᚣ	ᛠ
e	ng [ŋ]	d	l	m	œ [ø]	a	æ	y	ea

Vienna Codex

1	2	3	4	5	6	7	8	9	10	11	12	13	14	15	16	17	18
ᚠ	ᚢ	ᚦ	ᚩ	ᚱ	ᚳ	ᚷ	ᚹ	ᚻ	ᚾ	ᛁ	ᛄ	ᛇ	ᛈ	ᛉ	ᛋ	ᛏ	ᛒ
f	u	þ	o	r	c	g	w	h	n	i	j	ih	p	x [ks]	s	t	b

19	20	21	22	23	24	25	26	27	28
ᛖ	ᛗ	ᛚ	ᛝ	ᛞ	ᛟ	ᚪ	ᚫ	ᛠ	ᚣ
e	m	l	ng [ŋ]	d	œ	a	æ	ea	y

the Ruthwell Cross, Dumfries and Galloway, where the rune denotes a velar [k] followed by a front vowel in the Old English words *cyning* 'king' and *unket* 'us both'. No name is recorded for this rune.

The conversion of Anglo-Saxon England to Christianity led to the use of runes, as well as roman letters, in memorial inscriptions (see the text sample); to the employment of single runes as shorthand for their names in manuscripts; and for riddling purposes, as in the four "signed" poems of the early ninth-century poet Cynewulf, where runes are used to spell his name (Elliott 1991: 231–47). While inscriptions in Scandinavian runes were made in the British Isles, a few Anglo-Saxon pilgrims carved their names in runes in Italy between ca. 700 and 850. In Britain, Anglo-Saxon runic epigraphy probably ceased in the course of the tenth century.

Sample of Runic

1. Old English:	† ᛡᛁᛚᛋᚢᛁᚦ:	ᚪᚱᚫᚱᛞᛖ:	ᚫᚠᛏᛖ
2. Transliteration:	jilsuiþ:	arærde:	æfte(r)
3. Transcription:	jilswiθ	a:ræ:rdə	æftɛ(r)
4. Gloss:	Gilswith	raised	after

1. ᛒᛖᚱᚻᛏᛋᚢᛁᚦᛖ•	ᛒᛖᛣᚢᚾ
2. berhtsuiþe·	bekun
3. bɛrçtswiðə	bekʊn
4. Berhtswith	memorial

1. ᚠᚻᛒᛗᚱᚷᛁᚷᛗᛒᛁᛞᛞᚨᚦ

2. onbergigebiddaþ

3. on-bɛrgi-jɛbidaθ

4. on-mound-pray

1. ᚦᚫᚱ: ᛋᚪᚢᛚᛗ

2. þær: saule

3. ðæ:r   saʊlə

4. her   soul

> 'Gilswith erected a memorial for Berhtswith on (this) mound. Pray (for) her soul.'
>
> —*Early ninth century Anglo-Saxon inscription from Thornhill, Yorkshire.*

Bibliography

Antonsen, Elmer H. 1989. "The Runes: The Earliest Germanic Writing System." In *The Origins of Writing,* ed. Wayne M. Senner, pp. 137–58. Lincoln: University of Nebraska Press.

Bammesberger, Alfred, ed. 1991. *Old English Runes and Their Continental Background.* Heidelberg: Winter.

Derolez, René. 1954. *Runica Manuscripta: The English Tradition.* Brugge, Belgium: De Tempel.

Düwel, Klaus. 1983. *Runenkunde,* 2nd ed. Stuttgart: Metzler (1st ed. 1968).

Elliott, Ralph W. V. 1989. *Runes: An Introduction,* 2nd ed. Manchester: Manchester University Press; New York: St. Martin's (1st ed. 1959).

———. 1991. "Coming back to Cynewulf." In Bammesberger 1991: 231–47.

Jansson, Sven B. F. 1987. *Runes in Sweden,* trans. Peter G. Foote. Stockholm: Gidlunds.

Moltke, Erik. 1985. *Runes and Their Origin: Denmark and Elsewhere,* trans. Peter G. Foote. Copenhagen: National Museum of Denmark.

Page, Raymond I. 1973. *An Introduction to English Runes.* London: Methuen.

———. 1987. *Runes* (Reading the Past). London: British Museum; Berkeley and Los Angeles: University of California Press.

Ogham

DAMIAN MCMANUS

Ogham (Modern Irish [oːm], Old Irish *Ogam* [oɣəm], Modern English [ɔgəm] or [oːm]) is the earliest writing system known to have been used by the Irish, among whom it was the vehicle for funerary inscriptions. These are found on monuments in Ireland, Devon, Cornwall, Wales, and the Isle of Man (see Macalister 1945; on the Pictish Ogams of Scotland, see Jackson 1980) and date approximately from the fifth to the seventh centuries C.E. (McManus 1991: 78–100). The Oghams of Britain are often accompanied by an equivalent in Latin, but this is never the case in Ireland. So-called *scholastic* Oghams belong to the Irish manuscript period (i.e. post 7th century) and are found mainly in texts dealing specifically with the alphabet, such as *Auraicept na nÉces* 'The scholars' primer' (see Calder 1917, Ahlqvist 1982). By this time Ogham had ceased to be a functional script, though it continued to be studied in the native schools down to the seventeenth century.

The script (often styled the *Beithe-luis-nin*, after the names of its first, second, and fifth symbols) is made up of twenty tally-like symbols divided into four groups of five. The symbols of the first three groups, all representing consonants, appear as one to five scores cut to the right, left, and diagonally across the arris of the stone respectively. Those of the fourth group, which represent vowels, generally appear as notches cut on the arris itself, but also as horizontal short scores across it. A fifth group—called *Forfeda* 'supplementary letters', a mixture of vowels and consonants—appears in the manuscript tradition, but only the first of these is found regularly on the early inscriptions. This group was later modified to represent digraphs and diphthongs.

All symbols bear names which were meaningful words in the language and which operate on the acrophonic principle that the initial sound in the name corresponds to the value of the symbol (McManus 1988, 1989). These names were later transferred to letters of the conventional alphabet and continued in use down to the modern period.

The inscriptions are usually but not invariably written in boustrophedon fashion, beginning at the bottom left-hand side of the stone and continuing around the top and down the right-hand side. There is no word division or punctuation of any kind, nor is there any orthographic device for distinguishing length in vowels, quality (palatal or broad) in consonants, or the articulation of consonants as stops or fricatives; but because stops in initial position were subject to mutation to fricatives in certain pho-

TABLE 26.1: *Ogham Symbols*

Ogham	*Stone*	*Manuscript*	*Name*	
1. ᚁ	B	B	*Beithe*	'birch'
2. ᚂ	L	L	*Luis*	'blaze' or 'herb'
3. ᚃ	V	F	*Fern*	'alder'
4. ᚄ	S	S	*Sail*	'willow'
5. ᚅ	N	N	*Nin*	'fork' or 'loft'
6. ᚆ	?	H	*(h)Úath*	'fear(?)'
7. ᚇ	D	D	*Dair*	'oak'
8. ᚈ	T	T	*Tinne*	'rod of metal'
9. ᚉ	C	C	*Coll*	'hazel'
10. ᚊ	Q	Q	*Cert/Queirt*	'bush'
11. ᚋ	M	M	*Muin*	'neck'
12. ᚌ	G	G	*Gort*	'field'
13. ᚍ	?	NG	*(n)Gétal*	'wounding(?)'
14. ᚎ	?	Z	*Straif*	'sulfur'
15. ᚏ	R	R	*Ruis*	'red(ness)'
16. ᚐ, ᚐ	A	A	*Ailm*	?
17. ᚑ, ᚑ	O	O	*Onn*	'ash-tree'
18. ᚒ, ᚒ	U	U	*Úr*	'earth'
19. ᚓ, ᚓ	E	E	*Edad*	?
20. ᚔ, ᚔ	I	I	*Idad*	?
21. ᚕ	K/E	EA	*Ébad*	?
22. ᚖ		OI	*Ór*	'gold'
23. ᚗ		UI	*Uilen*	'elbow'
24. ᚘ		IA	*Pín/Iphín*	'pine'
25. ᚙ		AE	*Emancholl*	'double c'

netic environments in Irish, the use of a single symbol for both is not surprising (for *initial mutations* of this kind cf. Modern Irish *cú* [ku:] 'hound', but *a chú* [ə xu:] 'his hound' by *lenition* and *a gcú* [ə gu:] 'their hound' by *eclipsis*; see SECTION 59, "Irish" on page 656). Doubling of consonantal symbols is common but was never perfected as an orthographic device for distinguishing *unlenited* (e.g. [t k b l: n:]) from the corresponding *lenited* sounds (e.g. [θ x β l n]; McManus 1991: 124–26; Harvey 1987A). Scholastic Oghams, which are usually written horizontally from left to right, sometimes use an arrowhead (>) as a word separator.

Problems attach to three letters (nos. 6ᚆ, 13ᚍ, and 14ᚎ of TABLE 26.1), the early values of which are in doubt as they are not reliably attested in the monument period (McManus 1986, Sims-Williams 1993). The values accorded them by the manuscript tradition have to be treated with caution, as this tradition represents the language of its time, and redundant symbols were given a new lease on life by slight modification

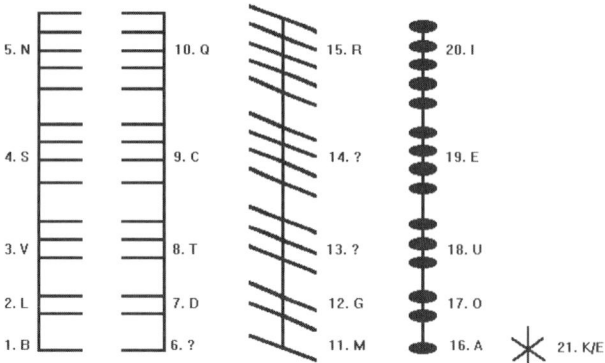

FIGURE 52. Ogham as it appears on stone, with conventional transliteration of attested symbols.

under the influence of Latin and Greek learning. Thus symbol 13 ⫻ is equated with Greek *Agma* in this tradition and is called *nGétal*; but there are grounds for believing that its original name was *Gétal* and that it represented the Primitive Irish labiovelar g^w (from Indo-European $*g^wh$), which had fallen together with [g] by the manuscript period.

Some scholars have sought the origins of Ogham in the Germanic runes, others in Greek, but the majority would now embrace Latin as the most likely and most probable candidate. The classification of the sounds of the Latin language by Latin grammarians (as opposed to the Latin alphabet itself) bears a number of similarities to the organization of the Ogham characters and is as close as one has come to an explanation of the latter, though considerable difficulties remain. For a full discussion see McManus 1991, chaps. 2 and 3.

Though it is likely to have been inspired by the Latin alphabet, the framers of Ogham showed remarkable independence of mind in their choice of script, their alphabetic sequence, and the sounds they chose to represent (witness for example the absence of [p], a sound not found in Primitive Irish, and the separate representation of [u] and [w]). The separation of vowels from consonants, the arrangement of the vowel sequence (the back vowels [a], [o], and [u] followed by front vowels [e] and [i]), and the pairing of phonetically related consonants ([d] and [t], [k] and [kʷ], [g] and [gʷ] or [ŋ]) show the creators of the system to have been students of their language, with an acute awareness of its requirements.

The script

Stone inscriptions

See FIGURE 52. The symbols ₁ *B*, ⊔ *D*, ⊔⊔ *T*, ⊔⊔⊔ *C*, ⊔⊔⊔⊔ *Q*, /*M*, and ⫻*G* represent [b/β], [d/ð], [t/θ], [k/x], [kʷ/xʷ], [m/ṽ], and [g/ɣ]. On British Oghams, ⊔⊔⊔ *T* and ⊔⊔⊔⊔ *C* can also represent [d] and [g]. Confusion of ⊔⊔⊔⊔ *C* and ⊔⊔⊔⊔ *Q* reflects the delabialization of the

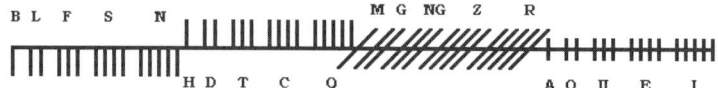

FIGURE 53. Ogham as it appears in the manuscript tradition, with contemporary transliteration.

latter, which took place during the monument period. � *S* represents [s], [ʃ], and the lenited form [h]. On bilingual inscriptions, ⫿ *V* is the equivalent of Latin *V*; it thus represents primitive Irish [w] (later > [f]). ⫿ *L*, ⫿ *N*, and ⫿*R* can represent both lenited and unlenited sounds (i.e. [l] and [l:] etc.) in initial position; in internal and final position, the unlenited sounds, which were probably articulated with greater energy as in later Irish, may be written double. The vowel symbols represent both long and short vowels (i.e. ı *A* = [a] and [a:], etc.). The inherited diphthongs [ai] and [oi] are represented by ⊢⊩ *AI* and ⊢⊩ *OI* (occasionally simply ı *A* and ⊩ *O*) respectively. Symbol 21 ✕ is used with the values [k/x] and [e].

Manuscript tradition

See FIGURE 53. For the most part the values are the same here as in the earlier tradition, but some significant sound changes had taken place in the interim. One of these was the change of [w] to [f] in absolute (unmutated) anlaut—with a corresponding change in the value of symbol 3 ⫿, now equated with Latin *f*. Symbol 6 ı has been equated with Latin *h* and is not pronounced in initial position; it combines with symbols 8 ⫿ and 9 ⫿ to render [x] and [θ]. Symbol 10 ⫿ is redundant for purposes of writing Irish; it is recommended instead of symbol 9 ⫿ when the latter is followed by [u], a rule based on Latin *qv*. Symbol 14 ⫿ is equated with Latin *z* and is used in Irish words for *st*; on symbol 13 ⫿, see above. The values assigned to the supplementary characters vary from one manuscript to the next (for details see McManus 1991: 141–46; Sims-Williams 1992).

Names

The names of the characters in normalized Old Irish (8th–9th century) spelling are included in TABLE 26.1. Contrary to popular belief, these, as will be clear, are not *all* names of trees (McManus 1988).

EXAMPLES OF OGHAM

ORTHODOX OGHAM

1. *Ogham:*	⁜ Ogham script ⁜			
2. *Transliteration:*	QRIMITIR	RONANN	MAQ	COMOGANN
3. *Transcription:*	kʷriṽʲiθʲirʲ	roːnaːnʲ	ṽakʷʲ	coṽəɣaːnʲ
4. *Gloss:*	priest	Rónán	son.of	Comogán

'(The stone of) the priest Rónán son of Comogán.'

—*Macalister 1945, no. 145.*

1.	⁜ Ogham script ⁜				
2.	CATTUVVIRR	MAQI	RITTAVECAS	MUCOI	ALLATO
3.	kaθuwirʲ	ṽakʷi	riθawexah	mukoi	alːaθoː
4.	Catuviros	son.of	Ritavix	of.the.tribe	of.Allatis

'(The stone of) Catuviros son of Ritavix of the tribe of Allatis.'

—*Macalister 1945, no. 250.*

1.	⁜ Ogham script ⁜		
2.	SAGRAGNI	MAQI	CUNATAMI
3.	saɣraɣni	ṽakʷi	xunadaṽi
4.	Sagragnos	son.of	Cunatamos

'(The stone of) Sagragnos son of Cunatamos.'   —*Macalister 1945, no. 449.*

SCHOLASTIC OGHAM

1.	⁜ Ogham script ⁜
2.	LATHEIRT
3.	lːaθʲərtʲ

'Hangover' (a 9th-century Irish scribe's excuse for errors in a morning's work!).   —*McManus 1991: 133.*

1.	⁜ Ogham script ⁜					
2.	GILLA	NA	NAEM	O	DEORAIN	SOND
3.	gilːə	nə	nːeːṽ	oː	dʲoːraːnʲ	son:
4.	Gilla	na	Naem	O	Deóráin	here.is

'I am Gilla na Naem O Deóráin' (a 16th-century scribal signature).

—*McManus 1991: 133.*

Bibliography

A detailed bibliography of works published before 1990 will be found in McManus 1991.

Ahlqvist, Anders. 1982. *The Early Irish Linguist* (Commentationes Humanarum Litterarum 73). Helsinki: Finnish Society of Sciences and Letters.

Calder, George. 1917. *Auraicept na nÉces: The Scholars' Primer.* Edinburgh: John Grant.

Carney, James. 1975. "The Invention of the Ogom Cipher." *Ériu* (Journal of the Royal Irish Academy) 26: 53–65.

Harvey, Anthony. 1987A. "The Ogam Inscriptions and Their Geminate Consonant Symbols." *Ériu* 38: 45–71.

———. 1987B. "Early Literacy in Ireland: The Evidence from Ogam." *Cambridge Medieval Celtic Studies* 14: 1–15.

Jackson, Kenneth H. 1980. "The Pictish Language." In *The Problem of the Picts,* ed. Frederick T. Wainwright, pp. 129–60. Perth: Melven.

Macalister, Robert A. S. 1945. *Corpus Inscriptionum Insularum Celticarum,* vol. 1. Dublin: Irish Manuscripts Commission.

McManus, Damian. 1986. "Ogam: Archaizing, Orthography and the Authenticity of the Manuscript Key to the Alphabet." *Ériu* 37: 1–31.

———. 1988. "Irish Letter-names and Their Kennings." *Ériu* 39: 127–68.

———. 1989. "Runic and Ogam Letter-names: A Parallelism." In *Sages, Saints and Storytellers: Celtic Studies in Honour of Professor James Carney,* ed. Donnchadh Ó Corráin, Liam Breatnach, and Kim McCone, pp. 144–48 (Maynooth Monographs 2). Maynooth: An Sagart.

———. 1991. *A Guide to Ogam* (Maynooth Monographs 4). Maynooth: An Sagart.

Mac Neill, Eoin. 1909. "Notes on the Distribution, History, Grammar and Import of the Irish Ogham Inscriptions." *Proceedings of the Royal Irish Academy* 27: 329–70.

Sims-Williams, Patrick. 1992. "The Additional Letters of the Ogam Alphabet." *Cambridge Medieval Celtic Studies* 23 (Summer): 29–75.

———. 1993. "Some Problems in Deciphering the Early Irish Ogam Alphabet." *Transactions of the Philological Society* 91: 133–80.

Thurneysen, Rudolf. 1937. "Zum Ogom." *Beiträge zur Geschichte der deutschen Sprache und Literatur* 61: 188–208.

The Slavic Alphabets

PAUL CUBBERLEY

The historical background

Traditionally the first Slavic writing is credited to Constantine—also known as (St.) Cyril, the name he took on becoming a monk—who, with his brother (St.) Methodius, led a mission from Byzantium to the Moravian Slavs in the early 860s. In preparation, they reputedly created an alphabet in which to write the liturgical texts in "Slavic." There is no factual evidence of any writing of a Slavic language before that time.

There are, however, many formal problems with this account, all centering around the fact that *two* alphabets were clearly "created" to fit Slavic needs: Glagolitic and Cyrillic (TABLE 27.1). Cyrillic presents little trouble: it is clearly based on uncial (capital) Greek, and its problems are reduced to determining the origin of the letters which could not have come from Greek, such as those representing the sounds [ʒ, ʃ, ʧ, ts], which Greek did not have.

The search for the formal origins of Glagolitic remains unsolved. One very popular view has been that Glagolitic is a *totally individual creation*, the corollary being that the creator was Constantine; the advantage of this view is that it obviates the need to find a formal model in some other alphabet. But most popular of all is the view that Glagolitic is based on Greek cursive forms, and that it predates Cyrillic. While there is much uncertainty about many of the derivations, the general principle seems provable—that is, most Glagolitic letters can be derived from Greek cursive forms in a way that is formally satisfying. Many other "sources" have been suggested for Glagolitic, in fact almost any alphabet which was around the relevant area at the time; however, none of these has been as generally accepted as the cursive Greek view.

Circumstantial arguments put forward to support the priority of Glagolitic over Cyrillic order include: the existence of palimpsests (reused manuscripts) with Cyrillic superimposed on Glagolitic, but none in the other direction; the identification of linguistic features which unite the western (Macedonian) area with Glagolitic (e.g. no Turkisms), and the eastern (Bulgarian) area with Cyrillic (presence of Turkisms); and the putative superiority of Glagolitic as representative of the early Slavic phonological system. None of these features is really of any clear significance, and all have been challenged.

The most likely scenario is as follows: Glagolitic was formed by the adaptation of cursive Greek by some Slavs during the couple of centuries preceding the 860s; it was formalized by Constantine, who also added letters for the non-Greek sounds; Constantine's disciples in Bulgaria (in the 890s) perceived Glagolitic as unsuitable for Church books and made up a new Slavic alphabet based on the "more dignified" uncial Greek. The remaining formal questions are then: Where did the added letters come from in Glagolitic? and, Can we satisfactorily derive the non-Greek Cyrillic ones from the Glagolitic?

Of the many Slavic sounds not existing in Greek, the most obvious are the palatals [ʒ, ʧ, ʃ]—but also [ts] and [b]; and of course many vowels, especially the nasals, the *jers* (mid-high ĭ, ŭ) and *jat'* (low front ě). Very little attempt has been made at finding sources for the vowel letters; most attempts at finding sources for the palatals and [ts] offer multiple sources, e.g. Coptic for [ʒ] and Hebrew for [ʃ], [ʧ], and [ts]. One might suppose that when Constantine created the new Glagolitic letters, he would have used some consistency in his choice of sources, and would as far as possible have sought a single source for all these sounds; one might argue for Armenian as such a source for the consonants, and Greek (variants) for the vowels (Cubberley 1982: 299–302).

As for the Cyrillic versions of these Slavic sounds, there are enough similarities to allow a derivation from Glagolitic. Thus we can derive Cyrillic ж ž, ц c, ч č from Glagolitic Ⱆ, Ⰴ, Ⱚ respectively; ш š is the same in both; for the vowels we derive ъ "/ĭ, ь '/ĭ, ѧ ę, ѫ ǫ from Ⱁ, Ⱁ, Ⰵ, ⰒⰅ respectively; while the symbol originally used for *jat'* (ě)—Cyrillic ѣ, Glagolitic Ⰰ—has been confused through the many changes and local reflexes of this Proto-Slavic sound (Cubberley 1984: 284–85).

The question of the naming of the two alphabets is a minor one and is probably most simply explained by a confusion in the reporting of the creation of "the alphabet," since no early source talks clearly of two alphabets or uses either of these names (except for one 11th-century one which appears to apply the name коуриловица *kurilovica* to Glagolitic). Sources usually talk only of the *bukvica* or *azbuka* (both 'alphabet'), with no further qualification. Only much later did either name, whether that of Cyril (*kiríllica* 'Cyrillic'), from Constantine's adopted monastic name, or Glagolitic (*glagólica*), from *glagol-* ('word, say'), become attached to one or the other alphabet.

_____

Forms of letters and phonological fit in old alphabets

The original Glagolitic letters are regarded as having been a good fit for the original system (Macedonian Slavic); unfortunately, it is likely that many of the original letters have been displaced through Cyrillic influence as well as confusion through the early spread to other dialectal areas (Moravia, Serbia, Bulgaria). Cyrillic certainly acquired one set of digraph and ligature from Greek, namely the forms оу/Ȣ for [u]. It expanded on this practice for non-Greek sounds, first in the case of the vowel [y], which in one of its origins came from a sequence like [ə] + [i], and this sound became written first as the digraph ъі or ъи, then the ligature ы (and still later ы). The original

TABLE 27.1: *Old Slavic Alphabets*

OCS Cyrillic	Num. Value	Glagolitic OCS	Glagolitic Croatian	Num. Value	Name	ISO	LC-1991	Sound (IPA)
а	I	Ⰰ	Ⰰ	I	azъ	a	a	[a]
б	–	Ⰱ	Ⰱ	2	buky	b	b	[b]
в	2	Ⰲ	Ⰲ	3	vědi/vědě	v	v	[v]
г	3	Ⰳ	Ⰳ	4	glagoli/glagolь	g	g	[g]
д	4	Ⰴ	Ⰴ	5	dobro	d	d	[d]
є	5	Ⰵ	Ⰵ	6	jestъ/estъ	e	e	[ɛ]
ж	–	Ⰶ	Ⰶ	7	živěte	ž	zh	[ʒʲ]
ѕ	6	Ⰷ	Ⰷ	8	(d)zělo	dz	ż	[dzʲ/zʲ]
з	7	Ⰸ	Ⰸ	9	zemlja	z	z	[z]
и	8	Ⰹ	Ⰹ	20	i, ižei	i	i	[i]
ї/і	10	Ⰺ / Ⱞ	Ⰺ / Ⱞ	10	iže	i	ī	[i]
ћ	–	Ⰼ	Ⰼ	30	ģervь/dervь	ģ	ģ	[gʲ/dʲ/j]
к	20	Ⰽ	Ⰽ	40	kako	k	k	[k]
л	30	Ⰾ	Ⰾ	50	ljudъje/ljudije	l	l	[l]
м	40	Ⰿ	Ⰿ	60	myslite/myslěte	m	m	[m]
н	50	Ⱀ	Ⱀ	70	našь	n	n	[n]
о	70	Ⱁ	Ⱁ	80	onъ	o	o	[ɔ]
п	80	Ⱂ	Ⱂ	90	pokoj	p	p	[p]
р	100	Ⱃ	Ⱃ	100	rьci	r	r	[r]
с	200	Ⱄ	Ⱄ	200	slovo	s	s	[s]
т	300	Ⱅ	Ⱅ	300	tvrdo/tverdo	t	t	[t]
оу/ꙋ	400	Ⱆ	Ⱆ	400	ukъ/ikъ	u	u/ū	[u]
ф	500	Ⱇ	Ⱇ	500	frtъ	f	f	[f]
х	600	Ⱈ	Ⱈ	600	chěrъ/cherъ	x	kh	[χ]
ѡ/ѿ	800	Ⱉ	Ⱉ	700	otъ	o	ō	[ɔ]
ц	900	Ⱌ	Ⱌ	900	ci	c	t͡s	[tsʲ]
ч	90	Ⱍ	Ⱍ	1000	črvь	č	ch	[tʃʲ]
ш	–	Ⱎ	Ⱎ	(800)	ša	š	sh	[ʃʲ]
щ	–	Ⱋ	Ⱋ	(800)	štja	št	sht	[ʃʲtʲ]
ъ	–	Ⱏ	Ⱏ	–	jerъ	″/ъ	″	[ŭ/ə]
ы/ъи	–	Ⱏⰻ / Ⱏⰺ		–	jery	y	y	[ɨ]
ь	–	Ⱐ	⟙	–	jerь	′/ь	′	[ĭ]
ѣ	–	Ⱑ	Ⱑ	–	ětь/jatь	ě	ě	[æ/e]
ю	–	Ⱓ	Ⱓ	–	ju	ju	i͡u	[ju]
ꙗ	–			–	ja	ja	i͡a	[ja]
ѥ	–			–	(je)	je	i͡e	[jɛ]
ѧ	900	Ⱔ		–	jusъ malyj	ę	ę	[ɛ̃]
ѩ	–	Ⱗ		–	jusъ malyj jotirovannyj	ję	i͡ę	[jẽ]
ѫ	–	Ⱘ		–	jusъ bolšij	ǫ	ǫ	[ɔ̃]
ѭ	–	Ⱙ		–	jusъ bolshij jotirovannyj	jǫ	i͡ǫ	[jɔ̃]
ѯ	60				ksi	ks	k͡s	[ks]
ѱ	700				psi	ps	p͡s	[ps]
Ω	9	Ⱚ		–	(thita)/fita	f	ḟ	[f]
ѵ	400	Ⱛ	Ⱛ		ižica	i/v	v̇	[i/v]

Slavic sequences of [i] + any vowel, which had by this time been reduced to [j] + vowel, then became written as ligatures of ɪ + vowel (ꙗ *ja*, ⱖ *je*, ꙙ *ję*, ꙛ *jǫ*). Interesting here is ю—which, despite its shape, represents [ju] and not [jo], the latter still being an impossible sequence at that time. Further, this is the only sequence of [j] + vowel with a letter (not apparently a ligature) in Glagolitic, ⱓ; and this may signify that it actually represented a different sound at first, most likely [u], until this was replaced by the ligature on the Cyrillic/Greek model (ꙋ *u* from ⱁ *o* + ⰲ *v*). The only obvious ligatures in Glagolitic are those with the nasal vowels ⱔ *ję*, ⱘ *ǫ*, ⱙ *jǫ*, and these too are taken to be later formations based on the Cyrillic model. One final form of interest is the letter ⱋ *št*, usually taken to be a ligature of ш *š* and т *t*, which looks possible for Cyrillic but not for Glagolitic; most likely this was an original Glagolitic form for a single sound (the reflex of Proto-Slavic **tj*), which became perceived as the letter for the sequence [ʃt] in the Bulgarian area and was interpreted as a ligature. Its numerical value also indicates that its original place was different.

Also inherited from Greek was the use of the letters for numerical value; note that the Glagolitic letters have the values in their Slavic order, while Cyrillic follows the inherited Greek order, including the Greek-only letters (the last four), with the non-Greek letters/sounds assigned no numerical value. The numerical value was indicated by a tittle over the letter(s), e.g. а̅ı̅ = 11. The tittle also had the inherited Greek function of indicating an abbreviated common word, e.g. х̅с̅ъ = христосъ *xristos″* 'Christ'.

As for the order of letters, it followed Greek for the common letters; two non-Greek letters, б *b*, ж *ž*, were seen as phonetic variants of Slavic sounds в *v* and ѕ *dz* and placed before them; the rest were added after the "omega" ω/ꙍ *o*, the consonants first, then the vowels; at the very end were placed the letters for non-Slavic sounds.

Glagolitic: Later history

After the initial period (to the end of the 9th century), Glagolitic continued to exist alongside Cyrillic in the Bulgarian/Macedonian area, around the centers of Preslav and Ohrid, until the beginning of the thirteenth century. However, Cyrillic steadily became dominant throughout the twelfth century. (It was during this period of coexistence of Cyrillic and Glagolitic that Glagolitic underwent the above-mentioned reverse influence from the increasingly popular Cyrillic in the shapes and variants of several letters.) Glagolitic also survived for a couple of centuries in Serbia and Bosnia; it was even used for limited periods, in some Church practice only, in the Polish and Czech areas (14th–16th centuries). Its subsequent history, though, belongs almost exclusively to the Croatian area, where it not only survived but flourished for many centuries—a somewhat paradoxical situation, in that these were the areas early dominated by the Roman church. In fact, Glagolitic became the symbol of some independence from Rome, and it was tolerated by Rome as a small concession permitting its continued influence in the Balkans; it even acquired official administrative status from the mid thirteenth century.

Formally, there was a gradual change in the lettershapes: from the original round style, there was a shift first to a slightly more square shape, and finally to the typical Croatian very square shape.

Glagolitic continued to be used in Croatia until the early nineteenth century, especially on the Adriatic islands; during that time it acquired a cursive form in its administrative functions, and was printed in Church books in several major centers, such as Venice, Tübingen, and Rome. As late as 1893 a Glagolitic Missal was printed in Rome. However, Glagolitic ceased to be very active outside the church from the seventeenth century.

Cyrillic: Later history

Cyrillic remained ensconced in the three basic areas in which it first developed: Bulgaria and Serbia, then Kievan Rus (from the late 10th century). Its further development is of a marginal nature—partly related to local phonological changes and partly to purely graphic ones. This section discusses only the changes which took place in the (Great) Russian area; for the other developments and adaptations of Cyrillic, see SECTION 60.

A general cause of trouble was the inheritance of an alphabet that was created for another language system, especially with the multiple vowel symbols brought in from Greek: the three letters for *i* (и, ї/і, v), the two for *o* (o, ω/ꙍ), and the variants for *u* (oy/ꙋ); there were similar problems with the Greek consonantal letters, with two each for *z* (ѕ, ꙁ) and *f* (ф, Ѳ).

In Russia the first attempt to come to grips with these problems was Peter the Great's "civil script" of 1708–10, introduced specifically to accommodate the printing of non-Church books. Not only did this settle on simpler forms of all letters for use in lay printing, but it also made a start on deleting redundant letters and shapes which were marked as "Church" variants (ω/ꙍ *o*, ꙗ *ja*, ѧ *ę*, ѱ *ps*); confirmed (by omission) the earlier abandonment of some (oy *u*, ѫ *ǫ*); fixed in place some earlier shape changes (y *u*, щ *šč*, ы *y*); and introduced some new forms (э *è*, я *ja*). Many of the "superfluous" letters or variants, however, remained: ѕ/ꙁ *z*, и/і/ї *i*, ꙋ *u*, ѯ *ks*, ф/Ѳ *f*, v *i/v*. The Academy of Sciences, initiated by Peter in 1724, made some fairly desultory attempts at reform in statements of 1735 and 1738 (the only positive and lasting change being the latter's introduction of the letter й for the sound [j] in postvocalic position); but the debate about shapes and variants continued in disordered fashion until 1918, there being as yet (there as elsewhere) no mechanism for the enforcing of a norm.

It was only the 1918 reform, promulgated by the new regime, that once and for all saw the removal of the redundant і, ѣ, and Ѳ in all cases, and of ъ in its redundant

TABLE 27.2: *Modern Russian*

Letter		"Italic" Form		Transliteration ISO	LC 1991	Sound (IPA)	Name (IPA)
А	а	*A*	*a*	a	a	[a]	a
Б	б	*Б*	*б*	b	b	[b]	bɛ
В	в	*В*	*в*	v	v	[v]	vɛ
Г	г	*Г*	*г*	g	g	[g]	gɛ
Д	д	*Д*	*∂*	d	d	[d]	dɛ
Е	е	*Е*	*е*	e	e	[(j)ɛ]	jɛ
(Ё)	(ё)[a]	*(Ё)*	*(ё)*	ё	i͡o	[(j)ɔ]	jɔ
Ж	ж	*Ж*	*ж*	ž	z͡h	[ʒ]	ʒɛ
З	з	*З*	*з*	z	z	[z]	zɛ
И	и	*И*	*и*	i	i	[i]	i
Й	й	*Й*	*й*	j	ĭ	[j][b]	i 'kratkəjɪ 'short i'
К	к	*К*	*к*	k	k	[k]	ka
Л	л	*1*	*л*	l	l	[l]	elʲ/ɛl
М	м	*М*	*м*	m	m	[m]	ɛm
Н	н	*Н*	*н*	n	n	[n]	ɛn
О	о	*О*	*о*	o	o	[ɔ]	ɔ
П	п	*П*	*п*	p	p	[p]	pɛ
Р	р	*Р*	*р*	r	r	[r]	ɛr
С	с	*С*	*с*	s	s	[s]	ɛs
Т	т	*Т*	*m*	t	t	[t]	tɛ
У	у	*У*	*у*	u	u	[u]	u
Ф	ф	*Ф*	*ф*	f	f	[f]	ɛf
Х	х	*Х*	*х*	x	k͡h	[x]	xa
Ц	ц	*Ц*	*ц*	c	t͡s	[t͡s]	tsɛ
Ч	ч	*Ч*	*ч*	č	ch	[t͡ʃʲ]	t͡ʃʲa
Ш	ш	*Ш*	*ш*	š	sh	[ʃ]	ʃa
Щ	щ	*Щ*	*щ*	šč	shch	[ʃʲt͡ʃʲ/ʃʲʃʲ]	ʃʲt͡ʃʲa/ʃʲʃʲa
Ъ	ъ	*Ъ*	*ъ*	″	″	–	'tvʲɔrdij znak 'hard sign'
Ы	ы	*Ы*	*ы*	y	y	ɨ	ɨ
Ь	ь[c]	*Ь*	*ь*	′	′	–	'mʲæxʲkʲɪj znak 'soft sign'
Э	э	*Э*	*э*	è	ė	ɛ	ɛ
Ю	ю	*Ю*	*ю*	ju	i͡u	(j)u	ju
Я	я	*Я*	*я*	ja	i͡a	(j)a	ja

a. The letter ё is used virtually only in dictionaries or language textbooks.
b. [j] between consonant and vowel is indicated with the hard/soft signs; e.g. Съя = C[ja]; Сья = Cʲ[ja].
c. Palatalization of consonants and [j] are indicated as follows:

Context	#	a	e	i	o	u
Hard (Plain)	C	Ca	(Се/Сэ)Сы	Co	Cy	
Palatalized	Сь	Ся	Се	Си	Се/Сё Сю	
[j]		й	я	е	е/ё	ю

final position. Other letters were omitted without comment, indicating that the loss of such as s, ω, ȝ, ψ, and v was by now assumed.

One reform frequently suggested (but to this day not implemented, mainly for morphophonological reasons) has concerned the need for a letter for [ɔ] after a soft consonant; Russian still officially uses the letter e for this function as well as for "normal" [e]; in pedagogical usage the form ë (first proposed in 1797) is used.

Orthography and phonotactics in Russian

Apart from occasional proposals of a phonetic principle, most Cyrillic areas (as indeed their Roman counterparts) have always applied the "morphological" principle in orthography, i.e. to retain visible morphological relations in spite of surface phonetic facts. Of the Slavic languages, Serbo-Croatian, because of its simple phonotactic rules, has been able to employ the phonetic principle, the only surface alternations that need to be accommodated being the assimilation of voice in median obstruent groups. Ukrainian is close behind, though it does not indicate such assimilation as it has. Of the rest, which all have several complicating factors, only Belarusian has chosen a phonetic representation of the vowels, though not of the consonants. The main other complicating phonotactic factors are, for the consonants, devoicing of word-final obstruents; and for the vowels, reduction in quality of unstressed vowels. Thus the word for 'town' in Russian is written город *gorod*, though pronounced ['gɔrət]—on the principle that in all the other forms of this word, the /d/ is realized as [d], the stress may shift, and so the root morpheme is {gorod}. The derived adjective is written городской *gorodskoj*, pronounced [gərʌt'skɔj]. The phonotactic rules are consistent enough for this not to be a problem for educated native speakers.

The phonological fit in Russian is complicated especially by the fact that palatalized consonants are often represented by the following vowel letter (often called *iotated*): е *e*, ё *jo*, и *i*, ю *ju*, я *ja*; whereas non-palatalized consonants are indicated by the parallel *non-iotated* letters э *è*, о *o*, ы *y*, у *u*, а *a*. The orthographic advantage of this system is that the twelve consonants which may occur also in palatalized form require only five extra letters; but it can cause problems, certainly for learners, e.g. тётя 'aunt' is phonologically /t'ot'a/, as opposed to тот 'that' /tot/. Where there is no following vowel, the soft sign ь is used, e.g. мать 'mother' /mat'/, свадьба 'wedding' /svad'ba/. In native Russian words, consonants before /e/ may not be unpalatalized; hence the absence of any spellings with the non-iotated letter э in this part of the lexicon. However, a large and increasing number of foreign borrowings, often well assimilated lexically, do contain a non-palatalized consonant in this context; but this remains unrecognized in the spelling, which retains the isolated letter e (e.g. фонетика [fʌ'net'ɪkə] 'phonetics'.

A further complication is the representation of the phoneme /j/: while a separate letter й does exist for this sound, it is used only in syllable final position, e.g. чай 'tea' /čaj/, чайка 'seagull' /čajka/; elsewhere the iotated vowel letters serve for the initial position, e.g. ясно 'clear' /jasno/, while they in addition to the hard sign ъ or soft sign ь are used after consonants, e.g. съезд 'congress' /sjezd/, статья 'article' /stat′ja/. This is now the only function of the hard sign, since elsewhere the absence of the soft sign implies "hard," e.g. тот 'that' /tot/ (see also TABLE 27.2 note c).

The only case of dislocation between orthography and pronunciation in a specific morphological context concerns the adjectival ending -ого (masculine/neuter genitive singular), in which the letter г is pronounced [v]. The reasons for the change in pronunciation from the original [g], which began at the time of the rise of Moscow (ca. 15th century), are unclear, the most likely being new contact between dialects. The reasons for retaining the former spelling stem partly from the profusion of dialects, since many of them did not undergo the pronunciation change; but mostly from the influence of the Old Church Slavonic pronunciation [g], especially during the formative period of the orthography in the nineteenth century. An additional factor is the usual resistance in the twentieth century arising from the inertia of established tradition.

Extra diacritics may be used in particular circumstances, for example to indicate suprasegmental features, or to aid disambiguation. For Russian these cases are: (a) The letter ё—phonetically representing stressed [ɔ] after a soft consonant—is used both in pedagogical functions and for disambiguation, e.g. to distinguish всё *vs′o* [fsʲɔ] 'all, every' (neuter singular) from все *vs′e* [fsʲɛ] 'all' (plural). (b) The use of an acute accent indicates stress position in dictionaries and textbooks, e.g. го́род *górod*. (c) The marking of the word что́ *čtó* with an acute accent indicates the object pronoun 'what' as opposed to the clitic conjunction 'that'.

TABLE 27.2 shows the distribution of the Cyrillic letters in modern Russian.

Sample of Old Church Slavonic

Place of stress and nature of pitch are insufficiently clear, so these have not been marked in the transcription.

1. *OCS Glagolitic:*	ⰵⰲⰰⰼⰵⰾⰹⰵ	ⱉⱅⱏ	ⰾⱆⰽⱏⰹ :
2. *OCS Cyrillic:*	євађєлиє	ωтъ	лꙋкы :
3. *Croatian Glagolitic:*	ⰵⰲⰰⰼⰵⰾⰹⰵ	ⱉⱅⱏ	ⰾⱆⰽⱏⰹ :
4. *Transliteration:*	evaǵelie	otъ	luky:
5. *Transcription:*	ɛvagʲɛliɛ	ɔt(ə)	lukɨ
6. *Gloss:*	gospel	from	Luke

1. ⱂⱁⱀⰵⰶⰵ	ⱆⰱⱁ·	ⰿⱀⱁⰷⰹ	ⱀⰰⱍⱔⱎⱔ·	ⱍⰹⱀⰹⱅⰹ
2. Понєжє	ꙋбо	мноꙅи	начѧшѧ ·	чинити
3. ⱂⱁⱀⰵⰶⰵ	ⱆⰱⱁ·	ⰿⱀⱁⰷⰹ	ⱀⰰⱍⱔⱎⱔ·	ⱍⰹⱀⰹⱅⰹ
4. Poneže	ubo	mnozi	načęšę.	činiti
5. pɔnɛʒɛ	ubɔ	mnɔzi	natʃɛ̃ʃɛ̃	tʃiniti
6. since	for	many	began	to.make

1. (Glagolitic)	(Glag.)	(Glagolitic)	(Glag.)	(Glag.)
2. повѣсть·	о	ιзвѣстьныхъ	въ	насъ
3. (Glagolitic)	(Glag.)	(Glagolitic)	(Glag.)	(Glag.)
4. pověstь.	o	izvěstъnyxъ	vъ	nasъ
5. pɔvest(ɪ)	ɔ	ɪzvest(ə)nɨx(ə)	v(ə)	nas(ə)
6. story	about	known	in	us

1. (Glagolitic)	(Glag.)	(Glagolitic)	(Glag.)	(Glagolitic)
2. вештехъ·	ѣкоже	прѣдаша	намъ·	бывъшеі
3. (Glagolitic)	(Glag.)	(Glagolitic)	(Glag.)	(Glagolitic)
4. veštekhъ.	ěkože	prědašę	namъ.	byvъšei
5. vɛʃtex(ə)	ekɔʒə	prɛdaʃɛ̃	nam(ə)	bɪv(ə)ʃei
6. things	just.as	passed.on	to.us	having.been

1. (Glagolitic)	(Glagolitic)	(Glag.)	(Glagolitic)	(Glagolitic)
2. ісконі	самовидьци·	і	слѹгы	словеси·
3. (Glagolitic)	(Glagolitic)	(Glag.)	(Glagolitic)	(Glagolitic)
4. iskoni	samovidьci	i	slugy	slovesi.
5. iskɔni	samovid(ɪ)ci	i	slugɨ	slɔvɛsi
6. from.the.beginning	eyewitnesses	and	servants	of.word

'The Gospel according to Luke: For inasmuch as many have begun to compile a narrative about things known to us. Just as they were handed down to us by those who were from the beginning eyewitnesses and servants of the word.'

—*Codex Zographensis (10th–11th c.), fol. 131.*
Original in Glagolitic; Cyrillic version from Jagić 1879.
(Ligatured form of /u/ is used in place of Jagić's separate form.)

SAMPLE OF MODERN RUSSIAN

1. Russian:	Орфография	русского	письма
2. Transliteration:	Orfografija	russkogo	pis′ma
3. Transcription:	ʌrfʌ'grafɪjə	'rusk-əvə	pʲɪ's^ʲma
4. Gloss:	orthography	Russian-GEN	of.writing

1. развивалась	в	сторону	все	более	последовательного
2. razvivalas′	v	storonu	vsë	boleje	posledovatel′nogo
3. rəzvʲɪ'valəsʲ	'fstɔrənu		'fsʲɔ	'bɔlʲɪjɪ	pʌ'slʲɛdəvətʲɪlʲn-əvə
4. developed	in	direction	always	more	consistent-GEN

1. применения	фонематического-морфологического	принципа.
2. primenenija	fonematičeskogo-morfologičeskogo	principa.
3. prʲɪmʲɪnʲenʲɪjə	fənɛmʌ'tʲitʃɪsk-əvə—mərfəlʌ'gʲitʃɪsk-əvə	'prʲintsɪpə
4. of.application	phonological-GEN—morphological-GEN	of.principle

1. Принцип   этот   требует   одинакового   написания   фонем,
2. princip   ètot   trebujet   odinakovogo   napisanija   fonem,
3. 'prʲintsɨp   'ɛtət   'trʲɛbujɪt   ʌdʲɪ'nakəv-əvə   nəpʲɪ'sanʲɪjə   fʌ'nʲɛm
4. principle   this   requires   identical-GEN   of.writing   of.phonemes

1. а   также   морфем   слов,   даже   если   произношение
2. a   takže   morfem   slov,   daže   jesli   proiznošenije
3. ʌ   'tagʒə   mʌr'fʲɛm   sləf   'daʒə   'jesʲlʲɪ   prʌɪznʌ'ʃenʲɪjɪ
4. and   also   of.morphemes   of.words   even   if   pronunciation

1. их   изменяется   в   различных   грамматических   формах   слов.
2. ix   izmenjajetsja   v   različnyx   grammatičeskix   formax   slov.
3. ɪx   ɪzmʲɪ'nʲæjɪttssə   vrʌz'lʲitʃnɨx   grəmʌ'tʲitʃɪskʲɪx   'fɔrməx   sləf
4. of.them   changes   in different   grammatical   forms   of.words

'The orthography of Russian writing developed in the direction of the ever more consistent application of the phonological-morphological principle. This principle requires the identical writing of the phonemes, and also the morphemes, of words even if their pronunciation changes in different grammatical forms of the words.'

—Istrin 1963: 166.

Bibliography

Comrie, Bernard, and Greville G. Corbett. 1993. *The Slavonic Languages.* London: Routledge.

Cubberley, Paul. 1982. "Glagolitic's Armenian Connection." *Wiener Slawistischer Almanach* 9: 291–304.

———. 1993. "Alphabets and Transliteration." In Comrie and Corbett 1993: 20–59.

De Bray, Reginald G. A. 1980A. *Guide to the East Slavonic Languages.* Columbus, Ohio: Slavica.

———. 1980B. *Guide to the South Slavonic Languages.* Columbus: Slavica.

Derwing, Bruce L., and Tom M. S. Priestly. 1980. *Reading Rules for Russian.* Columbus: Slavica.

Gardiner, Sunray C. 1984. *Old Church Slavonic: An Elementary Grammar.* Cambridge: Cambridge University Press.

Istrin, Viktor Aleksandrovich. 1963. *1100 let slavjanskoj azbuki* [1100 years of the Slavic alphabet]. Moscow: Akademia Nauk SSSR.

Jagić, V. 1879. *Quattuor evangeliorum codex olim Zographensis nunc Petropolitanus.* Berlin.

Jones, Daniel, and Dennis Ward. 1969. *The Phonetics of Russian.* Cambridge: Cambridge University Press.

Stilman, Leon. 1960. *Russian Alphabet and Phonetics,* 12th ed. (1st ed. 1949). New York: Columbia University Press.

The Armenian Alphabet

AVEDIS K. SANJIAN

The Armenian alphabet, known as *aybuben* (a term coined on the Greek model by combining the names of the first two letters of the Armenian script), was created in 406 or 407 C.E. by the cleric Mesrop Maštoc' († 17 Feb. 440; cf. Koriun 1964). This alphabet, comprising 36 characters, has been the medium for the expression of all three phases of the evolution of the Armenian language: Classical (*Grabar*), Middle, and Modern; the latter is represented by two mutually intelligible literary dialects, East and West Armenian. In devising the Armenian alphabet, Mesrop was guided by the principle that each letter should represent only one sound, and that all sounds in the language should be represented by one symbol each. (According to Koriun 1964: 37, 40–41, Mesrop also invented scripts for Georgian and for Caucasian Albanian [Kurdian 1956], but this claim is not confirmed by non-Armenian sources.)

The impetus for creating an Armenian script seems to have been to permit the Armenian people access to scriptural and liturgical texts, thitherto available only in Greek or Syriac. Until Mesrop's time, the Armenians used the Greek or Aramaic languages for all written materials; enigmatic references to a "Danielian" Armenian script, named for a Syrian bishop Daniel in Mesopotamia, have not been satisfactorily explained. No examples of such a script survive, and Granian's theory (1991–92) that it was pre-Christian, replaced by Greek, then rediscovered, and merely supplemented by Mesrop with vowels, is untenable.

Modeled presumably on the Greek alphabet (though other models, such as Syriac, Phoenician, and Pahlavi, have been suggested), Armenian writing proceeds from left to right. The extra letters for Armenian sounds not found in Greek are intercalated into the order of the Greek alphabet. So perfect has been the fit of the script to the phonology of the language that it has remained intact from its inception to the present day.

The symbols

The Armenian alphabet originally comprised 30 consonants and 6 vowels. The vowel *o* and the consonant *ֆ* were introduced in the twelfth century, the first to render the diphthong *aw*, the second the foreign sound *f*.

Classical Armenian texts are now read according to either the East or West literary dialect of Modern Armenian. The vowels are pronounced almost identically in both dialects. In the case of the consonants, however, the West dialect has retained only two series, voiced and aspirated, as opposed to the original three (voiced, voiceless, and aspirated) preserved in the East dialect.

There are two standard systems of Armenian transliteration: the Hübschmann-Meillet scheme (Meillet 1980), which utilizes diacritical marks (and is used here), and the Library of Congress system, which uses Roman digraphs to reflect certain consonants. Until the adoption of the Arabic numeral system in the seventeenth century, the Armenian script was also utilized to express numbers.

TABLE 28.1 provides the inventory of the Armenian characters in their standard order, the names of the individual letters, the two transliterations according to the phonology of East Armenian, and the numerical value assigned to the letters of the alphabet.

Evidence for the scholarly consensus that the Armenian script was basically modeled on the Greek is the order of letters and the use of the combination $o + w$ (Greek ου) for the vowel u; the shapes of certain letters seem derived from a variety of cursive Greek. The Greek alphabet could not supply all the characters that the phonological system of Armenian needed; hence it is assumed that Mesrop supplemented it either by borrowing from some other writing system, or by coining new symbols. It is generally agreed that Mesrop may be credited with the invention of the letters *p ə, d ž, ḷ l, ḫ x, ծ c, ՝ h, ձ j, ճ č, յ y, ՝ č', ọ ǰ, վ v, p r*, and *ɡ c'* (Godel 1975: 3). TABLE 28.2 compares the order of letters in the Greek and Armenian alphabets.

Since its inception in the fifth century, at least four distinct varieties of the script have been created for the writing of Armenian. The oldest is the uncial called *erkat'agir* 'iron-forged letters', also referred to as the "original Mesropian" or "Mesropian *erkat'agir*." This script was the standard from the fifth through the thirteenth centuries, and it remains the preferred script for epigraphic inscriptions. Created in the tenth century, the *bolorgir* 'cursive' became the popular hand from the thirteenth century onward and has been the standard script for printing of Armenian books and periodicals since the beginning of the sixteenth century. The *notrgir* (minuscule) script, created by speedwriters and notaries in the thirteenth century, was exclusively employed during the sixteenth to eighteenth centuries, especially in the colonies of the Armenian diaspora, and subsequently became a popular mode of printing. Finally, the *šełagir* 'slanted writing' has now become the most commonly used variety. Ligatures have been employed extensively in epigraphic inscriptions since the seventh century, but they are not attested in *erkat'agir* manuscripts. In contrast, the use of ligatures in *bolorgir* and *notrgir* codices is very common.

As a written language, Classical Armenian preserved its grammatical structure through the centuries, whereas the spoken dialects underwent gradual changes. It is generally assumed that the rules of pronunciation as formulated in medieval Armenian grammars date to the eleventh or twelfth century. The pronunciation rules given here are valid for Classical as well as for the two literary dialects of Modern Armenian.

TABLE 28.1: *The Armenian Alphabet*

| LETTER | | NAME | PRONUN-CIATION | TRANSLITERATION[a] | | NUMERICAL VALUE |
Capital	Minuscule			H-M	LC	
Ա	ա	ayb	[a]	a	a	I
Բ	բ	ben	[b]	b	b (p)	2
Գ	գ	gim	[g]	g	g (k)	3
Դ	դ	da	[d]	d	d (t)	4
Ե	ե	eč'	[jɛ-, -ɛ-]	e	e, y[b]	5
Զ	զ	za	[z]	z	z	6
Է	է	ē	[e]	ē	ē	7
Ը	ը	ət'	[ə]	ə	ě	8
Թ	թ	t'o	[tʰ]	t'	t'	9
Ժ	ժ	žē	[ʒ]	ž	zh[c]	10
Ի	ի	ini	[ɪ]	i	i	20
Լ	լ	liwn	[l]	l	l	30
Խ	խ	xē	[x]	x	kh[c]	40
Ծ	ծ	ca	[ts]	c	ts[c] (dz)	50
Կ	կ	ken	[k]	k	k (g)	60
Հ	հ	ho	[h]	h	h	70
Ձ	ձ	ja	[dz]	j	dz[c] (ts)	80
Ղ	ղ	łat[	[ɣ]	ł	gh[c]	90
Ճ	ճ	čē	[ʧ]	č	ch (j)	100
Մ	մ	men	[m]	m	m	200
Յ	յ	yi	[h-, -j-]	y	y, h[d]	300
Ն	ն	nu	[n]	n	n	400
Շ	շ	ša	[ʃ]	š	sh[c]	500
Ո	ո	o	[vo-, -o-]	o	o	600
Չ	չ	č'a	[ʧʰ]	č'	ch'	700
Պ	պ	pē	[p]	p	p (b)	800
Ջ	ջ	jē	[ʤ]	ǰ	j (ch)	900
Ռ	ռ	ṙa	[r]	ṙ	ṛ	1,000
Ս	ս	sē	[s]	s	s	2,000
Վ	վ	vew	[v]	v	v	3,000
Տ	տ	tiwn	[t]	t	t (d)	4,000
Ր	ր	rē	[ɹ]	r	r	5,000
Ց	ց	c'o	[tsʰ]	c'	ts'	6,000
Ւ	ւ	hiwn	[v, w]	w	w	7,000
Փ	փ	p'iwṙ	[pʰ]	p'	p'	8,000
Ք	ք	k'ē	[kʰ]	k'	k'	9,000
Ու	ու	u	[u]	u	u	–
Օ	օ	ō	[o]	ō	ō	–
Ֆ	ֆ	fē	[f]	f	f	–

a. H-M, Hübschmann-Meillet; LC, Library of Congress (West Armenian values in parentheses).

b. This value is used only when the letter is in initial position of a name and followed by a vowel, in Classical orthography.

c. A prime is placed between the two letters representing two different sounds when the combination might otherwise be read as a digraph (e.g. Դզնունի D'znuni).

d. This value is used only when the letter is in initial position of a word or of a stem in a compound, in Classical orthography.

TABLE 28.2: *Greek and Armenian Alphabetical Order*

Gk.	α β γ δ ε ζ η θ ι κ λ μ ν ξ ο π ρ σ τ υ φ χ ψ ω
Arm.	ա բ գ դ ե զ է ը թ ժ ի լ խ ծ կ հ ձ ղ ճ մ յ ն շ ո չ պ ջ ռ ս վ տ ր ց ւ փ ք
	a b g d e z ē ət' ž i l x c k h j ł čmyn š o č' p ǰ ŕ s v t r c'wp'k'

Symbol–sound correspondences

Most Armenian letters are pronounced straightforwardly as shown in TABLE 28.1. Some notes on the semivowels and vowels are necessary.

Semivowels

The semivowel *j y* occurs in all positions: *յոյս yoys* [hujs] 'hope', *այգ ayg* 'dawn'; it can occur before the unwritten shwa and the vowels *ա a* or *ո o*, but never intervocalically. In word-final position, the *j y* is, as a rule, not pronounced: *ծառայ caŕay* [tsara] 'servant'; but it is pronounced in final position after vowels in a few monosyllabic nouns, e.g. *խոյ xoy* 'ram', *թէյ t'ēy* 'tea'.

The consonants *վ v* and *ւ w* are in complementary distribution: *վ v* occurs in word-initial position: *ի վայր i vayr* 'down', and after the vowel *ո o*: *հոգւով hogwov* 'with spirit'. Both *վ v* and *ւ w* occur either between vowels or after a vowel in word- or syllable-final position. However, *վ v* is never found between a vowel and a syllable-final consonant, while *ւ w* frequently is. Moreover, both *վ v* and intervocalic or final *ւ w* are pronounced [v]: *հաւատալ hawatal* [havatal] 'to believe', *հովիւ hoviw* [hoviv] 'shepherd'. The vowel *ու ow > ու u*, when followed by another vowel, is also pronounced [v] or [əv]: *Աստուած Astowac* [astvats] 'God'; *նուէր nowēr* [nəveːɹ] 'gift'.

Vowels

It is presumed that Classical Armenian had no contrast between long and short vowels.

The vowel *ե e* never occurs in word-final position, except in the conjunctions *թե t'e* [tʰeː] and *եթե et'e* [etʰeː], both meaning 'that', which however were later spelled *թէ t'ē* and *եթէ et'ē*.

The vowel *է ē*, as a development of the former diphthong *ei/ey*, must have once been a long vowel. In Mesrop's day, it probably contrasted with *ե e* as a close [ɛ] to an open [e]; but about the tenth century *ե e* and *է ē* merged, except in initial position. The *է ē* occurs mostly in final syllables: *սիրէ sirē* 'he, she loves', and also before vowels: *Հրէաստան Hrēastan* 'Judaea'.

The *ի i* occurs in all positions and is pronounced [ɪ]. When representing a preposition with the accusative, locative, or ablative case, and followed by a word beginning with a vowel, *ի i* becomes an inseparable *յ y*: e.g., *ի աւանի i awani > յաւանի yawani* 'in a town', pronounced [havani].

The vowel *ո o* is pronounced [vo-] word-initially, *ոճ oč* [votʃ] 'style'; exceptions are such words as the interrogative *ով ov* [ov] 'who?', *ովկիանոս ovkianos* [ovkianos] 'ocean'. In all other positions it is pronounced [o]. As seen earlier, the vowel *o aw* was added to the alphabet in the twelfth century to replace the diphthong *աւ aw*: *աւր awr > օր or* 'day'. The *o aw* is often found in printed texts of Classical Armenian but does not represent the original sound. In Modern Armenian the *o aw* has merged with *ո o*, except word-initially.

The letter *ը ə* is rarely written, even though shwa is the most common vowel in spoken Armenian and must have been so in Mesrop's time as well. In this regard Armenian orthography did not and still does not reflect phonological reality, for *ə* occurs in many positions, especially in consonant clusters. (There are words in Armenian that contain clusters of as many as six consonants, which cannot be enunciated without the insertion of the unwritten shwa: *կրակ krak* [kərak] 'fire', *խնդալ xndal* [xəndal] 'to rejoice', *բժշկութիւն bžškut'iwn* [bəzəʃkutʰiwn] 'cure', *տրտնջիւն trtnǰiwn* [tərtəndʒiwn] 'murmur', *անխղճմտանք anxłčmtank'* [anxəɣtsmətankʰ] 'lack of scruple'.) The shwa is written word-initially in monosyllables and compounds derived from them before *մ m, ն n,* or *ղ ł* plus consonant: *ըմբեմ əmbem* 'I drink'; *ընտիր əntir* 'select', *ընկեր ənker* 'companion', *ըղձամ əłjam* 'I wish, long for'; it also occurs in the prepositions *ընդ ənd* 'to, at, toward' and *ըստ əst* 'according to, in relation to'.

The following pronunciations of vowel combinations should also be noted: *եա ea* [ja], as in *ատեան atean* [atjan] 'tribunal'; *եւ ew* [ev] before vowels and in final position (note that the spelling *իւ iw* for *եւ ew* is widely found in ancient Classical Armenian texts: e.g. *միւս miws* for *մեւս mews* 'another', *իւղ iwł* for *եւղ ewł* 'oil'); *իւ iw* [ju] when followed by a consonant, as in *նիւթ niwt'* [njutʰ] 'material', but this rule does not apply to nouns ending in *-իւ -iw, -այ -ay,* or *-ոյ -oy;* and *ոյ oy* [oj] before a consonant, as in *լոյս loys* [lujs] 'light', except in word-final position, in which case it is pronounced [-o]. Also to be noted are the trigraphs *եայ eay* and *իայ iay* [ja] as in *Հրեայ Hreay* [hrja] 'Hebrew', *կրիայ kriay* [krja] 'frog'; *եաւ eaw* [jav] as in *յարեաւ yareaw* [harjav] 'he arose'.

Orthographic change and script reform

The orthography of Armenian has undergone three stages in its development (see Gyulbudałyan 1973). In the first phase (5th–10th centuries), the orthography remained an almost perfect reflection of the phonological structure of Armenian. Beginning in the eleventh century, phonological changes in the spoken vernacular began to manifest themselves, but the orthography remained intact, excepting the diphthong *աւ aw,* which was replaced by the newly adopted vowel o.

The third phase was initiated by the government of Soviet Armenia in 1922, when it decreed "reforms," ostensibly to make the orthography of Armenian more phonetic (SECTION 65). The vowel *o ō* was eliminated from the alphabet; wherever it occurred in the traditional orthography, it was replaced by the vowel *ո o*. The use of *ւ w* was restricted to its combination with *ո o* to produce the vowel *ու u*. The vowel *է ē* was also replaced by *ե e* in all positions. Initial *է ē* and *ո o* were respectively spelled *յէ- ye-* and *վո- vo-*. The diphthongs *եա ea* and *իւ iw* were also changed to *յա ya* and *յու yu* respectively. Lastly, word-initial *յ y* was replaced by *հ h*, and silent word-final *յ y* was eliminated. In 1940, however, the Soviet authorities decreed the restoration of the vowels *o ō* and *է ē*; and word-initial *e* and *o* were again written *ե e* and *ո o*. It is significant to note that Armenians in the diaspora never adopted the "reformed" Soviet orthography and have continued to employ the traditional, classical spelling.

SAMPLE OF ARMENIAN

1. Armenian:	ի	սրտին	գործարանի	երեւութ‘ացեալ	հոգւոյն
2. Transliteration:	I	srtin	gorcarani	erewut‘ac‘eal	hogwoyn
3. Transcription:	i	səɹtin	goɹtsarani	eɹevutʰatsʰial	hogwoin
4. Gloss:	in	the.heart	of.the.organ	appearing	of.the.soul

1. աչաց	թաթ	ձեռին	աջոյ	գրելով	ի վերայ	վիմի.
2. ač‘ac‘	t‘at‘	jeřin	ajoy	grelov	i veray	vimi.
3. atʃʰatsʰ	tʰatʰ	dzeɹin	adʒo	gəɹelow	i veɹa	vimi
4. of.the.eyes	the.palm	of.the.hand	of.the.right	writing	on	the.rock

1. զի	որպէս	ի	ձեան	վերջք‘	գծին	կուտեալ ունէր	ք‘արն.
2. zi	orpēs	i	jean	veřjk‘	gcin	kuteal unēr	k‘arn.
3. zi	voɹpɛs	i	dzian	veɹdʒkʰ	gətsin	kutial unɛɹ	kʰaɹn
4. for	as	in	snow	traces	of.the.lines	had.retained	the.stone

1. եւ	յարուցեալ	յաղօթից‘ն	եստեղծ	զնշանագիրս	մեր,	հանդերձ
2. Ew	yaruc‘eal	yałot‘ic‘n	estełc	znšanagirs	mer,	handerj
3. jev	haɹutsʰial	hayotʰitsʰən	jesteɣts	əznəʃanagiɹəs	meɹ	handeɹʒ
4. and	arising	from.prayer	he.fashioned	the.letters	our	together

1. Հռոփիանոսիւ	կերպաձեւեալ	զգիրն	առ	ձեռն	պատրաստ	Մեսրոպայ,
2. Hṙop‘ianosiw	kerpajeweal	zgirn	ař	jeřn	patrast	Mesropay,
3. hrop ̣ʰianosiv	keɹpadzevial	əzgiɹən	ar	dzerən	patɹast	mesɹopa
4. with.Rufinus	by.giving.shape	the.letters	by	the.hand	prepared	of.Mesrop

1. *փոխատրելով* *զՀայերէն* *աթուաթայսն* *ըստ* *անսայթակութեան*
2. poxatrelov zhayerēn atʻutʻaysn əst ansaytʻakʻutʻean
3. poxatɹelov əzhajeɹen atʰutʰajsən əst ansajtʰakʰutʰian
4. altering the.Armenian the.letters according.to the.exactness

1. *սիղաբայից* *Հելլէնացւոց:*
2. siwłabayicʻ Hellenacʻwocʻ.
3. sjuɣabajitsʰ hellenatsʰvətsʰ
4. of.the.syllables of.the.Hellenes

'There appeared to the eyes of his soul a right hand writing on the rock; for the stone retained (the shapes) as tracks are traced in snow. And arising from prayer he fashioned our alphabet, with Rufinus, who gave shape to the script prepared by Mesrop, altering the Armenian letters according to the exactness of the Greek syllables.'　　—*Moses Khorenatsʻi, after Thomson 1978: 320–21.*

Bibliography

Abrahamyan, Ashot G. 1973. *Hayocʻ Gir ev Grčʻutʻyun* [The Armenian alphabet and paleography]. Erevan: State University Press.

Akinian, Nersēs. 1938. "Hayerēn Aybubeni Giwtə" [The discovery of the Armenian alphabet]. *Handes Amsorya* 9–12: 289–318.

———. 1949. *Der heilige Mashtotz Wardapet, sein Leben und sein Wirken*. Vienna: Mekhitarist Press.

Ačaṙian, Hračʻeay. 1926. "Hay Greru Jewapʻoxutʻiwnnerə" [The development of Armenian writing systems]. *Handes Amsorya* 9–10: 505–11, 11–12: 591–98.

———. 1968. *Hayocʻ Grerə* [The Armenian letters]. Erevan: Hayastan.

Godel, Robert. 1975. *An Introduction to the Study of Classical Armenian*. Wiesbaden: Reichert.

Gyulbudałyan, Sirak V. 1973. *Hayereni Ułłagrutʻyan Pamutʻyun* [History of Armenian orthography]. Erevan: Academy of Sciences Press.

Gṙanian, Andranik. 1991–92. "Hetapndelov Daniēlian Nšanagrerə" [In pursuit of the Danielian script]. *Haigazian Hayagitakan Handes* 11: 147–79, 12: 61–80. Beirut: Haigazian College Press.

Kʻolanǰyan, Suren. 1958. "Movses Xorenacʻu Noṙahayt Erkatʻagir Pataṙikn u Danielyan Nšanagreri Ōgtagorcman Žamanaki Harcʻə" [The newly discovered Erkatʻagir fragment from Movsēs Xorenacʻi and the question of the period when the Danielian script was used]. *Banber Matenadarani* 4: 163–82. Erevan: Armenian Academy of Sciences Press.

Koriun. 1964. *The Life of Mashtots*, trans. Bedros Norehad. New York: Armenian General Benevolent Union of America.

Kurdian, H. 1956. "The Newly Discovered Alphabet of the Caucasian Albanians." *Journal of the Royal Asiatic Society* 81–83.

Marquart, Josef. 1917. *Über das armenische Alphabet in Verbindung mit der Biographie des hl. Maštocʻ*. Vienna.

Meillet, Antoine. 1913. *Altarmenische Elementarbuch*. Heidelberg: Winter.

———. 1936. *Esquisse d'une grammaire comparée de l'arménien classique*, 2nd ed. Vienna: Imprimerie des PP. Mékhitaristes.

Moses Khorenatsʻi. 1978. *History of the Armenians*, ed. and trans. Robert W. Thomson. Cambridge: Harvard University Press.

Müller, Friedrich. 1864. "Über den Ursprung der armenischen Schrift." *Sitzungsberichte der Wiener Akademie des Wissenschaften* 46: 431–39.

———. 1888–90. "Zur Geschichte der armenischen Schrift." *Wiener Zeitschrift für die Kunde des Morgenlandes* 2: 245–48, 4: 284–88.

Nersoyan, Hagop. 1985–86. "The Why and When of the Armenian Alphabet." *Journal of the Society for Armenian Studies* 2: 51–71.

Peeters, Paul. 1929. "Pour l'histoire des origines de l'alphabet arménien." *Revue des Études Arméniennes* 9: 203–37.

Tašian, Yakobos. 1898. *Aknark Mə Hay Hnagrut'ean Vray* [An outline of ancient Armenian paleography]. Vienna: Mekhitarist Press.

Yovsēp'ian, Garegin. 1912. "Hayoc' Gri Glxawor Tesaknerə" [The major systems of Armenian writing]. *Taraz* (Tiflis) 10: 168–72.

———. 1913. *Grc'ut'ean Arvestə Hin Hayoc Mēǰ* [Paleographic Art Among the Ancient Armenians], part 3. Vałaršapat, Armenia: n.p.

The Georgian Alphabet

DEE ANN HOLISKY

The Georgian alphabet known as *mxedruli* (from *mxedari* 'warrior') is used for writing the Modern Georgian literary language. It contains 33 characters and is written from left to right with a space between words and a punctuation mark at the end of sentences. Extra spaces are added between the characters of a word to indicate emphasis. *Mxedruli* uses no diacritical marks and does not indicate stress, and in printed form the characters are not connected in any way (though cursive handwriting involves numerous ligatures). There are no capitals.

The general shape of *mxedruli* characters can be described in terms of their position within four imaginary horizontal lines. Four of the characters fill only the space between the two middle lines (e.g. ა *a*, თ *t*), twelve have ascenders that fill the space between the upper two lines as well (e.g. ბ *b*, მ *m*, რ *r*), twelve have descenders (e.g. დ *d*, ლ *l*, უ *u*), and five have both ascenders and descenders (e.g. ტ *t*, კ *k*, ჭ *c*). In titles and headlines it is usual to make all characters the same height, obliterating the distinction between ascenders and descenders: ქართული დამწერლობა versus ქართული დამწერლობა *kartuli damc̣erloba* 'Georgian writing'. An attempt by the linguist Akaki Shanidze (1887–1987) to introduce the characters of the Old Georgian alphabet *asomtavruli* to mark proper names and sentence beginnings was unsuccessful, though one finds *asomtavruli* characters used as capitals in his own works and in occasionally in works written in his honor.

Historically, Georgian had no special symbols to express numbers, the *mxedruli* characters being used for this purpose. The first nine characters expressed ones; the second nine, tens; the third nine, hundreds; and the fourth nine, thousands. The final symbol stood for 10,000.

TABLE 29.1 presents the characters of *mxedruli*. The transliteration system used by linguists of Georgian is similar to one published in *IKE* (differing *IKE* versions are given in parentheses). The character ყ (representing a glottalized uvular stop) is generally transliterated *q* (without a diacritic) because it has no nonglottalized counterpart. (In a less satisfactory transliteration for *mxedruli*, that adopted by the Library of Congress, lack of diacritic on voiceless consonants represents glottalization, while aspiration is indicated with a diacritic; see Aronson 1992–93 for a critical discussion of transliteration systems.)

The order of the characters of *mxedruli* follows that of the Greek alphabet, except when a Greek character does not have a Georgian equivalent. In such cases, a non-equivalent Georgian character has been inserted. Eleven other characters of Georgian that do not have equivalents in Greek appear at the end, between ქ *k* and the last character of the *mxedruli* alphabet, representing a sound equivalent to Greek omega; this character has since been lost.

Sound–symbol correspondences

The Georgian alphabet is almost perfectly phonemic, with each character standing for a single phoneme and each phoneme represented consistently by a single character. With a few exceptions (noted below) there are no silent letters, i.e., every letter that is written is pronounced.

Allophonic alternations are not usually represented in the orthography; e.g., both velarized [ɫ] and nonvelarized [l], allophones of the same phoneme (Robins and Waterson 1952: 63), are represented by the character ლ *l*. Similarly, [v], [w], and [β], which seem to be in free variation (ibid.), are represented by ვ *v*. Voiced consonants are subject to devoicing when initial, adjacent to a voiceless consonant, or final (ibid. 66), e.g. კბილს *ķbils* [k'bi̥s] 'tooth (dative)'. Though most devoicing is not represented in the orthography, word-final /d/ of the adverbial case ending *-ad* is sometimes written თ *t* and not დ *d*: კარგად *ķargad* [k'argat] 'well', also კარგათ *ķargat*.

One may encounter characters that are written but not pronounced, particularly ჰ *h* and ს *s* (when marking an indirect object) and მ *m*, რ *r*, and ლ *l* (in clusters). Silent ჰ *h* and ს *s* are an orthographic reflection of an ongoing grammatical change. Though required by prescriptive rules, these third person indirect object markers are frequently omitted in speech; hence they are often written but not pronounced (Robins and Waterson 1952: 61, Aronson 1990: 173): ჰკითხავ *hķitxav* [hk'itxav] or [k'itxav] 'you will ask him something', სწერს *sçers* [sc'ers] or [c'ers] 'he writes (it) to him'. Some speakers omit these markers in writing as well.

Silent მ *m*, რ *r*, and ლ *l*, on the other hand, are a reflection of phonological processes. Initial /m/ followed by a voiceless consonant is usually voiceless and sometimes not pronounced: მჭადი *mçadi* [mt͡ʃ'adi] or [t͡ʃ'adi] 'cornbread' (Vogt 1936: 13). Georgian /r/ is weakened and often deleted, particularly in medial position in clusters: დაბრჯანდით *dabrjandit* [dabrdzandit] or [dabdzandit] 'sit down' (ibid.). Loss of მ *m* and რ *r* is sometimes represented in the orthography, e.g. ჭადი *çadi* 'cornbread (a staple food made from maize)', with numerous examples in Tschenkéli's dictionary, e.g. ბრჯანებლ- *brjanebl* given as a variant of the verb root მბრჯანებლ- *mbrjanebl* 'ruler', -ბჯან- *bjan* as a variant of -ბრჯან- *brjan* 'order'. Like /r/, /l/ may be lost in clusters: სახლში *saxlši* [saxlʃi] or [saxʃi] 'at home' (Vogt 1936: 15). The results of these and other phonological processes, including fast speech phenomena, are not usually reflected in the orthography.

TABLE 29.1: *The Georgian Alphabet*

MXEDRULI		TRANSLITERATION					
Regular Character	*Headline*	GREEK EQUIVALENT	NAME	IPA VALUE	*Standard, (IKE)*	*Library of Congress*	NUMERICAL VALUE
ა	ⴀ	α	ani	[a]	a	a	1
ბ	ⴁ	β	bani	[b]	b	b	2
გ	ⴂ	γ	gani	[g]	g	g	3
დ	ⴃ	δ	doni	[d]	d	d	4
ე	ⴄ	ε	eni	[ɛ]	e	e	5
ვ	ⴅ		vini	[v]	v	v	6
ზ	ⴆ	ζ	zeni	[z]	z	z	7
ჱ		η	he	[ej > e]	ey/ē	ē	8
თ	ⴇ	θ	tani	[tʰ]	t	tʻ	9
ი	ⴈ	ι	ini	[i]	i	i	10
კ	ⴉ	κ	ḳani	[k']	ḳ	k	20
ლ	ⴊ	λ	lasi	[l]	l	l	30
მ	ⴋ	μ	mani	[m]	m	m	40
ნ	ⴌ	ν	nari	[n]	n	n	50
ჲ			je	[j]	y (j)	y	60
ო	ⴍ	o	oni	[o]	o	o	70
პ	ⴎ	π	ṗari	[p']	ṗ (p)	p	80
ჟ	ⴏ		žani	[ʒ]	ž	ž	90
რ	ⴐ	ρ	rae	[r/ɾ]	r	r	100
ს	ⴑ	σ	sani	[s]	s	s	200
ტ	ⴒ	τ	ṭani	[t']	ṭ	t	300
ჳ		υ	wie	[wi]	wi/ü	w	400
უ	ⴓ	ου	uni[a]	[u]	u	u	400
ფ	ⴔ	φ	pari	[pʰ]	p	pʻ	500
ქ	ⴕ	χ	kani	[kʰ]	k	kʻ	600
ღ	ⴖ		ğani	[ɣ]	ğ (ɣ)	ġ	700
ყ	ⴗ		qari	[q']	q/q̇ (q)	q	800
შ	ⴘ		šini	[ʃ]	š	š	900
ჩ	ⴙ		čini	[tʃ]	č	čʻ	1000
ც	ⴚ		cani	[ts]	c	cʻ	2000
ძ	ⴛ		jili	[dz]	j (ʒ)	ż	3000
წ	ⴜ		çili	[ts']	ç	c	4000
ჭ	ⴝ		čari	[tʃ']	ç	č	5000
ხ	ⴞ		xani	[x]	x	x	6000
ჴ			qari	[q]	q	ẋ	7000
ჯ	ⴟ		ǰan	[dʒ]	ǰ (ž̌)	j	8000
ჰ	ⴠ		hae	[h]	h	h	9000
ჵ		ω	oh (hoe)	[ow]	ow/ō	ō	10000

a. ⴓ *u* originated as a fusion of ⴍ *o* and ჳ *wi*, subsequently replacing ჳ and assuming its numerical value.

The development of *mxedruli*

The earliest example of Georgian writing is from 430 C.E., an inscription in a church in Palestine (Tsereteli 1961). It is written in a script completely unlike *mxedruli*, known as *asomtavruli* 'capital letter', also called *mrglovani* 'rounded' because of the rounded shapes of the characters in the earliest versions. *Asomtavruli* was in use from the fifth to the ninth century, after which it was gradually replaced by a more angular script called *nusxa-xucuri*, also known as *kutxovani* 'angular', used from the ninth to the eleventh century. *Nusxa-xucuri* developed into the rounder *mxedruli*, which appeared first in the tenth century and developed into a distinctly different shape by the thirteenth (Schanidse 1982: 11–13, Gamkrelidze 1990: 204–5).

Mxedruli was initially restricted to secular functions, while the two older scripts continued to be used in religious writings. At first, characters from both were mixed together, but eventually *nusxa-xucuri* prevailed, and *asomtavruli* was confined to use in titles and as the initial character of sentences. The two together are often called *xucuri* (from *xucesi* 'priest'). Ultimately *mxedruli* came to be used in religious writings as well as secular ones (Schanidse 1982: 18).

The *mxedruli* characters underwent remarkably little change in shape from eleventh-century manuscripts, to their first appearance in print in 1669, to the form standard in twentieth-century printing (see examples in Mačavariani 1989). Certain minor additions to the alphabet were introduced by Anton I in the eighteenth century, while more significant reform was conducted under the leadership of Ilia Chavchavadze in the 1860s (Dzidziguri 1986: 474). At that time five characters that no longer corresponded to sounds of Modern Georgian were dropped.

Although Armenian sources credit Mesrop Mashtots' with the creation of *asomtavruli*, this is effectively refuted by Gamkrelidze (1990: 194–95). Popular legends as well as some scholarly treatments place the creation of the alphabet in pre-Christian times, but Gamkrelidze (pp. 196–97) argues persuasively that it must have followed the advent of Christianity in Georgia (circa 337); the forms of the letters are freely invented in imitation of the Greek model.

Mxedruli is used almost exclusively for writing the Modern Georgian literary language, based on the Kartli dialect, but it has been used for writing in other Georgian dialects as well. It has been used occasionally for writing Mingrelian, a language related to Georgian, and was used at one time for writing Abkhaz, an unrelated language of the Northwest Caucasian language family (Hewitt 1989: 18).

SAMPLE OF GEORGIAN

1. Mxedruli:	სომხური	ისტორიული	წყაროები	ძველი	ქართული	ანბანის
2. Transliteration:	somxuri	isṭoriuli	çqaroebi	jveli	kartuli	anbanis
3. Transcription:	somxuri	isṭ'oriuli	ts'qaroɛbi	dzvɛli	kartuli	anbanis
4. Gloss:	Armenian	historical	sources	Old	Georgian	of.alphabet

1. შექმნას ... იმავე მესროპ-მაშტოცს მიაწერს. მაგრამ ამავე
2. šekmnas imave *mesrop-maštocs* miaçers. magram amave
3. ʃekmnas imavɛ mɛsrop'maʃtots miatsʼɛrs magram amavɛ
4. creation that.same Mesrop Mashtots' ascribes but this.same

1. ცნობების მიხედვით ირკვევა, რომ მესროპ-მაშტოცი
2. cnobebis mixedvit irkveva, rom *mesrop-maštocs*
3. tsnobɛbis mixɛdvit irk'vɛva rom mɛsrop'maʃtots
4. information according.to it.is.ascertained that Mesrop Mashtots'

1. თვით არ იყო დაუფლებული ქართულს, რაც სრულიად გამორიცხავს
2. tvit ar iqo dauplebeli kartuls rac sruliad *gamoricxavs*
3. tvit ar iqo dauplɛbɛli kartuls rats sruliad gamoritsxavs
4. self not was fluent Georgian which completely rules.out

1. შესაძლებლობას მის მიერ ქართული ანბანის შექმნისას.
2. šesajleblobas mis mier kartuli anbanis šekmnisas
3. ʃesadzlɛblobas mis miɛr kartuli anbanis ʃekmnisas
4. possibility him by Georgian of.alphabet of.creation

'Armenian historical sources ascribe the creation of the Georgian alphabet to
that very *Mesrop Mashtots'*, but according to the same source of information, it
can be ascertained that *Mesrop Mashtots'* himself was not fluent in Georgian,
which completely *rules out* the possibility that the Georgian alphabet was created by him.'   —*Gamkrelidze 1990: 195, cf. 1994: 81.*

―――――

Bibliography

Aronson, Howard I. 1989. *Georgian: A Reading Grammar.* Columbus, Ohio: Slavica.
―――. 1992–93. "Transliterating Georgian." *Annual of the Society for the Study of Caucasia* 4–5:
    77–84.
Boeder, Winfried. 1975. "Zur Analyse des altgeorgischen Alphabets." In *Forschung und Lehre, Ab-
    schiedsschrift zu Joh. Schröpfers Emeritierung,* ed. D. Gerhardt et al., pp. 17–34. Hamburg:
    Slawisches Seminar.
Deeters, Gerhard. 1955. "Das Alter der georgischen Schrift." *Oriens Christianus* 39: 56–65.
Dzidziguri, Shota. 1969. *The Georgian Language.* Tbilisi: Tbilisi University Press, esp. pp. 42–51,
    "The Origin of the Georgian Alphabet."
―――. 1974. *Literaṭurul-enatmecnieruli narḳvevebi.* Tbilisi: Merani, esp. pp. 253–69, "Kartuli an-
    banis çarmošoba" [The origin of the Georgian alphabet].
―――. 1986. "Kartuli damçerloba" [Georgian writing]. *Kartuli sabçota enciḳlopedia* 10: 473–74.
    Tbilisi.
Gamkrelidze [Gamqrelidze], Thomas V. 1990. *Çeris anbanuri sisṭema da jveli kartuli damçerloba*
    [Alphabetic writing and the Old Georgian script] (in Georgian and Russian with English sum-
    mary on dust jacket). Tbilisi: Tbilisi University Press. English version: Delmar, N.Y: Caravan
    Books, 1994.
Hewitt, B. George. 1989. *The Indigenous Languages of the Caucasus,* vol. 2, *The North West Cau-
    casian Languages,* Delmar, N.Y.: Caravan Books.

IKE = *Iberiul-Ḳavḳasiuri enatmecnierebis çeliçdeuli* [Annual of Ibero-Caucasian linguistics] vol. L.

Mačavariani, Elene. 1989. *Mçignobrobay kartuli* [Georgian writing]. Tbilisi: Kartuli sabčota en-
ciḳloṗedia.

Robins, Robert H., and Natalie Waterson. 1952. "Notes on the Phonetics of the Georgian Word."
Bulletin of the School of Oriental and African Studies 14: 55–72.

Schanidse [Shanidze], Akaki. 1982. *Grammatik der Altgeorgischen Sprache,* trans. Heinz Fähnrich.
Tbilisi: Tbilisi University Press.

Tschenkéli, Kita. 1960–74. *Georgisch-Deutsches Wörterbuch.* Zurich: Amirani-Verlag.

Tsereteli, George V. 1961. "The Most Ancient Georgian Inscriptions in Palestine." *Bedi Kartlisa* 11–
12: 111–30.

Vogt, Hans. 1936. "Esquisse d'une grammaire du géorgien moderne." *Norsk Tidsskrift for Sprog-
videnskap* 9–10: 5–188.

Part VI: South Asian
Writing Systems

WRITING PLAYED A SIGNIFICANTLY DIFFERENT CULTURAL ROLE in traditional South Asia (i.e. the Indian subcontinent) than in many other parts of the ancient world. In general, writing in traditional Indian culture never achieved the status and influence that it attained in many other cultures such as those of the ancient Near East, the Islamic world, or China. Oral traditions were usually more revered than written ones in India, and sacred texts such as the Vedas or the Buddhist canon were originally preserved by memory rather than in written form, which was felt to be less reliable. This low status may account in part at least for the uncertainties about the early history of writing in India, since its principal function may have been for ephemeral documents which have not survived.

The language of the Vedas is an ancestor of Classical Sanskrit known as Vedic; the language of the southern Buddhist scriptures is known as Pali, one of many Prakrits—vernacular languages descended from or closely related to Sanskrit. Dozens of languages of contemporary South Asia represent derivatives of the Prakrits. All these languages belong to the Indo-Aryan (or Indic) branch of the Indo-Iranian family, the southeasternmost component of Indo-European. Speakers of the earliest putative ancestor of these languages probably entered the region from the northwest in the mid second millennium B.C.E., apparently displacing southward the indigenous speakers of Dravidian languages (which cannot be grouped with any other language family). Dravidian left its mark on Indic as the source of the "retroflex" series of consonants that are so characteristic of Indian speech—and required the addition of numerous letters to the script on which those of India were modeled. A third sizable family of languages in India is the Munda, a branch of Austro-Asiatic, which is otherwise mainly confined to Southeast Asia. The Munda languages were not written until recently, and no Munda language is among the fifteen "scheduled" languages of the Indian Constitution (10 Indic, including Sanskrit; 4 Dravidian; and English); they are classed as "tribal."

371

The earliest writing of South Asia was the Indus script, which originated in the third millennium B.C.E. but seems to have died out in the following millennium. This script remains undeciphered, and in the current state of our knowledge there is no cogent evidence to connect it with later forms of writing in South Asia.

These later Indic scripts, namely Brāhmī and Kharoṣṭhī, appear much later in history; other than the Indus script, the earliest definitely datable written documents in South Asia are the inscriptions of the emperor Aśoka (mid-3rd century B.C.E.). Many scholars feel that the origins of these scripts must have gone back farther than this, but there is no conclusive proof. References to writing in literary sources from the pre-Ashokan period are mostly vague and inconclusive and difficult to date precisely. The clearest early reference to writing as such (Sanskrit *lipi*) is in Pāṇini's Sanskrit grammar, usually dated to about the fourth century B.C.E., but even here it is not certain what type of writing is referred to. Thus although many scholars are inclined to believe that the Indian scripts were developed around the fifth or fourth centuries B.C.E. or even earlier, some recent studies have denied any significant prehistory to these scripts and dated their origins to the late fourth to middle third centuries B.C.E. The source of the Brāhmī and Kharoṣṭhī scripts is also controversial, but the theory which attributes both of them directly or indirectly to a Semitic prototype, probably Aramaic, is clearly the most convincing one.

The later history of South Asian scripts consists essentially of the development and regional diversification of Brāhmī script, which became the ancestor of dozens of scripts of South, Southeast, and Inner Asia. Early regional varieties of Brāhmī eventually developed into distinct scripts, often associated with particular languages of the Indo-Aryan, Dravidian, and other families. But in systemic terms, the Indic scripts typically share the same basic principles of the *akṣara* system, i.e. a modified consonantal syllabary representing most vowels by diacritic signs attached to the consonants. In recent centuries, under Islamic influence, the Arabic script has become the written vehicle for some South Asian languages (e.g. Urdu, Sindhi, Kashmiri), and under still more recent European influence, the Roman script has been introduced for still others (e.g. Konkani, some Austro-Asiatic languages such as Khasi, and some Sino-Tibetan languages such as Lushai).

— RICHARD G. SALOMON

Brahmi and Kharoshthi

RICHARD G. SALOMON

Except for the much older and still undeciphered Indus Valley script (SECTION 11), the history of writing in India consists essentially of the Brāhmī and Kharoṣṭhī scripts and their derivatives. The oldest datable records in these scripts are the rock and pillar inscriptions of the Mauryan emperor Aśoka, from the middle of the third century B.C.E. There are a few minor inscriptions in Brāhmī which may be contemporary with or even somewhat earlier than the Aśokan inscriptions, but none of these are dated. Recently, Falk (1993) has suggested that Brāhmī script was most likely created during the Mauryan Empire, possibly under Aśoka himself. Kharoṣṭhī was probably somewhat older, probably having been developed in northwestern India in the fourth or even fifth century B.C.E.

The Brāhmī script is written from left to right (though several specimens running from right to left have been found). In its early forms, it has an angular, horizontally symmetrical, and pronouncedly monumental appearance (TABLES 30.1–30.4). From the earliest attested times, Brāhmī was used in all parts of India except for the northwestern regions, where Kharoṣṭhī prevailed. In the early period, Brāhmī was more or less unitary all over South Asia, but it evolved over the centuries into diverse regional variants which gradually came to be perceived as separate scripts. The earliest distinct regional varieties are those of South India, including the Brāhmī used in the Old Tamil inscriptions—which has a significantly different system of vowel notation, probably influenced by the phonetic structure of the Dravidian languages (Mahadevan 1971). By about the third century C.E., several distinct regional subvarieties had arisen, and these continued to differentiate until, by around 1000 C.E., the situation approximated the modern picture in which the Brāhmī-derived scripts have developed to the point that they are in effect independent scripts whose common ancestry may not be apparent to the casual observer. Particularly characteristic of the Indic scripts is the head-mark in its numerous varieties. This was originally an incidental serif arising from the use of a reed pen, which came to be perceived as an integral part of the letters and was extended in various distinctive ways in the regional scripts, such as the continuous top-line of Devanāgarī, the semi-circular "umbrella" of Oriya, and the "check-mark" of Kannada.

Brāhmī, as developed in India and as exported to other parts of Asia in the first millennium C.E., is the ultimate source not only of all of the indigenous scripts of South Asia but also of the major Southeast Asian scripts (Burmese, Thai, Lao, Khmer,

TABLE 30.1: *Brahmi Primary Vowels*

	SHORT		LONG	
	Initial	*Diacritic*	*Initial*	*Diacritic*
Unrounded low central	ꤰ a [ə]	_ ✚ ka	ꤰ ā [aː]	‾ ✚ kā
high front	∴ i [i]	⁻ ✚ ki	∷ ī [iː]	⁻ ✚ kī
Rounded high back	㇄ u [u]	⁼ ✚ ku	㇄ ū [uː]	⁼ ✚ kū

TABLE 30.2: *Brahmi Secondary Vowels*

	LONG		DIPHTHONGS	
	Initial	*Diacritic*	*Initial*	*Diacritic*
Unrounded front	▷ e	⁻ ✚ ke	▷ ai	⁼ ✚ kai
Rounded back	㇄ o	⁼ ✚ ko	–	⁼ ✚ kau

etc.), of Tibetan, and of other Central Asian scripts no longer in use. It thus constitutes one of the most important "parent" scripts of the world, rivaling Aramaic and Arabic in the number and range of its varieties and derivatives.

There is considerable confusion and inconsistency concerning the names of the pre-modern Indic scripts, mainly because the indigenous traditions provide little information on the subject; even the terms "Brāhmī" and "Kharoṣṭhī" themselves had to be recovered by modern scholars from rare references in Buddhist and Jaina texts.

TABLE 30.3: *Brahmi Occlusives*

	VOICELESS PLOSIVES		VOICED PLOSIVES		NASALS
	Unaspirated	*Aspirated*	*Unaspirated*	*Aspirated*	
Velar	✚ k [k]	⌐ kh	∧ g [g]	ⴑ gh	⊏ ṅ [ŋ]
Palatal	d c [c]	ⴐ ch	Ɛ j [ɟ]	Ρ jh	ℏ ñ [ɲ]
Retroflex	⊂ ṭ [ʈ]	⊙ th	⊣ ḍ [ɖ]	ⴳ ḍh	I ṇ [ɳ]
Dental	⋏ t [t]	⊙ th	⟩ d [d]	ⅅ dh	⅃ n [n]
Labial	㇄ p [p]	ⴱ ph	☐ b [b]	ⴖ bh	४ m [m]

TABLE 30.4: *Brahmi Sonorants and Fricatives*

	Palatal	*Retroflex*	*Dental*	*Labial*	*Other*
Sonorants	⅃ y [j]	┃ r [r]	⌡ l [l]	◊ v [ʋ]	
Sibilants	∧ ś [ç]	ⴲ ṣ [ʂ]	ⴕ s [s]		㇄ h [h]

TABLE 30.5: *Kharoshthi Vowels*

			Initial			Diacritic	
Unrounded	low central	૧	a	[ə]	–	⟩	ka
	high front	⟨	i	[i]	⟨	⟩	ki
Rounded	high back	⟩	u	[u]	=	⟩	ku
Syllabic vibrant		–			=	⟩	kṛ
Mid	front unrounded	⟨	e	[e]	⟨	⟩	ke
	back rounded	⟩	o	[o]	⟨	⟩	ko

In general, the modern practice is to refer to script forms up to about the fourth century C.E. as types of "Brāhmī," loosely divided into "early," "middle," and "late," and to later Brāhmī-derived scripts by regional or descriptive terms like "early Telugu-Kannada script" or "box-headed southern script."

Kharoṣṭhī, in striking contrast to Brāhmī, was essentially a regional script only, and died out in ancient times, leaving no modern descendants. In South Asia, Kharoṣṭhī was restricted to the regions of the northwest approximately corresponding to modern northern Pakistan and eastern Afghanistan, though some specimens are found in adjoining areas of India proper. Kharoṣṭhī was always written from right to left, and in contrast to the monumental appearance of early Brāhmī had a decidedly cursive look (TABLES 30.5–30.7). It is well attested from the Aśokan period until about the third century C.E., when it began to fall out of use in South Asia, being replaced by derivatives of Brāhmī. In the meantime, however, Kharoṣṭhī (along with Brāhmī) spread to Inner Asia, where it is abundantly attested around the second and

TABLE 30.6: *Kharoshthi Occlusives*

	VOICELESS PLOSIVES				VOICED PLOSIVES				NASALS	
	Unaspirated		*Aspirated*		*Unaspirated*		*Aspirated*			
Velar	⟩	k [k]	⟩	kh	⟩	g [g]	⟩	gh		
Palatal	⟩	c [c]	⟩	ch	⟩	j [ɟ]	⟩	jh	⟩	ñ [ɲ]
Retroflex	⟩	ṭ [ṭ]	⟩	ṭh	⟩	ḍ [ḍ]	⟩	ḍh	⟩	ṇ [ṇ]
Dental	⟩	t [t]	⟩	th	⟩	d [d]	⟩	dh	⟩	n [n]
Labial	⟩	p [p]	⟩	ph	⟩	b [b]	⟩	bh	⟩	m [m]

TABLE 30.7: *Kharoshthi Sonorants and Fricatives*

	Palatal		Retroflex		Dental		Labial		Other	
Sonorants	⟩	y [j]	⟩	r [r]	⟩	l [l]	⟩	v [ʋ]		
Sibilants	⟩	ś [ɕ]	⟩	ṣ [ʂ]	⟩	s [s]			⟩	h [h]

TABLE 30.8: *Representative Examples of Consonant Clusters*

Brahmi				Kharoshthi			
khya	𝟏	mha	𝟖	kṣa	Ƴ	rva	ꝫ
tva	𝛌	sta	𝑑𝑥	tra	ᒃ	sta	ꝥ
pta	𝐤	rva	𝟏	tva	ꟺ	spa	ꝑ
pra	ꝉ	sya	𝑑	pra	ᖯ	sya	ꭍ

third centuries in the oasis cities around the Tarim Basin (Xinjiang-Uyghur Autonomous Region, China) and in Uzbekistan and neighboring regions of western Inner
Asia. Certain documents, as yet poorly understood, from the northern Silk Route oa-
ses appear to be in local derivatives of Kharoṣṭhī, possibly as late as the seventh century; but other than this, Kharoṣṭhī died out without any survivals, and unlike Brāhmī
did not undergo any radical changes in form during the five centuries or so in which
it was in wide use.

Systemic features

Despite their superficial differences, Brāhmī and Kharoṣṭhī are systemically of essentially the same type, namely diacritically modified consonant syllabic scripts, or
alphasyllabaries. This characteristically Indian script type, particularly as developed
in Brāhmī, is remarkably stable, and nearly all the later Indic and extra-Indic scripts
derived from it follow essentially the same system. This system is based on the unit
of the graphic "syllable" or *akṣara*, which by definition always ends with a vowel
(type V, CV, CCV, etc.). Syllables consisting of a vowel only (usually at the beginning
of a word or sentence) are written with the *full* or *initial* vowel signs, e.g. ∴ *i*. But
when, as is much more frequently the case, the syllable consists of a consonant followed by a vowel, the vowel is indicated by a diacritic sign attached to the basic sign
for the consonant; e.g. Brāhmī ✦ *ki*. However, the basic consonantal character without any diacritic modification is understood to automatically denote the consonant
with the "inherent" vowel *a* [ə]; thus ✛ *ka*. A graphic "syllable" consisting of a cluster
of two or more consonants followed by a vowel (type CCV, CCCV, etc.) requires that
the consonants be joined together in a *conjunct* character to indicate the cancellation
of the inherent *a* vowel of the preceding consonant(s), thus ✚ *kta* (as opposed to ✛𝛌
kata); see TABLE 30.8. Common consonantal combinations, particularly those involving the sonorant *r*, tended to develop into special ligatures in the later forms of
both scripts and their derivatives.

Although they share the same basic system, there are significant systemic differences between Brāhmī and Kharoṣṭhī. Whereas Brāhmī has separate signs for short
and long vowels, both initial and post-consonantal/diacritic, Kharoṣṭhī indicates
vowel quality only, the same sign indicating both short and long vowels; thus ꓔ = *ka*

or *kā*, ✝ = *ki* or *kī*, etc. And while the initial vowel signs in Brāhmī are distinct for each vowel type (e.g. ℍ *a*, ∴ *i*, L *u*), in Kharoṣṭhī they are all based on the sign for *a*, to which are added the post-consonantal diacritics to indicate the other vowels (e.g. ጓ *a*, ⅃ *i*, ⅃ *u*). The system of representing consonantal clusters is essentially the same in the two scripts, but Kharoṣṭhī has several anomalous ligatures of uncertain origin, whereas all the combinations in early Brāhmī are visually transparent.

Linguistic features

All early documents in both Brāhmī and Kharoṣṭhī are written in various Middle Indo-Aryan ("Prakrit") dialects, and it appears that the scripts originally developed in connection with these languages. The early forms of these scripts thus lack signs for certain sounds, such as the vowels *r̥*, *l̥*, *ai*, and *au*, the velar nasal *ṅ*, and the *visarga* (unvoiced aspirate *ḥ*), which occur in Sanskrit but not in Prakrit. These characters begin to appear only around the first century B.C.E., when we first find Brāhmī inscriptions in Sanskrit. It is also then that vowelless consonants in final position are first represented, usually by a reduced form of the normal consonant with a horizontal line above. From this time onward the phonetic repertoire of Sanskrit comes to be the defining framework of Brāhmī and the Indic scripts derived from it. Virtually all of these, with the notable exception of Tamil script, which is heavily influenced by Dravidian phonetic structures, take the sound inventory and alphabetic order of Sanskrit as the basis of their graphic systems, with some necessary adaptations for writing other languages.

The Kharoṣṭhī script is specifically linked to the Middle Indo-Aryan dialect of the northwest, generally known as Gāndhārī, and some of its graphic features reflect the phonetic peculiarities of this language. For instance, intervocalic consonants often bear a diacritic sign which is thought to mark a fricative or otherwise modified pronunciation (e.g. ⴷ *ǵa* [ɣa]). An alternative character order known as Arapacana, widespread in Buddhist tradition, which incorporates conjunct as well as simple *akṣara*, probably originated in association with Kharoṣṭhī. *u ru pu cu nu la da ba ḍa ṣa va ta ya ṣṭa ka sa ma ga tha ja śva (sva) dha śa kha kṣa sta jña rtha (ha, pha, ita) bha cha sma hva tsa (sta) gha ṭha ṇa pha ska ysa śca ṭa ḍha (sta)* (Salomon 1990). Although there are a few specimens of Sanskrit written in Kharoṣṭhī, the script lacks characters for some Sanskrit sounds, such as the diphthongs *ai* and *au*. Some later Kharoṣṭhī documents have a diacritic stroke indicating a long vowel, which presumably developed in connection with the writing of Sanskrit and/or under the influence of Brāhmī.

Functions

The early forms of both Brāhmī and Kharoṣṭhī are known primarily from epigraphic materials, mostly inscriptions on stone and copper or other metals. They were undoubtedly also used for non-epigraphic purposes, but due to the destructive climate very few such documents survive in South Asia, though we do have early non-epi-graphic specimens on wood, leather, palm leaf, and birch bark from Inner Asia. The surviving documents are mostly religious records, Buddhist in the case of Kharoṣṭhī, and Buddhist, Brahmanical, or Jaina in Brāhmī.

The Indic scripts, especially later forms of Brāhmī from about the fourth century C.E., developed several notable calligraphic variants, some of which are so radically modified as to present serious difficulties in reading. Notable among the latter class of extreme calligraphic developments are the so-called "Ornate Brāhmī" and "Shell Script" or *śaṅkhalipi*.

Origins

The origin of Brāhmī is controversial, the theories generally falling into two camps: that which sees it as a derivative of a Semitic prototype, whether Phoenician, Arama-ic, or South Semitic, and that which views it as an indigenous Indian invention, often associated with the Indus Valley script. The Semitic theory, originally propounded by Albrecht Weber in 1856 and elaborated by Georg Bühler (1898), is fairly widely ac-cepted in the West, while the indigenous origin is generally preferred in South Asia. On the whole, the Semitic theory is much more strongly, though not conclusively, supported by the available data. Comparisons of the forms of early Brāhmī letters with presumed Phoenician or Aramaic prototypes are suggestive of a historical con-nection, but only about half the characters can be more or less clearly associated with corresponding Semitic letters.

More persuasive are systemic and comparative considerations; scripts of the In-dic alphasyllabic type can be readily explained as an adaptation of a consonant-syl-labic Semitic parent, whereas the invention of such a script type ex nihilo or by evolution from a (presumably) logosyllabic prototype (i.e. the Indus script) would be highly untypical of the normal patterns of historical development of scripts. More-over, certain patterns of early Brāhmī, for example the representation of the aspirate consonants *kha*, *gha*, and *tha* by forms that can be associated with Aramaic *qoph*, *ḥet*, and *ṭet* respectively, are suggestive of a Semitic background. Thus, although a final judgment should perhaps be withheld pending substantive progress toward the deci-pherment of the Indus script, some connection with the Semitic syllabaries is strongly supported by the evidence. More specifically, a connection with Aramaic, suggested by Diringer (1968: 262) among others, is much more plausible on historical and geo-graphical grounds than the Phoenician derivation propounded by Bühler. In all prob-ability, Brāhmī was developed at some indeterminate time, perhaps as late as the third century B.C.E., as a loose adaptation of Aramaic to Indic languages.

The origin of Kharoṣṭhī is much less problematic, as its formal and systemic re-lationship to Aramaic is patently evident. Unlike Brāhmī, the large majority of the characters of Kharoṣṭhī can be readily connected with the corresponding Aramaic let-ters. Moreover, the historical circumstances of such an origin are easily explained, since Kharoṣṭhī arose in the western reaches of India which from the late sixth century B.C.E. were under the control of the Achaemenian Empire, where Aramaic was widely used.

Development

The later history of South Asian scripts consists mainly of the development and regional diversification of Brāhmī, which became the ancestor of dozens of scripts of South, Southeast, and Inner Asia, while the Kharoṣṭhī script died out around the third or fourth century C.E. Brāhmī gradually developed regional varieties which became increasingly diverse and eventually developed into distinct scripts, many of which were associated with particular regional languages such as Bengali, Gujarati, Telugu, and Tamil. Most of the modern Indic scripts achieved their distinct forms between the tenth and fifteenth centuries. However, the Indian tradition itself does not record distinct names for most of the premodern scripts, so that there is no definitive standard terminology for them (cf. page 374).

Although the earliest forms of Brāhmī (known from the 3rd century B.C.E.) were more or less standardized throughout South Asia, by the early centuries of the Common Era a broad division between Northern and Southern styles had emerged. These developed in succeeding centuries into subvarieties which can be broadly divided into Western and Eastern varieties in the north and into Deccan and Peninsular varieties in the south. The dominant style in the north from about the seventh through tenth centuries, generally known as Siddhamātṛkā (one of the few traditional scripts for which we do have a traditional name), is the main source of the modern Devanagari, the dominant script of North India (SECTION 31); as well as of Bengali (SECTION 34) and Oriya (SECTION 35), the main scripts of eastern India; and of Tibetan (SECTION 40).

In the south, the derivatives of Brāhmī in the Deccan underlie the modern Kannada and Telugu scripts (SECTION 37), while the scripts of the far south led to the modern Tamil (SECTION 39) and Malayalam (SECTION 38). Other branches of the Brāhmī-derived family include the scripts of the western Himalayan regions, of which the modern Gurmukhi or Punjabi script is the only important modern survivor (SECTION 33). The Śāradā script of Kashmir, once important but now virtually defunct, also belongs to this group. The Sinhalese script (SECTION 36) underwent a largely separate process of development from early Brāhmī; it was imported from North India but was influenced at various stages of its development by peninsular south Indian scripts. Besides these major literary scripts, innumerable other local scripts and varieties are known from all periods of history, some of which are still in use in parts of modern South Asia. The modern Gujarati script (SECTION 32) is an example of a local variety of the Devanagari-based northern scripts which attained the level of a distinct regional writing.

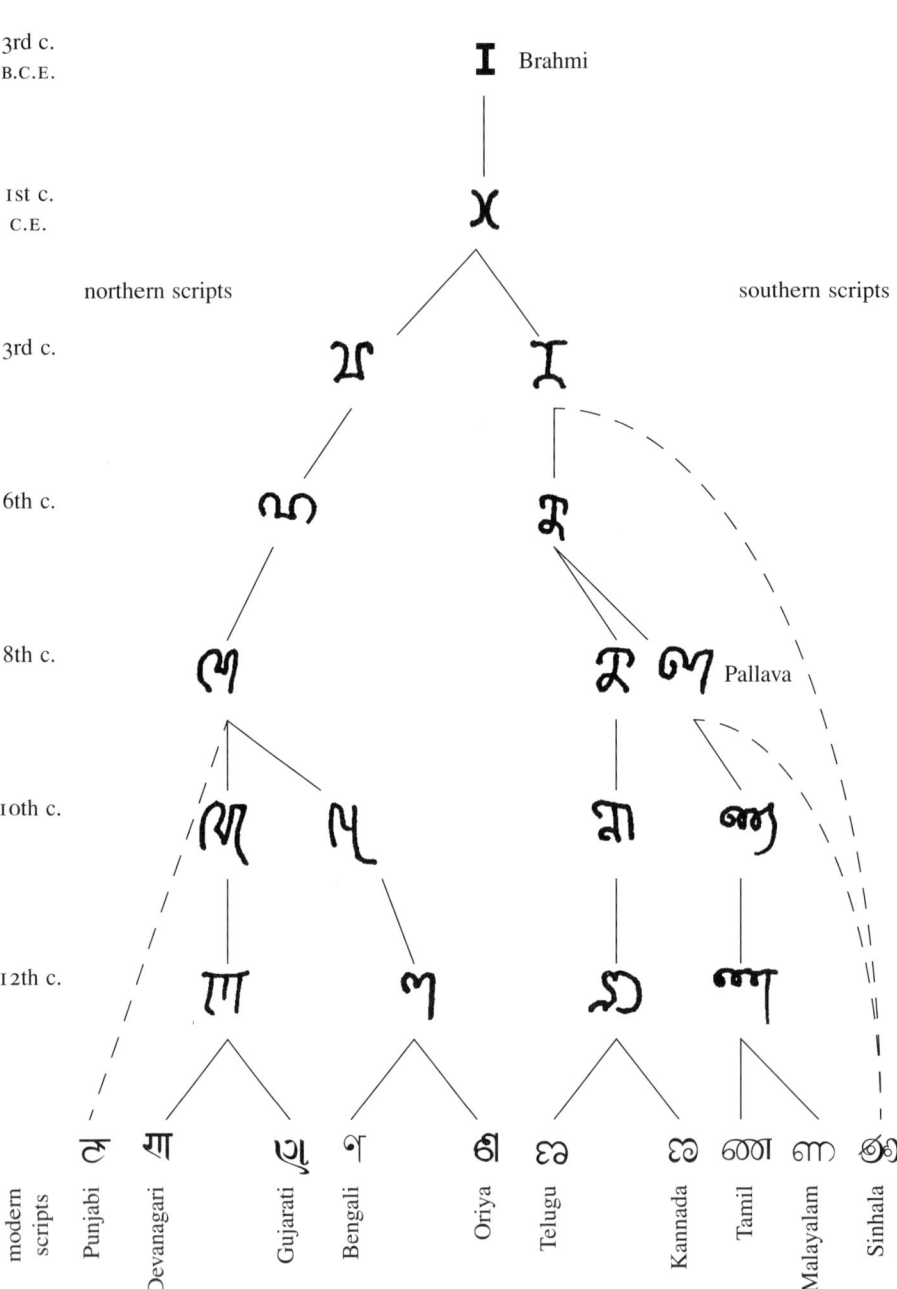

FIGURE 54. Development of *ṇa* in Brahmi and its modern standard descendants.

FIGURE 54 outlines the paleographic development of a single character, the consonant *ṇa*, from early Brāhmī to the major modern scripts. The changes illustrate the various processes of graphic alteration, such as cursivization, stroke reduction, and development of a characteristic ductus, which account for the gradual differentiation of the derivative scripts. Despite their very different superficial appearance, however, which often disguises their genetic relationships, nearly all the Brāhmī-derived scripts retain the basic systemic principles of the *akṣara* system, i.e. a diacritically modified consonantal signary. Among the major modern scripts, only Tamil has developed a major modification of this system, in using a diacritical mark to indicate a vowelless consonant, thereby obviating the need for the conjunct consonants which are characteristic of Indian scripts in general.

SAMPLE OF EARLY (AŚOKAN) BRĀHMĪ

1. Brāhmī:	꠱ꠦꠡꠧ	꠲ꠧꠡ	ꠥꠦꠑ
2. Transliteration:	devāna-piyena	piya-dasina	lājina
3. Transcription:	deːvaːnə-pijeːnə	pijə-dəsinə	laːɟinə
4. Gloss:	By.Beloved-of.the.Gods	of.Loving-Regard	the.King

1. ꠥ꠩꠪꠲ꠧꠡ	ꠑꠅ	ꠑꠧ꠪	ꠥꠦ꠪	꠲	ꠃꠃ	ꠦꠅ
2. vīsativasābhisitena	atana	āgāca	mahīyite	hida	budhe	jāte
3. viːsəti-vəsa:bʰisite:nə	ətənə	a:ga:cə	məhi:jite:	hidə	budʰe:	ɟa:te
4. twenty-years.anointed	himself	came	worshiped	here	the.Buddha	was.born

1. ꠅꠑ꠲ꠧ	ꠅ	꠲꠲ꠅꠧ꠪ꠦꠡ꠲	ꠤ꠲ꠅꠡ	꠲꠲ꠅꠟꠦ
2. sakyamunī	ti	silā-vigaḍa-bhīcā	kālāpita	silā-thabhe
3. səkjəmuni:	ti	sila:-vigəḍə-bʰi:ca:	ka:la:pitə	sila:-tʰəbʰe:
4. Śākyamuni	because	stone-inlaid-walls(?)	caused.to.be.made	stone-pillar

1. ꠖ	꠲ꠅꠧꠡꠡ	ꠑꠧ	ꠦ꠪ꠧꠅ	ꠦꠅ	ꠅ
2. ca	usapāpite	hida	bhagavaṃ	jāte	ti
3. cə	usəpa:pite:	hidə	bʰəɡəvə	ɟa:te:	ti
4. and	caused.to.be.erected	here	the.Lord	was.born	because

'The King, Beloved of the Gods, of Loving Regard, when he had been anointed for twenty years, came (here) in person and worshiped, because the Buddha Śākyamuni was born here. He caused walls inlaid with stone(?) to be constructed and caused (this) stone pillar to be erected, because the Lord was born here.'

— *The Rummindeī Pillar Edict in Old Ardha-Magadhi Prakrit*
(Hultzsch 1925: 164–65).

SAMPLE OF KHAROṢṬHĪ

re-ma-ku rma-va-dra-iṃ tre-pu sa-ga-te-stra sa-rma-va-śpa-vi←

mi-ba-thu mi-ka-a-ṇu-ta ti-ve-ṭha-ti-pra ra-ri-śa me-i e-rya-bha-sa

ta-i-ya-pu rya-bha-ga-te-stra ya ṇa-re-śi-śi go-te-stra rmo-va-śpa-vi

ta-i-ya-pu tra-pu-va-ji ya tra-mi-su-va ja-ra-ca-pa-a su-va-dra-iṃ

1. Transliteration:	viśpavarmasa	strategasa	putre	imdravarma	
2. Transcription:	viçpavarməsə	stra:te:gəsə	putre:	indrəvarma:	
3. Gloss:	Of Viśpavarma	Commander	son	Indravarma	

1.	kumare	sabharyae	ime	śarira	pratiṭhaveti	taṇuakami
2.	kuma:re	sə-bʰa:rja:e:	ime:	çəri:ra:	prətiṭʰəve:ti	təṇuəkəmi
3.	Prince	with-his.wife	these	bodily relics	establishes	in.his.own

1.	thubami	viśpavarmo	stratego	śiśirena	ya	
2.	tʰubəmi	viçpəvərmo:	stra:te:go:	çiçire:ṇa:	jə	
3.	stūpa	Viśpavarma	Commander	Śiśireṇa	and	

1.	strategabharya	puyaïta	imdravasu	apacaraja
2.	stra:te:gə-bʰa:rja:	pu:jəita:	īdrəvəsu	əpəcə-ra:ʝa:
3.	Commander-wife	honored	Indravasu	Apraca-king

1.	vasumitra	ya	jiva-putra	puyaïta
2.	vəsumitra:	jə	ʝi:vəputra:	pu:jəita:
3.	Vasumitrā	and	who.has.a.living.son	honored

'Prince Indravarma, son of Commander Viśpavarma, together with his wife establishes these bodily relics in his own *stūpa*. Commander Viśpavarma and Śiśireṇa, the wife of the Commander, are (hereby) honored. Indravasu, King of Apraca, and (his wife) Vasumitrā, who is the mother of a living son, are (hereby) honored.'

   —*Opening of an inscription in Northwestern or "Gāndharī" Prakrit*
    on a Buddhist reliquary of Prince Indravarma (Salomon 1996).

Bibliography

Bright, William. 1990. "Written and Spoken Language in South Asia." In his *Language Variation in South Asia*, pp. 130–47. New York: Oxford University Press.

Bühler, Georg. 1896. *Indische Palaeographie von circa 350 A. Chr. – circa 1300 P. Chr.* (Grundriss der indo-arischen Philologie und Altertumskunde, vol. 1, pt. 2). Strassburg: Trübner. Trans. J. F. Fleet, *Indian Paleography from about B.C. 350 to about A.D. 1300,* Appendix to *Indian Antiquary* 33 (1904).

———. 1898. *On the Origin of the Indian Brāhma Alphabet,* 2nd ed. Strassburg: Trübner. Repr. The Chowkhamba Sanskrit Studies, vol. 33. Varanasi: The Chowkhamba Sanskrit Series Office, 1963.

Dani, Ahmad Hasan. 1963. *Indian Palaeography.* Oxford: Clarendon Press. 2nd ed., Delhi: Munshiram Manoharlal, 1986.

———. 1979. *Kharoshthi Primer.* Lahore: Lahore Museum.

Das Gupta, Charu Chandra. 1958. *The Development of the Kharoṣṭhī Script.* Calcutta: K. L. Mukhopadhyay.

Diringer, David. 1968. *The Alphabet:A Key to the History of Mankind,* 3rd ed. New York: Funk & Wagnalls.

Falk, Harry. 1993. *Schrift im alten Indien: Ein Forschungsbericht mit Anmerkungen* (ScriptOralia 56). Tübingen: Narr.

Hultzsch, Eugen. 1925. *Inscriptions of Aśoka* (Corpus Inscriptionum Indicarum I). Oxford: Clarendon.

Mahadevan, Iravatham. 1971. "Tamil-Brahmi Inscriptions of the Sangam Age." In *Proceedings of the Second International Conference Seminar of Tamil Studies,* ed. R. E. Asher, pp. 73–106. Madras: International Association of Tamil Research.

Nowotny, Fausta. 1967. "Schriftsysteme in Indien." *Studium Generale* 20: 524–47.

Ojhā, Gaurīśaṃkara Hīrācaṃda. 1918. *Bhāratīya prācīna lipimālā* [The paleography of India], 2nd ed. Ajmer: Scottish Mission Industries Company.

Salomon, Richard G. 1990. "New Evidence for a Gāndhārī Origin of the Arapacana Syllabary." *Journal of the American Oriental Society* 110: 255–73.

———. 1996. "An Inscribed Silver Buddhist Reliquary of the Time of King Kharaosta and Prince Indravarman." *Journal of the American Oriental Society* 116.

Sircar, Dinesh Chandra. 1965. *Indian Epigraphy.* Delhi: Motilal Banarsidass.

———. 1965–83. *Select Inscriptions Bearing on Indian History and Civilization.* Vol. 1, 2nd ed., Calcutta: Calcutta University; vol. 2, Delhi: Motilal Banarsidass.

———. 1971. "Introduction to Indian Epigraphy and Paleography." *Journal of Ancient Indian History* 4: 72–136.

Upasak, Chandrika Singh. 1960. *The History and Palaeography of Mauryan Brāhmī Script.* Nalanda: Nava Nālandā Mahāvihāra.

Weber, Albrecht. 1856. "Über den semitischen Ursprung des indischen Alphabets." *Zeitschrift der Deutschen Morgenländischen Gesellschaft* 10: 389–406.

The Devanagari Script

WILLIAM BRIGHT

The script called *Nāgarī* (lit. 'of the city') or *Devanāgarī* ('divine Nagari') is phono-logically based, and is written from left to right. Historically, like other native scripts of South Asia, it derives from the Brahmi alphabet of the Ashokan inscriptions. Ty-pologically, it is what I call an *alphasyllabary*: that is, it writes each consonant-vowel sequence as a unit, called an *akṣara*, in which the vowel symbol functions as an oblig-atory *diacritic* to the consonant; in the terminology of Daniels (SECTION 1), it is an abugida.

Devanagari is currently used for Hindi, Nepali, and Marathi, and sometimes for local languages such as Bhojpuri. It is the script generally used for printing Sanskrit in modern times (in earlier times, Sanskrit manuscripts were written in a variety of local scripts). For an overview, see Masica 1991: 133–53.

The symbols

The traditional order of symbols in the Indian scripts is based primarily on articula-tory phonetics, as originally developed for Sanskrit by the ancient pandits. Implicit in the order is a series of phonological tables, organized in terms of articulatory features. First come the *primary* vowels, i.e. those recognized as simple vowels in Sanskrit grammar. TABLE 31.1 shows the independent or *initial* form for each vowel, followed by the diacritic or postconsonantal form, illustrated with the consonant प *p*. Phonetic values used in Sanskrit in ancient times are indicated by IPA symbols in brackets. The canonical order proceeds from each short vowel to the corresponding long vowel. The names of the letters consist of their sounds, sometimes followed by *kāra* 'making'; thus अ is called *a* or *a-kāra*. Symbols exist for short and long syllabic laterals (ऌ *ḷ* [l̩], ॡ *l̄*), but in Sanskrit the former is rare and the latter never occurs, and they are irrel-evant to the modern languages.

Next come the *secondary* vowels which, in Sanskrit, represent historical (and de-scriptively underlying) diphthongs, again in long and short pairs. However, what were originally *ai āi* and *au āu* came to be pronounced in Sanskrit as *e* [e:] *ai* [a:i̯]

ACKNOWLEDGMENTS: Thanks are due for the valuable suggestions of M. B. Emeneau, Yamuna Kachru, Colin Masica, and M. K. Verma.

TABLE 31.1: *Primary Vowels*

	SHORT		LONG	
	Initial	*Diacritic*	*Initial*	*Diacritic*
Unrounded low central	अ a [ʌ]	– प pa	आ ā [a:]	ा पा pā
high front	इ i [i]	ि पि pi	ई ī [i:]	ी पी pī
Rounded high back	उ u [u]	ु पु pu	ऊ ū [u:]	ू पू pū
Syllabic vibrant	ऋ r̥ [r̩]	ृ पृ pr̥	ॠ r̥̄ [r̩:]	ॄ पॄ pr̥̄

TABLE 31.2: *Secondary Vowels*

	LONG		DIPHTHONGS	
	Initial	*Diacritic*	*Initial*	*Diacritic*
Unrounded front	ऐ e	े पे ke	पे ai	ै पै kai
Rounded back	ओ o	ो पो ko	औ au	ौ पौ kau

and *o* [o:] *au* [a:u̯], respectively. TABLE 31.2 again shows the initial and diacritic forms.

Next in order come two symbols which are written only after vowels, and are normally listed in combination with *a*. In Sanskrit, they originally represented secondarily derived phonetic features. The first is a nasal feature called *anusvāra*; it is written with a dot above the *akṣara* and is transliterated as ṃ (e.g. अं aṃ). In Sanskrit it may originally have been a feature of nasalization, cooccurring with the preceding vowel. However, in later usage, it is often used for a nasal consonant homorganic with a following stop; e.g., *aṅga* 'limb of the body' is written either with a conjunct consonant symbol, as अङ्ग, or as *amga*, i.e. अंग. A variant form for this symbol is called *anunāsika* or *candrabindu* (e g अँ aṃ); it is used more explicitly to indicate nasalization of vowels, as in अँश *aṃśa* [ɔ̃cə] 'portion'.

After *anusvāra* comes an element of voiceless breath, [h], called *visarga* and transliterated ḥ. It is written with two dots after the *akṣara*, e.g. अः *aḥ* [əh]. (Note, by contrast, that the transliteration *h* represents voiced or murmured breath, [ɦ].)

Next follow the occlusive consonants, that is, the stops and nasals of Sanskrit. TABLE 31.3 shows the *independent* or *full* forms of each. (The canonical order of these and the remaining consonant symbols proceeds horizontally within each row.)

Among the nasals, velar *ṅ* and palatal *ñ* are secondarily derived in Sanskrit, and the symbols are relatively rare in the modern languages. Two letters have special variants used mainly in the Bombay area: झ *jha* is replaced by झ, and ण *ṇa* by ण.

There follow, again arranged from the back of the mouth toward the front, the oral sonorants and the voiceless sibilants, as shown in TABLE 31.4.

TABLE 31.3: *Occlusives*

	VOICELESS PLOSIVES		VOICED PLOSIVES		NASALS
	Unaspirated	*Aspirated*	*Unaspirated*	*Aspirated*	
Velar	क k [k]	ख kh	ग g [g]	घ gh	ङ ṅ [ŋ]
Palatal	च c [c]	छ ch	ज j [ɟ]	झ jh	ञ ñ [ɲ]
Retroflex	ट ṭ [ʈ]	ठ ṭh	ड ḍ [ɖ]	ढ ḍh	ण ṇ [ɳ]
Dental	त t [t]	थ th	द d [d]	ध dh	न n [n]
Labial	प p [p]	फ ph	ब b [b]	भ bh	म m [m]

The label *retroflex* as applied to *r* has some justification in terms of the underlying phonology of Sanskrit; however, it is phonetically an alveolar or dental vibrant. Note that combinations of *r* with *u ū* have special shapes: रु *ru* and रू *rū*.

Finally comes a miscellaneous category of sounds not classified in terms of articulation. In all the languages, this category contains ह *ha,* a voiced or murmured glottal fricative [ɦ]. In Vedic Sanskrit and in Marathi, the symbol ळ *ḷa* [ḷ], retroflex lateral, also occurs here.

In the modern languages, especially in Hindi, a subscript dot is used beneath certain consonants to represent additional sounds. Thus, with the addition of the dot, क *ka* becomes क़ *qa,* ख *kha* becomes ख़ *xa,* ग *ga* becomes ग़ *ya,* ज *ja* becomes ज़ *za,* ड *ḍa* becomes ड़ *ṛa* [ɽ], and ढ *ḍha* becomes ढ़ *ṛha.* The dot is ignored in the traditional ordering system.

In traditional writing, there was little systematic use of word space or of punctuation. The symbols I and II, respectively, were used in verse for minor and major prosodic boundaries. Modern practice has adopted conventions of word space and punctuation which are mainly based on European practice.

The numerals are shown in TABLE 31.5.

TABLE 31.4: *Sonorants and Fricatives*

	Palatal		*Retroflex*		*Dental*		*Labial*	
Sonorants	य y [j]		र r [r]		ळ l [l]		व v [ʋ]	
Sibilants	श ś [c]		ष ṣ [s]		स s [s]			

TABLE 31.5: *Numerals*

1	2	3	4	5	6	7	8	9	0
१	२	३	४	५	६	७	८	९	०

Specific features

A following short vowel *a* is considered inherent in each consonant symbol; thus, unless these letters are modified by other attached symbols, प is *pa*, and र is *ra*.

Each consonant is represented by a basic consonantal symbol, e.g. प *pa*, र *ra*. Consonants in sequence share a continuous horizontal headstroke across the top, thus पर *para*. (Letters with a break in this stroke are झ *jha*, थ *tha*, ध *dha*, and भ *bha*.) When people write on lined paper, they "hang" the symbols from the line; but in rapid handwriting on unlined paper, the headstroke may be omitted altogether.

Vowels other than *a,* when they follow a consonant, are written as obligatory diacritics. Some are on top of the associated consonant, some on the bottom, some on the left side, some on the right side, and some in a combination of positions. Thus the diacritic for *ā* is –ा on the right-hand side, as in पा *pā*. That for *i* is ि-, extending from the top of the consonant to its left-hand side, as in पि *pi*. That for *u* is ु written beneath the consonant, as in पु *pu*. That for *e* is -े, written above the consonant, as in पे *pe*; and that for *o* is –ो, written to the right of the consonant, as in पो *po*.

A vowel not occurring after a consonant—either in initial position, i.e. after a space, or after another vowel—is written not with a diacritic, but with an independent symbol; each one is considered an *akṣara* in its own right, and has its own headstroke. Thus initial *a* is written अ, initial *ā* is आ, initial *i* is इ, and so on. (In traditional Sanskrit usage, "initial" meant "at the beginning of a sentence or line of verse." In modern usage, it usually means "at the beginning of a word," with conventionally established word boundaries which reflect European practice.)

A consonant not occurring before a vowel—typically one in final position, i.e. before a space rather than before a vowel—is written with a subscript diagonal stroke which may be labeled *zero vowel*; in other words, it "kills" the vowel. The symbol is called *virāma*; a consonant so affected is called *halanta* (Lambert 1953: 15–16). Thus a final symbol प would be interpreted as *pa*; but with the added diacritic, प् corresponds to *p*.

Consonants may also occur in clusters, especially in Sanskrit and in words which the modern languages have borrowed from Sanskrit; these may involve both initial and medial sequences of two or three consonants, e.g. *ty, pr, kv, st, kṣ, str, kṣm.* In such cases, *conjunct* symbols are used to show that only the last consonant of the sequence is followed by a vowel. In traditional usage, most such compounds are formed by reducing consonant symbols other than the last one in the sequence to an abbreviated form, typically lacking the characteristic long vertical stroke on the right-hand side. These reduced forms, sometimes called *half* consonants, are written to the left of the final symbol. For example, प *p(a)* plus य *ya* combine as प्य *pya*; त *t(a)* plus क *ka* combine as त्क *tka*.

Some compound letters are combined not horizontally, as above, but vertically. This is especially common when the first symbol does not have a long vertical stroke, such as द *da* and ह *ha*. In such combinations, the second symbol is attached in modi-fied form beneath the first symbol; thus द *d(a)* plus व *va* combine as द्व *dva,* and ह *h(a)* plus य *ya* as ह्य *hya*. Some symbols are found in both horizontal and vertical arrange-ments, e.g. *jja* as either ज्ज or ज्ज.

Compounds in which one element is र *r(a)* are handled in special ways. As the first element in a cluster, *r* is written with ͡ (called *repha*) above the consonant which follows it; thus र *r* + प *pa* gives र्प *rpa*. As the second element in a cluster, *ra* is written with ੍ at the foot of the consonant which precedes it; thus प *p(a)* + र *ra* gives प्र *pra*.

A few consonant sequences correspond to special conjunct symbols which are less analyzable; the commonest are as follows.

क	k	+	ष	ṣa	=	क्ष	kṣa
ज	j	+	ञ	ña	=	ज्ञ	jña
त	t	+	त	ta	=	त्त	tta
त	t	+	र	ra	=	त्र	tra

These conjuncts may themselves occur in "half" forms when they are followed by yet another consonant; thus त्त *tt(a)* + व *va* gives त्त्व *ttva,* and क्ष *kṣ(a)* + म *ma* gives क्ष्म *kṣma*. (Some typewriters lack many of the special conjunct symbols; as a make-shift, a cluster like *tta* is then written with a "half" *t,* as त्त.)

Note that, where conjunct consonants are involved, the *akṣara* does not actually correspond to a spoken syllable: thus the word *sarva* 'all' would be syllabified as *sar + va* in pronunciation, but it is written with the two *akṣaras* स *sa* + र्व *rva.*

Correspondences

Correspondences of written symbols to spoken sounds, in the case of Sanskrit, are much as indicated by the descriptive labels and the transcriptions used above. Corre-spondences to the spoken sounds of the modern languages follow the lead of Sanskrit in many respects. The principal departures are as follows:

In all the modern languages, short *a* is normally not pronounced at the end of a word, or intervocalically in the environment VC__VC. Thus दास, in Sanskrit *dāsa* 'servant', is pronounced [daːs] in the modern languages; and उपदेश, in Sanskrit *upa-deśa* 'instruction', is pronounced [updeːś].

In both Marathi and Nepali, there is no distinction in pronunciation between et-ymological "short" इ *i* and "long" ई *ī,* or between "short" उ *u* and "long" ऊ *ū*. Among the low vowels, however, a qualitative distinction exists: "short" अ *a* is pronounced [ə], while "long" आ *ā* is [a].

In the modern languages, ऋ *ṛ,* ॠ *ṝ,* and ऌ *l* are pronounced as if they were *ri, rī,* and *li,* respectively.

In many varieties of Hindi, the diphthongs ऐ *ai* and औ *au* have come to be pro-nounced as monophthongs [æː ɔː].

In Hindi, the *anusvāra* अं is used mainly to write homorganic nasals before stops, as in अंग *aṅg* [əŋg] 'limb'. Before fricatives, many speakers pronounce it as [n], as in अंश *aṃś* [ənʃ] 'portion'. The related *anunāsika* अँ is used consistently to write nasalization of vowels, as in हाँ *hāṃ* [ɦã:] 'yes'. In Marathi, the *anusvāra* is again used to write homorganic nasals before stops; before fricatives, it is pronounced as [ṽ], as in *aṃś* [əṽʃ] 'portion'. In still other positions, it has mainly historical significance and is not pronounced as such.

What were originally palatal stops are in general pronounced as affricates in modern times; e.g., च *c* and ज *j* become [tʃ] and [dʒ] respectively. In Marathi, च *c,* ज *j,* and झ *jh* are pronounced as palatal affricates when followed by front vowels, and also in loanwords; but they are pronounced as [ts dz dzʰ] before back vowels in native words.

In Hindi, ज्ञ *jñ* is pronounced [gj] with a following nasalized vowel; in Marathi, it is pronounced [ɟɲ].

In Nepali, व *v* usually merges in pronunciation with ब *b*.

The sibilants श *ś* and ष *ṣ* are not usually distinguished in the pronunciation of the modern languages; both are pronounced as an alveo-palatal sibilant [ʃ]. In Nepali, they are further merged with स *s*.

Relations to other scripts

It should be noted that, inasmuch as Hindi and Urdu are virtually the same language on the colloquial level, much Hindi material which is written in Devanagari is interconvertible with Urdu material written in Perso-Arabic script (SECTION 62). With the adaptations to Devanagari letters which have been made to represent borrowed sounds of Perso-Arabic origin, it is possible for writing in Devanagari and in Urdu script to correspond to the same spoken text.

Proposals have been made in India to replace Devanagari script with Roman script, for modern languages such as Hindi. At present there seems little chance that such a change will ever be implemented. The use of Devanagari is increasing continually, with the spread of education, and it has been adapted to tribal languages in North India. Thus efforts to encourage literacy in Gondi, a Dravidian language spoken in Maharashtra State, have used the Devanagari script—appropriately, since Marathi is the dominant language of the area.

SAMPLE OF SANSKRIT

1. Devanagari:	नैनं	छिन्दन्ति	शस्त्राणि	नैनं	दहति	पावकः ।
2. Transliteration:	nainaṃ	chindanti	śastrāṇi	nainaṃ	dahati	pāvakaḥ
3. Transcription:	nainə̃	cʰindənti	çəstra:ɳi	nainə̃	dəɦəti	pa:ʋəkəh
4. Gloss:	not.this	they.cut	weapons	not.this	it.burns	fire

1. न   चैनं   क्लेदयन्न्यापो   न   शोषयति   मारुतः ॥
2. na cainaṃ kledayantyāpo   na   śoṣayati   mārutaḥ
3. nə cainə̃   kle:dəyəntja:po: nə   ço:ṣəjəti   ma:rutəh
4. not and.this they.moisten.waters not it.dries   wind

1. अच्छेद्यो   ऽयमदाह्यो   ऽयमक्लेद्यो   ऽशोष्य   एव   च ।
2. acchedyo   'yam adāhyo   'yam akledyo   'śoṣya   eva   ca
3. əcche:dyo: jəm əda:ɦyo: jəm əkle:dyo: ço:ṣjə   e:ʋə   cə
4. uncuttable this unburnable   this unwettable   undryable   just   and

1. नित्यः   सर्वगतः   स्थाणुरचलो   ऽयं   सनातनः ॥
2. nityaḥ   sarvagataḥ   sthāṇur acalo   'yam   sanātanaḥ
3. nitjəh   sərʋəgətəh   stʰa:ṇur əcəlo: jə̃   səna:tənəh
4. eternal   all.pervading   fixed immovable   this   primeval

'Weapons do not cut it [the soul], fire does not burn it.
Waters do not wet it, wind does not dry it.
It cannot be cut, or burned, or wetted, and cannot be dried.
It is eternal, all-pervading, fixed, immovable, primeval.'

—*Bhagavadgītā 2:23.*

Bibliography

Kellogg, S. H. 1938. *A Grammar of the Hindi Language*, 3rd ed. London: Routledge & Kegan Paul.
Lambert, Hester M. 1953. *Introduction to the Devanagari Script.* London: Oxford University Press.
Masica, Colin P. 1991. *The Indo-Aryan Languages.* Cambridge: Cambridge University Press.
Whitney, William Dwight. 1889. *Sanskrit Grammar.* Cambridge: Harvard University Press.

Gujarati Writing

P. J. MISTRY

The Gujarati script, used for writing Gujarati and Kacchi, is a variant of Devanagari (SECTION 31), differentiated by the loss of the head strokes and varying degrees of modifications in the remaining characters. The earliest available documents are, in handwriting, a 1592 manuscript and, in printing, a 1797 advertisement. Yet until the middle of the nineteenth century, the script was used primarily for correspondence and bookkeeping, while Devanagari was used for literary and scholarly works. Written from left to right, with symbols aligned at their heads, the script is organized in terms of the *akṣara* 'syllable'. It has been referred to as *śarāphi* 'banker's', *vāṇiāśāi* 'merchant's', and *mahājani* 'trader's'. Its 45 basic symbols are divided into *svara* 'vowels' and *vyaṃjana* 'consonants' (see Parikh 1974 for a history; Lambert 1953: 134–70 and Cardona 1965: 53–60 for description).

The symbols

Vowels, listed in their conventional order in TABLE 32.1, are grouped into historical *hrasva* 'short' and *dīrgha* 'long' classes, according to the *laghu* 'light' and *guru*

TABLE 32.1: *Vowel Symbols*

	SHORT				LONG				
	Initial		Diacritic		Initial			Diacritic	
Central	અ	a [ə]	–		આ	ā [a]	–ા	કા	kā
High front	ઇ	i [i]	િ	કિ	ki	ઈ	ī [i]	ી	કી	kī
High back	ઉ	u [u]	ુ	કુ	ku	ઊ	ū [u]	ૂ	કૂ	kū
High back vibrant	ઋ	r̥ [ru]	ૃ	કૃ	kr̥					
Mid front						એ	e [e, ɛ]	ે	કે	ke
Mid front diphthong						ઐ	ai [əy]	ૈ	કૈ	kai
Mid back						ઓ	o [o, ɔ]	ો	કો	kō
Mid back diphthong						ઔ	au [əʋ]	ૌ	કૌ	kau

391

TABLE 32.2: *Occlusives*

	VOICELESS PLOSIVES		VOICED PLOSIVES		NASALS
	Unaspirated	*Aspirated*	*Unaspirated*	*Aspirated*	
Velar	ક k [k]	ખ kh [kʰ]	ગ g [g]	ઘ gh [gʰ]	
Palatal	ચ c [t͡ʃ]	છ ch [t͡ʃʰ]	જ j [d͡ʒ]	ઝ jh [d͡ʒʰ]	
Retroflex	ટ ṭ [t]	ઠ ṭh [tʰ]	ડ ḍ [d]	ઢ ḍh [dʰ]	ણ ṇ [ɳ]
Dental	ત t [t]	થ th [tʰ]	દ d [d]	ધ dh [dʰ]	ન n [n]
Labial	પ p [p]	ફ ph [f]	બ b [b]	ભ bh [bʰ]	મ m [m]

'heavy' syllables they create in traditional verse. The historical long vowels *ī ū* are no longer distinctively long in pronunciation; only in verse do syllables containing ઇ *i*, ઈ *ī*, ઉ *u*, ઊ *ū*, and ઋ *r* assume the values required by a meter.

Consonant symbols are classified into *mūlākṣara* 'root letters' and *jodākṣara* 'conjunct letters', with the first group additionally subgrouped in terms of articulation. The basic consonant symbols are shown in TABLE 32.2.

The conventional order (from left to right in the tables) has 23 plosives, 4 sonorants, and 3 sibilants (TABLE 32.3), and four additional characters: હ *ha*, a glottal fricative; ળ *ḷa*, a retroflex lateral; and two conjuncts, ક્ષ *kṣa* and જ્ઞ *jña* [gn].

Other signs are: *anusvāra*, a dot above a character, representing a nasal element, as in ક *kū*; *visarga* :, a silent symbol in some Sanskrit words; and ઙ *ṅ* [ŋ], a velar nasal, also in Sanskrit. The symbols for numerals are shown in TABLE 32.4.

Specific features

A postconsonantal અ *a* has no overt mark; it is inherent in a consonantal symbol. Thus ક is *ka* (a slanting stroke, *virāma*, makes it *khodo* 'lame' and marks it as just a consonant; thus ક્ is *k*). Other vowel symbols have their full form in initial and post-

TABLE 32.3: *Sonorants and Fricatives*

	Palatal		Alveolar		Dental		Labial	
Sonorants	ય y	[j]	ર r	[r]	લ l	[l]	વ v	[ʋ]
Sibilants	શ ś	[ʃ]	ષ ṣ	[ʃ]	સ s	[s]		

TABLE 32.4: *Numerals and Their Names*

1	૧	ekado	3	૩	tragado	5	૫	pāmcado	7	૭	sātado	9	૯	navado
2	૨	bagado	4	૪	cogado	6	૬	chagado	8	૮	āṭhado	0	૦	mīṃduṃ

vocalic positions (e.g. આશા *āśā* 'wish', ભાઈ *bhāī* 'brother'). In postconsonantal position, they occur as diacritics juxtaposed on one or more sides of the consonant symbol (TABLE 32.1).

Many consonantal symbols contain a vertical line (e.g. પ *pa*, ચ *ca*), but some do not (e.g. ક *ka*, જ *ja*). In clusters, the first letter(s) lose the vertical line, and only the last one retains it, e.g., the combinations of ત *ta*, ક્ષ *kṣa*, and જ *ja* with ય *ya* are ત્ય *tya*, ક્ષ્ય *kṣya*, and જ્ય *jya*.

Special conjunct forms exist for the following:

1. શ *ś(a)* appears as ૪ preceding લ *la*, વ *va*, ન *na* (શ્મ *śma* but શ્લ *śla*), as well as ર *ra* (શ્ર *śra*) and ચ *ca* (શ્ચ *śca*).

2. ટ *ṭa* has a different shape when it is preceded by ષ *ṣ(a)*: ષ્ટ *ṣṭa*.

3. ર *r(a)*, as a first member, takes the form *repha* – over the following letter (e.g. ર્ક *rka*). As a last member, *ra* is a subscript ₋ with ટ *ṭ(a)*, ડ *ḍ(a)*, and ઠ *ṭh(a)* (e.g. ટ્ર *ṭra*). With other symbols, it is a diagonal stroke ₋ attached at the lower left (ક્ર *kra*, પ્ર *pra*). The conjuncts *hra*, *dra*, and *tra* appear as હ્ર, દ્ર, and ત્ર respectively. Affixing ₋ *u* and ₋ *ū* to ર *ra* results in રુ ~ રુ *ru* and રૂ *rū*.

4. હ *h(a)* combines with ય *ya*, મ *ma*, and ૠ *r̥* as હ્ય *hya*, હ્મ *hma*, and હૃ *hr̥*.

5. દ *d(a)* combines with ય *ya*, વ *va*, ધ *dha*, and મ *ma* to result in દ્ય *dya*, દ્વ *dva*, દ્ધ *ddha*, and દ્મ *dma*. It also combines with ૠ *r̥* as દૃ *dr̥*.

6. જા, જી, જુ ~ જુ, and જૂ ~ જૂ are *jā*, *jī*, *ju*, and *jū*, respectively.

7. Geminates *ṭṭa*, *ḍḍa*, *ṭhṭha*, and *ḍhḍha* combine vertically: ટ્ટ, ડ્ડ, ઠ્ઠ, and ઢ્ઢ (cf. ઠ *ṭṭha*). ત્ત *tta* and દ્દ *dda* are special forms.

Gujarati writing is essentially phonemic, with some exceptions. A word-final consonant which is written C*a* is pronounced as C; thus મન *mana* is [mən] 'mind'. Deletion of *a* in a base morpheme, under certain conditions (cf. ə-deletion in Mistry 1995), is not indicated in the written form; thus ત *ta* is pronounced [tə] in કાતરશે *kātaraśe* 'he will carve' but not in કાતરે *kātare* [katre] 'he carves'. *Anusvāra* has two values: either nasalization of a vowel (હું *huṃ* [hū] 'I') or a nasal consonant homorganic with a following occlusive (રંગ *raṃg* [rəŋg] 'color').

The use of *visarga*, *virāma*, the nasal ઙ *ṅ*, and ૠ *r̥* is restricted mainly to Sanskrit loans. Similarly, the distinction between ષ *ṣa* and શ *śa* is only a writing convention.

The system is underdifferentiated for open/close and clear/murmur distinctions in vowels (cf. Pandit 1966: 156–77): thus homographic મોરી *morī* for both [mori] 'gutter' and [mɔri] 'bland', and તારો *tāro* for both [taro] 'star' and [taṛo] 'your' with a murmured vowel.

The influx of English loans in recent years has made the representation of close and open mid vowels critical. To represent the open vowels, a practice of inverting the diacritics for *e* – and *o* –ો is gaining ground: બેટ [beṭ] 'island' vs. બૅટ [bæṭ] 'bat', બોલ [bol] 'speak!' vs. બૉલ [bɔl] 'ball'. The shortcomings of the system have been the basis for ongoing proposals for reform made by two individuals: Mahendra Meghani from the 1950s, mainly for typographical reasons, and Dayashankar Joshi from the early 1980s, with concern for literacy.

SAMPLE OF GUJARATI

1. Gujarati:	તાડપત્ર	પર	લખવાની	બે	પદ્ધતિઓ	હતી
2. Transliteration:	tāḍapatra	para	lakhavānī	be	paddhatio	hatī
3. Transcription:	taɖpətrə	pər	ləkʰʋani	be	pəddʰətio	həti
4. Gloss:	palm.leaf	on	of.writing	two	systems	were

1. (૧)	શાહીથી	પત્રો	પર	લખવાની	ઉત્તર	ભારતની	પદ્ધતિ
2. (1)	śāhīthī	patro	para	lakhavānī	uttara	bhāratanī	paddhati
3. ek	ʃahitʰi	pətro	pər	ləkʰʋani	uttər	bʰarətni	pəddʰəti
4. (1)	with.ink	leaves	on	of.writing	north	Indian	system

1. અને (૨)	પત્રમાં	ઝીણી	અણીવાળા	સોયા		વડે	અક્ષરો	કોતરીને
2. ane (2)	patramāṃ	jhīnī	aṇīvāḷā	soyā		vaḍe	akṣaro	kotarīne
3. əne be	pətrəma	ʥʰini	əɳiʋaɭa	soja		ʋəɖe	əkʃəro	kotrine
4. and (2)	in.leaf	small	edged	needle	with	letters	having.carved

1. પછીથી	તેમાં	શાહી કે	મેશ	પુરવાની	દક્ષિણ	ભારતની	પદ્ધતિ	
2. pachīthī	temāṃ	śāhī ke	meśa	puravānī	dakṣiṇa	bhāratanī	paddhati	
3. pətʃʰitʰi	tema	ʃahi ke	meʃ	purʋani	dəkʃiɳ	bʰarətni	pəddʰəti	
4. afterward	in.it	ink or	soot	of.filling	south	Indian	system	

1. ગુજરાતમાં	પહેલી	પદ્ધતિએ	તાડપત્રો	લખાયેલા	નજરે	પડે	છે
2. gujarātamāṃ	pahelī	paddhatie	tāḍapatro	lakhāyelā	najare	paḍe	che
3. guʤratma	pəɦeli	pəddʰətie	taɖpətro	ləkʰajela	nəʤəre	pəɖe	tʃʰe
4. in.Gujarat	first	by.system	palm.leaves	written	sight	fall	is

'There were two systems of writing on a palm leaf: (1) a north Indian system of writing on leaves with ink, and (2) a south Indian system of carving letters with a sharp needle and afterward filling the lines with ink or soot. In Gujarat one finds palm leaves written in the first system.'
  —*Parikh 1974: 61.*

Bibliography

Cardona, George. 1965. *A Gujarati Reference Grammar.* Philadelphia: University of Pennsylvania Press.

Lambert, Hester M. 1953. *Introduction to the Devanagari Script.* Oxford: Oxford University Press.

Mistry, P. J. 1995. "Gujarati Phonology." In *Phonologies of Selected Asian and African Languages,* ed. Alan S. Kaye. Wiesbaden: Harrassowitz.

Pandit, Prabodh B. 1966. *Gujarātī bhāshānū dhvani-svarūpa ane dhvani-parivartana* [Sound system and sound changes in Gujarati]. Ahmedabad: Gujarat University.

Parikh, Pravinchandra. 1974. *Gujarātmāṃ brāhmithī nāgarī sudhīno lipi-vikāsa* [Script development in Gujarat from Brāhmi to Nāgari]. Ahmedabad: Gujarat University.

The Gurmukhi Script

HARJEET SINGH GILL

The Gurmukhi script is used to write the Punjabi language, especially by members of the Sikh religion, in the Indian Punjab and elsewhere in India; in the Pakistani Punjab, Muslims continue to use the Persian script.

Gurmukhi evolved from the ancient Brahmi system, but it received its present definitive form from the second Guru of the Sikhs, Guru Angad (1504–1552); hence the nomenclature Gurmukhi, literally 'from the mouth of the Guru'. The name also refers to its use in the Adi Granth, which includes the numerous hymns and compositions of the Sikh Gurus of the fifteenth, sixteenth, and seventeenth centuries, and of a number of Sufi (Muslim) and Bhakti (Hindu) saint-poets. The earliest hymns are by the Sufi Farid Shakarganj of the twelfth century. The alphabet is sometimes called *paiṃtī* 'the thirty-five', from the fact that the basic repertoire of consonant and consonant-like symbols numbers 35.

Gurmukhi is written from left to right. The characters are normally aligned below the line of writing. The major symbols represent consonants. Vowels other than short *a* are indicated by diacritic symbols written above, below, or at the side of the consonant symbols. When a syllable begins with a vowel, a "vowel-bearer" is used: ਅ for *a ā ai au*, ੲ for *i ī e*, and ੳ for *u ū o*.

The most characteristic feature of the Punjabi language is its three-way tonal system: high, mid, low. The script has no separate symbols for tones, but they generally correspond to certain consonantal signs. This is the major function of the signs for voiced aspirates, for *h*, and for conjunct consonants including *h*. The use of these letters to indicate tones is often etymologically justified, and indeed the tones have probably developed from older **h* and from voiced aspirates.

The consonants

The basic consonantal graphs of the Gurmukhi script are as in TABLE 33.1, in canonical order (reading across the table). Some letters have a dot diacritic to represent marginal consonants, especially in loanwords (TABLE 33.2).

A limited number of consonant clusters are written with conjunct symbols similar to those of Devanagari, in which the second consonant (in current usage only *h*, *r*, and *w*) is subjoined; e.g. ਮ *m(a)* + ਹ *ha* = ਮ੍ਹ *mha*; ਪ *p(a)* + ਰ *ra* = ਪ੍ਰ *pra*; ਦ *d(a)* + ਵ *wa* = ਦ੍ਵ *dwa*. An abbreviated *ya* forms the second member of a cluster: ਦ *d(a)* + ਯ *ya* = ਦੵ *dya*.

TABLE 33.1: *Gurmukhi Letters*

	VOWEL-BEARERS					FRICATIVES			
	ੳ (back)		ਅ (low)		ੲ (front)	ਸ s	[s]	ਹ h	[h]
	OCCLUSIVES								
Velar	ਕ k	[k]	ਖ kh	[kʰ]	ਗ g	[g]	ਘ gh	[g]	ਙ ṅ	[ŋ]
Palatal	ਚ c	[tʃ]	ਛ ch	[tʃʰ]	ਜ j	[dʒ]	ਝ jh	[dʒ]	ਞ ñ	[ɲ]
Retroflex	ਟ ṭ	[t]	ਠ ṭh	[tʰ]	ਡ ḍ	[d]	ਢ ḍh	[d]	ਣ ṇ	[ɳ]
Dental	ਤ t	[t]	ਥ th	[tʰ]	ਦ d	[d]	ਧ dh	[d]	ਨ n	[n]
Labial	ਪ p	[p]	ਫ ph	[pʰ]	ਬ b	[b]	ਭ bh	[b]	ਮ m	[m]
	SONORANTS								
	ਯ y	[j]	ਰ r	[z]	ਲ l	[l]	ਵ w	[w]	ੜ ṛ	[t]

TABLE 33.2: *Gurmukhi Supplementary Consonants*

ਸ਼	ਜ਼	ਫ਼	ਖ਼	ਗ਼	ਲ਼
š [ʃ]	z [z]	f [f]	x [χ]	ɣ [ɣ]	! [l]

Vowels and accessory signs

Vowels other than short *a* are indicated by diacritics on the consonant signs. In TABLE 33.3, the vowels are shown in initial form (with the proper vowel-bearer) and with the consonant ਕ *k*.

TABLE 33.3: *Gurmukhi Vowels*

Initial	Diacritic		Transliteration	Phonetic Value
ਅ	–	ਕ	a	[ə]
ਆ	ਾ	ਕਾ	ā	[ɑ]
ਇ	ਿ	ਕਿ	i	[ɪ]
ਈ	ੀ	ਕੀ	ī	[i]
ਉ	ੁ	ਕੁ	u	[ʊ]
ਊ	ੂ	ਕੂ	ū	[u]
ਏ	ੇ	ਕੇ	e	[e]
ਐ	ੈ	ਕੈ	ai	[æ]
ਓ	ੋ	ਕੋ	o	[o]
ਔ	ੌ	ਕੌ	au	[ɔ]

Of the two signs for nasalization (transcribed *ṃ*), *ṭippī* ⌣ is used with the vowels *a i u* and with *ū* when final, e.g. ਮੁੰਡਾ *muṃḍā* [muṇḍa] 'boy'; *biṃdī* ⌣ is used with all other vowels, e.g. ਸ਼ਾਂਤ *šāṃt* [ʃãt] 'peaceful'.

Gemination is written by the sign ⌣ *addak* above and preceding the consonant to be doubled; ਪੱਕੀ *pakkī* [pəkki] 'ripe'. Clusters of unaspirated stop plus homorganic aspirated stop are written by the use of *addak* before the letter for the aspirate: ਪੱਖੀ *pakkhī* [pəkkhi] 'fan'. The two geminates *mm* and *nn* are written with *ṭippī*, the sign for nasalization: ਲੰਮੀ *lammī* [ləmmi] 'long'.

Tones

The most characteristic feature of the Punjabi language is its three-way system of high, low, and mid tonal accents. The high tone is phonetically a high rising-falling contour covering one or two syllables, transcribed [á]. The low tone is a low rising contour, again covering one or two syllables, transcribed [à]. The mid tone is a mid rising and falling contour not marked in transcription.

When the consonants that correspond to Devanagari voiced aspirates occur word-initially, they are pronounced as unaspirated voiceless stops plus low tone: ਘੋੜਾ *ghoṛā* [kòɽa] 'horse'. When stem-final, they are pronounced as unaspirated voiced stops with preceding high tone: ਮਾਘ *māgh* [mág] 'October'. In stem-medial position, after a short vowel and before a long vowel, these letters are pronounced as unaspirated voiced stops with following low tone: ਪਘਾਰਨਾ *paghārnā* [pəgàrna] 'to melt', ਮਘਾਣਾ *maghāṇā* [məgàṇa] 'to be lit'.

The letter ਹ *h(a)* represents [h] when initial: ਹਰੀ *harī* [həri] 'green'. In non-initial position, it has no consonantal value, but represents high tone on the preceding vowel: ਤੀਹ *tīh* [tí] 'thirty'.

The vowels *i* and *u* are normally pronounced [ɪ] and [ʊ], but *ih* and *uh* represent [é] and [ó] with high tone: ਕਿਹੜਾ *kihṛā* [kéɽa] 'who', ਕੁਹੜਾ *kuhṛā* [kóɽa] 'leper'. The combination of *a* + *h* + *i/u* is pronounced [ǽ]/[ɔ́]: ਕਹਿਣਾ *kahiṇā* [kǽṇa] 'to say', ਵਹੁਟੀ *wahuṭi* [wɔ́ʈɪ] 'bride'.

SAMPLE OF PUNJABI

1. Gurmukhi:	ਭੈਣਾਂ	ਮੈਂ	ਕਤਦੀ	ਕਤਦੀ	ਹੁੱਟੀ
2. Transliteration:	bhaiṇā	maiṃ	katadī	katadī	huṭṭī
3. Transcription:	pæ̀ṇa	mæ̃	kətdi	kətdi	huṭṭi
4. Gloss:	sister	I	weaving	weaving	tired

1.	ਪੜੀ	ਪੱਛੀ	ਪਿਛਵਾੜੇ	ਰਹਿ	ਗਾਈ
2.	paṛī	pacchī	pichawāṛe	rih	gaī
3.	pəɽi	pəʧʰi	piʧʰwaɽe	rǽ	gəi
4.	left	cotton-stick	behind	left	gone

1.	ਹੱਥ	ਵਿਚ	ਰਹਿ	ਗਈ	ਜੱਟੀ
2.	hatth	wic	rih	gaī	juṭṭī
3.	həthʰ	wɪʃ	ræ	gəi	dʒuṭṭi
4.	hand	in	left	gone	cotton

1.	ਅੱਗੇ	ਚਰਖਾ	ਪਿੱਛੇ	ਪੀਹੜਾ
2.	agge	carakhā	picche	pīhṛā
3.	əgge	tʃərkʰɑ	pɪtʧʰe	pírɑ
4.	in-front	spinning-wheel	behind	stool

1.	ਹੱਥ	ਮੇਰਿਉਂ	ਤੰਦ	ਟੁੱਟੀ
2.	hatth	meriom̐	tamd	ṭuṭṭī
3.	həthʰ	merɪõ	tə̃d	ʈuʈʈi
4.	hand	mine	strand	broken

'Sister, this weaving has tired me;
The cotton stick is left behind.
In my hand is left the cotton;
In front, the spinning wheel; behind, the stool.
The strand is broken in my hand.'

> —A poem by Bulleh Shah, from Sital 1970: 101 (copyrighted; reprinted by permission of Punjabi University).

Bibliography

Gill, Harjeet Singh, and Henry Allan Gleason, Jr. 1962. *A Reference Grammar of Panjabi.* Hartford, Conn.: Hartford Seminary Foundation; 2nd ed., Patiala: Punjabi University, Dept. of Linguistics, 1969.

Sital, Jit Singh. 1970. *Bulleh Shah.* Patiala: Punjabi University.

Uberoi, Mohan Singh. 1971. *A History of Panjabi Literature,* 3rd ed. Jullundur: Sadasiva Prakashan.

Bengali Writing

TISTA BAGCHI

The Bengali (or, to use the native term now frequently used among linguists and grammarians, Bangla) script is historically related and similar in design to the Devanagari script (SECTION 31): it has a comparable inventory of consonant and vowel characters and ligatures, with only one or two exceptions. The script-to-pronunciation correspondences are markedly different, however, because of the sound changes that the Bengali language has undergone and the independent development of the Bengali script from the Brahmi since early times (see Banerji 1919, Chakravarti 1938). For the inventory of Bengali vowel and consonant letters, see TABLES 34.1, 34.2, and 34.3. The Assamese script differs from the Bengali in just one or two consonant characters, although the correspondence between pronunciation and script is also different in a number of respects for Assamese; e.g. শ *sa* [ʃ] is pronounced [x] in Assamese.

Differences in inventory of characters

Of the differences between the inventories of characters in Bengali and Devanagari, it is worth noting the absence of distinct Bengali characters for [b] and [ʋ] (transliterated as *v*): the pronunciations of the two in words of Indic origin have collapsed into ব *ba*. But Bengali has [w], written as a combination of vowel characters (usually উ *u* or ও *o* followed by a vowel, or the semivowel letter য় *y* with vowel diacritic). Other Bengali characteristics are the absence of Sanskrit long syllabic *r* or *l*, the established use of *anunāsika* ँ for vowel nasalization (rather than *anusvāra* ं of Devanagari, realized in Bengali as ং *ṃ* [ŋ]); and the contrast of য় *ÿa* [ʤ] (when this is a reflex of earlier Indic *y*) with the semivowel য *ya* [j].

Script-to-pronunciation correspondences

Among the most salient peculiarities of the script-to-pronunciation correspondences is the pronunciation of the inherent vowel carried by a consonant vowel character when it is not accompanied by a vowel diacritic or by the *hasanta* 'silencing' symbol ্: this vowel is pronounced either [ɔ] or [o]. The rounded (lower-mid or mid) pronunciation of the inherent vowel contrasts with the pronunciation of the inherent vowel as [ə] in languages that employ the Devanagari script. But the inherent vowel is not always pronounced, and one can only partially predict whether its value is [ɔ],

TABLE 34.1: *Vowels*

Initial	Diacritic (k-)		Transliteration	Pronunciation
অ	–	ক	a	[ɔ, o]
আ	‑া	কা	ā	[a]
ই	ি‑	কি	i	[i]
ঈ	ী‑	কী	ī	[i]
উ	‑ু	কু	u	[u]
ঊ	‑ূ	কূ	ū	[u]
ঋ	‑ৃ	কৃ	r̥	[ri]
এ	ে‑	কে	e	[e, æ]
ঐ	ৈ‑	কৈ	ai	[oj]
ও	ে‑া	কো	o	[o]
ঔ	ে‑ৗ	কৌ	au	[ow]

[o], or silent in any given instance. For instance, the same spelling মত *mata* can represent either [mɔt] 'opinion, consent' or [moto] 'like, approximately' (postposition), whereas গত *gata* 'gone, past, dead' is invariably pronounced [ɡoto]. In native Bengali words and Sanskrit loanwords, the pronunciation tends to be [o] when followed by a high vowel or semivowel ([i], [j], [u], or [w]) immediately or in the following syllable; but [ɔ] otherwise.

TABLE 34.2: *Occlusives*

	VOICELESS PLOSIVES				VOICED PLOSIVES				NASALS		
	Unaspirated		*Aspirated*		*Unaspirated*		*Aspirated*				
Velar	ক	k [k]	খ	kh [kʰ]	গ	g [ɡ]	ঘ	gh [ɡʱ]	ঙ	ṅ [ŋ]	
Palatal	চ	c [ʧ]	ছ	ch [ʧʰ]	জ	j [ʤ]	ঝ	jh [ʤʱ]	ঞ	ñ [ɲ]	
Retroflex	ট	ṭ [t]	ঠ	ṭh [tʰ]	ড	ḍ [d]	ঢ	ḍh [dʱ]	ণ	ṇ [ɳ]	
Dental	ত	t [t]	থ	th [tʰ]	দ	d [d]	ধ	dh [dʱ]	ন	n [n]	
Labial	প	p [p]	ফ	ph [pʰ]	ব	b [b]	ভ	bh [bʱ]	ম	m [m]	

TABLE 34.3: *Sonorants and Fricatives*

	Palatal			Alveolar			Dental			Other		
Sonorants	য	ÿ	[ʤ]	র	r	[r]	ল	l	[l]			
Sibilants	শ	ś	[ʃ, s]	ষ	ṣ	[ʃ]	স	s	[ʃ, s]	হ	h	[ɦ]

TABLE 34.4: *Conjuncts (in order of second member)*

Conjunct	Transliteration & Pronunciation		Conjunct	Transliteration & Pronunciation		Conjunct	Transliteration & Pronunciation	
ক্ক	kk	[kk]	ন্ত	nt	[nt]	স্ন	sn	[sn]
স্ক	ṅk	[ŋk]	ন্তু, ন্তু	ntu	[ntu]	ল্প	lp	[lp]
র্ক	rk	[rk]	প্ত	pt	[pt]	স্প	sp	[sp,ᵃ ʃp]
স্ক	sk	[sk,ᵃ ʃk]	র্ত	rt	[rt]	দ্ম	dm	[dd(~)]
ঙ্গ	ṅg	[ŋg]	স্ত	st	[st]	ল্ম	lm	[lm]
ল্গ	lg	[lg]	স্ত্র	str	[str]	ষ্ম	ṣm	[ʃʃ, ʃmᵇ]
চ্চ	cc	[ttʃ]	থ্থ	tth	[ttʰ]	স্মৃ	smṛ	[srī/sri]
শ্চ	śc	[ʃtʃ]	ন্থ	nth	[ntʰ]	ক্র	kr	[kr]
চ্ছ	cch	[ttʃʰ]	স্থ	sth	[stʰ]	গ্র	gr	[gr]
চ্ছ্র	cchr	[ttʃʰr]	ব্দ	bd	[bd]	ত্র	tr	[tr]
জ্জ	bj	[bdʒ]	দ্ধ	ddh	[ddʰ]	প্র	pr	[pr]
জ্ঝ	jjh	[ddʒʰ]	ন্ধ	ndh	[ndʰ]	শ্র	śr	[sr]
ষ্ঠ	ṣṭh	[ʃʈʰ]	ক্ন	kn	[kn]	ক্ল	kl	[kl]
ণ্ড	ṇḍ	[ɳḍ]	ত্ন	tn	[tn]	গ্ল	gl	[gl]
ণ্ণ	ṇṇ	[nn]	দ্ন	dn	[dn]	শ্ল	śl	[ʃl, slᶜ]
ষ্ণ	ṣṇ	[ʃn]	ন্ন	nn	[nn]	ক্ষ	kṣ	[kʰ,ᵃ kkʰ]
ক্ত	kt	[kt]	প্ন	pn	[pn]	ক্ষ্ন	kṣṇ	[kʰn]
ত্ত	tt	[tt]	শ্ন	śn	[ʃn, snᶜ]	ক্স	ks	[kʃ]

a.   Initially.
b.   Learned.
c.   Casual.

The distinction between long and short high vowels ([i] and [u]) has been lost in the pronunciation of Bengali but persists in the spellings, e.g. দিন *dina* [din] 'day' vs. দীন *dīna* [din] 'indigent'; কুল *kula* [kul] 'lineage' vs. কূল *kūla* [kul] 'shore'.

The pronunciation of the letter এ or diacritic ে– *e* is either [æ] or [e], depending (historically, at least) on whether the vowel of an immediately following syllable is non-high ([e], [o], [æ], [ɔ], or [a]) or high ([i] or [u]), respectively.

Among the consonants, the pronunciation of the sibilant letters শ *śa*, ষ *ṣa*, and স *sa* is noteworthy: the "default" pronunciation of all these is a "hushing" sound [ʃ], but before non-retroflex coronals ([t], [n], [r], and [l]) they are all pronounced [s]. English *st* in loanwords is written in Bengali with স্ট *sṭa* [sṭ].

TABLE 34.5: *Numerals*

1	2	3	4	5	6	7	8	9	0
১	২	৩	৪	৫	৬	৭	৮	৯	()

The originally retroflex ণ *ṇa* and the dental ন *na* are now both pronounced the same, as alveolar or dental [n]. The palatal ঞ *ña* is pronounced as a nasalized glide [j̃] between vowels or word-finally, but as a post-alveolar [ɲ] before চ *ca*, ছ *cha*, জ *ja*, or ঝ *jha*.

Clusters

A number of consonant clusters are written as conjunct consonants as in Devanagari (for a sampling, see TABLE 34.4). Some of them have developed irregular pronunciations: জ্ঞ *jña*—initially, [g] plus nasalization of the following vowel, e.g. জ্ঞান *jñāna* [gæ̃n] 'knowledge'; elsewhere, [gg], e.g. বিজ্ঞ *bijña* [biggõ/biggo] 'wise'. হ্য *hya*—[ddʒʰ], e.g. সহ্য *sahya* [ʃoddʒʰo] 'tolerance, endurance'.

Clusters of C + ম *ma* are pronounced as [C] initially, plus nasalization of the following vowel, [CC] medially, e.g. স্মারক *smāraka* [ʃãrok] 'reminiscent (of), reminder', পদ্ম *padma* [pɔddo] 'lotus'.

Clusters of C + য *ya* (—্য) are pronounced as [C] initially, most often with modification of a following *a/ā* to the pronunciation [æ], e.g. ব্যয় *byaya* [bæɛ̯] 'expenditure', ব্যাকরণ *byākaraṇa* [bækɔron] 'grammar'; they are pronounced as [CC] inside a word, with or without modification of a following *a/ā* to [æ], e.g. অব্যয় *abyaya* [ɔbbɔɛ̯] 'indeclinable', হত্যা *hatyā* [hotta] 'murder' (also [hottæ]), প্রত্যেক *pratyeka* [prottek] 'each, every'.

Clusters of C + ব *ba* (—্ব) are pronounced as [C] initially, e.g. শ্বাস *śbāsa* [ʃaʃ] 'breath', [CC] inside a word, e.g. বিদ্বান *bidbān* [biddan] 'learned'.

These irregularities have arisen out of regular sound changes in Bengali and occur mostly in Sanskrit loanwords, in which the original spellings have been conserved.

The Bengali numerals are shown in TABLE 34.5.

SAMPLE OF BENGALI

1. Bengali:	ভারতবর্ষ	পাণিনির	জন্মভূমি।	তখনকার
2. Transliteration:	bhāratabarsha	pāṇinira	janmabhūmi.	takhanakāra
3. Transcription:	bʰarotbɔrʃo	paninir	dʒɔnmobʰumi	tɔkʰonkar
4. Gloss:	India	Panini.GEN	birth.ground	then.GEN

1. দিনে   প্রাকৃতকে   যাঁরা   লিপিবদ্ধ   করেছিলেন
2. dine   prākṛtake   ỹā̃rā   lipibaddha   karechilena
3. dine   prakritke   dʒā̃ra   lipibɔddʰo   koretʃʰilen
4. day.LOC   Prakrit.ACC   REL.PRON.PL script.bound   make.PAST.PERF.3HON

1. তাঁরা ছিলেন   পরম   পণ্ডিত।   অধচ   প্রাকৃতের   প্রতি   তাঁদের
2. tārā chilena   parama   paṇḍita. athaca   prākṛtera   prati   tā̃dera
3. tāra tʃʰilen   pɔrom   ponḍit   ɔtʰotʃo prakriter   proti   tāder
4. they be.PAST.3HON   great(ly) learned and.yet Prakrit.GEN   toward   their

1. অবজ্ঞা   ছিল   না।   সংস্কৃত   ব্যাকরণের   চাপে   তাঁরা
2. abajñā   chila   nā.   saṃskṛta   byākaraṇera   cāpe   tā̃rā
3. ɔbogga   tʃʰilo   na   ʃɔnʃkrito   bæ̃kɔroner   tʃape   tāra
4. contempt   be.PAST.3 NEG Sanskrit   grammar.GEN   pressure.LOC they

1. প্রাকৃতকে   লুপ্তপ্রায়   করেন   নি।   তার   কারণ
2. prākṛtake   luptaprāya   karena   ni.   tāra   kāraṇa
3. prakritke   luptopraɛ̃   kɔren   ni   tar   karon
4. Prakrit.ACC   obliterated.almost do.3HON PERF.NEG it.GEN reason

1. ভাষা   সম্বন্ধে   তাঁদের   ছিল   সহজ   বোধশক্তি।
2. bhāshā   sambandhe   tā̃dera   chila   sahaja   bodhaśakti.
3. bʰaʃa   ʃɔmbondʰe   tāder   tʃʰilo   ʃohodʒ   bodʰʃokti
4. language   relation.LOC their   be.PAST.3 natural   understanding.power

'India is the birthplace of Panini. The people who codified the Prakrits in writing in those days were extremely learned people. Yet they did not hold the Prakrits in contempt. They had not made the Prakrits disappear under pressure from Sanskrit grammar. This was because they had a natural ability to understand matters of language.'
                                                        —*Tagore 1935: 241.*

Bibliography

Banerji, Rakhal Das. 1919. *The Origin of the Bengali Script.* Calcutta: Calcutta University Press. Repr. Calcutta: Navabharat, 1973.

Chakravarti, S. N. 1938. "Development of the Bengali Script from the Fifth Century A.D. to the End of Muhammadan Rule." *Journal of the Royal Asiatic Society of Bengal: Letters* 4: 351–91.

Dimock, Edward C., Suhas Chatterjee, and Somdeb Bhattacharji. 1987. *Introduction to Bengali,* part 2: *A Bengali Prose Reader,* rev. Clinton B. Seely. Chicago: University of Chicago, South Asia Language and Area Center.

Lambert, Hester M. 1953. *Introduction to the Devanagari Script.* London: Oxford University Press.

Tagore, Rabindranath. 1935. *Bāṃlā śabdatattba* [Bengali lexicology]. Santiniketan, West Bengal: Visva-bharati.

Oriya Writing

B. P. Mahapatra

The Oriya [oṛia] script is derived from the Brahmi script of the Ashokan inscriptions; in Orissa state, specimens are found in the Dhauli and Jaugar inscriptions of the Emperor Ashoka (3rd century B.C.E.) and the Khandagiri inscriptions of King Kharabela (1st century C.E.). However, unlike these inscriptions, the language of which was Prakrit, the earliest inscription in Oriya is the Urjam inscription of 1051 C.E. This inscription is in Kalinga script, the variety of Brahmi from which modern Oriya script has evolved. It is syllabically based on the unit called the *akṣara* in Sanskrit, [ɔkhyɔrɔ] in Oriya. The script is written from left to right.

Since a large number of tribal languages, of both the Dravidian and Munda families, are spoken within the geopolitical limits of Orissa state, many of these languages have adopted the Oriya script in writing their languages. Sanskrit too is written in Oriya script in Orissa.

The specific features of the Oriya script are as follows.

The vowel *a*, phonetically [ɔ], is inherent in each consonant symbol, whether simple or conjunct, unless the letter is modified by the bottom stroke called *halanta*. Thus କ *ka* and ଗ *ga*, when marked wth this stroke as କ୍ , ଗ୍ , are read as *k* and *g* respectively.

Vowels other than *a*, when following a consonant, are written as obligatory diacritics. The diacritics for *ā* and *ī* are on the right side, as in କା *kā* and କୀ *kī*. The diacritic for *i* goes on top of the consonant letter, as in କି *ki*. The diacritics for *u*, *ū*, and *ṛ* go under the consonant, as in କୁ *ku*, କୂ *kū*, and କୃ *kṛ*. The diacritic for *e* precedes the consonant as in କେ *ke*. The diacritics for *o*, *ai*, and *au* are discontinuous, surrounding the consonant, as in କୈ *kai*, କୋ *ko*, and କୌ *kau*. Sometimes the vowel diacritics may be fused with consonants, e.g. କି *ki*, କୁ *ku*.

Similarly, secondary forms are used for consonants occurring in clusters; thus କ୍ *k* + ତ *ta* yields କ୍ତ *kta*, ସ୍ *s* + ଥ *tha* yields ସ୍ଥ *stha*. Homorganic nasal + stop clusters are generally written with distinct conjunct characters, such as ଙ୍କ *ṅka* and ଞ୍ଚ *ñca*, but the nasal may also be written with *anusvāra*, as in ଅଂକ for ଅଙ୍କ *aṅka*.

A fairly large number of other consonant clusters are also written with distinct conjunct characters which cannot be further analyzed; e.g., ନ୍ *n* + ଦ *da* = ନ୍ଦ *nda*, ଦ୍ *d* + ଧ *dha* = ଦ୍ଧ *ddha*. In borrowed words, however, clusters are written with *halanta* attached to the first member of the cluster, as in କ୍ ଚ *kca*, ପ୍ ଟ *pṭa*.

TABLE 35.1: *Vowels*

	Initial			Diacritic			
High neutral	ଅ	a	[ɔ]	–	କ	ka	[kɔ]
Low neutral	ଆ	ā	[a]	ା	କା	kā	[ka]
High unrounded	ଇ	i	[i]	ି	କି	ki	[ki]
High unrounded long	ଈ	ī	[i]	ୀ	କୀ	kī	[ki]
High rounded	ଉ	u	[u]	ୁ	କୁ	ku	[ku]
High rounded long	ଊ	ū	[u]	ୂ	କୂ	kū	[ku]
Syllabic vibrant	ଋ	r̥	[ru]	ୃ	କୃ	kr̥	[kru]
Mid unrounded	ଏ	e	[e]	େ	କେ	ke	[ke]
Mid rounded	ଓ	o	[o]	ୋ	କୋ	ko	[ko]
Diphthongs	ଐ	ai	[ɔi]	ୈ	କୈ	kai	[kɔi]
	ଔ	au	[ɔu]	ୌ	କୌ	kau	[kɔu]

The symbols

The traditional order of symbols in Oriya is based on articulatory phonetics, as originally developed for Sanskrit. First come the primary vowels, followed by five series of occlusives (including nasals) along the dimensions of voicing and aspiration. The rest of the consonants are non-occlusives. Nasalization of vowels is written with a diacritic *candrabindu* above the syllable, as in ଆ *ā* versus ଆଁ *ā̃* or କା *kā* vs. କାଁ *kā̃*.

TABLE 35.2: *Occlusives*

	Voiceless Plosives						Voiced Plosives						Nasals		
	Unaspirated			*Aspirated*			*Unaspirated*			*Aspirated*					
Velar	କ	k	[k]	ଖ	kh	[k^{h}]	ଗ	g	[g]	ଘ	gh	[g^{ɦ}]	ଙ	ṅ	[ŋ]
Palatal	ଚ	c	[ʧ]	ଛ	ch	[ʧ^{h}]	ଜ	j	[ʤ]	ଝ	jh	[ʤ^{ɦ}]	ଞ	ñ	[ɲ]
Retroflex	ଟ	ṭ	[ʈ]	ଠ	ṭh	[ʈ^{h}]	ଡ	ḍ	[ɖ]	ଢ	ḍh	[ɖ^{ɦ}]	ଣ	ṇ	[ɳ]
Dental	ତ	t	[t]	ଥ	th	[t^{h}]	ଦ	d	[d]	ଧ	dh	[d^{ɦ}]	ନ	n	[n]
Labial	ପ	p	[p]	ଫ	ph	[p^{h}]	ବ	b	[b]	ଭ	bh	[b^{ɦ}]	ମ	m	[m]

TABLE 35.3: *Sonorants and Fricatives*

	Palatal						*Retroflex*						*Dental*			*Labial*			*Other*		
Sonorants	ଯ	j́	[ʤ]	ୟ	y	[j]	ର	r	[r]	ଳ	ḷ	[ɭ]	ଲ	l	[l]	ୱ	v	[w]			
Sibilants	ଶ	ś	[s]				ଷ	ṣ	[s]				ସ	s	[s]				ହ	h	[h]

The set of vowels (*svara*), with their phonetic values, is given in TABLE 35.1.

The inventory of consonants (*vyañjana*) is given in TABLES 35.2 and 35.3. The palatal stops are phonetically affricates. The velar and the palatal nasals occur only in homorganic clusters. The retroflex voiced stops *ḍ*, *ḍh* have flapped variants [ɽ, ɽʰ] which occur intervocalically; a subscript dot is often used to mark these: ଡ଼ *ṛ*, ଢ଼ *ṛh*.

Conjunct consonants

Consonant clusters (*j′uktākṣara*) are written in Oriya in several ways. In many cases, the second member is reduced or simplified and attached to the bottom of the first member:

ଷ	ṣ	+	ପ	pa	=	ଷ୍ପ	ṣpa
ଣ	ṇ	+	ଠ	ṭha	=	ଣ୍ଠ	ṇṭha
ବ	b	+	ଦ	da	=	ବ୍ଦ	bda
ଦ	d	+	ଧ	dha	=	ଦ୍ଧ	ddha

In other cases, it is the first member which is reduced and attached to the second:

ଦ	d	+	ଭ	bha	=	ଦ୍ଭ	dbha
ଙ	ṅ	+	କ	ka	=	ଙ୍କ	ṅka

The consonant ତ *t* has two reduced forms, depending on whether it is first or second member. In first position ◌୍:

ତ	t	+	ପ	pa	=	ତ୍ପ	tpa
ତ	t	+	କ	ka	=	ତ୍କ	tka

In second position ◌୍:

ପ	p	+	ତ	ta	=	ପ୍ତ	pta
କ	k	+	ତ	ta	=	କ୍ତ	kta

In other combinations, however, ତ *t* has its full form:

ତ	t	+	ନ	na	=	ତ୍ନ	tna

Similarly, ର *r* has two reduced forms, in first position ◌୍:

ର	r	+	ପ	pa	=	ର୍ପ	rpa
ର	r	+	ବ	ba	=	ର୍ବ	rba

But in second position ◌୍:

ପ	p	+	ର	ra	=	ପ୍ର	pra
ଫ	ph	+	ର	ra	=	ଫ୍ର	phra

The consonant ଯ *y* in second position is written as ୟ after the first consonant:

କ	k	+	ଯ	ya	=	କ୍ୟ	kya

Finally, some clusters have idiosyncratic fused shapes:

କ	k	+	ଷ	ṣa	–	କ୍ଷ	kṣa
ନ	n	+	ଦ	da	=	ନ୍ଦ	nda

Distinctive characteristics

The Oriya script in its distinctive features resembles related scripts of the eastern Indic variety. Visually, the basic symbols for vowels and consonants can be grouped into five types on the basis of their sharing similar features. These are:

a. A top "hoop" attached to the distinctive shape, as in କ *ka* and ଚ *ca*.

b. A top curve with a tail (Matson's "handle") attached to the distinctive shape, as in ଇ *i* and ର *ra*.

c. A top curve with a side bar ("hatrack") attached to the distinctive shape, as in ଗ *ga* and ଶ *ṇa*.

d. A bottom curve with a side bar ("hook") attached to the distinctive shape, as in ଅ *a* and ଥ *tha*.

e. A few miscellaneous letters like ଏ *e* and ଠ *ṭha*.

SAMPLE OF ORIYA

1. Oriya:	ପ୍ରାଣୀଙ୍କ	ଆରତ	ଦୁଃଖ	ଅପ୍ରମିତ	ଦେଖୁ	ଦେଖୁ
2. Transliteration	prāṇiṅka	ārata	duḥkha	apramita	dekhu	dekhu
3. Transcription:	praṇinkɔ	arɔtɔ	dukhɔ	ɔprɔmitɔ	dekhu	dekhu
4. Gloss:	of.living.beings	misery	sorrow	unlimited	seeing	seeing

1.	କେବା	ସହୁ
2.	kebā	sahũ
3.	keba	sɔhu
4.	who	could.tolerate

1.	ମୋ	ଜୀବନ	ପଚେ	ନର୍କେ	ପଡ଼ିଥାଉ	ଜଗତ	ଉଦ୍ଧାର	ହେଉ
2.	mo	jībana	pache	narke	paṛithāu	jagata	uddhāra	heu
3.	mo	ʤibɔnɔ	pɔche	nɔrke	pɔṛithau	ʤɔgɔtɔ	uddhārɔ	heu
4.	my	life	even.if	in.hell	let.it.remain	world	saved	let.it.be

'Who could tolerate seeing the unbounded misery and sorrow of living beings? Let my life remain in hell, but let the world be saved.'

— *From a poem by Bhima Bhoi, an illiterate tribal saint of the 19th century.*

Bibliography

Bhima Bhoi. 1962. *Granthabali,* ed. Birakisore Das. Cuttack: J. Mahapatra & Co.

Das, Nilakantha. 1958. *Oriya bhāshā o sāhitya,* 2nd ed. Cuttack: New Students Store.

Mahapatra, B. P. 1993. "Oṛia akṣara." *Jhankara* (Cuttack) 45 (Bishuba issue): 1–6.

Matson, Dan. 1971. *Introduction to Oriya,* part 2: *Oriya Writing.* East Lansing: Michigan State University, Asian Studies Center.

Mohanty, Panchanan. 1992. "All That You Wanted to Know about Oriya Allographs." *Journal of the Board of Secondary Education, Orissa* 16/4: xxii–xxvii.

Tripathi, Kunjabihari. 1962. *The Evolution of Oriya Language and Script.* Cuttack: Utkal University.

Sinhala Writing

JAMES W. GAIR

Sinhala script is used for writing the Sinhala (Sinhalese) language, but in Sri Lanka also Pali, and sometimes Sanskrit. It is a Brahmi derivative, with a continuous inscriptional and literary history from the third–second century B.C.E., though it has undergone much change in form since then. The forms of its letters are distinctive, though manifestly influenced by the early Grantha script of South India (Fernando 1949, 1950). As in most Brahmi-derived South Asian alphabets, consonants imply a following inherent vowel *a*, unless marked for its absence by adding ͩ or ͨ, called *(h)al kirīma*, to the consonant; thus ප [pa] but ප් [p], and ම [ma] but ම් [m]. The "independent" vowel symbols අ *a*, ඉ *i*, උ *u*, etc. are used only word-initially. Vowels following a consonant are indicated by modifications to the consonant, which may occur above, below, or on either side of it; see TABLE 36.1. The existence of the vowels ඇ *æ*, ඈ *ǣ*, and a set of prenasalized stops (called "half-nasals") ඟ * n̆ga*, ඬ *n̆ḍa*, ඦ *n̆ḍa*, and ඹ *m̆ba* are special features of Sinhala phonology represented in the script.

Some conjunct symbols are used for writing consonant clusters (including doubled consonants) but most have recognizable parts, formed by truncating the first symbol, as in ඥ *nda* from ද + ද. A few, however, are less transparent, such as ඤ representing *ñja* (ඤ + ජ). Special symbols exist for ර *r* before a consonant, and for *r* and ය *y* following a consonant; thus, with ශ *śa*, we have ශ්‍ර *rśa*, ශ්‍ර *śra*, ශ්‍ය *śya*, ශ්‍ර්‍ය *rśya*. Consonant combinations may also be written by writing the "vowelless" symbol on all but the last, thus ද්‍ද *nda*, මබ *mba*; this device is common in current typed and printed works. (For a full account, see Gair and Karunatilaka 1976.)

The symbols

The full current Sinhala writing system actually contains an "alphabet within an alphabet." A subset of it, referred to as the *Eḷu hōḍiya* (boxed in the tables), reflects the classical language (*Eḷu*), as described in the classical grammar *Sidatsañgarā* (ca. 1300 C.E.). This is still widely regarded as authoritative, and the *Eḷu hōḍiya* is represented in current school charts and grammars even today. The character for *c* is generally not included, since the *Sidatsañgarā* does not list it (though employing it in examples). The full Sinhala alphabet, or *Miśra hōḍiya* ("mixed" alphabet) includes the symbols necessary for writing loanwords from Sanskrit and Pali, notably the aspirated consonants. A newer symbol ෆ has been introduced for *fa*; but often Roman

TABLE 36.1: *Vowels*

Independent	Diacritic (n-)		Transliteration	Pronunciation
අ	—	න	a	[a, ə]
ආ	—ා	නා	ā	[aː, a]
ඇ	—ැ ᵃ	නැ	æ	[æ]
ඈ	—ෑ ᵃ	නෑ	ǣ	[æː]
ඉ	⌐ ᵇ	නි	i	[i]
ඊ	⌐ ᵇ	නී	ī	[iː]
උ	⌐ ᵃ, ᶜ	නු	u	[u]
ඌ	⌐ ᶜ	නූ	ū	[uː]
ඍa	—a	නa	r̥	[ri, ru]
ඎaa	—aa	නaa	r̥̄	[riː, ruː]
එ	ෙ—	නෙ	e	[e]
ඒ	ෙ—ᵖ ᵃ, ᵈ	නේ	ē	[eː]
ඓ	ෙෙ—	නෛ	ai	[ɑj]
ඔ	ෙ—ා	නො	o	[o]
ඕ	ෙ—ෟ	නෝ	ō	[oː]
ඖ	ෙ—ෟ	නෞ	au	[ɑw]

a. With ර r, there are alterations in the shape of some vowel diacritics: රැ ræ, රෑ rǣ, රු ru, රූ rū, රෘ r.
b. The width of the diacritic varies with the consonant: දි di, පි pi, රි ri, etc.
c. Attached to certain letters with a stroke down and to the right (ක k, ග g, ත t, භ bh, ශ ś), the diacritics take the form ⌐, ⌐.
d. Attached to letters with a stroke up and to the left, like the *hal kirīma* the diacritic takes the form ⌐.

f is combined with ප *p*, as ෆ. TABLE 36.1 shows the vowel symbols, and TABLE 36.2 and TABLE 36.3 (reading across) the principal consonants, in canonical order. The "class nasal" ○ ṃ (Sinhala *binduva*) is listed following the vowels, but it usually represents a velar nasal [ŋ]. There was a limited indigenous system of punctuation, but it has now been superseded by the comma, period, etc. of English.

Correspondence of speech to writing

Sinhala is strongly diglossic; that is, it has sharply distinct written and spoken varieties (Gair 1992). Interestingly, the classical *Eḷu hōḍiya* suffices to represent the sounds of the current spoken language almost perfectly. The main differences are that the distinctions between ළ *la* and ල *ḷa* or න *na* and ණ *ṇa* are now purely orthographic, and

TABLE 36.2: *Occlusives*

| | VOICELESS PLOSIVES | | VOICED PLOSIVES | | NASALS | |
	Unaspirated	*Aspirated*	*Unaspirated*	*Aspirated*	*Pure Nasals*	*Half-nasals*
Velar	k [k]	kh [k]	g [g]	gh [g]	ṅ [ŋ]	ňg [ⁿg]
Palatal	c [tʃ]	ch [tʃ]	j [dʒ]	jh [dʒ]	ñ [ɲ]	
Retroflex	ṭ [t]	ṭh [t]	ḍ [d]	ḍh [d]	ṇ [n]	ňḍ [ⁿd]
Dental	t [t]	th [t]	d [d]	dh [d]	n [n]	ňd [ⁿd]
Labial	p [p]	ph [p]	b [b]	bh [b]	m [m]	m̌b [ᵐb]

that there are only two symbols for writing the three vowels *ə*, *a*, and *ā*. However, the distribution of those vowels is almost entirely predictable by rule: ℘ represents *a* in the first syllable, except in a few words. It represents *ə* word-finally and before single consonants (including the "half-nasals"), and represents *a* before double consonants or clusters. ℘ɔ represents *ā* everywhere except word-finally, where it may be either *ā* or *a* depending primarily on the syllable structure of the word. Similar length rules apply to *ē* and *ō* in final position, which may be pronounced short or long. In the written language, the representation of final vowels is essentially fixed; but there is some fluctuation in representing the colloquial forms, as in dialogs in fiction and drama.

Though the aspirated consonants are written in direct Sanskrit borrowings, they are generally not pronounced differently from their unaspirated counterparts, even in reading aloud, though speakers may attempt to distinguish them in formal settings.

The symbols ṣ *ṣ* and ś *ś* also represent a Sanskrit distinction not observed in Sinhala pronunciation, but both are pronounced as [ʃ]. In older village speech, they were not distinguished from ස *s*, which was the single sibilant, as represented in the classical alphabet. Widespread literacy and loanwords, including those from English, have now generally established a contrast between [s] and [ʃ] in speech; but there is some fluctuation in writing the latter sound as ṣ or ś when there is no Sanskrit form to use as a model.

An affix written as යි *yi*, with several functions, is generally pronounced as *y* and treated as a final consonant. Except for these few divergences, the fit of script to sound is straightforward when reading. Complications arise in the other direction, since a number of distinctions in the literary language pertain only to spelling.

TABLE 36.3: *Sonorants and Fricatives*

	Palatal	*Alveolar*	*Dental*	*Labial*	*Other*
Sonorants	y [j]	r [r]	l [l]	v [ʋ]	ḷ [l]
Sibilants	ś [ʃ]	ṣ [ʃ]	s [s]		h [ɦ]

SAMPLE OF SINHALA

1. Sinhala:	තුවර	යුගයට	පැමිණෙන්න	පෙර	දුවිඩ
2. Transliteration:	nuvara	yugayaṭa	pæmiṇenna	pera	draviḍa
3. Transcription:	nuvərə	jugəjəṭə	pæminennə	perə	draviḍə
4. Gloss:	Nuvara	period.DAT	reach.INF	before	Dravidian

1.	ආභාෂය	ලැබූ	ග්‍රන්ථයක්	ලෙස	නම්	කළ	හැක්කේ
2.	ābhāṣaya	læbū	granthayak	lesa	nam	kaḷa	hækkē
3.	a:ba:ʃəjə	læbu:	grantəjak	lesə	nam	kələ	hække
4.	reflection	got.REL	book.INDEF	as	name	do.PAST.REL	can.FOCUS

1.	සිදත්සඟරාවයි.	පාලි	සංස්කෘත	භාෂාවන්ගෙන්	ගත්
2.	sidatsaṅgərāvayi.	pāli	saṃskṛta	bhāṣāvangen	gat
3.	sidatsaⁿgəra:vaj	pa:li	saŋskrutə	ba:ʃa:vaŋgeŋ	gat
4.	Sidatsaṅgarāva.EMPH/AGR	Pali	Sanskrit	languages.ABL	taken

1.	නීති	රීති	ආදිය	ඇතත්	මේ	ග්‍රන්ථයේ	සැලැස්මත්
2.	nīti	rīti	ādiya	ætat	mē	granthayē	sælæsmat
3.	ni:ti	ri:ti	a:dijə	æta-t	me:	grantəje:	sælæsmat
4.	rules	regulations	etc.	be.also	this	book.LOC	organization.also

1.	සමහර	අදහසුත්	දුවිඩ	සාහිත්‍යයෙන්	ගෙන	තිබේ.	මෙය
2.	samahara	adahasut	draviḍa	sāhityayen	gena	tibē.	meya
3.	saməhərə	adəhasut	draviḍə	sa:hitjəjeŋ	genə	tibe:	mejə
4.	some	ideas.also	Dravidian	literature.ABL	taken	be.PRES	this

1.	වියරණ	ග්‍රන්ථයක්ම	නොවේ.	මෙහි	ප්‍රධාන	අදහස	කාව්‍ය
2.	viyaraṇa	granthayakma	novē.	mehi	pradhāna	adahasa	kāvya
3.	vijərəṇə	grantəjakmə	nove:	mehi	prəda:nə	adəhasə	ka:vjə
4.	grammar	book.EMPH	not.be	this.LOC	chief	idea	poetry

1.	රචනයට	උපදෙස් දීමයි.		වියරණ	නීති	රීතිත්	
2.	racanayaṭa	upades	dīmayi.	viyaraṇa	nīti	rītit	
3.	racənəjəṭə	upades	di:maj	vijərəṇə	ni:ti	ri:tit	
4.	composition.DAT	advice	giving.EMPH/AGR	grammar	rules	regulations.also	

1.	කාව්‍යාලංකාරත්	එක්	කොට	ගෙන	ඇති	මෙවැනිම	දුවිඩ
2.	kāvyalaṃkārat	ek	koṭa	gena	æti	mevænima	draviḍa
3.	ka:vjəlaŋka:rat	ek	koṭə	genə	æti	mevænimə	drəviḍə
4.	poetics	one	do.PCPL	take.PCPL	be	this.like.EMPH	Dravidian

1.	ග්‍රන්ථයක්	දකුණු	ඉන්දියාවේ	තිබේ.	'විරසොළියම්'	යනු	ඒ
2.	granthayak	dakuṇu	indiyāve	tibē.	'virasoḷiyam'	yanu	ē
3.	grantəjak	dakunu	indija:ve	tibe:	virəsolijam	janu	e:
4.	book.INDEF	South	India	be.PRES	Virasoliyam	QUOT.REL	that

1. ග්‍රන්ථයේ නමයි.

2. granthayē namayi.

3. grəntəje: namaj

4. book.LOC   name.EMPH/AGR

'As a book that received Dravidian influence before the Nuvara (Kandy) period, one can name the *Sidatsañgarāva.* Although there are grammatical rules etc. from Pali and Sanskrit, the organization and some ideas in this book have also been taken from Dravidian literature. This is not only a grammatical treatise. Its main idea is to give advice for the composition of poetry. A Dravidian work like this that unites grammatical rules and poetics exists in South India. The name of that book is "Virasoliyam."'   —*Baddēgama Vimalavaṃsa 1960: 56.*

Bibliography

Archaeological Survey of Ceylon/Sri Lanka. 1904–. *Epigraphia Zeylanica, Being Lithic and Other Inscriptions of Ceylon.* Vols. 1–4, London: Oxford University Press; subsequent vols., Colombo: Government Press.

Fernando, P. E. E. 1949. "Palaeographical Development of the Brāhmi Script in Ceylon from 3rd Century B.C. to 7th Century A.D." *University of Ceylon Review* 7: 282–301.

———. 1950. "Development of the Sinhalese Script from 8th Century A.D. to 15th Century A.D." *University of Ceylon Review* 8: 222–43.

Gair, James W. 1992. "Sinhala." *International Encyclopedia of Linguistics* 3: 439–45. New York: Oxford University Press.

Gair, James W., and W. S. Karunatilaka (Karunatillake). 1976. *Literary Sinhala Inflected Forms, with a Transliteration Guide to the Sinhala Script.* Ithaca, N.Y.: Cornell University, South Asia Program and Department of Modern Languages.

Vimalavaṃsa, Baddēgama. 1960. *Siṃhala grantha vicāraya* [A critical survey of Sinhala literary works]. Maradana: Anula Press.

Kannada and Telugu Writing

WILLIAM BRIGHT

The Kannada and Telugu scripts are closely related scripts used to write two Dravidian languages of South India: Kannada (Kanarese, Canarese), in the state of Karnataka, and Telugu in Andhra Pradesh. They are phonologically based, and are written from left to right. Historically, like other scripts native to South Asia, they derive from the Brahmi script of the Ashokan inscriptions. Over the centuries, Brahmi evolved in a variety of ways in different parts of the Indian subcontinent, with distinctive developments in the south (Dani 1986: 193–214). Among southern scripts, the Kadamba and Cālukya of the fifth to seventh centuries C.E. are especially important. After about the tenth century, these types took on a homogeneous form: the Old Kannada script, which was used across the entire Indian peninsula, in the areas where both Kannada and Telugu are now spoken. By around 1500, this script had diversified into two closely related varieties, the Kannada and Telugu scripts. In the early nineteenth century, separate scripts for Kannada and Telugu were standardized under the influence of printing presses established by Christian mission organizations.

Typologically, the Kannada and Telugu scripts are alphasyllabaries: that is, they write each consonant-vowel sequence as a unit, referred to by the Sanskrit term *akṣara* (Ka. *akṣara*, Te. *akṣaramu*), in which the vowel symbol functions as an obligatory diacritic to the consonant (for details, see SECTION 31). In the descriptions below, note that phonological representations reflect "reading pronunciations," used in relatively formal situations. Pronunciations used in informal, colloquial speech vary greatly depending on social and geographical dialect.

———

The symbols

The traditional order of symbols begins with the "primary" vowels, i.e. those recognized as simple vowels in Sanskrit grammar. TABLE 37.1 shows the independent or "initial" form for each vowel in Kannada and Telugu, followed by the "diacritic" or postconsonantal form, illustrated with the consonant ಕ/క *k*. The canonical order proceeds from each short vowel to the corresponding long vowel. The names of the let-

———

ACKNOWLEDGMENTS. Thanks are due for the valuable suggestions of Peri Bhaskararao, Bh. Krishnamurti, Harold Schiffman, and S. N. Sridhar.

TABLE 37.1: *Primary Vowels*

| | SHORT | | | | LONG | | | |
| | Initial | | Diacritic (k-) | | Initial | | Diacritic (k-) | |
	Ka.	Te.	Ka.	Te.	Ka.	Te.	Ka.	Te.
Unrounded low central	a [ʌ]				ā [aː]			
high front	i [i]				ī [iː]			
Rounded high back	u [u]				ū [uː]			
Syllabic vibrant	r̥ [ri/ru]				r̥̄			

TABLE 37.2: *Secondary Vowels*

| | SHORT | | | | LONG | | | | DIPHTHONGS | | | |
| | Initial | | Diacritic (k-) | | Initial | | Diacritic (k-) | | Initial | | Diacritic (k-) | |
	Ka.	Te.	Ka.	Te.	Ka.	Te.	Ka.	Te.	Ka.	Te.	Ka.	Te.
Unrounded front	e [e]				ē [eː]				ai [aj]			
Rounded back	o [o]				ō [oː]				au [aw]			

TABLE 37.3: *Occlusives*

| | VOICELESS PLOSIVES | | | | VOICED PLOSIVES | | | | NASALS | |
| | Unaspirated | | Aspirated | | Unaspirated | | Aspirated | | | |
	Ka. Te.		Ka. Te.		Ka. Te.		Ka. Te.		Ka. Te.	
Velar	ಕ క	k [k]	ಖ ఖ	kh	ಗ గ	g [g]	ಘ ఘ	gh	ಙ ఙ	ṅ [ŋ]
Palatal	ಚ చ	c [ʧ]	ಛ ఛ	ch	ಜ జ	j [ʤ]	ಝ ఝ	jh	ಞ ఞ	ñ [ɲ]
Retroflex	ಟ ట	ṭ [ʈ]	ಠ ఠ	ṭh	ಡ డ	ḍ [ɖ]	ಢ ఢ	ḍh	ಣ ణ	ṇ [ɳ]
Dental	ತ త	t [t]	ಥ థ	th	ದ ద	d [d]	ಧ ధ	dh	ನ న	n [n]
Labial	ಪ ప	p [p]	ಫ ఫ	ph	ಬ బ	b [b]	ಭ భ	bh	ಮ మ	m [m]

ters consist of their sounds, sometimes followed by -*kāra* 'making'; thus ಅ/అ is called *a* or *a-kāra* (Te. *a-kāramu*).

The "syllabic r" in borrowings from Sanskrit is pronounced [ri] or [ru], as in Ka. ಋತು *r̥tu* [ritu], Te. ఋతువు *r̥tuvu* [rutuvu] 'season'. Corresponding symbols for syllabic *r̥ l̥ l̥̄* exist, in imitation of Sanskrit, but are commonly omitted from the Kannada and Telugu inventories.

Next come the "secondary" vowels, comprising the mid vowels *e* and *o,* long and short, with their corresponding diphthongs. TABLE 37.2 again shows the initial and diacritic forms.

Next in order come two symbols which are written only after vowels, and are sometimes listed in combination with *a*. The first is a nasal feature called *anusvāra,* written as ం/ం and transliterated as *ṃ* (e.g. ಅಂ/అం *aṃ*). It is most often used for a nasal consonant homorganic with a following stop; e.g., *aṅga* 'limb of the body' is usually written not with a conjunct consonant symbol, but rather as *aṃga,* thus Ka. ಅಂಗ [ʌŋga] (Te. అంగము [ʌŋgəmu]). When *anusvāra* is followed by a consonant other than a stop, or when it is word-final, it is pronounced as [m]; e.g., ಸಿಂಹ/సింహ *siṃha* [sɛimha] 'lion', ಲಗಾಂ/లగాం *lagāṃ* [lʌgaːm] 'bridle'.

After *anusvāra* in the sequence comes an element called *visarga,* occurring principally in Sanskrit words. It is written as ః/ః, transliterated *ḥ*, and usually pronounced [ha]; e.g. ಪುನಃ/పునః *punaḥ* [punəha] 'again'.

Next follow the occlusive consonants, i.e. the stops and nasals. TABLE 37.3 shows the independent or "full" forms of each. The canonical order of these and the

TABLE 37.4: *Sonorants and Fricatives*

| | Palatal | | Alveolar | | Dental | | Labial | |
	Ka. Te.		Ka. Te.		Ka. Te.		Ka. Te.	
Sonorants	ಯ య	y [j]	ರ ర	r [r]	ಲ ల	l [l]	ವ వ	v [ʋ]
Sibilants	ಶ శ	ś [ɕ]	ಷ ష	ṣ [ʂ]	ಸ స	s [s]		

remaining consonant symbols proceeds horizontally within each row. Note that, among the nasals, velar *ṅ* and palatal *ñ* are associated with Sanskrit, and are relatively rare in Kannada or Telugu.

There follow, again in order from the back of the mouth toward the front, the oral sonorants and the voiceless sibilants, as shown in TABLE 37.4.

Finally comes a "miscellaneous" category of sounds not classified in terms of articulation, comprising ಹ/హ *ha* and ಳ/ళ *ḷa* [[a]].

In Kannada, when ಮ *m-* and ಯ *y-* occur with the vowels *o ō*, the consonants take reduced forms: ಮೊ *mo*, ಯೊ *yo*. To maintain the distinction between ಮ *m-* and ವ *v-*, the sequence *vo* is written as ವೊ (see next paragraph). In Telugu, the combinations of మ *m-* and య *y-* with *o ō* require a special form of the vowel: మొ *mo*, మో *mō*, యొ *yo*, యో *yō*.

When attached to the consonants ಪ/ప *p-*, ಫ/ఫ *ph-*, and ವ/వ *v-*, the vowels *u ū* take special forms that start beneath the consonant, e.g. ಪು/పు *pu*, ಪೂ/పూ *pū*. This means that ಮ/మ can only be interpreted as *ma*, since *vu* is ವು/వు. In Kannada, these special vowel forms are also used for *o ō*, e.g. ಪೊ *po*, ವೊ *vo*.

<hr>

Characteristic features

As in Devanagari (SECTION 31), a following short vowel *a* is considered inherent in each consonant symbol; thus Ka. ದ, Te. ద is *da,* and Ka. ರ, Te. ర is *ra.*

Each consonant is represented by a basic consonantal symbol, e.g. ದ/ద *da,* ರ/ర *ra.* Consonants lacking the characteristic headstroke at the top are ಖ/ఖ *kha,* ಙ/ఙ *ṅa,* ಜ/జ *ja,* ಞ/ఞ *ña,* ಟ/ట *ṭa,* ಣ/ణ *ṇa,* ಬ/బ *ba,* and ಲ/ల *la.* The headstrokes are absent from all consonants when the vowels *ā i ī* are attached, as is shown below.

Vowels other than *a,* when they follow a consonant, are written as obligatory diacritics, again as in Devanagari. Thus the diacritic for *ā* is Ka. –ಾ, Te. ా attached at the top right, as in ದಾ/దా *dā.* That for *i* is Ka. ಿ, Te. ి on top of the consonant, as in ತಿ/తి *ti.* That for *ī* is Ka. ೀ on top of the consonant plus –ೆ on the right, but Te. ీ on top, as in ತೀ/తీ *tī.*

A vowel occurring in initial position is written not with a diacritic, but with an independent symbol. Thus initial *a* is written Ka. ಅ, Te. అ; initial *ā* is Ka. ಆ, Te. ఆ; initial *i* is Ka. ಇ, Te. ఇ; and so on.

A consonant occurring without a following vowel in final position is written with Ka. –ಀ, Te. ్ above it. This is called *virāma* (Te. *virāmamu*), literally 'pause'; it "cancels" the inherent vowel. Thus a final symbol ದ/ద would be interpreted as *da*; but with the added diacritic, ದ್/ద్ corresponds to *d* alone.

Consonants may also occur in clusters, especially in words borrowed from Sanskrit; these may involve both initial and medial sequences of two or three consonants. In such cases, "conjunct" symbols are used. Most such combinations are formed by reducing consonant symbols other than the first one in the sequence to an altered form, adjoined beneath and/or to the right of the first consonant. For example, Ka. ತ,

Te. త *t(a)* plus యు/య *ya* combine as Ka. త్య *tya*, Te. త్య; Ka. క, Te. క *k(a)* plus ర/ర *ra* combine as Ka. క్ర, Te. క్ర *kra*. Other examples are Ka. క్క, Te. క్క *kka*; Ka. గ్గ, Te. గ్గ *gga*; Ka. చ్చ, Te. చ్చ *cca*; Ka. త్త, Te. త్త *tta*; Ka. న్న, Te. న్న *nna*; Ka. మ్మ, Te. మ్మ *mma*. A vowel following a consonant combination is adjoined to the first of the consonants, e.g. Ka. క్రి, Te. క్రి *kri*.

In Kannada, a consonant combination in which the first element is ర *r(a)* is often handled in a special way: the *r(a)* is written with –ర్ to the right of the consonant which follows it; thus ర *r(a)* + త *ta* gives ర్త *rta* (alternatively, ర్త).

Note that, where conjunct consonants are involved, the *akṣara* does not actually correspond to a spoken syllable: thus Ka. *rakta* 'blood' would be syllabified as *rak* + *ta* in pronunciation, but it is written with the two *akṣaras* ర *ra* + క్త *kta*.

―――

Correspondences

Correspondences of written symbols to spoken sounds are much as indicated by the descriptive labels and the transcriptions used above. Some exceptions are as follows:

In the consonant cluster జ్ఞ/జ్ఞ *jña*, the consonant *j* is pronounced as a palatal stop [ɟ], thus Ka. జ్ఞాన *jñāna* [ɟɳaːna] 'knowledge' (Te. జ్ఞానము [ɟɳaːnəmu]).

The sibilants శ/శ *śa* and ష/ష *ṣa* are not always distinguished in the pronunciation of the modern languages; both may be pronounced as an alveo-palatal sibilant [ʃ].

Consonant clusters involving హ/హ *h* as first member are sometimes pronounced with reversal of the two consonants; e.g., Ka. చిహ్న *cihna* 'sign' may be pronounced [ʧinha] (Te. చిహ్నము [ʧinhəmu]).

The Telugu vowel ఏ *ē* (and its secondary forms) corresponds to the pronunciation [æ:] when it occurs in the first syllable of a word which has *a* or *ā* in the following syllable, e.g. మేడ [mæːɽa] 'mansion'. However, the same vowel [æ:] is sometimes written with (diacritic forms of) ఆ *ā* when it occurs in the past tense suffix, e.g. తాగాను [taːgæːnu] 'I drank'.

In Telugu, చ *c(a)* and జ *j(a)* are pronounced as lamino-palatal affricates [ʧ ʤ] before the front vowels *i e* (long or short); but they are pronounced as alveolar affricates [ts dz] before the central and back vowels *a o u* in native Dravidian words, e.g. చాల [tsaːlaː] 'many', జాగు [dzaːgu] 'delay'. Nevertheless, in loanwords from Sanskrit, the palatal pronunciations are used, e.g. చలనము [ʧʌlənəmu] 'motion', జన్మము [ʤʌnməmu] 'birth'.

The numerals are shown in TABLE 37.5.

TABLE 37.5: *Kannada and Telugu Numerals*

	1	2	3	4	5	6	7	8	9	0
Kannada	೧	೨	೩	೪	೫	೬	೭	೮	೯	೦
Telugu	೧	೨	౩	౪	౫	౬	౭	౮	౯	౦

SAMPLE OF KANNADA

1. Kannada:	ಬಹಳ	ಹಿಂದಿನ	ಕಾಲದಲ್ಲಿ	ವಿದರ್ಭದಲ್ಲಿ	ಒಬ್ಬ
2. Transliteration:	bahaḷa	hindina	kāladalli	vidarbhadalli	obba
3. Transcription:	bʌhəḷa	hindina	ka:lədəlli	ʋidərbʰədəlli	obba
4. Gloss:	much	past	time.in	Vidarbha.in	one

1. ರಾಜನಿದ್ದ.	ಆ	ದೇಶದಲ್ಲಿ	ಬಹಳ	ದಿನಗಳಿಂದ	ಬಹಳವಾಗಿ
2. rājanidda.	ā	dēśadalli	bahaḷa	dinagaḷinda	bahaḷavāgi
3. ra:ʤənidda	a:	de:ɕədəlli	bʌhəḷə	dinəgəḷinda	bʌhəḷəʋa:gi
4. king.was	that	country.from	much	from.days	much.being

1. ಕಳ್ಳತನವಾಗಿತ್ತು.	ಇದನ್ನು	ಯಾರಿಂದಲೂ	ಕಂಡು	ಹಿಡಿಯಲು
2. kaḷḷatanavāgittu.	idannu	yārindalū	kaṇḍu	hiḍiyalu
3. kʌḷḷətənəʋa:gittu	idənnu	ja:rindəlu:	kʌɳɖu	hiɽijəlu
4. theft.had.become	this.OBJ	by.whomever	having.seen	to.catch

1. ಆಗದೆ	ಕೊನೆಗೆ	ರಾಜನೇ	ಒಂದು	ದಿನ	ಕಳ್ಳರನ್ನು
2. āgade	konege	rājanē	ondu	dina	kaḷḷarannu
3. a:gəde	konege	ra:ʤəne:	ondu	dina	kʌḷḷərənnu
4. not.having.become	to.end	king.self	one	day	thieves.OBJ

1. ಹಿಡಿಯುವುದಕ್ಕೆ	ಹೋಗುತ್ತಾನೆ.
2. hiḍiyuvudakke	hōguttāne.
3. hiɽijuʋudəkke	ho:gutta:ne
4. catch.purpose	he.goes

'A long time ago, in Vidarbha, there was a king. In that country, for a long time, there had been a lot of theft. Since whoever was doing this couldn't be caught, … finally one day the king himself goes to catch the thief.'
    —*Beginning of a children's story from the magazine* Candamāma, *April 1955.*

SAMPLE OF TELUGU

1. Telugu:	మీరు	అక్కడికి	వెళ్ళినతరువాత,	నాకు	ఉత్తరము
2. Transliteration:	mīru	akkaḍiki	veḷḷinataruvāta,	nāku,	uttaramu
3. Transcription:	mi:ru	ʌkkəɽiki	ʋeḷḷinətaruʋa:tə	na:ku	uttərəmu
4. Gloss:	you	to.there	after.having.gone	to.me	letter

1. వ్రాసి,	నేను	చేయవలసిన	పనులు	తెలియచేస్తే,	వారు
2. vrāsi	nēnu	cēyavalasina	panulu	teliyacēstē	vāru
3. ʋra:si	ne:nu	ʧe:jəʋələsina	pʌnulu	telijəʧe:ste:	ʋa:ru
4. having.written	I	must.do	works	if.inform	they

1. చేయవద్దని   చెప్పినప్పటికీ   మీరు   వ్రాసినప్రకారము   చేయడానకు
2. cēyavaddani   ceppinappaṭikī   mīru   vrāsinaprakāramu   cēyaḍānaku
3. ʧeːyəʋəddəni   ʧeppinəppəʈiki: mi:ru   ʋra:sinəprəka:rəmu   ʧe:jəʈa:nəku
4. "don't.do"   although.saying   you   according.to.writing   to.doing

1. ప్రయత్నము   చేస్తాను.
2. prayatnamu   cēstānu.
3. prʌjətnəmu   ʧe:sta:nu
4. effort   I.will.make

'After you have gone there, having written a letter to me, … if you inform me of the work I must do, … although they say not to do it, I will try to do as you have written.'   —*Arden 1937: 51.*

Bibliography

Arden, A. H. 1937. *A Progressive Grammar of the Telugu Language,* 4th ed. Madras: Christian Literature Society.

Dani, Ahmad Hasan. 1986. *Indian Palaeography,* 2nd ed. New Delhi: Munshiram Manoharlal.

Kittel, Ferdinand. 1903. *A Grammar of the Kannada Language in English.* Mangalore: Basel Mission Book and Tract Repository.

Krishnamurti, Bh., & J. P. L. Gwynn. 1985. *A Grammar of Modern Telugu.* Delhi: Oxford University Press.

Spencer, Harold. 1950. *A Kanarese Grammar,* rev. W. Perston. Mysore: Wesley Press.

Malayalam Writing

K. P. MOHANAN

The Malayalam script, like Devanagari, is written from left to right. In the traditional script, each character represents a syllable-sized unit, but recent innovations have introduced a few elements of alphabetic writing into the script.

The script is "phonemic" insofar as it encodes most contrasts at the classical phonemic level of representation. With a few exceptions, a character in the script (called an *akṣaram*) denotes a vowel by itself, or one or more consonants followed by a vowel. The inventory of fundamental *akṣaram* characters in Malayalam is given in their traditional order (reading left to right), vowels (*svaram*) in TABLE 38.1 and consonants (*vyanjanam*) in TABLE 38.2. Note that both written and spoken Malayalam, unlike most Indian languages, contrast dental [t̪], alveolar [t], and retroflex [ʈ] (albeit only when doubled). Also contrastive are nasals in seven articulatory positions: [m], [n̪], [ɳ], [ɲ], [ŋ] in the script, plus [n] and [ŋʲ] in pronunciation.

In TABLE 38.2, the transliteration symbols are given in terms of (abstract) consonants alone; when pronounced, the *akṣaram* is pronounced with following *a*, thus ക *k* = *ka*. The *akṣaram* ക്ഷ *kṣ* actually represents a conjunct consonant (see below), but is conventionally listed as a unit, near the end of the canonical order.

In simple cases, the *svaram* and *vyanjanam* characters can be simply strung together to form words: അറ *aṟa* 'room', ആന *āna* 'elephant', പക *paka* 'hostility'. The *svaram* characters are used only when the vowel occurs initially in a syllable, as in the initial syllables in 'room' and 'elephant'. Elsewhere, when the syllable begins with a consonant, the *vyanjanam* character indicates the consonant–vowel sequence.

A marginal contrast between velars ([k] etc.) and palatalized velars ([kʲ] etc.) is not reflected in the script; both series are indicated by the characters ക *k* ഖ *kh* ഗ *g* ഘ *gh* ങ *ṅ*. The symbol ന *n* represents dental [n̪] when initial, alveolar [n] elsewhere; but its geminate form ന്ന represents both dental [n̪n̪], as in പന്നി [pan̪n̪i] 'pig', and alveolar [nn], as in കന്നി [kanni] 'unmarried girl'. The symbol റ *ṟ* is pronounced, when doubled, as alveolar [tt], e.g. മാറ്റം *māṟṟam* [maːttam] 'change'; elsewhere it is alveolar [r], e.g. കറി *kaṟi* [kari] 'curry'.

A *vyanjanam* character by itself has the value of a syllable onset followed by the vowel *a*. When a syllable is followed by a vowel other than *a*, the vowel is indicated by a diacritic on the letter, rather than the full *svaram* character. The regular diacritics and their values are illustrated in TABLE 38.1 with the *vyanjanam* പ *p*. The shapes of *u ū* are irregular with some consonants, as shown in TABLE 38.3. However, in the

TABLE 38.1: *Vowel Symbols (svaram); Vowel–Consonant Combinations*

Svaram	Transliteration	Pronunciation	Diacritic (with p-)	
അ	a	[a]	—	പ
ആ	ā	[aː]	—ാ	പാ
ഇ	i	[i]	—ി	പി
ഈ	ī	[iː]	—ീ	പീ
ഉ	u	[u]	—	പു
ഊ	ū	[uː]	—	പൂ
ഋ	ṛ	[rɨ]	—	പൃ
എ	e	[e]	െ—	പെ
ഏ	ē	[eː]	േ—	പേ
ഐ	ai	[ai̯]	ൈ—	പൈ
ഒ	o	[o]	െ—ാ	പൊ
ഓ	ō	[oː]	േ—ാ	പോ
ഔ	au	[au̯]	േ—ൗ	പൗ
_a		[ə]	—	പ

a. The vowel [ə], which is never word-initial, has no independent symbol.

TABLE 38.2: *Consonant Symbols (vyanjanam)*

	VOICELESS PLOSIVES		VOICED PLOSIVES		NASALS
	Unaspirated	Aspirated	Unaspirated	Aspirated	
Velar	ക k [k]	ഖ kh [kʰ]	ഗ g [g]	ഘ gh [gʰ]	ങ ñ [ŋ]
Palatal	ച c [ʧ]	ഛ ch [ʧʰ]	ജ j [ʤ]	ഝ jh [ʤʰ]	ഞ ñ [ɲ]
Retroflex	ട ṭ [ʈ]	ഠ ṭh [ʈʰ]	ഡ ḍ [ɖ]	ഢ ḍh [ɖʰ]	ണ ṇ [ɳ]
Dental	ത t [t̪]	ഥ th [t̪ʰ]	ദ d [d̪]	ധ dh [d̪ʰ]	ന n [n̪]
Labial	പ p [p]	ഫ ph [pʰ]	ബ b [b]	ഭ bh [bʰ]	മ m [m]
Sonorants	യ y [j]	ര r [ɾ]	ല l [l]	വ v [ʋ]	
Fricatives	ശ ś [ç]	ഷ ṣ [ʃ]	സ s [s]	ഹ h [ɦ]	
Miscellaneous	ള ḷ [ɭ]	ക്ഷ kṣ [kʃ]	ഴ ḻ [ɻ]	റ ṟ [r]	

current revised script (see below), all these variants are replaced by uniform −ു *u* and
−ൂ *ū* afer the consonant.

The consonant *m*, when syllable-final, is represented as the symbol ം (called
anusvāram): ഔഷധം *auṣadham* 'medicine', വരും *varum* 'will come', ഹംസം
hamsam 'swan', സംയോഗം *samyōgam* 'joining together'.

Prepausal sonorant consonants (other than *m*) are represented by a special set of
characters which are called *cillakṣaram* 'letter fragments' (TABLE 38.4).

TABLE 38.3: *Irregular Shapes of -u and -ū*

ക	k + u =	കു	ku	ക	k + ū =	കൂ	kū
ഗ	g + u =	ഗു	gu	ഗ	g + ū =	ഗൂ	gū
ച	c + u =	ചു	cu	ച	c + ū =	ചൂ	cū
ജ	j + u =	ജു	ju	ജ	j + ū =	ജൂ	jū
ണ	ṇ + u =	ണു	ṇu	ണ	ṇ + ū =	ണൂ	ṇū
ത	t + u =	തു	tu	ത	t + ū =	തൂ	tū
ന	n + u =	നു	nu	ന	n + ū =	നൂ	nū
ഭ	bh + u =	ഭു	bhu	ഭ	bh + ū =	ഭൂ	bhū
ര	r + u =	രു	ru	ര	r + ū =	രൂ	rū
ശ	ś + u =	ശു	śu	ശ	ś + ū =	ശൂ	śū
ഹ	h + u =	ഹു	hu	ഹ	h + ū =	ഹൂ	hū

TABLE 38.4: *Cillakṣarams*

ണ	ṇ >	ൺ	ചാൺ	cāṇ	'handbreadth'
ന	n >	ൻ	അവൻ	avan	'he'
ര	r >	ർ	മലർ	malar	'popped rice'
ല	l >	ൽ	പകൽ	pakal	'day'
ള	ḷ >	ൾ	അവൾ	avaḷ	'she'

TABLE 38.5: *Consonant Diacritics*

ന	n	+	യ	y	=	ന്യ	ny	ന്യായം	nyāyam	'justice'
പ	p	+	ര	r	=	പ്ര	pr	പ്രീതി	prīti	'affection'
ശ	ś	+	വ	v	=	ശ്വ	śv	ശ്വാസം	śvāsam	'breath'

All word-internal sequences of consonants, except for *m* as mentioned above, are represented as *kūttakṣaram* 'conjunct characters'; these are of several types. First, when യ *y*, ര *r*, and വ *v* are second members in consonant clusters, they are represented as diacritics adjoined to the preceding consonant (TABLE 38.5). Many other conjuncts are formed by placing the character for the second sound beneath the character for the first sound; ല *l* takes the rather different shape ്ല (TABLE 38.6). But ് marks the doubling of a number of characters with the shape ു at the right, e.g. ച്ച *cc*, ബ്ബ *bb*, വ്വ *vv* (but പ്പ *pp*, ല്ല *ll*).

However, some of the most frequent conjuncts are formed by left-to-right combinations (TABLE 38.7).

In the 1970s and 1980s, the difficulties of printing Malayalam script gave rise to the introduction of a simplified script. The most important property of the modern

TABLE 38.6: *Vertical Conjuncts (in order of second member)*

സ	s	+	ക	k	=	സ്ക	sk	സ്കന്ധം	skandham	'shoulder'
ച	c	+	ഛ	ch	=	ച്ഛ	cch	അച്ഛൻ	acchan	'father'
ജ	j	+	ജ	j	=	ജ്ജ	jj	മജ്ജ	majja	'lymph'
ട	ṭ	+	ട	ṭ	=	ട്ട	ṭṭ	അട്ടി	aṭṭi	'pile'
ഷ	ṣ	+	ട	ṭ	=	ഷ്ട	ṣṭ	കഷ്ടം	kaṣṭam	'difficulty'
ഡ	ḍ	+	ഡ	ḍ	=	ഡ്ഡ	ḍḍ	ഇഡ്ഡലി	iḍḍali	'kind of cake'
ഷ	ṣ	+	ണ	ṇ	=	ഷ്ണ	ṣṇ	കഷ്ണം	kaṣṇam	'piece'
പ	p	+	ത	t	=	പ്ത	pt	സമാപ്തി	samāpti	'completion'
ബ	b	+	ദ	d	=	ബ്ദ	bd	ശബ്ദം	śabdam	'noise'
സ	s	+	ന	n	=	സ്ന	sn	സ്നേഹം	snēham	'love'
പ	p	+	പ	p	=	പ്പ	pp	അപ്പം	appam	'(sweet) bread'
ക	k	+	ല	l	=	ക്ല	kl	ക്ലേശം	klēśam	'pain'
പ	p	+	സ	s	=	പ്സ	ps	അപ്സര	apsara	'celestial dancer'
സ	s	+	സ	s	=	സ്സ	ss	മനസ്സ്	manassə	'mind'

TABLE 38.7: *Horizontal Conjuncts*

ക	k	+	ക	k	=	ക്ക	kk	പക്കം	pakkam	'side'
ക	k	+	ത	t	=	ക്ത	kt	ശക്തി	śakti	'power'
ങ	ṅ	+	ക	k	=	ങ്ക	ṅk	പങ്ക	paṅka	'fan'
ങ	ṅ	+	ങ	ṅ	=	ങ്ങ	ṅṅ	ചങ്ങല	caṅṅala	'chain'
ഞ	ñ	+	ഞ	ñ	=	ഞ്ഞ	ññ	കഞ്ഞി	kaññi	'rice gruel'
ഞ	ñ	+	ച	c	=	ഞ്ച	ñc	അഞ്ച്	añcə	'five'
ണ	ṇ	+	ട	ṭ	=	ണ്ട	ṇṭ	ചെണ്ട	ceṇṭa	'drum'
ണ	ṇ	+	ഡ	ḍ	=	ണ്ഡ	ṇḍ	മണ്ഡലം	maṇḍalam	'circle'
ത	t	+	ത	t	=	ത്ത	tt	കുത്തി	kutti	'stabbed'
ത	t	+	മ	m	=	ത്മ	tm	ആത്മാവ്	ātmāvə	'soul'
ന	n	+	ത	t	=	ന്ത	nt	ചന്തം	cantam	'beauty'
ന	n	+	ദ	d	=	ന്ദ	nd	ഇന്ദിര	indira	'Indira'
ന	n	+	ധ	dh	=	ന്ധ	ndh	അന്ധൻ	andhan	'blind'
ന	n	+	ന	n	=	ന്ന	[ṉṉ] or [nn]	മന്നൻ	mannan	'king'
ന	n	+	മ	m	=	ന്മ	nm	നന്മ	nanma	'goodness'
മ	m	+	മ	m	=	മ്മ	mm	ആമ്മ	amma	'mother'
ശ	ś	+	ച	c	=	ശ്ച	śc	ആശ്ചര്യം	āścaryam	'wonder'

script is the linearization of the diacritics in such a way that a complex character can be built by a left-to-right sequence of separate sorts for the main symbol and the diacritics (TABLE 38.8).

The second innovation is the breaking up of consonant clusters into sequences of atomic characters, using either a *cillakṣaram* as in ൻമ for ന്മ *nma*, or the diacritic ˘ (which otherwise writes [ə]) to indicate a consonant without a vowel (TABLE 38.9). Given these two changes, one would expect the modern script to become increasingly alphabetic, with each symbol representing a single segment. However, what has happened is that individual printers have opted for "modernizing" some characters but not others, thereby creating an inconsistent script with a large number of random options.

By and large, a space between two characters corresponds to a word boundary. However, Malayalam also allows a common style of writing in which the words of a phonological phrase are strung together such that the space between letters corresponds to a pause. For example, a *cillakṣaram*, as stated earlier, appears before a pause. When a sonorant consonant is followed by vowels in the same phonological phrase, the *cillakṣaram* is replaced by a regular character (TABLE 38.10). Similar observations apply to the encoding of phonological processes across words such as shwa insertion, glide insertion, gemination, nasal deletion, and so on (Mohanan 1986). The results of these processes are quite often represented in the script. When this happens, there is no space between the two words that participate in the phonological process.

The numerals are shown in TABLE 38.11.

TABLE 38.8: *Simplified Characters*

	Traditional	Modern
pra	൶	൶
pu	൹	൹
pū	൹	൹
pṛ	൹	൹

TABLE 38.9: *Simplified Consonant Clusters*

	Traditional	Modern
kta	ക്ത	ക ്ത
nta	ന്ത	ൻത (with *cillakṣaram*)
nma	ന്മ	ൻമ (with *cillakṣaram*)
pna	പ്ന	പ ്ന
ṣpa	ഷ്പ	ഷ ്പ
ska	സ്ക	സ ്ക

TABLE 38.10: *Spelling at Phrase Break*

In Pause			Scriptio Continua		
അവൻ	avan	'he'	അവനതാ	avanatā	'He is there.'
അവൾ	avaḷ	'she'	അവളെവിടെ	avaḷeviṭe	'Where is she?'
മലർ	malar	'popped rice'	മലരായി	malarāyi	'The popped rice is ready.'

TABLE 38.11: *Numerals*

1	2	3	4	5	6	7	8	9	0
൧	൨	൩	൪	൫	൬	൭	൮	൯	൦

SAMPLE OF MALAYALAM

1. Malayalam:	ആഹാരം	നിയന്ത്രിച്ചിട്ടും	വ്യായാമം	കൂട്ടിയിട്ടും
2. Transliteration:	āhāram	niyantriccittum	vyāyāmam	kūṭṭiyiṭṭum
3. Transcription:	aːɦaːṛam	ɳijanṭritʃiṭṭum	ʋjaːjaːmam	kuːṭṭijiṭṭum
4. Gloss:	food	controlled.despite	exercise	increased.despite

1. എന്തുകൊണ്ടാണ്	എദ്രോഗത്തിനൊരു	കടിഞ്ഞാൻ വീഴാത്തത്?	
2. entukoṇṭāṇə	hṛdrōgattinoru	kaṭiññāṇ	vīḻāttatə
3. eɳṭukoɳṭaːŋə	ɦɨḏroːgaṭṭinoṛu	kaʈiɳɳaːɳ	ʋiːɹaːṭṭatə
4. what.with.is	heart.disease.ACC.one	harness	fall.not.it

1. ദിനംപ്രതി അത്	കൂടുതലാളുകളെ	അടിമകളാക്കിക്കൊണ്ടിരിക്കുകയുമാണ്.	
2. dinamprati atə	kūtutalāḷukaḷe	aṭimakaḷākkikkoṇṭirikkukayumāṇə.	
3. ḏinamprati aṭɨ	kuːʈutalaːɭukaɭe	aʈimakaɭaːkkikkoɳʈirikkʰukajumaːɳə	
4. day.every it	more.people.ACC	slaves.make.have.continue.also.is	

1. ആരാണിതിനു	പിന്നിലെ	വില്ലൻ?
2. ārāṇitinu	pinnile	villan?
3. aːɹaːɳitinu	pinnile	ʋillan
4. who.is.its	behind.LOC.ACC	villain

'Despite controlling diet and increasing exercise, why is it that heart disease has not been restrained? Rather, it continues to enslave more and more people each day. Who is the villain behind this?'   — *Vasudevan 1994: 40.*

Bibliography

Frohnmeyer, L. J. 1913. *A Progressive Grammar of the Malayalam Language for Europeans.* Mangalore, India: Basel Mission.

Mohanan, K. P. 1986. *The Theory of Lexical Phonology.* Dordrecht: Reidel.

Sreekantheswaram Padmanabha Pillai, G. 1990. *Sabdataaraavali* [Malayalam dictionary], 14th ed. Kottayam, Kerala, India: National Book Stall.

Syamala Kumari, B. 1981. *An Intensive Course in Malayalam.* Mysore: Central Institute of Indian Languages.

Vasudevan, P. S. 1994. "Shastrakautukam." *Mathrubhumi Weekly* (20–26 March). Calicut.

Tamil Writing

SANFORD B. STEEVER

Historical background

The Tamil writing system, called *tamiẓ eẓuttu* 'Tamil letter', derives from the southern branch of Ashokan Brahmi. Its immediate predecessor, Grantha script, serves as the basis for the Tamil and Malayalam writing systems. Traditionally written with a stylus on palm leaves, *tamiẓ eẓuttu* evolved from angular to cursive characters, as angular strokes tend to rip leaves. Later, *tamiẓ eẓuttu* was engraved in stone and on copper plates. While no traditional texts treat Tamil orthography, the earliest grammar, *tolkāppiyam*, contains sutras that describe operations, not on sounds, but on the graphs representing them.

Printing arrived with Europeans, who adapted the handwritten script to movable type. European typography may have stimulated the linearization (see below) of *tamiẓ eẓuttu*.

Description

Tamil is written alphasyllabically (SECTION 31). Virtually unique within Indic scripts, *tamiẓ eẓuttu* has evolved toward an alphabet in one respect: it has eliminated most conjuncts, placing consonant clusters in a linear string. Some conjuncts remain in older official documents.

Vowel symbols (TABLE 39.1) have two basic allographs, initials and noninitials. Initials represent initial vowels and "overlong" vowels (e.g. initial இ *i* in இந்த *inta* 'this' and பெரிஇஇய *perīiya* 'reeeally big'). In premodern orthography, initials appear at the beginning of metrical groups; in modern orthography, influenced by European practice, at the beginning of words. The noninitials appear elsewhere, viz. in combination with consonant graphs, e.g. noninitial *i* ◌ி in கிளி *kiḷi* 'parrot'. Exceptions to this linearization process are the graphs எ *e*, ஏ *ē*, ஐ *ai*, ஒ *o*, ஓ *ō*, and ஔ *au*. The first three precede consonants, reversing phonemic order (e.g. கெ *e+k*, for phonemic *ke*); the last three are represented by "circumgraphs" around the consonant symbol (e.g. ப *p* + ◌ொ *o* = பொ *po*).

Each basic consonant graph (TABLE 39.2) includes the "inherent" vowel *a*, e.g., க is pronounced *ka*. Consonant graphs are phonemic, not phonetic: for example, க may represent [ka], [ga], or [ha], depending on distribution (see Asher 1985). (How-

TABLE 39.1: *Vowel Graphs*

Initial	Tranliteration	Value	Diacritic (p-)		Variations
அ	a	[ʌ]	–	ப	
ஆ	ā	[a:]	–ா	பா	(ணா) *ṇā*, (ரா) *rā*, (ணா) *ṇa*
இ	i	[i]	–ி	பி	டி *ṭi*
ஈ	ī	[i:]	–ீ	பீ	டீ *ṭī*
உ	u	[u,ɯ]	–ு	பு	கு *ku*, டு *ṭu*, மு *mu*, ரு *ru*, ழு *ẓu*, ளு *ḷu*
					ணு *ṇu*, து *tu*, நு *nu*, லு *lu*, று *ṟu*, னு *ṉu*
ஊ	ū	[u:]	–ூ	பூ	கூ *kū*, கு *cū*, டூ *ṭū*, மூ *mū*, ரூ *rū*, ழூ *ẓū*, ளூ *ḷū*
					ணூ *ṇū*, தூ *tu*, நூ *nū*, லூ *lū*, றூ *ṟū*, னூ *ṉū*
எ	e	[e]	ெ–	பெ	
ஏ	ē	[e:]	ே–	பே	
ஐ	ai	[ʌy]	ை–	பை	ணை *ṇai*, லை *lai*, ளை *ḷai*, னை *ṉai*
ஒ	o	[o]	ெ–ா	பொ	ணொ *ṇo*, ரொ *ro*, னொ *ṉo*
ஓ	ō	[o:]	ே–ா	போ	ணோ *ṇō*, ரோ *rō*, னோ *ṉō*
ஔ	au	[ʌʋ]	ெ–ள	பௌ	

ever, the graphs ந *na* and ன *ṉa* correspond to a subphonemic difference.) To represent consonants without vowels, as in clusters, a dot – called *puḷḷi* is placed over a consonant sign to suppress the inherent vowel, e.g. இந்த 'this' represents *inta*, not *inata*. This was optional in early writing.

The tables present Tamil vowel and consonant symbols in canonical order. Not all consonant+vowel combinations implied by these two charts are present in Tamil phonology, e.g., no Tamil word uses ளௌ *ḷau*.

Adequacy in representing Tamil phonology

Tamiẓ eẓuttu has three layers. The first adequately represents the core phonology of Tamil (see Steever 1987). The second adds the five *grantha* letters, which include signs to represent consonants and clusters borrowed from Sanskrit and, felicitously, English, e.g. ஸ *sa* and ஹ *ha*. The third reintroduces the ancient symbol *āytam* ஃ into modern orthography. When placed before a *p* or *j*, the combination represents a corresponding fricative, borrowed from other languages into the periphery of Tamil phonology; thus *āytam* + *p* = *f* (as in ஃபீச *fīcu* [fi:sɯ] 'fees'), and *āytam* + *j* = *z* (ஃஜிரொக்ஸ் *ziroks* 'Xerox'). However, there are no symbols or combinations to represent borrowed vowels, such as English [æ]. While *tamiẓ eẓuttu* has fewer graphs than other Indic systems—because Tamil lacks, for example, aspirated consonants—it has not borrowed available graphs from cognate orthographies to represent borrowed sounds.

TABLE 39.2: *Consonant Graphs*

Basic Form	Transcription	Value	Sample Forms with Vowels
க	k	[k, g, x, ɣ, h]	கா *kā*, கு *ku*, கூ *kū*
ங	ṅ	[ŋ]	ஙா *ṅā*, ஙு *ṅu*, ஙூ *ṅū*
ச	c	[ʧ, ʤ, ʃ, s]	சா *cā*, சு *cu*, சூ *cū*
ஞ	ñ	[ɲ]	ஞா *ñā*, ஞி *ñi*, ஞீ *ñī*
ட	ṭ	[ṭ, ḍ, ɽ]	டா *ṭā*, டி *ṭi*, டீ *ṭī*, டு *ṭu*, டூ *ṭū*
ண	ṇ	[ɳ]	ணா *ṇā*, ணு *ṇu*, ணூ *ṇū*, ணை *ṇai*
த	t	[t̪, d̪, ð]	தா *tā*, தி *ti*, தீ *tī*, து *tu*, தூ *tū*
ந	n	[n̪]	நா *nā*, நு *nu*, நூ *nū*
ப	p	[p, b, β]	பா *pā*, பு *pu*, பூ *pū*
ம	m	[m]	மா *mā*, மு *mu*, மூ *mū*
ய	y	[j]	யா *yā*, யு *yu*, யூ *yū*
ர	r	[ɾ]	ரா *rā*, ரி *ri*, ரீ *rī*, ரு *ru*, ரூ *rū*
ல	l	[l]	லா *lā*, லு *lu*, லூ *lū*, லை *lai*
வ	v	[ʋ]	வா *vā*, வு *vu*, வூ *vū*
ழ	ẓ, ḷ, r	[ɻ]	ழா *ẓā*, ழு *ẓu*, ழூ *ẓū*
ள	ḷ	[ɭ]	ளா *ḷā*, ளு *ḷu*, ளூ *ḷū*, ளை *ḷai*
ற	ṟ, R	[r, t, d]	றா *ṟā*, று *ṟu*, றூ *ṟū*, றொ *ṟo*, றோ *ṟō*
ன	ṉ, N	[n]	னா *ṉā*, னு *ṉu*, னை *ṉai*, னொ *ṉo*

GRANTHA LETTERS

Basic Form	Transcription	Value	Sample Forms with Vowels
ஜ	j	[ʤ]	ஜா *jā*, ஜி *ji*, ஜு *ju*, ஜூ *jū*
ஷ	ṣ	[ʂ]	ஷா *ṣā*, ஷி *ṣi*, ஷு *ṣu*, ஷூ *ṣū*
ஸ	s	[s]	ஸா *sā*, ஸி *si*, ஸு *su*, ஸூ *sū*
ஹ	h	[h]	ஹா *hā*, ஹி *hi*, ஹு *hu*, ஹூ *hū*
க்ஷ	kṣ	[kṣ]	க்ஷா *kṣā*, க்ஷி *kṣi*, க்ஷு *kṣu*, க்ஷூ *kṣū*

Trends

Tamiẓ eẓuttu has not undergone the reforms that Malayalam script recently has (see SECTION 38). Two minor changes have, however, occurred. First, government decree has sought to reduce the allographs for *ai*, which has two, ை– and ஐ–, depending on the consonant symbol with which it combines, e.g. கை *kai* but ஃல *lai* (this latter allograph is called *tumpikai* 'elephant's trunk'). Official documents now use only the first, e.g. கை *kai* and லை *lai*. Second, *āytam* ஃ is used to fricativize a following stop, as discussed above. Occasional proposals to change the individual symbols to purely alphabetic characters, by using vowel-initial allographs for all vowels, with consonant + *puḷḷi* for all consonants, have not been taken seriously; and they probably never will be, since the existing system represents Tamil syllables very well.

SAMPLE OF TAMIL

1. *Tamil:*   சிற்றில்   நற்றூண் பற்றி   நின் மகன்
2. *Tranliteration:* ciṟṟil   naṟṟūṇ paṟṟi   niṉ makaṉ
3. *Transcription:*   ʧiṭṭil   n̪ʌttu:ŋ pʌtti   n̪iṉ mʌɣʌn
4. *Gloss:*   small.house   pillar   leaning your son

1. யாண்டுளனே   என வினவுதி   என் மகன்
2. yāṇṭulaṉō   eṉa viṉavuti   eṉ makaṉ
3. ja:ɳɖuɭʌno: enʌ ʋinʌʋuði   en mʌɣʌn
4. where.is.he   that you.ask   my son

1. யாண்டு   உளன்   ஆயினும்   அறியேன்   ஒரும்
2. yāṇṭu   ulaṉ   āyiṉum   aṟiyēṉ   ōrum
3. ja:ɳɖu   uɭʌn   a:jinum   ʌrije:n   o:rum
4. where   he.is   that   I.don't.know once

1. புலி   சேர்ந்து   போகிய   கல்   அளை   போல
2. puli   cērntu   pōkiya   kal   aḷai   pōla
3. puli   ʧe:rn̪ɖu   po:ɣijʌ   kʌl   ʌɭʌy   po:lʌ
4. tiger   joining   going   stone lair   like

1. இன்ற   வயிரே   இதுவே
2. iṉṟa   vayiṟō   ituvē
3. ind'ʌ   ʋʌjiro: iðɯʋe:
4. begot   womb   this

1. தோன்றுவன்   மாதோ   போர்கள்ளத்   தானே
2. tōṉruvaṉ   mātō   pōrkaḷḷat   tāṉē
3. to:nd'ɯʋʌn   ma:ðo: po:rkaɭɭʌt   ta:ne:
4. appear   indeed   battlefield   only

'You stand against the pillar
of my hut and ask:
    Where is your son?
I don't really know.
My womb was once
a lair
for that tiger.
You can see him now
only in battlefields.'
—*Kāvaṟpeṇṭu, Puṟanāṉūṟu 86 (trans. A. K. Ramanujan 1985: 184).*

Bibliography

Arden, A. H. 1942. *A Progressive Grammar of the Tamil Language,* 5th ed. Madras: Christian Literature Society.

Asher, Ronald. 1985. *Tamil.* London: Croom Helm.

Burnell, A. C. 1878. *Elements of South Indian Palaeography,* 2nd ed. London: Trübner.

Lehmann, Thomas. 1989. *A Grammar of Modern Tamil.* Pondicherry: Pondicherry Institute of Linguistics and Culture.

Ramanujan, A. K., ed. 1985. *Poems of Love and War from the Eight Anthologies and the Ten Long Poems of Classical Tamil.* New York: Columbia University Press.

Steever, Sanford B. 1987. "Tamil and the Dravidian languages." In *The World's Major Languages,* ed. Bernard Comrie, pp. 725–46. London: Croom Helm; New York: Oxford University Press.

The Tibetan Script and Derivatives

Leonard W. J. van der Kuijp

The Tibetan script falls into two basic types, of which the first is called དབུ་ཅན་ *dbu can* 'with a head', the second དབུ་མེད་ *dbu med* 'acephalous'. The first is used in the earliest available monuments of Tibetan writing: inscriptions dating from the eighth and ninth centuries C.E., and manuscripts found in Dunhuang, Gansu Province, China (dating not later than about the middle of the 11th century); it was also used in later manuscripts and for the printing of texts. The earliest known specimen of a Tibetan printed text is one derived from printing blocks that were carved to completion on 16 December 1284 in present-day Beijing, under the patronage of the Mongol imperial family (van der Kuijp 1993). The *dbu med* script falls into several different types, such as དཔེ་ཡིག་ *dpe yig*, འཁྱུག་ཡིག་ *'khyug yig*, and འབམ་ཡིག་ *'bam yig*; the earliest extant texts using one or other type seem to date from the twelfth century (Csoma de Körös 1834: [2], [4], [31]). A number of ornamental scripts were also used in the Tibetan cultural area (SECTION 20); one of these, the "new Rin spungs script," seems to have been developed during the time that Central Tibet was more or less under the governance of the Rin spungs dynasty (1434–1565; Chandra 1982). The *dbu can* script is the basis for modern printed Tibetan, as presented here. All these scripts are phonologically based and, like Brahmi writing, are typologically alphasyllabaries (SECTION 31). Tibetan is written horizontally from left to right.

The Tibetan term for both the symbol and the sound representing it is ཡི་གེ་ *yi ge*, the basic, irreducible building block of Tibetan writing. This sometimes results in a confusion between graph and phoneme. The term *yi ge* is used as a translation of Sanskrit *akṣara* 'syllable', *vyañjana* 'consonant', and *varṇa* 'sound'. It is also used as an umbrella term for extra-phonological symbols.

For Tibetan Buddhists, the Tibetan script was traditionally created in the first half of the seventh century by a certain Thon mi Saṃbhoṭa. He is said to have been a minister under the first Buddhist king Srong btsan sgam po, who had sent him to northeastern India in order to devise a script for Tibetan. However, the Bon po religious tradition of Tibet does not accept this scenario, and suggests different origins, including Iranian or Central Asian ones (Tshul khrims phun tshogs 1985: 395ff.) In current scholarship there is a great deal of controversy surrounding the precise origins of the Tibetan *dbu can* script, and no definitive conclusion has been reached so far (for an overview, see Róna-Tas 1985: 183–242). Some investigators postulate that the *dbu med* script derives from *dbu can*, others maintain the reverse. Many indigenous Tibetan grammatological analyses of writing are based not only on the Indic grammatical traditions, but also on the more arcane linguistic speculations found in portions of the Buddhist tantra literature, where a close link is established between phonology and soteriology. What follows deals mainly with the *dbu can* script.

Symbols and specific features

A short vowel *a* is taken as inherent in each of the thirty consonant symbols, here called *radicals*, except the ༀ ་ཚ ་ *'a chung* (ༀ ་ *'a*) and ཨ ་ཚ ་ *a chen* (ཨ ་ *a*). The phonological realization for both these is *a*; but in the Lhasa dialect, the former has a high, and the latter a low tone. The *'a chung* can also represent a nasal; thus ་ཚ ་ *mtshams* 'boundary' and ་ཐུ ་ *mthun* 'agreement' are often written ་ཚ ་ *'tshams* and ་ཐུ ་ *'thun*. In current Central Tibetan pronunciation, neither initial *'a* nor *m* is realized. Further, *'a* may nasalize the juncture of two morphemes as in ་ཚ ་ ་ཚ ་ *dge 'dun* 'Buddhist community', pronounced [gendyn]. The name *'a chung* is a late, secondary invention of probable non-Tibetan origin, and is therefore not found in the Tibetan texts on orthography and orthotactics (cf. Blo ldan shes rab, Bsod nams rtse mo, Ngag dbang bstan dar). For the remaining consonants, we have names like *ka* for ཀ ་, *kha* for ཁ ་, etc.

Each radical is represented by a basic symbol. In the *dbu can* script, these hang from a superior baseline, which may be a single horizontal headstroke as in ཙ ་ *ca*, two short headstrokes as in པ ་ *pa*, or even three headstrokes as in ཨ ་ *a*. This seems to be the origin of the term *dbu can*, since such strokes are conspicuously absent in the *dbu med* scripts (for an example see FIGURE 30 on page 247). TABLE 40.4 shows the basic symbols for each of the thirty radicals and their phonological realization. Pronunciation follows the Central Tibetan dialect as described by Goldstein (1991: 3–5); the tones are high (acute accent), low (grave accent). As in Indic scripts, the traditional order of symbols in Tibetan is based in large measure on the articulatory phonetics of Sanskrit. A series of reversed symbols has been devised to represent the retroflex consonants in borrowed words: ཊ ་ *ṭ*, ཋ ་ *ṭh*, ཌ ་ *ḍ*, ཎ ་ *ṇ*, ཥ ་ *ṣ*.

The four vowel symbols other than *a* are written only diacritically, either above or below the radical or consonant clusters (TABLE 40.2). The diacritics ⌢ *i*, ⌢ *e*, and ⌢ *o* are written above the radical or complex ligatures; — *u* is written below them. Radicals, including *'u* and *a*, lose their *a*-value when they occur with one of these four

TABLE 40.1: *Consonants*

ཀ་	ka	[ká]	ཁ་	kha	[kʰá]	ག་	ga	[kà/kʰà]	ང་	ña	[ŋà]
ཙ་	ca	[t͡ɕá]	ཚ་	cha	[t͡ɕʰá]	ཛ་	ja	[t͡ɕà]	ཉ་	ña	[ɲà]
ཏ་	ta	[tá]	ཐ་	tha	[tʰá]	ད་	da	[tà/tʰà]	ན་	na	[nà]
པ་	pa	[pá]	ཕ་	pha	[pʰá]	བ་	ba	[pà/pʰà]	མ་	ma	[mà]
ཙ་	tsa	[tsá]	ཚ་	tsha	[tsʰá]	ཛ་	dza	[tsà]			
ཝ་	wa	[wà]	ཞ་	ža	[ʃà]	ཟ་	za	[sà]			
འ་	('a)	[à]	ཡ་	ya	[jà]	ར་	ra	[rà]	ལ་	la	[là]
			ཤ་	ša	[ʃá]	ས་	sa	[sá]			
ཧ་	ha	[há]	ཨ་	(a)	[á]						

vowel diacritics; thus '*u* and *u* are written ◌ and ◌. Strictly speaking, vowel symbols cannot occur in syllable-initial position.

   Long vowels occur only in loanwords. Traditionally, these are usually of Sanskrit origin, but the lexicon of Classical Tibetan also includes words borrowed from Mongolian, Chinese, and a few other languages. Tibetan used in the diaspora of the Indian subcontinent has an ever growing lexicon of Hindi and English loanwords, whereas the vernaculars used in China have adopted an enormous number of Chinese words. The long vowels are indicated by '*a chung* placed below the radical or complex ligature; thus *tā bla ma* 'grand lama' is written ཏ་བླ་མ་ (Tibetan *tā* reflects here Chinese *dā* 'grand') and Sanskrit *śrī* 'lustre, wealth' is written ཤྲི. Aside from loanwords, the Tibetan script admits diphthongs only in diminutive expressions; thus the diminutive form of མི་ *mi* 'person' is མེའུ་ *meu* 'dwarf'; of 'stone' རྡོ་ *rdo*, རྡེའུ་ *rdeu* 'pebble'.

TABLE 40.2: *Vowels*

Symbol		Example	
◌ི	i	ཀི	ki
◌ུ	u	ཀུ	ku
◌ེ	e	ཀེ	ke
◌ོ	o	ཀོ	ko

Tibetan script allows combinations of consonantal symbols of five types: (1) subscript, (2) prescript, (3) superscript, (4) postscript, and (5) post-postscript symbols. Depending on position, some lose their full graphic form, others do not; in all cases, they lose their inherent *a* and often undergo significant change in pronunciation. It is always the topmost consonant (whether or not this is the radical) that hangs from the baseline. Vowel diacritics are attached to the combination of symbols.

Subscript symbols

There are four consonants which, in modified form, can be affixed (*btags*) beneath a select number of radicals; these are *y*, *r*, *l*, and *w*. There are seven radicals beneath which *y* can appear, resulting in the following conjunct symbols: ཀྱ *kya*, ཁྱ *khya*, གྱ *gya*, པྱ *pya*, ཕྱ *phya*, བྱ *bya*, and མྱ *mya*. For the number of radicals to which *r* can be affixed, different listings are given. Blo ldan shes rab gives the following ten complex ligatures: ཀྲ *kra*, ཁྲ *khra*, གྲ *gra*, དྲ *dra*, པྲ *pra*, ཕྲ *phra*, བྲ *bra*, མྲ *mra*, སྲ *sra*, and ཧྲ *hra*. Ngag dbang bstan dar has a total of eleven, adding ཏྲ *tra* and ཐྲ *thra*, but omitting *mra*. A recent grammar of classical Tibetan registers all these plus ཤྲ *šra* (Hahn 1985: 7). The consonant *l* can be subscribed to six radicals, so that we have ཀླ *kla*, གླ *gla*, བླ *bla*, ཟླ *zla*, རླ *rla*, and སླ *sla*. However, Ngag dbang bstan dar remarks that some (including himself) claim that *rla* and *sla* involve the *r* and *s* superscripts; thus ལ *la* would be the radical, rather than *ra* and *sa*. Lastly, according to Tibetan sources, the *w* subscript can occur variously under twelve, fifteen, or sixteen radicals, e.g. ཀྭ *kwa* and ཁྭ *khwa*. Uniquely, it can also occur as a sub-subscript as in གྲྭ *grwa*.

Prescript symbols

The five symbols that can be written to the left of certain radicals are *g*, *d*, *b*, *m*, and *'a chung*. The consonant *g* may occur in front of eleven radicals, *d* in front of six, *b* in front of ten, *m* in front of eleven, and *'a chung* in front of ten. Examples are བསད *bsad* [sé] 'killed', དགའ *dga'* [gà] 'virtue'. There are six radicals that never occur with a prescript: *wa*, *ra*, *la*, *ha*, and *'a chung*.

Superscript symbols

According to later Tibetan traditions, only the radicals ར *r*, ལ *l*, and ས *s* may occur as superscripts. Of these, *r* can be placed above thirteen radicals, *l* above ten, and *s* above twelve. In clusters, the consonant *r* is written in full form only in རྙ *rnya* and རླ *rla*; otherwise it is represented by the symbol ˉ, as in རྐ *rka*, རྒ *rga*, རྔ *rña*, etc.

Postscript symbols

The ten radicals that occur as postscripts are *g, ñ, d, n, b, m, 'a chung, r, l,* and *s,* e.g. བདུན *bdun* [dỳn] 'seven'. However, a postscript consonant may represent not the second consonant in a cluster, but a syllable-final consonant; in that case, vowel diacritics are attached to the syllable-initial consonant, e.g. དོང *doñ* [tòŋ] 'pit', but དངོས *dños* [ŋờ:] 'real'. When the vowel is inherent *a,* the sequence CC is interpreted as CVC (དག *dag* [tàg] 'I'), whereas the sequence CCV is written with an added final *'a chung* (དགའ *dga'* [gà] 'virtue').

Post-postscript symbols

Two symbols can be post-postscribed, namely *s* and *d.* The consonant *s* can occur after the four postscribed symbols *g, ng, b,* and *m* (e.g. སེམས *sems* [sém] 'mind'); *d* can occur after *n, r,* and *l.* The latter is called *da drag*; it is found inconsistently in the Tibetan Dunhuang manuscripts as well as sometimes in later manuscripts. It was officially discontinued in the ninth century, but Blo ldan shes rab (1059–1109) states that some writers still chose to use it. Two examples of complex syllables are: བསྒྲུབས *bsgrubs* [ɖɹúb] 'established', གྱུརད *gyurd* [kjùr] 'became'.

━━━━━

Additional features

A supplementary symbol of Tibetan script is the བར་ཚེག *bar tsheg* 'intermediate dot', which serves to separate syllables from each other. It is found at the upper right-hand corner of the radical or, in the case of a more complex syllable, at the upper right-hand corner of the final element. This symbol permits the distinction between, e.g., བ ས *basa* and བས *bsa.* The entire syllabic complex with such an intermediate dot is sometimes called a ཚེག་ཁྱིམ *tsheg khyim* 'dot house'.

In Tibetan dictionaries, the canonical order applies first to the radical of each syllable—then to postscripts, subscripts, prescripts, and superscripts, in that order. Thus, under the radical ག *ga,* the syllables གད *gad,* གྱ *gya,* དགའ *dga'*, and རྒ *rga* occur in that order.

A special feature of Tibetan writing, particularly in manuscripts, is the frequent reduction of (a) a single symbol, (b) two symbols within one syllable, (c) a single syllable, and (d) a multi-syllabic unit to their barest graphic minimum. There is no hard and fast rule for this, and manuscripts frequently lack consistency. The best survey of abbreviations is still Bacot 1912.

The pronunciation of modern Tibetan differs greatly from that indicated by the written language, and shows much variation among dialects (the text sample below

TABLE 40.3: *Numerals*

1	2	3	4	5	6	7	8	9	0
༡	༢	༣	༤	༥	༦	༧	༨	༩	༠

displays the Central Tibetan vernacular). In general, syllable-initial and -final clusters are greatly reduced, and the vowel inventory is greatly increased (for details, see Goldstein 1991).

The Tibetan numerals are shown in TABLE 40.3.

SAMPLE OF TIBETAN

1. Dbu can script:	སྤྱིར	བསྟན	གྲངས	ངེས	ཚིག	ཕྲད	དང	
2. Transliteration:	spyir	bstan	grañs	ñes	tshig	phrad	dañ /
3. Pronunciation:	ʧíː	tén	ʈɹàŋ	ŋè	tsʰíg	tʰɹɛ́	tʰàŋ
4. Gloss:	general	in	number	DETERMINER	word	PARTICLE	and

1.	འཕུལ	དང	བརྟེན་པའི	སྤང	བླང	དང ༎	དམིགས་གསལ	སོ་སོར
2.	'phul	dañ	brten pa'i	spañ	blañ	dañ //	dmigs gsal	so sor
3.	pʰý	tʰàŋ	ténpáj	páŋ	láŋ	tʰàŋ	mígsé	sósór
4.	PREFIX	and	based.of	reject	accept	and	supplement	various

1.	དབྱེ་བ	སྟེ	རྣམ་པ	ལྔ	ཡིས	བསྡུས་པ	ཡིན
2.	dbye ba	ste /	rnam pa	lña	yis	bsdus pa	yin /
3.	jájwà	té	námpá	ŋá	ʤìː	dýpá	ʤìn
4.	ADV	division	rubric	five	by	summary	is

'In general [the subject-matter of this text] is summarized under five rubrics: the numerical determination [of graphs and ligatures], the particle[s], what is to be accepted or rejected about prefix[es] and postscript[s], and various classifications of additional matters.'   —*Blo ldan shes rab, fol. 1.*

The Lepcha script

According to tradition, the Lepcha (or Rong) script (TABLE 40.4) was devised in 1720 by Raja Phyag-rdor-rnam-rgyal of the Tibetan dynasty in Sikkim (India). It is based on Tibetan writing with some influence from Burmese script (SECTION 42), and exhibits Chinese influence in that it was formerly written in columns from right to left. The 90° turn accounts for the unusual indication of syllable-closing consonants with superposed diacritics rather than conjuncts (Haarh 1959; Chakraborty 1978).

TABLE 40.4: *The Lepcha Script*

ꓛ	ka	ꓴ	kha	ꓳ	ga	ꓘ	ña	ꓰ́	kak	ꓱ̃	kâ
ꓜ	ca	ꓢ	cha	ꓮ	ja	ꓤ	ña	ꓱ̈	kam	ꓯ	kā
ꓥ	ta	ꓦ	tha	ꓱ	da	ꓧ	na	ꓱ̂	kal	ꓲ	ki
ꓨ	pa	ꓝ	pha	ꓞ	ba	ꓬ	ma	ꓱ̃	kan	ꓳ̃	kī
ꓫ	tsa	ꓲ	tsha	ꓟ	za			ꓱ̆	kap	ꓵ	ko
ꓣ	ya	ꓩ	ra	ꓪ	la	ꓱ	wa	ꓱ̃	kar	ꓶ	kō
		ꓭ	ša	ꓷ	sa			ꓱ̄	kat	ꓼ	ku
ꓶ	ha	ꓮ	a	꓿	fa			ꓱ	kVñ[a]	ꓽ	kū
								ꓱ	kañ	꓾	ke

a. Must be used with a vowel sign; for short -*a*-, the form immediately below is used.

The 'Phags pa script

Historical background

The 'Phags pa script is named for its creator, the Tibetan monk 'Phags pa Blo gros rgyal mtshan (1235–1280), the fifth patriarch of the Sa skya pa school of Tibetan Buddhism. Having been appointed *guóshì* 'National Preceptor' in 1264 by emperor Qubilai ("Kubla Khan," r. 1260–1294), he was ordered to devise a script in which all the languages of his empire could be written, including Tibetan, Uyghur, Mongolian, and Chinese. 'Phags pa resided in Tibet from 1264 to 1267, and returned to the imperial court in 1268. According to such Chinese sources as the *Fózǔ lìdài tōngzhǎn* 'General record of successive Buddhist patriarchs' by the monk Nien Chang (1284–?) and the *Yuánshǐ* 'History of the Yuan' edited by Song Lian (1310–1381), he completed his work on this script in 1269. The available literature on its creation is scanty and fragmentary in the extreme, and it is very curious that neither of the main biographies of 'Phags pa by his Tibetan disciples comments on it; one of these was even commissioned by the heir apparent. Although this script is known in the secondary literature as the "'Phags pa script," this is not how it is known among the Tibetans or the Mongols. The former usually refer to it as the *hor gsar yig* 'new Mongolian script', and on one early occasion simply as the *hor yi ge* 'Mongolian script', as opposed to the *yu gur yi ge* 'Uighur script'. The Mongols themselves call it the *dörbelǰin üsüg* 'square or quadratic script'. In Chinese it is variously called *měnggǔ xīnzì* 'new Mongolian script', *měnggǔ zì* 'Mongolian script', *guózì* 'national script', and *měnggǔ chuānzì* 'Mongolian seal script'.

TABLE 40.5: *'Phags pa Consonants*

	k	[k]		k'	[kʰ]		g	[g]		q	[q]		γ	[ɣ]		ṅ	[ŋ]
	č	[ʧ]		č'	[ʧʰ]		ǰ	[dʒ]								ñ	[ɲ]
	c	[ts]		c'	[tsʰ]		ʒ	[dz]									
	t	[t]		t'	[tʰ]		d	[d]								n	[n]
	p	[p]		p'	[pʰ]		b	[b]						f	[f]		m	[m]
	y	[j]		i̢	[i̢]		r	[r]		l	[l]		w	[w]		u̢	[u̢]
	s	[s]		š	[ʃ]		z	[z]		ž	[ʒ]		h	[h]		ʾ	[ʔ]

General characteristics

The 'Phags pa script, although derived mainly from the Tibetan *dbu can* script, is written vertically, in columns from left to right. Typologically, 'Phags pa resembles its alphasyllabic Indic prototype in that the basic symbols denote consonants (TABLE 40.5) with the inherent vowel *a*, and initial vowels have special symbols (TABLE 40.6). However, vowel diacritics are not written above and below consonants, as in Indic and Tibetan; rather, they are written linearly, after the consonants which precede them in pronunciation, as in an alphabet. Thus ⌣ *o* is a diacritic over

the initial consonant cluster in the Tibetan word ⌣⌣ *rdo rje* 'diamond', written ⌣⌣ in 'Phags pa; in 'Phags pa, the symbol ∧ *o* follows the consonant cluster. In addition to the symbols adapted from Tibetan and Indic, 'Phags pa contains symbols to accommodate sounds peculiar to Chinese and Mongolian.

Geographic distribution

Although 'Phags pa was originally conceived as a script for Qubilai's multi-national empire, its use during Qubilai's time and the Yuan dynasty as a whole (until 1368) was sporadic at best. Documents surviving in it include epigraphic material, official tablets and seals, and some printed texts, mainly in Mongolian and Chinese. (For the

TABLE 40.6: *'Phags pa Vowels*

Initial	Not init.	Tr'lit.	Value	Initial	Not init.	Tr'lit.	Value	Initial	Not init.	Tr'lit.	Value	Initial	Not init.	Tr'lit.	Value
		'i	[i]			hi	[ɨ]			"ü	[y]			'u	[u]
		'e	[e]							"ö	[ø]			'o	[o]
		"a	[a]			"ä	[æ]			"ô̂	[ø:]			'ô	[o:]
		"äi	[i:]			"äe̢	[ei̢]			"üe̢	[yi̢]			'ue̢	[ui̢]
		"ayi	[ai]			"äyi	[ei]							'oyi	[ɔi]

most thorough study of the script in Mongolian documents, see Poppe 1957.) While discontinued elsewhere, it remained in use in the Tibetan cultural area, including those areas populated by Mongols who were Tibetan Buddhists, as an ornamental script and on seals of ranking dignitaries and religious hierarchs (Schuh 1981, Ou Zhaogui 1991). Some scholars believe that the Korean King Seycong (r. 1418–1450) was in part inspired by this script for his creation of the *onmun* 'vulgar script', now known as *hankul*, as opposed to Chinese characters (SECTION 17). However, he abandoned its relative graphic clumsiness and ambiguity, and went well beyond it in a number of ways (Ledyard 1966: 331–70).

SAMPLE OF MONGOLIAN

Prepared by GYÖRGY KARA

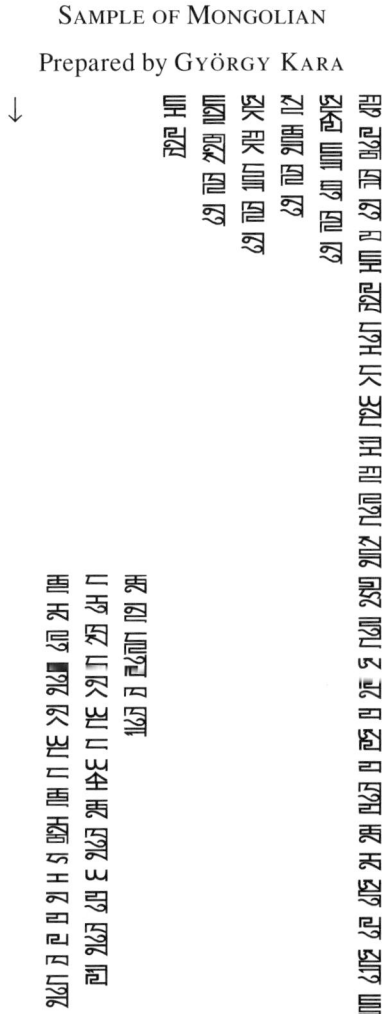

1. Transliteration:	če ri 'u dun	no yad da	če rig	ha ra na	ba la qa dun /
2. Normalization:	čeri'ü-dün	noyad-da	čerig	hara-na	balaqa-dun
3. Gloss:	soldiers-of	lords-to	soldier	man-to	cities-of

1. da ru qas da	no yad da	yor či qun	ya bu qun	ėl / či ne
2. daruqas-da	noyad-da	yorči-qun	yabu-qun	ėlči-ne
3. commanders-to	lords-to	proceeding-PL	going-PL	envoy-to

1. d'ul qa quė /	ǰar liq /	ǰiṅ gis	q' nu /	'eo keo deė	q' nu /	se čen
2. dülqaqui	ǰarliq	Jinggis	qānu	Öködei	qānu	Sečen
3. letting.hear	edict	Chinggis	emperor's	Ögödei	emperor's	Wise

1. q' nu /	'eol ǰeė tu	q' nu /	keu lug	q' nu	ba	ǰar liq dur
2. qānu	Ölǰeitü	qānu	Külüg	qānu	ba	ǰarliq-dur
3. emperor's	Fortunate	emperor's	Külüg	emperor's	also	edict-in

1. do yid	ėr ke 'ud	sen ši ṅud	' li ba	al ba	qub či ri
2. doyid	ėrke'üd	senšïngud	aliba	alba	qubčiri
3. Buddhist.monks	Christian.priests	Taoist.priests	any	levies	tax

1. 'eu lu	'eu ǰen
2. ülü	üǰen
3. not	seeing

'Edict to be obeyed by army officers, soldiers, commandants of cities, lords, and traveling envoys. In the edicts of the Chinggis Emperor (= Genghis Khan), of emperor Ögödei, of the Wise Emperor (= Qubilai Sechen), of the Fortunate Emperor (also: Temür), and also of emperor Külüg, [it is stated that] Buddhist monks, Christian priests, and Taoist priests [Chinese xiānshēng] are exempt from taxes.'

—*From one of the edicts of 1314 of the Mongol emperor Ayurbarvada*
(Ligeti 1972, no. 6, lines 4–12 = Poppe 1957, pl. II).

Bibliography

Bacot, Jacques. 1912. "L'Écriture cursive tibétaine." *Journal Asiatique* ser. 10, 19: 5–78.

Beyer, Stephan V. 1991. *The Classical Tibetan Language.* Albany: State University of New York Press.

Blo ldan shes rab (1059–1109). *Rngog Lo tsā ba: Dag yig nye mkho bsdus pa* [A summary of essentials of correct spelling], 9 folios. Beijing: Cultural Palace of Nationalities, ms. 004323(9).

Bsod nams rtse mo (1142–1182). "Yi ge'i bklag thabs byis pa bde blag tu 'jug pa" [The manner in which graphs are read aloud: An easy introduction for children]. In *Sa skya pa'i bka' 'bum* [Collection of texts belonging to the Sa skya pa school of Tibetan Buddhism], vol. 2. Tokyo: Toyo Bunko, 1968, p. 345, plate 4; p. 349, plate 4.

Chakraborty, Ashit. 1978. *Read Lepcha.* Calcutta: Kanakdhara.

Chandra, Lokesh. 1982. *Indian Scripts in Tibet.* New Delhi: Sharada Rani.

Csoma de Körös, Alexander. 1834. *A Grammar of the Tibetan Language in English.* Calcutta: Asiatic Society of Bengal. Repr. New York: Altai, 1969; New Delhi: Nawang Topgyal, 1983.

Goldstein, Melvyn. 1991. *Essentials of Modern Literary Tibetan.* Berkeley and Los Angeles: University of California Press.

Haarh, Erik. 1959. "The Lepcha Script." *Acta Orientalia* (Copenhagen) 24: 107–22.

Hahn, Michael. 1985. *Lehrbuch der klassischen tibetischen Schriftsprache* (Indica et Tibetica 10). Bonn: Indica et Tibetica Verlag.

Junast/Zhàonásītú. 1990–91. *Bāsībāzì hé měnggǔ yǔ wénxiàn, I–II* [The 'Phags pa script and the Mongolian language monuments]. Tokyo: Tōkyō Gaikokugo Daigaku.

Ledyard, Gari K. 1966. "The Korean Language Reform of 1446: The Origin, Background, and Early History of the Korean Alphabet." Ph.D. dissertation, Columbia University.

Ligeti, Louis. 1972. *Monuments en écriture 'phags-pa; Piéces de chancellerie en transcription chinoise.* Budapest: Akadémiai Kiadó.

Miller, Roy Andrew. 1956. *The Tibetan System of Writing.* Washington, D.C.: American Council of Learned Societies.

Ngag dbang bstan dar (1759– ca. 1840). *Yi ge'i bshad pa mkhas pa'i kha rgyan* [An explanation of graphs/phonemes: A scholar's mouth-ornament]. Beijing: Mi rigs dpe skrun khang, 1982.

Ou Zhaogui et al., eds. 1991. *Xīzàng lìdài zàng yìn* [Official seals in the history of Tibet]. Lhasa: Xizang renmin chubanshe.

Poppe, Nicholas. 1957. *Mongolian Monuments in hP'ags pa Script,* trans. John R. Krueger (Göttinger Asiatische Forschungen 8). Wiesbaden: Harrassowitz.

Róna-Tas, András. 1985. *Wiener Vorlesungen zur Sprach- und Kulturgeschichte Tibets.* Vienna: Arbeitskreis für Tibetische und Buddhistische Studien Universität Wien.

Scharlipp, Wolfgang Ekkehard, and Dieter Back. 1989. *Einführung in die tibetische Schrift.* Hamburg: Buske.

Schuh, Dieter. 1981. *Grundlagen tibetischer Siegelkunde: Eine Untersuchung über tibetische Siegelaufschriften in 'Phags-pa-Schrift* (Monumenta Tibetica Historica 5). Sankt Augustin, Austria: VGH Wissenschaftsverlag.

Tuna, Osman Nedim, and James Bosson. 1962. "A Mongolian 'Phags-pa text and Its Turkish Translation in the 'Collection of Curiosities'." *Journal de la Societé Finno-Ougrienne* 63: 3–16.

Tshul khrims phun tshogs (1783–?). "Bod kyi brda yang dag par sbyor tshul gyi bstan bcos brda sprod nyi shu bdun pa'i rang 'grel gshen bstan gsal ba'i nyi ma" [A treatise on the correct joining of Tibetan linguistic signs, an autocommentary on (a text on) linguistics consisting of twenty-seven (quatrains); A sun that illuminates Gshen's teachings]. In *Five Bonpo Texts for the Study of Grammar, Poetics and Lexicography,* pp. 383–583. Dolanji, Himachal Pradesh, India: Bonpo Monastic Centre, 1985.

van der Kuijp, Leonard W. J. 1993. "Two Mongol Xylographs (*hor par ma*) of the Tibetan Text of Sa skya Paṇḍita's Work on Buddhist Logic and Epistemology." *Journal of the International Association of Buddhist Studies* 16: 279–98.

Weiers, Michael. 1967. "Die Entwicklung der mongolischen Schriften." *Studium Generale* 20: 470–79.

Part VII: Southeast Asian Writing Systems

SOUTHEAST ASIA CONSISTS OF THOSE ASIAN TERRITORIES (together with their adjacent seas) that lie, so to speak, "between" India and China, i.e. to the east of India and to the south of China. It includes the modern states of Burma, Thailand, Laos, Cambodia, Vietnam, Malaysia, Indonesia, and the Philippines. The region is further divided into the mainland and the islands, and a further division exists between the coastal regions and the hinterlands. Yet another distinction is into the plains and river valleys, on the one hand, and the hills and mountains on the other. These geographical divisions have been important economically, politically, and culturally. For instance, states and writing systems are found only in the lowlands of mainland Southeast Asia, and on some of the islands.

As regards climate, the monsoons or seasonal winds have always been of immense significance. Not only do they bring the rains that are necessary to life, but the winds made it possible, before the age of motorized travel, to cross the seas by sail.

Early trade routes to Southeast Asia lay on the maritime route between China, on the one hand, and India, Persia, Arabia, and Europe on the other. Ships on this voyage had to pass the island of Sumatra, either up the east coast and through the Straits of Malacca, or through the Sunda Straits and up the west coast. Not only was it necessary for ships plying this route to call at ports in Southeast Asia, but Southeast Asia also had commodities of its own which were eagerly sought in the outside world; hence it was a trading destination in its own right.

The significance of Brahmi-based script in Southeast Asia can be appreciated from the fact that, until Islam introduced the Arabic script in the first half of the second millennium, derivatives of Brahmi were the only writing systems in existence, except in northern Vietnam (where the ancestors of the modern Vietnamese were then living), which originally used the Chinese script. Furthermore, the national scripts of modern Burma, Thailand, Laos, and Cambodia are simply local developments of Brahmi. What is more, the Brahmi script spread through Southeast Asia peacefully, so far as we can tell, in contrast to the Chinese script, which spread to Vietnam through Chinese conquest and forced Sinicization. Brahmi-based scripts are now used to write languages of several different families: Mon (of Burma) and Khmer (of

443

Cambodia) are Austro-Asiatic; Thai and Lao, as well as Shan (of Burma), are Tai languages; Karen (of Burma) and Burmese are Tibeto-Burman; Javanese and other languages of Indonesia and the Philippines are Austronesian.

The Brahmi script spread through Southeast Asia as part of the phenomenon of Indianization—the spread of Indian learning (and the Sanskrit and Pali languages in which it was expressed), Indian art and architecture, Indian epics, the Indian religions of Hinduism and Buddhism, Indian principles of state organization and law, Indian court ceremonies, and Indian alphabets. Because of these connections, mainland Southeast Asia has sometimes been called Farther India. We do not know exactly how this Indian influence began, since the dawn of Southeast Asian history presents us with already Indianized states. But the process continued for centuries into the historical period, and took place in several successive waves. All parts of India, but mostly the south, played a part. Curiously, the vocabulary of the ancient Indian vernaculars, as opposed to bookish and technical borrowings, has left virtually no trace in the languages of the Indianized states of Southeast Asia.

— CHRISTOPHER COURT

The Spread of Brahmi Script into Southeast Asia

CHRISTOPHER COURT

―――――

The beginnings of writing

As de Casparis (1975: 12) tells us, the earliest known examples of writing in Southeast Asia are some brief inscriptions on seals, intaglios, rings and similar precious objects, discovered at the ancient site of Oc-eo, not far from Rach-gia near the west coast of the Ca-mau peninsula in what is now southern Vietnam. However, since Oc-eo was an important trading center and most of the objects discovered there originate from elsewhere (often from the Indian subcontinent), there is no proof that the objects were actually inscribed in Southeast Asia. For this reason this script cannot properly be classified as Southeast Asian. The inscriptions are in Indian script and are datable to the period from the second to the fifth century C.E. The first Indian inscription of some length found in Southeast Asia is on the stela of Vo-canh—a granite block inscribed in Sanskrit on two faces, found near the village of Vo-canh in the province of Khanh-hoa, in present-day southern Vietnam. It has been assigned to the third century C.E. and either to the ancient state of Champa or to Funan. About the end of the fourth century or the beginning of the fifth, some inscriptions were written in Quang-nam, Phu-yen, and Tra-kieu in what is now Vietnam. These are in Sanskrit, except for a highly significant one that uses the same alphabet but is in the Old Cham language. Not only is the latter the oldest text in a language belonging to the Austronesian family (although its speakers lived, as their descendants still live, on the Southeast Asian mainland), but it is in exactly the same script as the Sanskrit inscriptions; this marks the first known instance of a Southeast Asian language being written, and written, in fact, in an Indian alphabet.

On the Malay peninsula, inscriptions go back no further than the fourth century, and these are in Sanskrit. In what is now Thailand (outside the Malay peninsula), the Sanskrit inscriptions found at Si Thep on the Sak River cannot be more recent than the fifth or sixth century, and are some of the earliest examples of Indian script from that territory. In the Indonesian archipelago, as Coedès says (1968: 18), the Sanskrit inscriptions of Mūlavarman in the region of Kutai, east Borneo, date back to the beginning of the fifth century, and those of Pūrṇavarman in the western part of Java, to the middle of the fifth century.

It should be noted that the types of script that have spread in Southeast Asia all seem to originate from the south of India. North Indian varieties have been employed here and there, but unlike the South Indian forms, they have not given rise to national alphabets (Damais 1955:368–69). As Damais goes on to say (pp. 369–70),

> The type of alphabet of South India which proved to be the most important, and whose destiny in Southeast Asia was to be so brilliant, is also the one which has delivered the most ancient specimens known in this region [apart from those of Oc-eo and Vo-canh]. It is called *Pallava* from the name of the Indian dynasty of the *Pallavas* which seems to have created it. It is to be found with minor variants in Fu-nan [in present-day southern Vietnam and Cambodia], in Champa [in the center and south of present-day Vietnam], in Cambodia, in the Mon country [in the Chaophraya River basin in Thailand], in Sunda (West Java), in Central and East Java, in East Kalimantan (Borneo), in Sumatra (where it lasted for a longer time), and in the Malay peninsula.

However, Nagaraju (1984) claims that we are dealing here not just with Pallava, but with a number of south Indian scripts (see also de Casparis 1979: 382–87). The variations in this script reflect not only the evolution of Pallava script in the course of four centuries but also the emergence of local Southeast Asian varieties (de Casparis 1975: 14).

Indigenization of Indian scripts

The first stage of adaptation of Brahmi-based scripts in Southeast Asia consists of the local writing of Indian languages in such scripts. Inscriptions prove that not only the languages—mostly Sanskrit but also Pali and Tamil—but also the scripts were indeed in use in Southeast Asia. The second stage, in which Southeast Asian languages are reduced to writing by using Indian or Indian-derived scripts, has been mentioned with regard to an early inscription in Old Cham; there are likewise inscriptions in Old Khmer, Old Malay, Old Javanese, Old Balinese, etc. The third stage of Indianization consists of local developments and variations in the scripts, with no counterpart in India. Thus one may note parallel or even identical developments of the letter shapes in different parts of Southeast Asia, which in some cases extend to south India and Sri Lanka as well; but these parallel developments seem to end by the late eighth century, when the scripts begin to diverge and adopt separate regional forms (de Casparis 1979: 387–88). A north Indian script which spread to the Deccan and South India, to Sri Lanka, and to parts of Southeast Asia was the Nagari script in an early form (also called Pre-Nagari or, by Damais 1955: 369, *siddhamātṛkā* or *siddham*). The spread of this alphabet into Southeast Asia was in most cases closely associated with Buddhism, especially in its Mahayana variant. There are, however, non-Buddhist examples, including inscriptions in Angkor, Cambodia: as stated by de Casparis (1979: 394), Angkor contains

a dozen digraphic Sanskrit inscriptions, all giving the same text in both Early
Nāgarī and Early Khmer script [a development stemming from South India],
dealing with the foundation by Yasovarman (ca. 889–900) of [Hindu] hermit-
ages. … This Cambodian Nāgarī, though essentially quite similar to the script
of the eighth-century Javanese [Early Nagari] inscriptions, shows some peculiar
stylistic features, notably the [characteristic] notched head marks. These are not
found in this form in Indian Nāgarī, as far as known to [the writer], but are
actually identical with the head marks of the contemporary Khmer script.

In other words, in Cambodia at that time a specifically Khmer script had evolved; and
even the coexisting, recently introduced, Early Nagari script had taken on a specifically Cambodian style.

Modern times bring the contemporary national scripts such as those of the Burmese, the Lao, and the Thai, as well as the obsolescent national scripts of the Mon,
Javanese, Sundanese, Balinese, Cham, etc., as well as tribal scripts in Sumatra and the
Philippines. For writing languages such as Khmer and Thai, with their non-Indic
vowels and consonants—and especially Thai with its tones—ingenious adaptations
of the scripts were undertaken. Thus Cambodian script, among other innovations,
records the distinction between ordinary voiced *b* [b] and *d* [d], now shifted to voiceless [p, t], and implosive *b* [ɓ] and *d* [ɗ] (SECTION 44). The Thai script, as well as
keeping a separate letter or sign for every sound of Sanskrit and Pali, shows additional
signs for vowels: long and short open *ae* [ɛ], long and short open *o* [ɔ], short close
e [e], long and short *oe* [ɤ], long and short *u'* [ɯ], the diphthongs *ia* [iə], *ua* [uə],
u'a [ɯə], and the corresponding "short" diphthongs [iəʔ, uəʔ, ɯəʔ] (SECTION 43).
Also distinguished are the Ancient Thai diphthong [aɯ] and the consonant [f], plus
the Ancient Thai consonant sounds [x], [ɣ], [z], and [v], plus four of the five modern
tones. What is more, the Thai alphabet dispensed with Indic subscript consonants and
independent vowel symbols. Such indigenous developments, like other aspects of Indian-derived culture in Southeast Asia, make clear that the Southeast Asians were no
mere passive imitators of things Indian, but creative selectors, developers, and adap-
tors.

For more on Indianization, see de Casparis 1975, 1979; Coedès 1966, 1968;
Damais 1955; Mabbett 1977; SarDesai 1989; and Sarkar 1968. A concise history of
the Southeast Asian scripts is given in Hosking and Meredith-Owens 1966: 35–41.
For samples of Indian script in Southeast Asia, see Chhabra 1965, Damais 1955,
Holle 1882, Jensen 1970: 387–98, Nagaraju 1984, and Filliozat 1953. Note that Jen-
sen 1970, though giving many fine illustrations of Southeast Asian scripts, is out of
date in some of its ethnic or language names, and in its derivation of all the Southeast
Asian scripts from North India.

For an illustration of the development of a Brahmi character in several Southeast
Asian scripts, see FIGURE 55.

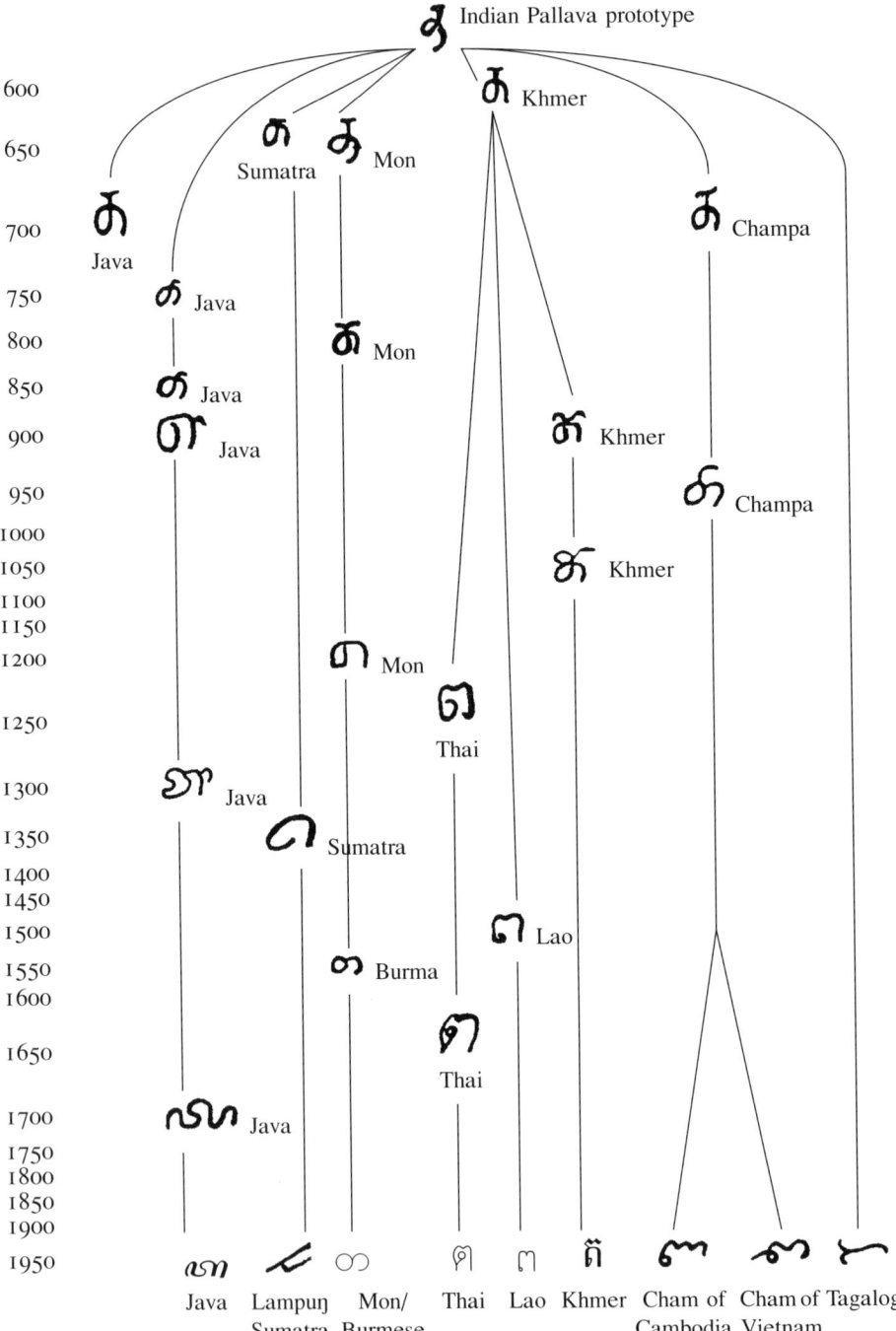

FIGURE 55. Family tree of the akshara *ta* in Southeast Asian scripts. Pallava prototype from Filliozat 1953: 697; other forms from Damais 1955, fig. 15.

Bibliography

Chhabra, Bahadur Chand. 1965. *Expansion of Indo-Aryan Culture during Pallava Rule.* Delhi: Munshi Ram Manohar Lal.

Coedès, Georges. 1966. *The Making of South East Asia.* London: Routledge & Kegan Paul.

———. 1968. *The Indianized States of Southeast Asia,* ed. Walter F. Vella, trans. Susan Brown Cowing. Honolulu: University Press of Hawaii.

Damais, Louis-Charles. 1955. "Les écritures d'origine indienne en Indonésie et dans le Sud-Est Asiatique continental." *Bulletin de la Société des Études Indochinoises* n.s. 30: 365–82.

de Casparis, J. G. 1975. *Indonesian Palaeography: A History of Writing in Indonesia from the Beginnings to c. A.D. 1500* (Handbuch der Orientalistik, division 3, vol. 4, fasc. 1). Leiden: Brill.

———. 1979. "Palaeography as an Auxiliary Discipline in Research on Early South East Asia." In *Early South East Asia: Essays in Archaeology, History and Historical Geography,* ed. Ralph B. Smith and William Watson, pp. 380–94. New York: Oxford University Press.

Filliozat, Jean. 1953. "Paléographie." Appendix I in *L'Inde classique: Manuel des études indiennes,* ed. Louis Renou and Jean Filliozat, vol. 2, pp. 665–712. Paris: Imprimerie Nationale.

Holle, Karel Frederik. 1882. *Tabel van Oud- en Nieuw-Indische Alphabetten.* Batavia: Bruining.

Hosking, R. F., and G. M. Meredith-Owens. 1966. *A Handbook of Asian Scripts.* London: British Museum.

Jensen, Hans. 1970. *Sign, Symbol and Script: An Account of Man's Efforts to Write,* 3rd ed., trans. George Unwin. London: George Allen and Unwin.

Mabbett, Ian W. 1977. "The 'Indianization' of Southeast Asia: Reflections on the Historical Sources." *Journal of Southeast Asian Studies* 8: 143–61.

Nagaraju, S. 1984. "The Palaeography of the Earliest Inscriptions of Burma, Thailand, Cambodia and Vietnam." In *Svasti Śrī: Dr. B. Ch. Chhabra Felicitation Volume,* ed. K. V. Ramesh et al., pp. 67–80. Delhi: Agam Kala Prakashan.

SarDesai, D. R. 1989. *Southeast Asia, Past and Present.* Boulder, Colo.: Westview.

Sarkar, Kalyan K. 1968. *Early Indo-Cambodian Contacts, Literary and Linguistic.* Santiniketan, West Bengal, India: Visva-Bharati.

Burmese Writing

JULIAN K. WHEATLEY

History

The Burmese script, attested in stone inscriptions at least as far back as the early twelfth century C.E., is a phonologically based script, adapted from Mon, and ultimately based on an Indian (Brahmi) prototype. (Several other scripts closely resemble the Burmese, including the Tai Yai script, which is the most widely used for the Shan language and is of considerable antiquity. Some Karen scripts devised in more recent times are explicitly modeled on Burmese.) Traditionally, it is thought that Mon scribes, brought to the city of Pagan after the sack of their capital by the Burmese king Anawrahta in 1057 C.E., provided the stimulus for adapting the Mon script to the writing of Burmese. There have been some changes since the inscriptional period, most notably: consistent use of the "rounded" rather than the "square" style of letters, changes in permissible combinations of vowel and final consonant signs, and stabilization of the system for marking tones.

Symbols

For the examples that follow, transliterations are given in a slightly modified version of the "standard" Blagden-Duroiselle system (summarized by Okell 1971). This system tends to go beyond the internal evidence of the Burmese script, assigning Mon and Indian values to the letters.

TABLE 42.1 shows the 33 consonant signs of Burmese arranged in traditional order (reading left to right), which, except for the final position of အ (the vowel support), accords with Indian phonetic order. Some works, including Judson's *Burmese–English Dictionary* (1966), place အ first rather than last. Letters generally have descriptive names (Roop 1972: 119–22), e.g. ထ ဆင် ခြောက်း *tha-chaṅ-thū:* 'elephant fetter [tʰá]', though some, including most of the sonorants, are simply named by their sound: မ is [má], အ is [á], etc.

Boxed consonants in the table are those that occur finally as well as initially in native syllables, though many others occur finally in Indic loanwords. (Final -*y* marks a tone.) The palatal nasal ည, rare as an initial, has come to be used to write only the nasalized reflexes of the -*añ* rhyme: thus ညဉ် *ññañ* [ɲī], but ညည်း *ññaññ:* [ɲì]

Certain of the -*m* rhymes are spelled with a superscript circle ◌ံ (*anusvāra*) rather than the ordinary consonant sign: သိမ်း *sim:* [θèí], but သုံး *sum:* [θòũ].

TABLE 42.1: *Consonants*

| | VOICELESS STOPS | | VOICED STOPS | | NASALS |
	Unaspirated	Aspirated	Unaspirated	Aspirated	
Velar	က k [k]	ခ kh [kʰ]	ဂ g [g]	ဃ gh [g]	င ṅ [ŋ]
Palatal	စ c [s]	ဆ ch [sʰ]	ဇ j [z]	ဈ jh [z]	ဉ ññ [ɲ]
					ည ñ [ɲ]
Retroflex	ဋ ṭ [t]	ဌ ṭh [tʰ]	ဍ ḍ [d]	ဎ ḍh [d]	ဏ ṇ [n]
Dental	တ t [t]	ထ th [tʰ]	ဒ d [d]	ဓ dh [d]	န n [n]
Labial	ပ p [p]	ဖ ph [pʰ]	ဗ b [b]	ဘ bh [b]	မ m [m]

	SONORANTS				
	ယ y [j]	ရ r [j]	လ l [l]	ဝ w [w]	သ s [θ]
		ဟ h [h]	ဠ ḷ [l]	အ Ø [ʔ]	

Dictionary order for rhymes is not as well established as for consonants. In general, dictionaries agree on the Indian order of vowels *a ā i ī u ū e ai o ō ui*, but they differ as to the order of tonal variants, and of irregular features such as the initial vowel signs and *anusvāra*. There are two major conventions: one takes the spoken language as basic, consistently listing tones in the order creaky, low, high, placing *anusvāra* with *-m*, placing the initial and diacritic versions of vowels together, and placing the *-ay* rhyme with *-ai*. The other tradition, current in most Burmese dictionaries, takes writing as basic, and thus orders tones differently, according to whether they are inherent or not; separates *anusvāra* from final *-m*, *-ay* from *-ai*; and so on (cf. Okell 1994 for details).

TABLE 42.2 shows the main vowel and tone combinations in open syllables; all diacritic vowels are given with the vowel support sign (pronounced [ʔ]). A tall version of the sign ‑ာ *ā* is used when the combinations of consonant and vowel would be confused with other consonants; thus ဝ *p* + ‑ာ *ā* is written ပါ *pā* [pa] to avoid confusion with ဟ *h*. The sharply reduced distribution of vowels and finals in regular rhymes is shown in TABLE 42.3.

General characteristics

The main features of Burmese script are as follows.

   (a) It is written left to right; spaces separate phrases, not words. Punctuation is usually limited to the symbols ၊ and ၁၊, borrowed from Indic scripts. These correspond roughly to comma (or semicolon) and period, respectively.

TABLE 42.2: *Vowels and Tones (open syllables)*

Tone	FRONT VOWELS Initial	Diacritic			CENTRAL VOWELS Initial	Diacritic			BACK VOWELS Initial	Diacritic		
					Primary Vowels							
creaky	အ	◌ိ	အိ	i [í]	အ	–		a [á]	ဥ	◌ု	အု	u [ú]
low	အီ	◌ီ	အီ	ī [i]	◌ာ	အာ	ā [a]		ဦ	◌ူ	အူ	ū [u]
high		◌ီး	အီး	i: [ì]	◌ား	အား	a: [à]		◌ူး	အူး	u: [ù]
					Mid Vowels							
High low	ဧ	ေ–	ေအ	e [e]					◌ို	အို	ui [o]
high		ေ–း	ေအး	e: [è]					◌ိုး	အိုး	ui: [ò]
creaky		ေ–	ေအ	ẹ [é]					◌ို့	အို့	uị [ó]
Low low	–ယ်	အယ်	ay [ɛ]						ေသာ်	ေ–ာ်	ေအာ်	ō [ɔ]
high	◌ဲ	အဲ	ai [ɛ̀]						ဩ	ေ–ာ	ေအာ	o [ɔ̀]
creaky	◌ဲ့	အဲ့	aị [ɛ́]						ေ–ာ့	ေအာ့	ọ [ɔ́]

(b) Consonants written without a vowel sign contain an inherent vowel: မ *ma*, လ *la*. However, the vowel may be canceled by a "killing stroke" over the consonant; thus မ် is syllable-final *m*. Other vowels are indicated with diacritics (cf. TABLE 42.2): မိ *mi*, မု *mu*, ေမ *me*, မာ *mā*, ေမာ် *mo* [mɔ̀], မို *mui* [mo], etc. The vowel signs also contain inherent tones. Burmese has three tones in non-checked syllables, called the "creaky" (*ma* [má], high, short with glottalized voice), the "low" (*mā* [ma], low, long), and the "high" (*ma:* [mà], high, long). Mon was not tonal, but for the vowels *a, i,* and *u* it does have short syllables ending in glottal stop that must have sounded very similar to Burmese creaky tone. Since these were written with what in Indic terms is the "short" version of the vowel, the same convention was carried over to Burmese to indicate creaky tone: မ *ma* [má], မိ *mi* [mí], မု *mu* [mú]. The "long" version is used for low- and high-toned open syllables: မာ *mā* [ma], မီ *mī* [mi], မူ *mū* [mu]; မား *mā:* [mà], မီး *mī:* [mì], မူး *mū:* [mù]. Historically closed syllables are written with the "short" vowels (မတ် *mat* [maʔ] etc.), and those ending in written nasals are inherently low-toned: မန် *man* [mā], မိန် *min* [meī], မုန် *mun* [moū].

Since only the three primary vowels *a i u* had two versions, tonal marking of the mid vowels used entirely different devices. The mid-high vowels in open syllables are inherently low-toned: ေမ *me* [me]; မို *mui* [mo]. But their mid-low counterparts in open syllables are inherently high-toned: လွဲ *lwai* [lwὲ], ေမာ *mo* [mɔ̀]. These are marked for low tone as follows: လွယ် *lway* [lwɛ], with a "killed" *y*; and ေမာ် *mō* [mɔ], with the "killing stroke," which in this case derives from a killed *w*, ဝ်. For all cases

TABLE 42.3: *Regular Rhymes*

	-ṅ	-ñ	-n	-m	-k	-c	-t	-p
a	အင်	အည်/ဉ်	အန်	အမ်	အက်	အစ်	အတ်	အပ်
	[ʔĩ]	[ʔĩ/i]	[ʔã]	[ʔã]	[ʔɛʔ]	[ʔiʔ]	[ʔaʔ]	[ʔaʔ]
i			အိန်	အိမ်			အိတ်	အိပ်
			[ʔeĩ]	[ʔeĩ]			[ʔeɪʔ]	[ʔeɪʔ]
u			အုန်	အုမ်			အုတ်	အုပ်
			[ʔoũ]	[ʔoũ]			[ʔoʊʔ]	[ʔoʊʔ]
o	အောင်				အောတက်			
	[ʔaũ]				[ʔaʊʔ]			
ui	အိုင်				အိုက်			
	[ʔaĩ]				[ʔaɪʔ]			

where the tones are not inherent, tones are specifically marked: High tone is marked by *visarga* (ः, Sanskrit *ḥ*), possibly in recognition of the slight breathiness sometimes associated with that tone; and creaky tone is indicated with a subscript dot: thus ေသ [se], ေသः [sè], ေသ့ [sé].

(c) In the written syllable, final consonants are distinguished from initial by a superscript hook (the "killer"), which suppresses the inherent vowel: တတ် *tat* [taʔ].

(d) In most native words, initial vowels are written as diacritics with the vowel support sign အ (အိ *ī*, အု *ū*, အော *o*, etc.).

Points (e)–(g) concern signs or combinations of signs that are mostly found in Indian loanwords.

(e) In some words—particularly Indian loanwords—special initial vowel signs (*akkharā*) are used: ဧ (= အေ) *e* in ဧရာဝတီ *erāwatī* 'Irawaddy river'; ဩ (= အော) *o* in ဩဂုတ် *ogut* 'August'; ဤ (= အီ) *ī*, the literary demonstrative 'this'. Only the historical monophthongs have special initial forms, and even then, not always with all tones (see TABLE 42.2).

(f) In addition to the initial vowels, a number of other signs appear primarily (though not exclusively) with Indian loanwords. These include the letters for the Indian retroflex and voiced aspirate series.

(g) The convention of preserving the original spelling of (mostly) Indian loanwords has also given rise to a number of "irregular rhymes," where "rhyme" refers to the vowel-plus-tone portion of a syllable. These have combinations of vowel and final consonant not usually found in native Burmese material, thus: ဓါတ် *dhāt* 'element' (cf. Pali *dhātu*), pronounced [daʔ], as if spelled ဒတ် *dat*; ဗိုလ် *buil* 'force' (cf. Pali *bala*), pronounced [bo], as if ဗို *bui*; ဥယျာဉ် *uyyāñ* 'garden' (cf. Pali *uyyāna*), read [úyĩ], as if အုယင် *uyaṅ*. Burmese scribes also follow the Indian practice of stacking geminate and homorganic consonants (cf. Okell 1994 for details): ဗုဒ္ဓ *buddha* (Pali *bud-*

dha) rather than ပုဒ္ဓ (regular rhyme, ဗုဒ်ဒ); မန္တလေး *mantale:* 'Mandalay' rather than မန်းတလေး. As the last example shows, the top member of a stack is neither "killed" nor marked for tone. In general, the second consonant of a cluster is pushed down to subscript position; but when -*ṅ* is the first consonant it is pushed up, and keeps its killing mark: အင်္ဂါနေ့ *aṅgāne* 'Tuesday' (rather than အင်ဂါနေ့). In some cases, the lower member of a stack is abbreviated or reoriented (cf. Okell ibid., "special stacks").

(h) The sonorant consonants ယ *ya*, ရ *ra*, ဝ *wa*, and ဟ *ha* have diacritical or medial variants, ျ, ြ, ွ, ှ. Thus: ချက် *khyak* [cʰɛʔ], မြန် *mran* [mjā], မွေး *mwe:* [mwè], မှာ *mha* [hmá], ရှ *rha* [ʃá]. Two medials may cluster on a single consonant: လျှ *lhya* [hljá] or [ʃá]. The Old Burmese of the inscriptions shows a subscript ္လ *-l-*, which attests to an earlier medial, later lost through mergers in the standard dialect.

Pronunciation

Particularly in the Central dialects of Burmese, which form the basis of the standard language, sound changes occurring since the language was reduced to writing have multiplied or changed the values of many letters. The peripheral dialects, such as Arakanese and Tavoyan, have preserved a number of initial clusters and final consonants and are a closer reflection of the orthography. The main developments in the standard language are as follows.

The sets of four final occlusives and four nasals represented in the orthography are reduced to a single occlusive and a single nasal value. In citation, these are realized as glottal stop [ʔ] and nasalization [̃] respectively; thus, လုပ် *lup* [louʔ]; လုံး *lum:* [lõũ].

Except for the vowel represented by *a*, vowels have diphthongized in historically closed syllables, resulting in divergent readings of the sort illustrated by the following pairs: မိ, မိန် spelled *mi, min*, but pronounced [mí], [meĩ]; နု, နုန် spelled *nu, nun*, but pronounced [nú], [noũ]; ပို, ပိုက် spelled *pui, puik*, but pronounced [po], [paɪʔ]; ‌ရော, ရောက် spelled *ro, rok*, but pronounced [jɔ̀], [jaʊʔ].

Combinations of velar (oral) stop and medial -*y*- or -*r*- in the orthography are pronounced as palatal stops: ကြက် *krak* 'chicken' [cɛʔ]; ကျပ် *kyap* (the unit of currency) [caʔ]. In all other combinations, *y* and *r* are read [j]. The palatalization of velars, reflected in the reading rule, can be regarded as the last step of a chain of developments affecting several series of consonants: [s] > [θ] (cf. သိပ် *sip* 'to put to sleep' [θeɪʔ]), making way for [c] > [s] etc. (cf. စား *cā:* [sà]), making way for [kj] > [c], etc.

A number of phonological processes (cf. Wheatley 1987) are not represented in the script. One is sandhi, which affects the realization of sounds at syllable boundaries in certain grammatically defined contexts. E.g., လူထု *lū-thu* 'crowd' is read [ludú] not [lutʰú], as suggested by the script. Another process is vocalic weakening, which affects the first syllables of certain words (mostly nouns and adverbs): ထမင်း *thamaṅ:* 'cooked rice' is read [tʰəmĩ] not [tʰámĩ]; ဘုရား *bhurā:* 'god; pagoda' is read [pʰəyà],

TABLE 42.4: *Abbreviations*

		Gloss		Source
၍	[ywé]	subordinate marker	ရယ်	ruy in Old Burmese
၏	[í]	genitive/declarative marker	ေအ်	ẹ in Old Burmese
၌	[hnaɪʔ]	locative marker	နှိက်	nhuik
၎င်း	[ləgàū]	'this, the same'	လည်းေကာင်း	laññ:-koṅ:

TABLE 42.5: *Numerals*

0	1	2	3	4	5	6	7	8	9	10
၀	၁	၂	၃	၄	၅	၆	၇	၈	၉	၁၀

not [pʰúyà]. The last example, in which initial *bh* is read [pʰ] rather than [b], is typical of the occasional irregularities that affect initial stops.

Miscellaneous signs and modifications

There are orthographic conventions for representing foreign sounds in the transcription, e.g., [f] is transcribed by ဖ *ph*, [v] by ဗ *b* or by the otherwise very rare ွ *bw*; cf. တီဗွီ *tī-bwī* [tivi] 'TV'. A second "killed" final consonant (sometimes in parentheses) can be placed after a first to indicate a foreign final sound: ဘတ်(စ်) *bhat(c)* [baʔ] + [s] to give [bas] 'bus'.

TABLE 42.4 shows four telescoped abbreviations current in the written literary language, followed by the spelled-out versions from which they derive. These are, in fact, logograms and are marked <L> in the text sample.

TABLE 42.5 shows the numerals.

SAMPLE OF BURMESE

1. Burmese: ပါဠိအေရးအသားသည် မြန်မာစာအေရးအသားကို
2. Transliteration: pāḷiare:asā:saññ mranmācāare:asā:kui
3. Transcription: palí-ʔəjèʔəθà-ði mjãma-sa-ʔəjèʔəθà-go
4. Gloss: Pali-writing-NOM Burmese-language-writing-ACC

1. အေတာ်ပင် လွှမ်းမိုးခဲ့ဟန်တူသည်။ အဘယ်ေကြာင့်ဆိုေသာ်
2. atōpaṅ lhwam:mui:khaḥhantūsaññ. abhaykroṅchuisō
3. ətɔbĩ hlũmmò-gé-hātu-ði əbɛ-cáū-sʰo-ðɔ
4. rather influence-DISPLACED-appear-DECL what-reason-say-ing

1. မြန်မာစကားလုံး   စစ်စစ်များကို   ရေးသားရာင့်ပင်
2. mranmācakā:luṁ: caccacmyā:kui re:sā:rā<L>paṅ
3. mjāma-zəgəlòū   si?si?-mjà-go   jèthà-ja-hnaɪ?-pī
4. Burma-words   real-many-ACC   writing-place-at-even

1. ပါဠိဟန်ကိုလိုက်၍   နှစ်လုံးဆင့်   ရေးသားလာခဲ့ကြသည်ကို
2. pāḷihankuiluik<L>   nhacluṁ:chaṅ re:sā:lākhaikrasaññkui
3. palí-hā-go-lai?-jwé   hnə-lòū-shî   jèthà-la-gé-já-ði-gō
4. Pali-appearance-ACC-follow-ing two-CLF-stack   write-come-DISP-PL-DECL-ACC

1. တွေ့ရသောကြောင့်   ဖြစ်၏။   သာဓက။   ပခုက္ကူမြို့၊   စက္ကူ၊   ကုက္ကို့ပင်။
2. twerasokroṅ   phrac<L>. sādhaka. pakhukkūmrui, cakkū, kukkuipaṅ.
3. twéjáðòcáū   phji?-?í   θadáká   pəkhou?kumjó   sɛ?ku   kou?kobī
4. meet-able-GEN-cause be-DECL   example   (a town)   paper   (a tree)

'Pali writing seems to have had considerable influence on Burmese writing. The reason we say this is that even when we write real Burmese words, we see that we follow the Pali model, writing letters one on top of the other [i.e. in stacks]. For example: (three examples of words with stacked consonants).'

— From the introduction of the Mranmā Abhidhān (vol. 1, p. e-5).

━━━━━

Bibliography

Burmese Language Commission. 1978. *Mranmā Abhidhān: akyañ:khyup* [Abridged Burmese dictionary]. Rangoon: Burmese Ministry of Education.

Judson, Adoniram. 1966. *Burmese–English Dictionary,* rev. ed. Rangoon: Baptist Board of Publications.

Okell, John. 1968. "Alphabetical Order in Burmese." *Journal of the Burma Research Society* 15: 145–71.

———. 1971. *A Guide to the Romanization of Burmese.* London: Luzac.

———. 1994. *Burmese: An Introduction to the Script.* DeKalb: Northern Illinois University, Center for Southeast Asian Studies.

Roop, D. Haigh. 1972. *An Introduction to the Burmese Writing System.* New Haven: Yale University Press.

Wheatley, Julian K. 1987. "Burmese." in *The World's Major Languages,* ed. Bernard Comrie, pp. 834–54. London: Croom Helm; New York: Oxford University Press.

Thai and Lao Writing

ANTHONY DILLER

Thai and Lao (Laotian) are closely related members of the same language family, and their writing systems are similar. The scripts are Indic in origin and written from left to right without regular word spacing. Instead, spaces are used to indicate sentences or phrasal units. European style paragraphing is used along with quotation marks, parentheses, and occasionally other punctuation marks. While the scripts are both phonologically based, the relationship of letters to sounds is complex, especially for Thai. Only the main features of written Thai and Lao are introduced here (see Haas 1956, Danwiwat 1987, and Kerr 1972 for comprehensive treatments).

The two scripts are directly convertible. Thus the majority of Lao speakers, as defined by linguistic criteria, actually reside in northeastern Thailand; they tend to write their spoken language using Thai script, whereas Lao script is standard in Laos proper. According to official estimates, over fifty million people are at least partly literate in these scripts taken together. In addition to the national languages Thai and Lao, the writing systems are used for several minority languages and non-standard dialects.

Consonant letters are considered the basis of both orthographies, with vowels added as required diacritics. An important feature of the writing systems, indicated in TABLE 43.1, is an apparently excessive number of consonant letters as compared to phoneme inventories. This relates to historical issues and modern tone marking explained below.

In both phonology and orthography, each language distinguishes the same nine pairs of long and short vowels. In the semi-official Thai-Lao transliteration system used here, vowel phonemes are transliterated as:

> high *i u' u*   mid *e oe o*   low *ae a o'*.

Authorities differ slightly over some phonetic equivalents, a consensus being:

> high [i ɯ u]   mid [e ɤ o]   low [æ a ɔ]

(see Henderson 1951, Haas 1956). Long vowels are transliterated here with a colon. Three diphthongs *ia*, *u'a*, and *ua* [iə ɯə uə] are counted as part of the core vowel systems and behave phonologically like long vowels, with rare short variants. Sounds transliterated here as *ay*, *aw* may appear elsewhere as *ai*, *ao* (e.g. in "Th**ai**," "**Lao**"). Stop + *h* represents aspirated stop (e.g. in "**Th**ai"); *c* = [tɕ]; *ng* = [ŋ]. Lao *v* varies among alternates [v ~ β ~ w], and *kh* among [kʰ ~ x ~ χ].

Transcriptions and transliterations for Thai and Lao show variation, with Lao sometimes transcribed in a French-inspired way ("Vientiane" for [víəŋ-tɕan]) and

TABLE 43.1: *Quantitative Comparison of Thai and Lao Inventories*

	Consonant Symbols	Consonant Phonemes	Simple Vowel Symbols	Core Vowel Phonemes
Thai	44	21	19	21
Lao	27	20	18	21

TABLE 43.2: *Sound Changes Affecting Interpretation of Thai and Lao Scripts*

			Thirteenth Century	Twentieth Century
(i)		ฬ	b	ph
	compare:	ฟ	ph	ph
(ii)		หม	m̥	m
	compare:	ม	m	m
(iii)		บ	ʔb	b
(iv)		ภ	bh(?)	ph

Thai often showing letter-by-letter Indic etymology rather than modern pronunciation, as explained below. The *Lao–English Dictionary* of Kerr (1972) uses a system close to that followed here, which differs only superficially from that of Haas (1956, 1964) for Thai, e.g. final stops are represented here as *-p*, *-t*, *-k* (rather than as *-b*, *-d*, *-g*, as in Haas).

Development

The diachronic background of the Thai and Lao orthographies is the key to understanding their modern complexity. Historically, written Thai and Lao can be traced back to South Indian writing systems of the Grantha type (SECTION 30), but the proximate source was a form of Old Khmer script. According to the traditional account, in 1283 King Ramkhamhaeng of Sukhothai, in what is now north-central Thailand, adapted this source script to a language of the Thai-Lao type. He is credited with the innovation of tone marks—arguably the first time that phonemic tone was regularly indicated in a writing system intended for common use.

The Sukhothai writing system underwent shifting and proliferation. In addition, according to most authorities, a set of important sound changes occurred in the spoken precursors of modern Thai and Lao over the following centuries (Li 1977). These changes are illustrated in TABLE 43.2 for selected Thai labial items.

Analogous changes occurred for other consonant groups and in general:

(i)   Unaspirated voiced occlusives > aspirated voiceless occlusives.
(ii)   Pre-aspirated or voiceless continuants > plain voiced continuants.

(iii)   Voiced preglottalized stops > plain voiced stops.

(iv)   However etymological voiced aspirates might have been pronounced in Sukhothai times, they have now merged with voiceless aspirates.

Along with the mergers implicit in TABLE 43.2 came a compensatory increase in tonal distinctions, somewhat differently in the Thai and Lao cases. Earlier spelling patterns were on the whole retained, so that letters in the writing system that had earlier indicated *consonantal distinctions* now came to function rather as *indirect markers of tone*, with tonal interpretations different in Thai and Lao. These changes provide the historical background for much of the consonant-letter proliferation of TABLE 43.1, and they motivate the column appearing in TABLE 43.3 which identifies particular consonants as class 1, 2, or 3 for purposes of modern tone rules (as in TABLE 43.9 on page 464). (Traditionally, these classes are labeled in Thai as กลาง *kla:ng* 'mid', สูง *sǔ:ng* 'high', and ต่ำ *tàm* 'low' respectively—probably referring to earlier tonal values.)

By the early sixteenth century a form of Sukhothai writing had spread to the Mekhong River basin, and subsequently several Thai–Lao orthographic differences began to develop (Gagneux 1983). Separate phonological changes also occurred, which further differentiated sounds represented by the writing systems. For Lao, changes included simplification of many consonant clusters, and shifts with merger of *r* > *h*, *ch* > *s*, and *y* > *ñ*; Thai had the reverse merger *ñ* > *y*.

More recently, different approaches to language standardization have been responsible for additional Thai–Lao divergences. Under successive regimes, Lao script has been scaled down to approach a phonemic representation. (An official order of 1960 provides the Lao text sample.) By contrast, written Thai tends to incorporate unpronounced etymological information. Forms meaning 'language' in both Thai and Lao are borrowed from Sanskrit *bhāṣā* 'speech' but are now pronounced segmentally as *pha:sa:* (with tones as assigned in TABLE 43.9). The text samples show that Lao has respelled this item phonemically, while Thai retains "extra" nonphonemic letters pointing back to the Sanskrit source consonants. Thai is also often romanized etymologically, especially for proper nouns of Indic origin: วชิราวุธ *Vajira:vudh*, pronounced [wachíra:wút].

Syllable-final stop proliferation of the above type calls for special attention in Thai schools. Phonologically, apart from final glottal stop (automatic with short vowels and not transcribed here), both Thai and Lao admit only three final stop-consonant sounds: -*p*, -*t*, and -*k*. Lao, as officially reformed, allows only three symbols: บ ด ก. (In initial position these represent *b*-, *d*-, *k*-.) Thai, by contrast, represents these three sounds by no less than 16 different letters, with the possibility of additional silent letters as well (see TABLE 43.3). A good example of extra finals is the word meaning 'etymology' itself, *nirúktisà:t*, as in the Thai text sample; compare Sanskrit *nirukti* 'derivation' + *śāstra* 'knowledge'.

For more historical detail see Hartmann 1986 and Li 1977. Aspects of this traditional view have been challenged in the debate presented by Chamberlain 1991.

TABLE 43.3: *Thai and Lao Consonants*

Indic Prototype	Thai Letter	Thai Sound as Initial	Lao Letter	Lao Sound as Initial	Class	Sound as Final
A. Velar and Palatal Letters						
k	ก	k-	ກ	k-	I	-k
kh	ข	kh-	ຂ	kh-	2	-k
	ฃ	(kh-)			2	
g	ค	kh-	ຄ	kh-	3	-k
	ฅ	(kh-)			3	
gh	ฆ	kh-			3	-k
ṅ	ง	ng-	ງ	ng-	3	-ng
c	จ	c-	ຈ	c-	I	-t
ch	ฉ	ch-			2	
j	ช	ch-	ຊ	s-	3	-t
	ซ	s-			3	-t , (-s)
jh	ฌ	ch-			3	-t
ñ	ญ	y-			3	-n
B. Retroflex and Dental (alveolar) Letters						
(ṭ)	ฎ	d-			I	-t
ṭ	ฏ	(t-)			I	-t
ṭh	ฐ	th-			2	-t
ḍ	ฑ	th-			3	-t
ḍh	ฒ	th-			3	-t
ṇ	ณ	n-			3	-n
(t)	ด	d-	ດ	d-	I	-t
t	ต	t-	ຕ	t-	I	-t
th	ถ	th-	ຖ	th-	2	-t
d	ท	th-	ທ	th-	3	-t
dh	ธ	th-		th-	3	-t
n	น	n-	ນ	n-	3	-n
C. Labial and Labiodental Letters						
(p)	บ	b-	ບ	b-	I	-p
p	ป	p-	ປ	p-	I	-p
ph	ผ	ph-	ຜ	ph-	2	-p
	ฝ	f-	ຝ	f-	3	
b	พ	ph-	ພ	ph-	3	-p
	ฟ	f-	ຟ	f-	3	-p, (-f)
bh	ภ	ph-		ph-	3	-p
m	ม	m-	ມ	m-	3	-m

TABLE 43.3: *Thai and Lao Consonants (continued)*

Indic Prototype	Thai Letter	Thai Sound as Initial	Lao Letter	Lao Sound as Initial	Class	Sound as Final
			D. Residual Consonant Letters			
y	ย	y-	ບ	ñ-	3	-y
			ຽ		1	-y
r	ร	r-, (l-)	ຣ	h-	3	-n
r			(ຣ)	l-	3	-n
l	ล	l-	ລ	l-	3	-n
v	ว	w-	ວ	v-, (w-)	3	-w
ś	ศ	s-			2	-t
ṣ	ษ	s-			2	-t
s	ส	s-	ສ	s-	2	-t, (-s)
h	ห	h-	ຫ	h-	2	
ḷ	ฬ	l-			3	-n
	อ	['-]	ອ	['-]	1	
	ฮ	h-			3	

Consonant symbols

In form, most Thai and Lao letters have small "heads" which are written first in hand-writing. The traditional order of Thai consonants, shown in TABLE 43.3, generally follows Devanagari (SECTION 31); but the sound changes mentioned above, as well as other innovations, disguise the parallelism. Some additional shifts characterize Lao order. Consonants are named by their sound followed by the vowel *o' :*. To differenti-ate consonant names in Thai, a token noun is used (see Haas 1954: 6–9).

Thai once distinguished velar fricatives, represented by ฅ and ฆ in TABLE 43.3A. The fricatives merged with stops, and the letters are no longer used; but they are still officially recognized. The Thai letter ช, representing an alveolar fricative *s*, is classi-fied among the palatals. In most Lao sources, two "residual" consonants (here moved to TABLE 43.3D) are included in the palatal series: ສ *s* (in the dictionary order of Thai ช *ch*) and ບ *ñ* (in the dictionary order of ຍ *y*).

In TABLE 43.3B, etymologically retroflex consonants are distinguished from dentals in written Thai but both series are pronounced as alveolars. Except for ฐ *th*, retroflex letters are unusual as initials. Parenthesized Indic prototypes indicate less common symbols.

How the Thai letter ร is pronounced is a strong sociolinguistic marker—norma-tively *r* but colloquially *l*. Similarly, the Lao letter ຣ, usually pronounced *l*, was for-merly used for Indic loans spelled with *r-*; but this (nonphonemic) letter has been

TABLE 43.4: *Compound and Conjunct Forms as Class-changing Alternates*

Thai Compound	Thai Sound	Lao Compound	Lao Conjunct	Lao Sound	Class
หง	ng-	ຫງ	–	ng-	2
หน	n-	ຫນ	ໜ	n-	2
หม	m-	ຫມ	ໝ	m-	2
หล	l-	ຫລ	ຼ	l-	2
หว	w-	ຫວ	–	v-, (w-)	2
หร	r- , (l-)	–	–		2
หย	y-	ຫຍ, ຫຽ	–	ñ-	2
อย	y-	–	(ຍ)	(y-)	1

officially discouraged, and ລ *l* is the prescribed substitute. Current use of ຣ may relate to political sympathies. The glottal-stop signs Thai อ and Lao ອ are required to begin written syllables in the absence of other consonants since, unlike Devanagari, Thai and Lao have no special syllable-initial symbols for vowels. Non-initial ຢ in Lao once had an alternate form ຽ, but officially this is now restricted to diphthongs; see TABLE 43.7.

Items in TABLE 43.4 are used for tone-marking purposes (TABLE 43.9). In Thai, silent ห- and อ- are prefixed to certain Class 3 items in TABLE 43.3 to create alternates in Classes 2 or 1. Lao makes similar shifts, with some freely varying conjunct alternates. Lao ຢ is etymologically associated with Thai อย.

■■■■■

Vowel symbols

In writing, some phonemes are represented directly by a simple vowel symbol. For others, symbols combine to form complexes. Vowel symbols may occur after, over, under, or before their associated consonant letter—that being the approximate dictionary order. TABLE 43.5 through TABLE 43.8 show syllable-final vowel forms. Some separate forms discussed in the following paragraphs are specified for medial position, i.e. in the presence of a final consonant.

Medially, short -*a*- is written as superscript ◌ั in both languages: Thai กัด *kàt* 'bite'; Lao ກັກ. For Thai, when a syllable ends in -*u' :* a silent อ is added: กือ *ku' :*. (In spelling pronunciation, syllables terminating in short vowels are given a glottal-stop closure and tone is assigned as in TABLE 43.9.)

In both languages, syllables in short *e* and *ae* occurring between consonants dispense with final ◌ะ. Instead, a superscript short sign is added over the initial consonant: Thai ◌็, Lao ◌็. Thus Thai เต็ม *tem* 'full'; Lao ເຕັມ. In the case of short *o* between consonants, Lao uses a special superscript symbol ◌ົ, while Thai opts for an unwritten in

TABLE 43.5: *Simple Short and Long Vowel Symbols*

Thai		Lao			Thai		Lao		
-ะ	กะ	-ະ	ກະ	ka	-า	กา	-າ	ກາ	ka:	
◌ิ	กิ	◌ິ	ກິ	ki	◌ี	กี	◌ີ	ກີ	ki:	
◌ุ	กุ	◌ຸ	ກຸ	ku	◌ู	กู	◌ູ	ກູ	ku:	
◌ึ	กึ	◌ຶ	ກຶ	ku' [kɯ]	◌ื	กื	◌ື	ກື	ku': [kɯ:]	

TABLE 43.6: *Short Vowel Indicated by Final ะ Added to Long-vowel Form*

Thai		Lao			Thai		Lao		
เ-ะ	เกะ	ເ-ະ	ເກະ	ke	เ-	เก	ເ-	ເກ	ke:
แ-ะ	แกะ	ແ-ະ	ແກະ	kae	แ-	แก	ແ-	ແກ	kae:
โ-ะ	โกะ	โ-ະ	ໂກະ	ko	โ-	โก	ໂ-	ໂກ	ko:

herent vowel. Thus Thai จน *con* 'poor'; Lao ຈິນ. In nonfinal syllables, the inherent
Thai vowel is usually -*a*-, whereas Lao marks all vowels overtly: Thai กบฎ *kabòt* 're-
bellion'; Lao ກະບົດ.

Medial *o'* and *o':* are rarely distinguished from each other (viz., with the short
signs mentioned above). They are written with letters elsewhere functioning as glottal
stop: Thai อ, Lao ອ. Thus Thai กอด *kò:t* 'to hug'; Lao ກອດ. As TABLE 43.7 indicates,
Thai uses this sign for syllable-final -*o':* as well, whereas Lao has a distinctive superscript. Thai อ, Lao ອ also appear as components in complex vowel signs. For medial
-*oe*- Thai uses a form analogous to Lao. For medial -*ia*- Thai adds the final consonant
to the complex in TABLE 43.7, whereas Lao uses the simple symbol ຽ alone: Thai
เทียน *thian* 'candle'; Lao ທຽນ. For medial -*ua*- both languages dispense with superscripts, employing consonant letters Thai ว, Lao ວ alone, with implied diphthong
function. Thus Thai สวน *sŭan* 'garden'; Lao ສວນ.

TABLE 43.7: *Compound Vowel Symbols; Consonant Symbols Used as Vowels*

Thai		Lao			Thai		Lao		
เ-าะ	เกาะ	ເ-າະ	ເກາະ	ko' [kɔ]	-อ	กอ	◌ໍ	ກໍ	ko': [kɔ:]
เ-อะ	เกอะ	ເ◌ິ	ເກິ	koe [kɤ]	เ-อ	เกอ	ເ◌ີ	ເກີ	koe: [kɤ:]
เ-ีย	เกีย	ເ◌ັຽ, ເ-ຍ	ເກັຽ, ເກຍ	kia [kiə]	เ-ือ	เกือ	ເ◌ືອ	ເກືອ	ku'a [kɯə]
◌ัว	กัว	◌ົວ	ກົວ	kua [kuə]	เ-า	เกา	ເ◌ົາ	ເກົາ	kaw [kaw]
เ-ย	เกย	ເ◌ັຽ, ເ-ຍ	ເກັຽ, ເກຍ	koe:y [kɤ:j]					

TABLE 43.8: *Symbols Standing for Other Vowel–Consonant Combinations*

Thai	Lao		Thai	Lao	
ไก	ໄກ	kay	ใก	ໃກ	kay (< *kaɯ)
ขำ	ກ຺ຳ	kam	กฤ	—	kri, kru'

Some miscellaneous symbols are shown in TABLE 43.8. The Thai symbol ฤ, after consonants as in พฤษภาคม *phrú'tsapha:khom* 'May', is traditionally counted among the vowel signs (compare Devanagari *ṛ*), but it occurs initially in a few words which are alphabetized in dictionaries after ร. It is pronounced as (i) *ru'*, as in ฤดู *rú'du:* 'season'; (ii) *ri*, as in ฤทธิ์ *rít* 'supernatural power'; (iii) *roe:*, as in ฤกษ์ *rôe:k* 'asterism'. In older manuscripts and certain archaizing texts, ฤ may be followed by า, the latter in this case sometimes given a matching downward prolongation ฦ. The value here is technically long *ru':*, but items now pronounced with the three other sounds noted above can be found in early texts spelled with ฤา. Similar principles apply to a parallel symbol ฦ *lu'*, encountered only in a few archaic contexts but still found on official lists of vowels.

▬▬▬

Tone rules

TABLE 43.9A shows how tone is assigned to a written syllable—differently for Thai and Lao—through a combination of four criteria: (i) class of initial consonant; (ii) whether the syllable is open, i.e. ends with a long vowel, nasal (*-m, -n, -ng*) or semivowel (*-w, -y*); or closed, i.e. ends with a stop sound (*-p, -t, -k*) or a glottal-stopped short vowel; (iii) whether the syllable is unmarked or bears a superscript tone marker (mainly used with open syllables); (iv) if closed, whether the vowel is long or short. Tones are more standardized for Thai than for Lao. Lao values in TABLE 43.9B like low falling and high falling apply to one common Vientiane dialect. The relation of

TABLE 43.9: *Main Tone Rules*

	OPEN SYLLABLES			CLOSED SYLLABLES	
	Unmarked	*Marker* –	*Marker* –	*Short Vowel*	*Long Vowel*
A. Main Thai Tone Rules (tones marked as in Haas 1964)					
Class 1	mid	low (ˋ)	falling (ˆ)	low (ˋ)	low (ˋ)
Class 2	rising (ˇ)	low (ˋ)	falling (ˆ)	low (ˋ)	low (ˋ)
Class 3	mid	falling (ˆ)	high (ˊ)	high (ˊ)	falling (ˆ)
B. Main Lao Tone Rules (tones marked as in Kerr 1972)					
Class 1	low	mid (ˉ)	high falling (ˋ)	high (ˊ)	low falling (ˆ)
Class 2	low rising (ˇ)	mid (ˉ)	low falling (ˆ)	high (ˊ)	low falling (ˆ)
Class 3	high (ˊ)	mid (ˉ)	high falling (ˋ)	mid (ˉ)	high falling (ˋ)

TABLE 43.10: *Numerals*

	1	2	3	4	5	6	7	8	9	0
Thai	๑	๒	๓	๔	๕	๖	๗	๘	๙	๐
Lao	໑	໒	໓	໔	໕	໖	໗	໘	໙	໐

tone to orthography in other Lao varieties and in regional Thai dialects is subject to the four criteria above, but specific tone values differ.

In addition to the two main tone markers ⟶ (*má:y-è:k*) and ⟶ (*máy-tho:*) shown in TABLE 43.9, two less frequent extra ones, of similar shape in Thai and Lao, are restricted to Class 1 consonants: ⟶ Thai high, Lao high falling; and ⟶ Thai rising, Lao low rising.

Markers are occasionally used with closed syllables, mainly for onomatopoetic effect, to override the closed-syllable values given by the tone rules: Thai อื๊ด *ó:t* 'buzz'. The exact alignment of tone markers varies, with Lao preferring placement directly over initial consonant and Thai often aligning markers right of center. When a tone marker occurs with a superscript vowel symbol, the tone marker is aligned on top: Thai นั้น *nán* 'that'; Lao ນັ້ນ *nàn*.

Numerals and other symbols

Thai and Lao have distinctive sets of numerals as in TABLE 43.10. These combine in normal decimal fashion. Other symbols: ๆ repeat sign; ฯ abbreviation sign; ฯลฯ et cetera sign; ์ silent letter diacritic.

SAMPLE TEXTS

Below are similar passages in Thai and Lao scripts, first in unspaced form as they would actually occur, then shown word-by-word. In the Thai transliteration, for convenience in identifying individual symbols, words of Indic or Khmero-Indic provenance are transliterated using "Indic prototype" source consonants as indicated in TABLE 43.3. For other (non-Indic) lexical items, and for Lao, standard alphabetic values are used. The tone-class of each syllable-initial consonant is indicated by subscript numbers, both as an aid to identification in TABLE 43.3 and to facilitate tone-rule application in TABLE 43.9. Tone markers *má:y-è:k* and *má:y-tho:* are indicated by superscript I and II respectively. The homophonous vowels ใ and ไ are similarly differentiated as ay_1 and ay_2 respectively. Silent-marked letters are parenthesized.

SAMPLE OF THAI

คำภาษาไทยให้เขียนตามหลักเกณฑ์นิรุกติศาสตร์

1. Thai:	คำ	ภาษา	ไทย	ให้	เขียน	ตาม	หลัก
2. Transliteration:	kh₃am	bh₃a:s₂a:	th₃ai₁y	h₂ai₂[II]	kh₂ian	t₁a:m	h₂lak
3. Transcription:	kham	pha:să:	thay	hây	khĭan	ta:m	làk
4. Gloss:	word	language	Thai	let	write	follow	basis

1.	เกณฑ์	นิรุกติศาสตร์
2.	k₁e:n̩(d̩)	n₃ir₃ukt₁iś₂a:st(r)
3.	ke:n	nirúktisà:t
4.	rule	etymology

'Words in the Thai language should be written on the basis of principles of etymology.'

SAMPLE OF LAO

ຄຳພາສາລາວໃຫ້ຂຽນຕາມສຽງເວົ້າ

1. Lao:	ຄຳ	ພາສາ	ລາວ	ໃຫ້	ຂຽນ	ຕາມ	ສຽງ	ເວົ້າ
2. Translit.:	kh₃am	ph₃a:s₂a:	l₃a:w	h₂ai₂[II]	kh₂ian	t₁a:m	s₂iang	vaw[II]
3. Transcr.:	khám	phá:să:	lá:w	hây	khĭan	ta:m	sĭaŋ	vàw
4. Gloss:	word	language	Lao	let	write	follow	sound	speak

'Words in the Lao language should be written according to pronunciation.'

Bibliography

Brown, J. Marvin. 1985. *From Ancient Thai to Modern Dialects and Other Writings on Historical Thai Linguistics.* Bangkok: White Lotus. (Original publications, 1965–79.)

Chamberlain, James R. 1991. *The Ramkhamhaeng Controversy.* Bangkok: Siam Society.

Danwiwat, Nanthana. 1987. *The Thai Writing System.* Hamburg: Buske.

Gagneux, Pierre-Marie. 1983. "Les écritures lao et leur évolution du XVe au XIXe siècles."*Asie du Sud-est et Monde Insulindien* 14 (1–2): 75–96.

Haas, Mary R. 1956. *The Thai System of Writing.* Washington, D.C.: American Council of Learned Societies.

———. 1964. *Thai-English Student's Dictionary.* Stanford, Calif.: Stanford University Press.

Hartmann, John F. 1986. "The Spread of South Indic Scripts in Southeast Asia." *Crossroads* 3.1:6–20. DeKalb, Ill: Northern Illinois University, Center for Southeast Asian Studies.

Henderson, Eugénie J. A. 1964. "Marginalia to Siamese Phonetic Studies." In *In Honour of Daniel Jones,* ed. David Abercrombie, pp. 415–24. London: Longmans.

Kerr, Allen D. 1972. *Lao–English Dictionary.* Washington, D.C.: The Catholic University of America Press.

Li, Fang Kuei. 1977. *A Handbook of Comparative Tai* (Oceanic Linguistics Special Publication 15) Honolulu: University Press of Hawaii.

Khmer Writing

ERIC SCHILLER

The signary used in the Khmer language is an Indic-based script which dates back about 1500 years. It was used in inscriptions as far back as the sixth century and remains in use throughout Cambodia. The system is highly complex. Much of the complexity is due to its long history, since the phonology of the language has changed radically while the writing system has remained fairly constant.

The writing system is alphasyllabic (see SECTION 31) and written from left to right. The primary graphic element represents a consonant, with vowels indicated by symbols on either side of the consonant or hovering above or below. The consonant is written first, and then the vowel is added, even if the vowel sign is written to the left of the consonant. The space below the primary consonant is used for secondary consonants. Diacritics which affect the interpretation of the consonant appear both above and below the consonant, sometimes shifting position depending on the shape of the consonant.

Modern Khmer writing uses a baseline approach, with the primary consonant sitting on the baseline; some letters have descenders below the line. The remnants of a historical "top line" are built into some letters, in the part known as the 'hair'. Khmer was originally carved in stone and written on palm leaves.

———

The symbols

Consonants

There are 33 consonant symbols, presented in TABLE 44.1, organized by phonological characteristics representing their Indic origin. The symbols are arranged in seven rows, five of which reflect the point of articulation of the consonant, proceeding forward from the back of the mouth; the sixth and seventh rows are reserved for miscellaneous items. One must keep in mind, however, that these phonological characteristics apply to an ancient form of the language, and that the presence of voiced aspirates at that stage is doubtful. Boxed letters are "series 1," others are "series 2," and this determines the pronunciation of vowels following them (see below).

Methods of transliteration vary, especially with regard to the retroflexes and *v/w*. Transliteration is generally based on the historical/Indic values of the letters, and therefore it can differ greatly from transcriptions, which are based on the modern pho-

TABLE 44.1: *Khmer Consonants*

| | VOICELESS PLOSIVES | | | | VOICED PLOSIVES | | | | | | NASALS | |
	Unaspirated		*Aspirated*			*Unaspirated*		*Aspirated*				
Velar	ñ	k [k]	ʒ	kh [kʰ]	ñ	g [k]	ឈ	gh [kʰ]	ង	ṅ [ŋ]		
Palatal	ប	c [c]	ឆ	ch [cʰ]	ណ	j [c]	ឈ	jh [cʰ]	ញ	ñ [ɲ]		
Retroflex	ដ	ṭ [ɗ]	ឋ	ṭh [tʰ]	ឌ	ḍ [ɗ]	ឍ	ḍh [tʰ]	ណ	ṇ [n]		
Dental	ត	t [t]	ថ	ṭh [tʰ]	ទ	d [t]	ធ	ḍh [tʰ]	ន	n [n]		
Bilabial	ប	p [ɓ]	ផ	ph [pʰ]	ព	b [p]	ភ	bh [pʰ]	ម	m [m]		

	SONORANTS AND OTHERS									
Misc. voiced	យ	y [j]	រ	r [r]	ល	l [l]	វ	v [w]	
Misc. voiceless	ស	s [s]	ហ	h [h]	ឡ	ḷ [l]	អ	ʔ [ʔ]	

nology. There are alternative forms of the consonants used in consonant clusters, derived from these basic shapes, as shown in TABLE 44.3.

Vowels

The vowel system of Modern Khmer is very complex, and there is still no consensus on the number of phonemes involved. From the standpoint of the writing system, the greatest complication is that each vowel symbol can have two different sound values, depending on the consonant to which it is attached. There are 21 dependent vowel signs, which must be used in conjunction with a consonant; they are transliterated in TABLE 44.2 with their traditional names, which begin with ñ *ʔ*. There are also some independent vowel signs, used when the vowel is not attached to any consonant.

When no vowel symbol is used, an inherent vowel is assumed, which can have three different values. If the vowel follows a consonant of the first series, it is pronounced [ɒː], while the second series value is [ɔː]. In Sanskrit and Pali loans, however, [a] is often used. Sometimes words which consist only of a single consonant and the inherent vowel are written with the diacritic *asdā* – in order to avoid confusion with longer words, since Khmer writing does not place spaces between words. An example is ñ [kɔː], a grammatical particle. The diacritic *saññōksañña* – is applied in cases where the inherent vowel is shortened (and may be later diphthongized) , e.g., ñ1ñ *gāt* [koɑt] 'a pronoun, usually third person singular'.

TABLE 44.2: *Khmer Vowel Signs and Transliterations*

Independent	Diacritic		Transliteration	Independent	Diacritic		Transliteration
អ	–	អ	ʔa		ឥ	ិ	ʔē
អា	–ា	អា	ʔā	ឫ	ឦ	ិ	ʔɛ
ឥ	–	ឥ	ʔi	ឩ	ឦ	ិ	ʔay
ឥ	–	ឦ	ʔī	ឨ, ឳ	ឱ	ិ	ʔō
	–	អ	ʔɨ	ឩ	ឱ	ិ	ʔaw
	–	អ	ʔɨ̄		ិ	អ	ʔum
ឩ	ិ	អ	ʔo		ិ	អ	ʔom
ឩ	ិ	អ	ʔū		ិ	អា	ʔam
ឩ	ិ	អា	ʔəw		ិ	អ៖	ʔah
	ិ	អ	ʔuə	ឫ	ិ	ិ	ŗ
	ិ	អ	ʔə̄	ឬ	ិ	ិ	r̄
	ិ	អ	ʔiə	ឭ	ិ	ិ	ḷ
	ិ	អ	ʔiə	ឮ	ិ	ិ	ḹ

Clusters

When a syllable begins with two consecutive consonants, the second consonant is written as a subscript to the first; in that case, a vowel that appears below the consonant is written underneath the subscript, e.g., ភ្ *phcuər* [phcuə] 'to plow'. In addition, geminate consonants in words borrowed from Sanskrit and Pali are often written as doubled consonants (see TABLE 44.3), though there is no phonological gemination in Khmer: អតេកច្ចបុក្កល *ʔatēkecchabokkal* [ʔateːkecchəbokuəl] 'fatalist'.

Special cases

There are a variety of special forms which apply to combinations of letters. Thus បា is used for the combination of [b] + [aː], to avoid confusion with ហា [haː]. The letter ហ្ (*h + ph*) is an artificial constuct used for the foreign sound [f], e.g., កាហ្វេ [kaːfeː] 'coffee'.

TABLE 44.3: *Khmer Consonants with Subscript Forms*[a]

Velar	ñ	k	ꞵ	kh	ñ	g	ꞵ	gh	ꞵ	ṅ
Palatal	ꞵ	c	ꞵ	ch	ꞵ	j	ꞵ	jh	ꞵ	ñ
Retroflex	ꞵ	ṭ	ꞵ	ṭh	ꞵ	ḍ	ꞵ	ḍh	ꞵ	ṇ
Dental	ñ	t	ꞵ	th	ꞵ	d	ꞵ	dh	ꞵ	n
Bilabial	ꞵ	p	ꞵ	ph	ꞵ	b	ñ	bh	ꞵ	m
Misc. voiced	ꞵ	y	ꞵ	r	ꞵ	l	ꞵ	v		
Misc. voiceless	ꞵ	s	ꞵ	h	ꞵ	ḷ	ꞵ	ʔ		

a. The full forms of consonants are for identification only; most of the clusters represented here do not occur in the language.

Correspondences

The modern pronunciation of these sounds is quite far from those of Old Khmer, and varies significantly in regional dialects. As the pronunciation of the Phnom Penh dialect is not very representative of Khmer as a whole, the Battambang dialect is used throughout this section. The sound system of Khmer has undergone several radical changes. A voicing contrast in initial consonants gave way to a contrast in phonation type of the following vowel. The voiced consonants lost their voicing but the following vowels retained a reflection of this voicing when they acquired a breathy phonation type ("register"). Eventually this breathy phonation type disappeared, leaving behind only an altered vowel quality. These changes are summarized in TABLE 44.4, which also shows the written form of these Khmer sounds. Note that the same vowel symbol now represents two different sounds in most cases.

It should be noted that details of both transliteration and transcription vary in orthography. The transcription of diphthongs in particular varies widely. In fact, one rarely finds two scholars using the same approach. The most common systems are those described in Henderson 1952, Jacob 1968, Huffman 1970, and Diffloth 1992. The system used here is based on Diffloth's.

The relationship betwen consonant series and vowel quality is made more elaborate by the use of diacritics that "switch" series. For example, to combine *m*, in series 2, with [aː], in series 1, one adds a diacritic, *trəysap* ″; compare ម៉ា *mā* [miə] 'uncle' and ម៉ាក *māk* [maːk] 'mark'. (For series 1 consonants, a *mūsekətoən* ̈ is used.) The situation is further complicated by the fact that vowels and elements of the consonant sometimes occupy the area above the main consonant. In the word ស៊ី [siː] 'to eat' the vowel [iː] is written on top of the *s*, so that there is no room for a *trəysap*. In such cases, a different diacritic is used, the *kbieh kraom*, which is identical to the vowel *u*, underneath the consonant symbol.

TABLE 44.4: *Khmer Vowel Series*

	FIRST SERIES			SECOND SERIES	
Written	*Transliteration*	*Transcription*	*Written*	*Transliteration*	*Transcription*
ក	ka	[kɒː]	គ	ga	[kɔː]
កា	kā	[kaː]	គា	gā	[kiə]
កិ	ki	[ke]	គិ	gi	[ki]
កី	kī	[kəi]	គី	gī	[kiː]
កឹ	kɨ	[kə]	គឹ	gɨ	[kɨ]
កឺ	kɨ̄	[kəɨ]	គឺ	gɨ̄	[kɨː]
កុ	ku	[ko]	គុ	gu	[ku]
កូ	kū	[kou]	គូ	gū	[kuː]
កួ	kuə	[kuə]	គួ	guə	[kuə]
កើ	kə̄	[kaə]	គើ	gə̄	[kəː]
កឿ	kɨə	[kɨə]	គឿ	gɨə	[kɨə]
កៀ	kiə	[kiə]	គៀ	giə	[kiə]
កេ	kē	[kei]	គេ	kē	[keː]
កែ	kɛ̄	[kae]	គែ	kɛ̄	[kɛː]
កៃ	kay	[kay]	គៃ	gay	[kɨy]
កោ	kō	[kao]	គោ	gō	[koː]
កៅ	kaw	[kau]	គៅ	gaw	[kɨw]
កុំ	kum	[kom]	គុំ	gum	[kum]
កំ	kəm	[kɒm]	គំ	gəm	[kum]
កាំ	kam	[kam]	គាំ	gam	[koə̯m]
កះ	kah	[kah]	គះ	gah	[keə̯h]

In addition, Indic loanwords obey a different set of pronunciation guidelines, which are not consistently followed. A detailed discussion is presented in Jacob 1968: 47–51. For example, the initial consonant transliterated as *b* ប is pronounced [p] in such loans as បារាសិត *bārāsit* [paːraːsət] 'parasite', but in Indic words which have become assimilated to the Khmer vocabulary it is pronounced [ɓ], for example បុណ្យ *boṇy* [ɓon] 'religious festival' (cf. Sanskrit *puṇya* 'merit'). Highly important religious terms are not immune to naturalization, so that the most sacred terms have been absorbed: ពុទ្ធ *buddh* [put] 'Buddha', ធម៌ *dharm* [tɔə̯] 'Dharma, law', សង្ឃ *saṅgh*

TABLE 44.5: *Khmer Numerals*

1	2	3	4	5	6	7	8	9	0
១	២	៣	៤	៥	៦	៧	៨	៩	០

[sɒŋ] 'Sangha, priesthood'. The word *dharm* also illustrates the symbol ~ *rəbāt*, used to write preconsonantal *r* in Indic loanwords.

Note that many final consonants are not pronounced. A sign used to indicate unpronounced elements of some loanwords is the *toəndəkhiet* 'kill sign' ˗, e.g. សិតិការណ៍ *sitəkārṇ* [sətəka:] 'smile'.

The lack of consistency with regard to matters of transcription and transliteration is even evident in the name of the country where most Khmer speakers reside. កម្ពុជា is, in transliteration, *kambujā*, but the modern pronunciation is [kampuciə]. This is reflected in the official name of the country, which was Kampuchea until quite recently, when the older form (Cambodia) has made a comeback due to political changes. The Khmer spelling has remained constant, however.

Punctuation and numerals

Words are not separated in Khmer script. A marker ។ *khan* is used to indicate change of topic and comes at the end of what amounts to a group of sentences, though often less than a paragraph. A special sign ២ *tō* indicates that the previous word or group of words is repeated. This is a common sign, because Khmer morphology applies reduplication for a variety of grammatical purposes.

Some colloquial words are written with a *kākbāt* ˗ on top, e.g., ចាស់ [cah] 'response particle used in women's speech'.

The numerals are shown in TABLE 44.5.

SAMPLE OF KHMER

ពេលនោះគាត់រុតបានត្រីរស់មួយហើយនិងបានទន្សាយលង់ទឹកមួយ

1. Khmer:	ពេល	នោះ	គាត់	រុត បាន	ត្រី រស់	មួយ
2. Transliteration:	pēl	nuh	gāt	rut bān	trī rah	muəy
3. Transcription:	pe:l	nuh	koət	rut ɓa:n	trəi rɒh	muəy
4. Gloss:	time	that	PRON	fish.with.basket	trei-rah	one

1.	ហើយ	និង	បាន	ទន្សាយ	លង់	ទឹក	មួយ
2.	hōy	niŋ	bān	dansāy	laŋ	dɨk	muəy
3.	haəj	nəŋ	ɓa:n	toənsa:j	loəŋ	tɨk	muəj
4.	already	then	get	rabbit	sink	water	one

'At that time, he fished out a trei-rah (kind of fish) and then got a rabbit which was drowning in the water.'   *—From a Khmer folktale.*

———————

Bibliography

Diffloth, Gérard. 1992. "Khmer." *International Encyclopedia of Linguistics,* ed. William Bright, vol. 2, pp. 271–75. New York: Oxford University Press.

Henderson, Eugénie J. A. 1952. "The Main Features of Cambodian Pronunciation." *Bulletin of the School of Oriental and African Studies* 1952: 149-74.

Huffman, Franklin E. 1970. *Cambodian System of Writing and Beginning Reader.* New Haven: Yale University Press.

Jacob, Judith M. 1968. *Introduction to Cambodian.* London: Oxford University Press.

———. 1974. *A Concise Cambodian–English Dictionary.* London: Oxford University Press.

Insular Southeast Asian Scripts

JOEL C. KUIPERS AND RAY MCDERMOTT

In 1593, two writing systems were united on the pages of the first book published in the Philippines, a *Doctrina Christiana*, which represented Spanish with a Roman (specifically Gothic Rotunda) script and Tagalog with an Indic script (Conklin 1991). About 2,500 years before, the two scripts had separated from their West Semitic ancestor and started to make their way around the world: one, Phoenician, headed west, took on new forms in Greece and Rome, spread throughout Europe, and continued to the Americas; the other, Aramaic, headed east, took on new forms in India, and spread, with continuing new forms, through most of mainland Southeast Asia (minus Vietnam) and the full extent of Indonesia before reaching the Philippines as late as 1300 C.E., probably by way of Sulawesi (Celebes). After circling the world in opposite directions, the two scripts were reunited when Spanish ships crossed the Pacific from Acapulco to Manila only years before the publication of the *Doctrina*.

The Insular Southeast Asian portion of the script circle developed over a millennium as the South Indian scripts of the Pallava dynasty joined commerce and religion in crossing the 3000 miles from the Straits of Malacca to the Philippines (de Casparis 1975, Noorduyn 1991, Scott 1984). Longstanding textual traditions have been attested by writings on stone and copper plates (Java and Bali, 9th century), bark books (Sumatra: Batak and Rejang, 18th century), latterday copies of earlier lontar leaf manuscripts (Sulawesi: Buginese and Makasarese, 14th century), and firsthand reports by travelers and missionaries (Philippines, 16th century). Some traditions of writing were extensive; missionary reports from the Philippines, for example, claim universal literacy for the sixteenth century (Reid 1988). Under Western colonial influence, the Indic script traditions of Insular Southeast Asia have been in all cases made marginal to Roman and sometimes Arabic scripts, but survive in traditional contexts under local circumstances and in schools for children in Java, Bali, Sulawesi, and the Philippines (Kaseng 1978, Postma 1989).

―――

Structure and historical continuity: The Holle charts

In 1877, K. F. Holle gathered 198 exemplars of scripts from India and much of Southeast Asia and displayed them in 52 pages of charts to show conclusively that they

ACKNOWLEDGMENTS: Harold C. Conklin, Joseph Errington, Nancy Florida, Robert H. Kasberg, Jr., Usud Kasidsid, Sirtyo Koolhof, and Lt. Col. Drs. Barsi Sidehabi contributed materials and wisdom to this survey.

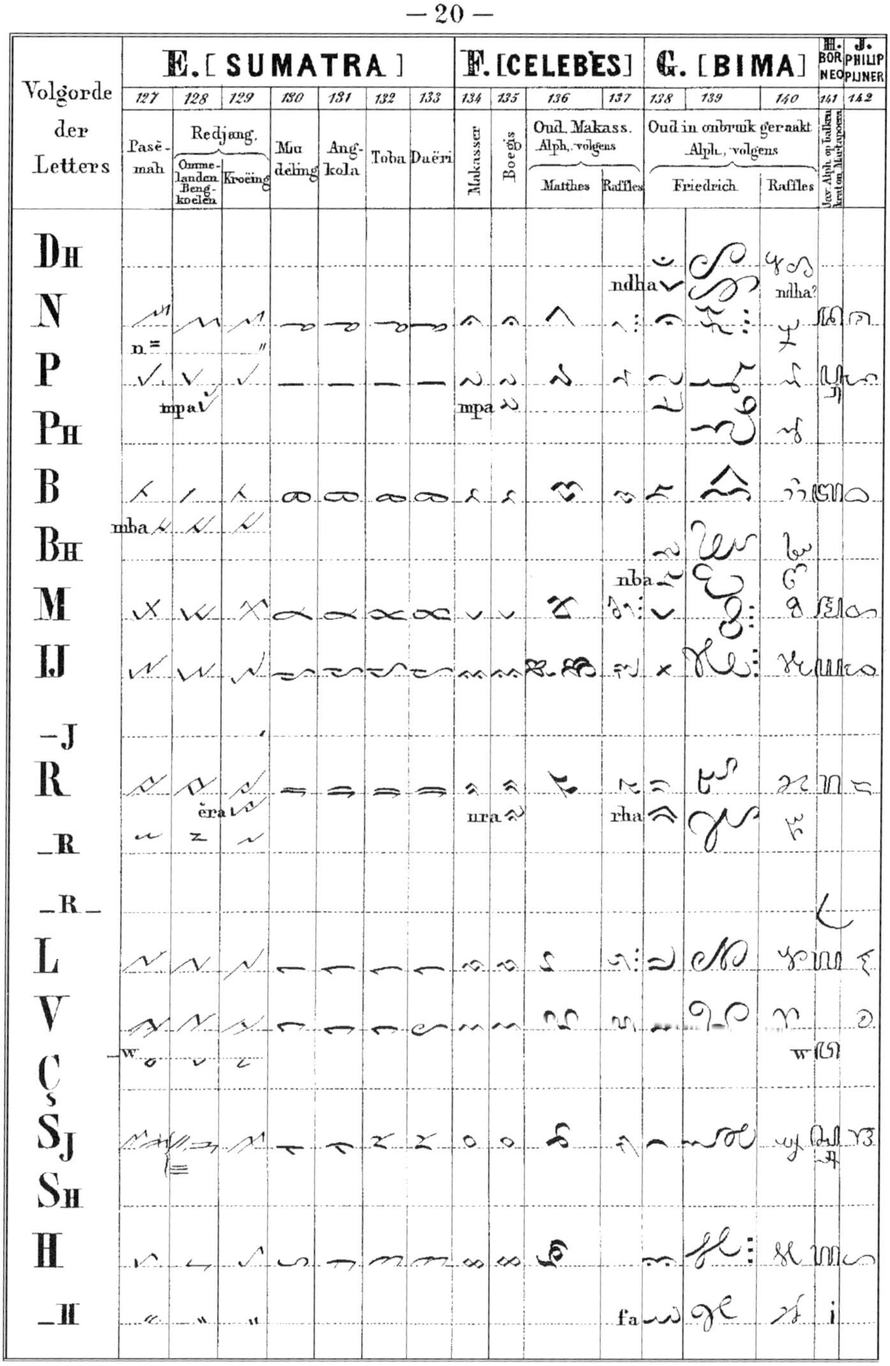
— 20 —
Volgorde der Letters
E. [SUMATRA]
F. [CELEBES]
G. [BIMA]
H. BORNEO
J. PHILIP PIJNER
127
128
129
130
131
132
133
134
135
136
137
138
139
140
141
142
Pasě-mah
Redjang.
Onme-landen Beng-koelen
Kroëing
Man-deling
Ang-kola
Toba
Daëri
Makasser
Boegis
Oud. Makass. Alph. volgens
Matthes
Raffles
Oud in onbruik geraakt Alph. volgens
Friedrich
Raffles
DH
N
P
PH
B
BH
M
IJ
–J
R
_R
_R_
L
V
Ç
SJ
SH
H
_H
ndha
ndha?
n =
mpa
mba
nba
ĕra
ura
rha
w
fa
i

FIGURE 56. Page 20 from Holle (1877), showing a continuity in sixteen scripts, listed west to east from Sumatra through Sulawesi to the Philippines.

comprised a single group of scripts. The charts were constructed by listing the names of Sanskrit letters in the left-hand column and lining the rows with the scripts in order from west to east; thus, columns 1–15 show scripts from India, column 20 gives us Tibet, 28 Khmer, 55–64 Old Javanese, 111 Bali, 132 Toba Batak, and 142 a few graphs from the Philippines. FIGURE 56 displays one chart showing both the similarities and the variations in graphic systems from Sumatra, Sulawesi, and the Philippines. Aside from the peculiarly florid Bima script columns, the other rows all exhibit easy-to-imagine continuities. Where the Rejang (129) give a diamond shape to the *ra* syllable, the Toba Batak (132) flatten it out, and the Buginese (135) elevate the middle. Such patterned variation provides internal coherence to individual systems of graphs, as well as systematic contrast between them. In a small volume explicating the charts, Holle (1882) advises that the differences among the scripts can be seen to "have taken place in gradual fashion," and, if the intermediary forms are included, "the sequence of changes and the relationship become clear."

Indic scripts are fairly thorough in representing consonant–vowel syllables (CV) or, more precisely, consonants which, when unmarked, end with an inherent *a* sound. Most systems also contain graphs for independent vowels, diacritics for altering the vowel sounds accompanying the initial consonants, and a few graphs for special purposes. From the scripts listed in FIGURE 56, for example, Rejang consists of 23 consonantal characters, plus 13 diacritics for changing or eliminating the inherent *a* (Jaspan 1964); Toba Batak consists of 16 consonantal characters, 3 vocalic characters, 4 named diacritics that change or delete the inherent *a*, another diacritic that gives a syllable a final velar nasal *ṅ*, and long curved punctuation marks indicating paragraph boundaries and textual structures (Tuuk 1867). In South Sulawesi, the Indic script includes three dots to mark off sentence boundaries and the use of red ink to mark the first graph of a personal name (Hilgers-Hesse 1967).

Writers working in languages with many closed syllables (CVC as a minimum form) have developed an interesting range of responses to the open-syllable graphs of the Indic scripts. The Sumatran scripts developed a special mark to eliminate the vowel of the previous syllable, thereby leaving a consonant in a syllable-final position. Old Javanese (Kawi) retains the Indic device of writing consonant clusters by putting one consonant symbol below another (see the sample of Javanese on page 479). The Sulawesi and Philippine scripts stand at the opposite extreme and leave their final consonants with no representation. This is not surprising in the first case, for the open-syllable languages of Sulawesi had little need to add syllable-final consonants; but the Philippine languages, rich in closed syllables, could have used such representation, but did not develop it. Together the two cases are taken as an argument for the Philippine scripts developing from the Sulawesi scripts: if Philippine writers had received a script with conventions for representing closed syllables, they would have kept them (Conklin 1949A, Scott 1984).

Cultural uses of the writing systems of Insular Southeast Asia

For graphic form, the Holle charts display both a continuity across time and space and a diversity under local conditions. Study of the cultural use of the scripts can show the same, although weaker pattern. At first glance, the continuities are overwhelming. In most examples—Kawi almanacs, Batak love magic, Rejang maxims, and South Sulawesi medical lore—a people use literacy to document their entreaties to the spirit world, to state the goals and rules governing social behavior, and to enjoy songs and other aesthetic pleasures. Record-keeping, taxation, and science—the usually acclaimed uses and consequences of literacy—are subordinate or absent (as in ancient India). There is diversity as well. Despite continuities in use across the cultures of Insular Southeast Asia, ethnographic accounts reveal the importance of local contexts.

Sumatra: Batak

Among the Batak, the *pustaha* 'tree bark manuscripts' are written in syllabary from left to right, and sometimes vertically. Used by *datu* 'priests' to write the Malay, Toba, Dairi, Asahan, Mandailing, and Angkola languages, the Batak script is devoted largely to recording magical formulae and calendrical information. Writing is said to be a predominantly male activity.

Sumatra: Rejang

The script used by the Rejang is often called *ka-ga-nga* for its first three syllables, listed in the usual Indic order. The Rejang use the script to represent love songs (in a literary language), spells, incantations, maxims, clan histories, and some closely guarded epics by inscribing them on materials such as bark cloth, bamboo, rattan, buffalo horn, and (now lost) copper plates. Jaspan (1964) found only a few hundred literates among 180,000 Rejang speakers.

Java and Bali

Kawi (literally 'poetry') refers to both a special register of Old (and sometimes Middle) Javanese and the script (*aksara jawa*) by which it is represented. In contemporary Java, the *kawi* speech register is used regularly only in *wayang* shadow puppet dramas when the puppeteer stops the action of the play to sing *kawi* verses called *suluk*. The audiences and even the performers rarely understand the words. Most *kawi* genres are literary and aesthetic: fables, epics, chronicles, but the script is used for almanacs as well. In Bali, *kawi* is a more productive literary medium; it is still the language of traditional ritual and in law courts.

TABLE 45.1: *Javanese Vowels*

Initial			*Diacritic* (k-)		*Name*
ꦄ	a	[a]	–	ꦏ	–
–	e, ĕ	[ə]	◌ꦼ	ꦏꦼ	pepet
ꦆ	i	[i]	◌ꦶ	ꦏꦶ	wulu
ꦈ	u, oe	[u]	◌ꦸ	ꦏꦸ	suku
ꦌ	e, é/è	[e, ɛ]	ꦺ◌	ꦏꦺ	taling
ꦎ	o	[o]	ꦺ◌ꦴ	ꦏꦺꦴ	taling-tarung

The Javanese script (written left to right) retains the essential property of its alphasyllabic antecedent (SECTION 31), placing vowel symbols (*sandhangan swara*; TABLE 45.1) around consonant symbols (*aksara*; TABLE 45.2). The conventional order of listing the consonants reflects a saying, ꦲꦤꦕꦫꦏ ꦢꦠꦱꦮꦭ ꦥꦝꦗꦪꦚ ꦩꦒꦧꦛꦔ *Hana caraka, data sawala, padha jayanya, maga bathanga* 'There were (two) emissaries, they began to fight, their valor was equal, they both fell dead' (Bohatta 1892: 7–8). Consonant clusters are noted only by means of "sub-

TABLE 45.2: *Javanese Consonants*

Letter	*"Subscript"*	*Capital*	*"Subscript"*	*Transliteration*	*Transcription*
ꦲ	꧀ꦲ	–	–	–, ha	Ø
ꦤ	꧀ꦤ	ꦟ	–	na	[na]
ꦕ	꧀ꦕ	–	꧀ꦖ	ca, tja	[ʧa]
ꦫ	꧀ꦫ	–	–	ra	[ra]
ꦏ	꧀ꦏ	ꦑ	꧀ꦑ	ka	[ka]
ꦢ	꧀ꦢ	–	–	da	[da]
ꦠ	꧀ꦠ	ꦡ	꧀ꦡ	ta	[ta]
ꦱ	꧀ꦱ	ꦯ, ꦰ	꧀ꦯ, ꧀ꦰ	sa	[sa]
ꦮ	꧀ꦮ	–	–	wa	[wa]
ꦭ	꧀ꦭ	–	–	la	[la]
ꦥ	꧀ꦥ	ꦦ	꧀ꦦ	pa	[pa]
ꦝ	꧀ꦝ	–	–	dha, ḍa	[ɖa]
ꦗ	꧀ꦗ	–	–	ja, dja	[ʤa]
ꦪ	꧀ꦪ	–	–	ya, ja	[ja]
ꦚ	꧀ꦚ	–	–	nya, ñaa	[ɲa]
ꦩ	꧀ꦩ	–	–	m	[ma]
ꦒ	꧀ꦒ	ꦓ	꧀ꦓ	ga	[ga]
ꦧ	꧀ꦧ	ꦨ	꧀ꦨ	ba	[ba]
ꦛ	꧀ꦛ	–	–	tha, ṭa	[ʈa]
ꦔ	꧀ꦔ	–	–	nga	[ŋa]
ꦉ	꧀ꦉ	–	–	rĕ	[rɔ]
ꦊ	꧀ꦊ	–	–	lĕ	[lɔ]

TABLE 45.3: *Javanese Punctuation*

Symbol	Name	Function
(꧋)	pada-luhur	introduces a letter to a person of lower rank
(꧋)	pada-madya	introduces a letter to a person of equal rank
(꧋)	pada-handhap	introduces a letter to a person of higher rank
(꧋) ꧅ (꧋)	purwa-pada	introduces a poem
(꧋) ꧅ (꧋)	madya-pada	demarcates a new song within a poem
(꧋) ꧅ (꧋)	wasana-pada	concludes a poem
꧇꧇	pada-bab	introduces a chapter or major part
꧈	pada-lungsi	comma
꧉	pada-lingsa	period
꧇	pada-handhegging-celathu	colon, quotation marks, designates numerals

TABLE 45.4: *Javanese Numerals*

0	1	2	3	4	5	6	7	8	9
꧐	꧑	꧒	꧓	꧔	꧕	꧖	꧗	꧘	꧙

script" forms written below or after the first consonant; except that following *-r-* takes the form of *cakra* (꧁. "Capital" forms (*aksara gedhe*) of some letters are used throughout proper names, etc. (not just initially). There are diacritics for four syllable-final consonants: *cecak* ꧆ *-ng*, *layar* ꧆ *-r*, *wignyan* ꧆ *-h*, and *pengkal* ꧆ *-y*. Vowelless-ness is marked with ꧆ *pangku*. Sounds borrowed from Arabic or Malay are indicated with the diacritic ꧆ over a similar-sounding Javanese letter. The distinctive punctua-tion marks of Javanese are shown in TABLE 45.3, and the numerals in TABLE 45.4.

Javanese script has largely been replaced by the Roman alphabet, and the equiv-alences are given as the transliterations; earlier, largely Dutch-based, practice is shown after the comma in the tables.

SAMPLE OF JAVANESE

1. *Javanese:*	꧍	꧍	꧍	꧍	꧍	꧍
2. *Transliteration:*	Haja	mung	seneng	yenlagi	darbe	panguwasa,
3. *Transcription:*	ɔ'ʤɔ	muŋ	sə'nəŋ	yɛn la'gi:	dar'be	pəŋuwɔ'sɔ
4. Gloss:	don't	only	happy	when.in.act.of	hold	power

1. ꧍	꧍	꧍	꧍	꧍	꧍
2. seri	kyen lagi	hora	darbe	panguwasa,	jalarran kuwi
3. səri?	yɛn la'gi:	ora	dar'be	pəŋuwɔ'sɔ	ʤalə'ran ku'wi
4. unhappy	when.in.act.of	not	hold	power	because it

1. ꦧꦏꦭ꧀ꦲꦤ   ꦧꦼꦧꦼꦢꦸꦤꦺ   ꦢ꧀ꦲꦺꦮꦺꦢ꧀ꦲꦺꦮꦺ꧈
2. bakal hana   bebedune   dhewedhewe.
3. ba'kal ɔ'nɔ   bəbədu'ne   ḍeweḍe'we
4. result will   burden   oneself

'Do not only be happy when holding power, or unhappy when you do not have power, for these attitudes have their own punishment.' —*Soeharto 1987: 188.*

South Sulawesi: Buginese and Makasarese

Writing is often called *lontara'*, after the palm leaves on which it is often inscribed. A wide range of genres is written by a *palontara'* 'writing specialist' on special occasions such as marriage. At one time both the Buginese and Makasarese extended reading and writing to contracts, trade laws, treaties, and maps to cover extensive commercial and maritime activities (Schwartzberg 1994).

The Buginese script comprises 18 consonant letters and one vowel letter (each with inherent -*a*; TABLE 45.5), as well as diacritics for five vowels (TABLE 45.6). Syllable-final consonants are unexpressed. There is one punctuation mark.

SAMPLE OF BUGINESE

1. *Buginese:*
2. *Transliteration:* eka'   eka'   garé.   eka'   séuwa   wetu.
3. *Transcription:* əŋka   əŋka   gare?   əŋka   seuwa   wəttu
4. *Gloss:*   was   was   story   was   one   time

1.
2. eka'   séuwa   aru   makunrai   ri   luwu.
3. əŋka   seuwa   aruŋ   makunrai   ri   luwu
4. was   one   princess   woman   in   Luwu

1.
2. masala   uli.
3. masala   uli
4. problem   skin

TABLE 45.5: *Buginese Letters*

	ka	[ka]		ga	[ga]		nga	[ŋa]		ka'	[ŋka]
	pa	[pa]		ba	[ba]		ma	[ma]		pa'	[mpa]
	ta	[ta]		da	[da]		na	[na]		nra'	[nra]
	ya	[ja]		ra	[ra]		la	[la]		wa'	[wa]
	sa	[sa]		a	[a]		ha	[ha]			

TABLE 45.6: *Buginese Vowels*

	é	[e]		e	[ə]		ó	[ɔ]		i	[i]		u	[u]

'Once there was a story, once upon a time, about a princess in Luwu with leprosy.'   —*After Damais 1948: 379.*

An arresting case: The Hanunóo of Mindoro, Philippines

With the arrival of the Spanish in the Philippines over four hundred years ago, the Indic scripts fell into disuse in all but the least accessible places. In 1947, Conklin (1949B) found the scripts still in use among three cultural groups, two in the mountains of Mindoro (Hanunóo, Buhid) and one on the island of Palawan (Tagbanua). The Hanunóo still use a distinctive Indic script to read, write, memorize, and exchange messages on a wide range of topics. They use the point of a knife to incise graphs onto bamboo—and, to a lesser extent, trees, house beams, and whatever else comes to hand. The main genre of writing, accounting for up to 85% of written communications, is love songs (Conklin 1949A, 1955, 1960; Postma 1989). The other major function of the script is correspondence. About 70% of the six thousand Hanunóo are literate enough to be full participants in the rounds of courtship and poetry that dominate Hanunóo leisure. Every family has a minimum of one person who can read and write.

Literacy has a central place in Hanunóo culture, and most adolescents achieve it quickly. Not learning carries no penalty, although it is apparently more fun to read, write, and court than just to court (Conklin 1959). In Conklin's (1960) account, a young girl, Maling, at the start of adolescent courtship took an interest in transcribing and memorizing love songs. Within a few months, not long after her original practice texts had likely been devoured by weevils, Maling could write down her own songs. The Hanunóo do not have a conventional order for memorizing their letters, and Maling worked first with the letters of her own name and gradually added new ones. If she had been left-handed, she could have worked in a mirror image, for the Hanunóo read with equal skill in all directions.

Words in Hanunóo are primarily disyllabic, and syllables can be closed by a final consonant in a CVC shape. The Hanunóo script, shown in TABLE 45.7, represents only vowel-final syllables.

Three graphs represent the vowels alone; fifteen graphs represent syllables consisting of a consonant–vowel pair; in addition, each of the fifteen CV syllables can have its final vowel changed by the addition of a *kulit*, a small diacritic on the left or

TABLE 45.7: *The Hanunóo Syllabary (after Conklin 1971)* [a]

	q-	h-	p-	k-	s-	l-	r-	t-	n-	b-	m-	g-	d-	y-	ṅ-	w-
-a~[b]	ⅴ	ⅴ	Ϗ	ⅴ	Ϟ	Ϟ	Ϟ	w	Ϟ	7	Ϗ	Ϟ	Ϟ	ⅴ	Ϗ	Ϟ
-u~	ⅴ	ⅴ	Ϗ	ⅴ	Ϟ	Ϟ	Ϟ	Ϟ	Ϟ	ⅼ	Ϗ	Ϟ	Ϟ	Ϟ	Ϗ	Ϟ
-i~	ⅴ	ⅴ	Ϗ	ⅴ	Ϟ	Ϟ	Ϟ	Ϟ	Ϟ	ⅰ̄	Ϗ	Ϟ	Ϟ	Ϟ	ⅴ	Ϟ

a. Listed in the 16th-century Tagalog sequence, with the addition of *r*-; no Hanunóo order is known today.

b. The symbol ~ represents any consonant or no consonant.

right of the syllable graph that changes, e.g., ⼈ *ba* to ⼈ *bi* or ⼈ *bu*. In TABLE 45.7, the graphs are oriented horizontally, and the *kulit* marks appear on the top and bottom; graphs can be read from any direction, but all the graphs in a single line must be similarly oriented. Each syllable can receive a final consonant, and a reader must use word context to choose from among sixteen possibilities; for example, ⼈ *ba* can be read as [ba], [ba?], [bab], [bad], [bag], [bak], [bal], [bam], [ban], [baŋ], [bap], [bar], [bas], [bat], [baw], or [baj] (Conklin 1953: 9).

Many of the love songs, called '*ambāhan*, take traditional form in a seven-syllable line. The sample text is a seven-line '*ambāhan* (from among thousands available, Postma 1989 offers a translation of 261 ranging in length from 3 to 135 lines). The example is written in columns, from bottom to top, away from the body, as is the usual but not required Hanunóo custom. A two-to-one closed-to-open syllable ratio holds for most '*ambāhan*, although an account of less formal writing would reverse the percentages. In this text, individual Hanunóo graphs are all oriented vertically with the *i* diacritic appearing on the left and the *u* diacritic appearing on the right.

SAMPLE OF HANUNÓO

This '*ambāhan* is sung as a lullaby ('*iyaya*) to a child. Reading proceeds from bottom to top, starting at the left.

1. Hanunóo:													

	1. Hanunóo:							

1. Hanunóo:					
2. Transliteration:	da-ṅa	ma-lu-mi-ma-lu-mi /	ki-ta	ma-nu-ga	ku-ti /
3. Transcription:	da:ŋa	maglumi-maglumi?	kita	madnugan	ku ti?
4. Gloss:	don't	keep.crying	we	will.be.heard	cat

1.					
2.	ku-ti	gi	sa	si-ya-ṅi /	ma-qi-ṅa	ma-ya-ya-ṅi /
3.	kuti	gin	sa	sijaŋi?	mag?iŋaw	magjaŋjaŋi?
4.	cat	coming	from	Siyangi	will.screech	scream

1.	𐑍 𝔀	𝔷	𝓧	𝓥, �7 𝓦	𑀬 𝔀	�7 𑀬	𝓣𝓯 �7 𝓲𝓰
2.	ki-ta	qu	ma	qi-ba-wi /	ka-ta	ba-ka	na-ba-ri /
3.	kita	ʔud	maj	ʔiba:wiʔ	kanta	baŋkaw	naba:riʔ
4.	we	do.not	have	effective.arms	our	spear	is.broken

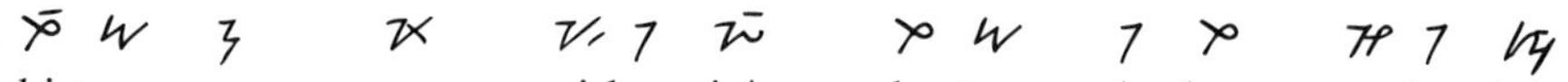

1.	𑀬 𝔀	𝔷 𝔀	𝓣𝓯 𝓲𝓰 �7
2.	ka-ta	qu-ta	na-lu-bi
3.	kanta	ʔutak	nalumbiʔ
4.	our	bolo	is.bent.in.two

'Don't cry anymore, or we'll be heard by the wild cat
The wild cat from Siyangi, who will let out a terrifying cry
And we can't do anything about it, because our hunting spear is broken
And our bolo is bent in two.'
— *From Conklin 1955, side 1, band 4 of the record; page 4 of the booklet.*

Bibliography

GENERAL

Behrend, T. E., and Willem van der Molen, eds. 1994. "Manuscripts of Indonesia." *Bijdragen tot de Taal-, Land- en Volkenkunde* 150: 407–629.

Damais, Louis-Charles. 1952. "Liste des principales inscriptions datées de l'Indonesia." *Bulletin de l'École Française d'Extrème-Orient* 46: 1–105.

———. 1955. "Les écritures d'origine indienne en Indonésie et dans le Sud-Est asiatique continentale." *Bulletin de la Societé des Études Indo-Chinoises* 30: 365–82.

de Casparis, J. G. 1975. *Indonesian Palaeography* (Handbuch der Orientalistik division 3, vol. 4, part 1). Leiden: Brill.

Holle, Karel Frederik. 1877. *Tabel van Oud- en Nieuw-Indische Alphabetten.* Batavia: Bataviaasch Genootschap van Kunsten en Wetenschappen.

———. 1882. *Tabel van Oud- en Nieuw-Indische Alphabetten: Bijdrage tot de Palaeographie van Nederlandsch-Indie.* Batavia: Bruining.

Reid, Anthony. 1988. *Southeast Asia in the Age of Commerce,* vol. 1: *The Lands beneath the Winds.* New Haven: Yale University Press.

Robson, Stuart. 1988. *Principles of Indonesian Philology.* Dordrecht: Foris.

Schwartzberg, Joseph E. 1994. "Southeast Asian Nautical Maps." In *The History of Cartography,* vol. 2, book 2: *Cartography in the Traditional East and Southeast Asian Societes,* ed. John Brian Harley and David Woodward, pp. 828–38 . Chicago: University of Chicago Press.

SUMATRA

Jaspan, Mervyn. 1964. *Redjang Ka-ga-nga Texts.* Canberra: Australian National University.

Tuuk, Hermanus N. van de. 1867. *A Grammar of Toba Batak.* Leiden: Brill. Repr. 1971.

Voorhoeve, Peter. 1950–51. "Batak Bark Manuscripts." *Bulletin of The John Rylands Library* 33: 283–98.

JAVA AND BALI

Bohatta, Hanns. 1892. *Praktische Grammatik der javanischen Sprache.* Vienna: Hartleben.

Damais, Louis-Charles. 1948. "Écriture javanaise." In *Notices sur les caracteres étrangers anciens et modernes,* ed. Charles Fossey, 2nd ed., pp. 353–74. Paris: Imprimerie Nationale de France.

Molen, Willem van der. 1993. *Javaans schrift.* Leiden: Vakgroep Talen en Culturen van Zuidoost-Azi en Oceani, Rijksuniversiteit Leiden.

Pigeaud, Theodor. 1975. *Die Handschriften van Bali und Java.* Wiesbaden: Springer.

[Soeharto]. 1987. *Butir-Butir Budaya Jawa* [Pearls of Javanese culture]. Jakarta: S. N.

Zurbuchen, Mary. 1987. *The Language of Balinese Shadow Theater.* Princeton: Princeton Univ. Pr.

SULAWESI

Damais, Charles. 1948. "Écriture bugie." In *Notices sur les caractères étrangers anciens et modernes,* ed. Charles Fossey, 2nd ed., pp. 375–79. Paris: Imprimerie Nationale de France.

Hilgers-Hesse, Irene. 1967. "Schriftsysteme in Indonesien: Makassaren und Buginesen." *Studium Generale* 20: 548–58.

Kaseng, Syahruddin. 1978. *Kedudukan dan fungsi bahasa Makassar di Sulawesi Selatan.* Jakarta: Pusat Pembinaan dan Pambangunan Bahasa.

Noorduyn, Jacobus. 1991. *A Critical Survey of Studies on the Languages of Sulawesi* (Bibliographical series 18). Leiden: Koninklijk Instituut voor Taal-, Land- en Volkenkunde.

Pelras, Christian. 1979. "L'oral et l'écrit dans la tradition bugis." *Asie du Sud-Est et Monde Insulindien* 10: 271–97.

Tol, Roger. 1990. *Een Haan in Oorlog/Toloqna Arung Labuaja: Een Twintigste-eeuws Buginees Heldendicht van de Hand van I Mallaq Daeng Mabela Arung Manajeng.* Dordrecht: Foris.

PHILIPPINES

Bernardo, Gabriel. 1953. *A Bibliography of the Old Philippine Syllabaries.* Quezon City: Library, University of the Philippines.

Conklin, Harold C. 1949A. "Bamboo Literacy on Mindoro." *Pacific Discovery* 2/4: 4–11.

———. 1949B. "Preliminary Report on Field Work on the Islands of Mindoro and Palawan." *American Anthropologist* 51: 268–73.

———. 1953. *Hanunóo-English Vocabulary* (University of California Publications in Linguistics 9). Berkeley and Los Angeles: University of California Press.

———. 1955. *Hanunóo Music from the Philippines.* Ethnic Folkways Library Album FE4466. New York: Folkways Records. Reissued in 1992 as Smithsonian Institution Folkways Casette 04466.

———. 1959. "Linguistic Play in Its Cultural Context." *Language* 35: 631–36.

———. 1960. "Maling, a Hanunóo girl in the Philippines." In *In the Company of Man,* ed. Joseph Casagrande, pp. 101–18. New York: Harper and Row.

———. 1971. "Indic Scripts of the Philippines." Paper presented at the Oriental Club of New Haven, 11 November 1971.

———. 1991. "*Doctrina Christiana, en lengua espanola y tagala,* Manila, 1593: Rosenwald Collection 1302." In *Vision of a Collector: The Lessing J. Rosenwald Collection in the Library of Congress/Rare Book and Special Collections Division,* ed. K. Mang and P. VanWingen, pp. 36–40, 119. Washington, D.C.: Library of Congress.

Gardiner, Fletcher. 1943. *Philippine Indic Studies.* San Antonio: Witte Memorial Museum.

Postma, Antoon. 1971. "Contemporary Mangyan scripts." *Philippine Journal of Linguistics* 2: 1–12.

———. 1986. *A Primer to Mangyan Script.* Panaytayan.

———. 1989. *Ambahan Mangyan.* Manila: Arnoldus Press.

Revel, Nicole. 1990–92. *Fleurs de paroles: Histoire naturelle Palawan,* 3 vols. Louvain: Peeters.

Romualdez, Norberto. 1914. "Alfabeto Tagbanua." *Cultura Filipina* 5: 53–82.

Scott, William Henry. 1984. *Prehispanic Source Materials for the Study of Philippine History,* 2nd ed. Quezon City: New Day Publisher.

Part VIII: Middle Eastern Writing Systems

In the Middle East, conditions prevailed that were opposite to those driving the spread of writing in Europe: religion, rather than politics, proved to be the principal vector. The first of the "peoples of the Book" were the Jews—a name that becomes appropriate with the post-Exilic period, a time when many scholars believe the text of the Hebrew Bible achieved its final form. The Hebrew language came to be, and still is, written in a form of Aramaic square script (the earlier Hebrew script being maintained only by the Samaritans). The Word of God inherited the sanctity of the Deity, to such an extent that even the slightest scrap of sacred text was to be treated with reverence and not destroyed. This attitude in part lay behind the sequestering of the documents known as the Dead Sea Scrolls, and a thousand or more years later to the keeping of a genizah—a place to store any written refuse, notably that in a Cairo synagogue which has yielded thousands of fragments of documents in several languages pertaining to everyday life as well as to sacred matters.

Christian scholars and missionaries evolved two prominent scripts from epigraphic Semitic predecessors. Cursive developments of the Aramaic branch of the Semitic abjad resulted in the script used for Mandaic and, in numerous Eastern churches, that of Syriac, which has been taken over for some of the related Aramaic languages that survive to the present. Other varieties came into use in (pagan) Iranian empires, successors to the Persian (Achaemenid) Empire of Darius—Arsacid (Parthian), Seleucid, and Sassanian—whence they were carried into Inner Asia. Meanwhile, in the Axumite kingdom of modern Ethiopia and Eritrea, immigrants using a South Arabian abjad erected imposing monuments. This was among the first kingdoms to be converted to Christianity; with the conversion, vowel notation was added to the script, yielding the abugida that has been used (with some systematic additions) until the present for several languages of the area.

Another cursivization of an Aramaic forerunner came to be used to write Arabic. When the revelations to Muhammad were written down (after the Prophet's time) to forestall the corruption of the ipsissima verba that was a perpetual danger with oral

485

transmission, the Arabic script became the medium of the new message. It soon developed strongly regional variations, and many of these became incorporated into the artistic repertoire of a culture that, forbidding graphic representation of living beings, developed calligraphy as a primary art form. The distinguishing dots, originally made necessary by the merging of the forms of many of the letters through their evolution, became part of the decorative resources of the civilization.

The sacred nature of the texts originally recorded in Hebrew, Syriac, and Arabic script, coupled with the need to supplement the abjad with indication of vowels—probably due to the introduction of unfamiliar foreign technical terms from languages like Greek and Persian—led scholars who used the three scripts to introduce vocalic notations that did not corrupt the consonantal text by invading the line of letters. The first script to receive this treatment was the Syriac, then the Arabic, and lastly the Hebrew; in each case scholars were aware of the achievements of their predecessors. To this day, the vocalizations are used only in sacred texts and to prevent confusion in unfamiliar or ambiguous words in secular contexts.

The languages written in this region belong to three major groups: Semitic (itself part of Afroasiatic), Indo-European, and Altaic. The demise of Akkadian left only representatives of West Semitic still in use. Ethiopic represents South(west) Semitic, and Hebrew and Aramaic together constitute Northwest Semitic; the position of Arabic between those two groups is now disputed. Mandaic and Syriac are Aramaic languages (while Hebrew is not)—the prominence of descendants of Aramaic script through much of Asia results from the use of (Imperial) Aramaic as the lingua franca of several ancient empires, including the Babylonian, Persian, and Iranian.

The Iranian group of languages, closely related to Indic (Indo-Aryan) within the Indo-Iranian branch of Indo-European, is diversely represented among the epigraphic remains of the ancient world. They fall into two periods: Old Iranian includes Old Persian, from southwest Iran, and Avestan, the language of the Avesta, the holy books of the Zoroastrians, from the northeast. Middle Iranian languages are attested from the first century B.C.E. (Bactrian, Parthian) to the ninth century C.E. (Khwarezmian to the 13th century). The Western group includes Parthian and Middle Persian (descendant of Old and ancestor of Modern Persian); Eastern includes Bactrian, Khwarezmian (most texts in a slightly modified Arabic script), Sogdian, Khotanese, and Tumshuqese (the last two written in variants of Brahmi).

The three principal language families of Inner Asia—Turkic, Mongolic, and Tungusic—are usually regarded as a single phylum, Altaic. The transmission and adaptation of Aramaic scripts can be followed from Turkic Uyghur to Mongolic Mongolian and Oirat to Tungusic Manchu; the influence of Chinese script can be seen in the vertical lines of writing, albeit ranged from left to right—as though a page of some earlier Aramaic script were rotated counterclockwise. Compare Syriac, written vertically but rotated clockwise for horizontal reading right to left; and Lepcha, rotated clockwise from the Tibetan left-to-right model to be read vertically right to left.

— PETER T. DANIELS

The Jewish Scripts

RICHARD L. GOERWITZ

The story of the Jewish scripts is the story of a clash between an older, Canaanite orthographic tradition and a broader, pan–Near Eastern Aramaic one. It is also the story of repeated readaptations of a simple consonant-only script (an abjad), and its ultimate expansion into a genuinely alphabetic writing system. The story of the Jewish scripts is thus a great deal more than the story of sectarian orthographic tradition: It is an important chapter in the history of writing.

From Phoenician to Aramaic to Jewish script

Although Hebrew probably existed in some distinct form as early as the mid second millennium B.C.E., texts broadly identifiable as such only begin to appear on the Palestinian archeological scene in the ninth century B.C.E. These texts are written in a distinctive right-to-left consonantal script that differs in its general appearance, but not in its basic twenty-two letter inventory, from what we find in the Dead Sea Scrolls, in medieval Jewish manuscripts, and even in today's modern Hebrew texts (TABLE 46.1; note later medial/final alternative forms).

This oldest Hebrew script was probably borrowed from Israel's northern coastal neighbors, the Phoenicians, whose script also consisted of twenty-two symbols (SECTION 5). While some Phoenician dialect might actually have possessed just twenty-two consonantal phonemes to go with these twenty-two symbols, the Hebrew of the early first millennium B.C.E. probably possessed at least twenty-five consonantal phonemes (see TABLE 46.2). Because the size of its consonantal inventory exceeded the number of symbols in the Phoenician script, we infer that some of the borrowed Phoenician letters must have taken on multiple values in Hebrew—the same way, for example, that English uses *th* to represent the values [θ] and [ð]. During this period, ﬠ ʿ, ח ḥ, and ש š/ś were probably bivalent ([ʕ, ɣ], [ħ, x], [ɬ, ʃ] respectively).

As it passed through successive generations of Israelite scribes, the Phoenician-derived Old Hebrew script took on certain traits that distinguished it from the scripts of its neighbors. Although the Old Hebrew script has persisted among the Samaritans—adherents to an ancient offshoot of Judaism—even into recent times (compare TABLE 46.2, col. 2, with TABLE 5.4 on page 95), among Jews this script did not outlive the many sociopolitical upheavals of the late first millennium B.C.E. and the early first millennium C.E., though in a few Dead Sea Scrolls it is used for the Name of God.

TABLE 46.1: *Old Hebrew and Jewish Scripts*[a]

Transliteration	Ca. 600 B.C.E.	Ca. 125 B.C.E.		Modern	
ʾ	𐤀	א		א	
b	𐤁	ב		ב	
g	𐤂	ג		ג	
d	𐤃	ד		ד	
h	𐤄	ה		ה	
w	𐤅	ו		ו	
z	𐤆	ז		ז	
ḥ	𐤇	ח		ח	
ṭ	𐤈	ט		ט	
y	𐤉	י		י	
k	𐤊	כ	ך	כ	ך
l	𐤋	ל		ל	
m	𐤌	מ	ם	מ	ם
n	𐤍	נ	ן	נ	ן
s	𐤎	ס		ס	
ʿ	𐤏	ע		ע	
p	𐤐	פ		פ	ף
ṣ	𐤑	צ		צ	ץ
q	𐤒	ק		ק	
r	𐤓	ר		ר	
š	𐤔	ש		ש	
t	𐤕	ת		ת	

a. In the last two columns, the right-hand letters are word-final forms. "600 B.C.E." reflects several texts; "125 B.C.E." represents a Hasmonean Dead Sea Scroll manuscript.

From about the twelfth century B.C.E. on, Aramaic-speaking peoples began to diffuse into the Levant, and later into Palestine itself, leading to a slow displacement of Canaanite-speaking peoples (of which the ancient Israelites were one, Hebrew being a southern or "inland" Canaanite dialect). A series of distinct and significantly Aramaized powers also seized control of Palestine. These were, in turn, the Assyrians, the Babylonians, and the Persians—the last of whom established one eastern dialect of Aramaic (what we now call "Imperial" Aramaic) as the administrative language of the entire Near East. Within a few decades, Imperial Aramaic, and its own Phoenician-derived script forms (see FIGURE 57), had achieved dominance throughout the region. We find it being used, for instance, in Aramaic papyri produced by a fifth-century B.C.E. Jewish military colony on Elephantine Island, opposite Aswan (Syene), Egypt. This domination persisted until the third century B.C.E.—the century after Alexander the Great conquered the Near East and ushered in a new era of Greek cultural hegemony over the eastern Mediterranean region.

Despite its replacement by Greek in official circles, Aramaic remained in use, both by local administrations and by the diverse populations who knew one or another dialect of it as their native language. No longer an official international medium of communication, Aramaic script forms became free to develop independently in the various locales that used them. It is out of this milieu that a distinctive Jewish script began to take shape. By the mid third century B.C.E., we begin to discern a local Judean variant emerging from the remnants of the Imperial Aramaic script. After a period of vacillation, during which the old Hebrew letter forms remained in use, Jews finally settled on a localized Aramaic script as their standard. This script was used for both Hebrew- and Aramaic-language documents.

Although many regional variations and stylizations have arisen over the years (e.g. the semi-cursive Italian "Rashi" script used for rabbinical commentaries, see TABLE 46.2, col. 3), the basic formal Jewish script has remained fundamentally the same all the way into modern times. Traditionally, Jews have taken great pride in their formal script, especially the often beautifully ornamented forms utilized in the Torah scrolls from which Rabbis read (actually, chant) scripture portions in the synagogue.

The standard reference for the history of the script is Naveh 1987; on the Hebrew language generally, see Sáenz-Badillos 1993. There is no similar volume on Aramaic.

From consonants to vowels

One notable trait of Phoenician orthography in the early first millennium B.C.E. was its defective character. In particular, it had no means of expressing vowels. Later on it also came to be written without any divisions between words. Hebrew and Aramaic scribes, when borrowing this script, maintained the older practice of marking word boundaries with a slash, dot, and—later on, in Aramaic—a space. They also worked out a way of representing vowels using "helping" consonants or *matres lectionis* 'mothers of reading', viz. ה *h*, [aː] and [ɛː], ו *w*, [uː] and later [oː], and י *y*, [iː] and later

TABLE 46.2: *Hebrew Consonants*[a]

Hebrew	Samaritan	Rashi	Num. Value	Trans-literation[b]	Reconstructed Mid 2nd Millennium	Tiberian	General Standard Israeli	Name
א	ࠀ	ɓ	I	ʾ	[ʔ]	[ʔ]	[ʔ, Ø]	ʾālep̄
ב	ࠁ	ɜ	2	b, ḇ	[b]	[b, v]	[b, v]	bēṯ
ג	ࠂ	ג	3	g, ḡ	[g]	[g, ɣ]	[g]	gímel
ד	ࠃ	ז	4	d, ḏ	[d]	[d, ð]	[d]	dā́leṯ
ה	ࠄ	ɔ	5	h	[h]	[h]	[h]	hē
ו	ࠅ	ו	6	w	[w]	[w]	[v]	wāw
ז	ࠆ	ſ	7	z	[z, dz][c]	[z]	[z]	záyin
ח	ࠇ	ɒ	8	ḥ	[ħ, x]	[ħ]	[x]	ḥēṯ
ט	ࠈ	ʋ	9	ṭ	[t']	[ɫ][d]	[t]	ṭēṯ
י	ࠉ	ʾ	10	y	[j]	[j]	[j]	yōḏ
כ ך	ࠊ	ɔך	20	k, ḵ	[k]	[k, x]	[k, x]	kap̄
ל	ࠋ	ɔ	30	l	[l]	[l]	[l]	lā́meḏ
מ ם	ࠌ	ɔ ס	40	m	[m]	[m]	[m]	mēm
נ ן	ࠍ	ɔ ſ	50	n	[n]	[n]	[n]	nūn
ס	ࠎ	ρ	60	s	[ts][e]	[s]	[s]	sā́meḵ
ע	ࠏ	ʋ	70	ʿ	[ʕ, ɣ]	[ʕ]	[ʔ, Ø][f]	áyin
פ ף	ࠐ	ɔ ٩	80	p, p̄	[p]	[p, f]	[p, f]	pēh
צ ץ	ࠑ	ſ ſ	90	ṣ	[ts', tʃ', tɬ']	[sˤ]	[ts]	ṣāḏēh
ק	ࠒ	ρ	100	q	[k']	[q]	[k]	qōp̄
ר	ࠓ	ɔ	200	r	[ɾ]	[ɾ]	[ʁ]	rēš
ש	ࠔ	ɒ	300	ś, š	[ɬ, s, tʃ]	[s, ʃ]	[s, ʃ]	śīn, šīn
ת	ࠕ	ɒ	400	t, ṯ	[t]	[t, θ]	[t]	tāw

a. In the first and third columns, a right-hand letter is the word-final form.
b. Over- and underbarred letters represent fricative versions (i.e. in pointed texts, without *dāgēš* or with *rāp̄ē*).
c. Perhaps [ʒ, dʒ]; Diakonoff 1992.
d. "Emphatic" consonant.
e. *ts* > *s*; Faber 1984, 1992.
f. See Blau 1982; Israeli ʿ varies widely.

[eː]; e.g. אדוני ʾdwny (Judges 13:8) ~ אדני ʾdny [ʔaðoːnaːj] 'lord'. At first, *matres* were used only for word-final long vowels (Cross and Freedman 1952; Zevit 1980.

Though the *matres* brought the Hebrew and Aramaic scripts considerably closer to what we think of as true alphabets, these scripts still fell short because they lacked distinct vowel symbols that could be used regardless of vowel length or position in the word. The Hebrew and Aramaic scripts, that is, still focused primarily on syllabic frames (e.g. **qām* appears as קם qm), representing their nuclei—that is, the vowels—only in restricted contexts, and using an imprecise modification of the consonantal system. The development of a full, voweled alphabet did, in fact, occur during the first

TABLE 46.3: *Tiberian Vowel Points*

Sign (with m)	Transliteration	Tiberian	Israeli	Name
מִ	i, ī; with yōḏ, î	[i(:)]	[i]	hîreq
מֵ	ē; with yōḏ, ê; with hē', ēh	[e:]	[e]	ṣērē
מֶ	e; with yōḏ, ệ; with hē', eh	[ɛ(:)]	[e]	səḡōl
מַ	a	[a(:)]	[a]	páṭaḥ
מָ	ā; with hē', â; o	[ɔ(:)]	[a, o]	qā́meṣ; as o, qā́meṣ ḥāṭūp̄
מֹ	ō; with wāw, ô; with hē', ōh	[o:]	[o]	ḥṓlem
מֻ, וּ — מ	u, ū; û	[u(:)]	[u]	qibbûṣ, šûreq
מֱ	ĕ	[ɛ]	[e]	ḥāṭēp̄ səḡōl
מֲ	ă	[a]	[a]	ḥāṭēp̄ páṭaḥ
מֳ	ŏ	[ɔ]	[o]	ḥāṭēp̄ qā́meṣ
מְ	ə, Ø	[ə, Ø]	[ə, Ø]	šəwā

millennium B.C.E.—but not among Canaanites or Arameans. Rather, it occurred farther west among the Greeks, who adapted and extended the Semitic script to suit their own dialects (SECTION 21).

Despite the contemporaneous development of a full alphabet among the Greeks, and later the Romans, etc., Hebrew scribes continued their consonant-dominated writing tradition, eschewing truly distinct vowel symbols. Though their system generally conveyed a given writer's basic intent, various diachronic phonological changes such as *h*-apocope, '-quiescence, *aw*- and *ay*-monophthongization, stress lengthening, etc., created a rift between spelling and pronunciation. As this rift widened, new and extended old uses of the *matres* arose to bridge the gap. We obtain our best view of these changes in the Dead Sea Scrolls of the late first millennium B.C.E., where Freedman and Mathews (1985) discern three spelling typologies: (a) the Proto-Rabbinic, (b) the Proto-Samaritan, and (c) the Hasmonean. A fairly conservative strand of the Proto-Rabbinic spelling system later became the dominant orthography for Jewish biblical manuscripts. Other forms of literature, being less constrained by tradition, tended to vary more widely (Weinberg 1985: 7–28).

As detail-conscious methods of biblical interpretation spread, and the correct reading of the biblical text became progressively more critical to Jewish liturgy and study, the nominally reformed biblical spellings became themselves insufficient, and additional extensions arose. In the early first millennium C.E., Greek transcriptions apparently came into use as adjuncts to the Hebrew, possibly in efforts to record the correct pronunciation of vowels not covered by the *matres* (cf. Vööbus 1971: 4–10). Later on, however (about 600 C.E.), a full solution was found: specialized *points* or diacritics (TABLE 46.3) that could be combined with the consonants used in traditional spellings (Yeivin 1980: 157–274).

As an example of how these diacritics worked, note the traditional spelling of the word 'Judah'. In the main medieval reading tradition, the Tiberian—that used in the northern Palestinian city of Tiberias—this word was probably pronounced [jəhu:ðɔ:], although scholars today typically transcribe it as *yəhûḏâ*.* The traditional consonantal writing of this word is יהודה, with the ו *w* and final ה *h* functioning as *matres* for [u] and [ɔ] respectively. Combined with the special diacritics for [ə], [u], and [ɔ], the Tiberian spelling of this word is יְהוּדָה, i.e. the original spelling augmented with some (sometimes redundant) dots and dashes. In a standard biblical text, יְהוּדָה would also carry a *cantillation mark* (or *accent*) to indicate stress position and musical motif (TABLE 46.4). Many medieval manuscripts also show a line over the ד, called *rāp̄eh*, which signals a voiced fricative [ð] rather than stop [d] pronunciation for the ד (so for all the nonemphatic stops, ב ג ד כ פ ת [v, ɣ, ð, x, f, θ], known by the mnemonic *begad kefat*). Had the ד been a stop, [d], it would have been marked with a *dāḡēš*, i.e., with a central dot דּ; similarly ת פ כ ג ב [b, g, k, p, t]). *Dāḡēš* also marks doubling, e.g., לּ stands for [ll]. The question of whether a *dāḡēš* indicates a geminate or stop articulation for a given consonant can ultimately be resolved, but often only by reference to (morpho)phonological processes that fall outside our scope. The two pronunciations of שׁ are distinguished as שׂ *ś* [s] and שׁ *š* [ʃ]. Another mark inserted into the consonantal text is the hyphen-like *maqqēp̄*, connecting a word with (usually) a particle that no longer bears primary stress: כֹּל אָדָם *kōl ʾāḏām* ~ כָּל־אָדָם *kol-ʾāḏām* 'every person'.

Three main Hebrew diacritic vowel/cantillation systems are known to scholars today. These are: (a) the Tiberian (mentioned above), (b) the Babylonian, and (c) the Palestinian. All developed between approximately 600 and 1000 C.E. Toward the end of this period, hybrid systems also proliferated. Aside from a few medieval manuscripts containing Aramaic Bible translations (called Targums), Jewish sacred literature (e.g. the Mishnah), or liturgical poetry (*piyyuṭim*), these diacritic systems—both hybrid and pure—occur only in biblical texts. Their purpose was to record one or another group's notion of how the biblical text ought to be correctly read; the scholars who devised and preserved the systems are known as Masoretes. Most of the differences between the three main Masoretic traditions are purely graphic; that is, they show the same overall cantillation patterns and vowels, but represent these by different signs. It is true, though, that a few of the vocalic differences reflect genuine underlying dialectal divergences. And, while the cantillation systems typically agree on the placement of the main clause and verse divisions (Aronoff 1985), they often differ substantially in their complexity and handling of lesser details.

Salient features of the major diacritic systems are described in Yeivin 1980, Revell 1970, 1977, and especially Yeivin 1985. There is still, however, a great deal of work left for the next generation of scholars. For example, Wickes 1881, 1887—the still standard monographs on the Tiberian cantillation marks—have not even been updated, still less replaced by more comprehensive studies. Medieval transcriptions of Tiberian Hebrew in Arabic characters are also for the first time being systematically

---

*A widely used transcription of Hebrew (and related languages) uses a circumflex accent for a long vowel marked by a *mater lectionis*, and a macron for a long vowel not so marked. A line under (or over, for *p* and *g*) a stop consonant indicates that it is pronounced as a fricative.

TABLE 46.4: *Tiberian Accents (cantillation marks)*[a]

IN THE TWENTY-ONE PROSE BOOKS			IN THE THREE POETICAL BOOKS[b]		
Accent	Name	Usage	Accent	Name	Usage
PAUSAL (DISJUNCTIVE) ACCENTS					
I. —	silluq	דָּבָר	I. —	sillûq	דָּבָר
2. —	aṭnāḥ	דָּבָר	2. —	ʿôleh wəyôrēd	דָּבָר
3. —	səḡôltā'	דָּבָר	3. —	'aṭnāḥ	דָּבָר
⊢	šalšélet	דָּבָר	4. —	great rəḇîaʿ	דָּבָר
4. —	great zaqēp̄	דָּבָר	—	little rəḇîaʿ	דָּבָר
—	little zaqēp̄	דָּבָר	5. —	rəḇîaʿ muḡrāš	דָּבָר
5. —	ṭip̄ḥā'	דָּבָר	6. —	ṣinnôr	דָּבָר
6. —	rəḇîaʿ	דָּבָר	7. —	dəḥî	דָּבָר
7. —	zarqā'	דָּבָר	8. —	pāzēr	דָּבָר
8. —	paštā'	דָּבָר	9. ⊢	great šalšélet	דָּבָר|
—	yəṯîḇ	מֶלֶךְ	10. ⊢	'azlâ ləḡarmēh	דָּבָר|
9. —	təḇîr	דָּבָר	⊢	məhuppāḵ ləḡarmēh	דָּבָר|
10. —	géreš	דָּבָר			
—	geršáyim	דָּבָר			
II. —	pāzēr	דָּבָר			
—	great pāzēr	דָּבָר			
12. —	great təlîšā'	דָּבָר			
13. ⊢	ləḡarmēh	דָּבָר|			
NON-PAUSAL (CONJUNCTIVE) ACCENTS					
I. —	mûnāḥ	דָּבָר	I. —	mêrəḵā'	דָּבָר
2. —	məhuppāḵ	דָּבָר	2. —	ṭarḥā'	דָּבָר
3. —	mêrəḵā'	דָּבָר	3. —	'azlā'	דָּבָר
—	double mêrəḵā'	דָּבָר	4. —	mûnāḥ	דָּבָר
4. —	darga'	דָּבָר	5. —	ʿillûy	דָּבָר
5. —	'azlā	דָּבָר	6. —	məhuppāḥ	דָּבָר
6. —	little təlîšā'	דָּבָר	7. —	galgal	דָּבָר
7. —	galgal	דָּבָר	8. —	little šalšélet	דָּבָר
[8. —	mâyəlā'	לְהַחֲלִי]	9. —	ṣinnôrît	דָּבָר

a. As enumerated in Wickes 1887: 10–11, 1881: 12.
b. Psalms, Proverbs, Job.

edited and published (Khan 1990). These promise to revolutionize much of what we know about the phonology behind the Tiberian diacritics (Khan 1987, 1990, with Garr 1990, form the basis of TABLE 46.3, col. 3; note also Goerwitz 1990 on long *pátaḥ* and *səḡōl*).

With the addition of specialized diacritics to the older consonantal system, a remarkable change took place in Hebrew writing: it became genuinely alphabetic. Medieval Hebrew script is, in fact, vastly more explicit and descriptive than printed Western scripts because its cantillation signs include detailed information about stress, pause (a word at the end of a syntactic unit usually assumes a somewhat different stress and vocalization pattern, closer to a historically earlier form), and musical pitch. The great irony here is that this system arose only after the Greeks had borrowed the Semitic consonantal script and extended it systematically to cover vowels as well. Liturgical Hebrew script simply reincorporates and extends these principles, finishing the "alphabetization" process that the Phoenician-derived scripts themselves had originally inspired. It remains unclear whether the Hebrew cantillation marks were adapted from Greek or Syriac antecedents, or whether they arose together against a common backdrop of Jewish, and subsequent Christian, modal chant.

Codification of the medieval script

By about 1200, the once diverse world of medieval Jewish pointing systems had become considerably more monolithic. The reason for this change is that the Tiberian system, by reason of its fullness and supposed greater accuracy, ended up superseding the others (Chiesa 1979: 9–17). Since that time, almost all biblical manuscripts have carried Tiberian vowel and cantillation marks. Adoption of the Tiberian system as the standard for all biblical manuscripts brought to completion the process of standardization that had begun over a millennium earlier, with the development of the national Jewish variant of the old Imperial Aramaic script. It is a remarkable but verifiable fact that anyone who can read a modern printed Hebrew Bible can, after a short period of adjustment, read not only medieval biblical manuscripts, but also for instance the Jewish-script manuscripts found among the Dead Sea Scrolls (see TABLE 46.1).

Although vowel and cantillation marks assume an important role in most medieval and later biblical manuscripts and editions, nonbiblical texts (as noted above) generally do not carry vowel or cantillation signs. Furthermore, nonbiblical texts show the same expansionistic uses of *matres lectionis* that were systematically excluded from the conservative biblical tradition. They also often differ in a few ancillary consonantal spelling conventions, such as the use of וו and יי for consonantal *w* and *y* respectively. Modern Israeli printed texts continue liberal, nonbiblical uses of the *matres*. Much work in developing standards for their use has in fact been done during the twentieth century (Weinberg 1985: 47–185). By way of contrast, vowel pointing or *niqqud* only appears (a) in school books, (b) in prayer books and poetry, and (c) in situations where a word, if left unpointed, might easily be misconstrued. Cantillation marks do not appear at all any more except in printed Bible editions. In effect, Israeli script, like most nonbiblical Hebrew orthographies, owes more to writing principles developed during the second millennium B.C.E. than to the medieval biblical scripts—whose diacritics supply nuances of pronunciation that serve no useful purpose in, and often even impede, everyday written communication.

SAMPLE TEXTS

IMPERIAL ARAMAIC

FIGURE 57. Introduction to a quitclaim written at Elephantine, 26 August 440 B.C.E.
(Sayce and Cowley 1906, papyrus F, lines 1–3).

←ב‎ ‎ ‾///\ / לאב הו יום ‎ ‾/// /// /// 19 לפחנס שנת = /// //‎ ‎ ארתחשסש מלכא
b← 14 b'l wh mwy 19 snhpl tnš 25 šsšhtr' 'klm

אמר פיא בר פחי ארדיכל לסון בירתא למבטחיה ברת מחסיה בר
rm' 'yp rb yhp lkydr' nwsl 'tryb hyhtbml trb hyshm rb

ידניא ארמיא זי סון לדגל וריזת על דינא זי עבדן בסון נפ‎֗/ˀת על כסף
'yndy 'ymr' yz nws lgdl tzyrw l' 'nyd yz ndb' nwsb t‎ʳ/dpn l' psk

1. *Transliteration:*   b   14   l'b   hw   ywm 19   lphns   šnt   25
2. *Normalization:*   ba   14   la-'ab   hū   yōm 19   la-pahons   šanat   25
3. *Gloss:*   on   14th   Ab   that   day 19   Pahons   year   25

1.   'rthšsš   mlk'   'mr   py'   br   phy   'rdykl   lswn
2.   'Artahšásta   malk-ā   'amar   Pī'a bar   Pahī   'aradēkal   la-Sūn
3.   Artaxerxes   king-the   said   Pia   son.of   Pakhi   builder   of-Aswan

1.   bytr'   lmbthyh   brt   mhsyh   br   ydny'
2.   bīrat-ā   la-Mibtahyā   barat   Mahsēyā   bar   Yadānyā
3.   fortress-the   to-Mibtachia   daughter.of   Machseia   son.of   Yedoniah

1.   'rmy'   zy   swn   ldgl   wryzt   'l   dyn'   zy
2.   'Aramāy-ā   dī   Sūn   la-dágəl   warīzat   'al   dīnā   dī
3.   Aramean-the   of   Aswan   of-division.of   Warizat   concerning   lawsuit   which

1.   'bdn   bswn   npd/rt   'l   ksp
2.   'abád-na   ba-Sūn   npʳ/dt   'al   kásəp
3.   did-we   in-Aswan   suit(?)   regarding   silver

'On the 14th of Ab, that is, day 19th of (the Egyptian month) Pahons, year 25 of
Artaxerxes the king, Pia son of Pakhi, a builder of Aswan, the fortress, said to
Mibtachia, daughter of Machseia son of Yedania the Aramean, belonging to the
the Warizat division at Aswan: "Concerning the lawsuit we undertook in
Aswan—a suit(?) regarding silver (and other belongings) …"'

    —AP 14, lines 1–3 (Cowley 1923: 41–43; Porten and Yardeni 1989: 38–39).

Note: The document goes on to state that Pia and Mibtachia's division of property is satisfactory to Pia, and that he will not litigate any further on this matter. Note the cosmopolitan setting: this document records a property settlement between a recently divorced Egyptian-named builder and his Jewish wife.

HEBREW WITH TIBERIAN VOCALIZATION

Stress falls on the last syllable of each word unless otherwise marked.

→וַיֹּאמְרוּ   אִם   מָצָאנוּ   חֵן   בְּעֵינֶיךָ   יִתֶּן   אֶת   הָאָרֶץ

ṣerā'āh   ṭe'   nattuy   āḵ̱ênê'əb   nēḥ   ûn'āṣām   mi'   ûrəm'ōyyaw←

הַזֹּאת   לַעֲבָדֶיךָ   לַאֲחֻזָּה   אַל   תַּעֲבִירֵנוּ   אֶת   הַיַּרְדֵּן

nēdrayyah   ṭe'   ûnērîḇă'at   la'   âzzuḥă'al   āḵ̱êḏāḇă'al   ṭ'ōzzah

1. Transliteration:	wayyō'mərû	'im	māṣā'nû	hēn	bə'ênêkā
2. Transcription:	waj-jo:m(ə)r-u:	?im	mɔ:'sɔ:-nu:	he:n	bəfe:'nɛ:xɔ:
3. Gloss:	and-said-they	if	found-we	favor	in-eyes-your

1.	yuttan	'et	hā'āreṣ	hazzō't	la'ăḇāḏêḵā	la'ăḥuzzā
2.	jutta:n	?eθ	hɔ:-'ʕɔ:rets	haz-zo:θ	la:-ʕavɔ:'ðɛ:-xɔ:	la:-?axuzzɔ:
3.	let.be.given	ACC	the-land	the-this	to-servants-your	as-possession

1.	'al	ta'ăḇîrēnû	'et	hayyardēn.
2.	?al	ta:-ʕavi:'re:-nu:	?εθ	haj-jarde:n
3.	not	may.you.cause-cross-us	ACC	the-Jordan

'Then they said, "If we have found favor with you, let this land be given to us, your servants, as a permanent possession. Do not make us cross the Jordan!"'
—*Numbers 32:5 (for the phonetics, see Khan 1990, ms. 1).*

ISRAELI HEBREW

→הַקוֹנְקוֹרְדַנְצִיָה לְתנ"ך הִיא עֲדַיִין בְּחֶזְקַת "סֵפֶר הֶחָתוּם" לְרוֹב

bôrl   "mûtāḥeh rps"   tqzḥb   nyyd'   'yh   k″ntl   hyṣnadrôqnôdh←

הַצִּיבּוּר, ... וַהֲרֵי לַאֲמִיתוֹ שֶׁל דָּבָר, הַקוֹנְקוֹרְדַנְצִיָה לְתנ"ך עֲשׂוּיָה לִהְיוֹת

tôyhl   hyûś' k″ntl   hyṣnadrôqnôdh   ,rbd   lš   ôtym'l yrhw ... rûbbyṣh

כְּלִי מַחֲזִיק בְּרָכָה וְסֵפֶר-עֵזֶר לְכָל אָדָם בְּיִשְׂרָאֵל, הַמִּתְעַנְיֵין

nyyn'tmh   ,l'rṣyb md'   lkl   rze'-rpsw   hkrb   qyzḥm   ylk

בְּכִתְבֵי-הַקוֹדֶשׁ שֶׁלָנוּ.

.ûnlš   šdôqh-ybtkb

1. Transliteration:	hqônqôrdansyh	ltn″k	hy'	'dyyn	bḥzqt
2. Transcription:	ha-konkordants'ja	la-ta'nax	hi	?a'dajin	b-xez'kat
3. Gloss:	the-concordance	to.the-Tanakh	that	still	in-presumption

1.	"spr	heḥatûm"	lrôb	hṣybbûr, ...	whry	l'mytô	šl	dbr,
2.	'sefer	he-xa'tum	l-rov	ha-tsi'bur	va-ha're	la-?ami'to	ʃel	da'var
3.	book	the-sealed	to-most.of	the-public	and-here	as.the-truth	of	thing

1. hqônqôrdanṣyh   ltn″k   ʿṣuyh lhyôt kli mḥzyq brkh
2. ha-konkordants'ja la-ta'nax ʔasuja li-hjot kli maxaziq braxa
3. the-concordance to.the-Tanakh made to-be tool holder.of blessing

1. wspr   ʿezr *lkl*   'dm byśrl,   hmtʿnyyn bktby
2. v-'sefer 'ʔezer l-xol ʔa'dam b-jisra'ʔel ha-mitʔanyen b-xitve
3. and-book.of help to-every person in-Israel the-interested in-scriptures.of

1. hqôdš   šlnû.
2. ha-'kodeʃ ʃe-'la-nu
3. the-holiness which-to-us

'A concordance of the Bible is still considered a "sealed book" by most of the public. … But the truth of the matter is that a concordance of the Bible can serve as a beneficial reference tool for anyone in Israel interested in our holy scriptures.'   *—Even-Shoshan 1985: 1.*

Note: *Tanakh* is an acronym for the three components of the Bible: *Torah, Nevi 'im, Ktuvim* 'the Law, the Prophets, and the Writings'.

Bibliography

Aronoff, Mark. 1985. "Orthography and Linguistic Theory: The Syntactic Basis of Masoretic Hebrew Punctuation." *Language* 61: 28–72.

Andersen, Francis I., and A. Dean Forbes. 1986. *Spelling in the Hebrew Bible* (Biblica et Orientalia 41). Rome: Biblical Institute Press.

Birnbaum, Solomon A. 1954–71. *The Hebrew Scripts.* 2 vols. Vol. 1, Leiden: Brill, 1971; vol. 2, London: Palaeographica, 1954–57.

Blau, Joshua. 1982. *Polyphony in Biblical Hebrew* (Israel Academy of Sciences and Humanities, Proceedings 4/2). Jerusalem.

Chiesa, Bruno. 1979. *The Emergence of Hebrew Biblical Pointing* (Judentum und Umwelt 1). Frankfurt am Main: Lang.

Cowley, A. 1923. *Aramaic Papyri of the Fifth Century B.C.* Oxford: Clarendon. Repr. Osnabrück: Zeller, 1967.

Cross, Frank Moore, Jr. 1961. "The Development of the Jewish Scripts." In *The Bible and the Ancient Near East,* ed. G. Ernest Wright, pp. 133–202. Garden City, N.Y.: Doubleday. Repr. Winona Lake, Ind.: Eisenbrauns, 1979.

Cross, Frank Moore, Jr., and David Noel Freedman. 1952. *Early Hebrew Orthography: A Study of the Epigraphic Evidence* (American Oriental Series 36). New Haven.

Diakonoff, Igor M. 1992. "Proto-Afrasian and Old Akkadian: A Study in Historical Phonetics." *Journal of Afroasiatic Languages* 4: 1–133.

Dolgopolsky, Aharon B. 1977. "Emphatic Consonants in Semitic." *Israel Oriental Studies* 7: 1–13.

Even-Shoshan, Abraham. 1985. *A New Concordance of the Bible* [in Hebrew]. Jerusalem: Kiryat Sefer.

Faber, Alice. 1984. "Semitic Sibilants in an Afro-Asiatic Context." *Supplement to Journal of Semitic Studies* 29/2, 189–224.

———. 1992. "Second Harvest: *šibbōleθ* Revisited (Yet Again)." *Journal of Semitic Studies* 37: 1–10.

Freedman, David Noel, A. Dean Forbes, and Francis I. Andersen. 1992. *Studies in Hebrew and Aramaic Orthography* (Biblical and Judaic Studies from the University of California, San Diego,

2). Winona Lake, Ind.: Eisenbrauns.

Freedman, David Noel, and K. A. Mathews. 1985. *The Paleo-Hebrew Leviticus Scroll.* N.p.: American Schools of Oriental Research.

Garr, W. Randall. 1990. "Interpreting Orthography." In *The Hebrew Bible and its Interpreters* (Biblical and Judaic Studies from the University of California 1), ed. William Henry Propp et al., pp. 53–80. Winona Lake, Ind.: Eisenbrauns.

Goerwitz, Richard L. 1990. "Tiberian Hebrew Segol: A Reappraisal." *Zeitschrift für Althebraistik* 3: 3–10.

Hanson, Richard S. 1964. "Paleo-Hebrew Scripts in the Hasmonean Age." *Bulletin of the American Schools of Oriental Research* 175: 26–42.

Khan, Geoffrey. 1987. "Vowel Length and Syllable Structure in the Tiberian Tradition of Biblical Hebrew." *Journal of Semitic Studies* 32: 23–82.

———. 1990. *Karaite Bible Manuscripts from the Cairo Genizah* (Cambridge University Library Genizah Series 9). Cambridge: Cambridge University Press.

Millard, Alan R. 1970. "'*Scriptio continua*' in Early Hebrew: Ancient Practice or Modern Surmise?" *Journal of Semitic Studies* 15: 2–15.

Naveh, Joseph. 1970. *The Development of the Aramaic Script* (Israel Academy of Sciences and Humanities, Proceedings 5/1). Jerusalem.

———. 1973. "Word Division in West Semitic Writing." *Israel Exploration Journal* 23: 206–8.

———. 1987. *Early History of the Alphabet,* 2nd ed. Jerusalem: Magnes.

Porten, Bezalel, and Ada Yardeni. 1989. *Textbook of Aramaic Documents from Ancient Egypt,* vol. 2: *Contracts.* Jerusalem: Hebrew University.

Revell, E. J. 1970. *Hebrew Texts with Palestinian Pointing* (Near and Middle Eastern Series 7). Toronto: University of Toronto Press.

———. 1971–72. "The Oldest Evidence for the Hebrew Accent System." *Bulletin of the John Rylands Library* 54: 214–22.

———. 1976. "Biblical Punctuation and Chant in the Second Temple Period." *Journal for the Study of Judaism* 7: 181–98.

———. 1977. *Biblical Texts with Palestinian Pointing and their Accents* (Society of Biblical Literature Masoretic Studies 4). Missoula, Mont.: Scholars Press.

Sáenz-Badillos, Angel. 1993. *A History of the Hebrew Language,* trans. John Elwolde. Cambridge: Cambridge University Press.

Sayce, Archibald H., and A. E. Cowley. 1906. *Aramaic Papyri Discovered at Assuan.* London: Moring.

Vööbus, Arthur. 1971. *The Hexapla and the Syro-Hexapla* (Papers of the Estonian Theological Society in Exile 22). Stockholm.

Weinberg, Werner. 1985. *The History of Hebrew Plene Spelling.* Cincinnati: Hebrew Union College Press.

Wickes, William. 1881. *A Treatise on the Accentuation of the Three So-Called Poetical Books of the Old Testament.* Oxford: Clarendon. Repr. with the following, New York: Ktav, 1970.

———. 1887. *A Treatise on the Accentuation of the Twenty-One So-Called Prose Books of the Old Testament.* Oxford: Clarendon. Repr. with the above, New York: Ktav, 1970.

Yeivin, Israel. 1980. *Introduction to the Tiberian Masorah,* ed. and trans. E. J. Revell (Society of Biblical Literature Masoretic Studies 5). Missoula, Mont.: Scholars Press.

———. 1985. *Mswrt hlšwn h'bryt hmštqpt bnyqwd hbbly* [The Hebrew language tradition as reflected in the Babylonian vocalization] (Academy of the Hebrew Language Texts and Studies 12). Jerusalem: Academy of the Hebrew Language.

Zevit, Ziony. 1980. *Matres Lectionis in Ancient Hebrew Epigraphs* (ASOR Monographs 2). Cambridge, Mass.: American Schools of Oriental Research.

Aramaic Scripts
for Aramaic Languages

PETER T. DANIELS

Aramaic was the lingua franca of Southwest Asia from early in the first millennium B.C.E. until the Arab Conquest in the mid seventh century C.E. Contemporary with the Roman Empire, several peoples used varieties of Aramaic script that had become cursive (no comprehensive survey of these "Late Aramaic" scripts has yet been published). These include the Palmyrans (Klugkist 1982)—Palmyra was a city-state in present-day eastern Syria—and the Nabateans (see TABLE 5.5 on page 97); the Manichean script, as well, belongs in this group (SECTION 48). The Nabateans (centered around Petra, in present-day southern Jordan) wrote in Aramaic but spoke Arabic, and the Arabic script (SECTION 50) emerged from the Nabatean (Abbott 1939, Gruendler 1993). Within this Arabic- (and Iranian- and Turkic-)speaking milieu, Aramaic has survived as the vernacular of several non-Muslim minorities (and three villages near Damascus which have become predominantly Muslim); and as the liturgical languages of two sects for which cursive scripts arose, Syriac for certain Christians and Mandaic for Mandeans. Syriac is the vehicle for a vast literature (its Golden Age was before the Conquest, its Silver Age after) and still serves in several contemporary churches; Mandaic, still used by a Gnostic group in Iraq, Iran, and elsewhere, is little known, but its script has undergone the most interesting development of any abjad.

Classical Syriac

The origin of Syriac script is not fully clear, though its development across the centuries of its flowering can be followed fairly easily thanks to dated colophons (Hatch 1946). The fullest discussion of Syriac paleography is Pirenne 1963.

Three kinds of consonants

There are three main varieties of Syriac writing. Oldest is the *Estrangelo*; during the Golden Age there came about a schism in the Syrian church, on Christological

ACKNOWLEDGMENT: I am extremely grateful to Bob Hoberman for his careful reading of and manifold improvements to the treatment of Classical Syriac.

TABLE 47.1: *Syriac Consonants*

				ESTRANGELO				SERTO			
TRANSLIT-ERATION	IPA	NAME	NUM. VALUE	Unconnected	Connected right	Connected left	Medial	Unconnected	Connected right	Connected left	Medial
ʾ	[ʔ]	ʾālap̄	1	ܐ	ܐ	–	–	ܐ	ܐ	–	–
b, ḇ/bh	[b, v]	bēṯ	2	ܒ	ܒ	ܒ	ܒ	ܒ	ܒ	ܒ	ܒ
g, ḡ/gh	[g, ɣ]	gāmal	3	ܓ	ܓ	ܓ	ܓ	ܓ	ܓ	ܓ	ܓ
d, ḏ/dh	[d, ð]	dālaṯ	4	ܕ	ܕ	–	–	ܕ	ܕ	–	–
h	[h]	hē	5	ܗ	ܗ	–	–	ܗ	ܗ	–	–
w	[w]	waw	6	ܘ	ܘ	–	–	ܘ	ܘ	–	–
z	[z]	zayn	7	ܙ	ܙ	–	–	ܙ	ܙ	–	–
ḥ	[ħ]	ḥēṯ	8	ܚ	ܚ	ܚ	ܚ	ܚ	ܚ	ܚ	ܚ
ṭ	[ṭ]	ṭēṯ	9	ܛ	ܛ	ܛ	ܛ	ܛ	ܛ	ܛ	ܛ
y	[j]	yūḏ	10	ܝ	ܝ	ܝ	ܝ	ܝ	ܝ	ܝ	ܝ
k, ḵ/kh	[k, x]	kāp̄	20	ܟ	ܟ	ܟ	ܟ	ܟ	ܟ	ܟ	ܟ
l	[l]	lāmaḏ	30	ܠ	ܠ	ܠ	ܠ	ܠ	ܠ	ܠ	ܠ
m	[m]	mīm	40	ܡ	ܡ	ܡ	ܡ	ܡ	ܡ	ܡ	ܡ
n	[n]	nūn	50	ܢ	ܢ	ܢ	ܢ	ܢ	ܢ	ܢ	ܢ
s	[s]	semkaṯ	60	ܣ	ܣ	ܣ	ܣ	ܣ	ܣ	ܣ	ܣ
ʿ	[ʕ]	ʿē	70	ܥ	ܥ	ܥ	ܥ	ܥ	ܥ	ܥ	ܥ
p, p̄/ph	[p, f]	pē	80	ܦ	ܦ	ܦ	ܦ	ܦ	ܦ	ܦ	ܦ
ṣ	[ṣ]	ṣāḏē	90	ܨ	ܨ	–	–	ܨ	ܨ	–	–
q	[q]	qōp̄	100	ܩ	ܩ	ܩ	ܩ	ܩ	ܩ	ܩ	ܩ
r	[r]	rēš, rīš	200	ܪ	ܪ	–	–	ܪ	ܪ	–	–
š	[ʃ]	šīn	300	ܫ	ܫ	ܫ	ܫ	ܫ	ܫ	ܫ	ܫ
t, ṯ/th	[t]	taw	400	ܬ	ܬ	–	–	ܬ	ܬ	–	–

grounds, with the Persian (East) Syrians becoming Nestorian Christians and the Roman (West) Syrians Monophysite (or Jacobite) Christians. From the fifth century, these two communities had nothing to do with each other, and the scripts of their manuscripts diverged, the forms being called *Nestorian* and *Serto* 'simple' respectively; there is also a very square variety used in Christian Palestinian Syriac manuscripts, which adds a reversed *p* ܦ for a Greek labial stop (Müller-Kessler 1991). Moller (1988), however, denies that every Syriac manuscript can be thus classified.

Each community applied its own system of vocalization to the consonantal script.

TABLE 47.2: *Syriac Vowels*

NESTORIAN (EASTERN)		JACOBITE (WESTERN)			
Diacritic	*With* b	*Diacritic*	*With* b	NAME	TRANSLITERATION
◢	⊐	–	⊃ or ⊅	ḥbāṣā	i, ī
⊤	⊐	⊃	⊃ or ⊅	rbāṣā karyā, zlāmā qašyā	ē
				rbāṣā	
⊤⊤	⊐	–		rbāṣā arrīkā, zlāmā pšīqā	e
⋅	⊐	⊢	⊃ or ⊅	pṭāḥā	a
⋅⋅	⊐	⊣	⊃ or ⊅	zqāp̄ā	ā
⊙	⊙⊐			'ṣāṣā rwīḥā	o, ō
		⊢	⊃ or ⊅	'ṣāṣā	u, ū
⊙	⊙⊐			'ṣāṣā allīṣā	

Syriac writes the same twenty-two consonants as Hebrew (SECTION 46), but the ductus has become cursive. Most of the letters of each word are connected, so that some letters take on slightly different shapes according as they are attached to their neighbors or not; eight of the letters never connect to the following letter (for the Estrangelo and Serto scripts, see TABLE 47.1; for the Nestorian script, see TABLE 47.3).

Words are separated by spaces, but sometimes common phrases can be written closed-up, and series of particles are often written as a unit. In Serto, 'alaph and lamadh assume each other's angle at the beginning or end of a word: *'l-* initially is ⋈, and *l '* finally is ⊔.

Certain vowels are consistently notated using the consonantal script alone: every final *ā* and *ē* is marked by ⋉ ', every *ī* by ⌐ *y*, and every *ū, u, ō,* and *o* by ◖ *w* (except in the two words ⋉ *kl* [kul] and ⋈⋈ *mṭl* [meṭṭul]). ◖ *w* and ⌐ *y* also represent the diphthongs *aw* and *ay*. In words of Greek origin, α *a* is often written ⋉ ', and ε *e* and αι *ai* sometimes ◖ *h*.

Arabic written in Syriac script is called Garshuni.

Diacritical points

A number of diacritics came into use to notate phonological and morphological properties of the Syriac language (Segal 1953). The outlines of *d* ⊣ and *r* ⊢ (which were very similar throughout the history of the Semitic abjad) converged, and the two letters are distinguished by a dot below or above, even in the oldest inscriptions. From earliest times, also, a plural noun or feminine(!) verb (but not an adjective) is in most instances marked by a pair of dots (*syāmē*)—if there is an *r* in the word, they replace its dot, ⊢; otherwise, they appear wherever they will fit: ⋉⋈ *malkā* 'king', ⋉⋈ *malkē* 'kings'. They are used even when the singular and plural are spelled differently.

Several native Semitic words could often be written with the same consonants, and where such forms represent nouns of common origin, or different forms of a single verb, some sort of differentiation was required. This at first took the form of a sin-gle dot placed over a letter to indicate a "fuller, stronger" syllable (usually with the vowel *a*), and under it to mark a "finer, weaker" vocalization, or none at all: ܥܒܕܐ *ʿbd'* [ʕvaːðaː] 'a work', ܥܒܕܐ *ʿbd'* [ʕavdaː] 'servant'; ܩܛܠ *qṭl* [qaːṭel] 'he kills' or [qaṭṭel] 'he murdered', ܩܛܠ *qṭl* [qṭal] 'he killed'. The latter sort of differentiation was generalized to mark morphological distinctions even when those specific vowels were not involved—ܣܡ *šm* [saːm] 'he placed'. This system is already in place in the earliest dated Syriac manuscript (411 C.E.); with the schism and the Conquest in the seventh century, further specification of vowel quality became essential, and the sys-tem of vowel points found in TABLE 47.2, first column, began to emerge. The system was perfected in East Syrian manuscripts of the ninth century.

In the West Syrian sphere, the pointing system was at first maintained; but Jacob of Edessa (later 7th century), showing how complicated it had become, proposed in-serting vowel letters into the consonantal text. This scheme was never used. Instead, the vowel letters of Greek could be placed alongside the Syriac consonant letters (TABLE 47.2, second column)—above or below as space dictated; the odd orientation of the vowel signs is explained by the Syriac scribal practice of writing downward on the page, left to right (90° counterclockwise from the direction of reading). The date of introduction of the Greek vocalization cannot be established more certainly than before 1000. The vocalization systems of Syriac (etc.) are described in Morag 1961.

A further sign sporadically found is the *linea occultans*, which occasionally marks a vowelless consonant, but more often an unpronounced consonant; it is placed above or (more recently) below the affected letter, ܡܕܝܢܬܐ *md(n)t'* [məðittaː] 'city'; but a line below could also represent a "fuller" pronunciation.

There are also two optional dots that indicate stop versus fricative pronunciation of the six plosive consonants *b g d k p t*: *quššāyā*, a dot above, marks the stop; *ruk-kāḵā*, a dot below, marks the fricative (Segal 1989). Only a stop following a vowel or an "underlying" vowel can be fricativized, so *rukkāḵā* is an important indicator of morphological information.

The first lines of the two Syriac samples might look as follows, fully vocalized:

SAMPLES OF CLASSICAL SYRIAC

ESTRANGELO

| nyhbw | 'tyr''b' | 'tw''t' | bkr | tymdq | 'nzk'd | nyrm' | nyš''n'w← |

| 'nr''ḥ' | 'r''psd | 'tw''t' | bkr | nwmylšw | 'nkh | ,'swmn | ms |

ܘܝܗܒ ܠܥܡ̈ܡܐ ܕܐܬܝܩܪ ܡܢܗܘܢ. ܘܩܕܡܝܬ ܕܣܘܪܝܝܐ ܗܘ ܕܝܗܒ
bhyd wh ʾyyrwsd tymdqw .nwhnm rqytʾd ʾmm″ʿl bhyw

ܠܚܝܪܡ ܕܨܘܪ
rwṣd mryḥl

1. Transliteration:	wʾnš″yn	ʾmryn	dʾkznʾ	qdmyt	rkb	ʾtw″tʾ
2. Normalization:	w-nāšîn	āmrîn	d-akznâ	qadm-āyat	rakkeb	ātwātâ
3. Gloss:	and-men	say	that-e.g.	first-ly	devised	letters.the

1.	ʿbr″ytʾ	wbhyn	sm	nmwsʾ,	hknʾ	wšlymwn	rkb
2.	ʿebrāyātâ	wa-b-hên	sām	nāmôs-â	hākannâ	wa-šlêmôn	rakkeb
3.	Hebrew	and-in-them	he.set	law-the	likewise	and-Solomon	devised

1.	ʾtw″tʾ	dspr″ʾ	ʾḥr″nʾ	wyhb	lʿm″mʾ	dʾtyqr
2.	ātwātâ	d-seprê	ḥrānê	w-yāb	l-ʿammê	d-etyaqqar
3.	letters.the	of-languages	others	and-gave	to-Gentiles	to-be.honored

1.	mnhwn.	wqdmyt	dswryyʾ	hw	dyhb	lḥyrm	dṣwr
2.	men-hôn	w-qadm-āyat	d-sûryāyâ	haw	d-yab	l-ḥîrām	d-Ṣôr
3.	by-them	and-first-ly	of-Syriac	DEMONST	that-he.gave	to-Hiram	of-Tyre

> 'Men say that as (Moses) first devised the Hebrew letters and wrote the law with them, so Solomon devised the letters of other languages and imparted them to the Gentiles in order to be held in honor by them. (He devised) first (the letters of) Syriac, which he gave to Hiram of Tyre.'
>
> —*From Ishodad of Merv's commentary on Genesis (9th century), quoted in Coxon 1970: 16.*

SERTO

ܣܦܪ̈ܐ ܗܠܝܢ ܕܠܘܬܢ. ܘܒܐܬܪ̈ܘܬܐ ܕܚܕܪ̈ܝܢ. ܡܢܗܘܢ ܡܢ ܡܫܡܠܝܢ
nylmšm nm nwhnm .nyr″dḥd ʾtwr″tʾbw .ntwld nylh ʾr″pes←

ܘܓܡܝܪܝܢ ܡܢܗܘܢ ܕܝܢ ܚܣܝܪܝܢ ܘܒܨܝܪܝܢ. ܘܣܦܪ̈ܐ ܡܫܡ̈ܠܝܐ ܠܟܠ
lkl ʾylmš″m ʾr″psw .nyryṣbw nyrysḥ nyd nwhnm nyrymgw

ܛܘܦܣܐ ܡܬܠܬܡܢܐ ܒܠܫܢܐ ܐܬܘܬܐ ܕܡܬܪܫܡܐ ܒܟܬܒܐ ܠܗܘܢ ܡܫܬܟܚܐ.
ʾḥktšm nwhl ʾbtkb ʾmšrtmd ʾtwtʾ ʾnšlb ʾnmtltm ʾspwṭ

ܐܟܡܐ ܕܠܝܘܢܝܐ ܘܪܘܡܝܐ ܘܐܓܘܦܛܝܐ ܘܐܪܡܢܝܐ. ܘܣܦܪ̈ܐ ܚܣܝܪ̈ܐ ܠܐ ܗܘܐ
ʾwh ʾl ʾr″ysḥ ʾr″psw .ʾynmrʾw ʾyṭpwgʾw ʾymwrw ʾynwyld ʾmkʾ

ܠܟܠ ܛܘܦܣܐ ܡܬܠܬܡܢܐ ܒܠܫܢܐ ܒܝܬܝܐ ܨܘܪܬܐ ܕܡܬܟܬܒܐ ܠܗܘܢ
nwhl ʾbtktmd ʾtrwṣ ʾytyb ʾnšlb ʾnmtltm ʾspwṭ lkl

ܡܫܬܟܚܐ. ܐܟܡܐ ܕܠܥܒܪܝܐ ܘܣܘܪܝܝܐ ܘܥܪܒܝܐ
ʾybrʿw ʾyyrwsw ʾyrbʿld ʾmkʾ .ʾḥktšm

1. *Transliteration:*	sepr″ʾ	hlyn	dlwtn.	dbʾtr″wtʾ	dḥdr″yn.
2. *Normalization:*	sep̄rē	hālēn	da-lwāṯ-an	d-ḇ-aṯrawwāṯā	da-ḥḏār-ayn
3. *Gloss:*	scripts	those	that-at-us	that-in-places	that-around-us

1. mnhwn.	mn	mšmlyn	wgmyryn	mnhwn	dyn	ḥsyryn
2. men-hôn	man	mšamlên	wa-ḡmîrîn	men-hôn	dên	ḥassîrîn
3. from-them	some	complete	and-perfected	from-them	however	incomplete

1. wbṣyryn.	wspr″ʾ	mš″mlyʾ	lkl	ṭwpsʾ	mtltmnʾ	blšnʾ
2. wa-bṣîrîn	w-sep̄rē	mšamlayyâ	l-ḵol	ṭûpsâ	meṯlaṯmānâ	b-leššānâ
3. and-imperfect	and-scripts	complete	to-each	type	pronounced	with-tongue

1. ʾtwtʾ	dmtršmʾ	bktbʾ	lhwn	mštkḥʾ	ʾkmʾ	dlywnyʾ
2. aṯûṯâ	d-meṯrašmâ	ba-ḵṯāḇâ	l-hôn	meštaḵḥâ	aḵmâ	da-l-yawnāyâ
3. letters	that-inscribed	in-writing	to-them	existing	such.as	that-of-Greek

1. wrwmyʾ	wʾgwptyʾ	wʾrmnyʾ.	wspr″ʾ	ḥsyr″ʾ	lʾ	hwʾ
2. w-rômāyâ	w-eḡupṭāyâ	w-armānāyâ	w-sep̄rē	ḥassîrê	lâ	wâ
3. and-Latin	and-Egyptian	and Armenian	and-scripts	incomplete	not	(was)

1. lkl	ṭwpsʾ	mtltmnʾ	blšnʾ	bytyʾ	ṣwrtʾ	dmtktbʾ
2. l-ḵol	ṭûpsâ	meṯlaṯmānâ	b-leššānâ	baytāyâ	ṣûrtâ	d-meṯkaṯbâ
3. to-each	type	pronounced	with-tongue	proper	form	that-written

1. lhwn	mštkḥʾ	ʾkmʾ	dlʿbryʾ	wswryyʾ	wʾrbyʾ
2. l-hôn	meštaḵḥâ	aḵmâ	da-l-ʿeḇrāyâ	wa-sûrāyâ	w-arbāyâ
3. to-them	existing	such.as	that-of-Hebrew	and-Syriac	and-Arabic

'As for the scripts (used) by us or our neighbors, some are complete and perfect, but others are incomplete and imperfect. For complete scripts, each distinct sound has its own written letter, as in Greek, Latin, Coptic, and Armenian; but incomplete scripts do not have, for each distinct sound, their own written form, as in Hebrew, Syriac, and Arabic.'

—*Bar Hebraeus (1225/6–1286), "Book of Rays," tractate 4, chap. 1, sec. 1 (Moberg 1922: 191–92, 1907: 3–4).*

Modern Aramaic

Robert D. Hoberman

Modern Aramaic languages—the ancestral languages have developed into as many as ten or more (Heinrichs 1990B)—have been written with the Syriac, Hebrew, Cyrillic, and Roman scripts, but only the Syriac script has gained widespread use, and it is the principal topic of this section.

TABLE 47.3: *Eastern (Nestorian) Syriac Letters*[a]

Letter	Translit.	Value	Soviet Orthog.	Turoyo Orthog.	Letter	Translit.	Value	Soviet Orthog.	Turoyo Orthog.
ܐ	ʾ	[ʔ]	–		ܠ	l	[l]	l	l
ܒ	b	[b, w]	в	b	ܡ ܡ	m	[m]	m	m
ܓ	g	[ɟ, ʔ, ɣ, j]	g, ç	g, ĝ	(ܢ) ܢ	n	[n]	n	n
ܕ	d	[d, ð]	d	d, d̲	ܣ	s	[s]	s	s
ܗ	h	[h]	h	h	ܥ	ʿ	[ʔ, ʕ]	–	c
ܘ	w	[w]	v	w	ܦ	p	[pʰ, p]	p	p
ܙ	z	[z]	z	z	ܨ	ṣ	[s]	s	ṣ
ܚ	ḥ	[x]	x	ḥ, x	ܩ	q	[q]	q	q
ܛ	ṭ	[t]	ṭ	ṭ	ܪ	r	[r]	r	r
ܝ	y	[j]	j	y	ܫ	š	[ʃ]	ṣ	ŝ
(ܟ) ܟ	k	[cʰ, c]	k	k	ܬ	t	[tʰ, t, θ]	t	t, t̲

a. Where more than one letter-shape is given, they are (from right to left) initial/medial, final, (final unconnected).

Until the nineteenth century, modern Aramaic was only sporadically written. During the nineteenth century, however, European missionaries working in Urmi, Iran, created an orthography for the modern Aramaic dialect of the Christians of that city, using the Syriac alphabet in its Eastern (Nestorian) variety. This orthography was deliberately etymological and designed to bridge, as much as possible, the great differences among dialects (Maclean 1895: xv–xvii). This remains the standard written language used today, and on it was based the spoken Aramaic koine of the Assyrians in Iraq (Odisho 1988).

The Modern Syriac writing system is phonologically based. It consists of twenty-two letters (TABLE 47.3) written from right to left, plus several varieties of diacritical marks, some of which are obligatory and others optional. Writing that includes the full set of diacritical signs is called *pointed*, while writing that includes only the letters and obligatory diacritics is called *unpointed*. Typologically, unpointed Modern Syriac is an abjad, meaning that, as in Arabic and Hebrew, (a) the letters chiefly represent consonants, though several letters can also represent vowels, and (b) some vowels are not indicated at all. In a pointed text, i.e. with the addition of the full set of diacritical marks, the writing indicates all the vowels as well as the consonants, and thus constitutes a full-fledged alphabet. Unlike Arabic and Hebrew, which are ordinarily written unpointed, Modern Syriac is nearly always fully pointed.

TABLE 47.4: *Modified Letters*

Letter	Translit.	Value
	STANDARD	WRITTEN LANGUAGE
ܓ	ǧ	[ʤ]
ܟ	č	[ʧ]
ܙ	ž	[ʒ]
ܬ	ž	[ʒ]
ܦ	p	[f], (with preceding *a* or *ă*) [o]
	OTHER	DIALECTS
ܛ	ṭ	[dˤ], [ðˤ]
ܨ	ṣ	[dˤ], [ðˤ]
ܦ	ṗ	[f]

Letters and obligatory diacritics

Within a word, the letters are connected at the baseline, except for eight letters, ܐ ʾ, ܕ *d*, ܗ *h*, ܘ *w*, ܙ *z*, ܨ *ṣ*, ܪ *r*, and ܬ *t*, which are connected to a preceding letter but never to a following one. A space is left between words. There are no one-letter words, as one-letter conjunctions and prepositions (ܘ *w*- 'and', ܕ *d*- 'that', ܠ *l*- 'to', ܒ *b*- 'at, by') are written connected to the following word. The letter *m* has different shapes depending on whether it is followed by another letter (ܡ) or at the end of a word (ܡ), and *k* and *n* have three shapes: ܟ *k*, ܢ *n* when connected to a following letter, ܟ *k* ܢ *n* when final and connected to the preceding letter, and ܟ *k* ܢ *n* when final and unconnected to the preceding (which is one of the eight non-connecting letters).

Furthermore, when *k*, *m*, or *n* appears in isolation (as in enumerating items in a list), it is doubled—written in both its connected form and its word-final form: ܟܟ, ܡܡ, ܢܢ. There are optional word-final ligatures: ܬ *-ta* and ܗ *-hi*.

All the letters represent consonants (including *y* and *w*). Three of the letters also represent vowels: normally [i] and [e] are written with ܝ *y*, [o] and [u] with ܘ *w*, and word-final [a] and [ı] with ܐ ʾ. The vowels [a] and [ı] in the middle of a word are normally not represented by any letter. No word begins with a vowel, but many begin with ܥ ʿ or ܐ ʾ, representing the glottal stop [ʔ].

When a consonant sound can be represented by two different letters, the choice is etymological. For example, in ܒܟܐ [baxı] 'cry' the [x] is written with *k*, while in ܡܚܐ [maxı] 'hit' [x] is written with *ḥ*.

The sounds [ʒ], [ʧ], and [ʤ], which did not exist in Classical Syriac, are indicated by adding to appropriate letters a tilde-like mark called *maǧliyana* (TABLE 47.4): *g* with *maǧliyana* is ܓ *ǧ* [ʤ]; *k* with *maǧliyana* is ܟ *č* [ʧ]; and *z* and *š* with *maǧliyana*

ܝ ܙ are both *ž* [ʒ] (Odisho 1993). In some dialects, pharyngealized [dˤ] or [ðˤ] are represented by adding a large dot on top of ܛ *ṭ* or ܨ *ṣ* (in imitation of the corresponding Arabic letters ظ and ض), and likewise [f] is sometimes represented by *p* with a large dot ڧ or a semicircle ڢ.

Two significant phonological features are only partially represented in writing. Each word in the language is either *emphatic* (pharyngealized, indicated in phonetic transcription with the symbol [~] before the word) or *plain*. The presence in a word of ܥ ‘, ܛ *ṭ*, or ܨ *ṣ* normally indicates that it is emphatic (note that ܚ *ḥ* or ܩ *q* do not!), but the spelling with ‘, *ṭ*, or *ṣ* is determined by etymology, correlating fairly well but not perfectly with the modern pronunciation: there are some plain words that contain one of the three letters, and many emphatic words that do not. Another feature only partly indicated in writing is aspiration. In emphatic words ܛ *ṭ* represents unaspirated [t] while ܬ *t* is usually aspirated [tʰ], again with exceptions; but other than this, aspiration is not indicated in writing.

Three additional signs are normally used in unpointed as well as pointed texts.

(a) Two large dots, called *syame* [sjamɪ], are placed above a letter in plural nouns and adjectives. In many cases the *syame* are the only written indication (in unpointed text) of plurality, for example ܡܠܟܐ *mlk’* [malcʰa] ‘king’, ܡܠܟ̈ܐ *mlk’’* [malcʰɪ] ‘kings’. If the word contains an ܪ *r*, the *syame* appear on it, replacing the dot which forms part of the r: ܪ̈ *r’’*. If there is no *r* in the word, the *syame* are placed above any letter, preferably near the end of the word and avoiding the ascenders ܠ *l* and ܐ ’.

(b) To help bridge the gaps between different contemporary dialects and between them and Classical Syriac, Modern Syriac orthography makes liberal use of the sign known as *talqana*, a diagonal line above a letter, indicating that it is not pronounced. For example, the word meaning ‘after’ is written ܒܬܪ *b(t)r* (the parentheses transliterate the *talqana*), suggesting on the one hand its Classical Syriac form [ba:θar] and the pronunciation [baθar] found in some modern dialects, and on the other hand the pronunciation [~bar] in Urmi and the koine. The letters ܐ ’, ܥ ‘, ܗ *h*, and ܝ *y*, written on an etymological basis, are frequently silent without being marked with *talqana*.

(c) A large dot is written over the *m* of ܡ̇ܢ *min* [man] ‘who’, distinguishing it from ܡ̣ܢ *min* [mɪn] ‘from’, written with the dot beneath the *m*. A large dot is likewise written over the *h* of the third person feminine singular suffix ܗ̇ܘ *-ûh* [-o] (dialectally also ܗ̇ *-ah* [-ah]), the personal pronouns masculine ܘܗ̇ *hw* [~aw] and feminine ܝܗ̇ *hy* [aj], and the identically spelled demonstratives, masculine [o], feminine [e]. These dots are a relic of Classical Syriac orthography.

The punctuation marks in traditional writing were : (comma), . (period), and ܀ (used at the end of a paragraph). Nowadays the full set of Western punctuation marks is used, with (as in Arabic) the question mark reversed (؟) and the comma inverted (،).

TABLE 47.5: *Vowel Diacritics*

Letter	Translit.	Value
\multicolumn{3}{c}{DIACRITICS ASSOCIATED WITH PARTICULAR LETTERS}		
ـ	î	[ij, i]
ة	ô	[u]
ة	û	[uj, u]
\multicolumn{3}{c}{DIACRITICS ADDED TO ANY LETTER (shown with *b*)}		
ـ	e	[i, ɪ, e]
ـ	ĭ	[ɪ]
ـ	a	[a]
ـ	ă	[a]

Optional diacritics

Pointed texts use seven additional diacritical marks, consisting of small dots, to specify the vowels (TABLE 47.5). The correspondences between the written symbols and the vowels as pronounced are complex, though virtually unambiguous.

The letter *y* with a dot beneath it ـ represents the vowel *î* [ij]. The letter *w* with a dot beneath it ة is *û* [uj] or [u], and with a dot above it ة is *ô* [u]. The other four vowel diacritics appear above or below any consonant letter (illustrated here with *b*); the consonant precedes the vowel in pronunciation: ـ *bĭ* [bɪ]; ـ *be* [bi], at the end of a word [bɪ]; ـ *bă* [ba]; ـ ba [ba]. The sound [e] is represented by *ay* or *ăy*, and [o] by *aw*.

The transliteration symbols *e*, *ô*, and *û* reflect the pronunciation of these vowels in an earlier historical period and in some present-day dialects. In Urmi, *î* and *e* are distinguished as [ij] and [i] (Polotsky 1961), but they have fallen together in the koine as [i], while *û* and *ô*, Urmi [uj] and [u], are both [u] in the koine.

The vowels *ĭ* and *ă* appear only in closed syllables, where all vowels are phonetically short; *î*, *e*, and *a* are used in open syllables, where vowels are long. Accordingly, *ĭ* and *ă* indicate that a following intervocalic consonant is doubled; compare ܣܡܐ *să-ma'* [samma] 'poison' and ܬܢܐ *tĭna'* [tʰɪnna] 'smoke' with ܣܡܐ *sama'* [saːma] 'portion' and ܬܐܢܐ *te'na'* [tʰiːna] 'fig'.

Another set of diacritical marks serves to specify modifications of the consonantal sounds of some of the letters. The letters *b*, *g*, and *k* represent two or three phonemes each: a stop, and a continuant or glide. The continuant or glide is indicated by a small dot under the letter (transliterated with a line under the letter): ـ *ḇ* [w]; ـ *ḡ* [ɣ], [ʔ], or [j]; ـ *ḵ* [x]. The stop variant may be indicated by a small dot above the letter (shown following the letter in transcription), ـ *b•* [b], ـ *g•* [ɟ], ـ *k•* [c], but this is omitted at the beginning of a word and often elsewhere. Speakers of dialects which have the interdental sounds [θ] and [ð] similarly indicate them with a small dot under ܬ *ṯ* and ܕ *ḏ*, and specify the corresponding stops by dots above these letters. The sequences *aḇ* and *ăḇ*, like *aw*, are pronounced [o]. Similarly, in a handful of words *ap* is pronounced [o], and the *p* is marked with a small semicircle underneath, as in ܛܠܦܚܐ *ṭlapḥ"eʾ* [~tloxɪ] 'lentils'.

Other scripts

In the Soviet Union, the same dialect of Modern Aramaic was written for a short time with an adapted Latin script (Friedrich 1959), and later Cyrillic (Polotsky 1961). The orthography was phonologically based, with letters corresponding nearly perfectly to the phonemes of the language. Emphatic or plain pronunciation was efficiently indicated by having two letters each for the phonemes [i] and [a]: in plain words these sounds are represented by *i* and *ə* respectively, and in emphatic words by *ь* and *a*; for example, *axьl* [~axil] 'eat', *kətiv* [cʰatɪv] 'write'. A different Latin-script orthography for the modern Aramaic language Ṭuroyo was developed in the 1980s by immigrants from Turkey in Sweden (Ishaq 1990). Both systems are included in TABLE 47.3.

Jewish speakers have written Modern Aramaic in the Hebrew alphabet, in a phonetic, non-etymological manner (Sabar 1976).

Sample of Modern Aramaic Koine

←ܩܘܝܡܐ ܕܟܠ ܚܕܐ ܐܘܡܬܐ ܬܠܝܐ ܝܠܗ ܒܠܫܢܗ، ܘܠܫܢܐ

ʾanašĭlw ,ḥônašĭlb hely ʾaylĭt ʾatmûʾ ʾadḥ lkd ʾamayûq←

ܒܟܬܝܒܬܘܗܝ ܘܒܣܦܪܝܘܬܘܗܝ. ܚܕ ܠܫܢܐ ܕܠܐ ܟܬܝܒܬܐ، ܐܝܟ ܚܕ

daḥ ḵyăʾ ,ʾetaḇî"tk ʾald ʾanašĭl dăḥ .yhûtûyarpĭsbw yhûtaḇî"tkb

ܟܪܡܐ ܝܠܗ ܕܠܐ ܢܛܘܪܐ. ܐܗܐ ܒܬ ܦܐܫ ܐܟܝܠܐ ܒܓܠܐ

ʾel"ĭgb ʾalîḵ(ʾ) šeʾap tĭb ʾahaʾ .ʾer"ôṭan ʾald hely ʾamrăk

ܫܐܕܢܐ، ܘܠܫܢܐ ܒܚܒܪܐ ܢܘܟܪܝܐ.

.ʾeyar"ḵûn ʾer"baḥb ʾanašilw ,ʾen"adʾeš

ܐܗܐ ܠܫܢܢ، ܐܦܢ ܡܘܣܟܢܐ، ܐܝܢܐ ܡܪܐ ܛܘܗܡܐ ܝܠܗ،

,hely ʾamhûṭ ʾeram ʾanîʾ ,ʾanĭksûm nĭpaʾ ,nănašĭl ʾahaʾ

ܘܐܝܬ ܠܗ ܕܝܠܝܬܐ ܚܩܝܪܐ. ܐܢ ܦܝܫܝ ܒܘܓܪܐ، ܟܐ ܗܘܝ

îwah ʾek ,ʾer"ğûb îšyap nĭʾ .ʾer"îqḥ ʾet"ayalîd hel tîʾw

ܡܦܬܘܝܐ ܘܓܪܘܣܐ ܘܡܩܘܡܐ ܒܣܕܪܐ ܕܐܢ ܠܫܢܐ ܣܦܪܝܐ

ʾeyar"pĭs ʾen"ašĭl naʾd ʾardĭsb ʾemûqămw ʾesûwragw ʾeyûtpam

ܘܪܗܛܪܝܐ ܕܕܘܢܝܐ.

.ʾeynûdd ʾeyar"ṭĭhrw

1. Transliteration: qûyama'   dkl   ḥda'   'ûmta'   tĭlya' yleh
2. Transcription: qujama   t-cʰul   xda   ʔumtʰa   tʰɪlje-lɪ
3. Gloss: subsistence   of-all   one   nation   depending-is

1. blĭšanôḥ,   wlĭšana'   bktî″ḇatûhy   wbsĭprayûtûhy.   ḥăd
2. b-liʃan-o   w-liʃana   b-cʰtʰiwatʰ-u   w-b-~sɪpʰrajutʰ-u   xa
3. in-language-its   and-language   in-writings-its   and-in-literature-its one

1. lĭšana'   dla'   ktîḇat″e',   'ăyḵ   ḥad   kărma' yleh   dla'   naṭôr″e'.
2. liʃana   dla   cʰtʰiwatʰɪ   ʔax   xa   cʰarmelɪ   dla   ~naturɪ.
3. language   without   writings   like   one   vineyard-is   without   keepers

1. 'aha'   bĭt   pa'eš   (')ḵîla'   bgĭl″e'   še'dan″e',   wlĭšana'
2. ʔaha   bɪt   pʰajiʃ   ~xila   b-ɟɪllɪ   ʃidanɪ   w-liʃana
3. this   FUTURE become   eaten   by-plants   crazy   and-language

1. bḥabr″e'   nûḵr″aye'.   'aha'   lĭšanăn,   'apĭn   mûskĭna',   'îna'
2. b-~xabrɪ   ~nuxrajɪ   ʔaha   liʃan-an   ʔapʰɪn   muscɪnna   ʔina
3. by-words   foreign   this   language-our   even.if   impoverished   but

1. mare'   ṭûhma' yleh,   w'ît leh   dîlayat″e'   ḥqîr″e'.   'în   payšî
2. marɪ   ~tuhme-lɪ   w-ʔɪtʰlɪ   dilayatʰɪ   ~xqirɪ   ʔin   pʰeʃi
3. possessor.of   pedigree-is   and-it.has   properties   glorious   if   become

1. bûǧr″e',   ke'   hawî   maptûye'   wgarwûse'   wmăqûme'   bsĭdra'
2. budʒrɪ   cʰi   hawi   mapʰtʰujɪ   w-ɟarwusɪ   w-maqqumɪ   b-~sɪdra
3. cultivated   PRESENT   be   expand   and-grow   and-stand   in-rank

1. d'an   lĭšan″e'   sĭpr″aye'   wrhĭṭr″aye'   ddûnye'.
2. d-ʔan   liʃanɪ   ~sɪpʰrajɪ   w-~rhɪtrajɪ   d-dunjɪ
3. of-those   languages   literary   and-eloquent   of-world

'The subsistence of every nation depends on its language, and language on its writings and its literature. A language without writings is like a vineyard without keepers. The latter will be eaten by weeds and the language by foreign words. This language of ours, even if it has become impoverished, is still of pedigree, and it has glorious properties. If they are cultivated, they expand and grow and stand in the ranks of the literary and eloquent languages of the world.'

   —From an editorial by Addai Alkhas in Gilgamesh *(Tehran), no. 1*
    (April 12, 1952), quoted in "Ba'uta" 1993.

Mandaic

PETER T. DANIELS

The Mandaic script changed very little over the centuries, and the earliest known documents employing it (including amulets on rolls of lead) are difficult to date. It has
therefore been difficult to determine its parentage and its relationships with the other
Late Aramaic scripts. The exchange between Coxon (1970), Naveh (1970), and
Macuch (1971) is an excellent example of philological dispute, showing how plausi-

TABLE 47.6: *The Mandaic Alphabet*

Letter	Transliteration[a]	Phonetic Value	Name
ₔ	a*	[a]	a
ⲭ	b	[b]	ba
⟩	g	[g]	ga
⟂	d	[d]	da
⟃	h	[h]	ha
⟂	u	[u, w]	wa
|	z*	[z]	za
ₔ	-ḥ		eh
⟂	ṭ	[ŧ]	ṭa
⟂	i*	[i, j]	ya
⟂	k	[k]	ka
⟂	l	[l]	la
⟂	m	[m]	ma
⟂	n	[n]	na
⟂	s	[s]	sa
⟂	ʿ	[e]	
⟂	p	[p]	pa
⟂	ṣ	[ʂ]	ṣa
⟂	q	[q]	qa
⟂	r	[r]	
⟂	š*	[ʃ]	ša
⟂	t	[t]	ta
⟂	ḏ-*		adu

a.   An asterisk indicates that the letter does not connect to the next one within a word.

ble conclusions drawn from limited evidence can be challenged when the same evidence is reviewed from a different perspective. Klugkist (1986) summarizes the arguments, concluding that the question is essentially undecidable.

Mandaic orthography has usually been regarded as alphabetic: the script employs the familiar 22 letters, plus a digraph for the relative particle *di* (TABLE 47.6), but it has extended the use of *matres lectionis* nearly as far as possible. The language has lost the glottal stop and the pharyngeal fricatives [ʔ ʕ ħ], so the letters ﻫ * ʾ and ﺟ * ʕ are available for other functions ([h] is spelled with ﻣ *ḥ, and ﺣ *h is used exclusively for the third person singular suffix). All [a]'s are represented by ﻫ *a, all [i]'s by ﻟ *i (final [i(:)] is ﻫﻟ), and all [u]'s by ﻟ *u ([j] and [w] rarely occur). But [o] is also written with ﻟ *u, and the use of ﺟ and the representation of [e] are complicated. ﺟ appears at the start of any word that begins with a vowel other than [a]: alone for [e] (but initial [e] seems only to be a prothetic vowel before the *t*-prefix in the passive verbs or before a monoconsonantal word), or before ﻟ or ﻟ for initial [i] or [u] respectively. Within a word, [e], like [i], is spelled with ﻟ—except that when two adjacent ﻟ's would result, they are replaced by ﺟ; and ﺟ is preferred to ﻟ after the consonants that have a point below the line (ﻙ *k, ﻥ *n, ﻑ *p, ﺹ *ṣ); and ﺟ can be used in place of ﻫﻟ when it represents word-final [i:] (and not [ja]).

The letters with descending points enter into ligatures when they precede letters with a vertical right edge, e.g. ﻙﻟ *kl, ﻥﻣ *nm. There are special forms ﻭﺗ for *wt* and ﻙﺩ for *kd*. The pronominal suffix ﺣ can be manipulated calligraphically in an otherwise pedestrian manuscript in order to fill out a line.

SAMPLE OF MANDAIC

ḥtqapn	amla	nm	ḥnim	tqapnd	amšin	kabuṭ	kabuṭ←

aišib	rudd	aruadl	ḥbtiuhd	airas	argaplu	amuliql

aigulpu	aniq	anisd	akušhd	amlal	aiṭah	hlukd	artal

1. Transliteration:	ṭubak	ṭubak	nišma	dnpaqt	minḥ	mn
2. Normalization:	ṭuba-k	ṭuba-k	nišma	di-npaq-t	min-eh	min
2. Gloss:		hail.to-you	hail.to-you soul	who-left-you	from-it	from

1. alma	npaqth	lqiluma	ulšagra	saria	dhuitbh
2. alma	npaq-t-eh	l-qiluma	u-l-pagra	saria	di-huit-b-eh
3. world	left-you-it	to-corruption	and-to-body	stinking	which-you.are-in-it

1. ldaura	ddur	bišia	latra	dkulh	haṭia	lalma
2. l-daura	di-dur	bišia	l-atra	di-kul-eh	haṭaiia	l-alma
3. for-dwelling	of-abode.of	evils	to-place	of-all-it	sins	to-world

1. ḏhšuka   ḏsina   qina   uplugia   …
2. di-hšuka   di-sina   qina   u-plugia
3. of-darkness   of-hatred   jealousy and-dissension …

> 'Hail to you, hail to you, soul who has departed from this world! You have left the corruption and the stinking body in which you dwelt, the abode of evils, the place of all the sins of the world, of darkness, of hatred, jealousy, and dissension …'   *—From a Masiqta hymn (Macuch 1967: 54, no. 5, lines 1–3).*

Note: The *masiqta* is a "sacramental meal (corresponding to the Christian mass), intended to assist the soul on its way to the regions of Light" (Macuch 1967: 75 s.v.).

Bibliography

ARAMAIC

Abbott, Nabia. 1939. *The Rise of the North Arabic Script and Its Ḳurʾānic Development with a Full Description of the Ḳurʾān Manuscripts in the Oriental Institute* (Oriental Institute Publications 50). Chicago: University of Chicago Press.

Gruendler, Beatrice. 1993. *The Development of the Arabic Scripts: From the Nabatean Era to the First Islamic Century According to Dated Texts* (Harvard Semitic Studies 43). Atlanta: Scholars Press.

Klugkist, A. C. 1982. "The Importance of the Palmyrene Script for Our Knowledge of the Development of the Late Aramaic Scripts." In *Arameans, Aramaic and the Aramaic Literary Tradition,* ed. Michael Sokoloff, pp. 57–74. Bar Ilan, Israel: Bar-Ilan University Press.

Rosenthal, Franz. 1939. *Die aramaistischen Forschungen seit Theodor Nöldeke's Veröffentlichungen.* Leiden: Brill.

Rosenthal, Franz, ed. 1967. *An Aramaic Handbook* (Porta Linguarum Orientalium 10). 2 vols. in 4 parts. Wiesbaden: Harrassowitz.

CLASSICAL SYRIAC

Brockelmann, Carl. 1960. *Syrische Grammatik,* rev. ed. Leipzig: VEB Verlag Enzyklopädie, repr. 1976 (1st ed., 1899).

Hatch, William Henry Paine. 1946. *An Album of Dated Syriac Manuscripts.* Boston: American Academy of Arts and Sciences.

Moberg, Axel. 1907–13. *Buch der Strahlen: Die grössere Grammatik des Barhebräus. Übersetzung nach einem kritisch berichtigten Texte mit textkritischem Apparat und einem Anhang: Zur Terminologie.* Vol. 1, *Einleitung, Traktat I–III,* 1913; vol. 2, *Einleitung und zweiter Teil,* 1907. Leipzig: Harrassowitz.

———. 1922. *Le livre des splendeurs: La grande grammaire de Grégoire Barhebraeus. Texte syriaque édité d'après les manuscrits avec une introduction et des notes* (Acta Reg. Societatis Humaniorum Litterarum Lundensis 4). Lund: Gleerup.

Moller, Garth I. 1988. "Towards a New Typology of the Syriac Manuscript Alphabet." *Journal of Northwest Semitic Languages* 14: 153–97.

Morag, Shelomo. 1961. *The Vocalization Systems of Arabic, Hebrew, and Aramaic: Their Phonetic and Phonemic Principles* (Janua Linguarum Series Minor 13). The Hague: Mouton.

Müller-Kessler, Christa. 1991. *Grammatik des Christlich-Palästinisch-Aramäischen,* part 1: *Schrift-*

lehre, Lautlehre, Formenlehre (Texte und Studien zur Orientalistik 6). Hildesheim: Olms.

Nöldeke, Theodor. 1904. *Compendious Syriac Grammar,* 2nd ed., trans. James A. Crichton. London: Williams & Norgate. (German orig., 1898; 1st ed., 1880.)

Pirenne, Jacqueline. 1963. "Aux origines de la graphie syriaque." *Syria* 40: 101–37.

Segal, Judah B. 1953. *The Diacritical Point and the Accents in Syriac* (London Oriental Series 2). London: Oxford University Press.

———. 1989. "*Quššaya* and *Rukkaḵa*: A Historical Introduction." *Journal of Semitic Studies* 34: 483–91.

MODERN ARAMAIC

ܒܥܘܬܐ "Ba'uta" [Appeal]. 1993. [Editorial]. *Journal of the Assyrian Academic Society* (Chicago) 7/1: Syriac section 79.

Friedrich, Johannes. 1959. "Neusyrisches in Lateinschrift aus der Sowjetunion." *Zeitschrift der Deutschen Morgenländischen Gesellschaft* 109: 50–81.

Heinrichs, Wolfhart. 1990A. "Introduction." In Heinrichs 1990B: ix–xvii.

Heinrichs, Wolfhart, ed. 1990B. *Studies in Neo-Aramaic* (Harvard Semitic Studies 36). Atlanta: Scholars Press.

Ishaq, Yusuf. 1990. "Turoyo: From Spoken to Written Language." In Heinrichs 1990B: 189–99.

Maclean, Arthur John. 1895. *Grammar of the Dialects of Vernacular Syriac.* Cambridge: Cambridge University Press. Repr. Amsterdam: Philo, 1971.

Marogulov, Q. I. 1976. *Grammaire néo-syriaque pour écoles d'adultes (dialecte d'Urmia),* trans. Olga Kapeliuk (Comptes Rendus du Groupe Linguistique d'Études Chamito-Sémitiques, Suppl. 5). Paris: Geuthner.

Odisho, Edward Y. 1988. *The Sound System of Modern Assyrian (Neo-Aramaic)* (Semitica Viva 2). Wiesbaden: Harrassowitz.

———. 1993. "*Majliyana:* An Orthographic Indicator of Phonological Change in Modern Assyrian." *Journal of the Assyrian Academic Society* (Chicago) 7/1: 76–83.

Polotsky, Hans Jakob 1961. "Studies in Modern Syriac." *Journal of Semitic Studies* 6: 1–32.

———. 1967. "Eastern Neo-Aramaic: Urmi and Zakho." In Rosenthal 1967, vol. 2, part 1, pp. 69–77.

Sabar, Yona. 1976. *Pəšaṭ Wayəhî Bəšallaḥ: A Neo-Aramaic Midrash on Beshallaḥ (Exodus): Introduction, Phonetic Transcription, Translation, Notes, and Glossary.* Wiesbaden: Harrassowitz.

MANDAIC

Coxon, P. W. 1970. "Script Analysis and Mandaean Origins." *Journal of Semitic Studies* 15: 16–30.

Drower, Ethel Stefana, Lady. 1937. *The Mandaeans of Iraq and Iran.* London: Oxford University Press.

Klugkist, A. C. 1986. "The Origin of the Mandaic Script." In *Scripta Signa Vocis: Studies about Scripts, Scriptures, Scribes and Languages in the Near East, Presented to J. H. Hospers by His Pupils, Colleagues and Friends,* ed. H. L. J. Vanstiphout, K. Jongeling, F. Leemhuis, and G. J. Reinink, pp. 111–20. Groningen: Forsten.

Macuch, Rudolf. 1965. *Handbook of Classical and Modern Mandaic.* Berlin: de Gruyter.

———. 1967. "Mandaic." In Rosenthal 1967, vol. 2, part 1, pp. 46–61; part 2, pp. 67–81.

———. 1971. "The Origins of the Mandaeans and Their Script." *Journal of Semitic Studies* 16: 174–92.

Naveh, Joseph. 1970. "The Origin of the Mandaic Script." *Bulletin of the American Schools of Oriental Research* 198 (April): 32–37.

Nöldeke, Theodor. 1875. *Mandäische Grammatik.* Halle: Waisenhaus. Repr. Darmstadt: Wissenschaftliche Buchgesellschaft, 1964.

Aramaic Scripts
for Iranian Languages

P. Oktor Skjærvø

During the Achaemenid period (549–330 B.C.E.), Aramaic was used as the chancery language throughout the Empire (hence the term "Imperial Aramaic"), and subsequently several Iranian states adopted the Aramaic alphabet for their languages. Exceptions occurred only where there was strong competion from other writing systems, such as the Greek script in Bactria and the Indian Brahmi (SECTION 30) used by the Iranians in Chinese Turkestan (Khotan and Tumshuq).

We do not know exactly when Iranians started writing their own languages using Aramaic script. We have Aramaic texts from the early days of the Achaemenid empire, while Iranian texts in Aramaic script are known only from the Parthian period (ca. 210 B.C.E. – 224 C.E.) onward. Although they are scarce, these Aramaic texts allow us to follow the development of the script in various parts of Iran from its earliest forms through its local variants. The most important are the Parthian, Middle Persian (TABLE 48.1), Avestan (TABLE 48.7), and Sogdian scripts (TABLE 48.2).

In addition, Iranian languages were written in varieties of the Syriac scripts (SECTION 47): the Manichean script derived from Estrangelo, used to write Parthian, Middle Persian, Sogdian, and Bactrian (1 fragment); and the Christian Sogdian derived from Nestorian script. The Manichean script was also used to write Old Turkish and Tokharian (2 fragments; most Tokharian manuscripts use forms of Brahmi). The Khwarezmian script is known from a few inscriptions; it was later replaced by the Arabic script.

Orthographic principles

Transliteration

There are various systems in use for transliterating the Aramaic letters (representing them by Roman letters in one-to-one correspondence).* Thus **w** is variously translit-

---

*Letters in bold type refer to the symbols (identified by their Hebrew names), with transliterations and transcriptions relevant to particular languages in italics. The Greek letters β, δ, γ represent fricatives *v* (labio-dental or bilabial), *ð*, *γ*.

erated as *w* or *v*, ḥ as *ḥ* or *h*, ṣ (in Iranian studies, represented by **c**) as *c* or *č*. Note that the letters **ḫ** (the symbol for **hē** has a bar under it to distinguish it from **h**, used for **ḥēt**), ʿ, and ṭ are found only in heterograms (see below), which are transliterated with capital letters **O** and **Θ**. The subscript dot of **h** may therefore be omitted without causing ambiguity.

Use of Aramaic letters

The Aramaic script, devised for Semitic languages, contained letters for numerous sounds not found in Iranian. Some of these were adopted to write sounds that were not found in Aramaic—ṣ for Iranian *č*, and **ḫ** for the velar fricative *x*; **l** in Sogdian for δ—but even so the Aramaic alphabet contained more letters than were needed, and ṭ, ʿ, and **q** were used only to write heterograms and numerals (differently in the Manichean and Christian Sogdian scripts, see below). In Middle Persian, ⟩ **l** is used more often than ⟨ **r** (= **w**) to write *r*.

In Aramaic documents from the mid-Parthian era, there is incipient confusion of **h** and **ḥ** (e.g., ḥmw for hmw and ʾhy for ʾḥy); and in the Parthian and Middle Persian heterograms, **ḫ** tends to be confined to final position while **ḥ** is written elsewhere, regardless of their etymologies.

Aramaic **ḫ** was used in Parthian and Sogdian for the feminine ending *-ă̄*, which resembled the Aramaic ending. This became a mere convention when the ending was lost in both Parthian (always; written only in female names) and Sogdian (in "heavy" stems—word stems containing at least one long vowel or a diphthong, including *ar*, *an*, *am*, which attracted the stress causing loss of short final vowels). In current transliterations of Parthian, the final **-ḫ** is variously rendered as *-ḫ*, *-H*, *-Ḥ*, or *-E*, e.g., ⲇⲧⲩⲏⲇ ʾnḥtyH/ʾnḥtyE (etc.) *Anāhīd*, a goddess (from OIran. *Anāhitāyāh, gen.-dat.). For Sogdian the final **-ḫ** is commonly transliterated as *-h*, e.g. ⲥⲃⲙⲇ δγwth δ(*u*)γutá 'daughter' but ⲥⲙⲇ δʾyh *dā́y* 'slave woman'.

For transliterating the Manichean alphabet, *h* is commonly used for **ḥ** and *ḫ* for **ḫ**.

For transliterating the Christian Sogdian alphabet, *ḥ*, *h*, or *ḫ* is used for **ḥ**, and *ḫ* or *h* for **ḫ**, both of which occur only in Syriac words and names. In Christian Sogdian, ⲩ **t** is used for *t* and ⲇ **t** is used for *θ* in Sogdian words, though in some manuscripts the practice is reversed.

Developments from Imperial Aramaic

The Aramaic script remained largely unchanged in Iran during the Achaemenid (549–330 B.C.E.), Seleucid (330 – ca. 210 B.C.E.), and early Parthian (ca. 210 B.C.E. – 224 C.E.) periods. The Achaemenid text corpus comprises the Aramaic letters from Egypt, the Aramaic inscriptions on ritual implements from Persepolis, and the Ashokan inscriptions from the northeast corner of the empire, modern Afghanistan and Pakistan.

There is a not yet completely interpreted inscription on the tomb of Darius (550–486), apparently from the Seleucid period and presumably in Aramaic. In the Seleucid period the coins of kings and satraps contain legends in Greek and Aramaic.

From the *Early Parthian* period (2nd–1st c. B.C.E.), there are a number of inscriptions on rock, metal objects (including coins), pottery, and parchment. Some of these are clearly in Iranian languages, presumably Parthian (e.g. the wine receipts from Nisa, east of the Caspian Sea; TABLE 48.1), although the fact is obscured by the extensive use of heterograms (see below). Other inscriptions, however, that have also been claimed to be Parthian are more likely to be in faulty bureaucratic Aramaic.

The official *Parthian script* (TABLE 48.1) had reached its standard form by the second century C.E. and continued into the Sassanian period (224–651 C.E.); the last Parthian inscription is from 292 (the Paikuli inscription).

The Persian variant of the Aramaic script evolved in southern Iran (Pars, modern Fars) in the late Parthian period, as can be seen from the coins of the line of *frataraka* kings, from which was to emerge Ardasher, the founder of the Sassanian dynasty. This variant became the official script for writing *Middle Persian* of the Sassanian empire (TABLE 48.1). It remained basically unchanged as a monumental script until the fifth century.

A variant of the Persian script used for writing on paper is the so-called *Psalter script*, known from a fragmentary manuscript of the Psalms of David found in Chinese Turkestan. In this script (TABLE 48.1) the letters are much changed, and many are now connected.

The Psalter script developed via a simplified epigraphic variant (known from numerous funerary inscriptions), here called *Early Cursive Pahlavi*, into the so-called *(Book) Pahlavi script*, so named because it is the script used in the Zoroastrian books (TABLE 48.1). The final stage is the almost indecipherable script used in the Pahlavi papyri of the late Sassanian/early Islamic period.

Avestan is a composite script based on the Psalter and Book Pahlavi scripts.

The *Sogdian script* is known in three principal forms (TABLE 48.2). The earliest form is used in letters written on paper, dating from the early fourth century C.E., and in a few short inscriptions from northern Pakistan. The common Sogdian script is a cursive variant found in secular documents, most importantly the royal archives discovered at Mount Mug, and in Buddhist and Manichean manuscripts, where two stages are distinguished: the *formal* or *sūtra* script, and the *Uyghur* variant (SECTION 49).

The main modern work on Iranian writing systems is found in Herzfeld 1924 and Henning 1958. For further bibliography see the contributions on individual languages in Schmitt 1989 , and, for the locations of Iranian languages, the map therein.

Heterograms (ideograms)

The transition from Aramaic to local Iranian as the written language was apparently a smooth one: the scribes gradually began inserting Iranian words into their texts,

TABLE 48.1: *Main West Iranian Scripts Developed from Aramaic*

Aramaic	Early Parthian (Nisa)	Parthian inscr's	Principal Phonetic Values (Parthian)	Middle Persian inscr's	Psalter	Early Cursive Pahlavi	Book Pahlavi	Principal Phonetic Values (MPers.)
ʾ			a, ā					a, ā
b			b, w					b, w
g			g, γ					g, y
d	ȝ = ʿ, r		d, δ					d, y
h (ḥ)								
w			w, ŏ, ŭ	2 = ʿ, r	ʟ = ʿ, r			w, ŏ, ŭ
z			z, ž					z
ḥ (h)			h, x					h, x
ṭ								
y			y, ẹ̆, ị̄					y, ẹ̆, ị̄, ǰ
k			k, g					k, g
l (δ)			l					l, r
m			m					m
n			n					n
s			s					s, h
ʿ	ɣ/ȝ = d, r	ȝ = r		2 = w, r	ʟ = w, r			Ø
p			p, b					p, b, f
ṣ (c)			č					č, ǰ, z
q								
r	ȝ = d, ʿ	ȝ = ʿ	r	2 = w, ʿ	ʟ = w, ʿ			r
š			š, ž					š
t			t, d					t, d

TABLE 48.2: *Main East Iranian Scripts Developed from Aramaic*

Aramaic	Sogdian Ancient Letters	Sogdian sutra script	Manichean Sogdian	Christian Sogdian	Principal Phonetic Values (Sogdian)
ʾ					a, ā
b					b, β
(β)					β
g					g, γ
(γ)					γ
d					d, δ
h (ẖ)					a, Ø
w					w, ŏ, ŭ
z					z
(j)					ž
(ž)					ž
ḥ (h)					γ, x, h
ṭ					t
y					y, ĕ, ĭ
k					k
(x)					x
l (δ)					δ
m					m
n					n
s					s
ʿ					Ø
p					p
(f)					f
ṣ (c)					č, ǰ
q					k
r					r
š					š
t					t, θ

turning the bureaucratic language into a "mixed" or "bastardized" Aramaic, but eventually the entire language was Iranian. They still wrote Aramaic words, however, but these became mere symbols (sometimes called "Semitic masks") for the corresponding Iranian words (compare the use of Latin abbreviations in English: *e.g.* = 'for instance', *etc.* = 'and so on'; and similar practices in the cuneiform scripts, SECTION 3). Thus they would write **mlk**⟩ for Parth., MPers. *šāh*, Sogd. *əxšēwanē* 'king'. These Semitic "masks" were until recently called "ideograms," but today *heterogram* or *Aramaogram* is the more common term.

It is customary to transliterate heterograms using capital letters: **MLKA**. In his Pahlavi dictionary (1971), D. N. MacKenzie introduced the convention of replacing ⟩, ⟨, **Ḥ**, and **Ḫ** in heterograms with **A, O, H,** and **E,** their historical descendants. H. Humbach later extended this convention to using Greek Θ for **Ṭ**. Thus one can dispense entirely with subscript diacritics.

Similar conventions have been applied to Sogdian, and a variety of systems can be seen in the scholarly literature. Today we usually find ⟩ (not **A**) and **H** (not **E**), but **X** for **Ḥ** (earlier also Γ), e.g. ܡܡ **⟩XRZY** (⟩ΓRZY, ⟩ḤRZY) *arti* 'and', ܡ **⟩XY** (⟩ḤY) *βrāt* 'brother', ܡ **MLK**⟩ *əxšēwanē* 'king', ܡܘ **KZNH** *māδ* 'thus'.

In Parthian, all the Aramaic letters were still used in the heterograms, but in Middle Persian **q** and **ṭ** were used only sporadically in the earliest inscriptions and were then replaced by **k** and **t**, e.g., Parth. ܡܡ **QΘLt** *ōžad* 'killed' = MPers. ܡܡ **YK-TLWN** *ōzad*; Parth. ܡܡ **ΘB** *nēw* 'good' = MPers. ܡ **ΘB,** later ܡܡ **TBw** *nēw*. In Middle Persian, the letter **q** became identical with **m** and survived only in ܡܡ **QDM** (= **MDM**) *abar* 'on'.

Aramaic ⟨ is still a distinct letter in the earliest Nisa documents, but in the later ones it is used only in the heterogram **OL** and is identical with **r** elsewhere. Similarly, in Sogdian it is found in the Ancient Letters in the heterograms ܡܡ **OD** *at* 'to' in the letter openings and in the sutra script in ܡܡ **ONYOW** *framāt* 'said' (respectful form; for **ONOYW** < ⟩*ny* 'to answer'?). In all other instances, ⟨ = **r**.

Phonetic complements

In Parthian and Middle Persian, heterograms may receive *phonetic complements* to identify the specific grammatical form of the underlying Iranian word (cf. the similar practice in cuneiform). See examples in TABLE 48.3; note also MPers. ܡܡ **LCDr** *tar* 'through, via'. The use of phonetic complements increased steadily with time.

TABLE 48.3: *Phonetic Complements in Parthian (†) and Middle Persian*

ܡܡ(ܢ)	**OBDW(t)**	*kar-ēd†*	'he does'		ܡܡ	**BRTE**	*duxt*	'daughter'
ܡܡ	**OBDWm**	*kar-ām†*	'I/we do'		ܡܡ	**BRTEr**	*duxt-ar* gen.-dat.
ܡܡ	**AHY**	*brād*	'brother'		ܡܡ	**HZYTN**	*dīd*	'saw'
ܡܡ	**AHYtl**	*brā-dar* gen.-dat.sg.; nom.pl.		ܡܡ	**HZYTNt**	*wēn-ēd* 3sg., 2pl.
ܡܡ	**AHYtlyn**	*brā-darīn* gen.pl.		ܡܡ	**HZYTNšn**	*wēn-išn* 'seeing'

Archaizing or "pseudo-historical" orthography

The Parthian and Middle Persian scripts are both strongly *archaizing*, i.e., the orthography remained largely unchanged from earlier stages of the languages (as in English or French) and therefore reflects outdated pronunciation. For instance, in both languages intervocalic voiceless stops were voiced between vowels ($p > b$, $t > d$, $k > g$), but the original *p t k* were still written. In both languages, intervocalic voiced stops first became spirants ($b > \beta$, $d > \delta$, $g > \gamma$); in Parthian β then became *w*, and in Middle Persian all three spirants developed into semivowels ($\beta > w$, δ and $\gamma > y$)—but the original *b d g* were still written. Two circumstances show that these retained orthographic conventions did not represent the actual pronunciation: the Manichean texts from the third and fourth centuries in the Manichean alphabet, which are written in a mostly phonetic orthography; and "pseudo-historical" spellings in Parthian and Middle Persian themselves.

Pseudo-historical (or wrongly archaizing) spellings occur when the scribe "makes a wrong guess" about the original spelling of a word. For instance, since Old Persian *bagadāta-* became Middle Persian *bayād* or *baʾād*, the scribes sometimes wrote ردیدر **bgdʾn** for *bayān* (*baʾān*, Man.MPers. ܒ‍ܐܐܢ *bʾʾn*) 'gods' from Old Persian *baganām*. Further examples are shown in TABLE 48.4.

In the Sogdian script, pseudo-historical orthography is found in the endings *-ē* and *-ō*, which developed from older *-akah, -akam, -akahya*, etc. In Sogdian, final *-ah* > *-i* (written **-y, -ʾy**) and *-am* > *-u* (**-w, -ʾw**); we therefore find **-y, -ʾy, -ʾky** for final *-ē*, and **-ʾw, -ʾkw** for final *-ō*. Occasionally **-ʾkw** seems to be used for *-ē* as well.

At some stage, probably toward the end of the Sassanian period, final *-g* [-ɣ] was lost in Middle Persian and Parthian (*-ag, -īg, -ōg, -ūg* > *-a, -ī, -ō, -ū*), as shown by transcriptions into Sogdian, although the final consonant was still commonly written (**-k**, Man. **-g**). This made possible the unetymological use of **-k** in Pahlavi to express Avestan long vowels, e.g., سلوک **ʾslwk** *āsrō* for Av. *āθrō* 'of the fire'.

The Manichean script shares with the Parthian and Middle Persian scripts the archaizing use of **c** (or **j**) for intervocalic Parth. *ž* and MPers. *z*.

TABLE 48.4: *Pseudo-historical Spellings in Parthian (†) and Middle Persian*

Iranian	Translit.	Notes	Normal.	Gloss	Manichean Equivalent
گ‍ت‍و	gtw	cf. Avestan گ‍اث‍و *gāθu*	*gāh*†	'throne'	Man.Parth. ܓ‍ܐܗ *gʾh*
اک‍م	ʾkm	Old Iranian *ākāmam	*āgām*†	'or'	Man.Parth. ܐܓ‍ܡ *ʾgʾm*
داتوبل	dʾtwbl	OIran. *dātōbara	*dāywar*	'judge'	Man.MPers. ܕ‍ܐ‍ܝ‍ܘ‍ܪ *dʾywr*
لوبان	lwbʾn	Av. *uruuąnəm*	*ruwān*	'soul'	Man.MPers. ܪܘܢ *rwʾn*
هدیبل	hdybl		*hayār*	'helper'	Man.MPers. ܗ‍ܝ‍ܪ *hyʾr*
راسی	rʾsy	Pahl. راه *rʾh* < *rāθiia*	*rāh*	'road'[a]	Man.MPers. ܪܐܗ *rʾh*
پوهلی	pwhly	or پولسی *pwlsy* < *pṛθu*	*puhl*	'bridge'	Man.MPers. ܦ‍ܘܗܠ *pwhl*
اسوموکی	ʾlswmwky	learned borrowing	*ahlomōɣ*	'heretic'	< Av. *ašǝmaoɣō*

a. Intervocalically both θ and *s* became *h*; cf. the next example.

SAMPLES OF PARTHIAN AND MIDDLE PERSIAN

PARTHIAN

W   mwyšhwt   ynktrk W WBC ntz'y   rp'   NL   nwgwš   sw'←

rtšh   tnw'   ENZ yprwyd' ntz'y   ytp W mYWH   trktsd   ntz'y

NL   NM RTAB WNM   šyWHL TDBO   ypBΘ W EMŠ   tNSHH W   tOBY

ynktrk   W   WBC   ntz'y   rp'   šyWHL   tYWH   whnrp W EYHY

tnWDBO   ytrktsd   W   tnEYHY   rwyd'   tz'y   KYA   dwyšhwt

1. Transliteration:	'ws	šwgwn	LN	'pr	y'ztn		CBW	W	krtkny
2. Normalization:	awās	čwāγōn	amāh	abar	yaz(a)dān	īr		ud	kerdagān
3. Gloss:	now	like	we	in	god.PL.OBL	matter		and	service

1.	twhšywm	W	y'ztn		dstkrt	HWYm W		pty	y'ztn	'dywrpy
2.	tuxšām	ud	yazdān		dastkerd	hēm	ud	pad	yazdān	aδyāwarīf
3.	we.toil	and	god.PL.OBL	property	we.are	and	by		god.PL.OBL	help

1.	ZNE	'wnt	hštr	YBOt	W	HHSNt	ŠME	W	ΘBpy	OBDt
2.	im	āwend	(x)šahr	wxāšt	ud	derd	nām	ud	nēwīf	kerd
3.	this	so.much	land	sought	and	held	name	and	bravery	made

1.	LHWyš	MNW	BATR	MN	LN	YHYE		W	prnhw
2.	haw-iž	kē	paš	až	amāh	bawāδ		ud	parrox
3.	he-too	who	after	from	us	he.shall.become		and	lucky

1.	HWYt	LHWyš	'pr	y'ztn	CBW	W	krtkny	twhšywd
2.	ahād	haw-iž	abar	yazdān	īr	ud	kerdagān	tuxšāδ
3.	he.shall.be	he-too	in	god.PL.OBL	matter	and	service	he.shall.toil

1.	AYK	y'zt	'dywr	YHYEnt		W	dstkrty	OBDWnt
2.	kū	yazd	aδyāwar	bawānd		ud	dastkerd	karānd
3.	so.that	god.PL.DIR	helper	they.shall.become	and	property	they.shall.make

'Now, as We toil (have toiled) in the matters and services of the gods and are (have been) the property of the gods and by the help of the gods have sought out and held (acquired) these many lands (and) made a name and (=of) bravery, (thus) he too who shall be after Us and shall be lucky, may he too toil in the matters and services of the gods so that the gods will be his helpers and and make (him their) property!'

—*From the trilingual (Parthian/Middle Persian/Greek) inscription of Šāpūr I at Naqš-e Rostam near Persepolis in southern Iran (Sprengling 1953, pl. 6).*

Middle Persian

ylt'tslpwh   n'tzy   KZ   NWWHY   YHORM   ENL   RHA   WNM   KYA←

yrbdh   nwgw'   ENZ   ytzy   cELO   KYA   dNWWHY   yltkm'kwhW

NWWHY   ENL   nwgyc   dNWWHY

1. Transliteration:	AYK	MNW	AHR	LNE	MROHY	YHWWN	ZK
2. Normalization:	kū	kē	pas	amāh	xwadāy	bawād	ān
3. Gloss:	so.that	who	after	us	lord	shall.become	he

1.	yzt'n	hwplst'tly	Whwk'mktly		YHWWNd	AYK
2.	yaz(a)dān	huparistātar	ud-hukāmagtar		bawād	kū
3.	god.PL.OBL	obedient.COMP	and-of.good.will.COMP		shall.become	so.that

1.	OLEc	yzty	ZNE 'wgwn	hdbry	YHWWNd	cygwn	LNE	YHWWN
2.	ōy-iz	yazd	ēn-ōwōn	hayār	bawānd	čiyōn	amāh	būd
3.	him-too	god.PL.DIR	this-thus	helper	shall.become	like	us	was

'So that whoever shall become lord after Us he will be more obedient and of better will toward the gods so that the gods will be his helpers too the way they have been Ours!'

—From the trilingual (Parthian/Middle Persian/Greek) inscription of Šāpūr I at Naqš-e Rostam near Persepolis in southern Iran (Sprengling 1953, pl. 9).

Psalter script

ykmh   šPA   ytyw'd   YHORM   tNWWHY   wy'   tt'yb'←

ytstp   sPA   YHORM   LO   tNETŠO   ydnkws   WNM   yhytlwbzn

LO KYMD   nNWBHY   AL ...   KYA   ypwk'y   YZ   ytdzy   LO   tNWLBY

YHORM   k'wyg   ńNWHKŠ   DO ywlb LO   ynšd'nw'   cALW   ENYA

ypwk'y   YZ   ytdzy   LO   n'dywW   yd'l

1. Transliteration:	'by'tt		'yw	YHWWNt	MROHY	d'wyty
2. Normalization:	ayād-it		ēw	bawēd	xwadāy	Dāwīd
3. Gloss:	memory-you.OBL	HORT	it.become	lord	David

1. APš		hmky	nzbwltyhy	MNW	swkndy	OŠTENt	OL	MROHY
2. u-š		hamag	nizburdīh	kē	sōgand	xward	ō	xwadāy
3. and.his.OBL		all	affliction	who	oath	ate	to	Lord

1. APš	ptsty		YBLWNt	OL	yzdty	ZY	yʾkwpy	AYK ...	LA
2. u-š	padist		burd	ō	yazd	ī	Yākūb	kū ...	nē
3. and-he.ENCL	promise		bore	to	God	of	Jacob	that	not

1. YHBWNn	DMYK	OL	AYNE	WLAc		ʾwnʾdšny	OL	blwy	OD
2. dahān	xwamn	ō	čašm	ud-nē-iz		ōnāyišn	ō	brū	tā
3. I.shall.give	sleep	to	eye	and-not-also		slumber	to	brow	until

1. HŠKHWNn	gywʾk	MROHY	lʾdy	Wwydʾn	OL	yzdty	ZY	yʾkwpy
2. windān	gyāg	xwadāy	rāy	ud-wiyān	ō	yazd	ī	Yākūb
3. I.shall.find	place	Lord	for	and-tent	to	God	of	Jacob

'Remember, O Lord, David and all his affliction, (he) who swore an oath to the Lord and promised the God of Jacob that: "I shall not give sleep to (my) eye(s) nor slumber to (my) brow until I find a place for the Lord and a tent for the God of Jacob.'

—*Psalm 131, from the Pahlavi Psalter found in Chinese Turkestan (Andreas and Barr 1933: 110 and pl. 9).*

Book Pahlavi script

In the Pahlavi script, numerous letters merged and became indistinguishable, while at the same time little effort was made to develop diacritical marks to distinguish them. When transliterating Pahlavi, therefore, it is customary to give the letters their origi-

TABLE 48.5: *Mergers of Letters in Pahlavi*

	Values	Notes
∿	ʾ = **h** = **yy**, etc.	
⌐	**b** = **d** = **g** = **y**	occasionally
s	**z** = **y**	occasionally, then often with the diacritic of **d** (ɜ transliterated **ẕ**)
ı	**w** = **r** (= ʿ) = **n** = -**ȳ**	transliterated as ı [a]
ɔɔ, ⱬⱬ	**yy** = **ẕd**, etc. = **s** or ʾ	
ⱳ	**E** = **mn**	
ⱳ	**š** = **yʾ**	in Indian manuscripts
ɔ	**y** = **b**	occasionally, then often with the diacritic of **d** (ɜ transliterated **ḇ**), e.g. ɜⱳ **TD** = **TḆ** *nēw* 'good' (inscr. ⌐ſ)
ⱳ	**t** = ⱳ **yyn** = **sn**, etc.	occasionally (transliterated **ṣn**, etc.)
ℓ	**p** and ⱬ **yc**	often confused

a. note that **ı** is the usual character for *r*, while **r** (= *w*) is found in a relatively small set of words, most of them heterograms.

TABLE 48.6: *Examples of Pahlavi writing*

Pahlavi	Transliteration	Normalization	Gloss	Notes
سسویہ	ʾsmʾnˈ	āsmān	'sky'	
۱۱سویہ	MDMENstnˈ	sahistan	'to seem'	
۱سویہ	gyhʾnˈ	gēhān	'world'	
۱سویویہ	ŠDYAʾnˈ	dēwān	'demons'	
هہ ہہ	QDM	abar	'on'	
سویہ	dmykˈ = ẕmykˈ	zamīg	'earth'	Psalter هہہ
۱سویہ a	yzdʾnˈ	yazdān	'god(s)'	inscr. ۵ویویہ
۱سویویہ b	ŠḎYAʾnˈ	dēwān	'demons'	inscr. ۵ویویہ
سویہ c	ʾwhrmẕd	Ohrmazd	'God'	inscr. ۵ویویویہ
۱سویہ	mʾ(y)yytˈ			can be read as **mẕdysnˈ** *mǎzdēsn* 'Mazdayasnian' (inscr. ویویہ) or **mh(y)stˈ** *mahist* 'greatest' (inscr. ویویہ *mhsty*)
۱سویہ d	YNSḆWN	stan-, stad	'to take'	inscr. ویویہ
۱۱سویہ e or ۱۱سویہ f	ŠDRWN, ŠḎRWN	frēst-	'to send'	inscr. ویویہ
سویہ g	ʾhlmnˈ	Ahrimen	'the Devil'	inscr. ویویویہ

a. Literally yʾʾww.
b. Or even ۱سویویہ, etc., lit. šʾʾʾww.
c. Literally ʾwʾwmʾ—traditional Parsi "school" pronunciation *anhuma*.
d. Literally YWYYYWW.
e. Literally ŠYWWW.
f. Literally ŠTWW.
g. Or—upside down—سویہ.

nal value as far as this can be ascertained from texts written in earlier forms of the alphabet and from etymological considerations. If one were to give each letter only one value, the words would be completely unrecognizable and the transliteration would not be useful. Nevertheless, in cases where the identity of a word is in doubt, one sometimes resorts to this kind of automatic transliteration. TABLE 48.5 shows the principal instances of merger of originally distinct letters.

Original final -*īy*, -*ēy*, -**ydy** (Ps. هوہ), is variously written سو ʾb, سو ʾy, سو -ʾʾ, or سو -ʾ (transliterated -**ydy**).

The verbal endings 3sg. -**yt(y)** and 3pl. -**(y)nd** are commonly written in "shorthand" as سو and سو. Various methods have been used to transliterate these signs. Two possibilities are to transliterate سو as -**yt** or x_I and سو as -**ynd** or x_2. The original value of the two signs is still seen in manuscripts of old texts, but with time their original use was forgotten, and x_I is used for both -**yt** and -**t**, and x_2 for both -**yt** and -**(y)nd**. The heterogram *BYN* is written in a "shorthand" ligature سو **B̲YN** = x_I. Examples of Pahlavi writing are given in TABLE 48.6.

In the script of the Pahlavi papyri, further simplifications take place, and the words have to be read as units (word symbols) rather than as sequences of letters.

Numerous systems of transcribing Pahlavi have been and still are in use. They fall into two main groups: the "archaizing" transcriptions attempt to follow the orthography as closely as possible; the "modernizing" transcriptions follow the pronunciation of the Sassanian period as indicated by the unambiguous Manichean spellings. The most important work employing "archaizing" transcription is Nyberg 1964–74. The "modernizing" transcription is found in MacKenzie 1971. Most of the time the two systems produce identical forms, with the possible exception of "archaic" **p, t, k, c, ž** vs. "modern" **b, d, g, z** and differences in vocalization in the case of *ī/ē* and *ō/ū*; but there are instances of wider discrepancies as well. Examples: **bwtk¹** *būtak ~ būdag* (Man. **bwdg**) 'something that has been', **t²cyk¹** *tāčīk ~ tāzīg* 'Arab', **bg, bgd²n** *bag, bagān ~ bay, bayān* (Man. **by, b²(²)n**), **bwd** *bōd ~ bōy* (Man. **bwy**) 'smell', **²dl** *adar ~ ēr* (Man. **²yr**) 'below', **drwc** *druž ~ druz* 'the Lie', **m²tgd²n** *mātag-dān, mādiyān ~ mādayān* (Man. **m²dy²n**) 'book'.

SAMPLE OF PAHLAVI

hys²k²	pswlh	NWP	kytsl²b	dzmrhw²	Y	k²typ	²nwgw²	nyd-LYPŠ	NWP←

KZ	²tNWWHY	y²mh	hynšwl	NYB̲	²kl²nk²	Y	²n²mz	hyhywW		

NWP	hykyl²t	NYB̲	²nmlh²	... dzmrhw²	Y	k²wygW	s²g	hynšwl		

tNWWHY	kd²plpwz	hykm²kl²tzW	hynšn²d	LHA

1. Transliteration:	PWN	ŠPYL-dyn	²wgwn¹	pyt²k	Y	²whrmzd	
2. Normalization:	pad	weh-dēn	ōwōn	paydāg	ī	Ohrmazd	
3. Gloss:	in	Good-Religion	thus	apparent	that	Ohrmazd	

1. b²lstyk	PWN	hlwsp ²k²syh	Wwyhyh	zm²n¹	Y	²kn²lk¹
2. bālistīg	pad	harwisp-āgāhīh	ud-wehīh	zamān	ī	akanārag
3. on.high	in	all-awareness	and-goodness	time	CONN	unlimited

1. BYN	lwšnyh	hm²y	YHWWNt¹	ZK	lwšnyh	g²s	Wgyw²k	Y
2. andar	rōšnīh	hamē	būd;	ān	rōšnīh	gāh	ud-gyāg	ī
3. in	light	ever	was	that	light	seat	and-place	of

1. ²whrmzd ...	²hlmn¹	BYN	t²lykyh	PWN	AHL	d²nšnyh
2. Ohrmazd ...	Ahrimen	andar	tārīgīh	pad	pas-dānišnīh	
3. Ohrmazd	Ahrimen	in	darkness	in	backward-knowledge	

1. Wzt²lk²mkyh	zwplp²dk	YHWWNt¹
2. ud-zadār-kāmagīh	zufr-pāyag	būd
3. and-destruction-desire	deep-station	was

'In the Good Religion it is revealed that Ohrmazd was on high in omniscience and goodness for an unlimited time in the light; that light (is) the throne and place of Ohrmazd ... Ahrimen was in darkness in backward knowledge and desire to destroy in the depth.'   —*From the Bundahišn (Codex DH 1970: 1)*.

The Avestan alphabet

The oldest Avestan texts are approximately contemporary with the *Rigveda* (2nd millennium B.C.E.), while the younger texts date from the first millennium B.C.E.; they were transmitted orally and written down only in the mid Sassanian period, the fifth–sixth centuries C.E. (though the oldest manuscripts date only from the 13th century).

TABLE 48.7: *Avestan Alphabet*

a		ā		å		ā̃		ą^a	ą^a
i		ī		e		ē		ə	ə̄
u		ū		o		ō			
b		β		p		f			m, m^b
d		δ		t		θ		ṯ^c	n
g, ġ^d		γ		k		x		h	ŋ
j				c					ń^e
Y^{f, g}		y^{f, g}				x́^h			ń^h
V^{i, g}						x^{v h}			ŋ^{v h}
r									ń^j
s	ṣ, s	z		š		ž		ś k, l	ṣ^{l, m}

a. Both nasal *ą*, used (apparently) indiscriminately in the extant manuscripts but may originally have represented nasal *ą* and *ə̨*.

b. Voiceless(?) variant of *m* after *h*, or substituted for *hm*.

c. Presumably unreleased (sometimes erroneously called "implosive") dental stop [t̚]

d. Rare; original value unknown.

e. Palatal [ɲ], found only before *i, ī*, but not used consistently.

f. Used only in initial position; the exact difference between **Y** and **y** is not known.

g. For *i* and *u* other than in initial position, the Avestan alphabet writes *ii* and *uu*, which are then to be analyzed as [iĭ] and [uŭ], cf. the Old Persian spellings *iy* and *uv*.

h. Palatalized and velarized velar fricatives and nasals; some scribes confuse **x́** with **x^v**, **ń** with **ŋ^v**.

i. Used only in initial position.

j. Written for *n* (sometimes *m*) before consonant (*ṇt, ṇc, ṇb*, etc.); corresponds to the unwritten pre-consonantal nasal in Old Persian (e.g., *ba^n daka*).

k. Historically < *či*.

l. The exact phonetic values and relationship to *š* at the time of the invention of the alphabet are not known. The original opposition may have been palatal *ś* vs. retroflex *š*, while *ṣ* was a voiceless lateral: *ṣ* is represented in Pahlavi by *hl* (e.g. *ašauua* 'righteous' > Pahl. *ahlaw*). In the extant manuscripts of Avestan texts the distinction between the original *š ~ ś ~ ṣ* is no longer observed.

m. Historically < *r^h t* (i.e. voiceless *r + t*).

A new alphabet based on the Psalter and the Pahlavi scripts was created for this purpose that also included letters for sixteen vowels (TABLE 48.7).

The Avestan alphabet is phonetic (presumably modeled on the Greek alphabet) and required a much larger number of letters than these two scripts could provide. Additional letters were therefore created by the use of diacritics (e.g. ꭹ ī and ꭹ ū from ꭵ i and ꭲ u; ꭿ β and ꭾ f from ꭳ p, which in Pahlavi had the phonetic values p, b, β, and f), and a few seem to have been simply invented. The Avestan letter ꭲ ə bears a striking resemblance to the Greek ε e.

"Pazand" refers to Pahlavi or Modern Persian written in the Avestan alphabet.

SAMPLE OF AVESTAN

←ꭲꭲꭲꭲꭲ . ꭲꭲ . (ꭲꭲꭲ) . ꭲꭲ . ꭲꭲꭲꭲ . ꭲꭲ . ꭲꭲꭲꭲꭲ←
. mərtšuθaraZ . ṭiāpu . ōmoah . ā . mūtar . ā . mīnauuāh←

:: ꭲꭲꭲꭲꭲꭲ . ꭲꭲꭲꭲꭲꭲ . ꭲꭲꭲꭲꭲ . ꭲꭲꭲ . ꭲꭲꭲꭲ
.mətṇaiiauuārs . acså̄θāg . mətṇaθadžoay . iriap . mərtā

ꭲꭲꭲꭲꭲ . ꭲꭲꭲ . ꭲꭲꭲ . ꭲꭲ . ꭲꭲ . ꭲꭲ . ꭲꭲꭲꭲꭲ . ꭲꭲꭲꭲ . ꭲꭲ . ꭲꭲ
. ehapsīv . məza . miY . īha . əran . ōk . ōrtšuθaraZ . ṭasərəp . mid . ā

ꭲꭲꭲꭲꭲ . ꭲꭲꭲꭲ . ꭲꭲꭲꭲꭲꭲ . ꭲꭲꭲꭲꭲ . ōtauutsa . šuəhṇa
. eheiiag . ehax^v . asəradad . mətšēars . ōtauutsa . šuəhṇa

:: ꭲꭲꭲꭲꭲ . ꭲꭲꭲꭲꭲ
.ehašəma . ōtauunax^v

1. *Transliteration:* hāuuanīm .   ā . ratūm .   ā . haomō . upāiṭ .
2. *Gloss:*   haoma.pressing at proper.time to haoma went.up.to

1. Zaraθuštrəm .   ātrəm .   pairi .   yaoždaθaṇtəm . gāθåsca .
2. Zarathustra.ACC   fire.ACC   around   purifying.ACC Gathas.ACC.and

1. srāuuaiiaṇtəm.   ā .   dim .   pərəsaṭ .   Zaraθuštrō. .   kō .
2. reciting.ACC   to   him.ACC   asked   Zarathustra.NOM   who.NOM

1. narə .   ahī .   Yim .   azəm .   vīspahe .   aŋhə̄uš .   astuuatō .
2. man.VOC   you.are whom.ACC I.NOM   all.GEN   world.GEN bone-ful.GEN

1. sraēštəm .   dadarəsa .   x^vahe .   gaiiehe .   x^vanuuatō .   aməšahe .
2. beautiful.SUP I.have.seen   own.GEN   life.GEN   sun-ful.GEN   immortal.GEN

'At the proper hour of the haoma pressing haoma went up to Zarathustra, who was ritually preparing the fire and reciting the Gathas. Zarathustra asked him: 'Who are you, man, whom I have (now) seen (to be) the most beautiful of my entire sunny immortal life?'

—*From the Avestan Hōm yašt 'hymn to haoma' (Yasna 9;*
Geldner 1896: 38–39).

Sogdian script

In the Sogdian script used in the "Ancient Letters" (TABLE 48.2), most of the letters are distinct and do not change shape when joined. In the "formal" and "Uyghur" Sogdian scripts, most of the letters are joined and, owing to the use of a broad pen, are frequently difficult to distinguish. In the earlier form, ᵓ is still distinguished from **n**; but in the later, ᵓ = **n**, ᵓ**n** = **n**ᵓ. Some scribes distinguish **z** from **n** by not connecting **z** to the preceding letter, but others make no distinction. In the later, increasingly cursive, form, other letters tend to become indistinguishable as well: γ/**x**/**s**/**š**, **r**/β/**y**. Some letters are distinguished only in final position (by some scribes), e.g., **n** ~ **z**, **x** ~ γ.

z is sometimes distinguished from **n** or **z** from **ž** by a diacritical point ⹁, and the foreign sound *b* was noted as ⸲ᵔ **ṗ**.

SAMPLES OF SOGDIAN

ANCIENT LETTERS

PLI	kkᵓnᵓk	wrᵓᵓβδynn	kkᵓrβ	wᵓtwx	wγβ		DO←

wnᵓᵓγβ	wMXyKZ	YZKYA ykwnᵓztᵓps wycᵓmn		MLŠ	rwyrβ

ktnβynn	ktnβ	δρyx	NM	tšyp	tryβ

1. Transliteration:	OD	βγw	xwtᵓw	βrᵓkk	nnyδβᵓᵓrw	kᵓnᵓkk
2. Normalization:	at	βaγu	xutāw	βarak	nanē-θβār	kanak
3. Gloss:	to	lord.ACC	master	Barak	Nana's-gift	Kanak

1.	ILP	βrywr	ŠLM	nmᵓcyw	spᵓtzᵓnwky	AYKZY
2.	(ēw-)zār	βrēwar	*āfrīwan	namācyu	spātzānūk	kaδ-uti
3.	thousand	ten.thousand	greeting(?)	reverence.ACC	bended.knee	when-that.and

1.	ZKyXMw	βγᵓᵓnw	βyrt	pyšt	MN	xypθ	βntk	nnyβntk
2.	wēšanu	βaγān(u)	βyart	pišt	con	xēpθ	βantē	nanē-βantē
3.	them.OBL	lords.OBL	received	written	from	own	servant	Nana's-servant

'To the Divine Master Barak(?) Nanethvar Kanak a thousand, ten thousand greetings, reverently with bended knees when received by their divinities. Written by his own servant Nanevante.'

—*From the Old Sogdian "Ancient Letters" found in a mailbag in the Great Wall*
(AL II, Reichelt 1931: 12 and pl. 2).

STORY OF RUSTAM

yšxr nnʾrβnδwβ wxʾ syʾʾ smytr kʾδywrp ymtswr yxʾy tnʾrtyw←

trʾγz ʾnβwx NM ymtswr wxʾ tpsnm šyrγyw ymtswr wKZ

wrp δγzʾβ tnyʾβyn ntsnwrδ nnδwγn mrc ʾknδrwp wKZ cnymytp

rʾs twyδ wk rʾβδʾp wšxr

1. Transliteration: wytrʾnt	yʾxy	rwstmy	prwyδʾk	rtyms
2. Normalization: wītarand	yaxī	Rustami	parwēδē	rti-mas
3. Gloss:	IMPF.they.departed brave	Rustam.GEN	to.seek	and-then

1. ʾʾys	ʾxw	βwδnβrʾnn	rxšy	ZKw	rwstmy
2. āyas	axu	βōδan-βarān	Raxši	awu	Rustami
3. came	the.NOM	perception-bearing	Raxš.NOM	the.ACC	Rustam.ACC

1. wyγryš	mnspt	ʾxw	rwstmy	MN	xwβnʾ	zγʾrt
2. wīγrēš	manspat	axu	Rustami	čon	xuβna	žγart
3. IMPF.he.woke	IMPF.arose	the.NOM	Rustam.NOM	from	sleep.ABL	quickly

1. ptymync	ZKw	pwrδnkʾ crm	nγwδnn	δrwnstn	nyβʾynt
2. ptīmēnč	awu	puʳδang-čarm	nγōδan	δrūn-stan	nīβēnd
3. IMPF.he.donned	the.ACC	leopard-skin	garment	bow-container	IMPF.he.tied

1. βʾzγδ	prw	rxšw	pʾδβʾr	kw	δywt	sʾr
2. βāžγaδ	par-ō	Raxšu	pāθfār	kū	δēwt	sār
3. IMPF.mounted	on-the.ACC	Raxš.ACC	IMPF.hurried	to-	demon.PL	-ward

'They (the demons) departed in search of the brave Rustam. Then came the perceptive(?) Rakhsh (his horse) and woke Rustam. Rustam arose out of his sleep, quickly donned (his) leopard-skin garment, tied on his bow-case, mounted Rakhsh, and hurried toward the demons.'

— *From a (Manichean?) version of the story of Rustam (Benveniste 1940A, pls. 193–94, 1940B: 135; Sims-Williams 1976: 54–57).*

Developments from Estrangelo Syriac

Manichean script (TABLE 48.2; Müller 1904: 5) is based on Estrangelo (SECTION 47). It is sometimes believed to have been invented by Mani, who founded the Manichean religion in the third century C.E., but it is probably older (Erika Hunter, personal communication).

This script was used to write Manichean texts in Persian, Parthian, Sogdian, and Bactrian (and also Turkish and Tokharian). As in the Sogdian script, Syriac **l** was used to write δ. In addition, diacritics are used to express specifically Iranian sounds. There is a new letter ܔ commonly transliterated as **j** (cf. Christian Sogdian, below).

In Manichean Middle Persian and Parthian, initial groups of sibilant + stop developed a prothetic vowel, which is written ˁ (MPers. ܠܡܐܒܐܢ ˁ**sp'h** ə/ispāh, Parth. ܠܡܐܒܐܢ ˁ**sp'd** ə/ispāδ 'army'). In Parthian inscriptions, this prothetic vowel is sometimes written ʾ (ܝܕܛܠܓܕܡܗܠ ʾ**sp'dpty** or ܡܗܠܓܒܡܗܠ **spdpty** əspāδbed 'general'). Occasionally, words with ē or ī and ō or ū are distinguished in spelling by the use of ʾ or ˁ, e.g. MPers. ܠܘܐܠ ʾ**yg** ēg 'then' ~ ܠܘܐܠ ˁ**yg** ī(g), relative particle; ܠܘܐܠ **zwr** zōr 'strength' ~ ܐܠܘܐܠ z**ˁwr** zūr 'deception', ܐܠܘܐܠ ʾ**dwr** ādur 'fire' ~ ܐܠܘܐܠ ʾ**dˁwr** *ādŭr 'excrement' (Tardieu 1980).

Sometimes, in order to fit a word on a line (rather than breaking it), letters marking long vowels are left out and the omission signified by superscript or subscript dots (thus also in the Psalter script). Note especially ܐ **ẅ** = ʾ**wd** and ܐ **š̈** = ʾ**w-š**. In Manichean Sogdian, *y* and *w* are frequently written double, and ʾ and **y** can be repeated to fill out a line.

SAMPLES OF MANICHEAN

MANICHEAN MIDDLE PERSIAN

ܟܐܡܐ	ܟܐܐ	ܟܐܝܪܐܟ	ܟܐܓ̇	ܘܐܐ	ܟܐܐܝ	ܖܐܘܝܐ	ܟܐܓ̇	ܝܐܐܠ	ܘܐܐ
dyʾp	dwʾ	dyrʾd	dwx	mwʾ	dywr	gʾbʾ	dwx	cnwn	mwʾ

ܟܐܓ̇	ܝܐܐܝܐܠܝܐ	ܟܐܐ	ܘܐܘܐܠܐܒ	ܝܐܐܝܐܠ	ܐ	ܘܐܐ	ܝܐܐܠ	ܟܐܠ	ܘܐܐ
drx	nʾmhwdrm	dwʾ	myšwq	nymrhʾ	ẅ	zʾʾ	gʾbʾ	rwz	dp	šwʾ

ܘܐܐܝܐܠ	ܝܐܐܝܐܠ	ܐ	ܝܐܐ	ܝܐܐ	ܝܐܘܘܐܐ	ܘܐܓܝܐܡܐܚ	ܝܐܘܐܐܠ	ܟܐܐ
myzwb	nymrhʾ	ẅ	zʾʾ	cʾ	nʾšwʾ	mycwmh	nšynʾd	dwʾ

	1. *Transliteration:*	ʾwm		nwnc	xwd	ʾbʾg	rwyd	ʾwm
	2. *Normalization:*	u-m		nūn iz	xwad	abāg	rawēd	u-m
	3. *Gloss:*	and-me.OBL		now-too	self	with	he.goes	and-me.OBL

	1.	xwd	dʾryd	ʾwd	pʾyd	ʾwš		pd	zwr	ʾbʾg	ʾʾz	ẅ
	2.	xwad	dārēd	ud	pāyēd	u-š		pad	zōr	abāg	Āz	ud
	3.	self	he.holds	and	protects	and-his.OBL		by	power	with	Āz	and

	1.	ʾhrmyn	qwšym	ʾwd	mrdwhmʾn	xrd	ʾwd	dʾnyšn	hmwcym
	2.	Ahrimen	kōšēm	ud	mardōhmān	xrad	ud	dānišn	hammōzēm
	3.	Ahrimen	I.fight	and	men	wisdom	and	knowledge	I.teach

	1.	ʾwšʾn	ʾc	ʾʾz	ẅ	ʾhrmyn	bwzym
	2.	u-šān	az	Āz	ud	Ahrimen	bōzēm
	3.	and-them.OBL	from	Āz	and	Ahrimen	I.save

'And even now he himself accompanies me, and he himself keeps and protects me. And by his power I fight with Az and Ahrimen and teach men wisdom and knowledge and save them from Az and Ahrimen.'

—*From Mani's autobiography in the Šābuhragān(?) (Andreas 1933: 307; facsimile in Sundermann 1981, pl. 42).*

MANICHEAN PARTHIAN

h'šrhym ẅ y'dwx nwšym dwb d'rb h'š n'h'š rhwb'š dyb←

šw' .dwb nymšwd tfykš° nyd ẅ gtšyrf w' ẅ .z'h' m'n

wk d'šwg tfykš° ẅ w'gr' wyn yk wy° tš'ryw n'tsydwb

ts' yn r'sw'h cyk

1. Transliteration:	byd	š'bwhr	š'h'n	š'h	br'd	bwd	myšwn
2. Normalization:	bid	Šābuhr	šāhān	šāh	brād	būd	Mēšūn
3. Gloss:	again	Shabuhr	king.PL.OBL	king	brother	was	Meshun

1.	xwd'y	u	myhrš'h	n'm	'h'z.	u	'w	fryštg	'wd	dyn	°škyft
2.	xwadāy	ud	Mihršāh	nām	ahāz.	ud	ō	frēštag	ud	dēn	iškeft
3.	lord	and	Mihrshah	name	was	and	to	apostle	and	religion	extremely

1.	dwšmyn	bwd.	'wš	bwdyst'n	wyr'št	°yw	ky	nyw
2.	dušmen	būd.	u-š	bōδ-estān	wirāšt	ēw	kē	nēw
3.	enemy	he.was	and-he.OBL	perfume-place	arranged	one	which	good

1.	'rg'w	u	°škyft	gwš'd	kw	kyc	h'ws'r	ny	'st
2.	aryāw	ud	iškeft	gušād	kū	keč	hāwsār	nē	ast
3.	lovely	and	extremely	opened	so.that	some	like	not	there.is

'Moreover, Shabuhr, king of kings, had a brother, lord of Meshun, and his name was Mihrshah. And he was extremely hostile to the religion of the apostle. And he had arranged a garden, which was good, lovely, and extremely large(?), so that there was none like it.'

—*From a text about Mani's life (Sundermann 1981: 102 and pl. 52).*

MANICHEAN SOGDIAN

nštr' cwsp yt' . yyr'j cn'wknmš nc 'nwk dn'rq yt'←

r'stp yṯr' .. nys r's nmδry'nšxwr wk r'stp

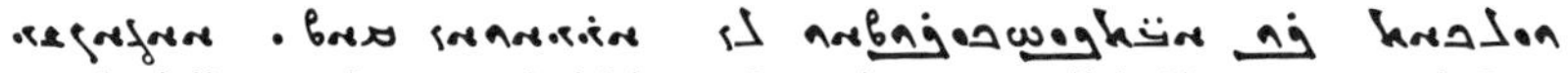

ܪܟܠܘܐ܂ ⸱ ܒܢܒ ܝܘܐܐܪܐ ܚܕ ܐܘܒܢܐ̈ܝܘܐܝܢ ܝܝ ܝܟܐܙܐܡ

dnzʾγ⁾⁾   . ṭʾm   nʾwʾdrʾ   nδ   wṭwx   ypšyktβʾ   wx   tʾpδyw

ܐܠܘܒܝܐܡܐ̈ ܝܚܐܘܒܐ ܘܘܝܝܐܒܢܐ ܚܝ ܒܢ ܝܘܐܝ ܒܢܘܝܘܐܝ

δδbmcfʾ   ʾnʾm-ʾw   mycʾstp   yṭ⁾   wnʾc   ṭryβn

1. *Transliteration:* ʾṭy qrʾnd   kwnʾ   cn   šmnkwʾnc   jʾryy .
2. *Normalization:* ati karānd   kuna   čan   šimnakwānč   žārī
3. *Gloss:*   and pure.PL you.make.IMV from Ahrimenian   poison.OBL

1. ʾṭy pswc   ʾrtšn   ptsʾr   kw   rwxšnʾγrδmn   sʾr   syn .. ʾrty
2. ati psōč   arti-šan   pat-sār   kū   roxšna-γarδman   sār   sēn   arti
3. and purify and-them.OBLafter-ward to- light-paradise   -ward raise   and

1. ptsʾr   wyδpʾt   xw   ʾβtkyšpy   xwṭʾw   δn   ʾrdʾwʾn
2. pat-sār   wēδ-pāt   xō   aβt-kišpi   xutāw   δan   ardāwān
3. after-ward that-time   the seven-clime master with righteousness.PL.OBL

1. mʾṭ .   ⁾⁾γʾznd   nβyrʾṭ   cʾnw   ʾṭy   ptsʾcym   wʾ-mʾnʾ   ʾfcmbδδ
2. māt   āγāzand   nβērāt   čānō   ati   patsāčēm   wā-mānā   afčambaδ
3. mother   they.began to.plan   how   and   we.arrange the-that   world

'Clean them of the poison of Ahrimen and purify them. Thereafter raise them to
Paradise! — Thereupon at that time the Lord of the Seven Climes and the
Mother of the Righteous began to plan: How shall we arrange that world?'
    —From a Manichean cosmological text (Henning 1948: 311–12).

Developments from Nestorian Syriac

The Christian Sogdian script is a variant of Nestorian (SECTION 47). It includes vowel
marks and contains a new letter ⲩ commonly transliterated ž. (Manichean ⲇ and
Christian Sogdian ⲩ probably have the same origin—and may be related to Tumshuqese Brahmi ž Manichean also has ⲉⲉ, however, which is commonly transliterated as
ž, and so ⲇ has been assigned the reading ǰ.) The letters ⵌ t and ⵅ ṭ are most often used
for θ and t respectively, but in a few manuscripts ⵌ t is t and ⵅ ṭ is θ. Vowels can be
marked using the Syriac pointing system, which makes this the only variety of Sogdian script in which the crucial distinctions between ǐ/ě and ǔ/ǒ are noted.

SAMPLE OF CHRISTIAN SOGDIAN

ܝܲ ⸱ ܚ ܗܐ ܐܘܲܙ̈ܪܕ ܘܟ ܛܚܝ ܟܝܐܘܐܘܪܣ ܝܝܐܘܪܣ ܟܘ ܐܡܠܘܐܠܡ ܚܕ⸱ܐ←

nd yq ʾs   wṭšyrf wq ṭnb   ṭpʾytpwʾ   ṭyṭšyrf tyn wnʾcnʾw raʾ←

ܗܘܐ ܚܘܡ ܚܟܚ ܐܝܬܚ ܟܝܚܝ ܚܝܟܚܟ ܝܚܚܝ ܗܝ ܚܘܐ ܐܡܪ̈ ܐܡܪܘ

frγ sm   ʾnγrf dymyrp   ʾynmž   yṭnmʾžyn   yṭs wrp nʾwr   yṭqryš

ܘܪܐܩܝܢܐܬܩ   ܪܦ   ܩܐܬܢܓ   ܙܐܢܘ   ܝܩ   ܐܣ   ܘܝܕ   ܕܝܘܝܩ   ܛܢܛܢܝܒܐ   ܛܘܝܥܕ

wrʾqynʾṭq   rp   qʾṭnγ   zʾnw   yq   ʾs   wyd   dywyq   ṭnṭnybʾ   ṭwyed

ܪܐܦܡܛ   ܢܥ   ܝܩ   ܐܝܢܡܙ   ܝܛܢܡܐܙܝܢ   ܢܐܘܪ

rʾpmṭ   nc   yq   ʾynmž   yṭnmʾžyn   nʾwr

1. Transliteration: ʾar   wʾncʾnw   nyṭ   fryšṭyṭ   ʾwptyʾpt   bnṭ
2. Normalization: ar   wān-čānō   nīt   frēštēt   āwpatyāpt   βant
3. Gloss: and   thus-like   other.PL   angel.PL   participant.PL   are

1. qw   fryšṭw   sʾ   qy   dn   šyrqty   rwʾn   prw   sty
2. kū   frēštō   sā   kē   δan   šīr-ktē   rwān   par-ō   stī
3. to-   angel.ACC   -ward   who   with   good-done.OBL   soul   on-the.ACC   is

1. nyžʾmnty   žmnyʾ   prymyd   frynʾ   ms   γrf   deywṭ   ʾbynṭnṭ
2. nīžāmandī   žamnyā   par-ēmēδ   fraγnā   mas   γarf   δēwt   āββendand
3. going.out.OBL   time.LOC   in-this   manner   also   many   demon.PL   are.bound

1. qywyd   deyw   sʾ   qy   wnʾz   γnṭʾq   pr   qtʾnyqʾrw   rwʾn
2. k-ēwēδ   δēw   sā   kē   wanāz   γandāk   par   ktānē-kārō   rwān
3. to-this   demon   -ward   who   made.IMPF   evil   in   sin-maker.ACC   soul

1. nyžʾmnty   žmnyʾ   qy   cn   ṭmpʾr
2. nīžāmand-ī   žamn-yā   kē   čan   tambār
3. going.out-OBL   time-LOC   which   from   body

'And as the other angels are fellows to the angel which is with the soul of the righteous man at the time of departure, so too many demons are associated with that demon which was performing evil in the sinful soul at the time of departing from the body.'

—*From Dādišōʿ Qaṭrāyāʾs commentary on the fifteenth homily of Abbā Isaiah*
(Sims-Williams 1985: 81, pl. 36).

Bibliography

Andreas, Friedrich C. 1933–37. "Mitteliranische Manichaica aus Chinesisch-Turkistan II," ed. Walter B. Henning. *Sitzungsberichte der Preußischen Akademie der Wissenschaften, Berlin* 292–363.

Andreas, Friedrich C., and Kaj Barr. 1933. "Bruchstücke einer Pehlevi-Übersetzung der Psalmen." *Sitzungsberichte der Preußischen Akademie der Wissenschaften, Berlin* 91-152.

Benveniste, Emile. 1940A. *Codices Sogdiani* (Monumenta Linguarum Asiae Majoris 3). Copenhagen: Munksgaard.

———. 1940B. *Textes sogdiens* (Mission Pelliot en Asie centrale 3). Paris: Geuthner.

The Codex DH: Being a Facsimile Edition of Bondahesh ... and Parts of Denkard. 1970(?). Tehran: Bonyād-e Farhang-e Irān.

Geldner, Karl F. 1896. *Avesta, the Sacred Book of the Parsis.* 3 vols. Stuttgart: Kohlhammer.

Henning, Walter B. 1948. "A Fragment of the Manichaean Cosmogony." *Bulletin of the School of Oriental and African Studies* 12: 306–18.

————. 1958. "Mitteliranisch." In *Iranistik* (Handbuch der Orientalistik, division 1, vol. 4, fasc. 1), pp. 20–130. Leiden: Brill.

Herzfeld, Ernst. 1924. "Essay on Pahlavi." In his *Paikuli: Monument and History of the Early Sassanian Empire I*, pp. 52–73. Berlin: Reimer.

Nyberg, Henrik S. 1964–74. *Manual of Pahlavi*, 2 vols. Wiesbaden: Harrassowitz.

MacKenzie, David Neil. 1971. *A Concise Pahlavi Dictionary*. London: Oxford University Press.

Müller, Friedrich W. K. 1904. *Handschriften-Reste in Estrangelo-Schrift aus Turfan, Chinesisch-Turkistan, II* (Abhandlungen der Preußischen Akademie der Wissenschaften). Berlin.

Reichelt, Hans. 1931. *Die soghdischen Handschriftenreste des Britischen Museums*, part 2: *Die nicht-buddhistischen Texte*. Heidelberg: Winter.

Schmitt, Rüdiger, ed. 1989. *Compendium Linguarum Iranicarum*. Wiesbaden: Reichert.

Sims-Williams, Nicholas. 1976. "The Sogdian Fragments of the British Library." *Indo-Iranian Journal* 18: 43–82.

————. 1985. *The Christian Sogdian Manuscript C2* (Berliner Turfantexte 12). Berlin: Akademie Verlag.

Sprengling, Martin. 1953. *Third Century Iran*. Chicago: University of Chicago, Oriental Institute.

Sundermann, Werner. 1981. *Mitteliranische manichäische Texte kirchengeschichtlichen Inhalts* (Berliner Turfantexte 11). Berlin: Akademie Verlag.

Tardieu, Michel. 1980. "*prātā* et *ādᶜur* chez les manichéens." *Zeitschrift der Deutschen Morgenländischen Gesellschaft* 130: 340–41.

Aramaic Scripts
for Altaic Languages

GYÖRGY KARA

Medieval Northern Iranians transmitted different forms of the Aramaic alphabet to the ancient Turks (6th–8th century C.E.) and perhaps to other non–Indo-European–speaking peoples of Inner Asia at earlier dates. A mid sixth century inscription found in Bugut, Mongolia, is an early monument showing Turkic usage of the Sogdian (Iranian) language and cursive script (SECTION 48). Non-cursive Sogdian script inspired the runiform alphabet of the ancient Turks, a highly original writing system of the region. Manichean Estrangelo (Aramaic) and Sogdian scripts were applied to the Turkic language of the Uyghurs and other Turks who were Manicheans or Nestorian Christians. The Sogdian and Brahmi (SECTION 30) scripts were used by their Buddhist countrymen. In the eleventh century, Arabic script came with Islam to the Turks of western and central Inner Asia (SECTION 61). No written document of the Huns or Avars of Inner Asia has been found, and only Chinese sources preserved the memory of the lost writing system of the Tabgach Empire (4th–6th century C.E.); its origin, type, and shape remain unknown. The vertical Uyghur variant of the Sogdian alphabet was applied to a Middle Mongolian dialect in Chinggis Khan's court (early 13th century); with some modification, it is still in use in Mongolia. The mid seventeenth century "Clear script," derived from the Mongolian "vertical" alphabet, became the writing system of the Western Mongols or Oirats (including the Kalmyks). In the Manchu Empire that embraced Manchuria, China, Mongolia, Tibet, and eastern Turkestan (from the 17th century to 1911), another modified form of the "vertical" alphabet was used to write the official Manchu language. The latest Inner Asian descendant of the Aramaic script is the Buryat alphabet (1905).

The runiform alphabet of the ancient Turks

Some early eighth century memorial inscriptions with the oldest known historical narratives in Turkic were discovered in the nineteenth century in the valley of the Orkhon River, Mongolia; hence the term *Orkhon* script. External resemblance of its characters to the Germanic runes (SECTION 24) evoked the name *runiform* alphabet or *Orkhon runes*. It has simple characters, easy to carve on wood or stone, but this does not entail the absence of curved elements. Rows read from bottom to top, char-

TABLE 49.1: *The Runiform Script of the Ancient Turks*

↑	a/e	⟩	n^1
Γ	ï/i/ë	๗	n^2
Ⴟ	ë (Yenisei)	☺	nt
⟩	o/u	⟩	nč
Ɲ	ö/ü	⟩	ñ
♪	b^1	⟩	ng (ṅ)
⤬	b^2	1	p
Ⴤ	γ	⅄	č
ϵ	g	Ⴤ	čⁱ
⅍	d^1	Ⱶ	q
×	d^2	◁	qⁱ
ꜧ	z	↓	q°
D	y^1	Ⴙ	r^1
ꝗ	y^2	↑	r^2
ⴗ	k	Ⴤ	s^1
Ⴙ	k°	I	s^2
⅃	l^1	¥, Ⴤ	š (or s^2 = š)
Ⴤ	l^2	⟐	t^1
M	lt	ꜧ	t^2
⟐	m	:	word/phrase end marker

acters run from right to left, and word division is marked by two dots like our colon. This system of some forty characters serves to render at least 26 phonemes. In this case, the discrepancy between characters and phonemes is not the result of applying a rich foreign script to a relatively simple set of sounds (though it is possible that the ancient Turks were not the first users of this script). Rather, it is the consequence of defective vowel representation. Four characters render at least eight vocalic phonemes: ↑ a = a/e [a/ɛ]; Γ i = ï/i [ɨ/i] and $ė$ [e], an allophone; ⟩ o = o/u [o/u]; and Ɲ $ü$ – ö/ü [ø/y]. These form two groups according to front versus back articulation, and a word contains vowels from only one of the two groups. This front/back harmony is combined with rules that predict the occurrence of the rounded/unrounded and high/mid/low vowels in the word. This system of vowels allows the simplification of vowel rendering, but vowels often remain unwritten. To decrease ambiguity, most consonants have two different characters, one used in back-vowel words, another used in front-vowel ones. Moreover, some letters indicate a high unrounded/rounded-vowel environment (e.g., the arrow-shaped ↓ q^o represents [ok/uk] or [ko/ku] (a pictogram? cf. Turkish *ok* 'arrow'). There is a single "neutral" character for each of the consonants *č* (beside another sign for *č* with a high unrounded vowel), *p, m, ñ, ng, z*, and for the intervocalic consonantal clusters *lt, nt, nč*; see TABLE 49.1.

   This writing system was later used in the early Uyghur empire (8th century) and in eastern Turkestan; its "Yenisei" variant is known from ancient Kirghiz inscriptions

(9th century). It has distant cognates in the various runiform alphabets found in the Talas Valley in western Turkestan, and in southeastern Europe.

SAMPLE OF ANCIENT TURKIC

1. *Transliteration:* ... t²ür²k°:　b²il²ga :qɣn¹ :　b¹üüd²ka : ul¹r¹t¹m :　s¹b¹mn¹ :
2. *Normalization:*　türk　bilge　qaɣan　bu ödke　olurtum　sabïmïn
3. *Gloss:*　Türk　Bilge　Khan　this time.at sat.I　word.my

1. t²ük°t²i : s²id²gl² :　ul¹y¹u :　in²y²gün²(m) ... / ...　b¹us¹b¹mn¹ :　d²güt²i :
2. tüketi　ešidgil　ulayu　iniyigün(üm)　　bu sabïmïn　edgüti
3. wholly　listen　further　(my).younger.brothers　this word.my　well

1. s²id² : qt¹ɣd¹i :　t¹iṅl¹a :　il²gr²ü :　kün² :　t¹uɣs¹qa :　b²ir²gr²ü :　kün² :
2. ešid　katïgdï　tïṅla.　ilgerü　kün　toɣsuq(q)a　birgerü　kün
3. listen　thoroughly　hearken　forward　sun　rising.at　to.the.right　sun

1. u ... / ...　　t²ür²k : qɣn¹ :　üt²k°n² :　y²iš :　ul¹r¹s¹r¹ :　il²t²a :
2. o(rtusïngaru)　türk　qaɣan　ötüken　y²iš　olursar　èlte
3. middle.its.toward　Türk　Khan　Ötüken　Range　sit.when　country.in

1. b¹uṅy¹q° : il²gr²ü : šṉtuṅ :　y¹ziqat²gi :　　s²ül² ... / ...　　m :
2. buṅ yoq　ilgerü　Šantuṅ　yazïqategi　sül(edim) ... / ...(süledi)m
3. need.less　forward　Shantung　plain.to reaching　campaigned.I　campaigned.I

1. y²ir¹ɣr¹u :　y²r² :　b¹y¹r¹q°u : y²ir²iṅa :　t²gi :　s²ül²d²m :　b¹unča :
2. yïrgaru　Yir　Bayïrqu　yiriṅ　etegi　süledim　bunča
3. to.the.left　Yir　Bayïrku　land.his.to　reaching　campaigned.I this.much

1. y²ir²ka : t²gi :　y¹ur¹t¹d¹ ... / ...　i :　q°ut¹y¹ : b¹uṅs¹z :　ṉčab²ir²ür² :
2. yirke　tegi　yorïtd(ïm) ... / ...　i　qutay　bungsuz　anča birür
3. land.to　reaching　proceeded.I　...　silk　need.less　so.much give

1. $t^1b^1\gamma\check{c}$:	$b^1ud^1n^1$:	s^1b^1i :	$s^1\ddot{u}\check{c}ig$:	γis^1i :	$y^2im\check{s}q$:	r^2ms^2
2. tabɣač	budun	sabï	$s^1\ddot{u}\check{c}ig$	aɣïs^{1}ï	yïmšak	ermiš
3. Chinese	people	word.his	sweet	poison.his	soft	was

'(I), the … Türk Bilge Khan, reigned at this time. Listen to my word perfectly, / and (you too) my younger brothers, listen well to this word of mine. Hearken thoroughly. / Forward, where the sun rises, and to the right, where the sun culminates, / When the Türk Khan reigned on the Ötüken Range, there was no need in the country. I campaigned forward (= eastward) up to the Shantung plain, … I campaigned / I campaigned to the left (= northward) up to the land of Yir Bayïrku. I proceeded to so many lands. / (They) give so much (goods), / silk plentiful. The Chinese people's word was sweet and its poison was smooth.'

— *From Köl Tegin's inscription, early 8th c., southern side*

(Radloff 1892, pl. XIX).

The Uyghur alphabet

Sogdian cursive script was adapted to the Turkic language of the Uyghur empire (8th–9th century) and was used by some Uyghur groups in Gansu (northwestern China) until the seventeenth century. The Sogdian alphabet borrowed by the Uyghurs is a reduced version of the Aramaic script; see TABLE 49.2. Used for Uyghur with slight modification, it later saw further changes. The originally horizontal lines are written vertically, in columns from left to right. Digraphs and trigraphs help to mark the rich set of Turkic vowels in initial syllables; thus aleph + aleph = initial *a*, aleph + yodh = initial *i/i*, aleph + waw = initial *o/u*, aleph + waw + yodh = initial *ö* or *ü*; while waw in any other syllable can render any rounded vowel according to vowel harmony.

The Semitic tradition of defective writing of vowels survives in words like *tnkry* for *tengri* 'heaven' (where *nk* is a digraph for a velar nasal), *kwnkwl* for *köngül* 'mind', or yodh + resh + hooked resh + gimel for *yarlïɣ* 'command'. Medial nun and aleph have the same form, and so do their main final forms. *d* is marked by lamedh (spirant *δ* in Sogdian), while hooked resh is used for *l* (this hook grows larger and larger, until it becomes a distinct symbol). Gimel and heth coincided and render the velar allophones of the voiced and unvoiced dorsal consonants (with or without diacritical dots). Kaph represents the palatal allophones of the same dorsal stops. Pe renders *b* and *p*. Samekh and shin merged as *s*. Tsadi marks the unvoiced palatal affricate *č*.

The written word has the shape of a vertical string of letters; positional variation of initial, medial, final, and independent forms is preserved. The sequence is interrupted by zain, which has no medial form and cannot be linked downward, and in the case of certain orthographical rules that prefer, e.g., an independent aleph after a gimel. Some nominal suffixes (case endings, etc.) are written separately after the stem, with the same space between stem and suffix as between words. Bold dots (sin-

TABLE 49.2: *Uyghur Script*[a]

Name[b]	Uyghur	Initial	Medial	Final	Separate	Ligatures	Uyghur
ʾaleph	e/vowel initial						ka/e
	a/e						pa/e
beth	w/v						
gimel	γ						
waw	o/u						
waw+yodh	ö/ü						
	o/u/ö/ü[c]						ko/u/ö/ü
							po/uö/ü
zain	z						
marked z	ž						
heth	x						
2-dotted	q						
yodh	y						ki/i
							pi/i
kaph	k/g						
lamedh	d/δ						
mem	m						ml
nun	n						
pe	b/p						
tsadi	č						
resh	r						
shin	s						
marked s	š						
tau	t						
hooked r	l						

a. Diacritics are often omitted. Some Uyghur alphabets have shin for samekh before pe; marked *z*, final *m*, and final *q* are added after hooked resh.

b. Hebrew name for the ancestral Aramaic letter.

c. In syllables other than the first.

gle, double, square, etc.) punctuate the text. In later Uyghur, strict distinction between the meaning of non-initial lamedh and taw is lost.

Uyghur calligraphy is based on Sogdian cursive; the Uyghurs developed their own cursive styles. The original alphabetical order of the Uyghur script is practically the same as that of Sogdian Aramaic. A mixed script is used in some texts where nouns appear in Chinese characters, while the rest is in the Uyghur alphabet. These logograms are to be read in Uyghur, as is clear from the suffixes attached to them. Interlinear Brahmi glosses often occur on the left side of Uyghur words of Indian origin.

SAMPLE OF UYGHUR (AND BUDDHIST HYBRID SANSKRIT)

1. *Transliteration:* nᵓmw pwδ : nᵓmw δᵓrm : nᵓmw sᵓnk : /   ywkwnwrmn
2. *Normalization:* namo bud   namo darm namo sang   yükünürmen
3. *Gloss:*   [Skt.] *namo buddhaya n. dharmaya n. sangghaya* [U.] prostrate.I

1. ᵓlqw pwrxn-lᵓr pwδystβ lᵓr / qwt lᵓr ynkᵓ :   ywkwnwrmn ᵓlqw
2. alqu burxan-lar bodistw-lar   qut-lar-ïnga :   yükünürmen alqu
3. all   buddha-s bodhisattva-s majestie-s-POSS.DAT prostrate.I   all

1. prti kᵓ / pwd lᵓr   twyz un šrᵓβᵓk-lᵓr   qwt lᵓr ynkᵓ : /   ywkwnwrmn
2. prati-ka- bud-lar   tözün šravak-lar qut-lar-ïnga   yükünürmen
3. pratyeka- buddha-s noble śrāvakas-s majestie-s-POSS.DAT prostrate.I

1. ʾʾlqw   ʾʾδʾ lʾr yq   yʾntwrdʾčy   ʾʾδyn / lʾr qʾ   ʾwtswqmʾʾq syz :   ʾʾδy
2. alqu   ada-lar-ïγ   yanturdačï   adïn-lar-qa   utsuqmaγ-sïz :   adï
3. all   danger-s-ACC   returner   other-PL-DAT   defeat-less   name.POSS

1. kwytrwlmyš   sytʾ / tʾpʾδry   qwtynkʾ :   ʾʾnčwlʾyw   ʾrwr :   mʾnynk /
2. kötrülmiš   Sitatapadri   qutïnga :   ančulayu   erür   mening
3. elevated   Sitātapatrā   majesty.POSS.DAT   thus   is   my

1. ʾšyδmyš ym :   ymʾ   pyr   ʾwydwn   ʾʾδy   kwytrwl/mys   strʾyʾstrys
2. ešidmiš-im :   yeme   bir   ödün   adï   kötrülmiš   Strayastris
3. heard.of-mine   also   one   time.by   name.POSS   elevated   Trayastrimśat

1. tnkry   yyr yntʾ   swdʾrʾm/šʾl tʾ   tnkry lʾr nynk   yyqylqw [l]wq yn
2. tengri   yėr-inte   Sudaramšal-ta   tengri-ler-ning   yïγïlγu-luq-ïn
3. god   land-POSS   Sudharmaśālā-LOC   god-PL-GEN   meeting.place

*'Homage to the Buddha. Homage to the Law. Homage to the Community. I bow
before the majesty of all buddhas and bodhisattvas. I bow before the majesty of
all pratyekabuddhas and noble shravakas. I bow before the majesty of Sitata-
patra whose name is exalted, who turns away all the dangers, and who is invin-
cible by others. Thus have I heard. At another time, He Whose Name Is Exalted
[resided] in the realm of the Thirty-three Gods, in Sudharmashala, in the
Assembly of the Gods.'*
*— Fragment of a Buddhist concertina-book with a Sitatapatra-text, printed in
the 14th century, found in eastern Turkistan (Müller 1910: 51–52).*

The Manichean script of the Uyghurs

Manichean Uyghurs also used another alphabet of Aramaic descent; see TABLE 49.3.
Its lines run from right to left, with more letters retained from the Aramaic and fewer
positional variants than in the Sogdian alphabet. Principles of vowel marking are the
same as in the Uyghur script, but initial *ï/i* can be either aleph + yodh or ʿain + yodh.
Gimel is transformed into two, slightly different, characters for *g*: one marks the velar, the other the palatal allophone of this voiced stop (or spirant). Kaph and qoph render *k*; either of them with one dot renders *x*, or with two dots, *q*. Daleth and lamedh
have their original values, but a second *d* is more often used than daleth. Samekh and
shin are distinguished. In writing a final vowel, yodh is often doubled, e.g. *ʿikii* 'two'.

SAMPLE OF UYGHUR IN MANICHEAN SCRIPT

••ᴄᴏᴧᵃᴊᵉᴇᴏ ••ᴄᴏᴧᵃᴊᴇᴧᵃᴇ ••ᴇᴧᴏᴊᵃ[ᴧ]	[ʾw]γwlyy bʾlgwsyy myngwsyy
ᵹᴇᴄᴇ ᴧᶜᴏᴧᴧ ᵭᴇᴏ ᴧᴧᵭ ᴇᴧᵹᴏᴧᴇ ᴿᴏᴧᴧ	ʾwd bwlïʾy •• bww yyr ʾwyzʾ nʾng
ᴡᴏᴧᴧᴧᴇᴧ ••ᴇᴏᴧᴏᴇ ᴊᴏᴧᵹ ᵭᴇ ᵹᴇᴄᴇᴧᴧ	ʾʾndʾγ tw kwyr yʾlwyy ʾʾrwyš
ᴧᴇᴏᴏᴇ ᴧᴧᴒᴏᴧᴏᴇᴧ ᴌᴏᴧ ᴜᴏᴇᴧ ᴜᴏᴧᴇ	ywq kym ʾwl ʾwmʾsʾr šmnw

TABLE 49.3: *Uyghur Manichean Script*

Name	Translit.	Initial	Final
ʾaleph	e/vowel initial		
ʾaleph+ʾaleph	a		
ʾaleph medial = ʾaleph initial	e-, -a/-e		
ʾaleph+waw	o/u		
ʾaleph+waw+yodh	ö/ü or oy/uy		
beth	b		
gimel[1]	γ		
gimel[2]	g		
daleth	d		
daleth[2]	ḍ		
he	h		
waw	w/v		
waw+yodh medial in 1st syll. after C	ö/ü		
	ö/ü		
waw in non-1st syll.	o/u/ö/ü/w/v		
zain	z		
teth	t		
yodh	y/i/i̇		
kaph[1]	k		
kaph[2]	x		
kaph[3]	q		
lamedh	l		
mem	m		
nun	n		
samekh	s		
ʿain	vowel initial, ʿ		
pe	p̣		
tsadi	č		
qoph[1]	k, x		
qoph[3]	q		
resh	r		
shin	š		
tau	t		

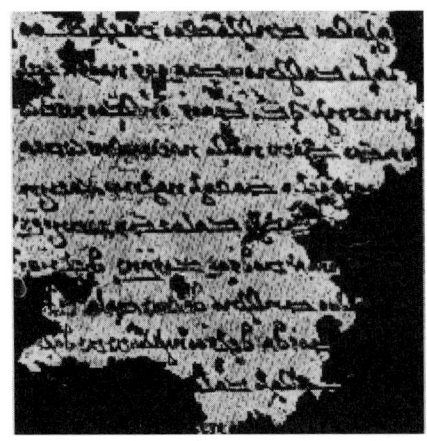

ܝܨܥܢ ܗܠܝܢ ܝܣܩܘܠ ܢܥܩܝܘܠ[ܝ]	[k]wyčyngʾ qwpwγ ʾwγʾy •• ʿynčʾ
ܢܩܘܝܣܘܗܥ ܢܩܣܐܠܩܘ ܝܣܘܢ [...]	[...] qmγ bwḍwnqʾ nwmčyqʾ
ܥܘܝܩܠܗ ܝܘܗܚܘܘ ܥܘܝܗܘ ܗܚܝ [...]	[...] rww mytryy bwrxʾn tngryy
[...]ܝܘܓ ܝܢܩܘܗ ܢܥܩܗܢܓܗ ܝܣܘܠ[ܓܘܝ]	[ʾwγ]lyy kʾlgʾy typʾn kyg[...]
[ ]ܝܓܘ ܝܣ ܝܣ ܝܘܨܓܢ ܝܬܠܩܗ ܝܗܝܬܝ ܝܣܘ [...]	[...] kyrtw tngryy ʾwγlyy mn mn tyg[ ]
[...ܝܘܩܥ]ܝܠܩܗ ܝܘܨܒܠ [...]	[...] ʿylyg bwḍw[nwγ ...]
[...]ܝܗܝܝ[ܝܘ]ܨ [...]	[...] ḍ[yn]dʾr [...]

1. Transliteration: [ʾw]γwlyy   bʾlgwsyy   myngwsyy /   ʾwḍ   bwlγʾy ••   bww
2. Normalization: oγulïï   belgüsii   mingüsii   ud   bolγay   boo
3. Gloss: son.POSS   token.POSS mount.POSS   bull   will.be   this

1. yyr   ʾwyzʾ   nʾng /   ʾʾndʾγ tw   kwyr   yʾlwyy   ʾʾrwyš /   ywq kym ʾwl
2. yėr   üze   neng   andaγ tev   kür   yelvii   arvïš   yoq kim ol
3. earth on   just   such   cheat fraud magic   spell   no   who he

1. ʾwmʾsʾr   šmnw /   [k]wyčyngʾ   qwpwγ   ʾwγʾy ••   ʿynčʾ / [...] qmγ
2. umasar   šïmnu   küčinge   qopuγ   uγay   ʿinča   qamaγ
3. cannot.if demon   force.POSS.DAT   all.ACC will.be.able   thus   all

1. bwḍwnqʾ   nwmčyqʾ /[...]rww mytryy   bwrxʾn   tngryy / [ʾwγ]lyy   kʾlgʾy
2. buḍunqa   nomčiqa   ruu Mitrii burxan   tengrii oγulïï   kelgey
3. people.DAT teacher.DAT   ...   Mithras Buddha   god   son.POSS   will.come

1. typʾn kyg[...]/[...] kyrtw   tngryy   ʾwγlyy   mn   mn   tyg[...]/[...]
2. tipen kig[...] ...   kirtü   tengrii oγlïï   men men tig[ ]
3. saying ...   true   god   son.POSS   I   I   ?say

1. ʿylyg   bwḍw[nwγ ...] / [...] ḍ[yn]dʾr [...]
2. ʿilig   buḍunuγ   ḍindar ...
3. country.ACC   people.ACC   elected

'The token and the mount of the [demon's] son will be a bull. On this earth
there is no such cheat and fraud, sorcery and spell that he will not be able [to
do]. He will be able [to do] all by the force of the demons. Thus […] for the
whole people and the teacher, […] saying that the son of the god, the Mithras
Buddha will come […] the true son of the god […] I [am], I [am …] the country
and the people […] the Elected […]."

— *Fragment of a Mithras-text from eastern Turkistan, 9th–10th century*
(von Le Coq 1919: 5, lines 7–17).

The Mongolian script

At the very beginning of the Mongol empire, the Uyghur alphabet became the writing
system of the Mongols; see TABLE 49.4. The whole set of symbols together with the
orthography was borrowed, and for several centuries no new letters were created for
the few Mongol phonemes unknown in Uyghur. This led to additional ambiguities
(e.g., initial yodh more often represents *ǰ* than *y*, while medial tsadi renders both *č* and
ǰ). Thus, in the orthography without diacritics, *qačar* 'cheek' and *γaǰar* 'place' have
the same written form. And though the Uyghur alphabet can distinguish *d* from *t,* no
initial *d* is marked, since this phoneme did not occur initially in Uyghur (so Mongolian *dalai* 'ocean' is written with initial taw). Medial and final taw was later used for
syllable-final *d,* medial lamedh (*d*) for both *d* and *t.* In the late, classical orthography
(17th–18th century), the angular tsadi marks *č,* the smooth tsadi renders medial *ǰ.* Initial yodh remained ambiguous until Manchu hooked yodh was accepted for initial *y*
(19th century). Zain had the same value as shin = *s*; it became obsolete for classical
Mongolian. As in Uyghur, several schools of orthography existed, with or without diacritics, and attempts were made to avoid ambiguity.

Dominance of this *vertical script* was challenged in 1269 by the introduction of
Emperor Qubilai's *square script* or *imperial alphabet* ('Phags pa, SECTION 40)—and
in the seventeenth century by the Manchu alphabet, the *clear script*, the *svāyambhu*
script, and the *horizontal square script* (the latter two were invented by Jñānavajra,
the Khalkha high priest). However, none of these offered the simplicity of the Uy-
ghur-Mongol vertical script. In 1587 Ayushi created an amplified version of this alphabet for the exact transcription of Sanskrit and Tibetan words; his new symbol for
foreign *h* was taken from Tibetan. A modern version of Ayushi's alphabet replaced the
older Mongol renderings of Mandarin syllables.

The Mongol script is known in various handwritten, shorthand, printed, and ornamental styles. There exist several alphabetical orders, different from the Aramaic.
In Inner Mongolia (China), this Mongol script now also serves for writing the Tungusic language Evenki. It was replaced by Cyrillic in 1946 in the Mongolian Republic, but recent political changes favor its revival. (For the use of Cyrillic in three
varieties of Mongolic, see below.)

TABLE 49.4: *The Mongolian Script*

Mongol. Value	Initial	Medial	Final	Separate	Miscellaneous	Mongol. Value
a						
e						ba/e
						k/ga/e
i (yodh)						bi
						k/gi
o/u (waw)						
ö/ü=waw+yodh						
in non-1st syll.						bo/u
n before vowel						k/go/u
n syll./wd. final						
q						
γ before vowel						
γ syll./wd. final						
b						
s						
š						
s final (Uyg. z)						
t/d (taw)						
d/t (lamedh)						
l						Mongγol
m						
č						
ǰ/y (medial: *top*, ǰ; *bottom*, y)						ml
k/g						ǰa
r						
w/v						
h						
p						
f						

SAMPLE OF MONGOLIAN

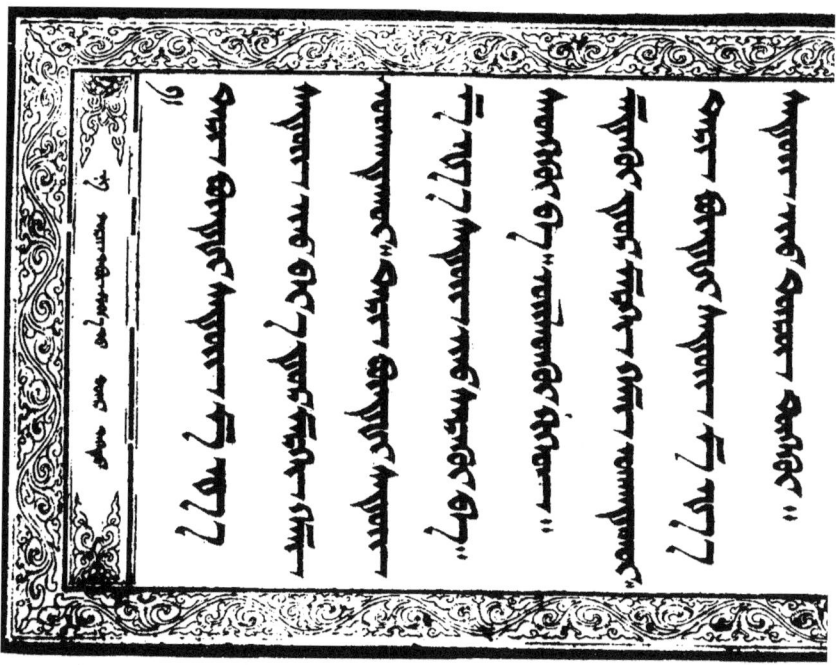

1. Transliteration: tʾrʾ pwβʾδhy sʾδwβʾmʾ hʾ ʾ /sʾδwβʾ ʾynw pʾy ʾ δwr mʾrkʾn
2. Normalization: tere bôdhi-saduva ma-hā-saduva inu bey-e-dür mergen
3. Gloss: that bodhisattva mahāsattva 3POSS body-DAT wise

1. kʾmʾn / ʾwqʾqδʾqwy : tʾrʾ pwβʾδhy sʾδwβʾ mʾ hʾ ʾ / sʾδwβʾ ʾynw serekü
2. kemen / uqaɣdaqui tere bôdhi-saduva ma-hā-saduva inu sereküi
3. saying should.know that bodhisattva mahāsattva 3POSS waking

1. ba : / sʾtkykwy pʾ : ʾwylʾtkwy kykʾt : / mʾδʾkwy dwr mʾrkʾn kʾmʾn
2. ba : / sedkiküi ba üiledküi kiɣed medeküi dür mergen kemen
3. and thinking and acting as.well knowing-DAT wise saying

1. ʾwqʾqδʾqwy : / tʾrʾ pwβʾδhy sʾδwβʾ mʾ hʾ ʾ/sʾδwβʾ ʾynw twyrwn twykʾkwy :
2. uqaɣdaqui tere bôdhi-saduva ma-hā-saduva inu törön tügeküi
3. should.know that bodhisattva mahāsattva 3POSS born spreading

'You should know: that bodhisattva and mahasattva is wise in (the knowledge of) body. You should know: that bodhisattva and mahasattva is wise in watch-fulness, thinking, acting as well as perceiving. That bodhisattiva (is wise in the knowledge of) the sense organs and sense objects (lit. what is being generated and what is spreading.'

—*From the printed Mongol Kanjur, vol. 49, folio 2A. Text without diacritics.*

Early 18th century blockprint.)

TABLE 49.5: *The Oirat "Clear Script"*

	Initial	Medial	Final	Miscellaneous	
a				after k or b	
e				after k or b	
i				after k or b	
o					
u					
ö				kö	
ü				kü	
vowel length (â)	–				
n				-ngg-	
b					
γ					
g				-q	
k				kâ	
x					
m					
l					
r					
t					
d					
y					
z-/ǰ				init. c/č med.	
s				š	
w/v				-ng	

The "Clear script"

Derived from the Mongol vertical script by the Zaya Pandita Oktorguin Dalai (1648)
to reflect the significant changes in the spoken language of his time, Clear script became the writing system of the Mongols of the West, the Oirats and Kalmyks; with
some changes, it is still used in Jungaria, eastern Turkestan (see TABLE 49.5). All ambiguities of the vertical script were eliminated with the aid of new diacritics, e.g. a
circle at the right for heth = γ; and new letters were derived from old variants. All
short vowels have their own symbols. Voiced and unvoiced consonants are strictly
distinguished. A new symbol (perhaps derived from an Indian alphabet) marks vowel
length of *a, e, o,* and *ö*. Long *i, u,* and *ü* are rendered by double letters (while *i* + long-

mark = *iaa/iee*, *u* + long-mark = *uaa*, etc.). Positional variation is mostly eliminated, but initial vowels still have the mandatory initial aleph. Plain waw = *ü*, while waw with a stroke = *u*; both have separate medial and final variants (but plain waw represents *u* after *x/γ* or *o*—a rational abbreviation). Word-final *ng* is marked by a ligature. The syllable-final velar stop *q* is represented by a new letter (γ with a crescent), regardless of vowel harmony. A modified kaph is used for a palatal *k* before long *a*. Initial yodh is *y*; angular tsadi is *ǰ* or *z*, and smooth tsadi is *č* or *c*. In modern usage, two symbols taken from the Oirat version of Ayushi's alphabet resolved this ambivalence: marked angular tsadi = *ǰ*, while marked smooth tsadi = *č*. In modern orthography, case endings are written separately, like postpositions or particles, with initial aleph if necessary (as also in the old, classical Oirat written language). The alphabetical order of this script differs from those of the Mongol vertical and the Aramaic scripts. Since the 1920s Kalmyks in the (former) Soviet Union have had a number of Latin and Cyrillic orthographies.

SAMPLE OF OIRAT

1. Transliteration: ... / yeke bodhidu   irō/müi : tögünčilen boluq/san dayini
2. Gloss: great bodhi.DAT pray   doing.so become enemy.ACC

1. darun   sai/tur dousuqsan oq/torγui coq kir ü/gei   tōsu arilγan üi/ledüqči
2. suppress well   completed heaven glory stain-less dust cleanse maker

1. burxandu / mürgümüi :: tögünčilen boluq/san dayini   darun   sayitur /
2. buddha   prostrate   doing.so   become   enemy.ACC suppress   well

1. dousuqsan   erdeniyin okiyin / gerel   padma bendury[a]/yin gerel   erdeni
2. completed   gem   top   light   lotus   lapis lazuli   light   gem

1. dür/sütü   beye   tögüsügsen
2. shaped   body   accomplished

   '(I) pray for the Great Enlightenment. (I) bow before the buddha, the Glory of Heaven, the Immaculate, he who became such (= Tathāgata), he who vanquished the enemy, he who well completed (his task), and he who succeeds in cleansing the dust (of passion); (I bow before) the Light of the Top of the Gem, he who became such, he who vanquished the enemy, he who well completed (his task), and he who is perfect with a body of the appearance of the lotus, the bright gem of lapis lazuli.'

 —From a 19th-century printing block in the Institute of Oriental Studies, St. Petersburg, with foreign h, p, ṇ, *and "subscript" Tibetan* y *with "inherent"* a.

The Manchu alphabet

In 1599 Nurhachi, founder of the Manchu Empire, ordered that a writing system be created for the Manchu language; see TABLE 49.6. Erdeni Bakshi added some new symbols to the Mongolian script, and this system, the "alphabet without dot and circle," was used until Dahai's reform of 1632, which introduced the "alphabet with dot and circle." Positional variation of the Mongolian letters is preserved, but all the ambiguities of Mongolian script are eliminated by diacritics and new symbols; hence this easternmost descendant of the Aramaic script is an ideal tool for recording Manchu phonemes and some allophones. Additional symbols make it possible to give an exact Manchu transcription of Mandarin Chinese. The new letters derived from those of the Mongol script are: f (hooked beth, before vowels other than u and i, where plain beth = w renders f); p (pe with indented bow); $š$ (modified shin); t^1 (round initial taw for t before a, o, and Chinese i); d^1 (smooth lamedh for medial d before a, o); t^2 (pointed initial taw for t before e or u); d^2 (pointed lamedh for medial t before e or u); y (hooked yodh, while plain initial yodh = $ǰ$); crossed kaph for foreign k before a or o; crossed shin = Chinese c (ts'); shin with vertical stroke = Chinese j (ts, pinyin z); zain = Chinese zh (pinyin r).

 A dot on the left marks n before a vowel. The diacritic dot and circle that appear on the right side of the letter cannot be combined with each other. Dotted aleph = e, dotted waw = u, dotted gimel = $γ$, dotted kaph = g, dotted taw or lamedh = d (e.g., dotted round taw + waw = do, while dotted pointed taw + waw = du).

 Gimel with circle = unvoiced velar spirant before a or o; kaph with circle = unvoiced velar spirant [x] before e, u, or i. Gimel with double dot on the left side = syllable-final q. Chinese $ï$, or the retroflex character of the preceding affricate (cf. pinyin *chi* and *zhi*), is marked by a circle below $č$ or $ǰ$. After s and the alveolar affricates, a diacritic similar to an inverted shin marks the appropriate foreign vowel. The vowel u is marked by the digraph waw + yodh after dotted gimel and dotted kaph. If u is the second element of a diphthong, no dot is added (so Manchu *geu* 'mare' is transcribed *geo*). Punctuation is single and double tear-shaped dots, for smaller and larger units.

 Competing with Chinese calligraphy, many styles were designed for seals and various ornamental purposes. The Manchu dialect of the Shibe people of China is still written in this script; it was formerly also the writing system for Mongolic Daur, spoken in China (now romanized).

TABLE 49.6: *Manchu Script*

	Initial	Medial	Final	Separate	Ligatures	
a						ba
						ke
e						be
i						bi, ki
o						bo
u						bu, gu
ô[a]						
n before V						
n syll. end						
ng						
q[b]						
q syll. end						
k						
γ						
g						k′a
k′						k′o, g′o
g′						
χ						
x						
b						
p						
s						
š						

TABLE 49.6: *Manchu Script (Continued)*

	Initial	Medial	Final	Separate	Ligatures
t^1					
t syll. end					
d^1					
t^2					
d^2					
l					
m					
č					
ǰ					
y					
r					
f					
w[c]					
c[d]					
cï; čï					
j; ǰï					Manǰu bitxe
ǰï					
ž					
sï					

a. The digraph *o* + *i* (waw + yodh) is considered a compound symbol *ô* (also transcribed *ū*) which denotes *u* after *q*, *γ*, or *χ*, where the dot of the usual *u* cannot be used.

b. The letters *q* and *k*, *γ* and *g*, and *χ* and *x* mark the velar and palatal allophones of *q/k*, *γ/g*, and *χ/x*. The letters derived from tau and lamedh, namely *t*, *t¹*, *t²*, *d¹*, and *d²*, also define the value of aleph and waw they precede.

c. The letter *w* renders [f] before *i* and *u*.

d. The last eight units represent Northern Chinese segments and syllables.

SAMPLE OF MANCHU

1. Transliteration: amba doro . amba qooli de gemu songqoloro / temgetu be
2. Transcription: amba doro amba kooli-de gemu songkoloro temgetu-be
3. Gloss: great rule great law-in all   following   seal-ACC

1. baχara . emu gisun emu γônin seme yooni doron tuwaqô / bisire be
2. bahara emu gisun emu gūnin seme yooni doron tuwakū bisire-be
3. obtaining one word one mind saying whole stamp model being-ACC

1. daχame . gurun i bitxe mingγan tangγô ǰalan de entexeme tutafi . /
2. dahame . gurun-i bithe minggan tanggū jalan-de enteheme tutafi
3. obeying state-of script 1000   100   age-in eternally having.held

1. šun usiχa . sungγari birai gese abqa na i   sidende   entexeme
2. šun usiha sunggari bira-i gese abka na-i   sidende   enteheme
3. sun star   Milky Way-of like sky earth-of between   eternally

1. tutambi dere :
2. tutambi dere
3. hold   likely

'Obtaining the Seal that wholly acts according to the Great Rule and the Great Law, fully obeying the given example unanimously and wholeheartedly, and keeping the script of the empire for thousands and hundreds of generations forever, it is likely to keep up between Heaven and Earth forever like the Sun, the stars, and the Milky Way.'

—From the emperor's preface of 1708 to the Manju gisun-i buleku bitxe [The Dictionary of Manchu] in the 1771 blockprint of its revised edition called Nonggime toqtobuχa Manju gisun-e buleku bitxe.

The Buryat alphabet

In 1905 in St. Petersburg, the learned lama Agwaan Dorzhiev (alias Vagindra) and the Buryat scholar Tsyben Zhamtsarano invented a script for modern Buryat (Northern Mongolian) on the basis of the Mongol vertical alphabet and the Western Mongolian clear script (TABLE 49.7). No positional variants are used; new letters, derived from the old ones for the Buryat sound system, have eliminated ambivalence. Vowel length and consonant palatalization are marked by diacritics (a vertical stroke and a small circle respectively). This alphabet was used in handwritten and typeset forms for some fifteen years, but was not able to replace the older, supradialectal, Mongol script, which remained in use until the introduction of a Roman and later (1939) a Cyrillic script for Buryat.

SAMPLE OF BURYAT

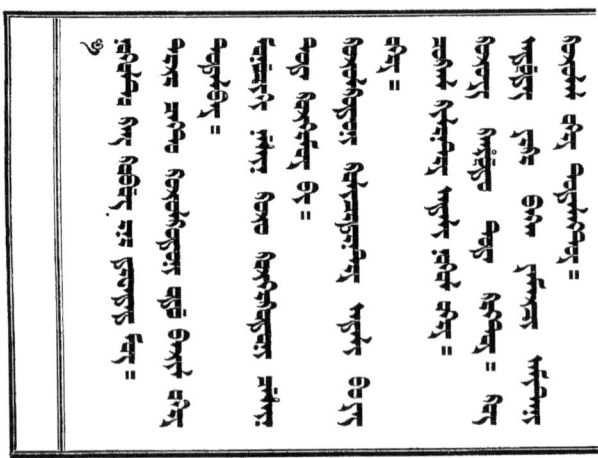

1. *Transliteration:* nügültü xang xübũng ene devadad   müng : / tere cagto
2. *Gloss:*   sinful king son   this Devadatta same   that time.DAT

1. xorolxodoni   üdô   baril ügey   tohalbay : / münôčigi nâšin   xoro
2. hurting.DAT.POSS revenge holding-less helped   now.too hither harm

TABLE 49.7: *The Buryat Alphabet*

Letter	Transliteration	Phonetic Value	Letter	Transliteration	Phonetic Value
ᛮ	a	[a]	ᛮ	â	[aː]
Л	e	[e]	Л	ê	[eː]
◀	i	[i]	◀	î	[iː]
◀	o	[o]	◀	ô	[oː]
◀	u	[u]	◀	û	[uː]
◀	ö	[ø]	◀	ô̊	[øː]
◀	ü	[y]	◀	û̊	[yː]
◔	g	[g]	◔	w′	[wʲ]
◔	k/x	[x]	◔	s′	[sʲ]
◔	ng	[ŋ]	◔	r′	[rʲ]
◔	ž	[ʒ]	◔	l′	[lʲ]
◔	č	[tʃ]	◔	h′	[hʲ]
◔	ñ	[ɲ]	◔	ḡ[a]	[g̊]
◔	d	[d]	◔	k̲	[kˀ]
◔	t	[t]	◔	ǰ	[ʤ]
◔	n	[n]	◔	d̲	[d̥]
◔	b	[b]	◔	p̄	[pˀ]
◔	p	[p]	◔	v	[v]
◔	m	[m]	◔	f	[f]
◔	z	[z]	◔	ǰ	[ʤ]
◔	c	[ts]	◔	šč	[ʃtʃ]
◔	w	[w]	◔	ï	[ɨ]
◔	š	[ʃ]		PUNCTUATION	
◔	s	[s]	ᴜ	question mark	
◔	y	[j]	ᴦ	exclamation point	
◔	r	[r]	‖	comma	
◔	l	[l]	ᵬ	period	
◔	h	[h]	◔	beginning of text	

a. The last ten letters represent Russian and other foreign sounds.

1. xürgexüdüni   câšin   toha xürgemüy bi : / xorolxodoni
2. sending.DAT.POSS thither help send   I   harm-doing.DAT.POSS

1. xülicehentey adali   boyang / ügey : / cuxal xilentey   adali   nügül
2. endured.SOC similar virtue   no   fury   hatred.SOC similar sin

1. ügey : / xoroyng   xar´ûdo   toha xegtüy : xüng / adûhang   yexe baga
2. no   harm.GEN response.DAT help do.OPT human beast   big   small

1. yamarči   amitani /   xorolal ügey   tuhalagtuy :
2. any.kind   being.ACC harm-doing-less help.OPT

> 'The Sinful Prince is this Devadatta. At that time, when he did harm to me, I did
> not feel vengeful, but helped him. Even now, when he does harm to me, I still
> help him. There is no (greater) virtue than patience against harm-doing. (And)
> there is no (greater) sin than hatred. In response to harm-doing, do favor. Help
> humans and beasts, big and small, all kinds of living beings, without doing
> harm.'
> —From a brochure typeset in St. Petersburg, Burxang bagšing gegênî xur´ângoy
> namtar bolong Buyanto xang xübûni namtar orošibay [(Here) abide the Holy
> Teacher Buddha's Short Vita and Prince Buyanto's Vita] (1906?).

Cyrillic script

Cyrillic script was introduced for Mongolic languages by Soviet authorities in 1939
(see SECTION 65), and in Mongolia in 1946 (TABLE 49.8).

Long vowels and diphthongs are written as vowel+vowel in Khalkha (i.e. Modern Mongolian) and Buryat; Kalmyk marks long vowels this way only in the first syllable of a word; in syllables after the first, short vowels are omitted, and long vowels
are represented by a single letter. In Khalkha, -ий represents long ii following a palatal or palatalized consonant; -ы represents long ii following a non-palatal consonant.
Khalkha orthography has complex rules specifying whether a short vowel in a syllable other than the first is to be written. "Buryat" is буряад bur´ād in Cyrillic Buryat,
буриад buriad in Khalkha, and buriyad in Classical Mongolian. "Kalmyk" is хальмг
khal´mg in Kalmyk, халимаг xalimag in Khalkha, and qalimaγ in Classical Mongolian.

Bibliography

Benzing, Johannes. 1985. *Kalmückische Grammatik zum Nachschlagen.* Wiesbaden: Harrassowitz.
Clauson, Sir Gerard. 1962. *Turkish and Mongolian Studies.* London: Royal Asiatic Society.
Deny, Jean, et al. 1959. *Philologiae Turcicae Fundamenta,* vol. 1. Wiesbaden: Steiner.
Fuchs, Walther, et al. 1968. *Tungusologie* (Handbuch der Orientalistik, division 1, vol. 5, part 3).
    Leiden: Brill.

TABLE 49.8: *Mongolic in Cyrillic Script*

Letter		Khalkha	Buryat	Kalmyk
А	а	a	a	a
Ә	ә	–	–	ä
Б	б	b	b	b
В	в	w	(v)	w
Г	г	g	g	g
Һ	h	–	–	γ (gh)
Д	д	d	d	d
Е	е	ye/yö	ye/yö	e/ye-
Ё	ё	yo	yo	
Ж	ж	ǰ	ǰ	ž (zh)
Җ	җ	–	–	ǰ
З	з	j (dz)	z	z
И	и	i	i	i
Й	й	i̭	i̭	y
К	к	(k)		k
Л	л	l	l	l
М	м	m	m	m
Н	н	n-, -ng	n-, -ng	n
Ң	ң	–	–	ng
О	о	o	o	o
Ө	ө	ö	ö	ö
П	п	p	p	p
Р	р	r	r	r
С	с	s	s	s
Т	т	t	t	t
У	у	u	u	u
Ү	ү	ü	ü	ü
Ф	ф	(f)		
Х	х	x	x	x (kh)
Һ	h	–	h	–
Ц	ц	c	(c)	c (ts)
Ч	ч	č	(č)	č (ch)
Ш	ш	š	š	š (sh)
Щ	щ	(šč)		
Ъ	ъ	mute shwa "hard sign"		
Ы	ы	long ii	ei/ii	
Ь	ь	i̭	palatalization	
Э	э	e	e	e initial
Ю	ю	yu/yü	yu/yü	yu initial
Я	я	ya	ya	ya initial

Gabain, Annemarie von. 1974. *Alttürkische Grammatik.* Wiesbaden: Harrassowitz.

Gabain, Annemarie von, et al. 1982. *Turkologie* (Handbuch der Orientalistik, division 1, vol. 5, part 1), 2nd ed. Leiden: Brill.

Hamilton, James. 1986. *Manuscrits ouïgours du IX–X siècle de Touen-houang.* 2 vols. Paris: Peeters.

Kara, György. 1972. *Книги монгольских кочевников* [Books of the Mongol nomads]. Moscow: Nauka.

Ligeti, Louis. 1952. "A propos de l'écriture mandchou." *Acta Orientalia* (Budapest) 2: 235–301.

Müller, Friedrich W. K. 1910. *Uigurica II.* Berlin: Preußiche Akademie der Wissenschaften.

Nadeliaev, V. M., et al. 1969. *Древнетюркский словарь* [Dictionary of Ancient Turkic; with comparative table of scripts]. Leningrad: Nauka.

Poppe, Nicholas. 1965. *Introduction to Altaic Linguistics.* Wiesbaden: Harrassowitz.

Poppe, N icholas, et al. 1964. *Mongolistik* (Handbuch der Orientalistik, division 1, vol. 5, part 2). Leiden: Brill.

Radloff, Wilhelm. 1892. *Atlas der Alterthümer der Mongolei,* vol. 1. St. Petersburg: Akademie der Wissenschaften.

Róna-Tas, A. 1991. "The Sources in Runic Script." In his *Introduction to Turkology,* pp. 51–61. Szeged, Hungary: University of Szeged.

Sims-Williams, Nicholas. 1981. "The Sogdian Sound-system and the Origin of the Uyghur Script." *Journal Asiatique* 269: 347–59.

Stary, Giovanni. 1980. *Die chinesischen und mandschurischen Zierschriften.* Hamburg: Buske.

Thomsen, Vilhelm. 1916. *Turcica: Etudes concernant l'interprétation des inscriptions turques de la Mongolie et de la Sibérie.* Helsinki: Société finno-ougrienne.

von Le Coq, Albert. 1919. *Türkische Manichaica aus Chotscho II.* Berlin: Preußiche Akademie der Wissenschaften.

Yartseva, V. N., et al. 1990. *Лингвистический энциклопедический словарь* [Linguistic encyclopedic dictionary]. Moscow: Sovietskaia Entsiklopediia.

Zieme, Peter. 1991. *Die Stabreimtexte der Uiguren von Turfan und Dunhuang.* Budapest: Akadémiai Kiadó.

Arabic Writing

THOMAS BAUER

The North Arabic script developed as a branch of Nabatean Aramaic script (see SEC-
TIONS 5 and 47). The earliest inscriptions date back to the fourth century C.E. Since
Aramaic has fewer consonants than Arabic, some letters came to stand for more than
one consonant. In order to eliminate these ambiguities, from the seventh century onward dots over or under some of the letters were introduced. These diacritical dots
form an integral part of the letter. Especially in order to comply with the need to guarantee an unequivocal reading of the Holy Qur'ān, further signs were introduced to denote the short vowels and consonant gemination. Yet even today, these signs are only
employed on rare occasions. After normalization and authoritative establishment by
the philologists and scribes in the first centuries of Islam, only minor developments
occurred in Arabic writing; thus the orthography of Classical Arabic and that of Modern Standard Arabic are essentially the same. This was only possible because the phonology and morphology of Modern Standard Arabic have been taken over from
Classical Arabic without change. Insofar as Modern Standard Arabic is considered to
be the only "valid" form of expression (though it is no one's mother tongue), there
have been only a few attempts to employ the Arabic writing systems for the modern
Arabic dialects (for Maltese, see SECTION 59, "Maltese" on page 686). But another
result of the significance of Arabic script is that it came to be used for many languages
of Islamic lands (SECTION 62).

The Arabic script runs from right to left. Since it is a cursive script, letters within
a word have to be joined wherever possible. However, the letters ‏ا‏ *u*, ‏د‏ *d*, ‏ذ‏ *ḏ*, ‏ر‏ *r*,
‏ز‏ *z*, and ‏و‏ *w* cannot be joined to the following letter; thus minimal spaces may occur
in the middle of a word. Words are set apart by greater spaces, but lexical units which
are represented by only one letter are joined to the following word. Other than the six
letters just mentioned, each letter may occur in four different positions: initial, medial, final, and isolated (as when a letter is the last letter of a word and is preceded by
one of the six letters not joinable on the left side). This may have consequences for
the shape of a letter—e.g., the curves of the final and isolated forms of letters like ‏ح‏ *h*
and ‏خ‏ *h* are omitted in initial and medial positions. Ligatures are quite often employed
in handwriting. The ligature ‏ل‏ *l* + ‏ا‏ *a* = ‏لا‏ *lā* is obligatory even in print and typewriting.

The importance of calligraphy (SECTION 20) in the Islamic arts is hardly paralleled in any other culture. Several calligraphic styles, developed from early times, are
not only used in books but became an integral element of architecture and crafts.

TABLE 50.1: *Arabic Letters*

Name	Trans-literation[a]	Transcrip-tion	Numerical Value	Isolated	Final	Initial	Medial
ʾalif	ʾ (a)	[ʔ]	1	ا	ـا	–	–
bāʾ	b	[b]	2	ب	ـب	بـ	ـبـ
tāʾ	t	[t]	400	ت	ـت	تـ	ـتـ
t̲āʾ	t̲, th	[θ]	500	ث	ـث	ثـ	ـثـ
ǧīm	ǧ, dj	[dʒ]	3	ج	ـج	جـ	ـجـ
ḥāʾ	ḥ	[ħ]	8	ح	ـح	حـ	ـحـ
ḫāʾ	ḫ, kh	[x]	600	خ	ـخ	خـ	ـخـ
dāl	d	[d]	4	د	ـد	–	–
d̲āl	d̲, dh	[ð]	700	ذ	ـذ	–	–
rāʾ	r	[r]	200	ر	ـر	–	–
zāy	z	[z]	7	ز	ـز	–	–
sīn	s, sh	[s]	60	س	ـس	سـ	ـسـ
šīn	š	[ʃ]	300	ش	ـش	شـ	ـشـ
ṣād	ṣ	[s̩]	90	ص	ـص	صـ	ـصـ
ḍād	ḍ	[d̵]	800	ض	ـض	ضـ	ـضـ
ṭāʾ	ṭ	[t̵]	9	ط	ـط	طـ	ـطـ
z̧āʾ	z̧	[z̧]	900	ظ	ـظ	ظـ	ـظـ
ʿayn	ʿ	[ʕ]	70	ع	ـع	عـ	ـعـ
ġayn	ġ (ḡ), gh	[ɣ]	1000	غ	ـغ	غـ	ـغـ
fāʾ	f	[f]	80	ف	ـف	فـ	ـفـ
qāf	q, ḳ	[q]	100	ق	ـق	قـ	ـقـ
kāf	k	[k]	20	ك	ـك	كـ	ـكـ
lām	l	[l]	30	ل	ـل	لـ	ـلـ
mīm	m	[m]	40	م	ـم	مـ	ـمـ
nūn	n	[n]	50	ن	ـن	نـ	ـنـ
hāʾ	h	[h]	5	ه	ـه	هـ	ـهـ, ـﻬ
wāw	w	[w]	6	و	ـو	–	–
yāʾ	y	[y]	10	ي	ـي	يـ	ـيـ

a. The main entry is the transliteration system of the Deutsche Morgenländische Gesellschaft, used in this book (except *u* is used for ʾalif for clarity throughout); the second is that of the *Encyclopedia of Islam*. Often mixtures between these two systems occur.

Basic characters

The Arabic script is composed of 28 letters, which are listed in TABLE 50.1. As can be seen from the table, each letter represents exactly one consonant of the Arabic language, and each consonant is represented by exactly one letter.

Yet there are some exceptions: The letters و *w*, ي *y*, and ا *a* represent not only the consonants [w], [y], and (historically) [ʔ], but also the three long vowels of Arabic, namely [u:], [i:], and [a:], respectively. The vowel [a:], however, may be represented in word-final position by ا *a* or ى *y* (with no dots in this case, but this differentiation is recent and only followed in some Arab countries), the choice being dependent on morphological conditions; they are called ʾ*alif maqṣūra biṣūrati l-*ʾ*alif* and ʾ*alif maqṣūra biṣūrati l-yā* ʾ, respectively.

In order to represent the glottal stop [ʔ], the sign ء, called *hamza*, was introduced. It may be used in addition to ا *a* in word-initial position, thus giving أ or إ (depending on the following vowel). It is obligatory today in word-medial and -final positions, where it is combined with ا *a*, و *w*, or ي *y* (without dots) or stands alone. The choice depends partly on phonological, partly on morphological, and partly on purely graphic considerations which are rather complicated and differ from country to country. However, since the five signs ا إ ء ئ ؤ أ can differentiate words (e.g. يأمن *y ʾmn* [yaʔmanu] 'he is safe' vs. يؤمن [yuʔmanu] 'he is made safe, one is safe'), they must be considered as separate "graphemes." A further addition to the graphic system must be noted, namely the sign ة (an *h* with two dots), which denotes the consonant [t] in its function as feminine ending (e.g. مرتبة *mrtbt* [martabat^(un)], where the second *t* is the feminine ending).* Its name is *tā* ʾ *marbūṭa*.

Though there are no basic characters for the short vowels, the common designation of the Arabic script as "consonantal" is incorrect, since the long vowels are represented but consonant gemination is not. Besides, the Arabic script gives a rather neat and unambiguous representation of the consonants and long vowels of the language. Only a few exceptions exist, e.g. in words like الله *allh* [aɫ-ɫa:h] 'God' and هذا *hda* [ha:ða:], where [a:] is not expressed in writing; or the suffix ه [-hu:, -hi:] 'him/his', where the long vowel is not indicated either.

Morphophonemic representation

In addition to the phonetically rather flat representation of consonants and long vowels, the Arabic script employs some devices to represent morphologically deeper structures. Thus the definite article, which is prefixed to nouns, is always written ال *al* /al-/, though the auxiliary syllable [a-] is dropped when the word occurs in the middle of a phrase and the /l-/ is often assimilated to the word-initial consonant of the noun:

---

*Various inflectional endings that are omitted when a word occurs at the end of an utterance are transcribed with raised letters.

TABLE 50.2: *Arabic Numerals*

1	2	3	4	5	6	7	8	9	0
١	٢	٣	٤	٥	٦	٧	٨	٩	.

كل الديوان *kl al-dywan* [kullu d-di:wa:n], written as if it were /kullu ʔal-di:wa:n/ 'all the-administration'. Another example of morphographic writing is the addition of an ا *a* (*ʾalif fāṣila*) to third person plural and imperative plural verbs, which end with the letter و *w* [-u:], where the ا *a* has no phonetic value: نحوا *nhwa* [naħħu:] 'remove (imper.)'. In masculine indefinite nouns, a final ا *a* is added to mark the accusative ending [-an]: بيتا *byta* [bayt^an] 'a house (acc.)'.

Optional signs

One of the most characteristic features of Arabic and related scripts (Hebrew, Aramaic) is the presence of an added system of diacritics to express short vowels and consonant gemination, neither of which is represented by the basic letters. These marks are placed above or below a basic letter. Taking as example the basic letter د *d*, we get دَ *da*, دِ *di*, دُ *du*, and دْ *d* (the ° — indicating vowellessness), using the signs called *fatḥa*, *kasra*, *ḍamma*, and *sukūn* respectively. The endings of the indefinite noun -*un* -*in* -*an*, which are omitted in pause, are indicated by doubling the vowel signs (*tanwīn*): in the nominative دٌ -*dun*, in the genitive دٍ -*din*. In the accusative, one gets ةً -*tan* with feminine nouns. In masculine nouns, where the accusative ending is already represented by the letter ا *a*, one may write دًا -*dan*. Gemination is expressed by the sign ّ (*šadda*), which may be combined with one of the short-vowel marks: دّ *dda*, دّ *ddi*, دّ *ddu*; دّ -*ddin*, دّ -*ddun*. There are further less important optional diacritics, such as دٰ *dā* in those few words where [a:] is not expressed by ا *a*; آ (*ʾalif madda*) in place of the sequence ءا *ʾā*; or a stroke placed over ا *a* (ٱ, *ʾalif waṣla*) to show that morphologically written ا is not to be pronounced. The first clause of the sample text (page 563) would read with optional diacritics:

نَظَرَ عَبْدُ ٱللّٰهِ بْنُ طَاهِرٍ إِلَى خَطِّ بَعْضِ كُتَّابِهِ

All these diacritics have in common that they are of very restricted use. They are used throughout the text only in the Qur'ān, less consistently in other authoritative religious texts, in editions of classical poetry and in textbooks for primary education, and occasionally in linguistically rather complex texts to avoid ambiguities. In book titles, letterheads, nameplates, etc., they may be used for decorative purposes. But they are virtually never applied in newspapers, ordinary books, or private documents.

The numerals are shown in TABLE 50.2; the letters can be used with their common Semitic numerical values (note that they reflect the ancestral order) for numbering pages, lists, etc.

The effects of defectiveness

In texts where optional diacritics are employed, every phoneme of the language is un-ambiguously represented; but in texts where only basic letters are used—i.e. in the overwhelming majority—a certain degree of ambiguity arises, since more than a quarter of the phonemes remain unexpressed. So the first word of the sample text, نظر *nẓr*, could be read as a verb in the active form, either as [naẓara] 'he looked' or as [naẓẓara] 'he made comparisons', and also as the corresponding passive forms [nuẓira] and [nuẓẓira], or as the nominal forms [naẓar] 'look, glance' or [niẓr] 'sim-ilar'. Yet in practice, the problems arising from the defectiveness of normal Arabic writing are not so great as one might suspect. First, a quarter of the non-expressed phonemes occur in endings which are syntactically determined and omitted in less formal speech anyway. Above all, the occurrence of short vowel phonemes is more easily predictable in Arabic than in many other languages, since its syllabic structure allows only syllables of the patterns CV, CVC, and C$\bar{\text{V}}$ (under certain circumstances also C$\bar{\text{V}}$C). Yet the fact remains that one can read an Arabic text correctly only if one knows the words. This means that Arabic writing is rather highly lexicalized.

The disadvantages of this system have often been complained about by Arab in-tellectuals, who have even proposed the introduction of Roman script. Since Standard Arabic is no one's mother tongue, it has to be learned at school. On the other hand, because of the defectiveness of the script, an Arabic text can be written and read de-spite a great amount of dialectal interference without disregarding any of the notated symbols—but this may certainly be an obstacle to learning correct Standard Arabic. However, Standard Arabic adhering completely to the written norm (which is that of Classical Arabic as laid down in medieval grammar books) is used only in rare and very formal communicative situations. So it is exactly the defectiveness of the Arabic script which makes texts readable more according to the reality of the living language, enabling one to avoid the artificial effect of case-endings and other obsolete Classical rules without violating the symbol–sound correspondences. Furthermore, these char-acteristics of the Arabic script enable people to read and write Arabic more or less cor-rectly even if they have only reached lower educational levels. Moreover, a more lexicalized script, as defective Arabic writing in fact is, permits not only quicker writ-ing but quicker reading as well. Above all, the fear of a complete break with tradi-tion—cultural as well as religious, since the Qur'ān, considered as eternal and uncreated, and thus sacrosanct not only in its wording but also in the form in which it is written—will make a drastic script reform impossible.

SAMPLE OF ARABIC

←نظر عبد الله بن طاهر إلى خط بعض كتابه فلم يرضه

rẓn←   db'   hlla   nb   rhaṭ   yl'   ṭh   d'b   hbatk   mlf   hḍry

فقال نحوا هذا عن مرتبة الديوان فإنه عليل الخط ولا يؤمن

| nm'y | alw | t̲hla | lyl' | hn'f | nawydla | tbtrm | n' | adh | awḥn | laqf |

أن يعدي غيره

| hryġ | yd'y | n' |

1. Transliteration:	nẓr	'bd	'llh	bn	t̲'hr	'ly	ḫt
2. Vocalization:	naẓara	'Abdullāhi	bnu	Ṭāhirin	'ilā	ḫatti
3. Transcription:	nʌʐʌrʌ	ʕabdʊl:aːhi	bnʊ	ɫaːhɪrɪn	ʔɪlʌ	xʌt:i
4. Gloss:	he.looked	'Abdallāh	son.of	Ṭāhir	at	handwriting.of

1.	b'ḍ	kt'bh	flm	yrḍh	fq'l	nḥw'	hḍ'
2.	ba'ḍi	kuttābihī	falam	yurḍihī	fa-qāla	naḥḥū	hāḏā
3.	baʕɖɪ	kʊtːæːbɪ-hiː	fʌ-lʌm	jʊrɖɪ-hiː	fʌ-qaːlʌ	nʌħħuː	hæːðʌ
4.	part.of	secretaries-his	and-not	it.pleased-him	and-he.said	remove	this

1.	'n	mrtbt	'ldyw'n	f'nh	'lyl	'lḫt
2.	'an	martabati	d-dīwāni	fa'innahū	'alīlu	l-ḫatti
3.	ʕʌn	mʌrtʌbʌti	d-diːwæːni	fʌ-ʔɪnnʌhʊ	ʕaliːlu	l-xʌtti
4.	from	office-of	the-administration	for-he	ill.of	the-handwriting

1.	wl'	y'mn	'n	y'dy	ġyrh
2.	wa-lā	yu'manu	'an	yu'diya	ġayrahū
3.	wʌ-læː	juʔmʌnu	ʔʌn	juʕdijʌ	ɣajrʌhu
4.	and-not	one-is-sure	that	he-infects	other-he

"Abdallāh ibn Ṭāhir looked at the handwriting of one of his secretaries but was
not content with it. So he said, "Remove this one from the administrative office,
for he suffers an illness in his handwriting, and one cannot be sure that he won't
infect others!""

—From aṣ-Ṣūlī 1922: 52f.

Dhivehi Writing

JAMES W. GAIR AND BRUCE D. CAIN

Dhivehi (or Divehi) is spoken by about 230,000 people in the Republic of the
Maldives in the Indian Ocean, where it is the official language. Approximately 10,000
more speakers live on the island of Minicoy (India), where it is known as Mahl or Mahal. It is an Indo-Aryan language, most closely related to Sinhala of Sri Lanka, but
not mutually intelligible with it. The earliest documents (ca. 1200 C.E.) are in *Evēlā*
'ancient' script, written from left to right, similar to the Sinhala script of the time.
This developed into a script called *Dives* (or *Divehi*) *Akuru* 'island letters', also written from left to right. It has been supplanted, since the early seventeenth century, by

TABLE 50.3: *Dhivehi Consonants (thaana)*

Letter	Translit.	Official	Value	Name	Letter	Translit.	Official	Value	Name
ノ	h	h	[h]	Haa	ه	t	th	[t]	Thaa
ィ	š	sh	[ṣ]	Shaviyani	ょ	l	l	[l]	Laamu
ノﾉ	n	n	[n]	Noonu	ぅ	g	g	[g]	Gaafu
メ	r	r	[r]	Raa	と	ñ	gn	[ɲ]	Gnaviyani
∞	b	b	[b]	Baa	ー	s	s	[s]	Seenu
ょ	ḷ	lh	[ḷ]	Lhaviyani	ё	ḍ	d	[ḍ]	Daviyani
ノ	k	k	[k]	Kaafu	ɛ	z	z	[z]	Zaviyani
ノ	–		Ø	Alifu	ɛ	ṭ	t	[ṭ]	Taviyani
ぅ	v	v	[v]	Vaavu	ﾉﾉ	y	y	[j]	Yaviyani
ふ	m	m	[m]	Meemu	ぅ	p	p	[p]	Paviyani
ょ	f	f	[f]	Faafu	ɛ	j	j	[ɟ]	Javiyani
ゅ	d	dh	[d]	Dhaalu	ﾉ	c	ch	[c]	Chaviyani

the current script known as *Gabuḷi Tāna*, or simply *Thaana (Tāna)*, which is written from right to left (like Arabic, which is also used among the Islamic population). The script has undergone changes in shape since then, but retains its essential character. During the administration of President Naseer, an official Roman script was developed, which proved unpopular; since the accession of President Gayoom, Thaana has been used almost exclusively.

While influences of Arabic and of other South Asian scripts are present, Thaana is unique in character. The basic alphabet has 24 consonantal characters, of which the first nine are derived from the numerals 1–9 of Arabic, and the second nine from an older set of local numerals. The remaining six letters are mainly adaptations of earlier ones or Perso-Arabic borrowings, and appear primarily in loanwords. The location of *p* and retroflex *ṭ* among this latter group can be attributed to a sound change by which inherited intervocalic [p] and [ṭ] became respectively [f] and [ṣ] (a retroflexed *sh*-like sound, and sometimes a retroflex voiceless flap), so that the present [p] and [ṭ] between vowels represent reborrowings.

The symbols

The consonantal characters are shown in TABLE 50.3. The current order of symbols is reflected in this table, but there have been changes from time to time (Geiger and

TABLE 50.4: *Dhivehi Vowels (fili)*

Fili	́	̋	—	—	̓	̏	̒	̏̏	̽	ℓ
Translit.	a	ā	i	ī	u	ū	e	ē	o	ō
Official	a	aa	i	ee	u	oo	e	ey	o	oa
Name	aba fili	aabaa fili	ibi fili	eebee fili	ubu fili	ooboo fili	ebe fili	eybey fili	obo fili	oaboa fili

Bell 1919, De Silva 1969). The manner of writing the independent vowels and the vowel order are shown in TABLE 50.4.

Like other South Asian languages, Taana writes vowels as diacritics on consonants. Atypically, however, consonant letters do not carry an inherent [a]. The presence of a vowel, including [a], is specified by a diacritic on the consonant character. There are ten vowel diacritics or *fili*. The *fili* for [i] and [i:] are written below the consonant character, e.g. ؍ *ni*, ؍ *nī*, all others above it, e.g. ؍ *na*, ؍ *nu*, ؍*ne*. The markings ◌́ *a*, — *i*, and ◌̋ *u* are direct borrowings from Arabic, and have been augmented for the vowel inventory of Dhivehi. Long vowels—except in the case of ◌̽ *o* and ℓ *ō*—are written by doubling the diacritic. A consonant with no vowel is indicated by the consonant symbol marked with an eleventh *fili* ◌̊, called *sukun*.

One symbol, ؍ alifu, though listed among the consonants, represents no specific sound, but is used as a neutral base for *fili*. When marked with a vowel diacritic, it is used to write that vowel word-initially or immediately following another vowel, thus, ؍؍؍؍ *irugai* 'time (locative)' (note the right-to-left order). Alifu with sukun ؍ writes a word-final glottal stop, as in ؍؍؍ *fa°* [faʔ] 'sawteeth'. Double consonants are generally written by using alif + sukun preceding the consonant being lengthened: ؍؍؍؍ *ba°dalu* [baddalu] 'meeting', ؍؍؍؍ *ba°ṭe°* [baṭṭeʔ] 'eggplant'. Double nasals, however, are written with *n* + sukun preceding the nasal: ؍؍؍ *en°me* [emme] 'only'.

The symbols ؍ *š* and ؍ *t* with sukun have special characteristics: they represent the glottal stop word-finally, but before another consonant represent doubling of that consonant. Thus ؍؍؍ *raš°* 'island' and ؍؍؍؍ *aš°ḍiha* '80' are pronounced [raʔ] and [aḍḍiha] (the change of *d* to retroflex *ḍ* results from the preceding retroflex consonant). However, in either position, a -*y*- offglide is pronounced on the vowel preceding *t* + sukun (؍). Thus ؍؍؍ *rat°* 'red' is [rayʔ], and ؍؍؍؍؍ *at°pulu* 'hand (honorific)' is *ayppulu* [ajppuḷu]. Like Sinhala (SECTION 36), Divehi has prenasalized voiced stops, which contrast with the corresponding nasal plus stop. These are written as *n* (without sukun) plus the stop, and sometimes without the nasal represented at all, even though it is there when spoken. Thus [kaⁿḍu] 'sea' is ؍؍؍ *kanḍu* or ؍؍ *kaḍu*.

Diphthongs are written by writing the second member as an independent vowel, i.e., alifu with the relevant diacritic. The first part is written in the usual way, i.e., as a diacritic on alifu (for word-initial diphthongs) or on the relevant consonant; hence ؍؍؍؍ *ais°* [ais] 'having come', ؍؍؍ *fai* [fai] 'leg'.

TABLE 50.5: *Additional Characters Used in Transliterating Arabic (tiki jehē tāna)*

Letter	Arabic	Transliteration	Letter	Arabic	Transliteration
ٮ	ح	ḥ	ٯ	ث	t̲
ٮ	خ	ḫ	ٯ	ط	ṭ
ٮ	ع	ʿ	ٯ	ق	q
ٮ	غ	ǵ	ٮ	ش	š
ٯ	و	w	ٮ	ص	ṣ
ٯر	ذ	d̲	ٮ	ض	ḍ

In writing Arabic loanwords, Arabic letters are commonly used, but there is an additional set of characters, called *tiki jehē tāna*, formed by adding dots to already existent Taana characters. that has been created for that purpose, and the government encourages its use in Taana documents. These are given in TABLE 50.5.

On the whole, Taana fits the phonology of the language very well, and M. W. S. De Silva has gone so far as to call it "perhaps the most scientific alphabet in South Asia" (1969: 208). As the text sample shows, the fit is very close, though there are some non-direct phonological representations as described earlier.

SAMPLE OF DHIVEHI

In normal speech, word-final glottal stop generally assimilates completely to the following consonant, except before vowels and *h*, where it becomes the velar nasal [ŋ], as illustrated in line 4.

īnavāmid °šakamak ūgadnu em°ne uri ēḷu °sog °šaham

°šakamak ūgadnu em°ne uri ēḷu °sog °šaham ?°emak °nok

ne .ēḷu e °negifihin °ne iaguri itad °ne īnav °šakamak

?°enihik īneḷu nafih

1. Transliteration:	mahaš°	gos°	uḷē	iru	en°me	undagū	kamakaš°
2. Transcription:	maha?	gos	uḷe:	iru	emme	u^{n}dagu:	kamaka?
3. Colloquial:	mahag	gos	uḷe:	iru	emme	u^{n}dagu:	kamakad
4. Gloss:	fish.to	going	being	time	most	difficult	thing.a.to

1. dimāvanī   kon°   kame°?   mahaš°   gos°   ul̪ē   iru   en°me   undagū
2. dima:va:ni: kon   kame?   maha?   gos   ul̪e: iru   emme   uⁿdagu:
3. dima:va:ni: koŋ   kame?   mahag   gos   ul̪e: iru   emme   uⁿdagu:
4. encountering which   thing   fish.to going being   time   most   difficult

1. kamakaš°   al̪ugand̪umen°naš°   vanī   en°   dati   irugai   en°
2. kamaka?   al̪ugaⁿd̪umenna?   vani: en   dati   irugai   en
3. kamakaŋ   al̪ugaⁿd̪umenna?   vani: en   dati   irugai   en
4. thing.a.to us.to   is   bait scarce time.in bait

1. nihifigen°   e   ul̪ē.   en°   hifan°   ul̪enī   kihine°?
2. nihifigen   e   ul̪e   en   hifan   ul̪eni: kihine?
3. nihifigeŋ   e   ul̪e   en   hifaŋ   ul̪eni: kihine?
4. not.having.caught that being bait to.catch is.being how

'When you go fishing, what is the most difficult situation you encounter?
—When we go fishing, the most difficult thing that happens to us is when the
bait fish are scarce and we don't get the bait. —How do (you) try to catch bait
fish?'   —*After De Silva 1969: 202.*

Bibliography

ARABIC

aṣ-Ṣūlī, Abū Bakr Muḥammad (d. 946 C.E.). 1922. *'Adab al-kuttāb* [The accomplishments of the secretaries], ed. M. Baḥğat al-Aṭarī. Cairo.

Endress, Gerhard. 1982. "Die arabische Schrift." In *Grundriß der arabischen Philologie,* vol. 1: *Sprachwissenschaft,* ed. Wolfdietrich Fischer, pp. 165–97. Wiesbaden: Reichert.

Fischer, Wolfdietrich. 1996. *A Grammar of Classical Arabic,* trans. Jonathan Rodgers. New Haven: Yale University Press. (German orig., 1972.)

Mitchell, Terence F. 1953. *Writing Arabic: A Practical Introduction to Ruq ʿah Script.* London: Oxford University Press.

Safadi, Yasin Hamid. 1978. *Islamic Calligraphy.* London: Thames and Hudson.

Wright, William. 1896–98. *A Grammar of the Arabic Language, Translated from the German of Caspari and edited with numerous additions and corrections,* 3rd ed., rev. W. Robertson Smith and M. J. de Goeje. 2 vols. Cambridge: Cambridge University Press. Repr. 1967.

DHIVEHI

Bell, Harry C. P. 1919. Appendixes to Geiger 1919: 123–82.

De Silva, M. W. Sugathapala. 1969. "The Phonological Efficiency of the Maldivian Writing System." *Anthropological Linguistics* 11: 199-208.

Geiger, Wilhelm. 1919. *Maldivian Linguistic Studies,* trans. Mrs. J. C. Willis, ed. H. C. P. Bell. *Journal of the Royal Asiatic Society of Great Britain* 27 (Extra Number).

Maniku, Hassan Ahmed, and Jayaratna B. Disanayaka. 1990. *Say It in Maldivian (Dhivehi).* Colombo, Sri Lanka: Lake House.

Nakanishi, Akira. 1980. *Writing Systems of the World,* pp. 31–32. Rutland, Vt.: Tuttle.

Ethiopic Writing

GETATCHEW HAILE

Approximately eighty languages belonging to three families—Semitic, Cushitic, and Nilo-Saharan—are spoken in Ethiopia. Prior to the twentieth century, not more than half a dozen of them had been reduced to writing. On the other hand, the morphology of one of the Semitic languages, Gəʿəz (also called Ethiopic, which is more properly the name of the subfamily of Semitic which is found in Ethiopia), has been transmitted both orally and through a writing system since at least the fourth century. Gəʿəz transmitted through this special writing system is, for its students, initially devoid of meaning: in the traditional system of training, the student learns the traditional pronunciation of Ethiopic from his teacher before he learns the language. Thus, at a certain level of his education, the student would read Ethiopic texts perfectly and fluently without understanding what he was reading. This training included identifying the proper stress, accent, and intonation. This section discusses this writing system, which has since been adopted by a few other Ethiopian languages, including Amharic, the official language of the country.

Consonants

To become a written language, Ethiopic needed a writing system which had characters to represent its consonants, as given in TABLE 51.1. For this it adopted the Sabean/Minean script or one that is closely related to it (see TABLE 5.7 on page 101).

In antiquity, ፀ was probably interdental ẓ, ሠ fricative š, and ኀ velar ḫ. Since then, ፀ and ሠ have become sibilants, and ኀ ḥ is laryngeal. Now, ፀ and ጸ are ṣ [ts]; ሐ ḥ and ኀ ḥ have become [h], like ሀ; and both አ ʾ and ዐ ʿ represent the glottal stop [ʔ]. These sets of letters tend to be confused in manuscripts; lexicographers must clarify them.

Characters

As the epigraphic sources witness, two writing systems were apparently available in the country at the time when the need for a system for writing Gəʿəz was felt. These were the South Arabian Sabean/Minean script or one related to it, and the Greek alphabet. In making the choice, the determining factor was obviously the relationship Ethiopia had had with South Arabia: Ethiopic and Sabean are both members of the family of the southern branch of the Semitic languages.

TABLE 51.1: *Consonants*[a]

	OCCLUSIVES			FRICATIVES			SONORANTS		SEMI-VOWELS
	vs	*vd*	*ej*	*vs*	*vd*	*ej*	*nas*	*nns*	*vd*
Labials	p	b	ṗ				m		w
Labiodentals				f	v				
Dentals	t	d	ṭ				n	l, r	
Sibilants				s, ś	z	ṣ, ḍ			
Palatals[b]	č	ǧ	č̣	š	ž		ñ		y
Velars	k	g	q	ḫ					
Labiovelars	kʷ	gʷ	qʷ	ḫʷ					
Laryngeals	ʾ			ʿ	h				

a. *vs,* voiceless; *vd,* voiced; *ej,* ejective; *nas,* nasal; *nns,* nonnasal.
b. Amharic only, except *y*.

The Sabean/Minean script (or one related to it) which Ethiopic adopted was able to represent all consonants except for [p] and [ṗ]. The symbols for these became ፐ and ጰ, respectively. ፐ seems to be a modification of the Greek Π, while ጰ is a derivative from the Ethiopic ጸ *ṣ*. For the labiovelars, the symbols for *g, ḫ, k,* and *q* (respectively) were modified. The mark of palatalization (for Amharic and other languages) is a horizontal line—broken in the middle in the case of ዥ *ž*—placed on the top of the related characters. ኀ is *h*, representing the laryngealized ኸ. In the case of *č̣*, the rule is violated: ጨ → ጨ.

By beginning with the letter ሀ (*h, hoy*), the alphabetical order of the Ethiopic writing system (TABLE 51.2) differs from those of the related systems, e.g. Arabic, Hebrew, Syriac, Greek, which begin with ʾ (aleph or alpha). Arguably, the name *alphabet* is a misnomer for Ethiopic because it does not begin with *alpha* or *alf* ኧ (ʾ) followed by *bet* ቡ (*b*). Several theories have been posited to explain why the characters of the Ethiopic alphabet have been arranged so differently, but none is satisfactory. It is much better to assume that Ethiopic preserves an early or ancient branch of the original. For the similar, though not identical, order of the ancient Sabean script, see SECTION 68. (In certain religious contexts, the North Semitic order—called *abugida*, from the first four consonants and the first four "orders"—which is known from the acrostic poems in the Gəʿəz translation of the Hebrew Bible, is also found.)

TABLE 51.2: *The Ethiopic Characters in Their Alphabetic Order (Amharic phonetics)*[a]

ሀ ለ ሐ መ ሠ ረ ሰ (ሸ) ቀ በ ተ (ቸ) ኀ ነ (ኘ) አ ከ ኸ (ኸ) ወ ዐ ዘ (ዠ) የ ደ (ጀ) ገ ጠ (ጨ) ጰ ጸ ፀ ፈ ፐ ፐ
h l ḥ m ś r s (š) q b t (č) ḫ n (ñ) ʾ k (h) w ʿ z (ž) y d (ǧ) g ṭ (č) ṗ ṣ ż f p
[h l h m s r s ʃ kʼ b t ʧ h n ɲ ʔ k h w ʔ z ʒ j d ʤ g tʼ ʧ pʼ ts ts f p]

ቈ	ኈ	ኰ	ጐ
qu [kʷ]	ḫu [ḫʷ]	ku [kʷ]	gu [gʷ]

a. *Upper row,* base forms; *lower row,* labialized forms; *in parentheses,* Amharic letters.

TABLE 51.3: *Vowels*

	Front	Central	Back
High	i	ə	u
Mid	e	o	
		3	
Low		a	

Vowels

A few inscriptions have been discovered which show Gəʿəz texts without vowel signs, just like the Sabean/Minean (and the other Semitic scripts). The characters in these inscriptions represented the consonant alone, or the consonant and any of the possible vowels. The reader had to guess, with the help of knowledge of the grammar, the necessary vowels and supply them. Therefore, one sign could be read, for example, as [b] or [b3] or [ba] or [bu] or [bi]. Thus [nəguʃ3 n3g3ʃt] 'king of kings' was written as **ንጉሥ/ንጉሥት** *ngś/ngśt*. The reader had to know the language and its grammar rather well to be able to read such texts. Many of the possible ways of reading a word are eliminated when the word is in a sentence. For example, **ንጉሥ** *ngś* in **ንጉሥ/ንጉሥት** *ngś/ngśt* cannot be other than [nəguʃ(3)]. However, as an isolated word, it could be [nəguʃ] or [n3gaʃi] or [n3gʃa] or [nəgʃ], since all these are real words which had to be written in the same way because of the absence of signs indicating the vowels.

At a certain stage of the language's written life, the difficulty of using the system without the help of vowel signs must have been felt by the majority of those who used it. Most probably that was when the number of students who used Gəʿəz as their second language had increased significantly. Obviously, large numbers of students could not begin their schooling by reading Gəʿəz written only in consonants. Creating vowel signs (and modifying the characters with them) became inevitable; the appearance of vowel signs in the epigraphic record coincides with the advent of Christianity in Ethiopia, about 350 C.E.

There are seven vowels, see TABLES 51.3 and 51.4; the seven forms of each consonant symbol are called *orders*.

Vowel signs

(1) The base character (called *gəʿəz*), the character which has no vowel sign (see TABLE 51.2), is understood as having the first vowel, *ä*. The character *gəʿəz* has thus

TABLE 51.4: *Vowels in Their Traditional Order*

"Order"	1	2	3	4	5	6	7
Transliteration	ä	u	i	a	e	ə	o
Transcription	[3]	[u]	[i]	[a, ʌ]	[e, ɛ]	[ə]	[o, ɔ]

lost its neutrality or ability to represent all the other possible readings. For example, በ is no longer *b*, but *bä*. In other words, the vowel [ə] is represented by a zero symbol. (In the case of the laryngeals, the vowel of the base is not [ə], but [a].)

(2) A short horizontal line attached to the middle of the right side of the character represents the vowel *u*. In the case of ሩ *ru*, ዉ *wu*, and ፉ *fu*, however, this system is violated.

All horizontal lines, whether they are vowel signs or part of the base character, bend down at the end.

(3) A short horizontal line attached to the lowest part of the right leg of the character represents the vowel *i*. In the course of time, a leg to carry the sign was added to ሂ *hi*, ሚ *mi*, ሢ *śi*, ዊ *wi*, ዒ *ʿi*, and ዚ *ẓi*. For ሪ *ri*, ዪ *yi*, and ፊ *fi*, the system is violated.

(4) A vertical line attached to the bottom of a character—to the right leg of the character, if the character has more than one leg—represents the vowel *a*. (The system includes the laryngeals, which have [a] in place of [ə].) If the character has only a single leg, the line is tilted to the left to make the addition clear. In the case of ራ *ra*, ና *na*, and ኛ *ña*, the rule is violated.

(5) A ring or half ring attached to the lower part of the right side of the character represents the vowel *e*. A leg to carry the sign is added to ሄ *he*, ሜ *me*, ሤ *śe*, ዌ *we*, ዔ *ʿe*, and ዜ *ẓe*; compare (3) above. In the case of ዬ *ye* and ቼ *če*, the ring is attached at the middle of the character with a short horizontal line.

(6) The sign for the vowel *ə* and the rule defining its place on the character are not generalized. In some cases, the sign is a short horizontal line placed on the left side of the character, but its placement on the left side is unpredictable. In the case of ር *rə*, ው *wə*, ድ *də*, ግ *ğə*, ፕ *pə*, ጽ *ṣə*, and ፍ *fə*, it is placed on the right side. In the case of ህ *hə*, ሕ *ḥə*, ቅ *qə*, ት *tə*, ን *nə*, እ *ʾə*, ዕ *ʿə*, and ዝ *ẓə*, it is placed on the head of the character. The signs for ል *lə*, ስ *sə*, ኅ *ḫə*, ይ *yə*, and ግ *gə* follow no rule; but those for ህ *hə*, ክ *kə*, ጥ *ṭə*, and ፕ *pə* do. These observations, however, are of little use for those who want to learn this column of characters. They have to be learned individually.

The modified character that represents the consonant with the vowel *ə* serves also to represent the vowelless consonant. For example, *bə* and *b* are represented by the same character, ብ. Tradition rightly identified the close relationship between the vowelless consonant and the consonant with the vowel [ə] (cf. the Hebrew shwa), but it is not clear why the base or *gəʿəz* characters were not chosen for this purpose—the characters without vowel signs, which are assigned to the consonant with the vowel *ä*.

(7) Two signs to represent the vowel *o* are discernible. The rule for their distribution is not clear. With some characters (of which only ሎ *lo* has two or more legs) it is a circle (taken from Greek omicron?) placed on or near the top of the character. If the character has two or more legs, the sign is a vertical line attached to the middle bottom of the character or to the end of the left leg. The rule is violated in the case of ሎ *lo*, ዮ *yo*, and ጎ *go*.

(8) A short horizontal line attached to the right leg of most of the characters indicates a combination of [u] (or [w]) and [a]. A leg to carry the sign is added to the char-

TABLE 51.5: *The Ethiopic Letters*

	Name	1 ä (a)	2 u	3 i	4 a	5 e	6 ə/ø	7 o	1 uä	3 ui	4 ua	5 ue	6 uə
h	hoy	ሀ	ሁ	ሂ	ሃ	ሄ	ህ	ሆ					
l	läwe	ለ	ሉ	ሊ	ላ	ሌ	ል	ሎ					
h/ḥ	ḥäwt	ሐ	ሑ	ሒ	ሓ	ሔ	ሕ	ሖ					
m	may	መ	ሙ	ሚ	ማ	ሜ	ም	ሞ					
ś	śäwt	ሠ	ሡ	ሢ	ሣ	ሤ	ሥ	ሦ					
r	rə's	ረ	ሩ	ሪ	ራ	ሬ	ር	ሮ					
s	sat	ሰ	ሱ	ሲ	ሳ	ሴ	ስ	ሶ					
š		ሸ	ሹ	ሺ	ሻ	ሼ	ሽ	ሾ					
q	qaf	ቀ	ቁ	ቂ	ቃ	ቄ	ቅ	ቆ	ቈ	ቊ	ቋ	ቌ	ቍ
b	bet	በ	ቡ	ቢ	ባ	ቤ	ብ	ቦ					
t	täwe	ተ	ቱ	ቲ	ታ	ቴ	ት	ቶ					
č		ቸ	ቹ	ቺ	ቻ	ቼ	ች	ቾ					
h/ḫ	ḫärm	ኀ	ኁ	ኂ	ኃ	ኄ	ኅ	ኆ	ኈ	ኊ	ኋ	ኌ	ኍ
n	nähas	ነ	ኑ	ኒ	ና	ኔ	ን	ኖ					
ñ		ኘ	ኙ	ኚ	ኛ	ኜ	ኝ	ኞ					
'	'älf	አ	ኡ	ኢ	ኣ	ኤ	እ	ኦ					
k	kaf	ከ	ኩ	ኪ	ካ	ኬ	ክ	ኮ	ኰ	ኲ	ኳ	ኴ	ኵ
h		ኸ	ኹ	ኺ	ኻ	ኼ	ኽ	ኾ					
w	wäwe	ወ	ዉ	ዊ	ዋ	ዌ	ው	ዎ					
ʿ/'	ʿäyn	ዐ	ዑ	ዒ	ዓ	ዔ	ዕ	ዖ					
z	zäy	ዘ	ዙ	ዚ	ዛ	ዜ	ዝ	ዞ					
ž		ዠ	ዡ	ዢ	ዣ	ዤ	ዥ	ዦ					
y	yämän	የ	ዩ	ዪ	ያ	ዬ	ይ	ዮ					
d	dänt	ደ	ዱ	ዲ	ዳ	ዴ	ድ	ዶ					
ğ		ጀ	ጁ	ጂ	ጃ	ጄ	ጅ	ጆ					
g	gäml	ገ	ጉ	ጊ	ጋ	ጌ	ግ	ጎ	ጐ	ጒ	ጓ	ጔ	ጕ
ṭ	ṭäyt	ጠ	ጡ	ጢ	ጣ	ጤ	ጥ	ጦ					
č̣		ጨ	ጩ	ጪ	ጫ	ጬ	ጭ	ጮ					
ṗ	ṗäyt	ጰ	ጱ	ጲ	ጳ	ጴ	ጵ	ጶ					
ṣ	ṣädäy	ጸ	ጹ	ጺ	ጻ	ጼ	ጽ	ጾ					
ṣ/ź	ḍäṗṗa	ፀ	ፁ	ፂ	ፃ	ፄ	ፅ	ፆ					
f	äf	ፈ	ፉ	ፊ	ፋ	ፌ	ፍ	ፎ					
p	psa	ፐ	ፑ	ፒ	ፓ	ፔ	ፕ	ፖ					

acters which need it, e.g. ‎ᄳ *mwa*. In the case of ‎ᄶ *rwa* and ‎ᄷ *fwa*, the sign is placed on the head of the character.

Vowel length is not recognized.

The array of Ethiopic letters is shown in TABLE 51.5.

Characters or diagrams

The combining of individual characters with vowel signs with so little systematization has resulted, in many cases, in the creation of a new character with an independent identity, a character virtually on the level of the base character. The vowel signs have become such an integral part of the body of the character that each of the seven forms, including the base form, is a symbol representing a consonant and a vowel. The system is not strictly syllabic because the symbols do not always represent syllables. The Ethiopic consonants may be 26 in number, but the characters are, in essence 26 (plus the derivatives) times 7, plus the signs for the labiovelars (which are 4 times 5—these four have only five vowels each: *ä, i, a, e,* and *ə*).

As a rule, Ethiopic characters do not extend below the line. In order not to violate this rule, either the vertical lines representing vowels are tilted to the left, in the case of some characters (especially those that have only one leg); or the base characters are written above the line in smaller size, so that the added vowel sign ends on the line. This method of modification gives the impression not of adding a sign to the base character but of creating a new character.

The Ethiopic writing system has no sign for gemination or the doubling of a consonant, although this is distinctive in the language. For example, the system does not distinguish between [səbħa] 'to be fat' and [səbbəħa] 'to praise'; both are written ሰብሐ. To make this distinction and to determine the presence or absence of the vowel *ə*, we must rely primarily on oral transmission of the pronunciation of the language(s). Except in these two points, the Ethiopic writing system can be characterized as phonetic, at least for Gəʻəz (and Amharic).

Numerals

The Gəʻəz numerals are developed from the Greek alphabet, borrowed possibly through Coptic, see TABLE 51.6. Time has of course changed them significantly. In writing modern Ethiopian languages, one usually uses the Arabic numerals.

TABLE 51.6: *Numerals*

፩	1	፮	6	፳	20	፸	70
፪	2	፯	7	፴	30	፹	80
፫	3	፰	8	፵	40	፺	90
፬	4	፱	9	፶	50	፻	100
፭	5	፲	10	፷	60	፼	10,000

Writing Ethiopic

In the inscriptions, words were separated with a vertical line, e.g. <ngśǀngśt>. In manuscripts and published books, this has been replaced with two dots which look like a colon (፡). This sign is being replaced with a blank space in writing the modern languages of the country. A semicolon is expressed by the two dots with a horizontal line above and below them (፤), a comma by the two dots with a horizontal line over or between them, and a full stop by doubling the two dots (፨).

Ethiopic is written from left to right. The characters should be drawn starting at the upper left side and proceeding forward and down to the lower right side; that is, the stroke of the pen should be, as a rule, from top to bottom, never from bottom to top or from right to left. No part should remain on the left or on top to be added. The stroke from top to bottom may be slightly angled at its two ends if necessary only to connect that part with the remaining body of the character.

SAMPLE OF GE'EZ

1. Ge'ez:	ወሶበ ፡	ሰምዐ ፡	ኢሳይያስ ፡	ዘንተ ፡	ነገረ ፡
2. Pronunciation:	wä-sobä	säm'a	'Isayəyyas	zänta	nägärä
3. Gloss:	and-when	heard.he	'Isayəyyas	this	statement

1.	እምአፉሆሙ ፡	ለአግብርተ ፡	ሰይጣን ፡	ቦአ ፡	ኀበ ፡	ንጉሥ ፡
2.	'əm-'afu-homu	la'agbərtä	säytan	bo'a	ḫabä	nəguś
3.	from-mouth-their	servants.of	Satan	went.he	to	king

1.	ወይቤሎ ፡	ለንጉሥ ፡ ...	ኦአግዚእየ ፡	ናሁ ፡	ይቤሉኒ ፡	አልብክ ፡
2.	wä-yəbel-o	lä-nəguś ...	'o-'əgzi'ə-yä	nahu	yəbelu-ni	al-bə-kä
3.	and-he.said-to.him	to-king ...	O-lord-my	behold	they.tell-me	not-in-you

1.	ሠናየ ፡	ንብረተ ፡	በመዋዕሊሁ ፡	ለዝ ፡	ንጉሥ ፡	ዘእንበለ ፡	በካልአ ፨
2.	śannäyä	nəbrätä	ba-mäwa'əli-hu	lä zo	nəguś	zä-'ənbälä	bä-kalə'.
3.	good	life	during-days-his	of-this	king	which-but	of-another

1.	ወይቤሎ ፡	ንጉሥ ፡	እለ ፡	መኑ ፡	ይብሉክ ፡	ከመዝ ፨
2.	wä-yəbel-o	nəgus	'əllä	männu	yəblu-kä	kämä-zə.
3.	and-he.said-to.him	king	those	who	say-to.you	like-this

1.	ወይቤሎ ፡	ኢሳይያስ ፡	ለንጉሥ ፡	ሰብአ ፡	ዚአየ ፡	ፍቁራንየ ፡
2.	wä-yəbel-o	'Isayəyyas	lä-nəguś	säb'ä	zi'a-yä	fəquran-əyä
3.	and-he.said-to.him	'Isayəyyas	to-king	people	of-me	dear.ones-my

1.	ይቤሉኒ ፡	ከመዝ ፨
2.	yəbelu-ni	kämä-zə
3.	they.said-to.me	like-this

'When 'Isayəyyas heard this statement from the mouth of the servants of Satan, he went to the king and said to the king, ..."O my lord, behold, they tell me, 'You will not have a good life during the days of this king but of another one.'" The king said to him, "Who are they who say such things to you?" 'Isayəyyas said to the king, "My people, my dear (friends), have spoken to me like this."'

—*Getatchew Haile 1991: 67, lines 21–26.*

Bibliography

Bender, M. Lionel, Sydney W. Head, and Roger Cowley. 1976. "The Ethiopian Writing System." In *Language in Ethiopia,* ed. M. L. Bender, J. D. Bowen, R. C. Cooper, and C. A. Ferguson, pp. 120–29. London: Oxford University Press.

Daniels, Peter T. 1991. "Ha, La, Ḥa or Hōi, Lawe, Ḥaut: The Ethiopic Letter Names." In *Semitic Studies in Honor of Wolf Leslau on the Occasion of his Eighty-fifth Birthday,* ed. Alan S. Kaye, pp. 275–88. Wiesbaden: Harrassowitz.

Dillmann, August. 1907. *Ethiopic Grammar,* 2nd ed. by Carl Bezold, trans. James A. Crichton. London: Williams & Norgate. Repr. Amsterdam: Philo, 1974.

Getatchew Haile, ed. 1991. *The Epistle of Humanity of Emperor Zär 'a Ya ʿəqob (Ṭomarä Təsbə 't)* (Corpus Scriptorum Christianorum Orientalium 522, Scriptores Aethiopici 95). Louvain: Peeters.

Grohmann, Adolf. 1918. "Über den Ursprung und die Entwicklung der äthiopischen Schrift." *Archiv für Schriftkunde* 1: 57–87.

Hartmann, Josef. 1980. *Amharische Grammatik.* Wiesbaden: Steiner.

Leslau, Wolf. 1957. "The Phonetic Treatment of the Arabic Loanwords in Ethiopic." *Word* 13: 100–23. Repr. in his *Fifty Years of Research: Selection of Articles on Semitic, Ethiopian Semitic and Cushitic,* pp. 43–66. Wiesbaden: Harrassowitz, 1988.

Ullendorff, Edward. 1955. *The Semitic Languages of Ethiopia: A Comparative Phonology.* London: Taylor's Foreign Press.

Part IX: Scripts Invented in Modern Times

WHY DOES SOMEONE INVENT A SCRIPT? What is the purpose of writing? The great majority of human societies have thrived without written records. What led some beyond memory alone?

There seem to be three different answers underlying the three most ancient writing systems we can interpret. In Mesopotamia, whether or not archaic counting devices are implicated, and whether or not the locus is sacral—what comes to be seen as "temple economies"—the primary impulse seems to be commerce: relations between cities, as well as administration of incipient or developed bureaucracy, of small groups or even legions of workers with a purpose other than individualistic enterprise.

In China, the earliest writings preserve the outcomes of oracular consultations with supernatural beings: if the gods must be consulted at every turn, there needs to be some certain way to preserve their responses.

In Mesoamerica, what is clearest about the interpretable remains is the astronomical information. Cycles spanning decades and centuries could perhaps be suspected, but only with records reaching beyond one observer's lifetime can the details be worked out.

What do these three cases have in common? Only, perhaps, the amount of information and its lack of certainty or predictability (astronomical patterns can only be discovered after much information has been determined). While it has perhaps not been forgotten by unlettered peoples, it was (re)discovered by the West close to a century ago that writing is not required to preserve literature and tradition. Homer and Moses did not need to write their stories down in order for them to be cherished from generation to generation. The poetic language and formulas of the one, the numinous power of the other, made them live forever. Written literature piggybacked on the mundane accountant's, or acolyte's, or observer's purely practical recording devices.

And their adaptation to recording ordinary, and then heightened, language had happened so recently in history (by definition, remember) that Plato could have Socrates decry the use of writing as detrimental to the power of memory. He was right.

It is in this sense that something happens to "civilization" when it takes up writing. It is not then that literature is invented; but it is then that it takes a new form. Only *prose* is added to the repertoire of the culture; is the *science* of Aristotle or of Galen more "advanced" than the *ethnoscience* that even today harvests efficacious medicines from the natural world? A good case can be made—taken up at the very end of this book—that only with printing, and the dissemination of identical, reliable copies of expository prose, did the existence of writing have a material, beneficial effect on human existence.

There is, of course, one exception, and it was adumbrated at the very beginning: the sphere of religion. The religions of the West, and some of those of the East, rely on Scripture. The dissemination of writing often serves the dissemination of scriptures. From earliest times, adherents have been called to both study and proselytize. The former activity produces new writings; the latter produces new scripts (but usually developed out of others).

But a motif found over and over in the stories of script inventors—grammatogenists—is divine inspiration, often in a dream, sometimes in retreat from the world. In almost every case, the script inventor wishes to benefit his people with a gift from heaven. In almost every remaining case, the inventor seeks to bring to his people the material benefits seen to be possessed by others who are able to talk to each other across distances that are beyond earshot, or across barriers that sound cannot penetrate. Their stories often refer to "leaves that can speak"; they were enmeshed in a world of communication by audition—and were freed by a sudden insight: *a* vision that revealed the potential *of* vision.

— PETER T. DANIELS

The Invention of Writing

PETER T. DANIELS

The normal way for a society to acquire its own script is by evolving, adapting, or adopting an existing writing system. Once in a while, though, some visionary, aware simply of the *existence* of writing among nearby peoples (often missionaries), sets out to devise his own system that will set his people apart from all others. The earliest such system we know of is the Old Persian cuneiform (SECTION 8); the earliest documented one is the Korean (SECTION 17); the most celebrated, and the earliest that was observed by interested outsiders, is the Cherokee. The scripts devised for Lepcha (SECTION 40), and the scripts of Cherokee, Cree, Vai, Munda languages, and Hmong, described below, are still in use, but they represent far from a complete list of modern "grammatogenies." The principal scholar of such things is Alfred Schmitt, whose comprehensive treatment was published posthumously in 1980.

Observable script inventions have much to teach about the possible scenarios of the three ancient grammatogenies (Sumerian, Chinese, Maya)—but only if we observe one distinction. There are grammatogenies by people already literate in some language, who possess at least some knowledge of phonetics—if only as much as is encoded in an existing script—a type I call *sophisticated*; and grammatogenies by people who cannot read in any language and who know nothing of phonetics—*unsophisticated* grammatogeny. It is the study of unsophisticated modern grammatogeny that may illuminate the ancient origins of writing.

Sophisticated grammatogenies

As with Korean and Cree, it is often the missionary impulse that leads someone to create a script for a culture. Its external characteristics may be determined by the availability of printing equipment (or even typewriters, in the minimal case of the adaptation of the English/French/Spanish etc. alphabet to local languages), or the inventor may feel free to design an entirely new set of characters. Either way, the resulting

ACKNOWLEDGMENTS: My data on the Pollard script come from T. R. Carlton of the University of Alberta, who was able to consult a preliminary version of Enwall 1994, and from Joakim Enwall (personal communications). Information on the Fraser script was provided by E. R. Hope of the United Bible Societies, Translation Centre for Southern Africa, and sample pages of text and dictionary by James Matisoff, University of California, Berkeley. I am extremely grateful to all four.

TABLE 52.1: *The Pollard Script*

⅃ [p]	T [t]	Δ [tl]	⊥ [ʈ]	⅃ [k]	J [q]	Y [ʔ, Ø]
⅃ʼ [pʰ]	Tʼ [tʰ]	Δʼ [tlʰ]	⊥ʼ [ʈʰ]	⅃ʼ [kʰ]	Jʼ [qʰ]	
	✝ [ts]		⊏ [ʈʂ, tɕ]			
	✝ʼ [tsʰ]		⊏ʼ [ʈʂʰ, tɕʰ]			
Γ [f]	S [s]	Lo [ɬ]	J [ʂ, ɕ]	ľ [χ]		⅂ [h]
V [v]	3 [z]	L [l]	R [ʐ]	I [ɣ]		
Ɔ [m̥]	Ꞇ [n̥]			ʗ [ŋ̊]		
) [m]	C [n]			C [ŋ]	ᵇ [ɯ (< ŋ)]	
U [w]			Λ [z, ɣ]			

∩ [i]	ꞌ [y]	ˢ [ɯ]	ᵁ [u]
˥ [ɪ]	ᵣ [ʏ]	ˀ [ə]	
ᶜ [e]	ˢ [œj]	ˉ [a]	° [o]
ᴸ [ei]	꞊ [ie]	ᶦ [ai]	‖ [au]

script is liable to betray some degree of phonetic sophistication—all and only the distinctive segments of the language will be provided for, and similarity in phonetic features may be reflected in similarity in shapes. Three examples may serve, two that achieved some importance in southern China, and one comprising invented scripts in contemporary imaginative literature. Mention should also be made of two scripts for Cushitic languages of the Horn of Africa: an Ethiopic-based abugida for Oromo, devised by Shaykh Bakri Saṗalō (Hayward and Hassan 1981), and an alphabet for Somali, called Osmanya from the name of the inventor, ʿIsman Yusuf, son and brother of the last two sultans of Olbia (Jensen 1969: 226f.). The former has been replaced by a modified Ethiopic, the latter by Roman orthography.

The Pollard script

Samuel Pollard (1864–1915) served as a Methodist missionary in southern China from 1887. In 1904 he went to the Ta Hwa Miao (Big Flowery Miao, A-Hmao) people, whose language is now called Western Hmong. He devised a script (Enwall 1994) comprising geometric symbols; it went through several stages of development, with that of 1936 apparently the one that has become standard (subsequent proposed improvements do not appear in a 1983 primer). Each consonant and vowel has its own symbol—each vowel is a diacritic, whose placement at the top, upper right, middle, or bottom of the consonant letter denotes different tones. (Some of the Hmong languages for which Pollard script has been used distinguish consonants by voicing rather than aspiration, and others replace those distinctions with a set of eight rather than four tones.) The order in which the 32(!) "big letters" are taught is: Y ʔ L ⅃ p T t ✝ ts Γ f ⅂ h C ts ⅃ k ⊥ t J q Ɔ n) m U w V v Λ z, y S s 3 z Δ tl Lo lh C ng I x J s R ẓ ⊔ mp Ƈ✝ nts CC nṭṣ ⊏ ngk ⊏T nt ⊏⊥ nṭ ⊏J ngq ⊏Δ ntl. The total of 37 "small letters" (i.e.

TABLE 52.2: *The Fraser Script*

P	[p]	T	[t]	F	[ts]	C	[c]	K	[k]		
ꓒ	[pʰ]	⊥	[tʰ]	Ⅎ	[tsʰ]	Ɔ	[cʰ]	ꓘ	[kʰ]		
B	[b]	D	[d]	Z	[dz]	J	[ɟ]	G	[g]	ꓨ	[ɦ][a]
ꓝ	[f]	S	[s]			X	[ʃ]	H	[x]	V	[h]
W	[v]	ꓤ	[z]			R	[ʒ]	ꓭ	[ɣ]		
M	[m]	N	[n]					Λ	[ŋ]		
		L	[l]								
W	[u̯]					Y	[i̯]				
		I	[i]	∩	[ü]	ꓶ	[ɯ]	U	[u]		
		E	[e]	Ǝ	[ø]	ɑ	[ə]	O	[ʊ]		
		Ɐ	[æ]			A	[ɑ]				
.	high tone	,	mid rising	.,	mid tone	..	mid tense	:	low tone	;	low tense
'	nasalization	_	[a̯]	–.	comma	=	period	–	in names	?	question

a. Used only with [ɑ] and low tone.

vowel and nasal finals) is arrived at by, again, counting compound symbols separately. The script has been adapted to about a dozen languages of Southeast Asia.

The Fraser script

About 1915, J. O. Fraser, a missionary working in China on the Tibeto-Burman language Lisu, created an Indic-style script using the Roman capital letters (upright and inverted) and punctuation marks to indicate tone. Regular Roman letters represent sounds that have close correspondences in English (vowels, semivowels, nasals, stops), though in some cases greater regularity was achieved by deviating from the traditional values. Inverted forms are used for phonetically similar sounds.

SAMPLE OF WESTERN HMONG

1. *Pollard Script:*	𖼀	𖼁	𖼂	𖼃	𖼄	𖼂	𖼅	𖼆	𖼇	𖼈	𖼉
2. *Transliteration:*	mì	nà	kú	žá	tsž	kú	tu	ṭau	mau	nió	tṣǜ
3. *Transcription:*	mi²¹	nʱa²¹	ku⁵⁵	ʑa⁵⁵	tsz̩⁵⁴	ku⁵⁵	tu⁵⁴	ʈau⁴⁴	mau⁴⁴	nʲo⁵⁴	ʥy²¹
4. *Gloss:*	you	look	I	shall	send	I	messenger			be	you

1.	𖼊	𖼋	𖼃	𖼌	𖼍	𖼉	𖼎	𖼏	𖼐	𖼈	𖼑 𖼒
2.	thà	nǜ	žá	ki	tsie	tṣǜ	tṣí	kù	māu	nió	ti tṣhiö̀
3.	tʰa²²	nʲʱy²²	ʑa⁵⁵	ki⁴⁴	tsie⁴⁴	ʥy²¹	tɕi⁵⁵	ku²²	mʱau²²	nʲo⁵⁴	ti⁵⁴ tɕʰœy⁴⁴ ²²
4.	in.front	he	shall	prepare		you	road	PART	walk	be	place

1. Ⅎₙ	)-	Ꞇˮ	Ꞔˊ	Jˉᵇ	Ɏˮ	Jˊ	Ƒᵘ	ꓹₙ	Ā	ꓱⁿ	ꓕⁿᶜ	Ꞓˉ
2. tṣià	mā		tï nï ṣang		a qï		xhu	hì	žá	ki	tsie	
3. dʑʰa²²	mʰa²⁴	tw⁵⁵ nw⁵⁵ ṣaw⁵⁴			a⁴⁴ qw⁴⁴		xu⁴⁴	hï²²	za⁵⁵	ki⁴⁴	tsie⁴⁴	tṣ̩⁵⁵
4. desert	exist	person			voice		call	say	shall	prepare		Lord

1. Ꞓᵖ	ꓱᵤ	)ⁱⁱ	ꓔ.	Ƒₙ	Ⳅ,	Ꞓᵖ	ꓱᵤ	ꓝ,	
2. tṣí	kù	maū	ṭeï	xhià	nù	tṣí	kù	nkè	
3. tɕi⁵⁵	ku²²	mʰau²²	ṭai²²	xa²²/xia²²	nʲʰy²²	tɕi⁵⁵	ku²²	ŋgʰə²²~⁴⁴	
4. road	PART	walk	then	build	he	road	PART	straight	

SAMPLE OF HWA (WESTERN) LISU

1. Fraser script:	NY..	N.-.	NU	MI:	ꓕꓦ:	SI..	KW	ʌW	FI	DU	FI
2. Transliteration:	nyā	ná,	nu	mì	thæ̀	sī	kwa	ŋwa	tsi	du	tsi

1.	ꓩU	KO_	LO-.	YI	NY	NU	J	GU	YE	T	VU..	NY,	Gꓶ_	BV_
2.	fu	kuą̈	lo,	ji	nya	nu	ɟa	gu	ye	ta	hū	nyǎ	guą̈	bhaą̈

1.	LO=	ꓕO:	ꓒ:	DE..	KW	L	ꓕO	ꓕI	RO	ꓫU.,	TY_	M	Sꓦ;	NY-.
2.	lo.	thò	phà	dē	kwa	la	tsho	thi	ʒo	khù	tyaą̈	ma	sæ̌	nya,

1.	SI..	ꓒ	J	GU	NU	W	YE	T	VU..	NY,-.	YI	Cꓱ.	Tꓱ,
2.	sī	pha	ɟa	gu	nu	va	ye	ta	hū	nyâ,	yi	cǿ	tǿ

1.	Tꓱ,;	BE	XY,-.	Bꓦ..	LO=
2.	tǿ	be	shyâ,	bǣ	lo.

[No analysis of the Hwa Lisu text is available.]

'See, I am sending my messenger ahead of you, who will prepare your way; the voice of one crying out in the wilderness: Prepare the way of the Lord, make his paths straight.'
— Mark 1:2–3 (Hmong: Enwall 1994, 1:189; Lisu: Nida 1972 no. 736).

Fictional scripts

Familiar to many English-speaking readers will be the Tengwar and Angertha ('letters' and 'runes') devised to accompany the languages invented by J. R. R. Tolkien as part of the creation of Middle Earth (Tolkien 1965, appendix E; see Tolkien 1931 on inventing languages generally). His calling as a philologist is obvious in the systematicity of both scripts. In the Tengwar, to be written with pen or brush, there are four basic forms—really variations on a single shape, with open or closed bowl, facing left or right; stops have a vertical descender, fricatives an ascender, and semivowels and nasals no extender. Voiced occlusives and nasals have a doubled bowl. Vowels and other consonants are written with letters that stand outside the pattern. The Angertha take over some shapes of Anglo-Saxon runes, but not their values. Here, voicing is marked with an added stroke; stops face right and fricatives face left; nasals involve some sort of doubling; vowels involve symmetry or doubled strokes. A sophisticated yet accessible account of Tolkien's languages and scripts is Noel 1980.

A writer whose connection with language science is by descent rather than by profession is Ursula K. LeGuin, daughter of the great anthropologist Alfred Kroeber. All her novels show her full command of the ways of human culture; in *Always Coming Home* (1985: 532–34), she provides an alphabet that is in a way more realistic than Tolkien's: some cases of graphic similarity reflecting phonetic similarity can be seen, but in other cases, letters seem to have diverged from a sophisticated original due to gradual change that came about through daily use of the script.

The Klingon language of the *Star Trek* universe has been elaborated by a linguist, but the Klingon script seen briefly in the first theatrical film seems to have been left in the ether, although a commercial computer font for Klingon is sold. No information is available on its creation, its phonetic (or logographic) nature, or its correspondence to the language as now studied.

Unsophisticated grammatogenies

Clearly, it is from the other kind of script invention that insights into the process may be gained. Rather unexpectedly, it turns out that virtually all unsophisticated grammatogenies share certain features: The resulting script is a *syllabary*. It includes only signs for *CV syllables*. The conventional order of the signs (when one exists) is *random*, and signs are not grouped together by phonetic similarity. Signs for phonetically similar syllables share *no* deliberate *graphic similarity*. Cherokee is the earliest documented script invention of this kind, and the Cherokee script exhibits all these characteristics.

Apparently some centuries older is a script used by ladies of the Chinese court, which is called "women's writing." It is said to be a syllabary, graphically similar to Chinese characters; whether the phonetic signs are based on appropriate Chinese logograms is unclear, as descriptions in Western languages are limited to newspaper accounts, and Chinese-language sources have proved unavailable in the U.S.

SECTIONS 53 and 54 describe unsophisticated grammatologies of scripts that are still in use. Herein I add some interesting examples that have not survived: besides Asia, scripts have been invented in Africa, North and South America, and Oceania.

The Bamum script

Early in the twentieth century, King Njoya [nʒɯəja] of the Bamum tribe of central Cameroon became aware of the writing of the missionaries, and resolved to provide his own people with a script (Schmitt 1967B). It came to him in a dream that the way to proceed was by inventing a picture for each object or action. He asked his subjects to provide drawings of all sorts of things, from which he would choose an inventory to write with. This proved impossible (we are not told why), despite some five attempts. Next, Njoya tried rebus writing: words could be written with the pictures that represented similar-sounding words. It happens that most Bamum words are monosyllables of the form CV(C), and the closing consonant can only be [p t m n ŋ]; many words thus share a shape, with differentiation by tones, so that a quite limited inventory of (logo)syllabic signs sufficed to write the language.

The Alaska script

The script created by Uyaqoq (also known by the translation of his name as Neck) between 1901 and 1905, at a Moravian mission in southwest Alaska (Schmitt 1967A), is unusual in being devised for an agglutinative language rather than a monosyllabic one—words in Inuit can reach seemingly unlimited lengths. The obvious strategy of assigning a symbol to each word immediately proved impossible, and Uyaqoq quickly settled on truncating a word to use its pictograph for just its initial CV portion. He also added a series of symbols for consonants that could close syllables. And in a practice reminiscent of Pahlavi writing (SECTION 48), he notated a few syllables with marks based on the cursive writing of English words, so that a squiggle resembling <*good*> represents the syllable [kut].

The Ndjuka script

Afaka, a "Bush Negro" of Dutch Guiana (modern Suriname), was also told in a dream to create a script (Gonggryp 1960). Before 1916, at the rate of a sign every two or three days, he came up with 56 characters with which to write. They are signs for CV syllables (including a few nasalized vowels). The Ndjuka language is an English-based creole (an English colony in Surinam was taken over by the Dutch in 1667, but the slaves and their descendants maintained their language; Holm 1989: 432–44), with the attendant phonological simplification (Huttar 1986), and the script was used only by a small fraction of the Christian minority.

The Caroline Islands script

Two distinct scripts were used to write the Woleaian language in the Caroline Islands, Micronesia, in the early twentieth century. Type 2 includes 19 characters, all of them clearly based on letters of the Roman alphabet, and Type 1, "at least 78" (Riesenberg and Kaneshiro 1960). All the characters in both scripts represent CV syllables. The values of the Type 2 characters (except for the plain vowels) are all of the form [Ci], representing the names of the letters of the Trukese alphabet, which had been brought to that neighboring island in 1878 by an English missionary and thence, imperfectly understood, to Woleiai in 1905. Within a couple of years, Type 1 was devised at Faraulep Island to remedy the perceived lack of means of expressing syllables containing vowels other than [i]. Some of its characters are pictographic, a few resemble appropriate katakana (SECTION 16), and some seem to be pure invention. The inventory could be increased as need was perceived for new characters.

The origin of writing

Accounts of unsophisticated grammatogeny reveal the characteristics of an independently invented script. Most striking is that the result of the process is always a *syllabary* emerging from logography, never an alphabet (valuable collections on early writing systems are Oates 1986 and Senner 1989 and, on a smaller scale, Joachim Jungius-Gesellschaft 1969). This phenomenon seems to originate in the way people use and process speech: various psycholinguistic and phonetic observations and experiments indicate that it is syllables and not any shorter stretches of speech (i.e. "segments," the result of phonological analysis and roughly equivalent to letters of the alphabet) that people can consciously hear—unless they have learned to read in an alphabetic script.

It is thus not surprising that the three known cases of independent script invention—for Sumerian (SECTION 3), for Chinese (SECTION 14), and for Mayan (SECTION 12)—resulted in logosyllabaries. But why did writing emerge only for these three civilizations? After all, the Incas of Peru enjoyed a highly developed civilization, yet could record only quantities, not language, with their knotted-cord quipus (Ascher and Ascher 1981). Moreover, many—perhaps all—preliterate cultures employ pictographic records as mnemonic devices (these are often, though misleadingly, listed as forerunners of writing).

The answer seems to me (Daniels 1988) to lie in the syllable. In Sumerian, Chinese, and Mayan, most morphemes and in particular independent words comprise single syllables. A word is the shortest stretch of speech that can be uttered by someone without linguistic training (an Inuit-speaker who makes a mistake can't break off in the middle of a word and correct part of it, but after breaking off must begin to say it at the beginning). Thus in "syllabically organized" languages like the three where writing was born, speakers can speak single syllables. So pictograms represent things with monosyllabic names. This in turn offers a means of representing those syllables that are not words for picturable objects—and that sort of representation is the defining characteristic of writing (SECTION 1). Using a picture of some object to represent the sound of a homophonous word is known as *rebus writing*. While rebuses today are party games, at the dawn of history they were the foundation of writing.

Bibliography

Ascher, Marcia, and Robert Ascher. 1981. *Code of the Quipu: A Study in Media, Mathematics, and Culture*. Ann Arbor: University of Michigan Press.
Daniels, Peter T. 1988 [pub. 1992]. "The Syllabic Origin of Writing and the Segmental Origin of the

Alphabet." In *The Linguistics of Literacy* (Typological Studies in Language 21), ed. Pamela Downing, Susan D. Lima, and Michael Noonan, pp. 83–110. Amsterdam: Benjamins.

Enwall, Joakim. 1994. *A Myth Become Reality: History and Development of the Miao Written Language.* Stockholm: Stockholm University, Institute of Oriental Languages.

Gonggryp, J. W. 1960. "The Evolution of a Djuka-Script in Surinam." *Nieuwe West-Indische Gids* 40: 63–72.

Hayward, R. J., and Mohammed Hassan. 1981. "The Oromo Orthography of Shaykh Bakri Saṗalō." *Bulletin of the School of Oriental and African Studies* 44: 550–66.

Holm, John. 1989. *Pidgins and Creoles*, vol. 2: *Reference Survey* (Cambridge Language Surveys). Cambridge: Cambridge University Press.

Huttar, George. 1986. "The Afaka Script: An Indigenous Creole Syllabary." *13th LACUS Forum*, pp. 167–77.

Jensen, Hans. 1969. *Sign, Symbol and Script*, trans. George Unwin. New York: Putnam's.

Joachim Jungius-Gesellschaft der Wissenschaften, Hamburg. 1969. *Frühe Schriftzeugnisse der Menschheit.* Göttingen: Vandenhoeck & Ruprecht.

LeGuin, Ursula K. 1985. *Always Coming Home.* New York: Harper & Row. Repr. New York: Bantam, 1986.

Nida, Eugene A., ed. 1972. *The Book of a Thousand Tongues*, rev. ed. London: United Bible Societies.

Noel, Ruth S. 1980. *The Languages of Tolkien's Middle Earth.* Boston: Houghton Mifflin.

Oates, Joan, ed. 1986. Early Writing Systems [special issue]. *World Archaeology* 17/3.

Riesenberg, Saul H., and Shigeru Kaneshiro. 1960. *A Caroline Islands Script.* Smithsonian Institution Bureau of American Ethnology *Bulletin* 173: 273–333 (= *Anthropological Papers* 60).

Schmitt, Alfred. 1967A. "Die Alaska-Schrift." *Studium Generale* 20: 565–74.

———. 1967B. "Die Bamum-Schrift." *Studium Generale* 20: 594–604.

———. 1980. *Entstehung und Entwicklung von Schriften*, ed. Claus Haebler. Cologne: Böhlau.

Senner, Wayne M., ed. 1989. *The Origins of Writing.* Lincoln: University of Nebraska Press.

Tolkien, J. R. R. 1931. "A Secret Vice." In his *The Monster and the Critic and Other Essays*, ed. Christopher Tolkien, pp. 198–223. Boston: Houghton Mifflin, 1980.

———. 1965. *The Return of the King* (The Lord of the Rings 3). Boston: Houghton Mifflin.kj

Cherokee Writing

JANINE SCANCARELLI

Cherokee is written with a syllabary invented by Sequoyah (ca. 1770–1843), a mono-lingual Cherokee speaker. Also known by the English name George Guess (or Gist or Guyst), he was illiterate until he invented his syllabary. He noticed that marks on pa-per could be used to represent English, and from that observation he went on to invent a writing system for Cherokee (see Foreman 1938). In their present form many of the syllabary characters resemble Roman, Cyrillic, or Greek letters or Arabic numerals, but there is no apparent relationship between their sounds in other languages and in Cherokee. Sequoyah gave a public demonstration of the syllabary in 1821, and by 1824 knowledge of his invention had spread widely among the Cherokees. (On the early history of the syllabary see Walker and Sarbaugh 1993.) Materials written in the syllabary are sometimes said to be written "in Sequoyan."

The characters of the Cherokee syllabary and their arrangement

TABLE 53.1 shows the 85 characters of the syllabary as arranged by Samuel A. Worcester, a missionary to the Cherokees who played an important role in the devel-opment of Cherokee printing and who devised a commonly used transliteration of the syllabary. To the right of each character is Worcester's transliteration, which is its name and reflects what can be considered the basic pronunciation of the character. Charts similar to TABLE 53.1 are well known to almost all Cherokees.

Cherokee is written from left to right. It is common to place hyphens between the transliterations of the characters in a word.

The characters in TABLE 53.1 are arranged by sound: the columns correspond to the six distinctive Cherokee vowel qualities, and the rows correspond to consonants that can begin syllables. The order of the vowels corresponds to the English alphabet-ical order of the transliteration (v is phonetically [ə] but commonly written v in lin-guistic literature, as in Worcester's transliteration). The order of the consonants in the remaining twelve rows likewise corresponds to the English alphabetical order of the transliteration, with the velar stop of the second row alphabetized as g, and the alve-olar stop of the ninth row treated as t. In the transliteration, qu (line 7) represents a labialized velar stop [kʷ], dl and tl (line 10) represent an alveolar affricate with lateral release ([tˡ], a sound not present in all dialects of Cherokee), and ts (line 11) repre-sents an affricate which may be pronounced as alveolar or palato-alveolar [ts, tʃ].

TABLE 53.1: *The Characters of the Cherokee Syllabary*

	a			*e*		*i*		*o*		*u*		*v* = [ə̃]
1.	D a			R e		T i		Ꮹ o		Ꮎ u	i	v
2.	S ga	Ꮙ ka		Ᏺ ge		Ᏻ gi		Ꭺ go	Ꭻ gu	Ꮩ gv
3.	Ꭿ ha			Ꮪ he		Ꭹ hi		Ꮁ ho	Ꮀ hu	Ꮂ hv
4.	W la			Ꮯ le		Ꮅ li		Ꮃ lo	Ꮄ lu	Ꮈ lv
5.	Ꮖ ma			Ꮊ me		Ꮌ mi		Ꮋ mo	Ꮽ mu	
6.	Ꮎ na	Ꮏ hna	Ꮐ nah	Ꭸ ne		Ꮑ ni		Ꮓ no	Ꮔ nu	Ꮕ nv
7.	Ꮖ qua			Ꮗ que		Ꮘ qui		Ꮙ quo	Ꮚ quu	Ꮛ quv
8.	Ꮝ s	Ꮜ sa		Ꮞ se		Ꮟ si		Ꮠ so	Ꮢ su	Ꮢ sv
9.	Ꮣ da	Ꮤ ta		Ꮥ de	Ꮦ te	Ꮧ di	Ꮨ ti	Ꮩ do	Ꮪ du	Ꮫ dv
10.	Ꮬ dla	Ꮭ tla		Ꮮ tle		Ꮯ tli		Ꮰ tlo	Ꮱ tlu	Ꮲ tlv
11.	Ꮳ tsa			Ꮴ tse		Ꮵ tsi		Ꮶ tso	Ꮷ tsu	Ꮸ tsv
12.	Ꮹ wa			Ꮻ we		Ꮼ wi		Ꮼ wo	Ꮽ wu	Ꮾ wv
13.	Ꮿ ya			Ᏸ ye		Ᏹ yi		Ᏺ yo	Ᏻ yu	Ᏼ yv

a. Ꮝ *s* is listed in the *a* column; in some syllabary charts, Ꮝ *s* appears to the right of Ꮜ *sa*.

TABLE 53.2: *Orthographic Equivalences[a]*

Worcester	Phonemic	Feeling
g	k; kh	g; k
k	kh	k
h	h	h
l	l; hl = [ɬ]	l; hl
m	m	m
n	n; hn	n; hn, nh
qu	kw = [kʷ]; kwh	gw; kw
s	s	s
d	t; th	d; t
t	th	t
dl	tl = [tˡ]	dl
tl	tl; tlh, hl	dl; tl, hl
ts	c = [ts, tʃ]; ch	j; ch
w	w; hw	w; hw, wh
y	y = [j]; hy	y; hy, yh

a. Sequoyah's characters in general represent a wider range of consonants than Worcester's transliteration suggests. Column 1 lists the consonants used by Worcester to represent syllable onsets. Column 2 lists in a phonemic notation the sounds that may correspond to characters transliterated with those consonants. The third column lists the symbols used in Feeling's practical orthography to represent those sounds.

R	D	W	Ᏺr	G	ꮬ	ꮻ	P	Λ	ꮞ	У	ꭹ	Ᏼ	P	ꭴ	M	ꮯ	ꮀ
e	a	la	tsi	nah	wu	we	li	ne	mo	gi	yi	si	tlv	o	lu	le	ha

ꮼ	ꮣ	W	B	ꮄ	ꮑ	ꭲ	ꮒ	Γ	Λ	ꮫ	ꮅ	4	ꮤ	C	ꭰ	ꮂ	Ᏺ
wo	tlo	ta	yv	lv	hi	s	yo	hu	go	tsu	mu	se	so	tli	qui	que	sa

Ꮫ	Z	ꭴ	Ᏻ	R	ꮒ	S	V	ꮖ	Ꮮ	E	Ꮎ	T	ꮻ	ꭹ	ꮹ	ꮏ	J
qua	no	ka	tsv	sv	ni	ga	do	ge	da	gv	wi	i	u	ye	hv	dv	gu

K	ꮾ	ꭹ	Ꮎ	G	Ᏻ	Ꮴ	Ꭻ	ꭹ	S	ꮪ	Ꮹ	i	ꭴ	Ꮏ	ꮉ	ꮝ	ꭱ
tso	quo	nu	na	lo	yu	tse	di	wv	du	de	tsa	v	nv	te	ma	su	tlu

ꭾ	ꮁ	H	ꮤ	ꭹ	Ᏻ	Ꭲ	L	ꮭ	ꮻ	ꭷ	Ꭰ	Ꮟ
he	ho	mi	tla	ya	wa	ti	tle	na	quu	dla	me	quv

FIGURE 58. Sequoyah's alphabetical order (read left to right).

TABLE 53.2 shows the consonants of Worcester's transliteration with their equivalents in a phonemic orthography and in the practical orthography used in the important dictionary of Feeling 1975.

The sound [m] is rare in Cherokee; there is no character for *mv*. The symbol G *nah* is not much used, and there is some controversy among speakers as to what sounds it represents.

The Cherokee characters have been alphabetized in various ways. Usually alphabetical order runs across each row of the syllabary chart, starting at the top and working down the page (D R T ꭴ ꮼ i S ꭴ ꮖ …). Another order runs down each column, starting at the left and working across the page (D S ꭴ 4 W ꭱ Ᏻ ꭲ G …). Sequoyah arranged the characters in a different order, shown in FIGURE 58.

The appearance of written Cherokee

In printed Cherokee, words are separated by spaces, and punctuation marks are used as in English. In some publications, larger versions of the characters serve as capital letters, which are used as in English. Handwritten characters are similar in appearance to the printed characters shown in TABLE 53.1. In manuscript materials, words may be separated by spaces or by raised periods, punctuation may or may not be used, periods are sometimes raised rather than appearing on the baseline, and capital letters are generally not used. Sequoyah invented a numeral system, but it was never adopted: Cherokee writers use Arabic numerals or spell out Cherokee number names in the syllabary.

The sound and spelling of Cherokee

Except for Ꮝ *s*, each character can represent a syllable. The characters in the first line represent vowels (at the beginnings of words, as in ᎠᎹ *a-ma* [ama] ‘water’) or [ʔV] syllables (in other environments, as in ᎯᎠ *hi-a* [hiʔa] ‘this’). The rest of the characters represent a wider range of sounds than the transliterations in TABLE 53.1 might suggest (Scancarelli 1992).

Each character can represent syllables with long or short vowels pronounced on any of several different pitches. (In the transcriptions presented here, long vowels are written with a following colon; pitch is not marked.) Thus ᎠᎹ *a-ma* represents both [ama] ‘water’ (with low pitch on the first syllable) and [a:ma] ‘salt’ (with high pitch on the first syllable).

Each character can represent syllables that end with vowels, long or short, or with [h] or [ʔ]. Thus ᏑᏗ *su-di* represents [suhti] ‘fishhook’ and ᏔᎵ *ta-li* represents [t^haʔli] ‘two’.

Most characters can represent syllables that begin with plain consonants or clusters of plain consonants with [h]. Sequences of stop or affricate plus [h], pronounced as aspirates, are distinguished from their unaspirated counterparts in just five cases: Ꭶ *ga* = [ka], Ꭷ *ka* = [k^ha]; Ꮣ *da* = [ta], Ꮤ *ta* = [t^ha]; Ꮥ *de* = [te], Ꮦ *te* = [t^he]; Ꮧ *di* = [ti], Ꮨ *ti* = [t^hi]; Ꮬ *dla* = [t^la], Ꮭ *tla* = [t^{lh}a]. Thus the syllabary distinguishes the first two syllables in ᎧᎦᎵ *Ka-ga-li* [k^ha:kaʔli] ‘February’; but a single spelling, ᎪᎳ *go-la*, represents both [ko:la] ‘winter’ and [k^ho:la] ‘bone’. Sequences of [h] plus sonorant are distinguished from plain sonorants in just one case: Ꮎ *na* = [na], Ꮏ *hna* = [hna]. Thus the syllabary distinguishes ᎬᎾ *gv-na* [kə̃:na] ‘I'm alive’ from ᎬᏁ *gv-hna* [kə̃:hna] ‘she/he is alive’, but a single spelling, ᎬᏂᎭ *gv-ni-ha*, represents both [kə̃:niha] ‘I'm striking it’ and [kə̃:hniha] ‘she/he is striking it’.

The letter Ꮝ *s* represents [s] in syllables that begin with [sC] clusters, as in ᏍᎪᎯ *s-go-hi* [sko:hi] ‘ten’. It also represents [s] at the end of a syllable, as in ᎯᏴᏫᏯᏍ *hi-yv-wi-ya-s* [hijə̃:wi:ja:s] ‘Are you an Indian?’.

To represent a consonant other than [h], [ʔ], or [s] at the end of a syllable, a character is used that represents the appropriate consonant with some dummy vowel, which is not pronounced. In some cases, the symbol that is chosen may reflect an underlying or etymological vowel: the second symbol in the word ᏔᎵᏍᎪᎯ *ta-li-s-go-hi* [t^haʔlsko:hi] ‘twenty’ reflects the vowel that appears in the related word ᏔᎵ *ta-li* [t^haʔli] ‘two’. In other cases the choice of vowel may be arbitrary, with *a*, *i*, and *v* commonly used: ᎦᎵᏉᎩ *ga-li-quo-gi* is the common spelling for [kaɬk^wo:ki] ‘seven’.

Similarly, consonant clusters at the beginnings of syllables (except clusters with [h] and [s]) are written with symbols representing dummy vowels, as in ᎬᏙᎠ *gv-do-a* [kt^ho:ʔa] ‘it is hanging (of a long object)’.

Some other conventions: The symbol 'Ꮫ' is often pronounced [kʷu] rather than [kʷo] (see sample text). In some manuscript materials, including those attributed to Sequoyah, [sV] syllables are written with Ꮝ *s* before the *s*V symbol. Thus Sequoyah spelled his name ᏍᏏᏉᏯ *s-si-quo-ya*. Syllables beginning with [ɬ] may be written with either the *l*V or *tl*V characters. Spellings of words may vary, reflecting particular pronunciations or individual choices in representing consonant clusters (see discussion in Chafe and Kilpatrick 1963).

Uses of the syllabary

Since 1828 the syllabary has been used in legal, political, religious, and informational publications. Manuscript materials include letters, diaries and other records, and notebooks of medical formulas. In the late twentieth century, Cherokee is more often read than written. The ability to read Cherokee plays an important role in traditional Cherokee medicine and in Cherokee Christian church services. Two publications in the syllabary are widely owned and read, the Cherokee New Testament and a hymnal. Both are facsimiles of nineteenth-century editions prepared by Worcester with Cherokee collaborators. These books are familiar even to non-Christians. For some Cherokees, the spellings and grammatical constructions that appear in these texts define a standard for formal language. One sometimes hears spelling pronunciations, in which a word is pronounced in accordance with Worcester's transliteration regardless of ordinary usage.

SAMPLE OF CHEROKEE

The sample exhibits two verses of a beloved Cherokee hymn. The words are often sung to the tune of "Amazing Grace." In line 3, the words are transcribed as they are sung, although speakers will differ in details of pronunciation. Length of vowels is not marked, since in singing length is determined by the tune. In line 4, the words appear as they would ordinarily be pronounced. Virginia Carey assisted with the transcription and translation.

1. Cherokee:	ᏲᎾᎳᏅᎯ	ᎤᏪᏥ	ᎢᎦᎬᏴᎮᎢ,
2. Transliteration:	U-ne-la-nv-hi	U-we-tsi /	I-ga-gu-yv-he-i, /
3. Sung:	uneɫanə̃hi	uwetsi	ikakʰujə̃heji
4. Spoken:	u:ne:ɫanə̃hi	u:wetsi	i:kakʷʰijə̃:he:ʔi
5. Gloss:	God	his.offspring(SG)	he.paid.it.for.us

1.	ᎿᏊ	ᏦᏒ	ᎮᎤᎣᏎ	ᎢᎦᎬᏴᎰᏅ.
2.	Hna-quo	tso-sv	wi-u-lo-se /	I-ga-gu-yv-ho-nv.
3.	nakʷu	tsosə̃	wijulose	ikakʰujə̃hohnə̃
4.	na:kʷu	tso:sə̃	wu:lo:se	i:kakʷʰijə̃:hohnə̃
5.	then	heaven	he.went	he.paid.it.all.for.us

1.	**ᎠᏎᏃ**	**ᎢᎤᏁᏤᎢ**	**ᎢᏳᏃ**	**ᏚᎴᏅ,**
2.	A-se-no	i-u-ne-tse-i /	I-yu-no	du-le-nv, /
3.	asehno	ijuhnetseji	ijuhno	tulehnə̃
4.	a:se:hno	iʔu:hne:tse:ʔi	iju:hno	tu:le:hnə̃
5.	but	he.spoke.again	when	he.arose

1.	**ᏔᎵᏁ**	**ᏛᏥᎷᏥᎵ,**	**ᎤᏛᏁ**	**ᎤᏁᏨ.**
2.	Ta-li-ne	dv-tsi-lu-tsi-li, /	U-dv-ne	u-ne-tsv.
3.	t^{h}aline	tə̃tsilutsiɬi	utə̃hne	unetsə̃
4.	t^{h}aʔli:ne	tə̃:tsiluhtsi:ɬi	u:tə̃:hne	u:hne:tsə̃
5.	second	I.am.going.to.return	he.said.it	when.he.spoke

'God's son paid for us [paid for our sins],
Then he went to heaven, he paid it all for us.

But he spoke again when he arose,
"I am going to come back a second time," he said when he spoke.'

—*From Worcester and Boudinot n.d.: 57.*

Bibliography

Chafe, Wallace L., and Jack Frederick Kilpatrick. 1963. "Inconsistencies in Cherokee spelling." In *Symposium on Language and Culture: Proceedings of the 1962 Annual Spring Meeting of the American Ethnological Society*, ed. Viola E. Garfield, pp. 60–63. Seattle: University of Washington.

Feeling, Durbin. 1975. *Cherokee–English Dictionary*, ed. William Pulte. Tahlequah: Cherokee Nation of Oklahoma.

Foreman, Grant. 1938. *Sequoyah* (The Civilization of the American Indian 16). Norman: University of Oklahoma Press.

Scancarelli, Janine. 1992. "Aspiration and Cherokee Orthographies." In *The Linguistics of Literacy*, ed. Pamela Downing, Susan D. Lima, and Michael Noonan (Typological Studies in Language 21), pp. 135–52. Amsterdam: Benjamins.

Walker, Willard. 1981. "Native American Writing Systems." In *Language in the U.S.A.*, ed. Charles A. Ferguson and Shirley Brice Heath, pp. 145–74. Cambridge: Cambridge University Press.

Walker, Willard, and James Sarbaugh. 1993. "The Early History of the Cherokee Syllabary." *Ethnohistory* 40: 70–94.

[Worcester, Samuel A., and Elias Boudinot.] n.d. *Cherokee Hymn Book*. Philadelphia: American Baptist Publication Society.

Scripts of West Africa

JOHN VICTOR SINGLER

Surveys of indigenous writing systems among the Niger-Congo languages of West Africa have identified as many as sixteen scripts. The best known of these, the Vai system, was invented in the 1830s, with the others all created in the twentieth century. The principal scholarly work on writing systems in the region is that of Dalby 1967, 1968, 1969, 1970. The recency of several of the systems described by Dalby indicates that the creation of writing systems is a continuing occurrence in modern West Africa.

Dalby divides the systems geographically: Liberia–Sierra Leone (Vai, Kpelle, Mende, Loma, Bassa, Gola); Cameroun–Nigeria (Bamum, Bagam, Ibibio-Efik, Yoruba); Guinea–Senegal–Mali (Manding [Mandekan], Wolof, two Fula); and Côte d'Ivoire (Bete, Guro). Of the fifteen systems for which information was available to Dalby, eight were alphabets, and seven syllabaries. Three of the alphabets and one of the syllabaries were written from right to left, while the remainder were all written from left to right. The two with the largest current use and the greatest body of written literature are Vai and N'ko, the Manding alphabet, and they are described here.

The N'ko alphabet

According to Dalby (1969: 162), the N'ko alphabet for Mandekan was created by Soulemayne Kante in Kankan, Guinea, in the years following World War II. Mandekan (what Dalby calls Manding) encompasses Bambara, Maninka, Mandinka, Dyula, Malinke, Kuranko, Mandingo, and various other dialects spoken widely across the West African Sahel and the regions south of the Sahel. N'ko (literally 'I say' in all the dialects) reads from right to left. There are eighteen consonants and seven vowels. A diacritic placed below a vowel indicates nasalization, and diacritics placed above a vowel or syllabic nasal signals length, tone, and "differences of tonal behaviour resulting from different grammatical contexts" (Dalby 1969: 165). This last, according to Dalby, primarily points to the difference in Mandekan tone patterning between nouns and verbs.

Vai script

The Vai script was developed in approximately 1833 by Momolu Duwalu Bukele, who told the German linguist S. K. Koelle that the inspiration for the Vai script had come to him in a dream (Dalby 1967). Bukẹlẹ and five friends then devised the characters for the script. Evidently Bukẹlẹ was aware of the existence of the Arabic and Roman writing systems, and possibly Cherokee as well (Dalby 1968, Holsoe 1971). The script was standardized in 1899 and again in 1962, this last at a conference at the University of Liberia. The conference is said to have been dominated by Western-trained Vai scholars rather than by the people who actually use the script on a daily basis (and who are not literate in English). The script's primary use is for correspondence and record-keeping. Since knowledge of the script is acquired informally rather than formally, there has been no mechanism for the imposition of the standardized version. Items are occasionally published that use the script—e.g. a 1989 translation of the Gospel of Mark in Vai with the Roman alphabet on the left and the script on the right—but the basis for the enduring popularity of Vai has been its personal uses rather than more public ones.

Orthographic principles

The Vai writing system is a left-to-right system. While it has always been described as syllable-based, the basic unit of the system is more accurately the mora. The weight of the syllable determines the number of characters that will be used to represent it. The only closed syllables are those ending with a velar nasal. If a syllable ends with a velar nasal consonant, the nasal is written with a separate character 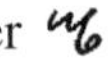, e.g.  *ke-ń* [kéŋ] 'house'. The velar nasal can itself be syllabic, e.g.  [ŋ́] 'first person singular'. (The velar nasal is subject to assimilation processes and is not always pronounced as a velar; but however it is pronounced, it is always written as 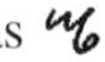.) Apart from these cases involving a nasal consonant, every syllable ends with a vowel. When an open syllable contains only a short vowel, the syllable is written with a single character, e.g. *jí* 'water'. When it contains a long vowel or a diphthong, it is written with two characters.

There is variation as to the spelling of syllables containing a long vowel or a diphthong. For example, [táá] 'go' is ordinarily written 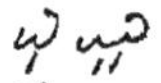 *ta-ha* and not  *ta-a*. Similarly, [lákóa] 'about' is most often written  *la-ko-wa*. Apart from loanwords, the only Vai words which begin with a vowel are pronouns, interjections, and conjunctions. Of these, only the pronouns are truly common in speech or writing, and they begin with either *i* or *a*: [í] 'you (singular)', [à] 'he, she', and [ànú] 'they'. The character for *a* is . Ordinarily it is reserved for those instances when it starts a word; when it occurs as the second half of a long vowel or diphthong,  *ha* or  *wa* is used instead. By contrast,  *i* appears both word-initially and otherwise. In the script chart devised at the 1962 conference, a distinction is made between the characters for *w*V syllables and for V syllables. However, except for *wa* versus *a*, this is largely an artificial distinction and is not strictly observed. Thus, while it is certainly possible to write [kùú] 'compound, home' as 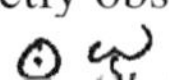 *ku-u*, instead it is usually written 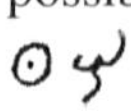 *ku-wu*.

TABLE 54.1: *The Vai Syllabary, 1962 Version*

Translit.[a]	Value	e	i	a	o	u	ɔ (ọ)	ε (ẹ)
p	[p]							
b	[b]							
ɓ	[ɓ]							
mɓ	[mɓ]							
kp	[kp]							
mgb	[mgb]							
gb	[gb]							
f	[f]							
v	[v]							
t	[t]							
d	[d]							
l	[l]							
ḍ	[d]							
nḍ	[nd]							
s	[s]							
z	[z]							
c	[c]							
j	[ɟ]							
nj	[nɟ]							
y	[j]							
k	[k]							
ṅg	[ŋg]							
g	[g]							
h	[h]							
w	[w]							
—								

ⱴ Syllabic nasal

Nasal syllables

		ĩ	ã	ũ	ɔ̃	ε̃
hʋ	[h̃]					
m	[m]					
n	[n]					
ny	[nj]					
ṅ	[ŋ]					

a. The transliterations are not official or standard, and reflect typographic convenience.

A series of phonetic changes in progress in Vai is affecting the fit of the written language to the spoken language. In the case of [ŋ] between like vowels, the consonant is disappearing, while the surrounding vowels are becoming nasalized, e.g. /kaŋa/ 'box', now ordinarily pronounced [kã́ã́]. Even though in most cases this change is largely complete, the affected words continue to be written as if the nasal consonant were still present, e.g. ⟨ka-ña⟩ 'box'. A less advanced but far more pervasive change is the variable deletion of [l], both word-medially and as the first segment of grammatical elements such as postpositions. (The greater importance of the change involving [l] is a consequence of the segment's widespread presence word-internally in Vai.) In writing, the use of characters containing [l] is more conservative and arguably more formal than the use of [l]-less ones. There is also geographic variation in this, reflecting the degree of completion of the phonetic change in different areas. Thus /kálố/ 'moon', most often pronounced [ká́ố], is spelled both ⟨ka-lo⟩ and ⟨ka-wo⟩ (and also ⟨ka-o⟩).

The discussion thus far has implied that vowel length is always indicated; but in fact it is sometimes omitted, particularly in grammatical elements. This omission includes instances where the long vowel has been created by the disappearance of [l]. This can be seen, for example, in the sample of Vai script below; the assignment of phonological length there follows Welmers 1976.

Vai has lexical tone, with two level tones and two contours (transcribed ´ high, ˉ low, ˆ falling, ˇ rising). The writing system does not indicate tone. However, as Welmers notes, "Pairs or larger groups of stems that differ from each other only in tone are not particularly common, especially within a single grammatical category" (1976: 31).

As suggested above, Vai has a strict (C)V(N) syllable pattern. The final nasal is expressed by a separate character, and vowel length also involves distinct characters. Because of the restriction of possible syllable shape and the conventions regarding the final nasal and vowel length, the number of possible "syllables" to be represented by the Vai script is comparatively small, slightly more than 200.

There is no division between words. Many writers signal the end of a sentence by writing ⟨hé⟩. Script users familiar with other writing systems, i.e. Roman or Arabic, tend to replace ⟨ ⟩ with ✳. As noted by Scribner and Cole (1981: 142–50), the lack of division between words makes reading the script difficult. Vai literates report that the script is easier to write than to read. Still, various script conventions and distributional patterns among Vai's consonants make the task less arduous than it might be otherwise (Singler 1983: 897).

The characters

The table of characters given in TABLE 54.1 emerged from the 1962 conference at the University of Liberia. Most literates find the need for only forty to sixty characters. In many ways, the participants at the 1962 conference "filled in the blanks," creating symbols where none had existed before. Thus the conference largely intro-

duced into the writing system distinctions between pairs of syllables beginning with
s and z, f and v, wV and V, and the palatal consonants c, j, nj, and y. Very often, a contrast already existed between pairs of consonants with some vowels; now it was extended to all seven oral vowels. Thus most of the seeming systematicity in the shape
of characters is artificial, imposed in 1962 and never in fact widely accepted by script
users. (According to Welmers 1976: 11, the system did not originally distinguish between [ɓ] and [mɓ], [ɗ] and [nɗ], or [k] and [ŋg]; these distinctions were only introduced into the writing system around 1900.) A further point about the relationship of
the chart to ordinary use is that the usual form of some characters represents an inversion, reversal, or turning of the version in the chart (as Gail Stewart notes in an unpublished paper). For example, the chart lists ʄ *fe*, but most Vai literates write it ↬.

SAMPLE OF VAI

1. Transliteration:	mḅe-i	3	de	ḍi-fi-yẹ		lọ	nã	ki-ḅa-lo	mũ	kẹ	a	mẹ
2. Transcription:	mɓéì		dè	ḍìfí-ĕ		lɔ̀	ná	kìɓálò	mù	ké	à	mè
3. Gloss:		May	3 day	night-the	in		I	dream	REL	do	it	this

1.	nã	ku-lu-ṅ	mũ-su	wa	fẹ-lẹ	a	nã		ṅ	ḅa-la
2.	ná	kúlúŋ	mùsú	wá	fèlè	à	ná-à		ŋ́	ɓàlà
3.	I	Kru	woman	EMPH	see	she	come-COMP		me	to

1.	ṅ	wo-ha	mḅe	a	ti	nã	kpẹ-la-ḍe-ṅ	ko	ke-wu-yẹ	lọ
2.	ŋ́	wòló-à	mɓɛ̀	à	tĭ	ná	kpìlàɗéŋ	kó	kèù-ĕ	lɔ̀
3.	I	want-COMP	I	her	be	my	lover		be	dream-the	in

'The night before May third, this is the dream I had: I saw a Kru woman. She
came to me. In the dream I wanted to her to be my lover.'
—*From a journal originally in the collection of Oldman Gbondo Senwan in the
village of Laa, Tombe Chiefdom, Grand Cape Mount County, Liberia. The journal dates from the beginning of the twentieth century. In it the author recorded
business transactions, major events, and dreams. Sample, translation, and analysis provided by Mohamed B. Nyei.*

Note: In four instances the form of the characters used in this passage has changed over time. ↬ *ḍi* is now
written •⁌; ⌇ *kẹ* is written 𝒴; ⁝ *mẹ* is written ////; and ↫ *wu* is written 𝒴. In addition the author of the
passage does not distinguish syllables beginning with implosives from those beginning with prenasalized stops.
The assignment of tone and vowel length follows Welmers 1976.

Bibliography

Dalby, David. 1967. "A Survey of the Indigenous Scripts of Liberia and Sierra Leone: Vai, Mende, Loma, Kpelle and Bassa." *African Language Studies* 8: 1–51.

———. 1968. "The Indigenous Scripts of West Africa and Surinam: Their Inspiration and Design." *African Language Studies* 9: 156–97.

———. 1969. "Further Indigenous Scripts of West Africa: Manding, Wolof and Fula Alphabets and Yoruba 'Holy' Writing." *African Language Studies* 10: 161–81.

———. 1970. "The Historical Problem of the Indigenous Scripts of West Africa and Surinam." In *Language and History in Africa*, ed. David Dalby, pp. 109–19. New York: Africana.

Holsoe, Svend E. 1971. "A Case of Stimulus Diffusion? (A Note on Possible Connections between the Vai and Cherokee Scripts)." *The Indian Historian* 4/3: 56–57.

Maáki. Kamba lá kú'ẹ súndá bẹ́ẹbẹ́ẹ mú Maáki la a nyei Masího Ísa lá kóa [The good news Mark wrote about Jesus the Messiah]. 1989. Monrovia: The Institute for Liberian Languages.

Nyei, Mohamed B. 1981. "A Three Script Literacy among the Vai: Arabic, English and Vai." *Liberian Studies Journal* 9: 13–22.

Scribner, Sylvia, and Michael Cole. 1981. *The Psychology of Literacy*. Cambridge: Harvard University Press.

Singler, John Victor. 1983. Review article on Scribner and Cole 1981. *Language* 59: 893–901.

Welmers, William E. 1976. *A Grammar of Vai*. Berkeley and Los Angeles: University of California Press.

The Cree Syllabary

JOHN D. NICHOLS

The Cree syllabary, or *syllabics*, is a shorthand-based script written left to right, employing geometric characters, some representing syllables and some representing single segments. Created in 1840 for two Algonquian languages of Canada, Cree and Ojibwe, it was adapted in Canada for Athabaskan and Inuit (Eskimo) languages, and, in China, influenced the Pollard script (SECTION 52; Enwall 1994). Until recently it chiefly appeared in printed translations of Christian sacred texts and liturgies, and in handwritten letters and personal records. Syllabic typewriters and, beginning in the 1980s, personal computers have allowed control of the printing technology to shift from missionaries to native speakers; many schoolbooks, periodicals, and official documents now appear in the indigenous languages written in syllabics. Syllabics are particulary valued for the ease and speed with which minimal literacy can be achieved, and for their distinctiveness from the scripts of the dominant colonial languages. Syllabic text looks indisputably Indian or Inuit. In the 1990s, syllabic scripts were being documented for inclusion in international standard character coding for computers.

Algonquian syllabaries

The Cree syllabary was devised by James Evans (1801–1846), a Wesleyan missionary, at Norway House in then Rupert's Land, now Manitoba. Evans had developed a Roman orthography for Ojibwe in Ontario, based on a sophisticated analysis of its sound system, and had presented it in a primer-style syllabary chart. Struck by reports in the mission press of the success of the Cherokee syllabary, and familiar with non-Roman shorthand and Devanagari scripts, Evans experimented with alphabetic and syllabic non-Roman characters for writing Ojibwe.

Arriving at a new mission station at Norway House in 1840, he revised his syllabary for Cree, the local language closely related to the Ojibwe he knew, drawing on British shorthand for most of the characters. In 1841 he printed a hymnbook entirely in syllabics using handmade type, later replaced by type from England made to his specifications. The syllabary was rapidly indigenized, being spread by its first Native

ACKNOWLEDGMENT: The author would like to thank Doug Hitch for help with Inuktitut and Athabaskan.

TABLE 55.1: *Algonquian Syllabics*[a]

W E (e)			W E (i)			W E (ii)			W E (o)			W E (oo)			W E (a)			W E (aa)			W E (final)		
C	O	IPA	C	O	IPA	C	O	IPA	C	O	IPA	C	O	IPA	C	O	IPA	C	O	IPA	C	O	IPA
ê	e	[e:]	i	i	[i]	î	ii	[i:]	o	o	[o]	ô	oo	[o:]	a	a	[a]	â	aa	[a:]	h	h, '	[h, ʔ]
pê	pe	[pe:]	pi	pi	[pi]	pî	pii	[pi:]	po	po	[po]	pô	poo	[po:]	pa	pa	[pa]	pâ	paa	[pa:]	p	p	[p]
tê	te	[te:]	ti	ti	[ti]	tî	tii	[ti:]	to	to	[to]	tô	too	[to:]	ta	ta	[ta]	tâ	taa	[ta:]	t	t	[t]
kê	ke	[ke:]	ki	ki	[ki]	kî	kii	[ki:]	ko	ko	[ko]	kô	koo	[ko:]	ka	ka	[ka]	kâ	kaa	[ka:]	k	k	[k]
cê	ce	[tʃe:, tse]	ci	ci	[tʃi, tsi]	cî	cii	[tʃi:, tsi:]	co	co	[tʃo, tso]	cô	coo	[tʃo:, tso:]	ca	ca	[tʃa, tsa]	câ	caa	[tʃa:, tsa:]	c	c	[tʃ, ts]
mê	me	[me:]	mi	mi	[mi]	mî	mii	[mi:]	mo	mo	[mo]	mô	moo	[mo:]	ma	ma	[ma]	mâ	maa	[ma:]	m	m	[m]
nê	ne	[ne:]	ni	ni	[ni]	nî	nii	[ni:]	no	no	[no]	nô	noo	[no:]	na	na	[na]	nâ	naa	[na:]	n	n	[n]
sê	se	[se:]	si	si	[si]	sî	sii	[si:]	so	so	[so]	sô	soo	[so:]	sa	sa	[sa]	sâ	saa	[sa:]	s	s	[s]
šê	she	[ʃe:]	ši	shi	[ʃi]	šî	shii	[ʃi:]	šo	sho	[ʃo]	šô	shoo	[ʃo:]	ša	sha	[ʃa]	šâ	shaa	[ʃa:]	š	sh	[ʃ]
yê	ye	[je:]	yi	yi	[ji]	yî	yii	[ji:]	yo	yo	[jo]	yô	yoo	[jo:]	ya	ya	[ja]	yâ	yaa	[ja:]	y	y	[j]
wê	we	[we:]	wi	wi	[wi]	wî	wii	[wi:]	wo	wo	[wo]	wô	woo	[wo:]	wa	wa	[wa]	wâ	waa	[wa:]	w	w	[w]
rê	re	[re:]	ri	ri	[ri]	rî	rii	[ri:]	ro	ro	[ro]	rô	roo	[o:]	ra	ra	[ra]	râ	raa	[ra:]	r	r	[r]
lê	le	[le:]	li	li	[li]	lî	lii	[li:]	lo	lo	[lo]	lô	loo	[lo:]	la	la	[la]	lâ	laa	[la:]	l	l	[l]
ve, fe		[ve:, fe:]	vi, fi		[vi, fi]	vii, fii		[vi:, fi:]	vo, fo		[vo, fo]	voo, foo		[vo:, fo:]	va, fa		[va, fa]	vaa, faa		[va:, fa:]	v, f		[v, f]
the		[ðe:]	thi		[ði]	thii		[ði:]	tho		[ðo]	thoo		[ðo:]	tha		[ða]	thaa		[ða:]	th		[ð]

a. W, Western syllabics; E, Eastern syllabics. C, Cree orthography; O, Northern Ojibwe orthography. IPA, pronunciation.

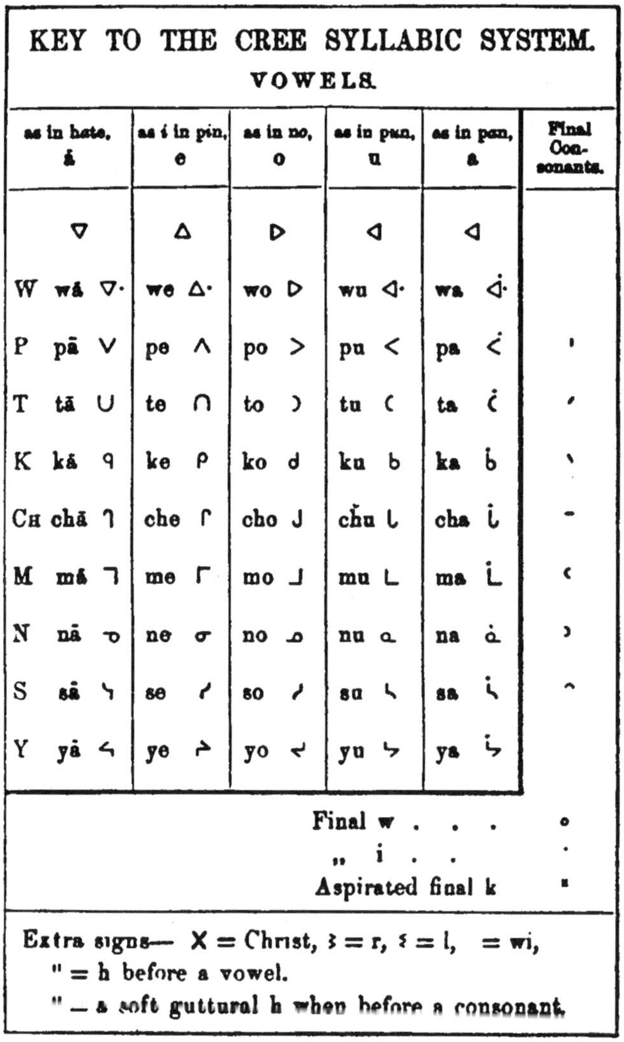

KEY TO THE CREE SYLLABIC SYSTEM.

VOWELS.

	as in hate, á	as i in pin, e	as in no, o	as in pun, u	as in pan, a	Final Consonants.
	ᐁ	ᐃ	ᐅ	ᐊ	ᐊ	
W	wá ᐌ	we ᐎ	wo ᐅ	wu ᐗ	wa ᐚ	
P	pā ᐯ	pe ᐱ	po ᐳ	pu ᐸ	pa ᐹ	ᑊ
T	tā ᑌ	te ᑎ	to ᑐ	tu ᑕ	ta ᑖ	ᐟ
K	kā ᑫ	ke ᑭ	ko ᑯ	ku ᑲ	ka ᑳ	ᐠ
Ch	chā ᒉ	che ᒋ	cho ᒍ	chu ᒐ	cha ᒑ	ᐨ
M	mā ᒣ	me ᒥ	mo ᒧ	mu ᒪ	ma ᒫ	ᒼ
N	nā ᓀ	ne ᓂ	no ᓄ	nu ᓇ	na ᓈ	ᐣ
S	sā ᓭ	se ᓯ	so ᓱ	su ᓴ	sa ᓵ	ᐢ
Y	yā ᔦ	ye ᔨ	yo ᔪ	yu ᔭ	ya ᔮ	

Final w . . . ᐤ
" i . . ·
Aspirated final k ᐦ

Extra signs— X = Christ, ᕐ = r, ᓬ = l, = wi,
" = h before a vowel.
" — a soft guttural h when before a consonant.

FIGURE 59. Western Algonquian syllabary (*Book of Common Prayer* n.d).

users prior to its introduction by other missionaries, who were often reluctant to adopt it. It has been given an indigenous origin in Cree legend (Dusenberry 1962: 267–69), although some have seen its sources in quill and bead work designs.

The Western Algonquian syllabary, in which the Cree dialects west of James Bay are usually written, is the direct descendent of Evans's syllabary. In 1865, changes introduced to this around James Bay (in the 1850s) were standardized, and additional characters were added, to create the Eastern Algonquian syllabary, used to write Cree and Naskapi east of James Bay, as well as Ojibwe. The most used characters of both sets are given in TABLE 55.1 and as syllabary charts in FIGURE 59 (Western), FIGURE 60 (a Roman Catholic variant of Western), and FIGURE 61 (Eastern).

▽ e	△ i	▷ o	◁ æ	•○	ⱳ
7 me	⌐ mi	⌐ mo	∟ ma	c	m
∪ te	∩ ti	⊃ to	⊂ ta	′	t
� ke	P ki	⅃ ko	ϑ ka	◝	k
⌐ᴏ ne	σ ni	ᴏ no	ᴏ na	ϡ	n
⊽ le	∩ li	⅃ lo	⊂ la	s	l
ϡ re	∧ ri	⋏ ro	ϡ ra	z	r
ϟ se	∫ si	∫ so	∖ sa	∧	s
⦛ ye	⟩ yi	⟨ yo	⟩ ya	+	y
∩ tce	∩ tci	⌐ tco	∟ tca	−	tc
⋎ pe	∧ pi	⟩ po	⟨ pa	ι	p
▽· we	△· wi	▷· wo	◁· wa	○	ⱳ
▽·○ wew	△·○ wiw	▷·○ wow	◁·○ waw		

FIGURE 60. Western Algonquian syllabary, Roman Catholic variant (*Anamie Nagamonan* 1965).

In every community in which syllabics are written, there are local and personal styles in character inventory, shape, and writing conventions. There is no standardized spelling for any dialect of Cree or Ojibwe; however, fitting the shorthand origins of the system, writers may use *plain* syllabics, indicating only the bare outline of syllable structure, or *pointed* syllabics, adding diacritics all the way up to phonemic transcription, the full realization of which is rare. Many writers put spaces or dots between words or prefixes; others write all the characters equally far apart with no word division. The period ₓ is the only distinctive common punctuation mark, the others being as in English.

Characteristic features

Vowels that begin syllables are written with a triangle syllabic, rotated through four positions to show the vowel quality. Front vowels have a vertical axis and are related by inversion thus: ▽ *e*, △ *i*; back vowels have a horizontal axis and are related by re-

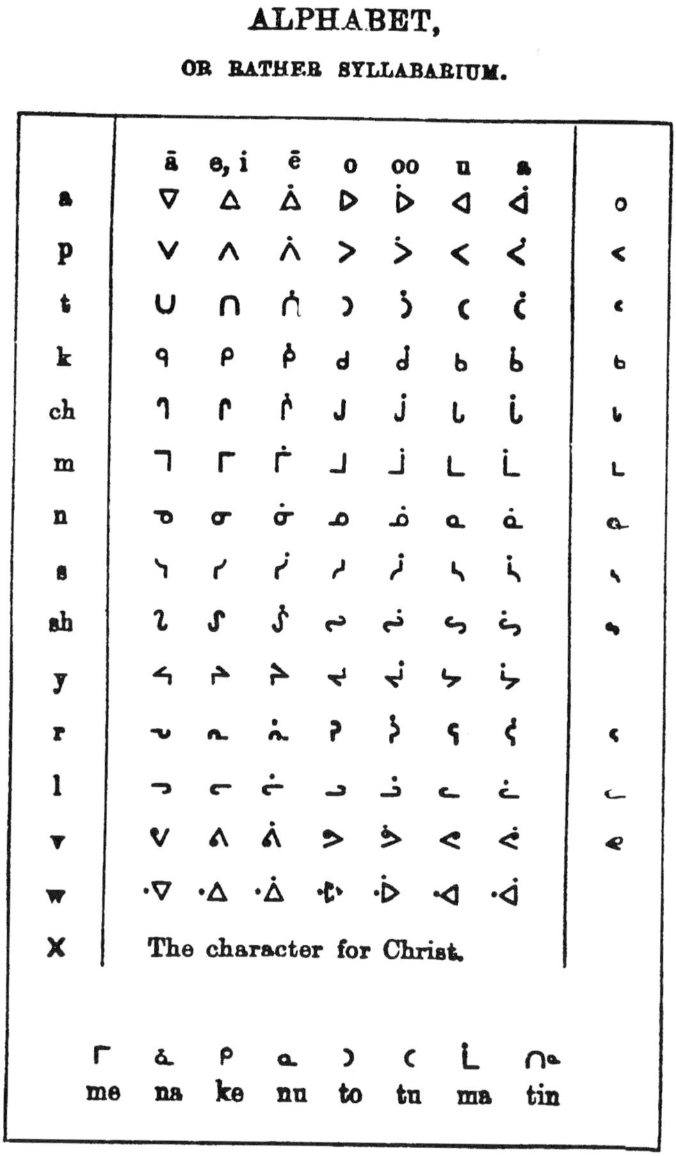

ALPHABET,

OR RATHER SYLLABARIUM.

FIGURE 61. Eastern Algonquian syllabary (Horden 1925).

flection thus: ▷ o, ◁ a. The vowels form the first row of the chart in that order, following the alphabetical order of Evans's Ojibwe Roman orthography, which used the letters a e o u for the same sounds.

Consonant-initial syllables (except those beginning with [w]) are written with syllabics in which the shape shows the consonant, and the orientation shows the vowel. There are two orientation patterns. First, symmetrical shapes for [p] and [t] share the vowel orientations of the vowel triangle, e.g. ∨ pe, ∧ pi, > po, < pa, as does the nonsymmetrical shape for [ʃ]: ꙁ *še*, ꙅ *ši*, ~ *šo*, ᴝ *ša*. Second, the nonsymmetrical shapes for [k], [tʃ], [m], [n], [s], and [j]—consisting of a vertical line (in the case of [n], a circle) with a differentiating angle, curve, line, or circle at one quadrant—have the front vowels related to the back vowels by inversion, with the vowels within each set distinguished by reflection, e.g. ꙏ *se*, Ꙑ *si*, ꙑ *so*, Ꙓ *sa*. As Cree dialects from Manitoba west do not have [ʃ], its row is usually left out of Western syllabaries, although it appears in the original syllabary intended for Ojibwe. The order of the consonant rows in the syllabary charts derives from that in Evans's Ojibwe Roman orthography chart.

The consonants [l] and [r], needed in certain Cree dialects and in foreign words and names, are written in the original Western syllabary with an alphabetic character, reflected to distinguish the two as ꙍ *l* and ꙝ *r*. The Eastern syllabary has full syllabics for [l], namely Ꙏ *le*, ꙏ *li*, Ꙑ *lo*, ꙑ *la* in the second orientation pattern; and for [r], namely ꙓ *re*, ᴖ *ri*, ꙕ *ro*, ꙗ *ra*, with a unique orientation pattern. These sets are ordered at or near the end of the chart. The Western Roman Catholic syllabary in FIGURE 60 has different syllabics for [r] and [l], and a different order of the rows.

Prevocalic [w] is written with a dot at mid line (some local styles use two dots, one above the other). The symbol follows the syllabic in Western, but precedes it in Eastern, and in Western as written on James Bay. The [w] syllabics thus are Western ▽· *we*, △· *wi*, ▷· *wo*, ◁· *wa*, and Eastern ·▽ ·△ ·▷ ·◁. The [w] row may be added to the chart after the vowel row or following the [j] row; or the [w] dot may be treated on the side as a diacritic, or left off the chart entirely. A C*w*V syllable is written in the same way, with the [w] dot written outside the syllabic although it sounds inside the syllable, e.g. Western ▽· *pwe*, Eastern ·▽.

Consonants closing a syllable are written with small alphabetic characters, called *finals*, originally at mid line, but now usually superscripted; local usage in writing position and relative size varies. The finals are given as a fifth column of the chart following the four vowel columns.

The shape of the Western finals indicates the manner of articulation of the consonant, with the orientation (and in one instance, size) providing further differentiation. A straight line represents oral stops, thus ˈ *-p*, ʹ *-t*, ˋ *-k*, ˉ *-c*. A vertical semicircle represents nasals, with ˈ *-m* and ˈ *-n* distinguished by reflection. A horizontal semicircle represents sibilants, with ˄ *-s* and ˅ *-š* distinguished by inversion. A circle represents semivowels, large and at midline as o *-w*; and small and above, or as a superscript to a syllabic, as ° *-y*, now usually written with the final ˈ *-y* in Western Canada.

All but the [w] and [j] finals are replaced in the Eastern syllabary with small *a*-orientation syllabics, e.g. ᴏ *-n*, sometimes handwritten as superscripted or full-size *i*-position syllabics, e.g. ᴼ *-n* or σ *ni*. As in the Western syllabary, a large midline circle o stands for final [w] and a small superposed or superscripted circle ° for final [j], although many writers use either size of circle for both [w] and [j], or replace the [j] circle with an *a*-position [j] syllabic ˀ or an *i* position [j] syllabic ˀ. Added for word-final C*w* clusters in a Quebec Cree dialect are small *o*-position syllabics, e.g. ᵈ *-kw*.

The initial member of a consonant cluster can be written with a final, e.g. Cree ᒥᐢᑎᐠ *mistik* 'tree', ᐊᒥᐢᐠ *amisk* 'beaver'. In Ojibwe, writing the initial nasal of a consonant cluster is optional.

[h] or [ʔ] before vowels, or the preaspiration of consonants, may be written with the final ᐦ *-h*, e.g. Cree ᒪᐦᐄᐦᑲᐣ *mahîhkan* 'wolf', ᐊᐢᑭᐦᐠ *askihk* 'kettle, pail'. This character is often treated as the final for the vowel row in syllabary charts but is sometimes omitted from them; writing [h] is an optional feature, used mainly in pointed syllabics. In some styles the most common word-final clusters may be written with ᕽ, [hk] in Cree and [nk] in Ojibwe.

Vowel length may be marked with a dot over a syllabic, except that [e:] does not contrast with a short vowel and is never so marked. In the earliest syllabic printing, long vowels were shown by slashed or bold syllabics; the superposed dot was intended as the vowel length diacritic only in handwriting. The marking of vowel length is now optional, a feature of pointed syllabics. Some charts add an [a:] column (FIGURE 59), some add three long vowel columns (FIGURE 61), and some treat it on the side as a diacritic or omit it.

Modified *p* and *t* syllabics are available in Eastern for [f] and [ð] in foreign words. Barred *y* syllabics have recently been proposed for Cree dialects with [ð], only one of several recent local innovations in character inventory and shape.

SAMPLE OF NORTHERN OJIBWE IN THE EASTERN SYLLABARY

1. Plain:	ᐊᐱᒋ	ᐌᑕᓐ	ᐁᓂᑕᑾᔥᑵᐱᒋᐱᐃᑫᒃ
2. *Transliteration:*	a-pi-ci	we-tan	e-ni-ta-wkash-wke-pi-ci-pi-i-kek
3. *Pointed:*	ᐋᐦᐱᒋ	ᐌᓐᑕᓐ	ᐁᓂᐦᑖᒀᔥᑵᐱᒋᐲᐦᐃᑫᓐᒃ
4. *Transliteration:*	āh-pi-ci	wen-tan	e-nih-tā-wkāsh-wke-pi-ci-pīh-i-kenk
5. *Orthography 1:*	aahpici	wentan	e-nihtaa-kwaashkwepicipii'ikenk
6. *Orthography 2:*	Aapiji	wendan	e-nitaa-gwaashkwebijibii'igeng
7. *Transcription:*	a:hpidʒi	we:ndan	e:nihta:gwa:ʃkwe:bidʒibi:ʔige:ng
8. *Gloss:*	very.much	is easy	knowing.how.to.write.syllabics

1. ᐸᑕᓂᑕᐊᓂᔑᓇᐯᒧᒃ,	ᐁᑕ	ᒣᐑᔕ	ᓂᒪᒪ
2. pa-ta-ni-ta-a-ni-shi-na-pe-mok,	e-ta	me-wi-sha	ni-ma-ma
3. ᐹᐦᑖᓂᐦᑖᐊᓂᐦᔑᓈᐯᒧᓐᒃ,	ᐁᐦᑕ᙮	ᒣᐑᓐᔕ	ᓂᒫᒫ
4. pāh-tā-nih-tā-a-nih-shi-nā-pe-monk,	eh-ta.	me-win-sha	ni-mā-mā
5. paahtaa-nihtaa-anihshinaapemonk,	ehta.	mewinsha	nimaamaa
6. baataa-nitaa-anishinaabemong,	eta.	Mewinzha	nimaamaa
7. ba:hta:nihta:ʔanihʃina:be:mong	e:hta	me:winʒa	nima:ma:
8. being.able.to.speak.Ojibwe	only	long.ago	my.mother

1. ᓂᑭᓂᑕᐅᔑᐱᐊᒪᑎᒥ°   ·ᐊᖬ
2. ni-ki-ni-ta-o-shi-pi-a-ma-ti-min   wa-sa
3. ᓂᐱ̇ᓂ"ᐨᐅᔑᐱ̇"ᐊᖾᒪᑎᒥ°   ·ᐟᖬ ᖬ
4. ni-kī-nih-tā-o-shi-pīh-a-mā-ti-min   wāh-sa
5. nkii-nihtaa-oshipii'amaatimin   waahsa
6. ngii-nitaa-ozhibii'amaadimin   waasa
7. ŋgi:nihta:ʔoʒibi:ʔama:dimin   wa:hsa
8. we.used.to.write.to.each.other   far

1. ᑭᑕᔑᑭᑭᓄᐊᒪᑯᔭ<ᵃₓ   ᐊᒥ   ᐁᐨ   ᐃ·ᐁ   ᐅᔑᐱᐃᑲᖬ
2. ki-ta-shi-ki-ki-no-a-ma-ko-ya-pan.   a-mi   e-ta   i-we   o-shi-pi-i-kan
3. ᑭ̇ᑕᔑᑭ"ᑭᓄ"ᐊᖾᑯᔭᖬ̇<ᵃₓ   ᐊᒥ̇   ᐁ"ᐨ   ᐃ·ᐁ   ᐅᔑᐱ̇"ᐃᑲᖬ
4. kī-ta-shi-kih-ki-noh-a-mā-kō-yām-pān.   a-mī   eh-ta   i-we   o-shi-pīh-i-kan
5. kii-tashi-kihkino'amaakooyaampaan.   amii   ehta   iwe   oshipii'ikan
6. gii-dazhi-gikino'amaagooyaambaan.   Amii   eta   iwe   ozhibii'igan
7. gi:daʒigihkino?ama:go:ja:mba:n   ami: e:hta   iwe: oʒibi:ʔigan
8. I.used.to.be.taught.there   and.so   only   that   letter/writing

1. ᑲᐅᒋᑭᑫᑕᒪ°   ᐊᓂᐣ   ᐁᔑᐁᐸᐟ   ᑲᐃᔑᑕᔭᐣₓ
2. ka-o-ci-ki-ke-ta-man   a-ni-n   e-shi-we-pak   ka-i-shi-ta-yan.
3. ᑲᐅ̇ᒋᑭ"ᑫᐟᑕᒪ°   ᐊ̇ᓂᐣ   ᐁᔑᐁᐸᐟ   ᑲ̇ᐃᔑᑕ̇ᔭᐣₓ
4. kā-on-ci-kih-ken-ta-mān   ā-nīn   e-shi-we-pak   kā-i-shi-tā-yān.
5. kaa-onci-kihkentamaan   aaniin   eshiwepak   kaa-ishitaayaan.
6. gaa-onji-gikendamaan   aaniin   ezhiwebag   gaa-izhidaayaan.
7. ga:ondʒigihke:ndama:n   a:ni:n   e:ʒiwe:bag   ga:ʔiʒida:ja:n
8. by.which.means.I.knew   how   things.were.happening   where.I.lived

1. ᓂᵃ   <ᕆᓯᐳ   ᓂᑭ·ᐁᕒ
2. nin   pa-ci-shi-ya   ni-ki-we-si
3. ᓂ̇ᵃ   <ᕆᓯᐳ   ᓂᵃᑭ·ᐁᵃᕒ
4. nīn   pa-ci-shi-ya   nin-ki-wen-si
5. niin   Pacishiya   Ninkiwensi
6. Niin   Bajishiya   Ningiwenzi
7. ni:n   badʒiʃija   ningiwe:nzi
8. I   Patricia   Ningewance

'It's easy to write in syllabics, only once you are fluent in Ojibwe. Long ago my mother and I used to write to each other when I went to school far away (from home) Letters were the only way I knew what was happening back home. I'm Patricia Ningewance.'

— *Original text by Patricia Ningewance of Lac Seul, Ontario and Winnipeg, Manitoba, lecturer in Ojibwe at the University of Manitoba.*

Note: "Orthography 1" is Northern Ojibwe; "Orthography 2" is Southern Ojibwe (the writer's preference).

TABLE 55.2: *Inuit Cultural Institute Inuktitut Syllabic and Roman Orthographies*

ᐃ i [i]	ᐄ ii [i:]	ᐅ u [u]	ᐆ uu [u:]	ᐊ a [a]	ᐋ aa [a:]	ᐦ h [h]
ᐱ pi [pi]	ᐲ pii [pi:]	ᐳ pu [pu]	ᐴ puu [pu:]	ᐸ pa [pa]	ᐹ paa [pa:]	ᑉ p [p]
ᑎ ti [ti]	ᑏ tii [ti:]	ᑐ tu [tu]	ᑑ tuu [tu:]	ᑕ ta [ta]	ᑖ taa [ta:]	ᑦ t [t]
ᑭ ki [ki]	ᑮ kii [ki:]	ᑯ ku [ku]	ᑰ kuu [ku:]	ᑲ ka [ka]	ᑳ kaa [ka:]	ᒃ k [k]
ᒋ gi [ɣi]	ᒌ gii [ɣi:]	ᒍ gu [ɣu]	ᒎ guu [ɣu:]	ᒐ ga [ɣa]	ᒑ gaa [ɣa:]	ᒡ g [ɣ]
ᒥ mi [mi]	ᒦ mii [mi:]	ᒧ mu [mu]	ᒨ muu [mu:]	ᒪ ma [ma]	ᒫ maa [ma:]	ᒻ m [m]
ᓂ ni [ni]	ᓃ nii [ni:]	ᓄ nu [nu]	ᓅ nuu [nu:]	ᓇ na [na]	ᓈ naa [na:]	ᓐ n [n]
ᓯ si [si]	ᓰ sii [si:]	ᓱ su [su]	ᓲ suu [su:]	ᓴ sa [sa]	ᓵ saa [sa:]	ᔅ s [s]
ᓕ li [li]	ᓖ lii [li:]	ᓗ lu [lu]	ᓘ luu [lu:]	ᓚ la [la]	ᓛ laa [la:]	ᓪ l [l]
ᔨ ji [ji]	ᔩ jii [ji:]	ᔪ ju [ju]	ᔫ juu [ju:]	ᔭ ja [ja]	ᔮ jaa [ja:]	ᔾ j [j]
ᕕ vi [vi]	ᕖ vii [vi:]	ᕗ vu [vu]	ᕘ vuu [vu:]	ᕙ va [va]	ᕚ vaa [va:]	ᕝ v [v]
ᕆ ri [ʁi]	ᕇ rii [ʁi:]	ᕈ ru [ʁu]	ᕉ ruu [ʁu:]	ᕋ ra [ʁa]	ᕌ raa [ʁa:]	ᕐ r [ʁ]
ᕿ qi [qi]	ᖀ qii [qi:]	ᖁ qu [qu]	ᖂ quu [qu:]	ᖃ qa [qa]	ᖄ qaa [qa:]	ᖅ q [q]
ᖏ ngi [ŋi]	ᖐ ngii [ŋi:]	ᖑ ngu [ŋu]	ᖒ nguu [ŋu:]	ᖓ nga [ŋa]	ᖔ ngaa [ŋa:]	ᖕ ng [ŋ]
ᖠ ɬi, &i [ɬi]	ᖡ ɬii, &ii [ɬi:]	ᖢ ɬu, &u [ɬu]	ᖣ ɬuu, &uu [ɬu:]	ᖤ ɬa, &a [ɬa:]	ᖥ ɬaa, &aa [ɬa:]	ᖦ ɬ, & [ɬ]

Scripts for Inuit (Eskimo) languages

Anglican missionaries introduced syllabics to the Inuit in Canada's Eastern Arctic as early as 1856; the current form, used for most dialects of Eastern Canadian Inuktitut and for the Natsilingmiut dialect of Western Canadian Inuktun, derives from the 1865 reforms that also standardized the similar Eastern Algonquian syllabary (Harper 1985: 143–45, 1992: 1–2). Characters were added for some Inuktitut sounds that are not in Cree (FIGURE 62), but the system remained underdifferentiating until reformed

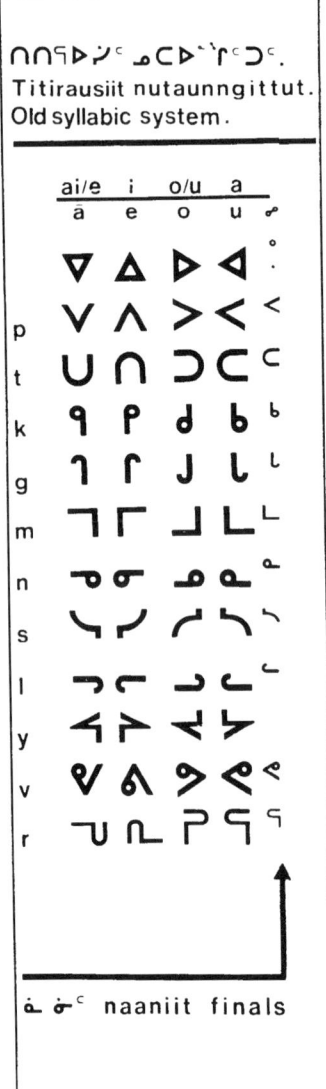

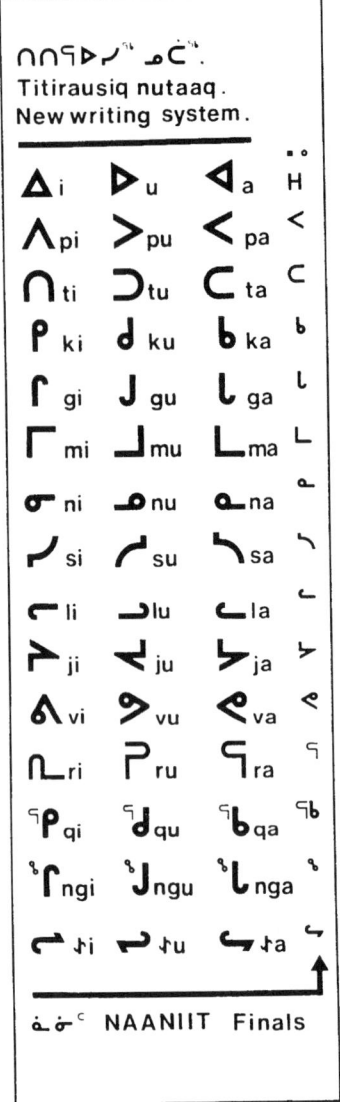

FIGURE 62. Pre-1976 Inuktitut syllabary; Inuit Cultural Institute syllabary, from Harper 1983B: 59.

in 1976 by the Inuit Cultural Institute (along with a parallel Roman orthography). In this standard orthography, presented in TABLE 55.2 and FIGURE 62, new compound characters allow full phonemic specification. Other reforms in writing conventions made the first column of characters for [ai] redundant.

Syllabics remain the normal script for the Inuit of the Eastern Arctic; however, some reforms have not been accepted locally, and revisions are still under way to accommodate additional dialects. Nonphonemic Roman orthographies are used in Labrador and the Western Arctic.

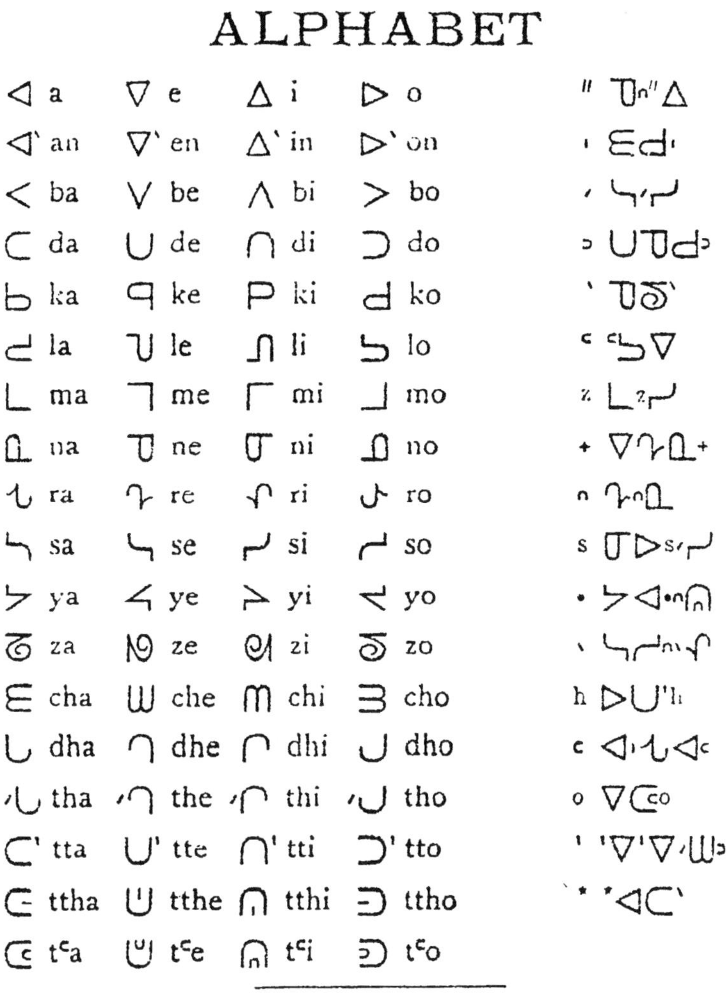

ALPHABET

◁ a	▽ e	△ i	▷ o	″	⊤ₙ″△
◁‘ an	▽‘ en	△‘ in	▷‘ on	ˌ	Ɛ◁ˌ
< ba	V be	∧ bi	> bo	⸒	↳⸒⌐↲
⊂ da	∪ de	∩ di	⊃ do	˓	∪⊤◁˒
␑ ka	ᑫ ke	P ki	◁ ko	‘	⊤ᔕˋ
⊐ la	⊍ le	⊓ li	␖ lo	ᶜ	ᶜᔕ▽
∟ ma	⊓ me	Γ mi	⊐ mo	ᶻ	∟ᵿ⌐↲
⨅ na	⊍ ne	⨃ ni	⨂ no	✢	▽ᵧ⨅✢
⎍ ra	ᵧ re	✓ ri	↵ ro	⌐	ᵧₙ⨅
↳ sa	↳ se	⌐↲ si	↱ so	ₛ	⊓▷ₛˌ⌐↲
⋗ ya	⋖ ye	⋗ yi	≺ yo	•	⋗◁•ₙ⨅
ᗰ za	ℕ⊙ ze	⊙◁ zi	ᗧ zo	ˏ	↳⌐↲ₙˌ✓
Ɛ cha	Ⅲ che	⋔ chi	Ⅎ cho	ʰ	▷∪ˌʰ
⎿ dha	⌐ dhe	⌐ dhi	⨆ dho	ᶜ	◁ˌ⎍◁ᶜ
⸝⎿ tha	⸝⌐ the	⸝⌐ thi	⸝⨆ tho	ᵒ	▽Ⅽᶜᵒ
Cˈ tta	∪ˈ tte	∩ˈ tti	⊃ˈ tto	ˈ	ˈ▽ˈ▽⸝Ⅲ⸒
Ⅽ ttha	∪ tthe	∩ tthi	⊃ ttho	ˋ	ˋ˒◁C˓
Ⅽ tᶜa	∪ tᶜe	∩ tᶜi	⊃ tᶜo		

FIGURE 63. Chipewyan syllabary, ca. 1870 (*Chipewyan Hymn Book* 1984).

Roman orthographies have been used by the Inuit of Greenland since the eighteenth century and a significant body of written literature created. The revised standard orthography of 1973 for Greenlandic is essentially the same as the Inuit Cultural Institute Roman orthography (TABLE 55.2) except that ł is not required. The new standard carries over some overdifferentiating features from the earlier orthography: *e* and *o* are written for variants of [i] and [u] before the uvulars *q* and *r*, and double *ff* for the voiceless geminate form of [v]. Two additional characters are available for sounds occurring in some dialects: *N* for [ɴ] (appearing only in a restricted morphological context) and *S* for [ʃ] (Kleivan 1984: 595, Fortescue 1990: 233–37).

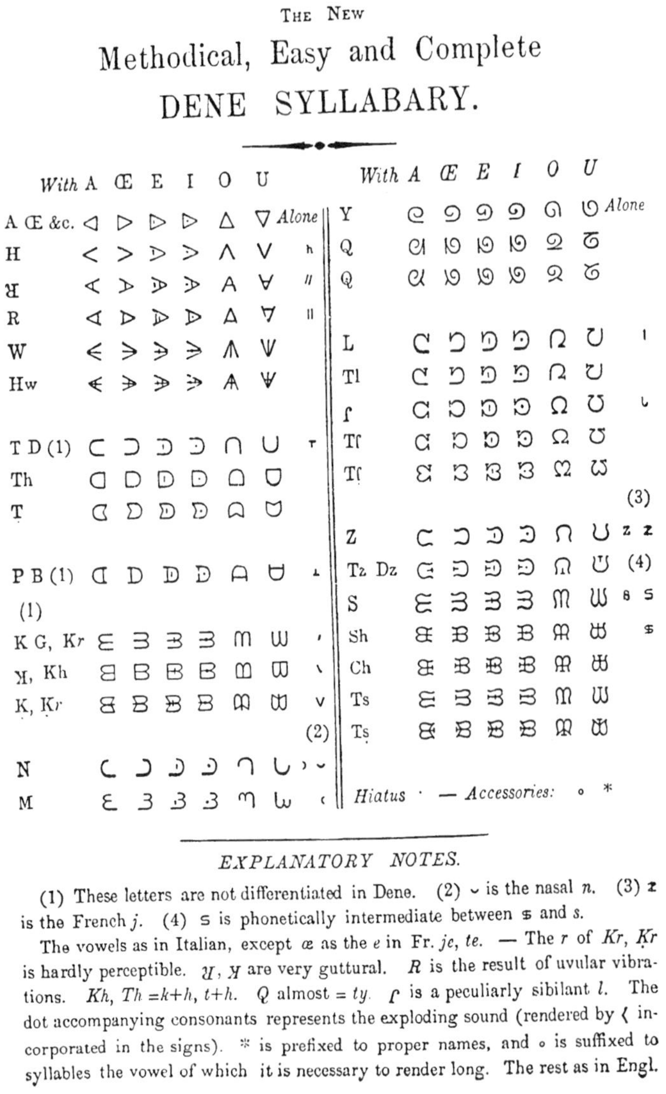

THE NEW

Methodical, Easy and Complete
DENE SYLLABARY.

The Carrier syllabary chart, arranged in columns headed *With A Œ E I O U* (left half) and *With A Œ E I O U* (right half), with consonant rows including A Œ &c., H, Ꚇ, R, W, Hw, T D(1), Th, T, P B(1), K G, Kr, Ꝗ Kh, Ꝗ Kr, N, M (left) and Y, Q, Q, L, Tl, ſ, Tꝛ, Tſ, Z, Tz Dz, S, Sh, Ch, Ts, Tṣ (right). *Hiatus · — Accessories: o *

(1) (2) (3) (4)

EXPLANATORY NOTES.

(1) These letters are not differentiated in Dene. (2) ◡ is the nasal *n*. (3) **z** is the French *j*. (4) **s** is phonetically intermediate between **s** and *s*.

The vowels as in Italian, except æ as the *e* in Fr. *je, te.* — The *r* of *Kr, Ḳr* is hardly perceptible. Ꝗ, ɤ are very guttural. *R* is the result of uvular vibrations. *Kh, Th* =k+h, t+h. *Q* almost = *ty*. *ſ* is a peculiarly sibilant *l*. The dot accompanying consonants represents the exploding sound (rendered by ⟨ incorporated in the signs). * is prefixed to proper names, and o is suffixed to syllables the vowel of which it is necessary to render long. The rest as in Engl.

FIGURE 64. Carrier syllabary (Morice 1890, repr. in Pilling 1892).

Syllabics for Sub-Arctic Athabaskan languages

Evans had attempted to write Chipewyan using a variant of his original syllabary. Other missionaries remodeled the Evans syllabary for Chipewyan, Slavey, and other Athabaskan languages. Although new and altered characters were added for the rich inventory of consonants in these languages, underdifferentiation of both vowels and consonants is frequent. A traditional syllabary for Chipewyan is given in FIGURE 63 and a greatly elaborated syllabary created for Carrier in FIGURE 64.

Bibliography

Anamie Nagamonan [Hymns]. 1965. Kenora, Ont.: n.p.

The Book of Common Prayer ... Translated into the Language of the Cree Indians. n.d. Toronto: General Board of Religious Education.

Burnaby, Barbara, ed. 1985. *Promoting Native Writing Systems in Canada.* Toronto: OISE Press.

A Chipewyan Hymn Book for the Keewatin and Mackenzie Districts. 1984. Brochet, Manitoba: n.p. (repr. of 1960 ed.).

Dusenberry, Verne. 1962. *The Montana Cree: A Study in Religious Persistence* (Acta Universitatis Stockholmiensis 3). Stockholm: Almqvist and Wiksell.

Enwall, Joakim. 1994. *A Myth Become Reality: History and Development of the Miao Written Language.* Stockholm: Stockholm University, Institute of Oriental Languages.

Evans, James (1801–1846). Papers. University of Western Ontario Library, London, Ontario.

Fiero, Charles. 1985. "Style Manual for Syllabics." In Burnaby 1985: 49–104.

Fortescue, Michael, ed. 1990. *From the Writings of the Greenlanders/Kalaallit atuakkiaannit.* N.p.: University of Alaska Press.

Harper, Kenn. 1983A. "Writing in Inuktitut: An Historical Perspective." *Inuktitut* 53: 3–35.

———. 1983B. "Inuktitut Writing Systems: The Current Situation." *Inuktitut* 53: 36–84.

———. 1985. "The Early Development of Inuktitut Syllabic Orthography." *Études/Inuit/Studies* 9:141–62.

———. 1992. *Current Status of Writing Systems for Inuktitut, Inuinnaqtun and Inuvialuktun.* Yellowknife: Northwest Territories Culture and Communications.

Horden, John, comp. 1925. *A Collection of Psalms and Hymns in the Language of the Cree Indians of North-West America*, rev. ed. London: S.P.C.K.

Kleivan, Inge. 1984. "West Greenlandic before 1950." In *Handbook of American Indians*, vol. 5: *Arctic*, ed. David Damas, pp. 595–621. Washington, D.C.: Smithsonian Institution.

Mallon, S. T. 1985. "Six Years later: The ICI Dual Orthography for Inuktitut, 1976–1982." In Burnaby 1985: 137–57.

Morice, Adrien Gabriel. 1890. *The New Methodical, Easy and Complete Dene Syllabary.* Stuart Lake, B.C.: Stuart's Lake Mission.

Murdoch, John Stewart. 1981. "Syllabics: A Successful Educational Innovation." M.Ed. dissertation, University of Manitoba.

———. 1985. "A Syllabary or an Alphabet: A Choice between Phonemic Differentiation or Economy." In Burnaby 1985: 127–36.

Nichols, John D. 1984. "The Composition Sequence of the First Cree Hymnal." In *Essays in Algonquian Bibliography in Honour of V. M. Dechene*, ed. H. C. Wolfart, pp. 1–21. Winnipeg: Algonquian and Iroquoian Linguistics.

Pilling, James Constantine. 1892. *Bibliography of the Athapascan Languages* (Bureau of American Ethnology Bulletin 14). Washington, D.C.: Smithsonian Institution.

Scripts for Munda Languages

NORMAN ZIDE

Central India of the first half of the twentieth century was a place where many new scripts were devised by members of "tribal" language communities (i.e. minority groups outside mainstream Hindu society). Apparently it was felt by the newly conscious speakers of these languages that a full-fledged language in the Indian context needed a script of its own, clearly different from those of its neighbors. More than a dozen were made for less than half that many languages; for some, e.g. Ho, more than four scripts were devised. Most of these scripts are no longer used, or even remembered. Several of the tribal communities were, sooner or later, satisfied to use a regional or international script (on factors in script choice in India, see SECTION 65), and speakers of these languages saw—and were pressured to see—the advantages of learning, and in some cases replacing their native languages with, the dominant regional languages: Hindi, Bengali, Oriya, Telugu, Marathi. Most of the Christian missions—in the earlier periods the chief, often the only, advocates and promoters of literacy in the tribal and regional languages—and the communities influenced by them in this area used the Roman script until fairly recently, when (except in northeast India and the Nicobars) it was replaced by a local regional script.

The three scripts discussed here, Sorang Sompeng for Sora, Ol Cemet' for Santali, and Varang Kshiti for Ho (all languages of the Munda family, which with Mon-Khmer makes up Austro-Asiatic), were devised by charismatic community leaders as parts of a comprehensive cultural program, and each was offered as an improvement over scripts used by Christian missionary linguists and their "tribal" associates. All the devisers of these scripts were familiar with one or more scripts used in their provinces. These three scripts survive, are used in primary and adult education, and are published in a variety of printed materials. Santali is spoken over a wide area by more than three million people; it was—and is—written in four "older" scripts: Devanagari, Bengali, Oriya, and Roman. Ol Cemet' has been the most successful of the three scripts, and there have been recent attempts by Santals to induce other "tribal" groups in the Chota Nagpur area, both Munda and Dravidian, to adopt this improved script.

Sorang Sompeng

We know less about Sorang Sompeng than about the other two scripts; the one history and description of this script is found in a short paper by Khageshwar Mahapatra

TABLE 56.1: *The Characters of Sorang Sampeng with Transliterations*

						s	t	b	c	d	g
						m	ṅ	l	n	v	p
						y	r	h	k	j	ñ
						a	e	i	u	o	ę

(1978–79). Sora has been written in a Roman-based script originated by Baptist missionaries, and also in Telugu and Oriya characters. Mahapatra describes controversy between the promoters of Oriya and those of Telugu for the predominant influence on the Sora people living between the Oriya- and Telugu-speaking populations in what later became the Orissa–Andhra border area. Some "self-conscious tribal leaders," Mahapatra writes, "instead of choosing a side to merge themselves, endeavoured to maintain their identity by inventing a new script for themselves." Malia Gomango, an influential leader of the non-Christian Sora, led the movement for a separate script, and "inspired his son-in-law, Mangei Gomango," to devise a proper script for Sora. Mangei, "an educated person ... conversant in Oriya, Telugu and English," retreated to the hills, where on June 18, 1936, he received in a vision the 24 letters of Sorang Sompeng. He founded a religious order dedicated to Akshara Brahma. The script was widely taught, though it is unclear to what extent it is used; all the publications listed by Mahapatra are by Mangei, though the press has also issued many ephemera.

The 24 characters are arranged in a four-row by six-column diagram, with the six vowels in the bottom row. (The shwa vowel is "inherent" in the letter.) The letters get their names from 24 gods in the Sora pantheon, e.g. *s* for Sundaṅ, *t* for Tənod; no rationale is apparent for the ordering. The names of the consonant characters are derived by adding *a ʾ* to the consonant sound, i.e. *sa ʾ, ta ʾ*, etc. Mahapatra suggests that the general shapes of the characters owe something to English cursive letter shapes; perhaps the loops and curlicues were influenced by the Telugu script.

Divine providence does not guarantee a script linguistic efficiency. Mangei's script does not represent the phonemes of Sora (TABLE 56.2) as well as it might in an efficient writing system. But it should be noted that we don't know as much about the

TABLE 56.2: *Sora Phonemes*

p	t	c	k	ʔ	i	ɨ	u
b	ḍ	j	g		e	ə	o
m	n	ɲ	ŋ		ɛ	a	ɔ
	r ṛ	l	w				

script as we need to, so we may be missing morphophonemic and, perhaps, dialecto-logical information built into Mangei's writing system. Sorang Sompeng uses the *h* symbol for the glottal stop [ʔ] (there is no aspiration in Sora outside loanwords), but seems not to write glottal stop in some of the instances where it does occur. The ret-roflex [ɽ] is written *rd*. Mahapatra claims that there is no use for *c* and *v* in Sora. The letter *i* is used for [i] and [ɨ], and *o* for [o] and [ɔ]. Consonant clusters are written not with conjunct characters (as in the Indic scripts), but by simply juxtaposing consonant letters, so the reader must recognize the presence or absence of [ə] in any particular instance. There is no *halanta*-like "killer" diacritic.

Ol Cemet'

The Ol Cemet' or, as it is usually called now, Ol Ciki (or just Ol) script of Santali is alphabetic; it has none of the syllabary properties of the Indic scripts. The Santali di-alect represented in Ol is the southern one, spoken in the Mayurbhanj district of Oris-sa. The chief phonological peculiarity is that this dialect has six vowels, whereas the dialect of Santal Parganas (described by Bodding and others) has eight or nine. Liter-ature from the Ol Press says nothing about how to write the additional vowels, but Mahapatra and Mahapatra (1979) show that this is done with the vowel characters in the table plus diacritic marks. Pandit Raghunath Murmu, the inventor of Ol Cemet', arranges the written characters in a diagram with the vowels in the first column. Vowel letters are named with *l*V, and consonant letter names have the vowel found at the be-ginning of their row. Thus the letters of the first row are called *lǫ*, *ǫt*, *ǫk'*, *ǫń*, and *ōl*.

Raghunath devised and advertised his script as "easy to learn," as compared with Santali written in the Oriya, Bengali, Devanagari, or Roman scripts, which he called *Ol Urum* 'dusty', i.e. superannuated, writing. Among the features making it easier to learn, the following are mentioned:

TABLE 56.3: *The Letters of Ol Cemet' with Transliterations and Transcriptions*

ꡃ	O	ꁇ	ꀂ	ꀞ	ǫ [ɔ]	t [t]	k' [k', g]	ṅ [ŋ]	l [l]
ꡂ	ꃀ	ꁷ	ꀯ	ꡂ	a [a]	k [k]	c' [c', j]	m [m]	w [w]
ꡒ	ꃅ	ꁱ	q	ꁅ	i [i]	s [s]	h [ʔ, h]	ñ [ɲ]	r [r]
ꡕ	ꃐ	ꁌ	ꁢ	ꁇ	u [u]	c [c]	t' [t', d]	ṇ [ɳ]	y [j]
ꁜ	ꃨ	ꁍ	ꏝ	ꁘ	e [e]	p [p]	ḍ [ɖ]	n [n]	ṛ [ɽ]
ꡕ	ꁘ	ꁉ	ꁟ	ꀍ	o [o]	ṭ [ʈ]	p' [p', b]	w̃ [w̃]	(C)h [ʰ]

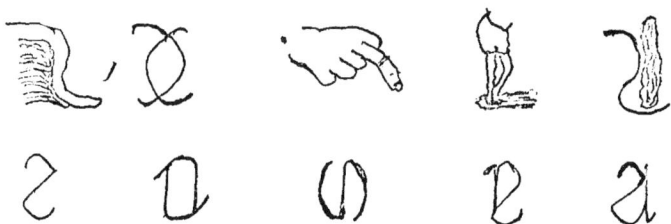

FIGURE 65. The pictorial origin of the letters in the *e* row of Ol Cemet' (Zide 1967: 187, 1968: 251).

(a) The script makes use of signs and symbols long familiar to the Santals, e.g. marks made on stones or trees to indicate 'danger' or 'meeting place'.

(b) The letters are "scientifically" arranged, which "facilitates the children to learn the names of letters as there is a flow being headed by the same vowel."

(c) The shapes of the letters are not arbitrary, but reflect the names of the letters, which are words, usually the names of objects or actions represented—in conventionalized form—in the pictorial shapes of the characters.

Most of the characters can be described in terms of a small set of components and can be seen as contained in a more-or-less oval envelope, the letter shape tracing some part of this envelope (Zide 1968).

Some examples of these features are seen in FIGURE 65: *le* 'swelling'; *ep* 'to meet, collide'; *eḍ* 'to point out a place', a symbol (previously) used for 'meeting place'; *en* 'to thresh grain', from a picture of two legs threshing; *eṛ* 'to avoid', from a picture of a path that turns to avoid an obstruction or a dangerous place.

One ingenious—"scientific"—and unique feature of Ol Cemet' that certainly increases the efficiency of writing Santali is the deglottalizing *ọhọṭ'* diacritic. This neatly preserves the morphophonemic relationships between the glottalized and voiced equivalents: the former occurs word-finally and at certain word-internal preconsonantal junctures, the latter prevocalically, but never morpheme-initially in these alternations. Thus, *oḱ'* is the name of a letter that represents both [k'] and [g]. Two further diacritics include a horizontal loop added at the top right of the character for the aspiration of consonants, and a raised dot for vowel nasalization.

When, thirty years ago, I asked knowledgeable people in Bihar and Orissa what they thought of the chances of a wide—if not pan-Santal—acceptance of Ol Cemet', almost all were skeptical. The competition of Oriya, Devanagari, etc., was too powerful. But in fact, Ol Cemet' has become more and more widely accepted. Official recognitions have been made. Pandit Raghunath Murmu has been honored by the Orissa government. More recently, various Santal organizations have tried to promote the script for other languages of Chota Nagpur, mostly Munda languages, but for the Dravidian Kuḍux as well—without much success.

Ho

Ho is a North Munda language, fairly closely related to Santali. It is less conservative in its vowel inventory than Santali, and has the standard areal five-vowel system (but, unlike Indo-Aryan or Dravidian, without vowel length). The Varang Kshiti script of Lako Bodra, the script to be described here, is a script for Ho Hayam—very roughly 'hieratic Ho'—and the key question here has do with the difference between Ho Hayam and Ho Kaji 'ordinary Ho'. The amount of overlap is unclear. The authority on the matter—and on all aspects of Lako Bodra's script—is H.-J. Pinnow. Pinnow (1972) suggests three possibilities as to what HoH may be: (a) a (regional?) dialect of Ho; (b) an arbitrary mixture of Ho, Mundari, Santali, and other elements; or (c) an old, sacerdotal language kept secret until now. These alternatives are not mutually exclusive.

Pinnow writes that the script exhibits highly syncretistic features, many borrowings from a variety of older scripts (I suspect that he overestimates the degree of borrowing), and clear borrowings from Brahmi (he sees 14 of the Ho characters as fairly directly borrowed). Several of the letter shapes—the non-cursive forms in particular—resemble English. They are *not*—and this is no accident—similar to Devanagari characters. Lako Bodra was not unaware of the Brahmi similarities. According to Pinnow, Lako Bodra's claim was that the script was "invented in the 13th Century by a certain Dhawan Turi and rediscovered in a shamanistic vision and modernized by Bodra himself." My own conversations with followers of Lako Bodra in the late 1970s brought out further assertions of an even greater antiquity of the script, and the claim that the Ho script was the most ancient in the subcontinent and the (only?) survivor of an ancient flood. There is an Institute of Ancient Culture and Science Society concerned with promoting the Varang Kshiti script and related matters. Ho—any variety of Ho, presumably—must be written in its proper script, according to Bodra's followers. The similarities between Varang Kshiti and other Indian scripts are the result of

TABLE 56.4: *The Consonants of Varang Kshiti with Transliterations*

૩	3	⌒	ℳ	먹	ℓ	ṅ	g	k
∞	♂	E	ℰ	력	ℓ	ñ	j	c
ℕ	ℳ	⌐	ℓ	L	⟨	ṇ	ḍ	ṭ
1	⌐	⋓	℅	O	℮	m	b	p
♁	ℐ	◇	◇	U	℧	h	l	ṛ
℧	ℳ	⋑	ℐ	5	ℑ	r	ṣ	s
T	Ɣ	℧	ℳ	ℓ	ℑ			

TABLE 56.5: *The Vowels of Varang Kshiti with Transliterations*

V	ν	ʃ	ſ	ᵮ	ꜰ	L	ι	∇	ʊ	Z	ᴢ
Y	y	ꓱ	ß	E	ꓼ	⊦	ꓶ				

m	a	i	u	e	o
ꞌ	y	ī	ū		

borrowing *from*, not *by*, Ho, according to Bodra's followers and probably Lako Bodra himself; but according to outside observers, the script is his in that he invented it, not rediscovered it.

Varang Kshiti is written from left to right, with the vowel characters in the order they are spoken; the complications of vowel placement and variant forms found in Brahmi-derived scripts are eschewed. The characters are now given in a standard tabular form (TABLE 56.4, from Lako Bodra 1963), the consonants being ranged in rows of three, the first five of these triads having systematic phonetic properties of a kind familiar from the standard arrangement of the Devanagari characters. The last two rows are—again largely on the Devanagari pattern—miscellaneous.

Lako Bodra has created certain extra characters—there is no call in Ho for *ṣ* distinct from *s*—apparently because he wants an archaic, Sanskrit-like cast to Varang Kshiti. The letter *h* after a vowel indicates vowel lengthening. The sequence *hb* represents *w*, whose interpretation ([v]? [w]?) is unclear. There is a special symbol for the mystical syllable *oṃ*.

Varang Kshiti has ten vowel characters: simple vowels, mixed vowels, and ligatures (TABLE 56.5, from Lako Bodra 1963). The four simple vowels (*īpan bor(o)ñ*) are *a*, *i*, *u*, and *ṃ* (nasalization, cf. Hindi *candrabindu* and *anusvara*), plus the inherent vowel as in Devanagari and other Indic scripts. The inherent vowel is not always to be pronounced [a], but sometimes [o] or [e]. The two mixed vowels (*sell ip(a)ñ bor(o)ñ*) are *e* and *o*, presumably following Sanskrit notions according to which these are not "simple." The ligatures (*dobri bor(o)ñ*), neither vowels nor consonants, are four; the characters are composite.

TABLE 56.6: *The Numerals of the Munda Scripts*

	1	*2*	*3*	*4*	*5*	*6*	*7*	*8*	*9*	*0*
Sorang Sompeng	ſ	ｌ	ꝫ	ｊ	↓	ｂ	⸖	L	♭	O
Ol Cemet'	∿	૨	ੲ	৬	৪	℮	ᶎ	૯	૬	O
Varang Kshiti (Pinnow 1972)	ᶑ 1 ᷓ 10 ᶑᶑ 11	ᷓ 2 ⤬ 20 ᷚᶆ 23	ᶆ 3 ⤬ 30	ꓩ 4 ꓵ 40	⤳ 5 ⤳ 50	ꝩ 6 ꝩ 60	ᷓ 7 ᷓ 70	ꓫ 8 ♭ 80 ⤳ᷓ 57	Ϛ 9 Ϛ 90	

Bibliography

SORA

Baṅsa ɔnoblegaṅji [Proverbs in Saora]. N.D. Bible Society of India and Ceylon.

Mahapatra, Khageshwar. 1978–79. "'SoraN SompeN': A Sora Script." Unpublished conference paper (Delhi, Mysore). Oriya version in his *Oṛia lipi o bhāṣā,* pp. 147–55. Cuttack, 1977.

Mattiu [Matthew]. 1961. Bible Society of India and Ceylon.

Three booklets in the Sorang Sompeng script. 1965, 1967.

SANTALI

Bodding, P. O. 1923. *Materials for a Santali Grammar,* part 1: *Mostly Phonetic.* Benegaria, Bihar, India: Santal Mission Press.

Mahapatra, B. P., and Ranganayaki Mahapatra. 1979. "Santal Script and Texts." Work paper for the post-plenary session of the Tenth International Congress of Anthropological and Ethnological Sciences, Mysore, pp. 1–15.

Zide, Norman H. 1967. "The Santali Ol Cemet' Script." In *Languages and Areas: Studies Presented to George V. Bobrinskoy,* pp 180–89. Chicago: University of Chicago, Division of the Humanities.

———. 1968. "Graphemic System in the Ol Cemed Script." *Papers from the Fourth Regional Meeting of the Chicago Linguistic Society,* pp. 238–54.

A number of pamphlets on Ol Cemet' published in the 1950s and 1960s, mostly by the Ol Press, P.O. Rairangpur, Mayurbhanj District, Orissa, India, for the Adibasi Cultural Association. [The author had very helpful correspondence in the 1960s with people at the Association, in particular with Mr. B. Hansdah.]

HO

Burrows, Lionel. 1915. *Ho Grammar (with Vocabulary).* Calcutta: Catholic Orphan Press. Repr. Delhi: Cosmo, 1980.

Deeney, John J. 1975. *Ho Grammar and Vocabulary.* Chaibasa, Bihar, India: Xavier Ho.

———. 1978. *Ho–English Dictionary.* Chaibasa: Xavier Ho.

Lako Bodra. 1963. *Ho Hayam Paham Puti.* Jhinkpani.

———. N.D. *Ho Halaṅ Galaṅ* (a trilingual dictionary, manuscript in the possession of Mr. B. Pat Pingua of Ranchi, a follower of Lako Bodra, who provided information on Lako Bodra's movement and the script). Jhinkpani.

———. [Pinnow lists several additional publications not seen by the author.]

Pinnow, Hans-Jürgen. 1972. "Schrift und Sprache in den Werken Lako Bodras im Gebiet der Ho von Singbhum (Bihar)." *Anthropos* 67: 822–55.

Zide, Norman. 1991. "The Munda Languages." In *Wörterbücher: Ein internationales Handbuch zur Lexicographie,* vol. 3, pp. 2533–47. Berlin: Mouton de Gruyter.

The Pahawh Hmong Script

MARTHA RATLIFF

Pahawh Hmong (ᖲᖁ ᖰᎲ ᖴᏌ *Phajhauj Hmoob* [pʰâ hâu ʰmɔ́ŋ]) is the name of a phonological writing system for the Hmong language of Southeast Asia (Hmong-Mien or Miao-Yao family) created by an uneducated and, at the time of its creation, apparently illiterate Hmong peasant, Shong Lue Yang. Pahawh Hmong is unique among the writing systems invented in modern times, because it is a system based upon subsyllabic phonological units and it exhaustively represents every such unit in the language. (Transliterations in this section are in the Romanized Popular Alphabet, another widely used system for writing Hmong. Final consonants in RPA indicate tones.)

The development of this writing system and the movement to preserve and disseminate it are linked to a history of native messianic movements. Many Hmong believe that, throughout time, God has given them power and validation through the gift of writing. The loss of writing is understood as divine retribution. Shong Lue Yang believed that he himself was divine, and that the Pahawh was divinely revealed to him for the benefit of the Hmong people. The original version of this writing system was created by, or through, Shong Lue Yang in 1959 in the borderlands of northern Laos and Vietnam. During the next twelve years, he and his disciples taught the Pahawh widely as part of a larger revival of Hmong cultural values. Shong Lue Yang worked incessantly on modifications to the Pahawh, producing three increasingly sophisticated versions of the script, until in 1971 government soldiers, fearful of his growing influence, assassinated him. He also developed a writing system for the Khmu language (Mon-Khmer family), but this script has not been preserved. A full account of the development and significance of the script is given in Smalley et al. 1990; an account of the life of Shong Lue Yang is presented in Vang et al. 1990.

Features of the system

Hmong, like other languages of the area including Chinese, is an isolating language with monosyllabic morphemes. It has eight tones, a rich system of initial consonants, and only one syllable-final consonant: [ŋ]. The most widely used Third Stage Reduced Version of Pahawh Hmong (ᖲᖁ ᖰᎲ ᗅᏦ ᗯᎲ ᖴᖲ *Phajhauj Ntsiab Duas Peb* [pʰâ hâu ntʃía ʔdùa pé] 'kernel Pahawh, stage three') represents demisyllables: the onset (consonant or consonant cluster) and the rime (vowel, final [ŋ], and tone

619

TABLE 57.1: *104 Rime (vowel-tone) Symbols of the Third Stage Pahawh Hmong with Romanized Popular Alphabet Equivalents*

	´ high level	˰ low glottalized	ˬ low rising	^ high falling	ˇ mid rising	– mid level	˴ low level	ˍ falling-breathy
[ɛŋ]	keeb	keem	keed	keej	keev	kee	kees	keeg
[i]	kib	kim	kid	kij	kiv	ki	kis	kig
[au]	kaub	kaum	kaud	kauj	kauv	kau	kaus	kaug
[u]	kub	kum	kud	kuj	kuv	ku	kus	kug
[e]	keb	kem	ked	kej	kev	ke	kes	keg
[ai]	kaib	kaim	kaid	kaij	kaiv	kai	kais	kaig
[ɔŋ]	koob	koom	kood	kooj	koov	koo	koos	koog
[aɨ]	kawb	kawm	kawd	kawj	kawv	kaw	kaws	kawg
[ua]	kuab	kuam	kuad	kuaj	kuav	kua	kuas	kuag
[ɔ]	kob	kom	kod	koj	kov	ko	kos	kog
[ia]	kiab	kiam	kiad	kiaj	kiav	kia	kias	kiag
[a]	kab	kam	kad	kaj	kav	ka	kas	kag
[ɨ]	kwb	kwm	kwd	kwj	kwv	kw	kws	kwg

combination). In this version, illustrated here, the rime symbols are developing unique associations with vowel qualities, while the rime diacritics are developing unique associations with tonal values. This line of development is fully realized in the last version of Pahawh Hmong which Shong Lue Yang created shortly before his death: in this Final Version (ᖔᖆ ᖆᒐ ᖅᖇ *Phajhauj Txha* [pʰâ hâu tsʰa] 'core Pahawh'), each vowel quality is associated with one symbol, and each tone with one diacritic. However, the Final Version is not used by supporters of the Pahawh; although more linguistically advanced, it is not as important culturally, and is reserved for note-taking.

The onset and rime elements of each syllable are written in reverse order from the way they are pronounced, that is, rime–onset, although the monosyllabic morphemes themselves are written from left to right across the page. Spaces are used to separate morphemes, which are thus typically represented by pairs of symbols.

The fit between Pahawh Hmong and the spoken language is perfect; all distinctive sounds are symbolized, including the opposition between the "hard" glottal stop onset **À** and the "soft" onset for vowels **ᴛ**, which is here the distinctive absence of sound. Other features of the system include the following.

The rime–onset order of the symbols in a writing system that is otherwise left-to-right indicates that Shong Lue Yang perceived vowels and associated tones (**ᴜ͏ꞏꞏᴡ** *yub* [jú]) to be primary and consonants (**Ữᴜꞏ** *las* [là]) to be secondary.

The final [ŋ] is not symbolized separately with the available onset symbol for [ŋ] (**Ữ̇**); rather, it is perceived as a feature of the rime (see TABLE 57.1).

The eight tones are indicated by a combination of diacritic and choice of vowel symbol. The first four tones are indicated by the choice of the first vowel symbol (**ᴜꞏᴡ ᴠᴣ̇** *yub teeb* [jú téŋ] 'placement vowel') in combination with tone diacritics; the second four tones are indicated by the choice of the second vowel symbol (**ᴜꞏᴡ ᴔᴠ̇** *yub txauv* [jú tsӑu] 'replacement vowel') in combination with a separate set of tone diacritics (see TABLE 57.1). Diacritic symbols also form part of consonant symbols, but in this case the diacritics have no independent significance (see TABLE 57.2). Both tone and consonant diacritics appear centered above the basic symbols.

Initial [k] is not symbolized. The absence of an onset symbol indicates that the word is pronounced with an initial [k].

Similarly, [au] with mid level tone is usually not symbolized. The absence of a rime symbol indicates that a word is pronounced with mid level [au]. However, the symbol **ᴔ̇** corresponds to mid level [au], and is used for disambiguation when the symbol to the left is a rime symbol with inherent [k]. Without such an option, the rime from the first word and the onset from the second might be incorrectly read as though they belonged together (Smalley et al. 1990: 58).

Hmong Daw 'White Hmong' is the dialect used for exemplification here. However, the other major Hmong dialect of Southeast Asia, Hmong Leng or Hmong Njua 'Green Hmong', has regular correspondences with Hmong Daw and is equally well represented by Pahawh Hmong, since Shong Lue Yang invented two special symbols for the Hmong Leng clusters [ndl] and [ndʰl] (**ᴦ̇** and **ᴄ̄**), which do not have counterparts in Hmong Daw.

The symbols

Shong Lue Yang's presentation of the Pahawh symbols did not vary from one version of the writing system to the next. He displayed vowel–tone combination symbols in charts where rows correspond to vowel quality and columns correspond to tone (TABLE 57.1). Although consonant symbols are differentiated by diacritics in each row, neither the rows (symbols) nor the columns (diacritics) correspond to any phonological feature of the Hmong consonant inventory (TABLE 57.2). Shong Lue Yang and his associates also developed logographic symbols for numerals (TABLE 57.3) and certain common words, as well as punctuation marks modeled on Western writ-

TABLE 57.2: *Sixty Onset (consonant) Symbols of the Third Stage Pahawh Hmong with Romanized Popular Alphabet Equivalents*

Symbol	IPA	Name	Symbol	IPA	Name	Symbol	IPA	Name
C	[v-]	vau	Ġ	[ɳʈ-]	nrau	C̈	[f-]	fau
∩	[ŋk-]	nkau	ṅ	[nts-]	ntxau	n̈	[tʰ-]	rhau
A	[s-]	xau	Ȧ	[ʔ-]	au	Ä	[ɲ-]	nyau
∀	[c-]	cau	V̇	[ntʃʰ-]	ntshau	V̈	[ts-]	txau
ɯ	[l-]	lau	ɯ̇	[ʔd-]	dau	ɯ̈	[ʔdʰ-]	dhau
K	[ntʃ-]	ntsau	K̇	[tʃ-]	tsau	K̈	[pʰ-]	phau
Ч	[ʰl-]	hlau	Ч̇	[ʒ-]	zau	Ӵ	[ntsʰ-]	ntxhau
ʯ	[ʈ-]	rau	ʯ̇	[mpʰ-]	nphau	ʯ̈	[mpʰl-]	nphlau
Ħ	[ʰn-]	hnau	Ħ̇	[kʰ-]	khau	Ħ̈	[nt-]	ntau
m	[pʰl-]	plhau	ṁ	[tʃʰ-]	tshau	m̈	[p-]	pau
M	[ntʰ-]	nthau	Ṁ	[mpl-]	nplau	M̈	[ŋkʰ-]	nkhau
ɔ	[cʰ-]	chau	ɔ̇	[ç-]	xyau	ɔ̈	[t-]	tau
∪	[n-]	nau	U̇	[ɴq-]	nqau	Ü	[ɴqʰ-]	nqhau
ʊ	[ml-]	nlau	ʊ̇	[ʰml-]	hnlau	ʊ̈	[ŋ-]	gau
E	[qʰ-]	qhau	Ė	[ʰɲ-]	nyhau	Ë	[ʰm-]	hmau
⼕	[h-]	hau	⼕̇	[tʰ-]	thau	⼕̈	[pl-]	plau
Ꝺ	[ɲcʰ-]	nchau	Ꝺ̇	[ɳʈʰ-]	nrhau	Ꝺ̈	[mp-]	npau
R	[m-]	mau	Ṙ	[tsʰ-]	txhau	R̈	[q-]	qau
ɰ	[j-]	yau	ẇ	[ɲc-]	ncau	ẅ	[ʃ-]	sau
ʊ	Ø	'au	ʊ̇	[ndl-]	ndlau	ʊ̈	[ndʰl-]	ndlhau

TABLE 57.3: *Numerals*

O	Ч	З	ᕊ	⅄	Ӡ	C	ᴚ	ᴋ	K	Ɩ	Ӿ
0	1	2	3	4	5	6	7	8	9	10s	100s

ing conventions. Two symbols created to reflect important aspects of Hmong style are ħ, used following a word to indicate reduplication, and :·, used at the end of a line of writing to indicate that the line be chanted rather than read (see Smalley et al. 1990, chapter 6, for details).

Use

Although it has ardent supporters, Pahawh Hmong is not as widely used as the RPA system developed by missionary linguists, chief among them William Smalley, in the 1950s. Limited access to the equipment necessary to produce the script, lack of adequate published materials, and association of the script with a movement of political resistance in Laos have kept Pahawh Hmong from supplanting the RPA. However, most Hmong take great pride in the accomplishment of Shong Lue Yang and in the existence of a script created by one of their own people.

SAMPLE OF HMONG DAW

1. *Pahawh Hmong:*	ⴙⵦ̈	ᵀⴑ	ⴟⵙ	ⵖⴑ	ᵓⴑ	ᱼⵄ	ᵓ̇	ᱼᴚ̇	ᵴ
2. *RPA:*	Soob	Lwj	yog	leej	neeg	tsis	tau	mus	kawm
3. *Transcription:*	ʃɔ́ŋ	lɨ̂	jɔ̰	lêŋ	nɛ̂ŋ	t͡ʃì	tau	mù	ka̰ɨ
4. *Gloss:*	Shong	Lue	be	CLF	person	not	get	go	study

1.	ⴙ	ᴨⱯ	ᴕᴋ	ⴟⴑ	ᴨᱼ̇	ᵀⴑ	ⴒⴖ	ᵓⴑ,	ᵓⴟ̇	ᱼⵦ̈
2.	kev	txawj	ntse	los	ntawm	lwm	haiv	neeg,	tab	sis
3.	kě	tsâɨ	nt͡ʃe	lɔ̀	nta̰ɨ	lɨ̰	hǎi	nɛŋ	tá	ʃì
4.	wɑy	be.able	clever	source	at		another	group	person	but

1.	ᴊⴒ	ᴨᴿ	ⵖⴟ̇	Ɐᴀ	ᴨᵀⱴ̌	ᴕᴋ	ⴟⴑ	ᴨᱼ̇	ᵓⵞ	ⵖⴑ	ᴊⱴ̌.
2.	nws	muaj	tsheej	xeeb	txawj	ntse	los	ntawm	Vaj	Leej	Txi.
3.	nɨ̀	mûa	t͡ʃʰêŋ	sɛ́ŋ	tsâɨ	nt͡ʃe	lɔ̀	nta̰ɨ	vâ	lêŋ	tsi
4.	he	have	knowing	heart	be.able	clever	source	at		king	CLF	father

1.	ᴊⴒ	ⵃⴟ̇	ⴧⴀ̇	ⵦⴟ̇	ᵓⵦ	ᴕᴋ̇	ⵘⴟ̇	ⵕ	ⴒⴖ	ᴨⴖ̇	ⴒ̇ⵦ̇	ⴒⴒ	ⵦⴟ̇	ⴟⵙ
2.	Nws	paub	ib	puas	yam	tsav	nyob	hauv	lub	ntiaj	teb	no	uas	yog
3.	nɨ̀	páu	ʔí	pùa	ja̰	t͡ʃǎ	ɲɔ́	hǎu	lú	ntîa	té	nɔ̰	ʔùa	jɔ̰
4.	he	know	one	hundred	kind	plus	exist	in	CLF	face	earth	this	which	be

1. ꗃꗂ ꖴꘇ ꖜꕙ ꗵ ꖶꖷ ꗥꖷ. ꖳꗛ ꖵꘇ ꕰꗙ ꘇꗛ ꗃꖰ, ꘇꗛ

2. Vaj   Leej Txi   tau   tsim   tseg. Thiab nws   txawj tshuab raj, tshuab

3. vâ   lêŋ   tsi   tau   tʃi̬   tʃe̬   tʰía   nì̵   tsâ̵   tʃʰúa   ʈâ   tʃʰúa

4. king CLF father get   create leave and   he   be.able blow   flute blow

---

1. ꖷꗃ,   ꖩꖰ   ꗃꗰ   ꖵꗛ   ꗛꗙ   ꖶꖷ   ꗃꗰ ꗵꕰ   ꖽ   ꘇꕰ

2. ncas,   tshov qeej   thiab txawj tsim   Phaj Hauj rau   haiv

3. ncà   tʃʰɔ̌   qêŋ   tʰía   tsâ̵   tʃi̬   pʰâ hâu   ʈau   hǎi

4. mouth.harp   play   pipes and   be.able create Pahawh   for   group

---

1. ꖽꗵ   ꖷꗰ   ꘇꕰ   ꖩꖰ ꗵꗰ   ꕰ,   ꗥꕰ   ꗳ   ꖳꖰ   ꗵꗵ   ꗙꕙ   ꗵ

2. Hmoob thiab haiv   Pub Thawj kawm, es   kom   lawv nyias ceev tau

3. ʰmɔ́ŋ   tʰía   hǎi   pu tʰâ̵   kại   ʔè   kɔ̣   lǎ̵   ɲìa   cĕŋ   tau

4. Hmong and   group Khmu   study PART cause they each   concern get

---

1. ꗵꗵ   ꖴꖰ   ꗱꕰ   ꕰ.

2. nyias li   moj   kuab.

3. ɲìa   li   mô   kúa

4. each   own   importance

'Shong Lue was a man who had no education from any foreign country, but was
educated by the Father. He knew everything in the universe that was created by
the Father. He also knew how to play the flute, the [mouth harp] and the bamboo pipes. And he knew how to create the Pahawh for the use of the Hmong
and the Khmu' people, so that they could preserve their own languages.'

—*Text and free translation from Vang et al. 1990: 38.*

Bibliography

Smalley, William A., Chia Koua Vang, and Gnia Yee Yang. 1990. *Mother of Writing: The Origin
    and Development of a Hmong Messianic Script.* Chicago: University of Chicago Press.
Vang Chia Koua, Gnia Yee Yang, and William A. Smalley. 1990. *The Life of Shong Lue Yang:
    Hmong "Mother of Writing" (Keeb Kwm Soob Lwj Yaj: Hmoob 'Niam Ntawv',* ꖰ ꖵ ꖽꗵ
    ꖵꖰ ꗃꖷ: ꖽꗵ "ꖰꖰ ꖷꗵ"), trans. Mitt Moua and Yang See (Southeast Asian Refugee Stud-
    ies Occasional Papers 9). Minneapolis: University of Minnesota, Center for Urban and Region-
    al Affairs.

Part X: Use and Adaptation of Scripts

THREE KINDS OF DIVERSIFICATION OF SCRIPTS—functional, religious, and political —can be observed at work in society. First to be treated in this Part is functional diversity, whereby new ways of using writing are devised as new needs arise.

Historically, the most common impetus for the adaptation of existing scripts to previously unwritten languages is the missionary impulse. The liturgy of Western (Roman) Christianity was conducted in Latin, whatever the vernacular of the community of worshipers, and it was the alphabet of Latin that was adapted for writing those vernacular languages. Contrast the situation in areas evangelized by Eastern (Greek, principally) Christianity, described in Part V, where worship was conducted in the vernacular, and alphabets based on or inspired by the Greek alphabet were devised for these languages. The sanctity of the Word in Judaism and Islam leads to a prohibition of translation—the faithful Jew and Muslim are expected to study Scripture in the original—and these People of the Book, too, more readily adapt the script of the sacred language for the vernacular, rather than devising one that seems to set aside the holy tradition.

In recent decades, in secular societies, it is politics rather than religion that has prompted the choice of script on which to base writing systems for new languages. Most notably, the Soviet Union undertook a vigorous campaign to bring Cyrillic script to dozens of unlettered nationalities, in a few cases decoupling languages of Islamic peoples from existing Arabic-based scripts, distancing them from coreligionists in the rest of the world—and in each case distancing them from First-World, Latin-script culture.

Contemporary Christian missionaries, who do most of the ongoing work on unwritten languages, are probably motivated more by practicality than by a sense of either a sacred script or a political purpose in nearly always devising Roman-based orthographies. Technology is best equipped for Roman-alphabet work; the IPA, which can be mined for additional letters as they are needed, is Roman-based.

— PETER T. DANIELS

625

A Functional Classification

JOHN MOUNTFORD

In any advanced literate society, a variety of different *writing systems* will be found in use—different writing systems for different languages, as well as different writing systems for one and the same language, distributed variously among intersecting groups with bilingual and monolingual members. In profiling the literacy of individuals (or of groups) in such a society, account must be taken not only of biliteracy, i.e. literacy in more than one language, but of bisystemacy, i.e. literacy in more than one writing system for any given language. Executives are rarely able to read the shorthand their secretaries write.

The basic sociolinguistic question here is: "Who uses which writing system to whom, in what context, and for what purpose?" Here the "whom" (in literacy even more than in oracy) may be undetermined and indefinitely numerous; or, at the other end of the scale, it may be no one other than the writer (addresser = addressee—the reporter's pad is usually read only by the reporter).

The purposes for which different writing systems are used, or designed to be used, served as the basis of a functional classification of writing systems proposed in Mountford 1973 as a contribution to library science (adopted and amplified in Wellisch 1978, see below). Libraries exist, historically, to store (and to make available!) written texts. Since all written texts, whether handwritten or machine-written, are in one (or more) language(s), and each language is realized in one (or more) writing system(s), writing systems were seen as a linguistic variable requiring principled attention in cataloguing and in bibliographical description. A functional classification by purpose was seen as theoretically independent of the structural classifications familiar in the historical study of writing and in linguistics.

Functional kinds of writing system

Five classes, or *functional kinds*, are distinguished: (i) orthographies, (ii) stenographies, (iii) cryptographies, (iv) pedographies, and (v) technographies.

(i) *Orthographies* are the vast majority of writing systems. They have, understandably and rightly, monopolized the attention of general historians of writing, and of students of writing in its many compartmentalized disciplines. These are the most elaborated kind of writing system: elaboration (see below) is a distinguishing feature of modern orthographies. The reason for this is the sheer versatility that a standard orthography (or, in Sampson's words, "the ordinary writing system of a society" [1985: 123]) must sustain in order to serve the multitudinous needs, from monumental to ephemeral, of modern economies and cultures over centuries of development. The only purposes which orthographies do not serve are those provided for by the four specialized functional kinds which follow.

(ii) *Stenographies*, or shorthands, have no particular precedence among the specialized kinds; but they provide a sharp contrast to orthographies, a contrast which is known to the general public, at least in the Western tradition (see SECTION 70). Stenographies are designed specifically so that they can be written faster than "the ordinary writing system"—fast enough to take down speech verbatim, whether by hand or machine. In decline since the advent of convenient sound-recording, shorthand is still an essential tool for some personnel in press-reporting, commercial and professional correspondence, court proceedings, etc., as well as being the preferred medium of composition for some individual professional writers (Bernard Shaw was a great advocate of Pitman's Shorthand for this purpose).

(iii) *Cryptographies* are similarly known, as "codes," to the layperson (if only by repute). These are designed to conceal what "the ordinary writing system" would reveal; they are routinely and extensively used in diplomatic and military communications and, increasingly, in industrial and commercial activity when secrecy is at a premium. Beside the institutionalized and highly sophisticated world of ciphers, there are the "secret codes" of private individuals (Bertrand Russell and Beatrix Potter are among those who have kept private journals in a writing system of their own invention).

(iv) *Pedographies* (cf. "pedagogical") are *systèmes d'apprentissage* designed for learners as stepping-stones to standard orthographies, whether of a first or of a second language. Less familiar now than in the decades from the 1880s to the 1960s, such writing systems were used, in Western education, in the teaching of "modern languages" (especially transcriptions using the IPA, to assist the acquisition of, typically, French pronunciation by English speakers); in teaching English as a foreign language; and in the teaching of initial literacy in English (notably the experiments with the Initial Teaching Alphabet [i.t.a.] in the United Kingdom and the United States in the 1960s). The needs of learners can be borne in mind in the design of new orthographies for unwritten languages; but the "ordinary writing systems" of many long-established standard languages contain traditional spelling systems which may well be user-friendly for some users, but which cannot be described as learner-friendly.

(v) *Technographies* are *systèmes de métier,* tools designed and used by linguists engaged in linguistic analysis (see Abercrombie 1967, Trager 1974, and SECTION 71). Their purpose is scientific: they were seen by Bloomfield in sharp contrast to "ordinary systems of writing," and this contrast is embodied in the controversy over "scientific" vs. "practical alphabets" which arose in the nineteenth century (Berry 1977, Venezky 1977). The commonest technographies are the systems of phonemic transcription used for particular languages in linguistic publications, but a great variety of such writing systems are employed for purposes ranging from phonetic fieldwork to the decipherment of texts in lost languages.

General-purpose versus special-purpose writing systems

The main thrust of the classification just outlined is to bring out the nature of "ordinary systems of writing" by contrasting them with non-ordinary ones. In a modern society, the standard languages in use are served by standard orthographies (much language planning is concerned with the creation, elaboration, and reform of orthographies), and a single orthographic writing system serves all institutionalized and individual activities which make use of writing. One institutionalized activity is education, and education systems have the job of imparting and developing literacy in the appropriate orthographies, which can be defined as general-purpose writing systems.

The other functional kinds are special-purpose writing systems, each of which is used, typically, *in addition to* an orthography. Letters, speeches, or dictated novels, taken down in shorthand, are "typed up" in orthography; enciphered text is deciphered into "plaintext," i.e. orthography. If children learn to read with a pedography, it is in order to graduate to "the ordinary system of writing"—for Chinese children, this may mean a roman-letter system as a stepping-stone to the traditional orthography based on characters. Finally, linguists' technographic texts are embedded in orthographic ones.

Terminology

In using *orthography* in this way (and not just as a synonym for "spelling"), account must be taken of a change in terminology in this field of linguistics. Bloomfield did not use the term *writing system* in his major work *Language* published in 1933; it did not become current until the 1950s, when it emerged as a specifically linguistic term, not borrowed from the existing disciplines concerned with the study of writing. Since then, it has steadily gained ground. For example, within linguistics, an early paper by David Abercrombie, "The Visual Symbolization of Speech," delivered at an International Shorthand Congress in 1937 and containing a functional classification in germ, was reprinted by him in 1965 retitled "Writing Systems." In the historical study of writing, I. J. Gelb's well-known book *The Study of Writing*, first published in 1952, did not contain the term *writing system*, but Gelb made use of it later in his article "Forms of writing" in the 1974 edition of the *Encyclopædia Britannica*. (Both book and article have since been superseded by works such as Sampson 1985 and Coulmas 1989, and by Olson 1988.)

The advantages to be derived from the term *writing system*, however, do not lie only in its role as a superordinate term in the above classification. It is equally well suited to fill the role of superordinate in a composition schema of whole and parts (cf. the dimensions of "range" and "scope" in Mountford 1990: 720).

———

The composition of writing systems in relation to function

Just as *orthography* can be desynonymized from *spelling*, so *writing system* can be desynonymized from *spelling system*. If we take the Standard Orthography of English (SOE), which is the matrix writing system of this volume, it is clear that it consists of a number of parts. These can be summarized as spelling, elaboration, and script.

In *spelling*, stenographies like Pitman's Shorthand, pedographies like i.t.a., and technographies on IPA principles all differ from SOE: they are "more phonemic." (i.t.a., being quasi-orthographic, reflected the spelling system of SOE by preserving some digraphs, and also in distinguishing some homonyms—a logographic property of many standard orthographies.) Cryptographies for English may also employ their own spelling systems, typically "more phonemic" ones, but the huge edifice of encipherment is built on forms of symbol substitution—originating in the schoolchild's B for A, C for B, etc. This does not change the spelling system at all (cf. Mountford 1990: 706): the changes are only at the level of script.

Elaboration is a cover term not only for all the resources (see Vachek 1989) of shape differentiation and spatial disposition, e.g. those deployed in this volume, but also for other significant components of orthographies which often get overlooked through concentration on spelling systems. In the case of SOE, these include punctuation, numeric, and other non-letter symbols—and, as an indexing device, crucial to information retrieval, an institutionalized alphabetical order. Systems of numeric symbols are integral to writing (children learn both their letters and their numbers in initial literacy): SOE has two at its disposal—Arabic and Roman, with roman vs. italic type and other contrasts available for both, and even upper and lower case for the latter. The special functional kinds do not require such resources. Of the features we take for granted in SOE, word spacing may be inimical to technographies and cryptographies, while case contrast is superfluous to stenographies and pedographies.

Third, and very briefly, *script*. The most obvious contrast between SOE and Pitman's Shorthand is not the spelling systems, but the visual difference between a Latin-letter script and a geometric script—just as the great systems of writing the world over are characterized by their distinctive scripts. The choice of script in different functional kinds may be variously motivated, e.g. by cursivity in a shorthand, by iconicity in a technography, and by political considerations in an orthography.

———

Multiplicity of writing systems

Many writing systems of all functional kinds, including spelling reformers' orthographies, have been used, or designed to be used, for English. A grammatological profile of other major languages will yield a similar plethora. Shorthands for Russian based on Cyrillic script, as well as on Pitman's script, give a tiny hint of the profusion of possible stenographies in the world: the same possibilities of multiple writing systems, based on domestic or borrowed scripts, exist for the other special-purpose functional kinds. The same is true, of course, for orthography—a cultural borrowing par excellence.

More functional kinds?

One informative study in which the proliferation of orthographic writing systems can be explored in terms of cultural borrowing is Hans Wellisch's *The Conversion of Scripts: Its Nature, History and Utilization* (1978), written from the viewpoint of library science. Wellisch starts by bringing the functional classification used above into the computer age with the addition of *machinographies*, designed for the (typically electronic) storage and transmission of texts. His ultimate object of study, however, is *transliteration* (and the interplay of script and spelling system) in application—a topic of importance to others besides librarians (cartographers, archivists, descriptive bibliographers, etc., as well as language scholars). Do transliterations constitute a functional kind ("convertographies"?) or is transliteration merely a means to an end in one or another of the proposed functional kinds? Wellisch accords it the latter, secondary, status. His work is a reminder that five, or six, functional kinds may not be exhaustive. Nor must they be thought of as mutually exclusive: technographies and pedographies overlap (see Abercrombie 1964); and Samuel Pepys, a skilled bisystemate writer of "tachygraphy" in the early heyday of English shorthand, must have taken comfort from the secrecy it bestowed on his *Diary*.

Conclusion

Crystal (1987: 194) has offered an interpretation of *technography* as "a system that enables a specialized field to perform its function, such as phonetic transcription, chemical notation, cartography, or computer coding." This is a different view of *technography* from the one adopted here, but Crystal's coverage of "Graphology," richly illustrated, is warmly recommended. Trager (1974) accords "Special writing systems" more attention than most linguists writing on graphology.

Bibliography

Abercrombie, David. 1937. "The Visual Symbolization of Speech." *Pitman's Business Education* 4: 689–90, 698. Repr., with a few omissions, as "Writing Systems" in his *Studies in Phonetics and Linguistics,* pp. 86–91. London: Oxford University Press, 1965.

———. 1964. *English Phonetic Texts.* London: Faber & Faber.

———. 1967. *Elements of General Phonetics.* Edinburgh: Edinburgh University Press.

Berry, Jack. 1977. "'The Making of Alphabets' Revisited." In Fishman 1977: 3–16.

Bloomfield, Leonard. 1933. *Language.* New York: Holt, Rinehart & Winston. British ed. London:

Allen & Unwin, 1935.

Butler, E. H. 1951. *The Story of British Shorthand.* London: Pitman.

Coulmas, Florian. 1989. *Writing Systems of the World.* Oxford: Blackwell.

Crystal, David. 1987. *The Cambridge Encyclopedia of Language.* Cambridge: Cambridge University Press.

Denning, Dorothy. 1982. *Cryptography and Data Security.* Reading, Mass.: Addison-Wesley.

Downing, John. 1967. *Evaluating the Initial Teaching Alphabet.* London: Cassell.

Fishman, Joshua A., ed. 1977. *Advances in the Creation and Revision of Writing Systems.* The Hague: Mouton.

Gelb, I. J. 1952. *A Study of Writing* (2nd ed., 1963). Chicago: University of Chicago Press.

———. 1974. "Writing, forms of." *Encyclopædia Britannica,* 15th ed., *Macropædia* 19:1033–45.

Kahn, David. 1967. *The Codebreakers: The Story of Secret Writing.* New York: Macmillan.

MacMahon, M. K. C. 1994. "Shorthand." In *The Encyclopedia of Language and Linguistics,* ed. R. E. Asher and J. M. Y. Simpson, pp. 3877–82. Oxford: Pergamon.

Mountford, John. 1973. "Writing-system: A Datum in Bibliographical Description." In *Toward a Theory of Librarianship: Papers in Honor of Jesse Hauk Shera,* ed. Conrad H. Rawski, pp. 415–49. Metuchen, N.J.: Scarecrow.

———. 1990. "Language and Writing-systems." In *An Encyclopaedia of Language,* ed. N. E. Collinge, pp. 701–39. London: Routledge.

Olson, David R. 1988. "Writing: The Nature and Origin of Writing." *Encyclopædia Britannica,* 15th ed. revised, 29:1025–34.

Pitman, James, and John St. John. 1969. *Alphabets and Reading: The Initial Teaching Alphabet.* London: Pitman.

Sampson, Geoffrey. 1985. *Writing Systems: A Linguistic Introduction.* London: Hutchinson.

Trager, George L. 1974. "Writing and Writing Systems." In *Current Trends in Linguistics,* ed. Thomas A. Sebeok, vol. 12, *Linguistics and Adjacent Arts and Sciences,* pp. 373–496. The Hague: Mouton.

Vachek, Josef. 1989. *Written Language Revisited,* selected, edited, and introduced by Philip A. Luelsdorff. Amsterdam: Benjamins, esp. "Some Remarks on the Stylistics of Written Language," pp. 43–52.

Venezky, Richard L. 1977. "Principles for the Design of Practical Writing Systems." In Fishman 1977: 37–54.

Wellisch, Hans. 1978. *The Conversion of Scripts: Its Nature, History and Utilization.* New York: Wiley.

Adaptations of the Roman Alphabet

Romance languages

EDWARD TUTTLE

Transition from Latin to early Romance

Among modern European languages, the Roman alphabet was most organically inherited by the neo-Latin vernaculars; but ease of transmission has also carried the handicap of culturally ordained, etymological accretions encumbering any trim, even semi-phonemic ideal. An enduring tension between functional denotation and varying amounts of connotative reminiscence—i.e., between optimal economy and clarity of representation and inertially prestigious, archaizing abstractions—has recurred since the primordial ninth-century attempts at Romance spelling. The graphemes of Late Antiquity were seamlessly transmitted by early Romance scribes who, as Wright (1982) has emphasized, merely endowed them with their own evolving phonic values. Before the ninth century, it seems that, as a diastratic or socially graded *sermo plebeius* 'common speech' was evolving into an ever more geographically diversified *rustica romana lingua* 'rustic Roman language', scant heed was paid to the divide between speech and writing. Then, however, efforts to reform and purify the resulting barbarous Latin (*latinum circa romancium*), especially in its oral liturgical role (e.g., Alcuin's *De Orthographia*) had as their result an awareness of Romance autonomy and, in consequence, of internal dialect diversity. Unconscious bilingualism (DeVoto's phrase, 1953) gave way to acknowledged diglossia, wherein the rustic code was forever sundered into regionally discrete varieties. Regional scripts arose by variously adapting graphs from common sources.

Lineal descent and internal realignment

Much of the new wine entered old bottles with little outward difficulty, local phonetic values being smoothly projected onto ancestral graphic correspondents. Instances of fusion admitted of easy resolution. Thus (following the convention that Classical and Vulgar Latin forms are printed in small capitals, while both reconstructions and attested Romance-language forms are in italics), -GN- had already merged with NJ as /ɲ/ = [ɲː] in Italo-Romance by the time laymen began to write, and it became the preferred unified digraph (IUNIU → Florence 1211 *giu(n)gn(i)u* → mod. *giugno* 'June', UĪNEA → *vin(g)nia* → *vigna* 'vineyard', on the model of *cogno* 'wedge' < CUNEU, *legno* 'firewood' < LIGNU, *pugno* 'fist' < PUGNU, *segno* 'sign' < SIGNU, etc.). In cases of phonemic split, however, ready linear accomodation left a gap that demanded some tinkering, and thus fostered diverse solutions. These are most conspicuous for the Romance palatalizations. E.g., Latin C [k] was fronted, affricated, and assibilated before front vowels (as [ʧ] or as [ts], i.e. merged in most areas with locally extant [ts] from TJ/CJ). Direct continuation of Latin spelling (CĒNA > *cena* 'supper', CENTU > *cento* 'hundred' vs. CANE > *cane* 'dog', CŌTE > *cote* 'whetstone') left no simple mode for representing [ke] and [ki]. Kappa, eschewed in Classical Latin for all but a few lexemes, was widely resuscitated from Italy to Iberia, only to be abandoned with the advent of Humanism. Q(U), transmitted by Classical Latin only in labiovelar contexts, could fill the breach where its vernacular simplification ($k^w > k$) was lexically well diffused. Thus we have Hispano-Romance *queso* 'cheese' [késo] < CASEU, *que* 'which' [ke] < QUID; this required a later *cu* for [k^w]: sixteenth-century *cuando* 'when' < QUANDO, and in tandem *gu* = [g] versus *gü* = [g^w]. But where, as in Italy, competing conservative pronunciations came to prevail, [k] before [e, i] required another representation, namely *ch* (cf. older, substandard *kando* replaced by *quando*, vs. *che* < QUID).

Treatment of empty vestiges

Latin H was silent; but in the Graeco-Latin rendering *ch* (for the aspirate χ 'chi'), it was revitalized in Italy to represent [ke/ki] (*chiedere* 'to ask' < QUÆRERE, analogously *ghe/ghi* = [ge/gi]) and even extended superfluously (*chasa* 'house' for *casa*). In most western dialects, this digraph was used for palatal /ʧ/, and thence it was extended in Old Provençal to palatalized L [ʎ] = *lh* and N [ɲ] = *nh*. In northernmost Spain, Galician imitators of the Provençal lyric established the palatalized triad *ch/lh/nh* for what was to become the Portuguese tradition.

Graphemes from external sources

Adapting Hellenisms, especially in the Christian period, led to the introduction of *z* (e.g., *baptizare* 'baptize'), which probably represented palatal [ʤ] or alveolo-dental [dz]/[z]. Its use flourished despite the admonitions of later grammarians, e.g. Isidore of Seville (ca. 560–636): "Although *tj* as in IUSTITIA ['justice'], MALITIA ['malice'], etc. represents the sound *z*, since the words are Latin [and not Greek-derived], they ought to be written with *t*" (1911, book I, chap. 27). Thence Christian transcribers of Germanic languages, without any orthographic precedents, utilized *cz* for [ts]. Bilingual monastic scriptoria favored transfer of *cz*; e.g., the *Eulalie* sequence (ca. 882), like the *Ludwigslied* associable with the St. Amand community, documents *czo* 'this' < *ecce hoc* and *canczons* 'songs' < CANTIONES. (Compare the more recent adaptation of German digraphs by Rumantsch writers in the Swiss Grisons; e.g. Engadine *cotschen* 'red' [kɔ́ʧən], Sursilvan *tgietschen* [tɕíəʧən] < COCCINU.) When scribally condensed as a ligature, the *cz* digraph was abbreviated ç.

Abbreviations as diacritics

To return to the palatalized sonant pair, Hispano-Romance [ʎ/ɲ] also derived from ambisyllabic or fortis LL and NN, and these sources provided their graphic representation. However, in the symbol ñ the tilde is no longer sensed as a second *n*. By Late Antiquity, scribal practice had spawned thousands of shorthand symbols and ligatures. Since the Carolingian reforms, such Tironian notes (Isidore attributed their systematization to a freeman of Cicero, Tirō; see SECTION 70) have been progressively suppressed. Besides the *titulus* (> *tilde*) just mentioned, only the subscript *zedilla* 'little *z*, "*zed*"' was pressed into orthophonic service. Fused with *c* to form *ç*, it represented Gallo-Romance and Spanish [ts] before non-front vowels, later [s] (and regionally [z] between vowels); it was imitated in Galego-Portuguese and, in the nineteenth century, utilized by Rumanian.

Collateral extension of the foregoing sources

As noted above, perceived phonetic affinities gave rise to graphic analogies and thus encouraged the extrapolation of paired or kindred spellings (e.g. It. *ch/gh*, Prov. *ch/lh/nh*). Beside *gn* = [ɲ], Florentine merchants developed *gl* = [ʎ] (*luglio*, var. *lulglio* 'July' < IULIU). Regarding such medieval variants, private mercantile and notarial usage provided a seedbed for hyperphonemic experiments (recall that Italian medial /ʎ/ and /ɲ/ are ambisyllabic, hence *lgl* and *ngn*). Silent reading arose only in the Renaissance and then only among an elite. Medieval writers "sounded out" their text at a slow tempo; thus, in a manner reminiscent of children, they were curiously faithful to sandhi phenomena and other subphonemic distinctions (e.g., Old Castilian *DonRramiro*, *honrra* 'honor', Old Florentine *centto* '100', *Dantte*).

Orthographic reforms

The advent of print, the public orthoepic medium par excellence, which favored analytic word-spacing as well as fixed phonologic lexical representation, tended to prune away such overly detailed allographs. The fixing of standards, given relative social stability within the literate caste, has prompted periodic movements to bring orthography back into step with pronunciation. Aside from Humanistic Latinate backtracking in Renaissance France, almost all such reforms aim at optimality or systematic clarity and economy.

Rumanian

The only massive reform in modern times has been that of Rumanian. Cut off in its Balkan isolation, Daco-Romance clove with its Slavic and Byzantine neighbors, in alphabet as in certain other areal linguistic affinities. For official and liturgical use, Middle Bulgarian (Slavic) supplanted Greek, after the tenth century (cf. Niculescu 1981). The earliest Rumanian documents adapt Cyrillic, e.g. a 1521 letter of the boyar Neacsu di Cîmpulung (< *CAMPU-LONGU). Venetian printing technology, arriving via Serbia, served to confirm Transylvanian Cyrillic, e.g. in a 1559 Orthodox catechism from Braşov (Brassó, Kronstadt, Oraşul Stalin), the response to a similar Protestant initiative (1544) now lost. A Protestant hymnal of 1570 represents a first attempt at transcription into the Roman alphabet, adapting Hungarian graphemes (*cz* [ts], *sz* [s], *s* [ʃ], *zs* [ʒ], etc.; see page 681). It was not until the nineteenth century that Italophile and Francophile intellectuals graphically reoriented Wallachia toward the Occident (cf. Close 1974, Onu 1989), although Moldavia (now Moldova) and Bessarabia remain anchored in the Cyrillic tradition. Thus the pioneer Transylvanian School introduced *j* [ʒ] *à la française* and the Italian opposition *c/g* = [tʃ/dʒ] versus *ch/gh* [k/g] before *i, e*, promptly accepted in Bucharest by Ion Heliade Radulescu (1802–1872), the arbiter of national culture. The Rumanian Academy's first standard (1869) was mildly etymologizing, the better to assert Latin ancestry, a key political rallying point; thus *di, si, ti/ci* rather than *j* [ʒ], *ş* [ʃ], *ci* [tʃ], and *â, ê, î, û* rather than neutralized *î* [ɨ] (symbolically, *român* 'Rumanian' still defies the phonetic principle [= *romîn*]). However, because of Heliade's enthusiasm for contemporary Franco-Italian civilization, the etymologizing tendency was less marked than in proposals of a generation before (e.g. *claue* for *cheie* 'key' (CLAUE), *glácie* for *gheaţa/ghiaţa* 'ice' (GLACIĒS), *lacte* for *lapte* 'milk' (LAC[TE])). Subsequent reforms, promoted largely by linguists and writers of democratic inclination—e.g. Titu Maiorescu (1840–1917), Alexandru Lambrior (1845–1883), and Hariton Tiktin (1850–1936)—aimed at greater phonologic economy and fidelity. Thus, by 1904, the Academy dispensed with final *-u* (*unu omu mortu* → *un om mort* 'a dead man'), acknowledged diphthongs and other vowel shifts (*mórte* 'death' → *moarte* 'death', *ómeni* → *oameni* 'men', *în tóta téra* → *în toata tara* 'throughout the land'), and abandoned morphemic criteria grounded on Latinate analogies (*stela/stele* → *steala/stele* 'star/stars'). Interbellum debate and the reform of 1932 are associated with Ovid Densusianu (1873–1938) and Sextil Puscariu (1877–1948), that of 1953 with Alexandru Rosetti (1895–1989).

Contemporary orthography

TABLE 59.1 shows the phonological correspondences with letters of the Roman alphabet (including diacritics, as well as digraphs and trigraphs) in the principal modern Romance languages. The grave accent mark in Italian, and the acute in Spanish, indicate word accent only; the asterisk (*) is a reminder of this. Accent marks in Portuguese and Catalan may indicate combinations of word stress and vowel quality; in French and Rumanian, they refer mainly to vowel quality.

Conventions used in TABLES 59.1 and 59.4: Only the most general and regular values are indicated; many exceptions are neglected. The symbol "/ __" means 'preceding …'; $ is syllable boundary; C is consonant; V is vowel; I is any front vowel. A comma between phonetic values indicates that contrasting sounds are written with the same letter; the symbol ~ indicates that phonetic variants are in predictable distribution.

TABLE 59.1: *Values of Letters in Standard Romance Languages*

	Italian	Spanish	Portuguese	Catalan	French	Rumanian
a	[a]	[a]	[á; ɐ]	[á; ə]	[a, ɑ]	[a]
ãe			[ɜ̃ɪ̯̃]			
ai	[ai]	[ai]	[ai]	[ai]	[ɛ]	[ai]
ain /__$					[ɛ̃]	
an /__$					[ã]	
ão			[ɜ̃ũ̯]			
au	[au]	[au]	[au]	[au]	[o]	[au]
â		[ə]			[ɑ]	[ɨ]
ă						[ə]
ã			[ã]			
b	[b]	[b ~ β]	[b]	[b ~ β]	[b]	[b]
c /__i, e	[tʃ]	[θ] (Am. [s])	[s]	[s]	[s]	[tʃ]
c (elsewh.)	[k]	[k]	[k]	[k]	[k]	[k]
ch	[k] /__i, e	[tʃ]	[ʃ]	[k] (rare)	[ʃ]	[k] /__i, e
ç			[s] /__i, e	[s] /__i, e	[s] /__i, e	
d	[d]	[d ~ ð]	[d]	[d ~ ð]	[d]	[d]
e	[e, ɛ]	[e]	[é, ɛ́; i]	[é, ɛ́; ə]	[e, ɛ, ə]	[e]
è	*			[ɛ́]	[ɛ]	
ê			[é]		[ɛ]	
é		*	[ɛ́]	[é]	[e]	
eau					[o]	
ei	[ei]	[ei]	[ei]	[ei]	[ɛ]	[ei]
ein /__$					[ɛ̃]	
en /__$					[ã]	
eu	[eu]	[eu]	[eu]	[eu]	[ø, œ]	[eu]
f	[f]	[f]	[f]	[f]	[f]	[f]
g /__i, e	[dʒ]	[χ]	[ʒ]	[dʒ ~ ʒ]	[ʒ]	[dʒ]
g (elsewh.)	[g]	[g ~ ɣ]	[g]	[ɣ ~ ɡ]	[g]	[ɡ]
gh	[g] /__i, e					[g] /__i, e
gl	[ʎ(ː)]					
gn	[ɲ(ː)]				[ɲ]	
gu /__i, e	[gw]	[g]	[g]	[g]	[g]	[gw]
gu (elsewh.)	[gw]	[gw]	[gw]	[gw]		[gw]
gü		[gw]	[gw]	[gw]		
h	Ø	Ø	Ø	Ø	Ø	[h]
i	[i̯] /__V, [i] elsewh.	[i̯] /__V, [i] elsewh.	[i̯] /__V, [i] elsewh.	[i̯] /__V, [i] elsewh.	[i̯] /__V, [i] elsewh.	[i̯] /__V, [i] elsewh.
î					[i]	[ɨ]
j		[χ]	[ʒ]	[dʒ ~ ʒ]	[ʒ]	[ʒ]
k (in loans)	[k]	[k]	[k]	[k]	[k]	[k]

TABLE 59.1: *Values of Letters in Standard Romance Languages (Continued)*

	Italian	Spanish	Portuguese	Catalan	French	Rumanian
l	[l]	[l]	[l]	[l]	[l]	[l]
lh			[ʎ]			
ll		[ʎ] (Am. [j])		[ʎ]		
l.l				[l]		
m	[m]	[m]	[m]	[m]	[m]	[m]
n	[n]	[n]	[n]	[n]	[n]	[n]
nh			[ɲ]			
ñ		[ɲ]		[ɲ]		
o	[o, ɔ]	[o]	[ó, ɔ́; u]	[ó, ɔ́; u]	[o, ɔ]	[o]
ò	*			[ɔ́]		
ô			[ó]		[o]	
ó		*	[ɔ́]	[ó]		
õ			[õ]			
õe			[õĩ̯]			
œ(u)					[œ]	
oi	[oi]	[oi]	[oi]	[oi]	[wa]	[oi]
on /__$					[ɔ̃]	
ou			[ou]		[w] /__V, [u] elsewh.	
p	[p]	[p]	[p]	[p]	[p]	[p]
qu /__i, e	[kw]	[k]	[k]	[k]	[k]	
qu (elsewh.)	[kw]				[k]	
r	[r]	[r: ~ ɾ]	[r: ~ ɾ]	[r: ~ ɾ]	[ʁ]	[r]
rr		[r:]	[r:] (Am. [χ])	[r:]		
s	[s ~ z]	[s]	[ʃ] /__$, [s ~ z] elsewh.	[s ~ z]	[s ~ z]	[s]
ss			[s]	[s]		
ş						[ʃ]
t	[t]	[t]	[t]	[t]	[t]	[t]
ţ						[ts]
u	[u̯] /__V, [u] elsewh.	[u̯] /__V, [u] elsewh.	[u̯] /__V, [u] elsewh.	[u̯] /__V, [u] elsewh.	[ɥ] /__V, [y] elsewh.	[u̯] /__V, [u] elsewh.
un /__$					[œ̃]	
v	[v]	[b ~ β]	[v]	[b ~ β]	[v]	[v]
w (in loans)	[v, w]	[w]	[v, w]	[w]	[v, w]	[v, w]
x	[ks]	[ks]	[ʃ, ks]	[ʃ, ks]	[ks]	[ks]
y (mainly in loans, except in Spanish)	[j]	[i] /__#, [j] elsewh.	[j]	[j]	[i, j]	[j]
z	[ts, dz]	[θ] (Am. [s])	[z]	[z]	[z]	[z]

SAMPLES OF ROMANCE LANGUAGES: THE TOWER OF BABEL

ITALIAN

1. *Italian:*   E   il   Signore disse,   Ecco   un   medesimo popolo, ed
2. *Transcription:* e   l̦   siɲóre dísse   ékko   un   medézimo pópolo ed
3. *Gloss:*   and the lord   said   here.is one   same   people and

1. essi tutti hanno un   medesimo linguaggio. … Orsù,   scendiamo,
2. éssi tútti ánno   un   medézimo liŋguáddʒo   orsú   ʃendi̦ámo
3. they all   have   one   same   language   now.then   let.us.descend

1. e   confondiamo quivi la   lor   favella; sicché l'uno   non   capisca
2. e   konfondi̦ámo ku̦ívi la   lor   favélla sikké   lúno   non   kapíska
3. and   let.us.confuse here the their speech   so.that the.one not   understand

1. il   parlare   dell'altro. … Così l'Eterno   li   disperse di   là   sulla
2. il   parláre   dell-áltro   kozí l-etérno   li   dispérse di   lá   sulla
3. the   speaking of.the-other   thus the-eternal them scattered from there on.the

1. faccia di tutta la   terra. … Perciò a   questa fu   dato il   nome   di
2. fáttʃa di tútta la   térra   pertʃɔ̀ a   ku̦ésta fu   dáto il   nóme   di
3. face   of all   the earth   therefore to this   was   given the name   of

1. Babel, perché   l'Eterno   confuse   quivi   il   linguaggio.
2. babél perké   letérno   konfúze   ku̦ívi   l̦   liŋgu̦áddʒo
3. Babel because the.eternal confused here   the language

SPANISH (CONTINENTAL)

1. *Spanish:*   Y   se   dijo: "He   aquí un pueblo uno, tienen   todos
2. *Transcription:* i   se   ðíχo e   akí um pu̦éβlo úno ti̦énen   tóðos
3. *Gloss:*   and self said behold here a   people one they.have all

1. una lengua   sola. … Bajemos,   pues, y   confundamos su   lengua,
2. úna léŋgua   sóla   baχémos   pu̦es i   konfundámos su   léŋgua
3. a   language alone   let's.descend then and let's.confuse their language

1. de modo   que   no   se   entiendan   unos a   otros." Y
2. de móðo   ke   no   se   enti̦éndan   únos a   ótros   i
3. of manner that not   self they.may.understand   ones to   others and

1. los dispersó   de   allí Yavé   por   toda la   haz de   la tierra.
2. loz ðispersó   ðe   aʎí jaβé   por   tóða la   aθ   ðe   la ti̦érːa
3. them scattered from there LORD   through all   the face of   the earth

1. ... Por   eso   se   llamó   Babel,   porque allí   confundió Yavé   la
2. por   éso   se   ʎamó   βaβél   porke   aʎí   konfundi̯ó jaβé   la
3. through that   self   called   Babel   because there confused   Yahweh the

1. lengua   de   la   tierra   toda. ...
2. léŋgu̯a   ðe   la   ti̯ér:a   tóða
3. language of   the   earth   all

FRENCH

1. French: Et   l'Éternel   dit: Voici,   ce n'est   qu'un seul et   même
2. Transcription: e   leteʁnel   di   vwasi   sə nɛ   kœ̃   sœl   e   mɛm
3. Gloss: and   the.eternal said   behold   it is.not   but.a   sole   and same

1. peuple: ils   ont   un   même   langage ... Venez   donc, descendons,   et
2. pœpl   ilz   ɔ̃   œ̃   mɛm   lãgaʒ   vəne   dɔk   desãdɔ̃   e
3. people   they have one   same   language   come   then   let's.descend and

1. confondons   là   leur   langage,   afin   qu'ils   n'entendent   point
2. kɔ̃fɔ̃dɔ̃   la   lœʁ   lãgaʒ   afɛ̃   kil   nãtãd   pwɛ̃
3. let's.confuse   there their   language   in.order that.they   not.understand   at.all

1. le   langage   l'un   de   l'autre.   Ainsi l'Éternel   les   dispersa de   là
2. lə   lãgaʒ   lœ̃   də   lotʁ   ɛ̃si   leteʁnel   le   dispeʁsa də   la
3. the   language the.one of   the.other   thus   the.eternal them scattered from there

1. par   toute la   terre. ... C'est   pourquoi   son   nom fut   appelé Babel; car
2. paʁ   tut   la   tɛʁ   sɛ   puʁkwa   sɔ̃   nɔ̃   fy   aple   babɛl kaʁ
3. through all   the earth   that.is why   its   name was   called Babel for

1. l'Éternel   y   confondit le   langage   de   toute la   terre. ...
2. leteʁnel   i   kɔ̃fɔ̃di   lə   lãgaʒ   də   tut   la   tɛʁ
3. the.eternal there confused   the   language of   all   the   earth

PORTUGUESE (SÃO PAULO, BRAZIL)

1. Portuguese: Eis   aqui   um   povo,   que   não   tem   senão
2. Transcription: ei̯z   a'ki   ũ   'povu   ki   nɔ̃ũ̯ tẽi̯   si'nɔ̃ũ̯
3. Gloss: here.is here   a   people that   not   has   but

1. una   mesma   linguagem; ...   Vinde   pois,   desçamos,   e
2. 'umə   'mezmə   lĩ'gwaʒẽi̯   'vĩdi   poi̯s   de'səmus   i
3. a   same   language   come   then   let's.descend   and

1. ponhamos   nas   suas   línguas   tal   confusão,   que   êles
2. po'ɲəmuz   nas   'suəz   'lĩgwəs   tau̯   kõfu'zɔ̃ũ̯   ki   'elis
3. let's.put   in.the   their   languages such   confusion   that   they

1. se	não	entendam	uns	aos	outros.	Desta	maneira	é
2. si	nə̃ũ̯	ĩ'tẽdə̃ũ̯	ũz	au̯z	'ou̯trus	'dɛstə	ma'nei̯rə	ɛ
3. REFL	not	understand	ones	to.the	others	of.this	manner	is

1. que	o	Senhor	os	espalhou	daquele	lugar	para	todos
2. ki	u	se'ɲor:	uz	ispa'ʎou̯	da'keli	lu'gar:	parə	'toduz
3. that	the	Lord	them	scattered	from.that	place	to	all

1. os	países	da	terra ...	E	por	esta	razão é	que lhe
2. us	pa'iziz	da	'tɛr:ə	i	por	'ɛstə	r:a'zə̃ũ̯ ɛ	ki ʎi
3. the	lands	of	earth	and	for	this	reason is	that to.it

1. foi	pôsto	o	nome	de	Babel,	porque	nela é	que sucedeu
2. foi̯	'postu	u	'nomi	di	ba'bɛu̯	purki	'nɛlə ɛ	ki suse'deu̯
3. was	placed	the	name	of	Babel	because	in.it is	that happened

1. a	confusão	de	tôdas	as	linguas	do	mundo.
2. ɑ	kõfuzə̃ũ̯	di	'todəz	az	'lĩgwəz	du	'mũdu
3. the confusion	of	all	the	languages	of.the world

ACKNOWLEDGMENT: The editors would like to thank Prof. Milton Azevedo for his assistance.

RUMANIAN

prepared by KOSTAS KAZAZIS

1. Rumanian:	Şi	Domnul	a	zis:	„Iată,	ei	sînt	un	singur
2. Transcription:	ʃi	'domnul	ɑ	zis	'jatə	jei̯	sɨnt	un	'siŋgur
3. Gloss:	and	Lord.the	has	said	behold	they	are	one	single

1. popor,	şi	toţi	au	aceeaş	limbă; ...	Haidem!	să Ne
2. po'por	ʃi	'totsʲ	au̯	a'tʃejaʃ	'limbə	'hai̯dem	sə ne
3. people	and	all	have	the.same	language	let.us	that us

1. pogorîm	şi	să	le	încurcăm	acolo	limba,	ca
2. pogo'rɨm	ʃi	sə	le	iŋkur'kəm	a'kolo	'limbu	ku
3. we.descend	and	that	to.them	we.confuse	there	language.the	in.order

1. să	nu-şi	mai	înţeleagă	vorba	unii
2. sə	nuʃ	mai̯	intse'lɛagə	'vorbɑ	'uni
3. that	not-to.them	any.more	they.understand.SUBJ	word.the	the.ones

1. altora." ...	Şi	Domnul	i-a	împrăştiat	de	acolo pe
2. 'altora	ʃi	'domnul	ja	imprəʃ'tjat	de	a'kolo pe
3. of.the.others	and	Lord.the	them-has	scattered	from	there on

1. toată	faţa	pămîntului;	De aceea	cetatea a	fost	numită Babel,
2. 'tɔatə	'fatsa	pə'mɨntului̯	de a'tʃeja	tʃe'tatɛa ɑ	fost	nu'mitə ba'bel
3. all	face.the	earth.of.the	therefore	city.the has	been	named Babel

1. căci	acolo	a	încurcat	Domnul	limba	întregului
2. kətʃ	a'kolo	a	iŋkur'kat	'domnul	'limba	ɨn'tregului̯
3. because	there	has	confused	Lord.the	language.the	entire.of.the

1. pămînt, şi	de	acolo	i-a	împrăştiat	Domnul	pe	toată
2. pə'mɨnt ʃi	de	a'kolo	ja	imprəʃ'tjat	'domnul	pe	'to̯atə
3. earth	and	from	there	them-has	scattered	Lord.the	on	all

1. faţa	pămîntului.
2. 'fatsa	pə'mɨntului̯
3. face.the	earth.of.the

> 'And the LORD said, Behold, the people is one, and they have all one language. ... Go to, let us go down, and there confound their language, that they may not understand one another's speech. So the LORD scattered them abroad from thence upon the face of all the earth. ... Therefore is the name of it called Babel; because the LORD did there confound the language of all the earth.'
>
> *—Genesis 11:6–9 (Authorized Version, 1611).*

Germanic languages

WAYNE M. SENNER

The Germanic languages are traditionally classified into three branches. The Eastern branch consists of Gothic, now extinct (SECTION 22). West Germanic includes Old English, with its English descendants; Old Saxon, with its descendant Dutch; and Old High German, with its Middle and New High German descendants. North Germanic has a Western (Scandinavian) branch, including Norwegian and Icelandic, and an Eastern branch, which includes Swedish and Danish.

German

The adaptation of Roman script to German has historically been complicated by the lack of a standard language and a dialectal hodgepodge of orthographies which in some cases existed from the Carolingian period until the late eighteenth century.

Two profound linguistic changes further conditioned the adaptation of the Latin alphabet. The first was vowel mutation (umlaut), an assimilatory process by which a following unstressed front vowel caused the fronting of a preceding, stressed back vowel. This feature, shown in TABLE 59.2, is also found in North Germanic languages. Standardization of the umlaut dots for mutated vowels (e.g. *ü*) was not achieved until the New High German period.

My gratitude to my colleagues for their critical comments and suggestions: Jesse Byock of UCLA, Daniel Brink and Marit Carlsen of Arizona State University, and Jan Sjåvik of the University of Washington.

TABLE 59.2: *Vowel Mutation in Old, Middle, and New High German*

OHG gast (sg.)	OHG gesti (pl.)	NHG Gäste	'guests'
OHG fuoren	MHG füeren	NHG führen	'to lead'
OHG sconi	MHG schoene	NHG schön	'beautiful'
OHG gabi	MHG gaebe	NHG gäbe	'would give'
OHG husir	MHG huiser	NHG Häuser	'houses'

TABLE 59.3: *OHG Consonant Shift: p, t, k*

Old Norse	Mod. Norweg.	OHG	NHG	
planta	plante	phlanza	Pflanze	'plant'
hjálpa	hjelpe	helphan	helfen	'to help'
tíu	ti	zëhan	zehn	'ten'
bíta	bite	beizan	beißen	'to bite'
bók	bok	buoh	Buch	'book'

The second change was the OHG consonant shift, which distinguishes German from the other Germanic languages. It involved the voiceless stops *p, t, k*, which in most cases became fricatives in syllable-final and affricates in syllable-initial position, as shown in TABLE 59.3.

In the twentieth century, orthography was standardized in Germany, Austria, and Switzerland and is based on the authority of *Dudens Rechtschreibung*. The NHG and other modern Germanic alphabets are shown in TABLE 59.4 (see conventions on page 636).

In spite of the authority of Duden, German orthography does not have a separate symbol for each structurally significant class of sounds in the language. The following represent some of the major complications in the orthographic system.

First, consonantal doubling after vowels indicates vowel shortness: *Betten* ['bɛtn̩] 'beds', *beten* ['beːtn̩] 'to pray'. However, it is not used in a large number of short function words: *Mann* [man] 'man', *man* [mɑn] 'one'.

Second, German avoids homography for homophonous words: [moːr] *Mohr* 'Moor', *Moor* 'moor'; [heːr] *her* 'hither', *hehr* 'exalted', *Heer* 'army'; [maːlən] *malen* 'to paint', *mahlen* 'to grind'.

Third, German retains the historical and etymological pairs *e* and *ä* for [eː, ɛ], *eu* and *äu* for [ɔj], *ie* and *i* for [i], *ü* and *y* for [y]: [ɛ] *Enge* 'narrowness', *Länge* 'length'; [ɔj] *heute* 'today', *läuft* 'runs'; [i] *Liebe* 'love', *Stil* 'style'; [y] *üben* 'to practice', *lyrisch* 'lyrical'.

Fourth, some phonemes are represented by various spellings: [k] by *k* in *Kind* 'child', *ck* in *decken* 'to cover', *q* before *u* in *Quelle* 'source', *ch* before *s* in *wachsen* 'to grow'; [ç] by *ch* in *ich* 'I', *g* after *i* in *mächtig* 'mighty'.

Fifth, voiced obstruents *b, d, g, v, s,* and *g* are devoiced at the end of syllables (TABLE 59.5).

TABLE 59.4: *Values of Letters in Standard Germanic Languages*

	German	Dutch	Icelandic	Norwegian (bokmål)
a	[a, aː]	[a, ɑ]	[a]	[ɑ]
á	–	–	[au̯]	–
ä	[ɛ, eː]	–	–	–
å	–	–	–	[ɔ]
aa	[aː]	[a]	–	–
aai	–	[aːi̯]	–	–
au	[au̯]	–	[øɥ]	[æʉ̯]
äu	[ɔi̯]	–	–	–
auw	–	[ɔu̯]	–	–
ay	[ai̯]	–	–	–
æ	–	–	[ai̯]	[ɛ, æ]
b	[p] /__$	[p] /__$	[b̥]	[b]
	[b] elsewh.	[b] elsewh.		
ch	[ç] /I, C__	[x]	–	–
	[x] elsewh.			
ck	[k][a]	–	–	–
d	[t] /__$	[t] /__$	[d̥]	[d]
	[d] elsewh.	[d] elsewh.		
ds	[dz] (in loans)	–	–	–
dsch	[dʒ] (in loans)	–	–	–
ð	–	–	[ð]	–
e	[ɛ, eː], [ə] unacc.	[e, ɛ], [ə] unacc.	[ɛ]	[e, ɛ, æ], [ə] unacc.
ee	[eː]	[e]	–	
eg	–	–	–	[æi̯]
eeuw	–	[eːu̯]	–	–
ei	[ai̯]	[ɛi̯]	[ei̯]	[æi̯]
er	[ɐ] unacc.			
eu	[ɔi̯]	[ø]	–	–
ey	–	–	[ei̯]	–
f	[f]	[f]	[f, v]	[f]
g	[ç] /I__$, [ʒ] in loans,	[x] /__$	[gj] /__I, [x] /__{l,	[j] /__I
	[k] /__$, [g] elsewh.	[ɣ] elsewh.	s}, [ɣ] /V__V, [g]	[g] elsewh.
h	[ː] /V__; [h] elsewh.	[h]	[h]	[h]
hj	–	–	[ç]	
i	[ɪ, iː]	[i, ɪ]	[ɪ]	[i]
í	–	–	[ii̯]	–
ie	[iː]	[i]	–	–
ieuw	–	[iːu]	–	–
ij	–	[ɛi̯]	–	–
j	[j], [ʒ] in loans	[j]	[j]	–
k	[k]	[k]	[kj] /__I	[ç] /__I
			[k] elsewh.	[k] elsewh.
kk	–	–	[ʰkj] /__I	–
			[ʰk] elsewh.	
l	[l]	[l ~ ɫ]	[l]	[l]
m	[m]	[m]	[m]	[m]
n	[n]	[n]	[n]	[n]

TABLE 59.4: *Values of Letters in Standard Germanic Languages (Continued)*

	German	Dutch	Icelandic	Norwegian (bokmål)
ng	[ŋ]	[ŋ]	[ŋ]	[ŋ]
nj	–	[ɲ]	–	–
o	[ɔ, oː]	[ɔ, oː]	[ɔ]	[o, ɔ]
ó	–	–	[ou̯]	–
ö	[œ, øː]	–	[ø]	–
ø	–	–	–	[ø]
oe	–	[u]	–	–
øg	–	–	–	[øɥ]
øy	–	–	–	[øɥ]
oo	[oː]	[o]	–	–
ooi	–	[oːi̯]	–	–
ou	–	[ɔu̯]	–	–
p	[p]	[p]	[p]	[p]
pf	[pf]	[f]	–	–
ph	[f] (in loans)	–	–	–
pp	–	–	[ʰp]	–
qu	[kv] (in loans)	–	–	–
r	[r ~ ʀ ~ ʁ], [ɐ] /V__	[r, ʁ]	[r]	rd, rl, rn, rs, rt: retro- flex dental [ɖ, ɭ, ɳ, ʂ, ʈ]; [r, ʀ] elsewh.
s	[z] /V__V, [ʃ] /__{t, p} [s] elsewh.	[s]	[s]	[s]
sch	[ʃ]	–	–	–
sj	–	[ʃ]	–	[ʃ] /__I
sk	–	–	–	[ʃ] /__I
ß (ss)	[s]	–	–	–
t	[t]	[t]	[t]	[t]
tj	–	[tʲ]	–	–
ts	[ts]	–	–	–
tsch	[t͡ʃ] (in loans)	–	–	–
tt	–	–	[ʰt]	–
þ	–	–	[θ]	–
u	[uː, ʊ]	[y, ʏ]	[ʏ]	[ʉ, ɵ]
ú	–	–	[uu̯]	–
ü	[ʏ, yː]	–	–	–
ui	–	[œɥ]	–	–
uu	–	[y]	–	–
uw	–	[yːu̯]	–	–
v	[f], in loans [v]	[v]	[v]	[v]
w	[v]	[ʋ]	–	–
y	[ʏ, yː]	–	[ɪ]	[y]
ý	–	–	[ii̯]	–
z	[ts]	[z]	–	[z]

a. When a word divides at *ck*, *-k-* ends the first line and *k-* begins the second.

TABLE 59.5: *Obstruent Devoicing*

	Non-final			Syllable-final	
Liebe	[li:bə]	'love'	lieblich	[li:plɪç]	'lovely'
Tode	[to:də]	'deaths'	Tod	[to:t]	'death'
Tage	[ta:gə]	'days'	Tag	[ta:k]	'day'
brave	[bra:və]	pl. 'honest'	brav	¡bra:f]	sg. 'honest'
beiges	[be:ʒəs]	sg.neut. 'beige'	beige	[be:ʃ]	undecl. 'beige'
Felsen	[fɛlzn̩]	'rock'	Fels	[fɛls]	'rock'

Orthographic inconsistencies are particularly evident for the voiceless sibilant [ʃ]: *Sch Schnee* 'snow', *S+t Stuhl* 'chair', *S+p Spiel* 'game', *Ch Chance* 'chance', *Sh Shorts* 'shorts', *Sc Crescendo* 'crescendo'.

Finally, although NHG has generally replaced *Fraktur*, known in English as Gothic script, with the Roman script (see SECTION 63), the fourteenth-century ligature *ß* [s], a substitute for the older *sz*, has been retained when word-final or preconsonantal, and after a long vowel: *Haß* [ha:s] 'hatred', *haßt* [hast] 'hates', *Buße* [bu:sə] 'repentance' (cf. *s* [z] in *Busen* [bu:zen] 'breast'). The sole example of words differentiated only by *ss/ß* is *Masse* ['masə] 'crowd' versus *Maße* ['ma:sə] 'measures'.

SAMPLE OF GERMAN

1. German:	Das	Wort	„deutsch"	erschien	zuerst		in	der
2. Transcription:	das	vɔʁt	dɔjtʃ	ʔɛʁˈʃi:n	tsu:-ˈʔe:ʁst		ʔɪn	deʁ
3. Gloss:	the	word	"deutsch"	appeared	to-first		in	the

1. lateinischen	Schriftsprache	als	„theodiscus"	und	bedeutete
2. laˈtaɪnɪʃn̩	ˈʃʁift-ʃpʁa:xə	als	teoˈdɪskus	ʔunt	bəˈdɔɪtətə
3. Latin	writing-language	as	"theodiscus"	and	meant

1. ursprünglich	etwa	„zum	Volk	gehörig"	und	bezog	sich
2. ʔu:ʁ̩ˈʃpʁʏŋlɪç	ˈʔetva:	tsum	fɔlk	gəˈhø:ʁɪç	ʔunt	bəˈtso:k	zɪç
3. originally	somewhat	"to.the	folk	belonging"	and	referred	self

1. im	frühen	Mittelalter	zuerst	nicht	auf	das	Land,	sondern
2. ʔɪm	ˈfʁy:ən	ˈmɪtl̩-ʔaltɐ	tsu:-ˈʔeʁst	nɪçt	auf	das	lant	ˈzɔndɐn
3. in.the	early	middle-age	to-first	not	on	the	country	but

1. auf	die	Volkssprache,	im	Gegensatz	sowohl	zum	Latein	der
2. auf	di:	ˈfɔlks-ʃpʁa:xə	ʔɪm	ˈge:gn̩zats	zoˈvo:l	tsum	laˈtaɪn	deʁ
3. on	the	people-language	in.the	contrast	in.fact	to.the	Latin	of.the

1. Gelehrten	als	auch	zum	„Walhisk"	(„Welsch")	der	romanischen
2. gəˈle:ʁtn̩	als	aux	tsum	ˈva:lɪsk	vɛlʃ	deʁ	roˈma:nɪʃn̩
3. educated	as	also	to.the		foreign	of.the	Romance

1. oder	romanisierten	Nachbarn	im	Fränkischen	Reich.
2. 'o:dɐ	ʁoma:nɪ'zi:ɐ̯tn̩	'na:xba:ɐ̯-n	ɪm	'fʁɛŋkɪʃn̩	raiç
3. or	Romanized	neighbor-s	in.the	Franconian	kingdom

'The word "German" appeared first in written Latin as *theodiscus* and originally meant something like 'in the vernacular' and in the early Middle Ages at first did not refer to the country but to the language of the people in contrast both to the Latin of scholars as well as to "Walhish" ('foreign tongue') of the Romance or Romanized neighbors in the Franconian kingdom.'   *—Bach 1965: 144.*

Dutch and Afrikaans

Dutch is the oldest name for the language; the English word comes from *Duutsc*, which ultimately derives from the Latin *theodiscus*, also the source for *Deutsch* 'German'. Although Dutch is historically closely related to Low German, favorable economic and cultural conditions helped entrench the language and prevent it from yielding to the advance of High German, as Low German did. Afrikaans arose within two generations after a seventeenth-century party of Dutch established a colony at the Cape of Good Hope. The drastic modifications of the spoken language (e.g. loss of inflections) probably were caused by the use of pidgin with non-European slaves. By the third decade of the twentieth century, Afrikaans had supplanted Dutch as an official language in South Africa.

Long vowels are "overlong" before *-r*. Single vowels in Dutch are short in closed syllables and before double consonants. In closed syllables long vowels are doubled. There are a few additional features that complicate the orthography and pronunciation of Dutch. Written consonants are doubled in polysyllabic words after a short vowel: *pil* [pɪl] 'pill', *pillen* ['pɪlən] (pl.); *bus* [bʏs] 'bus', *bussen* ['bʏsən] (pl.). Written double vowels are simplified in polysyllabic words but retain their length: *laan* [la:n] 'avenue', *lanen* ['la:nən] (pl.); *boom* [bo:m] 'tree', *bomen* ['bo:mən] (pl.). Clusters of consonants are entirely voiced or voiceless, with stops controlling spirants: *hoofden* ['ho:vdən] 'heads'; *ijsbreker* ['ɛiz,brɛkər] 'icebreaker'. In stop clusters, voicing dominates, but in spirant clusters voicelessness is dominant: *uitbreiden* ['œyd,brɛidən] 'to expand'; *afzetten* ['af,sɛtən] 'to take off'. At the end of a syllable *d* is unvoiced and between vowels frequently disappears: *oud* [ɔu̯t] 'old', *oude* ['ɔu̯də] (masc.); *goede* ['ɣu:jə] 'good'.

SAMPLE OF DUTCH

1. Dutch:	Er	worden	in	Nederland	naast	het	beschaafde
2. Transcription:	ɛr	'ʋordən	ɪn	'ne:dər,lant	'na:st	hɛt	bə'sxa:vdə
3. Gloss:	there	are	in	Netherlands	next.to	the	cultivated

1. Nederlands   een   groot   aantal   dialecten   gesproken.   In   de
2. 'neːdər.lɑnts   eːn   'ɣroːt   'aːntɑl   diːaː'lɛktən   ɣə'sproːkən   ɪn   də
3. Dutch   a   large   number dialects   spoken   in   the

1. gemeenschap waarin   het   gangbaar   is,   doet   een   dialect   als
2. ɣə'meːnsxɑp ʋaː'rɪn   hɛt   'ɣɑŋbaːr   ɪs   'duːt   eːn   diːaː'lɛkt   ɑls
3. communities wherein   it   current   is   does   a   dialect   as

1. communicatiemiddel   niet   onder   voor   het   beschaafde   Nederlands.
2. kɔmyːnɪ'katsiː-,mɪdəl   niːt   'ɔndər   voːr   hɛt   bə'sxaːvdə   'neːdər,lɑnts
3. communication-means   not   under   before   the   cultivated   Dutch

1. De   dialectklanken   zijn   op   zichzelf   ook   niet   minder   mooi
2. də   diːaː'lɛkt-,klɑŋkə   zei̯n   ɔp   zɪx'sɛlf   'oːk   'niːt   'mɪndər   moːi̯
3. the   dialect-sounds   are   on   themselves   also   not   less   beautiful

1. dan   die   van   het   beschaafde   Nederlands.
2. dɑn   'diː   vɑn   hɛt   bə'sxaːvdə   'neːdər,lɑnts
3. than   those of   the   cultivated   Dutch

> 'In Holland, next to cultivated Dutch, there are a large number of dialects spo-
> ken. In the communities where it is current a dialect does not yield as a means
> of communication to cultivated Dutch. Dialect sounds are in themselves also
> not less beautiful than those of cultivated Dutch.'   —*van den Berg 1958: 108.*

Scandinavian languages

ICELANDIC AND NORWEGIAN. Vowel mutation is also characteristic of the Scandinavian languages and was first described linguistically in a twelfth century Old Icelandic manuscript, *First Grammatical Treatise*, which describes the "blended" vowels
as follows: ǫ, "a blending of" *a* and *o* (*rǫ* 'yard'); ę, "a blending of" *a* and *e* *(fę̨r*
'sheep'); ø "made up from the sounds of *e* and *o*" (*øra* 'to upset'); y "made up from
the sounds of *i* and *u*" (*syna* 'laps').

Although most of the characters used to mark vowel mutation in Old Icelandic
have disappeared or have been replaced by other signs, the practice of employing
many ligatures, abbreviations, and gemination signs continued until the nineteenth
century in Iceland, where manuscripts played a major role in the dissemination of cultural information; e.g., ŋ = *ng*, N = *nn*, R = *rr*, d. = *dag* 'day', sa = *svaraþe* 'answered'
(normalized: *svaraði*), kngr = *konungr* 'king', h = *hann* 'he', ka = *kona* 'woman'.

During the Middle Scandinavian period, political and linguistic changes profoundly influenced the development of the Scandinavian languages. The consumma-
tion of the Kalmar Union in 1397 brought Iceland (until 1944), Norway (until 1814),
and Sweden (until 1523) under Danish dominion; as a result, Icelandic remained isolated and retained its ancient writing traditions, while Old Norwegian gradually yielded to written Danish. The strong influence of Low German helped bring the

Scandinavian languages together, and today unity is more conspicuous than the differences. The exception to this is modern Icelandic.

MODERN ICELANDIC. Although Icelandic has changed pronunciation greatly, it has retained the orthography (and the grammar and lexicon) of Old Icelandic thoroughly enough to allow Icelanders to read medieval texts more easily than any other European people. This is particularly evident in the vowel system: the acute accents of the *FGT* are retained to mark long vowels, but now serve to mark diphthongs as well.

Vowel quantity is independent of quality: short vowels precede geminates and clusters except *pp*, *tt*, and *kk*.

Two rules produce additional diphthongs. First, a homorganic glide is inserted after short vowels before *ng* and *nk*: *þing* [θiiŋg] 'thing', *enginn* ['eiŋgɪn] 'nobody', *ýngri* ['iˈŋgri] 'younger', *kongur* ['kouŋgʏr] 'king', *ungur* ['uuŋgʏr] 'young' (masc.). Second, *gi* (or *gj* before a vowel) is pronounced [j], and before this [j] a vowel is diphthongized to [Vi̯]: *stigi* ['stiijɪ] 'ladder', *segja* ['seija] 'to say', *lygi* ['liijɪ] 'lie', *lögin* ['loijɪn] 'the law', *daginn* ['daijɪn] 'the day', *bogi* ['boijɪ] 'bow', *hugi* ['hʏijɪ] 'mind'.

Although Icelandic has undergone fewer changes in the consonant system than in the vowel system, several features complicate phonetic–graphic relationships. Thus dissimilation and devoicing of sonorants occur: *fjall* [fjaḍl̩] 'mountain', *steinn* [steiḍn̩] 'stone', *karl* [karḍl̩] 'man', *horn* [horḍn̩] 'horn', *efla* ['eb̥la] 'to strengthen', *hefna* [heb̥na] 'to avenge'; *hnífur* ['hn̥ii̯vʏr] 'knife', *höfn* [høb̥n̩] 'harbor'. Palatalization of *g, k, sk* before front vowels is illustrated by *géta* ['gjeta] 'to be able to', *kenna* ['kjena] 'to teach', *skera* ['sgjera] 'to cut'.

Finally, many consonants (e.g. *b*, *d*, *f*, *g*, *k*, *n*, *r*, *t*, *v*) are lost in certain consonantal environments: *b*, when after *m* and before *d, t, s, g*—*kembdi* ['kjʰɛmdɪ] 'combed'; *d*, when after *l, n* and before *g, n, l, k, s*—*holdgun* ['hɔlgʏn] 'incarnation'; *f*, when after *l* and before *n, r, s, t*—*hálfna* ['haulna] 'to halve'—and when after *á, ú, ó*—*húfa* [huua] 'cap'; *n*, when after *r, t* and before *s*—*barns* [b̥as] 'child' (gen.).

SAMPLE OF MODERN ICELANDIC

1. Icelandic:	Ísland	hefur	alltaf	átt	mörg	skáld	og
2. Transcription:	'iisland̩	'hɛvʏr	'al̩tav	'auʰt	'mørg̊	'skauld̩	ɔɣ
3. Gloss:	Iceland	has	always	had	many	poets	and

1.	rithöfunda	að	tiltölu	við	fólkfjölda.	Á	tólftu	og
2.	'rɪt,høvʏnda	að	'tɪltølʏ	vɪð	'foulks,fjøld̩a	au	'toulftʏ	ɔɣ
3.	writers	to	proportion	with	population	in	twelfth	and

1.	þrettándu	öld	var	Ísland	miðstöð	menningar	á	Norðurlöndum,
2.	'θrɛʰtaund̩ʏ	'øld	'var	'iisland̩	'mɪðstøð	'mɛniŋgar	au	'nɔrðʏr,lønd̩ʏm
3.	thirteenth	centuries	was	Iceland	center	of.culture	in	Scandinavia

1. og   enn   byrjar   bókmenntasaga   allra   þjóða   á   Norðurlöndum,
2. ɔɣ   'ɛn   'bɪrjar̩   'boṳkmɛnta-ˌsaɣa   'aḓlra   'θjoṳða au   'norðʏr̩ˌlønḓʏm
3. and   still   begins   literature-history   of.all   nations in   Scandinavia

1. og   einkum   Norðmanna,   á   bókmenntum   Íslendinga.   Eddukvæði
2. ɔɣ   'eiŋkʏm   'norðˌmana   au   'boṳkmɛntʏm   'iislɛnḓiiŋga   'ɛdɣ-ˌkvaiḓɪ
3. and   especially   of.the.Norsemen   in   literature   of.Icelanders   Edda-poems

1. og   sögurnar   eru   kunnar um   allan   hinn   menntaða heim.
2. ɔɣ   'søɣʏrḓnar ɛrʏ   'kʏnar   ʏm   'aḓlan   hɪn   'mɛntaða heịm
3. and   sagas   are   known   through all   the   civilized   world

'Iceland has always had many poets and writers in proportion to the population. In the twelfth and thirteenth centuries Iceland was the center of culture in Scandinavia, and the history of literature of all nations in Scandinavia, and especially of the Norsemen, begins with the literature of the Icelanders. The Edda poems and sagas are known all throughout the civilized world.'

—Einarsson 1961:270.

MODERN NORWEGIAN (BOKMÅL). Historically, Norwegian and Danish shared a written language; however, spoken Norwegian retained a conservative phonology, while spoken Danish underwent many sound changes. In the nineteenth century, two standard varieties of Norwegian evolved: *bokmål*, based on the old Dano-Norwegian, and *nynorsk*, based on comparative reconstruction from Norwegian dialects. Spelling reforms have brought these two standards closer together, but *bokmål* remains predominant, and is the basis for the following description.

In pronouncing Norwegian it should be noted that, as in all Germanic languages, the stress is generally on the first syllable. The stressed vowel is usually long when followed by a single, short consonant or none.

A few rules are needed to explain the differences between spellings and their phonetic values. First, before front vowels, *g*, *k*, and *sk* are palatalized, as are consonants followed by a *j*: *kirke* [çɪr̀kə] 'church', *gift* [jɪft] 'married', *skip* [ʃip] 'ship', *gjore* [gjøːˋrə] 'to do', *sju* [ʃʉ:], 'seven', *hjelpe* [jɛl̀pə] 'to help'. Note also *rs* and *sl* and the vocalization of *g*: *slags* [slɑks] 'kind of', *ellers* [ɛləʃ] 'otherwise', *jeg* [jæi̯] 'I'. In some dialects *r* assimilates to a following alveolar: *vers* [væss] 'verse', *vært* [vætt] 'been'.

Some consonants are written but not pronounced, such as final *t*, *d*, and *g*; and *h* before another consonant: *huset* [hʉːˊsə] 'the house', *hva* [vɑ:] 'what', *tolv* [tɔl] 'twelve', *ledig* [leːˋdi] 'vacant', *kveld* [kvɛl] 'evening'.

Finally, two suprasegmental features—pitch accent in Norwegian and Swedish, and the glottal catch in Danish, not indicated orthographically—complicate the pronunciation of these languages. Accent 1 (ˊ) in Norwegian is like the basic stress in other Germanic languages, but Accent 2 (ˋ) involves a rising pitch on the next syllable.

SAMPLE OF MODERN NORWEGIAN

1. Norwegian: Det   norske   språksamfunnet   er   lite   og   det
2. Transcription: dɛ   nor`skə       sprɔːkˊ-sam`funə   ær   liːˋtə   ɔg   dɛ
3. Gloss: the   Norwegian   language-community   is   small   and   it

1. er   begrenset   hvor   mange   bøker   det   kan   ta   imot   hvert
2. ær   bəgrɛnˊsət   vorˊ   maŋˋgə   bøːˊkər   dɛ   kanˊ   taːˊ   imoːtˊ   værtˊ
3. is   limited   how   many   books   it   can   take   toward   each

1. år.   På den   annen   side   er   den   moderne   bok,   en   vare
2. ɔːrˊ   pɔː dɛn   aːəˋn   siːˋdə   ær   dɛn   moderˊnə   boːkˊ   en   vaːˋrə
3. year   on the   other   side   is   the   modern   book   a   commodity

1. som   egner   seg   best   for   masseproduksjon.   Det   er   neppe
2. sɔm   æiɲˋər   sæiˌ   bestˊ   for   maˊsə-produkʃoːnˊ   dɛ   ær   nɛˋpə
3. which suits   itself best   for   mass-production   it   is   hardly

1. den   beste   forutsetning   for   dikterisk   innsats   å   vite   at   man
2. dɛn   bɛsˋtə   forˊʉtsɛtniŋ   for   dikˋtɛrisk   inˊsats   ɔː   viːˋtə   aːt   man
3. the   best   condition   for   poetic   motivation to   know   that one

1. skriver   for   en   håndfull   mennesker.
2. skriːˋvər   for   en   hɔndˋfʉl   mɛˋnɛskər
3. writes   for   a   handful   people

'The Norwegian language community is small and it is limited in how many
books it is able to receive each year. On the other hand the modern book is a
commodity which is best suited for mass production It is hardly the best condition for poetic motivation to know that one is writing for a handful of people.'
                                                        —*Dahl 1975: 363.*

English

PETER T. DANIELS

HISTORY OF ENGLISH SPELLING. The first writings in English are the *Old English* or
Anglo-Saxon glosses in Latin church documents (see FIGURE 45B on page 318). The
earliest are from the late seventh century C.E.; literary as well as ephemeral manuscripts survive only from the time of King Alfred (r. 871–899).

   The spelling system of English—often stigmatized as chaotic—reflects quite
well several unique circumstances that have befallen the language. Old English absorbed loanwords (and their spellings) in a normal way from Scandinavian invaders
and Greek- and Latin-speaking missionaries. But then the Norman Conquest of 1066
(the conventional boundary of *Middle English*) began an influx of Romance (Norman

French) words, which pertained to more cultivated levels of society—domestic animals have Germanic names but their flesh is eaten in French (*cow*/*beef*, *calf*/*veal*, *sheep*/*mutton*), for instance. Ever since, the vocabulary of science and other intellectual pursuits has been formed from Latin and Greek roots rather than Germanic ones (as has been preferred in German—it's not as if the native resources would have been inadequate). As is often the case (cf. SECTION 62), the spelling conventions of the originating language have been retained as words are borrowed.

The second unusual circumstance concerned the timing of the introduction of printing to England, by William Caxton in 1476 (taken as the start of *Modern English*). He is largely responsible for establishing norms of spelling based on the usage of the capital, London. Unfortunately, just when printers had settled on an orthographic system conforming with the general European use of the vowel letters, the vowels were undergoing a change in pronunciation, the Great English Vowel Shift—whereby, e.g., mid front [e:] became high front [i:]. (Such wholesale reorganizations are not unusual in the world's languages, and indeed a very similar shifting can be observed in progress in present-day American English.) Certain other vowels merged (*meat* and *meet* do not rhyme in many nonstandard dialects, for instance). Spelling, however, was not reformed (the arguments against rendering all the past's literature obsolete are powerful), so English vowel orthography is now inconsistent with that of every other language that uses the Roman alphabet. (Seeming consonant anomalies, such as *rough*/*ruff*/*through*/*threw*, result from quite normal changes, here the loss of velar fricatives in different contexts.) The large number of identifiable, regular spellings of vowels that have merged differentially in different dialects provide a convenient metric for categorizing the worldwide variety of English dialects (Wells 1982 uses the 24 keywords KIT, DRESS, TRAP, LOT, STRUT, FOOT, BATH, CLOTH, NURSE, FLEECE, FACE, PALM, THOUGHT, GOAT, GOOSE, PRICE, CHOICE, MOUTH, NEAR, SQUARE, START, NORTH, FORCE, and CURE).

Lastly, the birth of the new American nation afforded the rare opportunity to carry out a spelling reform, led by Noah Webster: it involved mostly the omission of unnecessary letters such as the *u* in *-our* and the change of *-re* to *-er*. This innovation, coupled with a certain conservatism in pronunciation (such as the retention of postvocalic *r* in many American dialects), means that American spelling reflects the pronunciation of English a bit more faithfully than English spelling does.

SYMBOLS. English has always used the Roman alphabet, but a number of sounds not found in Latin have been accommodated in two different ways (Cummings 1988: 207–12). Early on, either *ð* (called *edh*) or *þ* (*thorn*) was used for either [θ] or [ð], a symbol (*wen*) with a shape intermediate between *p* and *þ* was [w] (an example appears in FIGURE 45B), and *ȝ* (*yogh*) was [ɣ]; these letters are said to have Runic origins (cf. SECTION 25). Subsequently, Norman scribes, adapting Latin usage for rendering borrowed Greek sounds, created digraphs with *h* for unfamiliar English sounds: *ch* represents [tʃ] (Old English *c*)—after a short vowel spelled *cch*, which became *tch*; *gh* represents [ɣ]—which persists in spelling long after the sound was lost (*gh* for [g] is later and irregular); *ph* [f], the Latin version of Greek φ, alternates with native *f*; *sh* [ʃ] (Old English *sc*) was probably simplified from *sch*; *th* [θ, ð] is the Latin version of Greek θ; and *wh* [ʍ] (sometimes becoming [w] or [hw]) also represents [h] *whole*. (*W* is the doubling of the *v* shape of *u* for the consonantal value [u̯], i.e. [w]; cf. *y*, the Latin adaptation of Greek Y [y], which alternated with *i* for both [i] and [i̯], i.e. [j]. *X* and *z* received their current pronunciations, differing from the Greek originals, in Latin.)

There have been a number of attempts to catalog the correspondences between sound and spelling of English. The most successful is that of Edward Carney, who presents both speech-to-text correspondences (1994: 134–255) and text-to-speech correspondences (pp. 280–380, summary pp. 381–94) for British spelling. Cummings (1988) presents the former sort of correspondence, though not exhaustively (omitting the spellings of shwa and other unstressed vowels, p. xxvi), for American spelling. Venezky (1970) presents the latter sort, very compactly—but the laurel for compression must go to W. A. Ainsworth, whose 159 rules for driving a minimal speech synthesizer from written input can be reproduced on a single page (Carney 1994: 265). (Contemporary speech synthesizers rely on a list of exceptional correspondences in addition to an algorithm for generating pronunciations from spellings deemed to be regular.)

SPELLING, SPELLING REFORM, AND READING INSTRUCTION. Calls are continually heard for the wholesale reform of English spelling, so that one letter would correspond to one phoneme—it is argued that an alphabet ought to reflect the pronunciation of its language. But it is not difficult to demonstrate that current spelling does this quite well, on the whole; the reflection, though, is of a slightly abstracted form of the language, at the level of the morpheme rather than of the spoken word. A standard example is *photograph*, which is pronounced several ways depending on its surroundings. It is /fówtəgræf/ (alone), /fətágrɨf/ (in *photography*), and /fòwtəgrǽf/ (in *photographic*). If the spelling reflected the pronunciation of the words rather than the identity of their base, their relationship would be obscured.

Another benefit of the extended resources of English orthography is the availability of different spellings for homophones, such as *to*, *two*, and *too*; *its* and *it's*; and *presence* and *presents*. Furthermore, the native versus Romance versus Classical (i.e. Latin/Greek) origin of the word, as marked by some feature of its spelling, can indicate which suffixes may be applied, on the pattern of *similarity*, not *similarness*, cf. *sameness*. An example of native versus Classical spelling is *f* versus *ph* for [f]; and [ʒ] occurs nearly exclusively in words of Romance origin (*beige*, *genre*) as well as resulting from the palatalization of [z] before [j] (*confusion*, *usual*).

Words that do not obey any of the rules for these subsystems are of two kinds. They can be borrowings from non-European languages, such as *gnu* and *Iraq* (English is unusually hospitable to foreign words, one of the features that suits it to be an international language—see Strevens 1985, little known but very insightful). Or they can result from meddling by sixteenth- and seventeenth-century pedants who tried to assimilate English to the Classical languages, as in *debt*, historically *dett* but awarded a *b* by analogy with Latin *debitus*.

To the extent that the historic richness of English vocabulary and spelling result in sets like *bomb/comb/tomb* and *cove/love/move*, where each word has to be learned separately, English writing can be considered logographic. But the spelling never deviates far from the pronunciation—*tomb* can never be read 'grave', for instance. It is thus generally agreed among linguists that strategies for teaching reading that do not incorporate the study of phonics (correspondence between spelling and sound) are at least inefficient, and probably ineffective as well. Spelling/sound correspondence is highly amenable to computerization, and was in fact one of the first linguistic phenomena to be so studied (Hanna et al. 1966). However, the Hanna study (despite its title) used not a phonemic analysis of American English, but the pronunciation key in a standard dictionary, as its input, and suffers from conceptual weaknesses as well as the sorts of problems that beset early, massive computerized investigations (Carney 1994: 86–96). Its indeed rather chaotic findings ("English spelling is 50% regular"!) ought not to have been cited against the phonics approach to teaching reading.

Carney (1994: 473–88) updates Mencken's (1936: 397–407, 1948: 287–316) survey of spelling reform proposals. Some of the suggestions of reformers have been more or less widely accepted—e.g. *catalog* for *catalogue*, *thru* for *through*—but most have not. The case of the reformers is not advanced when they construct, by ignoring etymology and morphophonemics, examples even more ridiculous than G. B. Shaw's specious *ghoti* [fiʃ]: *gh* can only be [f] at the end of a word after *ou*, *o* is [ɪ] only in the truly anomalous *women*, and *ti* is [ʃ] only in Latinate suffixes such as *-tion*. Crystal (1995: 273) reprints an epic piece of doggerel by one G. N. Trenité, writing as "Charivarius," which both makes and breaks the case for spelling reform: H. I. Aronson suggests that in memorizing the poem, one learns every irregularly spelled English word! The first stanza: "Dearest *creature* in *Creation*, / Studying English pronunciation, / I will teach you in my verse / Sounds like *corpse*, *corps*, *horse* and *worse*."

SAMPLE OF ENGLISH

The passage is followed by transcriptions into British "Received Pronunciation" (by M. K. C. MacMahon) and "General American" (by P. T. Daniels, reflecting New York origin and Chicago influence). RP is a prestigious accent spoken by a minority and admired by many; General American is often used in formal speaking and broadcasting, largely devoid of regional characteristics. Stress marks note only the location of stress within polysllabic words; nothing is indicated of sentence-accent or intonation.

1. English:	All	attempts	to	connect	particular	types	of
2. RP:	ɔl	əˈtɛmpts	tə	kəˈnɛkˀt	pəˈtɪkjələ	tajps	əv
3. Gen. Amer.:	ɔl	əˈtɛmts	tə	kəˈnɛkˀt	pɹ̩ˈtɪkjələ˞	tajps	əv

1. linguistic   morphology   with   certain   correlated   stages   of
2. lɪŋ'gwɪstɪk   mɔ'fɒlədʒɪ   wɪð   'sɜtⁿn̩   'kɒrə,lejtɪd   'stejdʒɪz   əv
3. lɪŋ'gwɪstɪk   mɔɹ'falɨdʒij   wɪð   'sɹt?n̩   'kɔɹə,lejtɨd   'stɛjdʒɨz   əv

1. cultural   development   are   vain.   Rightly   understood,   such
2. 'kʌltʃərəɫ   dɪ'vɛləpⁿmənt   ə   'vejn   'rajtlɪ   ˌʌndə'stʊd   sʌtʃ
3. 'kʌltʃɹ̩ɫ   də'vɛləpⁿmn̩t   aɹ   vɛjn   'ɹajtlɪj   ˌʌndɹ̩'stʊd   sʌtʃ

1. correlations   are   rubbish. ...   When   it   comes   to   linguistic
2. ˌkɒrə'lejʃn̩z   ə   'rʌbɪʃ   wɛn   ɪt   kʌmz   tə   lɪŋ'gwɪstɪk
3. ˌkɔɹə'lejʃn̩z   aɹ   'ɹʌbɪʃ   ʍɛn   ɪt   kʌmz   tʊw   lɪŋ'gwɪstɪk

1. form,   Plato   walks   with   the   Macedonian   swineherd,
2. fɔm   'plejtəw   wɔks   wɪð   ðə   ˌmæsɪ'dəwnɪən   'swajn,hɜd
3. fɔɹm   'plɛj,tʰow   wɔks   wɪð   ðə   'mæsə,downijən   'swajn,hɹd

1. Confucius   with   the   head-hunting   savage   of   Assam.
2. kən'fjuwʃəs   wɪð   ðə   'hɛd,hʌntɪŋ   'sævɪdʒ   əv   æ'sæm
3. kn̩'fjʊwʃɨs   wɪð   ðə   'hɛd,hʌntɪŋ   'sævɨdʒ   av   ˌæs'sæːm

—Sapir 1921: 219.

Note: Sapir was mistaken in placing headhunters in Assam; they occupied a neighboring area.

Celtic languages

DAMIAN MCMANUS

Three Continental Celtic languages are distinguished, namely Gaulish, Lepontic, and Celtiberian. Lepontic inscriptions (from the area of Lake Lugano) are written in a North Etruscan (North Italic) script, as are three Gaulish inscriptions from Italy. Celtiberian inscriptions are written in an Iberian alphabet. Gaulish inscriptions from Gallia Narbonensis are in the Greek alphabet while those from eastern and central Gaul, which are chronologically later, are usually in the Latin alphabet.

Insular Celtic languages are Irish with its offshoots Scottish Gaelic and Manx; and Welsh, Cornish, and Breton, all deriving ultimately from British. Scottish Gaelic orthography corresponds in essence to that of Early Modern Irish and has not undergone the third stage in the history of the evolution of Irish orthography (i.e. the Modern Irish Caighdeán Oifigiúil; see below). There are examples of Scottish Gaelic written according to English orthographic conventions, the most notable being in the Book of the Dean of Lismore (16th century). Manx, known to us mainly from seventeenth- and eighteenth-century translations of religious texts, is also written in an orthography based on English orthographical conventions.

Early British is known to us in the main from Classical sources and from Latin inscriptions belonging to the Romano-British period in the Imperial province. The main sources for Late British, Primitive Welsh, and Cornish are the Early Christian inscriptions of post-Roman Britain written for the most part in the Latin alphabet. Old Welsh, Cornish, and Breton appear mainly in glossed Latin texts dating from the eighth and ninth centuries and, like Late British, are written in an adaptation of Latin orthographical conventions based on a British pronunciation of Latin. In later sources the influence of Anglo-Saxon and Anglo-Norman conventions are found particularly in Cornish and Breton.

Irish

Christianity gained a secure foothold in Ireland during the fifth century, and Ogham (SECTION 26), inspired doubtless by contact with the Roman alphabet, is the earliest writing system known to have been used by the Irish. Experimentation with the Latin alphabet itself, as opposed to the Ogham script, may have been on-going during the early centuries of the Christian period, but our oldest surviving texts date from the seventh century, and Classical Old Irish (8th and 9th centuries) is the best starting point for a discussion of the adaptation of the Roman alphabet to Irish.

The Irish adopted 18 Roman characters: the vowel symbols *a, e, i, o, u*; the consonant symbols *b, c, d, f, g, l, m, n, p, r, s, t*; and *h*, which for them was for the most part a *nota aspirationis*—though it could also appear as a mute letter at the beginning of short words and loans (e.g. *hi* [i] 'in', *húar* [uər] 'hour' < Latin *hora*). The vowel symbols may be said to have their Latin values, both long and short, in Old Irish; the long vowels are served by the use of the Latin *apex* (acute accent), i.e. *á, é, í, ó, ú*. The Irish consonants are more complicated, as each of these had a *broad* (velar) and *slender* (palatal) quality (for the most part contrastive), and in initial position each had *mutated* and *unmutated* (radical) forms. The most important developments in the evolution of Irish orthography focus on establishing an unambiguous system of representing this variety in the consonantal system. As the first stage in this evolution, Old Irish orthography is the least unambiguous and thus the most complicated.

TABLE 59.6: *Glides Indicating Consonant Quality*[a]

Old	Modern	Pronunciation	
Fintan	Fiontan	fʲoNtən	'Fintan'
Déclán	Déaglán	dʲeːglaːn	'Declan'
úa Cellig	Ó Ceallaigh	oː kʲaLə(ɣʲ)	'O'Kelly'
úa Cennétig	Ó Ceinnéidigh	oː kʲeNʲeːdʲəɣʲ	
	Ó Cinnéide	oː kʲiNʲeːdʲə	'O'Kennedy'
Érenn	Éireann	eːrʲəN	'of Ireland'

a. A consonant marked with [ʲ] is slender, otherwise it is broad.

A system of writing on- and off-glides, which had begun early, was perfected in time to distinguish palatal and velar quality. The front vowels *i* and *e* were associated with the former; *a*, *o*, and *u* with the latter. By the Early Modern period (1200–1650), the rule *Caol le caol, leathan le leathan* 'Slender with slender, broad with broad' had been evolved whereby consonants had to be followed, preceded, and/or flanked by glides indicating their quality. Some examples illustrate this (TABLE 59.6).

Modern Irish spelling, then, is characterized by the use of digraphs such as *ea/éa/eá, io/ío, ai/ái, oi/ói, ui/úi*, etc. One member of each set serves solely to mark the quality of a preceding or following consonant; the other serves primarily as the main vowel but also, by its nature, indicates the quality of an adjacent consonant. The first letter of the digraph represents the main vowel if it is long; otherwise the second usually predominates, thus *féar* [fʲeːr] 'grass' but *fear* [fʲar] 'man'; *Séamus* [sʲeːməs] 'James' but *Seán* [sʲaːn] 'John'.

In word-initial position, consonants in Irish may have their radical form; or they may be mutated by *lenition* (spirantization)* or *nasalization* (nasalization and subsequent absorption of voiced stops, voicing of voiceless stops, and lengthening of voiced continuants etc.). A good example of lenition is furnished by the name *Séamus* [sʲeːməs], vocative *a Shéamuis* [ə heːməsʲ], whence Scottish *Hamish*. The final sound of a preceding closely connected word was the governing factor in Primitive Irish (pre-5th century): a vowel lenited a following consonant, a nasal nasalized it, any other consonant left it unmutated. But initial mutations are a feature of grammar in the period of recorded Irish, as the final syllables which caused them were lost in or around the fifth century. Thus the nominative, accusative, and genitive singular respectively of 'man' (Modern Irish *fear, fear, fir*) are *fer, fer,* and *fir* in Old Irish, but were **wiros, *wiron*, and **wirī* at an earlier stage. Though they have the same auslaut in Old Irish, the nom. causes no mutation, the acc. nasalizes, and the gen. lenites the initial consonant of a following closely connected word. Similarly, the possessive adjectives *a* 'his', *a* 'her', and *a* 'their' are identical in shape in Old and Modern Irish but have different effects on a following initial, *a* 'his' leniting (< **esyo*), *a* 'her' causing no mutation to a consonant (< **esyās*), and *a* 'their' causing nasalization (< **eysōm*). Modern Irish *capall* [kapəL], then, becomes *chapall* [xapəL] 'horse' after *a* 'his', remains unchanged after *a* 'her', and becomes *gcapall* [gapəL] after *a* 'their'. Representing these mutations unambiguously was a major challenge to Irish orthography, and TABLE 59.7 illustrates the Old and the Modern systems.

The most significant feature of the Old Irish system is its failure to mark the nasalization (voicing) of voiceless stops (i.e. its *t-* for Modern *dt-* etc.) and the lenition of their voiced counterparts and *m* (i.e. its *d-* for Modern *dh-* etc.). This, however, is more apparent than real, as the Old Irish system is based on traditional Latin spelling serving British (i.e. British Celtic) pronunciation. In British Latin the words *populus,*

---

*The unlenited forms of *l*, *n*, and *r* are represented in transcriptions by the small capital versions L, N, and R of those letters; for phonetic details see Thurneysen 1946 § 135.

TABLE 59.7: *Orthographic Representation of Mutations*

		Radical		Lenited		Nasalized	
t-	Old	[t]		th-	[θ]	t-	[d]
	Modern	[t]		th-	[h]	dt-	[d]
c-	Old	[k]		ch-	[x]	c-	[g]
	Modern	[k]		ch-	[x]	gc-	[g]
p-	Old	[p]		ph-	[ɸ]	p-	[b]
	Modern	[p]		ph-	[f]	bp-	[b]
d-	Old	[d]		d-	[ð]	nd-	[N]
	Modern	[d]		dh-	[ɣ]	nd-	[N]
g-	Old	[g]		g-	[ɣ]	ng-	[ŋ]
	Modern	[g]		gh-	[ɣ]	ng-	[ŋ]
b-	Old	[b]		b-	[β]	mb-	[m]
	Modern	[b]		bh-	[v]	mb-	[m]
m-	Old	[m]		m-	[β̃]	m(m)-	[m]
	Modern	[m]		mh-	[v]	m-	[m]
l-ᵃ	Old	[L]		l-	[l]	l(1)-	[L]
	Modern	[L]		l-	[l]	l-	[L]
s-	Old	[s]		ṡ-	[h]	s-	[s]
	Modern	[s]		sh-	[h]	s-	[s]
f-	Old	[f]		ḟ-	(no sound)	f-	[β]
	Modern	[f]		fh-	(no sound)	bhf-	[v]

a. *n* and *r* are treated similarly to *l*.

pater, and *locus* were pronounced (by British "lenition") with intervocalic [b], [d], and [g], while *scribo*, *idolum*, *legendum*, and *dominicus* had intervocalic [β], [ð], [ɣ], and [β] respectively by the same process. In writing, the Irish simply adopted traditional Latin spelling with this pronunciation, so these words, which were borrowed into Irish, appear in Old Irish as *popul* [pobul] 'people', *paiter* [padʲər] 'the Lord's prayer, a paternoster', *loc* [loɡ] 'place'; and *scríbaid* [skrʲiːβəðʲ] 'writes', *ídol* [iːðəl] 'idol', *léigend* [leːɣʲənd] 'reading', *domnach* [doβnəx] 'Sunday'. The letters *p*, *t*, and *c*, on the one hand, and *b*, *d*, *g*, and *m*, on the other, had two sets of values in initial position in British, depending on whether they were "lenited" or not. This British "lenition" corresponded to Irish lenition in the case of the voiced stops (and *m*) and to Irish nasalization in the case of the voiceless ones; and Old Irish (like Early Welsh) simply applied the dual-value principle across word boundary (a boundary often ignored in writing). Thus, as the intervocalic *p* in *popul* [pobul] represented [b], the initial *p* could also represent [b] (its nasalized counterpart) in *a popul* [ə bobul] 'their people' (Modern *a bpobal*); and as intervocalic *d* represented [ð] in *ídol*, the initial *d* in *dán* 'poem' [daːn] could represent [ð] (its lenited counterpart) in *a dán* [ə ðaːn] 'his poem' (Modern *a dhán* [ə ɣaːn]).

The same mutations were indicated unambiguously, however, in the case of other sounds. Thus the lenition of voiceless stops, unlike their voiced counterparts, was represented by Latin *ch*, *th*, and *ph*; that of *f* and *s*, which involved the complete loss of the sound in the case of the former, and reduction to [h] or no sound in some sequences in the case of the latter (e.g. Old Irish *mac int śacairt* [mak iNt agəʀdʲ] 'son of the priest' = 'Mac Entaggart'), came to be marked during the Old Irish period by the Latin *punctum delens* (i.e. *ḟ*, *ś*), a scribal device for indicating an erroneously written letter. Similarly, the nasalization of the voiced stops *b*, *d*, and *g*, unlike their voiceless counterparts, was represented by Latin *mb*, *nd*, and *ng*.

By a process of cross-fertilization (operating in the direction indicated by the arrows in TABLE 59.7), the Old Irish devices just mentioned were gradually extended to the ambiguous notation discussed above so that lenited initial and internal *b* [β], *d* [ð], *g* [ɣ], and *m* [β̃] came to be written *ḃ* or *bh*, *ḋ* or *dh*, *ġ* or *gh*, and *ṁ* or *mh* (the latter in each case winning out completely in the Modern Irish standard, where even *ḟ* and *ś* have yielded to *fh*, *sh*). Similarly, as *mb-*, *nd-*, and *ng-* were pronounced [m], [N], and [ŋ], the principle that the first letter indicated the sound to be pronounced, the second the radical, was extended to nasalized (i.e. voiced) initial *p-*, *t-*, *c-*, and *f-*, giving *bp-*, *dt-*, *gc-*, and *bhf-* (after an intermediate experimentation with *pp-*, *tt-*, etc.). When not in word-initial position, *p* [b], *t* [d], and *c* [g] gave way to *b*, *d*, and *g*; e.g. Old Irish *Pátraic* [pa:drəgʲ] (< British Latin *Patricius* [padrigiu̯s]) > Modern *Pádraig* [pa:drəgʲ], [pa:rəgʲ] in some dialects). These developments were on-going during the Early Modern period, 1200–1650, and manuscripts of the time often have both systems side by side. Some examples will illustrate the changes: Old *hi cocad* [i gogəð] > Modern *i gcogadh* [i gogə] 'in a fight', Old *a tech* [ə dʲex] > Modern *a dteach* [ə dʲax] 'their house', Old *a gobae* [ə ɣoβe] > Modern *a ghabha* [ə ɣau] 'his smith'.

The Official Modern Irish Standard (the *Caighdeán Oifigiúil*) established in the twentieth century fixed these developments; if it did not represent a new departure in orthographic convention, it did constitute a major break with tradition in taking the modern pronunciation as its basis. Scottish Gaelic orthography did not pass through this third stage.

SAMPLE OF IRISH WORDS AND NAMES

The following words and surnames (formerly patronymics) illustrate the conventions of the three periods in Irish orthography (Old and Middle, 8th–12th c.; Modern, 13th–20th c.; *Caighdeán Oifigiúil*, 1958–).

1. Old and Middle Irish:	buiden	[buðʲən]	slegán	[sʲlʲeɣa:n]
2. Modern Irish:	buidhean	[biɣʲən]	sleaghán	[sʲlˠaɣa:n]
3. Caighdeán Oifigiúil:	buíon	[bi:n]	sleán	[sʲlˠa:n]
4. Gloss:	host		slane, turf-spade	

1. celebrad	[kʲelʲəβrəð]	mac Mathgamno	[mak maθɣəβno]
2. ceileabhradh	[kʲelʲəβrəð]	Mac Mathghamhna	[mak mahɣəβnə]
3. ceiliúradh	[kʲelʲuːrə]	Mac Mathúna	[mak mahuːnə]
4. celebration		son of *Mathgamain* 'bear' > McMahon	

1. úa Domnaill	[uə doβnəLʲ]	úa Ségdai	[uə sʲeːɣði]
2. Ó Domhnaill	[oː doβnəLʲ]	Ó Séaghdha	[oː sʲeːɣðə]
3. Ó Dónaill	[oː doːnəLʲ]	Ó Sé	[oː sʲeː]
4. grandson/descendant of *Domnall* 'world leader' > O'Donnell		grandson/descendant of *Ségdae* 'the propitious one' > O'Shea	

Welsh

Eric P. Hamp

The orthography of Modern Welsh is the long-range result of adapting the Roman alphabet to the Celtic languages of Britain. The Roman alphabet corresponds to the sounds of Modern Welsh as shown in TABLE 59.8 (differences between South Walian and North Walian are indicated by the abbreviations SW and NW). Digraphs consisting of consonant plus *h* indicate, in part, changes resulting from morphophonemic processes called *mutation* (see below). In addition to the symbols shown, the letter *j* [dʒ] is sometimes used in words borrowed from English, e.g. *garej* 'garage', *jeli* 'jelly'. The letter *z* is occasionally used for [z] in borrowed words, but *s* is more usual: *sŵ* [zuː] 'zoo'. The Welsh palatal fricative [ʃ] is represented by the digraph *si* before a vowel: *siarad* ['ʃarad] 'talk'.

An important difference between North and South Walian pronunciation is that the former has the additional vowels [ɨ, ɨː], written with *u* and *y*. In South Welsh these have merged with [ɪ, iː], although the orthographic distinction remains. This holds for the offglide segments of diphthongs as well. The pronunciation of *y* varies according to its position in the word: it is SW [ɪ, iː], NW [ɨ, ɨː] in most monosyllables (e.g. *dŷn* 'man', *tŷ* 'house'), and in final syllables of polysyllabic words. But it is [ə] for both dialects in non-final syllables, thus *mynydd* ['mənɨð] 'mountain', pl. *mynyddoedd* [mə'nəðoɨð]. The pronunciation [ə] is also used in some unstressed monosyllabic elements, e.g. the definite article forms *y* and *yr, fy* 'my', *dy* 'your', *yn* 'in', *yn* 'predicative particle', and *yn* 'preverbal particle'.

The standard literary representation and pronunciation of Modern Welsh involves short and long vowels (except *y*, when pronounced [ə]). Length is partly predictable in terms of following consonants, but the circumflex accent is often used to indicate unpredictable vowel length (often in loans): *llên* 'literature', *pêl* 'ball', *côr* 'choir', *plât* 'plate'. The circumflex is omitted in certain common (native) words with long

ACKNOWLEDGMENT. The editors are grateful for the help of Kathryn Klar, Dorian Llewellyn, and Robert Thiel.

TABLE 59.8: *Welsh Orthography*

Letter	Name	Value	Notes
a	â	[a, a:]	*ae* = [a̱ɨ]; *ai* = [aɪ̯]; *au* = NW [a], SW [ɛ]; *aw* = [au̯]
b	bi	[b]	
c	ec	[k]	
ch	ech	[x]	
d	di	[d]	
dd	edd	[ð]	
e	ê	[ɛ, e:]	*ei* = [əɪ̯]; *eu/ey* = NW [ə̱ɨ], SW [əɪ̯]; *ew* = [ɛu̯]
f	ef	[v]	
ff	eff	[f]	
g	eg	[g]	
ng	eng	[ŋ]	Occasionally represents [ŋg], as in *Bangor*; mutated form *ngh* is [ŋ̥ŋ]
h	hets	[h]	Letter name pronounced [he:tʃ]
i	î	[ɪ, i:]	Before a vowel, *i* may represent [i̯]. Letter name in SW is *î-dot*
l	el	[l]	
ll	ell	[ɬ]	
m	em	[m]	Mutated *mh* = [mm̥]
n	en	[n]	Mutated *nh* = [nn̥]
o	ô	[ɔ, o:]	*oe, oi* = [ɔ̱ɨ]; *ou* = NW [ɔ̱ɨ], SW [ɔɪ̯]
p	pi	[p]	
ph	ffi, yff [ff]		Mutated form of *p*; pronounced the same as *f*
r	ri	[r]	
rh	rhi	[r̥]	
s	es	[s]	Before a vowel, *si* = [ʃ]
t	ti	[t]	
th	eth	[θ]	
u	û	NW: [ɨ, ɨ:] SW: [ɪ, 1.]	*uw* = [ɨu:] *uw* = [ɪu:]; letter name is *û-bedol*
w	ŵ	[ʊ, u:]	*wy* = [uɨ]; sequence *gw* may be [gu̯] before vowel
y	ŷ	NW: [ɨ, ɨ:] SW: [ɪ, i:]	In monosyllables, non-final syllables, and particles, both NW and SW have [ə]

vowels, and one must simply learn the correct pronunciation: *hen* [he:n] 'old', *dyn* [dɨ:n] 'man'.

Stress falls generally on the penult, and is not usually indicated by any written mark (even when it falls elsewhere). Examples of unwritten ultimate stress include *Cymraeg* [kəm'ra̱ɨg] 'the Welsh language'; the emphatic pronouns 1sg. *myfi*, 2sg. *ty-di*, etc.; and the class of verbal nouns ending in *-(h)au*, such as *parhau* 'to continue, endure' and *mwynhau* 'to enjoy'. Stress is written (exceptionally) in certain suffixes,

TABLE 59.9: *Welsh Initial Consonant Mutation*[a]

Initial	Lenited	Nasalized	Spirantized	Example	Gloss	'his ...'	'my ...'	'her ...'
p	b	mh	ph	pen	'head'	ei ben	fy mhen	ei phen
t	d	nh	th	tad	'father'	ei dad	fy nhad	ei thad
c	g	ngh	ch	ci	'dog'	ei gi	fy nghi	ei chi
b	f	m	*	braich	'arm'	ei fraich	fy mraich	ei braich
d	dd	n	*	dant	'tooth'	ei ddant	fy nant	ei dant
g	Ø	ng	*	gardd	'garden'	ei ardd	fy ngardd	ei gardd
m	f	*	*	mam	'mother'	ei fam	fy mam	ei mam
ll	l	*	*	llais	'voice'	ei lais	fy llais	ei llais
rh	r	*	*	rhosyn	'rose'	ei rosyn	fy rhosyn	ei rhosyn

a. Asterisk indicates no change.

e.g. in *caniatáu* 'to allow, permit'; and the derivative nouns are written with a circumflex in positions where vowel length can be distinctive (*caniatâd* 'permission').

Sometimes the circumflex accent is used to distinguish the sequences *gwy* [gu̯ɨ], *gwŷ* [gu̯ɨ:], and *gwy* [gu̯ɨ]: thus *gwŷdd* [gu̯ɨ̯ð] 'goose', *gwydd* [gu̯ɨ:ð] 'woods, trees', *gwyn* [gu̯ɨn] 'white'. The letter *i* may be a semivowel when followed by a vowel: thus *iach* [i̯ax] 'healthy', *iaith* [i̯ai̯θ] 'language', *ceiniog* ['kəi̯ni̯ɔg] 'penny'. This is also true of *w*, but only as a result of word-initial lenition (see below): *gwaith* [gwai̯θ] 'work', but *ei waith* [i 'wai̯θ] 'his work'.

Like the other Celtic languages, Welsh has a set of morphophonemic alternations that affect word-initial sounds; these are referred to as *initial mutations* and are conditioned by grammatical factors (with details differing slightly from Irish). The consonantal changes in pronunciation, which are reflected straightforwardly in the spelling, are shown in TABLE 59.9, along with examples. (The order of presentation here, from labials to velars, is that generally used by foreign linguists; however, in Welsh pedagogy, the order *c p t g b d ll m rh* is more usual.) The type of mutation called *aspiration* has the effect of inserting an *h* before a word beginning with a vowel: thus *enw* 'name', *ei henw* 'her name'; *arian* 'money', *eu harian* 'their money'.

Spoken dialects of Welsh show many phonological reductions and contractions which, in the twentieth century, are increasingly represented in writing. All dialects show a tendency for word-final *f* [v] to be dropped, so that *tref* 'town' becomes [tre:]; South Welsh shows a similar tendency with word-final *dd* [ð].

SAMPLE OF WELSH

1. Welsh:	Yr	oedd	dau	gyfaill	rywbryd	yn	meddwl	cerdded
2. Transcription:	r	ɔi̯ð	dai̯	'gəvai̯ɬ	'rubrɨd	ən	'mɛðʊl	'kɛrðɛd
3. Gloss:	PTCL	was	two	friends	once	at	thinking	walking

1.	trwy	goed.	Cofiodd		un	ohonynt	fod	y	lle	yn
2.	truɨ	'gɔɨd	'kɔvi̯ɔð		ɨn	ɔ'hɔnɨnt	vod	ə	ɬe	ən
3.	through	wood	remembered		one	of.them	being	the	place	PTCL

1.	enwog	am	eirth,	a	dywedodd	wrth	ei	gyfaill,	"Beth
2.	'ɛnu̯ɔg	am	'əi̯rθ	a	də'u̯ɛdɔð	urθ	i	'gəvai̯ɬ	beθ
3.	famous	for	bears	and	said	at	his	friend	what

1.	a	ddigwydd	inni	os	daw	arth	i'n	cyfarfod?"
2.	a	'ðigu̯ɨð	ɪ'nɪ	ɔs	'dau̯	'arθ	ɪn	kə'varvɔd
3.	PTCL	happens	to.us	if	comes	bear	to.our	meeting

'There were two friends once thinking of walking through a wood. One of them remembered the place to be famous for bears, and said to his friend, "What will happen to us if a bear comes to meet us?"'

— From a folktale, in Vinay and Thomas 1948: 88.

Languages of Eastern and Southern Europe

BERNARD COMRIE

Baltic and Slavic

Roman script is used for the Baltic languages Lithuanian and Latvian, and for the following Slavic languages: Polish, Czech, Slovak, Upper Sorbian, Lower Sorbian, Slovene, and (alongside Cyrillic script) Serbo-Croatian (cf. SECTION 64).

VOWELS, STRESS, AND TONE. Most languages use the five basic vowels of Roman script—*a, e, i, o, u*—in their usual continental values. Latvian, which lacks a mid back rounded vowel in native words, uses *o* to represent the diphthong [uo]; but the mid back rounded vowel is found in loanwords, and is also written *o*.

ACKNOWLEDGMENTS: I am grateful for information provided by Marie Alexander, Albert J. Borg, Wayles Browne, Helena Halmari, Tooru Hayasi, Robert Hetzron, José Ignacio Hualde, István Kenesei, Katalin É. Kiss, Joseba Lakarra, Jules Levin, Ronald Lötzsch, Jolanta Machevichius, Kazuto Matsumura, Leonard Newmark, Tom Priestly, David Short, Aleksandra Steinbergs, Gerald C. Stone, Tiit-Rein Viitso, and Nigel Vincent. Remaining errors are my own responsibility. Work on this article proceeded while I was a Visiting Professor at the Institute for the Study of Languages and Cultures of Asia and Africa, Tokyo University of Foreign Studies. ALPHABET TABLES: Capital letters are shown as they would appear when required at the beginning of a sentence. For letters that do not occur word-initially, capital forms are shown as they would appear in a text written in capitals throughout. Indented letters are not considered distinct for purposes of alphabetical ordering. Letters in parentheses occur only in unassimilated loanwords. The tones on long vowels and diphthongs are marked in the phonetic transcription as follows: rising [ʌ], level/rising [˦], falling [˅], broken (glottal) [V̰]. SAMPLE TEXTS: Low-level morphophonemic processes, such as word-final devoicing and voice assimilation in Polish and Czech, and palatalization assimilation in Lithuanian, are not shown orthographically. The texts that follow are sometimes slightly adapted from the originals.

Phonemically distinct more and less open non-high vowel qualities are distinguished in Upper Sorbian as *e* versus *ě* and *o* versus *ó*; in Lower Sorbian as *e* versus *ě*; in Slovak as *ä* versus *e* (but in Slovak the distinction is usually neutralized, even in standard speech); in Lithuanian as *e* versus *ė*. Slovene does not distinguish orthographically between its phonemically distinct open and close non-high vowels, nor does Latvian between its open and close non-high front vowels. In Slovene, *e* also represents phonemically distinct [ə].

In Polish and the Sorbian languages, *y* represents a vowel somewhat retracted from that represented by *i*, though both are arguably allophones of a single phoneme. In Czech and Slovak, the *i/y* opposition has no direct phonetic correlate, though it plays a role in the indication of palatal consonant quality (see below).

Vowel length is phonemic in Czech and Slovak (including syllabic *r* and *l* in Slovak), where it is indicated by means of an acute accent; in Serbo-Croatian and Slovene (including syllabic *r*—in Slovene the pronunciation is [ər]), where it is not indicated orthographically; and in Latvian, where it is written with a macron. In Lithuanian, short and long [i] are distinguished as *i* and *y*, short and long [u] as *u* and *ū*; *a* and *e* represent both long and short vowels, though the distribution is largely (not entirely) predictable. The Polish spelling *ó* (homophonous with *u*) originally represented a long [o]; Czech *ů*, used for [u:] except word-initially (where *ú* is used), originally represented a diphthong [uo].

In Polish, nasal vowels are indicated by a subscript hook, although in contemporary pronunciation they are realized as a sequence of oral vowel + homorganic nasal before stops, and are denasalized before *l* and *ł* (*ę* usually also word-finally). The hook diacritic originally indicated vowel nasalization in Lithuanian, but hooked vowels are now simply long counterparts of the corresponding simple vowels.

The position of stress is usually predictable, and is not marked, in Polish, Upper Sorbian, Lower Sorbian, Czech, Slovak, and Latvian. It is unpredictable, but not marked orthographically, in Serbo-Croatian, Slovene, and Lithuanian. In Serbo-Croatian, Lithuanian, and Latvian there are phonemic tone distinctions, and also in one variety of standard Slovene (even on syllabic *r* in Serbo-Croatian and, as [ər], in Slovene); these are also not represented orthographically.

CONSONANTS. Polish makes extensive use of digraphs, but the other languages prefer diacritics, in particular the *háček*, which was an innovation (originally a superscript dot) of Jan Hus. The only widely used digraph is *ch* for [x], and even here *h* is used by Serbo-Croatian, Slovene, and (usually) Latvian. The affricates [d͡z] and [d͡ʒ] are also represented as digraphs, *dz* and *dž* (Polish *dż*, Sorbian *dź*), even in those languages where they are clearly unitary phonemes. By contrast, the affricate [t͡s] is represented as *c*. The palato-alveolar fricatives [ʃ] and [ʒ] and the affricate [t͡ʃ] are represented by means of a diacritic *háček* as *š*, *ž*, *č*—except in Polish, which uses digraphs *sz* for [ʃ], *cz* for [t͡ʃ], and either a diacritic *ż* (with the original Hussite dot) or a digraph *rz*, depending on etymology, for [ʒ]. Czech also has a fricative trill, represented by *ř*.

The complications of Roman-script Slavic orthographies stem basically from the representation of palatal and palatalized consonants. Only Serbo-Croatian and Latvian have one-to-one correspondence between phoneme and symbol (counting digraphs as single symbols): Serbo-Croatian *ć, đ, lj*, and *nj* correspond to [t͡ɕ], [d͡ʑ], [ʎ], [ɲ] respectively; and Latvian *ģ, ķ, ļ, ņ*, and obsolescent *ŗ* correspond to [ɟ], [c], [ʎ], [ɲ], and [rʲ] respectively. (In Slovene, *lj* and *nj* represent sequences of two phonemes before a vowel, and simple [l], [n] elsewhere.) In Czech and Slovak, only [t], [d], [n] (and in Slovak [l]) have phonemically distinct palatal counterparts; orthographically, they are distinguished by the vowel symbols in the case of *y* (after non-palatal) versus *i* (after palatal), in Czech also by *e* (after non-palatal) versus *ě* (after palatal). (In Slovak, with a number of exceptions not indicated orthographically, only the palatals occur before *e*). Elsewhere, a *háček* or an apostrophe-like diacritic indicates the palatal member of the pair. In other positions in Czech and Slovak, *y* and *i* are phonetically indistinguishable, and written on the basis of etymology, while Czech *ě* is pronounced [je] (after *m*, [ɲe]). In Polish, palatalized consonants (including the alveo-palatals) are indicated in three ways: by an acute accent word-finally or before a consonant; by a following *i* rather than *y*; and by the letter *i* after the consonant before other vowels. The Sorbian languages follow essentially the same conventions as Polish, but with *j* rather than *i* between a palatalized consonant and a vowel, and with acute accent even before vowels on *ś, ź, ć*, and *dź*. Lithuanian, in which the palatalized opposition occurs only before back vowels, adopts that part of the Polish convention that uses the letter *i* between a palatalized consonant and a back vowel.

As reflexes of Proto-Slavic or Proto-Baltic **v*, most languages use *v*, but Polish and the Sorbian languages use *w*. In Polish and the Sorbian languages, the *l* versus *ł* opposition originally represented palatalized versus non-palatalized; but now *l* is [l], and *ł* is either [ɫ] (in archaic and regional Polish) or [w], in the Sorbian languages merging with *w*. In Czech, Slovak, Upper Sorbian, Lower Sorbian, and Lithuanian, *h* represents [ɦ]; this pronunciation is also found in archaic and regional Polish, but in other varieties of Polish merges in pronunciation with *ch* as [x]. In Latvian, an earlier norm distinguished voiced *h* from voiceless *ch*, but the norm consolidated during the Soviet period merges these as the voiceless sound, written *h*.

ALPHABETICAL ORDER. Whether letters with diacritics and digraphs are considered separate letters for purposes of alphabetical ordering depends on the individual language, and sometimes on the individual letter. Diacriticized letters and digraphs are usually placed after or with the corresponding simple letter. Sometimes, however, they are placed after or with phonetically or morphophonemically related letters: *ch* after *h* in Upper Sorbian, Lower Sorbian, Czech, and Slovak (and older Latvian); *ć* after *t* in Upper Sorbian (usually); and *y* with *i* in Lithuanian.

TABLE 59.10: *Polish Alphabet*

Letter[a]		Phonetic Value[b]	Name
A	*a*	[a]	[a]
Ą	*ą*	[õ]; [o] before *l*, *ł*; [o] + homorganic nasal before stop	[õ]
B	*b*	[b]	[be]
C	*c*	[t͡s] (when palatalized, [t͡ɕ])	[t͡se]
Ć	*ć*	[t͡ɕ]	[t͡ɕe]
D	*d*	[d]	[de]
E	*e*	[e]	[e]
Ę	*ę*	[ẽ]; [e] before *l*, *ł* and word-finally; [e] + homorganic nasal before stop	[ẽ]
F	*f*	[f]	[ef]
G	*g*	[g]	[gʲe]
H	*h*	[x], archaic–regional [ɦ]	[xa], [ɦa]
I	*i*	[i]	[i]
J	*j*	[j]	[jot]
K	*k*	[k]	[ka]
L	*l*	[l]	[el]
Ł	*ł*	[w], archaic–regional [ɫ]	[ew], [eɫ]
M	*m*	[m]	[em]
N	*n*	[n] (when palatalized, [ɲ])	[en]
Ń	*ń*	[ɲ]	[eɲ]
O	*o*	[o]	[o]
Ó	*ó*	[u]	[o kreskovane] 'lined o'
P	*p*	[p]	[pe]
R	*r*	[r]	[er]
S	*s*	[s] (when palatalized, [ɕ])	[es]
Ś	*ś*	[ɕ]	[eɕ]
T	*t*	[t]	[te]
U	*u*	[u]	[u]
W	*w*	[v]	[vu]
Y	*y*	[ɪ]	[igrek]
Z	*z*	[z] (when palatalized, [ʑ])	[zet]
Ź	*ź*	[ʑ]	[zet]
Ż	*ż*	[ʒ]	[ʒet]

a. The following digraphs are not considered single letters of the alphabet:

Ch	ch	[x]
Cz	cz	[t͡ʃ]
Dz	dz	[d͡z] (when palatalized [d͡ʑ])
Dź	dź	[d͡ʑ]
Dż	dż	[d͡ʒ]
Rz	rz	[ʒ]
Sz	sz	[ʃ]

b. Consonants are palatalized before *i* [i], and are represented as C + *i* before other vowels. The palatalized consonant symbols with acute accents are used only before consonants and word-finally.

TABLE 59.11: *Upper Sorbian Alphabet*

Letter[a]		Phonetic Value	Name
A	a	[a]	[a]
B	b	[b]	[bɛj]
C	c	[t͡s][b]	[t͡ʃɛj]
Č	č	[t͡ʃʲ]	[t͡ʃʲɛj]
Dź	dź	[d͡ʒʲ]	[d͡ʒʲɛj]
E	e	[ɛ]	[ɛj]
Ě	ě	[e] ~ [ie]	[et], [jet]
F	f	[f]	[ɛf]
G	g	[g]	[gɛj]
H	h	[h]	[ɦa]
Ch	ch	[x], morpheme-initial [kʰ]	[xa]
I	i	[i][c]	[i], [ji]
J	j	[j][d]	[jɔt], [jot]
K	k	[k]	[ka]
Ł	ł	[w]	[ɛw]
L	l	[l]	[ɛl]
M	m	[m]	[ɛm]
N	n	[n]	[ɛn]
Ń	ń	[jn]	[ɛjn]
O	o	[ɔ]	[ɔ]
Ó	ó	[o]~[uo]	[ot]
P	p	[p]	[pɛj]
R	r	[ʀ]	[ɛʀ]
Ř	ř	[ʃʲ] after *k, p*; [sʲ] after *t*	[ɛʀʃʲ]
S	s	[s]	[ɛs]
Š	š	[ʃʲ]	[ɛʃʲ]
T	t	[t]	[tɛj]
Ć	ć	[t͡ʃʲ]	[t͡ʃʲet]
U	u	[u]	[u]
W	w	[w] (in loanwords, [v])	[wɛj]
Y	y	[ɨ][c]	[ɨ]
Z	z	[z]	[zɛt]
Ž	ž	[ʒʲ]	[ʒʲɛt]

a. For purposes of alphabetical ordering, *ó* is usually not considered distinct from *o*; and *ć* may be ordered before or after *č*.

b. An additional phoneme, [t͡sʲ], is represented by various digraphs: *tř, tč, tš, dš, dč*.

c. [i] and [ɨ] are allophones of a single phoneme.

d. Labials, *n*, and *r* are palatalized before *i* and *ě*, and their palatalization is represented as C + *j* before other vowels.

TABLE 59.12: *Lower Sorbian Alphabet*

Letter		Phonetic Value	Name
A	a	[a]	[a]
B	b	[b]	[bɛj]
C	c	[t͡s]	[t͡sɛj]
Č	č	[t͡ʃ]	[t͡ʃet]
Ć	ć	[t͡ʃʲ]	[t͡ʃʲet], [t͡ʃʲɛj]
D	d	[d]	[dɛj]
DŽ	dž	[d͡ʒʲ][a]	[d͡ʒʲɛj]
E	e	[ɛ]	[ɛj]
Ě	ě	[e] ~ [ie]	[et]
F	f	[f]	[ɛf]
G	g	[g]	[gɛj]
H	h	[h]	[ɦa]
Ch	ch	[x]	[xa]
I	i	[i][b]	[i]
J	j	[j][c]	[jɔt]
K	k	[k]	[ka]
Ł	ł	[w]	[ɛw]
L	l	[l]	[ɛl]
M	m	[m]	[ɛm]
N	n	[n]	[ɛn]
Ń	ń	[nʲ][c]	[ɛjn][d]
O	o	[ɔ]; [o][e]	[ɔ]
P	p	[p]	[pɛj]
R	r	[ʀ]	[ɛʀ]
Ŕ	ŕ	[ʀʲ][c]	[mʲɛkɛ ɛjʀʲ][d]
S	s	[s]	[ɛs]
Š	š	[ʃ]	[ɛʃ]
Ś	ś	[ʃʲ]	[ʃʲɛj]
T	t	[t]	[tɛj]
U	u	[u]	[u]
W	w	[w]	[wɛj]
Y	y	[ɨ][b]	[ɨ]
Z	z	[z]	[ʑɛl]
Ž	ž	[ʒ]	[ʒet]
Ź	ź	[ʒʲ][a]	[ʒʲɛj]

a. [d͡ʒʲ] is an allophone of /ʒʲ/.

b. [i] and [ɨ] are allophones of a single phoneme.

c. Labials, *n*, and *r* are palatalized before *i* and *ě*; their palatalization is represented as C + *j* before other vowels—and, in the case of *n* and *r*, by an acute accent word-finally and before consonants.

d. Or German: *weiches n/r* 'soft *n/r*'.

e. [o] is largely a positional variant of [ɔ], with [o] occurring after labials (but not orthographic *ł*) and velars if not also followed by a labial or velar; there is thus a contrast between *ło* [wɔ] and *wo* [wo] if no labial or velar follows.

TABLE 59.13: *Czech Alphabet*

Letter		Phonetic Value	Name[a]
A	a	[a]	[aː]
Á	á	[aː]	[dlou̯ɦe: aː] 'long *a*'
B	b	[b]	[beː]
C	c	[t͡s]	[t͡seː]
Č	č	[t͡ʃ]	[t͡ʃeː]
D	d	[d]; as palatal [ɟ]	[deː];
Ď	d'	[ɟ]	[ɟeː], [de: z ɦa:t͡ʃkem] '*d* with hook'
E	e	[e]	[eː]
É	é	[eː]	[dlou̯ɦe: eː] 'long *e*'
Ě	ě	[e]; [je], see text	[e: z ɦa:t͡ʃkem] '*e* with hook'/[ije]
F	f	[f]	[ef]
G	g	[g]	[geː]
H	h	[ɦ]	[ɦaː]
Ch	ch	[x]	[xaː]
I	i	[i]	[iː], [mɲeke: iː] 'soft *i*'
Í	í	[iː]	[dlou̯ɦe: iː], [dlou̯ɦe: mɲeke: iː] 'long (soft) *i*'
J	j	[j]	[jeː]
K	k	[k]	[kaː]
L	l	[l]	[el]
M	m	[m]	[em]
N	n	[n]; as palatal [ɲ]	[en]
Ń	ń	[ɲ]	[eɲ]
O	o	[o][b]	[oː]
Ó	ó	[oː]	[dlou̯ɦe: oː] 'long *o*'
P	p	[p]	[peː]
(Q	q	[kv])	[kveː]
R	r	[r]	[er]
Ř	ř	[r̝]	[er̝] (fricative trill)
S	s	[s]	[es]
Š	š	[ʃ]	[eʃ]
T	t	[t]; as palatal [c]	[teː]
Ť	t'	[c]	[ceː], [te: z ɦa:t͡ʃkem] '*t* with hook'
U	u	[u]	[uː]
Ú	ú	[uː]	[dlou̯ɦe: uː] 'long *u*'
Ů	ů	[uː]	[u: s krou̯ʃkem] '*u* with circle', (informal) [krou̯ʃkovane: uː] 'circled *u*'
V	v	[v]	[veː]
(W	w	[v])	[dvojite: veː] 'double *v*'
(X	x	[ks])	[iks]
Y	y	[i]	[ipsilon], (informal) [tvrde: iː] 'hard *i*'
Ý	ý	[iː]	[dlou̯ɦe: ipsilon] 'long *y*', (informal) [dlou̯ɦe: tvrde: iː] 'long hard *i*'
Z	z	[z]	[zet]
Ž	ž	[ʒ]	[ʒet]

a. For the consonants, combinations of the consonant sound plus [ə] are more frequently used than the letter names, e.g. in oral spelling. Short vowels may be distinctively named as [kra:tke: aː] 'short *a*', etc.

b. The digraph *ou* [ou̯] is not considered a single letter of the alphabet.

TABLE 59.14: *Slovak Alphabet*

Letter			Phonetic Value	Name[a]
A	a		[a]	[aː]
Á	á		[aː]	[dlhe: aː] 'long *a*'
Ä	ä		[æ], [e]	[a z dvoma botkami] '*a* with two dots'
B	b		[b]	[beː]
C	c		[t͡s]	[t͡seː]
Č	č		[t͡ʃ]	[t͡ʃeː]
D	d		[d]; as palatal [ɟ]	[deː]
Ď	d'		[ɟ]	[ɟeː], [mæke: deː] 'soft *d*'
Dz	dz		[d͡z]	[d͡zeː]
Dž	dž		[d͡ʒ]	[d͡ʒeː]
E	e		[e]	[eː]
É	é		[eː]	[dlfie: eː] 'long *e*'
F	f		[f]	[ef]
G	g		[g]	[geː]
H	h		[ɦ]	[ɦaː]
Ch	ch		[x]	[xaː]
I	i		[i]	[iː]
Í	í		[iː]	[dlfie: iː] 'long *i*'
J	j		[j]	[jeː]
K	k		[k]	[kaː]
L	l		[l]; as palatal [ʎ]	[el]
Ĺ	ĺ		[lː]	[dlfie: el] 'long *l*'
Ľ,L'	l'		[ʎ]	[eʎ], [mæke: el] 'soft *l*'
M	m		[m]	[em]
N	n		[n]; as palatal [ɲ]	[en]
Ň	ñ		[ɲ]	[eɲ]
O	o		[o][b]	[oː]
Ó	ó		[oː]	[dlfie: oː] 'long *o*'
Ô	ô		[u̯o]	[o z voka:ɲom] '*o* with *vokáň*'
P	p		[p]	[peː]
(Q	q		[kv])	[kveː]
R	r		[r]	[er]
Ŕ	ŕ		[rː]	[dlfie: er] 'long *r*'
S	s		[s]	[es]
Š	š		[ʃ]	[əʃ]
T	t		[t]; as palatal [c]	[teː]
Ť	t'		[c]	[ceː], [mæke: teː] 'soft *t*'
U	u		[u]	[uː]
Ú	ú		[uː]	[dlfie: uː] 'long *u*'
V	v		[v]	[veː]
(W	w		[v])	[dvojite: veː] 'double *v*'
(X	x		[ks])	[iks]
Y	y		[i]	[ipsilon]
Ý	ý		[iː]	[dlfie: ipsilon] 'long *y*'
Z	z		[z]	[zet], [zeː]
Ž	ž		[ʒ]	[ʒet]

a. Short vowels may be distinctively named as [kra:tke a:] 'short *a*', etc. For the consonants, combinations of the consonant sound plus [ə] are more frequently used than the letter names, e.g. in oral spelling.

b. The digraph *ou* [ou̯] is not considered a single letter of the alphabet.

TABLE 59.15: *Slovene Alphabet*

Letter		Phonetic Value	Name[a]
A	a	[a]	[aː]
B	b	[b]	[beː]
C	c	[t͡s]	[t͡seː]
Č	č	[t͡ʃ]	[t͡ʃeː]
D	d	[d][b]	[deː]
E	e	[ɛ], [e], [ə]	[eː]
F	f	[f]	[ɛf]
G	g	[g]	[geː]
H	h	[x]	[xaː]
I	i	[i]	[iː]
J	j	[j]	[jeː]
K	k	[k]	[kaː]
L	l	[l]	[ɛl]
M	m	[m]	[ɛm]
N	n	[n]	[ɛn]
O	o	[ɔ], [o]	[oː]
P	p	[p]	[peː]
(Q	q)	[kv]	[kuː]
R	r	[r]	[ɛr]
S	s	[s]	[ɛs]
Š	š	[ʃ]	[ɛʃ]
T	t	[t]	[teː]
U	u	[u]	[uː]
V	v	[v]	[veː]
(W	w)	[v]	[ˈdvoːjni 'veː]]c] 'double v'
(X	x)	[ks]	[ˈiːks]
(Y	y)	[j], [i]	[ˈiːpsilon], [ipˈsiːlon]c]
Z	z	[z]	[zeː]
Ž	ž	[ʒ]	[ʒeː]

a. An alternative, much more frequently used system of letter names for the consonants (except *x* and *y*) uses the sound of the consonant followed by [ə], e.g. [bə]; in this system, *q* is [kvə] and *w* is [ˈdvoːjni 'və].
b. The digraph *dž* [d͡ʒ] is not considered a single letter.
c. Rising and falling tones on stressed long vowels have been indicated, although this prosodic distinction is not required in standard pronunciation; long stressed vowels whose tone is not indicated may be either rising or falling; short stressed vowels can only have falling tone.

TABLE 59.16: *Serbo-Croatian (Latin) Alphabet[a]*

Letter		Value	Name
A	a	[a]	[ˈaː]
B	b	[b]	[ˈbeː]
C	c	[t͡s]	[ˈt͡seː]
Č	č	[t͡ʃ]	[ˈt͡ʃeː]
Ć	ć	[t͡ɕ]	[ˈt͡ɕeː]
D	d	[d]	[ˈdeː]
Dž	dž	[d͡ʒ]	[ˈd͡ʒeː]
Đ	d	[d͡z]	[ˈd͡zeː]
E	e	[e]	[ˈeː]
F	f	[f]	[ˈef]
G	g	[g]	[ˈgeː]
H	h	[x]~[h]	[ˈxaː] ~ [ˈhaː]
I	i	[i]	[ˈiː]
J	j	[j]	[ˈjeː], [ˈjot], [ˈjə]
K	k	[k]	[ˈkaː]
L	l	[l]	[ˈel]
Lj	lj	[ʎ]	[ˈeʎ]
M	m	[m]	[ˈem]
N	n	[n]	[ˈen]
Nj	nj	[ɲ]	[ˈeɲ]
O	o	[o]	[ˈoː]
P	p	[p]	[ˈpeː]
R	r	[r]	[ˈer]
S	s	[s]	[ˈes]
Š	š	[ʃ]	[ˈeʃ]
T	t	[t]	[ˈteː]
U	u	[u]	[ˈuː]
V	v	[v]	[ˈveː]
Z	z	[z]	[ˈzeː]
Ž	ž	[ʒ]	[ˈʒeː]

a. Cf. TABLE 60.4 on page 704.

TABLE 59.17: *Lithuanian Alphabet*

Letter[a]			Phonetic Value	Name[b]
A	a		[a], [aː]	[\a]
Ą	ą		[aː]	[\a \noːsʲinʲeː] 'nasal *a*'
B	b		[b]	[\bʲɛ]
C	c		[t͡s]	[\t͡sʲɛ]
Ch	ch		[x]	[\xə]
Č	č		[t͡ʃ]	[\t͡ʃʲɛ]
D	d		[d]	[\dʲɛ]
E	e		[ɛ],[c] [ɛː]	[\ɛ]
Ę	ę		[ɛː]	[\ɛ \noːsʲinʲeː] 'nasal *e*'
Ė	ė		[eː]	[\eː]
F	f		[f]	[\ɛf]
G	g		[g]	[\gʲɛ]
H	h		[ɦ]	[\ɦaʃ]
I	i		[i][d]	[\i trum\poːji] 'short *i*'
Į	į		[iː]	[\i \noːsʲinʲeː] 'nasal *i*'
Y	y		[iː]	[\i il\goːji] 'long *i*'
J	j		[j]	[\jot]
K	k		[k]	[\ka]
L	l		[l]	[\ɛl]
M	m		[m]	[\ɛm]
N	n		[n]	[\ɛn]
O	o		[oː]; [o] in loanwords	[\o]
P	p		[p]	[\pʲɛ]
R	r		[r]	[\ɛr]
S	s		[s]	[\ɛs]
Š	š		[ʃ]	[\ɛʃ]
T	t		[t]	[\tʲɛ]
U	u		[u]	[\u trum\poːji] 'short *u*'
Ų	ų		[uː]	[\u \noːsʲinʲeː] 'nasal *u*'
Ū	ū		[uː]	[\u il\goːji] 'long *u*'
V	v		[v]	[\vʲɛ]
Z	z		[z]	[\zʲɛ]
Ž	ž		[ʒ]	[\ʒʲɛ]

a. The following digraphs are not considered single letters of the alphabet:

Dz	dz	[d͡z]
Dž	dž	[d͡ʒ]
Ie	ie	[ie]
Uo	uo	[uo]

plus diphthongs consisting of *a* or *e* plus *i, u, l, r, m, n*.

b. An alternative system of letter names for the consonants uses the sound of the consonant followed by [ə], e.g. [bə]. A traditional system gives names of the form [Cʲeː] to those letters here shown as [Cʲɛ].

c. Some speakers pronounce short *e* as [e] in loanwords.

d. Consonants are automatically palatalized before front vowels. Before back vowels, palatalization of a consonant is indicated by the letter *i* between the consonant and the back vowel.

TABLE 59.18: *Latvian Alphabet*

Letter		Phonetic Value	Name[a]
A	a	[a]	[˦a:]
Ā	ā	[a:]	
B	b	[b]	[˦be:]
C	c	[t͡s]	[˦t͡se:]
Č	č	[t͡ʃ]	[˦t͡ʃe:], [˦t͡ʃa:]
D	d	[d]	[˦de:]
Dz	dz	[d͡z]	[˦d͡ze:]
Dž	dž	[d͡ʒ]	[˦d͡ʒe:], [˦d͡ʒa:]
E	e	[ɛ], [e]	[˦e:]
Ē	ē	[ɛ:], [e:]	
F	f	[f]	[ef]
G	g	[g]	[˦ga:]
Ģ	ģ	[ɟ]	[mi̭ːk˦stais ˦ga:] 'soft *g*'
H	h	[x]; older [ɦ]	[˦xa:], [˦ɦa:]
(Ch	ch	[x])[b]	[˦xa:])
I	i	[i]	[˦i:]
Ī	ī	[i:]	
J	j	[j]	[jot]
K	k	[k]	[˦ka:]
Ķ	ķ	[c]	[mi̭ːk˦stais ˦ka:] 'soft *k*'
L	l	[l]	[el]
Ļ	ļ	[ʎ]	[eʎ], [mi̭ːk˦stais el] 'soft *l*'
M	m	[m]	[em]
N	n	[n]	[en]
Ņ	ņ	[ɲ]	[eɲ], [mi̭ːk˦stais en] 'soft *n*'
O	o	[uo]; in loanwords [o], [o:]	[˦o:]
P	p	[p]	[˦pe:]
R	r	[r]	[er]
(Ŗ	ŗ	[rʲ])[b]	[mi̭ːk˦stais er] 'soft *r*'
S	s	[s]	[es]
Š	š	[ʃ]	[eʃ]
T	t	[t]	[˦te:]
U	u	[u]	[˦u:]
Ū	ū	[u:]	
V	v	[v]	[˦ve:]
Z	z	[z]	[˦ze:]
Ž	ž	[ʒ]	[˦ʒe:], [˦ʒa:]

a. The long vowels may be distinctively named as [˦a: ar garum\zi:mi] '*a* with length-sign' or [ga˦rais ˦a:] 'long *a*', etc.

b. The letters *ch* and *ŗ* were abolished in Soviet Latvia, and their status since the reestablishment of independence is controversial (SECTION 67).

SAMPLES OF SLAVIC AND BALTIC LANGUAGES

POLISH

1. Polish:	Już	w	rękopisach	wytworzył	się	swoisty	
2. Transcription:	juʃ	w	reŋkopʲisax	vɪtfoʒɪw	ɕe	sfojistɪ	
3. Gloss:	already	in	manuscripts	created	self	characteristic	

1. typ	ortografii,[a]	w szczegółach zaś	wykrystalizował	się	we
2. tɪp	ortografji	f ʃtʃeguwax zaɕ	vɪkrɪstalʲizovaw	ɕe	ve
3. type	of.orthography	in details	however crystallized	self	in

1. wzorowych drukowniach	krakowskich.	Polega	on	na	łączeniu
2. vzorovɪx drukovɲax	krakofskʲix	polega	on	na	wontʃeɲu
3. leading printing-houses	Cracowian	relies	it	on	combination

1. liter	alfabetu	łacińskiego	i	na użyciu litery	i	jako znaku
2. lʲiter	alfabetu	watɕiɲskʲego	i	na uʒɪtɕu lʲiterɪ	i	jako znaku
3. of.letters	of.alphabet	Latin	and	on use of.letter *i*	as	sign

1. miękkości.[b]	Próby	radykalnej	zmiany	minęły	bez	echa.
2. mʲeŋkoɕtɕi	prubɪ	radɪkalnej	zmʲanɪ	mʲinewɪ	bez	exa
3. of.softness	attempts	of.radical	change	passed	without	echo

'Already in the manuscripts there arose a characteristic type of orthography; however, it was crystallized in its details in the leading Cracow printing-houses. It is based on the combination of letters of the Latin alphabet and on the use of the letter *i* as a sign of softness. Attempts at radical change have passed by without trace.'   —*Encyklopedia Powszechna 1975: 586.*

Notes:

[a]The word *ortografii* shows the letter *i* representing [j] before a vowel, a possibility found in loanwords.
[b]The adjective *miękki* 'soft' and its derivatives are spelled with double *k*, but pronounced with single [kʲ].

CZECH

1. Czech:	Třebas	nová	Pravidla	českého	pravopisu	vyšla
2. Transcription:	třebas	nova:	pravidla	tʃeske:ɦo	pravopisu	viʃla
3. Gloss:	although	new	rules	of.Czech	orthography	came.out

1. až	v průběhu	sazby	slovníku,	bylo	ještě	možno
2. aʃ	f pru:bjeɦu	sazbi	slovɲi:ku	bilo	jeʃce	moʒno
3. until	in course	of.setting	of.dictionary	it.was	still	possible

1. přihlédnout	k nim	všude	tam,	kde	připouštějí	u slov
2. přiɦle:dnout	k ɲim	fʃude	tam	gde	připouʃceji:	u slof
3. to.take.account	to them	everywhere	there	where	they.admit	at words

1. jedinou pravopisnou podobu. Kde   uvádějí   podobu dvojí
2. jeɟinou pravopisnou podobu ɡde   uvaːɟejiː   podobu dvojiː
3. single orthographic form   where   they.introduce form   double

1. (zvláště   u výpůjček z   cizích jazyků),   tam   byl ponechán
2. zvlaːʃce   u viːpuːjtʃek s   t͡siziːx jazikuː   tam   bil ponexaːn
3. especially at loans   from foreign languages there   was left

1. pravopisný způsob   dosud   obvyklý.
2. pravopisniː spuːsop   dosut   obvikliː
3. orthographic manner   hitherto usual

> 'Although the new Rules of Czech Orthography came out during the typesetting
> of the dictionary, it was still possible to take account of them wherever they
> admit of a single orthographic form for words. Where they introduce two forms
> (especially with loans from foreign languages), the hitherto usual way of spell-
> ing has been left.'   —*Poldauf 1959: vi.*

SERBO-CROATIAN (CROATIAN STANDARD)

1. Croatian: Ako riječ   ima   više   različitih   značenja
2. Transcription: \ako \rijeːt͡ʃ /imaː   \viʃeː   /raːzlit͡ʃitiːx /znaːt͡ʃeɲaː
3. Gloss: if   word   has   several different   meanings

1. odnosno ako meðu   značenjima   postoje   znatnije   smisaone
2. /odnosno \ako \med͡zu   /znaːt͡ʃeːɲima po/stoje   /znatnijeː   \smiːsaoneː
3. or   if   among   meanings   exist   more.significant semantic

1. nijanse, to   su hrvatski prijevodi   odijeljeni točkom   i
2. ni/janse \to: su /xrvaːtski: pri/jeːvodi /odije/ʎeni \tot͡ʃkoːm i
3. nuances   then are Croatian translations separated   by.dot   and

1. zarezom,   dok   su sinonimi, odnosno riječi   sličnog   značenja,
2. /zaːrezom \dok   su si/nonimi /odnosno \rijeːt͡ʃi \slit͡ʃnoːɡ /znaːt͡ʃeɲa
3. by.comma while are synonyms or   words   of.similar meaning

1. odijeljeni zarezom.   Fraze,   idiomi,   uzrečice i   poslovice
2. /odije/ʎeni /zaːrezom /fraːze idi/oːmi /uzret͡ʃitse i /poslovit͡se
3. separated   by.comma   phrases idioms   sayings and proverbs

1. odvojene su od prijevoda dvjema   tankim   uspravnim   crtama.
2. /odvojene su od pri/jeːvoda /dvjeːma /tankiːm \uspraːvniːm \t͡sr̩tama
3. separated are from translation by.two   thin   vertical   lines

> 'If a word has several different meanings or if among the meanings there are
> more significant semantic nuances, then the Croatian translations are separated
> by a semicolon, while synonyms, or words of similar meaning, are separated by

a comma. Phrases, idioms, sayings, and proverbs are separated from the translation by two thin vertical lines.' *—Poljanec and Madatova-Poljanec 1973: v.*

LITHUANIAN TEXT

1. Lithuanian:	Tai	buvo	nedidelė	balta	katytė.	Jos	menkas
2. Transcription:	/ˈtai	\ˈbuvo:	nʲɛ\dʲidʲɛlʲe:	bal\ta	ka\tʲiːtʲe:	/jo:s	/mʲɛnkas
3. Gloss:	it	was	small	white	kitten	its	poor

1.	suliesėjęs	kūnelis	visas	drebėjo	nuo	šalčio	ir	baimės;
2.	sulʲiɛ\sʲeːjɛːs	ku:/nʲɛːlʲis	\vʲisas	dʲrʲɛ\bʲeːjo:	nuo	/ʃalʲtʲo:	ir	\baimʲeːs
3.	emaciated	body	all	shivered	from cold	and	fear

1.	jos	plaukai,	lietaus	sušlapinti	ir	purvais	apskretę,	visi
2.	/jo:s	plau/kai	lʲiɛ/taus	su/ʃlaːpʲinʲtʲi	ir	pur/vais	ap/skrʲɛːtʲɛː	vʲi\sʲi
3.	its	hairs	of.rain	soaked	and	with.mud	covered	all

1.	kabėjo	sustirę	ir	pasišiaušę.	Radau	aš	ją	lauke,
2.	ka\bʲeːjo:	su\sʲtʲirʲɛː	ir	pasʲi\ʃʲauʃʲɛː	ra/dau	\aʃ	/ja:	lau\kʲɛ
3.	hung	stiff	and	disheveled	found	I	it	outside

1.	patvory	pritūpusią,	susirietusią,	nelaimingą.
2.	patvo:/rʲi:	pʲrʲi/tu:pusʲa:	susʲi/rʲiɛtusʲa:	nʲɛlai\mʲinga:
3.	at-fence	squatting	cowering	unhappy

'It was a small white kitten. Its whole poor emaciated body shivered with cold and fear; all its fur, soaked and covered with mud, hung stiff and disheveled. I found it outside, squatting by the fence, cowering, unhappy.'
—G. Niliūnas, "Kliudžiai" [I hit the mark], in Vinogradov et al. 1968: 524.

Albanian

Various means of writing Albanian were used into the twentieth century, adapting Latin, Greek, Cyrillic, or Arabic script, depending on the models immediately at hand to the user. The Congress of Monastir (Bitola) in 1908 was a landmark in the adoption of the currently used Latin script. Albanian dialects differ markedly from one another, with a major division between Tosk (southern) and Geg (northern, also spelt Gheg); the dividing line is roughly the Shkumbin River. A standard written language, based primarily on central Tosk, has been developed since World War II; it is accepted as such in Albania and (since 1968) in Kosovo, an administrative division of Serbia with an ethnic and linguistic Albanian majority. In the early twentieth century, various dialects were used in writing; however, a variety based on the southern Geg dialect of Elbasan was proposed as a standard, and was used as such by some people in the 1920s and 1930s. Written Geg is most readily recognizable in the use of the circumflex diacritic for nasalized vowels, which are phonemic in Geg but absent from Tosk.

TABLE 59.19: *Albanian Alphabet*

Letter[a]		Phonetic Value	Name
A	a	[a]	[a]
B	b	[b]	[bə]
C	c	[t͡s]	[t͡sə]
Ç	ç	[t͡ʃ]	[t͡ʃə]
D	d	[d]	[də]
Dh	dh	[ð]	[ðə]
E	e	[ɛ]	[ɛ]
Ë	ë	[ə]	[ə]
F	f	[f]	[fə]
G	g	[g]	[gə]
Gj	gj	[ɟ]	[ɟə]
H	h	[h]	[hə]
I	i	[i, j][b]	[i]
J	j	[j]	[jə]
K	k	[k]	[kə]
L	l	[l]	[lə]
Ll	ll	[ɫ] ("dark" *l*)	[ɫə]
M	m	[m]	[mə]
N	n	[n]	[nə]
Nj	nj	[ɲ]	[ɲə]
O	o	[ɔ]	[ɔ]
P	p	[p]	[pə]
Q	q	[c]	[cə]
R	r	[ɾ]	[ɾə]
Rr	rr	[r]	[rə]
S	s	[s]	[sə]
Sh	sh	[ʃ]	[ʃə]
T	t	[t]	[tə]
Th	th	[θ]	[θə]
U	u	[u]	[u]
V	v	[v]	[və]
X	x	[d͡z]	[d͡zə]
Xh	xh	[d͡ʒ]	[d͡ʒə]
Y	y	[y]	[y]
Z	z	[z]	[zə]
Zh	zh	[ʒ]	[ʒə]

a. The diphthongs [iɛ], [ua], [yɛ] are written as vowel sequences: *ie, ua, ye*. The nasalized vowels of Geg, when written, take a circumflex diacritic, but are not considered distinct letters of the alphabet.

b. *i* is normally syllabic, *j* nonsyllabic; but in some instances nonsyllabic [j] is written *i*, e.g. to preserve morphological parallelism and to distinguish [nj] *ni* from [ɲ] *nj*, [gj] *gi* from [ɟ] *gj*.

Spoken Albanian, including even the reading of a text written in standard written Albanian, is more likely than not to reveal phonetic features that deviate from a literal interpretation of the written standard; thus to say that the current orthography is generally phonemic is in a sense true, but fails to note that it is a phonemic representation of a highly idealized pronunciation—one might even argue that this idealized pronunciation is a reflection of the orthography, rather than vice versa. Thus many speakers omit word-final unstressed *ë* [ə] after a single consonant (and Geg speakers will typically lengthen the preceding vowel, thus giving rise to phonemic vowel length, not normally marked orthographically even when Geg is written). The pronunciation of stressed *ë* will normally follow that of the speaker's native dialect, ranging from [ɔ] for Geg speakers to [æ] for southeast Tosk speakers. Word-final voiced obstruents are likely to be devoiced by Tosk speakers, but not by Geg speakers. In this case the orthography is actually closer to Geg, since for Tosk speakers it is either morphophonemic (where there is morphological alternation between word-final voiceless and word-medial voiced obstruents) or historical (where there is no such alternation). Stress is partly, but not fully, predictable, given morphological information; it tends to fall on the last syllable of the stem of the word. In particular, stress is not in general subject to change when inflectional suffixes are added.

The date of the Monastir alphabet means that its originators had a wide range of models to choose from. Most of the non-digraph letters of the alphabet have standard values found in other languages of eastern Europe, while *ç* [t͡ʃ] and *q* [c] continue an older Albanian tradition. The use of *j* in digraphs to mark palatals is a logical choice, adopted in part also by Serbo-Croatian (Latin script), while the uses to which *h* is put in digraphs closely follow the English model. Letter names of vowels are simply the sounds of the vowels; those of consonants are the sounds of the consonants followed by shwa, a system also found in some other languages of the Balkans (Bulgarian, Macedonian, Serbo-Croatian [Cyrillic script]).

SAMPLE OF ALBANIAN

1. Albanian:	Perëndia,	i	paçim	uratën,	si	bëri
2. Transcription:	pɛrən'dia	i	'pat͡ʃim	u'ratən	si	'bəri
3. Gloss:	God	to.him	may.we.have	the.blessing	as	he.made

1.	në	pesë	ditë	tokën,	diellin	dhe	yjet,	dritën,
2.	nə	'pɛsə	'ditə	'tɔkən	'diełin	ðɛ	'yjɛt	'dritən
3.	in	five	days	the.earth	the.sun	and	the.stars	the.light

1.	ditën	e	natën,	bimët,	malet,	kafshët	e
2.	'ditən	ɛ	'natən	'bimət	'malɛt	'kafʃət	ɛ
3.	the.day	and	the.night	the.plants	the.mountains	the.animals	and

1.	gjithë	ç'na		sheh	e	nuk	na	sheh	syri,	të
2.	'ɟiθə	t͡ʃna		'ʃɛh	ɛ	'nuk	na	'ʃɛh	'syri	tə
3.	all	what.for.us		it.sees	and	not	for.us	it.sees	the.eye	the

1.	gyashtën,	si	pa	që	këto të	mira[a]		do të shkonin[b]
2.	'ɟaʃtən	si	pa	cə	kə'tɔ tə	'mira		dɔ tə 'ʃkɔnin
3.	the.sixth	as	he.saw	that	these	good.things		they.would.go

1.	kot,	ra	në	mendime	të	thella[a]	e	më	në	fund
2.	'kɔt	'ra	nə	mɛn'dimɛ	tə	'θɛɫa	ɛ	mə	nə	'fund
3.	in.vain	he.fell	in	thoughts		deep	and	more	in	end

1.	i	dha	udhë	të	krijonte	robin.
2.	i	'ða	'uðə	tə	kri'jɔntɛ	'rɔbin
3.	to.him	it.gave	path	that	he.might.create	the.person

'God, may we have his blessing, as in five days he made the earth, the sun and the stars, the light, the day and the night, the plants, the mountains, the animals, and all that our eye sees and does not see for us, and as, on the sixth, when he saw that these good things would go for naught, he fell into deep thought and finally it occurred to him that he might create Man.'

—*Jakov Xoxa, "Lumi e vdekur" [Blessed and dead], in Camaj 1984: 299.*

Notes:
[a]In *të mira* and *të thella*, the particle *të* is required before the adjective.
[b]In *do të shkonin*, the sequence *do të* 'wish that' plus the imperfect of the main verb expresses the conditional (future in the past).

Uralic languages

Europe's Uralic literary languages, Finnish, Estonian, and Hungarian, all have high and mid front rounded vowels, Finnish and Estonian also [æ], represented orthographically by an umlaut—except that Finnish, like Swedish, uses *y* rather than *ü*. Although archaic and rural varieties of standard Hungarian distinguish low and mid front unrounded vowels, they are not distinguished orthographically (or in current urban speech).

All three languages have distinctive vowel and consonant length. Consonant length is shown by doubling the consonant (or the first element of a digraph in Hungarian, e.g. *ssz* for long *sz* [s]). Doubling is also used for vowel length in Finnish and Estonian; but Hungarian uses an acute accent, and combines umlaut and acute to give the distinctive diacritic in *ő ű*.

Estonian has a distinction between light and heavy stressed syllables, involving a combination of tenseness, segment length, and pitch, but this is usually not shown orthographically. However, for long intervocalic obstruents (except [s]) Estonian writes *p, t, k, f, š* in light stressed syllables, and *pp, tt, kk, ff, šš* in heavy stressed syllables, e.g. *kapi* [kappi] 'cupboard (genitive)', *kappi* ["kappi] 'cupboard (illative)', where ["] symbolizes heavy stress. The short obstruents are written *b, d, g, ž* word-

TABLE 59.20: *Finnish Alphabet*

Letter[a]		Value	Name
A	a	[ɑ]	[ɑ:]
(B	b)	[b]	[be:]
(C	c)	[k], [s]	[se:]
D	d	[d]	[de:]
E	e	[e]	[e:]
(F	f)	[f]	[æf], [ef]
G	g	[g][b]	[ge:]
H	h	[h]	[ho:]
I	i	[i]	[i:]
J	j	[j]	[ji:]
K	k	[k]	[ko:]
L	l	[l]	[æl], [el]
M	m	[m]	[æm], [em]
N	n	[n]	[æn], [en]
O	o	[o]	[o:]
P	p	[p]	[pe:]
(Q	q)	[kv]	[ku:]
R	r	[r]	[ær], [er]
S	s	[s]	[æs], [es]
T	t	[t]	[te:]
U	u	[u]	[u:]
V	v	[v]	[ve:]
(W	w)[c]	[v]	['kaksois,ve:] 'double *v*'
(X	x)	[ks]	[æks], [eks]
Y	y	[y]	[y:]
(Z	z)	[ts]	[tset]
Ä	ä	[æ]	[æ:]
Ö	ö	[ø]	[ø:]

a. The following are not considered separate letters of the alphabet:
  NG ng [ŋŋ]
  (Š, Sh š, sh [ʃ])
b. *g* has the value [g] only in unassimilated loanwords.
c. *w* is not treated as distinct from *v* for purposes of alphabetical ordering.

TABLE 59.21: *Estonian Alphabet*

Letter		Value	Name[a]
A	a	[ɑ]	["ɑ:]
B	b	[p]	["be:], ["nərkk "pe:] 'weak *b*'
(C	c)	[t͡s]	["t͡se:]
(Č	č)[b]	[t͡ʃ]	["t͡ʃe:]
D	d	[t]	["de:], ["nərkk "te:] 'weak *d*'
E	e	[e]	["e:]
F	f	[f]	["eff]
G	g	[k]	["ge:], ["ke:]
H	h	[h]	["hɑ:]
I	i	[i]	["i:]
J	j	[j]	["jott]
K	k	[kk]	["kɑ:]
L	l	[l]	["ell]
M	m	[m]	["emm]
N	n	[n]	["enn]
O	o	[o]	["o:]
P	p	[pp]	["pe:], [tukev "pe:] 'strong *p*'
(Q	q)	[kv]	["ku:]
R	r	[r]	["ærr]
S	s	[ss]	["ess]
Š	š	[ʃʃ]	["ʃɑ:]
Z	z	[s]	["se:]
Ž	ž	[ʃ]	["ʃe:]
T	t	[tt]	["te:], [tukev "te:] 'strong *t*'
U	u	[u]	["u:]
V	v	[v]	["ve:]
(W	w)	[v]	[kaksisve:] 'double *v*'
Õ	õ	[ɤ]	["ɤ:]
Ä	ä	[æ]	["æ:]
Ö	ö	[ø]	["ø:]
Ü	ü	[y]	["y:]
(X	x)	[ks]	["ikks]
(Y	y)	[j], [y]	[ypsilon]

a. Heavy-stressed syllables are shown by the diacritic ["] before the syllable. An older system used *pehme* ["pehme] 'soft' and *kõva* ["kvvɑ] 'hard' rather than *nõrk* ["nɤrkk] 'weak' and *tugev* ['tukev] 'strong', respectively. The names of the letters *b*, *d*, *g*, *z*, and *ž* are spelled *(nõrk) bee*, *(nõrk) dee*, *gee*, *zee*, *žee*, respectively.
b. The status of *č* is controversial; it is often replaced by *tš*.

TABLE 59.22: *Hungarian Alphabet*

Letter		Value	Name[a]	Letter		Value	Name[a]
A	a	[ɒ]	[ɒ:]	Ny	ny	[ɲ]	[ɛɲ]
Á	á	[a:]	[a:]	O	o	[o]	[o]; [røvid o:] 'short *o*'
B	b	[b]	[be:]	Ó	ó	[o:]	[o:]; [hossu: o:] 'long *o*'
C	c	[t͡s]	[t͡se:]	Ö	ö	[ø]	[ø]; [røvid ø:] 'short *ö*'
Cs	cs	[t͡ʃ]	[t͡ʃe:]	Ő	ő	[ø:]	[ø:]; [hossu: ø:] 'long *ö*'
D	d	[d]	[de:]	P	p	[p]	[pe:]
DZ	dz	[dz]	[dze:]	(Q	q)		[ku:]
Dzs	dzs[b]	[d͡ʒ]	[d͡ʒe:]	R	r	[r]	[ɛr]
E	e	[ɛ]	[ɛ:]	S	s	[ʃ]	[ɛʃ]
É	é	[e:]	[e:]	Sz	sz	[s]	[ɛs]
F	f	[f]	[ɛf]	T	t	[t]	[te:]
G	g	[g]	[ge:]	Ty	ty	[c]	[ce:]
Gy	gy	[ɟ]	[ɟe:]	U	u	[u]	[u]; [røvid u:] 'short *u*'
H	h	[h]	[ha:]	Ú	ú	[u:]	[u:]; [hossu: u:] 'long *u*'
I	i	[i]	[i]; [røvid i:] 'short *i*'	Ü	ü	[y]	[y]; [røvid y:] 'short *ü*'
Í	í	[i:]	[i:]; [hossu: i:] 'long *i*'	Ű	ű	[y:]	[y:]; [hossu: y:] 'long *ü*'
J	j	[j]	[je:]	V	v	[v]	[ve:]
K	k	[k]	[ka:]	(W	w)		[duplave:] 'double *v*'
L	l	[l]	[ɛl]	(X	x)		[iks]
Ly	ly	[j]	[ɛl ipsilon]	(Y	y)		[ipsilon]
M	m	[m]	[ɛm]	Z	z	[z]	[ze:]
N	n	[n]	[ɛn]	Zs	zs	[ʒ]	[ʒe:]

a.   The names of the vowels *a* and *e* are usually phonetically long, being distinguished qualitatively from the names of *á* and *é*. For the other vowels, where qualitative distinctions are less marked, there are variant systems, as indicated in the table.

b.   Dictionaries usually, but not invariably, place words beginning with *dzs* at the end of the *d* section, rather than as a separate section; there are no words beginning with *dz* (other than the letter name *dzé*) and its status as a unitary phoneme is dubious, whence it is transcribed here as a sequence of sounds rather than as an affricate. Since *z* and *zs* are the last letters of the alphabet, there are no examples where treating *dz* and *dzs* as single letters or as sequences of *d-z* and *d-zs* would affect alphabetical order.

medially and -finally (short [f] does not occur here), but *p, t, k, f, š* word-initially, as in *kabi* [kɑpi] 'hoof'.

Finnish uses the digraph *ng* to represent [ŋ] (which occurs only long and intervocalically, other than through assimilation of /n/ to a following velar), this being the only use of *g* in native words.

Estonian has an extra vowel [ɤ], written *õ*, and also has phonemically distinct (pre-)palatalized [tʲ], [nʲ], [sʲ], and [lʲ] in very restricted environments, the palatalization not being shown orthographically.

Hungarian has a more complicated consonant inventory, including palatals and affricates, and like Polish it makes widespread use of digraphs: [t͡s] is represented by *c*, as in most central and eastern European languages. A digraph with *y* represents a palatal in the case of *gy* [ɟ], *ty* [c], *ny* [ɲ]; *ly* originally represented a palatal lateral, but has now merged with [j]. A digraph with *s* represents a palatal in the case of *cs* [t͡ʃ] and *zs* [ʒ]. Among the voiceless fricatives, Hungarian has *s* for [ʃ] but the digraph *sz* for [s]—a unique distribution among the modern languages of central and eastern Europe, but one found elsewhere in earlier periods. All languages have basically non-phonemic stress, though Estonian has exceptions in words of foreign origin; stress is not indicated orthographically. Finnish and Estonian show Scandinavian influence in placing the special vowel letters at or near the end of the alphabet.

SAMPLES OF URALIC LANGUAGES

FINNISH

1. *Finnish:*	Kesäinen	sade[a]	rapisee	pärekattoon.[a]		Räystään
2. *Transcription:*	'kesæinen	'sader	'rɑpise:	'pærek,katto:n		'ræystæ:n
3. *Gloss:*	summery	rain	patters	into.shingle.roof		of.eaves

1.	alta	seinänrakoisista	käy	hienoinen	tuulenhenkäys	ja
2.	ɑlta	'seinæn,rɑkoisista	'kæy	'hienoinen	'tu:len,heŋkæys	ja
3.	from under	from,wall.cracks	comes	gentle	wind.draft	and

1.	hämähäkinverkot	katto-orsissa	keinuvat	ja	heiluvat.	Joskus
2.	'hæmæhækin,verkot	'katto,orsissa	'keinuvat	ja	'heiluvat	'joskus
3.	cobwebs	in.roof.poles	swing	and	sway	sometimes

1.	varpuset	käyvät	hyppimässä	katolla.	Hämärällä	ullakolla	vallitsee
2.	'varpuset	'kæyvæt	'hyppimæssæ	'katolla	'hæmærællæ	'ullɑkolla	'vallitse:
3.	sparrows	come	hopping	on.roof	dark	on.garret	reigns

1.	salaperäinen	tunnelma.
2.	'sɑla,peræinen	'tunnelma
3.	mysterious	atmosphere

'The summer rain patters onto the shingle roof. From under the eaves a gentle draft comes through the cracks in the wall and the spiders' webs swing and sway on the roof-poles. Sometimes sparrows come hopping on the roof. A mysterious atmosphere reigns in the dark garret.'

— *Veikko Huovinen, "Havukka-ahon ajattelija" [The thinker of Havukka-aho],*
in Ravila 1965: 135.

Note:
[a]The words *sade* [sade], [sade?] 'rain' and *päre* [pære], [pære?] 'shingle' ended historically (and still for some speakers) in a glottal stop; for all speakers, they geminate a following consonant, as in *sade rapisee* and *pärekattoon.*

HUNGARIAN

1. Hungarian:	Szeretnők,	ha	nemcsak	a	magyar		nyelv
2. Transcription:	sɛrɛtnøːk	hɒ	nɛmt͡ʃɒk	ɒ	mɒɟɒr		ɲɛlv
3. Gloss:	we.would.like.it	if	not.only	the	Hungarian		language

1. történetének	búvárai,		hanem	népünk	széles	rétegei	is
2. tørteːnɛteːnɛk	buːvaːrɒi		hɒnɛm	neːpynk	seːlɛʃ	reːtɛgɛi	iʃ
3. of.its.history	its.investigators		but	our.people	broad	its.strata	also

1. tudatában	lennének	annak	a	hősi	küzdelemnek,	melyet
2. tudɒtɒːbɒn	lɛnneːnɛk	ɒnnɒk	ɒ	høːʃi	kyzdɛlɛmnɛk	mɛjɛt
3. in.its.consciousness	would.be	of.that	the	heroic	of.struggle	which

1. Petőfi	vívott	irodalmi	s	elsősorban	költői	nyelvünk
2. pɛtøːfi	viːvott	irodɒlmi	ʃ	ɛlʃøːʃorbɒn	køltøːi	ɲɛlvynk
3. Petőfi	fought	literary	and	in.first.place	poetic	our.language

1. megújhodásáért.
2. mɛguːjhodaːʃaːeːrt
3. for.its.revival

'We would be happy if not only investigators of the history of the Hungarian language, but also broad strata of our people, would be conscious of the heroic struggle that Petőfi fought for the revival of our literary and, especially, poetic language.'   —*Gáldi et al. 1973: 135.*

Turkish

On the order of Kemal Atatürk in 1928, the Republic of Turkey switched virtually overnight from the Arabic-based script of Ottoman Turkish (TABLE 62.8 on page 758) to a Roman alphabet script (Heyd 1954, Bazin 1983). Turkish has an eight-vowel system; the front rounded vowels are indicated by means of an umlaut, the high back unrounded vowel by dropping the dot from the letter *i* (the upper case equivalent of *i* is *İ*, that of *ı* is *I*.) Vowel length is distinctive, in particular in loans from Arabic–Persian, but is only rarely indicated by means of a circumflex accent. In native words,

TABLE 59.23: *Turkish Alphabet*

Letter		Phonetic Value	Name
A	a	[a]	[a]
B	b	[b]	[be]
C	c	[d͡ʒ]	[d͡ʒe]
Ç	ç	[t͡ʃ]	[t͡ʃe]
D	d	[d]	[de]
E	e	[e]	[e]
F	f	[f]	[fe]
G	g	[g], [gʲ]	[gʲe]
Ğ	ğ	(see text)	[jumuˈʃak ˌgʲe] 'soft *g*'
H	h	[h]	[he], [ha]
I	ı	[ɯ]	[ɯ]
İ	i	[i]	[i]
J	j	[ʒ]	[ʒe]
K	k	[k], [kʲ]	[kʲe], [ka]
L	l	[l], [lʲ]	[lʲe]
M	m	[m]	[me]
N	n	[n]	[ne]
O	o	[o]	[o]
Ö	ö	[ø]	[ø]
P	p	[p]	[pe]
R	r	[r]	[re]
S	s	[s]	[se]
Ş	ş	[ʃ]	[ʃe]
T	t	[t]	[te]
U	u	[u]	[u]
Ü	ü	[y]	[y]
V	v	[v]	[ve]
Y	y	[j]	[je]
Z	z	[z]	[ze]

vowel length arises through the historical loss of a voiced velar fricative syllable-finally, and is represented by the etymological spelling of vowel + ğ (between vowels, ğ is silent). The representation of consonants is basically in terms of a one-to-one phoneme–letter correspondence. Among palatals, *y* represents [j] while *j* (as in French) is [ʒ]; [ʃ] and [t͡ʃ] are indicated by means of a cedilla (*ş*, *ç*), while [d͡ʒ] makes idiosyncratic but efficient use of the letter *c*. There is contrast in loanwords between front and back *k*, *g*, *l* before back vowels (in the case of *l*, also word-finally); this is not usually shown orthographically, although a circumflex accent is sometimes used on *a* and *u* to indicate a preceding front velar or lateral. Stress is phonemic, in particular in proper names and in loanwords, but is not indicated orthographically.

SAMPLE OF TURKISH

1. Turkish: Bin   dokuz   yüz   yirmi   sekiz   yılında   kabul
2. Transcription: 'bin   do'kuz ˌjyz jirˌmi se'kʲiz juɫun'da   ka'bulʲ
3. Gloss: 1000   9   100   20   8   in.its.year acceptance

1. edilmiş   olan   Yeni   Türk   Alfabesi   her   ses   için   ayrı
2. edilʲˌmiʃ olan   jeˌni 'tyrkʲ alfabe'si   'her   ˌses   itʃin aj'rɯɯ
3. done   being   new   Turk   its.alphabet each   sound for   separate

1. bir harf   ve   her   harf   için yalnız   bir   ses   esasları   üzerine
2. bir 'harf ve   'her ˌharf itʃin 'jalnɯz 'bir ˌses   esasla'rɯɯ   yzerine
3. a   letter and   each letter for   only   one   sound its.principles onto

1. Lâtin   harfleriyle   tertip   edilmiştir. Bütün   harfler   okunur.
2. lʲa'tin harflʲe'rijlʲe   ter'tip   edilʲˌmiʃtir by'tyn harf'lʲer   oku'nur
3. Latin   with.its.letters organization was.done   all   letters   are.read

1. Yalnız   yumuşak   ge   harfinin   okunmadığı   ve   yerine
2. 'jalnɯz jumu'ʃak 'gʲe harfi'nin   o'kunmadɯɯ   ve   jeri'ne
3. however soft   *g* its.letter not.to.be.read and to.its.position

1. göre   farklı   söylendiği   olur.   Türk   alfabesi
2. gʲøre   fark'lɯ   søjlʲendi'i   olur   'tyrkʲ   alfabe'si
3. according different to.be.pronounced happens   Turk   its.alphabet

1. sade   ve   kullanışlıdır.
2. sa:'de   ve   kullanɯʃ'lɯɯdɯr
3. simple   and   convenient.is

> 'The New Turkish Alphabet, which was approved in the year 1928, is organized
> according to the principle of a separate letter for each sound and only one sound
> for each letter using Latin letters. All letters are read. However, it happens that
> soft *g* is not read, and is pronounced differently according to its position. The
> Turkish alphabet is simple and convenient.'   —*Banguoğlu 1959: 26.*

Basque

Basque is spoken in many dialects over an area of northern Spain and southwestern
France; it is not known to be related to any other languages. Standard Basque has a
five-vowel system, using the symbols of Roman script in their usual values; some dialects also have a high front rounded vowel, represented by *ü* when these dialects are
written. The representation of consonants is selectively based on principles that are
or were current in other languages of the Iberian peninsula. Noteworthy is the phonemic distinction between apical and laminal alveolars (fricative and affricate), indicated orthographically by *s*, *ts* versus *z*, *tz*. The corresponding palatals are *x* and *tx*; these
are complemented by nasal *ñ* and lateral *ll*, and also by palatal stops, voiceless *tt* and

TABLE 59.24: *Basque Alphabet*

Letter[a]		Phonetic Value	Name
A	a	[a]	[a]
B	b	[b]~[β]	[be]
(C	c)	[k], [s̺] (laminal)	[s̺e]
D	d	[d]~[ð]	[de]
E	e	[e]	[e]
F	f	[f]	[efe]
G	g	[g]~[ɣ]	[ge]
H	h	Ø	[at͡ʃe]
I	i	[i]~[i̥]	[i]
J	j	[j]~[x]~[ʝ]~[ɟ]	[jota]
K	k	[k]	[ka]
L	l	[l]	[ele]
Ll	ll	[ʎ]	[eʎe]
M	m	[m]	[eme]
N	n	[n]	[ene]
Ñ	ñ	[ɲ]	[eɲe]
O	o	[o]	[o]
P	p	[p]	[pe]
(Q	q)	[k]	[ku]
R	r	[ɾ], [r]	[ere]
RR	rr[b]	[r]	[ere]
S	s	[s̺] (apical)	[es̺e]
T	t	[t]	[te]
Ts	ts	[t͡s̺] (apical)	[tees̺e]
Tx	tx	[t͡ʃ]	[teekis̺]
Tz	tz	[t͡s̪] (laminal)	[tes̪eta]
U	u	[u]~[ɯ̥]	[u]
(V	v)	[b]~[β]	[ube]
(W	w)	[u̯]	[ube bikoit̺s̺a] 'double *v*'
X	x	[ʃ]	[ekis̺], [iʃa]
(Y	y)	[i]~[i̥]	[i ɡrekoa] 'Greek *i*'
Z	z	[s̪] (laminal)	[s̪eta]

a. The following digraphs are not considered single letters of the alphabet:
  Dd   dd   [ɟ]
  Tt   tt   [c]
b. *rr* occurs only intervocalically, the only position where [r] and [ɾ] contrast.

voiced *dd* (for some speakers, the latter has fricative allophones, paralleling the other voiced stops). There is also a distinction intervocalically between tap *r* and trill *rr*. (An earlier variant orthography used an acute accent rather than doubling of consonant symbols.) Except in some dialects spoken in France, *h* is silent, serving a purely etymological function; dialects with phonemic [h] also have phonemically distinct aspirated voiceless stops, indicated as *th*, etc., when these dialects are written. The symbol *j* represents, according to dialect, [j], [ĵ], [ɟ], or [x], some of which overlap with other phonemes. Some, but not all, Basque dialects have phonemic pitch-accent systems; no such distinctions are represented orthographically.

SAMPLE OF BASQUE

1. Basque:	Ia	urtebete	da	Miren	Lasa	Gernikatik
2. Transcription:	ia	ur̥tebete	da	mir̥en	las̪a	gernikatik
3. Gloss:	about	whole.year	is	Miren	Lasa	from.Guernica

1. goizean	goiz	atera	eta	ahizpa	ikusten	baserrian	izan
2. gois̪ean	gois̪	atera	eta	ais̪pa	ikusten	bas̪erian	is̪an
3. in.the.morning	morning	left	and	sister	seeing	on.the.farm	being

1. zela.	Ez	zaio,	haatik,	egun	hura	oraindik	ahaztu.	Harez
2. s̪ela	es̪	s̪aio	aatik	egun	ur̥a	oraindik	aas̪tu	ar̥es̪
3. that.she.was	not	it.is.to.her	however	day	that	still	forgotten	that

1. gero	Begoña	etengabe	ari	zaio	eskutitzez	eta
2. gero	begoɲa	etengabe	ar̥i	s̪aio	es̪kutits̪es̪	eta
3. after	Begoña	constantly	occupied	she.is.to.her	by.letter	and

1. telefonoz,	har	dezala	iaz	bezala	egun	bat	eta	joan
2. telefonos̪	ar̥	des̪ala	ias̪	bes̪ala	egun	bat	eta	joan
3. by.telephone	take	that.she.it	last.year	like	day	one	and	going

1. dakiola	berriz	ikusi	bat	egitera.
2. dakiola	beris̪	ikus̪i	bat	egiter̥a
3. she.may.to.her	again	visit	one	in.order.to.do

> 'It is about a year since Miren Lasa left Guernica early in the morning and visited her sister on the farm. However, she has still not forgotten that day. Since then, Begoña has continually been contacting her by letter and telephone so that she might take a day like last year and go to visit her again.'
> —*Patxi Altuna, in Shimomiya 1979: 216.*

Maltese

Maltese is an Arabic language spoken by the Christian community of Malta, and has come under much Italian influence—even to being written with the Roman alphabet

TABLE 59.25: *Maltese Alphabet*

Letter[a]		Phonetic Value	Name[b]
A	a	[a]	[a]
B	b	[b]	[bɛ]
Ċ	ċ	[t͡ʃ]	[t͡ʃɛ]
D	d	[d]	[dɛ]
E	e	[ɛ]	[ɛ]
F	f	[f]	[fɛ], ['ɛffɛ]
Ġ	ġ	[d͡ʒ]	[d͡ʒɛ]
G	g	[g]	[gɛ]
Għ	għ	(see text)	[aˤjn][c]
H	h	(see text)	['akka]
Ħ	ħ	[ħ]	[ħɛ]
I	i	[i]	[i]
Ie	ie	[iɛ][d]	[iɛ]
J	j	[j]	[jɛ]
K	k	[k]	[kɛ]
L	l	[l]	['ɛllɛ]
M	m	[m]	['ɛmmɛ]
N	n	[n]	['ɛnnɛ]
O	o	[o]	[o]
P	p	[p]	[pɛ]
Q	q	[ʔ]	[ʔɛ]
R	r	[r]	['ɛrrɛ]
S	s	[s]	['ɛssɛ]
T	t	[t]	[tɛ]
U	u	[u]	[u]
V	v	[v]	[vɛ]
W	w	[w]	[wɛ]
X	x	[ʃ]	['ɛʃʃɛ]
Ż	ż	[z]	[zɛ]
Z	z	[t͡s]; [d͡z]	[t͡sɛ]

a. There is some variation in the ordering of letters; in particular, some dictionaries place *gh* after *n*, place *ħ* before *h*, or place *ż* after *z* (but *ġ* usually precedes *g*).

b. Aquilina (1990: 1652–53) gives some letter names different from those given here (and provided by Marie Alexander), namely (in Maltese orthography): *ħ he, ż żeta, z zeta*. Some speakers use English letter names, with Maltese designations of diacritics (e.g. *ħ* is *ejċ maqtugħa* 'cut *h*', *h* is *ejċ mhix maqtugħa* 'uncut *h*').

c. The name of the letter *gh* is spelled *għajn*.

d. *ie* is not always considered a separate letter.

and following, to some extent, Italian spelling conventions. Maltese vowels may be short, long, or pharyngealized; the pharyngealized vowels are also long, and in urban speech merge with the corresponding unpharyngealized long vowels. Vowel length is not usually indicated orthographically. Vowel pharyngealization is indicated by the digraph *għ* before or after the vowel symbol, or between identical vowel symbols— according to etymology and/or morphophonemics. The vowels *i* and *u* are diphthongized to [aj] and [ow] after *għ* (in addition to being pharyngealized in dialects that retain pharyngealization), e.g. *għid* [aˤjt] 'say'. The short vowels are represented by *a*, *e*, *i*, and *o/u*, while the spelling uses both *o* and *u* for short vowels in both native and loanwords, this does not correspond to a consistent difference in pronunciation. The long vowels are represented by *a*, *e*, *i*, *o*, *u*, *ie*, the last ranging from [iɛ] to [ɪː].

The representation of consonants is basically one-to-one between phoneme and symbol. Some of the choices of phoneme–symbol correspondences show Italian influence: thus *z* represents [t͡s] (and [d͡z] in a handful of Italian loanwords), while [z] is represented by adding a dot. Similarly, *ġ* for [d͡ʒ] is a modified *g* (cf. the "soft" pronunciation of *g* in Italian), while *ċ* for [t͡ʃ] redundantly has the same superscript dot (there is no undotted *c*). The use of *x* for [ʃ] reflects a practice once widespread in the Mediterranean area. The use of *q* for [ʔ] (deriving from Arabic [q]) and of *ħ* for [ħ] reflect Semitic transliteration practices. The digraph *għ* basically functions synchronically as an indicator of pharyngealization (or length); but word-finally and under obstruent cluster devoicing, it is [ħ]. The letter *h* has similar, but more restricted, functions, being often simply silent. A word-final apostrophe after *a* reflects an etymological *għ*, but has no phonetic realization.

Stress is not entirely predictable, but is not normally marked orthographically, except for the use of a grave accent on word-final stressed vowels—a possibility that only occurs in loans from Italian and follows Italian practice.

SAMPLE OF MALTESE

1. Maltese:	Il-gżejjer	Maltin	għandhom	storja	kbira	li
2. Transcription:	il'gzɛjjɛr	mal'tiːn	'aˤndum	ˌstoːrja	ˌgbiːra	li
3. Gloss:	the-islands	Maltese	they.have	history	big	that

1.	tifrex	tul	il-medda	ta'	ħafna	snin.	Fiha	naraw	li	minn
2.	'tifrɛʃ	tuːl	il'mɛdda	ta	'ħafna	'sniːn	'fiːa	na'raw	li	min
3.	stretches	across	the-space	of	many	years	in.it	we.find	that	from

1.	żminijiet	qodma	l-poplu	beda	jinfirex	f'inħawi	differenti
2.	zmini'jiət	'ʔodma	l'poːplu	'bɛda	jin'firɛʃ	fin'ħawi	diffe'rɛnti
3.	times	old	the-people	began	it.spread	in.directions	different

1.	biex	jifforma	komunitajiet	żgħar	li	bil-mod	il-mod
2.	biɛʃ	jif'forma	kumunita'jiət	'zaˤr	li	bil'moːd	il'moːt
3.	in.order.that	it.form	communities	small	that	with.the-way	the-way

1. bdew   joktru   u   jikbru.
2. 'bdɛw   'joktru   u   'jigbru
3. began   they.multiply   and   they.grow

'The Maltese islands have a long history that stretches across the space of many years. In it we find that from ancient times the people began to spread in different directions to form small communities that little by little multiplied and grew.'   — *Guillaumier 1987: first unnumbered page of introduction.*

Notes:

[a]Low-level morphophonemic processes like word-final devoicing and obstruent voice assimilation are not shown orthographically.

[b]In normal speech, short [o] and [u] are allophonically distributed.

African languages

JOHN BENDOR-SAMUEL

Approximately one third of the world's languages are spoken in Africa. Of these two thousand or so distinct languages, over five hundred now have a written form, the vast majority using a Roman-based orthography.

This has come about because, at the beginning of the colonial era, very few African languages had developed a written form (for earlier uses of Arabic script for African languages, see SECTION 62). Officials needed to compile records which involved writing down for the first time the names of places and people, and indeed a whole range of geographic and ethnographic details. At the same time missionaries gave high priority in their work to translating the Bible into these hitherto unwritten languages. With these translations came the need for literacy materials. Inevitably at that time the systems of writing that were developed followed the conventions of the colonial languages, and these were all Roman-based. Since the sounds and sound systems of the African languages vary very considerably from the sound systems found in the European languages, the Roman alphabet had to be adapted considerably in order to provide a system of symbols which would be adequate.

The primary colonial powers in Africa were Britain and France. They followed different principles in developing orthographical systems for the African languages. The British were influenced by the Royal Geographical Society's decision in 1836 to adopt the principle "The vowels as in Italian and the consonants as in English." The French, however, tended to stick more closely to the orthographic traditions of French.

In 1848 the Church Missionary Society, which worked primarily in the British colonies, published "Rules for Reducing Unwritten Languages to Alphabetical Writing in Roman characters, with reference especially to the languages spoken in Africa." These Rules set down fixed values for the letters of the Roman alphabet, avoiding two-letter compounds for single sounds and making use of the subscript dot. It recommended *ṣ* for *sh* [ʃ], *ṭ* for *th* [θ], *ẹ* for [ɛ], *ọ* for [ɔ], and *ạ* for [ə]. In the mid 1850s there was a series of alphabetical conferences which resulted in what was called "The Standard Alphabet" devised by Richard Lepsius (see SECTION 71) and later adapted for African use by Professor Carl Meinhof. These alphabets continued very much along the lines of the CMS's "Rules." Diacritical marks continued to be used for sounds which were outside the twenty-six letters of the Roman alphabet.

When the International African Institute was founded in 1926, one of its first endeavors was to develop an "Africa" alphabet. In 1928 the Institute published "The Practical Orthography of African Languages." The orthographic system it proposed moved away from the Meinhof–Lepsius system primarily in advocating the use of a number of "phonetic" letters in preference to a Roman letter with a diacritic, for example *ɛ* in place of *ẹ*, *ɔ* in place of *ọ*, *ə* in place of *ạ*, *ŋ* in place of *ng*, *ʃ* in place of *ṣ*, etc. Diacritics were to be used for marking tone and nasalization.

This "Africa" alphabet has spread widely over Sub-Saharan Africa, though it is not used universally. In southern Nigeria, for instance, the use of diacritics to mark vowel quality with the dot under the standard Roman symbols still prevails, rather than the use of separate symbols. Swahili, the language in Africa spoken more widely than any other indigenous language, still follows the CMS's "Rules" as regards the principle "Vowels as in Italian, consonants as in English," but uses digraphs such as *sh, ng, ch, ny,* instead of diacritics. While there is still a great deal of diversity across Africa, in the last twenty years several countries, particularly in the Francophone area, have taken steps toward standardizing the orthographies for their indigenous languages.

Problems in adapting consonants

Although the 1848 "Rules" with its slogan "Consonants as in English" has been widely followed throughout Africa, there have always been problems because of the consonantal sounds in African languages which do not correspond to any English sounds. In general three solutions have been used. The first is to develop a digraph, e.g. *kh* for [χ] and *gh* for [ɣ]. The second solution is to use a diacritic, as in *ṣ* for [ʃ]. The third solution is to use a "phonetic" letter, introducing it as an additional symbol in the alphabet, for example *ŋ*.

It is interesting to note that in a sample of some two hundred alphabets, mainly developed in the last twenty years, the first solution is by far the most widely used. Double-articulated plosives such as bilabial velars are nearly always symbolized by digraphs (*kp, gb*). Similarly, digraphs are used for aspirated, labialized, and palatalized sounds (e.g. *ph, th, kh, bh, bw, sw, tw, gw, fy, gy, ly,* etc.). The only "phonetic" symbol used at all widely is the *ŋ*, followed by the hooked letters *ɓ* and *ɗ*. No other phonetic letters have found a place in most of these alphabets. Diacritics are found only rarely, e.g. *ṣ* in southern Nigeria.

Problems in adapting vowels

Comparatively few African languages have as few as five vowels, so that in most languages the five Roman vowel symbols are inadequate. Again three solutions have been used; additional diacritical marks, additional "phonetic" letters, and very occasionally digraphs. A fourth solution has also been used fairly widely, namely, not distinguishing certain vowels in the alphabet even though they are known to be phonemically distinct! It seems rather clear that the trends in recent years have been away from the use of diacritics and toward the use of special symbols. Where the system of using diacritics is well established, as in Yoruba, this continues to prevail and to be extended to new systems developed for languages in geographical proximity. Outside these geographical areas, however, there are few instances of this system being adopted. In some of the francophone countries the acute and grave accents are still used for vowel quality, and Côte d'Ivoire symbolizes central vowels *ä, ï, ö*. Fairly common too in Cameroon are the barred symbols *ɨ, ʉ*. The vowel symbols *ɛ, ɔ, ə* are found very widely across the continent.

Vietnamese

Nguyễn Đình-Hoà

The currently used conventional orthography in Vietnam is a Roman script called *(chữ) quốc-ngữ* 'national language'. To letters of the Latin alphabet its inventors added diacritical marks to indicate vowel quality and/or one of the six tones of the standard dialect—that of Hanoi, the capital city. The two earlier systems of writing which native scholars had at their disposal until the first decades of the twentieth century are *chữ nôm* 'southern' or 'demotic script'—a system of "square characters" derived from written Chinese—and *chữ Hán, chữ nho* 'Han' or 'scholarly script', i.e. the characters learned from the Chinese, who ruled Vietnam from 111 B.C.E. to 939 C.E.

The codifier of the *quốc-ngữ* system was Alexandre de Rhodes (1591–1660), a brilliant French Jesuit scholar/missionary from Avignon, who continued the work of other Catholic missionaries in the creation of an alphabetic system for the new converts to Christianity. Indeed, he said that he based his Vietnamese–Portuguese–Latin dictionary, published in Rome in 1651, on earlier works by Gaspar de Amaral and Antoine de Barbosa, both from Portugal (cf. Rhodes 1991). Although the Roman script was initially used only in religious writings, including catechisms and prayer books, it eventually spread beyond the world of European missionaries and their local followers, who found it fairly easy to learn. However, its official use began only in 1910, when a decree issued by the French Résident Supérieur of the protectorate of Tonkin (northern Vietnam, where Rhodes first served) required that all public documents be transcribed into *quốc-ngữ*. Orthographic changes were later suggested by French scholars and colonial administrators, and after independence were recommended at

TABLE 59.26: *The Eleven Vowels*

i	[i]			ư	[ɯ]	u	[u]
ê	[e]	â	[ə]	ơ	[ɤ]	ô	[o]
e	[ɛ]	ă	[a]	a	[ɑ]	o	[ɔ]

several scholarly conferences and meetings held during the 1954–75 partition. These changes have been focused on the representation of vocalic elements. In general, the system reflects the phonological system of a northern dialect, which has been called "Middle Vietnamese" (Gregerson 1969); the initial consonant letters more closely reflect the dialects of southern Vietnam, while the final consonants correspond more closely to those of northern dialects. Despite a few inconsistencies, the *quốc-ngữ* system is easy to learn and has helped to promote literacy.

Letters of the alphabet

The shape of individual letters is not much different from that recorded in the 1651 dictionary. A typical syllable, formerly written with either one Chinese character or one *nôm* character, consists of a minimal vocalic nucleus V optionally preceded by an initial onset C_1 and optionally followed by a coda C_2, which can be a semivowel [j, w]. Alphabetical order is *a ă â b c ch d đ e ê g gi h i k kh l m n ng nh o ô ơ p ph q r s t th tr u ư v x y*.

The so-called rhyme, i.e. what follows C_1, is affected by one of the six phonemic tones T, and the syllabic structure can be represented as $C_1 + V^T + C_2$. Examples are: V, *à* 'oh!'; CV, *há* 'to open [mouth]'; CVC, *hán* 'Han, Chinese'; *w*V, *oà* 'to burst into tears'; C*w*V, *hoá* 'to change (into)'; C*w*VC, *hoán* 'to exchange'. The basic CVC norm can be maximally expanded to $C_1wV\partial C_2$, as in *khuyên* [xu̯īən] 'to advise'.

The syllabic nucleus must be one of the eleven vowels, as shown in TABLE 59.26, or one of the three combinations of high vowel + glide.

The vowel [i] is written arbitrarily *i* in some words, *y* in others. The three vowel combinations [iə ɯə uə] are written *ia ưa ua* in open syllables, but in closed syllables they are spelled *iê- ươ- uô-*.

A front or central vowel may be followed by a [w] offglide, spelled *-u* or *-o* to indicate the quality of the preceding vowel: *hiu* [hīw] '(of breeze) gentle', *hiểu* [hĭəw] 'to understand', *kêu* [kēw] 'to call, shout', *heo* [hɛ̄w] 'pig', *nâu* [nə̄w] 'brown', *cau* [kāw] 'areca nut', *cao* [kāw] 'tall'.

A central or back vowel may be followed by a [j] offglide, spelled *-y* or *-i* to indicate the quality of the preceding vowel: *cửi* [kǔj] 'loom', *cười* [kùəj] 'to laugh', *mời* [mỳj] 'to invite', *túi* [túj] 'pocket', *tuổi* [tŭəj] 'year (of age)', *tôi* [tōj] 'I, me', *toi* [tɔj] '(of cattle, poultry) to die', *tai* [tāi] 'ear', *tây* [tə̄j] 'west', *tay* [tāj] 'hand, arm'.

The twenty-two onsets C_1 are shown in TABLE 59.27. (The digraphs *ch th tr kh ph gi gh ng nh* represent not clusters, but single sounds, as indicated in phonetic brackets.)

TABLE 59.27: *The Onsets*

p	*t*	*tr* [ʈ]	*ch* [c]	*c/k/q* [k]	
	th [tʰ]				
b	*đ* [d]				
ph [f]	*x* [s]	*s* [ʃ]		*kh* [x]	*h*
v	*d* [z]	*gi* [ʒ]		*g(h)* [ɣ]	
m	*n*		*nh* [ɲ]	*ng(h)* [ŋ]	
	l				
	r				

The influence of Romance orthography is clear in the writing of the velar stop; it is *k* before a front vowel *i ê e*, but *c* before the other vowels, and *q* before [w]: *kim* [kīm] 'needle', *kê* [kē] 'millet', *kem* [kēm] 'cream, ice cream', *cam* [kām] 'orange', *cơm* [kɤm] 'cooked rice', *câm* [kɜm] 'mute, dumb', *căm* [kām] 'to resent', *cúm* [kúm] 'flu', *cốm* [kóm] 'green rice', *còm* [kɔm] 'gaunt, skinny', *quỳ* [kwì] 'to kneel down', *quê* [kwē] 'village', *que* [kwē] 'stick, twig'.

The voiced dental stop [d] is written with barred *đ*, as opposed to non-barred *d*, which represents the voiced spirant [z]: compare *đa* [dā] 'banyan' and *da* [zā] 'skin' (modern [z] < 17th-century [d] *d*, whereas [d] < implosive [ɗ] *đ*, hence the odd-seeming assignment of the letters).

The consonants [ʈ ʃ ʒ] are typical of the central and southern dialects, in which *s* represents [ʃ] and *gi* represents [ʒ]: *sa* [ʃā] 'to fall down', *xa* [sā] 'far'; *gia* [ʒā] 'household'; cf. *da* [zā] 'skin' (modern [s] probably < 17th-century laminal [s̺], and [ʃ] < apico-alveolar [s̺], which the missionaries equated with Portuguese *x* and *s* respectively). Although the Hanoi dialect does not distinguish *d* from *gi* in pronunciation, there is a contrast in spelling: *dành* 'to save, put aside' and *giành* 'to dispute' are both pronounced [zàɲ].

In most northern dialects, the *s/x* and *ch/tr* contrasts are neutralized: *sa* 'to fall' and *xa* 'far' are both pronounced [sā], *chê* 'to denigrate' and *trê* 'catfish' are both pronounced [cē]. Some speakers even confuse *lào* [làw] 'Laos, Laotian' and *nào* [nàw] 'which'.

For the velar spirant [ɣ] and nasal [ŋ], a letter *h* is added after *g* or *ng* if the nucleus is a front vowel *i ê e*: thus *ga* [ɣā] 'station, depot', but *ghi* [ɣī] 'to record'; *ngô* [ŋō] 'corn, maize', but *nghi* [ŋī] 'to suspect'.

The initial sequence [kw] is always written *qu*, as in *qua* [kwā] 'to cross over', *quỳ* [kwì] 'to kneel down', *quê* [kwē] 'village', *quét* [kwét] 'to sweep'. In other contexts, however, [w] is spelled *o* before *a, ă, e*, as in *hoà* [hwà] 'peace', *toan* [twān] 'to intend', *hoặc* [hwàˀk] 'or', *ngoặc* [ŋwàˀk] 'brackets', *khoẻ* [xwɛ̌] 'strong, healthy', *xoè* [swɛ̀] 'to spread (wings)'; but *u* before *i, ê, â, ơ* as in *tuy* [twī] 'although', *khuy* [xwī] 'button', *thuê* [tʰwé] 'tax', *tuần* [twɜ̀n] 'week', *khuân* [xwɜn] 'to lug' (heavy object)', *thuở* [tʰwɤ̌] 'time (in the past)'.

TABLE 59.28: *Tone Marking*

Tone	Orthography	Phonetic Value	Gloss
level	ma	[mā]	'ghost'
high rising	má	[má]	'cheek'
low (falling)	mà	[mà]	'but'
dipping-rising	mả	[mǎ]	'tomb'
high rising glottalized	mã	[má^ʔ]	'horse'
low glottalized	mạ	[mà^ʔ]	'rice seedling'

In syllable-final position C$_2$ can appear one of the stops *p t ch* [c] *c* [k], or one of the nasals *m n nh* [ɲ] *ng* [ŋ], apart from the offglides described above. Some orthographic irregularities occur: thus *ach anh* are pronounced [aik aiŋ] (*ǎch ǎnh* do not occur), e.g. *sách* [sáik] 'book', *anh* [āiŋ] 'elder brother'. (After the rounded vowels *u ô o*, the velars take on the roundness feature, and the resulting labiovelars [k͡p ŋ͡m] may be perceived as [p m] though spelled *k ng*.)

The diphthongs pronounced [ɑj ɑw] are spelled *ai ao*, while those pronounced [aj aw] are spelled *ay au*; e.g., *hai* [hāj] 'two' versus *hay* [hāj] 'interesting', *sao* [sāw] 'star' versus *sau* [sāw] 'behind'.

Of the six phonemic tones, the high or mid level tone is unmarked, whereas the other five are indicated by diacritics placed above or below the vowel letter (TABLE 59.28).

SAMPLE OF VIETNAMESE

1. Vietnamese: Việc   sáng-tác   chữ   quốc-ngữ   chắc   là
2. Transcription: vì^{ʔ}ək   sáŋ-ták   cuí^ʔ kúək-ŋuí^ʔ cák   là
3. Gloss: task   create   script   national-language   certain   be

1. một   công-cuộc   chung   của   nhiều   người,   trong   dó   có
2. mò^{ʔ}t   kōŋ-kùʔək   cūŋ   kửə   ɲìəw   ŋùəj   ʈɔ̄ŋ   dɔ́   kɔ́
3. one   undertaking   collective   of   many   people   inside   which   have

1. cả   các   giáo-sĩ   người   Tây-ban-nha,   Bồ-dào-nha   và   Pháp-lan-tây.
2. kả   kák   ʒáw-síʔ   ŋùəj   tōj-bān-ɲā   bò-dàw-ɲā   và   fáp-lān-tōj
3. even PL   missionary   people   Spain   Portugal   and France

1. Nhưng   người   có   công   nhất   trong   việc   ấy   là   cố
2. ɲūŋ   ŋùəj   kɔ́   kōŋ   ɲə́t   ʈɔ̄ŋ   vì^{ʔ}ək   ə́j   là   kó
3. however   person   have credit   uppermost   inside   task   that   be   father

1. Alexandre de Rhodes   vì   chính   ông   là   người   dâu-tiên   dem
2. aleksādrə də ʁo:dz   vì   cíɲ   ōŋ   là   ŋùəj   də̀w-tīən   dēm
3. Alexandre de Rhodes   because   exactly   he   be   person   first   take

1.	in	những	sách	bằng	chữ	quốc-ngữ,		thứ	nhất	là
2.	ĭn	ŋúˀŋ	sác	bàŋ	cúˀ	kúək-ŋúˀ		tʰú	ŋə́t	là
3.	print	PL	book	use	script	national-language		order	first	is

1.	một	cuốn	tự-điển,	khiến	cho	người	sau	có	tài-liệu	mà
2.	mò̂ˀt	kúən	tù̀ˀ-dĭən	xíən	cɔ̄	ŋùəj	sāw	kɔ́	tàj-lìˀəw	mà
3.	one	CLF	dictionary	cause	give	people	later	have	materials	in.order.to

1.	học	và	kê-cứu.
2.	hɔ̀ˀk	và	kē-kúɨw
3.	study	and	research

'The creation of a script for the national language was certainly a collective undertaking of many people, including missionaries from Spain, Portugal and France. However, the person who deserved the most credit in that task was Father Alexandre de Rhodes, because it was he who first had several books printed in the national language script, especially one dictionary, so that later people could have materials to study and do research.'

—*Dương Quảng-Hàm 1941: 191.*

Bibliography

ROMANCE LANGUAGES

Allen, W. Sidney. 1965. *Vox Latina: The Pronunciation of Classical Latin.* Cambridge: Cambridge University Press.

Close, Elizabeth. 1974. *The Development of Modern Rumanian: Linguistic Theory and Practice in Muntenia 1821–1838.* Oxford: Oxford University Press.

DeVoto, Giacomo. 1953. *Profilo di storia linguistica italiana.* Florence: La Nuova Italia.

Harris, Martin, and Nigel Vincent, eds. 1988. *The Romance Languages.* London: Routledge; New York: Oxford University Press.

Isidore of Seville. 1911. *Etymologiarum sive Originum,* ed. Wallace M. Lindsay. Oxford: Clarendon.

Niculescu, Alexandru. 1981. *Outline History of the Romanian Language.* Bucharest: Editura Ştiintifica şi Enciclopedica.

Onu, Liviu. 1989. "Le roumain: Langue et écriture." In *Lexicon der romanistischen Linguistik,* ed. Günter Holtus et al., 3:305–24. Tübingen: Niemeyer.

Wright, Roger. 1982. *Late Latin and Early Romance in Spain and Carolingian France.* Liverpool: Francis Cairns.

GERMANIC LANGUAGES

Bach, Adolf. 1965. *Geschichte der deutschen Sprache.* Heidelberg: Quelle & Meyer.

Benediktsson, Halinn. 1959. "The Vowel System of Icelandic: A Survey of Its History." *Word* 15: 282–312.

Benware, Wilbur A. 1986. *Phonetics and Phonology of Modern German.* Washington, D.C.: Georgetown University Press.

Dahl, Willy. 1975. *Var Egen Tid,* vol. 6: *Norges Litteratur Historie,* ed. Edvard Beyer. Oslo: Cappelens.

Donaldson, Bruce C. 1981. *Dutch Reference Grammar.* The Hague: Nijhoff.

Einarsson, Stefan. 1961. *Icelandic: Grammar, Texts, Glossary.* Baltimore: The Johns Hopkins Press.

Hall, Christopher. 1992. *Modern German Pronunciation: An Introduction for Speakers of English.* Manchester: Manchester University Press.

Haugen, Einar. 1976. *The Scandinavian Languages: An Introduction to Their History.* Cambridge: Harvard University Press.

———. 1982. *Scandinavian Language Structures: A Comparative Historical Survey.* Minneapolis: University of Minnesota Press.

Keller, Rudolf E. 1978. *The German Language.* New Jersey: Humanities Press.

König, Ekkehard, ed. 1994. *The Germanic Languages.* London: Routledge.

Shetter, William Z. 1975. *Introduction to Dutch.* The Hague: Nijhoff.

van den Berg, Berend. 1958. *Foniek van het Nederlands.* The Hague: Van Goor Zonen.

Waterman, John T. 1976. *A History of the German Language,* rev. ed. Seattle: University of Washington Press.

ENGLISH

Carney, Edward. 1994. *A Survey of English Spelling.* London: Routledge.

Crystal, David. 1995. *The Cambridge Encyclopedia of the English Language.* Cambridge: Cambridge University Press.

Cummings, Donald Wayne. 1988. *American English Spelling: An Informal Description.* Baltimore: Johns Hopkins University Press.

Finegan, Edward. 1987. "English." In *The World's Major Languages,* ed. Bernard Comrie, pp. 77–109. London: Croom Helm; New York: Oxford University Press.

Hanna, Paul R., Jean S. Hanna, Richard E. Hodges, and Edwin H. Rudorf, Jr. 1966. *Phoneme–Grapheme Correspondences as Cues to Spelling Improvement.* Washington, D.C.: U.S. Department of Health, Education, and Welfare. Office of Education.

Hogg, Richard M., ed. 1992– . *The Cambridge History of the English Language.* 6 vols. Cambridge: Cambridge University Press.

Mencken, H. L. 1936. *The American Language,* 4th ed.; *Supplement II,* 1948. New York: Knopf.

Sapir, Edward. 1921. *Language.* New York: Harcourt, Brace & World.

Strang, Barbara M. H. 1970. *A History of English.* London: Methuen. Repr. London: Routledge.

Strevens, Peter. 1985. "The State of the English Language in 1982: An Essay in Geo-linguistics." In *Language Standards and Their Codification: Process and Application* (Exeter Linguistic Studies 9), ed. J. Douglas Woods, pp. 15–28. Exeter: University of Exeter.

Venezky, Richard L. 1970. *The Structure of English Orthography* (Janua Linguarum Series Minor 82). The Hague: Mouton.

Wells, J. C. 1982. *Accents of English.* 3 vols. Cambridge: Cambridge University Press.

CELTIC LANGUAGES AND IRISH

Ball, Martin J., and James Fife, eds. 1993. *The Celtic Languages.* London: Routledge.

Black, R. 1994. "Bog Loch and River: The Nature of Reform in Scottish Gaelic." In *Language Reform: History and Future 6,* ed. István Fodor and Claude Hagège, pp. 123–48. Hamburg: Buske.

Harvey, Anthony. 1989. "Some Significant Points of Early Insular Celtic Orthography." In *Sages, Saints and Storytellers: Celtic Studies in Honour of Professor James Carney,* ed. Donnchadh Ó Corráin, Liam Breatnach, and Kim McCone, pp. 56–66 (Maynooth Monographs 2). Maynooth, Ireland: An Sagart.

Jackson, Kenneth H. 1953. *Language and History in Early Britain.* Edinburgh: University Press.

MacAulay, Donald, ed. 1990. *Celtic Languages.* Cambridge: Cambridge University Press.

Meid, Wolfgang. 1992. *Gaulish Inscriptions* (Archaeolingua Series Minor 1). Budapest: Hungarian Academy of Sciences.

McCone, Kim. 1992. "Relative Chronologie: Keltisch." In *Rekonstruktion und relative Chronologie: Akten der VIII. Fachtagung der Indogermanischen Gesellschaft, Leiden, 1987,* ed. Robert Beekes, Alexander Lubotsky, and Jos Weitenberg, pp. 11–39. Innsbruck: Institut für Sprachwissenschaft.

Ó Baoill, Dónall. 1988. "Language Planning in Ireland: The Standardization of Irish." *International Journal of the Sociology of Language* 70: 109–26.

Ó Cuív, Brian. 1969. "The Changing Form of the Irish Language." In *A View of the Irish Language,* ed. B. Ó Cuív, pp. 22–34. Dublin: Stationery Office.

Ó Murchú, Máirtín. 1985. *The Irish Language.* Dublin: Bord na Gaeilge.

Thomson, R. L. 1992. "Manx Language and Literature." In *The Celtic Connection,* ed. Glanville Price, pp. 154–70. Gerrards Cross, England: Colin Smythe.

Thurneysen, Rudolf. 1946. *A Grammar of Old Irish,* trans. D. A. Binchy and Osborn Bergin. Dublin: Dublin Institute for Advanced Studies.

WELSH

Evans, D. Simon. 1964. *A Grammar of Middle Welsh.* Dublin: Institute for Advanced Studies.

Hamp, Eric P. 1951. "Morphophonemes of the Keltic Mutations." *Language* 27: 230–47.

———. 1975. "Labial Continuant Graphs in Llanstephan 1 and Havod 2." *Archivum Linguisticum* 6: 71–76.

Jones, Morgan D. 1976. *A Guide to Correct Welsh.* Llandysul, Dyfed: Gomer Press.

King, Gareth. 1993. *Modern Welsh: A Comprehensive Grammar.* London: Routledge.

Morris-Jones, John. 1921. *An Elementary Welsh Grammar.* Oxford: Oxford University Press.

Pwyllgor Llên Bwrdd Gwybodau Celtaidd Prifysgol Cymru [Literature Committee of the Board of Celtic Studies of the University of Wales]. 1942. *Orgraff Yr Iaith Gymraeg.* Cardiff: University of Wales Press.

Rhys-Jones, T. J. 1977. *Living Welsh.* Sevenoaks, Kent: Hodder and Stoughton.

Vinay, J. P., and W. O. Thomas. 1948. *The Basis and Essentials of Welsh.* London: Nelson.

Williams, Stephen J. 1980. *A Welsh Grammar.* Cardiff: University of Wales Press.

BALTIC AND SLAVIC LANGUAGES

Comrie, Bernard, & Greville G. Corbett, eds. 1993. *The Slavonic Languages.* London: Routledge.

De Bray, Reginald G. A. 1980A. *Guide to the South Slavonic Languages.* Columbus, Ohio: Slavica.

———. 1980B. *Guide to the West Slavonic Languages.* Columbus, Ohio: Slavica.

Encyklopedia Powszechna PWN [General encyclopedia of the State Scientific Publishing House]. 1975. Vol. 3. Warsaw: Państwowe Wydawnictwo Narodowe.

Endzelins, Janis. 1922. *Lettische Grammatik.* Riga: A. Gulbis. [Also Heidelberg, 1923: Winter.]

Poldauf, Ivan. 1959. *Česko–anglický slovník středního rozsahu/Czech-English Dictionary, Medium.* Prague: Státní Pedagogické Nakladatelství.

Poljanec, R. F., and S. M. Madatova-Poljanec. 1973. *Rusko-hrvatski rječnik* [Russian–Croatian dictionary]. Zagreb: Školska knjiga.

Senn, Alfred. 1957–66. *Handbuch der litauischen Sprache.* 2 vols. Heidelberg: Winter.

Vinogradov, V. V., et al., eds. 1968. *Jazyki narodov SSSR* [Languages of the peoples of the USSR], vol. 1. Moscow: Nauka.

ALBANIAN

Camaj, Martin. 1984. *Albanian Grammar.* Wiesbaden: Harrassowitz.

Lambertz, Max. 1954–59. *Lehrgang des Albanischen.* 3 vols. Halle (Saale): Niemeyer.

Newmark, Leonard, Philip Hubbard, and Peter Prifti. 1982. *Standard Albanian: A Reference Grammar for Students*. Stanford: Stanford University Press.

Pogoni, Bardhyl. 1967. "Albanian Writing Systems." Ph.D. dissertation, Indiana University.

URALIC LANGUAGES

Benkő, Lórand, and Imre Samu, eds. 1972. *The Hungarian Language* (Janua Linguarum Series Practica 134). The Hague: Mouton; Budapest: Akadémiai Kiadó.

Gáldi, László, et al., comp. 1973. *Petőfi-szótár* [Petőfi dictionary], vol. 1. Budapest: Akadémiai Kiadó.

Kurman, George. 1968. *The Development of Written Estonian* (Indiana University Publications Uralic and Altaic Series 90). Bloomington: Indiana University; The Hague: Mouton.

Lehikoinen, Laila, and Silva Kiuru. 1989. *Kirjasuomen kehitys* [The development of written Finnish]. Helsinki: Helsingin Yliopiston Suomen Kielen Laitos.

Ravila, Paavo. 1965. *Finnish Literary Reader*. Bloomington: Indiana University Press; The Hague: Mouton.

Sulkala, Helena, and Merja Karjalainen. 1992. *Finnish*. London: Routledge.

Tauli, Valter. 1973. *Standard Estonian Grammar*, part 1: *Phonology, Morphology, Word-Formation* (Acta Universitatis Upsaliensis, Studia Uralica et Altaica Upsaliensia 8). Uppsala.

TURKISH

Banguoğlu, Tahsin. 1959. *Türk grameri, Birinci bölüm: Sesbilgisi* [Turkish grammar, first part: phonology]. Ankara: Türk Tarih Kurumu Basimevi.

Bazin, Louis. 1983. 'La réforme linguistique en Turquie." In *Language Reform: History and Future*, vol. 1, ed. István Fodor and Claude Hagège, pp. 155–77. Hamburg: Buske.

Heyd, Uriel. 1954. *Language Reform in Modern Turkey* (Notes and Studies 5). Jerusalem: Israel Oriental Society.

Lewis, G. L. 1967. *Turkish Grammar*. Oxford: Oxford University Press.

BASQUE

Hualde, José Ignacio. 1991. *Basque Phonology*. London: Routledge.

Shimomiya, Tadao. 1979. *Baskugo nyuumon* [Introduction to Basque]. Tokyo: Taishukan.

MALTESE

Aquilina, Joseph. 1961. "Systems of Maltese orthography." In his *Papers in Maltese Linguistics*, pp. 75–101B. [Floriana]: Royal University of Malta.

———. 1987–90. *Maltese–English Dictionary*, 2 vols. Valletta: Midsea.

Guillaumier, Alfie, comp. 1987. *Bliet u Rhula Maltin* [Maltese towns and villages], vol. 1. Malta: Valletta Publishing.

Schabert, Peter. 1976. *Laut- und Formenlehre des Maltesischen anhand zweier Mundarten*. Erlangen: Palm & Enke.

AFRICAN LANGUAGES

Hartell, Rhonda L., ed. 1993. *Alphabets of Africa*. Dakar: UNESCO and Summer Institute of Linguistics.

Lepsius, C. Richard. 1863. *Standard Alphabet for Reducing Unwritten Languages and Foreign Graphic Systems to a Uniform Orthography in European Letters*, 2nd ed., recommended for adoption by the Church Missionary Society. London: Williams and Norgate; Berlin: Hertz. Repr. Amsterdam: Benjamins, 1981.

Mann, Michael, and David Dalby. 1987. *A Thesaurus of African Languages: A Classified and Annotated Inventory of the Spoken Languages of Africa, with an Appendix on Their Written Representation.* London: Zell.

The Practical Orthography of African Languages. 1928, rev. 1930 (International Institute of African Languages and Cultures, Memorandum 1). London: Oxford University Press.

Rules for Reducing Unwritten Languages to Alphabetical Writing in Roman Characters with Reference Especially to the Languages Spoken in Africa. 1848. London: Church Missionary House. Repr. Spencer 1966: 89–91.

Smalley, William A., et al. 1964. *Orthography Studies: Articles on New Writing Systems* (Helps for Translators 6). London: United Bible Societies.

Spencer, John. 1966. "S. W. Koelle and the Problem of Notation for African Languages, 1847–1855." *Sierre Leone Language Review* 5: 83–105.

Tucker, Archibald N. 1971. "Orthographic Systems and Conventions in Sub-Saharan Africa." In *Current Trends in Linguistics,* ed. Thomas A. Sebeok, vol. 7, *Linguistics in Sub-Saharan Africa,* pp. 618–53. The Hague: Mouton.

VIETNAMESE

Dương Quảng-Hàm. 1941. *Việt-nam văn-học sử-yếu* [Outline history of Vietnamese literature] (7th printing, 1960). Saigon: Bộ Quốc-gia Giáo-dục.

Emeneau, Murray B. 1951. *Studies in Vietnamese (Annamese) Grammar* (University of California Publications in Linguistics 8). Berkeley and Los Angeles: University of California Press.

Gregerson, Kenneth J. 1969. "A Study of Middle Vietnamese Phonology." *Bulletin de la Société des Etudes Indochinoises* 44: 135–93.

Hashimoto, Mantaro. 1978. "The Current State of Sino-Vietnamese Studies." *Journal of Chinese Linguistics* 6: 1–26.

Haudricourt, André-Georges. 1949. "Origine des particularités de l'alphabet vietnamien." *Dân Việt-Nam* 3: 61–68.

Nguyễn Đình-Hoà. 1955. *Quốc-ngữ: The Modern Writing System in Vietnam.* Washington, D.C.: Author.

———. 1986. "Alexandre de Rhodes' Dictionary." *Papers in Linguistics* 19: 1–18.

———. 1990. "Graphemic Borrowings from Chinese: The Case of *chữ nôm,* Vietnam's Demotic Script." *Bulletin of the Institute of History and Philology, Academia Sinica* 61: 383–432.

Rhodes, Alexandre de. 1991. *Từ điển Annam–Lusitan–Latinh,* trans. Thanh Lãng, Hoàng Xuân Việt, and Đỗ Quang Chính. Hanoi: Khoa-học Xã-hội (Latin orig., *Dictionarium Annamiticum Lusitanum et Latinum,* 1651).

Thompson, Laurence. 1984–85. *A Vietnamese Reference Grammar,* 2nd ed. (Mon-Khmer Studies 13–14). Honolulu: University of Hawaii Press.

Uỷ-ban Khoa-học Xã-hội Việt-nam. 1983. *Ngữ-pháp tiếng Việt* [Vietnamese grammar]. Hanoi: Khoa-học Xã-hội.

Adaptations of the Cyrillic Alphabet

BERNARD COMRIE

Cyrillic script (SECTION 27) is used for the Slavic languages Russian, Belarusian, Ukrainian, Bulgarian, Macedonian, and (alongside Roman script, cf. SECTION 64) Serbo-Croatian, and also for a number of non-Slavic languages of the former Soviet Union (cf. SECTION 67) and (alongside Vertical Mongolian script, SECTION 49) for Mongolian. In addition, a highly idiosyncratic adaptation of Cyrillic was introduced by Bishop Stephen of Perm for Old Permic, i.e. Old Komi, in the late fourteenth century; it fell into disuse in the seventeenth century (Lytkin 1952).

Slavic languages

Serbo-Croatian (Cyrillic) and Macedonian have one-to-one correspondence between sounds and symbols, using alphabets stemming from Vuk Karadžić's modification of Cyrillic for Serbo-Croatian. For phonemes not represented by single letters in Russian, Serbo-Croatian uses ħ ć, a derivative of an Old Church Slavonic Cyrillic letter ħ, for [t͡ɕ], and a modification thereof, ђ đ, for the voiced equivalent [d͡z]; Macedonian uses diacritics for its etymological equivalents, ѓ ǵ and ќ ḱ. The palatal nasal and lateral are indicated by combining the ordinary consonant symbol with the "soft sign" ь, to give њ nj and љ lj. The use of џ dž for [d͡ʒ] is an original innovation, while Macedonian ѕ dz for [d͡z] revives an Old Church Slavonic Cyrillic letter ѕ. The symbol ј j for [j] is a borrowing from Roman script, simplifying the complex representations of [j] in older Cyrillic and completing the phonemic spelling of palatals.

Belarusian, Ukrainian, and Bulgarian writing systems are closer to Russian, although Bulgarian has an additional vowel phoneme [ə], whose usual written equiva-

ACKNOWLEDGMENTS: I am grateful for information provided by Mikhail E. Alekseev, Raisa M. Batalova, Christopher Beckwith, Wayles Browne, Paul Cubberley, Donald Dyer, Victor Friedman, Martin Haspelmath, Tooru Hayasi, Talant Mawkhanuli, Peter J. Mayo, John R. Payne, Ramazan Rajabov, Ernest C. Scatton, George Y. Shevelov, and Draga Zec. Remaining errors are my own responsibility. Work on this article was conducted while the author was a Visiting Professor at the Institute for the Study of Languages and Cultures of Asia and Africa, Tokyo University of Foreign Studies.
ALPHABET TABLES: Upper-case letters are shown as they would appear when required at the beginning of a sentence. For letters that do not occur word-initially, upper-case forms are shown as they would appear in a text written in upper case throughout. Transliterations used here and in the sample texts are symbol-by-symbol transliterations, not scientific transcriptions, for the languages in question. Letters in parentheses are used only in Russian loans. Indented letters are not considered distinct letters for purposes of alphabetical ordering. In the transcriptions, $ stands for syllable boundary, # for word boundary, I for front vowels, and U for back vowels.
SAMPLE TEXTS: The texts are sometimes slightly adapted from the originals.

TABLE 60.1: *Belarusian Alphabet*

Letter[a]		Translit.	Value		Name
А	а	a	[a]	[a]	
Б	б	b	[b]	[be]	
В	в	v	[v]	[ve]	
Г	г	h	[ɣ]; [g][b]	[ɣe]	
Д	д	d	[d]	[de]	
Е	е	e	[je]; [e] /Cʲ__	[je]	
Ё	ё	ë	[jo]; [o] /Cʲ__	[jo]	
Ж	ж	ž	[ʒ]	[ʒe]	
З	з	z	[z]	[ze]	
I	i	i	[i][c]	[i]	
Й	й	j	[j][d]	['i nʲeskɫa'dovaje] 'non-syllabic *i*', ['i ka'rotkaje] 'short *i*'
К	к	k	[k]	[ka]	
Л	л	l	[l]	[elʲ]	
М	м	m	[m]	[em]	
Н	н	n	[n]	[en]	
О	о	o	[o]	[o]	
П	п	p	[p]	[pe]	
Р	р	r	[r]	[er]	
С	с	s	[s]	[es]	
Т	т	t	[t]	[te]	
У	у	u	[u]	[u]	
Ў	ў	w	[w][e]	['u nʲeskɫa'dovaje] 'non-syllabic *u*', ['u ka'rotkaje] 'short *u*'
Ф	ф	f	[f]	[ef]	
Х	х	x	[x]	[xa]	
Ц	ц	c	[t͡s]	[t͡se]	
Ч	ч	č	[t͡ʃ]	[t͡ʃe]	
Ш	ш	š	[ʃ]	[ʃa]	
Ы	ы	y	[ɨ][c]	[ɨ]	
Ь	ь	'	—[d]	[jer], ['mʲakʲkʲi 'znak] 'soft sign'
Э	э	è	[e]	[e]	
Ю	ю	ju	[ju]; [u] /Cʲ__	[ju]	
Я	я	ja	[ja]; [a] /Cʲ__	[ja]	

a. The following digraphs are not considered separate letters of the alphabet for alphabetical ordering:

Дж	дж	[d͡ʒ]
Дз	дз	[d͡z]

b. [g] occurs only in onomatopoeia and loanwords.
c. [i] and [ɨ] are arguably allophones of a single phoneme.
d. Palatalization of consonants and [j] are indicated as follows:

	—	[a]	[e]	[i]	[o]	[u]
Plain	С	Са	Сэ	Сы	Со	Су
Palatalized	Сь	Ся	Се	Сi	Сё	Сю
[j]		й	я	е		ё	ю

[j] between a vowel and a consonant is indicated by an apostrophe followed by a yotated vowel, e.g. С'я C[ja].
e. [w] is not a distinct phoneme, reflecting the neutralization of word-final and pre-consonantal /v/ and /l/.

TABLE 60.2: *Ukrainian Alphabet*

Letter[a]		Transliteration	Phonetic Value	Name
А	а	a	[a]	[a]
Б	б	b	[b]	[be]
В	в	v	[w]~[v]	[we]
Г	г	h	[ɦ]	[ɦe]
Ґ	ґ	g	[g][b]	[ge]
Д	д	d	[d]	[de]
Е	е	e	[e]	[e]
Є	є	je	[je]; [e] after Cʲ	[je]
Ж	ж	ž	[ʒ]	[ʒe]
З	з	z	[z]	[ze]
И	и	y	[ɪ]	[ɪ]
І	і	i	[i]	[i]
Ї	ї	ji	[ji]	[ji]
Й	й	j	[j][c]	[jot]
К	к	k	[k]	[ka]
Л	л	l	[l]	[el]
М	м	m	[m]	[em]
Н	н	n	[n]	[en]
О	о	o	[o]	[o]
П	п	p	[p]	[pe]
Р	р	r	[r]	[er]
С	с	s	[s]	[es]
Т	т	t	[t]	[te]
У	у	u	[u]	[u]
Ф	ф	f	[f]	[ef]
Х	х	x	[x]	[xa]
Ц	ц	c	[t͡s]	[t͡se]
Ч	ч	č	[t͡ʃ]	[t͡ʃe]
Ш	ш	š	[ʃ]	[ʃa]
Щ	щ	šč	[ʃt͡ʃ]	[ʃt͡ʃa]
Ю	ю	ju	[ju]; [u] after Cʲ	[ju]
Я	я	ja	[ja]; [a] after Cʲ	[ja]
Ь	ь	ʹ	—[c]	[mjaˈkɪj ˈznak] 'soft sign'

a. The following digraphs are not considered separate letters of the alphabet for alphabetical ordering:

    Дж   дж   [d͡ʒ]
    Дз   дз   [d͡z]

b. During the Soviet period, the separate letter ґ *g* was not used, and г *h* served for both [ɦ] and [g], the latter occurring only in onomatopoeia and loanwords. With national independence, ґ *g* has been reintroduced.

c. Palatalization of consonants and [j] are indicated as follows:

	—	[a]	[e]	[i]	[o]	[u]
Plain		C	Ca	Ce	Cи	Co	Cy
Palatalized		Cь	Cя	Ce	Ci	Cьо	Cю
[j]		й	я	є	ї	йо	ю

[j] between a vowel and a consonant is indicated by an apostrophe followed by a yotated vowel, e.g. C'я C[ja].

TABLE 60.3: *Bulgarian Alphabet*

Letter		Transliteration	Phonetic Value	Name
А	а	a	[a][a]	[a]
Б	б	b	[b]	[bə]
В	в	v	[v]	[və]
Г	г	g	[g]	[gə]
Д	д	d	[d]	[də]
Е	е	e	[e]	[e]
Ж	ж	ž	[ʒ]	[ʒə]
З	з	z	[z]	[zə]
И	и	i	[i]	[i]
Й	й	j	[j][b]	['i 'kratko] 'short *i*'
К	к	k	[k]	[kə]
Л	л	l	[l]	[lə]
М	м	m	[m]	[mə]
Н	н	n	[n]	[nə]
О	о	o	[o]	[o]
П	п	p	[p]	[pə]
Р	р	r	[r]	[rə]
С	с	s	[s]	[sə]
Т	т	t	[t]	[tə]
У	у	u	[u]	[u]
Ф	ф	f	[f]	[fə]
Х	х	x	[x]	[xə]
Ц	ц	c	[t͡s]	[t͡sə]
Ч	ч	č	[t͡ʃ]	[t͡ʃə]
Ш	ш	š	[ʃ]	[ʃə]
Щ	щ	št	[ʃt]	[ʃtə]
Ъ	ъ	ã	[ə][a]	['ɛr go'l'am] 'big *er*'
Ь	ь	′	_[b]	['er 'malək] 'little *er*'
Ю	ю	ju	[ju]; [u] after Cʲ	[ju]
Я	я	ja	[ja]; [a] after Cʲᵃ	[ja]

a. In certain grammatical suffixes, [ə] is written with a after plain consonants, and with я after palatalized consonants and [j]; [ə] does not otherwise occur after palatalized consonants or [j].

b. Palatalization of consonants and [j] are indicated as follows:

	—	[a]	[o]	[u]	[ə]
Plain		Ca	Co	Cy	Cъ (Ca)
Palatalized		Cя	Cьo	Cю	Cя
[j]	й	я	йo	ю	я

TABLE 60.4: *Serbo-Croatian (Cyrillic) Alphabet*

Letter		Translit.[a]	Value	Name[b]
А	а	a	[a]	[‚a:]
Б	б	b	[b]	[‚bə]
В	в	v	[v]	[‚və]
Г	г	g	[g]	[‚gə]
Д	д	d	[d]	[‚də]
Ђ	ђ	đ	[d͡z]	[‚d͡zə]
Е	е	e	[e]	[‚e:]
Ж	ж	ž	[ʒ]	[‚ʒə]
З	з	z	[z]	[‚zə]
И	и	i	[i]	[‚i:]
Ј	ј	j	[j]	[‚jə]
К	к	k	[k]	[‚kə]
Л	л	l	[l]	[‚lə]
Љ	љ	lj	[ʎ]	[‚ʎə]
М	м	m	[m]	[‚mə]
Н	н	n	[n]	[‚nə]
Њ	њ	nj	[ɲ]	[‚ɲə]
О	о	o	[o]	[‚o:]
П	п	p	[p]	[‚pə]
Р	р	r	[r]	[‚rə]
С	с	s	[s]	[‚sə]
Т	т	t	[t]	[‚tə]
Ћ	ћ	ć	[t͡ɕ]	[‚t͡ɕə]
У	у	u	[u]	[‚u:]
Ф	ф	f	[f]	[‚fə]
Х	х	x	[x]~[h]	[‚xə]~[‚hə]
Ц	ц	c	[t͡s]	[‚t͡sə]
Ч	ч	č	[t͡ʃ]	[‚t͡ʃə]
Џ	џ	dž	[d͡ʒ]	[‚d͡ʒə]
Ш	ш	š	[ʃ]	[‚ʃə]

a. The Roman transliteration symbols given are those of the Serbo-Croatian Latin-script alphabet; cf. TABLE 59.16 on page 670.
b. The phonetic tone mark [‚] indicates falling tone.

TABLE 60.5: *Macedonian Alphabet*

Letter[a]		Translit.	Value	Name
А	а	a	[a]	[a]
Б	б	b	[b]	[bə]
В	в	v	[v]	[və]
Г	г	g	[g]	[gə]
Д	д	d	[d]	[də]
Ѓ	ѓ	ǵ	[gʲ]~[d͡z]	[gʲə]
Е	е	e	[e]	[e]
Ж	ж	ž	[ʒ]	[ʒə]
З	з	z	[z]	[zə]
Ѕ	ѕ	dz	[d͡z]	[d͡zə]
И	и	i	[i]	[i]
Ј	ј	j	[j]	[jə]
К	к	k	[k]	[kə]
Л	л	l	[ɫ]; [l] before [i], [e], [j]	[ɫə]
Љ	љ	lj	[l] (non-standard [ʎ])	[lə]
М	м	m	[m]	[mə]
Н	н	n	[n]	[nə]
Њ	њ	nj	[ɲ]	[ɲə]
О	о	o	[o]	[o]
П	п	p	[p]	[pə]
Р	р	r	[r]	[rə]
С	с	s	[s]	[sə]
Т	т	t	[t]	[tə]
Ќ	ќ	ḱ	[kʲ]~[t͡ɕ]	[kʲə]
У	у	u	[u]	[u]
Ф	ф	f	[f]	[fə]
Х	х	x	[x]	[xə]
Ц	ц	c	[t͡s]	[t͡sə]
Ч	ч	č	[t͡ʃ]	[t͡ʃə]
Џ	џ	dž	[d͡ʒ]	[d͡ʒə]
Ш	ш	š	[ʃ]	[ʃə]

a. There is also a marginal phoneme [ə], used in dialect words and the names of the letters of the alphabet, and represented by an apostrophe.

lent is ъ *ǎ*. In particular, the three languages use essentially the same devices for indicating palatalization and [j], although the actual symbols used differ from language to language; for details, see TABLES 60.1–60.3. Bulgarian lacks palatalization oppositions except before nonfront vowels. Belarusian and Ukrainian use an apostrophe, rather than the "soft sign" ь or the "hard sign" ъ, to indicate [j] following a consonant; this sequence does not occur in Bulgarian. Otherwise, the main characteristics of Belarusian are a separate letter ў *ŭ* for [w] (though this is not a distinct phoneme), the absence of щ *šč* (for which шч *š-č* is used), and the orthographic representation of vowel reduction in unstressed syllables, e.g. вада *vada* [vaˈda] 'water' (cf. Russian вода *voda* [vʌˈda]). Ukrainian has a special letter ї *ji* to represent [ji], and a special letter ґ *g* to indicate the voiced plosive [g] in onomatopoeia and loanwords, contrasting with the voiced fricative г *h* [ɦ].

Macedonian has basically antepenultimate stress, while the other languages have free stress. Serbo-Croatian has phonemic vowel length on stressed and post-tonic vowels, and stressed vowels distinguish rising and falling tone. Serbo-Croatian and Macedonian have syllabic [r]. None of these prosodic features are marked orthographically.

SAMPLES OF SLAVIC LANGUAGES

UKRAINIAN

1. Ukrainian:	Вода	при	березі	починала	каламутитись	і
2. Transliteration:	Voda	pry	berezi	počynala	kalamutytysʹ	i
3. Transcription:	woˈda	prɪ	ˈberezʲi	poʧɪˈnala	kalaˈmutɪtɪsʲ	i
4. Gloss:	water	by	shore	began	to.grow.turbid	and

1. жовкнути,	разом	z	піском	хвиля	викидала	зо	дна	моря
2. žovknuty,	razom	z	piskom	xvylja	vykydala	zo	dna	morja
3. ˈʒowknutɪ	razom	s	pʲisˈkom	ˈxwɪlʲa	wɪkɪˈdala	zo	ˈdna	ˈmorʲa
4. to.yellow	together	with	sand	wave	threw.out	from	bottom	of.sea

1. на	берег	каміння	і,	тікаючи	назад,	волікла	іх	по	дну
2. na	bereh	kaminnja	i,	tikajučy	nazad,	volikla	jix	po	dnu
3. na	ˈberefi	kaˈmʲinnʲa	i	tʲiˈkajuʧɪ	naˈzad	wolʲikˈla	jix	po	ˈdnu
4. onto	shore	stones	and	running	back	dragged	them	along	bottom

1. з	таким	гуркотом,	наче	там	щось	велике	скреготало
2. z	takym	hurkotom,	nače	tam	ščosʹ	velyke	skrehotalo
3. s	taˈkɪm	ˈfiurkotom	ˈnaʧe	ˈtam	ˈʃʧosʲ	weˈlɪke	skrefioˈtalo
4. with	such	noise	as.if	there	something	huge	gnashed

1. зубами	й	гарчало.	
2. zubamy	j	harc"alo.	
3. zuˈbamɪ	j	fiarˈtʃalo	
4. with.teeth	and	growled	

'The water by the shore began to grow turbid and yellow, together with the sand the wave threw stones out from the sea bottom onto the shore and, running back, dragged them along the bottom with such a noise, as if something huge were there gnashing its teeth and growling.'

—M. *Kocjubyns´kyj*, *На Камені* [*On the stone*], in Vinogradov 1966–68, *1:66*.

Notes:
[a]Low-level assimilations, such as voice assimilation in obstruent clusters, are not shown by the orthography.
[b]The [e]~[ɪ] opposition tends to be neutralized in unstressed position.

SERBO-CROATIAN (EASTERN STANDARD, CYRILLIC SCRIPT)

1. Serbian:	Српскохрватски	правопис	био	је	до	Вука	
2. Transliteration:	Srpskohrvatski	pravopis	bio	je	do	Vuka	
3. Transcription:[a]	srpsko/xr̥va:tski:	\pravopi:s	\bio	je	do	\vu:ka	
4. Gloss:	Serbo-Croatian	orthography	been	is	before	Vuk	

1. углавном	етимолошки,	а	Вук	је	увео	нов,	фонетски
2. uglavnom	etimološki,	a	Vuk	je	uveo	nov,	fonetski
3. u/glavno:m	eti/moloʃki:	a	\vu:k	je	/uveo	\nov	/fonetski:
4. mainly	etymological	but	Vuk	is	introduced	new	phonetic

1. правопис	по	принципу	»Пиши	као	што	говориш,	а
2. pravopis	po	principu	"Piši	kao	što	govoriš,	a
3. \pravopi:s	po	prin/tsi:pu	/piʃi	\kao	ʃto	/govori:ʃ	a
4. orthography	according.to	principle	write!	as	that	you.speak	and

1. читај	како	је	написано«;	смисао	тога	је да	се	промене
2. čitaj	kako	je	napisano";	smisao	toga	je da	se	promene
3. /tʃita:j	\kako je		/napi:sa:no	\smi:sao	\toga	je da	se	\promene
4. read!	as	is	written	meaning	of.this	is that	self	changes

1. гласова	обележавају	само	у	засебним	речима,	а	
2. glasova	obeležavaju	samo	u	zasebnim	rečima,	a	
3. \glaso:va:	obele/ʒa:vaju:	\samo	u	/za:sebni:m	/retʃima	a	
4. of.sounds	they.indicate	only	in	separate	words	but	

1. промене	гласова	у	блиско	везаним	речима	у	реченици
2. promene	glasova	u	blisko	vezanim	rečima	u	rečenici
3. \promene	\glaso:va:	u	\blisko	\ve:za:ni:m	/re:tʃima	u	re/tʃenitsi
4. changes	of-sounds	in	closely	linked	words	in	sentence

1. не	обележавају	се.	
2. ne	obeležavaju	se.	
3. ne	obele/ʒa:vaju:	se	
4. not	they.indicate	self	

'Serbo-Croatian orthography was mainly etymological before Vuk, but Vuk introduced a new phonetic orthography based on the principle 'Write as you speak and read as is written'; the meaning of this is that changes of sounds should be indicated only in separate words while changes of sounds in closely linked words in a sentence should not be indicated.'
–*Мала Енциклопедиja Просвета* [*Small Prosveta encyclopedia*] *1978, 2:896.*

Note:
[a]Phonetic symbols used for tone are [Λ] rising and [\\] falling.

Non-Slavic languages

Given the number of non-Slavic languages using Cyrillic script—over fifty in the early 1990s—and the typological diversity of their phonologies, the following treatment is necessarily selective as regards both languages and phenomena. The languages that appear here are classified into the following families: *Indo-European*—(Romance) Moldovan, (Iranian) Tajik; *Uralic*—(Permic) Komi; *Turkic*—Azeri, Turkmen, Tatar, Kazakh, Uzbek, Kirghiz; *Northwest Caucasian*—Abkhaz, Kabardian; *Northeast Caucasian*—Avar; and *Chukotko-Kamchatkan*—Chukchee. The aim is to give some idea of the kinds of solutions adopted in dealing with phonological problems different from those found in the Russian alphabet, which forms the basis for the alphabets of all the languages concerned. Two basic classes of solutions can be discerned.

   (i) Some new letters are modifications of Russian letters or add diacritics to them, such as ү *ü* for [y] in several Turkic and Mongolic languages, ң or ҥ *ŋ* for [ŋ] in various languages, or ӯ *ū* for [o] in Tajik.

   (ii) Digraphs (and even trigraphs and tetragraphs) are used, such as ку *ku* for [kʷ], къу *k"u* for [qʷ], and кхъу *kx"u* for [qʷ] in Kabardian.

   In general, solution (i) is preferred across most of the former USSR, but solution (ii) is preferred for languages of the northern Caucasus—with the notable exception of Abkhaz, which has the largest number of modified letters of any Cyrillic alphabet in widespread current use. The difference between the two solutions can be seen in orthographic representations of [q]: the usual solution is қ *ķ*, as in Kazakh, Uzbek, Uyghur, Tajik, and Chukchee (with a variant ҡ in Bashkir). Digraphs are found not only in the North Caucasian languages (for which see below), but also, in the shape of къ *k"*, in the Turkic languages Kumyk, Karachay-Balkar, and Crimean Tatar. In addition, letters are occasionally borrowed from other scripts, the most frequent being I (the numeral "one" on a Russian typewriter) in alphabets of the northern Caucasus. More sporadic are i (from Roman or pre-1918 Russian Cyrillic script) and h (from Roman script); the last is found for [h] in Azeri, Tatar, Bashkir, Kazakh, Uyghur, Buryat, and Kalmyk. The modified Cyrillic letter х *χ* is used in Tajik, Karakalpak, and Uzbek; the digraph гъ *g'* occurs in Kumyk, Avar, Lak, Dargwa, Lezgian, and Tabasaran.

TABLE 60.6: *Moldovan Alphabet*

Letter		Tr'lit.	Value	Name
А	а	a	[a]	[a]
Б	б	b	[b]	[be]
В	в	v	[v]	[ve]
Г	г	g	[g]	[ge]
Д	д	d	[d]	[de]
Е	е	e	[je] /$__, [je]
			[e] /C__
Ж	ж	ž	[ʒ]	[ʒe]
Ӂ	ӂ	ǯ	[d͡ʒ]	[d͡ʒe]
З	з	z	[z]	[ze]
И	и	i	[i]	[i]
Й	й	j	[j]	[i skurt] 'short *i*'
К	к	k	[k]	[ka]
Л	л	l	[l]	[el]
М	м	m	[m]	[em]
Н	н	n	[n]	[en]
О	о	o	[o]	[o]
П	п	p	[p]	[pe]
Р	р	r	[r]	[er]
С	с	s	[s]	[es]
Т	т	t	[t]	[te]
У	у	u	[u]; [w]	[u]
Ф	ф	f	[f]	[ef]
Х	х	x	[x]	[xa]
Ц	ц	c	[t͡s]	[t͡se]
Ч	ч	č	[t͡ʃ]	[t͡ʃe]
Ш	ш	š	[ʃ]	[ʃe]
Ы	ы	y	[ɨ]	[ɨ]
Ь	ь	′	[j][a]	['semnul 'mo̯ale] 'soft sign'
Э	э	è	[ə]	[ə]
Ю	ю	ju	[ju]	[ju]
Я	я	ja	[ja]; [e̯a]	[ja]

a. Non-vocalic [j] and [e̯] after a consonant are indicated by the devices that usually indicate palatalization in Cyrillic orthographies, e.g. бунь *bun′* [bunj] 'good (plural)', пятрэ *pjatrè* ['pjatrə], 'stone', нямц *njamc* [ne̯amt͡s] 'German', уд-льоаркэ *ud-l′oarkè* ['ud 'lʲo̯arkə] 'dripping wet'. Otherwise, sequences of [j] plus vowel are indicated as follows: [ja] as я, [je] as e (but ье after a consonant), [jo] as йо, [ju] as ю. Elsewhere, [j] is written й.

TABLE 60.7: *Tajik Alphabet*

Letter		Tr'lit.	Value	Name
А	а	a	[a]	[a]
Б	б	b	[b]	[be]
В	в	v	[v]	[ve]
Г	г	g	[g]	[ge]
Д	д	d	[d]	[de]
Е	е	e	[je] /$__; [je]	
			[e] /C__	
Ё	ё	ë	[jɒ]	[jɒ]
Ж	ж	ž	[ʒ]	[ʒe]
З	з	z	[z]	[ze]
И	и	i	[i]	[i]
Й	й	j	[j][a]	['ii ko'tɒh] 'short *i*'
К	к	k	[k]	[ka]
Л	л	l	[l]	[el]
М	м	m	[m]	[em]
Н	н	n	[n]	[en]
О	о	o	[ɒ]	[ɒ]
П	п	p	[p]	[pe]
Р	р	r	[r]	[er]
С	с	s	[s]	[es]
Т	т	t	[t]	[te]
У	у	u	[u]	[u]
Ф	ф	f	[f]	[ef]
Х	х	x	[χ]	[χa]
(Ц	ц	c)		[tse]
Ч	ч	č	[t͡ʃ]	[t͡ʃe]
(Щ	щ	šč)		[ʃt͡ʃa]
Ъ	ъ	″	[ʔ][b]	[alɒ'mati sak'ta] 'sign of pausing'
(Ы	ы	y)		[je'rɨ]
Ь	ь	′	__[a]	[alɒ'mati d͡ʒudɒ'i] 'sign of separation'
Э	э	è	[e] /$__	[e]
Ю	ю	ju	[ju]	[ju]
Я	я	ja	[ja]	[ja]
Ғ	ғ	ḡ	[ʁ]	[ʁe]
Ӣ	ӣ	ī	[i] / '_#	['ii zada'nɒk] 'accented *i*'
Қ	қ	ḳ	[q]	[qe]
Ӯ	ӯ	ū	[o]	[o]
Ҳ	ҳ	ḫ	[h]	[he]
Ҷ	ҷ	č̣	[d͡ʒ]	[d͡ʒe]

a. [ja], [jɒ], [je], and [ju] are indicated as я, ё, е, ю, respectively, initially and after a vowel; after a consonant, ь is written before the yotated vowel. Elsewhere, [j] is written й, including йӯ [jo].
b. ъ after a vowel is usually realized as vowel length.

TABLE 60.8: *Komi (Komi-Zyryan) Alphabet*

Letter[a]		Translit.	Phonetic Value	Name
А	а	a	[a]	[a]
Б	б	b	[b]	[be]
В	в	v	[v]	[ve]
Г	г	g	[g]	[ge]
Д	д	d	[d]; as palatal, [dʲ]	[de]
Е	е	e	[je]; [e] after C except [t, d, s, z, n, l]	[je]
Ё	ё	ë	[jo]; [o] after [tʲ, dʲ, sʲ, zʲ, nʲ, lʲ]	[jo]
Ж	ж	ž	[ʒ]	[ʒe]
З	з	z	[z]; as palatal, [zʲ]	[ze]
И	и	i	[i]	[nʲebɨd i] 'soft *i*'
І	і	ï	[i] after [t, d, s, z, n, l]	[t͡sʲorɨd i] 'hard *i*'
Й	й	j	[j][b]	[i kratkəj]
К	к	k	[k]	[ka]
Л	л	l	[l]; as palatal, [lʲ]	[el]
М	м	m	[m]	[em]
Н	н	n	[n]; as palatal, [nʲ]	[en]
О	о	o	[o]	[o]
Ö	ö	ö	[ə]	[ə]
П	п	p	[p]	[pe]
Р	р	r	[r]	[er]
С	с	s	[s]; as palatal, [sʲ]	[es]
Т	т	t	[t]; as palatal, [tʲ]	[te]
У	у	u	[u]	[u]
(Ф	ф	f)	[f]	[ef]
(Х	х	x)	[x]	[xa]
(Ц	ц	c)	[t͡s]	[t͡se]
Ч	ч	č	[t͡sʲ]	[t͡sʲe]
Ш	ш	š	[ʃ]	[ʃa]
(Щ	щ	šč)		[ʃt͡ʃa]
Ъ	ъ	ʺ	_[b]	[t͡sʲorɨd znak] 'hard sign'
Ы	ы	y	[ɨ]	[ɨ]
Ь	ь	ʹ	_[b]	[nʲebɨd znak] 'soft sign'
Э	э	è	[e] /$__ and after [t, d, s, z, n, l]	[e]
Ю	ю	ju	[ju]; [u] after [tʲ, dʲ, sʲ, zʲ, nʲ, lʲ]	[ju]
Я	я	ja	[ja]; [a] after [tʲ, dʲ, sʲ, zʲ, nʲ, lʲ]	[ja]

a. The following digraphs are not considered separate letters of the alphabet:

Дз	дз	dz	[d͡zʲ]
Дж	дж	dž	[d͡ʐ]
Тш	тш	tš	[t͡ʂ]

b. The distinction between palatal and non-palatal and the representation of [j] follow the system below:

	—	[a]	[e]	[i]	[o]	[u]	[ə]	[ɨ]
Non-palatal	С	Са	Сэ	Сі	Со	Су	Сö	Сы
Palatal	Сь	Ся	Се	Си	Сё	Сю	Сьö	Сьы
[j]		й	я	е	йи	ё	ю	йö	йы

Between a consonant and a yotated vowel, [j] is represented by ъ, e.g. каръяс *karʺjas* [karjas] 'towns'.

Representation of vowels

Orthographic representation of the "extra" (relative to Russian) front vowels [y ø æ] gives a good indication of the range of different solutions to essentially a single problem. The most frequent solution is with modified Russian letters, namely ү *ü*, ө *ö*, and ә *ä*; this is the solution found in the major Turkic languages and in the Mongolic languages. Use of an umlaut to give ÿ (in Chuvash, ӳ), ö, and ä is found sporadically — in Gagauz, Khakas, Altay, Mari, and Chuvash. In languages of the northern Caucasus, the preferred solution is a digraph, with the "soft sign" ь after the corresponding back vowel, to give уь, оь, аь; some or all of these digraphs are used not only in Northeast Caucasian languages (Chechen, Ingush, Lak, Lezgian, Tabasaran), but also in Turkic languages of the area (Kumyk, Nogay). Yet a fourth solution is to use the Russian yotated vowels ю *ju*, ё *ë*, and я *ja* in this function, as in Karachay–Balkar and Crimean Tatar. The third and fourth solutions are even combined in some Northeast Caucasian and Turkic languages, with the yotated vowel symbol being used after consonants and the digraph elsewhere, as in Kumyk уьч *üč* [yt͡ʃ] 'three' but гюз *gjuz* [gyz] 'autumn'.

Solutions to the orthographic representation of the minimal vowel inventories of the Northwest Caucasian languages are of interest. On at least one analysis, the languages have three basic vowels, [a], [ə], and [aː], with such vowel qualities as [e] and [o] being combinatory variants. The spelling systems of Abkhaz, Abaza, Kabardian, and Adyghe all agree in representing these secondary vowel qualities. For the basic vowel qualities, Abkhaz and Abaza use а *a*, ы *y*, and аа *aa*, while Kabardian and Adyghe use э *è*, ы *y*, and а *a*, respectively—another instance of different orthographic solutions to the same phonological problem.

Representation of palatalization

Orthographic representations of [j] show considerable variation, depending largely on the extent to which Russian orthographic norms are followed. A few languages have a uniform symbol for [j]—adopting the Roman letter j as in Azeri, or using Cyrillic й *j* as in Yakut, or using и *i* as in Abkhaz. But nearly all other languages carry over the Russian conventions of using the symbol й only between a vowel and a consonant or word boundary, of using the yotated vowels to represent [j] word-initially or after a vowel, and usually also of using some variant of ь or ъ plus a yotated vowel to represent [j] between a consonant and a vowel. This Russian system gives rise to further problems when the language in question has sequences of [j] plus vowel that do not occur in Russian. Typically, the Russian system is used where Russian provides a model, but й plus vowel where it does not, e.g. Chukchee йигйит *jigjit* [jiɣjit] 'small intestine'. In some cases, phonemic oppositions are simply merged orthographically after [j], as in the use of ю *ju* to represent both [ju] and [jy] in Tatar and Mongolian. In the (relatively few) languages that have a phonemic opposition of palatalization, or of palatal versus non-palatal, the Russian yotated vowels can be used as in Russian,

TABLE 60.9: *Azeri Alphabet*

Letter		Tr'lit.	Value	Name
А	а	a	[a]	[a]
Б	б	b	[b]	[be]
В	в	v	[v]	[ve]
Г	г	g	[g]	[ge]
Ғ	ғ	ḡ	[ɣ]	[ɣe]
Д	д	d	[d]	[de]
Е	е	e	[e]	[e]
Ə	ə	ä	[æ]	[æ]
Ж	ж	ž	[ʒ]	[ʒe]
З	з	z	[z]	[ze]
И	и	i	[i]	[i]
Ы	ы	y	[ɯ]	[ɯ]
Ј	ј	j	[j]	[je]
К	к	k	[kʲ], [k]ᵃ	[kʲe]
Қ	к	ķ	[gʲ]	[gʲe]
Л	л	l	[l]	[el]
М	м	m	[m]	[em]
Н	н	n	[n]	[en]
О	о	o	[o]	[o]
Ө	ө	ö	[ø]	[ø]
П	п	p	[p]	[pe]
Р	р	r	[r]	[er]
С	с	s	[s]	[se]
Т	т	t	[t]	[te]
У	у	u	[u]	[u]
Ү	ү	ü	[y]	[y]
Ф	ф	f	[f]	[fe]
Х	х	x	[x]	[xe]
Һ	h	h	[h]	[he]
Ч	ч	č	[t͡ʃ]	[t͡ʃe]
Ҹ	ҹ	ç	[d͡ʒ]	[d͡ʒe]
Ш	ш	š	[ʃ]	[ʃe]
'	'	'	_ᵇ	[apo'strof] 'apostrophe'

a. In words of Arabic or Russian origin к can represent [k]; in indigenous words it represents [kʲ].

b. The apostrophe occurs in loans from Arabic and corresponds to an Arabic word-medial glottal stop. Its pronunciation in Azeri varies; after a vowel it is usually realized as vowel length.

TABLE 60.10: *Turkmen Alphabet*

Letterᵃ		Tr'lit.	Value	Name
А	а	a	[a]	[a]
Б	б	b	[b]	[be]
В	в	v	[β]	[βe]
Г	г	g	[g]~[ʁ]	[ge]
Д	д	d	[d]	[de]
Е	е	e	[je] /$__; [je] [e] /C__	
Ё	ё	ë	[jo]	[jo]
Ж	ж	ž	[ʒ]	[ʒe]
Җ	җ	ǰ	[d͡ʒ]	[d͡ʒe]
З	з	z	[ð]	[ðe]
И	и	i	[i]	[i]
Й	й	j	[j]ᵇ	[ju]
К	к	k	[k]~[q]	[ka]
Л	л	l	[l]	[el]
М	м	m	[m]	[em]
Н	н	n	[n]	[en]
Ң	ң	ņ	[ŋ]	[eŋ]
О	о	o	[o]	[o]
Ө	ө	ö	[ø]	[ø]
П	п	p	[p]	[pe]
Р	р	r	[r]	[er]
С	с	s	[θ]	[eθ]
Т	т	t	[t]	[te]
У	у	u	[u]	[u]
Ү	ү	ü	[y]	[y]
Ф	ф	f	[ɸ]	[eɸ]
Х	х	x	[h]~[x]	[xa]
(Ц	ц	c)		[t͡se]
Ч	ч	č	[t͡ʃ]	[t͡ʃe]
Ш	ш	š	[ʃ]	[ʃa]
(Щ	щ	šč)		[ʃt͡ʃa]
(Ъ	ъ	″)		[ajɯɯ'ɯɯa belgi'si] 'sign of separation'
Ы	ы	y	[ɯ]	[ɯ]
(Ь	ь	′)		[jumʃak'lɯk belgi'si] 'sign of softening'
Э	э	è	[e] /$__	[e]
Ә	ә	ä	[æ:]	[æ:]
Ю	ю	ju	[ju]	[ju]
Я	я	ja	[ja]	[ja]

a. Vowel length is not in general marked, although [y:] is written уй; [æ:] is nearly always long, [e] nearly always short.

b. [ja], [je], [jo], [ju] are written я, е, ё, ю, even—at least in the case of я and ё—after a consonant. Elsewhere, [j] is written й; thus [jy] is йү.

TABLE 60.11: *Tatar (Volga Tatar, Kazan Tatar) Alphabet*

Letter		Transliteration	Phonetic Value	Name
А	а	a	[a]	[a]
Б	б	b	[b]	[be]
В	в	v	[w] /$__	[we]
Г	г	g	[g]; [ʁ][a]	[ge]
Д	д	d	[d]	[de]
Е	е	e	[je]; [jɣ] /$__; [e] /C__	[je]
(Ё	ё	ë)		[jo]
Ж	ж	ž	[ʒ]	[ʒe]
З	з	z	[z]	[ze]
И	и	i	[i]	[i]
Й	й	j	[j][b]	[qɯs'qa 'i] 'short *i*'
К	к	k	[k]; [q][a]	[qa]
Л	л	l	[l]	[el]
М	м	m	[m]	[em]
Н	н	n	[n]	[en]
О	о	o	[o]	[o]
П	п	p	[p]	[pe]
Р	р	r	[r]	[er]
С	с	s	[s]	[es]
Т	т	t	[t]	[te]
У	у	u	[u]; [w] /U__$	[u]
Ф	ф	f	[ɸ]	[eɸ]
Х	х	x	[x]	[xa]
(Ц	ц	c)		[t͡se]
Ч	ч	č	[t͡ʃ]	[t͡ʃe]
Ш	ш	š	[ʃ]	[ʃa]
(Щ	щ	šč)		[ʃt͡ʃa]
Ъ	ъ	"	[ʔ] /__U[a, b]	[qalɣn'lɣk bilge'se] 'sign of hardness'
Ы	ы	y	[ɣ]	[ɣ]
Ь	ь	'	[ʔ] /__I[a, b]	[net͡ʃkæ'lek bilge'se] 'sign of thinness'
Э	э	è	[e] /$__; [ʔ] /__$	[e]
Ю	ю	ju	[ju]; [jy]	[ju]
Я	я	ja	[ja]; [jæ]	[ja]
Ә	ә	ä	[æ]	[æ]
Ө	ө	ö	[ø]	[ø]
Ү	ү	ü	[y]; [w] /I__$	[y]
Җ	җ	ǯ	[d͡ʒ]	[d͡ʒe]
Ң	ң	ŋ	[ŋ]	[eŋ]
һ	һ	h	[h]	[he]

a. Tatar has no special symbols to distinguish velars from uvulars. In general, velars occur in front-vowel environments, uvulars in back-vowel environments. A uvular before a front vowel is indicated by writing the corresponding back vowel, e.g. кардәш *kardäš* [qær'dæʃ] 'kinsman'. The front value of the vowel is usually retrievable from vowel harmony; if not, ь is added at the end of the syllable, e.g. шагыйрь *šagyjr´* [ʃa'ʁir] 'poet'. Exceptional syllable-final velars are indicated by means of ь, exceptional syllable-final uvulars by means of ъ, e.g. пакь *pak´* [pak] 'pure', вәгъдә *väg″dä* [wæʁ'dæ] 'promise'.

b. [ja] and [jæ] are both written я, [ju] and [jy] both ю, [jɣ] and [je] both e; after a consonant, ь is inserted before the yotated vowel in front-vowel environments, ъ in back-vowel environments. The ambiguity between front- and back-vowel pronunciations is usually resolved by vowel harmony; if not, ь is added syllable-finally to specify the front value of the vowel, e.g. юнь *jun´* [jyn] 'cheap'. In all other cases, [j] is written й.

TABLE 60.12: *Kazakh Alphabet*

Letter		Transliteration	Phonetic Value	Name
А	а	a	[a]	[a]
Ә	ә	ä	[æ]	[æ]
Б	б	b	[b]	[be]
(В	в	v)		[ve]
Г	г	g	[g]	[ge]
Ғ	ғ	ḡ	[ʁ]	[ʁa]
Д	д	d	[d]	[de]
Е	е	e	[e]	[je]
(Ё	ё	ë)		[jo]
Ж	ж	ž	[ʒ]	[d͡ʒe]
З	з	z	[z]	[ze]
И	и	i	[ɯj], [ij]	[ij]
Й	й	j	[j]ᵃ	[qɯs'qa 'i] 'short *i*'
К	к	k	[k]	[ka]
Қ	қ	ķ	[q]	[qa]
Л	л	l	[l]	[el]
М	м	m	[m]	[em]
Н	н	n	[n]	[en]
Ң	ң	ṇ	[ŋ]	[eŋ]
О	о	o	[o]	[o]
Ө	ө	ö	[ø]	[ø]
П	п	p	[p]	[pe]
Р	р	r	[r]	[er]
С	с	s	[s]	[es]
Т	т	t	[t]	[te]
У	у	u	[uw], [yw], [w]	[uw]
Ұ	ұ	ṻ	[u]	[u]
Ү	ү	ü	[y]	[y]
Ф	ф	f	[f]	[ef]
Х	х	x	[χ]	[χa]
Һ	h	h	[h]	[he]
(Ц	ц	c)		[t͡se]
(Ч	ч	č)		[t͡ʃe]
Ш	ш	š	[ʃ]	[ʃa]
(Щ	щ	šč)		[ʃt͡ʃa]
(Ъ	ъ	")		[ajɯ'ruw belgi'si] 'sign of separation'
Ы	ы	y	[ɯ]	[ɯ]
I	i	ï	[i]	[i]
(Ь	ь	')		[d͡ʒiŋiʃke'lik belgi'si] 'sign of thinness'
(Э	э	è)		[e]
Ю	ю	ju	[ju], [jy]	[ju]
Я	я	ja	[ja]	[ja]

a. [j] occurs only intervocalically and syllable-finally. [ja] is written я, both [ju] and [jy] are written ю; before other vowels, [j] is written й, as is also done syllable-finally except for the special case of [ɯj] and [ij], both written и. The Kazakh representation of the high vowels is unique among languages using Cyrillic script.

TABLE 60.13: *Uzbek Alphabet*

Letter[a]		Transliteration	Phonetic Value[b]	Name
А	a	a	[a]	[a]
Б	б	b	[b]	[be]
В	в	v	[w]	[we]
Г	г	g	[g]	[ge]
Д	д	d	[d]	[de]
Е	e	e	[je] /$__; [e] /C__	[je]
Ё	ё	ë	[jo]	[jo]
Ж	ж	ž	[d͡ʒ]	[d͡ʒe]
З	з	z	[z]	[ze]
И	и	i	[i]	[i]
Й	й	j	[j][c]	[qis'qa 'i] 'short *i*'
К	к	k	[k]	[ka]
Л	л	l	[l]	[el]
М	м	m	[m]	[em]
Н	н	n	[n][d]	[en]
О	о	o	[ɒ]	[ɒ]
П	п	p	[p]	[pe]
Р	р	r	[r]	[er]
С	с	s	[s]	[es]
Т	т	t	[t]	[te]
У	y	u	[u]	[u]
Ф	ф	f	[ɸ]	[eɸ]
Х	х	x	[χ]	[χa]
(Ц	ц	c)		[t͡se]
Ч	ч	č	[t͡ʃ]	[t͡ʃe]
Ш	ш	š	[ʃ]	[ʃa]
Ъ	ъ	ʺ	[ʔ][e]	[qattiq'liq belgi'si] 'sign of hardness', [ad͡ʒra'tiʃ belgi'si] 'sign of separation'
(Ь	ь	ʹ)		[jumʃɒq'lik belgi'si] 'sign of softness'
Э	э	è	[e] /$__	[e]
Ю	ю	ju	[ju]	[ju]
Я	я	ja	[ja]	[ja]
Ў	ў	ŭ	[o]	[o]
Қ	қ	ķ	[q]	[qa]
Ғ	ғ	ḡ	[ʁ]	[ʁe]
Ҳ	ҳ	ẖ	[h]	[ha], [he]

a. Uzbek does not use щ *šč* or ы *y* in loans from Russian; it substitutes шч *š-č* and и *i* respectively.

b. The Uzbek variety represented lacks phonemically distinct front rounded and high back unrounded vowels.

c. [ja], [je], [jo], and [ju] are written я, e, ё, and ю, even—at least in the case of ё—after a consonant, e.g. дарё *darë* [dar'jo] 'river'. Elsewhere, [j] is written й.

d. The digraph нг *ng* [ŋ] is not considered a separate letter of the alphabet.

e. Whether and how ъ is realized varies with speech style.

TABLE 60.14: *Kirghiz Alphabet*

Letter		Transliteration	Phonetic Value[a]	Name
А	а	a	[a]	[a]
Б	б	b	[b]	[be]
(В	в	v)		[ve]
Г	г	g	[g] ~ [ʁ]	[ge]
Д	д	d	[d]	[de]
Е	е	e	[je] /$__; [e] /C__	[e]
Ё	ё	ё	[jo]	[jo]
Ж	ж	ž	[d͡ʒ]	[d͡ʒe]
З	з	z	[z]	[ze]
И	и	i	[i]	[i]
Й	й	j	[j][b]	[ij]
К	к	k	[k]~[q]	[ka]
Л	л	l	[l]	[el]
М	м	m	[m]	[em]
Н	н	n	[n]	[en]
Ң	ң	ṇ	[ŋ]	[uŋ]
О	о	o	[o]	[o]
Ɵ	ɵ	ö	[ø]	[ø]
П	п	p	[p]	[pe]
Р	р	r	[r]	[er]
С	с	s	[s]	[es]
Т	т	t	[t]	[te]
У	у	u	[u]	[u]
Ү	ү	ü	[y]	[y]
(Ф	ф	f)		[ef]
Х	х	x	[χ]	[χa]
(Ц	ц	c		[t͡se]
Ч	ч	č	[t͡ʃ]	[t͡ʃe]
Ш	ш	š	[ʃ]	[ʃa]
(Щ	щ	šč)		[ʃt͡ʃa]
(Ъ	ъ	″)		[ad͡ʒɯtaˈru: belgiˈsi] 'sign of separation'
Ы	ы	y	[ɯ]	[ɯ]
(Ь	ь	′)		[it͡ʃkerˈty: belgiˈsi] 'sign of thinness'
Э	э	è	[e] /$__	[e]
Ю	ю	ju	[ju]	[ju]
Я	я	ja	[ja]	[ja]

a. Long vowels are indicated by doubling the vowel letter. If the first vowel symbol is yotated, the second is the unyotated equivalent, e.g. [aˈju:] 'bear' is аюу.

b. [j] occurs only intervocalically and syllable-finally. [ja, je, jo, ju] are written я, е, ё, ю; otherwise, [j] is written й.

e.g. in Komi сайсянь *sajsjan´* [sajsʲanʲ] 'from behind'. Other solutions must be found if the opposition extends to vowels before which it is not found in Russian: Komi uses i (and the closely related Udmurt uses ӥ *ï*) to indicate non-palatal quality before [i], as in ci *sï* [si] 'fiber', cf. си *si* [sʲi] 'hair'. Before Komi ы *y* [ɨ] and ö *ö* [ə], ь must be used after the palatal consonant, as in preconsonantal or word-final position, e.g. сьӧд *s´öd* [sʲəd] 'black'. In the languages of the northern Caucasus that have digraphs comprising consonant plus ь (and also Yakut), this spelling remains even before a vowel, as in Avar гьабуна *g´abuna* (not *гябуна *gjabuna*) [habuna] 'made'.

Representation of consonants

The indication of a phonemic opposition between ejective and non-ejective (typically aspirated) consonants, confined to the northern Caucasus, shows partial, but by no means complete, uniformity. The usual solution is consonant plus I *l* for the ejective, as in Abaza, Kabardian, Adyghe, Chechen, Ingush, Avar, Lak, Dargwa, Lezgian, and Tabasaran пI *pl* [pʼ]. With the uvulars, however, Kabardian distinguishes ejective къ *k″* [qʼ] from non-ejective кхъ *kx″* [q], probably reflecting a correct assessment of markedness relations (some languages of the area have an ejective but no non-ejective uvular stop). The Northeast Caucasian languages typically have a single ejective кь *k´* [qʼ] (but in Avar this represents [t͡ɬʼː]), a single non-ejective (aspirated) хъ *x″* [q], and a geminate къ *k″* [qː] or [qʼː]. Abkhaz goes its own way in writing the ejective by means of a diacritic (usually a subscript tail) in the case of affricates, but the non-ejective (aspirated) by means of the same diacritic in the case of plain stops, e.g. ejective ҷ *ç̌* [t͡ʃʼ] and ӄ *k* [kʼ] versus non-ejective ч *č* [t͡ʃ] and қ *ḳ* [k]; again, this may reflect judgments about markedness. Ossetic also goes its own way by consistently using a digraph with ъ for ejectives, e.g. пъ *p″* [pʼ]. However, ъ is used for [ʔ] in Abaza, Avar, Lak, Dargwa, Lezgian, Tabasaran, and (outside the Caucasus) several Turkic languages, in Tajik, and (in some environments) in Chukchee. By contrast, Adyghe, Kabardian, Chechen, and Ingush use I *l* for [ʔ]. The symbol I is also used in the digraph гI *gl* [ʕ] in Abaza, Chechen, Ingush, Avar, Lak, and Dargwa.

Representation of prosodic phenomena

Prosodic phonemes are generally not marked, whatever their functional load. Thus phonemic tone is not marked in Dunganese, and phonemic stress is not normally marked in any of the relevant languages—as indeed it is not in Russian. Tajik idiosyncratically but usefully distinguishes the frequent stressed derivational suffix -[i] from the frequent unstressed grammatical linker -[i] by writing the former as ӣ *ī* word-finally, the latter as и *i*. Vowel length is indicated in some languages by doubling the vowel letter (e.g. the Mongolic languages, Kirghiz, Tuvan, Yakut); but it remains without orthographic representation in others, even where it contains a high functional load (e.g. Nenets, Turkmen, the Tungusic languages).

TABLE 60.15: *Abkhaz Alphabet*

Letter[a]		Translit.	Value[b]	Name	Letter[a]		Translit.	Value[b]	Name
А	а	a	[a]	[a]	М	м	m	[m]	[mə]
Б	б	b	[b]	[bə]	Н	н	n	[n]	[nə]
В	в	v	[v]	[və]	О	о	o	[o]	[o]
Г	г	g	[g]	[gə]	Ҩ	ҩ	o̧	[ɥ]	[ɥə]
Гь	гь	g′	[gʲ]	[gʲə]	П	п	p	[p']	[p'ə]
Ҕ	ҕ	ġ	[ɣ]	[ɣə]	Ԥ	ԥ	ṗ	[p]	[pə]
Ҕь	ҕь	ġ′	[ɣʲ]	[ɣʲə]	Р	р	r	[r]	[rə]
Д	д	d	[d]	[də]	С	с	s	[s]	[sə]
Дә	дә	dᵒ	[dʷ]	[dʷə]	Т	т	t	[t']	[t'ə]
Џ	џ	j	[d͡z]	[d͡zə]	Тә	тә	tᵒ	[tʷ]	[tʷə]
Џь	џь	j′	[d͡z]	[d͡zə]	Ҭ	ҭ	ṭ	[t]	[tə]
Е	е	e	[e]	[e]	Ҭә	ҭә	ṭᵒ	[tʷ]	[tʷə]
Ҽ	ҽ	ċ	[t͡ʂ]	[t͡ʂə]	У	у	u	[w, u]	[u]
Ҿ	ҿ	ç	[t͡ʂ']	[t͡ʂ'ə]	Ф	ф	f	[f]	[fə]
Ж	ж	ž	[ʐ]	[ʐə]	Х	х	x	[x]	[xə]
Жь	жь	ž′	[z]	[zə]	Хь	хь	x′	[xʲ]	[xʲə]
Жә	жә	žᵒ	[ʐʷ]	[ʐʷə]	Ҳ	ҳ	x̧	[ħ]	[ħə]
З	з	z	[z]	[zə]	Ҳә	ҳә	x̧ᵒ	[ħʷ]	[ħʷə]
Ҙ	ҙ	ӡ	[d͡z]	[d͡zə]	Ц	ц	c	[t͡s]	[t͡sə]
Ҙә	ҙә	ӡᵒ	[d͡zʷ]	[d͡zʷə]	Цә	цә	cᵒ	[t͡sʷ]	[t͡sʷə]
И	и	i	[j, i]	[i]	Ҵ	ҵ	c̄	[t͡s']	[t͡s'ə]
К	к	k	[k']	[k'ə]	Ҵә	ҵә	c̄ᵒ	[t͡sʷ']	[t͡sʷ'ə]
Кь	кь	k′	[kʲ]	[kʲə]	Ч	ч	č	[t͡ɕ]	[t͡ɕə]
Қ	қ	ķ	[k]	[kə]	Ҷ	ҷ	ç	[t͡ɕ']	[t͡ɕ'ə]
Қь	қь	ķ′	[kʲ]	[kʲə]	Ш	ш	š	[ʂ]	[ʂə]
Ҟ	ҟ	ḳ	[q']	[q'ə]	Шь	шь	š′	[ɕ]	[ɕə]
Ҟь	ҟь	ḳ′	[qʲ]	[qʲə]	Шә	шә	šᵒ	[ʂʷ]	[ʂʷə]
Л	л	l	[l]	[lə]	Ы	ы	y	[ə]	[ə]

a. The following digraphs, in which y *u* indicates labialization, are not considered separate letters (contrast those where labialization is marked by ə):

Ку	ку	ku	[kʷ']
Қу	қу	ķu	[kʷ]
Гу	гу	gu	[gʷ]
Ҟу	ҟу	ḳu	[qʷ']
Ҕу	ҕу	ġu	[ɣʷ]
Ху	ху	xu	[xʷ]

b. The vowels [i], [u], [e], and [o] are derivatives of the basic vowels [ə] and [a] in palatal and labial environments. [a:] is written aa.

TABLE 60.16: *Kabardian (East Circassian) Alphabet*

Letter[a]		Translit.	Value[c]	Name	Letter[a]		Translit.	Value[c]	Name
А	а	a	[aː]	[aː]	М	м	m	[m]	[mə]
Э	э	è[b]	[a]	[a]	Н	н	n	[n]	[nə]
Б	б	b	[b]	[bə]	О	о	o	[o]	[o]
В	в	v	[v]	[və]	П	п	p	[p]	[pə]
Г	г	g	[ɣ]	[ɣə]	ПI	пI	p1	[p']	[p'ə]
Гу	гу	gu	[gʷ]	[gʷə]	Р	р	r	[r]	[rə]
Гъ	гъ	g″	[ʁ]	[ʁə]	С	с	s	[s]	[sə]
Гъу	гъу	g″u	[ʁʷ]	[ʁʷə]	Т	т	t	[t]	[tə]
Д	д	d	[d]	[də]	ТI	тI	t1	[t']	[t'ə]
Дж	дж	dž	[gʲ]	[gʲə]	У	у	u	[w, u]	[wə]
Дз	дз	dz	[d͡z]	[d͡zə]	Ф	ф	f	[f]	[fə]
Е	е	e	[ja]	[je]	ФI	фI	f1	[f']	[f'ə]
(Ё	ё	ë)		[jo]	Х	х	x	[x][e]	[xə]
Ж	ж	ž	[ʒ]	[ʒə]	Ху	ху	xu	[xʷ]	[xʷə]
Жь	жь	ž′	[z]	[zə]	Хь	хь	x′	[ħ]	[ħə]
З	з	z	[z]	[zə]	Хъ	хъ	x″	[χ]	[χə]
И	и	i	[i]	[i]	Хъу	хъу	x″u	[χʷ]	[χʷə]
Й	й	j	[j][d]	[jə]	Ц	ц	c	[t͡s]	[t͡sə]
(К	к	k)		[kə]	ЦI	цI	c1	[t͡s']	[t͡s'ə]
Ку	ку	ku	[kʷ]	[kʷə]	Ч	ч	č	[kʲ]	[kʲə]
КI	кI	k1	[kʲ']	[kʲ'ə]	Ш	ш	š	[ʃ]	[ʃə]
КIу	кIу	k1u	[kʷ']	[kʷ'ə]	Щ	щ	šč	[ɕ]	[ɕə]
Къ	къ	k″	[q']	[q'ə]	ЩI	щI	šč1	[ɕ']	[ɕ'ə]
Къу	къу	k″u	[qʷ']	[qʷ'ə]	Ы	ы	y	[ə]	[ə]
Кхъ	кхъ	kx″	[q]	[qə]	(Э	э	è)[b]		[e]
Кхъу	кхъу	kx″u	[qʷ]	[qʷə]	(Ю	ю	ju)		[ju]
Л	л	l	[ɮ]	[ɮə]	Я	я	ja	[jaː]	[jaː]
Лъ	лъ	l″	[ɬ]	[ɬə]	I	I	1	[ʔ]	[ʔə]
ЛI	лI	l1	[ɬ']	[ɬ'ə]	Iу	Iу	1u	[ʔʷ]	[ʔʷə]

a. ъ and ь are not considered letters of the Kabardian alphabet, although they are used in writing loans from Russian.

b. Note that э has a different alphabetical order in native words than in Russian loans.

c. The vowels [i], [u], [e], and [o] are derivatives of the basic vowels [ə] and [a] in palatal and labial environments.

d. [ja] is written e, though this letter represents [e] after a consonant, and [jaː] is written я.

e. x represents [h] in the plural suffix -хэ -[ha].

TABLE 60.17: *Avar Alphabet*

Letter		Translit.	Value[a]	Name	Letter		Translit.	Value[a]	Name
А	а	a	[a]	[a]	П	п	p	[p]	[pe]
Б	б	b	[b]	[be]	Р	р	r	[r]	[er]
В	в	w	[w][b]	[we]	С	с	s	[s]	[es]
Г	г	g	[g]	[ge]	Т	т	t	[t]	[te]
Гъ	гъ	g″	[ʁ]	[ʁe]	ТI	тI	tl	[t']	[t'e]
Гь	гь	g′	[h]	[he]	У	у	u	[u]	[u]
ГI	гI	g1	[ʕ]	[ʕe]	(Ф	ф	f)	[f]	[ef]
Д	д	d	[d]	[de]	Х	х	x	[χ]	[χa]
Е	е	e	[je], C+[e]	[je]	Хъ	хъ	x″	[q:]	[q:a]
Ё	ё	ë	[jo]	[jo]	Хь	хь	x′	[x]	[xa]
Ж	ж	ž	[ʒ]	[ʒe]	ХI	хI	x1	[ħ]	[ħa]
З	з	z	[z]	[ze]	Ц	ц	c	[t͡s]	[t͡se]
И	и	i	[i]	[i]	ЦI	цI	c1	[t͡s']	[t͡s'e]
Й	й	j	[j][c]	[j]	Ч	ч	č	[t͡ʃ]	[t͡ʃe]
К	к	k	[k]	[ka]	ЧI	чI	č1	[t͡ʃ']	[t͡ʃ'e]
Къ	къ	k″	[q':]	[q':a]	Ш	ш	š	[ʃ]	[ʃa]
Кь	кь	k′	[t͡ɬ':]	[t͡ɬ':a]	Щ	щ	šč	[ʃ:]	[ʃ:a]
КI	кI	k1	[k']	[k'a]	Ъ	ъ	″	[ʔ]	[jer]
Л	л	l	[l][d]	[el]	(Ы	ы	y)		[jerɨ]
Лъ	лъ	l″	[ɬ]	[eɬ]	(Ь	ь	′)		[jerʲ]
М	м	m	[m]	[em]	Э	э	è	[e] initial	[e]
Н	н	n	[n]	[en]	Ю	ю	ju	[ju]	[ju]
О	о	o	[o]	[o]	Я	я	ja	[ja]	[ja]

a. The diacritic [:] indicates an "intensive" (strong, geminate) consonant; some other consonants have intensive counterparts; the feature is sporadically indicated by doubling the corresponding simple letter, e.g. кк [k:], кIкI [k':]. Gemination in the consonants [q':], [t͡ɬ':], and dialectal [t͡ɬ:] is nonphonemic, and there is variation in whether or not they are phonetically geminate.

b. Labialization of consonants is indicated by adding в *v* after the consonant symbol, e.g. хьв [xʷ].

c. [ja], [je], [jo], [ju] are written я, е, ё, ю. Elsewhere [j] is written й, i.e. syllable-finally and in йи [ji]; other than in Russian loans, [j] does not occur after a consonant.

d. Some dialects have an additional phoneme [t͡ɬ:], indicated by лI *ll* when forms from such dialects are written.

TABLE 60.18: *Chukchee Alphabet*

Letter		Transliteration	Phonetic Value[a]
А	а	a	[a]
(Б	б	b)	
В	в	v	[β]
Г	г	g	[ɣ]
(Д	д	d)	
Е	е	e	[je]; [e] after л, ч
Ё	ё	ë	[jo]; [o] after л
(Ж	ж	ž)	
(З	з	z)	
И	и	i	[i]
Й	й	j	[j][b]
К	к	k	[k]
Ҟ	ҟ	ķ	[q]
Л	л	l	[ɬ]
М	м	m	[m]
Н	н	n	[n]
Ӈ	ӈ	ŋ	[ŋ]
О	о	o	[o]
П	п	p	[p]
Р	р	r	[ɹ]
С	с	s	[s][c]
Т	т	t	[t]
У	у	u	[u]
(Ф	ф	f)	
(Х	х	x)	
(Ц	ц	c)	
Ч	ч	č	[t͡c][c]
(Ш	ш	š)	
(Щ	щ	šč)	
Ъ	ъ	″	[ʔ] after consonants except л, ч
Ы	ы	y	[ə]
Ь	ь	′	[ʔ] after л, ч
Э	э	è	[e]
Ю	ю	ju	[ju]; [u] after л
Я	я	ja	[ja]; [a] after л
ʼ	ʼ	ʼ	[ʔ] after vowel[d]

a. The orthographic position of the symbols representing the glottal stop does not always correspond to their phonetic position, at least in more conservative varieties of Chukchee; see further Comrie (1994).

b. [ja], [je], [jo], [ju] are written я, е, ё, ю; after a consonant, ь is inserted before the yotated vowel symbol. Elsewhere, [j] is written й.

c. [s] and [t͡c] are allophones of a single phoneme.

d. Although the apostrophe is not listed as a letter of the alphabet in Moll and Inènlikèj 1957, it is treated as the last letter of the alphabet for purposes of alphabetical ordering.

Letter names and alphabetical order

There are two systems of naming letters. One is essentially that of modern Russian: the vowels have names corresponding to their sound, while the consonants have names of the form C[e], [e]C, or C[a]. A few letters have common words in their names ('short *i*', 'hard sign', 'soft sign'); these last are translated into the language in question. Such a system is used by the East Slavic languages and by most of the Cyrillic writing systems of the former USSR, with some minor variations, especially in names for й *j*; however, Azeri names all consonants C[e], except that liquids and nasals have [e]C. The second system again has names for the vowels corresponding to their sound, but all consonants are named C[ə]; this system is used by the South Slavic languages that have Cyrillic writing systems, and also by the Northwest Caucasian languages.

The alphabetical order of those letters that occur in the Russian alphabet follows that of Russian, with very sporadic exceptions: Ukrainian places ь at the end of the alphabet; Kabardian orders э *è* immediately after а *a* when it represents the indigenous phoneme [a], but follows the Russian order when э represents [e] in words of Russian origin. Special letters are either placed after the letter to which they are most similar (in shape or sound), or are grouped together at the end of the alphabet. Digraphs etc. are treated as single letters or as sequences of letters, with different languages having different rules.

SAMPLE OF TAJIK

1. Tajik:	Кампир	ба	сари	оташдон	рафт.
2. Transliteration:	Kampir	ba	sari	otašdon	raft.
3. Transcription:	ˌkam'pir	ba	'sari	ɒtaʃ'dɒn	raft
4. Gloss:	old.woman	to	head.LINK	fireplace	went

1.	Дилбар	дастурхонро	гирифта	ба	пеши	падараш	кушод,
2.	Dilbar	dasturxonro	girifta	ba	peši	padaraš	kušod,
3.	dil'bar	ˌdastur'xɒnrɒ	girif'ta	ba	'peʃi	pa'daraʃ	ku'ʃɒd
4.	Dilbar	tablecloth	taking	to	front.LINK	his.father	spread

1.	баъд	ба	сари	оташдон	рафта	косахои	шӯрборо	овардан
2.	ba "d	ba	sari	otašdon	rafta	kosaxoi	šūrboro	ovardan
3.	'ba:d	ba	'sari	ɒtaʃ'dɒn	raf'ta	kɒsa'hɒi	ʃor'bɒrɒ	ɒvar'dan
4.	then	to	head.LINK	fireplace	going	cups.LINK	soup.ACC	to.bring

1.	гирифт.	Дар	вақти	шӯрбохӯрӣ	занак	ба	шавхараш	нилох
2.	girift.	Dar	vaқti	šūrboxūrī	zanak	ba	šavxaraš	nilox
3.	girift	dar	vaqti	ʃor,bɒxo'ri	za'nak	ba	ʃav'haraʃ	ni'lɒh
4.	began	in	time.LINK	soup.drinking	woman	to	husband	glance

1. карда	бо	овози	паст	гуфт:	—Дадеш,	як	маслиҳат.	
2. karda	bo	ovozi	past	guft:	—Dadeš,	jak	masliχat.	
3. kar'da	bɒ	ɒ'vɒzi	'past	'guft	da'deʃ	jak	masli'hat	
4. doing	with	voice.LINK	low	said	father	one	conversation	

'The old woman went to the fireplace. Dilbar took the tablecloth and spread it in front of his father. Then he went to the fireplace and began to bring the cups of soup. During the soup-drinking the woman glanced at her husband and said in a low voice: "Father, a word with you."'

—*J. Ukrâmî, Шодū [Joy], in Vinogradov 1966–68, 1:234.*

SAMPLE OF KOMI (KOMI-ZYRYAN)

1. Komi:	Важөн	оліс-вылiс	вöралысь	морт.	Сылöн	вöлi
2. Transliteration:	Važön	olïs-vylïs	võralys´	mort.	Sylön	völï
3. Transcription:	vaʒən	olis vɨlis	vəralɨsʲ	mort	sɨlən	vəli
4. Gloss:	long.ago	lived.was	hunting	man	his	was

1. куим	пи, зэв	ёнось.	Найö	нёльöн	кайисны	ылö	вöрö	вöравны,
2. kuim	pi, zèv	ënos´.	Najö	nël´ön	kajisny	ylö	vörö	vöravny,
3. kuim	pi zev	jonosʲ	najə	nʲolʲən	kajisnɨ	ɨlə	vərə	vəravnɨ
4. three	son very	strong	they	four	went.up	distant	to.forest	to.hunt

1. сьöла	да	ур	кыйны.	Налы	прöмыс	кутіс	ёна
2. s´öla	da	ur	kyjny.	Naly	prömys	kutïs	ëna
3. sʲəla	da	ur	kɨjnɨ	nalɨ	prəmɨs	kutis	jona
4. hazel.grouse	and	squirrel	to.catch	to.them	catch	began	strongly

1. шедны.	Няньыс	быри.	Гортö	лэччыны	зэв	ылын,	да
2. šedny.	Njan´ys	byri.	Gortö	lèččyny	zèv	ylyn,	da
3. ʃednɨ	nʲanʲɨs	bɨri	gortə	lettʃʲinɨ	zev	ɨlɨn	da
4. to.be.obtained	the.bread	ran.out	to.home	to.go.down	very	far	and

1. и	лым	уси	быдса	весьт.	Бать	юавны	кутіс	пиянлысь:
2. i	lym	usi	bydsa	ves´t.	Bat´	juavny	kutïs	pijanlys´:
3. i	lɨm	usʲi	bɨdsa	vesʲt	batʲ	juavnɨ	kutis	pijanlɨsʲ
4. and	snow	fell	whole	quarter-arshin	father	to.ask	began	from.sons

1. «Коді	ветлас	гортö	няньла?»	
2. "Kodï	vetlas	gortö	njan´la?"	
3. kodi	vetlas	gortə	nʲanʲla	
4. who	will.go	to.home	for.bread	

'Long ago there was a hunter. He had three sons, very strong. The four of them went to a distant forest to hunt, to catch grouse and squirrels. Their catch began to be successful. The bread ran out. To go home was very far, and moreover the

snow fell a full seven inches deep. The father began to ask his sons: "Who will
go home for bread?'"   — *V. I. Lytkin in Vinogradov 1966–68, 3:298.*

SAMPLE OF TATAR

1. Tatar:	Ләкин	сезгә	куркыныч	юк.	Дулкын	ничаклы
2. Transliteration:	Läkin	sezgä	kurkynyč	juk.	Dulkyn	ničakly
3. Transcription:	'lækin	sez'gæ	qurqɤ'nɤt͡ʃ	'juq	dul'qɤn	'nit͡ʃaqlɤ
4. Gloss:	but	to.you	danger	not.exist	wave	how.much

1.	каты	булса	да,	ул	сезнең	биек	тау	итәгендәге
2.	katy	bulsa	da,	ul	sezneŋ	biek	tau	itägendäge
3.	qa'tɤ	bul'sa	da	'ul	sez'neŋ	bi'jek	'taw	itægendæ'ge
4.	strong	would.be	even	it	your	high	mountain	at.its.foot.LINK

1.	urynygyzga	килеп	җитә	алмаячак.	Сезгә	тыныч	булырга,
2.	urynygyzga	kilep	žitä	almajačak.	Sezgä	tynyč	bulyrga,
3.	urɤnɤʁɤz'ʁa	ki'lep	d͡ʒi'tæ	'almajat͡ʃaq	sez'gæ	tɤ'nɤt͡ʃ	bulɤr'ʁa
4.	to.place	come.and	reaching	will.not.take	to.you	peaceful	to.be

1.	тәрәзәләрегезне	ачып,	диңгез	тавышын	тыңларга	да	аннан
2.	täräzäläregezne	ačyp,	diŋgez	tavyšyn	tyŋlarga	da	annan
3.	tæræzælæregez'ne	a't͡ʃɤp	diŋ'gez	tawɤ'ʃɤn	tɤŋlar'ʁa	da	an'nan
4.	your.windows	open.and	sea	its.voice	to.listen	also	from.that

1.	соң	рәхәт-рәхәт	тагын	йокыгызга	чымарга	мөмкин.
2.	soŋ	räxät-räxät	tagyn	jokygyzga	čumarga	mömkin.
3.	soŋ	ræ'xæt-ræxæt	ta'ʁɤn	joqɤʁɤz'ʁa	t͡ʃumar'ʁa	møm'kin
4.	after	rest.rest	again	to.your.sleep	to.plunge	possible

'But there is no danger for you. However strong the wave may be, it cannot
come and reach your place at the foot of the high mountain. You may be peaceful, you may open your windows and listen to the sea and after that again
plunge restfully into your sleep.'
—G. Ibrahimov, *Безнең көннөр [Our days], in Vinogradov 1966–68, 2:152.*

SAMPLE OF KABARDIAN

1. Kabardian:	Нартхэр	зыхуей	псоу	яхуищӏпи
2. Transliteration:	Nartxèr	zyxuej	psou	jaxuišč1ri
3. Transcription:	na:rtħar	zə'xʷaj	'psawə	ja:hʷəjç"rəj
4. Gloss:	Narts.ABS	which.need	alive	and.he.not.did.it.for.them

1.	Лъэпщ	ищӏэн	имыгъуэтыжу	къанери
2.	L"ępšč	išč1èn	imyg"uètyžu	k"aneri
3.	'ɬapʃ	jə'ç'an	jəməʁʷa'təʒəw	q'a:na'rəj
4.	Tlepsh	he.knew.it.NONFIN	he.not.found.it	and.he.remained.in.it

1.	зэш	хъуащ.	Хыэмышэчыж	щыхъум,	Сэтэней
2.	zèš	x″uašč.	Xuèmyšèčyž	ščyx″um,	Sètènej
3.	'zaʃ	'χʷa:ɕ	xʷaməʃa'kʲəʒ	'cəχʷəm	'satanaj
4.	he.yearn	it.happened	he.not.endure.it	it.happen.to.him	Satanaya

1.	гуащэм	деж	кIуэри	елъэIуащ
2.	guaščèm	dež	k1uèri	el″è1uašč.
3.	'gʷa:ɕam	'dajʒ	kʷa'rəj	jaɬa'ʔʷa:ɕ
4.	lady.OBL	near.her	and.he.went	he.asked.her.for.something

'Tlepsh could not make what the Narts needed in life. He could not find the knowledge. He remained thus until he grew desperate. He could not bear it, he went to Lady Satanaya and begged her.'   —*Colarusso 1992: 203, 208, 219.*

SAMPLE OF AVAR

1. *Avar:*	Гъадида	цо	хIанил	кесек	батана.	ХIанги
2. *Transliteration:*	G″adida[a]	co	x1anil	kesek	batana.	X1angi
3. *Transcription:*	ʁa'dida	t͡so	'ħanil	ke'sek	'batana	'ħangi
4. *Gloss:*	at.crow	one	of.cheese	piece	found	and.cheese

1.	кIалдиб	ккун,	гьев	цо	гъотIоде	бахана.	Царада	гьеб
2.	k1aldib	kkun,	g′eb	co	g″ot1ode	baxana.	Carada[a]	g′eb
3.	'k'aldib	'k:un	heb	t͡so	ʁo't'ode	'baχana	t͡sa'rada	heb
4.	in.mouth	having.seized	it	one	to.tree	ascended	at.fox	it

1.	бихьана	ва	гьелъ	гьеб	гуккизе	къасд	гьабуна.	Цер	гъотIоде
2.	bix′ana	va	g′el″[a]	g′eb	gukkize	k″asd	g′abuna.	Cer	g″ot1ode
3.	'bix:ana	wa	heɬ:	heb	'guk:ize	'q':as:d	ha,buna	'tser	ʁo't'ode
4.	saw	and	by.it	it	to.cheat	decision	made	fox	to.tree

1.	гIагарлъана	ва	рачIги	хьвагIулаго	гьелъ	кIалъазе	байбихьана:
2.	g1agarl″ana	va	rač1gi	x′vag1ulago	g′el″	k1al″aze	bajbix′ana:
3.	ʕa'garɬana	wa	'rat͡ʃ':gi	'xʷ:aʕulago	heɬ:	k'a'ɬaze	'bajbix:ana
4.	approached	and	and.tail	shaking	it	to.speak	began

1.	–Дир	хирияб	гъедо!
2.	—Dir	xirijab	g″edo!
3.	'dir	χ:i'rijab	'ʁedo
4.	my	dear	crow

'A crow found a piece of cheese and, having seized it in its mouth, ascended to a tree. A fox saw it and decided to cheat it. The fox approached the tree and, shaking its tail, began to speak: "My dear crow!"'

—*B. G. Hewitt in Comrie 1981: 235.*

Note:
[a]The locative cases гъадида, царада and the ergative case гьелъ indicate transitive subjects.

SAMPLE OF CHUKCHEE

1. Chukchee:	Кыткытръогъэ.	Тиркытир	а’қагнэтыңогъэ.	Пэтле
2. Transliteration:	Kytkytr″og″è.	Tirkytir	a’ḳagnètyŋog″è.	Pètle
3. Transcription:	kətkət'ɹʔoɣʔe	'tiɹkətiɹ	'aʔqaɣnetəŋoɣʔe	'petɬe
4. Gloss:	spring.began	sun	began.to.warm	soon

1. рагръоӈӈоӈыт	рэквытти.	Авынқаагынрэтыльын	иквъи:
2. ragr″oŋŋoŋyt	rèkvytti.	Avynḳaagynrètyl′yn	ikv″i:
3. ɹaɣ'ɹʔoŋŋoŋət	'ɹekβatti	aβən'qaaɣənɹetəɬʔən	'ikβʔi
4. will.begin.to.calve	does	head.deer.herdsman	said

1. Вэтыкун	льоолқыл	таӈавээн.	Ынрэчымче	қуливээмык	ы’льыл
2. Vètyḳun	l′oolḳyl	taŋavèèn.	Ynrèčymče	ḳulivèèmyk	y’l′yl
3. 'βetəqun	'ɬʔoolqəɬ	taŋa'βeen	ən'ɹetɕəmtɕe	quɬi'βeemək	'ʔəɬʔəɬ
4. without.fail	must.find	good.pasture	nearby	at.one.river	snow

1. агтымкыкыльэн,	ы’лгиӈкы-ым	нытвақэн	кытуркин	въаглыӈын.
2. agtymkykyl′èn,	y’lgiŋky-ym	nytvaḳèn	kyturkin	v″aglyŋyn.
3. 'aɣtəmkəkəɬʔen	'ʔəɬɣiŋkə-əm	nət'βaqen	kə'tuɹkin	'βʔaɣɬəŋən
4. not.deep	snow.bottom-and	was	last.year's	grass

'Spring was beginning. The sun was beginning to warm. Soon the female reindeer would be calving. The head herdsman said: We must without fail find good pasture. Nearby, by one river, the snow was not deep, and under the snow was last year's grass.'   —*P. Ja. Skorik in Vinogradov 1966–68, 5:270.*

———

Bibliography

Colarusso, John. 1992. *A Grammar of the Kabardian Language.* Calgary: University of Calgary Press.

Comrie, Bernard. 1981. *Languages of the Soviet Union.* Cambridge: Cambridge University Press.

———. 1994. "An Evaluation of Chukchee Orthography." In *Linguistic Studies in the Non-Slavic Languages of the Commonwealth of Independent States and the Baltic Republics,* ed. Howard I. Aronson, pp. 55–64. Chicago: Chicago Linguistic Society.

Comrie, Bernard, and Greville G. Corbett, eds. 1993. *The Slavonic Languages.* London: Routledge.

De Bray, Reginald G. A. 1980A. *Guide to the East Slavonic Languages.* Columbus, Ohio: Slavica.

———. 1980B. *Guide to the South Slavonic Languages.* Columbus, Ohio: Slavica.

Hanser, Oskar. 1977. *Turkmen Manual: Descriptive Grammar of Contemporary Literary Turkmen, Texts, Glossary* (Beihefte zur *Wiener Zeitschrift für die Kunde des Morgenlandes* 7). Vienna: Verlag des Verbandes der Wissenschaftlichen Gesellschaften Österreichs.

Hebert, Raymond, and Nicholas Poppe. 1963. *Kirghiz Manual* (Indiana University Publications, Uralic and Altaic Series 33). Bloomington: Indiana University; The Hague: Mouton.

Householder, Fred W., Jr., with Mansour Lotfi. 1965. *Basic Course in Azerbaijani* (Indiana University Publications, Uralic and Altaic Series 45). Bloomington: Indiana University; The Hague: Mouton.

Kuipers, Aert H. 1960. *Phoneme and Morpheme in Kabardian (Eastern Adyghe)* (Janua Linguarum

Series Minor 8). The Hague: Mouton.

Lytkin, V. I. 1952. *Drevnepermskij jazyk* [The Old Permic language]. Moscow: Izdatel´stvo Akademii Nauk SSSR.

———. 1961. *Komi–russkij slovar´* [Komi–Russian dictionary]. Moscow: Gosudarstvennoe Izdatel´stvo Inostrannyx i Nacional´nyx Slovarej.

Mala Enciklopedija Prosveta. 1978. [Small Prosveta encyclopedia]. Belgrade.

Moll, T. A., & P. I. Inènlikèj. 1957. *Čukotsko–russkij slovar´* [Chukchee–Russian dictionary]. Leningrad: Gosudarstvennoe učebno-pedagogičeskoe izdatel´stvo Ministerstva Prosveščenija RSFSR.

Poppe, Nicholas. 1963. *Tatar Manual* (Indiana University Publications, Uralic and Altaic Series 25). Bloomington: Indiana University; The Hague: Mouton.

———. 1970. *Mongolian Language Handbook.* Washington, D.C.: Center for Applied Linguistics.

Rastorgueva, V. S. 1963. *A Short Sketch of Tajik Grammar,* trans. and ed. Herbert H. Paper (*International Journal of American Linguistics* 29, no. 4, part 2). Bloomington: Indiana University; The Hague: Mouton. (Russian orig. "Kratkij očerk grammatiki tadžikskogo jazyka," in M. V. Raximi & L. V. Uspenskaja, eds., *Tadžiksko–russij slovar´* [Tajik–Russian dictionary], Moscow: Gosudarstvennoe Izdatel´stvo Inostrannyx i Nacional´nyx Slovarej, 1954.)

Sjoberg, Andrée F. 1963. *Uzbek Structural Grammar* (Indiana University Publications, Uralic and Altaic Series 18). Bloomington: Indiana University; The Hague: Mouton.

Street, John C. 1963. *Khalkha Structure* (Indiana University Publications, Uralic and Altaic Series 24.) Bloomington: Indiana University; The Hague: Mouton.

Vinogradov, V. V., ed. 1966–68. *Jazyki narodov SSSR* [Languages of the peoples of the USSR]. 5 vols. Moscow & Leningrad: Nauka.

Adaptations of Hebrew Script

BENJAMIN HARY

Jewish "languages" or ethnolects

It is probably impossible to offer a purely linguistic definition of a Jewish "language," as it is difficult to find many common linguistic criteria that can apply to Judeo-Arabic, Judeo-Spanish, and Yiddish, for example. Consequently, a sociolinguistic definition with a more suitable term, such as *ethnolect*, is in order. An ethnolect is an independent linguistic entity with its own history and development that refers to a language or a variety and is used by a distinct language community. A Jewish ethnolect, then, is a spoken and/or written form serving for the most part the Jewish population of a specific area. Our knowledge of Jewish ethnolects is inadequate, as in many cases scholars began to investigate them when it was too late and only a handful of speakers were still using them; in worse cases, some of these ethnolects had already disappeared.

Jewish ethnolects share many characteristics: they incorporate Hebrew and Aramaic elements, not restricted to the sphere of cultural vocabulary but also found throughout the lexicon as well as in phonology, morphology, and syntax. They have developed distinct spoken forms as well as unique ways of translating sacred Hebrew texts verbatim (Hary 1995) into the various Jewish ethnolects. The most obvious external characteristic of Jewish ethnolects, however, is the consistent use, in their written forms, of Hebrew characters (SECTION 46). Very frequently, Jews adopted the spelling conventions of Talmudic orthography, employing the final forms of Hebrew letters and sometimes adding vowel signs using existing consonants and/or symbols. Thus, the Hebrew script symbolizes the Jewish nature of the ethnolect. It is not uncommon to use script as a religious identification for a language, as with the Arabic script of Persian and Urdu, for example, which symbolizes the Muslim nature of the languages.

Jewish ethnolects developed in the diaspora from local languages and were used in both their written and spoken forms by Jews within the Jewish community. They developed as one result of a migration, the dispersion of the Jews throughout Asia and Europe during the early centuries of the Common Era (Birnbaum 1971: 68). The creation of these ethnolects began as a way of assimilation into the non-Jewish environment but later came to be a hallmark of "continuing Jewish consciousness and identity" (Ben-Sasson 1971: 771). That is, the initial adoption of a local language was an attempt to assimilate into the surrounding environment and to speak like the local inhabitants; but later, in order to become a symbol of Jewish identity and an actual obstacle to assimilation, the language established itself as Jewish with its Hebrew script and Hebrew and Aramaic linguistic elements.

Jewish languages are numerous, and the list reflects Jewish history and geography. Beside Hebrew, the primary Jewish language (although see Ornan 1985), Jewish forms of Aramaic began to develop even before the beginning of the Common Era. Before the end of the Second Temple period, Hellenistic Jews began to employ the Greek Koiné in its Jewish form —Yevanic, which many centuries later became known in the Balkans as Judeo-Greek. After the seventh century, when Islam began to spread across the Middle East and North Africa, Judeo-Arabic began to develop, and Jews from Spain to Iraq adopted forms of this ethnolect. In North Africa, Judeo-Berber emerged; and in Iran, Judeo-Persian. On the other side of the Jewish world, Latin produced six different ethnolects: Judeo-Italian (Italkian) in Italy; Judeo-Provençal (Shuadit) in southern France, and Judeo-French (Zarphatic) more to the north; Judeo-Catalan in the eastern part of the Iberian Peninsula, and Judeo-Portuguese in the western part; and Judeo-Spanish (Ladino, Jidyó, Judezmo) in between. After the expulsion of the Jews from the Iberian Peninsula toward the end of the fifteenth century, Judeo-Spanish spread to the east through the Balkans, Turkey, and Palestine, and to the south throughout North Africa. Yiddish originated in the tenth century among central European Jews and spread to eastern Europe and, centuries later, to the Americas, South Africa, Australia, and Palestine. Before the Holocaust, three quarters of world Jewry spoke Yiddish. In the east, Kurdish Jews use Judeo–Neo-Aramaic, Judeo-Arabic dialects, as well as Kurdish with mixed Hebrew, Turkish, and Arabic elements. In Central Asia Judeo-Tajik is employed, Judeo-Tat (of the Iranian family) is used by Jews in Daghestan in the eastern Caucasus, and Judeo-Georgian is used by Jews in Georgia in the southern Caucasus. Judeo-Crimchak (of the Turkic family) is employed by Crimean Jews, both Rabbanites and Karaites.

Of these languages, Judeo-Arabic, Judeo-Spanish, and Yiddish have had the largest impact on Jewish culture and civilization since the dispersion of the Jews. Among these, Judeo-Arabic holds a significant place: it has the longest recorded history of the three, from pre-Islamic times to the present; additionally, it spans the widest geographical area, from Spain to Yemen and Iraq, and "it was the medium of expression for one of the foremost periods of Jewish cultural and intellectual creativity" (Stillman 1988:3–4). Judeo-Arabic is thus here the primary example of the use of the Hebrew script; Yiddish and Judeo-Spanish are treated as well.

Judeo-Arabic

Judeo-Arabic is an ethnolect which has been spoken and written in various forms by Jews throughout the Arabic-speaking world; its literature is concerned for the most part with Jewish topics and is written by Jewish authors for Jewish readers. Judeo-

TABLE 61.1: *Judeo-Arabic/Arabic Consonant Correspondences*

Arabic	Judeo-Arabic	Phonetic Value
ا	א	[Ø, ʔ]
ب	ב	[b]
ت	ת, ﺗ	[t]
ث	ﺗ, ﺙ, ת	[t, θ]
ج	ג, ﬞג	[g, ʤ]
ح	ח	[ħ]
خ	ח/ﬞך, כ	[x]
د	ד	[d]
ذ	ﬞד, ד	[d, ð]
ر	ר	[r]
ز	ז	[z]
س	ס	[s]
ش	שׁ	[ʃ]
ص	צ/﬩, ס	[ʂ]
ض	צ/﬩, ﬞד	[ɖ, ẓ]
ط	ט	[ʈ]
ظ	ד, צ/﬩, ﬞט	[ɖ, ẓ]
ع	ע	[ʕ]
غ	ר, ﬞג, ג	[ɣ]
ف	פ, ﬞפ	[f]
ق	ﬞק, ק	[q]
ك	כ/ך	[k]
ل	ל	[l]
م	ס/מ	[m]
ن	ﬞ/ג	[n]
ه	ה	[h]
ة	ﬞה, ה, ת	[t, h]
و	ו, וו	[w]
ي	י, ײ	[j]

TABLE 61.2: *Vowel Representation*

[i] Ø, sometimes ʾ	[i:] usually ʾ		[u] Ø, frequently ו	[u:] usually ו
[e] Ø, sometimes ʾ	[e:] usually ʾ		[o] Ø, frequently ו	[o:] usually ו
		[a] Ø [ā] usually א		

Arabic has had a long history, with a dramatic change occurring around the fifteenth century C.E., when the Jewish world severed its contact with the Muslim world and its Arabic language and culture. This was especially true in North Africa and less so in Yemen, where strong contact was maintained for some time. To refine and more accurately describe the history of Judeo-Arabic, I periodize it as follows: Pre-Islamic, Early (8th/9th–10th centuries), Classical (10th–15th centuries), Later (15th–19th centuries), and Modern Judeo-Arabic (20th century). This scheme, however, should not distract us from the major change that occurred in the fifteenth century: the first three periods constitute Medieval Judeo-Arabic; the latter two, Late.

Three script usages can be identified for Judeo-Arabic: "Phonetic," "Arabicized," and "Hebraized." Of the three, Arabicized orthography has had the greatest influence. In general terms, TABLE 61.1 represents the transcription of Judeo-Arabic consonants irrespective of the three orthographic traditions. The final varieties of Hebrew letters (shown to the right of the slant) are used in word-final position. The vowels are represented as in TABLE 61.2. (Note that most Judeo-Arabic manuscripts are written in Rashi letters, whereas printed editions use square Hebrew as well as Rashi script.)

Arabicized orthography

Arabicized orthography, for the most part uniform, is based on imitation of the spelling of Classical Arabic (SECTION 50, which see for the technical terms used below); and since there are fewer Hebrew characters than Judeo-Arabic phonemes, Arabicized orthography very often uses diacritic points that copy those of the Arabic letters. This is the case for צ *ḍ*, ט *ẓ*, ד *ḏ*, ח *ḥ/t*, ת *ṭ*, ג *ǧ*, ק *q*, and פ *f* (although this could be interpreted as belonging with the following set). Sometimes a phonetic principle is used, as in the case of כ *x*, ג *ǧ*, and occasionally ת *t*—allophones of כ, ג, and ת respectively.

The conventions of Talmudic spelling, influential in most orthographies of Jewish ethnolects, are represented in Arabicized orthography in a slight tendency to mark short [u] with ו *w* and in rendering (especially geminated) consonantal [w] and [y] with וו *ww* and יי *yy* respectively. As a whole, however, Arabicized orthography is primarily based on the spelling of Classical Arabic: the long vowels are marked with vowel letters; the definite article (')al is always written morphophonemically, regardless of its pronunciation—even when the ' is not pronounced and the *l* is assimilated to the following consonant, the definite article is written אל *ʾl*. The same holds true for *ʾalif waṣla*, and sometimes even for *ʾalif fāṣila* as well as keeping the distinction between *ʾalif maqṣūra biṣūrati l- ʾalif* and *ʾalif maqṣūra biṣūrati l-yā ʾ*. Even short vowels, *tašdīd*, and the *madda*, when marked, are sometimes written with the Arabic signs over the Hebrew characters. This orthography is typical of Classical Judeo-Arabic, but is also used during Early Judeo-Arabic, and to a lesser degree, during Later and Modern Judeo-Arabic.

Phonetic orthography

Phonetic orthography, on the other hand, is used only during Early Judeo-Arabic. It is based on phonetic principles, free from the influence of Classical Arabic orthography. Moreover, Blau and Hopkins (1987: 124) claim, "There is no orthographical feature [in this tradition] which has to be explained as an imitation of literary Arabic spelling habits." The main characteristic of (broad) Phonetic orthography are as follows.

(i) Marking *ḍ* and *ẓ* with ד *d*, as it represents the closest phoneme in Hebrew to the pronunciation of ض and ظ (e.g. קבד *qbd* [qabaḍa] 'he received', cf. قبض *qbḍ*; חפדך *ḥpdk* [ḥafiẓaka] 'may He preserve you', cf. حفظك *ḥpẓk*, ibid. 133).

(ii) Marking the definite article phonetically, not morphophonemically as in Arabicized orthography (e.g. בילקמח *bylqmh* [bilqamḥ] 'with the grain', cf. بالقمح *b ʾlqmh*; ארחים *ʾrḥm* [arraḥi:m] 'the Merciful', cf. الرحيم *ʾlrḥym*; בתמן *btmn* [bittaman] 'with the price', cf. بالتمن *b ʾltmn*, ibid. 147–48).

(iii) Use of *plene* 'full' and "defective" writing phonetically. E.g., both short [u] and [i] are frequently marked with ו *w* and י *y* respectively, contrary to Classical Arabic usage; "defective" writing of medial *ā* (i.e. without an equivalent of Classical *ʾalif*); and the spelling of *ʾalif maqṣūra biṣūrati l-yāʾ* with א.

Both Phonetic and Arabicized orthographies were used side by side in Early Judeo-Arabic. Scribes who were educated in Classical Arabic used Arabicized orthography, and those who were not used Phonetic. This, of course, explains the fact that almost no literary texts were written in Phonetic orthography (Blau and Hopkins 1984: 26–27). The possibility exists, though, that even scribes who were educated in Classical Arabic, and knew the principles of Arabicized orthography, may have still used Phonetic orthography when attempting to reach a readership among the lower strata of the Jewish population who did not know Classical Arabic and had mastered only the Hebrew script, as was traditionally the case with Jews.

During the tenth century, Phonetic orthography vanished rapidly and was replaced by Arabicized. Blau and Hopkins attribute this sudden disappearance to the publication of Saʿadya Gaon's *tafsīr* 'translation/commentary' of the Pentateuch. Saʿadya (882–942) was educated in Classical Arabic and subsequently used Arabicized orthography. Since his work was widely distributed and prestigious among all the Jewish communities in the Arab world, it opened the way for Arabicized orthography to be adopted by Judeo-Arabic scribes. From then on, the orthography of Saʿadya's translation of the Pentateuch, which happened to be Arabicized orthography, became the model for Judeo-Arabic. The scribes did not need to be further educated in Classical Arabic or even to be familiar with its orthography; they only needed to be familiar with Saʿadya's work in order to use Arabicized orthography.

Hebraized orthography

After the fifteenth century, during the period of Later Judeo-Arabic, another script type began to develop, best termed *Hebraized*. During this period, Hebraized orthography existed alongside Arabicized orthography; it is characterized by three main features.

(i) Hebrew/Aramaic influence on spelling. E.g., *'alif maqṣūra biṣūrati l-yā'* was not spelled with י *y* as was the case in Arabicized orthography. Rather, it was spelled with ה *h* in imitation of Hebrew orthography (e.g. נווה *nwwh* [nawwa] 'intended', cf. نوى *nw'*; אלבושרה *'lbwšrh* [ilbuʃra] 'the good news', cf. البشرى *'lbšr'*, Hary 1992: 87–88); or with א *'*, as influenced by the orthography of the Babylonian Talmud (for example, נוא *nw'* 'intended', יוסמא *ywsm'* [jusamma] 'is named', cf. يسمى *ysm'*, ibid. 88). Moreover, final *'alif* was often spelled with ה *h* (e.g. אנה *'nh* [ʔana] 'I', cf. انا *'n'*; תעטינה *t'tynh* [tuʕtiːna] 'you will give us', cf. تعطينا *t'tyn'*, ibid.) in imitation of standard Hebrew orthography; and feminine nouns were spelled with a final א *'*, possibly a reflection of the Babylonian Talmud, which used this kind of spelling in both Hebrew and Aramaic (e.g. קלעא *ql'* [qalʕa] 'citadel', cf. قلعة *ql't*; קהווא *qhww'* [ʔahwa] 'coffee', cf. قهوة *qhwt*; ibid. 89–90).

(ii) Closer phonetic representation. For example, the use of *plene* writing to represent short vowels phonetically; marking consonantal *w* and *y* with וו *ww* and יי *yy* respectively; marking *'alif mamdūda* according to its phonetic representation (*-a*) with ה *h* or א *'*; occasional phonetic spelling of the definite article (e.g. אנאס *'n's* [innaːs] 'the people', cf. الناس *'ln's*; פלריף *flryf* [firriːf] 'in the country', cf. في الريف *fy 'lryf*, ibid. 92–93); occasionally marking *ḍ* with ד *d* for phonetic reasons (e.g. בעד *[baʕḍ]* 'some', cf. بعض *b'ḍ*; דאק *d'q* [ḍaːq] 'was annoyed', cf. ضاق *ḍ'q*, ibid. 94); frequently spelling the enclitic conjunction *fe-* 'and' as a separate word פֿי *fy*, probably to indicate the pronunciation; and frequently writing the accusative *tanwīn* with ן *n* (e.g. חזן *ḥzn* [ħazzᵃⁿ] 'pleasure', cf. حظ *ḥẓ*; כופֿן *kwfn* [xoːfᵃⁿ] 'fear', cf. خوف *xwf*, ibid. 297).

(iii) The continued influence of Arabicized orthography.

In sum, Hebraized orthography differs from the Phonetic and Arabicized orthographies in different ways. Whereas the influence of Classical Arabic orthography is not seen in Phonetic orthography, it is one element of Hebraized, albeit via Arabicized. Hebraized differs as well from Arabicized orthography in that it shows greater phonetic representation, and spelling conventions of Hebrew and Talmudic orthography. In other words, the tradition of Hebraized orthography is based neither on the orthographic model of Classical Arabic exclusively, as with Arabicized, nor on phonetic considerations exclusively, as with Phonetic. In some ways, Hebraized orthography is a combination of Phonetic and Arabicized.

SAMPLE OF LATER JUDEO-ARABIC

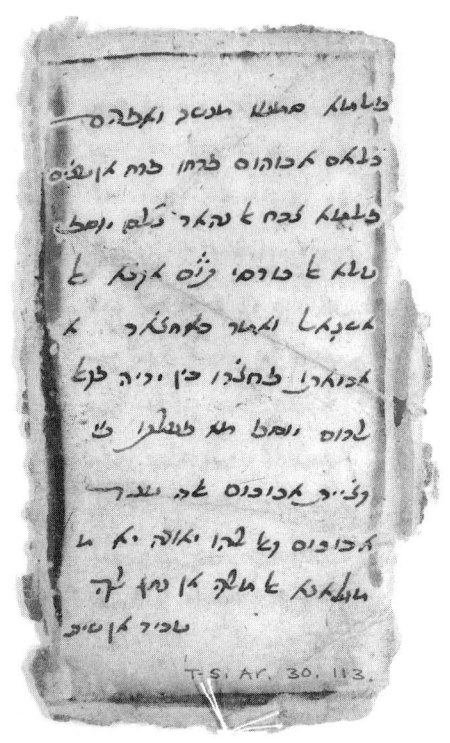

FIGURE 66. Cairo Genizah Ms. T-S Ar 30.113, recto
Published here with the kind permission of the
Syndics of Cambridge University Library

פלמא סמעו מנשה ואפרים←
myrf'w   hšnm   w'ms   'mlf←

כלאם אכוהום פרחו פרח אן
n'   ḥrf   wḥrf   mwhwk'   m'lk

פלמא צבח אל נהאר גלס יוסף
fswy   slǧ   r'hn l'   ḥbṣ   'mlf

עלא אל כורסי תֻם אקצא אל
l'   'ṣq'   mwṯ   ysrwk l'   'l'

אשגאל ואמר באחצאר א
'   r'dḥ'b   rm'w   l'ǧš'

אכואתו פחצרו בין ידיה פקאל
l'qf   hydy   nyb   wrdḥf   wt'wk'

להום יוסף מא פעלתו פי
yf   wtl'f   'm   fswy   mwhl

קצّ'ית אכוכום אלדי ענד
dn'   ydl'   mwkwk'   tyydq

אבוכום קאל להו יאודה יא מ
m'y   hdw'y   whl   l'q   mwkwb'

מולאנא אל מלך אן נחן לך
kl   nḥn   n'   klm l'   'n'lwm

עביד אן שית
tyš   n'   dyb'

1. *Normalization:*   f°lama   sim'u   menaše   wiefrayim   kalām
2. *Transcription:*   fə-lama   sɪmʕ-u   mɛnaʃɛ   wɪ-ɛfrajɪm   kala:m
3. *Gloss:*   and-when   heard-they   Menashe   and-Efrayim   words.of

1. axūhom   faraḥu   farḥan   'azīm   f°lama   ṣibih
2. axu:-hɔm   faraħ-u   farħ-an   ʕaẕi:m   f°-lama   ṣibiħ
3. brother-their   rejoiced-they   happiness-ACC   great   and-when   began

1. °lnahār   jalas   yūsuf   'ala lkursi   ṯumma   aqṣa   il
2. ən-naha:r   dʒalas   yu:suf   ʕala l-kursi   θumma   aqṣa   il
3. the-daytime   sat   Joseph   on   the-chair   afterward   went.deep   the

1. ašǧāl   wi'amar   bi'iḥdār   a   ixwāto   f°-ḥudru   bēn
2. aʃɣa:l   wi-ʔamar   bi-ʔiħda:r   ə   ixwa:t-ɔ   fə-ħudr-u   be:n
3. concerns   and-ordered   in-bringing   brothers-his   and-came-they   between

1. yadēh	f°'āl	lahom	yūsuf	ma	faʿalto	fi	'adiyyet	
2. yade:-h	fə-ʔa:l	la-hɔm	ju:suf	ma	faʕal-tɔ	fi	ʔadijjet	
3. hands-his	and-said	to-them	Joseph	what	did-you	in	problem.of	

1. axūkom	illazi	ʿand	axūhom	'āl	lahu	ye'uda	ya m
2. axu:-kɔm	illazi	ʕand	axu:-hɔm	ʕa:l	la-hu	jəʔuda	ya m
3. brother-your	who	with	brother-your	said	to-him	Judah	Oh, …

1. mawlāna	ilmalik	inna	naḥnu	lak	ʿabīd	in	šīt
2. mawla:-na	il-malik	inna	naḥnu	la-k	ʕabi:d	in	ʃi:-t
3. master-our	the-king	indeed	we	to-you	slaves	if	wanted-you

'And when Menashe and Ephraim heard their brother's words, they became very glad. And when the morning came, Joseph sat on the chair, went into deep thoughts and ordered to bring his brothers to come in front of him. Joseph then said to them, "What did you do regarding your brother who is with your father?" Judah answered to him, "Oh, master, we are truly slaves to you, and if you wish, …"'

—*Egypt, ca. 1600 C.E.; from the literature on Joseph and His Brothers.*

Judeo-Spanish (Ladino)

Judeo-Spanish is also written in Hebrew characters, although there are texts written in the Latin alphabet. TABLE 61.3 indicates the Judeo-Spanish phonetic equivalents of the Hebrew letters used in standard Judeo-Spanish spelling. The final varieties of letters are used in the same way as in Judeo-Arabic and Yiddish at the end of words. The following Hebrew letters are used in Judeo-Spanish, but usually limited to Hebrew words: כ [k], ע Ø, צ [s], and ת [t].

In different Judeo-Spanish manuscripts, the letters that are here followed by an apostrophe ('ב for [v], for example) may exhibit other diacritics, such as a line above the letter ב̄, a supralinear *segol* ב̤, or even ב̤.

TABLE 61.3: *Judeo-Spanish*

Letter	Value	Letter	Value	Letter	Value
א	[Ø, a]	ז	[z]	ן נ	[n]
ב	[b]	'ז	[ʒ]	ני	[ɲ]
'ב	[v]	ח	[ʃ, ʒ]	ס	[s]
ג	[g]	ט	[t]	פ	[p]
'ג	[ʧ, ʤ, ʃ, ʒ]	יי, י	[j]	'פ	[f]
ד	[d, ð]	ל	[l]	ק	[k]
ה	[a]	לי	[ʎ]	ר	[r]
ו	[v]	ם מ	[m]	ש	[s, ʃ]

Yiddish

HOWARD I. ARONSON

Yiddish is first attested in glosses to Hebrew manuscripts dating from the twelfth century. The first printed work in Yiddish is dated 1534. Like all Jewish languages, modern Yiddish uses the square Hebrew script. Yiddish has never had the official status of being a language of state (the so-called "Jewish Autonomous Oblast'" in Soviet Birobidzhan can hardly be viewed as an exception). Consequently there has never been a generally accepted central authority that could legislate a normative orthographic system; this has resulted in wide variation. All the orthographic systems are, however, basically alphabetic and can be viewed as either historically based or, preferably, interdialectal. (There is also no single normative orthoepy; native speakers generally speak in one of the three major dialects of the language.) Variation in the systems of orthography is shown in FIGURE 67.

These variations are largely correlated with different religious and political groups, with *phonemic* spelling of Hebrew and Aramaic words being typical of Soviet Yiddish as well as of non-Soviet Yiddish in the usage of radical left-wing organizations. *Pseudo-etymological* spelling is today found in some ultra-Orthodox Yiddish usage. The overwhelming majority of Yiddish publications today combine the traditional spelling of Hebrew and Aramaic words with the interdialectal morphophonemic spelling; these we call *standard* systems.

Standard orthographies

The overwhelming majority of modern Yiddish publications combine the traditional spelling of most Hebrew and Aramaic words with the interdialectal morphophonemic spelling of words of non-Semitic origin. There are many sub-varieties of this orthography. Perhaps the most widely used in literary works today is the so-called YIVO orthography proclaimed by the אינסטיטוט וויסנשאַפטלעכער ייִדישער (ייִוואָ) *Yidisher visnshaftlekher institut (YIVO)* 'Yiddish Scientific Institute' and the צענטראַלע ייִדישע

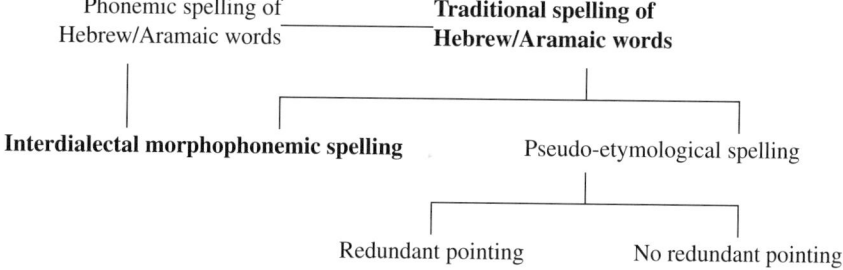

FIGURE 67. Yiddish orthographic systems (most common components of standard systems in **bold**).

TABLE 61.4: *The Yiddish Alphabet*

Letter[a]	Name	Value[b]	YIVO[c]	Other	Notes[d]
א	(shtumer) alef	–	– (’)		silent; occurs initially before *i, u, ey, ay, oy*
אַ	pasekh alef	[a]	a	א	*
אָ	komets alef	[ɔ]	o	אַ	*
ב	beys	[b]	b	בּ	
בֿ	veys	[v]	v (b̲)	ב	only in Semitic words; never word-initial
ג	giml	[g]	g		
ד	daled	[d]	d		
ה	hey	[h]	h		
ו	vov	[ʊ]	u (w)		
וּ	melupm vov	[ʊ]	u	ו	*; occurs after וו *v*; occurs before י *y*
וו	tsvey vovn	[v]	v		*
וי	vov-yud	[ɔj]	oy		*
ז	zayen	[z]	z		
זש	zayen-shin	[ʒ]	zh		*
ח	khes	[x]	kh (ḥ)		only in Semitic words
ט	tes	[t]	t (ṭ)		
טש	tes-shin	[ʧ]	tsh		*
י	yud	[j]	y		before or after vowel
		[ɪ]	i		between consonants
		[–ʲ]	y		after *t, d, s, z, l, n* and before a vowel indicates the palatals in words of Slavic origin
יִ	khirik yud	[ɪ]	i	י	*; occurs after initial י *y*; occurs after vowels
יי	tsvey yudn	[ɛj]	ey		*
ייַ	pasekh tsvey yudn	[aj]	ay	יי	*
כ	kof	[k]	k	כ	only in Semitic words
כ, ך	khof, lange khof	[x]	kh (k̲)		
ל	lamed	[ɫ, l, ʎ]	l		
מ, ם	mem, shlos mem	[m]	m		
נ, ן	nun, lange nun	[n]	n		
ס	samekh	[s]	s		
ע	ayin	[ɛ]	e (‘)		unstressed = [ɛ̆] or [ɪ̆], depending on dialect
פּ	pey	[p]	p		
פ, ף	fey, lange fey	[f]	f (p̲)	פ	
צ, ץ	tsadek, lange tsadek	[ts]	ts (ṣ)		
ק	kuf	[k]	k (q)		
ר	reysh	[ʀ]	r		
ש	shin	[ʃ]	sh (š)		
שׂ	sin	[s]	s (ś)	ש	only in Semitic words
תּ	tof	[t]	t	ת	only in Semitic words
ת	sof	[s]	s (t̲)		only in Semitic words; never word-initial

a. A letter after a comma is the final form.
b. The values given do not necessarily apply to words of Semitic origin, which follow a distinct set of rules.
c. YIVO transliteration; the Hebrew transliteration of the letter is shown in parentheses.
d. An asterisk indicates that the letter/digraph is not treated by YIVO as a separate item for alphabetization.

שול-אָרגאַניזאַציע (ציישאָ) *Tsentrale yidishe shul-organizatsye (TsIShO)* 'Central Yid-dish School Organization' in Poland on September 1, 1936, and first published in 1937 in Vilno under the title *Takones fun yidishn oysleyg* 'Rules of Yiddish orthogra-phy'. In what follows, the YIVO system is described along with the major deviations from it in the more commonly used standard systems. TABLE 61.4 gives the tradition-al order of the Yiddish alphabet.

Variant orthographies

Most words of Semitic origin (Hebrew and Aramaic) are spelled in the traditional way in most Yiddish orthographies, e.g., אמת *'mt* ['ɛmɛs] 'truth', מלך *mlk* ['mɛjlɛx] 'king', סך-הכל *sk-hkl* [s(ɛ)'xakl] 'total'. However, Soviet Yiddish authors and many pro-So-viet radical organizations spelled such words according to the phonemic principle: סאכאקל, מיילעך or מיילעך, עמעס (the Hebrew system may have represented for them "obsolete" religion; cf. Hary 1990: 79, 1992: 112–13 on orthographic manifestation of competing political, religious, or cultural preference). As a consequence, the letters that occur only in words of Semitic origin (ב *b*, ח *ḥ*, כ *k*, שׂ *ś*, ת *t*, ת *ṯ*) were not found there. In earlier Soviet Yiddish, the final letters ך *kh*, ם *m*, ן *n*, ף *f*, ץ *ts* were replaced by the non-final letters: כ, מ, נ, פ, צ. In 1961 the final letters were reintroduced into most Soviet Yiddish (with the main exception of publications from Birobidzhan).

Yiddish orthography in the late nineteenth and early twentieth centuries showed a tendency to reproduce as literally as possible German orthography. We shall call such spelling *pseudo-etymological* (TABLE 61.5). In the same period certain texts contained, in addition to the regular vowel letters of Yiddish (אַ *a*, אָ *o*, ו *u*, י *i*, ע *e*; יי *ey*, ײַ *ay*, וי *oy*), the Hebrew vowel points below the consonant: in what follows, (a) is a text with redundant vowel pointing and (b) is the corresponding YIVO orthography (words in italics are from Hebrew).

(a) דִי וָוס הָאבְן אַ בטָחוֹן אוֹף גָאט וֶועלְן זֵיי זַיין אַזוֹי וִוי דער בַאַרג ציון

(b) די וואָס האָבן אַ בטחון אויף גאָט וועלן זיי זײַן אַזוי ווי דער באַרג ציון

Di vos hobn a *bitokhn* oyf Got veln zey zayn azoy vi der barg *Tsien*.

'They that have confidence in God, they will be just like (the) Mount Sinai.'

Such orthography was found in secular works in the nineteenth century; today, when found, it tends to be in works published by ultra-Orthodox groups.

TABLE 61.5: *Pseudo-etymological vs. Morphophonemic Spelling*

German	Pseudo-etymological		Pronunciation	Morphophonemic		Gloss
T(h)ür	טהור	thur	['tɪr]	טיר	tir	'door'
Jude	יוד	yud	['jɪd]	ייִד	yid	'Jew'
sehr	זעהר	zehr	['zɛjɛr]	זייער	zeyer	'very'
ver-	פֿער-	fer-	[far]	פֿאַר-	far-	(verbal prefix)
ab-	אַב-	ab-	[ɔp]	אָפּ-	op-	(verbal prefix)

TABLE 61.6: *Dialect Variation in Vowel Realization*

Letter	YIVO	Northeast	Central	South
אַ	[a]	[a]	[a]	[a]
אָ	[ɔ]	[ɔ]	[ʊ, ʊː/ɔ, ɔː]	[ʊ/ɔ]
י	[ɪ]	[ɪ]	[ɪ, ɪː]	[ɪ]
ו	[ʊ]	[ʊ]	[ɪ, ɪː/ʊ, ʊː]	[ɪ/ʊ]
ע	[ɛ]	[ɛ]	[ɛ/ɛj]	[ɛ/ɛj]
יי	[ɛj]	[ɛj]	[aː]	[a]
יַי	[aj]	[aj]	[aː(j)]	[ɛj]
וי	[ɔj]	[ɛj/ɔj]	[ɔj, ɔːj, ɔw]	[ɔj, ɔw, ʊ]

Vowel representation

As indicated above, YIVO orthography does not reflect the phonology of any of the three major dialects of Yiddish, though it closely approximates that of Northeast Yiddish. Dialect differences are found mainly in the vocalic system. TABLE 61.6 gives the most common values of the vowel letters in the YIVO norm and in the three major dialects.

Of the Yiddish vowel letters, only אַ *a*, אָ *o*, and ע *e* can occur word-initially, as in אַלט *alt* 'old', אָרעם *orem* 'poor', עסן *esn* 'eat'. The remaining vowel letters cannot occur at the very beginning of a word, but must, in this position, be preceded by the letter א, the so-called *shtume(r) alef* 'silent alef'. Note that the *shtumer alef* has no marking below the line; this differentiates it from the vowels אַ *a* and אָ *o*. In initial position the remaining vowels have the forms אי *i*, איי *ey*, אײַ *ay*, אוי *oy*, או *u*, as in איך *ikh* 'I', איין *eyn* 'one', אײַזן *ayzn* 'iron', אויג *oyg* 'eye', אונטער *unter* 'under'. As a rule, when a word beginning with one of these vowels is preceded by a prefix, the *shtumer alef* remains, e.g., אייביק ['ɛjbɪk] 'eternal', פֿאַראייביקן [far'ɛjbɪkn̩] 'immortalize'.

Consonant representation

The spelling of words of non-Semitic origin generally does not indicate such phonologically conditioned alternations as voice assimilation, assimilation of nasals, simplification of C₁C₁ clusters, etc.; e.g., איך ליב *ikh lib* ['ɪx 'lɪb] 'I love' in the north, ['ɪx 'lɪp] in the south, and דו ליבסט *du libst* ['dʊ 'lɪpst]; האָבן *hobn* ['hɔbm̩] 'to have', אָנפּאַקן *onpakn* ['ɔm'pakn̩] 'cram'; אָפּפּוצן *opputsn* ['ɔ'pʊtsn̩] 'polish'.

Palatal *ty, dy, sy, zy,* and *ny* (occurring almost exclusively in words of Slavic origin) are marked by טי, די, סי, זי, ני before vowels; palatal *ly* before vowels is marked by לי in words of Slavic origin, but is generally unmarked in words of Western European origin. Syllable-final palatals are not marked. Examples: טיאָך *tyókh* 'throb', דיעגעכץ *dyégekhts* 'tar', גאָטיניו *gótinyu* 'God (dim.)', ליולקע *lyúl'ke* '(tobacco) pipe', לינאָליי *linol'éy* 'linoleum'.

The orthography does not indicate stress, which is distinctive.

TABLE 61.7: *Differences between YIVO and Other Orthographies*

	YIVO	Non–YIVO	Transliteration	Gloss
(a)	וווּ	וואו	vu	'where'
	ווּונדער	וואונדער	vunder	'wonder'
	געוווּסט	געוואוסט	gevust	'known'
(b)	נאַיִוו	נאַאיוו	naiv	'naive'
	רויִק	רואיק	ruik	'calm'
(c)	ייִד	איד	yid[a]	'Jew'
	ייִנגל	אינגל	yingl[a]	'boy'
(d)	שיין	שיין	sheyn	'beautiful'
	שײַן	שיין	shayn	'glow'
	וויין	וויין	veyn	'(I) cry'
	ווײַן	וויין	vayn	'wine'
	ניין	ניין	neyn	'no'
	נײַן	ניין	nayn	'nine'
(e)	כּיבור	כיבוד	kibed	'tribute'
	תּרבות	תרבות	tarbes	'politeness'
(f)	שׂמחה	שמחה	simkhe	'party'
	שעה	שעה	sho	'hour'
(g)	בבֿל	בבל	bovl	'Babylonia'
	פֿאָר	פאָר	for	'(I) travel'
	פּאָר	פּאָר	por	'pair'
(h)	געגנבֿעט	גע'גנב'עט	ge-ganv-et	'stolen'
(i)	משהס	משה'ס	Moyshe-s	'Moses''
	זעלדעס	זעלדע'ס	Zelde-s	'Zelda's'

a.   In some dialects these words are pronounced [ɪd], [ɪŋɫ].

Special spellings

TABLE 61.7 exemplifies a number of spelling differences between YIVO and other systems. (a) Sequences of *v+u* are spelled with the letter וּ for [u] in YIVO spelling, while other orthographies generally have a *shtumer alef* before the וּ. (b) After a vowel YIVO uses the letter יִ to indicate [ɪ], while most other systems again use a *shtumer alef* here. (c) The letter יִ is also used after initial י to mark the initial sequence [jɪ]; most other systems use the sequence אי.

Other differences between YIVO and other systems include: (d) lack of distinction between ײַ *ay* and יי *ey*; (e) in many publications, absence of the *dagesh* (dot) distinguishing כּ [k] from כ [x] and תּ [t] from ת [s]; frequently, lack (f) of the dot distinguishing שׂ [s] from ש [ʃ] in YIVO spelling, and (g) of the *rafe* (bar above a letter) that serves to distinguish בֿ [v] from ב [b] and, in addition to the *dagesh*, to distinguish פֿ [f] from פּ [p]. (h) Non–YIVO systems tend to separate non-Semitic affixes from Semitic roots by means of apostrophes. Similarly, (i) the possessive *s* is often separated from the noun, as in English, by an apostrophe.

SAMPLE OF YIDDISH

The transliteration here deviates from the YIVO system in two respects: words of Semitic origin are transliterated according to Hebrew transliteration (italicized), with the YIVO transliteration in line 2; and the *shtumer alef* is indicated by a hyphen. (In the right-to-left transliterations, the equivalents that are digraphs are underlined merely for clarity.)

←נאָך דער חתונה פֿון גרשמען מיט נחמהען האָט זיך דאָס פּאַרפֿאָלק
klofrop sod khiz toh nehmhn tim nemšrg nuf hntẖ red khon←

געלעבט שטיל און באַשיידן. צו דער ריכטיקער צײַט איז נחמה געלעגן
ngeleg hmhn zi- tyats rekitkhir red uts .ndyeshab nu- litsh tbeleg

געוואָרן, געהאַט אַ יינגעלע און דער ברית איז פֿאַרגעקומען כּדת משה
hšm tdk nemukegrof zi- tyrb red nu- elegniy a taheg ,nroveg

וישׂראל. די שטיל געבענטשטע ליבע האָט זיך אַרויסגעריסן פֿון דער
red nuf nsiregsyora khiz toh ebil etshtnebeg litsh id .l'rśyw

פֿרום־צניעתדיקער געצוימטקייט און האָט געאַנקערט אַן ני- דער פֿרייד
dyerf red ni- treknaeg toh nu- tyektmyotseg rekidt 'ynṣ-murf

פֿון זייער בשותפֿותדיקן יינגעלע מענדעלע-- אַזוי האָבן יעז מי- אַ
a mi- yez nboh yoza —eldnem elegniy nkidtwpṭwšb reyez nuf

נאָמען געגעבן. די עלטערן פֿון ביידע צדדים, סיי פֿון קאָצק
kstok nuf yas ,mydds edyeb nuf nretle id nbegeg nemon

און סיי פֿון כעלעם, האָבן געהאַט פֿון זיי נחת.
nu- yas nuf ,melekh nboh taheg nuf yez .tẖn

1. *Transliteration:*	nokh	der	*htnh*	fun	*gršmen*	mit	*nhmh*en
2. *Normalization:*	nokh	der	khasene	fun	Gershemen	mit	Nekhomen
3. *Transcription:*	nɔɣ	dɛr	'xasɛnɛ	fuŋ	gɛr'ʃemen	mɪt	nɛ'xɔmɛn
4. *Gloss:*	after	the	marriage of		Gershom.DAT	with	Nekhame.DAT

1.	hot zikh	dos	porfolk	gelebt	shtil -un	basheydn. tsu	der
2.	hot zikh	dos	porfolk	gelebt	shtil un	basheydn. tsu	der
3.	'hɔtsɛx	dɔs	pɔr'fɔlk	gɛ'lɛpt	ʃtɪɫ ʊn	ba'ʃɛjdn̩	tsu dɛr
4.	has REFL	the	married.couple	lived	quiet and	modest	to the

1.	rikhtiker	tsayt	-iz	*nhmh*	gelegn gevorn,	gehat	a	yingele -un	der
2.	rikhtiker	tsayt	iz	Nekhome	gelegn gevorn,	gehat	a	yingele un	der
3.	'rɪxtɪkɛr	'tsajt	ɪz	nɛ'xɔmɛ	gɛ'lɛgn̩ gɛ'vɔrn̩,	gɛ'hat	a	'jɪŋgɛlɛ ʊn	dɛr
4.	correct	time	is	Nekhame	gave.birth	had	a	boy	and the

1. *bryṭ*   -iz   forgekumen *kdṭ*   *mšh*   *wyśr ʾl*
2. bris   iz   forgekumen kedas   Moyshe ve-Yisroel
3. 'brɪs   ɪs   'fɔrgeʼkumɛn kɛ-'das   'mɔjʃɛ vɛ-jɪs'rɔɛɫ
4. ritual.circumcision is   occurred   according.to-law.of Moses   and-Israel

1. di   shtil   gebentshte   libe hot zikh   aroysgerisn fun   der   frum–
2. di   shtil   gebentshte   libe hot zikh   aroysgerisn fun   der   frum–
3. dɪ   'ʃtɪɫ   geʼbɛntʃtɛ   'lɪbe 'hɔtsɛx   aʼrɔjzgeʼrɪsn fon   dɛr   'frum-
4. the   quietly   blessed   love has REFL   wrested   from the   pious-

1. ṣny ʿṭdiker   getsoymtkeyt -un   hot   geankert -in   der   freyd   fun
2. tsniesdiker   getsoymtkeyt un   hot   geankert in   der   freyd   fun
3. 'tsnɪɛsdɪkɛr   geʼtsɔjmtkɛjt on   (h)ɔt geʼaŋkɛrt ɪn   dɛr   'frɛjt   fon
4. virtuous.DAT   restraint   and   has   anchored in   the   joy   from

1. zeyer *bšwṭp̄wṭdikn*   yingele mendele—   azoy hobn   zey -im a
2. zeyer beshutfesdikn   yingele mendele—   azoy hobn   zey im   a
3. 'zɛjer beʼʃutfesdɪkŋ   'jɪŋgelɛ 'mɛndɛlɛ   aʼzɔj 'hɔbm̩   'zɛj ɪm   a
4. their joint   boy   Mendele   so   they.have   they him a

1. nomen   gegebn.   di   eltern   fun beyde *ṣddym*,   say fun kotsk
2. nomen   gegebn.   di   eltern   fun beyde tsdodim,   say fun kotsk
3. 'nɔmɛn   geʼgɛbm̩   dɪ   'ɛɫtɛr-n̩ fom 'bɛjdɛ 'tsdɔdɪm   'saj foŋ 'kɔtsk
4. name   given   the   parent-s from both   side-s   both from Kotsk

1. -un   say fun khelem,   hobn   gehat   fun   zey *nḥt.*
2. un   say fun khelem,   hobn   gehat   fun   zey nakhes.
3. on   'saj fun 'xɛɫem   'hɔbm̩ geʼhat fon   'zɛj 'naxɛs
4. and   both from Khelem   have   had   from   they pleasure

'After the marriage of Gershom and Nekhome, the married couple lived quietly
and modestly. At the proper time Nekhame gave birth, had a boy, and the ritual
circumcision occurred according to the law of Moses and Israel. A quietly
blessed love arose from their pious and virtuous restraint and became anchored
in the joy of their common boy Mendele—so they had named him. Their par-
ents on both sides, both from Kotsk and from Khelem (two Polish towns), had
pleasure from them.'   —*Erlikh 1977: 49.*

━━━━━━

Bibliography

Bar-Asher, Moshe. 1988. "The Sharḥ of the Maghreb: Judeo-Arabic Exegesis of the Bible and
    Other Jewish Literature—Its Nature and Formation" [in Hebrew]. In *Studies in Jewish Lan-
    guages: Bible Translations and Spoken Dialects,* ed. Moshe Bar-Asher, pp. 3–34. Jerusalem:
    Misgav Yerushalayim.
Ben-Sasson, Haim Hillel. 1971. "Assimilation." *Encyclopaedia Judaica* 3: 770–83.
Birnbaum, Solomon Asher. 1971. "Jewish Languages." *Encyclopaedia Judaica* 10: 66–69.

———. 1979. *Yiddish: A Survey and a Grammar.* Toronto: University of Toronto Press.

Blanc, Haim. 1981. "Egyptian Arabic in the Seventeenth Century: Notes on the Judeo-Arabic Pas-sages of *Darxe No'am* (Venice, 1697)." In *Studies in Judaism and Islam Presented to Shelomo Dov Goitein,* ed. Shelomo Morag, I. Ben-Ami, and Norman Stillman, pp. 185–202. Jerusalem: Magnes.

Blau, Joshua. 1980. *A Grammar of Medieval Judeo-Arabic,* 2nd ed. [in Hebrew]. Jerusalem: Magnes.

———. 1981. *The Emergence and Linguistic Background of Judaeo-Arabic,* 2nd ed. Jerusalem: Ben-Zvi Institute.

———. 1988. *Studies in Middle Arabic and Its Judaeo-Arabic Variety.* Jerusalem: Magnes.

Blau, Joshua, and Simon Hopkins. 1984. "On Early Judaeo-Arabic Orthography." *Zeitschrift für arabische Linguistik* 12: 9–27.

———. 1987. "Judaeo-Arabic Papyri: Collected, Edited, Translated and Analysed." *Jerusalem Studies in Arabic and Islam* 9: 87–160.

Erlikh, B. E. 1977. *Khelemer dertseylungen.* Tel-Aviv: Farlag Mikhoel.

Fishman, Joshua A., ed. 1985. *Readings in the Sociology of Jewish Languages.* Leiden: Brill.

Hary, Benjamin. 1990. "The Importance of the Orthography in Judeo-Arabic Texts." *Proceedings of the Tenth World Congress of Jewish Studies,* division D, vol. 1, pp. 77–84. Jerusalem: World Union of Jewish Studies.

———. 1991. "The Tradition of Later Egyptian Judeo-Arabic Orthography" [in Hebrew]. *Massorot* 5–6: 119–37.

———. 1992. *Multiglossia in Judeo-Arabic. With an Edition, Translation and Grammatical Study of the Cairene Purim Scroll* (Études sur le judaïsme médiéval 14). Leiden: Brill.

———. 1995. "Judeo-Arabic in Its Sociolinguistic Setting." *Israel Oriental Studies,* vol. 15: *Lan-guage and Culture in the Near East: Diglossia, Bilingualism, Registers,* ed. R. Drory and Shlo-mo Izre'el.

Katz, Dovid. 1987. *Grammar of the Yiddish Language.* London: Duckworth.

Komisye durkhtsufirn dem eynheytlekhn yidishn oysleyg. 1961. *Yidisher ortografisher vegvayzer.* New York: Tsiko-bikher-tsentrale. [Contains the 1937 *Takones.*]

Marcus, Simon. 1965. *The Judeo-Spanish Language.* Jerusalem: Kiryat Sefer.

Ornan, Uzzi. 1985. "Hebrew Is Not a Jewish Language" [in Hebrew]. *Leshonenu* 48/49: 199–206. Summarized in Fishman 1985: 22–24.

Sephiha, Haïm Vital. 1986. *Le Judéo-Espagnol.* Paris: Editions Entente.

Stillman, Norman A. 1988. *The Language and Culture of the Jews of Sefrou, Morocco: An Ethnol-inguistic Study.* Louvin: University of Manchester.

———. 1991. "Language Patterns in Islamic and Judaic Societies." In *Islam and Judaism: 1400 Years of Shared Values,* ed. Steven Wasserstrom, pp. 41–55. Portland, Ore.: Institute for Judaic Studies in the Pacific Northwest.

Weinreich, Uriel. 1968. *Modern English–Yiddish Yiddish–English Dictionary.* New York: YIVO In-stitute for Jewish Research.

———. 1976. *College Yiddish.* New York: YIVO Institute for Jewish Research.

Weinriech, Uriel, and Beatrice Weinreich. 1959. *Yiddish Language and Folklore: A Selective Bibli-ography for Research.* The Hague: Mouton.

Wexler, Paul. 1981. "Jewish Interlinguistics: Facts and Conceptual Framework." *Language* 57: 99–149.

Adaptations of Arabic Script

ALAN S. KAYE

The Arabic writing system (SECTION 50) has been and is used to write many non-Semitic languages. It is now, after the Roman alphabet, the most used segmental script in the world. The Arabic alphabet or abjad (see SECTION 1) is employed today to write the literary variety of Arabic (Classical or Modern Standard); but Maltese, historically a form of Arabic, is written in the Roman alphabet (SECTION 59, page 686). Arabic has also been written in Syriac script (Karshuni or Garshuni, SECTION 47), and Middle Arabic—the Judeo-Arabic and Christian Arabic dialects—has a long literary tradition written in Hebrew and Arabic script respectively (see SECTION 61). There is also a continuing trend of writing colloquial Arabic dialects, particularly Egyptian, in Arabic script: cartoons, plays, advertisements, etc.

Among the more important non-Semitic languages using Arabic script are: the Berber languages of North Africa, except Tuareg with Tifinigh (SECTION 5, "The Berber Scripts" on page 112); the Iranian languages Persian, Pashto, Kurdish, and Balochi; Indo-Aryan Urdu (see SECTION 65), Sindhi, and Kashmiri; Dravidian Moplah (a dialect of Malayalam); and Austronesian Sulu, Malagasy, and Malay. For the Turkic and Caucasian languages using Arabic script—besides Osmanli (Ottoman) Turkish from about 1300 C.E. to 1928, and (along with Hebrew script) the literary language Karaite (Diringer 1968, 1:439–40)—see TABLE 67.1 on page 782. In some republics of the former Soviet Union, Arabic script is now once more competing with Cyrillic for writing Turkic and Iranian languages (SECTION 67). Thus the Arabic script has become much more widespread than the Arabic language itself.

Spread of Arabic script

With the spread of Islam from Spain to Indonesia and much of Africa—and along with it the Holy Qur'ān, which according to custom and tradition must be studied in the original Arabic along with the faithful's Classical Arabic prayers—there soon developed a powerful influence of both the Arabic language and its script on the new converts. Under the first three caliphs, Islam reached Damascus (633), Jerusalem (637), Cairo (641), and Persia (646). Under the Umayyads (661–750), who ruled in Damascus, the Maghreb and Andalusia were added to the Empire (e.g. Tunis, 699). In 750, the Umayyads fell to the Abbasids (750–1258), whose capital was Baghdad. During the rule of the Ottomans (1412–1918) and of the Safavids of Persia (1500–

1779), Turks and Afghans conquered India, establishing the Mughal Empire (1526–1730). From India, Islam spread to Malaysia and Indonesia. Arabic script replaced local scripts wherever it reached—notably in Iran, and among the Islamic peoples of South and Southeast Asia. Unlike the Copts of Egypt, however, these peoples have not given up their languages in favor of Arabic; they have absorbed many loanwords.

Still other languages used to be commonly written in the Arabic script and may occasionally still be, especially by well-educated Muslim scholars and by others as well. Particular mention should be made of Swahili, Kanuri, Hausa, and Fulani. Still other languages have been so written by Muslims (e.g. Semitic Harari in Ethiopia; Albanian; Slavic Serbo-Croatian in Bosnia, Polish, and Belarusian, for which see Wexler 1971; and even Japanese, Naim 1971: 117 n. 7). It is the reverence Muslims have for Arabic and its script that explains, on the one hand, the appreciation and high regard for Arabic calligraphy; and, on the other, why the Muslims of Spain, having come to speak Spanish as a native language, wrote it in Arabic characters (*aljamiado* is the term for the Arabic script used to write Spanish). Political factors as well can impact that reverence, as when the Roman-Turkish alphabet replaced centuries of Arabic-script tradition for Ottoman Turkish on November 28, 1928 (modern-day Turks are still Muslims); but during the course of its long history Ottoman Turkish was also written in Armenian, Cyrillic, Greek, and Hebrew characters. Although an older generation of Turks knew Osmanli Turkish, few Turkish-speakers today are literate in it.

Note also that a language such as Somali fits the circumstances for being written in Arabic script (Somalia is predominantly Muslim, has some Arabic–Somali bilinguals, and is even a member of the Arab League); yet the attempt by Shaikh Awes (d. 1909) did not succeed (Diringer 1968, 1:236). However, the order of the letters and long vowel representations of the Osmanya script (SECTION 52) are based on the Arabic script, and some letters indeed look like Arabic. Somali is today written in the Roman alphabet.

―――――

Minor adaptations of the Arabic script

This section does not deal with the intricacies of all the languages which have been written in the Arabic script, nor with the various highly prized calligraphic styles (see SECTION 20). Note also the very unusual case of Divehi (SECTION 50), which uses the Arabic numerals and certain other signs from Arabic in its script.

The Malagasy script

Malagasy, the native language of Madagascar, is the only Austronesian language spoken in Africa. Diringer (1968, 1:232–33), noting that Malagasy's first script, *sorabe*, was based on Arabic (Munthe 1987 gives a sample of English so written), cites a letter from Bishop Ronald O'Ferrall of Madagascar (dated 1940): "The Latin script introduced by missionaries early in the nineteenth century soon drove out the Arabic script, and it is now only used in a few out-of-the-way villages, though the books are still used by diviners." A peculiarity of the Arabic script is that it is written from top to bottom (the bishop does not state whether it is read horizontally, cf. Syriac practice). That development may be, according to Diringer, due to Chinese influence.

The Yezidi cryptic script

Diringer (1968, 1:233–34—repeating verbatim his 1948: 296 account) describes the 25,000 Yezidis, who live in Iraq, Syria, Turkey, and the Caucasus. They speak both Kurdish and Arabic. Their two holy books are written "probably in a cryptic" script, which "is based partly on the Perso-Arabic writing, and partly on the Latin alphabet." Diringer also believes that it is possible that these texts were first written in the Perso-Arabic alphabet before being "transcribed in the new cryptic script."

General characteristics of Arabic-based writing systems

Arabic script has been quite flexible as it was adapted to the phonological structure of other languages. All the Arabic characters are borrowed, so that Arabic loanwords can preserve their original spelling, whereas their pronunciation will differ depending on the borrowing language. Since, according to Arab tradition, Arabic (*luġat uḍḍād*) is the only language in the world with a voiced emphatic dental stop, ض *ḍād* [ɖ], this consonant must, of necessity, change—it is pronounced [z] in Persian, Urdu, etc. The Arabic emphatic, interdental, and pharyngeal consonants are quite rare in the languages of the world, so various Arabic letters have acquired different pronunciations. Even in Arabic dialects, ض may be [ð] (Iraq) or [z̧] (Egypt).

Ottoman Turkish, or Swahili in Arabic characters, had several noticeable deficiencies in the script, perhaps moreso than other languages which have borrowed it. Some may claim that, in fact, these deficiencies were so severe that they led to the demise of the Arabic script for such languages. For example, Arabic ك *kāf* renders, in addition to [k], Ottoman Turkish [g] (the Persian گ *gāf*, the *kāf* with an additional stroke on top, is not common) and *ñ* [ŋ] (it can also be ڭ with three dots, although they are rarely used). The Swahili drawbacks (see Maw 1981: 227–29) are problematic even for native-speaker learners. There are no distinct symbols, e.g., in the more traditional orthography for [p], [g], [tʃ], [v], [ɲ], and [ŋ]; the Persian forms پ *p* and چ *č* plus non-Persian غ *g* and ڤ *v*, or ش *č*, a variant of چ, are used in the early learning period, but rarely beyond. Also, the *kasra* diacritic can represent either [i] or [e], while *ḍamma* may render [o] or [u]. Furthermore, as with all languages employing the Arabic script, there is a choice of two or more symbols for the same phoneme (cf. Persian or Urdu [s], which may be written with س, ث, or ص; or [z], which may be written with ز, ذ, ض, or ظ). For example, Swahili has no uvular point of articulation, so there is little synchronic justification for writing *rafiki* 'friend' with *q* rather than *k* other than paying homage to the Arabic etymon رفیق *rfyq* [rafiːq]. Since early Swahili writers were bilingual in Arabic, this was unproblematic.

In addition to borrowing all 28 or 29 Arabic letters, new ones needed to be creat-ed, depending on the language, for the different non-Arabic phonemes. Particular di-acritics were often employed to create these new letters, which have assisted the new, expanded writing system to become more "feature"-oriented (Daniels 1992). In Urdu, for example, پ *p* is ب *b* with three dots below the basic configuration, and چ *č* is ج *ǧ* with three dots below the basic configuration; ژ *ž* is ز *z* with three dots above the basic configuration (as Arabic ش *š* modifies س *s* by marking palatality with three dots); a superscript ط *ṭ* (or sometimes two or four dots in various publications) marks retrof-lexion consistently, as in ٹ *ṭ* [ʈ], ڈ *ḍ* [ɖ], or ڑ *ṛ* [ɽ]; lastly, connected *h* allographs rep-resent the aspirated phonemes: بھ *bh*, پھ *ph*, تھ *th*, ٹھ *ṭh*, جھ *jh*, چھ *čh*, دھ *dh*, ڈھ *ḍh*, ڑھ *ṛh*, کھ *kh*, and گھ *gh*. Daniels is quite correct to stress "the regularities involved in the additions." He also notes: "Since Persian polities were responsible for much of the spread of Islam into Asia, these additional Persian letters are found in most of the Ar-abic scripts of the continent."

Scripts of Islamic literary languages

Each table includes the transliteration according to the Library of Congress system (Barry 1991) and an IPA transcription. Since the LC system does not transliterate alif, in the discussion and texts here ا is rendered *a*. The major languages are in roughly chronological order of assuming the script; related languages are grouped with them.

Persian

TABLE 62.1 presents the Persian script (Paper and Jazayery 1955).

The following revaluations of Arabic letters are found in Persian, and hence widely in the Islamic world: (a) ذ *d̲*, ظ *z̲*, and ض *ḍ* → [z]; (b) ث *t̲* and ص *ṣ* → [s]; (c) ط *ṭ* → [t]; (d) ح *ḥ* → [h]; (e) و *w* → [v]; (f) ع *ʿ* and ا *a* → [ʔ] or [Ø] (ع *ʿ* may often represent a preceding long vowel, especially in informal styles).

(g) Arabic *tanwīn* (nunation) and *šadda* (gemination mark) are normally not writ-ten. However, they need to be marked in a transcription since they are often pro-nounced: حقیقتا *ḥqyqta* [haqi:qatan] 'really' (Arabic حقیقة); اول *avl* [avval] 'first' (Arabic أوَّل). Gemination, however, is a feature of the higher registers. The Arabic short vowels are rarely written.

(h) Other "irregularities" in the phoneme–symbol correspondences are men-tioned by Naim (1971: 119), such as the fact that [e] finally is "irregularly" ه *h* (خانه *khanh* [xa:'ne] 'house'). Barry (1991: 147–50) also presents "irregularities" ([a:] may be written as ی *y*, e.g. مصطفی *mṣṭfy* [mostafa:] 'Mustafa'; و *v* is not pronounced after خ *kh*, e.g. خوابیدن *khwabydn* [xa:bi:dan] 'to sleep').

(i) The new letters not occurring in Arabic are پ *p*, گ *g*, چ *č*, and ژ *ž*. All add three dots to the Arabic letters (گ may be analyzed as ک with the three dots evolved into a parallel stroke).

TABLE 62.1: *The Persian Abjad*

LC Transliteration	Transcription	Isolated	Final	Initial	Medial
–	[ʔ, ɔ, æ, Ø]	ا	ـا	–	–
b	[b]	ب	ـب	بـ	ـبـ
p	[p]	پ	ـپ	پـ	ـپـ
t	[t]	ت	ـت	تـ	ـتـ
s̲	[s]	ث	ـث	ثـ	ـثـ
j	[dʒ]	ج	ـج	جـ	ـجـ
ch	[tʃ]	چ	ـچ	چـ	ـچـ
ḥ	[h, Ø]	ح	ـح	حـ	ـحـ
kh	[x]	خ	ـخ	خـ	ـخـ
d	[d]	د	ـد	–	–
z̲	[z]	ذ	ـذ	–	–
r	[r]	ر	ـر	–	–
z	[z]	ز	ـز	–	–
zh	[ʒ]	ژ	ـژ	–	–
s	[s]	س	ـس	سـ	ـسـ
sh	[ʃ]	ش	ـش	شـ	ـشـ
ṣ	[s]	ص	ـص	صـ	ـصـ
z̤	[z]	ض	ـض	ضـ	ـضـ
ṭ	[t]	ط	ـط	طـ	ـطـ
ẓ	[z]	ظ	ـظ	ظـ	ـظـ
ʻ	[ʔ, Ø], preceding V → V:	ع	ـع	عـ	ـعـ
gh	[ɣ]/V_V; [q, ɢ, x]	غ	ـغ	غـ	ـغـ
f	[f]	ف	ـف	فـ	ـفـ
q	[q, ɢ]	ق	ـق	قـ	ـقـ
k	[k]	ك	ـك	كـ	ـكـ
g	[g]	گ	ـگ	گـ	ـگـ
l	[l]	ل	ـل	لـ	ـلـ
m	[m]	م	ـم	مـ	ـمـ
n	[n]	ن	ـن	نـ	ـنـ
v	[v, u, o, ow]	و	ـو	–	–
h	[h, Ø, ɛ, æ], Arab. fem. [t]	ه، ة	ـه، ـة	هـ	ـهـ
y	[j, i, e]	ى	ـى	يـ	ـيـ

TABLE 62.2: *The Consonants of the Kurdish Alphabet*

LC Transliteration	Transcription	Isolated	Final	Initial	Medial
–	[ʔ]	ا	ـا	–	–
b	[b]	ب	ـب	بـ	ـبـ
p	[p]	پ	ـپ	پـ	ـپـ
t	[t]	ت	ـت	تـ	ـتـ
j	[ʤ]	ج	ـج	جـ	ـجـ
ch	[ʧ]	چ	ـچ	چـ	ـچـ
ḥ	[ħ]	ح	ـح	حـ	ـحـ
kh	[x]	خ	ـخ	خـ	ـخـ
d	[d]	د	ـد	–	–
r	[r]	ر	ـر	–	–
ṛ	[ɽ]	ڕ	ـڕ	–	–
z	[z]	ز	ـز	–	–
zh	[ʒ]	ژ	ـژ	–	–
s	[s]	س	ـس	سـ	ـسـ
sh	[ʃ]	ش	ـش	شـ	ـشـ
ṣ	[sˤ]	ص	ـص	صـ	ـصـ
ʿ	[ʕ]	ع	ـع	عـ	ـعـ
gh	[ɣ]	غ	ـغ	غـ	ـغـ
f	[f]	ف	ـف	فـ	ـفـ
v	[v]	ڤ	ـڤ	ڤـ	ـڤـ
q	[q]	ق	ـق	قـ	ـقـ
k	[k]	ك	ـك	كـ	ـكـ
g	[g]	گ	ـگ	گـ	ـگـ
l	[l]	ل	ـل	لـ	ـلـ
ḷ	[ɫ]	ڵ	ـڵ	لـ	ـڵـ
m	[m]	م	ـم	مـ	ـمـ
n	[n]	ن	ـن	نـ	ـنـ
w	[w]	و	ـو	–	–
h	[h, ə]	ە	ـە	هـ	ـهـ
y	[j, iː, eː]	ی	ـی	یـ	ـیـ

TABLE 62.3: *The Vowels of the Kurdish Alphabet*

a	[ə]	ە (ﻩ)	ـە	ه	ـهـ
ā	[ɑ]	ا	ـا	–	–
u	[uː, ʉ, o]	و	ـو	–	–
ū	[uː]	وو	ـوو	–	–
ī	[iː]	یی	ـیی	یـ	ـیـ
ē	[eː]	ی	ـی	–	ـیـ
o	[o]	ۆ	ـۆ	–	ـۆ

SAMPLE OF PERSIAN

خیام اگر ز باده مستی / خوشباش با ماه رخی اگر نشستی خوشباش

shabshvx   ytsshn rga ykhr ham ab shabshvkh / ytsm hdab z rga maykh←

چون عاقبت کار جهان نیستی است / انگار که نیستی چو هستی خوشباش

shabshvx   ytsh vch ytsyn hk ragna   / tsa ytsyn nahj rak tbqa' nvch

1. Transliteration:	khyam	agr	z	badh	msty	khvshbash
2. Normalization:	xayyām	agar	ze	bāde	mastī	xošbāš
3. Transcription:	xæjjɔm	ægær	zɛ	bɔdɛ	mæsti	xoʃbɔʃ
4. Gloss:	Khayyam	if	from	wine	drunk.you.are	happy.be

1. ba	mah	rkhy	agr	nshsty	xvshbash
2. bā	māh	roxī	agar	nešastī	xošbāš
3. bɔ	mɔh	roxi	ægær	nɛʃæsti	xoʃbɔʃ
4. with	moon	face.a	if	you.are.sitting	happy.be

1. chvn	'aqbt	kar	jhan	nysty	ast
2. čūn	'āqebate	kāre	jahān	nīstī	'ast
3. tʃun	ʔɔɣɛbæte	kɔrɛ	dʒæhɔn	nisti	ʔæst
4. since	end.of	work.of	world	nonexistence	is

1. angar	kh	nysty	chv	hsty	xvshbash
2. 'engār	ke	nīstī	čo	hastī	xošbāš
3. ʔɛŋgɔr	kɛ	nisti	tʃo	hæsti	xoʃbɔʃ
4. suppose	that	nothing	when	you.are	happy.be

'And if the Wine you drink, the Lip you press,
End in the Nothing all Things end in—Yes—
Then fancy while Thou art, Thou art but what
Thou shalt be—Nothing—Thou shalt not be less.'
— *From the Rubaiyyat of Omar Khayyam (Tajvidi 1963: 120);*
trans. Edward Fitzgerald, no. 42 (1st ed.).

Kurdish

The Kurdish script (Naim 1971, following McCarus 1958) is a true alphabet, since notating all vowels is obligatory. TABLE 62.2 shows the consonants of the Kurdish alphabet, and TABLE 62.3 the vowels.

Pashto

TABLE 62.4 presents the Pashto script (MacKenzie 1987: 552–53).

(a) Features (a)–(d) and (f) under Persian also apply for Pashto.

(b) The *g* occurs in two varieties: the Persian *gāf* گ or the *kāf* with a circle added below the upper stroke ګ.

TABLE 62.4: *The Pashto Abjad*

LC Transliteration	Transcription	Isolated	Final	Initial	Medial
–	[ʔ, Ø, ə, ɑ(ː), i, u]	ا	ـا	–	–
b	[b]	ب	ـب	بـ	ـبـ
p	[p]	پ	ـپ	پـ	ـپـ
t	[t]	ت	ـت	تـ	ـتـ
ṭ	[ʈ]	ټ	ـټ	ټـ	ـټـ
s̱	[s]	ث	ـث	ثـ	ـثـ
j	[dʒ]	ج	ـج	جـ	ـجـ
ch	[tʃ]	چ	ـچ	چـ	ـچـ
ḥ	[h, Ø]	ح	ـح	حـ	ـحـ
ṡ	[ts]	څ	ـڅ	څـ	ـڅـ
ż	[dz]	ځ	ـځ	ځـ	ـځـ
kh	[x]	خ	ـخ	خـ	ـخـ
d	[d]	د	ـد	–	–
ḍ	[ɖ]	ډ	ـډ	–	–
ẕ	[z]	ذ	ـذ	–	–
r	[r]	ر	ـر	–	–
ṛ	[ɽ]	ړ	ـړ	–	–
z	[z]	ز	ـز	–	–
zh	[ʒ]	ژ	ـژ	–	–
ẕh	[ʐ]	ږ	ـږ	–	–
s	[s]	س	ـس	سـ	ـسـ
sh	[ʃ]	ش	ـش	شـ	ـشـ
ṣh	[ʂ]	ښ	ـښ	ښـ	ـښـ
ṣ	[s]	ص	ـص	صـ	ـصـ
ẓ	[z]	ض	ـض	ضـ	ـضـ
ṭ	[t]	ط	ـط	طـ	ـطـ
ẓ	[z]	ظ	ـظ	ظـ	ـظـ
ʿ	[ʔ, Ø, ɑ], preceding V→V:	ع	ـع	عـ	ـعـ
gh	[ɣ]	غ	ـغ	غـ	ـغـ
f	[f]	ف	ـف	فـ	ـفـ
q	[q]	ق	ـق	قـ	ـقـ
k	[k]	ك	ـك	كـ	ـكـ
g	[g]	ګ	ـګ	ګـ	ـګـ
l	[l]	ل	ـل	لـ	ـلـ
m	[m]	م	ـم	مـ	ـمـ
n	[n]	ن	ـن	نـ	ـنـ
ṇ	[ɳ]	ڼ	ـڼ	ڼـ	ـڼـ
w	[w, o, u(ː)]	و	ـو	–	–
h	[h, a, ə, Ø], Arab. fem. [t]	ه، ة	ـه، ة	هـ	ـهـ
y	[j, e, aj, i(ː)]	ی، ي	ـی، ي	یـ	ـیـ

(c) The following have been invented specifically for Pashto: ټ *ṭ* [ṭ], څ *ś* [ts], ځ *ż*
[dz], ډ *ḍ* [ḍ], ړ *ṛ* [ṛ], ږ *ẓh* [ẓ], ڼ *ṣh* [ṣ], and ڼ *ṇ* [ṇ]. Furthermore, ي is used for [e], and
ئ for [əj]. The latter occurs only finally and is not used in Peshawar (Penzl 1962: 5).
According to MacKenzie (1987: 553), ی is used for nominals, whereas ئ is used for
verbals. MacKenzie also notes that [e] and [aj] are written with the Urdu ے in Pakistani Pashto. Penzl remarks that the distinction of [i] ي and [e] ي "is not as yet systematically carried through in all Pashto publications" (1962: 8).

(d) The short vowels are normally not written. Final [a] or [ə] is written ه *h*.

(e) In Pakistan, Pashto retroflexes ټ *ṭ*, ډ *ḍ*, and ړ *ṛ* can be written in Urdu fashion—ٹ, ڈ, and ڑ respectively.

(f) The *hamza* is occasionally used in the standard script to represent [ə], e.g. ژٴ
zh' [zə] 'I' (MacKenzie 1987: 553).

(g) Plene spelling is an option, with ي indicating [i] or [e], and و for short [u] or
[ʊ]. Thus, انځر or اينځر [indzə́r] 'fig', دِ or دي [de] 'your', ګل or ګول [gul] 'flower'
(ibid.).

SAMPLE OF PASHTO

شک کېنښ حال دی به ، و ، شوی خراب ټيلفون مدير يوه د ټوکه←
s̱ẖk laẖ ẏd hp ,w ywsẖ barkẖ nwflyṭ rydm hwy d hkwṭ←

د دی د مدير نو پېژاندی. نه مدير مګر راغی ورته سری یو
d ẏd d rydm wn ydnazhẏp hn rydm rgm yghar htrw ẏrs wy

تر مخه د کې ښکاره فعال خان ته سرې دی و چه پاره
rt hkhm d ẏk hrakṣẖ la'f naż ht ẏrs ẏd w hch hrap

زکرم — لبېک :ھرک یی یغ ، کړه کې، پورته ټيلفون یی پوښتنی
zkrm —lbẏk :ḥrk yy ghẓẖ ,yk htrwp nwflyṭ yy yntṣẖwp

راکه. ریاست مطبوعاتو د
hkar tsayr wta'wbṭm d

1. Transliteration:	ṭwkh.	d	ywh	mdyr	ṭyltwn	khrab	sl̤iwy
2. Vocalization:	ṭokə.	də	yəwə	mudīr	ṭilifūn	xarāb	shəwəy
3. Transcription:	'ṭokə	də	jəwə	mu'dir	ṭili'fun	xaˈra:b	'ʃəwəj
4. Gloss:	joke	of	one	director	telephone	out.of.order	got

1.	w,	ph	dy	ḥal	kṣh	yw	sry	wrth	raghy	mgr
2.	wu,	pə	dē	hāl	kṣi	yaw	saṛay	wərtə	rāghəy	magar
3.	wu	pə	'de	ha:l	kṣi	jaw	sa'ṛaj	wər-tə	ra:ɣəj	'magar
4.	had	in	this	condition	in	one	man	him.to	he.came	but

1.	mdyr	nh	pyzhandy.	nw	mdyr	d	dy	d parh	chh	w
2.	mudīr	nə	pežāndəy.	nō	mudīr	də	dē	də pārə	či	wə
3.	mu'dir	nə	peʒa:n'dəj	no	mu'dir	də	de	də pa:rə	tʃi	wə
4.	director	not	he.knew	then	director	of	this	for.the.sake	that	to

1.	dy	sṛy	th	żan	faʿl	shkarh	ky		d mkhh	tr	pwshtny
2.	dē	səṛī	tə	żān	faʿāl	ṣkāra	kī		də maxa	tər	puṣtənī
3.	'de	sə'ṛi	tə	dzaːn	faaːl	ṣkaː'ra	ki		də 'maxa	tər	puṣ'təni
4.	this	man	to	oneself	active	clear	he.makes		before		question

1.	yy	ṭylfwn	pwrth	ky		żh gh	yy	krh	kybl—
2.	yē	ṭilifūn	pōrtə	kəy		żagh	yē	kṛə	kēbəl—
3.	je	ṭili'fun	'portə	kəj		'żɑɣ	je	kṛə	ke'bəl
4.	by.him	telephone	upward	he.made		sound	by.him	was.made	cable

1.	mrkz...!	d	mṭbwʿatw	ryast	rakh.
2.	markaz...!	də	matbo'ātu	riyāsat	rākə
3.	mar'kaz	də	matboaːtu	riyaː'sat	raːkə
4.	center	of	publications	department	give.to.me

'A Joke—The telephone of a director had gotten out of order. At this time a man came to him, but the director did not know him. Then the director, in order to reveal himself to this man as active, before (any) question lifted the telephone (receiver). He shouted: "Operator, operator! Give me the Press Department.'

—*From Penzl 1962: 18–21, 26.*

Kashmiri

TABLE 62.5 presents the Kashmiri script (Barry 1991: 72–75, Zaxarin and Edelman 1971). The aspirated stops are as in Urdu (پھ *ph*, تھ *th*, ٹھ *ṭh*, چھ *ch*, کھ *kh*) plus ژھ *tsh*. Undotted ی palatalizes the preceding consonant, e.g. اپیر *apyr* [əpʲər].

Urdu

TABLE 62.6 presents the Urdu script (Bright and Khan 1958).

(a) Since Urdu script is adapted from that of Persian (rather than directly from Arabic), many features of Persian script and pronunciation, as described above, also apply to Urdu.

(b) The retroflex phonemes use a small superscript ط (or 2–4 dots as variations) modifying the closest non-retroflex counterpart: ٹ *t*, ڈ *d*, and ڑ *r*. There are also three aspirated retroflexes ٹھ *ṭh*, ڈھ *ḍh*, and ڑھ *ṛh*. The latter two are allophones, however (Naim 1971: 134).

(c) Aspiration is marked with digraphs of the consonant and *h*, listed on page 746 (see Naim 1971: 132, and for criticisms of Naim's account, Daniels 1992, n. 25).

(d) All the nasalized vowels, which are phonemic, are written with ں, undotted *n*, finally. Elsewhere, they are written as ن *n*, e.g. اونچا *awnča* [ũtʃa] 'tall, high'.

(e) In words of Arabic origin, etymological ة *t* is sometimes replaced by ت *t*.

(f) Final *ē* is generally written ے, e.g. لڑکے *lrke* [ləṛke] 'boy(s)'. Final *i* is ی, e.g. لڑکی *lrky* [ləṛki] 'girl'.

TABLE 62.5: *The Kashmiri Alphabet*

LC Translit.	Value	Isolated	Final	Initial	Medial	LC Translit.	Value	Isolated	Final	Initial	Medial
b	[b]	ب	ب	ب	ب	k	[k]	ك	ك	ک	کـ
p	[p]	پ	پ	پ	پ	g	[g]	گ	گ	گ	گ
t	[t]	ت	ت	ت	ت	l	[l]	ل	ل	ل	ل
ṭ	[ʈ]	ٹ	ٹ	ٹ	ٹ	m	[m]	م	م	مـ	مـ
s̱	[s]	ث	ث	ث	ث	n	[n]	ن	ن	ن	ن
j	[ʤ]	ج	ج	ج	ج	v	[w]	و	و	–	–
c	[ʧ]	چ	چ	چ	چ	h	[h]	ھ	ہ، ھ	ھ	ھ
ḥ	[h]	ح	ح	ح	ح	y	[j]	ے	ے	یـ	یـ
kh	[kʰ]	خ	خ	خ	خ	a	[a]	آ	ـَ	آ	ـَ
d	[d]	د	د	–	–	ā	[a:]	آ	ا	آ	ا
ḍ	[ɖ]	ڈ	ڈ	–	–	ạ	[ə]	أ	ـٔ	أ	ـٔ
ẕ	[z]	ذ	ذ	–	–	ą̄	[ə:]	آٔ	آٔ	آٔ	آٔ
r	[r]	ر	ر	–	–	i	[i:]	ا	–	ا	–
ṛ	[ʈ]	ڑ	ڑ	–	–	ī	[ɪ]	اَی	ـَی	ایـٕ	ـیـٕ
z	[z]	ز	ز	–	–	u'	[ɨ:]	إ	ـٕ	إ	ـٕ
ts	[ts]	ژ	ژ	–	–	ū'	[ɨ]	اٗ	ـٗ	اٗ	ـٗ
s	[s]	س	س	سـ	ـسـ	u	[u:]	اُ	ـُ	اُ	ـُ
ś	[ʃ]	ش	ش	شـ	ـشـ	ū	[ʊ]	اۆ	ـۆ	اۆ	ـۆ
ṣ	[s]	ص	ص	صـ	ـصـ	o	[o:]	اۆ	ـۆ	اۆ	ـۆ
ẓ	[z]	ض	ض	ضـ	ـضـ	ō	[o]	او	و	او	و
ṭ	[t]	ط	ط	ط	ط	ọ	[ɔ]	او	و	او	و
ẓ̱	[z]	ظ	ظ	ظ	ظ	ọ̄	[ɔ:]	اوآ	وآ	–	–
ʿ	[ʔ, Ø]	ع	ع	عـ	ـعـ	e	[e]	لے	ـٚ	ایٚ	ـیـٚ
gh	[g]	غ	غ	غـ	ـغـ	ē	[e:]	لے	ے	ایـ	ـیـ
f	[f, pʰ]	ف	ف	فـ	ـفـ	ẏ	[ʲ]	لے	ی	–	ـیـ
q	[k]	ق	ق	قـ	ـقـ						

TABLE 62.6: *The Urdu Abjad*

LC Transliteration	Transcription	Isolated	Final	Initial	Medial
–	/C_ [ɑ]; [ə]	ا	ﺎ	–	–
b	[b]	ب	ﺐ	ﺑ	ﺒ
p	[p]	پ	ﭗ	ﭘ	ﭙ
t	[t]	ت	ﺖ	ﺗ	ﺘ
ṭ	[ṭ]	ٹ	ﭩ	ﭨ	ﭪ
s̲	[s]	ث	ﺚ	ﺛ	ﺜ
j	[ʤ]	ج	ﺞ	ﺟ	ﺠ
c	[ʧ]	چ	ﭻ	ﭼ	ﭽ
ḥ	[h]	ح	ﺢ	ﺣ	ﺤ
kh	[x]	خ	ﺦ	ﺧ	ﺨ
d	[d]	د	ﺪ	–	–
ḍ	[ḍ]	ڈ	ﮉ	–	–
z̲	[z]	ذ	ﺬ	–	–
r	[r]	ر	ﺮ	–	–
ŗ	[ṭ]	ڑ	ﮍ	–	–
z	[z]	ز	ﺰ	–	–
zh	[ʒ]	ژ	ﮊ	–	–
s	[s]	س	ﺲ	ﺳ	ﺴ
sh	[ʃ]	ش	ﺶ	ﺷ	ﺸ
ṣ	[s]	ص	ﺺ	ﺻ	ﺼ
ẓ	[z]	ض	ﺾ	ﺿ	ﻀ
ṭ	[t]	ط	ﻂ	ﻃ	ﻄ
ẓ	[z]	ظ	ﻆ	ﻇ	ﻈ
ʿ	/C_ [ɑ]; [Ø, ʔ, ə]	ع	ﻊ	ﻋ	ﻌ
gh	[ɣ]	غ	ﻎ	ﻏ	ﻐ
f	[f]	ف	ﻒ	ﻓ	ﻔ
q	[q]	ق	ﻖ	ﻗ	ﻘ
k	[k]	ك	ﻚ	ﻛ	ﻜ
g	[g]	گ	ﮓ	ﮔ	ﮕ
l	[l]	ل	ﻞ	ﻟ	ﻠ
m	[m]	م	ﻢ	ﻣ	ﻤ
n	[n]; nasalization	ن	ﻦ	ﻧ	ﻨ
n̲	nasalization	ں	ﮟ	ﻧ	ﻨ
v	[v, u, ʊ, o, ow]	و	ﻮ	–	–
h	/_# [ɑ]; [h, Ø]	ہ	ﻪ	ﻫ	ﻬ
t	[t] (Arabic feminine)	ة	ﺔ	–	–
y	[j, i, e, ɛ]	ى	ﻰ	ﻳ	ﻴ

(g) There are many irregularities (see Barry 1991: 204–8), including: (1) in some words of Arabic origin, a final ی *y* is pronounced [a]; (2) [a] is sometimes omitted in writing; (3) final ہ *h* is often not pronounced.

(j) The two variants of medial *h* used in Arabic have been assigned different functions in Urdu. As seen above, the "eyeglass" shape of *h* ھ marks the aspirated consonants (and is used in final position as well); whereas the pointed shape ہ represents consonantal *h* (with the Arabic-style final form ہ). Typical of handwriting is an alternative initial form of *h*: ہ, thus ھندوستان or ہندوستان *hndwstan* [hindusta:n] 'India'.

Sample of Urdu

←ھندوستان جنوبی ایشیا کا ایك بڑا ملك ھے۔ اس کی لمبائی
y’abml yk sa .eh klm aṛb kya ak aysh̲ya ybvnj natsvdnh←

شمال میں کشمیر سے لیکر جنوب میں کیپ کمورن تك لگ بھگ
gbh̲ gl kt nrvmk pyk ṉym bvnj rkyl es rymsh̲k ṉym lamsh̲

دو ھزار میل ھے۔ ملك کے شمال میں ھملیه پہاڑ ھیں جن پر
rp nj ṉyh ṛahp hylmh ṉym lamsh̲ ek klm .eh lym razh vd

سال بھر برف رھتی ھے۔ ان پہاڑوں سے بہت سے ندیاں نکلتی ھیں
ṉyh ytlkn ṉaydn es thb es ṉvṛahp na .eh ythr frb rbh̲ las

اور شمالی میدان میں بہتی ھیں۔
.ṉyh ythb ṉym nadym ylamsh̲ rwa

1. Transliteration:	hndvstan	jnvby	ayshya	ka	ayk	bṛa	mlk	hy.	’s
2. Normalization:	Hindustān	janūbī	Ēshiā	kā	ēk	baṛā	mulk	hai.	us
3. Transcription:	hɪndʊstɑn	ʤənubi	eʃjɑ	kɑ	ek	bəɽɑ	mʊlk	hɛ	ʊs
4. Gloss:	India	southern	Asia	of	one	big	country	is	it

1. ky	lmba’y	shm’l	myṉ	kshmyr	sy	lykr	jnvb	myṉ	kyp
2. kī	lambā’ī	shimāl	mẽ	Kashmīr	sē	lēkar	janūb	mẽ	Kēp
3. kɪ	ləmbɑi	ʃɪmɑl	mẽ	kaʃmir	se	lekər	ʤənub	mẽ	kep
4. of	length	north	in	Kashmir	from	starting	south	in	Cape

1. kmvrn	tk	lg bhg	dv	hz’r	myl	hy	mlk	ky	shm’l	myṉ
2. Kamorin	tak	lag bhag	do	hazār	mīl	hai	mulk	kī	shimāl	mẽ
3. kəmorɪn	tək	ləg bʱəg	do	həzɑr	mil	hɛ	mʊlk	ki	ʃɪmɑl	mẽ
4. Comorin	up.to	approx.	two	thousand	mile	is	country	of	north	in

1. hmlyh	ph’ṛ	hyṉ	jn	pr	s’l	bhr	brf	rhty	hy.	’n
2. himāliyā	pahāṛ	hẽ	jin	par	sāl	bhar	barf	rahtī	hai.	un
3. hɪmalɪja	pəhaɽ	hẽ	ʤɪn	pər	sɑl	bʱər	bərf	rəhti	hɛ	ʊn
4. Himalaya	Mountain	are	which	on	year	full	snow	stay	is	those

1. pharvn̲	sy	bht	sy	ndyan̲	nklty	hyn̲	awr	shmly
2. pahāṛō	sē	bahut	sī	nadiyã	nikaltī	hẽ	awr	shimālī
3. pəhaṛō	se	bəhot	si	nədɪjã	nɪkəlti	hẽ	ɔr	ʃɪmali
4. mountains	from	many	INTENS	rivers	emerge	are	and	northern

1. myd'n	myn̲	bhty	hyn̲.
2. mēdān	mẽ	bahtī	hẽ.
3. medan	mẽ	bəhti	hẽ
4. plains	in	flow	are

'India is a large country of South Asia. Its length from Kashmir in the north to Cape Comorin in the south is approximately two thousand miles. In the north of the country are the Himalaya Mountains on which snow stays year round. Many, many rivers emerge from those mountains and flow in the northern plains.'
— *From Gumperz and Naim 1960: 123.*

Sindhi

TABLE 62.7 presents the Sindhi abjad, which has created new letters using the basic Arabic shapes plus diacritics for its aspirated and implosive series—fifteen of them (Yegorova 1971, Barry 1991: 168–69, Naim 1971: 128–30).

Ottoman Turkish

TABLE 62.8 presents the Ottoman Turkish script (Németh 1962: 28–32); the IPA transcription is based on a probable older pronunciation of the language.

(a) Features (a–g) under Persian also apply for Ottoman Turkish.

(b) The گ *g* and ڭ *ñ* are, more often than not, written without the upper stroke and three dots, respectively.

(c) The letters for Arabic emphatic consonants are associated with back vowels, and the corresponding plain letters with front vowels: ص *ṣ*, ط *ṭ*, ق *q* versus س *s*, ت *t*, ك *k*.

(d) Arabic and Persian loanwords are almost always spelled as they were spelled in those languages. There are, thus, from the Turkish point of view, many irregularities and inconsistencies (underlined romanizations used here are modern orthography): واقعا is *yakıâ* 'in fact', لكن is *lâkin* 'but', بعده is *badehu* 'thereafter'; however, معتاد is [muːtat] 'customary' = *mûtad*. Some Turkish pronunciations of the loanwords point to colloquial Arabic as the donor rather than Classical Arabic; however, the words are spelled in Classical fashion (e.g. *sahra* 'desert' written صحرا ء *shra'*, sometimes without the hamza). A word such as *siret* 'moral character' can be spelled سيرت (< Persian) or سيرة (< Arabic) *syrt*; however, note جب *cep* [dʒep] 'pocket' for Arabic جيب *ğyb* [dʒajb], فقرا *fqra* for Arabic فقرا ء [fuqaraːʔ] 'poor people', or قران *Kur'an* 'Qur'ān' for Arabic قران [qurʔaːn].

TABLE 62.7: *The Sindhi Abjad*

LC Translit.	Value	Isolated	Final	Initial	Medial	LC Translit.	Value	Isolated	Final	Initial	Medial
–	/C_ [ɑ]	ا	ـا	–	–	z	[z]	ز	ـز	–	–
b	[b]	ب	ـب	بـ	ـبـ	s	[s]	س	ـس	سـ	ـسـ
ḇ	[ɓ]	ڃ	ـڃ	ڃـ	ـڃـ	sh	[ʃ]	ش	ـش	شـ	ـشـ
bh	[bʰ]	ٻ	ـٻ	ٻـ	ـٻـ	ṣ	[s]	ص	ـص	صـ	ـصـ
t	[t]	ت	ـت	تـ	ـتـ	ẓ	[z]	ض	ـض	ضـ	ـضـ
th	[tʰ]	ٿ	ـٿ	ٿـ	ـٿـ	ṭ	[t]	ط	ـط	طـ	ـطـ
ṭ	[ʈ]	ٽ	ـٽ	ٽـ	ـٽـ	ẓ	[z]	ظ	ـظ	ظـ	ـظـ
ṭh	[ʈʰ]	ٺ	ـٺ	ٺـ	ـٺـ	ʿ	[Ø]	ع	ـع	عـ	ـعـ
s̱	[s]	ث	ـث	ثـ	ـثـ	gh	[ɣ]	غ	ـغ	غـ	ـغـ
p	[p]	پ	ـپ	پـ	ـپـ	f	[f]	ف	ـف	فـ	ـفـ
j	[dʒ]	ج	ـج	جـ	ـجـ	ph	[pʰ]	ڦ	ـڦ	ڦـ	ـڦـ
ǰ	[ʒ]	ڄ	ـڄ	ڄـ	ـڄـ	q	[k]	ق	ـق	قـ	ـقـ
jh	[dʒʰ]	جھ	ـجھ	جھـ	ـجھـ	k	[k]	ڪ	ـڪ	ڪـ	ـڪـ
ñ	[ɲ]	ڃ	ـڃ	ڃـ	ـڃـ	kh	[kʰ]	ک	ـک	کـ	ـکـ
c	[tʃ]	چ	ـچ	چـ	ـچـ	g	[g]	ڳ	ـڳ	ڳـ	ـڳـ
ch	[tʃʰ]	ڇ	ـڇ	ڇـ	ـڇـ	ǧ	[ɠ]	ڱ	ـڱ	ڱـ	ـڱـ
ḥ	[h]	ح	ـح	حـ	ـحـ	gh	[gʰ]	ڱ	ـڱ	ڱـ	ـڱـ
kh	[x]	خ	ـخ	خـ	ـخـ	ṅ	[ŋ]	ڱ	ـڱ	ڱـ	ـڱـ
d	[d]	د	ـد	–	–	l	[l]	ل	ـل	لـ	ـلـ
dh	[dʰ]	ڌ	ـڌ	–	–	m	[m]	م	ـم	مـ	ـمـ
ḍ	[ɖ]	ڏ	ـڏ	–	–	n	[n]	ن	ـن	نـ	ـنـ
ḍ	[ɗ]	ڊ	ـڊ	–	–	ṇ	[ɳ]	ڻ	ـڻ	ڻـ	ـڻـ
dh	[dʰ]	ڍ	ـڍ	–	–	v	[v, u, o]	و	ـو	–	–
ẕ	[z]	ذ	ـذ	–	–	h	[h]	ه، ھ	ه	ھـ	ـھـ
r	[r]	ر	ـر	–	–	y	[j, i, e]	ي	ـي	يـ	ـيـ
ṛ	[ʈ]	ڙ	ـڙ	–	–						

(e) There are variations in vowels, as [o] could be spelled either plene or not; e.g. *ordu* 'army' is اردو *ardw* or اوردو *awrdw*, and *dört* 'four' is دورت *dwrt* or درت *drt*. There is also variation in [y], e.g. آيی *ʾayy*/ايو *ʾayw* [ajy] (= Modern Turkish *ayı*) 'bear'. *kara* 'black' can be spelled قرا *qral*/قاره *qarh*/قره *qrh*. The word خدمت *ḥdmt* 'service' was pronounced *hizmet* (originally, a graphic error for ذ *ḏ*?). The [e] in ضربه *ḍrbh darbe* [dɑrbe] 'stroke' is indicative of a loanword from colloquial Arabic *ḍarbe*.

TABLE 62.8: *The Ottoman Turkish Abjad*

LC Transliteration[a]	Transcription	Isolated	Final	Initial	Medial
–	[ɑ, Ø]; sometimes [o, e]	ا	ـا	–	–
b	[b, p]	ب	ـب	بـ	ـبـ
p	[p]	پ	ـپ	پـ	ـپـ
t	[t]	ت	ـت	تـ	ـتـ
s̠	[s]	ث	ـث	ثـ	ـثـ
c	[ʤ, ʧ]	ج	ـج	جـ	ـجـ
ç	[ʧ]	چ	ـچ	چـ	ـچـ
ḥ	[h]	ح	ـح	حـ	ـحـ
ḫ	[h]	خ	ـخ	خـ	ـخـ
d	[d, t]	د	ـد	–	–
ẕ	[z]	ذ	ـذ	–	–
r	[r]	ر	ـر	–	–
z	[z]	ز	ـز	–	–
j	[ʒ]	ژ	ـژ	–	–
s	[s]	س	ـس	سـ	ـسـ
ş	[ʃ]	ش	ـش	شـ	ـشـ
ṣ	[s]	ص	ـص	صـ	ـصـ
ż	[z, d]	ض	ـض	ضـ	ـضـ
ṭ	[t, d]	ط	ـط	طـ	ـطـ
ẓ	[z]	ظ	ـظ	ظـ	ـظـ
ʿ	[Ø, ɑ]	ع	ـع	عـ	ـعـ
ġ	[ɣ, g, k, h]	غ	ـغ	غـ	ـغـ
f	[f]	ف	ـف	فـ	ـفـ
ḳ	[k]	ق	ـق	قـ	ـقـ
k	[k, j]	ك	ـك	كـ	ـكـ
g	[g, k]	گ	ـگ	گـ	ـگـ
ñ	[ŋ]	ڭ	ـڭ	–	ـڭـ
l	[l]	ل	ـل	لـ	ـلـ
m	[m]	م	ـم	مـ	ـمـ
n	[n]	ن	ـن	نـ	ـنـ
v	[v, Ø, u, ɯ, i, y, o, œ]	و	ـو	–	–
h	[h, ɑ, i, e], Arab. fem. [t]	ه, ة	ـه, ـة	هـ	ـهـ
y	[j, i, y, e, ej, ɑ, u, ɯ]	ى	ـى	يـ	ـيـ

a. These are the letters used in contemporary orthography (cf. TABLE 59.23 on page 683), except that ǧ is more or less the equivalent of غ.

SAMPLE OF OTTOMAN TURKISH

خواجه‌← مركبني ضايع ايتمش هم آرار هم شكر ايدر ايمش
hcavḥ←   ʿyaż ynbkrm   şmtya   mh   rara'   mh   rkş   rdya   şmya

سبب تشكرى صورمشلر اوزرنده بولنمديغمه شكر ايدييورم. اكر
bbs   yrkşt   .rlşmrvş   hdnrzva   hmġydmnlwb   rkş   .mrvyydya   rga

بولونايدم، بن ده برابر غائب اولوردم، دیمش.
mdyanvlvb   nb   hd   rbarb   b'aġ   mdrvlva   şmyd

1. Transliteration:	ḥvach	mrkbny	żayʿ	aytmş	hm		'arar
2. Mod. Turkish:	Hoca	merkebini	zayi	etmiş	hem		arar
3. Transcription:	hoʤ'ɑ	mɛrkɛbɪ'ni	zaji	ɛt'miʃ	'hɛm		a'rar
4. Gloss:	teacher	his.donkey	lost	he.made	both		searching.for

1.	hm	şkr	aydr	aymş	sbb	tşkry	şvrmşlr.
2.	hem	şükr	eder	imiş	sebebi	teşekkürü	sormuşlar.
3.	'hɛm	ʃykr	ɛdɛr	ɪ'mɪʃ	sɛ'bebi	tɛʃɛk:yry	sormuʃ-'lar
4.	and	thanks	he.made	PAST	the.cause.of	thanks	asked-they

1.	avzrndh	bwlnmdyġmh	şkr	aydyyvrm.	agr
2.	üzerinde	bulunmadığıma	şükr	ediyorum.	eğer
3.	yzɛr-ɪndɛ	bʊlʊnmaduyu'ma	ʃykr	ɛdɪ'jorum	e:'ɛr
4.	it-on	my.because.of.not.being	thanks	I.am.making	if

1.	bvlvnaydm	bn	dh	brabr	ġa'b	avlvrdm	dymş
2.	bulunaydım	ben	de	beraber	kayıp	olurdum	demiş
3.	bulu'najdum	bɛn	dɛ	bɛra'bɛr	'kajɯp	o'lurdʊm	dɛ'mɪʃ
4.	I.had.been	I	also	together	lost	would.have.been	he.replied

'The teacher lost his donkey. He was both searching for it and was expressing his thanks. They asked the cause of being grateful. "Because of my not being on it, I am expressing my thanks. If I had been (on it), I, too, together (with it) would have been lost," he replied.'   —From Németh 1966: 18–19.

Uyghur

TABLE 62.9 presents the Uyghur alphabet (Hahn 1991: 97). Uyghur is exceptional among Islamic languages in not preserving the Arabic spelling of Arabic loanwords.

Malay

TABLE 62.10 presents the Malay script (Lewis 1958), now largely replaced by the Roman alphabet. Malay represented the common Austronesian morphological feature of reduplication with a raised numeral 2: نكَرِي ٢ *ngry*[2] [nəgəri-nəgəri] 'countries'. Arabic loanwords could receive pronunciation-spellings (Naim 1971: 137–39).

TABLE 62.9: *The Uyghur Alphabet*

LC Transliteration	Transcription	Isolated	Final	Initial	Medial
a	[ɑ]	ا	ﺍ	–	–
ă	[ə]	ﻩ	ﻪ	–	–
b	[b]	ﺏ	ﺐ	ﺑ	ﺒ
p	[p]	ﭖ	ﭗ	ﭘ	ﭙ
t	[t]	ﺕ	ﺖ	ﺗ	ﺘ
j	[ʤ]	ﺝ	ﺞ	ﺟ	ﺠ
ch	[ʧ]	ﭺ	ﭻ	ﭼ	ﭽ
kh	[x]	ﺥ	ﺦ	ﺧ	ﺨ
d	[d]	ﺩ	ﺪ	–	–
r	[r]	ﺭ	ﺮ	–	–
z	[z]	ﺯ	ﺰ	–	–
zh	[ʒ]	ﮊ	ﮋ	–	–
s	[s]	ﺱ	ﺲ	ﺳ	ﺴ
sh	[ʃ]	ﺵ	ﺶ	ﺷ	ﺸ
gh	[ɣ]	ﻍ	ﻎ	ﻏ	ﻐ
f	[f]	ﻑ	ﻒ	ﻓ	ﻔ
q	[q]	ﻕ	ﻖ	ﻗ	ﻘ
k	[k]	ﻙ	ﻚ	ﻛ	ﻜ
g	[g]	ﮒ	ﮓ	ﮔ	ﮕ
ng	[ŋ, n]	ﯕ	ﯖ	ﯗ	ﯘ
l	[l]	ﻝ	ﻞ	ﻟ	ﻠ
m	[m]	ﻡ	ﻢ	ﻣ	ﻤ
n	[n]	ﻥ	ﻦ	ﻧ	ﻨ
h	[h]	ﻩ	ﻪ	ﻫ	ﻬ
o	[o]	ﯗ	ﯘ	–	–
u	[u]	ﯗ	ﯘ	–	–
ö	[ø]	ﯙ	ﯚ	–	–
ü	[y]	ﯜ	ﯝ	–	–
v	[v]	ﯞ	ﯟ	–	–
e	[e]	ﯤ	ﯥ	ﺋ	ﺌ
i	[i]	ﻯ	ﻰ	ﺋ	ﺌ
y	[j]	ﻱ	ﻲ	ﻳ	ﻴ
ʾ				ﺋ	ﺌ
la	[la]	ﻻ	ﻼ	–	–

TABLE 62.10: *The Malay (or Jawi) Abjad*

Transliteration	Transcription	Isolated	Final	Initial	Medial
–	[Ø]	ا	ـا	–	–
b	[b]	ب	ـب	بـ	ـبـ
t	[t]	ت	ـت	تـ	ـتـ
th	[s]	ث	ـث	ثـ	ـثـ
j	[ʤ]	ج	ـج	جـ	ـجـ
ch	[ʧ]	چ	ـچ	چـ	ـچـ
ḥ	[h]	ح	ـح	حـ	ـحـ
kh	[x, k]	خ	ـخ	خـ	ـخـ
d	[d]	د	ـد	–	–
dz	[dz]	ذ	ـذ	–	–
r	[r]	ر	ـر	–	–
z	[z, ʤ]	ز	ـز	–	–
s	[s]	س	ـس	سـ	ـسـ
sh	[ʃ, s]	ش	ـش	شـ	ـشـ
ṣ	[s]	ص	ـص	صـ	ـصـ
ḍ	[z, ʤ]	ض	ـض	ضـ	ـضـ
ṭ	[t]	ط	ـط	طـ	ـطـ
ẓ	[z]	ظ	ـظ	ظـ	ـظـ
ʿ	[Ø]	ع	ـع	عـ	ـعـ
gh	[ɣ, r]	غ	ـغ	غـ	ـغـ
ng	[ŋ]	ڠ	ـڠ	ڠـ	ـڠـ
f	[f, p]	ف	ـف	فـ	ـفـ
p	[p]	ڤ	ـڤ	ڤـ	ـڤـ
k	[k]	ق	ـق	قـ	ـقـ
k	[k]	ك	ـك	كـ	ـكـ
g	[g]	ڬ	ـڬ	ڬـ	ـڬـ
l	[l]	ل	ـل	لـ	ـلـ
m	[m]	م	ـم	مـ	ـمـ
n	[n]	ن	ـن	نـ	ـنـ
w	[w]	و	ـو	–	–
h	[h]	ه	ـه	هـ	ـهـ
la	[la]	لا	ـلا	–	–
ʾ	[Ø]	ء	ء	–	ـئـ
y	[j]	ي	ـي	يـ	ـيـ
ny	[ɲ]	ث	ـث	ثـ	ـثـ

Bibliography

Barry, Randall K., comp. 1991. *ALA–LC Romanization Tables: Transliteration Schemes for Non-Roman Scripts.* Washington, D.C.: Library of Congress.

Bright, William, and Saeed A. Khan. 1958. *The Urdu Writing System.* Washington, D.C.: American Council of Learned Societies. Repr. Ithaca, N.Y.: Spoken Language Services, 1976.

Daniels, Peter T. 1992. "The Protean Arabic Abjad." Paper presented at North American Conference on Afroasiatic Linguistics, Cambridge, Mass. To appear in *Humanism, Culture, and Language in the Near East: Studies in Honor of Georg Krotkoff,* ed. A. Afsaruddin, M. Zahnisser, and K. Stowasser. Winona Lake, Ind.: Eisenbrauns.

Diringer, David. 1968. *The Alphabet: A Key to the History of Mankind,* 3rd ed. 2 vols. London: Hutchinson.

Gumperz, John J., and C. Mohammed Naim. 1960. *Urdu Reader.* Berkeley, Calif.: Center for South Asian Studies.

Hahn, Reinhard F. 1991. *Spoken Uyghur.* Seattle: University of Washington Press.

Lewis, M. B. 1958. *A Handbook of the Malay Script.* London: Macmillan.

MacKenzie, D. N. 1987. "Pashto." In *The World's Major Languages,* ed. Bernard Comrie, pp. 547–65. London: Croom Helm.

Maw, Joan. 1981. "Arabic and Roman Writing Systems for Swahili." In *Towards a History of Phonetics: Papers Contributed in Honour of David Abercrombie,* ed. R. E. Asher and Eugénie J. A. Henderson, pp. 225–47. Edinburgh: Edinburgh University Press.

McCarus, Ernest N. 1958. *A Kurdish Grammar: Descriptive Analysis of the Kurdish of Sulaimaniya, Iraq* (Program in Oriental Languages, Series B, Aids 10). New York: American Council of Learned Societies.

Munthe, Ludwig. 1987. "The Arab Influence on Madagascar." In *Religion, Development and African Identity* (Seminar Proceedings 17), ed. Kirsten Holst Pertersen, pp. 103–10. Uppsala: Scandinavian Institute of African Studies.

Naim, C. Mohammed. 1971. "Arabic Orthography and Some Non-Semitic Languages." In *Islam and Its Cultural Divergence: Studies in Honor of Gustave E. von Grunebaum,* ed. Girdhari L. Tikku, pp. 113–44. Urbana: University of Illinois Press.

Németh, J. 1962. *Turkish Grammar* (Publications in Near and Middle East Studies, Series B 1), trans. T. Halasi-kun. The Hague: Mouton.

———. 1966. *Turkish Reader for Beginners* (Publications in Near and Middle East Studies, Series B 2), trans. T. Halasi-kun. The Hague: Mouton.

Paper, Herbert H., and Mohammed Ali Jazayery. 1955. *The Writing System of Modern Persian.* Washington, D.C.: American Council of Learned Societies. Repr. Ithaca, N.Y.: Spoken Language Services, 1976.

Penzl, Herbert. 1962. *A Reader of Pashto.* Ann Arbor: University of Michigan Press.

Tajvidi, Mohammed, ed. 1963. *Rubaiyyat of Omar Khayyam,* 2nd ed. Tehran: Amir-Kabir. *The Rubaiyát of Omar Khayyám, Comprising the Metrical Translations by Edward Fitzgerald & E. H. Whinfield and the Prose Version of Justin Huntly McCarthy; with an Appendix Showing the Variations in the First Three Editions of FitzGerald's Rendering,* ed. with an introduction by Jessie B. Rittenhouse. Boston: Little, Brown, 1900.

Wexler, Paul. 1971. Review of *Belorusskie teksty, pisannye arabskim pis'mom, i ix grafiko-orfografičeskaja sistema,* by A. K. Antonovič. *General Linguistics* 11: 43–53.

Yegorova, R. P. 1971. *The Sindhi Language,* trans. E. H. Tsipan. Moscow: Nauka.

Zaxarin, B. A., and D. I. Edelman. 1971. *Jazyk kashmiri* {The Kashmiri language]. Moscow: Nauka.

Part XI: Sociolinguistics
and Scripts

LINGUISTS, SOCIAL ANTHROPOLOGISTS, AND SOCIOLOGISTS have long recognized
that a special relation exists between language and society. Language provides its
speakers with the terminology and the communicative machinery which allow social
life as we know it to exist. Through language, we learn social traditions from the generations that have preceded us. In turn, society provides the mechanisms that permit
the transmission of language; the development of language as a tool and its change
over time are both mediated by social structures. The importance of areas of study labeled "sociology of language" or "language in society" is well established.

Since the 1960s, however, an interdisciplinary field called "sociolinguistics" has
come to the fore, in which contemporary modes of analysis, both of language and of
society, have been brought to bear. The focus has been on the importance of linguistic
diversity: the types of variation in linguistic behavior that are related to the social
identity of the "sender" (in oral communication, the speaker), or the social identity of
the "receiver" (or hearer), or the social situation in which communication occurs. Examples of such phenomena are the differences between the speech of upper-class vs.
lower-class speakers, the differences between polite and non-polite language, and the
linguistic differences between a formal situation (such as that of a business letter) and
a non-formal situation (as in letters among friends). In bilingual or multilingual societies—say Quebec or Belgium or India—the choice may be not between two varieties
of a single language, but between two different languages. In all such cases, linguistic
and social factors are in constant interaction; e.g., in communication between two
strangers, choice of language or style serves to set up a social relationship, but is itself
simultaneously determined by that evolving relationship. If the communication occurs in Montreal or Brussels or Delhi, the choice of language may not only have in-
terpersonal importance, but be politically significant as well.

Pioneering research in sociolinguistics tended to focus in particular on spoken
usage. However, it is clear that variation involving written language is equally important. In some parts of the world, formal and informal speech are conducted in lan-

763

guage variants so different that they are not mutually intelligible; such a situation of "diglossia" exists, for example, in the Arab world, where the language of formal address or of religious worship is relatively uniform over a large geographic area, but is not intelligible in terms of the many regional dialects used for informal conversation. But formal spoken Arabic is closely linked to "Classical" written Arabic—for which the Qur'an, a written document, is the ultimate standard.

The development of sociolinguistics in recent years has been increasingly focused on the social role of written language as compared to spoken language; on the mutual influence of written and spoken language; on the social values associated with internal variation within specific written languages, or with the choice among them; on the relationships of literacy (or its absence) to psychological, cultural, and social phenomena; and on the nature of the confrontation between literate and non-literate societies which has been going on through history and seems likely to continue into the indefinite future. Discussion of all these topics could fill another book at least as large as the present one. In this book, however, we merely offer some case studies dealing specifically with sociolinguistic choices among competing scripts. We hope to make the reader aware that the choices people make when they put language into written form—in effect, the choices represented by the writing systems described elsewhere in this volume—are not purely linguistic ones. They involve questions of social interaction; they are complex; they often involve controversy, and sometimes conflict.

— WILLIAM BRIGHT

Germany: Script and Politics

GERHARD AUGST

While the humanist minuscule script was spreading throughout Europe in the sixteenth century, Fraktur writing was developed in the German-speaking countries, emerging as a modification of Textura, an angular script. From the sixteenth to the twentieth centuries, then, there were two forms of writing in Germany. This Fraktur script, together with the handwritten "Kurrent" script, is typically called "German script"—in contrast to Antiqua, whose printed and handwritten form is also called the Latin script.

There is no difference in orthography between Fraktur and Antiqua; see TABLE 63.1. Lower-case *s* in Fraktur distinguishes the long *s* (ſ) and syllable-final *s* (ꞩ). Another noticeable difference in Fraktur is a number of ligatures (characters containing two letters united, e.g. ſt *st*, ch *ch*, ck *ck*, tz *tz*). A new character, ß, was developed from the ligature combining long *s* ſ with ʒ *z*. This character was also adopted in the Latin script as *ß*.

The cooccurrence of two forms of writing assumed the following distribution: all foreign texts and foreign quotes, and often even foreign words and names, were written in Antiqua. In the Baroque period, German poetic works were published in Fraktur, while technical and scientific publications more often appeared in Antiqua. By the eighteenth and nineteenth centuries, Fraktur had become the normal writing system employed in printing; Antiqua represented a divergent form, being associated with attributes such as "international," "educated," "cosmopolitan," and "scientific."

The writing system of the German language is also characterized by a second peculiarity. The capitalization of proper names, which is found in all European languag-

TABLE 63.1: *Latin Script, Fraktur Script, and Kurrent Script*

A	𝔄	a	𝒜	𝒶	I	ℑ	i	𝒥	𝒾	Q	𝔔	q	𝒬	𝓆	Y	𝔜	ŋ	𝒴	𝓎
B	𝔅	b	ℒ	ℓ	J	ℑ	j	𝒥	𝒿	R	ℜ	r	ℛ	𝓇	Z	ℨ	ʒ	𝒵	𝓏
C	ℭ	c	𝒞	𝒸	K	𝔎	ſ	𝒦	𝓀	S	𝔖	ſs	𝒫	𝓈	Ä	𝔄̈	ä		
D	𝔇	d	𝒟	𝒹	L	𝔏	l	ℒ	ℓ	T	𝔗	t	𝒯	𝓉	Ö	𝔒̈	ö		
E	𝔈	e	ℰ	𝓃	M	𝔐	m	ℳ	𝓂	U	𝔘	u	𝒰	𝓊	Ü	𝔘̈	ü		
F	𝔉	f	ℱ	𝒻	N	𝔑	n	𝒩	𝓃	V	𝔙	v	𝒱	𝓋	ß		ß		
G	𝔊	g	𝒢	ℊ	O	𝔒	o	𝒪	ℴ	W	𝔚	w	𝒲	𝓌	tz		tz		
H	ℌ	h	ℋ	𝒽	P	𝔓	p	𝒫	𝓅	X	𝔛	x	𝒳	𝓍					

765

es, was extended in the sixteenth century to include all nouns. By the eighteenth century this process was complete, and capitalizing nouns became the norm, as exemplified by its codification in grammars such as Gottsched's (1762).

There is no satisfactory explanation of why writing in the German-speaking areas developed in this particular way. The most plausible answer lies in the influence of Protestantism: For instance, the retention of Fraktur also persisted longer in the Scandinavian countries of Norway, Sweden, and Denmark—countries also strongly influenced by Lutheranism and Luther's Bible. This also pertains to the adoption and retention of capitalizing the first letter of nouns, which also experienced a great impetus through Luther's translation of the Bible. Fraktur has noticeably large majuscules, and it is possible—although research has not yet confirmed this—that the practice of capitalizing the first letter of nouns and the retention of this orthographic peculiarity in the German-speaking areas, as well as in the Scandinavian countries, is closely linked to the retention of Fraktur.

Throughout the centuries there have been many attempts on the part of scholars and other leading figures to put an end to these exceptional developments in the German-speaking countries. Fraktur was ultimately discarded, but the capitalization of nouns was retained. Seen in the larger context of German intellectual history, however, the fight for the retention of Fraktur and the capitalization of nouns are both integrally linked with the fight to rid the German language of foreign words. The following aspects are relevant: In the nineteenth century Fraktur became increasingly associated with German national pride. The fight to keep Fraktur and to continue capitalizing nouns, as well as the fight to rid the language of foreign words, were all part of this era. Friedrich Soennecken's *Verein für Altschrift* 'Association for Antiqua Script', an organization created in 1886 and devoted to the abolition of Fraktur, was countered by Adolf Reinecke, who founded the *Allgemeiner Deutscher Schriftverein* 'General German Writing Association' in 1890; its name was changed in 1918 to *Bund für Deutsche Schrift und Sprache* 'Association for German Writing and Language'. Initially, those supporting the retention of Fraktur had the upper hand. In 1911 the German Reichstag voted 75% in favor of this writing.

In Nazi Germany, Fraktur became the graphic symbol of a nationalistic movement, and the number of books printed in Fraktur increased tremendously (42% in 1932, 60% in 1936). In the schools, only German writing (Fraktur and Kurrent) was taught, and rune-like variations of Fraktur were created, having highly emotionalized national-socialist names like *Tannenberg, Potsdam, National*. A radical change occurred in March 1940, however, when Joseph Goebbels ordered that all propaganda material to appear abroad be published in Antiqua "normal" writing. On January 3, 1941, the use of German writing was prohibited nationwide on the tactical but incorrect grounds that it was a *Schwabacher Judenletter* 'Schwabacher Jewish script'. The motive here is clear: Fraktur was illegible in those countries conquered by the Nazis. The emotional fight between Antiqua and Fraktur was thus abruptly halted, and the 450-year period of coexistence came to an end. Since 1945 Fraktur has not been taught in schools. Today the handwritten form (Kurrent) is practically unknown, and printed Fraktur serves as a marked form used for special occasions (advertisements, certificates, etc.). It is now associated with attributes such as "ornamental," "old," "traditional," and "conservative," as well as with German national pride. It is also closely tied to the memory of the Third Reich. Because of this stigma, an organization supporting the reintroduction of Fraktur is not likely to enjoy any success.

The capitalization of nouns was attacked most decisively in the nineteenth century by historical linguists, above all by Jakob Grimm. However, at Orthographic Conferences held at Berlin in 1876 and 1901, pragmatically minded participants were able to push their ideas through. German orthography became official and thus binding in all German states, in spite of the fact that no sweeping reform had been accomplished. Subsequent to these conferences there were again many proposals calling for the abolition of noun capitalization. Such proposals came mainly from printers and teachers, who felt that the rules were too complex. All proposals presented, for example at Stuttgart in 1954 and Wiesbaden in 1959, ultimately failed because of conservative politicians supported by conservative circles in German society. Even the latest proposal (1992), calling for an international study group with representatives from all German-speaking countries, has been rejected by the governments of Germany, Austria, and Switzerland.

SAMPLE TEXT

1. Fraktur: Neben der lateinischen Ausgangsschrift kann man für die
2. Transliteration: Neben der lateinischen Ausgangsschrift kann man für die

Schreibung der deutschen Sprache auch die sogenannte deutsche Schrift
Schreibung der deutschen Sprache auch die sogenannte deutsche Schrift

verwenden. Unter diesen Überbegriff werden die drei Gattungen gebrochener
verwenden. Unter diesen Überbegriff werden die drei Gattungen gebrochener

Druckschrift = Gotisch, Schwabacher und Fraktur = sowie die deutschen spitzen
Druckschrift - Gotisch, Schwabacher und Fraktur - sowie die deutschen spitzen

Schreibschriften zusammengefaßt. Bis in den Zweiten Weltkrieg hinein wurde ein
Schreibschriften zusammengefaßt. Bis in den Zweiten Weltkrieg hinein wurde ein

Großteil des deutschen Schrifttums in diesen Schriften gedruckt, doch sind sie ab
Großteil des deutschen Schrifttums in diesen Schriften gedruckt, doch sind sie ab

1941 auf Befehl Hitlers allmählich von ihrem alten Platz verdrängt und durch die
1941 auf Befehl Hitlers allmählich von ihrem alten Platz verdrängt und durch die

lateinische Schrift ersetzt worden.
lateinische Schrift ersetzt worden.

'Besides the Latin script, what is called "Deutsche Schrift" can also be used to write German. This cover term refers to three types of broken-line printed scripts: Gothic, Schwabacher, and Fraktur, and also includes German angular handwriting. Until World War II, most published material appearing in Germany was printed in these scripts. Beginning in 1941, though, they were gradually displaced, on Hitler's orders, by the Latin script.'

—Poschenrieder and Stang 1993: 91.

Bibliography

Augst, Gerhard. 1983. "Spelling-Reform in Germany and its Implications in German-Speaking Countries: A Historical Overview and Some Recent Trends." *Folia Linguistica* 4: 81–99.

Gottsched, Johann Christoph. 1762. *Vollständigere und neuerläuterte deutsche Sprachkunst.* Leipzig: Breitkopf.

Heiderhoff, Horst. 1971. *Antiqua oder Fraktur? Zur Problemgeschichte eines Streits.* Frankfurt am Main: Polygraph.

Internationaler Arbeitskreis. 1992. *Deutsche Rechtschreibung: Vorschläge zu ihrer Neuregelung.* Tübingen: Narr.

Poschenrieder, Thorwald, and Christian Stang. 1993. *Gutachten zu ausgewählten des Rechtschreib-Erneuerungsentwurfes.* Hannover: Bund für deutsche Schrift.

Reunecke, Hans Otto. 1988. "Zur Geschichte der Schwabacher." *Die deutsche Schrift: Vierteljahrsschrift zur Förderung von Gotisch, Schwabacher, Fraktur* 55: 2–14.

Stiebner, Erhardt, and Leonard Walter. 1980. *Bruckmann's Handbuch der Schrift,* 2nd ed. Munich: Bruckmann.

Strunk, Hiltraud. 1992. *Stuttgarter und Wiesbadener Empfehlungen: Entstehungsgeschichte und politisch-institutionelle Innenansichten gescheiterter Reformversuche von 1950 bis 1965.* Frankfurt: Lang.

Serbo-Croatian:
A Biscriptal Language

LAURIE BETH FELDMAN AND DRAGANA BARAC-CIKOJA

Linguistic conditions in several regions of the former Yugoslavia (Republics of Bosnia-Herzegovina, Montenegro, Croatia, and Serbia) provide an interesting example of two writing systems in concurrent use. Until recently, the Roman and Cyrillic alphabets were used interchangeably and fluently by most skilled readers to write Serbo-Croatian, the official language. In fact, according to the educational policy in effect until the republics separated, all school children were required to demonstrate and maintain proficiency in both alphabets by varying the script in which they wrote classroom exercises. In most cases the alphabets were interchangeable, although they were seldom mixed within one text. Convention dictated that, in a Cyrillic document, names of Western authors were transliterated into Cyrillic, and the original spelling in Roman was optionally added in brackets; however, in Roman documents, names were preserved in their original spelling. Although official policy as laid out by the *Novosadski Dogovor* 'Novi Sad agreement' of 1954 held the scripts to be equivalent (*Pravopis srpskohrvatskog jezika* 1970), some regional differences were evident. In the eastern (Serbian) region, Cyrillic predominated. In the western (Croatian) region, Roman predominated. Alphabetic preference reflected the influence of the Slavic Orthodox church in the east, and of the Catholic Church in the west. Government policy was sensitive to regional differences; thus the order in which the alphabets were taught in the first and second grades of school, as well as the script used for official documents, street signs, and daily publications, varied by region. Reinterpreted in terms of the current political situation, alphabet use in the former Yugoslavia was tied to national identities and religion. With evolving nationalism, the process of institutionalizing regional tendencies has emerged; and as tolerance between ethnic groups deteriorates, the association between alphabet and ethnic group is exaggerated. For example, Cyrillic has been eliminated from schools in Croatia (except in regions where Serbs predominate), and the use of Roman script in Serbia is diminishing.

The Cyrillic script is an adaptation of the Greek uncial alphabet of the ninth century C.E., and the Roman script is a variation of the Latin alphabet. In both cases, the scripts had to be modified to represent sounds not present in the original language (see SECTIONS 59 and 60). The orders of letters in the Cyrillic and Roman alphabets are not identical (see TABLE 64.1) and reflect their respective origins.

In both Croatia and Serbia, the writing system was reformed in the Pan-Slav movement of the nineteenth century so that the mapping of letter to sound is consistent and regular. However, many dialect variations are represented in script, so that spelling as well as pronunciation varies across regions. For example, the word for 'milk' is written *mleko* in the dialects spoken near Belgrade (Serbia), but *mlijeko* in those near Split (Croatia). Accent (rising/falling, long/short) is not captured in writing, even though it can differentiate two semantic interpretations of a letter string. For example, *luka* can mean 'port' with a long rising accent (*lúka*), 'onion' with a short falling accent (*lùka*), or be a personal name with a long falling accent (*Lûka*). This means that Serbo-Croatian is a semi-tonal language (Lehiste 1970). Nevertheless, Serbo-Croatian is frequently cited in the psycholinguistic literature as an example of a "shallow" orthography, one which tends to maintain a consistent and simple mapping between letter and phoneme. But in some respects it is morphophonemic; e.g., the first D in *predsednik* 'president' is unvoiced to /t/.

Although most letters of the Roman and Cyrillic alphabets are unique to one alphabet or the other, a subset is shared by the two alphabets. Of the shared characters, the *common* letters (A, E, J, K, M, O, T) receive the same phonemic interpretation in both alphabets, whereas the *ambiguous* letters (B, C, H, P) represent different phonemes in Cyrillic and in Roman (see TABLE 64.1 and FIGURE 68). Comparisons between isolated words composed exclusively of shared letters (i.e. words with two phonemic interpretations) and words that include at least one non-shared letter (i.e. alphabetically unique words) provide the basis for studies of phonological processing in reading (Feldman and Turvey 1983; Turvey, Feldman, and Lukatela 1984). For example, *CAMOBAP* is bivalent because, by treating it as Cyrillic, it can be read as /samovar/ 'samovar', and by treating it as Roman it is /tsamobap/, which has no

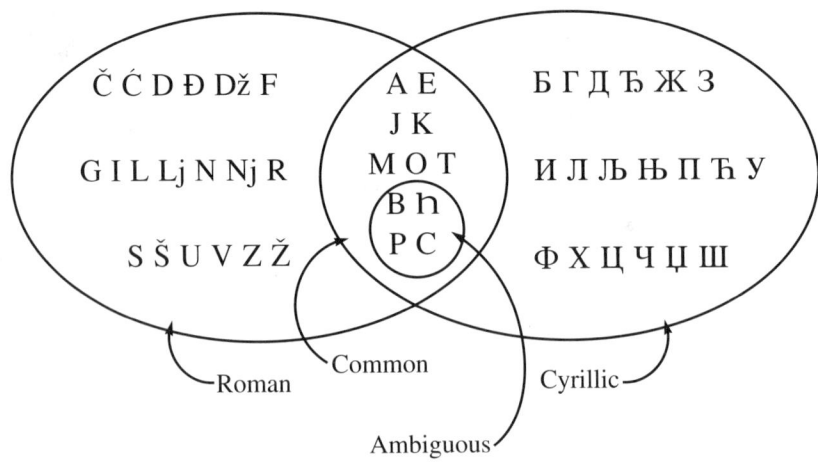

FIGURE 68. Letters unique to the Roman and/or Cyrillic alphabets and letters shared by the two. Shared letters with a single phonemic interpretation are classified as *common*; shared letters with two phonemic interpretations are *ambiguous*.

TABLE 64.1: *Letters Unique to the Roman and/or Cyrillic Alphabets and Letters Shared by the Roman and Cyrillic Alphabets*

Roman letter	Roman phoneme	Cyrillic phoneme	Classification[a]	Cyrillic letter	Cyrillic phoneme	Roman phoneme	Classification[a]
A	a	a	common	А	a	a	common
B	b	v	ambiguous	Б	b		Cyrillic
C	ts	s	ambiguous	В	v	b	ambiguous
Č	tʃ		Roman	Г	g		Cyrillic
Ć	tʃʲ		Roman	Д	d		Cyrillic
D	d		Roman	Ђ	ʤʲ		Cyrillic
Đ	ʤʲ		Roman	E	e	e	common
Dž	ʤ		Roman	Ж	ʒ		Cyrillic
E	e	e	common	З	z		Cyrillic
F	f		Roman	И	i		Cyrillic
G	g		Roman	J	j	j	common
H	h	n	ambiguous	К	k	k	common
I	i	i	common	Л	l		Cyrillic
J	j	j	common	Љ	lj		Cyrillic
K	k	k	common	М	m	m	common
L	l		Roman	Н	n	h	ambiguous
Lj	lj		Roman	Њ	nj		Cyrillic
M	m	m	common	О	o	o	common
N	n		Roman	П	p		Cyrillic
Nj	nj		Roman	Р	r	p	ambiguous
O	o	o	common	С	s	ts	ambiguous
P	p	r	ambiguous	Т	t	t	common
R	r		Roman	Ћ	tʃʲ		Cyrillic
S	s		Roman	У	u		Cyrillic
Š	ʃ		Roman	Ф	f		Cyrillic
T	t		Roman	Х	h		Cyrillic
U	u		Roman	Ц	ts		Cyrillic
V	v		Roman	Ч	tʃ		Cyrillic
Z	z		Roman	Џ	ʤ		Cyrillic
Ž	ʒ		Roman	Ш	ʃ		Cyrillic

a. Shared letters with one phonemic interpretation are *common*; shared letters with two phonemic interpretations are *ambiguous*.

meaning. The form *SAMOVAR* can only be read in Roman as /samovar/ 'samovar'. When words are presented in isolation and readers must either read them aloud or make judgments as to their meaningfulness, readers are slower for bivalent forms than for forms with only one reading. This outcome indicates that phonological complexity influences the reading process. In a typical text, bivalent words are presented in the context of other words that render the form meaningful by specifying alphabet. In experimental reading tasks that limit the availability of alphabet information, however, alphabetic contexts defined by another word or a meaningless letter string do not fully eliminate the effect of phonological bivalence (Lukatela et al. 1989). Alphabetic context has no effect on words that are not ambiguous with repect to pronunciation, however (Feldman and Moskovljević 1987).

The psycholinguistic implications of the experimental results described above are that skilled readers of Serbo-Croatian rely on phonology, and that the alphabet context serves to constrain the mapping between letter and phoneme when it is ambiguous. Sociolinguistically, the maintenance of two scripts reflects more than idiosyncratic linguistic preferences or arbitrary convention; it attests the interaction between two cultures. Whereas the coexistence of two alphabets for Serbo-Croatian reflected the influence of two churches in the past, more recently it has been undermined by a state-mandated policy whose goal is to highlight differences between Serbian and Croatian cultures.

Bibliography

Feldman, Laurie B., and Jasmina Moskovljević. 1987. "Repetition Priming Is Not Purely Episodic in Origin." *Journal of Experimental Psychology: Learning, Memory and Cognition* 13: 573–81.

Feldman, Laurie B., and Michael T. Turvey. 1983. "Word Recognition in Serbo-Croatian Is Phonologically Analytic." *Journal of Experimental Psychology: Human Perception and Performance* 9: 288–98.

Lehiste, Ilse. 1970. *Suprasegmentals*. Cambridge: MIT Press.

Lukatela, Georgije, Laurie B. Feldman, Michael T. Turvey, Claudia Carello, & Leonard Katz. 1989. "Context Effects in Bi-alphabetic Word Perception." *Journal of Memory and Language* 28: 214–36.

Pravopis srpskohrvatskog jezika sa pravopisnim rečnikom [Orthography of the Serbian language with spelling dictionary]. 1960. Novi Sad, Zagreb: Matica Srpska, Matica Hrvatska.

Turvey, Michael T., Laurie B. Feldman, and Georgije Lukatela. 1984. "The Serbo-Croatian Orthography Constrains the Reader to a Phonologically Analytic Strategy." In *Orthographies and Reading*, ed. Leslie Henderson, pp. 81–89. London: Erlbaum.

South Asia: Coexistence of Scripts

COLIN P. MASICA

From the standpoint of writing systems, South Asia presents a striking paradox. On the one hand, with the exception mainly of the relatively recent Islamic component (and even this has been affected), it has been a civilization which has valued the oral above the written word. Its most sacred texts have been transmitted orally, through memorization, rather than by copyists. (One exception is the relatively recent sacred book of the Sikhs, the *Guru Granth Sahib* [early 17th century], the very existence and status of which undoubtedly owes something to Islamic models. However, the adherents of the Jain religion in western India have treasured books and maintained libraries in a tradition quite independent of Islamic influence.) Writing seems to have been more a practical affair of merchants and administrators than one of priests, although the Brahmans, in their capacity as a class not only of priests but also of scholars and literati, were not slow to take advantage of this tool and to play a major role in turning it to higher purposes.

On the other hand, nowhere else in the world do we find such a profusion of scripts—each originally with a distinctive set of numerals besides (although some have now made a concession to the machinery of wider communication, and employ international numerals). To be sure, all except those of Perso-Arabic and Roman derivation stem ultimately from "Northern" or "Southern" variants of ancient Brahmi; but superficially at least they appear far more divergent than Greek, Latin, and Cyrillic. What accounts for this development? A history of political disunity is not the whole story: this has also been true of Europe, even that part of it which uses the Roman alphabet. However, there have been periods when much of the South Asian subcontinent was united under great empires. Nor is sheer creative exuberance the explanation, although it too undoubtedly played a role. Many of these scripts are aesthetically very pleasing—although, again paradoxically, the art of calligraphy is not cultivated (but see SECTION 20), certainly not to the extent it is in Islamic (including South Asian Islamic) or East Asian cultures (cf. King 1974: 30).

This seemingly impractical variety of scripts—which does impose an additional barrier to communication (note the contrast with the situation in China) in an area with many languages, to say nothing of adding to the cost and complication of printing and education—does appear to have a function. That function would seem to be to mark boundaries (and identities) in a region with a solid shape conducive to the existence of dialectal continua, and quite different from that of Europe with its distinctive peninsulas and islands. The crossing of an invisible geographic and often rather arbitrary linguistic boundary is marked by a very visible shift in script. Where this solution has not prevailed, e.g., in the wide swath of northern India known as the "Hindi area," the distinction between language and dialect remains unclear.

In South Asia there is indeed a widespread feeling that a self-respecting language should have its own unique script to confirm its status as a language, a feeling which has led to recent attempts to create special scripts for Munda (see SECTION 56) and Konkani. It is characteristic that foreigners, who are less influenced by this consideration or by indigenous cultural components of linguistic identity, have tended to discern more "languages" in the "Hindi area" than have Indians. William Carey's missionary press in Serampore was barely two decades old when it brought out Bible translations in such languages as Bikaneri, Magahi, Awadhi, Bagheli, Kanauji, Harauti, Kumaoni, Garhwali, and Marwari (Kesavan 1988, 1:426–27). Hence the myth of an India wallowing in a linguistic chaos of "thousands of dialects."

The introduction of printing played a major role in producing the situation we have today. On the one hand—after a last-minute rush in the nineteenth century to give status to local dialects by casting as many exotic typefaces as possible, many of which (mainly in small Himalayan kingdoms) did not endure—it eventually brought a halt to further differentiation (except by deliberate design as noted above), and a standardization to the major scripts, which had often exhibited considerable local and personal variation (Kesavan 1988, 1:176). On the other hand, it froze in place for all time the differentiation that had already taken place, including such minor differentiation as separates the Kannada and Telugu scripts (SECTION 37).

Printing from movable type established itself in different parts of the subcontinent (originally at the behest of missionaries and colonial administrators) at widely different times: as early as 1556 in Goa, thence elsewhere in the Peninsula, and more than two hundred years later in Calcutta. Tamil was the first Indian script to be printed (1579); Sinhala type was cast in the 1720s; Bengali type was first used in 1778 (for Nathaniel B. Halhed's *Grammar*); Nagari type was first used in India in 1796 (for John B. Gilchrist's *Grammar*, published in Calcutta). Only with the establishment of Fort William College in 1800 did the printing revolution begin to make inroads into the remainder of the subcontinent; it gained momentum with the repeal of the Press Act in 1835, allowing natives of India to own presses, and was in full swing by mid-century, along with its concomitant shaking-out process. Gujarati opted to discard the Nagari script employed up to that point, in favor of its present distinctive script (SECTION 32); but Marathi opted for Nagari (SECTION 31) over the distinctive regional Modi, still used for private letter-writing by some.

Nagari had an uphill battle for acceptance even in its own ostensible heartland—northern India, where the Perso-Arabic script (SECTION 62) held sway with official support through the nineteenth century, except in remote Kumaon-Garhwal and parts of present-day Madhya Pradesh—and the cursive Kaithi continued to be a potent rival (Grierson 1899). But the Nagari script has continued to gain adherents in this century:

it has replaced traditional scripts of both Maithili (a language of northern Bihar and adjoining parts of Nepal) and Newari (a major Tibeto-Burman language in Nepal). However, this process has probably gone about as far as it is going to in the foreseeable future; the logical and practical extension of Nagari to all South Asian languages does not appear to be in the offing, although this has had its advocates among a nationalist elite. (The idea of adopting the Roman script, advocated by a few European officials and scholars and even some Indians, e.g. S. K. Chatterjee, never got off the ground.) Resistance to Nagari is much stronger in Bengal and in South India, where old traditions of distinctive writing (and printing) are entrenched. It might also reasonably be claimed that the various scripts have evolved to suit the languages for which they are employed. Even in Punjab, where the language is closely allied to Hindi—and partly for that very reason (demarcation again)—Nagari is unlikely to replace the Gurmukhi script. Where it has prevailed, as in Nepal and Maharashtra, local identity is safeguarded by an international boundary in the former case, and by distance in the latter, as well as by distinctive letters and/or spelling conventions.

It is with Hindi and Urdu that script plays the ultimate differentiating role. Although some registers of each language are strongly differentiated by choice of vocabulary also, it is ultimately the choice of the Devanagari or the Perso-Arabic script that is the most important factor in identifying the language as "Hindi" or "Urdu" (King 1974: 121–22; Shackle and Snell 1990).

The traditional tools of writing—the pen in the north and the stylus in the south—influenced the original forms of South Asian scripts, leading to rounded forms where the latter was used (including Orissa, whose script is actually akin to Bengali and not to southern scripts, despite superficial resemblances to the latter; SECTION 35). Similarly, modern tools of writing subsequent to the printing press—the typewriter and the word processor in particular—have begun to influence the form of South Asian scripts. For example, about twenty years ago, Malayalam, the South Asian language with the highest percentage of literacy, replaced, at least in print, complicated old ligatures of consonant + long and short *u*, which varied from consonant to consonant and sorely taxed the ingenuity of keyboard designers (although they were no problem for manual typesetters, and even a convenience for handwriting), with a more linear and uniform representation of these vowels, after the consonant and separate from it (SECTION 38).

Perso-Arabic script, especially in its favored *nasta'līq* form, has presented special difficulty for typing and typesetting. Although word processing programs have recently been worked out, this has meant that Urdu books and newspapers, representing a tradition more oriented toward the written word, ironically continued to be lithographed from handwritten text long after this process (itself invented only in the 1790s) was abandoned for Brahmi-based scripts.

Large portions of the population of South Asia, however, are not concerned with these matters: they have, as it were, leapt directly from a preliterate to a postliterate stage without passing through a literate stage in between—that is, they have gone from a culture rich in oral literature and performance to a culture of films, videotapes, and audiocassettes. Vendors and renters of these are ubiquitous in South Asia as well as in South Asian communities abroad; but booksellers in South Asian languages (as contrasted with those catering to the English-reading minority) are—except in certain language areas—few, especially in the "Hindi area," despite a prodigious output of published titles and official encouragement. Visitors even to remote Hunza in Pakistan report that local tape libraries have sprung up, catering to Burushaski connoisseurs of their own oral literature—a more congenial vehicle for its dissemination and enjoyment, apparently, than writing it down and then deciphering it from that alien medium would be. In any case, although the reading public is very large in absolute terms, it is the film, audiocassette, and television, rather than the book, that are becoming the premier vehicles of mass cultural consumption today. To be sure, South Asia may not be unique in this respect. On a more traditional note, poetry—essentially an oral art—continues to maintain a popular appeal in South Asia that is probably unparalleled elsewhere. Meanwhile, printing has obviously facilitated the establishment of an interesting new "tradition," namely the ritual reading, particularly by women, of devotional texts.

Bibliography

Blumhardt, James Fuller. 1892. *Catalogue of Marathi and Gujarati Printed Books in the Library of the British Museum.* London: Quaritch.

Grant, Sir Alexander. 1867–69. *Catalogue of Native Publications in the Bombay Presidency up to 31st December 1864.* Bombay: Education Society's Press, Byculla.

Grierson, George A. 1899. *A Handbook to the Kaithi Character.* Calcutta: Thacker, Spink.

Kesavan, B. S. 1988. *History of Printing and Publishing in India: a Story of Cultural Re-awakening,* vol. 1: *South Indian Origins of Printing and Its Efflorescence in Bengal;* vol. 2, *Origin of Printing and Publishing in Karnataka, Andhra, and Kerala.* New Delhi: National Book Trust, India.

King, Christopher Rolland. 1974. "The Nagari Pracharini Sabha of Benares, 1893–1914: A Study in the Social and Political History of the Hindi Language." Ph.D. dissertation, University of Wisconsin, Madison.

Priolkar, Anand Kukba. 1958. *The Printing Press in India: Its Beginning and Early Development,* 3 vols. Bombay: Marathi Samshodhana Mandala.

Shackle, Christopher, and Rupert Snell. 1990. *Hindi and Urdu since 1800: A Common Reader.* London: University of London, School of Oriental and African Studies.

Singh, Arvind Kumar. 1991. *Development of the Nagari script.* Delhi: Parimal.

Christian Missionary Activities

ALLAN GLEASON

Since 1500, Christian missionaries—Catholic, Protestant, and Orthodox—have established writing systems for more than a thousand languages; exact figures are not available. Perhaps two thirds of these date from the twentieth century and another quarter from the nineteenth. Activity is on-going. By "established" is here meant that literature was published and circulated, and at least some part of the community became literate enough to use it for at least some time.

The quality has been very uneven. Some are poor or worse; some from early in the nineteenth century are very good, even when judged in the light of phonologic ideas they anticipated by a century or more. Some, perhaps with minor revision from time to time, have persisted; others were soon abandoned or replaced. Success or failure depends on many factors beyond linguistic adequacy.

The earliest of these missionaries simply applied Spanish conventions as best they could to the Amerindian languages they were recording. They seem to have been unable or extremely reluctant to depart very far, though; for example, some wrote *h* (silent in Spanish) for *ʔ*; others did not take even that liberty. Some early grammars comment to the effect that *ll* is to be pronounced as in Latin, not as in Spanish. That same pattern has been repeated by missionaries of other backgrounds. However, there seems to be increasing freedom by the nineteenth century. Some missionaries were able to use that freedom constructively; some could not.

Though we have plentiful records of what was produced, we have little of why or how. However Schütz (1985: 18–54) has pieced together a fairly detailed and very revealing account of the course of development in Fijian (brought to near final form in 1839). This is one of the good and successful ones, coming about as near as orthographies ever do to being phonemic, economical, and practical.

It would seem that productive innovations were generally the result of some combination of high competence through long immersion in the language and culture, some special language aptitude, sensitivity to native reactions as preliminary versions were taught, an occasional fortunate accident, and increasing understanding of the nature of language.

Academic interest in non-European languages grew steadily through the nineteenth century. Much of the data came from missionary grammars and dictionaries. In turn many missionaries followed with interest some of the new discoveries. Similarly, some missionaries followed the development of phonetics—largely, but not exclusively, as an aid to language learning for new missionaries. These academic inputs did not, before the World Wars, provide much in the way of specific techniques for language analysis or orthography design; but combined with information running through the missionary networks, they did markedly broaden views of language.

Most of the systems were modifications of existing scripts. In South and Southeast Asia, and in a few other areas, it was usually, but not always, an indigenous script: Devanagari, Burmese, Thai, Amharic, etc. In areas with Muslim dominant populations, it was often the Arabic script. Across northern Asia it was Cyrillic (and into America for the Aleut language). Elsewhere it was usually the Latin alphabet, sometimes with radical reassignment of letters, modification of some letter shapes, addition of letters, or diacritics. For samples of writing systems as used in Bible translations, see Nida 1972; cf. also Smalley 1976.

Usually the basis from which modification started is apparent. So, for example, in Kâte (developed in pre–World War I German New Guinea), *w* is used for [v], *j* for the palatal semivowel, and *z* for [ts], but *c* is reassigned for [?] and *q* for [kp]; one diacritic is used for a low back vowel *â* (particularly appropriate because *a* and *â* interchange in various contexts); and three new letters are added. The result is quite satisfactory orthography.

English missionaries came to work very generally on the slogan "Consonants as in English; vowels as in Italian." Many of them seem to have been aware of, and influenced by, the dictum that an ideal orthography would allocate one letter for each sound and one sound for each letter. Trivial as these things may seem, they apparently opened up new possibilities.

Attempts to establish uniform conventions in British and French Africa (and there were several) were largely unsuccessful, even sometimes for the same language. Partly this was because of different backgrounds for the missionaries, but also (and perhaps more importantly) as response to government preferences or dictates.

There seem to be only three successful attempts to create fundamentally new systems, though all three were subsequently adapted to neighboring languages. The first is the Evans syllabary, described in SECTION 55. It has been reported that within ten years the community was essentially 100% literate, so that this is not just one of the most innovative of the missionary-designed systems, but also one of the most successful. For the Pollard and Fraser scripts, see SECTION 52. Pollard (first publication 1907), which was developed for a Miao (Hmong) language in Southwest China, is apparently still in use, but is being supplanted by a more recently designed Latin-based system. The Fraser script was developed about 1915 for a dialect of Lisu in the Burma-Thailand-China border area.

When a language has had a traditional writing system, that has usually been used by missionaries and the churches. In some instances, missionary presses cut the first types, thus helping to establish the modern form of a script. In India, printing in the native scripts was started when Lutherans sent out a printer and three typecasters.

The last half of the twentieth century has seen significant changes: most missionaries involved in language work now have some background in linguistics. Often this is one or two summers of intensive field-oriented training, often provided by the Summer Institute of Linguistics at several sites across the world. Sometimes it is university work leading to an M.A. or Ph.D. degree. Generally those expecting to work in "new" languages, and those expecting to do pioneer translation work—which includes almost all that will have any part in writing system development—get at least enough to profoundly affect their attitudes and instill a willingness to seek help when needed.

The Bible Societies through the nineteenth century were passively involved as publishers of translations prepared by others. In the twentieth they have moved into research, publication of various helps, and operations on the field where translation is occurring. The latter is through a corps of highly trained consultants who have access to, among other things, a large mass of research and practical experience on orthographic problems. Landmarks in this are Nida 1947, with a chapter on orthography (pp. 100–29), and Smalley 1964.

From the beginning missionaries worked with native helpers; then the helpers became colleagues. Today, in all language work, the missionary is more likely to be a consultant to a committee of native speakers. Missionaries are no longer exclusively westerners: Asians are working in Africa, and Latin Americans in the Pacific. That is not wholly new; the first publication of the British and Foreign Bible Society, in 1804, was the Gospel of John in Mohawk translated by a Cherokee!

In 1550, Charles V decreed that all work with natives of Mexico should be in Spanish. The religious orders successfully lobbied for repeal. That pattern has persisted through all the colonial empires and the independent states that have succeeded them (cf. Heath 1972). Where missions are allowed, they are almostly always circumscribed, pariculary in language matters. But increasingly, governments have been specifying not only what language might be used by churches and missions, but many details, including how they should be written.

The design of writing systems, today, is often a process involving missionaries, academic linguists, and government bureaucrats. The latter may have (and take) good technical advice, or they may operate solely on the basis of political expediency. In either case, government has the last word. Even when the team seems to be working on its own, very tight constraints are often imposed by government or by influential elements in the ambient society. In this sort of situation, it is becoming less and less easy to identify writing systems created by missionaries; but the input from church workers—local people or missionary consultants—may still be significant. In the near future, we may expect a dozen or so new writing systems each year in which church workers have made a major contribution.

Bibliography

Heath, Shirley Brice. 1972. *Telling Tongues: Language Policy in Mexico, Colony to Nation.* New York: Teachers College.

Nida, Eugene A. 1947. *Bible Translating: An Analysis of Principles and Procedures with Special Reference to Aboriginal Languages.* New York: American Bible Society.

Nida, Eugene A., ed. 1972. *The Book of a Thousand Tongues,* rev. ed. London: United Bible Societies.

Schütz, Albert J. 1985. *The Fijian Language.* Honolulu: University of Hawaii Press.

Smalley, William A., ed. 1964. *Orthography Studies: Articles on New Writing Systems.* London: United Bible Societies.

———, ed. 1976. *Phonemes and Orthography: Language Plann ing in Ten Minority Languages of Thailand* (Pacific Linguistics, C-43). Canberra: Australian National University.

Wonderly, William L., and Eugene A. Nida. 1964. "Linguistics and Christian Missions." *Anthropological Linguistics* 5 (1): 104–44.

Script Reform in and after the
Soviet Union

BERNARD COMRIE

In the early 1980s, some sixty languages were officially used, to differing degrees, as written languages in the Soviet Union. In some cases, these written languages directly continued pre-Soviet written traditions; in others they resulted from policies initiated in the 1920s and 1930s to spread native-language literacy. The loosening of internal controls from the 1980s meant that some other languages acquired limited status as written languages, e.g. for the recording of folkloric material, using either Cyrillic or Roman script. Since the breakup of the Soviet Union, responsibility for script policy has devolved on the individual, newly independent states.

Script replacement

Script usage for most of the official written languages of the Soviet Union is given in TABLE 67.1. Some languages used the same script throughout the life of the Soviet Union and continue to do so today.

Most of the other written languages of the former Soviet Union used Roman script from the late 1920s or early 1930s (occasionally earlier), replacing this with Cyrillic script in the late 1930s or early 1940s (occasionally later). In some cases Roman script was the first script used for the language; in others, an earlier script was replaced—most commonly Arabic, but also vertical Mongolian, and even Cyrillic. The shift from Roman to Cyrillic script followed the ideological shift from the earlier commitment to world revolution, with Roman script as a symbol of internationalism, to the later commitment to socialism in one country, with Cyrillic script as a symbol of Sovietness. The structural argument advanced by advocates of Cyrillic, that the Cyrillic alphabet contains more letters than the Roman alphabet, is spurious: some of the letters (e.g. yotated vowels) are usually redundant outside Slavic, while the existence of special letters like ш, ж, ч for [ʃ], [ʒ], [t͡ʃ] is balanced by the absence of letters

ACKNOWLEDGMENTS: I am grateful for information provided by Ju. D. Dešeriev, Andrej Kibrik, Tooru Hayasi, Lars Johanson, John Perry, and Aleksandra Steinbergs. Remaining errors are my own responsibility. Work on this article was conducted while I was a Visiting Professor at the Institute for the Study of Languages and Cultures of Asia and Africa, Tokyo University of Foreign Studies.

TABLE 67.1: *Script Use for Selected Languages in the Former USSR*

Languages with No Change of Script

    Cyrillic script:

        Russian, Belorussian (Belarusian), Ukrainian; Mari (Cheremis), Mordvin (Erzya, Moksha), Udmurt (Votyak); Chuvash, Gagauz[a]

    Roman script:

        Latvian, Lithuanian; Estonian

    Armenian script:

        Armenian

    Georgian script:

        Georgian

    Hebrew script:

        Yiddish

Languages with Roman, then Cyrillic Script

        Khanty (Ostyak), Mansi (Vogul), Nenets (Yurak Samoyed); Tuvan, Yakut (Sakha); Even (Lamut), Evenki (Tungus), Nanay (Gold); Abaza;[b] Tabasaran;[b] Chukchee; Eskimo (Siberian Yupik)

Languages with Arabic, then Roman, then Cyrillic Script[c]

        Tajik; Azeri (Azerbaijani), Bashkir, Crimean Tatar, Karachay–Balkar, Karakalpak, Kazakh, Kirghiz, Kumyk, Nogay, Tatar (Volga Tatar, Kazan Tatar), Turkmen, Uyghur, Uzbek; Adyghe (West Circassian), Kabardian (East Circassian); Avar, Chechen, Ingush, Dargwa, Lak, Lezgian; Dunganese (Hui)

Languages with Cyrillic, then Roman, then Cyrillic Script

        Ossetic (in Russia); Komi; Altay, Khakas, Shor

Languages with Vertical Mongolian, then Roman, then Cyrillic Script

        Buryat, Kalmyk (Oirat)

Special Cases (scripts in chronological order)

    Abkhaz:

        Cyrillic, Roman, Georgian, Cyrillic

    Kurdish (in Armenia):

        Armenian, Roman, Cyrillic

    Moldavian (Moldovan):

        as language distinct from Rumanian, Cyrillic only

    Ossetic (in Georgia):

        Cyrillic, Roman, Georgian, Cyrillic

---

a. Gagauz only from 1957.

b. Abaza and Tabasaran were sporadically written in Arabic script.

c. Some of these languages are written in Arabic script outside the former Soviet Union.

for [h], [d͡ʒ], [q], and [w]. One interesting aspect of the shift to Cyrillic was the decision, valid for most languages, that loanwords from Russian should be written exactly as in Russian.

Finally, three languages went through a period of using a different script: Abkhaz and (in Georgia) Ossetic used Georgian script from the late 1930s to the mid 1950s; in Armenia, Kurdish used Armenian script in the 1920s.

Intra-script reform

Major orthographic reforms not involving script changes were (a) an experiment undertaken in the 1920s, with languages then using Arabic script, of using only independent forms of Arabic letters, rather than distinct independent, initial, medial, and final forms; and (b) an attempt during the period of Roman script to unify the alphabets of the Soviet Union (the "New Alphabet"), with partial success in, for instance, the Unified Turkic Alphabet introduced from the late 1920s, replacing alphabets idiosyncratic to individual Turkic languages. (By contrast, the Cyrillic orthographies introduced from the 1930s often involve different solutions to the same phonetic problem in different languages; SECTION 60.) In addition, various changes took place in the orthographic systems of languages of the Soviet Union to improve the fit between spelling and pronunciation. Russian itself gave a lead by reforming its writing system in 1918, removing some historically motivated spellings. Soviet Armenian orthography was simplified by abolishing some etymological spellings. In Yiddish as used in the Soviet Union, the spelling of words of Hebrew–Aramaic origin was modified to fit the pronunciation. The Latvian alphabet was modified by dropping the letter *ŗ* (in favor of *r*) and the digraph *ch* (in favor of *h*), reflecting the merger for some (not all) speakers of the oppositions [r], [rʲ] and [x], [ɦ]. Other changes have less obvious motivation, such as the replacement of ҝ and ҹ by к and ч, for [gʲ] and [d͡ʒ] respectively, in Azeri in 1958, although the same reform also introduced j as a uniform solution to the writing of [j].

Post-Soviet developments

Developments in the late Soviet and immediate post-Soviet period can be characterized in terms of tension between, on the one hand, wanting to reverse features that are viewed as obviously Soviet (especially where these contradict usage outside the former Soviet Union, or traditions that are still valued), and, on the other hand, the feeling that there has already been enough tampering with script and orthography, making this at least a lower priority than other pressing social and economic problems. Major changes and proposed changes include the following.

In Moldova, the notion of a language separate from Rumanian, and therefore the use of Cyrillic rather than Roman script, were abandoned in 1989. In Tajikistan, a pre-independence language law of 1989 specifies that Arabic script is to be promoted, while a post-independence language law of 1992 promises to revive and teach Arabic script in all educational institutions and to revert to Arabic script officially in the near future; at present both Cyrillic and Arabic scripts are in use. The newly independent

Turkic-speaking republics (Azerbaijan, Kazakhstan, Kyrgyzstan, Turkmenistan, Uzbekistan) are considering adopting Roman script, in the form of the Ortak Türk Alfabesi 'Common Turkic Alphabet', i.e. the Turkish alphabet with the addition of five letters for use in those languages that need them: *ä* [æ] (though in Azeri ə is used), *x* [x], *q* [q] (but in Azeri [g], while [gʲ] is *g*), *ñ* [ŋ], and *w* [w] (Final Communiqué; *MTAS*). This alphabet is currently in use, alongside Cyrillic script, for Azeri in Azerbaijan. Latin script is also being introduced for Chechen in Chechnya. As an example of less far-reaching consideration, in Latvia controversy has arisen over whether the letter *ŗ*, and perhaps even the digraph *ch*, should be reintroduced, while in Ukraine the separate letter ґ has been reintroduced to represent [g] in onomatopoeia and loanwords. In the early 1990s, many such situations are very fluid.

Bibliography

Bokarev, E. A., & Ju. D. Dešeriev. 1959. *Mladopis'mennye jazyki narodov SSSR* [New written languages of the peoples of the USSR]. Moscow & Leningrad: Izdatel'stvo Akademii Nauk SSSR.

Comrie, Bernard. 1981. *Languages of the Soviet Union.* Cambridge: Cambridge University Press.

Fierman, William. 1991. *Language Planning and National Development: The Uzbek Experience.* Berlin: Mouton de Gruyter.

Final Communiqué, Conference on Alphabet and Spelling, Ankara, 8–10 March 1993.

MTAS 1992. = *Milletlerarası Türk Alfabeleri Sempozyumu 18–20 Kasım 1991* [International symposium on Turkic alphabets 18–20 November 1991] (Marmara Üniversitesi Yayınları, 509, Türkiyat Araştırmaları, 1.) Istanbul: Marmara University.

Perry, John. FORTHCOMING. "From Persian to Tajik to Persian: Culture, Politics and Law Reshape a Central Asian Language." In *NSL-8: Linguistic Studies in the Non-Slavic Languages of the Commonwealth of Independent States and the Baltic Republics,* ed. Howard I. Aronson. Chicago: Chicago Linguistic Society.

Vinogradov, V. V., ed. 1966–68. *Jazyki narodov SSSR* [Languages of the peoples of the USSR], 5 vols. Moscow & Leningrad: Nauka.

Wurm, Stefan. 1954. *Turkic Peoples of the U.S.S.R.: Their Historical Background, Their Languages and the Development of Soviet Linguistic Policy.* London: Central Asian Studies Centre.

Part XII: Secondary Notation Systems

IN THIS PART are grouped uses and adaptations of the Roman alphabet whose purposes are other than strictly the recording of language: the alphabet as a vehicle of literacy, as an ordering tool, as a mnemonic device; its embodiment other than on a conventional page. In legal and commercial contexts, scripts have been devised—usually alphabet-based—that could be written at the speed of speech, nearly. Linguists need a medium for recording the phonetic detail of any language without a prism of phonological analysis, and phonetic notation has often (though not always) been alphabet-based. Lastly, language is not the only communicative system that can be notated: priority goes to numerical notation systems. As Western art music developed, so did a complicated, partly iconic, but universally employed notation system. Emerging out of the need to record dance movement, systems have been devised that now exhibit sufficient rigidity to write the emic units of American Sign language, and sufficient flexibility to record both dance and gesture language. These topics occupy the sidelines of the pageant of writing, but sometimes the sidelines are the best place to look for insight into the principal action.

— PETER T. DANIELS

785

The Alphabet as a Technology

M. O'CONNOR

Writing systems are used to convey and preserve language across time and space, and this primary function of writing systems has been the principal subject of this volume. There are two related problems to be addressed. First, how do people learn to write, i.e., how do they master the system so that they can use it? Second, how do people use elements of writing systems to order the world around them, i.e., how are writing systems adapted to purposes other than conveying and preserving language? (On script as a native-speaker analysis of a language, see O'Connor 1983.) These two problems are intertwined in various ways, most importantly in the matter of the order of the alphabet.

Most people think of the alphabet as a writing device in terms of the order in which they learned it; and they look at other orders of the alphabet, e.g. the order in which the letters of the Western European alphabets are set out on typewriter keyboards, as deviant or weird. In fact, there is nothing that intrinsically binds an alphabet to the conventional order in which its elements are learned. Every alphabet has an order and has had nearly since the beginning of alphabetic writing, but the alphabet and its order are distinct phenomena. The alphabetic order is a crucial element in attaining literacy; the fact that it is so often taken for granted does not gainsay its importance.

How do people learn how to write?

Learning to write is a demanding process that involves numerous aids. Chief among these is a large class of devices that give memorable shape to the units or characters of the writing system. The major types of writing system use a variety of such devices.

If the writing system is logosyllabic (e.g. Chinese or Mesopotamian cuneiform), the mnemonic devices include both semantic (or broadly referential) and graphic patterns across groups of characters, as well as schemes for counting the strokes or wedges and for visualizing the writing of their characters, i.e. their growth (by giving, say, "left" priority over "right," "top" priority over "bottom," a longer containing line priority over shorter contained groups of lines, etc.). Such devices, intended to aid the learning of the writing system, do not aim at providing a scientific breakdown of its parts. These pedagogic devices work—Chinese people learn to write Chinese characters, as do Japanese and other East Asians (according to a variety of schemes), and ancient Mesopotamian scribes learned the cuneiform system. Such devices are not used exclusively for learning the writing systems; they also form the basis of dictionaries and specialized word lists as well as other indexing and arranging schemes.

If a writing system is syllabographic (or includes a syllabographic component, as Japanese does), the devices involved in learning the system are apt to be simpler and more reliable, although because the type of system itself is simpler, some syllabographic systems have no standard order. The representations may be graphic, as are the grids conventionally used by linguists to exemplify syllabic systems. Non-graphic representations can also come into play. The Ethiopic syllabographic abugida, for example (SECTION 51), has a fixed order of consonants and another of vowels; both these series are susceptible of memorization. The system of writing can be learned easily because it can be learned in part aurally. The Japanese syllabary (SECTION 16) was traditionally taught through the "Iroha uta," a short piece of rhythmic prose that uses all but one of the syllabographs; the graphic features of the kana play little part in this device (FIGURE 34 on page 250; Uwano 1983). The "Iroha" order is used in numbering schemes e.g. of front matter in books; such use is also familiar to alphabetic readers.

The types of writing system in which each sign, i.e. each written unit, in principle represents a simple linguistic segment—namely, the abjad and the alphabet—present a curious profile when we seek to examine the device (or devices) by which they are learned. The device and the system itself tend to merge in the eyes and ears of an alphabetic culture. Those raised on the alphabet tend to conceive of the writing system as fused with the device by which we learn the system, i.e. the alphabetic order (Faber 1992, Daniels 1992). The fixed order of the alphabet is a metalinguistic fact, not involved in the structure of the sound–symbol mapping. This fusion in understanding is not limited to naive users of the alphabet; it has also affected historians of writing, who tend to regard the invention of the alphabet as coincident with the invention of the alphabetic order. Even if the issues were as simple as they are sometimes taken to be, this view is historically groundless: the earliest form of the ancestor of the alphabet (SECTION 5) is associated with two different alphabetic orders.

The order of the alphabet

The orders of the various alphabets of the European languages are derived from what we can call the Levantine order; *the Levant* is a general term for the eastern end of the Mediterranean Sea, the region in which segmental writing arose. This is the order used, with variations, for the Hebrew abjad and its close relatives and for the alphabets of Greek (from which Cyrillic orders derive) and Latin (from which Western European alphabet orders derive). Some of the sources for the various forms of this order are epigraphic, and some are literary.

Abecedaries or ABC texts are found in the earliest major body of segmental writing; the texts from late second millennium Ugarit in northern Syria use the wedge (cu-

TABLE 68.1: *Order of the Reduced Levantine Abjad*

ʾ	b	g	d	h	w	z	ḥ	ṭ	y	k	l	m	n	s	ʿ	p	ṣ	q	r	š	t
1	2	3	4	5	6	7	8	9	10	11	12	13	14	15	16	17	18	19	20	21	22

TABLE 68.2: *Ancestral and Modern Orders of the English Alphabet*

Hebrew		English	
ʾ	1	a	1
b	2	b	2
g	3	c	3
d	4	d	4
h	5	e	5
		f	6
w	6		
		g	7
		h	8
z	7		
ḥ	8		
ṭ	9		
y	10	i	9
		j	10
k	11	k	11
l	12	l	12
m	13	m	13
n	14	n	14
s	15		
ʿ	16	o	15
p	17	p	16
ṣ	18		
q	19	q	17
r	20	r	18
ś/š	21	s	19
t	22	t	20
		u	21
		v	22
		w	23
		x	24
		y	25
		z	26

neiform) abjad (Bordreuil 1982). The order of the Phoenician–Hebrew linear abjad, which is known from abecedaries and from acrostic poems (in which the first lines form an alphabet) in the Hebrew Bible (Christian Old Testament), is shown in TABLE 68.1.

There are 22 letters in the abjad. Letter #21 had two values in one major dialect of ancient Hebrew; the graphic differentiation between these two values is preserved by making letter #21 two different characters (SECTION 46), and 𝒲 *ś* is conventionally ordered before 𝒲 *š*. Older, Late Bronze Age forms of the abjad had 27 units or 30 units (TABLE 5.2 on page 92; Kochavi 1977, Demsky 1977). The 22-unit abjad was the source of the Phoenician–Hebrew script and also the oldest Aramaic abjad.

Other forms of the Levantine alphabet can be derived from the 22-letter Phoenician–Hebrew form. Two general conditions are important. First, the Semitic gutturals (ʾ, *h*, *ḥ*, ʿ) are adapted for use as vowel signs (*a*, *e*, Greek *ē*, *o*), as is the consonant *y* (*i*) (SECTION 21). Second, "extra" letters are "added," usually at the end (Ryckmans 1987: 316). For the sake of simplicity, we can take the English alphabet as typical (TABLE 68.2).

Some of the differences can be explained briefly. English letters #9 and #10 were a single letter in Latin and have been separated only since the European invention of printing, with #9 used as a vowel and #10 as a consonant; English letter #25 was derived from *j* at about the same time, and German, for example, uses the *j* the way English uses *y*. (English letters #21 and #22 are a similarly late split; in older English spelling *i* and *j*, and *u* and *v* interchange.) Hebrew letter #3 is similar in sound to English letter #3—the split between *c* and *g* was introduced in Latin; *g* was inserted later in the order (SECTION 23). The sibilants, sounds of hissing and hushing (English letters #19, 26), form a confusing group, and it would be difficult to trace their wanderings through the alphabet.

TABLE 68.3: *Order of the South Semitic Abjad*

h	l	ḥ	m	q	w	š	r	b	t	s¹	k	n	ḫ	s³	p	ʾ	ʿ	ḍ	g	d	ġ	ṭ	z	ḏ	y	ṯ	ṣ	ẓ
1	2	3	4	5	6	7	8	9	10	11	12	13	14	15	16	17	18	19	20	21	22	23	24	25	26	27	28	29

Until recently, the alphabetic order attested in several South Semitic forms (Old South Arabian, Ethiopian) was thought to be a late phenomenon, one unrelated to the early history of the alphabet (Daniels 1991). It has recently been shown that a Late Bronze Age text has a form of the South Semitic order (TABLE 68.3), which is thus more or less as old as the Levantine order (Lundin 1987; Puech 1986, 1991; Ryckmans 1985). One important byproduct of distinguishing the alphabet from the alphabetic order is that it allows us to recognize the Levantine order and the South Semitic order, which must be independent of each other, as being of comparable antiquity (Ryckmans 1985: 358, 1987: 324). The Ethiopians also use a form of the Phoenician–Hebrew order (called *abugida*) for indexing, counting, and arranging purposes (SECTION 51).

It would seem that graphic similarities, such as were mentioned above in connection with learning logographic systems, would be a logical way to learn an alphabet as well. The major alphabetic order used in Arabic (SECTION 50) is based on a mixture of the standard Levantine order and such graphic similarities. Like the Ethiopians, Arabs use a form of the Phoenician–Hebrew order (called *abjad*) for outlines, counting, etc.

Letter names

How does the alphabetic order work as a mnemonic device? Most significantly, it works by brevity: a series of 22, 25, 27, or 30 words or syllables is easily learned. Remarkably enough, it seems that the linguistic character of the words or syllables themselves is of little importance.

There are two major sets of letter names associated with the earliest alphabetic order: the names in the Jewish tradition (first attested in the fourth century C.E.), some of which are Hebrew words or similar to Hebrew words; and the names in the Greek and Arabic tradition, which are mostly derived from the Jewish names. It is sometimes said that the letter names in Phoenician, Hebrew, and related languages are transparent, i.e., that they are ordinary common nouns (e.g. Millard 1985: 41*). This is true in some cases, but other names are obscure. The Greeks and Arabs took over for the most part the Northwest Semitic names; because in Greek and Arabic these were meaningless, they were simplified. The Romans, evidently unwilling to continue with such names, created a new and simpler set, similar to those we use in English (Gordon 1973). In any language, however, letter names are a type of name, and all names have a certain degree of autonomy from ordinary language usage, the degree of their comprehensibility notwithstanding (Swiggers 1986).

Unlike Greek and Arabic, most languages that have taken over the alphabet have not adopted the letter names but have elaborated their own, rather uniform system. The Latin names [a:], [be:], [ke:], [de:], etc. (which have come into English as [e:j], [bi:j], [si:j], [di:j]), are good for rhyming but otherwise without meaning. The Latin names presumably replaced the Greek ones because the Greek ones had no great mnemonic value.

Some letter names are adjectival. In Greek we find *ò mikrón* 'short (lit. little) o' distinguished from *ō méga* 'long (lit. big) o'; and *è psilón* 'naked e', distinguished from *êta*; there is no partner for *u psilón* 'naked u'. Adjectival letter names in modern languages are not perceived as notably different from other letter names: English *w* (*double u*) and French *y* (*i grec* 'Greek i') fit right in the flow of the other names.

Elements of writing systems used for various purposes

A variety of uses for parts of writing systems is found in the speech and daily life of literate peoples. In China, a Phillips-head screwdriver is called a 'number 10 screwdriver' because the cross shape on the head looks like the number 10.

Modern alphabet users are familiar with various alphabetic marking systems (e.g., "Insert tab A into slot B"). Such use is extremely archaic. Ancient Near Easterners used fitters' marks, single letters of the alphabet apparently used to indicate the order in which various building materials are to be assembled. Various decorative ivory pieces from Nimrud, Iraq, were letter-coded to show the order in which they were to be inserted into furniture (Millard 1962: 49–51). In a temple at Petra, Jordan, archeologists found "large, individually letter-coded, ashlar blocks spread along the floor of [a] room … in the temple structure" (Hammond, Johnson, and Jones 1986: 77). In a 1971 salvage expedition of a ship downed off Marsala, Italy, Honor Frost discovered "letters at key places where wood was to be joined … the ship assembly [was thus] a colossal game of carpentry by letters, like a modern paint-by-numbers project" (Soren, ben Khader, and Slim 1990: 96). A related use is quality labeling: jar-label inscriptions in Phoenician include an 'aleph, the first letter of the alphabet, standing independently, presumably indicating that the commodity in the jar is first-class (Naveh 1987).

Letter names can be used in various strictly linguistic codes. In the military "phonetic" alphabet—the "NATO alphabet"—common nouns and proper names replace the letter names because they are longer and thus clearer in long-distance transmission. Demanding communication situations have led to various transformations of the alphabet. At sea the semaphore system of two-flag units (one flag per hand) in various combinations was developed to convey alphabetic messages, and it has been adapted to other settings. Telegraphy prompted a greater simplification, using only three elements instead of a roster of flags: Samuel F. B. Morse (1791–1872) devised a code system based on the dot, dash, and space to convey letters (and numbers) by flashes or sounds. These representations of the alphabet are shown in TABLE 68.4.

TABLE 68.4: *Secondary Forms of the English Alphabet*

Military Phonetic or NATO alphabet[a]	Semaphore[b]	Morse Code[c]	Braille[d]	American Finger-Spelling
Alpha		• —		
Bravo		— • • •		
Charlie		— • — •		
Delta		— • •		
Echo		•		
Foxtrot		• • — •		
Golf/Gulf		— — •		
Hotel		• • • •		
Indigo		• •		
Juliet		• — — —		
Kilo		— • —		
Lima		• — • •		
Mike		— —		
November		— •		
Oscar		— — —		
Papa		• — — •		
Quebec		— — • —		
Romeo		• — •		
Sierra		• • •		
Tango		—		
Uniform		• • —		
Victor		• • • —		
Whiskey		• — —		
X-Ray		— • • —		
Yankee		— • — —		
Zulu		— — • •		

a. Earlier forms: World War II era—Able, Baker, David, Easy, Fox, Now, Peter, Year, Zebra; pre-Vietnam era—Apple, India, Kangaroo.

b. Numeral sign ⚑, word break ⚑.

c. Numerals: 0 — — — — —, 1 • — — — —, 2 • • — — —, 3 • • • — —, 4 • • • • —, 5 • • • • •, 6 — • • • •,
7 — — • • •, 8 — — — • •, 9 — — — — •; period • — • — • —, comma — — • • — —, question • • — — • •.

d. See TABLE 70.1 on page 816.

The various sign languages used by deaf and hearing-impaired people are, it is generally agreed, true languages, independent of the spoken languages used in the environment those people live in (and are, in Western Europe and the Americas, literate in). In sign language, frequently-used names have signs of their own. Sign languages in literate regions generally supplement their own sign systems with a finger-spelling system. Finger-spelling is used when a name is newly introduced in a conversation or is rare, or when an unusual word, for which no sign exists (or is known to both signers), is required. Most sign languages are two-handed systems, i.e. signs are regularly formed with both hands, and the signs are defined over the signing space (the face and torso, as well as the space slightly above and to the sides); for a notation system for American Sign Language (ASL), see FIGURE III on page 863. Finger-spelling is simpler; first, it is indifferent to location in the signing space (you can spell in front of your mouth as well as in front of your chest); second, it can be one-handed, as is ASL finger-spelling (British finger-spelling, in contrast, is two-handed).

There are also religious uses of the alphabet. The acrostic poems of the Hebrew Bible reflect the comprehensive or encyclopedic ambitions of the wisdom tradition (Ceresko 1985). The completeness of the poem (as praise of God and of God's creation) is signaled by the use of the alphabet as a structural device. It is not clear what such usage means for general literacy. Some scholars, observing the wide distribution of abecedary texts in the ancient world, have wondered if they were not only learning tools but also magical or religious devices (Millard 1985:39* with references; Patrich 1985).

Whether or not ancient abecedaries were magical devices in the sense of tools to manipulate a transcendent reality is difficult to say. Certainly abecedaries and similar devices based on writing systems are tools useful for manipulating mundane reality. They provide points of guidance in such practical matters as assembling ships and toys. They complement counting systems, often providing a backup system that can easily be kept separate from a main series of numbers. Most importantly, they supplement language, clarifying speech when it is being exchanged under adverse or unusual conditions and rounding out sign language. As a matter of principle, linguists claim that speech (or rather, the primary medium, be it speech or signing) is integral and that writing is dependent on it, but in the everyday lives of literate people, elements of writing systems are often called on to make speech (or signing) more effective.

Bibliography

Bordreuil, Pierre. 1982. "Quatre documents en cunéiformes alphabétiques mal connus ou inédits." *Semitica* 32: 5–14.

Ceresko, Anthony R. 1985. "The ABCs of Wisdom in Psalm xxxiv." *Vetus Testamentum* 35: 99–104.

Daniels, Peter T. 1991. "Ha, La, Ḥa or Hôi, Lawe, Ḥaut: The Ethiopic Letter Names." In *Semitic Studies in Honor of Wolf Leslau*, ed. Alan S. Kaye, pp. 275–88. Wiesbaden: Harrassowitz.

———. 1992. "The Syllabic Origin of Writing and the Segmental Origin of the Alphabet." In Downing, Lima, and Noonan 1992: 83–110.

Demsky, Aaron. 1977. "A Proto-Canaanite Abecedary Dating from the Period of the Judges and Its Implications for the History of the Alphabet." *Tel Aviv* 4: 14–27.

Downing, Pamela, Susan D. Lima, and Michael Noonan, eds. 1992. *Linguistics and Literacy* (Typological Studies in Language 21). Amsterdam: Benjamins.

Faber, Alice. 1992. "Phonemic Segmentation as Epiphenomenon: Evidence from the History of Alphabetic Writing." In Downing, Lima, and Noonan 1992: 111–34.

Gordon, Arthur E. 1973. *The Letter Names of the Latin Alphabet* (University of California Publications: Classical Studies 9). Berkeley and Los Angeles: University of California Press.

Hammond, Philip C., David J. Johnson, and Richard N. Jones. 1986. "A Religio-legal Nabataean Inscription from the Atargatis/al-'Uzza Temple at Petra." *Bulletin of the American Schools of Oriental Research* 263: 77–80.

Kochavi, Moshe. 1977. "An Ostracon from the Period of the Judges from 'Izbet Ṣarṭah." *Tel Aviv* 4: 1–13.

Lundin, A. G. 1985. "Quelques lettres des alphabets sémitiques." In Robin 1985: 239–44.

———. 1987. "L'abécédaire de Beth Shemesh." *Le Muséon* 100: 243–50.

Millard, Alan R. 1962. "Alphabetic inscriptions on ivories from Nimrud." *Iraq* 24: 41–51.

———. 1985. " 'BGD ...—Magic Spell or Educational Exercise?" *Eretz-Israel* 18: 39*–42*.

Naveh, Joseph. 1987. "Unpublished Phoenician Inscriptions from Palestine." *Israel Exploration Journal* 37: 25–30.

O'Connor, M. 1983. "Writing Systems, Native Speaker Analyses, and the Earliest Stages of Northwest Semitic Orthography." In *The Word of the Lord Shall Go Forth: Essays in Honor of David Noel Freedman in Celebration of His Sixtieth Birthday,* ed. Carol L. Meyers and M. O'Connor, pp. 439–65. Winona Lake, Ind.: Eisenbrauns.

Patrich, Joseph. 1985. "Inscriptions araméennes juives dans les grottes d'El-'Aleiliyât." *Revue biblique* 92: 265–73.

Puech, Emile. 1986. "Origine de l'alphabet: documents en alphabet linéaire et cunéiforme du IIe millénaire." *Revue biblique* 93: 161–213.

———. 1991. "La tablette cunéiforme de Beth Shemesh: Premier témoin de la séquence des lettres du sud-sémitique." In *Phoinikeia Grammata: Lire et écrire en Méditerranée,* ed. Claude Baurain, Corinne Bonnet, and Véronique Krings, pp. 33–47. Namur, Belgium: Société des Études Classiques.

Robin, Christian, ed. 1985. *Mélanges linguistiques offerts à Maxime Rodinson* (*Comptes Rendus du Groupe Linguistique des Etudes Chamito-Sémitiques* Supplément 12). Paris: Geuthner.

Ryckmans, Jacques. 1985. "L'Ordre alphabétique sud-sémitique et ses origines." In Robin 1985: 343-59.

———. 1987. "Aux origines de l'alphabet." *Bulletin des Séances/Académie Royale des Sciences d'Outre-Mer / Mededelingen der Zittingen/Koninklijke Academie voor Overzeese Wetenschappen* (Brussels) 32: 311–33.

Soren, David, Aicha ben Abed ben Khader, and Hedi Slim. 1990. *Carthage: Uncovering the Mysteries and Splendors of Ancient Tunisia.* New York: Simon & Schuster.

Swiggers, Pierre. 1986. "La Nature du nom propre selon Joseph Vendryes." *Beiträge zur Namenforschung* 21: 267–71.

Uwano Zendō. 1983. "Iroha poem." *Kodansha Encyclopedia of Japan* 3:332. Tokyo: Kodansha.

Numerical Notation

JOHN SÖREN PETTERSSON

Forerunners of numerical notation

Notches in bones, some more than 20,000 years old, and in sticks are commonly regarded as the earliest representation of numerals (Marshack 1972). Pebbles have also been used for numerical record-keeping, and illiterate herdsmen of some cultures still use them (see TABLE 69.1 for classification of ways of expressing numbers).

Knotted cords have been used in many parts of the world for storing numerical information, and the practice is still used in some places. An extremely elaborate system, the *quipu*, was used by the Incas of South America before the Spanish arrived. A quipu consisted of a main cord with a few to several thousand subsidiary cords (including subsidiaries to subsidiaries, and so on). On each substring, one or two numbers were represented by knots. A base 10 positional system was used, but how calculations were performed is not known. Quipus with interrelated numerical content have been found. From extant quipus it has been inferred that the Incas computed, at the least, addition, division into equal or proportional parts, and multiplication of integers by integers or by fractions (Ascher and Ascher 1981: 151–52).

For numerical memory aids in literate cultures, different notational devices may coexist: the tally stick was used by the British Royal Treasury until 1826 (Menninger 1969: 236–40). In old Sumerian cuneiform tablets, numbers were written either by cuneiform signs or by punch marks (for cuneiform, see SECTION 3; for punch marks, see FIGURES 70 and 71). The occurrence of the latter has been connected with a simultaneous use of counters, the punch marks being representations of pebbles. For later times as well, when writing was exclusively in cuneiform, it has been concluded that accounting was done simultaneously in writing and by storing assemblages of counters (Oppenheim 1959).

Denise Schmandt-Besserat (1992) tried to go even further. She investigated small clay objects from ancient sites in the whole of the Middle East. These *tokens*, as she calls them, are of fairly simple forms like disks, ovoids, and tetrahedra. They start to appear as early as 8000 B.C.E.—that is, at the dawn of agriculture and animal husbandry. Schmandt-Besserat views the tokens as a simple accounting device of early farmers, using different shapes for different commodities. Further, she connects an increase in types of token during the fourth millennium with a probable increase in types of goods during the contemporary formation of town and state constellations.

TABLE 69.1: *Terminology*

Number. A unit belonging to an abstract mathematical system, subject to laws of succession, addition, and multiplication.

Numeral. A conventional symbol that represents a number.

Additive. A simple grouping system, like the Roman numeral system where I = 1, II = 2, III = 3.

Sign-value notation. To express large numbers, different symbols are used; again the Roman system serves as an example with its I = 1, V = 5, X = 10, L = 50, C = 100, D = 500, M = 1,000. Thus Roman XXXVIII = 38.

Subtractive. The Romans also employed a *subtraction principle*: IX = 9 ≠ XI = 11 (however, IX for VIIII did not become standard until the time of the printing press).

Multiplicative. In some sign value notations, small numerals denote the number of the bigger units of the system; if the Romans had written XXXVIII thus, it could have looked like this: $X^{III} V^{I} I^{III}$. Similar notations have actually been used, with M and C as superscripts over I's and V's.

Positional systems utilize the concept of *place value*; they are like a multiplicative system but without explicit signs for the higher ranks (cf. the abacus). To illustrate: rewriting XXXVII by use of place value, it would look like this: III I II, where the first position, from right to left, denotes ones, the second five, and the third tens. When initial and medial positions are not used, they must be marked by empty spaces (as on an abacus) or by a special sign, called *zero*.

Base of a numerical system is a magnitude greater than 1 that has a particular expression in the system, and powers of which are also marked specifically. Base systems are named as follows:

binary	*quinary*	*octal*	*decimal*	*hexadecimal*	*vigesimal*	*sexagesimal*
2	5	8	10	16	20	60

Examples:

Modern Western: The digits 0, 1, 2, …, 9, used in the ordinary way, constitute an example of a non-additive, decimal positional system. (Non-additive systems are sometimes called *ciphered*.)

Aztec: additive vigesimal: • = 1, •• = 2, …, •••••••••••••••••• = 19, and special signs are used for three powers of 20 (an axe for 20, an object that looks like a feather for 400, and a purse for 8,000; see Ifrah 1985: 224).

Mayan: The additive Mayan system may be called either vigesimal (positional) or quinary vigesimal. 1–6: •, •, •, •, |, ⊦; 15: ‖; 19: ⫴.0: ⬮, 20: •⬮. The head variants for the numerals are shown in FIGURE 69. The Maya also had several systems for counting time (none quite vigesimal), including ciphered systems.

Interestingly, the numerals and number words used by a people rarely fit well: e.g., Aztec number words for 1–19 are quinary, and Maya words for 1–19 are decimal (Menninger 1969: 53, 59–64).

Then the ancients began to secure the count of tokens by enclosing them in hollow lumps of clay with seal impressions covering the entire surface. Gradually, impressions of the tokens began to appear on the outside of the clay balls, obviously to make the tokens sealed inside countable. Finally, the envelopes collapsed into tablets

FIGURE 69. Head variants for the Maya numbers (with equivalents in spoken Yucatec).
Coe notes that '13' through '19' are "skull variants" of '3' through '9'.
Reproduced with permission from Coe 1992: 113; artist: John Montgomery. © Michael D. Coe.

with token (or blunt stylus) impressions and sealings. (The relationship between early envelopes and numerical tablets was originally elaborated by Pierre Amiet and Maurice Lambert, as cited in Schmandt-Besserat 1992: 9.)

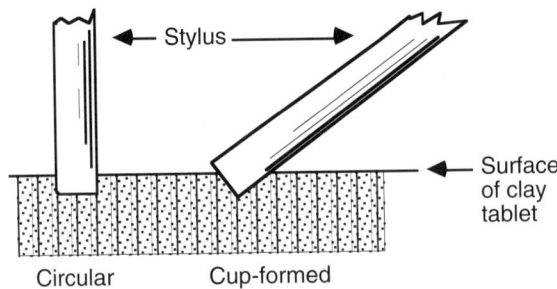

FIGURE 70. The making of circular and cup-shaped numerals.

FIGURE 71. Two sizes resulting in four different signs.

Secondarily, incised signs, which evolved into cuneiform signs, were added to the numerical notations to specify the type of goods and the sender or receiver. When the notation no longer mixes number and item in the same sign, the numerical signs are true numerals, as they stand for abstract numbers. For more on the suggestions of Schmandt-Besserat and criticism of them, see SECTION 2.

The following presents material in a more or less chronological order so as to suggest possible (but as yet unclear) influences among cultures.

Ancient Near East

Mesopotamia

From the protoliterate period on (see SECTION 10), several different systems of counting were used, each system being connected with specific types of measurement. Eventually, the sexagesimal system became dominant in the cuneiform world (see "Sexagesimal System S" in FIGURE 14 on page 162). When cuneiform signs started to replace the numerical punch marks (see FIGURES 70 and 71), the size of the wedge for 60 was larger than the wedge for 1, and 3,600 was written as an outline of the earlier large circular punch seen in FIGURE 14. That is, the technique of sign-value notation was still used.

A true positional system, including fractions, evolved around 2000 B.C.E. (TABLE 69.2). Originally, no zero existed; furthermore, the ideal use of blank space, as exemplified in TABLE 69.2 for 3,601, 61, and 2, was not always followed by the scribes. Signs to denote an empty position became common in the third century B.C.E., but except for astronomical tables, they were not used at the beginning of fractions nor at the end of numbers. This failure to mark the size of the numbers should perhaps be seen as a consequence of a parallel use of tabulated standard calculations

TABLE 69.2: *Mesopotamian Sexagesimal Place-value Notation*

I	2	3	4	...	9	10	11	12	...	50	60
𒁹	𒐀	𒐁	𒐂		𒐘	𒌋	𒌋𒁹	𒌋𒐀		𒐐	𒁹

The numerals for 1–50 show a decimal system at work within the sexagesimal system:

Number:	216,000	36,000	3,600		600	60		10	I
Old sign value:	𒁹	𒁹	𒁹		𒁹	𒁹		𒌋	𒁹

Place value:

Sign:	𒁹		𒌋	𒁹		𒌋	𒁹		𒌋	𒁹
Position:	4th (60³)			3rd (60²)			2nd (60¹)		1st (60⁰)	

Note 2, 61, 3,601: 𒐀, 𒁹 𒁹, 𒁹 𒁹

The subtraction principle could be used: 𒌋 𒁹 𒁹 = 20 − 1 = 19; earlier, OO𒁹 D.

In Akkadian cuneiform, only 1–99 were written with numerals, while special signs for 100 and 1,000 made it possible to express numbers in decimal notation, conforming to the structure of number words in Semitic languages. An example:

3601: 𒐁 𒌋 𒌋 𒁹 𒁹   '3 thousand 6 hundred 1'

TABLE 69.3: *Example of How Calculation Was Aided by Standard Tables*

$a/b \rightarrow a \times (1/b)$ previously calculated

A division 7/5 was transformed to a multiplication $7 \times (1/5)$. For 1/5, standard tables of recipro-
cals would be employed; such a table gives 1/5 = 𒌋 𒐀, i.e. 12 rather than 0;12 (= 12/60)
[the semicolon separates representations of units from sixtieths].

Product table for 7 then gives $7 \times 12 = 𒁹 𒌋 𒐘$ '1 24', where the 𒁹 signifies 60, and by considering the size of the original numbers, one realizes that the correct quotient is 1;24 (= 1.4 in our notation). (For sexagesimally non-finite fractions, the Babylonians used approximations.)

(see TABLE 69.3); by not respecting the size of the original numbers, standard lists could be applied in a wide range of computations. Did the lack of a medial zero hamper earlier Babylonian accountancy and mathematics? Probably not. Sixty as a base is much greater than ten, and thus the risk for confusion was small. However, several precautions were taken by the scribes: numerals could be written in columns, for instance, or words were used to give the size of specific numerals. The Babylonian sexagesimal system has survived in our present-day minutes and seconds.

Egypt

The Egyptian system had ten as its base but did not need the zero, since it was built up like the older Mesopotamian systems with different symbols for different magnitudes; see TABLE 69.4. Fractions are also shown: note that they are *unit fractions* 1/*n*, where *n* is a whole number. Special signs could be used for ½, ⅔, and ¾. A frequent problem in the Rhind papyrus (1600 B.C.E.), one of the principal sources of knowledge about ancient Egyptian mathematics (Robins and Shute 1987), is doubling of

TABLE 69.4: *Egypt*

	I	IO	IOO	1,000	10,000	100,000	1,000,000
	l	∩	ρ	⌇	∫	⬃	𓁨

$\frac{1}{3}$	$\frac{1}{4}$	$\frac{1}{5}$	$\frac{1}{10}$	...		$\frac{1}{2}$
⌒ ııı	⌒ ıııı	⌒ ı ı ı	⌒ ∩			⌒ ı

$$\frac{47}{60} = \frac{1}{5} + \frac{1}{4} + \frac{1}{3} \qquad\qquad \frac{2}{7} = \frac{1}{28} + \frac{1}{4}$$

⌒ ⌒ ⌒   ıııı ⌒ ⌒
ııı ıııı ııı   ıııı ○○ ıııı
ı ı

TABLE 69.5: *The Egyptian Horus-eye*

◁	○	⌢	▷	⌣๑	ʅ	𓂀
$\frac{1}{2}$	$\frac{1}{4}$	$\frac{1}{8}$	$\frac{1}{16}$	$\frac{1}{32}$	$\frac{1}{64}$	

unit fractions (for some reason these are never written additively as 1/n 1/n). For fractions of the *hekat*, a unit of volume, the Egyptians used parts of the Horus eye; see
TABLE 69.5. Multiplications and divisions were not computed in the Mesopotamian
fashion but "by breaking up any higher multiple into a sum of consecutive duplica-
tions" (Neugebauer 1957: 73f.). In the hieratic hand, the individual occurrences of the
basic signs were simplified to small strokes, dots, or angles on cursive variants of the
basic signs. In this way, special symbols emerged for each number 1–9, 10–90, 100–
900, 1,000–9,000. The demotic system was also non-additive. During the Monarchic
period of ancient Israel/Judah, hieratic-inspired numerals were used in the Old Hebrew script (SECTION 5).

Linear A and B

The structure of the numerical system for whole numbers in Linear A and B (SECTION
7) resembles the Egyptian; the shapes of the signs are shown in TABLE 69.6. The

TABLE 69.6: *Linear A and Linear B*

	I	IO	IOO	1,000	10,000
Linear A	l	• or ⁻	○	◇	?
Linear B	l	⁻	○	◇	◇

Cretan hieroglyphic writing displays a similar system (with • for 10).

Concrete fractions in Linear B: ⚹ıııⳤıı◁ıı

The example shows a measure of olive oil: 3 units (of ~30 liters), 2 thirds, and 2 eighteenths (i.e.
the second fraction is one-sixth the first fraction). From Knossos tablet Fp1 (Chadwick 1987: 14).

stroke for 'one' and the word-divider are often distinguishable from each other by the former being raised to the top of the line. In Linear A tablets, a great many signs for true fractional numbers have been found, although they have not yet been definitively interpreted. In Linear B tablets, on the other hand, another way of dealing with parts is encountered: the ordinary unit signs are used together with special signs for fractional measures, which differ depending on whether volume or weight is measured. However, several of the Linear B fractional signs are derived from Linear A (for details, see Ventris and Chadwick 1973: 53–60).

Northwest Semitic

In (North) West Semitic writing, numbers were often written out in words. True numerals in the Aramaic script begin to appear from the eighth century B.C.E. (see FIGURE 57 on page 495) and are then found in Phoenician and other inscriptions. These numerals are vertical strokes for 1–9 (grouped in threes for easier reading), pairs of the horizontal 10-stroke to denote tens (thus 50 was written as –==), and special signs for hundred, thousand, and ten thousand (to be used multiplicatively).

South and East Asia

Indus script

It is reasonable to propose an original base eight system for the undeciphered Indus script (SECTION 11), since one to seven strokes appear fairly often (see FIGURE 72), while larger assemblages of strokes are very rare. Surprisingly, numerals appear in seal inscriptions. Perhaps they were used syllabically (rebus-style) to write names, or else they may be signs for gods, which are often parts of mortals' names (in mystic religious cuneiform texts, one actually finds ordinary god names replaced by numbers; S. Parpola 1993). Fairservis (1992) has proposed identifications of signs used for 8–12 and suggests, specifically, that these were used to denote the months of the year. This is, however, a highly uncertain interpretation. It is probably safer to interpret numerals on Indus pottery and bronzes as signifying volume and weight. However, the state of preservation of inscribed objects makes it hard to check even this hypothesis. It seems as if semicircles signified 'eight' or 'ten', and strokes 'one', but there were also tilted rows of four strokes: were these for fractions (halves?) or for non-numerical concepts?

FIGURE 72. Two variants in the Indus script of the number '7' in a frequently attested context. Many of the actual contexts for '7' are longer than indicated here, although most Harappan inscriptions are very short.

TABLE 69.7: *China*

		Example:
一	1	$279,514 = (2 \times 10 + 7]) \times 10,000 + 9 \times 1,000 + 5 \times 100 + (1 \times) 10 + 4$
二	2	二
三	3	十
四	4	七
五	5	萬
六	6	九
七	7	千
八	8	五
九	9	百
十	10	(一)
百	100	十
千	1,000	四
萬 or 万	10,000	

China

The earliest known Chinese notational system is contemporary with the earliest script remains, the oracle bones (see SECTION 14). Present-day Chinese numerals (also used in Japan and Korea) are shown in TABLE 69.7. However, today the "Arabic" digits 0–9 are in common use in East Asia—though the abacus is still widely used, and for simple commercial calculations is competitive in speed with electronic calculators. The Chinese system constitutes a multiplicative system, as the example in TABLE 69.7 shows. Additional signs have been employed in scientific works to express large numbers. Not later than the third century B.C.E., a bamboo-stick arithmetic had been established (FIGURE 73). These *rod numerals* were adapted to writing. Negative num-

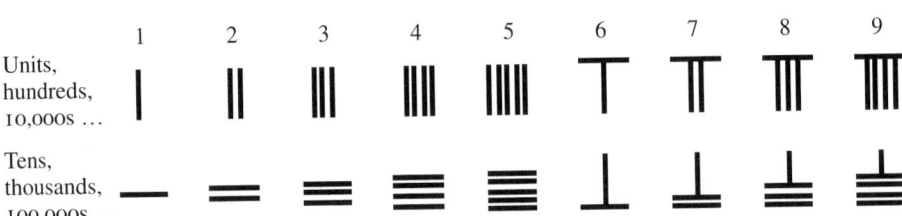

The Chinese rod system used five small sticks of bamboo or wood to form two sequences of the numbers 1–9. Such numbers were laid in the squares of a checkered counting board which facilitated representation of position (powers of 10). Because there were two sequences, there was no pressing need for a special sign for zero when rod numerals were adapted to writing. In this example, the 6 cannot be interpreted as 60, nor can the 3 stand for 300:

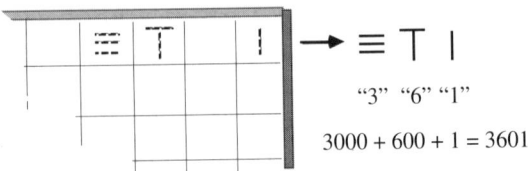

"3" "6" "1"

$3000 + 600 + 1 = 3601$

FIGURE 73. Chinese rods

bers were perhaps introduced as early as the rod arithmetic. From about 1200 C.E. there are, in writing, different notations of negativity: positive numbers written in red color, negative in black; or negative numbers are indicated by a diagonal stroke over the last numeral of the number. Fractions were for a long time written in words. From the eighth century on, empty position (zero) was marked by a blank space, and from the thirteenth century a circle was used, paving the way for positional fractions (e.g. 005 meaning 0.05). Lam Lay-yong (1988) has argued that the conceptual (although not the graphic) origin of our decimal system is the Chinese rod system.

Classical Greece and Rome

Greece

The Greek acrophonic system, called Attic or Herodianic, used the first letter of the words ΠENTE *pente* 'five', ΔEKA *deka* 'ten', HKATON *hekaton* 'hundred', XIΛIOI *khilioi* 'thousand', MYPIOI *myrioi* 'ten thousand'. In its structure, it resembles the Roman system (in TABLE 69.8, note that there existed composite graphs for 50, 500, 5,000, and 50,000).

However, possibly to make it easier to write numbers, the Greeks invented another system, the alphabetic (see SECTION 22). Strokes were used to indicate thousands (‚ε = 5,000, for instance). Without multiplication being simplified, computing addition required more skill in the alphabetic system than in the acrophonic system. In any event, this system, at first frequently found only in scientific texts, became common in the second century B.C.E. and supplanted the acrophonic totally, lasting into the Byzantine era. The Greek letter numerals were used, and occasionally still are, in Ethiopia (SECTION 51), where, however, only the first nineteen letters (1–9, 10–90, 100) are employed, higher numerals being expressed by the multiplicative principle.

Probably under Greek influence, other alphabets (see under each of these scripts in PARTS V and VIII) began to be used as numerals: Hebrew from before the Common Era, Gothic from around the fourth century C.E., Georgian and Syriac (Serto and Nestorian) from the seventh century C.E., and Arabic from the eighth century (where the 28th letter is used for 1,000 and multiples of 1,000 are expressed multiplicatively). A curious use of the numerical value of the letters is Hebrew *gematria*, where the val-

TABLE 69.8: *Greek (Attic system)*

I	I	⊢	500
Π	5	X	1,000
Δ	10	⊠	5,000
Δ⌐	50	M	10,000
H	100	M	50,000

TABLE 69.9: *Roman*

I)	500		C|)	1,000
I)	5,000		CC|)	10,000
I))	50.000		CCC|))	100,000

ues of the letters in a word or name are computed and manipulated and compared; 'the number of the beast' of the Book of Revelations is similar. There have been several kinds of gematria systems.

Rome

For the Roman numerals, see the illustration in TABLE 69.1. The Roman numerals are not acrophonic even though C for 100 (*centum* in Latin) and M for 1,000 (*mille*) may suggest this. In fact, the source of the original graphs is not clear, but they were obviously later adapted to the shapes of the letters of the Roman alphabet. Early forms of thousands, some used as late as the nineteenth century, are shown in TABLE 69.9. A composite way of denoting thousands was especially employed in the Middle Ages: a bar over I denoted 1,000, a bar over II denoted 2,000, and so on. Although Roman numbers (and acrophonic Greek) may seem long and complicated, they are very suitable for addition (and subtraction); it was just a matter of heaping similar symbols and then replacing them by greater powers as needed.

0 – 9

Our ordinary numerals, 0–9, are often called *Arabic*, but some historians of mathematics prefer *Hindu-Arabic* because the Arabic numerals were originally Indian. The original numerals spread not only to Europe and the Arab world, but in different guises also to Central and Southeast Asia (see FIGURE 74 for a diagram presenting the history of one of them). They first appeared in the Brahmi script (SECTION 30) in the second century B.C.E. At this stage the numerals 1–3 were still one to three strokes, while 4–9 were actually ciphered. There were signs for 10–90, 100, and 1000; thus no zero was needed, nor any principle of position. Around 600 C.E., the numerals 1–9 appear in a positional system. Finally, the concept of zero also entered this system. Around the year 800 the Indian decimal system, with zero, was introduced in Muslim areas. The earliest European use of "Arabic" numerals is found at the end of the first millennium, but the gradual replacement of abaci and other devices did not begin before the twelfth century, and not until the fifteenth century did the digits 0–9 become common (and graphically standardized). The European forms have spread worldwide, and their sole global rival is … the bar code!

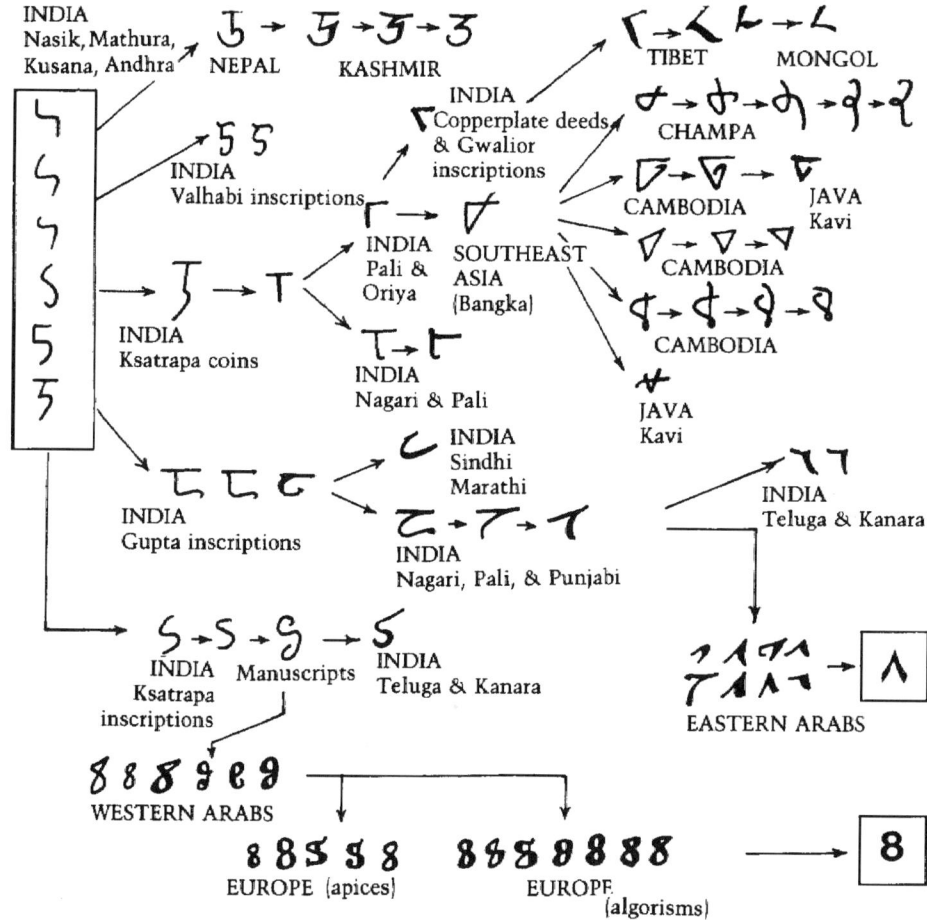

FIGURE 74. Origin and evolution of the numeral 8
(reproduced with permission from Ifrah 1985: 488).

Further reading

Ifrah 1985 is a highly commendable volume on numerals through all of history (though it contains an unfortunate attempt at deciphering Proto-Elamite numerals, and has nothing on the enigmatic Indus numerals). The French original (1981) may be consulted for its comprehensive bibliography. A book which focuses on both number symbols and number words is Menninger 1969. Cajori 1928–29 gives the history of mathematical notations. For mathematics and its applications, one can profitably turn to Newman 1956, Neugebauer 1957, Needham 1959, and Gillispie 1978, though there are many other good works on the history of mathematics.

Bibliography

Ascher, Marcia, and Robert Ascher. 1981. *Code of the Quipu.* Ann Arbor: University of Michigan Press.

Cajori, Florian. 1928–29. *A History of Mathematical Notations.* 2 vols. Chicago: Open Court. Repr. in 1 vol., New York: Dover, 1993.

Chadwick, John. 1987. *Linear B and Related Scripts* (Reading the Past). London: British Museum; Berkeley and Los Angeles: University of California Press.

Coe, Michael D. 1992. *Breaking the Maya Code.* New York: Thames and Hudson.

Damerow, Peter, and Robert K. Englund. 1987. "Die Zahlzeichensysteme der Archaischen Texte aus Uruk." In *Zeichenliste der Archaischen Texte aus Uruk,* pp. 117–66. Berlin: Mann.

Dilke, O. A. W. 1987. *Mathematics and Measurement* (Reading the Past). London: British Museum; Berkeley and Los Angeles: University of California Press.

Fairservis, Walter A. 1992. *The Harappan Civilization and its Writing.* Leiden: Brill.

Friberg, Jöran. 1990. "Mathematik" [in English]. *Reallexikon der Assyriologie und vorderasiatischen Archäologie* 7: 531–85. Berlin: de Gruyter.

Gillispie, Charles Coulston, ed. 1978. "Topical Essays." In *Dictionary of Scientific Biography* 15 suppl. 1: 529–818. New York: Scribner's. Repr. as vol. 8, 1981.

Ifrah, Georges. 1985. *From One to Zero: A Universal History of Numbers.* New York: Viking Penguin (French orig., *Histoire universelle des chiffres,* 1981).

Lam Lay-yong. 1988. "A Chinese Genesis: Rewriting the History of Our Numeral System." *Archive for the History of Exact Sciences* 38: 101–8.

Marshack, Alexander. 1972. *The Roots of Civilization: The Cognitive Beginnings of Man's First Art, Symbol and Notation.* New York: McGraw-Hill.

Menninger, Karl. 1969. *Number Words and Number Symbols: A Cultural History of Numbers,* trans. Paul Broneer. Cambridge: MIT Press (German orig., 1958). Repr. New York: Dover, 1992.

Needham, Joseph. 1959. *Mathematics and the Sciences of the Heavens and the Earth* (Science and Civilization in China 3). Cambridge: Cambridge University Press.

Nemet-Nejat, Karen Rhea. 1993. *Cuneiform Mathematical Texts as a Reflection of Everyday Life in Mesopotamia* (American Oriental Series 75). New Haven: American Oriental Society.

Neugebauer, Otto. 1957. *The Exact Sciences in Antiquity,* 2nd ed. Providence: Brown University Press. Repr. New York: Dover, 1969.

Newman, James R., ed. 1956. *The World of Mathematics.* New York: Simon and Schuster. Repr. New York: Microsoft Press, 1988.

Oppenheim, A. Leo. 1959. "On an Operational Device in Mesopotamian Bureaucracy." *Journal of Near Eastern Studies* 18: 121–28.

Parpola, Simo. 1993. "The Assyrian Tree of Life: Tracing the Origins of Jewish Monotheism and Greek Philosophy." *Journal of Near Eastern Studies* 52: 161–208.

Robins, Gay, and Charles Shute. 1987. *The Rhind Mathematical Papyrus: An Ancient Egyptian Text.* London: British Museum Publications; New York: Dover.

Schmandt-Besserat, Denise. 1992. *Before Writing,* vol. 1: *From Counting to Cuneiform.* Austin: University of Texas Press.

Ventris, Michael, and John Chadwick. 1973. *Documents in Mycenaean Greek,* 2nd ed. Cambridge: Cambridge University Press.

Shorthand

PETER T. DANIELS

Only one even somewhat detailed history of shorthand seems to have appeared in English in the last century (and the literature in other languages is hardly more promising). That was a long series of short articles by John Robert Gregg (1867–1948) in his magazine *The Business Education World* published between 1933 and 1940. (The series, brought down to the end of the 18th century, was interrupted by "more pressing war work," and inquiries as to whether any continuation survives among his papers have gone unanswered.) This survey is perforce largely based on those reports.

Shorthand may be characterized as a notation system for recording words as fast as they are spoken. A written shorthand record is called *notes*, and the act of making shorthand notes is *reporting*. The process is not complete until the report is transcribed into ordinary orthography, and even the best reporter needs to do the transcription before the material reported has totally vanished from recall, as elimination of redundancy, and even the introduction of ambiguity, may make the report virtually unrecoverable. A secondary advantage of shorthand in the workplace or lawcourt is confidentiality: while another reporter may be able to decipher someone's notes, they are fairly secure from casual interception.

Historical survey

The earliest known materials that might be considered shorthand are a genre of Mesopotamian cuneiform documents in which virtually all the phonographic characters have been eliminated; only logograms are left to carry the content of the text, with the grammatical relations largely unexpressed. This seems to have been done less for concision than to maintain secrecy; the texts involved are magical and technical, recording confidential procedures and recipes.

Classical era

The search for means of writing more quickly seems almost as old as Greek alphabetic writing: two stones inscribed with experimental schemata for abbreviated writing have been found, which were dedicated one at Athens and one at Delphi, dating from the fourth century B.C.E. (Boge 1974 surveys Classical and Medieval shorthand, with detailed bibliography. He contends that Greek shorthand developed out of the Roman system of *Tironian notæ*, named for Tirō, ex-slave, secretary, and companion

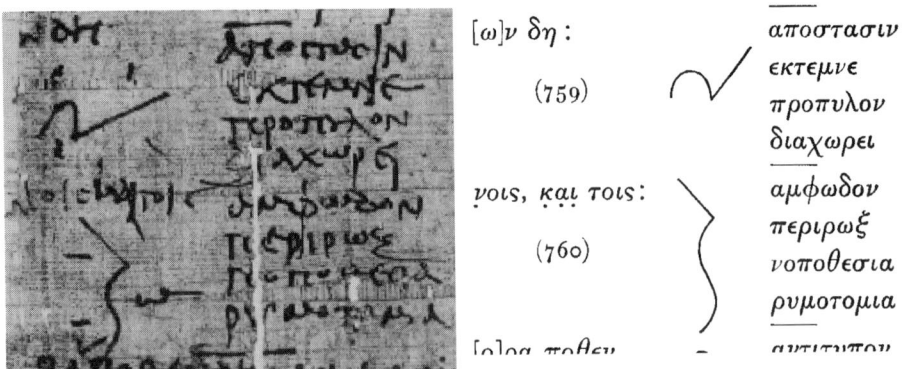

FIGURE 75. Excerpt from the Greek shorthand manual, Commentary (Milne 1934, pl. I and p. 64).

to the great orator M. Tullius Cicero [106–43 B.C.E.], who is said to have devised it.)

The system known as Greek *tachygraphy* 'fast writing' consisted of a Syllabary and a Commentary, to which were added signs for complete phrases. The Syllabary included signs for vowels (four of the seven the same as the ordinary letters), for diphthongs (compounded from parts of the vowel signs), for syllables—vowel plus consonant, consonant plus vowel, and more elaborate combinations—and for grammatical inflections. In the Commentary, groups of four words, usually chosen arbitrarily, are associated with symbols whose shapes can sometimes be related to the Syllabary. Each of these four words is notated with the word-symbol accompanied by a sign related to the word's last syllable placed in a particular location alongside it (FIGURE 75). Manuals of the system survive among papyri discovered at Oxyrhynchus (in Egypt) from the third or fourth century C.E., and the edition of those fragments gives 810 signs with their tetrads (Milne 1934: 21–67).

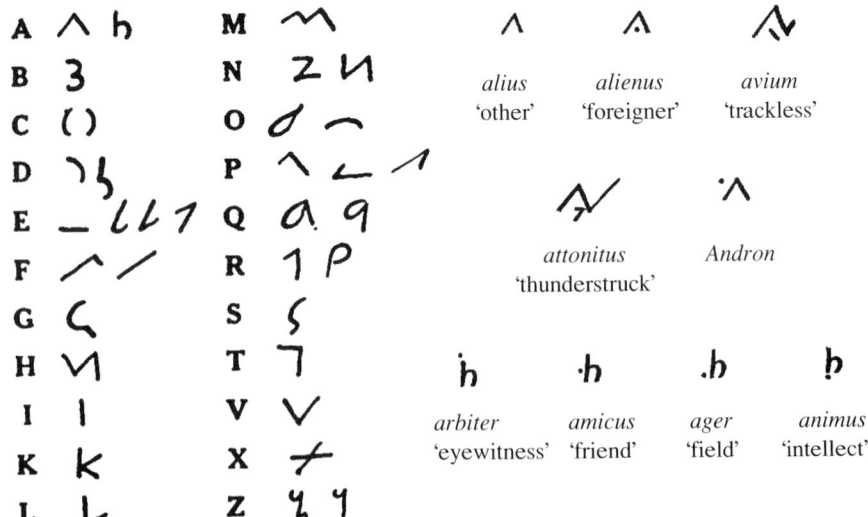

FIGURE 76. The Tironian alphabet and some wordsigns beginning with *a* (*BEW* Feb. 1934: 284–85).

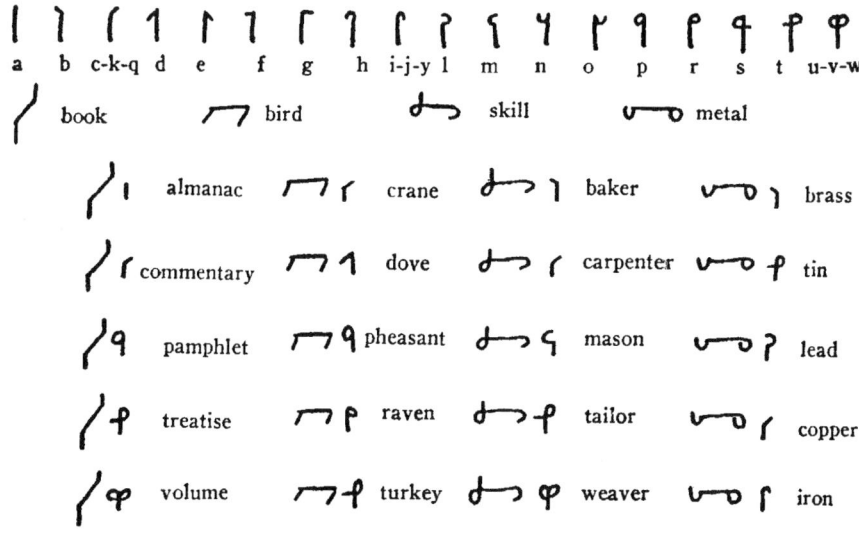

FIGURE 77. Alphabet and composite words in Bright's Characterie (*BEW* May 1934: 532–33).

The acme of Greek tachygraphy was in the Byzantine administration, in the several centuries before the Arab Conquest (7th century C.E.). A more detailed system was in use during the ninth through twelfth centuries.

In Rome, public affairs and business matters were recorded by stenographers employing Tironian notæ. The system shows similarity to the Greek. The main principle is that a word is recorded according to its initial letter, the symbol for which is slanted in different degrees to denote the following vowel; supplementary dots, dashes, and other marks distinguish particular words (FIGURE 76). Roman stenography continued in limited use by the Merovingian and Carolingian chanceries, and by scholars until the tenth century. The most complete study remains Kopp 1817–29, supplemented by the important work of Schmitz 1893 (Thompson 1912: 73–74; I am indebted to Michael K. C. MacMahon for information and references).

Renaissance

Medieval manuscripts are full of abbreviatory devices (Cappelli 1929), but these served to save precious writing materials (and a bit of time), rather than to facilitate swift reporting; they are largely transparent and would not have presented any difficulty to the reader. It is not until Elizabethan England that shorthand again appears: in 1588, Timothe Bright, M.D., published *Characterie*. This worked somewhat like Roget's Thesaurus: 537 signs for basic concepts (the shapes taken from arbitrary symbols of their initial letters) served as key, or master, words; to note a related word, a sign was written with beside it the initial of the desired word, synonyms to the left, antonyms to the right. Many words were treated as genus and species (FIGURE 77). Almost nothing written in Characterie has survived, but Friedrich (1918) suggests that it was the means by which the texts of Elizabethan plays were recorded for publication; he substantiates his claim with a detailed study of variants between the editions of Shakespeare's *Merry Wives of Windsor*. This is followed by an even more detailed study of the publication history of *Romeo and Juliet* (Schöttner 1918).

Bright seems to have been aware of Renaissance research into the nature of the Tironian notæ, but did not himself incorporate any of the ancient symbols into his own system. This was first done by John Willis, author of the first phonetically grounded shorthand system, *The Art of Stenographie* (1602). Willis wrote the sign for the initial letter full size; the following vowel was indicated by writing the next consonant small in one of six positions around the main letter. Subsequent consonants of a cluster were attached to the bottom of the letter (FIGURE 78).

Gregg recognizes John Willis's importance in creating phonetic shorthand, but credits Edmond Willis with the first practical shorthand (1618), inasmuch as its symbols are much easier to write. He adapts some of the earlier devices, for instance simplifying vowel representation by not using positions to the left of the main letter.

Gregg devotes several pages each to a number of seventeenth- and eighteenth-century innovators, whose achievements must be reduced to a few words apiece: Thomas Shelton (1626) found a new way to write diphthongs (his is the system used by the famous diarist Samuel Pepys and advocated by Thomas Jefferson). Jeremiah Rich (1646) used the dot of "i" to stand for *i*, apparently stimulating others to use simple, separate signs for vowels; and he used length of stroke to distinguish two letters, *m* and *n*. William Mason (1672, 1682, 1707) almost completely abolished the use of "arbitraries" or "symbolicals," wordsigns that had nothing to do with phonetics. Through such characters, shorthand systems became enmeshed in the Enlightenment

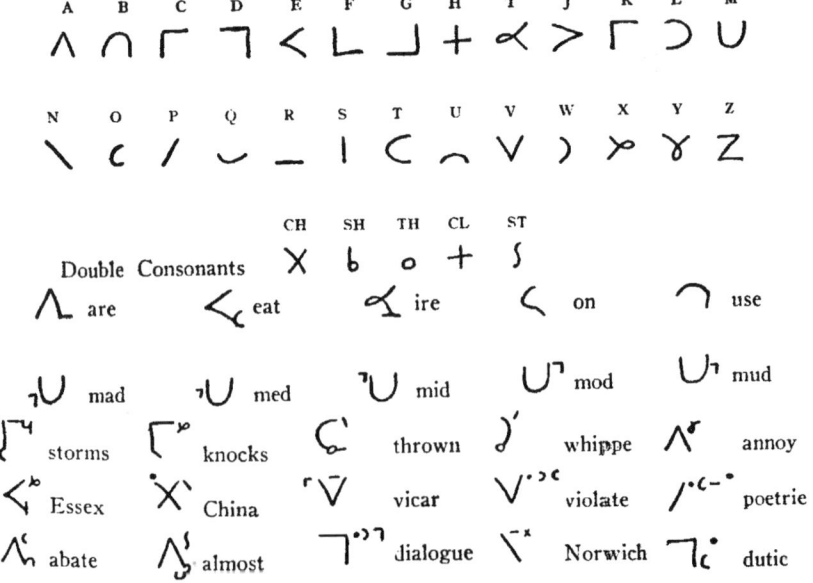

FIGURE 78. Consonants, vowels, and words in J. Willis's Stenographie (*BEW* Oct. 1934: 96–97).

search for a "universal language," wherein great scholars such as Leibniz and Newton applied themselves to such endeavors (Slaughter 1982).

Modern

It was the practical needs of reporting Parliamentary debates that gave rise to the shorthand systems whose descendants have not yet quite given way to mechanical court stenography and to office voice-recording devices. The House of Gurney had been, at the time of Gregg's writing, Official Shorthand Writers to the House of Commons and the House of Lords for well over a century—they were appointed in 1813 (the first time any such office had been recognized anywhere); the system they used was based, by Thomas Gurney (1750), on that of William Mason. The most celebrated user of Gurney's was Charles Dickens, who worked as a Parliamentary reporter between the ages of 18 and 20.

Gregg identifies a second stream in the development of shorthand beginning with John Byrom (1720), who introduced geometric shorthand, with signs based on segments of circles; grouped consonants phonetically; and used dots exclusively for vowels. All consonants were joined together, and vowels were largely optional. William Williamson (1775) applied the theories of Byrom in a more practical way. Gregg includes two more names in this group—Samuel Taylor (1786) and William Mavor (1789)—but this is where his narrative breaks off. Instead of continuing with the achievements of Isaac Pitman and his descendants (they were his chief rivals in the sale of shorthand instruction, and perhaps he wished to avoid the appearance of confrontation), he skips to the First International Shorthand Congress, held in London in 1887. (The 19th century saw shorthand come to France, with the brothers Abbé Émile and Gustave Duployé; to Germany, with F. X. Gabelsberger; and elsewhere.) He then takes up the theoretical bases of shorthand, and does not fully succeed in avoiding polemics. Polemics pervade discussions of shorthand, for it must not be forgotten that the shorthand industry was a huge business through most of the twentieth century.

Isaac Pitman (1813–1897) used Taylor's system for seven years, and "was invited" to prepare for publication a system of his own in 1837 (Abercrombie 1937: 101). This he did within a few months (FIGURE 79), and Pitman Shorthand is the leading system used in Great Britain, and the second most popular in the United States. Pitman is probably the first shorthand creator who was a sophisticated phonetician (Kelly 1981), and he incorporates the graphic device of shading (lighter and heavier lines), along with length differences, to indicate phonetic similarity. (For another shorthand created by a linguist, the celebrated phonetician Henry Sweet, see MacMahon 1981; Karlgren 1978: 133 n. 1 claims it is difficult to write with Sweet's system, since he has not ensured that vowels can be conveniently connected to consonants!)

John Robert Gregg (Leslie 1964, Cowan 1984)—born in rural Ireland, raised in Glasgow—as a youth suffered a disciplinary blow to the head that partly deafened him and gave him a reputation for dull-wittedness. When a wise old friend pointed

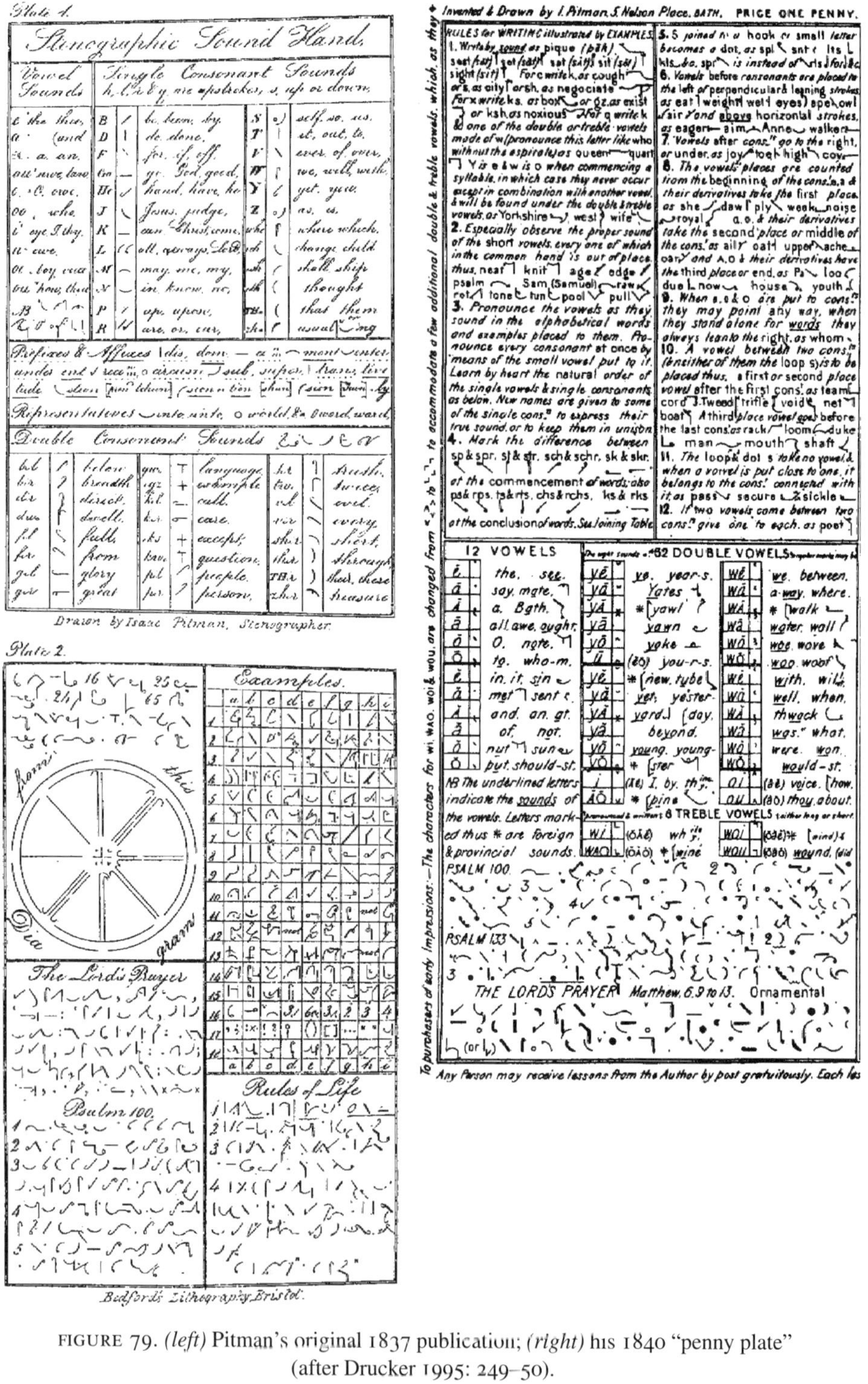

FIGURE 79. (left) Pitman's original 1837 publication; (right) his 1840 "penny plate" (after Drucker 1995: 249–50).

out that he was "dull o' hearing, … but no dull o' brain," he resolved to do something with his life (he was ten years old). As everyone in his family had studied shorthand and failed, he resolved to study shorthand and succeed. He began (as Pitman had) with a version of Taylor's; but he was obsessed, and tried to master every system he could find. His wide experience with more or less suitable systems, and his study of various learnèd analyses, drove him to devise one of his own that would incorporate as many reasonable principles as possible. He eschewed shading, and differentiation by positioning; he adopted cursive rather than geometric styling; he admitted more

CONSONANTS

Written forward:

K   G   R   L   N   M   T   D   TH

⌐   ⌒   ⌣   ⌣   ‒   —   ╱   ╱   ⌐ or ⌐

Written downward:

P   B   F   V   CH   J   S   SH

((   )   )   ╱   ╱   ⌐ or ⌐   ╱

H   NG   NK

•   ⟍   ⟍

VOWELS

ă   ○   ĭ   ｡   ŏ   ⌣   ŭ   ⌐
ä   ○   ĕ   ｡   aw   ⌣   ŏŏ   ⌐
ā   ○   ē   ｡   ō   ⌣   ōō   ⌐

DIPHTHONGS

Composed of		Composed of	
ū	ē-ōo as in *unit* ⌐	oi	aw-ē as in *oil* ꜱ
ow	ä-ōo as in *owl* ⌐	ī	ä-ē as in *isle* ○

BLENDED CONSONANTS

The consonants are so arranged that two strokes joining with an obtuse or blunt angle may assume the form of a large curve, thus:

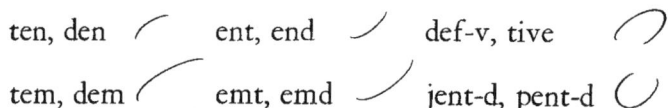

ten, den ⌐   ent, end ⟋   def-v, tive ⌒

tem, dem ⌐   emt, emd ⟋   jent-d, pent-d ⌣

FIGURE 80. The Alphabet of Gregg Shorthand (Gregg 1929: xvi).

than one shape per sound, to permit facile combinations; and above all he studied the frequency of combinations of sounds in English—the easiest shapes should render the most common sounds, so that for Gregg a particularly natural stroke sequence is *pr*, which for Pitman is *ln*, and for Sloan-Duployé (an adaptation of the principal French system, at one time strong competition for Pitman and Gregg) is *ws*.

Gregg migrated first to Liverpool, where his system was published in 1888 (FIGURE 80), then to Boston, Chicago, and finally New York. Within a few years, his system had become preeminent in the U.S. (except, oddly, in New York City), due not only to its inherent quality but also to his energetic self-promotion and salesmanship.

In the wake of Gregg's American success, there seems to have been a decline in publication of competing shorthand systems (though for "Teeline," recently popular in Great Britain, see MacMahon 1994); instead, a large number of alphabet-based shorthands is available. The best known has been "Speedwriting," whose ubiquitous advertising slogan "if u c rd ħs u c gt a gd jb" stimulated many a joke; "Notescript" includes instructions for "Notetyping" (Hawkins 1964: 109).

Typology

Some authors (e.g. MacMahon 1994; also, apparently, J. R. Gregg) see shorthand falling into two categories: *geometric* and *cursive*. The former covers systems whose signs are based on circles, straight lines, etc.; the latter refers to those whose shapes are taken from those found in current handwriting. Pitman and Gregg exemplify the two types, respectively.

I prefer (as elsewhere in this volume) to classify systems by function rather than form: by whether they encode words, letters ("literal"), or sounds. This division also corresponds to the historical order of the development of shorthand.

Logographic

Although even Greek tachygraphy and Tironian notæ rested ultimately on a literal foundation, they were primarily logographic, and the eventual catalog of some 8,000 signs was far too cumbersome for efficient use. Bright's Characterie likewise overwhelmed the user, and logography was soon abandoned as the exclusive basis for shorthand. Nonetheless, every shorthand system includes at least a few wordsigns for the most common particles, since it would be folly not to take advantage of the statistics of speaking (the 15 most frequent words in any text make up 25% of it; the first 100, 60%; and the first 1000, 85%: Crystal 1987: 87).

Alphabetic

Since everyone interested in writing faster is already competent in writing, it makes sense to build on existing ability. Words are composed of letters, and letters are what are written, so we ought merely to find a faster way of writing letters. Such was the practice of the pioneers like Willis and Shelton. But there is an additional wrinkle: not until the early nineteenth century was there a standard means of distinguishing two meanings of *letter*, viz. 'speech sound' and 'written character' (Abercrombie 1949). Essentially, the shorthand inventor who made shapes for "letters" was recording both speech and writing.

It is recent alphabetic systems that take advantage of existing knowledge of writing, in that they take the standard spelling of English, rather than its pronunciation, as the base, and offer systematic instructions for omitting redundant letters. We know that whole-word-shape plays a part in word recognition, so that *know* is easier to read than KNOW—we know that *know* is tall at the front, so we do not omit the "silent" *k*; in Notescript, for instance, *know* and its derivatives are "*kn.*". Note that Karlgren 1978: 119 denies that "abbreviated longhand" is a form of shorthand at all.

TABLE 70.1: *The 63 Braille Shapes Arranged by Dot Pattern (Loomis 1942)*[a]

A	B	C	D	E	F	G	H	I	J
1	2	3	4	5	6	7	8	9	0
a	but	can	do	every	from	go	have		just

K	L	M	N	O	P	Q	R	S	T
knowl-edge	like	more	not		people	quite	rather	so	that

U	V	X	Y	Z	Ç	É	À	È	Ù
us	very	it	you	as	and	for	of	the	with

Â	Ê	Î	Ô	Û	Ë	Ï	Ü	Ö Œ	W
child		shall	this	which					will
ch	gh	sh	th	wh	ed	er	ou	ow	

,	;	:	.		!	( )	? "		"
	bb	cc	dd	en		gg; were		in	

Ì	Ò		Ä Æ	'	-
fraction line		numeral			
st	ing	sign	ar		

numerical index accent	literal index	recurring decimal mark wordlets		italic sign decimal point	letter sign	capital sign

a. Numerous rules govern the use of various grades of braille.

BRAILLE. (American) braille is not simply a transposition of English words, letter by letter, into patterns of embossed dots that are perceived by a blind person's fingertips. Not just 26 of the possible combinations of six dot positions (TABLE 68.4 on page 792) are used, but all 63. (The 64th possibility, absence of all dots, is the space character.) Some of the "extra" characters index the following one(s) as e.g. numerals or capitals or "italics"; some are punctuation marks; many represent common letter combinations; and there is a large complement of "contractions" and abbreviations that function very like the equivalents in written shorthands (AAWB et al. 1984; TABLE 70.1). In Hamp and Caton 1984, "an analysis of American English braille as a written code was undertaken from a linguistic viewpoint. The object was to view and analyze the braille code internally and not as an encipherment of printed lan-

TABLE 70.2: *Outline of Braille Terms (after Hamp and Caton 1984)*

1. Letters
   a. Alphabetic letters (26)
   b. Nonalphabetic letters (12)
      i. 0–9
         decimal point
         fraction bar
      ii. other braille units with abstract letterlike function
         accent sign
         apostrophe
         asterisk ⠡⠔
         ellipsis
         hyphen or dash—when used to indicate missing letters in words
2. Grams[a]
   a. Phonograms (e.g. *ed* in *red* ⠫, *for* in *forest* ⠿, *gh* in *ghost* ⠣)
   b. Morphograms (e.g. *in* in *indecent* ⠔ or *input* ⠔, *th* in *seventh* ⠮)
   c. Logograms
      i. letter word (24) (*a, but, can, ..., it, you, as*)
      ii. wordlet (*about* ⠁⠃, *above* ⠁⠃⠧, *day* ⠙, *there* ⠮, *these* ⠮, *their* ⠮, ...)
3. Modulations
   a. Punctuation
      i. look back
         | colon | period |
         | comma | question mark |
         | exclamation point | semicolon |
      ii. enclose
         bracket or brace (in pairs)
         comma (in pairs)
         parenthesis (in pairs)
         quotation marks, single (in pairs)
         quotation marks, double (in pairs)
      iii. link
         | bar | long dash |
         | hyphen | bracket or brace (one) |
         | dash | |
   b. Register[b]
      | capital sign, single | letter sign |
      | capital sign, double | number sign |
      | italic sign, single | termination sign |
      | italic sign, double | |

a. Grams are segmental in value, but they have no single counterpart in print.
b. Register signs "look forward," and have no segmental counterpart in print.

guage" (cited from an augmented version kindly provided, along with other relevant material, by Eric P. Hamp, to whom I here express my appreciation). This analysis classifies the units of the code—including those comprising more than one shape that are recognized as units—as in TABLE 70.2. The purpose of the analysis was improvement of materials for the education of braille users (for whom braille is *not* a variety of English orthography, which they have never learned to read, but rather an independent writing system), and it has been put into practice in Caton et al. 1993.

Phonotypic

Phonotypy is Isaac Pitman's word for a featural script (SECTION 1)—whether shorthand or reformed spelling—in which the shapes of characters correspond to phonetic features of the sounds they stand for (Kelly 1981). Thus, in Pitman, *t* is a light downward vertical, and *d* is a heavy downward vertical; in Gregg, *t* is a short upward straight line (sloping to the right), and *d* is a longer upward straight line (and *ted* is a very long upward straight line). No one seems, even in the heyday of shorthand research in the mid twentieth century, to have investigated whether phonotypy, as opposed to the random assignment of sounds to shapes, has a practical effect on speed or accuracy of shorthand reporting or transcription. One might expect a *decrease*, since confusion might arise with (near) homonyms being (near) homographs as well. Such questions are touched on by Karlgren (1978)—apparently the only article on shorthand in the entire linguistic literature?—citing earlier European shorthand scholars. (As between alphabetic and phonotypic shorthand, one instructor reported that Speedwriting is easier to learn than Gregg, but Gregg is easier to use; see Daniels 1992: 88, with n. 15 on the needlessness of teaching phonetics to shorthand students.)

An earnest pamphlet (O'Keefe 1920 for the New York State Shorthand Reporters' Association Committee on Shorthand Standards) may help account for the primacy of Pitman in New York. Ostensibly a review of the sort of exaggerated claims by shorthand advertisers that used to pollute the print media, its supposedly objective evaluations of the two principal systems and three heavily promoted rivals are based on Dewey 1920. Godfrey Dewey was the son of the library scientist and spelling reformer Melvil Dewey; his objective data on the frequency of English sounds and spellings come from an analysis of 100,000 words of connected English (the basis of Dewey 1923, 1970). But his terribly scientific arrangement of "axioms and definitions," "canons," and "theorems"—which are the subdivisions of "General considerations," "Fonetic or sounds," "Geometric or signs," "Assignment of signs to sounds," "Manual or writing," "Visual or reading," and "Mental or remembering"—belies the fact that his every statement is unsupported, unargued opinion. Thus he presents his analysis of English sounds into 40 of what were soon to be recognized as phonemes; asserts that they fall into a particular set of what are now called natural classes; insists that any shorthand must provide representation for each sound so identified; and requires that sounds in any of the classes must be assigned similar signs. (Some of his rules are attributed to an otherwise unidentified Dr. R. G. Latham writing "more than half a century" earlier; p. 26. This was an English philologist, 1812–1888.)

The analyses take into account that there are potentially three types of shorthand uses: professional reporting (in court or legislature; a few thousand practitioners), commercial dictation (a few hundred thousand stenographers), and general personal use (then, very few; now, almost the only users). For Pitman, they include two pages of "strength" and three pages of "weakness"; for Gregg, one and five respectively. (For Pitman: "The very valuable device of position is hopelessly overburdened," p. 61; for Gregg: "Exclusion of position subtracts more ... than it adds," p. 70.) Yet Dewey's criteria are clearly designed to favor Pitman, even sometimes explicitly; and the two main "weaknesses" of Gregg would now be recognized as particular strengths: it does not provide distinct signs for certain sounds of low functional load (such as [ð] and [ʒ]); and it groups the vowels more according to their spelling than according to their sound (thus accommodating speakers of various dialects of English, rather than requiring them to report at great speed in essentially a non-native language).

Gregg's (1923: 141) seven basic principles of shorthand follow. As John Robert Gregg was probably unique in combining practical experience of a wide variety of shorthands, a lifetime of intense thought about the problems involved, and creation of a highly successful system, his conclusions should underlie any future research on the nature of shorthand:

1. Based on the ellipse or oval—on the slope of longhand
2. Curvilinear motion
3. Elimination of obtuse angles by natural blending of lines
4. Joined vowels
5. One thickness—elimination of shading
6. One position—elimination of "position writing"
7. Lineality—the easy, continuous flow of the writing along the line

---

Bibliography

Specific shorthand publications are not cited here, unless they have been directly quoted; for bibliography, see Rockwell 1884, Brown and Haskell 1932–34.

Abercrombie, David. 1937. *Isaac Pitman[: A Pioneer in the Scientific Study of Language]*. London: Pitman. Abridged repr. in Abercrombie 1965: 92–107.

——. 1949. "What Is a 'Letter'?" *Lingua* 2: 54–63. Repr. in Abercrombie 1965: 76–85.

——. 1965. *Studies in Phonetics and Linguistics* (Language and Language Learning 10). London: Oxford University Press.

American Association of Workers for the Blind; Association for Education of the Visually Handicapped; and National Braille Association. 1984. *English Braille American Edition 1959, revised 1972*. With *Addenda 1980, 1987*. Louisville, Ky.: American Printing House for the Blind.

Asher, R. E., and Eugénie Henderson. 1981. *Towards a History of Linguistics: Papers Contributed in Honour of David Abercrombie*. Edinburgh: Edinburgh University Press.

Boge, Herbert. 1974. *Griechische Tachygraphie und Tironische Noten* (Altertumswissenschaftliche Texte und Studien 2). Hildesheim: Olms.

Brown, Karl, and Daniel C. Haskell. 1932–34. "The Shorthand Collection in the New York Public Library" (28 parts, April 1932 – October 1934). *Bulletin of the New York Public Library*.

Cappelli, Adriano. 1929. *Dizionario di abbreviature latine ed italiane*. Repr. Milan: Ulrico Hoepli, 1973.

Caton, Hilda, et al. 1993. *Patterns: The Primary Braille Spelling and English Program Level B, Teacher's Edition to Accompany Building Blocks*. Louisville, Ky.: American Printing House for the Blind.

Cowan, Leslie. 1984. *John Robert Gregg*. Oxford: The Pre-Raphaelite Press at Oxford.

Crystal, David. 1987. *The Cambridge Encyclopedia of Language*. Cambridge: Cambridge Univ. Pr.

Cylke, Frank Kurt, comp. 1990. *World Braille Usage*. Paris: UNESCO; Washington, D.C.: Library of Congress, National Library Service for the Blind and Physically Handicapped.

Daniels, Peter T. 1992. "The Syllabic Origin of Writing and the Segmental Origin of the Alphabet." In *The Linguistics of Literacy* (Typological Studies in Language 21), ed. Pamela Downing, Susan D. Lima, and Michael Noonan, pp. 83–110. Amsterdam: Benjamins.

Dewey, Godfrey. 1920. "The Science of Shorthand." In O'Keefe 1920: 13–44.

———. 1923. *Relativ Frequency of English Speech Sounds*. Cambridge: Harvard University Press (rev. ed., 1950).

———. 1970. *Relative Frequency of English Spellings*. New York: Teachers College Press.

Drucker, Johanna. 1995. *The Alphabetic Labyrinth: The Letters in History and Imagination*. London: Thames and Hudson.

Friedrich, Paul. 1918. "Studien zur englischen Stenographie im Zeitalter Shakespeares: Timothe Brights Characterie entwicklungsgeschichtlich und kritisch betrachtet." *Archiv für Schriftkunde* 1: 88–140, 147–88.

Gregg, John Robert. 1923. *The Basic Principles of Gregg Shorthand*. New York: Gregg.

———. 1929. *Gregg Shorthand: A Light-line Phonography for the Million,* anniversary edition. New York: Gregg.

———. 1933–40. "The Story of Shorthand" (45 parts, September 1933 – November 1940). *The Business Education World* (published 9 times a year).

Hamp, Eric P., and Hilda Caton. 1984. "A Fresh Look at the Sign System of the Braille Code." *Journal of Visual Impairment and Blindness* 78: 210–14. Augmented version to appear in *Four Analytic Studies of the American Literary Braille Code,* by Eric P. Hamp, Hilda Caton, et al. Louisville, Ky.: American Printing House for the Blind.

Hawkins, Laurence F. 1964. *Notescript*. N.p.: Barnes & Noble.

Karlgren, Hans. 1978. "On the Arbitrariness of Shorthand Signs." *Studia Linguistica* 32: 119–36.

Kelly, John. 1981. "The 1847 Alphabet: An Episode of Phonotypy." In Asher and Henderson 1981: 248–64.

Kopp, Ulrich Friedrich. 1817–29. *Palaeographia critica*. 4 vols. Mannheim.

Leslie, Louis A., ed. 1964. *The Story of Gregg Shorthand Based on the Writings of John Robert Gregg*. New York: McGraw-Hill, Gregg Division.

Loomis, Madeleine Seymour. 1942. *The Braille Reference Book [for Grades I, I¹/₂, and II]*. New York: Harper.

MacMahon, Michael K. C. 1981. "Henry Sweet's System of Shorthand." In Asher and Henderson 1981: 265–81.

———. 1994. "Shorthand." *The Encyclopedia of Language and Linguistics* 7: 3877–82. Oxford: Pergamon.

Milne, H. J. M. 1934. *Greek Shorthand Manuals: Syllabary and Commentary* (Graeco-Roman Memoir 24). London: Egypt Exploration Society.

O'Keefe, David H., comp. 1920. *Shorthand Systems Analyzed: Gregg Pitman K. I. Paragon and Boyd Syllabic*. Brooklyn, N.Y.: author.

Rockwell, J. E. 1884. *The Teaching and Practice of Shorthand*. United States Department of the Interior, Education Bureau, Circular of Information 2. Washington, D.C.: Govt. Printing Office.

Schöttner, Adolf. 1918. "Über die mutmaßliche stenographische Entstehung der ersten Quarto von Shakespeares 'Romeo und Julia.'" *Archiv für Schriftkunde* 1: 229–340.

Schmitz, W. 1893. *Commentarii Notarum Tironianarum ....* Leipzig.

Slaughter, M. M. 1982. *Universal Languages and Scientific Taxonomy in the Seventeenth Century*. Cambridge: Cambridge University Press.

Thompson, E. Maunde. 1912. *An Introduction to Greek and Latin Paleography*. Oxford: Clarendon.

Phonetic Notation

MICHAEL K. C. MACMAHON

The term *phonetic notation* refers both to the repertoire of phonetic symbols and diacritics used in the transcription of spoken language, and to the employment of such symbols and diacritics in creating a transcription of pronunciation. Because of its scientific basis, it has come to be regarded as superior to more traditional methods of notating speech, namely the use of an alphabetic orthography or (for certain languages like Chinese and Japanese) a syllabary. Phonetic notation focuses exclusively on the articulatory dimension of speech, i.e. the postures and movements of the speech organs. There is no equivalent notational system for the acoustic dimension, i.e. the patterns of air-pressure changes set in motion by the movements of the speech organs and transmitted to the listener's ears.

A comparison of four words in traditional orthography and in phonetic notation will illuminate the difference between the two methods of transcription. The English word *hat*, consisting of three letters, suggests that—certain regional dialects excepted—there are three sounds in the word; the phonetic notation [hat] indeed confirms this. The word *hath*, with four letters, contains, however, only three sounds; hence the phonetic notation [haθ]. *That*, with four letters but only three sounds, has a different *th* sound at the beginning compared with the *th* at the end of *hath*: the phonetic notation is therefore [ðat]. A phonetic notation of *hate*, with its four orthographic characters, will show that there are only three sound-units in the word: [h], a vowel, and [t]. The notation of the vowel, however, will depend on the speaker's pronunciation. It could be transcribed as [het], [heːt], [heɪt], [hɛɪt] or [hæɪt]; yet other possibilities exist. (The double-vowel notation in the last three transcriptions indicates that the sound-unit is a diphthong, i.e. a sound in which there is movement of the tongue—and sometimes also the lips. In *hat* the vowel is, for most speakers, a monophthong, a stationary vowel.)

━━━━━

The International Phonetic Alphabet (IPA)

The alphabet devised and promulgated by the International Phonetic Association (also IPA) is the main phonetic alphabet in use today throughout the world, and contains an extensive set of symbols and diacritics (FIGURE 81). In the transcription of any one language, however, only a subset of these will be required.

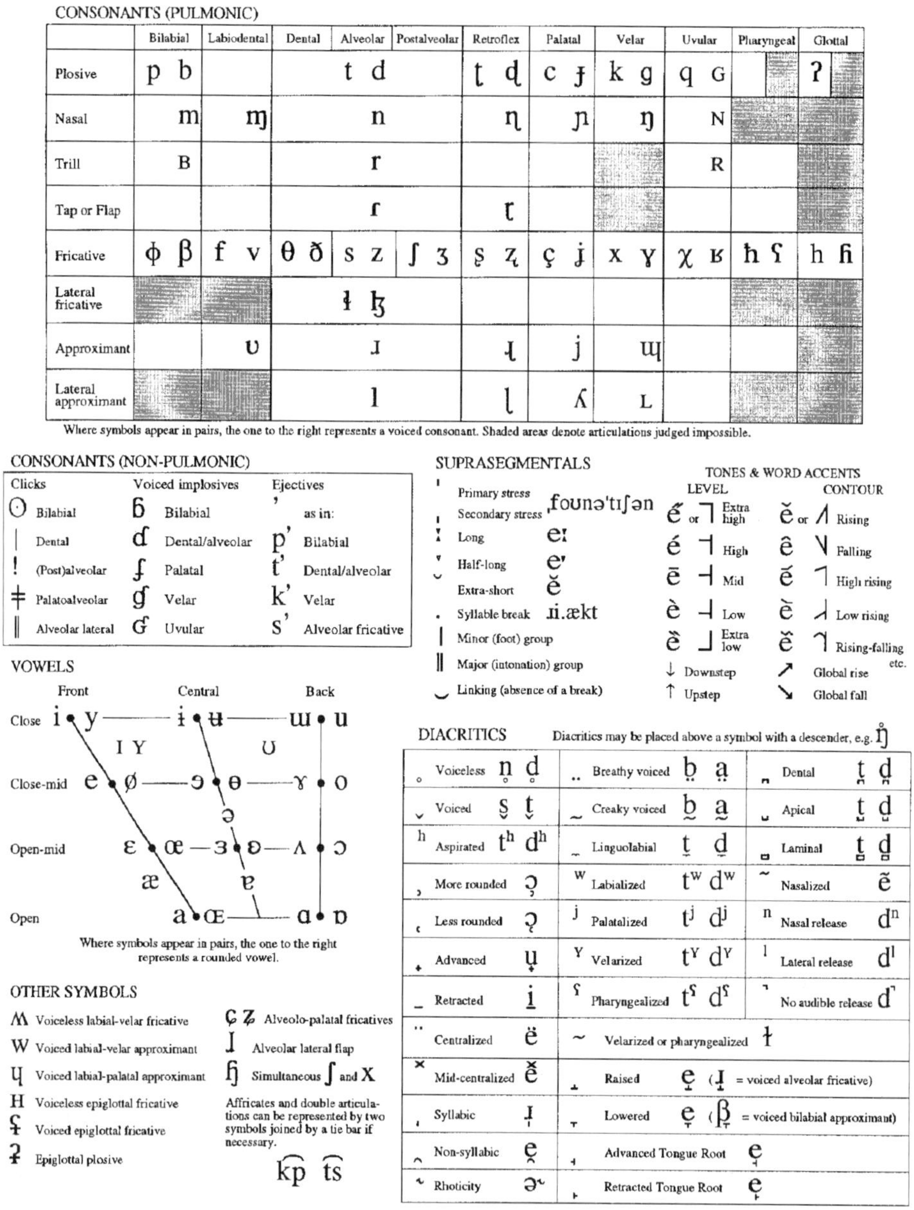

CONSONANTS (PULMONIC)

	Bilabial	Labiodental	Dental	Alveolar	Postalveolar	Retroflex	Palatal	Velar	Uvular	Pharyngeal	Glottal
Plosive	p　b			t　d		ʈ　ɖ	c　ɟ	k　ɡ	q　ɢ		ʔ
Nasal	m	ɱ		n		ɳ	ɲ	ŋ	N		
Trill	B			r					R		
Tap or Flap				ɾ		ɽ					
Fricative	ɸ　β	f　v	θ　ð	s　z	ʃ　ʒ	ʂ　ʐ	ç　ʝ	x　ɣ	χ　ʁ	ħ　ʕ	h　ɦ
Lateral fricative				ɬ　ɮ							
Approximant		ʋ		ɹ		ɻ	j	ɰ			
Lateral approximant				l		ɭ	ʎ	L			

Where symbols appear in pairs, the one to the right represents a voiced consonant. Shaded areas denote articulations judged impossible.

CONSONANTS (NON-PULMONIC)

Clicks		Voiced implosives		Ejectives	
ʘ	Bilabial	ɓ	Bilabial	’	as in:
ǀ	Dental	ɗ	Dental/alveolar	p’	Bilabial
ǃ	(Post)alveolar	ʄ	Palatal	t’	Dental/alveolar
ǂ	Palatoalveolar	ɠ	Velar	k’	Velar
ǁ	Alveolar lateral	ʛ	Uvular	s’	Alveolar fricative

VOWELS

Where symbols appear in pairs, the one to the right represents a rounded vowel.

OTHER SYMBOLS

ʍ Voiceless labial-velar fricative
w Voiced labial-velar approximant
ɥ Voiced labial-palatal approximant
ʜ Voiceless epiglottal fricative
ʢ Voiced epiglottal fricative
ʡ Epiglottal plosive

ɕ ʑ Alveolo-palatal fricatives
ɺ Alveolar lateral flap
ɧ Simultaneous ʃ and x

Affricates and double articulations can be represented by two symbols joined by a tie bar if necessary.

k͡p t͡s

SUPRASEGMENTALS

ˈ	Primary stress	ˌfoʊnəˈtɪʃən
ˌ	Secondary stress	
ː	Long	eː
ˑ	Half-long	eˑ
̆	Extra-short	ĕ
.	Syllable break	ɹi.ækt
ǀ	Minor (foot) group	
ǁ	Major (intonation) group	
‿	Linking (absence of a break)	

TONES & WORD ACCENTS

	LEVEL			CONTOUR	
e̋ or ˥	Extra high		ě or ˩˥	Rising	
é ˦	High		ê ˥˩	Falling	
ē ˧	Mid		e̋ ˩˧	High rising	
è ˨	Low		ȅ ˧˩	Low rising	
ȅ ˩	Extra low		e̋ ˩˧˩	Rising-falling	
↓	Downstep		↗	Global rise	etc.
↑	Upstep		↘	Global fall	

DIACRITICS   Diacritics may be placed above a symbol with a descender, e.g. ŋ̊

̥	Voiceless	n̥ d̥	̤	Breathy voiced	b̤ a̤	̪	Dental	t̪ d̪
̬	Voiced	s̬ t̬	̰	Creaky voiced	b̰ a̰	̺	Apical	t̺ d̺
ʰ	Aspirated	tʰ dʰ	̼	Linguolabial	t̼ d̼	̻	Laminal	t̻ d̻
̹	More rounded	ɔ̹	ʷ	Labialized	tʷ dʷ	̃	Nasalized	ẽ
̜	Less rounded	ɔ̜	ʲ	Palatalized	tʲ dʲ	ⁿ	Nasal release	dⁿ
̟	Advanced	u̟	ˠ	Velarized	tˠ dˠ	ˡ	Lateral release	dˡ
̠	Retracted	i̠	ˤ	Pharyngealized	tˤ dˤ	̚	No audible release	d̚
̈	Centralized	ë	̴	Velarized or pharyngealized	ɫ			
̽	Mid-centralized	ě̽	̝	Raised	e̝ (ɹ̝ = voiced alveolar fricative)			
̩	Syllabic	l̩	̞	Lowered	e̞ (β̞ = voiced bilabial approximant)			
̯	Non-syllabic	e̯	̘	Advanced Tongue Root	e̘			
˞	Rhoticity	ə˞	̙	Retracted Tongue Root	e̙			

FIGURE 81. The International Phonetic Alphabet (revised to 1993).

A number of important principles of phonetic notation emerge from the exposition so far.

(1)   Some of the symbols used in phonetic notation—at least those of IPA—are the same as in traditional orthography, e.g. [h], [a], [t], [e], but their sound values may differ from those normally associated with the orthographic characters.

(2)   Each symbol has, generally, a specific sound-value associated with it. Thus the [a] of [kat] *cat* cannot be used for the vowel in *hate*. For this, [e] or [e:] etc. must be used (see above).

(3)   Some symbols hark back to an older, extended Roman alphabet for English, still sometimes used—as well as, simultaneously, to the modem Scandinavian alphabets. The phonetic symbols [æ] and [œ], for example, occasionally occur today in words like *encyclopædia* and *homœopathic*.

(4)   Some symbols are taken from the Greek alphabet, e.g. [θ] and [ɛ].

(5)   Some symbols are modified versions of Roman letters or punctuation marks, e.g. [ɪ] and [ʔ].

(6)   Other symbols derive from more specialized alphabets. For example, [ʃ], used for the *sh* sound in e.g. *she*, is very like the integral symbol in mathematics. And the [″] diacritic, marking extra-high tone, is taken from the Hungarian version of the Roman alphabet, where it marks a long rounded front vowel.

(7)   A final category, not so far illustrated, consists of phonetic characters which are not based on any specific alphabet but have been created de novo: e.g. the diacritic for a dental articulation [ṋ], and the diacritic for no audible release [̚].

Transcriptions of *caught* [kɔ:t] and *team* [ti:m] show [ɔ], the reversed form of the phonetic symbol [c], and [:] (which indicates that the preceding vowel is long), a more elaborate version of the orthographic colon :. The word *nurse*, as pronounced by most speakers in England, would be transcribed [nɜ:s]. The [ɜ] is both a reversed Greek epsilon ɛ and a Russian zemla ɜ *z*. A transcription of most American pronunciations of *nurse* will require an additional element [ˇ] to indicate the positioning of the tongue for an *r* sound; the word is transcribed [nɝs]. Because of different historical changes in pronunciation, the English of England has, by and large, lost any trace of an *r* before the [s], and the pronunciation is thus more out of line with the orthography than is the case with the majority of American English accents.

The structure of the International Phonetic Alphabet

An examination of the 1993 International Phonetic Alphabet (FIGURE 81) shows that: (a) Many of the symbols and diacritics are direct or partial derivatives of symbols and punctuation marks of the Roman alphabet. (b) Lower-case forms predominate; where upper-case letters are used, they are normally in the form of small capitals. (c) All characters are in Roman type; italic type is not used. (d) There is, generally, little systematic connection between the shape of a symbol and the sound it represents. Exceptions are the symbols for nasal sounds (*top box, second row*), which are all based on the letter *n*; the symbols for retroflex sounds (*top box, middle column*), which all have a descender ending in a curl to the right below the baseline; and the symbols for voiced implosives and ejectives (*left side, middle box*), which respectively have a right-turning hook on top and a following apostrophe. Some phonetic alphabets, however, but not IPA, do consistently reflect articulatory features in their symbol-shapes—see "Iconic notation" on page 838. (e) Considerable care has been taken in the design of the font to ensure that there is visual harmonization of the symbols.

Ever since the first IPA chart was published, in 1888, one of its underlying principles has been that a sound should be symbolized only if it has phonemic status in at least one language in the world. What this means is that, even if a particular sound is used in a language, it will not be assigned an individual symbol unless it contrasts meaningfully with an articulatorily similar sound in the same language. (Technically, there has to be a *phonemic contrast* between the two sounds.) Thus there are symbols for the [s] and [z] sounds in IPA because of the meaningful contrast between [pi:s] *piece*, *peace*, and [pi:z] *peas*; but no separate symbol for the third sound in the word *cupful*, if it is pronounced slightly differently from the [p] sound in *cup*—i.e. with the upper teeth and lower lip in contact, rather than the two lips. However, since IPA serves the needs of all languages, it is inevitable that separate symbols will have been created for contrasts in certain languages which can be utilized in transcriptions of languages where the sounds in question do not contrast phonemically. For example, the [ɱ] symbol, for a voiced labiodental nasal, can be used to transcribe this sound in many speakers' pronunciations of the *m* in words like *symphony* and *triumph*, whereas for the labiodental plosive in *cupful*, an arbitrary notational solution has to be sought: namely adding a dental diacritic [◌̪] to a bilabial [p] symbol—thus [p̪]. To indicate that a phonetic symbol represents a phoneme, slant brackets / / enclose the transcription; square brackets [ ] indicate a sound regardless of its phonemic status. The same symbol, therefore, can sometimes have noticeably different interpretations. For example, /t/ in English refers not just to an alveolar place of articulation, but to dental, and postalveolar—and even glottal. But [t] in English can mean only an alveolar sound. In French, /t/ will represent a dental sound. In Malayalam, where the distinction between [t̪], [t], and [ʈ] is phonemic, separate phoneme symbols are required (cf. SECTION 38).

Strictly speaking, then, the IPA is not a universal phonetic alphabet in the sense of an alphabet that will provide a notation for every conceivable sound used in a natural language. Rather, it is a selective phonetic alphabet which is constrained by the requirement of phonemic contrastivity.

Consonant and vowel sounds

The top box on the IPA chart follows the traditional method of setting out the articulatory features, together with their symbols, of consonant sounds which utilize air from the lungs (*pulmonic*). Eleven *places of articulation* run in columns—i.e. areas of the vocal tract where there can be a degree of constriction to the airflow, from the lips on the left to the larynx on the right—and eight *manners of articulation*, in rows, which define the extent of the constriction and how the air is channeled out of the vocal tract. The meanings of the terms are set forth in TABLE 71.1. An empty cell, e.g. at the intersection of Labiodental and Trill, or Retroflex and Lateral fricative, indi-

TABLE 71.1: *Labels for Consonant Sounds*

	Definition	Examples[a]
Alveolar	The alveolar ridge (= teeth-ridge behind the upper front teeth) is one of the articulators	[d] _den_, [z] bu_sy_
Alveolo-palatal	A more forward place of articulation than palatal	[ɕ], [ʑ] Polish _wieś_ 'village', _źle_ 'badly'
Approximant	The gap between the articulators is greater than for a fricative, and the sound does not cause turbulence (friction)	[j] _yes_, [w] _wet_
Bilabial	Both lips are used as the articulators	[b] _big_, [m] _hammer_
Click	A sound made by reducing the air pressure quickly in the mouth during the closure for a stop sound; lung air is not used	[ǀ] (pre-1989 symbol [ʇ]) _tsk_, [ǁ] (pre-1989 symbol [ʖ]) _Xhosa_ (an African language), [ǃ] (pre-1989 symbol [ʗ]) Zulu [ǃaǃa] 'explain'
Dental	The back of the upper front teeth is one of the articulators	[n̪] _tenth_, [θ] _think_, [t̪] French _ton_
Ejective	Air is jerked out of the mouth by pushing the larynx upward quickly	[k'] Quechua [k'ujuj] 'to twist'
Epiglottal	Using as an articulator the epiglottis, the cartilage which folds over the neck of the larynx during swallowing	the _'ain_ [ʕ] in several forms of Arabic and of Oriental Hebrew
Fricative	Because there is a small gap between two articulators, the airflow becomes turbulent and the effect of "friction" is heard	[s] _sing_, [ʃ] _shin_, [x] Scots _loch_
Glottal	The glottis is the space between the vocal cords (folds), depending on the position of the vocal cords. When the cords are completely together, a glottal plosive ("stop") is produced	[ʔ] in many pronunciations of _kitten_, _what_
Implosive	The opposite motion from an ejective: air is sucked inward by downward movement of the larynx	[ɠ] Sindhi [ɠaɳu] 'handle'; sometimes heard in English, e.g., if a stutterer attempts to say the [g] in _get_ and prolongs the sound
Labial-palatal	There are two constrictions to the airflow through the mouth: at the lips and at the hard palate	[ɥ] French _lui_
Labial-velar	There are two constrictions to the airflow through the mouth: at the lips and at the softpalate	[ʍ] in many pronunciations of _when_, [w] in all pronunciations of _wet_, French _Louis_
Labiodental	The lower lip and the upper front teeth are the articulators	[ɱ] _symphony_, Italian i_n_vidia 'envy'; [f] _find_, [ʋ] German _Quelle_ 'source'

TABLE 71.1: *Labels for Consonant Sounds (Continued)*

	Definition	Examples[a]
Lateral approximant	The gap between the articulators is greater than for the equivalent fricative, and the air leaves the mouth over the sides of the tongue	[l] *lend*, [ʎ] Italian *figlio* 'son'
Lateral fricative	The friction occurs between the edges of the tongue and the roof of the mouth	[ɬ] Welsh *llan* 'church, parish', [ɮ] Zulu *dhla* 'eat'
Nasal	The soft palate (velum) is lowered and all the air is directed into the nose	[m] *map*, [n] *pin*, [ŋ] *song*. Note that a word like *finger* contains both a nasal [ŋ] and a plosive [g]
Palatal	The hard palate, situated between the alveolar ridge and the soft palate, is one of the articulators	[ɟ] Hungarian *nagy* 'big', [c] Persian *yak* 'one'
Pharyngeal	The pharynx is the upper half of the throat. Generally, pharyngeal sounds involve creating constrictions of several muscles in the throat	[ħ], [ʕ] Arabic [ħamma:m] 'bath', [ʕamm] 'uncle'
Plosive	There is a brief and complete blockage to the flow of air in the mouth. When the blockage is removed, a mild "ex*plos*ion" of air results	[p] *pin*, [g] *aghast*
Postalveolar	The area behind the alveolar ridge is one of the articulators	[ʃ] *bash*, [ʒ] *measure*
Retroflex	This describes the shape of the tongue: the tip and blade are curled back	[ɻ] in many, especially American, pronunciations of *red*, [ʈ] Swedish *kort* 'card'. Retroflex sounds are common in many languages of the Indian subcontinent, e.g. Hindi, Malayalam
Stop	A general term often used for click, ejective, implosive, and plosive	
Tap or Flap	A brief tapping sound made by an articulator against another	[r] often heard in varieties of British English in words like *three* and *bring*; in American English, a typical pronunciation in *latter* and *ladder*
Trill	An articulator beats rapidly but loosely against another	[r] an exaggerated stage pronunciation in words like *ragged*, *grow*; or in some forms of French, *regrette rien* 'regret nothing'
Uvular	The uvula, the grape-like object which forms the very end of the soft palate, is one of the articulators	[ʁ] French *rue* 'street', [ɢ] Arabic *qom*, [ɴ] Eskimo *enina* 'melody'
Velar	The soft palate (velum) is one of the articulators	[k] *cat*, [g] *get*, [ŋ] *sang*, [x] Scots *loch*, [ɣ] Spanish *abogado* 'lawyer'

a. English, unless otherwise indicated.

cates that the sound in question is not known to be used as a separate phoneme in any of the world's languages. If subsequent research shows the contrary, then the IPA will consider creating appropriate symbols for such sounds. The shaded cells indicate intersections of place and manner which are judged to be physiologically impossible: e.g. Velar + Trill, which would involve the rapid and fairly loose movement of the back of the tongue against the soft palate—something that the human articulatory apparatus cannot achieve. Where two symbols occur in a cell, that on the right represents a sound produced with *voicing*, i.e. vibration of the vocal cords (= vocal folds), and the sound is described as being *voiced*; that on the left, a sound without voicing: the sound is *voiceless*. Compare the [z] (voiced) and [s] (voiceless) sounds in the words *razor* and *racer*.

The smaller box below the pulmonic consonant box gives the place (and sometimes also the manner) of consonants which do not utilize air from the lungs in their production (*non-pulmonic*). The *click* sounds in the *tsk-tsk* expression of disapproval/annoyance in English would be written [| |].

For more detailed symbolizations of consonant sounds—usually at the level of narrow transcription—the box at the lower right of the chart provides a set of special diacritics. A diacritic is placed, depending on its phonetic value and shape, either below the symbol, e.g. [d̥]; through it, e.g. [ɫ]; above it, e.g. [ë]; or as a superscript to the right of the symbol, e.g. [tʰ].

As with most consonants, the symbols for vowel sounds (*left side, two-thirds down*) employ traditional Roman (or modified Roman) symbols; but there is little systematicity in the choice of symbols. Again, there is a historical reason for this, namely the preference for certain symbols during thc early years of the IPA's existence. The trapezoidal shape devised by the British phonetician Daniel Jones on which the vowel symbols are located is known as the Cardinal Vowel chart (D. Jones 1962: 31–39)— although for technical reasons not all the symbols indicated there are Cardinal Vowels (see Catford 1988: 138–71).

Beneath the vowels is a set of additional symbols with their descriptors. In some cases (e.g. alveolar lateral flap, which contains three significant features), they cannot easily be fitted into the two-dimensional Consonants box at the top of the chart; in other cases, the symbols are very recent (e.g. those for the epiglottal fricatives and plosive).

Prosodic features

Prosodic features, also called *suprasegmentals*, are features of pronunciation which extend beyond the domain of a single segment, e.g. stress, intonation, and rhythm. Pronouncing aloud the words *impish* and *impossible* will reveal a different pattern of stress (or emphasis) between the two words. The IPA convention is to mark the beginning of the stressed syllable (*not* the vowel in the stressed syllable, as in many dictionaries) by means of a raised vertical mark: thus, ˈimpish, imˈpossible. The word

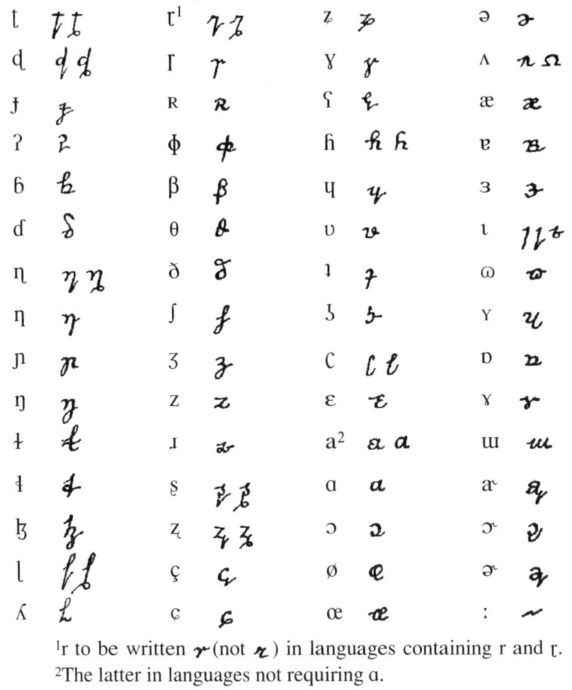

¹r to be written 𝒓 (not 𝒙) in languages containing r and ɽ.
²The latter in languages not requiring ɑ.

FIGURE 82. The International Phonetic Alphabet (revised to 1949): Cursive forms.

examination, if said fairly slowly, will require an extra mark to indicate a secondary degree of stress, i.e. ex‚ami'nation. Sometimes, to indicate a particularly heavy stress (*emphatic* stress), a double " is used, e.g. *She "can't come*, although this symbolization is no longer sanctioned by the IPA.

Intonation, i.e. the melody of the voice, can be notated using diacritics for tones and word accents—some of them IPA (*middle, right side*), others arbitrary—or with more precision by means of an iconic transcription, an arrangement of the segmental notation, be it phonetic, phonemic, or orthographic. An example is:
Diacritical:

I ＼don't think °they'll be ˅pleased.

/aɪ ＼doʊnt θɪŋk °ðeɪl bɪ ˅pliːzd/
Iconic:

aɪ ᵈoʊnt θɪŋk ðeɪl bɪ pliːzd

The IPA chart lacks a dedicated set of symbols or diacritics for notating the rhythmic structure of speech. Conventions from the work of earlier prosodists (e.g. ◡ for a short syllable, and – for a long syllable), are generally employed, although these do not have, as yet, IPA approval. Furthermore, misunderstandings can occur: e.g., the diacritic ◡̆ on the chart stands for an extra-short sound, not a short syllable.

Extensions to the IPA

One area in which IPA notation has been used extensively is the speech and language pathology clinic. For the notation of various forms of pathological speech, however, the limitations inherent in the available repertoire of symbols and diacritics, together with articulatory categories, have led to the devising of extra symbols and diacritics, which have the approval of the IPA (Duckworth et al. 1990, Ball 1991: 39–40).

Relatively recent studies of voice quality have led to the creation of additional notational features. Voice quality is the auditory effect of the long-term settings of the vocal tract that individual speakers employ. For example, one speaker may use, virtually consistently, a nasalized voice ("talking through the nose"), another one a whispery voice, etc. Symbols for certain voice qualities are provided by the IPA (e.g. for creaky voice and nasalized voice); appropriate symbolizations of many other voice qualities can be found in Laver 1994: 423. Specifically for the notation of phonation types (i.e. modes of vibration of the vocal cords and the ventricular (= false) cords), as well as for the indication of loudness levels and types of pauses in speech, additional symbols and diacritics are now also available (Ball 1991: 41).

All the IPA's symbols and diacritics, including those in the "extensions" set, have been assigned an individual ISO computer code, to permit the unambiguous electronic transmission of phonetic notation (Esling and Gaylord 1993, Ball 1991). Also, the method of mapping of many (but not all) of the phonetic symbols onto the ASCII character set has been regularized (Wells 1987, Laver 1994: 103). At the other end of the technology spectrum, handwritten symbols have been devised for the printed symbols and diacritics of the IPA, but they are rarely used nowadays (FIGURE 82).

Using IPA notations

A variety of professionals use phonetic notation on a day-to-day basis, e.g. phoneticians, linguists, speech and language therapists, speech scientists, dialectologists, foreign-language teachers, lexicographers, and persons engaged in certain sorts of Bible translation work. There are, however, a number of different ways in which the symbols and diacritics can be employed.

The IPA allows some latitude in the choice of symbols, especially in a phonemic transcription. Thus an English English pronunciation of *What a fool not to see the good and the bad things* might be symbolized in several ways:

(1)   /wot ə fuːl not tə siː ðə gud ənd ðə bad θiŋz/
(2)   /wɒt ə fuːl nɒt tə siː ðə gʊd ənd ðə bæd θiŋz/
(3)   /wɔt ə fuːl nɔt tə siː ðə gud ənd ðə bæd θiŋz/
(4)   /wot ə fuul not tə sii ðə gud ənd ðə bad θiŋz/

Yet further notations can be devised (Abercrombie 1964). The choice of symbols depends largely on the purpose of the notation. For example, the needs of a student learning a foreign language are quite different from those of a dialectologist con-

		Bi-labial	Labio-dental	Dental and Alveolar	Retroflex	Palato-alveolar	Alveolo-palatal	Palatal	Velar	Uvular	Pharyngal	Glottal
CONSONANTS	Plosive	p b		t d	ʈ ɖ			c ɟ	k g	q ɢ		ʔ
	Nasal	m	ɱ	n	ɳ			ɲ	ŋ	ɴ		
	Lateral Fricative			ɬ ɮ								
	Lateral Non-fricative			l	ɭ			ʎ				
	Rolled			r						ʀ		
	Flapped			ɾ	ɽ					ʀ		
	Fricative	ɸ β	f v	θ ð s z ɹ	ʂ ʐ	ʃ ʒ	ɕ ʑ	ç j	x ɣ	χ ʁ	ħ ʕ	h ɦ
	Frictionless Continuants and Semi-vowels	w ɥ	ʋ	ɹ				j (ɥ)	(w)	ʁ		

		Bi-labial	Front	Central	Back
VOWELS	Close	(y ʉ u)	i y	ɨ ʉ	ɯ u
	Half-close	(ø o)	e ø	ə	ɤ o
	Half-open	(œ ɔ)	ɛ œ æ	ɐ	ʌ ɔ
	Open	(ɒ)		a	ɑ ɒ

(Secondary articulations are shown by symbols in brackets.)

OTHER SOUNDS.—Palatalized consonants: ƫ, ȡ, etc. Velarized or pharyngalized consonants: ɫ, ɗ, ᵶ, etc. Ejective consonants (plosives with simultaneous glottal stop): p', t', etc. Implosive voiced consonants: ɓ, ɗ, etc. ř fricative trill. σ, ϱ (labialized θ, ð, or s, z). ʅ, ʓ (labialized ʃ, ʒ). ʇ, ʗ, ʖ (clicks, Zulu *c*, *q*, *x*). ɺ (a sound between r and l). ʍ (voiceless w). ɪ, ʏ, ʊ (lowered varieties of i, y, u). ɜ (a variety of ə). ɵ (a vowel between ø and o).

Affricates are normally represented by groups of two consonants (ts, tʃ, dʒ, etc.), but, when necessary, ligatures are used (ʦ, ʧ, ʤ, etc.), or the marks ⁀ or ‿ (t͡s or t‿s, etc.). c, ɟ may occasionally be used in place of tʃ, dʒ. Aspirated plosives: ph, th, etc.

LENGTH, STRESS, PITCH.—ː (full length). ˑ (half length). ˈ (stress, placed at beginning of the stressed syllable). ˌ (secondary stress). ¯ (high level pitch); _ (low level); ˊ (high rising); ˏ (low rising); ˋ (high falling); ˎ (low falling); ˆ (rise-fall); ˇ (fall-rise). See *Ecriture Phonétique Internationale*, p. 9.

MODIFIERS.—˜ nasality. ̥ breath (l̥ = breathed l). ̬ voice (s̬ = z). ʻ slight aspiration following p, t, etc. ̣ specially close vowel (ẹ = a very close e). ̨ specially open vowel (ę = a rather open e). ̫ labialization (n̫ = labialized n). ̪ dental articulation (t̪ = dental t). ˙ palatalization (ż = ʑ). ˔ tongue slightly raised. ˕ tongue slightly lowered. ˒ lips more rounded. ˓ lips more spread. Central vowels ï (= ɨ), ü (= ʉ), ë (= ə˔), ö (= ɵ), ɛ̈, ɔ̈. ̩ (e.g. n̩) syllabic consonant. ̯ consonantal vowel. ʃˢ variety of ʃ resembling s, etc.

FIGURE 83. The International Phonetic Alphabet (revised to 1932).

cerned with capturing certain phonetic and phonological features as accurately as possible. The student would probably find version (1) valuable; the dialectologist is more likely to prefer version (2).

The term *phonemic transcription* indicates that analysis of the speech data has already led to setting up a system of contrasting sounds (*phonemes*). Hence the term *systematic* transcription is often used in its place. An *allophonic* (sometimes called a *narrow*) transcription notates the individual sounds, regardless of which phoneme or phonemes they are associated with. A third type of transcription, known as *impressionistic*, makes no reference whatever to the phonemic status of the sound—or indeed, if necessary, to the segmentation of the stream of speech. Nor need word boundaries be marked. The focus is exclusively on the characteristics of the articulatory adjustments taking place in the vocal tract. An example of an impressionistic transcription of a pronunciation of the sentence *When shall I come?* is: [ʉ̥ʉəɛ̃nnʷʃʷɵlˡɐ̈ëʔk̥ɐ̰̃mm̥].

Different IPA alphabets

During the last hundred years and more, nearly a dozen IPA alphabets have been published, each slightly different from the preceding one. A comparison of, for example, the 1932 alphabet (FIGURE 83), the 1989 (ENDPAPERS), and the 1993 version (FIGURE 81) shows that there have been: (1) slight changes to the typefaces for some of the symbols; (2) changes of name for some phonetic categories; (3) additions to the Alphabet (e.g. [ɺ], [ɶ], and various diacritics; (4) deletions from the Alphabet (e.g. [ơ], [ʠ]). Going further back still, to the earliest official Alphabet, in 1888 (Passy 1888, see FIGURE 84), one finds, in comparison with 1993, only two symbols which have since been removed, [ʌ] and [û], some different terminology ("glottal catch" and "narrow" vowel), and different allocations for some of the symbols (e.g. [q] would be [ɣ] in 1993, and [q] is now used for a sound unsymbolized in 1888). Because overall the changes have largely been minimal, it is comparatively easy to read IPA phonetic notation from earlier periods.

The immediate source for many of the IPA symbols when the alphabet was being created in 1888 was the Revised Romic system—"Romic" is equivalent to "Roman"—devised for English and various other languages by the English phonetician Henry Sweet (1880–81, 1971: 270–85). This in turn is based on the Phonotypic Alphabet, devised by Isaac Pitman (of shorthand fame, see SECTION 70) and Alexander J. Ellis, an English phonetician and philologist, in 1847 (Kelly 1981). Indeed, much earlier examples of some of the symbols are attested: [ð] is an Old English and Old Icelandic symbol; [ŋ] was first used by the English schoolteacher Alexander Gill the Elder, in 1619; and [ɪ] by the English grammarian Charles Butler a few years later, in 1633 (see also Kemp 1994, Abercrombie 1981).

Other alphabetic notations

Interest in phonetic notation can be traced back, in England, to the late sixteenth century and the work of the diplomat and scholar Sir Thomas Smith and the phonetician John Hart, both of whom published examples of their notations. An unpublished notational system used for transcribing Algonkian, devised in the late sixteenth century

in əkɔrdəns, əz mœtc əz pɔsəbl, wið ðiz prinsiplz, wĭ v tcouzn ðə fɔloiɴ list əv sainz (ðə letərz markt wið ə star˙ ər proviჳənl ceips, ən wil bĭ rĭpleist hwen serkəmstənsiz wil əlau).

ceip				vælju	
		iɴglic	*frenc*	*dჳœrmən*	*œðər læɴgwidჳiz*
p	az in	*p*ut	*p*as	*p*ferd	
b		*b*ut	*b*as	*b*oot	
t		*t*en	*t*ant	*t*ot	
d		*d*en	*d*ent	*d*a	
k		*k*ind	*k*épi	*k*uh	
g		*g*ood	*g*ai	*g*ut	
m		*m*y	*m*a	*m*ein	
n		*n*o	*n*on	*n*ein	
ɴ			rè*g*ne		ital. re*g*no.
˙ɴ		thi*ng*		di*ng*	ital. a*n*che.
l		*l*ull	*l*a	*l*ang	
˙ʎ			fi*ll*e (in ðə sau θ)		sp. *ll*ano, ital. *g*li.
r		*r*ed	*r*are	*r*ot	(tœɴ-pɔint *r*)
ʀ			*r*a*r*e	*r*ot	(bak *r*). — dan. t*r*æ
u				q*u*er	flem. *w*rocht, span. *b*i*b*ir.
ɥ			b*u*is		
w		*w*el	o*u*i		ital. q*u*esto
f		*f*ull	*f*ou	*v*oll	
v		*v*ain	*v*in	*w*ein	
θ		*th*in			span. ra*z*on
ð		*th*en			dan. ga*d*e
s		*s*eal	*s*el	wei*ss*	
z		*z*eal	*z*èle	wei*s*e	
˙c		*sh*e	*ch*at	fi*sch*	swĕd. *s*kæl, dan. *sj*æl, ital la*sc*ia
ჳ		lei*s*ure	*j*eu	*g*enie	
ç				i*ch*	
j		*y*ou	*y*ak	*j*a	swed. *j*a, ital. *j*ena.
x			a*ch*		span. *j*ota
q			wa*g*en		

FIGURE 84. *(above & right)* The first IPA (Passy 1888); note the text in English, transcribed in IPA.

by the English explorer Thomas Harriot, has recently come to light (see Salmon 1992). However, it is the period from the end of the eighteenth century to the early part of the twentieth that witnessed the greatest activity in devising phonetic notations. Each system was devised with a specific purpose in mind. One of these was the need to incorporate information about pronunciation into dictionaries; this led to a number of special notations. Some, like that employed in the famous *Critical Pronouncing Dictionary* of 1791 by the English elocutionist, actor, and phonetician John Walker, involved the use of superscript numbers placed on top of orthographic vowel

h	*h*igh	(*h*aut)	*h*och	
u	f*u*ll	c*ou*	n*u*ss	
o	s*o*ul	p*o*t	s*o*ll	
ɔ	n*o*t	n*o*te		ital. n*o*tte
ʌ		p*a*s	v*a*ter	swid. s*a*l
ˈa	f*a*ther			ital. m*a*no, swid. m*a*nn.
a	*eye, how*	p*a*tte	m*a*nn	
æ	m*a*n			
ɛ	*air*	*ai*r	b*æ*r	
e	m*e*n	n*é*	n*e*tt	
i	p*i*t	n*i*	m*i*t	
ˈœ	b*u*t, f*u*r			
œ		s*eu*l	k*œ*nnen	
ˈœ		p*eu*	s*œ*hne	
y		n*u*	d*ü*nn	
ˈü			f*ü*r	
ə	n*e*ver	j*e*	gab*e*	
'		glotl kætc		

-u, u-,	wik strest *u*	⎫	ðiz mədifikeicənz
·u, u·, ù,	stroN strest *u*	⎬	əplai
u:,	loN *u*	⎭	tu ɔl letərz
æ̃	neizl *æ* (or eni œðər vauəl)		
ũ	loN ən næro *u* (or əni œðər vauəl)		
hl, lh	voislis *l* (or eni œðər kənsənənt)		
:	mark əv leNθ.		

letters to indicate particular sounds (Walker 1791). Thus, a̍ represents the vowel sound in *fate*, a̎ the stressed vowel in *father*, a̎ the vowel sound of *fall*, and a̎ the vowel of *fat*. The notation by James Murray for the first edition of the *Oxford English Dictionary* is closer to, though not identical, to IPA (MacMahon 1985); the latest edition (*OED2*), however, does use IPA.

The quickening of interest toward the end of the eighteenth century in the study of the languages and cultures of Asia led, inevitably, to the question of whether their pronunciation could be represented by the characters of the Roman alphabet. Sir William Jones, a British judge based in Calcutta and the linguist who first gave currency to the Indo-European hypothesis of language family relationships, proposed in 1788 a system whereby Roman letters, modified where necessary by a set of diacritics, could be used for the notation of many Asian languages. His repertoire of symbols is reproduced in FIGURE 85. An example of his transcriptional technique is his reduction of an extract of the *Zend* into a romanized orthography (FIGURE 86).

The indigenous languages of North and Central America, well removed in structure from English and the other major Indo-European languages, also attracted attention. Following Jones's example, the American lawyer-cum-linguist John Pickering produced an equivalent Roman-based orthography for several North American languages (Pickering 1818). His main modification was to use the cedilla hook with

Soft and hard Breathings

	a *or* e	h a	hha	
Vowels	*Diphthongs*	*and*	*Semivowels*	
ă ā.	a, à	e	è	y a
i	ì	o	ò	w a
u	ù	a i	a u	r a
r ĭ	r ī	lrĭ	lrī	l a
â ã	ê è	î ì	û ù	á â

Consonants

c a	c'ha ⎫	g a	g'ha ⎫	ṅ a
k a	kha ⎭		g ha ⎭	
s a	s ha	z a	z ha	ś a
t́ a	t́'ha ⎫	d́ a	d́'ha ⎫	ñ a
	⎭		dh a ⎭	
t a	⎧ t'ha ⎫	d a	⎧ d'ha ⎫	n a
	⎩ t ha ⎭		⎩ dha ⎭	
p a	⎧ p'ha ⎫	b a	⎧ b'ha ⎫	m a
	⎩ f a ⎭		⎩ v a ⎭	

Compounds.

| c ha | ch.ha | j a | jha | ṅva |
| ża | ż a | ż a | c sha | jṅya |

FIGURE 85. "The System of Indian, Arabian, and Persian Letters" of Sir Wm. Jones (1788/99, pl. 1).

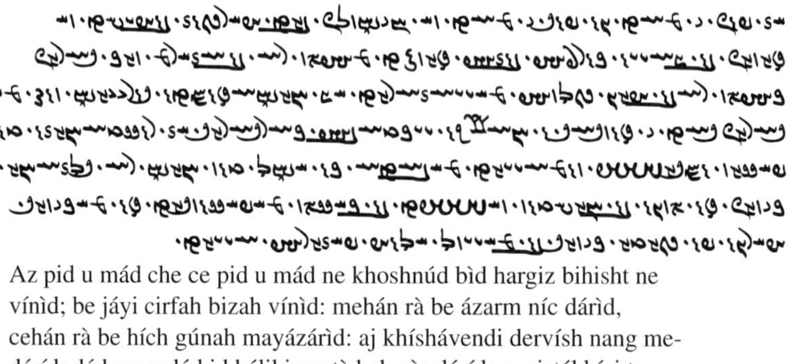

Az pid u mád che ce pid u mád ne khoshnúd bìd hargiz bihisht ne
vínìd; be jáyi cirfah bizah vínìd: mehán rà be ázarm níc dárìd,
cehán rà be hích gúnah mayázárìd: aj khíshávendi dervísh nang me-
dáríd: dád u vendád i kháliki yectà beh càr dárìd; az ristákhízi ten
pasín endísheh nemáyìd; mabádá ce ashù ten khísh rà dúzakhí
cunìd, va ánche be khíshten nasháhad be casán mapasendìd va ma cunìd:
herche be gitì cunìd be mainù [az] aúeh pazírah áyed.

'If you do that with which your father and mother are not pleased, you shall never see heaven; instead of good spirits, you shall see evil beings: behave with honesty and with respect to the great ; and on no account injure the mean: hold not your poor relations a reproach to you: imitate the justice and goodness of the Only Creator: meditate on the resurrection of the future body; lest you make your souls and bodies the inhabitants of hell; and whatever would be unpleasing to yourselves, think not that pleasing to others, and do it not: whatever good you do on earth, for that you shall receive a retribution in heaven.'

FIGURE 86. Sir William Jones's transcription and translation of a Persian text in Avestan alphabet (after W. Jones 1788/1799, pl. 7 and p. 217).

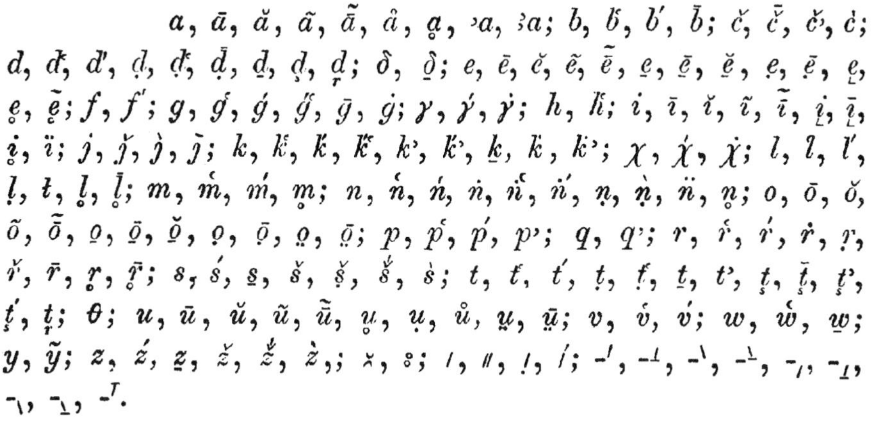

$$a, \bar{a}, \breve{a}, \tilde{a}, \tilde{\bar{a}}, \mathring{a}, ạ, {}^{\jmath}a, {}^{\jmath}a; \; b, \;\hbar, \; b', \; \underline{b}; \; \check{c}, \; \bar{\check{c}}, \; \check{c}', \; \dot{c};$$

$$d, \; \hbar, \; d', \; ḍ, \; \hbar, \; ḍ̱, \; \underline{d}, \; \d, \; ḍ; \; \delta, \; \d\delta; \; e, \; \bar{e}, \; \check{e}, \; \tilde{e}, \; \tilde{\bar{e}}, \; ẹ, \; \bar{ẹ}, \; \breve{e}, \; ẹ, \; \bar{e}, \; ẹ,$$

$$ẹ, \; \bar{ẹ}; \; f, \; f'; \; g, \; \dot{g}, \; \acute{g}, \; \check{g}, \; \bar{g}, \; \dot{g}; \; \gamma, \; \acute{\gamma}, \; \dot{\gamma}; \; h, \; \hbar; \; i, \; \bar{i}, \; \breve{i}, \; \tilde{i}, \; \tilde{\bar{i}}, \; ị, \; \bar{ị},$$

$$ị, \; \ddot{i}; \; j, \; \acute{\jmath}, \; \dot{\jmath}, \; \bar{\jmath}; \; k, \; \hbar, \; \hbar, \; \hbar, \; k', \; k^{\flat}, \; \underline{k}, \; \d{k}, \; k^{\flat}; \; \chi, \; \dot{\chi}, \; \acute{\chi}; \; l, \; \bar{l}, \; l',$$

$$\d{l}, \; \hbar, \; \underline{l}, \; \check{l}; \; m, \; \dot{m}, \; \acute{m}, \; \d{m}; \; n, \; \dot{n}, \; \acute{n}, \; \grave{n}, \; \hat{n}, \; \ddot{n}, \; \eta, \; \grave{\eta}, \; \ddot{\eta}, \; \d{\eta}; \; o, \; \bar{o}, \; \breve{o},$$

$$\tilde{o}, \; \tilde{\bar{o}}, \; ọ, \; \bar{ọ}, \; \breve{ọ}, \; ọ, \; \bar{ọ}, \; ọ, \; \d{ọ}; \; p, \; \acute{p}, \; p', \; p^{\flat}; \; q, \; q'; \; r, \; \grave{r}, \; \acute{r}, \; \dot{r}, \; ṛ,$$

$$\hat{r}, \; \bar{r}, \; \d{r}, \; \bar{ṛ}; \; s, \; \acute{s}, \; ṣ, \; \check{s}, \; \check{ṣ}, \; \acute{\check{s}}, \; \dot{s}; \; t, \; \hat{t}, \; t', \; ṭ, \; \hbar, \; \underline{t}, \; t^{\flat}, \; \d{t}, \; \hbar, \; t^{\flat},$$

$$\acute{t}, \; \d{t}; \; \theta; \; u, \; \bar{u}, \; \breve{u}, \; \tilde{u}, \; \tilde{\bar{u}}, \; \d{u}, \; ụ, \; \mathring{u}, \; ụ, \; \bar{ụ}; \; v, \; \acute{v}, \; \dot{v}; \; w, \; \mathring{w}, \; \underline{w};$$

$$y, \; \tilde{y}; \; z, \; \acute{z}, \; ẓ, \; \check{z}, \; \check{\acute{z}}, \; \dot{z},; \; \chi, \; \varepsilon; \; {}^{\prime}, \; {}^{\prime\prime}, \; {}_{\prime}, \; {}^{\prime}; \; {-}^{\prime}, \; {-}^{\perp}, \; {-}^{\backslash}, \; {-}_{\perp}, \; {-}_{\prime}, \; {-}_{\perp},$$

$${-}_{\backslash}, \; {-}_{\perp}, \; {-}^{\top}.$$

FIGURE 87. The inventory of characters in Lepsius's Standard Alphabet (1863: 18); cf. FIGURE 84.

vowel letters (e.g. Ą, Q) for nasalized vowel sounds (ibid. 353). A similar work was the *Analytic Orthography* of Samuel Haldeman, a professor of zoology and later comparative philology at the University of Pennsylvania (Haldeman 1860). It combines a discussion of articulations in various languages, questions concerning the choice of phonetic notation, and examples of the notation in practice. Like Jones and Pickering, Haldeman used a modified Roman alphabet.

Missionary and linguistic activity by various branches of the Christian church in the nineteenth century in Africa and elsewhere led to the devising of several different Roman-based alphabets for the notation of native languages, until eventually, in the early 1850s, moves were made to standardize a single set of symbols and diacritics for use in the mission-fields (cf. SECTION 66; "African languages" on page 689 in SECTION 59). An "Alphabetical Conference" was convened in London in 1853 at which the German Egyptologist (Carl) Richard Lepsius presented the notational system he had been working on. This was quickly accepted and adopted as the Church Missionary Society's standard and was published, first in German (1853), then in English (1854), under the title "Standard Alphabet" (Lepsius 1863/1981). It is based almost entirely on the italic shapes of the Roman alphabet—some Greek characters are included—with the addition of numerous diacritics (FIGURE 87). To this extent, it bears a certain resemblance in its basic design principles to IPA. It consists altogether of 186 characters. The second edition, in 1863, included sample transcriptions, together with accompanying commentaries, for over a hundred languages. Despite its success, it was later eclipsed by IPA, because the modern-language teachers who formed the nucleus of the International Phonetic Association felt that its range of symbols and diacritics was unnecessarily complex for their particular requirements.

The study of the local dialects of various languages of Europe led to the development of several language-specific notational systems (cf. Heepe 1928: 31–95). For transcribing English dialects, the English phonetician and philologist Alexander J. Ellis created several systems (Palaeotype, Glossic, and variants), some of which he con-

10.	1	i	wʋr	ʋgíʋt	ʋ	waanɪn	—	sez	shʋ		fʋr
	2	,,	wʋz			wáɪnɪn	ʋwéeʋ	,,	shii		,,
	3	,,	waar	ʋgíʋt	,,	wíɪnɪn	—	,,	shʋ		fʋ
	4	,,	wʋr	,,	,,	waanɪn	—		,,	sez	fʋr
	5	,,	waar	,,	,,	wíɪnɪn	—	sez	shéɪ		,,
	6	,,	wʋr	,,	,,	wáɪnɪn	—	,,	shʋ		fʋ
	7	ii	,,	,,	,,	waanɪn	—	,,	,,		,,
	8	,,	,,	ʋgéeʋt	,,	,,	—	,,	,,		fʋr
	9	i,	wʋz	—		plɪʋnɪn	ʋwéeʋ	— —			,,
	10	,,	,,	—		grʋʋnɪn	—	— shʋ	sez		,,

1	éeʋl	t'	waald	laak	tʋv	ʋ	sɪʋk	béeʋn	ʋr		ʋ
2	aal	,,	wold	léɪk		,,	badlɪ	,,	,,		,,
3	ɹal	,,	waald	laak		,,	sɪʋk	bɪɪʋn	,,		,ɪ
4	aal	,,	,,	,,		,,	,,	béeʋn	,,		,,
5	óoʋl	,,	wold	léɪk		,,	,,	baan	,,		,,
6	ɹal	th	waald	sɪɪʋm	ʋz	,,	,,	béeʋn	,,		,,
7	,,	t'	,,	laak		,,	siik	béeʋn	,,		,,
8	ʌʌ'ʋl	,,	,,	,,		,,	sɪʋk	béeʋn	,,		,,
9	óoʋl	,,	wold	léɪk		,,	badlɪ	,,	,,	els	,,
10	ool		woold	lə'ɪk		,,	,,	,,	,,		,,

1	laal	las	ɪv	ʋ	tívɪ.
2	lɪt'l	,,	,,	,,	frɪɪʋt.
3	laal	,,	,,	,,	tívɪ.
4	,,	,,	ʋt)	s	pɪɪʋvɪsh.
5	láɪl	,,	i	ʋ	tɹóʋfɪn.
6	laal	,,	,,	,,	ɹíumʋ.
7	láɪl	,,	,,	,,	puuk.
8	lɪɪʋl	,,	,,	,,	múʋndɹ.
9	laat'l	,,	— —		wɪmprɪn.
10	,,	gɹel	— —		fretɪn.

FIGURE 88. The sentence *He was whining away, says she, for all the world like a sick child, or a little girl in a fret* in ten Yorkshire dialects, transcribed in Dialectal Palaeotype (Ellis 1889: 509–10).

sidered to be candidates for a reformed orthography of English. His "dialectal Palaeotype," used for a major survey of (mainly) rural pronunciations in Britain in the 1880s, is based on the Roman alphabet—hence *palaeotype*, the 'old alphabet'—extended by means of different fonts, turned letters, and punctuation marks. The result is a very extensive symbol-repertoire of over 250 characters (Ellis 1889: 78*–88*). FIGURE 88 shows an example of the notation in practice: a transcription of part of a test sentence pronounced in ten Yorkshire dialects. See FIGURE 89A for the symbols of his earlier Palaeotype of 1869.

Since about 1925, the IPA's alphabet has had few competitors, although there have been deliberate (but usually relatively small) adjustments to it for specific purposes, for example for notating pronunciation in dictionaries. Among certain linguists in North America, a modified IPA alphabet has been in use for many years. This differs from IPA mainly in using the symbols [š] and [ž] for IPA [ʃ] and [ʒ], [č] and [ǰ] for IPA [tʃ] and [dʒ], [y] for IPA [j] and hence [ü] for IPA [y]; and in the names of certain phonetic categories (e.g. *low* vowel, rather than the IPA's *open* vowel). A convenient listing of phonetic symbols, IPA and non-IPA, is Pullum and Ladusaw 1986.

a.

	1	2	3	4	5	6	7	8	9	0	
a	kh	ɟh	rh	ph	'	æ	ʏ	i	ʜ'	·	a
b	kʍh	s	sh	wh	r	ɹ	ə	e	'	doub-ling.	b
c	ʎh	ljh	lh	f	i, ɟ	ɶ	əh	ʀ	;	,	c
d	lʍh	th	ťh	fh	ɹ	ʀ	ɣ	i	‚	.,	d
e	k	tj	t	p	ɯ	a	ah	e	ʌ	⁞	e
f	qh	njh	nh	mh	ʜ	ɑ	ɷ	æ	ʜʍh	⁞	f
g	gh	ɹ	r	bh	'w	u	ʊ	ɪ	d̨	ʜ:	g
h	gʍh	z	zh	w	rw	o	oh	ɘ	'‚'	‡	h
i	ʎ	lj	l	v	y	ʌ	ah	əh	┤	┼	i
k	lw	dh	ďh	vh	ɹw	u	ʋh	y	┝	┼	k
l	g	dj	d	b	u, w	o	oh	œ	.	§§	l
m	q	nj	n	m	'h	ɔ	oh	æh	,,	*	m
	1	2	3	4	5	6	7	8	9	0	

b.

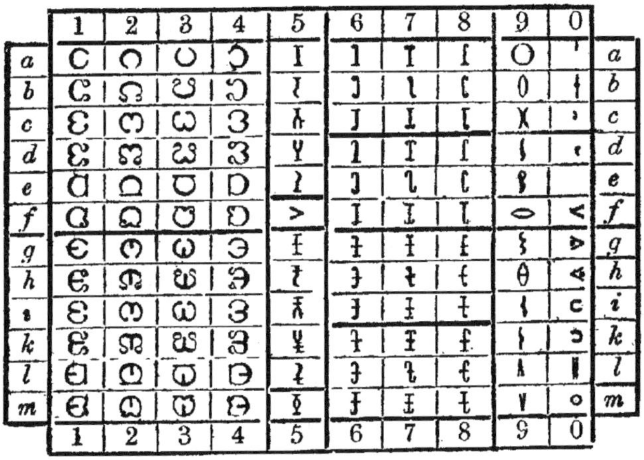

c.

	1	2	3	4	5	6	7	8	9	0	
a	x	ç	ɾ̥	ɸ	ˇ	ɯ	ɨ	i	h	ˈ	a
b	xʷ	s	ʃ	ʍ	ʁ̝	ʌ	ɘ	e	ʰ	ː	b
c	ʟ̥	ʎ̝̊	l̥	f	j	ɑ	ɜ	ɛ	ʔ	hiatus	c
d	ʟ̥ʷ	θ	ɬ	fˠ	ɹ	ɣ	ë	ɪ	(˜)	abrupt	d
e	k	c	t	p	β	ʋ̥	ʋ	e̞	˜	˞	e
f	ŋ̊	ɲ̊	n̥	m̥	‥	ɑ	ʋ̝	æ̝	whistle	ingress. airflow	f
g	ɣ	j̊	r	β	ɦʷ	u	ʉ	ʏ	trilled	˞	g
h	ɣʷ	z	ʒ	w	ʁ̝ʷ	o	θ	ø	ɦ	click	h
i	ʟ	ʎ	l	v	y	ɔ	ʋ̞ʷ	œ	_	ˬ	i
k	ʟʷ	ð	ɭ	vˠ	ɹʷ	ʊ	ʉ̝	y	˔	ˌ	k
l	g	ɟ	d	b	ʷ	o̞	ö	œ	˕	lateral artic.	l
m	ŋ	ɲ	n	m	ˬ	ɒ	ö	ɶ	ˌ	coartic-ulated	m
	1	2	3	4	5	6	7	8	9	0	

FIGURE 89. The characters of (a) Paleotype and (b) Visible Speech (Ellis 1869: 15), with (c) transliteration into IPA (1993).

Iconic notation

Iconic notations involve the use of symbol-shapes which convey explicit information about particular articulatory features of the sounds (cf. Korean *hankul* in SECTION 17). The most famous is Alexander Melville Bell's *Visible Speech* of 1867 (FIGURE 89B), although it has predecessors in the systems of e.g. Bishop John Wilkins (1668), Francis Lodwick (1686), Charles de Brosses (1765), and Ernst von Brücke (1863); see Kemp 1994: 3044. Bell was a Scottish phonetician and the father of Alexander Graham Bell, the Scottish-Canadian inventor of the telephone.

In the subtitle of *Visible Speech* are the words "self-interpreting physiological letters," which reveal much about the concept behind the notation. Each symbol displays sufficient *visual* information about the articulation for the reader to be able to work out what the symbolized sound is. In other words, a knowledge of the values of the component elements of the symbols allows the reader to interpret all and any of the symbols.

For example, Bell's iconic symbol for [n], ☺, contains the following pieces of information. The bowl-like shape represents a turned letter C—for *consonant*. Its potential open area, though closed here, points upward toward the roof of the mouth: the alignment indicates an alveolar articulation. The small vertical represents the appearance of the vocal folds when they are vibrating—they are practically together. The line along the top of the C-bowl contains two separate elements: a straight line to the left, which represents total closure—in this case between the blade of the tongue and the alveolar ridge—and a wavy line, which if turned through 90° would suggest the appearance of the soft palate in its lowered position. Putting these features together, one can calculate that the sound must be a voiced alveolar nasal consonant. (It should be noted that Bell viewed the vocal tract from the *right* side of the head and neck, not the *left* as in IPA. As a result, sounds involving the lips are on the right side.)

Bell's system won wide support in America in the nineteenth century in schools for the deaf as a means of illustrating the component properties of sounds to deaf children learning to speak. Among phoneticians, the degree of support was less enthusiastic—mainly on the grounds that the notation bore no observable connections with an alphabetic system of notation. However, it is a relatively easy system to use once the underlying principles have been grasped. Bell claimed that it was a *general* phonetic alphabet: that is, like the IPA alphabet, it can be used in the notation of any language on earth. However, unlike IPA, it allows for many more shades of pronunciation to be symbolized. It can be handwritten in cursive form using special modified symbols (Bell 1867, pl. XII).

A revision of Visible Speech was published in 1880, not by Bell but by his one-time pupil Henry Sweet, under the title Revised Organic Alphabet (Sweet 1880–81: 203–35). One of his revisions (which were based on many years of practical experience of the system) was to make some of Bell's symbols easier to read. For example,

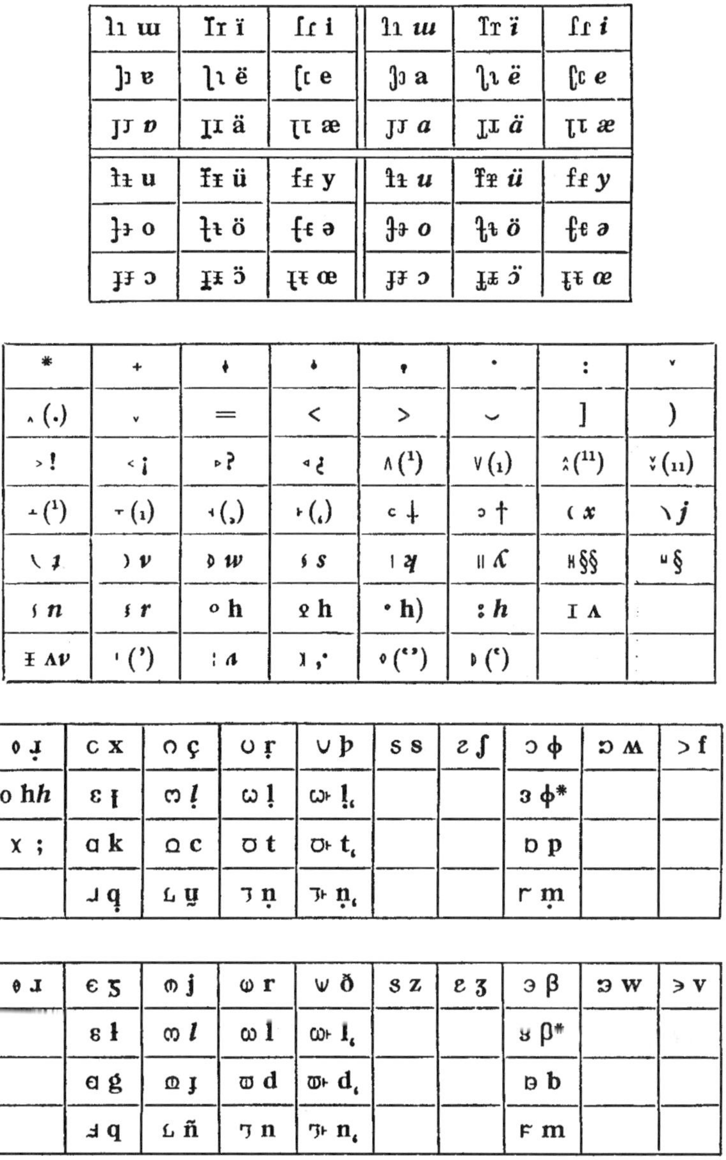

ʮ ɯ	Ɪr ï	ʃr i	ʮ *ɯ*	Ɪr *ï*	ʃr *i*
]ɪ ɐ	ʮ ë	[ɪ e	ʓɔ a	ʮ *ë*	[ɪ *e*
ɟʀ ɒ	ɪɪ ä	ʈɪ æ	ɟʀ *a*	ɪɪ *ä*	ʈɪ æ
ʮ u	Ɪr ü	fʃ y	ʮ *u*	Ɪʀ *ü*	fʃ *y*
}ʓ o	ʮ ö	{ɛ ə	ʓʓ *o*	ʮ *ö*	{ɛ *ə*
ʓʀ ɔ	ɪɪ ɔ̈	ʈɪ œ	ʓʀ *ɔ*	ɪɪ *ɔ̈*	ʈɪ œ

*	+	◆	◆	▾	•	:	˅
ʌ (.)	˅	=	<	>	⌣	]	)
>!	<¡	▸?	◂ɩ	ʌ(¹)	ᴠ(ɪ)	⌃(¹¹)	˅(ɪɪ)
◂(¹)	▾(ɪ)	◂(,)	▸(ɪ)	c+	ɔ†	(x	\j
\ɟ	)ʋ	▸w	ʃs	ɪɣ	‖ʌ	н§§	ᵘ§
ʃn	ʃr	oh	ᵹh	•h)	:h	I ʌ	:
₮ ʌʋ	ꞌ(ʼ)	:ɑ	ɹ,˙	ꞏ(˙ˀ)	▸(ˀ)		·

o ɹ	c x	ɔ ç	ᴜ ɽ	ᴜ þ	s s	ʒ ʃ	ɔ φ	ɔ ʍ	> f
o hh	ɛ ɩ	ɷ ḷ	ω ḷ	ω₊ ḷ,			ʒ φ*		
x ;	ɑ k	ɑ c	ᴜ t	ᴜ₊ t,			ᴅ p		
	⌐q	ʟ ṳ	ʇ ṇ	ʇ₊ ṇ,			ᴦ ṃ		

o ɹ	ɛ ʒ	ɷ j	ω r	ᴜ ð	ꜱ z	ɛ ʒ	ɘ β	ɘ w	> v
	ʒ ɩ	ɷ l	ω ɫ	ω₊ ḷ,			ʒ β*		
	ꙅ g	ɷ ɟ	ᴜ d	ᴜ₊ d,			ɘ b		
	⌐q	ʟ ñ	ʇ n	ʇ₊ n,			ꜰ m		

FIGURE 90. The Revised Organic Alphabet, with equivalents in Romic. *Top,* vowels; *middle,* "general symbols"; *bottom (two boxes),* consonants (Sweet 1880–81: 220–21, 1971: 282–83).

Sweet removed the C bowl element in nasal sounds and notated [n] solely as ʇ. The horizontal line still indicates, as in Visible Speech, total closure between the blade of the tongue and the alveolar ridge, and the wavy line the soft palate in its lowered position. The marker for voicing is, of course, retained, though repositioned. See FIGURE 90 for the complete character set; also Sweet 1971: 256–85, esp. 283–85. In Britain, Sweet's Organic Alphabet soon came to be used more than Bell's Visible

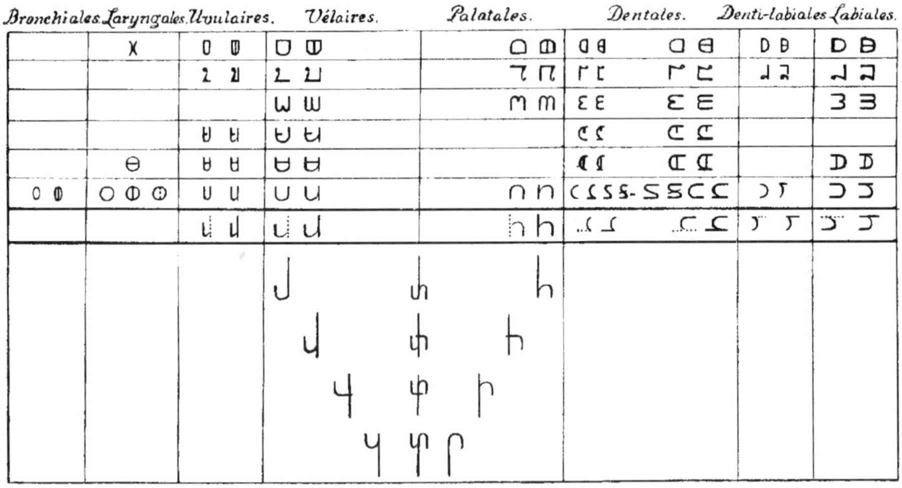

Bronchiales. Laryngales. Uvulaires.   Vélaires.   Palatales.   Dentales.   Denti-labiales Labiales.

Bron-chiales	Laryn-gales	Uvu-laires	Vélaires	Palatales	Dentales			Denti-labiales	Labiales
	ʔ	q ɢ	k g	c ɟ	t̪ d̪	t̺ d̺		p̪ b̪	p b
		ɴ ɴ	ŋ̊ ŋ	ɲ̊ ɲ	n̪̊ n̪	n̺̊ n̺		m̪̊ m̪	m̥ m
			ɫ̥ ɫ	ʎ̥ ʎ	l̪̥ l̪	l̺̥ l̺			* *
		ʀ̥� ʀ̆	ʀ̥ʜ ʀ̺ʜ		r̪̥ r̪	r̺̥ r̺			
	*	ʀ̥ ʀ	ʀ̥ ʀ̺		r̪̥ r̪	r̺ r̺			* *
ʜ ʢ	h ɦ ɦ̬	χ ʁ	x ɣ	ç j	ɬ ɮ	ʃ ʒ s z θ ð		f v	ɸ β
		χ̺ ʁ̺	x̺ ɣ̺	ç̺ j̺	ɬ̺ ɮ̺	θ̺ ð̺		f̺ v̺	ɸ̺ β̺
			ɯ ï i						
			ʌ ë e						
			ʌ ä ɛ						
			ɑ ɑ̈ a						

FIGURE 91. The Organic Alphabet, with key *(below)* in IPA (Passy and Jones 1907: 2–3).

Speech—at least by the country's small coterie of phoneticians. A later alphabet, not by Sweet but also called the Organic Alphabet, which bears only partial resemblances to either Bell's or Sweet's system, was published in 1907 by Paul Passy and Daniel Jones (FIGURES 91 and 92). It seems to have been little used by phoneticians generally.

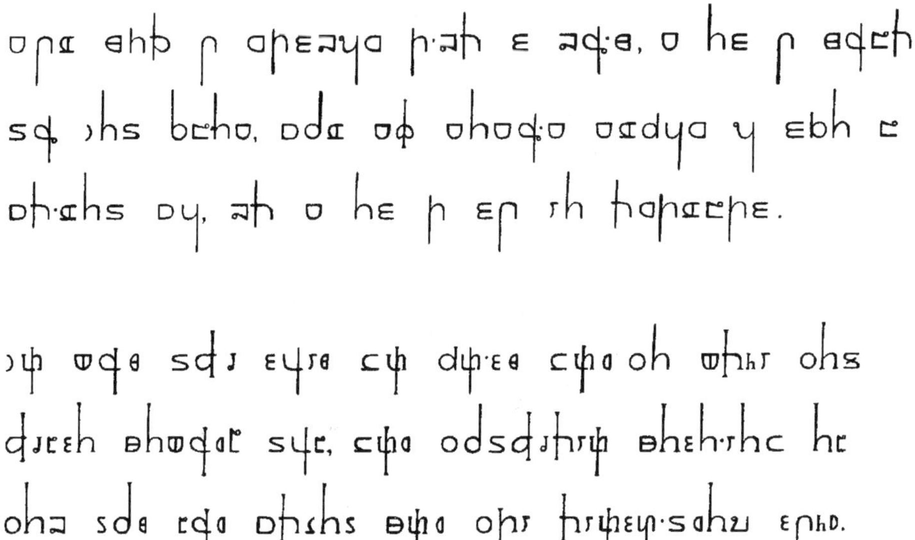

kar djø a tɛlmɑ̃t ɛ:me l mɔ̃:d, k il a dɔne / sɔ̃ fis ynik, pur kə kikɔ̃:k krwɑt ɑ̃ lɥi n / pe:ris pɑ, me k il ɛ la vi etɛrnɛl.

'Car Dieu a tellement aimé le monde, qu'il a donné son fils unique, pour que quiconque croit à lui ne périsse pas, mais qu'il ait la vie éternelle.'

fə gɔd sou lʌvd ðə wä:ld ðət hi geiv hiz / ounli bigɔtn sʌn, ðət husouevə bili:viθ in / him ʃud nɔt periʃ bət hæv evəlɑ:stiŋ laif.

'For God so loved the world that he gave his only begotten son, that whosoever believe in him should not perish but have everlasting life.'

FIGURE 92. Samples of French and English in the Organic Alphabet, with key *(below)* in contemporary IPA (Passy and Jones 1907: 6).

Linear and parametric notations

The transcription that a phonetician makes may be either *linear* (i.e., it notates the stream of speech as though it consisted of discrete sound segments that follow one another in time), as in the example of [hat] discussed above, or *parametric* (i.e., it represents *parameters*—potentially variable features of speech production, which may last less than or more than the duration of the allegedly single, discrete segment). Almost all phonetic notation, both now and in the past, has been made on a linear basis.

The parallelism noted earlier between orthographic *hat* and phonetic [hat] suggests that a phonetic notation will be based on the perceived number of sounds in a word. This is not necessarily so. Native users of English will comment that the pronunciation [hat] contains three sounds, which make up a single syllable; phoneticians will show that depending on the purpose of one's phonetic analysis and notation, a varying number of sounds can be uncovered. For example, the [h] at the beginning of *hat* has precisely the same tongue position as the following [a] vowel sound—the difference lies in the absence of voicing in the [h]. In terms of what the entire vocal tract

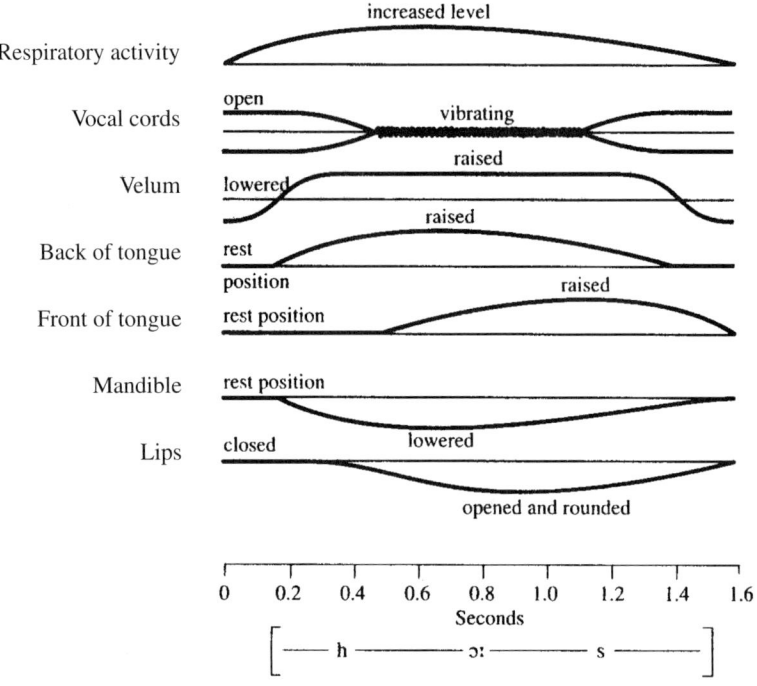

FIGURE 93. Parametric analysis of the articulatory actions of some of the vocal organs in the production of the English (RP) word *horse* /hɔːs/ (Laver 1994: 102).

does in the production of *hat*, only two major settings must be achieved: the body of the tongue positioned for [h] and [a]; and second, the totally new setting of the tip and blade of the tongue against the alveolar ridge behind the upper front teeth for the [t].

An alternative parametric interpretation, however, which pays much closer attention to the finer adjustments of the vocal tract in the pronunciation of *hat*, would show that, during the [a] vowel, the tip and blade of the tongue begins to rise upward toward the alveolar ridge. The concept of an [a] followed by a [t] is, strictly speaking, erroneous. Sounds flow into and out of one another, and there is usually no precise dividing line between them. No standardization of parametric notation has been attempted. An example of a parametric notation is seen in FIGURE 93.

Analphabetic notation

By *analphabetic* notation is meant those notations which delineate the individual phonetic features of a sound by means of (usually) a long, sequential notation often involving different symbol systems; an analogy is chemical formulas such as H_2O for 'water'. Several such systems have been devised since the early eighteenth century, including one by Erasmus Darwin, grandfather of Charles Darwin, in 1803 (Kemp 1994: 3048). Later examples are the Analphabetic Notation of the Danish phonetician

TABLE 71.2: *Qualities of the 'a' Vowel in Several Languages (Jespersen 1889: 80)*

		Analphabetic Notation				IPA (1993)[a]
English	father	$\alpha{<}8^b$	βgf	$\gamma7_j$	$\delta0\ \epsilon1$	[ɑ̞]
German	Gabe	$\alpha8^b$	βgf	$\gamma{>}7_j$	$\delta0\ \epsilon1$	[ɑ̞]
French	pas	$\alpha{>}8^{ba}\,\beta$g		$\gamma7_{jk}$	$\delta0\ \epsilon1$	[ɑ̞]
Swedish	hatt	$\alpha{<}8^{bc}\,\beta$f		$\gamma7_{ij}$	$\delta0\ \epsilon1$	[ä]
Danish	mand	$\alpha{<}8^b\ \beta$f		$\gamma7_{ji}$	$\delta0\ \epsilon1$	[ˈä̠ʼ]
	mane	$\alpha{<}8^b\ \beta$fe		$\gamma{<}7_{ij}$	$\delta0\ \epsilon1$	[ʌ̈]
	rat	$\alpha8^b$	βgf	$\gamma8_{kj}$	$\delta0\ \epsilon1$	[a]

a. IPA cannot notate the slightly different lip and tongue-tip positions (α and β) for these vowels; a verbal description is therefore necessary.

Otto Jespersen (1889) and the Functional Analphabetic Symbolism of the American phonetician Kenneth Pike (1943).

For IPA [n], Jespersen writes $\alpha_{,,}\beta0^f\gamma_{,,}\delta2\epsilon1\zeta3$. This provides information about what he calls the "elements of sounds," i.e. the component features (Jespersen 1889: 7). The symbol α denotes the lips, β the tip of the tongue, γ the upper surface of the tongue, δ the soft palate, ϵ the vocal folds, and ζ the lungs. Note the systematic progression from the lips back to the lungs employing the first six letters of the Greek alphabet—precisely as in the left-to-right arrangement of the IPA chart (except that the latter does not have a specific "place of articulation" for the lungs). The letters or numbers after the Greek letters provide more specific information about the activity (or otherwise) of the particular speech organs. The symbol ,, indicates a "neutral or passive" state of an articulator or articulators. 0 indicates complete closure between two articulators. Superscript ^{f} indicates the alveolar ridge. 2 is the *third* position of an articulator: in the case of $\delta2$, this is the lowered position of the soft palate for nasal consonants like [m], [n], and [ŋ]. ($\delta0$ would be complete closure between the soft palate and the posterior pharyngeal wall; and $\delta1$ would indicate the "nasal twang" of certain American accents.) 1, a symbol taken from Bell's Visible Speech and Sweet's Organic Alphabet, stands for voicing in chest register. 3 is the middle degree of stress (in the sence of the respiratory reinforcement of syllables) on a scale from 1 (weak) to 5 (extra strong).

Although inevitably baffling at first sight, the analphabetic notation has an excellent internal logic, since any phonetic analysis needs to be able to specify the precise component elements in an articulation, quite independently of being able to provide a notation for the sound; Jespersen achieves both at the same time. An alphabetic notation like the IPA, even with diacritics associated with its symbols, does not have ready-made the same precise (and expandable) repertoire of classificatory subtleties that are available in an analphabetic notation. Few phoneticians, however, have used Jespersen's notation. TABLE 71.2 shows how the notation can highlight slightly different articulations.

Pike's notation of IPA [n̩] as

*M*alldDe*C*VoeIpvnnAP*paa*tdtl*tn*ransn*s*f*S*p*va*vdtlv*tn*ransss*s*f*T*p*gag*dtlwv*ti*tv*r*ansn*s*f*S*rp*F*Ss

is based on precisely the same principles as Jespersen's, but Pike makes the analysis even more detailed—and uses only Roman letters. The notation, which, like Jespersen's, is totally indecipherable without a knowledge of the coding principles behind it, lists information about the airstream mechanism (in this case, air being expelled from the lungs), the position of the soft palate (lowered away from the back wall of the pharynx), the precise setting of the blade of the tongue against the alveolar ridge, and the role of the sound within a syllable. Pike is describing here an [n] which is operating as a syllable in its own right, as in the pronunciation of the word *and*, said very quickly in a phrase like *back and forth*, where the *and* is simply a single [n] sound with no vowel before it and no consonant after it (Pike 1943: 155).

Summary

The relationships between the various, and sometimes radically different, styles of phonetic notation that have evolved over the past 400 years can be shown as in FIG-URE 94. Of these, the type that has formed the basis of most phonetic notations has been the Linear, particularly a linear alphabetic notation which provides a single symbol for each identifiable sound segment (or phoneme).

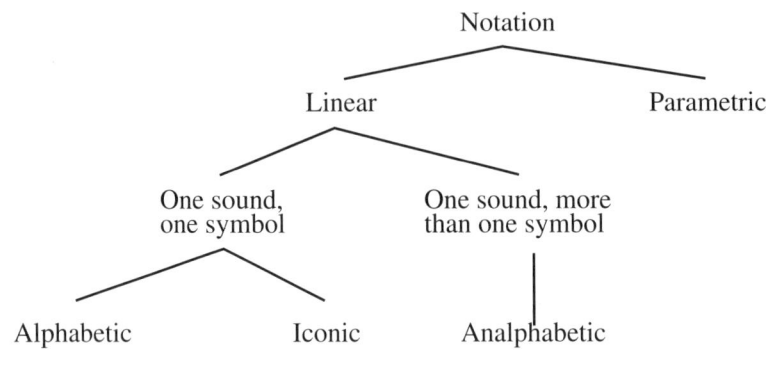

FIGURE 94. Styles of phonetic notation.

Bibliography

Abercrombie, David. 1964. *English Phonetic Texts.* London: Faber and Faber.

———. 1981. "Extending the Roman Alphabet: Some Orthographic Experiments of the Past Four Centuries." In Asher and Henderson 1981: 207–24.

Asher, Ron E., and Eugénie J. A. Henderson, eds. 1981. *Towards a History of Phonetics.* Edinburgh: Edinburgh University Press.

Ball, Martin J. 1991. "Computer Coding of the IPA: Extensions to the IPA." *Journal of the International Phonetic Association* 21: 36–41.

Bell, Alexander Melville. 1867. *Visible Speech: The Science of Universal Alphabetics; or, Self-interpreting Physiological Letters, for the Writing of All Languages in One Alphabet.* London: Simpkin, Marshall.

Catford, J. C. 1988. *A Practical Introduction to Phonetics.* Oxford: Clarendon.

Duckworth, M., G. Allen, W. Hardcastle, and M. J. Ball. 1990. "Extensions to the International Phonetic Alphabet for the Transcription of Atypical Speech." *Clinical Linguistics and Phonetics* 4: 273–80.

Ellis, Alexander J. 1869–89. *On Early English Pronunciation.* Part 1, London: Asher. Part 5, London: Trübner.

Esling, John H., and Harry Gaylord. 1993. "Computer Codes for Phonetic Symbols." *Journal of the International Phonetic Association* 23: 83–97.

Haldeman, Samuel S. 1860. *Analytic Orthography: An Investigation of the Sounds of the Voice, and Their Alphabetic Notation; Including the Mechanism of Speech, and Its Bearing upon Etymology.* Philadelphia: Lippincott.

Heepe, Martin. 1928. *Lautzeichen und ihre Andwendung in verschiedenen Sprachgebieten.* Berlin: Reichsdruckerei. Repr. Hamburg: Buske, 1983.

International Phonetic Association. 1932. "The International Phonetic Alphabet (revised to 1932)." *Le Maître Phonétique* 37 (January–March) loose insert.

———. 1949. *The Principles of the International Phonetic Association, Being a Description of the International Phonetic Alphabet and the Manner of Using It, Illustrated by Texts in 51 Languages.* Supplement to *Le Maître Phonétique* 91, January–June.

———. 1989. "The International Phonetic Alphabet (revised to 1989)." *Journal of the International Phonetic Association* 19/2 centerfold.

———. 1993. "The International Phonetic Alphabet (revised to 1993)." *Journal of the International Phonetic Association* 23/1 centerfold.

Jespersen, Otto. 1889. *The Articulations of Speech Sounds Represented by Means of Analphabetic Symbols.* Marburg: Elwert.

Jones, Daniel. 1962. *An Outline of English Phonetics,* 9th ed. Cambridge: Heffer.

Jones, William. 1788. "A Dissertation on the Orthography of Asiatick Words in Roman Letters." *Asiatick Researches; Or, Transactions of the Society, Instituted in Bengal, for Inquiring into the History and Antiquities, the Arts, Sciences, and Literature, of Asia* 1: 1–56. Repr. in his *Works,* vol. 1, pp. 175–228. London: G. G. and J. Robinson; R. H. Evans, 1799.

Kelly, John. 1981. "The 1847 Alphabet: An Episode of Phonotypy." In Asher and Henderson 1981: 248–64.

Kemp, J. Alan. 1981. Introduction. In Lepsius 1863/1981: 1*–99*.

———. 1994. "Phonetic Transcription: History." In *The Encyclopedia of Language and Linguistics,* ed. Ron E. Asher and J. M. Y. Simpson, vol. 6, pp. 3040–51. Oxford: Pergamon.

Laver, John. 1994. *Principles of Phonetics.* Cambridge: Cambridge University Press.

Lepsius, Richard. 1863. *Standard Alphabet for Reducing Unwritten Languages and Foreign*

Graphic Systems to a Uniform Orthography in European Letters, 2nd ed. London: Williams & Norgate. Repr. Amsterdam: Benjamins, 1981.

MacMahon, Michael K. C. 1985. "James Murray and the Phonetic Notation in the *New English Dictionary.*" *Transactions of the Philological Society* 72–112.

Passy, Paul. 1888. "Our Revised Alphabet." *The Phonetic Teacher* August–September, pp. 57–60.

Passy, Paul, and Daniel Jones. 1907. *Alphabet phonétique organique, avec les formes correspondantes de l'alphabet phonétique usuel.* Suppl. to *Le Maître Phonétique* May–June, pp. 1–8.

Pickering, John. 1818. "On the Adoption of a Uniform Orthography for the Indian Languages of North America." *Memoirs of the American Academy of Arts and Sciences* 4/2: 319–60. Separatim, *An Essay on a Uniform Orthography* .... Cambridge, Mass., University Press, Hilliard and Metcalf, 1820.

Pike, Kenneth L. 1943. *Phonetics: A Critical Analysis of Phonetic Theory and a Technic for the Practical Description of Sounds.* Ann Arbor: University of Michigan Press.

Pullum, Geoffrey K., and William A. Ladusaw. 1986. *Phonetic Symbol Guide.* Chicago: University of Chicago Press.

Salmon, Vivian. 1992. "Thomas Harriot (1560–1621) and the Origins of Algonkian Linguistics." *Historiographia Linguistica* 19: 25–56.

Sweet, Henry. 1880–81. "Sound Notation." *Transactions of the Philological Society* 177–235, *191 (see also Sweet 1971: 256–85).

————. 1971. *The Indispensable Foundation: A Selection from the Writings of Henry Sweet,* ed. Eugénie J. A. Henderson (Language and Language Learning 28). London: Oxford University Press.

Ternes, Elmar. 1983. Einleitung. In Heepe 1928/1983: vii–xxviii.

Walker, John. 1791. *A Critical Pronouncing Dictionary and Expositor of the English Language* .... London: G. G. J. and J. Robinson.

Wells, John C. 1987. "Computer-coded Phonetic Transcription." *Journal of the International Phonetic Association* 17: 94–114.

Music Notation

JAMES D. MCCAWLEY

This section is concerned only with the notational tradition of European classical music. The family of notational systems standardly used within that tradition has evolved as means of indicating what performers are to sing or play in performing the works in question. They thus provide detailed information as to the notes, their timing and duration, and their dynamics, though at most indirect information about musical structure.

Pitch

Notes are represented on the lines and spaces of a *staff* of five parallel horizontal lines, supplemented when necessary by subsidiary partial lines and spaces above and below the staff, with acoustically "higher" notes (= greater number of vibrations per second: the unit of measure is the Hertz, Hz) represented on graphically higher lines and spaces. The notes making up a *diatonic scale*, i.e. notes corresponding at least roughly to the white keys on a piano, appear on consecutive lines and spaces of the staff. Other notes are represented with ♯ and ♭ (*sharp* and *flat*), which indicate respectively raising or lowering the pitch by an increment equal to the difference between the large and small intervals of the diatonic scale. (In a diatonic scale, there are five instances of a large interval—C–D–E and F–G–A–B—and two instances of a small interval—E–F and B–c.)*

In the "12 equal interval" tuning system that has been standard in European art music since about 1800, in which the large interval is exactly twice the small interval, the increment corresponding to ♯ and ♭ can appropriately be called a "semitone"; however, that term is avoided here, since the use of ♯ and ♭ is exactly the same even with reference to tuning systems in which there is no such thing as a semitone—as in the "Pythagorean" tuning scheme that was standard in medieval music, in which the small interval of the diatonic scale is less than half the large interval, and the "meantone" tuning scheme that was standard in Renaissance and baroque music, in which the small interval is more than half the large interval. The differences among these

---

*In a commonly used system for designating particular octaves (*registers*), C stands for the lowest note on a pipe organ keyboard, with a wavelength of ca. 64 Hz; c stands for the next higher octave, c′ is "middle C" (ca. 256 Hz), a′ is "A 440", c″ is the note near the middle of a soprano's range, and so on (Read 1969: 44).

treble clef   soprano clef   alto clef   tenor clef   bass clef

FIGURE 95. Clefs

tunings reflect differences in the tuning of the interval of a *fifth*—the interval from C up to G: in Pythagorean tuning, the fifth is tuned "pure," i.e. to a frequency ratio of $3/2 = 1.5$, with the consequence that the major third—the interval from C up to E— is painfully sharp; in meantone tuning, the major third is tuned pure, that is, to a frequency ratio of $5/4 = 1.25$, which makes the fifth somewhat flat (frequency ratio 1.4953); in twelve equal interval tuning, the fifth is tuned flat enough (frequency ratio 1.4983) to make the large diatonic interval twice the small interval, which makes the major third slightly sharp (frequency ratio 1.2599). As a consequence of the relative sizes of the large and small diatonic intervals, F♯ is higher than G♭ in Pythagorean tuning, lower than it in meantone tuning, and equal to it in twelve equal interval tuning.

The five-line staffs of standard notation are marked with a *clef* that identifies one of the lines of the staff with a particular note. The clefs that are in standard use originated as script letters G, C, and F, marking those notes on particular lines; middle C is represented as in FIGURE 95 with different clefs.

Tonal music is generally written with a *key signature* to the right of the clef; e.g., in a piece in the key of A major, the clef will be followed by ♯s on lines and spaces corresponding to the notes F, C, and G, indicating that the notes of the A major scale are to be played (thus F♯ rather than F, C♯ rather than C, and G♯ rather than G) except where the contrary is indicated. Deviations from the scale indicated by the key signature are indicated by a ♯, ♭, or ♮ (*natural*, canceling out a ♯ or ♭) to the left of the note in question.

Duration

Temporal sequence is represented iconically on the left–right dimension; notes precede those that appear to their right. Vertical alignment indicates simultaneity, both within a single staff and on multiple staffs that are grouped together into a *system* (as in a score in which the parts for the different instruments are written on separate staffs, or in piano music, which is generally written on two staffs). This interpretation of vertical alignment applies not only to notes but also to the various diacritics that are written above or below the staff, indicating such things as dynamics, accents, and changes of tempo, e.g. a *ff* indicates that the note or chord below/above which it is written is to be played *fortissimo* (very loud).

The metrical organization of a piece of music is partially indicated by vertical *bars* that divide the music into *measures* (also called *bars*). Each measure begins with

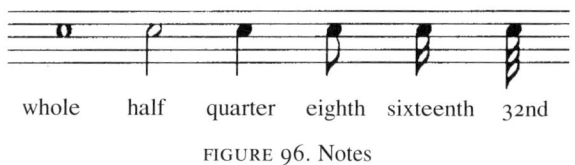

whole   half   quarter   eighth   sixteenth   32nd

FIGURE 96. Notes

FIGURE 97. Beams (the three groups represent identical pitch and duration)

a metrically strong beat. At the beginning of the piece (or at a point where the meter changes), there is a *time signature* indicating the metrical composition of the measures (e.g. **4/4** indicates that each measure is to consist metrically of four quarter-notes, **6/8** that each measure is to consist metrically of six eighth-notes, etc.). The time signature is usually written with the "numerator" on the upper lines of the staff and the "denominator" on the lower lines.

Each note is represented by an oval centered on the appropriate line or space of the staff. The duration of the note is represented by various typographical adornments of the basic circle (FIGURE 96). The unadorned oval is a "whole note"; an oval with a vertical *stem* represents a half-note, whose duration is half that of a whole note; a filled-in oval with a vertical stem represents a quarter-note; and adding "hooks" (called *flags*) to the quarter-note converts it successively into an eighth-, sixteenth-, thirty-second- (etc.) note.

When there are successive eighth-, sixteenth- (etc.) notes, they may be connected by *beams* that replace the flags; e.g., two eighth-notes followed by two sixteenth-notes can be represented in various ways (FIGURE 97).

A dot to the right of a note (or of another dot) increases its duration by half; e.g., in a passage that is counted in quarter notes, a dotted whole note is held for six beats, a dotted half-note for three beats, a dotted quarter note for one and a half beats, and a double-dotted quarter note for $1\frac{3}{4}$ beats. Numerical diacritics are used to represent other ways of dividing beats. Thus, when one beat of **4/4** time is to be divided in three, three eighth-notes are written and bracketed with a **3** and when a measure of **2/4** time is to be filled by a sequence of five notes of equal duration, five eighth-notes are written and bracketed with a **5** (FIGURE 98).

FIGURE 98. Chopin, Nocturne no. 5

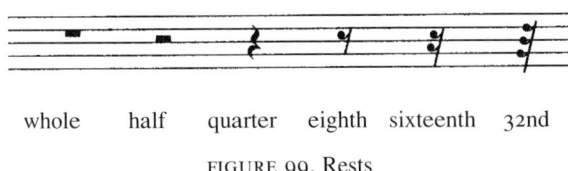

whole   half   quarter   eighth   sixteenth   32nd

FIGURE 99. Rests

Each of the notational devices for the duration of notes has a counterpart in the notation for *rests* (i.e. for places where nothing is to be played in the given part),with a different kind of "hook" used in the notation for eighth-, sixteenth- (etc.) rests, and dots again used to increase the duration of a rest by half (FIGURE 99).

The grouping that is indicated by beams is sometimes a metrical grouping (as when four sixteenth-notes that make up one beat of **4/4** time are beamed together), and sometimes melodic constituent structure (as when a "pick-up" to a beat is beamed together with a note that is on the beat). In the latter case, beams sometimes cross bar lines. Beams sometimes skip over rests, as when sixteenth-notes on either side of a sixteenth-rest are beamed together (FIGURE 100).

In runs of sixteenth and shorter notes, breaks in the multiple beams are sometimes used to indicate grouping of the notes, as in FIGURE 101, where the sixteenth-notes are grouped in threes.

A *ligature* (called a *tie*) joining the head of a note in one measure to the head of a note on the same line or space at the beginning of the next measure indicates that the former note is simply prolonged into the next measure and not re-struck; this device thus allows one to indicate that a note that begins in one measure ends in a later measure. A very different use of the ligature (called a *slur*) is to indicate phrasing; in this case, the ligature usually does not connect two note heads, but is rather written over or under a sequence of notes that are to be played as a phrase (FIGURE 102). Here the upper ligature is a tie indicating that the note is prolonged into the first full bar, while the lower ligature is a slur indicating that the triplet and the following note are to be played as a phrase.

The direction of the stems of notes is sometimes distinctive, sometimes not. When a staff contains a single voice, the stems of notes are generally pointed up or

FIGURE 100. Schumann, Grosse Sonate no. 1

FIGURE 101. Chabrier, Pièces Pittoresques

FIGURE 102. Brahms, Intermezzo, op. 118, no. 4

down in such a way as to minimize the extent to which they extend above or below the staff; i.e., for notes above the middle line of the staff, the stem will point down, and for notes below the middle line it will point up. However, when two or more voices are written on a single staff, one voice will be written with stems up and the other with stems down, so as to keep the identity of the voices clear, as in the Brahms intermezzo. FIGURE 103 illustrates two ways in which musical overlap can be represented by overlapping notational devices. A single note-head with two stems indicates a note that belongs simultaneously to two voices, and a white note-head combined with a beam indicates a half-note whose beginning is simultaneously the first of a sequence of eighth-notes in a different voice.

Dynamics and articulation

Dynamics are indicated below or above the staff by boldface initials of corresponding Italian words (e.g. **p f mp** for *piano* 'soft', *forte* 'loud', *mezzo-piano* 'medium soft'), with repetition of the letter to indicate added degrees (**pp** for *pianissimo* 'extra soft', and **ppp** or even **pppp** for still lower volume). Increases or decreases in loudness are indicated either by the words *crescendo* and *diminuendo* respectively (often abbreviated) or by a symbol whose two lines either spread apart as the volume increases, or narrow to a point as the volume decreases. The latter symbol extends from (below or above) the note where the crescendo or diminuendo begins to the place where it ends, as in FIGURE 100.

The "scopes" of symbols such as *cresc.* and *dim.* are often indicated by a broken line that extends from the symbol to the end of its scope; i.e., the maximum or minimum volume is to be reached at the point where the broken line ends. However, the scopes of these symbols, as of many others, are often not explicitly indicated, but are subject to the convention that a symbol for a state or process remains operative until

FIGURE 103. Schumann, Davidsbündlertänze

FIGURE 104. Beethoven, Bagatelle, op. 119, no. 7

another symbol supersedes it. Thus markings for dynamic levels remain in effect until the next symbol that calls for a different dynamic level; e.g., **pp** will appear at the beginning of a (possibly long) passage that is to be played *pianissimo*. By contrast, symbols for events such as *sf* (*sforzando*, lit. 'forcing', indicating a loud onset and rapid decay) apply only to the notes on which they are marked, except when there is an explicit marking (such as *sempre staccato*) indicating that the same mode of attack is to be used throughout a passage.

Structure

Sections of a piece that are to be repeated are marked by a bold-face double bar whose function as a bracket around the repeated part is marked by dots after the "left bracket" and before the "right bracket" (FIGURE 104).

The status of repeat signs as brackets is often emphasized by extending the double bar above and below the staff, and bending it in the direction of the repeated matter. A repeated section often has to have different endings, as when a repeated passage that leads from tonic to dominant has to return to the tonic the first time it is played, but stay in the dominant the second time. In such cases, a **1** is written above the staff where the "first ending" begins, and a horizontal line runs from the **1** to the repeat sign where the first ending ends; the second ending is marked similarly, with a **2** and a horizontal line. Obvious extensions of this notation are used for cases where a section is to be played more than twice in succession. The notation is sometimes supplemented by ad hoc devices indicating where the player is to go at the end of each repetition; such ad hoc notations are used extensively in many Beatles songs.

When the beginning of the repeated matter is the beginning of the piece itself, the "left bracket" is omitted entirely; i.e., on coming to a "right repeat sign," the player goes back to the corresponding "left repeat sign" if there is one, otherwise to the beginning of the piece. When a repeated section is immediately followed by another re-

FIGURE 105. Mendelssohn, String Octet, fourth violin part

peated section, the abutting repeat signs are generally superimposed, i.e. there are not four vertical lines but only two—but with dots on both sides of the double bar, indicating the end of one repeated section and the beginning of another.

The symbol ⁒ indicates repetition of a measure or even part of a measure; it is used, e.g., in keyboard music when one hand repeats an accompanying figure. Overlapping symbols can also be used to indicate repetitions, as when repeated sixteenth notes are indicated by a quarter- or half-note whose stem is crossed by a double beam, or when a tremolo is indicated by half-notes connected by beams (FIGURE 105). In both cases, the beams indicate the duration of the individual notes, while the note heads indicate the duration of the repeated figure—which in one case is a single note, and in the other case a sequence of two notes; the beams implicitly connect the note(s) to an appropriate number of copies of itself/themselves.

Small print is used for notes that are extrametrical either in the sense that the note simply doesn't count metrically (as when the meter is interrupted by a *fermata*—a diacritic on a note or rest instructing the performer to prolong it at will—and the notes precede the resumption of the normal meter) or the sense that it serves as an ornament (either on the beat, usurping part of the duration of its host note, or before the beat, usurping part of the duration of the preceding note). The latter types of ornament sometimes appear with slashes through the stems, emphasizing their extrametricality. In FIGURE 106, a slash is combined with small type to indicate two levels of extrametricality—the first d′ is an extrametrical onset to a group of notes that is itself an extrametrical onset to what follows.

Modifications

The standard notational system is modified in numerous ways in particular musical genres and milieus. For example, "Sprechstimme," in which a vocalist uses a voice quality closer to speech than to singing, is notated in an adaptation of standard notation that represents rhythms precisely, but indicates only approximate pitches: noteheads are either omitted or replaced by ×'s, and the relative heights of the stems and ×'s indicate relative pitch. Composers such as Hindemith have sometimes indicated isolated deviations from the ambient meter by writing a time-signature above the be-

FIGURE 106. Chopin, Nocturne no. 11

ginning of the measure that is metrically special, e.g. a single **3/8** measure in the middle of a **2/4** passage. The various musical instruments have spawned numerous diacritics that indicate techniques of playing those instruments, e.g. the different ways of using the bow on a string instrument and the different ways of tonguing wind instruments.

Bibliography

Boretz, Benjamin, and Edward T. Cone. 1976. *Perspectives on Notation and Performance.* New York: Norton.

Blackwood, Easley. 1985. *The Structure of Recognizable Diatonic Tunings.* Princeton: Princeton University Press.

Cole, Hugo. 1974. *Sounds and Signs: Aspects of Musical Notation.* Oxford: Oxford University Press.

Donato, Anthony. 1963. *Preparing Music Manuscript.* Englewood Cliffs, N.J.: Prentice-Hall. Repr. New York: Amsco, n.d. (Everybody's Favorite Series 130).

Kaufmann, Walter. 1967. *Musical Notations of the Orient.* Bloomington: Indiana University Press.

McCawley, James D. 1992. "Linguistic Aspects of Musical and Mathematical Notation." In *The Linguistics of Literacy* (Typological Studies in Language 21), ed. Pamela Downing, Susan D. Lima, and Michael Noonan, pp. 169–90. Amsterdam: Benjamins.

Read, Gardner. 1969. *Music Notation: A Manual of Modern Practice,* 2nd ed. New York: Crescendo. Repr. London: Gollancz, 1974; New York: Taplinger, 1979.

Ross, Ted. 1970. *The Art of Music Engraving and Processing.* Miami Beach, Fla.: Hansen.

Movement Notation Systems

BRENDA FARNELL

In contrast to notation systems for writing vocal gestures (speech), movement writing systems provide the means to write bodily actions whose modality is visual rather than vocal. Like the history of writing systems for speech, however, the history of movement writing reveals a tremendous variety of solutions to problems of transcription, and several ways of identifying basic units that form the basis for a script. In contrast to various forms of mnemonic devices, such as word glosses or static pictographic representations of the human body in diagrams or photographs, movement scripts represent a genuine technological breakthrough because they provide the means to become literate in relation to the medium; that is, they provide a means to apperceive, read, write, reconstruct, think, and analyze in terms of graphic symbols that represent the movement itself (see Farnell 1994, 1995; Williams and Farnell 1990).

Extant records show that at least 87 movement writing systems have been used in Europe and North America since the fifteenth century. Many were invented to record one specific movement system, such as an idiom of dancing or a gestural system, and disappeared from use when the movement system itself changed or disappeared. It is only in the mid twentieth century that generalized systems have emerged that are adaptable to wider needs. The scholarship in this field remains extremely meager, and we know virtually nothing of movement writing systems in areas of the world outside Europe and North America. Hutchinson-Guest (1984) and Key (1977) provide useful discussions and bibliographies of known systems

Historical developments in Europe

Historical records show that, in fifteenth-century Europe, movement notation systems began to appear as mnemonic devices for social dances. Renaissance dancing masters in the courts of Italy, France, and Spain were highly esteemed as purveyors of an elaborate etiquette that involved displays of wealth and power in the form of elegant dress, stately dances, and correct deportment. The earliest known treatises on dance technique (e.g., Ebreo 1463, written in Milan; Cornozano 1465) recorded dances then popular at court. Known as *Basse danses* 'low dances', each dance was composed of different combinations of five basic step patterns, each of which had a name. Transcribing a particular dance sequence was easily accomplished by listing the initial let-

855

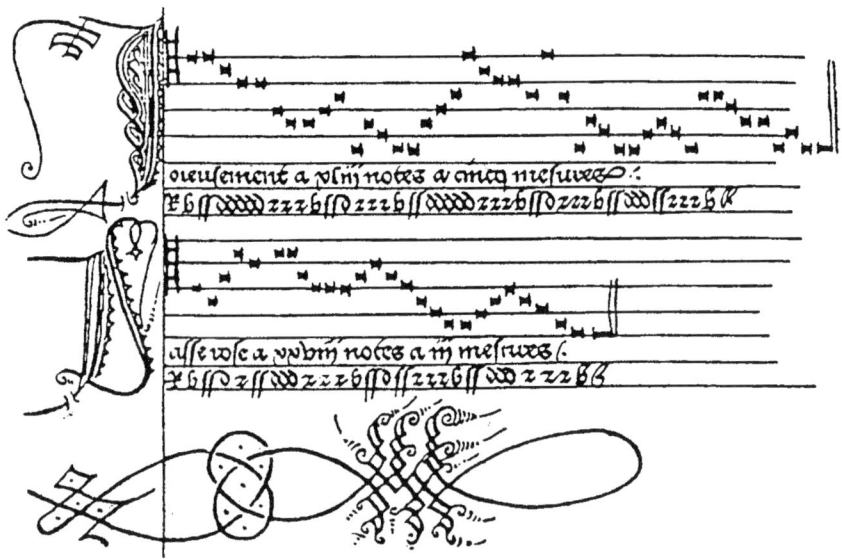

FIGURE 107. From *The Dance Book of Margaret of Austria* (ca. 1460), also known as the Golden Manuscript and the Burgundian Manuscript (Royal Library, Brussels); reprinted, with permission, from Hutchinson-Guest 1984: 44. It first belonged to Marie de Bourgogne and later to her daughter Margaret of Austria. The steps are: *R*, *reverencia* 'reverence', a bow to start the dance; *b*, *branle*, a swaying step; *s*, *simple*, a step forward followed by closing the feet together; *d*, *double*, three forward steps followed by closing feet together; *r* (looks like *z*), *represa* 'reprise', a backward step.

ter of each step. FIGURE 107 shows an example from a collection of dances written ca. 1460, in which the steps are written by placing the appropriate letter under the musical notes. The most widely translated and reprinted book that uses this letter system is *Orchésographie* (1589/1967) by Thoinot Arbeau, a pseudonym for one Jehan Tabout, a Jesuit priest, who, unlike most of his fellow clerics, was in favor of dancing.

This primitive system served its limited mnemonic purpose well at the time, but many essential elements of correct performance were assumed to be common knowledge and so were not recorded. This has left historians of Renaissance court dances unable to reconstruct fully the actions of the arms, head, and torso, as well as essential features such as correct gaze, posture, precise choreographic forms, and floor patterns. An unidentified Catalonian dancing master of the same period provides the earliest known example of using arbitrary but iconically motivated signs to represent movement in these court dances (FIGURE 108).

The movement notation found in John Playford's popular *The English Dancing Master* (1651) represents a transitional stage, in that he used some of these letter abbreviations but added graphic signs for repeats, as well as diagrams of basic floor patterns with signs that distinguished male and female dancers. However, the actual sequences of movements were described in words. Many books written about the popular European dances of the eighteenth and nineteenth centuries follow this pattern, showing floor plans and accompanying music, with the steps described briefly

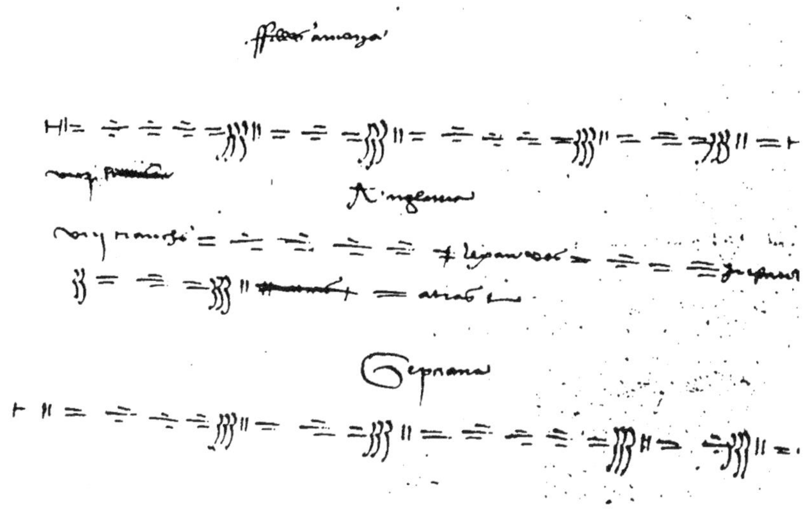

FIGURE 108. A mid 15th c. dance step notation system from Catalonia. Anonymous ms., Cervera Municipal Archives, Spain; reprinted, with permission, from Hutchinson-Guest 1984: 45. The letters normally used to represent dance steps have been replaced with a horizontal stroke that represents forward movement. Two horizontal lines represent two 'simple' steps; three horizontal lines the 'double' step; and |—, the *reverencia*, represents the forward body movement of a bowing action. A vertical stroke represents a step in place; e.g. || for the *branle* step (swaying from side to side equals two steps in place). A stylized *z, ʒ*, represents the *represa*.

in words. They too, however, act primarily as mnemonic devices and do not facilitate accurate reproduction.

As European dance forms changed and more detail was required, other notation systems were invented, such as the Beauchamps-Feuillet system used in France circa 1700. Although invented by Pierre Beauchamps, a famous ballet-master, it was the younger Raoul Auger Feuillet who first published a book on the subject. King Louis XIV's passion for dancing set a social climate in which a system of notation for dancing could flourish. As dancing was a required social grace at court and among the educated classes, instruction in the art became necessary. The Académie Royale de la Danse was established by the King in 1661, and there followed a period when the ability to read dances using the Beauchamps-Feuillet notation was an expected skill of any educated person in the courts of Europe. Feuillet's books were quickly translated into English and German, and collections of the latest dance compositions by famous teachers were published almost yearly between 1700 and 1722. Indeed, as Joseph Addison wrote in *The Tatler* in 1709, "there is nothing so common as to communicate a dance by letter" (cited in Hutchinson-Guest 1984: 64).

This excursion into movement literacy lasted almost a hundred years but declined along with the demise of the French aristocracy during the French Revolution. The emergent French middle class practiced the simpler *contredanses* 'country dances' from England. In contrast, theatrical dance forms, which were basically the same

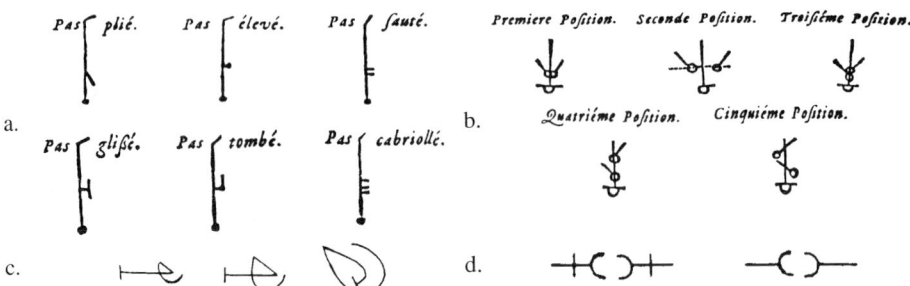

FIGURE 109. The Beuchamp-Feuillet notation system for the court dances of Europe (Feuillet 1700A). *Above: (a)* Variations in steps, *(b)* positions of the foot, *(c)* arm movements, *(d)* taking and releasing the hands. *Right:* An example of a dance.

as the court dances in the early eighteenth century, developed into classical ballet. Such dance forms became elaborate and highly skilled, and altogether separate from social dancing. In this milieu, movement literacy declined because professional theatrical dancers were not members of literate elites. In addition, not all influential teachers were in favor of writing dances (e.g. Jean George Noverre). As a consequence, the Beauchamps-Feuillet notation system was never developed sufficiently to accommodate the new complexities of an enlarged ballet vocabulary, and by the turn of the century the tradition of literacy had been broken. Theatrical dancing reverted to an oral-visual tradition, with disastrous consequences for our knowledge of the historical development of European choreography.

The Beauchamps-Feuillet writing system is based upon a center line that traces the dancer's path across the floor (FIGURE 109). Indications for steps are somewhat iconic; a dot indicates the start of a step, a line traces the direction of its path, and an angular line at the end represents the foot. Strokes added to the basic step sign allow for ornamentation such as bending the knee, rising on toe, a springing step, or a gliding step. Positions of the feet in relation to each other can be written, along with some arm movements, and there are signs for indicating the taking or releasing of hands. As with the earlier notation systems, focus was on the intricate footwork, while knowledge of elegant carriage and graceful use of the arms was taken for granted. The Beauchamps-Feuillet system did not distinguish steps (weight-bearing) from leg gestures in the air, nor did it accommodate ornamental and pantomimic arm gestures and use of the torso and head. Theatrical dances of the period increasingly involved a large number of dancers moving simultaneously, and so the track system, upon which the Beauchamps-Feuillet system was based, became unworkable (Hutchinson-Guest 1984: 62–66).

During the nineteenth century, several new dance notation systems emerged, some of which centered on stick-figure representations of the body, others on adaptations of musical notation (e.g. Saint-Léon 1852, Zorn 1887). Most notable in this period, perhaps, is the system invented by Vladimir Ivanovitch Stepanov (1892). Although a dancer of the Maryinsky Theater in St. Petersburg, Stepanov also studied

anatomy and anthropology at the University of St. Petersburg, and was sent to Paris to further his studies. Alexander Gorsky refined the system after Stepanov's untimely death in 1896, but it was Gorsky's assistant Nikolai Grigorevich Sergeyev who put it to work. He and his assistants recorded a large number of ballets and used the notation to reconstruct the latest choreography on new companies such as the Diaghilev Ballets Russes, the Latvian National Theater, the Paris Opera, and London's Vic-Wells (now the Royal Ballet).

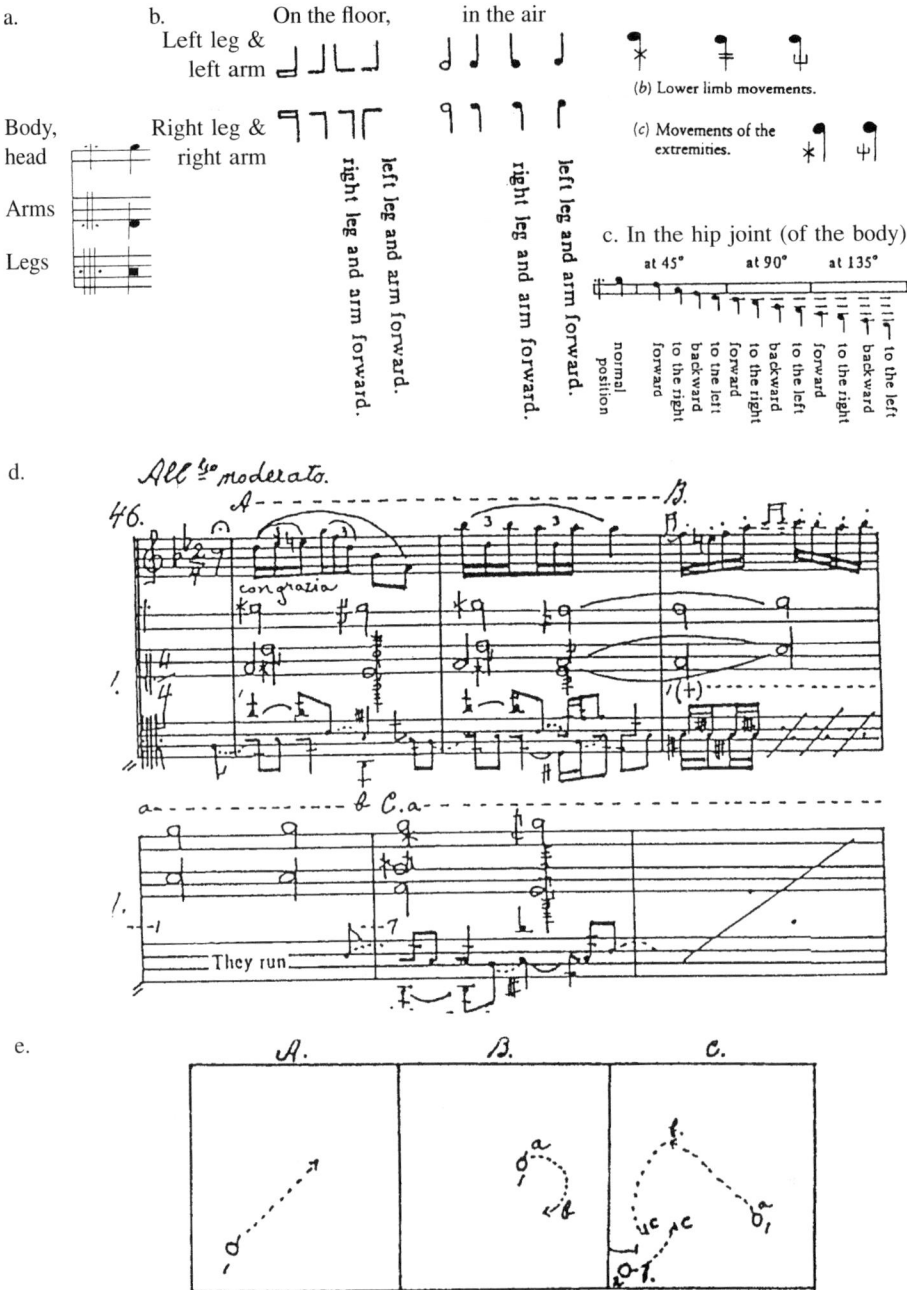

FIGURE 110. Stepanov system (1892). *(a)* Staff for the placement of body parts, *(b)* different forms of the note signs, *(c)* notation of flexion and extension of hip joint, *(d)* an example of writing, *(e)* floor plans. Redrawn after Gorsky 1978: 11, 13, and 56; and Hutchinson-Guest 1984: 73.

Stepanov was the first to base a notation system on an understanding of the anatomical structure of the human body. Musical notes form the basic signs (an idea used previously by Bernard Klemm in 1855), and the time value of a note is the same as in music. A modified musical staff provides sections on which to indicate movements of the legs, arms, body, and head (FIGURE 110). Square-headed music notes indicate steps in contact with the ground, whereas round-headed notes indicate leg gestures. Note stems that go upward represent the left leg or arm; note stems going down, the right leg or arm. Additional notations on the stem indicate movements involving flexion, extension, adduction, abduction, twisting, turns, and circular movements. As these terms indicate, Stepanov's taxonomy of the body and classification of movement is clearly based on his anatomical training. An innovation was to indicate the degree of turn with numbers distributed around a circle, and floor plans were also included.

Despite that fact that Stepanov's system was officially tested and approved by his Russian superiors before being put to practical use, by 1920 it was moribund. The reasons for its demise are complex, but they certainly involve the personalities and politics of the day, as well as its technical shortcomings (see Hutchinson-Guest 1984: 74, Wiley 1978: xii–xvii). An important factor, however, and one which continues today in European and American professional dance subcultures, was skepticism toward, or complete rejection of, the very idea of notation by principal figures. There was (and is) an overwhelming focus on the continual invention of new choreography, and so ballet-masters desired to create their own versions of the classics according to the skills and strengths of new dancers, rather than copy their predecessors. Thus classic works that carried the same name frequently contained entirely new choreography. For example, Marius Petipa, a leading nineteenth-century Russian choreographer, was "completely convinced (pray God that I may be wrong) that worthy ballet masters will not use [Stepanov's] method of notation" (Petipa 1892, cited in Wiley 1978: xiii). One can only wonder whether Petipa's prayer suggests a faint glimmer of awareness about the long-term consequences that such self-serving attitudes would have for the history and subsequent academic status of his art form.

Dancing is not the only context in which the notation of movement has been attempted. A system was developed in 1806 by Gilbert Austin for the notation of gestures and body positions during public speaking, and this was combined with notations for vocalizations. Austin used letter abbreviations that referred to a specific classification of gestural actions (see FIGURE 111). Many subsequent studies in nonverbal communication have repeated this type of abbreviation, using checklists of graphic signs or word glosses that represent different positions of head, eyes, lips, and mouth as movement possibilities to be checked off if and when they occur (see examples in Key 1977). It should be noted that these methods tend to focus on position rather than movement, and their aim is usually statistical analysis according to these predetermined units, rather than movement literacy and a score that would allow full reproduction of the flow of movement. In addition, Birdwhistell (1952) invented a

a.

b.

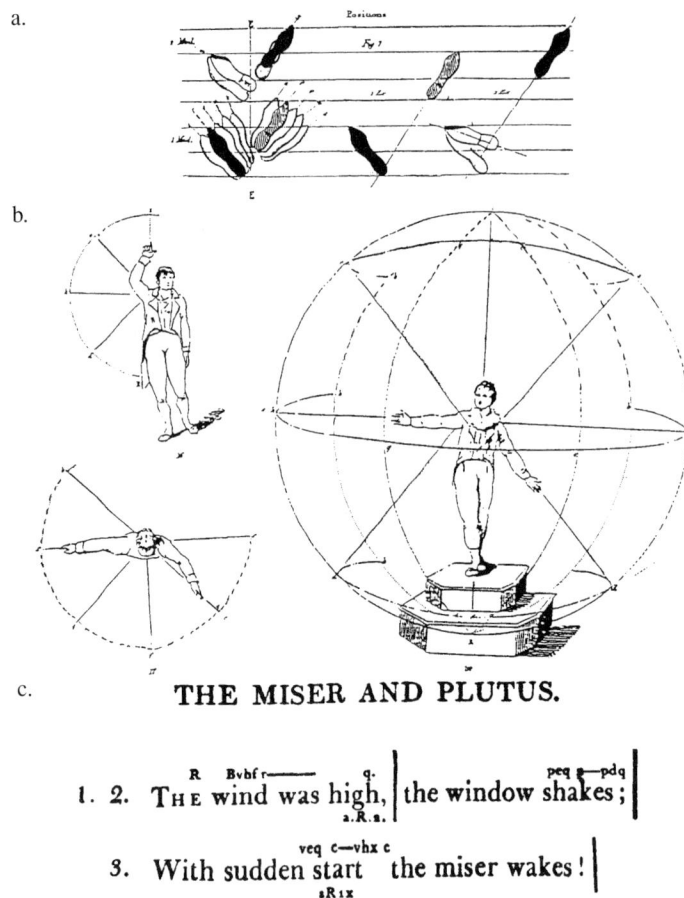

c.　　　　　　**THE MISER AND PLUTUS.**

1. 2. The wind was high, | the window shakes;

3. With sudden start　the miser wakes!

FIGURE III. Austin's notation system for gesture and speech in oratory (1806: 363–69). *(a)* Foot patterns with weight distribution are shown by degrees of shading; *(b)* arm movement is described with coordinates determined by placing the body in an imaginary circle divided into vertical and horizontal planes; *(c)* letter abbreviations classify hand, arm, head, and eye movements: e.g. (letters above the spoken text) R, round look of eyes; B, both hands; v, vertical presentation of palms; h, horizontal arms; f, arms forward in transverse direction; r——, motion right; q, arms stop at oblique position; (letters below the spoken text) a,R.2., advance right foot to second position.

movement notation system for use in functional-anatomical descriptions of "behavior" in an approach to movement research known as *kinesics*.

　　Also of note are systems invented since the 1960s for writing signed languages. FIGURE II2 shows a script for American Sign Language (ASL) invented by William Stokoe (1960) and adapted for the notation of Australian Aboriginal sign languages by Adam Kendon (1989). Valerie Sutton (1973) devised a pictographic system for writing ASL called Sign Writing. This application, largely a mnemonic device, followed her attempt to create a "shorthand" for writing classical ballet. La Mont West, Jr. (1960) also invented a notation system for Plains Indian sign language.

Tab symbols

1. Ø zero, the neutral place where the hands move, in contrast with all places below
2. ○ face or whole head
3. ∩ forehead or brow, upper face
4. ⊔ mid-face, the eye and nose region
5. ∪ chin, lower face
6.) cheek, temple, ear, side-face
7. π neck
8. [] trunk, body from shoulders to hips
9. \ upper arm
10. ⌿ elbow, forearm
11. ɑ wrist, arm in supinated position (on its back)
12. ꭰ wrist, arm in pronated position (face down)

Dez symbols, some also used as tab

13. A compact hand, fist; may be like 'a', 's', or 't' of manual alphabet
14. B flat hand
15. 5 spread hand; fingers and thumb spread like '5' of manual numeration
16. C curved hand; may be like 'c' or more open
17. E contracted hand; like 'e' or more clawlike
18. F "three-ring" hand; from spread hand, thumb and index finger touch or cross
19. G index hand; like 'g' or sometimes like 'd'; index finger points from fist
20. H index and second finger, side by side, extended
21. I "pinkie" hand; little finger extended from compact hand
22. K like G except that thumb touches middle phalanx of second finger; like 'k' and 'p' of manual alphabet
23. L angle hand; thumb, index finger in right angle, other fingers usually bent into palm
24. 3 "cock" hand; thumb and first two fingers spread, like '3' of manual numeration
25. O tapered hand; fingers curved and squeezed together over thumb; may be like 'o' of manual alphabet
26. R "warding off" hand; second finger crossed over index finger, like 'r' of manual alphabet

27. V "victory" hand; index and second fingers extended and spread apart
28. W three-finger hand; thumb and little finger touch, others extended spread
29. X hook hand; index finger bent in hook from fist, thumb tip may touch fingertip
30. Y "horns" hand; thumb and little finger spread out extended from fist; or index finger and little finger extended, parallel
31. 8 (allocheric variant of Y); second finger bent in from spread hand, thumb may touch fingertip

Sig symbols

32. ^ upward movement ⎫
33. ˅ downward movement ⎬ vertical action
34. ᴺ up-and-down movement ⎭
35. > rightward movement ⎫
36. < leftward movement ⎬ sideways action
37. ᶻ side to side movement ⎭
38. ᵀ movement toward signer ⎫
39. ⊥ movement away from signer ⎬ horizontal action
40. Ɪ to-and-fro movement ⎭
41. ɑ supinating rotation (palm up) ⎫
42. ꭰ pronating rotation (palm down) ⎬ rotary action
43. ω twisting movement ⎭
44. ꞃ nodding or bending action
45. □ opening action (final dez configuration shown in brackets)
46. ♯ closing action (final dez configuration shown in brackets)
47. ꝛ wiggling action of fingers
48. ⊘ circular action
49. ⟩(convergent action, approach ⎫
50. × contactual action, touch ⎪
51. Ɪ linking action, grasp ⎪
52. ˙ crossing action ⎬ interaction
53. ⊙ entering action ⎪
54. ÷ divergent action, separate ⎪
55. ⟨⟩ interchanging action ⎭

TAB (< Tabula) = location
DEZ (< Designator) = handshape
SIG (< Signation) = movement

orientation represented by subscripts on handshape compound notation used to represent signs with two locations

I. BASIC FORMS
Each sign must have one TAB, one DEZ, and one SIG in that order TD^S

$$[\,]A^X \qquad \_A^X \qquad ØW^꭪$$

Some signs have two handshapes TDD^S

$$ØBB^{>^\cdot} \qquad ØL^{\cdots^\vee} \qquad GL^{\cdots X}$$

Some signs have two *simultaneous* movements TD^S_S or TDD^S_S

$$[\,]¥ ^{¥}_X \qquad DI^꭪_X \qquad {}^-¥^\vee_X$$

Some signs have two *sequential* movements TD^{SS} or TDD^{SS}

$$\sqrt{V}^{v^{v^\cdot v}} \qquad {}^-I^{V^>} \qquad {}^-V^{XᵒX} \text{ or } {}^-V^{XᴰX}$$

Some signs have both sequential and simultaneous movements TD$^{SS}_S$ etc.

$$[\,]K^{X>X}_v \qquad \backslash B^{Tᴰᵥ}_{ᴰX\ X} \qquad {}^-55^{XW}_\perp$$

Repeated movement is shown by a dot following the sig symbol TD$^{S\cdot}$

$$DI^{X\cdot} \qquad ƎA^{\dot{\vert}}_X \qquad ØYY^{W\cdot}$$

Alternating movement is shown by a tilde (~) following the sig symbol

$$^-II^{\theta\cdot}_\perp \qquad ØGG^{\theta\cdot}_T \qquad [\,]AA^{\vee\cdot}_T$$

II. ORIENTATION
Orientation of the hands to the signing space is shown by a subscript on the DEZ symbol. Orientation symbols look like SIG symbols, but they mean starting position, not movement. TD$_o^S$

$$ØB_ɑB_ɑ^{N\cdots} \qquad Ø3_ᴰ3_ᴰ^{N\cdots} \qquad {}^-O^\cdot_{TX} \\ {}^-Y^\cdot_\perp \qquad {}^X_ᴰV^{\cdots}{}^{\vee}_ᴰX \qquad ØX^\cdot_{\dot\sim}{}'X^{\cdot X}_< $$

III. RELATIONSHIPS BETWEEN THE TWO HANDS
In signs involving both hands, symbols are sometimes used to show the positions of the hands as related to each other.

$$\overline{X}X^{Lᵒ}_v \qquad \sqrt{}X^\cdot \qquad A_▲A^X \qquad ØH^+H^꭪$$

Some signs use the non-dominant hand as the TAB. In these cases the first DEZ symbol represents the non-dominant hand, and the second indicates the dominant.

$$5^ᵒG^ɑ \qquad I_>{}'I^{\ >}_< \qquad I^♯X^꭪_\wedge$$

Some signs show the change in handshape as part of the movement notation, and also indicate the final shape in raised brackets.

$$^-5_ᴰ^{♯[ᵒ]} \qquad [\,]5^{♯[ᵒ]}_<$$

IV. COMPOUND SIGNS
Signs which require contact at two locations are often notated in compound form. Many of these are historically decomposable into two separate meaning components.
Compound symbol ‖

Examples
$$^-5_ᴰ^{♯}‖[\,]5^X \text{ or } ^-5^X‖[\,]5^X \\ [\,]5_\perp^X‖O5_ᴰ5_ᴰ^\emptyset$$

V. Miscellaneous leftovers
A few signs require simultaneous contact in two different locations. The two necessary notations are shown in vertical arrangement and are joined together by square brackets.

$$\begin{bmatrix} {}_\perp↑Gᵛ \\ ØA_ᴰ^ɑ \end{bmatrix}$$

Diacritical marks are additions to the symbol set that modify in small ways the symbols that are seen as basic.

A B H R   among others can show thumb extension
D⋯ 5⋯ V⋯ O⋯ among others can show curved or 'bent' fingers

A dot (·) *above* a movement symbol means sharp, strong single movement TD^S TD$^{S\cdot}$ *to the right* of a movement symbol means repetition …

▲   shows one hand in front of the other; however it can be interpreted in two ways. TD$_▲$D^S

Ø   When this TAB appears before signs with two DEZ symbols that the movement applies to both hands.
$$ØGG_X^{\dot\vert}$$

If no Ø is present and the sign has two DEZ symbols, then the first is the base hand and the second is the active hand. Only the active hand moves.

$$GG_f^X$$

FIGURE 112. *(above)* Table of symbols from William Stokoe's writing system for ASL (Stokoe, Casterline, and Croneberg 1965: x–xii); *(below)* instructions for use (after Frishberg 1983: 28).

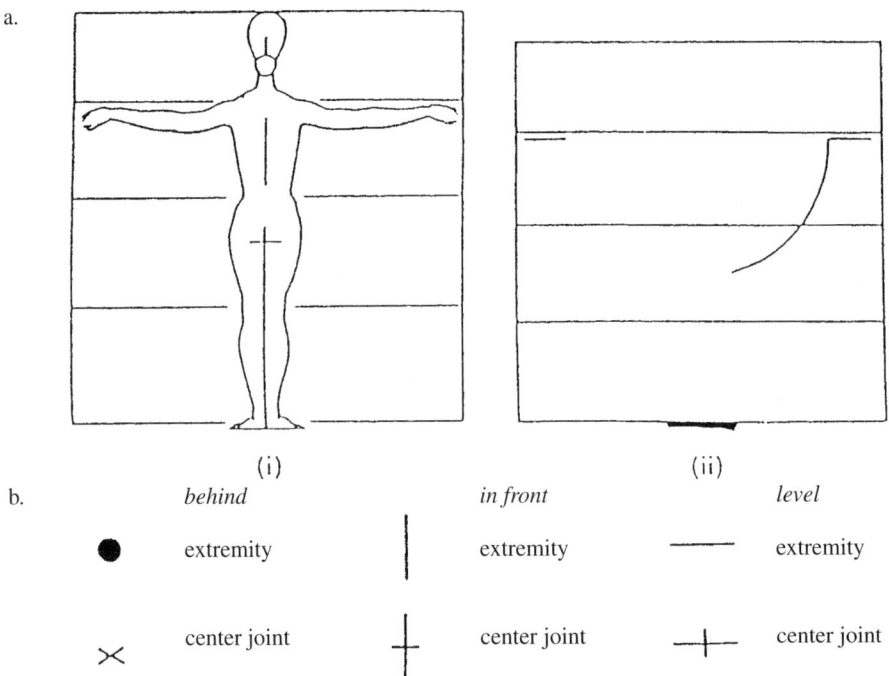

FIGURE 113. Benesh notation system: *Above: (a)* body parts and staff: (i) matrix representing the performer; (ii) arm raised sideways (redrawn after Benesh and Benesh 1956: 11. *(b)* direction symbols for the third dimension. *Right: (c)* Signs under the staff indicate stage direction faced, turning, stage location, and direction traveled (redrawn after Hutchinson-Guest 1984: 99, 100). *(d)* An example of writing from McGuinness-Scott 1983: 117.

The emergence of general movement scripts

The writing systems mentioned so far have been little used because they were developed to meet the needs of one particular movement system, dance style, or research project. The problem facing investigators has been to develop a script capable of writing all anatomically possible bodily action that would preserve the identity of the movement, make possible accurate reproduction of it, and maintain its semantic content. This entails a concern with recording action rather than gross physical movement (see Best 1974: 193, Williams 1991: 19–20, Farnell 1994). It is only in the twentieth century that such generalized systems have emerged, and in this they aim to provide the movement equivalent of an International Phonetic Alphabet (SECTION 71); such systems are not dance notation systems, any more than the Roman alphabet is a poetry writing system. Three such comprehensive movement writing systems are currently in use: Labanotation, also known as Kinetography Laban (Laban 1928); Benesh Choreology (Benesh and Benesh 1956); and Eshkol-Wachmann notation (Eshkol and Wachmann 1958). It is important to note that the inventors of these three systems had different aims, came from different cultural backgrounds, and were fa-

c.   face the audience   a half-turn right,
end facing upstage

   6   a file of six persons   6   a line of six traveling
sideways to the right

   a line downstage
on left stage   entering upstage
through right wing

d. Ribbons

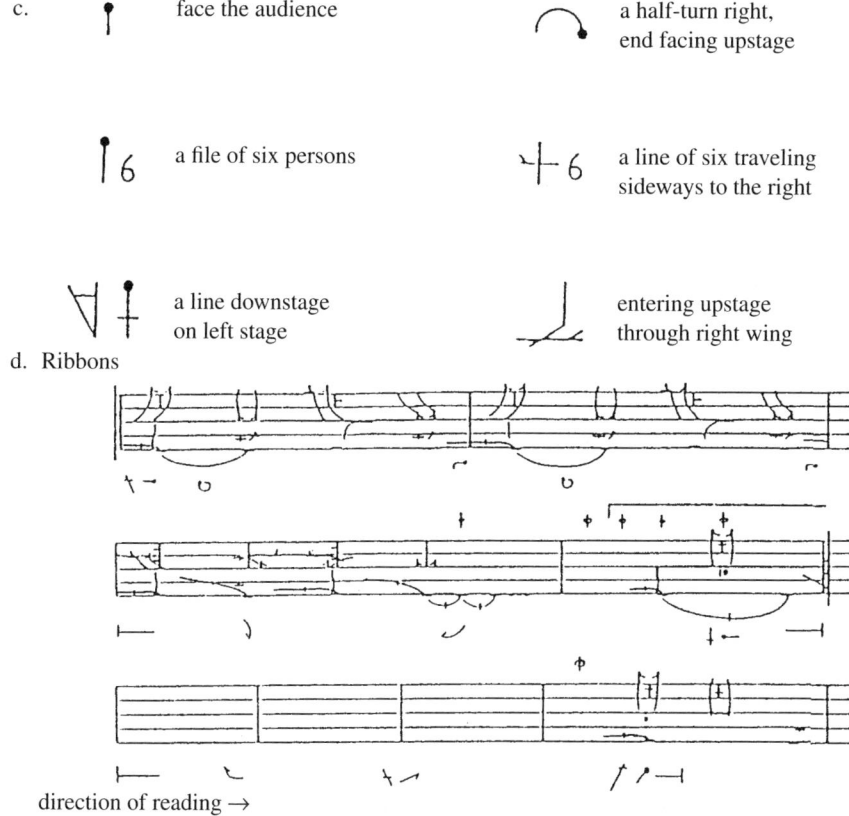

direction of reading →
time: bar lines follow the same convention as a musical score

miliar with different movement systems. These factors influenced the choices they
made in solving basic problems of transcription.

English ballet dancer Joan Benesh and her husband Rudolph designed their system at the outset to record ballet, and so the writing system itself underscores a concern with line and the visual results of movement. The *Benesh system* relies on an
iconic visualization of the body placed within a horizontal five-line staff (FIGURE
113). In addition to ballet, however, the Benesh system has been expanded and applied to other forms of dancing, as well as to physical therapy.

Eshkol-Wachmann notation was invented by Israeli modern dance choreographer
Noa Eshkol and Israeli architect Abraham Wachmann. Both were interested in the
complex articulations of any moving object in space. The system utilizes numbers derived from a planal division of space, together with a few other graphic signs such as
arrows, all of which are written on horizontal columns assigned to major divisions of
the body (FIGURE 114). The Eshkol-Wachmann system has been used in non-human
contexts such as computer graphics, architectural design, and animal behavior studies, as well as the recording of traditional Israeli dances, contemporary choreography,
and Israeli sign language.

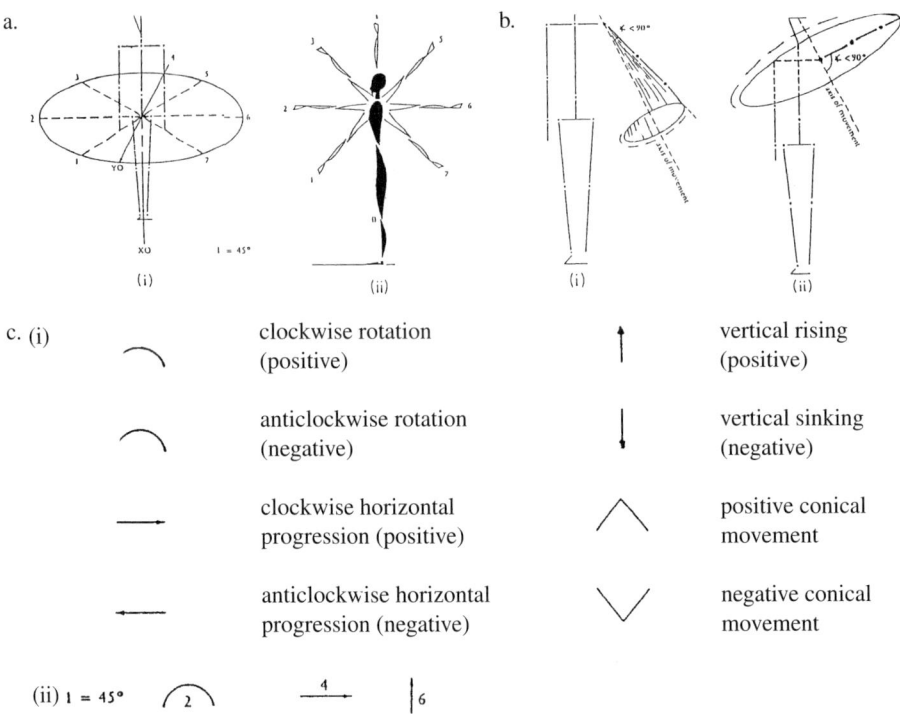

FIGURE 114. Eshkol-Wachmann notation system. *Above: (a)* Organization of space: (i) coordinates of the horizontal plane, (ii) coordinates of the vertical plane (redrawn after Hutchinson-Guest 1984: 112). *(b)* Circular motion: (i) Conical movement, (ii) planal movement (redrawn after Eshkol and Wachmann 1958: 10, 11). *(c)* Symbols: (i) Signs for motion, (ii) numbers added to each of the signs for motion to state the degree of displacement (redrawn after Hutchinson-Guest 1984: 111). *Right: (d)* The full staff: body parts (redrawn after Eshkol and Wachmann 1958: 8). *(e)* An example of writing (redrawn after Hutchinson-Guest 1984: 109).

Labanotation was invented by the Austro-Hungarian choreographer and dancer Rudolf Laban (1879–1958), who set out to devise a system that could record any human movement. He was intrigued by Greek concerns with mathematics, the motions of planetary spheres, and crystal forms, as well as the Bauhaus movement in visual art and architecture in Germany. He studied human movement in many diverse situations, from manual labor in industrial settings to mime. Current applications include the creation of a historical library of Western theater choreography and the traditional folk dances of Eastern Europe, socio-cultural anthropology, religious studies, Plains Indian sign language, and kinesiology. A related system for analyzing movement dynamics, known in the United States as Effort-Shape, has been applied to child development, dance in education, dance therapy, and personality analysis (Dell 1977). Labanotation is the system I have chosen to use, and it is used here to illustrate how some of the fundamental issues involved in the process of transcribing movement have been solved.

d.

	Left	Hand								20
		Forearm								19
		Upper Arm								18
		Shoulder								17
	Right	Hand								16
		Forearm								15
		Upper Arm								14
		Shoulder								13
	Head									12
	Neck									11
	Torso (upper part)									10
	Pelvis									9
	Right	Thigh								8
		Lower Leg								7
		Foot								6
	Left	Thigh								5
		Lower Leg								4
		Foot								3
	Weight									2
	Front									1

time →

e.

reading direction →

Problems in the transcription of human movement

A comprehensive movement writing system has to resolve several difficult technical issues. Human actions take place in three dimensions of space and one dimension of time and mobilize many parts of the body simultaneously. An inventory of graphic signs is therefore required to represent (1) all parts and surfaces of the body; (2) the three-dimensional space in which those parts move; (3) time; (4) dynamics; and (5) relationships between the moving body parts of one person, and between persons and objects in the form space of the dance or movement event. In addition, orthographic conventions must be established to distinguish simultaneous action from sequential actions through time, and to provide syntactic order. The task is complex, surely, but not insurmountable. The conventions of Labanotation furnish the illustrations.

Body

FIGURE 116 illustrates how Labanotation solves the problem of representing the joints, limbs, and surfaces of the body. The graphic signs are arbitrary, but iconically motivated. They thus offer an aid to memory but the number of signs required is greatly reduced in comparison to a system that attempts a pictographic representation of the body. Such specification also provides a system of finite differentiation between body parts. Taxonomies of the body differ across cultures, and the degree of flexibility offered by the Laban system, rather than being redundant, accommodates such anthropological concerns.

Vertical columns assigned to major body parts create a basic staff that also provides syntactic order (FIGURE 117). This basic staff can be adapted, if necessary, to the needs of a specific system. For example, FIGURE 117 shows the basic Labanotation staff adapted to the needs of writing Plains (Indian) Sign Talk (Farnell 1995).

Space

In order to create a finite model of the space in which the body moves, Laban, using a Euclidean view, conceived of the body as being surrounded by a sphere of space as if inside a balloon. This spherical space is divided along three dimensions by three

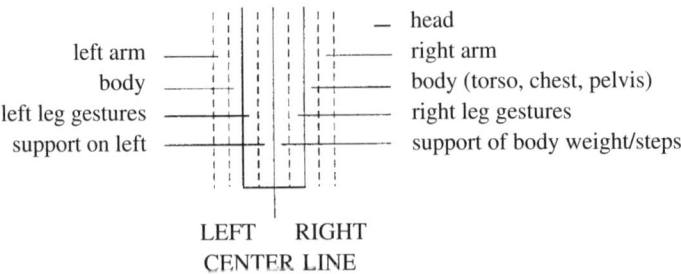

FIGURE 115. The basic Labanotation staff provides syntactic order for the symbols of the script.

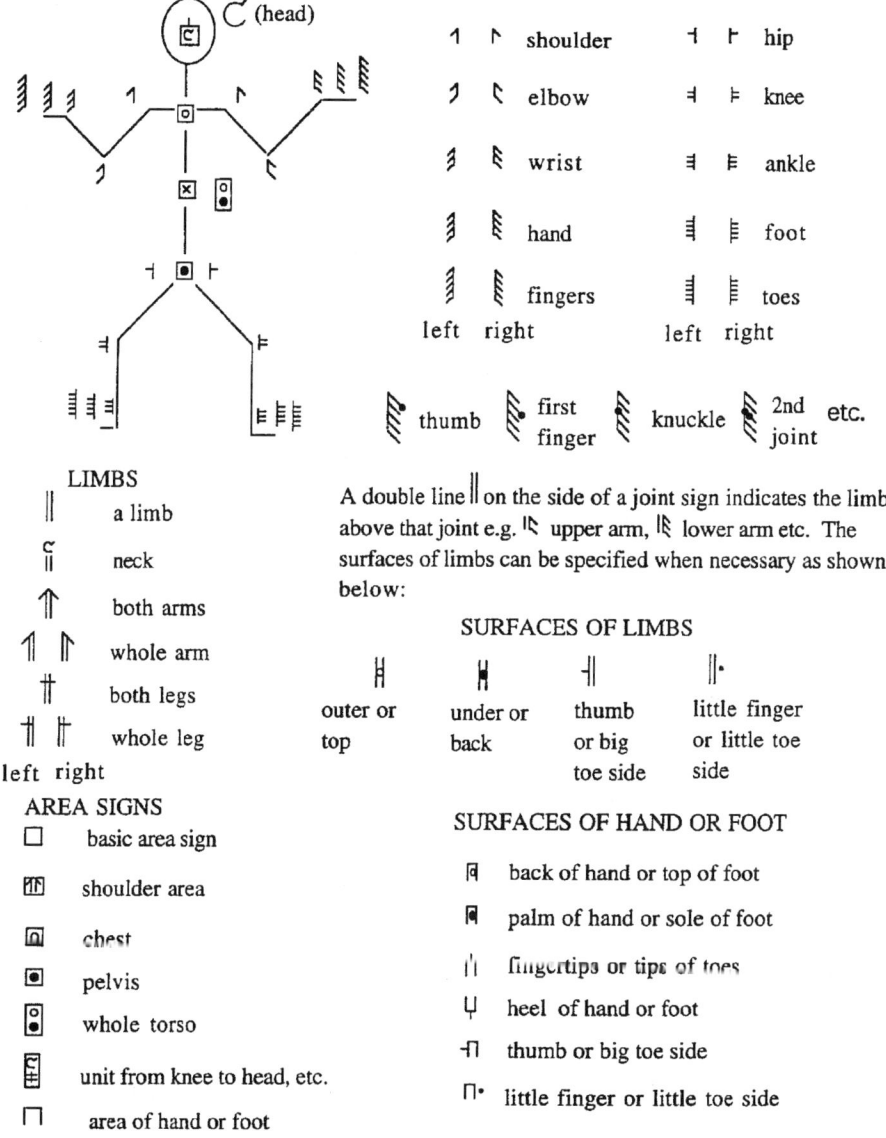

LIMBS

‖   a limb

c̦̦   neck

⇈   both arms

↿ ↾   whole arm

⇊   both legs

⇃ ⇂   whole leg

left right

AREA SIGNS

□   basic area sign

▦   shoulder area

▣   chest

▣   pelvis

▤   whole torso

▦   unit from knee to head, etc.

⊓   area of hand or foot

A double line ‖ on the side of a joint sign indicates the limb above that joint e.g. ⱦ upper arm, ⱦ lower arm etc. The surfaces of limbs can be specified when necessary as shown below:

SURFACES OF LIMBS

‖	‖	⊣‖	‖•
outer or top	under or back	thumb or big toe side	little finger or little toe side

SURFACES OF HAND OR FOOT

◨   back of hand or top of foot

◧   palm of hand or sole of foot

⌐̸   fingertips or tips of toes

Ч   heel of hand or foot

⊣⌐   thumb or big toe side

⌐•   little finger or little toe side

Sides of an area can be specified using a set of minor directional pins ↓ low, ⊥ middle ↑ high: e.g. ▣ upper front side of chest, ▱ lower left back diagonal side of pelvis, ⊡ front middle area of head, i .e. face. Signs for parts of the face are also built out of these units e.g. ⊚ eyes, ⊂ right ear, ⊂ chin.

FIGURE 116. Labanotation system: graphic signs for body parts and surfaces
(Farnell 1995, with permission).

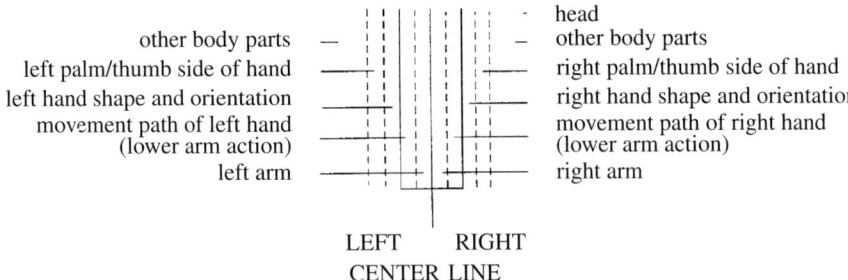

FIGURE 117. The Labanotation staff adapted for writing Plains Sign Talk.

axes perpendicular to each other (up/down, right/left, front/back), with the body at the center. Each of these major directions and their intermediate divisions is assigned a graphic sign, as shown in FIGURE 118. The script utilizes this simple set theory rather than mensurational measuring. Each graphic sign that refers to spatial direction is built out of the basic rectangle ⊔. A change of shape denotes the dimensions ⊔ front versus ⊓ back and ◁ left versus ▷ right, and—in ▨ high, ⦁ middle, ■ low—a change of shading accommodates the up/down dimension.

This same spatial scheme provides a framework for indicating the direction of pathways for the whole body (as when a person moves from one location to another). Locating a smaller imaginary cross of axes at each joint specifies the direction of individual limbs and smaller body parts. Spatial direction for any body part is judged by the relationship between the distal (far) end of a limb and the proximal end (nearest to torso). For example, if one raises one's right arm in front of the torso, so that the hand is higher than the shoulder, then the movement is designated as being in a forward high direction ▨ . If the hand is then moved until it is the same level as the shoulder, the movement of the arm would be described as going toward forward middle ⦁ , and if it continued moving until it was lower than the shoulder it would be ■ forward low. When the arm rests at the side of the torso, it is in a "default" position (assumed unless stated otherwise) and is described as ■ , having moved to, or being in, "place low."

As with taxonomies of the body, there are cultural and linguistic variations to spatial orientation as well as to the semantic values attached to spatial directions. Such features can become components of movement texts written with Labanotation through the use of spatial orientation keys. These inform the reader which particular conception of space is in operation, much as the key of C# minor might operate at the start of a musical score: N W⊞E S = S E⊠W N   . This key refers to a difference between Euro-American and Assiniboine (Nakota) conceptions of the four cardinal di-

Spatial direction is determined by both the shape of the graphic sign and by different shading.

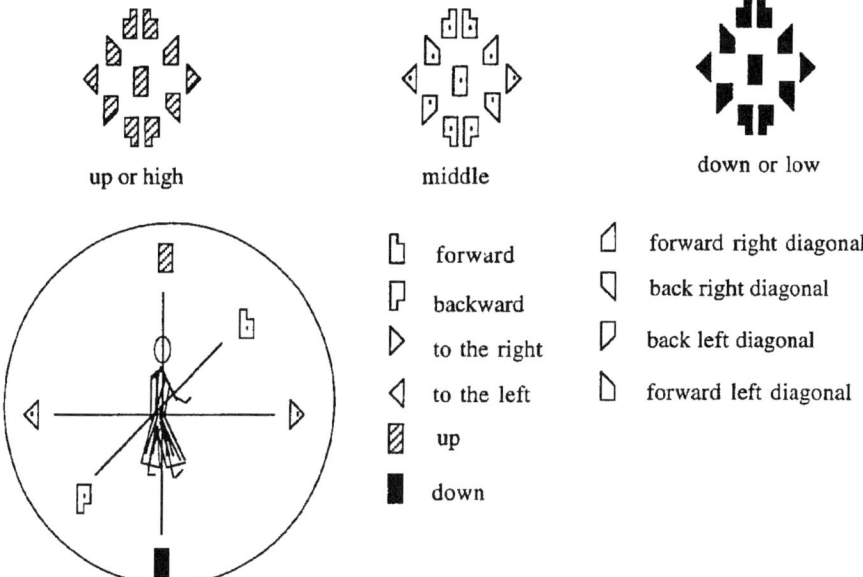

up or high   middle   down or low

The three dimensional cross of axes that organizes spatial direction: the body is in the centre of this kinesphere

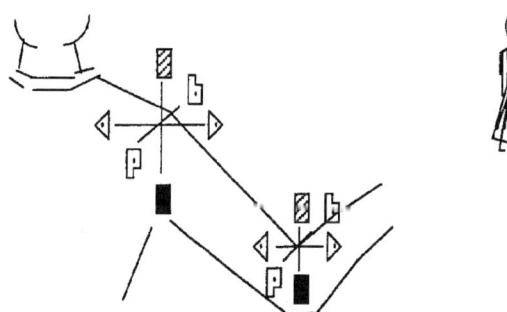

Gestural data: a smaller cross of axes is imagined at the centre of each joint so that direction for each part of a limb can be specified.

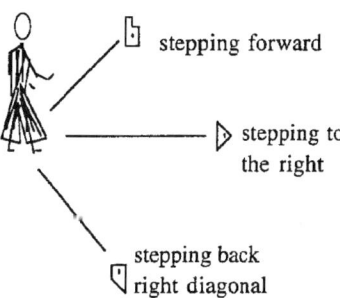

Track data: direction symbols for moving the whole body from one place to another. These would be placed in the central support column on the staff.

FIGURE 118. Labanotation system: graphic signs for specifying spatial direction (Farnell 1995, with permission).

Relationships:

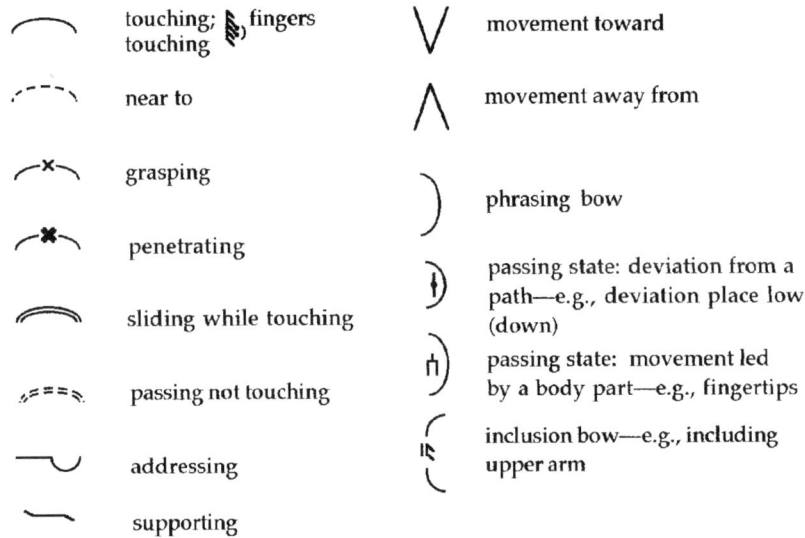

Minor direction signs and relationships:

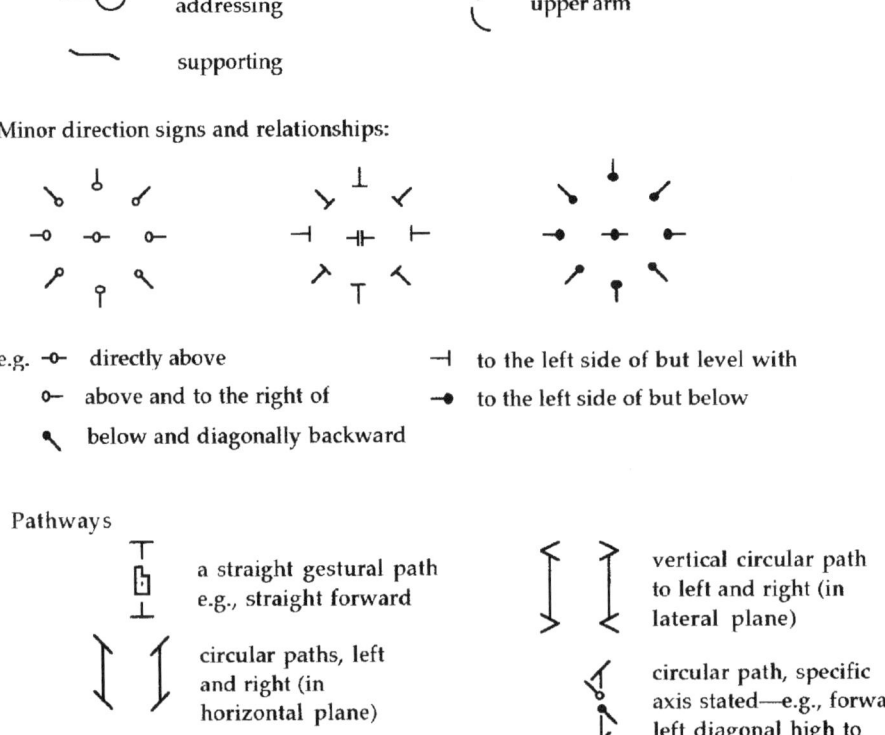

Pathways

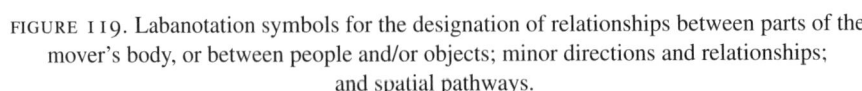

FIGURE 119. Labanotation symbols for the designation of relationships between parts of the mover's body, or between people and/or objects; minor directions and relationships; and spatial pathways.

rections. Assiniboine people consider south to be the most salient direction and view nort, south, east, and west as four quarters or areas *from* which certain kinds of power come toward a person. This contrasts with the conventional Euro-American perspective in which mapmaking conventions locate north at the top of a page and each direction is conceived to be a straight line pointing out from a central location. FIGURE 120 shows how this key is used on the first page of my transcription and translation of an Assiniboine storytelling performance with Plains Sign Talk (PST): 'Long ago, the people who live here now, did not always live here.' PST, like ASL, is a sign language that is fully developed grammatically. It served as a lingua franca across the Plains of North America until English gradually assumed this function early in the twentieth century. PST survives in storytelling and ceremonial contexts in many Plains Indian cultures (Farnell 1995).

Another important feature of the Laban system is that action is written from the mover's perspective rather than from the standpoint of an observer, and so one records and reads from an agentive perspective.

Time

Scripts of all kinds deal with time by assigning a direction for reading—an axis for the sequential flow of sound or action. Labanotation reads from bottom to top. This was not an arbitrary choice for Laban: he originally devised a script that read from left to right but changed it in order to retain an iconicity between left and right sides of the reader's body and left and right sides of the written text of the action. Labanotation is written from the mover's perspective, not an observer's, so the reader imagines performing the action while reading along. Graphic signs for forward spatial direction point upward, while signs for backward point down (FIGURE 118). This iconicity assists rapid reading as the flow of time appears to move forward and up as one reads (a direction which is itself iconic of Western metaphors concerning "time" and "progress" moving forward and up). The horizontal axis provides for actions that occur simultaneously, and actions that occur sequentially are shown in vertical succession. When the timing of actions is controlled by music or other rhythmic divisions, the time axis of the staff can be divided up in a manner similar to standard music notation (SECTION 72). Spatial direction signs normally lengthen vertically to indicate the time taken for performance, but they can also be given a standard length in action sign systems where absolute timing is not important (e.g. sign languages).

Additional dynamics

A body movement always involves some degree of muscular tension or strength; so that dynamics such as acceleration or deceleration, the impetus or initial point for the action, accents, vibration, and phrasing may also be added to the description.

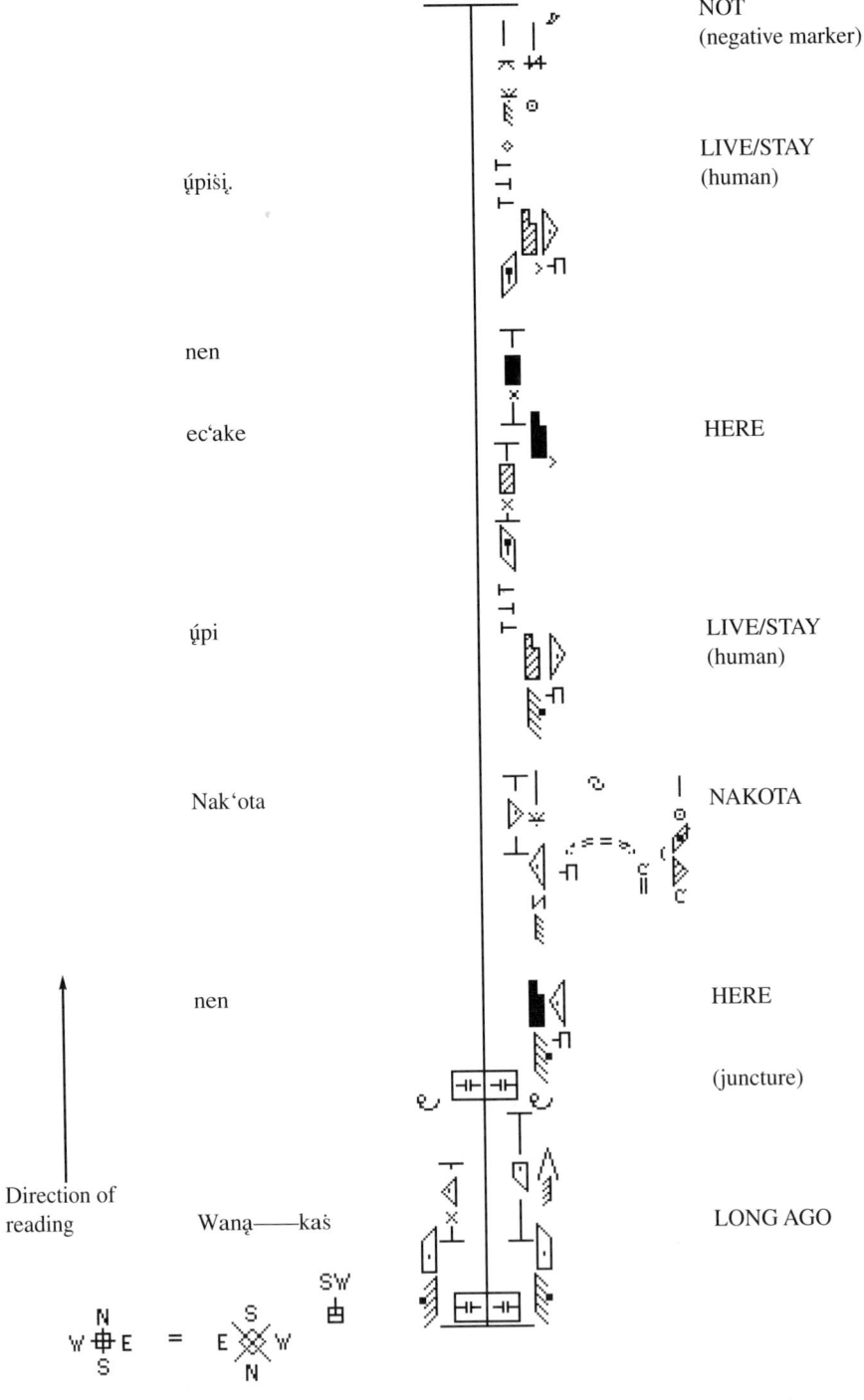

FIGURE 120. Assiniboine storytelling with Plains Sign Talk and spoken Nakota:
page one of the Labanotated score (Farnell 1995, with permission).

Relationships

Relationships between body parts, and between the person acting and objects or other people, are important components of social action and can be described with a series of relationship signs such as $\bigvee$ 'moving toward', $\bigwedge$ 'moving away from', $\frown\!\!\!\!\smile$ 'addressing' something or someone, $\frown$ 'touching', $\mathrel{\rlap{\raise2pt{\hbox{$\scriptstyle\mathord{=}$}}}{\nearrow}}$ 'passing near to', and $\frown\!\!^{\times}\!\!\searrow$ 'grasping' (FIGURE 119).

Reading the action

A detailed exegesis of the utterance shown in FIGURE 120 will provide an example of how these parameters are utilized when writing actions with the Laban script. A "sign" in a sign language such as Plains Sign Talk can be viewed as a combination of four parameters: (a) handshape(s), (b) hand orientation(s), (c) location in the sign space, and (d) movement(s). In order to read FIGURE 120, note that the center line divides the right side of the body from the left side, and that the direction of reading is from the bottom of the page upward. The utterance consists of seven signs.

1) LONG AGO

movement path: toward side left

movement path: toward back right diagonal

left hand orientation: forward right diagonal

right hand orientation: forward left diagonal

left handshape: index finger extended

right handshape: index finger extended

location of sign: center of signing space

The first sign involves making the same handshape with both hands. The index finger $\text{\small (e.g. right index finger) points toward the forward left diagonal}$. The orientation of the palm does not need to be written because it is in a "default" position, that is, the wrist is not rotated in any way. Both hands are located in the center of the signing space , in front of the torso. The right hand moves along a straight horizontal path toward the back right diagonal , while the left hand takes a shorter ✕ horizontal path toward side left ◁ . The length of the movement path sign ⊥ indicates timing—the longer the path sign, the more time it takes to perform.

Additional graphic signs add further information. For example, the movement of the right hand involves an important semantic component. The intention is to move the right hand away from the left hand, in contrast, say, to a conception of moving the hand into the back right diagonal. Such a difference in the action is not observable, of course, but highlights the difference between writing *actions* as opposed to merely

gross physical movements. This component of the action is written 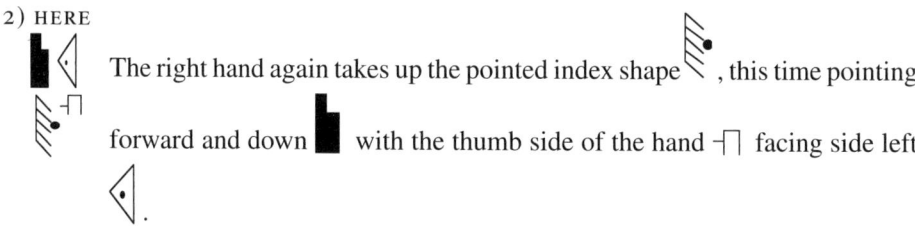 : the graphic sign for the left hand ⅋ is followed by a sign indicating 'movement away from'. After the movement paths are complete, both hands relax ℰ⌣ and return to the center of the signing space ⊞ . The left hand plays no further role in this utterance.

2) HERE

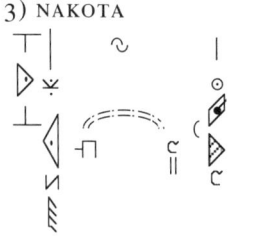 The right hand again takes up the pointed index shape ⧆ , this time pointing

forward and down ▮ with the thumb side of the hand ⊓ facing side left

◁ .

3) NAKOTA

The tribal sign for the Nakota people follows, as the right hand ⧇ extends ⋈ with the fingers oriented toward (point-ing to) side left ◁ . This hand is located so that the thumb side of the hand ⊓ takes up a 'passing near to' relationship with the neck ∥ , as the hand makes a movement path that slides toward side right ⊥ . Additional information shows that the hand folds three degrees ⊻ (i.e. bends at the knuckles) during the latter half of the move-ment path, and that the 'passing near to' relationship ceases thereafter ↻ (release sign). The head ℂ is also involved in this performance. The signer tilts his head to side right high ⬙ while turning it slightly ⬗ (i.e. ⅛ turn to the right). The tilt and turn of the head take place simultaneously, and this is indicated by the small connecting bow ℂ . The head then returns to its normal upright position ⊙.

4) LIVE/STAY

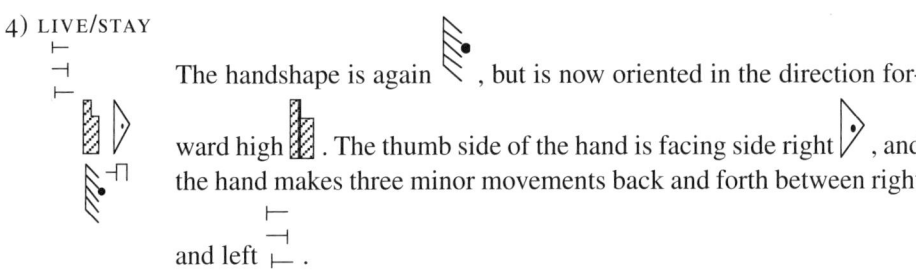

The handshape is again , but is now oriented in the direction forward high . The thumb side of the hand is facing side right , and the hand makes three minor movements back and forth between right and left .

5) HERE

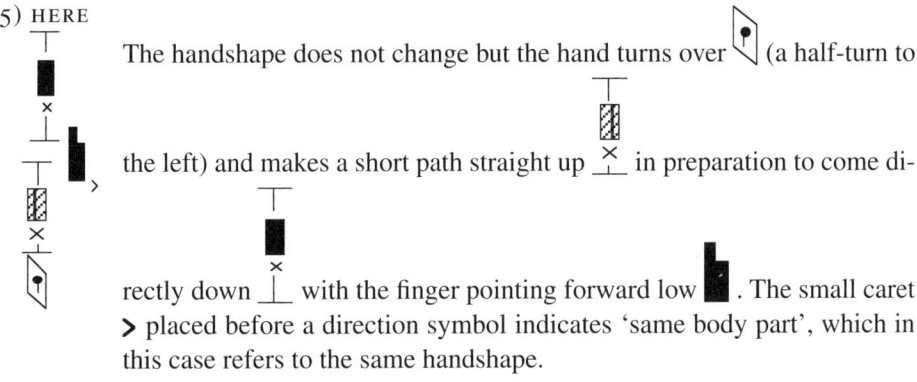

The handshape does not change but the hand turns over (a half-turn to the left) and makes a short path straight up in preparation to come directly down with the finger pointing forward low . The small caret > placed before a direction symbol indicates 'same body part', which in this case refers to the same handshape.

6) LIVE/STAY

The fourth sign in the utterance is now repeated, but is preceded by a half-turn to the right which returns the hand to its previous orientation.

7) NOT

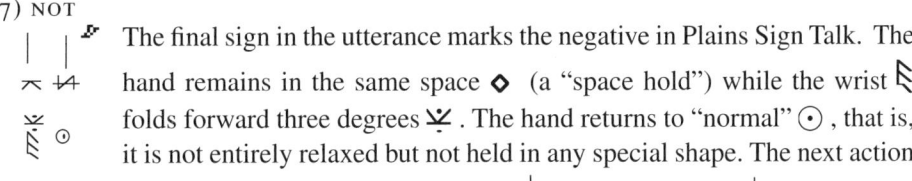

The final sign in the utterance marks the negative in Plains Sign Talk. The hand remains in the same space ◊ (a "space hold") while the wrist folds forward three degrees . The hand returns to "normal" ⊙ , that is, it is not entirely relaxed but not held in any special shape. The next action then folds the wrist over backward (outward) while the hand extends and spreads (a three-dimensional extension). This action is performed with a slight accent or emphasis .

This example illustrates how a writing system creates concepts specific to the medium. While descriptions of gestures in words are certainly possible, representation in graphic signs that do not relate to the medium under investigation distort that medium and make accurate reproduction or analysis of structure and semantics impossible. In emphasizing this, I am not suggesting that spoken language concepts are not involved. When learning any notation system, of course, spoken language descriptions are necessary as part of the learning process (as illustrated by the exegesis above). The point is that, once the reader is literate, this intermediary function is abandoned and a direct reading of the action occurs. The parameters of the body, space, time, dynamics, and relationships, and the Labanotation signs that specify them, provide a means with which to record "talk" *from* the body—to record the agentive production of meaning using the semiotics of body movement. A movement script, therefore, offers much more than a new methodology for inquiry into human movement. The possibility of movement literacy opens up an important theoretical alternative to objectivist talk *about* the body or phenomenological-subjectivist talk *of* the feeling of body movement (see Farnell 1994, Varela 1993).

Bibliography

Arbeau, Thoinot. 1589. *Orchesography.* Trans. Mary Stewart Evans, with a new introduction and notes by Julia Sutton, and a new Labanotation section by Mireille Backer and Julia Sutton. New York: Dover, 1967. (French orig., *Orchésographie et traicté en forme de dialogue, par lequel toutes personnes peuvent facilement apprendre & practiquer l'honneste exercise des dances.* Lengres.)

Austin, Gilbert. 1806. *Chironomia: Or a Treatise on Rhetorical Delivery: Comprehending Many Percepts, Both Ancient and Modern, for the Proper Regulation of The Voice, The Countenance, and Gesture: Together with an Investigation of the Elements of Gesture, and a New Method for the Notation Thereof: Illustrated by Many Figures.* London: T. Cadell and W. Davies. Repr. Carbondale: Southern Illinois University Press, 1966.

Benesh, Joan, and Rudolph Benesh. 1956. *An Introduction to Benesh Dance Notation.* London: A.& C. Black.

Best, David. 1974. *Expression in Movement and the Arts: A Philosophical Enquiry.* London: Lepus.

Birdwhistell, Ray L. 1952. *Introduction to Kinesics: An Annotation System for Analysis of Body Motion and Gesture.* Washington, D.C.: Foreign Service Institute.

Cornozano, Antonio. 1465. *Il Libro dell'arte del danzare.* Ms. Bib. Vatican, Italy.

Dell, Cecily. 1977. *A Primer for Movement Description.* New York: Dance Notation Bureau Press.

Ebreo, Guglielmo. 1463. *De Practica seu arte tripulii vulgare opusculum.* Ms. Bibliotheque Nationale, Paris.

Eshkol, Noa, and Abraham Wachmann. 1958. *Movement Notation.* London: Weidenfeld and Nicholson.

Farnell, Brenda. 1994. "Ethno-graphics and the Moving Body." *Man* 29: 929–74.

———. 1995. *Do You See What I Mean? Plains Indian Sign Talk and the Embodiment of Action.* Austin: University of Texas Press.

Feuillet, Raoul A. 1700A. *Choreographie, ou L'Art de Decrire la Danse.* Paris: Author and M. Brunet. Repr. Hildesheim: Olms, 1979.

———. 1700B. *Recueil de Dances Composées par M. Pecour.* Paris: Author.

Frishberg, Nancy. 1983. "Writing Systems and Problems for Sign Language Notation." *Journal for the Anthropological Study of Human Movement* 2: 169–95.

Gorsky, Alexander. 1978. *Two Essays on Stepanov Dance Notation,* trans. R. J. Wiley. New York: CORD Special Publication.

Hutchinson-Guest, Ann. 1977. *Labanotation,* 3rd ed. New York: Routledge/Theatre Arts Books.

———. 1984. *Dance Notation: The Process of Recording Movement on Paper.* New York: Dance Horizons.

Kendon, Adam. 1989. *Sign Languages of Aboriginal Australia.* Cambridge: Cambridge University Press.

Key, Mary Ritchie. 1977. *Non-Verbal Communication: A Research Guide and Bibliography.* Metuchen, N.J.: Scarecrow.

Klemm, Bernard. 1855. *Katechismus (Handbuch) der Tanzkunst.* Leipzig: J. J. Weber.

Laban, Rudolph (von). 1928. *Schrifttanz: Kinetographie Methodik.* Vienna: Universal Edition.

———. 1956. *Principles of Dance and Movement Notation.* London: Macdonald & Evans.

McGuinness-Scott, Julia. 1983. *Movement Study and Benesh Movement Notation.* London: Oxford University Press.

Playford, John. 1651. *The English Dancing Master.* London (18 editions 1651–1728). Repr. London: Schott, 1957.

Saint-Léon, Arthur. 1852. *La Sténochoréographie.* Paris and St. Petersburg: Author (microfilm in New York Public Library, Library of the Performing Arts, Lincoln Center).

Stepanov, Vladimir I. 1892. *L'alphabet des mouvements du corps humain.* Paris: M. Zuckerman.

Stokoe, William. 1960. *Sign Language Structure* (*Studies in Linguistics,* Occasional Paper 8). Buffalo, N.Y.: University of Buffalo. Repr. Silver Spring, Md.: Linstok Press, 1978.

Stokoe, William, Dorothy Casterline, and Carl Croneberg. 1965. *A Dictionary of American Sign Language.* Washington, D. C.: Gallaudet College Press.

Sutton, Valerie. 1973. *Sutton Movement Shorthand Book 1.* Irvine, Calif.: The Movement Shorthand Society.

Varela, Charles. 1993. "Ethogenics and Semasiology: The Proper Alignment of Causal Powers and the Action Sign." *Journal for the Anthropological Study of Human Movement* 7: 219–48.

West, La Mont, Jr. 1960. "The Sign Language: An Analysis." Ph.D. dissertation, Indiana University.

Wiley, Roland J. 1978. Translator's Preface. In Gorsky 1978: ix–xix.

Williams, Drid. 1991. *Ten Lectures on Theories of the Dance.* Metuchen, N.J.: Scarecrow.

Williams, Drid, and Brenda Farnell. 1990. *The Laban Script: A Beginning Text on Movement Writing for Non-Dancers.* Canberra: Australian Institute for Aboriginal Studies.

Zorn, Friedrich A. 1887. *Grammatik der Tanzkunst.* Leipzig: J. J. Weber. English trans., *Grammar of the Art of Dancing,* ed. A. J. Sheafe. Boston: Heintzemann, 1905. Repr. New York: Dance Horizons, 1975.

Part XIII: Imprinting
and Printing

BEFORE WRITING, ALL LEARNING WAS PASSED ON ORALLY. A culture's tradition consisted of what its wisest members could remember. Poetry and formula and mnemonic devices played a part; but the sum total was limited. The innovation of writing made it possible for a culture to include more knowledge than a single mind could encompass. Records of all kinds could be kept, both important and ephemeral.

The growth of populations created a demand for multiple copies of visual materials. There were illustrations, then there was text accompanying illustrations. Text could be recreated in toto each time it was needed; eventually, in Korea and China, then in Europe, ways were found to reproduce texts by printing from movable type. This was not so much a single invention, as the insight to combine the techniques of numerous crafts—the press from wine-making or oil production, the ink from chemists, the paper from ragpickers, and especially the precisely machined and matched, intricate, minuscule pieces of type from the jeweler's or goldsmith's skill.

Printing was essential for several intellectual revolutions: the spread of religious reform, as the essential texts, and their commentaries, became available to believers; the development of science, as observations could be reproduced accurately for those who could not travel to distant lands; the distribution of classics and the composition of literature to be savored by readers who could not afford individually produced manuscripts.

It is possible that the present dissemination of electronic communication is as significant as the print revolution of the fifteenth century. It is barely possible that physical books will no longer be produced. It is impossible that writing itself—the recording of language in a phonetically based, durable form—will be superseded.

— PETER T. DANIELS

Analog and Digital Writing

PETER T. DANIELS

There are 26 letters in the English alphabet. The number is an accident of history (Greek has 24, Hebrew 22, Russian 32, Arabic 28), but its size—its order of magnitude—is of the utmost significance to modern civilization. We could do with a few more: around 40, so we would not need to use digraphs for single segments like *th* [θ, ð] and *sh* [ʃ], and it would take at least 60 to include all the information given by our supposedly awkward and inefficient way of spelling English; but 26 is what have been used for about two centuries.

Just two centuries! The first edition of the *Encyclopædia Britannica*, in 1768, alphabetized I and J, and U and V, together. It was only then that I and U were coming to be used for vowels only, and J and V for consonants; previously they had been simply graphic variants. At the time of Shakespeare and the Authorized Version of the Bible, in 1611, *love* looked like *loue*, because the lower-case letter was rounded on the bottom and the capital was pointed. (*J* started as a variant of lower-case *i* at the end of a word. Regular *s* likewise appeared only at the end of a word, long *s* everywhere else.) Were there, then, 26 letters, or 27, or only 24? In 1768, that was not a particularly important question—but now it is.

Dichotomy

To understand the importance of the small number of letters in our alphabet, we can use a pair of words from computer technology: *analog* and *digital*. An analog computer represents numbers by varying some physical quantity in proportion to a number being represented. An old crank-operated adding machine was an analog computer, because the digits it manipulated were represented by how far a gear-wheel turned. A rotary telephone dial is also an analog computer: turning the dial a certain arc clockwise loads a spring; upon release, the wheel turns back again, making and breaking an electrical contact that sends as many pulses into the system as contacts the wheel crosses during its counterclockwise spin.

ACKNOWLEDGMENTS: I experimented with a Hammod typewriter courtesy of Matthew W. Stolper, Oriental Institute, and with a VariTyper courtesy of Bernard A. Lalor, formerly Geography Department, both University of Chicago. This section originated as an invited lecture in the symposium "The Alphabet as a Technology," organized by Ephraim Isaac, Institute of Semitic Studies, Princeton, N.J., April 9, 1989.

On the other hand, a digital computer, which is what virtually all electronic computers now in use are, represents quantities not by some proportionate amount of electricity, but by turning the measured quantities—the data being manipulated—into numbers that can be represented by electronic switches. The easiest things for a switch to do, of course, are to turn on and turn off; so electronic computers are based on binary arithmetic—just zeros and ones, offs and ons. A digital computer, however, need not be binary-based. A push-button telephone works by sending out two of seven pure tones, one assigned to each row and column of the keypad. The electronic switching equipment interprets the twelve unique two-note chords as the ten digits and two symbols used for phone numbers and instructions.

What does this have to do with the size of the alphabet? The topic under consideration is the mechanization of writing. There are two kinds of ways to do that: analog ways and digital ways. Analog mechanization, which has been with us for five thousand years and more, reproduces a whole text of some sort all at once. The most familiar example is the *print*. An artist carves an image in a block of wood, applies ink to it, presses paper onto it, and lifts the paper off with a copy of the image. The image, of course, can include or can be writing.

Digital mechanization, which goes back maybe twice as far as analog, reproduces a text character by character, so that individual pieces of it are individually accessible. Analog looks at an entity as a whole, without analyzing it into meaningful components; digital encodes the separate significant parts. Other names for these two classifications might be the linguist's *synthetic* and *analytic*, respectively, or the pop-psychology terms "right-brain" and "left-brain."

History

Fifty centuries ago, Sumerians made analog reproductions of pictures and writings when they impressed *stamp seals* on clay surfaces—no different from official seals impressed in wax on official documents to this day—or when they rolled *cylinder seals* across the clay to make a permanent continuous record of the information carved onto the side of the cylinder. Each cylinder was unique in its carving and served to identify its owner, as a signature; but it produced the same design each time it was used. Thus at or even before the beginning of history, we have the two characteristics of analog printing: *reproducibility* and *immutability.*

And even before we can recognize Sumerians specifically in the Mesopotamian cradle of civilization, going back perhaps ten thousand years, from Iran to Syria, there was digital record-keeping in the form of *tokens*. Three sheep and two goats might be represented by three of one kind of token and two of another. The next day's shepherding might involve a record of two sheep and six goats; a new "document" could be produced to memorialize that situation. Again, the characteristics of digital printing: ease of assembling the elements of the text—the characters—and uniqueness of the resulting document.

We now return from ancient history to recent history, keeping in mind the analog and digital ways of looking at text reproduction. Until printing with movable type, invented first in China in the mid eleventh century by Pi Sheng and, perhaps independently, in Germany in the fifteenth, by Johannes Gutenberg or his associates, there was only analog reproduction: In the first place, creating a document individually—with ink and pen or brush on any receptive surface, or with stylus on soft clay, or with chisel on stone. Secondarily, making a print as described above, from a carved original on wood or (in the Orient) on ceramic; or by making a rubbing, where charcoal or a similar substance is rubbed on paper laid over a raised or depressed carving.

Printing with movable type represents the introduction of a digital technique into text reproduction. The typesetter selects the individual characters one by one and places them in a frame in the significant order that represents the text in a language. Mistakes can be corrected, changes made. When the text is finalized, the array of characters is locked into place and the type matrix has become an analog device to make a print from.

With hand-set type—the only option for over four hundred years—it did not matter how many different characters the typesetter had to choose from. In East Asia, Chinese texts could involve thousands of different characters. These necessitated a very large cabinet and a good memory for its organization; yet it was apparently more efficient to use movable type than to carve entire texts, a page at a time, on woodblocks—the technique of printing that had been used in China for centuries before the new invention. Even Gutenberg, setting the Bible in Latin, with its 24 letters—double that to count the capitals, and add a few numbers and punctuation marks—used not 70 or so sorts (a *sort* is an individually designed piece of type), but over 400. He wanted to imitate handwritten manuscripts, complete with abbreviations and ligatures. Instead of that kind of complexity, modern printing require *italic*, SMALL CAPITAL, **bold**, and decorative types. As long as one person was picking out individual pieces of cast lead (or whatever) from a typecase, there could be any number of sorts.

This made it possible for printing to follow, or even accompany, missionaries from Christian Europe to literate civilizations throughout the world and disseminate the Scriptures in translation. The first specimen sheets for foreign alphabets (called *exotic* types) were produced by the papal printers in the early 1500s. (Books were printed from Hebrew type in the 1480s.) By the early nineteenth century, one could print from type just about any language that possessed an indigenous script.

Certain scripts, though, most notably the Arabic, have a long and superb tradition of calligraphy. Even the most workaday Arabic hands use ligatures that do not cling to a horizontal line: they possess a fluidity and grace that could not easily be incorporated into the blocky nature of rectangular type. The appearance of Arabic types was a less than happy compromise between art and technology. Nonetheless, by the late nineteenth century books were being printed in Bulaq, modern Cairo, that transcend the rectangular frames of the pieces of type and are close to indistinguishable from unornamented handwriting.

People

As the scope of digital printing expanded, so did the techniques of analog: after wood engraving came steel engraving, and etching, and lithography. Each of these could be and was used for reproducing texts, but always texts of a special kind: William Blake's poems, whose first incarnations incorporated the author's drawings; the illustrations in scholarly journals of newly discovered inscriptions in languages that did not yet have type cut for them or, in some cases, whose scripts had not even been deciphered. (Yet even the most intricate new writings were soon reduced to type—Mesopotamian cuneiform type, scarcely used by Assyriologists; and Egyptian hieroglyphic type, still found on virtually every page of an Egyptological publication.) The most widespread analog process of all, though, was photography—an amalgamation of physics, chemistry, technology, and art that might be seen as a pinnacle of the Industrial Revolution.

"Industrial Revolution" may be too simplistic a notion for modern historians to tolerate. But it is useful for considering the technology of writing. The handset type described so far was fine for an age with time to spare: Reaching for each individual letter, and much more so for each individual Chinese character, takes time. The society that had invented mechanical printing presses and wood-pulp paper (the bane of archivists, but quick of manufacture compared to rag paper) could not long wait for the hand typesetter to laboriously turn out page after page. The machine tool industry developing in Britain meant that precision equipment would be available as needed. The United States was expanding westward across a continent. Business offices were becoming swamped as clerks like Dickens's Bob Cratchit spent their ill-lit days hand-copying documents. Even language scholars—philologists and the new profession of linguists—could not be assumed to be able to read every foreign script.

Yet none of these proved to be the impetus for the first effective digitization of writing. That honor goes to a scholar working for those who could not perceive an analog representation of a text: Louis Braille, who in 1830 invented writing for the blind. Various schemes for embossing letter shapes had been tried, but the intricate curves proved too difficult to perceive with the fingertips. It occurred to Braille, as it had apparently not occurred to anyone else, that the letters of the alphabet could be represented by arbitrary combinations of more easily perceptible shapes. He chose a rectangle of six dots: three high, two wide. This number of dots, each one either present or absent, allows 64 different characters, and the simplicity of the pattern makes it easy for the practiced reader to feel each character with a fingertip. (The principle is identical to that used in a computer, where *bytes* of eight *bits*—characters of eight dots—allow sets of 256 characters.) Braille documents at first were simply transpositions of print, letter by letter, to the new mode, but shortcuts were soon adopted that turned braille into a quite distinct orthography that is very like alphabetic shorthand. Students learn English orthography only after mastering the other.

Something similar was devised in the first digitization of the alphabet to widely affect society in general: the *telegraph*, of 1838. Not only did Samuel F. B. Morse have to figure out how to transmit an electrical impulse across many miles of wire; he had to devise a way for that electrical impulse to carry a message. The only signal he had to work with was the click ON or OFF of his apparatus. He could have simply decreed that each letter was to be represented by a different number of clicks, from 1 to 26; but obviously this would have been less than practical or practicable. Braille was free to arrange his single unit of significance, the dot, in a two-dimensional matrix, height by width; but Morse had only a single dimension—time, or a straight line—in which to accommodate his message. So Morse chose to use two different units of significance, a short click and a long click, or a dot and a dash. It was now possible to devise an alphabet where each letter took no more than four symbols, dots and dashes, in a single dimension. A little extra time separates the letters.

Quite a different sort of digitization achieved standardization during the nineteenth century, in the form of phonetic notation. As mentioned above, with the growth of knowledge of the languages of the world, it was no longer possible for a scholar to be familiar with all the world's scripts. It had long been the practice, of course, to write approximations of foreign words in familiar orthography: *Hindu* was long spelled *Hindoo* because *oo* spelled [u] in English (only). The still-current *Moslem* in place of the more accurate *Muslim* is a relic of those days. The name of the state of [ˌɪlɨˈnɔj] is the English pronunciation of the French spelling *Illinois* [iliˈnɥa] of the Algonquian word *elenwa* meaning, apparently, 'one who sounds normal'. Scholars, though, had conventions by which they represented the sounds of foreign languages in the Roman alphabet—or, more often, by which they represented the characters of their scripts in a transliteration. But different languages tend to have different sounds in them, and the orthography for one language, in general, cannot simply be applied to another. For instance, Polish has three voiceless sibilants, English two, but Latin only one—so that the Roman alphabet has only one letter for all of them, *s*. Among the spellings for the sibilants are *s*, *ś*, *š*, *sch*, *sh*, and *sz*. Clearly, much confusion could arise as linguists from different native orthographies tried to communicate about foreign languages. The phonetic notations devised during the period of digitization at once assigned unique significance to letters and diacritics, and laid the foundation as well for demonstrating that the languages of the world could be described in terms of a limited number of symbols, rather than as completely unique entities.

Machines

Consider again the 26 letters. In the middle of the nineteenth century, all type was still being set by hand: the typesetter reached to the typecase for each successive character. It did not matter how many different characters were needed for a text, so long as they were carefully arranged and accessible. It might take as long to locate the single sort for a syllable in the larger typecase as it did to locate the two or more characters that compose it in an alphabetic transliteration. Until printing was mechanized, then, the typology of writing was not an important factor in typesetting efficiency. Even so, with a widely agreed universal alphabet, it was no longer necessary to maintain the large stock of exotic types for reproducing foreign texts. Let us return, however, from the scholar's study to that outer office where Bob Cratchit copied documents all day for Ebenezer Scrooge. Perhaps his handwriting was crabbed. Perhaps he occasionally made a mistake or a blot. Perhaps he got tired of writing the same thing several times over for hours at a time. He needed a *typewriter.*

The first practical typewriter was invented in 1867 by Christopher Latham Scholes—one historian says his was the 52nd idea for a personal writing machine—and was placed on sale in 1873 by Remington. It had 44 keys, accommodating the capital letters, the numbers, and some punctuation. Suddenly, the number of characters in a script became important to the business world. If a language was to benefit from the efficiency inherent in digitalization, its script had to fit into the confines of the typewriter. Of course the shift key was soon added, and ordinary typewriters could handle 88 to 92 characters.

It was in fact the alphabet that made the typewriter possible. China was famed for its mechanical wonders from the time of Marco Polo on. It was certainly not beyond the inventive capability of a Chinese mechanical engineer to devise the combinations of levers and springs involved in a typewriter. But would the idea ever occur that one could assemble enough of those mechanisms to provide a key for each needed character? Similarly, in Japan or India or Ethiopia, who might suppose that hundreds or even scores of symbols could be accommodated in a manageable box? The small size of the alphabet made possible—and thinkable—a mechanical device for printing the script.

Soon after, analog technology followed along: *carbon paper* appeared before 1880. It was now possible to make more than one copy of a business document at a time—or of any document produced by a pressure device: drawings as well as type-script. The *telephone*, too, is an analog information transmission device. The telegraph sent a digitized message over the wires; the phone sends an analog representation of the sound waves that lie behind the written message and converts it back to sound.

Other visual analog devices began to appear, perhaps less ubiquitous than carbon paper used to be, but of considerable importance: office duplicators. These fall into two categories. One kind uses a stencil through which ink is squeezed onto paper, or which picks up ink on areas from which a water-repellent coating has been removed, and offsets it to the paper. This is the *mimeograph* machine. The other kind creates a master with the pigment added in the desired patterns, and transfers an infinitesimal layer of it to paper moistened with a solvent. This is the purple *ditto* once so common in schools.

Mark Twain was the first writer to submit the manuscript of a novel in typescript. Suddenly an author could turn out a text faster than a typesetter could typeset it! However, this advantage was not to last long. In the 1880s, Ottmar Mergenthaler devised the *Linotype*, which was the first successful typecasting machine. It and Tolbert Lanston's *Monotype* work by casting new type each time a character is used (the machine arranges the molds for the type into the lines of text, and then injects the molten lead—*hot type*—creating the printing plate). This equipment can accommodate a larger selection of sorts than the typewriter—Linotype holds 180 sorts, Monotype 220—in ordinary work, they would be roman, italic, boldface, and small capitals—but do not approach what is needed for the syllabaries or logographies of the world.

Again, it is clear that the alphabet drives the technology, and the technology serves the alphabet. Now and then, there were compromises. The imperialist West recognized that it might sometimes be practical to use a native orthography; so for instance a four- or five-digit numerical code was assigned to each Chinese character so that telegrams could be sent in Chinese. The message was encoded; the telegraph operator transmitted the numbers; the numbers were decoded at the recipient's end.

Another typewriter inventor, James B. Hammond, was disconcerted that his news reports from Civil War battlefields were misinterpreted by telegraphers and typesetters in the process of getting into the newspapers. He wished for a portable printing machine, and began to cogitate and sketch. In 1881 he produced the Hammond typewriter, which worked totally differently from the Scholes design (which uses type elements on levers that, as their keys are struck, swing to hit an ink-impregnated ribbon that impacts the paper) that became the model for nearly all typewriters until the IBM Selectric (which places 92 characters on a spheroid, whose whirling and tilting is electronically controlled). Hammond's typewriter incorporates what is called a type *shuttle*: an arc, a segment of a cylinder, maybe half an inch high, about a third of the circumference of a circle, with three rows of type characters around it. Pressing the key for a letter rotates the shuttle around its circular frame so the appropriate character is at the striking point, and makes a lever bang the paper forward gently to receive the impression of the character through an ink-bearing ribbon. There are three levels of shift, with 30 characters per level; two shuttles can be mounted in the machine simultaneously; and they can be changed with almost no effort.

Therein lies the importance of the Hammond typewriter. Now it was possible for any office to write in any script. Type shuttles were prepared for dozens of scripts. Hammond came as close as anyone to integrating the analog and digital approaches to mechanical writing.

Unfortunately, the Hammond was never very popular; it languished until the company was succeeded by VariTyper, which marketed the technology not as an office or scholar's typewriter, but as a machine for producing print copy for offset reproduction. It added more and more features to imitate the capability of hot-metal typesetting, such as varying widths of characters (*proportional spacing*, always a property of metal type, which had been sacrificed in the design of typewriters) and justified margins. VariTypers were in use until 1970 or so, when the company had switched to electronic phototypesetting—among the last components of the story.

Photography had been around since 1837. Gradual improvements in optics and in photosensitive chemicals have made it possible to create print materials with no type at all. Older phototypesetting machines, driven by primitive computers, used precisely calibrated lenses and whirling opaque glass disks with transparent letter designs arranged in circles. Light was sent through each letter in turn and focused on photographic paper to produce black images in the desired size. This paper was passed through developing and fixing chemicals to become a photo-offset master. In later models, the beam of light was controlled not by a transparent image in a black disk, but entirely electronically: a beam of electrons was sent to a cathode-ray tube, and the glow of the screen was what flashed onto the paper—not one character at a time, but several inches of text. Filmsetters now create entire 16-page signatures from computer files without human intervention.

Thus in the newest typesetting equipment, analog and digital again have merged, but with the intermediary of the electromechanical or the electronic interface. The first home computers similarly sent digital signals—selected from the 256 bytes—to a *daisy-wheel* or *dot-matrix* printer, which translated them into a spinning wheel or a pattern of dots impressed on paper; the present-day *ink-jet* printer is similar.

In recent decades, still another analog technology was introduced: the photocopier. Here, any image at all is reproduced when it is projected onto a polished metal drum, causing patterns of electric charge (as in magnetic tape recording). Black powder is attracted to this drum, and then heat-bonded onto paper as it rolls past. In desktop publishing equipment, the same sort of electronic pattern is painted by a computer onto the drum of the laser printer, which turns out high-quality pages; in using Adobe Systems' PostScript page description language, the transition from digital to analog is made within the computer, and not at an external interface. Scanning and printing devices have been attached to telephones to produce fax machines. In an inadvertent homage to the first digital writing, a braille panel can be driven by a computer, so the user's fingers can read each line—but software is now available that can turn written standard English (or other languages) into readily intelligible, synthesized speech. A few years ago, this involved massively subsidized, dedicated hardware available only to the blind; now it is a component of a mid-price word processing program. Communication at a distance is again analog.

Consequences

Two other aspects of the alphabet, one very new, one very old, take us from a technical to a humanistic approach to writing. Very new is the place of the computer, the word processor, in the act of creative writing. It has both advantages and drawbacks. The obvious advantages include the spelling checker and the elimination of erasing and of retyping. Drawbacks include the insistence on immediate improvement rather than careful consideration of the text, and the lack of earlier drafts to consult.

The development of the computer network brings its own share of rewards and problems. One reward is access to vast quantities of information stored in databases around the world, available to anyone who can navigate through the labyrinth of cyberspace. Another is the virtually instant communication with people anywhere within reach of the interconnections. But the problems arise in the very vastness and instantaneity of the system. There is the risk of being overwhelmed by quantities of information, all clamoring equally for attention, in the absence of a librarian skilled at retrieving the most reliable materials and at suggesting caution in the use of the rest. The databases themselves are mutable in a way physical documents are not: they can be updated, yes, but they can also be undetectably falsified. One cannot be certain of retrieving the same content tomorrow as yesterday. The availability of immediate reply to an interlocutor brings the practice—in hindsight, inevitable—already dubbed *flaming*: the instant transmission of a hostile response. Reconsideration is not available; one cannot tear up an e-letter on the way to the e-mail, nor recall it from the recipient's mailbox. A new etiquette must evolve to forestall such hurt.

A pair of essays published a few weeks apart in *The New Yorker* celebrate both the old way and the new way of recording information. In "This Living Hand" (January 16, 1995), Edmund Morris meditates on the letter in which Ronald Reagan revealed his affliction with Alzheimer's disease:

> Script's primary power is to convey the cursive flow of human thought, from brain to hand to pen to ink to eye—every waver, every loop, every character trembling with expression. Type has no comparable warmth; matrix dots and laser sprays and pixels of L.C.D. interpose their various screens between writer and reader. If Mr. Reagan's letter … had been keyboarded to the world, instead of handwritten and issued in facsimile, its poignancy would have been reduced by half. (p. 66)

In "Byte Verse" (February 20 & 27), Anthony Lane delights in the power of a four–CD-ROM set of *English Poetry*, which contains the complete works of some twelve hundred fifty poets—approximately 165,000 poems.

> You can call up all the poems by one writer, or every poem from one era, you can hunt for something half remembered if you can cough up a first line, a title, or even a particular word. And that word itself can come from anywhere: from the text, the dedication, the epigraph. Oh, and you can read a poem, which is always nice. … The uncharitable view of "English Poetry" is that it will turn students into sluggards (which is hardly a major overhaul); that it relieves them of the need to grapple with literature, and encourages them to wing it instead; and that, most perilous of all, they will forget the physical textures and habits, the ageless stuff, of which reading is made. The download killeth, say the purists, but the letter giveth life. The charitable view, on the other hand, is that nothing dies, and that the database will send you back to books feeling none the worse—pretty well tuned, in fact. It doesn't do the work for you, it does the legwork; time previously devoted to the long grind can now be freed up for the

really scary part, which is called *thinking*. Once you have a printout of your ... findings, the onus is then on you, as never before, to wonder what on earth they might mean; the computer hasn't a clue. (pp. 103, 104)

One last aspect of the 26 letters—the very old one—is recalled by one more *New Yorker* essay. The miniaturist Nicholson Baker, in the 27 indignant pages of "Discards" (April 4, 1994), describes the process by which library catalogs are transferred from card files to computers—and much information is lost (notably, the ability to find what one was *not* looking for). The card catalog itself was only about a century old; previously, a library's holdings were listed in bound books that were continually interleaved and on occasion completely redone. The advantage of cards derives directly from the magnitude of the number 26—and from the fact of a canonical order of the letters. Any list of words can be *alphabetized*. An alphabetical list is infinitely expandable. But scripts with more than a fewscore characters lose this property. There was no list of all the cuneiform characters; there are many competing lists of Chinese characters, and they are arranged by differing principles, so that compilers of Chinese lists may finally concede to the alphabet and order the characters by their pinyin equivalents, as Japanese directories order the kanji by their kana equivalents.

Cultural historians quarrel over the importance of writing itself, and of alphabetical writing in particular, for the development of the modern world. With printing, though, factual information could for the first time be widely disseminated in identical copies—so long as publication required the hand copying of treatises, their distribution was necessarily limited; but also, accuracy of data could not be assured from copy to copy. Modern science relies on facts that are reliable—and procedures that are reproducible. It could come about only when every researcher began with the same database, and proceeded through reliable publication. Publications began to mount up, and their information had to be retrieved. Alphabetical lists were the key.

Writing makes civilization possible. Printing makes science possible. Indexing makes them accessible.

Bibliography

The history of recent printing technology and business machines has not been told, to my knowledge. I have found useful the summaries in the 15th edition of *Encyclopædia Britannica* (1974), under "Office Machines," "Printing," and "Telegraph."

Beeching, Wilfred A. 1974. *Century of the Typewriter.* New York: St. Martin's.

Eisenstein, Elizabeth L. 1979. *The Printing Press as an Agent of Change: Communications and Cultural Transformations in Early-modern Europe.* Cambridge: Cambridge University Press.

Olson, David R. 1994. *The World on Paper: The Conceptual and Cognitive Implications of Writing and Reading.* Cambridge: Cambridge University Press.

Steinberg, S. H. 1966. *Five Hundred Years of Printing.* Harmondsworth: Penguin. (1st ed., 1955.)

Tsien Tsuen-hsuin. 1985. *Paper and Printing* (*Science and Civilisation in China*, by Joseph Needham, vol. 5, *Chemistry and Chemical Technology*, part 1). Cambridge: Cambridge University Press.

Index

Colophon

(In approximate order of use)

Ecological Linguistics fonts
CuneiformOriental family
IPATimes family
EuroTimes family
EuroIranica family
VietnamTimes family
Assyrian family (cuneiform)
Meroitic
Ugaritic
FRHebrewRoman
SouthArabian
Iberic
Numidian family
Tifinagh
Mycenaean family
Cypriot
PersianCun (Old Persian)
GreekTimes
CopticG
GothicAlph
Runes
OghamPD
TambovCyrillic family
TambovOCS
Glagolitic
Armenian
GeoIllya (Georgian)
TbilisiMaj (Georgian)
BrahmiRGS
KharoshthiPD
NepaliExt
DevanagariExt
GujaratiLaser
BengaliCS
OriyaPD
SriLankaLaser (Sinhala)
CanareseOldKG (Kannada)
AndhraKG (Telugu)

MalayalamLaser
TamilTimesGH
Tibetan96
Lepcha
Phagspa family
BurmanTimesJO
Chiengmai (Thai)
LaossPost (Lao)
KhmerJrieng
Javanese
Buginese
Hanunoo
SamaritanUSA
RashiUSA
EstrangeloUSA
SertoUSA
EastSyriacUSA
MandaicUSA
ALSogdian
Avestan
BSogdian
CSogdian
FunPahlavi
Manichean
NisaParthian
Pahlavi
Parsig
Parthian
Psalter
Orkhon
BuryatUSA
BaghdadUSA (Arabic)
Cyprea (Dhivehi)
EthiopicCDS
Pollard
Fraser
Cherokee
CreeCanadaK
CreeWCanadaK

InuitCanadaS
PahawhHmong
AbkhazCIS
AzerbaijanCIS
KashmiriUSA
KurdishUSA
PashtoUSA
SindhiUSA
Uyghur/MalayUSA
Semaphore
Braille
GallaudetTT
DaysCodex (Maya)

Adobe Systems fonts
TimesRoman family
Times Small Caps & Old
  Style Figures
Helvetica
Wittenberger Fraktur

Oriental Institute fonts
Cleo family (Hieroglyphs)
Cleo Mirrored family
Demotic

Proprietary fonts
Indus

Apple Computer, Inc., fonts
Li Sung Light (Chinese)
Song (Simplified Chinese)
Hon Mincho (Japanese)
Myungjo (Korean)

Shareware fonts
Constantin and Methodius

Softkey fonts
Koffee

THE INTERNATIONAL PHONETIC ALPHABET (revised to 1989)

CONSONANTS

	Bilabial	Labiodental	Dental	Alveolar	Postalveolar	Retroflex	Palatal	Velar	Uvular	Pharyngeal	Glottal
Plosive	p b			t d		ʈ ɖ	c ɟ	k g	q ɢ		ʔ
Nasal	m	ɱ		n		ɳ	ɲ	ŋ	N		
Trill	B			r					R		
Tap or Flap				ɾ		ɽ					
Fricative	ɸ β	f v	θ ð	s z	ʃ ʒ	ʂ ʐ	ç ʝ	x ɣ	χ ʁ	ħ ʕ	h ɦ
Lateral fricative				ɬ ɮ							
Approximant		ʋ		ɹ		ɻ	j	ɰ			
Lateral approximant				l		ɭ	ʎ	L			
Ejective stop	p'							k'	q'		
Implosive	ƥ ɓ			ɗ			ʄ	ƙ ɠ	ʠ ʛ		

Where symbols appear in pairs, the one to the right represents a voiced consonant. Shaded areas denote articulations judged impossible.

DIACRITICS

Voiceless	n̥ d̥	More rounded	ɔ̹	^{w} Labialized	tʷ dʷ	~ Nasalized	ẽ			
Voiced	s̬ t̬	Less rounded	ɔ̜	^{j} Palatalized	tʲ dʲ	^{n} Nasal release	dⁿ			
^{h} Aspirated	tʰ dʰ	Advanced	u̟	^{ɣ} Velarized	tˠ dˠ	^{l} Lateral release	dˡ			
Breathy voiced	b̤ a̤	Retracted	i̠	^{ʕ} Pharyngealized	tˤ dˤ	No audible release	d̚			
Creaky voiced	b̰ a̰	Centralized	ë	~ Velarized or pharyngealized	ɫ					
Linguolabial	t̼ d̼	Mid-centralized	ě	Raised	e̝ (ɹ̝ = voiced alveolar fricative)					
Dental	t̪ d̪	Syllabic	ɹ̩	Lowered	e̞ (β̞ = voiced bilabial approximant)					
Apical	t̺ d̺	Non-syllabic	e̯	Advanced Tongue Root	e̘					
Laminal	t̻ d̻	Rhoticity	ɚ	Retracted Tongue Root	e̙					